W9-ALK-411

MCSA 70-687 Cert Guide: Configuring Microsoft Windows 8.1

Don Poulton
Randy Bellet
Harry Holt

800 East 96th Street
Indianapolis, Indiana 46240 USA

MCSA 70-687 Cert Guide: Configuring Microsoft Windows 8.1

ISBN-13: 978-0-7897-4879-9
ISBN-10: 0-7897-4879-7

Library of Congress Control Number: 2014944426

Printed in the United States of America

First Printing: July 2014

Trademarks

Warning and Disclaimer

Special Sales

For information about buying this title in bulk quantities, or for special sales opportunities (which may include electronic versions; custom cover designs; and content particular to your business, training goals, marketing focus, or branding interests), please contact our corporate sales department at corpsales@pearsoned.com or (800) 382-3419.

For government sales inquiries, please contact governmentsales@pearsoned.com.

For questions about sales outside the U.S., please contact international@pearsoned.com.

Associate Publisher
Dave Dusthimer

Acquisitions Editor
Betsy Brown

Development Editors
Christopher Cleveland
Eleanor Bru

Managing Editor
Sandra Schroeder

Project Editor
Seth Kerney

Copy Editor
Chuck Hutchinson

Indexer
Heather McNeill

Proofreader
Anne Goebel

Technical Editor
Chris Crayton

Editorial Assistant
Vanessa Evans

Multimedia Developer
Lisa Matthews

Book Designer
Gary Adair

Page Layout
TnT Design, Inc.

Contents at a Glance

Introduction

CHAPTER 1 Introducing Windows 8.1 2

CHAPTER 2 Installing Windows 8.1 68

CHAPTER 3 Migrating Users and Applications to Windows 8.1 130

CHAPTER 4 Configuring Devices and Device Drivers 164

CHAPTER 5 Installing, Configuring, and Securing Applications in Windows 8.1 198

CHAPTER 6 Configuring Internet Explorer 248

CHAPTER 7 Configuring Hyper-V 286

CHAPTER 8 Configuring TCP/IP Settings 326

CHAPTER 9 Configuring Networking Settings 378

CHAPTER 10 Configuring and Maintaining Network Security 404

CHAPTER 11 Configuring and Securing Access to Files and Folders 440

CHAPTER 12 Configuring Local Security Settings 512

CHAPTER 13 Configuring Authentication and Authorization 550

CHAPTER 14 Configuring Remote Management and Remote Connections 590

CHAPTER 15 Configuring and Securing Mobile Devices 640

CHAPTER 16 Configuring Windows Update 700

CHAPTER 17 Disk Management 722

CHAPTER 18 Managing and Monitoring System Performance 760

CHAPTER 19 Configuring System Recovery Options 810

CHAPTER 20 Configuring File Recovery 842

APPENDIX A Answers to the "Do I Know This Already?" Quizzes 864

GLOSSARY 900

INDEX 922

On The CD:

APPENDIX B Memory Tables

APPENDIX C Memory Tables Answer Key

PRACTICE EXAM 1

ANSWERS TO PRACTICE EXAM 1

PRACTICE EXAM 2

ANSWERS TO PRACTICE EXAM 2

Table of Contents

Introduction xviii

Chapter 1 Introducing Windows 8.1 2

"Do I Know This Already?" Quiz 3

Foundation Topics 7

Leading Up to Windows 8.1 7

Windows 8.1 8

Windows 8.1 Editions 9

New Features of Windows 8 and Windows 8.1 12

Productivity Improvements 12

Security Improvements 15

A Quick Tour of Windows 8.1 18

Windows 8.1 Search 20

Configuring the Windows 8.1 Taskbar 23

Taskbar Properties 24

Navigation Properties 25

Jump Lists Properties 27

Toolbars 27

Windows 8.1 Apps 28

Libraries 29

Windows 8.1 Settings 30

PC and Devices 31

Accounts 34

OneDrive 36

Search and Apps 37

Privacy 39

Network 40

Time and Language 42

Ease of Access 42

Update and Recovery 44

Administrative Tools 45

Control Panel 46

System and Security 47

Network and Internet 49

Hardware and Sound 50

Programs 52

User Accounts and Family Safety 53

Appearance and Personalization 54

Displaying File Extensions 55

Clock, Language, and Region 55
Ease of Access 55
The Computer Management Snap-in 55
Evaluating Hardware Readiness and Compatibility 57
Windows 8.1 Hardware Requirements (Including Screen Resolution) 57
Hardware Compatibility 58
Using 32-Bit or 64-Bit Windows 59
Choosing Between an Upgrade and a Clean Installation 60
Software Compatibility 63
Determining Which SKU to Install 65
Determining Requirements for Windows Features 65
Exam Preparation Tasks 66
Review All the Key Topics 66
Complete the Tables and Lists from Memory 67
Definitions of Key Terms 67
Chapter 2 Installing Windows 8.1 68
"Do I Know This Already?" Quiz 69
Foundation Topics 75
Performing a Clean Installation 75
Performing an Attended Installation 75
Performing an Unattended Installation of Windows 8.1 81
Dual-Booting Windows 8.1 90
Refreshing Windows 8.1 92
Troubleshooting Failed Installations 92
Upgrading to Windows 8.1 from a Previous Version of Windows 95
Preparing a Computer to Meet Upgrade Requirements 97
Upgrading the Computer to Windows 8.1 97
Upgrading from Windows 8 to Windows 8.1 99
Upgrading from One Edition of Windows 8.1 to Another 100
Installing as Windows To Go 102
Preparing USB Drives for Windows To Go 103
Using Windows To Go on a Host Computer 107
Using a VHD 108
Understanding VHDs 109
Types of Virtual Hard Disks 109
Tools Used with Virtual Hard Disks 110
Configuring a VHD for Native Boot 111
Installing Windows 8.1 to a VHD 114
Booting VHDs 118

Installing Additional Windows Features 120
Client Hyper-V 121
Miracast Display 122
Pervasive Device Encryption 123
Virtual Smart Cards 123
Secure Boot 124
Configuring Windows for Additional Languages 124
Exam Preparation Tasks 126
Review All the Key Topics 126
Complete the Tables and Lists from Memory 128
Definitions of Key Terms 128

Chapter 3 Migrating Users and Applications to Windows 8.1 130
"Do I Know This Already?" Quiz 131
Foundation Topics 135
Migrating Users and Their Profiles 135
User State Migration Tool 135
Windows Easy Transfer 142
Configuring Folder Redirection 147
Benefits of Folder Redirection 147
Redirecting Library Folders 148
Implementing Domain-Based Folder Redirection 150
Configuring Profiles 154
Implementing Roaming Profiles 158
Establishing Mandatory Profiles 161
User Profiles and Operating System Versions 162
Exam Preparation Tasks 163
Review All the Key Topics 163
Definitions of Key Terms 163

Chapter 4 Configuring Devices and Device Drivers 164
"Do I Know This Already?" Quiz 165
Foundation Topics 169
Installing and Configuring Device Drivers 169
Device Setup 170
Device Stage 171
Updating Drivers 174
Using Device Manager 175
Maintaining Device Drivers 179
Managing and Troubleshooting Drivers and Driver Signing 180
Managing Driver Packages 183

Resolving Driver Issues 185
Using Device Manager to Resolve Driver Conflicts 185
Using Windows 8.1 Rollback to Resolve a Problem Driver 189
Configuring Driver Settings 191
Driver Verifier 191
Configuring Driver Settings 193
Advanced Driver Settings 194
Exam Preparation Tasks 196
Review All the Key Topics 196
Complete the Tables and Lists from Memory 197
Definitions of Key Terms 197
Chapter 5 Installing, Configuring, and Securing Applications in Windows 8.1 198
"Do I Know This Already?" Quiz 199
Foundation Topics 203
Installing and Configuring Desktop Applications 203
Configuring Application Compatibility Mode 203
Using the Application Compatibility Toolkit (ACT) 205
Using Windows Installer 207
Configuring File Associations and Default Program Settings 213
Managing App-V Applications 220
Using Windows Store Applications 225
Introduction to Windows Store Apps 225
Installing and Updating Windows Store Apps 226
Managing Windows Store Content 228
Configuring Application and Hardware Restrictions 230
Setting Software Restriction Policies 231
Application Control Policies 236
Configuring Assigned Access 245
Exam Preparation Tasks 246
Review All the Key Topics 246
Complete the Tables and Lists from Memory 247
Definitions of Key Terms 247
Chapter 6 Configuring Internet Explorer 248
"Do I Know This Already?" Quiz 249
Foundation Topics 253
Configuring Internet Explorer 11 and Internet Explorer for the Desktop 253
Internet Explorer Interfaces 255

Configuring Compatibility View 256

Deleting Browsing History 257

Using Group Policy to Configure Compatibility View 258

Configuring Security Settings 260

Configuring Internet Explorer Security Zones 261

Configuring Protected Mode in Internet Explorer 263

Configuring the SmartScreen Filter 263

Privacy Tab Settings 266

Content Tab Settings 269

Advanced Tab Settings 269

Managing Add-ons 271

Configuring Providers 273

Using Accelerators 275

Using InPrivate Browsing Mode 275

Configuring WebSockets 277

Configuring WebSockets in Windows 8.1 279

Using Group Policy to Configure WebSockets 280

Configuring Download Manager 280

Working with Download Manager 281

Using Group Policy to Configure Download Manager 284

Exam Preparation Tasks 284

Review All the Key Topics 284

Complete the Tables and Lists from Memory 285

Definitions of Key Terms 285

Chapter 7 Configuring Hyper-V 286

"Do I Know This Already?" Quiz 288

Foundation Topics 292

Understanding VHDs 292

Creating and Configuring VHDs 292

Mounting VHDs 296

Creating Virtual Machines 297

Enabling Client Hyper-V in Windows 8.1 298

Deploying Virtual Machines 311

Using Virtual Machine Checkpoints 315

Creating and Configuring Virtual Switches 318

Using an External Virtual Switch 321

Using Internal Virtual Switches 322

Using Private Virtual Switches 323

Connecting Virtual Machines 323

Exam Preparation Tasks 325
Review All the Key Topics 325
Definitions of Key Terms 325
Chapter 8 Configuring TCP/IP Settings 326
"Do I Know This Already?" Quiz 327
Foundation Topics 332
Understanding the TCP/IP Protocol Suite 332
Configuring TCP/IP Version 4 334
Configuring TCP/IP Version 6 339
Dynamic IP Addressing 343
Connecting to Wired Networks 344
The Network and Sharing Center 344
Using the Network and Sharing Center to Set Up a TCP/IPv4 Connection 346
Implementing APIPA 350
Connecting to a TCP/IP Version 6 Network 351
Configuring Name Resolution 354
Configuring TCP/IPv6 Name Resolution 356
Disabling IPv6 357
Configuring Network Locations 357
Setting Up New Network Connections 358
Connecting to Existing Networks 359
Setting Up Network Sharing and Discovery 359
Using Internet Connection Sharing to Share Your Internet Connection 361
Resolving Connectivity Issues 365
Windows 8.1 Network Diagnostics Tools 365
Using TCP/IP Utilities to Troubleshoot TCP/IP 367
Troubleshooting IPv4 and IPv6 Problems 372
Exam Preparation Tasks 376
Review All the Key Topics 376
Complete the Tables and Lists from Memory 377
Definitions of Key Terms 377
Chapter 9 Configuring Networking Settings 378
"Do I Know This Already?" Quiz 379
Foundation Topics 384
Connecting to Wireless Networks 384
Wireless Networking Protocols 385
Setting Up a Wireless Network Connection 386
Managing Wireless Network Connections 389

Managing Preferred Wireless Networks 392

Wireless Network Profiles 393

Configuring Network Adapters 396

Troubleshooting Network Adapter Issues 398

Configuring Location Aware Printing 401

Exam Preparation Tasks 403

Review All the Key Topics 403

Complete the Tables and Lists from Memory 403

Definitions of Key Terms 403

Chapter 10 Configuring and Maintaining Network Security 404

"Do I Know This Already?" Quiz 405

Foundation Topics 410

Configuring Windows Firewall 410

Basic Windows Firewall Configuration 411

Configuring Windows Firewall with Advanced Security 416

Configuring Multiple Firewall Profiles 418

Configuring New Firewall Rules 420

Configuring New Connection Security Rules 424

Modifying Rule Properties 426

Configuring Notifications 427

Group Policy and Windows Firewall 428

Configuring Authenticated Exceptions 430

Configuring Network Discovery 432

Managing Wireless Security 435

Exam Preparation Tasks 438

Review All the Key Topics 438

Complete the Tables and Lists from Memory 439

Definitions of Key Terms 439

Chapter 11 Configuring and Securing Access to Files and Folders 440

"Do I Know This Already?" Quiz 442

Foundation Topics 449

Configuring Shared Folder Permissions 449

Using the Network and Sharing Center to Configure File Sharing 449

Sharing Files, Folders, and Printers 450

Modifying Shared Folder Properties 452

Use of the Public Folder for Sharing Files 457

Mapping a Drive 457

Command-Line Administration of Shared Folders 458

Password-Protected Sharing 459

Media Streaming 459

Configuring Homegroup Settings 460
Creating a Homegroup 460
Joining a Homegroup 462
Modifying Homegroup Settings 463
Configuring NTFS Permissions 464
NTFS File and Folder Permissions 465
Applying NTFS Permissions 466
Specifying Advanced Permissions 468
NTFS Permissions Inheritance 472
Taking Ownership of Files and Folders 474
Effective Permissions 474
Viewing a User's Effective Permissions 475
Copying and Moving Files and Folders 476
Copying Files and Folders with NTFS Permissions 476
Moving Files and Folders with NTFS Permissions 477
Using the Mouse to Copy or Move Objects from One Location to Another 478
Practical Guidelines on Sharing and Securing Folders 478
Configuring Data Encryption 479
Encrypting File System Basics 480
Preparing a Disk for EFS 482
Encrypting Files 483
Backing Up EFS Keys 484
Decrypting Files 485
EFS Recovery Agents 486
Configuring File Libraries 487
Configuring OneDrive (formerly SkyDrive) 492
OneDrive app 493
OneDrive Desktop 496
OneDrive Settings 497
File Storage 497
Camera Roll 498
Sync Settings 498
Metered connections 499
Configuring Near Field Communication 500
Configuring Disk Quotas 502
Some Guidelines for Using Quotas 505
Configuring Object Access Auditing 506
Enabling Object Access Auditing 506
Specifying Objects to Be Audited 508

Exam Preparation Tasks 510
Review All the Key Topics 510
Complete the Tables and Lists from Memory 511
Definitions of Key Terms 511
Chapter 12 Configuring Local Security Settings 512
"Do I Know This Already?" Quiz 513
Foundation Topics 518
Configuring Local Security Policy 518
Configuring Account Policies 519
Password Policies 520
Account Lockout 521
Unlocking an Account 523
Configuring Local Policies 523
Audit Policies 523
Security Options 526
Configuring User Account Control 528
Features of User Account Control 529
Application Prompts 532
Running Programs with Elevated Privileges 534
User Account Control Options 535
User Account Control Policies 537
Configuring Secure Boot 541
Enabling UEFI Secure Boot 542
UEFI Partition Requirements 544
Using SmartScreen Filters 545
Exam Preparation Tasks 548
Review All the Key Topics 548
Definitions of Key Terms 549
Chapter 13 Configuring Authentication and Authorization 550
"Do I Know This Already?" Quiz 552
Foundation Topics 557
Controlling Windows Logon 557
Windows 8.1 Lock Screen and Logon Prompts 557
Configure Picture Password 559
Managing Credentials 563
Adding, Editing, and Removing Credentials in Credential Manager 565
Windows Credentials Backup and Restore 567
Web Credentials 568
Managing Certificates 569
Requesting Certificates 572

Configuring Smart Cards and PINs 574
Virtual Smart Cards 575
Smart Card Group Policies 577
Configuring Biometrics 578
Biometric Devices 578
Group Policies for Biometrics 579
Configuring PINs 579
Managing the Use of PINs 581
Configuring User Rights 581
Managing Local Accounts and Groups 581
Controlling User Rights 584
Setting Up and Configuring a Microsoft Account 585
Signing In Using a Microsoft Account 585
Domain Accounts 587
Managing the Use of a Microsoft Account 588
Exam Preparation Tasks 589
Review All the Key Topics 589
Definitions of Key Terms 589
Chapter 14 Configuring Remote Management and Remote Connections 590
"Do I Know This Already?" Quiz 591
Foundation Topics 596
Configuring Remote Authentication 596
Remote Authentication Planning 596
Remote Access Authentication Protocols 597
NTLM and Kerberos Authentication 599
Remote Authentication Group Policies 600
Configuring Remote Assistance and Easy Connect 601
Configuring Remote Assistance 602
Configuring and Using Easy Connect 608
Configuring Remote Desktop and Remote Management Settings 609
Remote Desktop 609
Establishing a Remote Desktop Connection with Another Computer 610
Configuring the Server Side of Remote Desktop 612
Selecting a Nondefault Port 613
Using Windows Remote Management Service 614
Using Windows Remote Shell 616
Using Windows PowerShell and MMCs for Remote Management 616
PowerShell and PowerShell ISE 617

PowerShell Remoting 620
Using MMC Snap-ins for Remote Management 623
Configuring VPN Authentication and Settings 624
Understanding Remote Access 625
Establishing VPN Connections and Authentication 626
VPN Connection Security 630
Enabling VPN Reconnect 631
Managing Broadband Connections 632
RD Gateway and DirectAccess 632
RD Gateway 633
RD Gateway Policies 635
DirectAccess 635
Exam Preparation Tasks 637
Review All the Key Topics 637
Complete the Tables and Lists from Memory 638
Definitions of Key Terms 638
Chapter 15 Configuring and Securing Mobile Devices 640
"Do I Know This Already?" Quiz 641
Foundation Topics 646
Configuring Offline File Policies 646
Client Computer Configuration 646
Server Configuration 649
Use of the Sync Center 650
Offline File Policies 653
Using the Always Offline Mode 655
Configuring Transparent Caching of Offline Files 657
Configuring Power Policies 658
Configuring Power Options 659
Power Plans 660
Additional Power Plan Options 661
Advanced Power Settings 663
Battery Meter 665
Power Management and Group Policy 667
Windows Mobility Center 668
Configuring Wi-Fi Direct 670
Configuring BitLocker and BitLocker To Go 671
BitLocker Drive Encryption 672
Enabling BitLocker 674
Managing BitLocker 677

BitLocker To Go 678
BitLocker Policies 680
Operating System Drives 680
Fixed Data Drive Policies 682
Use of Data Recovery Agents 683
Configuring Startup Key Storage 687
Preparing a Computer Without a TPM to Use BitLocker 687
Syskey Startup Keys 690
Configuring Remote Wipe 692
Device Management with Windows Intune 693
Configuring Location Settings 694
Configuring System Location 695
Configuring Windows App Location Settings 696
Location Settings Group Policies 697
Exam Preparation Tasks 698
Review All the Key Topics 698
Definitions of Key Terms 699

Chapter 16 Configuring Windows Update 700
"Do I Know This Already?" Quiz 701
Foundation Topics 704
Configuring Updates to Windows 8.1 704
Configuring Windows Update Settings 705
Checking for New Updates 709
Using a WSUS Server with Windows 8.1 710
Configuring Windows Update Policies 710
Reviewing Update History and Rolling Back Updates 714
Updating Windows Store Applications 715
Other Tools for Managing Windows App Updates 718
Exam Preparation Tasks 720
Review All the Key Topics 720

Chapter 17 Disk Management 722
"Do I Know This Already?" Quiz 723
Foundation Topics 728
Managing Disks and Volumes 728
Basic and Dynamic Disks 729
Working with Basic Disks 731
Converting Basic Disks to Dynamic 736
Working with Dynamic Disks 737
Troubleshooting Disk Problems 739

RAID Volumes 741
Creating a RAID-0 Volume 742
Creating a Spanned Volume 744
Creating a Mirrored Volume 744
Creating a RAID-5 Volume 745
Using DiskPart to Create Striped, Mirrored, and RAID-5 Volumes 745
Managing and Troubleshooting RAID Volumes 746
Managing File System Fragmentation 747
Optimizing Drives 747
The `Defrag.exe` Command-Line Tool 750
Error Checking 751
Managing Storage Spaces 751
Creating a Storage Space 752
Managing Storage Pools and Storage Spaces 754
Managing Storage Spaces with PowerShell 757
Exam Preparation Tasks 758
Review All the Key Topics 758
Complete the Tables and Lists from Memory 759
Definitions of Key Terms 759
Chapter 18 Managing and Monitoring System Performance 760
"Do I Know This Already?" Quiz 761
Foundation Topics 766
Configuring and Working with Event Logs 766
Viewing Logs in Event Viewer 767
Customizing Event Viewer 769
Creating Tasks from Events 770
Using Event Log Subscriptions 771
Configuring Computers to Forward and Collect Events 771
Configuring Event Log Subscriptions 772
Managing and Optimizing Computer Performance 775
Reliability Monitor 775
Resource Monitor 777
CPU Tab 779
Memory Tab 779
Disk Tab 779
Network Tab 780
Performance Monitor 780
Data Collector Sets 784

Creating Data Collector Sets 784
Using Performance Monitor to Create a Data Collector Set 788
Optimizing and Troubleshooting Memory Performance 789
Optimizing and Troubleshooting Processor Utilization 792
Optimizing and Troubleshooting Disk Performance 792
Command-Line Utilities 794
Configuring Task Manager 794
Configuring Additional Performance Settings 798
System Configuration Utility 799
General Tab 799
Boot Tab 800
Services Tab 800
Startup Tab 801
Tools Tab 801
Action Center 802
Configuring Services and Programs to Resolve Performance Issues 803
Configuring Indexing Options 805
Exam Preparation Tasks 808
Review All the Key Topics 808
Complete the Tables and Lists from Memory 809
Definitions of Key Terms 809
Chapter 19 Configuring System Recovery Options 810
"Do I Know This Already?" Quiz 811
Foundation Topics 815
Creating a USB Recovery Drive 815
Performing System Restore 817
Rolling Back Drivers 821
Performing a Push-Button Reset 822
Refreshing Your Computer 823
Resetting Your Computer to Original Installation Condition 827
Advanced Startup Options 830
Performing a System Image Recovery 833
Using the USB Recovery Drive 836
Configuring Restore Points 837
Exam Preparation Tasks 840
Review All the Key Topics 840
Definitions of Key Terms 840

Chapter 20 Configuring File Recovery 842

"Do I Know This Already?" Quiz 843

Foundation Topics 846

Using File History to Protect Your Data 846

Setting Up File History 847

Adding Additional Folders to File History 851

Creating a System Image 852

Using `Wbadmin` to Back Up Data 854

Restoring Previous Versions of Files and Folders 855

Using File History to Restore Damaged or Deleted Files 856

Using `Wbadmin` to Recover Data 858

Recovering Files from OneDrive 859

OneDrive and the Recycle Bin 859

OneDrive Version History 861

Exam Preparation Tasks 863

Review All the Key Topics 863

Definitions of Key Terms 863

Appendix A Answers to the "Do I Know This Already? Quizzes 864

Glossary 900

Index 922

On The CD:

Appendix B Memory Tables

Appendix C Memory Tables Answer Key

Practice Exam 1

Answers to Practice Exam 1

Practice Exam 2

Answers to Practice Exam 2

Introduction

MCSA 70-687 Cert Guide: Configuring Microsoft Windows 8.1 is designed for network administrators, network engineers, and consultants who are pursuing the Microsoft Certified Solutions Associate (MCSA) certification for Windows 8.1. This book covers the "Configuring Windows 8.1" exam (70-687), which is the first of two exams required for earning the MCSA: Windows 8, certification. The exam is designed to measure your skill and ability to implement, administer, and troubleshoot computers running all editions of Windows 8.1. Microsoft not only tests you on your knowledge of the desktop operating system (OS), but also has purposefully developed questions on the exam to force you to problem-solve in the same way that you would when presented with a real-life errors. Passing this exam demonstrates your competency in administration.

This book covers all the objectives that Microsoft has established for exam 70-687. It doesn't offer end-to-end coverage of the Windows 8.1 OS; rather, it helps you develop the specific core competencies that you need to master as a desktop support specialist. You should be able to pass the exam by learning the material in this book, without taking a class.

Goals and Methods

The number-one goal of this book is a simple one: to help you pass the Configuring Windows 8.1 Certification Exam (exam number 70-687). It is the first step in obtaining the MCSA certification in Windows 8.1, and is a stepping stone toward the Microsoft Certified Solutions Expert (MCSE) in any of several Windows fields.

Because Microsoft certification exams stress problem-solving abilities and reasoning more than memorization of terms and facts, our goal is to help you master and understand the required objectives for the 70-687 exam.

To aid you in mastering and understanding the MCSA certification objectives, this book uses the following methods:

- **Opening Topics List:** This defines the topics to be covered in the chapter.
- **Do I Know This Already? Quizzes:** At the beginning of each chapter is a quiz. The quizzes, and answers/explanations (found in Appendix A), are meant to gauge your knowledge of the subjects. If the answers to the questions don't come readily to you, be sure to read the entire chapter.
- **Foundation Topics:** The heart of the chapter. Explains the topics from a hands-on and a theory-based standpoint. This includes in-depth descriptions, tables, and figures geared to build your knowledge so that you can pass the exam. The chapters are broken down into several topics each.

- **Key Topics:** The key topics indicate important figures, tables, and lists of information that you should know for the exam. They are interspersed throughout the chapter and are listed in table form at the end of the chapter.
- **Memory Tables:** These can be found on the CD-ROM within Appendix B, "Memory Tables." Use them to help memorize important information.
- **Key Terms:** Key terms without definitions are listed at the end of each chapter. Write down the definition of each term and check your work against the complete key terms in the glossary.

Study and Exam Preparation Tips

It's a rush of adrenaline during the final day before an exam. If you've scheduled the exam on a workday, or following a workday, you will find yourself cursing the tasks you normally cheerfully perform because the back of your mind is telling you to read just a bit more, study another scenario, practice another skill so that you will be able to get this exam out of the way successfully.

The way that Microsoft has designed its tests lately does not help. I remember taking Microsoft exams many years ago and thoroughly understanding the term "paper certified." Nowadays, you can't get through a Microsoft exam without knowing the material so well that when confronted with a problem, whether a scenario or real-life situation, you can handle the challenge. Instead of trying to show the world how many MCSAs or MCSEs are out there, Microsoft is trying to prove how difficult it is to achieve a certification, thereby making those who are certified more valuable to their organizations.

Learning Styles

To best understand the nature of preparation for the test, you need to understand learning as a process. You are probably aware of how you best learn new material. You might find that outlining works best for you, or, as a visual learner, you might need to "see" things. Or, as a person who studies kinesthetically, the hands-on approach serves you best. Whether you might need models or examples, or maybe you just like exploring the interface, or whatever your learning style, solid test preparation works best when it takes place over time. Obviously, you shouldn't start studying for a certification exam the night before you take it; it is very important to understand that learning is a developmental process. Understanding learning as a process helps you focus on what you know and what you have yet to learn.

People study in a combination of different ways: by doing, by seeing, and by hearing and writing. This book's design fulfills all three of these study methods. For the kinesthetic, there are key topics scattered throughout each chapter. You will also discover step-by-step procedural instructions that walk you through the skills you need to master in Windows 8.1. The visual learner can find plenty of screen shots explaining the concepts described in the text. The auditory learner can reinforce skills by reading out loud and copying down key concepts and exam tips scattered throughout the book. You can also practice writing down the meaning of the key terms defined in each chapter, and in completing the memory tables for most chapters found on the accompanying CD-ROM. While reading this book, you will realize that it stands the test of time. You will be able to turn to it over and over again.

Thinking about how you learn should help you recognize that learning takes place when you are able to match new information to old. You have some previous experience with computers and networking. Now you are preparing for this certification exam. Using this book, software, and supplementary materials will not just add incrementally to what you know; as you study, the organization of your knowledge actually restructures as you integrate new information into your existing knowledge base. This leads you to a more comprehensive understanding of the tasks and concepts outlined in the objectives and of computing in general. Again, this happens as a result of a repetitive process rather than a singular event. If you keep this model of learning in mind as you prepare for the exam, you will make better decisions concerning what to study and how much more studying you need to do.

Study Tips

There are many ways to approach studying, just as there are many different types of material to study. However, the tips that follow should work well for the type of material covered on Microsoft certification exams.

Study Strategies

Although individuals vary in the ways they learn information, some basic principles of learning apply to everyone. You should adopt some study strategies that take advantage of these principles. One of these principles is that learning can be broken into various depths. Recognition (of terms, for example) exemplifies a rather surface level of learning in which you rely on a prompt of some sort to elicit recall. Comprehension or understanding (of the concepts behind the terms, for example) represents a deeper level of learning than recognition. The ability to analyze a concept and apply your understanding of it in a new way represents further depth of learning.

Your learning strategy should enable you to know the material at a level or two deeper than mere recognition. This will help you perform well on the exams. You will know the material so thoroughly that you can go beyond the recognition-level types of questions commonly used in fact-based multiple-choice testing. You will be able to apply your knowledge to solve new problems.

Macro and Micro Study Strategies

One strategy that can lead to deep learning includes preparing an outline that covers all the objectives and subobjectives for the particular exam you are planning to take. You should delve a bit further into the material and include a level or two of detail beyond the stated objectives and subobjectives for the exam. Then you should expand the outline by coming up with a statement of definition or a summary for each point in the outline.

An outline provides two approaches to studying. First, you can study the outline by focusing on the organization of the material. You can work your way through the points and subpoints of your outline, with the goal of learning how they relate to one another. For example, you should be sure you understand how each of the main objective areas for Exam 70-687 is similar to and different from another. Then you should do the same thing with the subobjectives; you should be sure you know which subobjectives pertain to each objective area and how they relate to one another.

Next, you can work through the outline, focusing on learning the details. You should memorize and understand terms and their definitions, facts, rules and tactics, advantages and disadvantages, and so on. In this pass through the outline, you should attempt to learn detail rather than the big picture (that is, the organizational information that you worked on in the first pass through the outline).

Research has shown that attempting to assimilate both types of information at the same time interferes with the overall learning process. If you separate your studying into these two approaches, you will perform better on the exam.

Active Study Strategies

The process of writing down and defining objectives, subobjectives, terms, facts, and definitions promotes a more active learning strategy than merely reading the material does. In human information-processing terms, writing forces you to engage in more active encoding of the information. Simply reading over the information leads to more passive processing. Using this study strategy, you should focus on writing down the items highlighted in the book: bulleted or numbered lists, key topics, notes, cautions, and review sections, for example.

You need to determine whether you can apply the information you have learned by attempting to create examples and scenarios on your own. You should think about how or where you could apply the concepts you are learning. Again, you should write down this information to process the facts and concepts in an active fashion.

Common-Sense Strategies

You should follow common-sense practices when studying: You should study when you are alert, reduce or eliminate distractions, and take breaks when you become fatigued.

Pretesting Yourself

Pretesting enables you to assess how well you are learning. One of the most important aspects of learning is what has been called *meta-learning*. Meta-learning has to do with realizing when you know something well or when you need to study some more. In other words, you recognize how well or how poorly you have learned the material you are studying.

For most people, this can be difficult to assess. Memory tables, practice questions, and practice tests are useful in that they reveal objectively what you have learned and what you have not learned. You should use this information to guide review and further studying. Developmental learning takes place as you cycle through studying, assessing how well you have learned, reviewing, and assessing again until you feel you are ready to take the exam.

You might have noticed the practice exam included in this book. You should use it as part of the learning process. The Pearson IT Certification Practice Test engine included on this book's CD-ROM also provides you with an excellent opportunity to assess your knowledge.

You should set a goal for your pretesting. A reasonable goal would be to score consistently in the 90% range.

Exam Prep Tips

After you have mastered the subject matter, the final preparatory step is to understand how the exam will be presented. Make no mistake: An MCSA exam challenges both your knowledge and your test-taking skills. Preparing for the 70-687 exam is a bit different from preparing for those old Microsoft exams. The following is a list of things that you should consider doing:

- **Combine Your Skill Sets into Solutions:** In the past, exams would test whether you knew to select the right letter of a multiple-choice answer. Today, you need to know how to resolve a problem that might involve different aspects of the material covered. For example, on exam 70-687, you could be presented with a problem that requires you to understand how to incorporate drivers in an unattended installation, as well as what errors you might see if you installed a computer that used a device driver incompatible with Windows 8.1. The skills themselves are simple. Being able to zero in on what caused the problem and then to resolve it for a specific situation is what you need to demonstrate. In fact, you should not only be able to select one answer, but also multiple parts of a total solution.

- **Delve into Excruciating Details:** The exam questions incorporate a great deal of information in the scenarios. Some of the information is ancillary: It will help you rule out possible issues, but not necessarily resolve the answer. Some of the information simply provides you with a greater picture, as you would have in real life. Some information is key to your solution. For example, you might be presented with a question that lists a computer's hard disk size, memory size, and detailed hardware configuration. When you delve further into the question, you realize that the hardware configuration is the problem. Other times, you will find that the hardware configuration simply eliminates one or more of the answers that you could select. For example, a portable laptop does not support dynamic disks, so if the hardware configuration is a portable laptop and one of the answers is a dynamic disk configuration, you can eliminate it. If you don't pay attention to what you can eliminate, the answer can elude you completely. Other times, the hardware configuration simply lets you know that the hardware is adequate.

- **TCP/IP Troubleshooting Is Built Right In:** Because TCP/IP is a core technology to the Windows 8.1 operating system, you are expected to know how to configure the operating system, how to recognize IP conflicts, and how to use the TCP/IP tools to troubleshoot the problem. Furthermore, Microsoft expects you to know how to work with the new version 6 of TCP/IP along with the traditional version 4 that has been used for many years. You should also be able to discern between an IP problem and something wrong with the OS or hardware, or even some combination that involves IP along with some other element.

- **It's a GUI Test:** Microsoft has expanded its testing criteria into interface recognition. You should be able to recognize each dialog box, properties sheet, options, and defaults. You will be tested on how to navigate the new interface: for example, the new Start screen and apps used by Windows 8.1, as well as the Category View shown in Control Panel. If you have not yet learned the new interface, you might end up selecting answers that are deliberately placed to confuse a person used to the old Windows desktop. Of course, if you know the difference between the two, you'll be able to spot the old ones and avoid them.

- **Practice with a Time Limit:** The tests have always been time restricted, but it takes more time to read and understand the scenarios now and time is a whole lot tighter. To get used to the time limits, test yourself with a timer. Know how long it takes you to read scenarios and select answers.

Microsoft 70-687 Exam Topics

Table I-1 lists the exam topics for the Microsoft 70-687 exam. This table also lists the book parts in which each exam topic is covered.

Table I-1 Microsoft 70-687 Exam Topics

Chapter	Title	70-687 Exam Topics Covered
Chapter 1	Introducing Windows 8.1	**Evaluate hardware readiness and compatibility** ■ Choose between an upgrade and a clean installation; determine which SKU to use, including Windows RT; determine requirements for particular features, including Hyper-V, Miracast display, pervasive device encryption, virtual smart cards, and Secure Boot
Chapter 2	Installing Windows 8.1	**Install Windows 8.1** ■ Install as Windows To Go, migrate from previous versions of Windows to Windows 8.1, upgrade from Windows 7 or Windows 8 to Windows 8.1, install to VHD, install additional Windows features, configure Windows for additional languages
Chapter 3	Migrating Users and Applications to Windows 8.1	**Migrate and configure user data** ■ Migrate user profiles; configure folder location; configure profiles, including profile version, local, roaming, and mandatory
Chapter 4	Configuring Devices and Device Drivers	**Configure devices and device drivers** ■ Install, update, disable, and roll back drivers; resolve driver issues; configure driver settings, including signed and unsigned drivers; manage driver packages
Chapter 5	Installing, Configuring, and Securing Applications in Windows 8.1	**Install and configure desktop apps and Windows Store apps** ■ Install and repair applications by using Windows Installer, configure default program settings, modify file associations, manage access to Windows Store
Chapter 6	Configuring Internet Explorer	**Configure Internet Explorer 11 and Internet Explorer for the desktop** ■ Configure compatibility view; configure Internet Explorer 11 settings, including add-ons, downloads, security, and privacy

Chapter 7	Configuring Hyper-V	**Configure Hyper-V** ■ Create and configure virtual machines, including integration services; create and manage checkpoints; create and configure virtual switches; create and configure virtual disks; move a virtual machine's storage
Chapter 8	Configuring TCP/IP Settings	**Configure IP settings** ■ Configure name resolution, connect to a network, configure network locations
Chapter 9	Configuring Networking Settings	**Configure networking settings** ■ Connect to a wireless network, manage preferred wireless networks, configure network adapters, configure location-aware printing
Chapter 10	Configuring and Maintaining Network Security	**Configure and maintain network security** ■ Configure Windows Firewall, configure Windows Firewall with Advanced Security, configure connection security rules (IPsec), configure authenticated exceptions, configure network discovery
Chapter 11	Configuring and Securing Access to Files and Folders	**Configure shared resources** ■ Configure shared folder permissions, configure HomeGroup settings, configure libraries, configure shared printers, set up and configure OneDrive **Configure file and folder access** ■ Encrypt files and folders by using Encrypting File System (EFS), configure NTFS permissions, configure disk quotas, configure file access auditing
Chapter 12	Configuring Local Security Settings	**Configure local security settings** ■ Configure local security policy, configure User Account Control (UAC) behavior, configure Secure Boot, configure SmartScreen filter
Chapter 13	Configuring Authentication and Authorization	**Configure authentication and authorization** ■ Configure user rights, manage credentials, manage certificates, configure biometrics, configure picture password, configure PIN, set up and configure Microsoft account, configure virtual smart cards, configure authentication in workgroups or domains, configure User Account Control (UAC) behavior

Chapter 14	Configuring Remote Management and Remote Connections	**Configure remote management** ■ Choose the appropriate remote management tools; configure remote management settings; modify settings remotely by using MMCs or Windows PowerShell; configure Remote Assistance, including Easy Connect **Configure remote connections** ■ Configure remote authentication, configure Remote Desktop settings, configure virtual private network (VPN) connections and authentication, enable VPN reconnect, configure broadband tethering
Chapter 15	Configuring and Securing Mobile Devices	**Configure mobility options** ■ Configure offline file policies, configure power policies, configure Windows To Go, configure sync options, configure WiFi direct **Configure security for mobile devices** ■ Configure BitLocker and BitLocker To Go, configure startup key storage
Chapter 16	Configuring Windows Update	**Configure and manage updates** ■ Configure update settings, configure Windows Update policies, manage update history, roll back updates, update Windows Store apps
Chapter 17	Disk Management	**Manage local storage** ■ Manage disk volumes and file systems, manage storage spaces
Chapter 18	Managing and Monitoring System Performance	**Monitor system performance** ■ Configure and analyze event logs, configure event subscriptions, configure Task Manager, monitor system resources, optimize networking performance, configure indexing options
Chapter 19	Configuring System Recovery Options	**Configure system recovery** ■ Configure a recovery drive, configure system restore, perform a driver rollback, perform a refresh or recycle, configure restore points
Chapter 20	Configuring File Recovery	**Configure file recovery** ■ Restore previous versions of files and folders, configure file history, recover files from OneDrive

How This Book Is Organized

Although this book could be read cover to cover, it is designed to be flexible and enable you to easily move between chapters and sections of chapters to cover just the material that you need more work with. If you do intend to read all the chapters, the order in the book is an excellent sequence to use.

- **Chapter 1, "Introducing Windows 8.1":** This introductory chapter is designed to ease readers who are new to Windows 8.1 into this book. It provides a broad description of the components of the Windows 8.1 operating system, including the major items that are new or recently updated, the Start screen and desktop interfaces, and the Control Panel components. It then goes on to identify the requirements for running Windows 8.1 on your computer.
- **Chapter 2, "Installing Windows 8.1":** This chapter covers installing Windows 8.1 on a new computer without an operating system.
- **Chapter 3, "Migrating Users and Applications to Windows 8.1":** This chapter discusses the procedures available for getting users of older computers working on new Windows 8.1 computers with a minimum of delay. It then describes procedures involved in redirecting the location of standard library folders and configuring user profiles.
- **Chapter 4, "Configuring Devices and Device Drivers":** This chapter covers procedures you might use to set up and configure a variety of hardware devices, including use of the drivers that interface these devices with the Windows operating system.
- **Chapter 5, "Installing, Configuring, and Securing Applications in Windows 8.1":** Applications are the heart of any work done by users with Windows 8.1 computers. This chapter discusses methods you might use to set up applications and configure or troubleshoot options with these applications, including the new Windows Store applications included by default with every Windows 8.1 computer. It also describes policies that you can employ to limit the applications that users can run on their Windows 8.1 computers.
- **Chapter 6, "Configuring Internet Explorer":** Windows 8.1 includes two versions of Internet Explorer 11—the Start screen version and Internet Explorer for the Desktop. This chapter describes the differences between these versions and shows you how to configure various security settings that limit the ability of malicious Internet content to display on the computer.
- **Chapter 7, "Configuring Hyper-V":** Virtualization is becoming increasingly prevalent in the corporate world these days, and this chapter discusses methods available for creating and using virtual machines, virtual hard disks, and virtual network switches.

- **Chapter 8, "Configuring TCP/IP Settings":** This chapter discusses versions 4 and 6 of the TCP/IP protocol together with setting up network connections and name resolution. It also discusses network connectivity problems.
- **Chapter 9, "Configuring Networking Settings":** This chapter describes the methodology involved in connecting to and managing wireless networks. It then goes on to discuss issues that might occur with network adapters and concludes with a discussion of location-aware printing.
- **Chapter 10, "Configuring and Maintaining Network Security":** This chapter discusses the methods available for configuring and maintaining Windows Firewall, as well as network discovery and wireless network security.
- **Chapter 11, "Configuring and Securing Access to Files and Folders":** This chapter covers sharing of files, folders, and printers and restricting access to these resources by users and groups. It also covers the use of the Encrypting File System (EFS) to provide an extra layer of security to sensitive documents.
- **Chapter 12, "Configuring Local Security Settings":** This chapter discusses various local security settings that help to protect your Windows 8.1 computer, including User Account Control, Secure Boot, and SmartScreen Filters.
- **Chapter 13, "Configuring Authentication and Authorization":** This chapter describes methods available for verifying the identity of objects, services, and users that are connecting to Windows 8.1. It shows you how to manage credentials, certificates, smart cards, and PINs used in authenticating users to Windows 8.1 and authorizing their connections to various resources.
- **Chapter 14, "Configuring Remote Management and Remote Connections":** More and more users need to connect to corporate networks from diverse locations such as home, hotels, and client locations. This chapter covers all methods used for creating, authenticating, and troubleshooting these remote connections.
- **Chapter 15, "Configuring and Securing Mobile Devices":** This chapter covers topics of special interest to users with portable computers, including data protection, network access, power options, Wi-Fi Direct, startup key storage, Remote Wipe, and Windows Location Services.
- **Chapter 16, "Configuring Windows Update":** This chapter covers methods you might use to ensure that computers are kept up-to-date with the latest Microsoft patches, hotfixes, and service packs.
- **Chapter 17, "Disk Management":** This chapter discusses methods you would use for installing and managing disks and disk volumes and troubleshooting problems you might encounter with disks.

- **Chapter 18, "Managing and Monitoring System Performance":** This chapter focuses on computer performance and looks at factors that might cause degraded performance and steps you might take to restore performance to an acceptable level.
- **Chapter 19, "Configuring System Recovery Options":** This chapter covers methods you can use to recover computers that have encountered startup and other problems.
- **Chapter 20, "Configuring File Recovery":** This chapter discusses the new File History feature in Windows 8.1 that is now the primary application for backing up and recovering data on your computer. It also shows you how to recover files and previous versions of files from OneDrive.

In addition to the 20 main chapters, this book includes tools to help you verify that you are prepared to take the exam. The CD includes the glossary, practice tests, and memory tables that you can work through to verify your knowledge of the subject matter.

About the Authors

Don Poulton (A+, Network+, Security+, MCSA, MCSE) is an independent consultant who has been involved with computers since the days of 80-column punch cards. After a career of more than 20 years in environmental science, Don switched careers and trained as a Windows NT 4.0 MCSE. He has been involved in consulting with a couple of small training providers as a technical writer, during which time he wrote training and exam prep materials for Windows NT 4.0, Windows 2000, and Windows XP. Don has written or contributed to several titles, including *Security+ Lab Manual* (Que, 2004); *MCSA/MCSE 70-299 Exam Cram 2: Implementing and Administering Security in a Windows 2003 Network (Exam Cram 2)* (Que, 2004); *MCSE 70-294 Exam Prep: Planning, Implementing, and Maintaining a Microsoft Windows Server 2003 Active Directory Infrastructure* (Que, 2006); *MCTS 70-620 Exam Prep: Microsoft Windows Vista, Configuring* (Que, 2008); *MCTS 70-680 Cert Guide: Microsoft Windows 7, Configuring* (Que, 2011); *MCTS 70-640 Cert Guide: Windows Server 2008 Active Directory, Configuring* (Que, 2011); and *MCTS 70-642 Cert Guide: Windows Server 2008 Network Infrastructure, Configuring* (Que, 2012).

In addition, he has worked on programming projects, both in his days as an environmental scientist and more recently with Visual Basic, to update an older statistical package used for multivariate analysis of sediment contaminants.

When not working on computers, Don is an avid amateur photographer who has had his photos displayed in international competitions and published in magazines such as *Michigan Natural Resources Magazine* and *National Geographic Traveler*. Don also enjoys traveling and keeping fit.

Don lives in Burlington, Ontario, with his wife, Terry.

Randy Bellet: After establishing himself as a retailer in Richmond, Virginia, curiosity about the fledgling small computer industry brought Randy Bellet into the IT field in 1981. Beginning with the TRS-DOS operating system on a Radio Shack Model III and "sneaker-net," he automated his and other businesses, initially programming spreadsheets using one of the original versions of VisiCalc. Hardware consisted of 32K of RAM, monochrome monitors, and no hard drives. Data was stored on floppy disks that really flopped. After the PC-XT and its clones arrived, he followed the market and extended his skills into the networking of PCs and XENIX servers and wrote applications for the retail and pager industries.

As PCs became commonplace and their connectivity a necessity, Randy configured Windows client-server networks for small and medium-sized businesses, and wrote n-tier applications on various Windows platforms ranging from Windows 3.1 through Windows 2008 Server for the medical, insurance, food, and leisure industries. As organizations expanded and scaled their uses of PCs, extracting data from mainframes for use in Windows applications became a specialty.

Since 1999, Mr. Bellet has been on the faculty of ECPI University, delivering and developing courses in Network Security and Programming, and writing ancillary instructor materials. Certifications include CompTIA Network +, MCSE, MCSD, and MCDBA. He holds a bachelor's degree in economics and marketing from New York University, and a master's degree in IT from Virginia Tech.

Harry Holt started his career in the early 1980s while working in trust accounting, where he discovered the advantages of Lotus 123 over paper spreadsheets, and how much better D:Base was at tracking transactions than a cabinet full of 3x5 index cards. That prompted a career change, and Harry took advantage of the burgeoning IT program at Virginia Commonwealth University's prestigious School of Business to hone his knowledge.

Harry gained experience over the years in most technical roles in the industry—from computer operator, programmer, LAN administrator, to network engineer, DBA, and project manager, among others. He has used his skills to improve efficiencies in a range of organizations including Fortune 500 companies, financial institutions, government agencies, and even small partnerships and sole proprietorships.

Exploring aspects of the computer industry both professionally, as a hobby, and as a volunteer for various non-profit organizations, Harry gained a working knowledge of many types of systems from large IBM z/OS mainframes, VAX systems, and Unix platforms, to Windows, Macintosh, and Linux systems. He can program in a variety of development languages and platforms, and enjoys collaborating in open source projects. Harry has a bachelor's degree in IT with a PMP certification, and is currently working as a Cyber Applications Manager in Richmond, Virginia.

Dedications

I would like to dedicate this book to my newest grandson Blake, who holds a world of international love in his future with his Chinese/Canadian heritage.
—Don Poulton

Dedicated to Evelyn, Rachel, and Sarah, all of whom supported my career choices at every turn.
—Randy Bellet

Dedicated to Donna, who taught me about healthy eating, which really helped while working on this book.
—Harry Holt

Acknowledgments

I would like to thank all the staff at Pearson IT Certification and, in particular, Betsy Brown, for making this project possible. My sincere thanks go out to Chris Crayton for his helpful technical suggestions, as well as development editors Ellie Bru and Chris Cleveland for their improvements to the manuscript. Thanks especially to Randy Bellet and Harry Holt for their contributions, without which this entire project would never have been possible.

—Don Poulton

Thanks to everyone at Pearson including Betsy Brown, who brought me on board; Chris Crayton and Chris Cleveland, who did everything to move this project along, even though the technology changed as we were writing; and to Vanessa Evans. Thanks especially to Don Poulton, who set the standard, and to Harry Holt, whose tireless efforts and research made this all something special.

—Randy Bellet

Thanks to all the professional folks at Pearson for their help, including Chris Crayton and Chris Cleveland. Without their patience and attention to detail, the project could not have happened. Thanks also to Betsy Brown for her support on the project. Special thanks is owed to Don Poulton, who had the experience to set the foundation we built upon, and to Randy Bellet, who helped keep me focused on task and made the work a pleasant experience.

—Harry Holt

We Want to Hear from You!

As the reader of this book, *you* are our most important critic and commentator. We value your opinion and want to know what we're doing right, what we could do better, what areas you'd like to see us publish in, and any other words of wisdom you're willing to pass our way.

We welcome your comments. You can email or write to let us know what you did or didn't like about this book—as well as what we can do to make our books better.

Please note that we cannot help you with technical problems related to the topic of this book.

When you write, please be sure to include this book's title and authors as well as your name, email address, and phone number. We will carefully review your comments and share them with the authors and editors who worked on the book.

Email: feedback@pearsonitcertification.com

Mail: ATTN: Reader Feedback
Pearson IT Certification
800 East 96th Street
Indianapolis, IN 46240 USA

Reader Services

Visit our website and register this book at www.pearsonitcertification.com/register for convenient access to any updates, downloads, or errata that might be available for this book.

This chapter covers the following subjects:

- **Leading Up to Windows 8.1:** Windows 8.1 is the latest in a long hierarchy of Microsoft operating systems. This section traces the history of Windows as it has unfolded in the past 25-plus years.
- **New Features of Windows 8 and Windows 8.1:** Windows 8.1 presents a brand-new user interface, together with many new and improved features designed to help users work smartly and securely. This section provides a brief overview of new and improved features in Windows 8.1.
- **A Quick Tour of Windows 8.1:** This section introduces the Windows 8.1 Start button and screen, charms, and desktop. It also provides a brief introduction to the features of the Control Panel.
- **Evaluating Hardware Readiness and Compatibility:** This section discusses factors that you need to know prior to installing Windows 8.1, such as hardware requirements, screen resolution, upgrades versus clean installs, and so on.

CHAPTER 1

Introducing Windows 8.1

In recent years, more and more individuals have been attracted to mobile devices such as smartphones and tablets marketed by manufacturers such as Apple, BlackBerry, and Android, equipped with touch screens that have become increasingly simple to use and navigate. Accompanying these devices is an increasing number of simple applications (known simply as apps) that enable the user to perform tasks such as locating restaurants while in a strange city, or knowing when her kids arrive home from school. At the same time, computer manufacturers have come out with laptops and mobile devices equipped with touch-sensitive displays; additionally, touch-sensitive monitors have become available for the still ubiquitous desktop computer.

Windows 7 brought with it significant enhancements in the usability and security of Microsoft's flagship operating system. Included was an array of touch-sensitive options, but they lacked considerably behind those being offered by competitors in the mobile device business. Windows 8 represents Microsoft's efforts to add a level of touch-sensitive capability and easily used apps, while at the same time catering to the masses who still employ the traditional mouse-based desktop and laptop computers.

"Do I Know This Already?" Quiz

The "Do I Know This Already?" quiz allows you to assess whether you should read this entire chapter or simply jump to the "Exam Preparation Tasks" section for review. If you are in doubt, read the entire chapter. Table 1-1 outlines the major headings in this chapter and the corresponding "Do I Know This Already?" quiz questions. You can find the answers in Appendix A, "Answers to the 'Do I Know This Already?' Quizzes."

Table 1-1 "Do I Know This Already?" Foundation Topics Section-to-Question Mapping

Foundation Topics Section	Questions Covered in This Section
Leading Up to Windows 8.1	1
New Features of Windows 8 and Windows 8.1	2
A Quick Tour of Windows 8.1	3–5
Evaluating Hardware Readiness and Compatibility	6–10

1. What is the version of Windows 8.1 designed for running on mobile platforms called?
   - a. Windows PE
   - b. Windows RT 8.1
   - c. Windows NT
   - d. Windows 8.1 Home Basic

2. Which of the following actions requires that you install Windows 8.1 Pro or Windows 8.1 Enterprise as opposed to the basic version of Windows 8.1? (Choose all that apply.)
   - a. Joining a Windows Server domain
   - b. Running Windows Media Center
   - c. Using more than one monitor on your computer
   - d. Encrypting files using Encrypting File System (EFS)

3. How do you access the Windows 8.1 charms from the Start screen?
   - a. Swipe your finger into the screen from either the top-left or bottom-left corner on a touch-screen device; on a conventional computer, move the pointer to either of these corners.
   - b. Swipe your finger into the screen from either the top-right or bottom-right corner on a touch-screen device; on a conventional computer, move the pointer to either of these corners.
   - c. Click **Start** and then type `charms` in the Search dialog box.
   - d. Right-click a blank area on the Start screen and choose **charms** from the pop-up menu that appears.

4. Which of the following tasks can you perform from the new PC Settings screen in Windows 8.1? (Choose all that apply.)
   - a. Select lock screen, start screen, and wallpaper images
   - b. Create new user accounts

   c. Specify time zone and language options
   d. Install hardware devices
   e. Configure accessibility options
   f. Create a new HomeGroup or join an existing HomeGroup

5. How do you add icons for Windows 8.1 Administrative Tools to the Start screen?
   a. Open the Charms bar and select **Search**. Type the name of the administrative tool(s) that you require and then press **Enter**.
   b. Open the Charms bar and select **Search**. From the list of applications that appears, select the administrative tool(s) that you require and then press **Enter**.
   c. From File Explorer, click **Tools > Settings**. In the dialog box that appears, toggle the switch under **Administrative Tools** to **On**.
   d. Open the Charms bar and select **Settings**. From the Settings bar, select **Tiles** and then toggle the switch under **Administrative Tools** to **On**.

6. What is the minimum processor speed required for a Windows 8.1 computer?
   a. 1 GHz
   b. 2 GHz
   c. 3 GHz
   d. 4 GHz

7. What is the minimum amount of hard drive space required for a 64-bit Windows 8.1 installation?
   a. 10 GB
   b. 15 GB
   c. 16 GB
   d. 20 GB
   e. 40 GB

8. Which of the following is true about the use of the 64-bit Windows operating system? (Choose all that apply.)
   a. Most 32-bit programs can run efficiently on a 64-bit machine, with the exception of some antivirus programs.
   b. The 32-bit programs will not run on a 64-bit machine; you must upgrade all 32-bit programs to 64-bit.

   c. Programs specifically designed to run on a 64-bit machine won't work on 32-bit Windows.
   d. You need 64-bit device drivers to use all your hardware devices with 64-bit Windows. Drivers designed for 32-bit Windows won't work on a machine running 64-bit Windows.
   e. Any device driver written for 32-bit Windows will work perfectly well on a 64-bit Windows machine.

9. Which of the following is true regarding the performing of an upgrade installation of Windows 8.1 versus a clean installation?
   a. A clean installation maintains all Windows settings, personal files, and applications from the previous Windows installation, whereas an upgrade installation of Windows 8.1 requires that you reinstall all programs and re-create all Windows settings.
   b. An upgrade installation maintains all Windows settings, personal files, and applications from the previous Windows installation, whereas a clean installation of Windows 8.1 requires that you reinstall all programs and re-create all Windows settings.
   c. An upgrade installation maintains Windows settings from the previous Windows installation but requires that you reinstall all programs. A clean installation maintains programs from the previous Windows installation but requires that you re-create all Windows settings.
   d. Both a clean installation and an upgrade installation require that you reinstall all programs and re-create all Windows settings.

10. What is the major difference between a Windows 8.1 upgrade SKU and a Windows 8.1 full edition SKU?
   a. The upgrade SKU contains only the Windows components that have changed since Windows 7; it picks up unchanged components from the current Windows installation.
   b. The two SKUs have identical features, but the upgrade SKU searches the computer for evidence of an older Windows installation before allowing installation of Windows 8.1 at all.
   c. The two SKUs have identical features, but the upgrade SKU requires that you provide a correct product code for a valid earlier Windows version before installation will begin.
   d. The two SKUs have identical features, but the upgrade SKU searches the computer for evidence of an older Windows installation before allowing the new Windows 8.1 to be activated.

Foundation Topics

Leading Up to Windows 8.1

Computers running some version of Microsoft Windows have been with us since the mid-1980s, when Windows 1.0 was first released. Most people first discovered Windows with versions 3.1 and Windows for Workgroups 3.11 in the early 1990s. As this decade progressed, Microsoft released Windows 95, which sported the first graphical user interface (GUI) that is the oldest original ancestor to the GUI used in much the same form to the most recent Windows 7.

At the same time, Microsoft developed an industrial-strength, 32-bit networking system known as Windows NT. Starting with Windows NT 3.1 and progressing to Windows NT 3.5 and Windows NT 3.51, this operating system used the same GUI as displayed by the consumer-oriented Windows versions. In 1996, Microsoft released Windows NT 4.0, which brought the Windows 95-style GUI to the NT system of Windows operating systems. Following soon afterward was Windows 2000 Professional. Also available were server versions of each of these operating systems.

At this point, Microsoft brought the home and corporate user versions together under the Windows NT kernel. The home user version became Windows XP Home edition, while the corporate version was Windows XP Professional. They differed in that Windows XP Professional contained additional components (many of which had been present in Windows 2000) designed for integration into corporate, server-based networks. Microsoft also added a complete entertainment software package including support for watching and recording TV shows and working with digital music and videos to Windows XP Professional to create the Windows XP Media Center edition.

The early 2000s were plagued with security problems, which forced Microsoft to work hard on enhancing the security behind Windows XP, a task that included the introduction of many security patches and three service packs. This resulted in numerous delays in the next release of the Windows operating system, originally code-named "Longhorn" and finally named Windows Vista when it was released to the public on January 30, 2007. But Windows Vista had its own problems that resulted in large segments of the population having a negative opinion of the operating system for numerous reasons such as the need for more powerful hardware, added features that required a steep learning curve, business applications not running properly, and the lack of appropriate device drivers for many hardware devices in use at that time. Consequently, Windows Vista was not widely accepted; many purchasers used the downgrade license that was provided to run Windows XP, particularly within corporations.

So Microsoft placed high priority in readying a new version of its flagship operating system with the strong hope of alleviating these concerns and developing a secure, well-planned version of Windows that would be much more well accepted by individuals and corporations around the world. The result was Windows 7, which Microsoft released to manufacturers on July 22, 2009, and to the general public on October 22, 2009.

At the same time, cellular phone manufacturers were increasing the capability of their devices, turning them into miniature computers that could surf the Internet and run many applications that had previously been unthought of. Users became able to access apps and surf the Internet with a mere touch of the screen. Although Windows 7 brought touch capabilities to computers equipped with the appropriate hardware, the usability of these devices lagged considerably behind the new smartphones. Further, Microsoft was entering the smartphone market with its new Windows Phone 7 operating system. Based on Windows 7, these phones lacked the capability of those running Apple iOS, BlackBerry, or Android devices. Developers at Microsoft were aware of these shortcomings even before Windows 7 was released, and started development of Windows 8. A total redesign of the user interface was in the works with the new touch-enabled devices and smartphones brought to the forefront of developer action. The result of this feverish activity is a new interface that replaces the familiar Start button with a completely new Start screen (also known as the Metro screen), which includes by default a large range of apps similar to those you would see on an iOS, BlackBerry, or Android device. Microsoft released a Consumer Preview (beta) of the new operating system on February 29, 2012, and followed with the release to manufacturing of the final version on August 1, 2012, and general availability of Windows 8 on October 26, 2012.

Windows 8.1

Consumer reaction to modified features introduced in Windows 8 was swift; in particular, most users of the new operating system lamented the disappearance of the Start button and the fact that the computer now booted up into an unfamiliar Start screen containing tiles rather than the familiar desktop and icons. Sales of Windows 8 computers lagged considerably in its first few months of availability, compared to those of Windows 7 after its introduction. Debates about the future of Windows 8 raged, with some detractors suggesting that Windows 8 was faring even worse in its first few months than Windows Vista had at a similar point in time after initial release. Several third-party software providers introduced Start menu substitutes designed to provide an experience closer to that of Windows 7. Microsoft responded in early 2013 by beginning development on a new Windows build initially codenamed "Blue." By April 2013, it was announced that Windows Blue would be named Windows 8.1, and that upgrades would be free for existing users of Windows 8. Microsoft then released a Consumer Preview of Windows 8.1 on June 26, 2013, followed by the release to manufacturing of the final version of Windows 8.1 on August 24, 2013, and general availability of Windows 8.1 on October 18, 2013.

NOTE As this book was in the final writing stages, Microsoft announced the impending release of Windows 8.1 Update 1 for April 8, 2014. This update is intended to improve the familiarity of the operating system to individuals who are used to working with Windows 7 or older computers, especially those who do not use touch screens. This update will include a new right-click context menu for Windows Store apps, which enables you to pin them to the taskbar, unpin from the Start screen, or uninstall. You can also resize or turn off live tiles from this menu. The top of these apps will now include a title bar.

Windows 8.1 Editions

Many consumers found the large number of Windows 7 editions confusing, so Microsoft opted to reduce the number of editions available in Windows 8 and Windows 8.1. Available are the following four editions:

- **Windows RT 8.1:** This mobile operating system is especially designed to run on mobile devices utilizing the ARM architecture, such as smartphones and tablets. Windows RT 8.1 succeeds Windows RT; it is only available preinstalled on ARM-based devices or by upgrading from Windows RT. ARM is a hardware platform originally developed by ARM Industries in England, and provides ultraminiaturized system chips that enable thinner, more powerful devices with improved battery life. Limited to running built-in apps or apps downloaded from the Windows Store, however, Microsoft Office 2013 RT is included with these computers and includes Office 2013 RT versions of Word, Excel, PowerPoint, OneNote, and Outlook.
- **Windows 8.1:** Descended from the Home Basic and Home Premium editions of Windows 7, this edition is designed for home users who do not require domain membership or enhanced security features.
- **Windows 8.1 Pro:** This full-fledged version of Windows 8.1 supports enterprise requirements such as the need to join Active Directory domains.
- **Windows 8.1 Enterprise:** Similar to Windows 8.1 Pro, this edition is available only to Software Assurance customers via the Volume License Service Center. You can also obtain evaluation versions by means of your TechNet Professional Subscription or MSDN Subscription.

NOTE Throughout this Cert Guide, we use the term Windows 8.1 to include all editions of Windows 8.1, only identifying the RT/Pro/Enterprise editions as required when features specific to these editions are discussed.

Table 1-2 provides additional detail on the components included in the various editions of Windows 8.1. We introduce many of these features in the following sections.

Table 1-2 Components Included in Windows 8.1 Editions

Component	Windows RT 8.1	Windows 8.1	Windows 8.1 Pro	Windows 8.1 Enterprise
Internet Explorer 11	x	x	x	x
Windows Search	x	x	x	x
Windows Update	x	x	x	x
Windows Defender	x	x	x	x
Windows Firewall	x	x	x	x
Messaging	x	x	x	x
Mail app	x	x	x	x
BitLocker drive encryption	**		x	x
Action Center	x	x	x	x
Parental Controls		x	x	x
Taskbar Thumbnail Previews	x	x	x	x
Create ad-hoc wireless networks	x	x	x	x
Task Manager	x	x	x	x
HomeGroup membership	x	x	x	x
Windows SkyDrive	x	x	x	x
Improved support for multiple monitors	x	x	x	x
Remote Desktop client	x	x	x	x
3D printing support	x	x	x	x
Automatic updating of Windows Store apps	x	x	x	x
Windows Store apps can open multiple instances or launch other apps	x	x	x	x
Assigned access	x		x	x
Biometric fingerprint enrollment	x	x	x	x

Component	Windows RT 8.1	Windows 8.1	Windows 8.1 Pro	Windows 8.1 Enterprise
Bring your own device (BYOD) multifactor authentication	x	x	x	x
Desktop wallpaper set as Start screen background	x	x	x	x
Device enrollment	x	x	x	x
Miracast wireless display support	x	x	x	x
Mobile hotspot/Wi-Fi tethering	x	x	x	x
Lock screen photo slide show	x	x	x	x
Open MDM support	x	x	x	x
Open up to four variable-sized windows at once	x	x	x	x
PC Settings improvements	x	x	x	x
Portrait mode improvements	x	x	x	x
Remote business data removal	x	x	x	x
Search powered by Bing	x	x	x	x
New Windows 8.1 Start button	x	x	x	x
Ability to customize multiple Start screen tiles and four sizes	x	x	x	x
Wi-Fi Direct wireless printing support	x	x	x	x
Work folders	x	x	x	x
Workplace join	x	x	x	x
Storage Spaces		x	x	x
Internet Connection Sharing		x	x	x
Ability to create a HomeGroup		x	x	x
System Restore		x	x	x
Windows Media Center		x	x	x
File History		x	x	x
Ability to join a domain			x	x
Remote Desktop host			x	x
File encryption using Encrypting File System (EFS)			x	x
VDI enhancements				x

Component	Windows RT 8.1	Windows 8.1	Windows 8.1 Pro	Windows 8.1 Enterprise
Advanced security capabilities, including AppLocker, DirectAccess, and BranchCache				x
Start screen control				x
Windows To Go				x

NOTE Although Windows RT 8.1 does not include support for BitLocker, it does support its own form of device encryption based on a Trusted Platform Module (TPM), like BitLocker. The main difference is that BitLocker can be managed by an IT administrator using group policies on a domain. Because Windows RT 8.1 does not support joining a domain or utilizing group policies, you cannot use these administrative tools to manage Windows RT 8.1 devices.

New Features of Windows 8 and Windows 8.1

Windows 8.1 includes virtually all the new features introduced in Windows Vista and 7, improving many of these features in ways that enhance your productivity and security with the new operating system. At the same time, after you become familiar with the new Start screen and desktop interfaces (introduced in more detail in the next section), you will find that you can perform most actions in much the same way as you did with recent versions of Windows.

Productivity Improvements

Windows 8 and 8.1 include a number of new features and enhancements that are designed to improve the way users interact with their computers. The basic productivity enhancements included with most editions of Windows 8 and 8.1 include the following:

- **Enhanced capabilities on touch-screen devices:** Windows 8 and Windows 8.1 enable users on laptops and tablets equipped with touch screens to tap icons and tiles to access programs, folders, and so on, in much the same fashion that they would do on a smartphone or tablet.
- **Start screen:** Windows 8 and Windows 8.1 replace the Start button and menu, which have existed in much the same format ever since Windows NT 4.0 and

Windows 95, with the Start screen. This screen is the new home base from which you can open apps, websites, folders, and other items. Tiles included on the Start screen enable you to obtain news, weather, and sports headlines and other quick information. More about the Start screen later in this section.

- **New Windows 8.1 Start button:** Windows 8.1 reintroduces the Start button that was removed in the original Windows 8. When you click this button, you are taken to the Start screen. Right-click the button to access a menu that provides access to most of the functions previously found on the Windows 7 Start menu.
- **Charms:** Windows 8 and Windows 8.1 introduce a set of five charms, which lie along the right side of your screen. You can access these charms by hovering your mouse pointer over the top-right corner of the screen, or on a touch screen by swiping your finger in from the top-right corner. These charms enable you to perform several common tasks, as follows:
  - **Search:** Enables you to search for files, folders, or programs on your computer. You can even look up items on the Internet. Windows 8.1 integrates the previously separated search categories for apps, settings, and files into a single search operation.
  - **Share:** Enables you to share files and folders with other users or send data to another program without leaving the program you're running. You can also email photos to others, update your Facebook page, or send links to other programs.
  - **Start:** Enables you to jump to the Start screen. If you're on the Start screen, you can return to the last app you were working with.
  - **Devices:** Enables you to work with all peripheral devices on the computer. For example, you can print files, sync data with a smartphone, or stream a home movie to your TV.
  - **Settings:** Enables you to access the Control Panel (when on the desktop) and modify settings for the computer and its apps. You can also shut down or restart your computer from the Power icon accessed via this charm.
- **Improved Help and Support:** You can obtain help about using Windows 8 and Windows 8.1 by opening the Search charm from either the Start screen or the desktop, typing `help`, and then clicking **Help and Support**. When using an app, you can obtain app-specific help by following the same procedure.
- **Windows OneDrive:** Originally called SkyDrive, this cloud-based feature enables you to make images, documents, and other types of files available on any computer or smartphone without the need for syncing or special cables. This includes computers running Windows Vista/7 and Mac OS X Mavericks. You

can share data with others with whom you work, regardless of your physical location. Anyone who signs up for a SkyDrive account has access to 7 GB of free storage, and more storage is available at economical rates.

- **Client Hyper-V:** This feature provides computer virtualization technology that was previously available only on servers. It improves on the capability of Windows XP Mode that was previously available in Windows 7, and enables you to install a virtual copy of an older Windows version on computers running Windows 8.1 Pro or Windows 8.1 Enterprise and run older business software that might not run properly on Windows 8.1.
- **Windows To Go:** You can install a copy of Windows 8.1 on a USB thumb drive and use this on a computer that meets the Windows 7 or Windows 8.1 hardware requirements regardless of the operating system installed on the computer. This enables an additional Windows workspace that operates in a manner similar to an ordinary Windows installation with few exceptions.
- **The Windows Store:** New to Windows 8 and 8.1 is the Windows Store, accessible from http://windows.microsoft.com/en-us/windows-8/apps#Cat=t1. You can browse new or featured apps, many of which are available free or at low prices. Apps are arranged in categories to facilitate the location of apps for specific purposes. When you first access the Windows Store, you set up an account that keeps track of all apps that you own; you can install any of these apps on up to five different computers. We provide more information on installing and using Windows Store apps in Chapter 5, "Installing, Configuring, and Securing Applications in Windows 8.1."
- **Workplace Join:** In Windows 8.1, a user can bring his own device to the corporate network and work on this device with access to corporate resources. You can provide fine-grained control for such a user to only those resources required for his work functions. In addition, the Work Folders feature enables a user to sync data to his device from his user folder to a file server. Copies of this data are automatically synchronized to the folder on the server.
- **Mobile device management:** In Windows 8.1, users enrolling their own device join the device to the Windows Intune management service. You can manage these devices using existing Windows Intune utilities; this includes both Windows RT 8.1 devices and mobile Windows 8.1 computers.
- **Web Application Proxy:** Windows Server 2012 R2 provides a new Web Application Proxy role service, which enables you to publish access to corporate resources, with enforced multifactor authentication and the capability of using conditional access policies that verify the identity of the user and her device.

- **Printing enhancements in Windows 8.1:** You can tap a Windows 8.1 device against an enterprise NFC printer to automatically connect to this printer without the need to search for an appropriate printer on the network. You can also connect to Wi-Fi Direct printers without the need for additional drivers or software.
- **Mobility enhancements in Windows 8.1:** Windows 8.1 provides improved support for virtual private network (VPN) clients, mobile broadband, broadband tethering, and automatic prompts for signing into VPN networks. Users on Windows To Go can access the Windows Store to obtain apps and roam to other machines.

Security Improvements

As you know, previous Windows versions have been subjected to a never-ending flow of new vulnerabilities. Microsoft has introduced several new features designed to improve the security of computing in Windows 8.1:

- **Picture password:** You can use a picture password for a more personal option when logging on to your user account. This involves tracing a series of up to three gestures on an image that you select. This type of password is actually more secure than a traditional password.
- **Trusted Boot and Secure Boot:** New to Windows 8.1 and Windows Server 2012 and continued in Windows 8.1 and Windows Server 2012 R2, Trusted Boot verifies the integrity of all Windows boot components such as the digital signature kernel, boot drivers, startup files, and the Early Launch Anti-Malware (ELAM) component. Secure Boot helps prevent unauthorized firmware or operating systems from loading at boot time. It functions by maintaining databases of software images and software signers that are authorized to run on the individual computer. The ELAM driver starts before other drivers and evaluates other drivers including third-party software as they attempt to start up. Any malicious drivers are blocked. Also available is Measured Boot, which allows non-Microsoft software on a remote server to verify the security of all startup components, so that malware is unable to execute.
- **AppLocker:** First introduced in Windows 7, this is an easily administered tool that enables administrators to specify what programs are allowed to run on the desktop in a domain-based environment. You can specify applications that are allowed or denied execution, and you can create exceptions to these rules as desired. Added to Windows 8.1 and Windows Server 2012 R2 is the ability to set rules for Packaged apps and Packaged app installers, as well as control of additional file formats.

- **BitLocker and BitLocker To Go:** First introduced in Vista and enhanced in Windows 7 and Windows 8 and 8.1, BitLocker enables you to encrypt any hard drive partition to prevent unauthorized individuals from accessing data contained therein. BitLocker To Go extends this protection to removable devices such as USB flash drives and portable disks. Even if a thief removes a protected drive from its computer and installs it in another computer, he cannot access the data contained on the drive. New to Windows 8/8.1 and Windows Server 2012 R2 is support for server clusters and the ability to link a BitLocker key protector to an account in Active Directory. Windows 8.1 adds pervasive device encryption, which automatically encrypts data on consumer devices when a Microsoft account is used.

- **BranchCache:** Additional performance, manageability, scalability, and availability improvements have been included in Windows 8, 8.1, and Windows Server 2012 R2. They include support for a single Group Policy Object (GPO) for client computer configuration, additional integration with the File Server role in Windows Server 2012 R2, disk storage savings by avoiding the storage of duplicated content, offline creation of content information, encryption of cached content, and several other features. You can now manage BranchCache using PowerShell or Windows Management Instrumentation (WMI).

- **Enhanced auditing capabilities:** Auditing capabilities have been enhanced in Windows 8/8.1 and Windows Server 2012 R2 to include features such as the use of expression-based audit policies and resource properties, thereby enabling scenarios that were difficult to impossible to work with in previous Windows versions. You can also audit removable storage devices as well as obtain additional information from user logon and file access attempts.

- **Enhanced smart card features:** Smart cards and their associated personal identification numbers (PINs) are gaining in popularity as a secure, cost-effective form of two-factor authentication. New to Windows 8/8.1 and Windows Server 2012 R2 is the support of virtual smart cards using the TPM chip in place of a physical smart card and reader, improved detection of smart cards and PINs, changes to the start and stop behavior of the Smart Card service, and support of new types of desktop applications.

- **Virtual smart cards:** New to Windows 8.1, virtual smart cards offer security benefits that are similar to those of physical smart cards but with more convenience to users. They function similarly to a physical smart card that is always inserted in the computer, and enable authentication to external resources, secure data encryption, and integrity by means of reliable signing. Cryptographic capabilities are the same as those provided by conventional smart cards.

- **New Internet Explorer 11 Security Features:** Microsoft has improved and secured Web browsing with new capabilities including enhancements to Protected Mode, which was first introduced in Internet Explorer 7. Smart Screen filters help detect phishing websites and prevent the downloading and installation of malware from rogue websites. InPrivate browsing mode hides your browsing history when using public computers. Tracking Protection functionality helps protect users from being tracked online. Improved support for enhanced web standards such as HTML5, Cascading Style Sheets level 3, Document Object Model, Indexed Database API, and Scalable Vector Graphics is included. Many new Group Policy settings have also been added. Internet Explorer 11 in Windows 8.1 takes security features further, including enhanced antimalware, which scans input for inappropriate binaries before passing data for execution. Usability enhancements in Internet Explorer 11 include faster page load times, side-by-side browsing, enhanced pinned site notifications, and app settings such as favorites that sync across multiple devices.
- **Improvements to Windows Firewall with Advanced Security:** New to Windows 8.1 and Windows Server 2012 R2 are the support of Internet Key Exchange version 2 (IKEv2) for IPSec transport mode connections, control of the use of Windows Store apps, and additional Windows PowerShell configuration and management options.
- **Remote business data removal:** Windows 8.1 and Windows Server 2012 R2 enable you to mark corporate data for deletion from personal devices when a user leaves your company.
- **Improved biometric capability:** Windows 8.1 provides enhanced biometric authentication capabilities including fingerprint-based biometrics and the prevention of spoofing.
- **Enhanced malware resistance:** In Windows 8.1, Windows Defender includes network behavior monitoring that helps detect and prevent the execution of known and unknown malware.

Chapter 5, Chapter 7, "Configuring Hyper-V," Chapter 10, "Configuring and Maintaining Network Security," and Chapter 12, "Configuring Local Security Settings," provide details of most of these features.

NOTE For more information on new and improved Windows 8.1 features, refer to "What's New in Windows 8.1" at http://technet.microsoft.com/en-us/windows/dn140266. For more information on enhanced security technologies, refer to "What's Changed in Security Technologies in Windows 8.1" at http://technet.microsoft.com/en-us/library/dn344918.aspx.

A Quick Tour of Windows 8.1

From the very beginning when you first start up your computer, Windows 8.1 presents an entirely new look with the new Start screen containing a series of tiles, each connecting to a default application (app) included with the new operating system (see Figure 1-1). These tiles are not simply icons that you double-click to open a program; each tile connects to a person, app, website, folder, playlist, or other important object, and they can automatically provide information such as news or weather data. You can add additional tiles to the Start screen or move them around to arrange them in whatever fashion you prefer. Many programs such as Microsoft Office automatically add tiles to the Start screen when you install them.

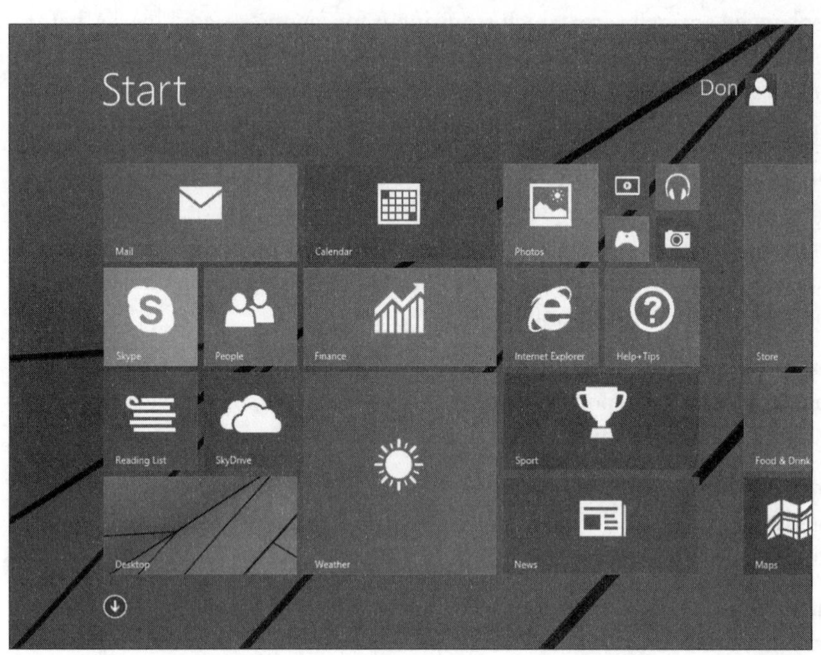

Figure 1-1 The Windows 8.1 Start screen as seen when you first install Windows 8.1.

Initially referred to as "Metro," the new Start screen performs well with touch-enabled monitors that are standard on tablet devices and fast becoming available on laptops and conventional desktop monitors. But users with conventional mouse-based systems are not forgotten either.

The familiar Windows desktop is not gone; you can access it from the Start screen by clicking the **Desktop** tile to reveal it, as shown in Figure 1-2. Here, you can place icons that provide shortcuts to programs or folders in much the same way as done with previous versions of Windows.

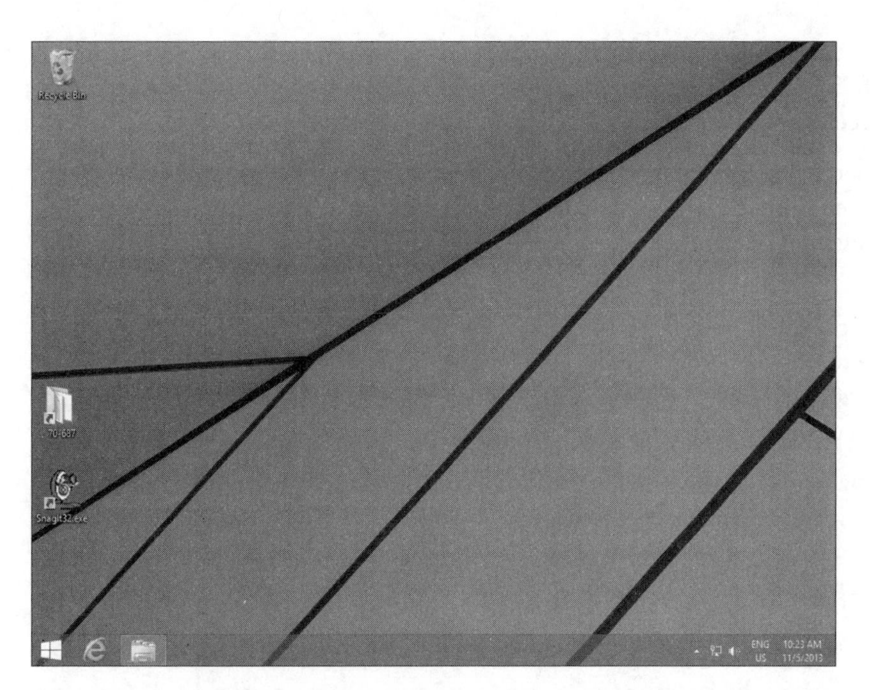

Figure 1-2 You can place icons relating to installed programs or folders on the Windows 8.1 desktop.

The following introduces new actions that you can perform from the Start screen:

- To access the desktop, tap the Desktop tile on a touch-screen device; on a conventional computer, click this icon.
- To return to the Start screen from the desktop, tap the lower-left corner on a touch-screen device; on a conventional computer, move the pointer to the lower-left corner to see a thumbnail image of the Start screen and then click this thumbnail. You can also press the **Windows** key on the keyboard.
- To access the Charms panel, which is a thin vertical panel of icons along the right side of the Start screen, swipe your finger into the screen from either the top-right or bottom-right corner on a touch-screen device; on a conventional computer, move the pointer to either of these corners.
- To access additional tiles on the Start screen, swipe to the right; then swipe to the left to return to the tiles first visible on the screen. On a conventional computer, use the scroll wheel on the mouse or drag the bar at the bottom of the screen. To view tiles for the desktop apps installed on your computer (both default apps and those you've installed), click the small down arrow near the bottom-left corner (refer back to Figure 1-1).

- To jump from one Start screen app to the next, swipe into the screen from the left border. On a conventional computer, point to the upper-left corner of the screen or use the **Windows + Tab** key combination.
- To switch between open programs on a touch-screen device, swipe into the screen from the left border and then back out again. This displays a vertical column of open program icons. On a conventional computer, press **Alt + Tab** or **Windows + Tab** as in previous Windows versions.
- To close a tile-based app on a touch-screen device, swipe down from the middle of the top border, almost all the way down the screen. On a conventional computer, point to the top of the window to obtain a grabber handle and drag this down the screen toward the bottom.
- To zoom an image, map, or web page accessed from the Start screen, spread or pinch two fingers on a touch-screen device just as you would do on a smart phone or tablet. On a conventional computer, press the **Ctrl** key with the **+** or **–** key or hold down the **Ctrl** key while turning the scroll wheel.

NOTE Using a touch-screen device, tap any icon found on the Start screen to open the associated program or folder, or double-tap any icon found on the desktop. In the remainder of this Cert Guide, when we instruct you to "click" an icon or tile, this action also assumes you can tap the icon or tile when using a touch-screen device.

When you've installed a large number of apps and other programs, the Start screen can fill up such that you can have difficulty locating a particular program. Many of the tiles can become hidden from view unless you scroll across large distances. But you can zoom the display outward to shrink the tiles and view a larger number. On a touch screen, squeeze the display with two fingers; on a standard display, hold down the **Ctrl** button while using the mouse wheel to zoom out (see Figure 1-3).

Windows 8.1 Search

Clicking the **Search** button on the Charms panel brings you to the new Windows 8.1 Search screen shown in Figure 1-4.

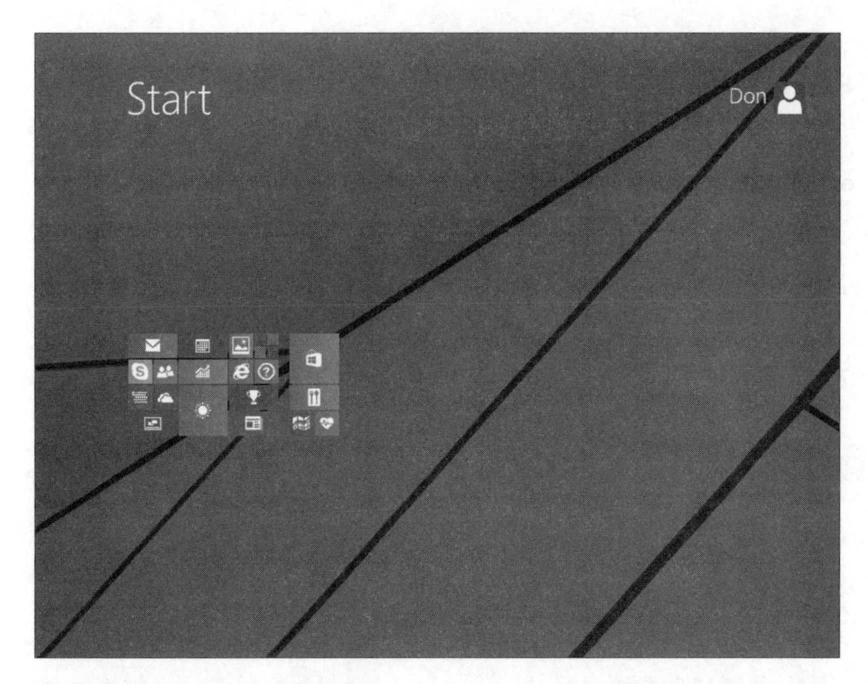

Figure 1-3 You can zoom the Start screen out to enable display of a large number of program tiles.

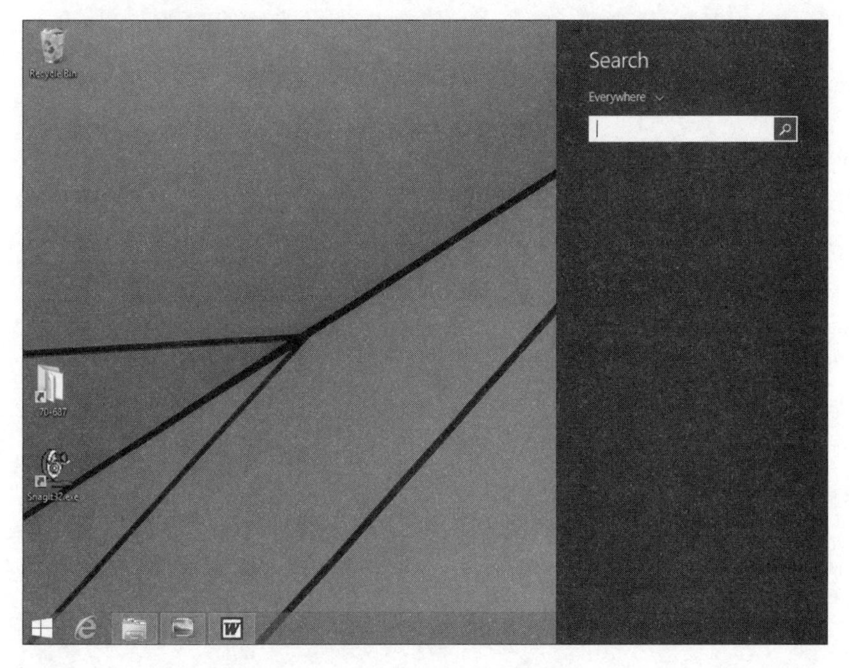

Figure 1-4 The Windows 8.1 Search screen enables you to search for apps, settings, folders, or files on your computer or the Internet.

Type any program, web page, or filename in the space provided. You need only type a portion of a name in the space, and Windows will attempt to locate matches from your computer or the Internet. You can also click **Everywhere** to display a list of search item types, including Everywhere, Settings, Files, Web images, and Web videos. Doing so enables you to choose the type of item being searched for and consequently can speed up your search. You can also open a network share by typing the Universal Naming Convention (UNC) path to the share, for example, **`\\server1\documents`**.

Search results can include both local and Internet results; for example, typing **`computer management`** yielded the results shown in Figure 1-5.

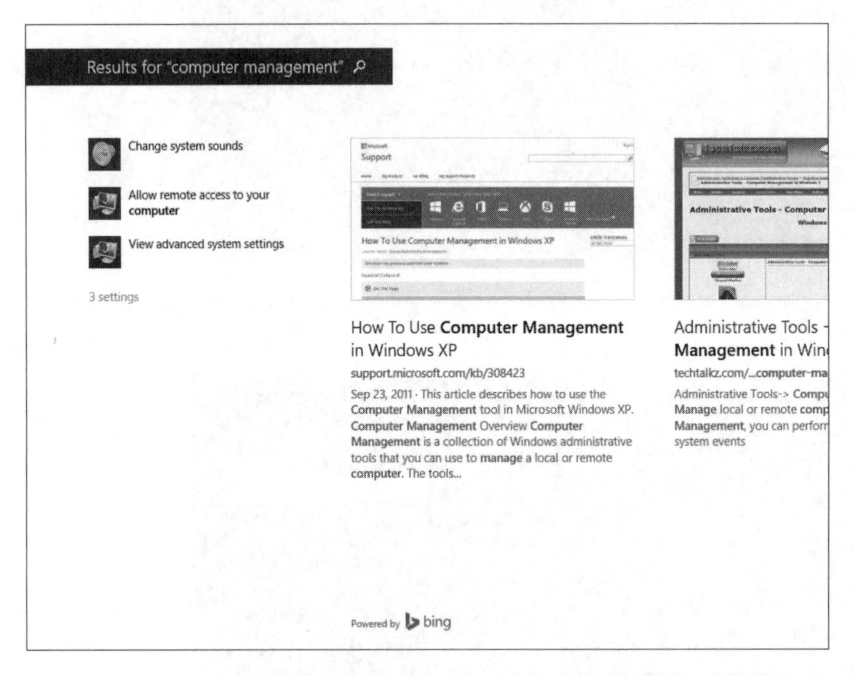

Figure 1-5 Search results in Windows 8.1 can include both local and Internet results.

Configuring the Windows 8.1 Taskbar

The new Windows 8.1 taskbar is similar to the Windows 7 taskbar, combining features of the taskbar and Quick Launch area formerly present in older Windows versions. By default, when you first install Windows 8.1, the taskbar contains the revised Start button plus two buttons at the far left side, which represent Internet Explorer and File Explorer. Each time you open an application, a button representing this application is added to the taskbar. You can add applications to the taskbar; simply find the desired application from the tiles on the Start screen (using Search if desired), right-click it, and choose **Pin to Taskbar**. These remain on the taskbar whether the program is running or not; if you want to remove a button from the taskbar later, simply right-click it and choose **Unpin this program from taskbar**.

Taskbar buttons can take on any of the three following appearances:

- For a pinned program that is not running, a simple icon for the program appears. Click the button to open the program.
- If a single instance of the program (or a single File Explorer window or Internet Explorer tab or page) is running, the button is enclosed by a single rectangular frame. Mouse over the button to view a thumbnail of the application; click it to bring it to the front. If the application is already in the front on your desktop, clicking its taskbar button minimizes the application.
- If multiple instances of the program (or of Explorer windows or Internet Explorer tabs or pages) are running, the button takes on a pseudo-3D appearance that looks like stacked frames. If you mouse over the button, a series of icons representing each instance or tab appears; click the desired one to bring it to the front.

Windows 8.1 provides several options for configuring the properties of the taskbar. Right-click the taskbar and choose **Properties** to bring up the Taskbar and Navigation Properties dialog box, which enables you to configure properties related to the taskbar, navigation, jump lists, and toolbars.

Taskbar Properties

Selecting the **Taskbar** tab of the Taskbar and Navigation Properties dialog box enables you to configure the items shown in Figure 1-6.

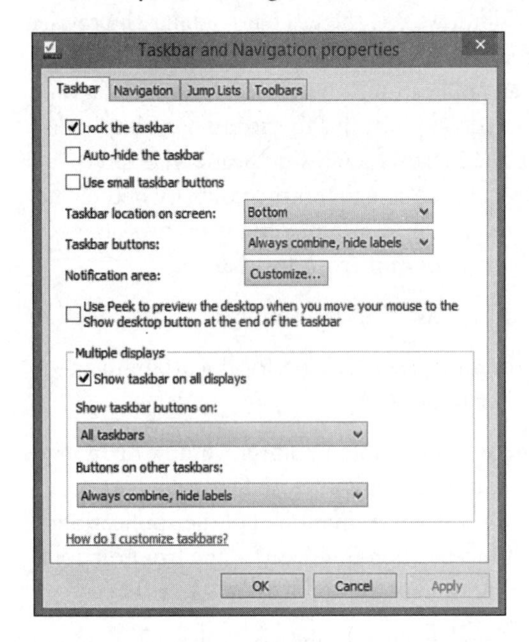

Figure 1-6 The Taskbar tab enables you to configure several taskbar properties.

Most of the properties on this tab function as they have done in recent Windows versions:

- **Lock the taskbar:** Determines whether the taskbar is always visible at the bottom of the display.
- **Auto-hide the taskbar:** Determines whether the taskbar disappears automatically after a program is started.
- **Use small taskbar buttons:** Shrinks the size of icons on the taskbar buttons.
- **Taskbar location on screen:** Enables you to choose between top, bottom, left, or right.
- **Taskbar buttons:** Provides the following three options for display of taskbar buttons.
  - **Always combine, hide labels:** Provides the default Windows 8.1 view already described.
  - **Combine when taskbar is full:** Displays icons in a similar fashion to that of Vista with descriptive labels that are combined only when a large number of applications are open.

  - **Never combine:** Offers a similar display but does not combine icons for open programs.

- **Notification area:** Click **Customize** to display the Notification Area Icons applet of Control Panel, which enables you to choose what items are displayed in the notification area (formerly known as the system tray). Some third-party programs add options to this applet when installed.
- **Use Peek to preview the desktop when you move your mouse to the Show desktop button at the end of the toolbar:** Enables the view of the desktop by hovering the mouse over a small area to the right of the clock at the end of the taskbar.
- **Multiple displays:** Provides options for displaying taskbars and their buttons when more than one monitor is attached to the computer. You can choose which taskbar application buttons appear on and whether to combine taskbar buttons on other taskbars.

Navigation Properties

New to Windows 8.1, the Navigation tab shown in Figure 1-7 enables you to configure your computer to modify the default tasks performed when you navigate to corners of the display or access the Start screen.

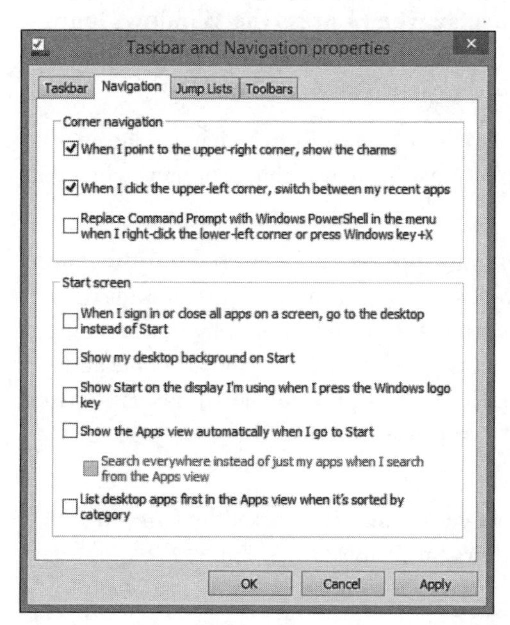

Figure 1-7 The Navigation tab enables you to configure several properties related to pointing at corners of the screen or displaying the Start screen.

You have the following options:

- **When I point to the upper-right corner, show the charms:** If you deselect this option, the charms appear only when you point to the lower-right corner of the display.
- **When I click the upper-left corner, switch between my recent apps:** When this option is selected, you can switch between Start screen or Windows Store apps by clicking this corner. This is similar to pressing Alt+Tab, except that traditional desktop apps are not displayed. Clearing this option disables this action.
- **Replace Command Prompt with Windows PowerShell in the menu when I right-click the lower-left corner or press Windows key+X:** Enables direct access to Windows PowerShell rather than the command prompt. You can still access the command prompt by accessing the Search charm and typing `cmd`.
- **Go to the desktop instead of Start when I sign in:** Enables you to boot directly to the desktop, similar to previous Windows versions.
- **Show my desktop background on Start:** When you click **Start**, the Start screen tiles appear above the desktop image rather than the solid color background previously shown in Figure 1-1.
- **Always show Start on my main display when I press the Windows logo key:** Select this option to always have the Start screen appear on the main display when using a computer equipped with two or more monitors.
- **Show the Apps view automatically when I go to Start:** Changes the appearance of the Start screen to display a list of all available programs when you click **Start**.
- **Search everywhere instead of just my apps when I search from the Apps view:** When this option is deselected, searching from the Apps view (as opposed to the Search charm) searches only for installed apps on your computer, including desktop programs. When it is selected (this is made available and selected by default when you select **Show the Apps view automatically when I go to Start**), the search box on the Apps view behaves the same as in the Search charm.
- **List desktop apps first in the Apps view when it's sorted by category:** Displays desktop apps before Windows Store apps.

Jump Lists Properties

Many of the items on the left side of the Start menu link to jump lists, which are lists of program features associated with the primary item, or of documents that you have recently opened from the indicated program. Right-click an icon in the taskbar to display the jump list. You can then click any item in the jump list to open it. From the Jump Lists tab (see Figure 1-8), you can specify the number of recent items to be displayed in a jump list and specify whether recently opened programs or files are stored and displayed in jump lists.

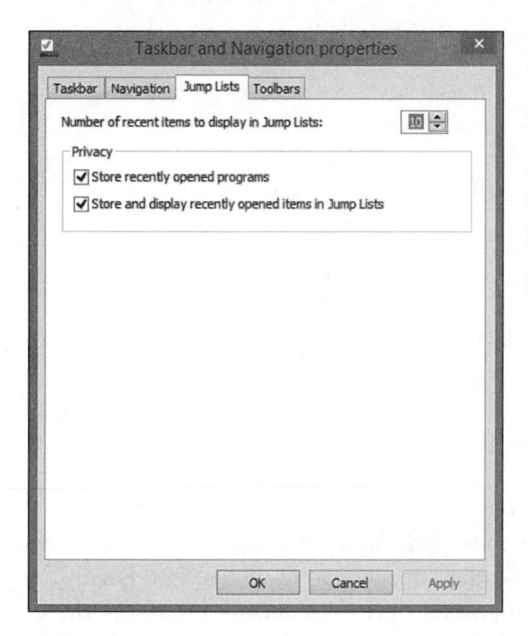

Figure 1-8 You can customize the behavior of jump lists from the Jump Lists tab.

Toolbars

Click the **Toolbars** tab to configure the taskbar to display toolbars for Address, Links, Touch Keyboard, and the Desktop, as shown in Figure 1-9. These toolbars appear on the right side of the taskbar, next to the Notification area.

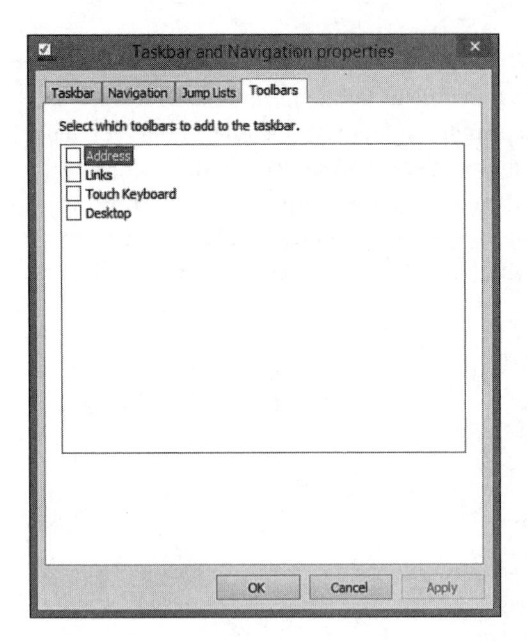

Figure 1-9 The Toolbars tab enables you to display several toolbars on the desktop.

Windows 8.1 Apps

As already introduced, Windows 8.1 comes with a series of Start screen apps (originally called Metro apps), which enable you to perform many simple tasks easily. They include mail, messaging, people, weather, music, photos, video, travel, maps, and so on (refer back to Figure 1-1). Windows 8.1 provides updates to most of these basic apps and adds several new ones, including Fresh Paint, which is an overhauled version of the Paint utility that has been provided for many years. In addition, Windows 8.1 enables you to have up to four apps visible on the screen at the same time; you can size and arrange these apps in any manner desired. Using these apps is simple and intuitive; simply click or tap the desired app on the Start screen. You can obtain additional apps from the Windows Store; many of these are free and most of the others are available for a small charge.

Once started, Windows 8.1 apps remain open in the background and, in most cases, do not consume much computer resources. Windows automatically closes any app that hasn't been accessed after a certain length of time. If you want to close an app sooner, perhaps because it is not responding or is consuming too much resources, you can do any of the following:

- Point your mouse to the top center of the app screen so that it takes the form of a hand. Then drag downward so that the app shrinks in size and follows your pointer downward. When it is near the bottom of the screen, it should disappear.
- If more than one app is running, point your mouse to the top-left corner of the screen. When you see a thumbnail view of the app you want to close, right-click it and choose **Close**.
- When the app is onscreen, press **Alt+F4**.
- On a touch-screen device, touch the top center of the app screen and drag your finger downward toward the bottom edge of the screen. When your finger is near the bottom of the screen, the app should disappear.

Libraries

Windows 8.1 continues the concept of libraries, first introduced in Windows 7. These are collections of Windows folders, such as Documents, Pictures, Videos, and Music. They replace the special shell folders such as My Documents that were found in Windows versions prior to 7 and provide access to files and folders with a common theme. Each library is simply a pointer that opens a window containing all subfolders and files within the library. By default, the following four libraries are provided:

- **Documents:** Includes the My Documents and Public Documents folders.
- **Music:** Includes the My Music and Public Music folders.
- **Pictures:** Includes the My Pictures and Public Pictures folders.
- **Videos:** Includes the My Videos and Public Videos folders.

To access your libraries in Windows 8.1, open a File Explorer window and click the **Desktop** icon under **Favorites** at the top-left corner of the window. Double-click the **Libraries** icon to display these four default libraries.

You can add additional folders to a library at any time. Right-click the desired library and choose **Properties** to display the dialog box shown in Figure 1-10. To add a folder, click **Add** and browse to the desired folder. To remove a folder, select it and click **Remove**.

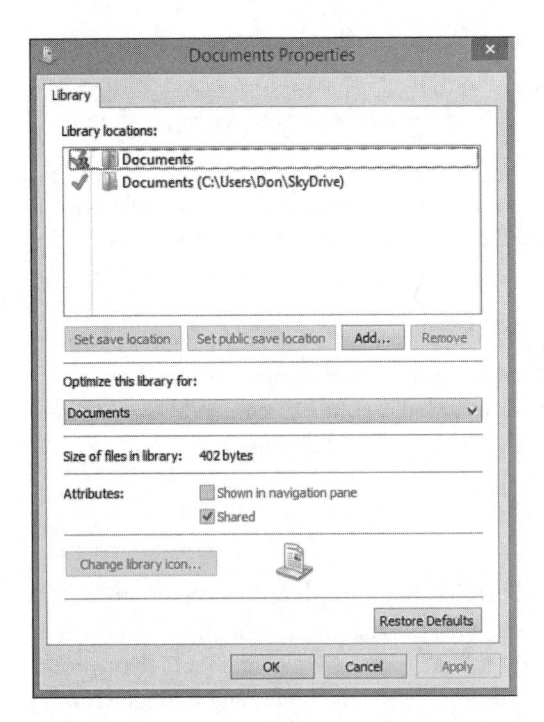

Figure 1-10 Each library has a Properties dialog box that enables you to perform actions such as adding and removing folders accessed from the library.

You can also create new libraries at any time. Right-click a blank area in the Libraries window and choose **New > Library**. Provide a name for the library and then follow the procedure in the preceding paragraph to add folders to your library.

By default, all libraries are shared when the computer is in a HomeGroup or workgroup. You can modify this behavior as desired. We discuss sharing of libraries and folders in more detail in Chapter 11, "Configuring and Securing Access to Files and Folders."

Windows 8.1 Settings

Clicking the **Settings** button on the Charms panel and selecting **Change PC settings** brings you to the new Windows 8.1 PC Settings screen shown in Figure 1-11. You can also access the PC Settings screen by pointing the mouse to the upper-left corner of the screen. From this screen, you can access a variety of utilities that enable you to configure various functions on your computer, as discussed in the following sections.

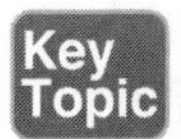

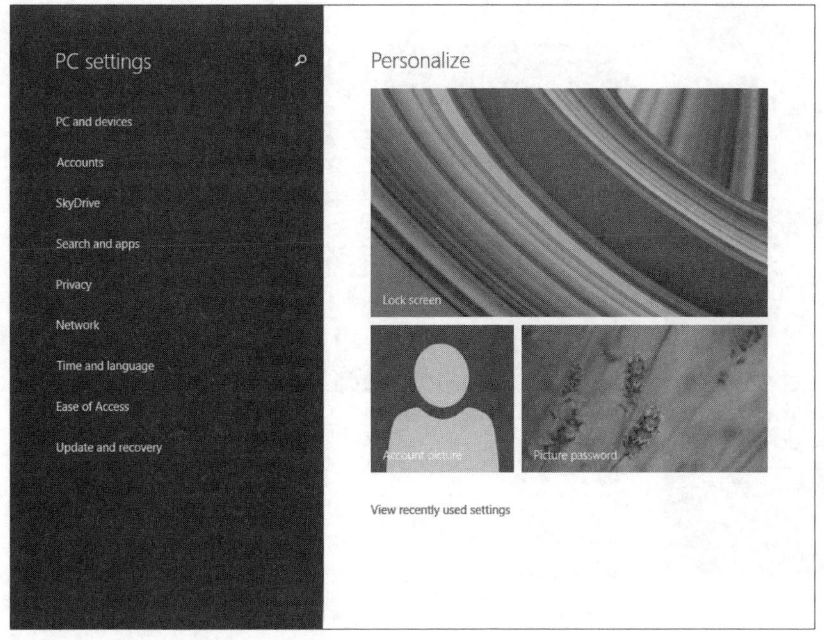

Figure 1-11 The new PC Settings utility enables you to configure a series of Windows settings on your computer.

PC and Devices

The PC and Devices utility, shown in Figure 1-12, enables you to configure a series of options related to the use of the computer and the appearance of the desktop. The options provided enable you to perform the following tasks:

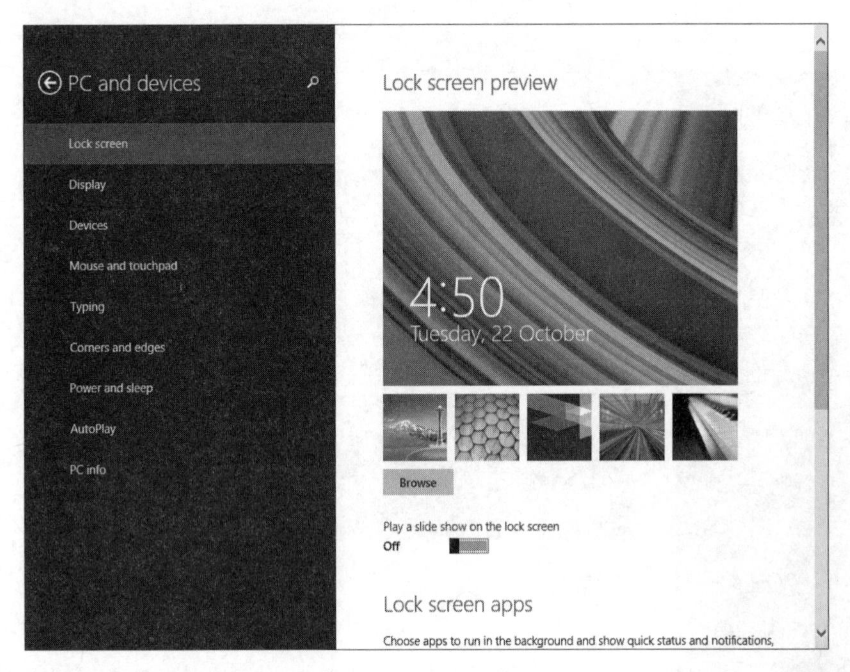

Figure 1-12 The PC and Devices utility enables you to perform several desktop personalization actions.

- **Lock screen:** The lock screen is the image that appears before you log on or after you have logged off. By default, the lock screen also appears when you resume your computer from sleep mode (this behavior can be changed if desired; see Chapter 15, "Configuring and Securing Mobile Devices," for more information). You can select from any of the sample images displayed here or click **Browse** to use one of your own images. Doing so takes you to the Pictures library, from which you can drill down through its subfolders to locate an image to be used. You can also choose to play a slide show from the chosen location on the lock screen (disabled by default).
- **Display:** This utility enables you to customize the appearance of your display, including setting the screen resolution and extending your desktop view to multiple monitors. When using multiple monitors, you can also select which monitor is your main display and choose to use only a specified display or to mirror your display on both monitors.

- **Devices:** As shown in Figure 1-13, this utility displays a list of hardware devices attached to your computer. Click **Add a Device** to enable Windows to search for new hardware devices. If using a metered Internet connection (where you pay according to the length of time connected to the Internet), you can toggle the Download over Metered Connections option to **Off** to limit the connection time used for downloading updates, drivers, and so on. We discuss hardware devices in more detail in Chapter 4, "Configuring Devices and Device Drivers."

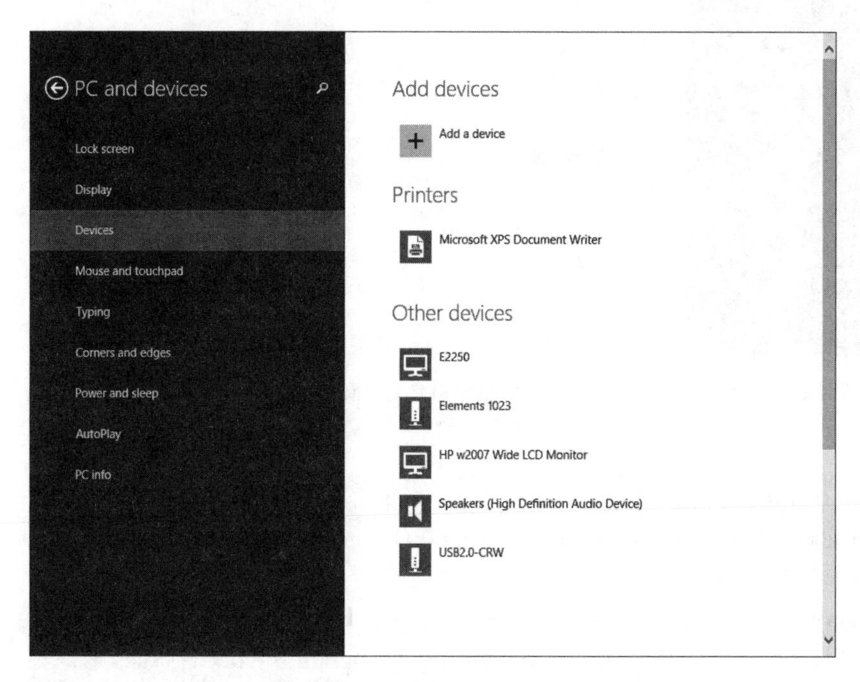

Figure 1-13 The Devices utility enables you to add hardware devices.

- **Mouse and touchpad:** Enables you to configure the primary mouse button or the number of lines scrolled by the mouse wheel. Left-handed users can choose to use the right mouse button as the primary button from this utility.
- **Typing:** Enables you to highlight and autocorrect misspelled words as you type. By default, both of these options are turned on.
- **Corners and Edges:** Enables you to configure the options shown in Figure 1-14 related to switching between apps and navigating to the corners.

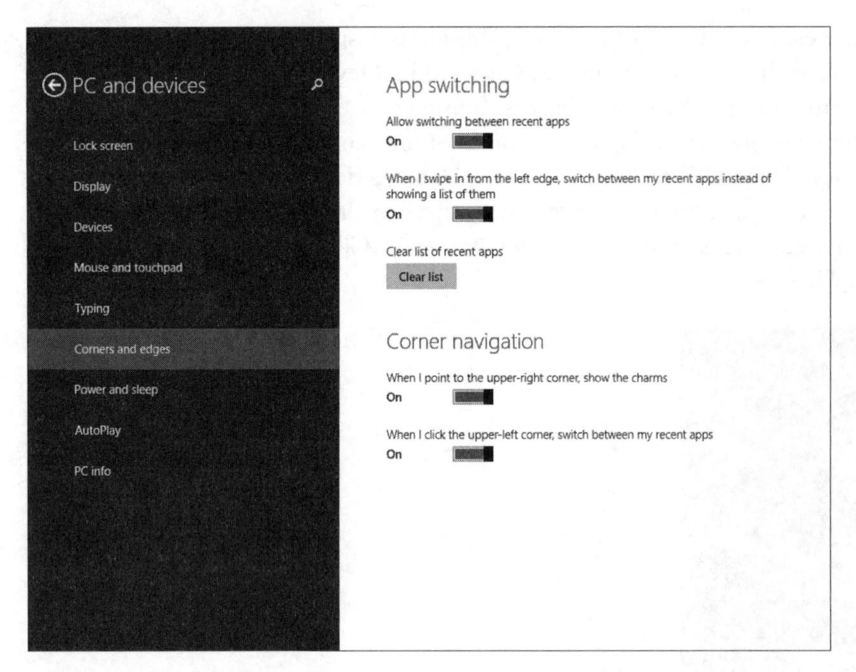

Figure 1-14 The Corners and Edges utility enables you to configure the behavior of the computer when you point to or swipe from the edges or corners of your display.

- **Power and sleep:** Enables you to specify the length of inactive time after which the computer will shut the screen off (10 minutes by default) and go to sleep (30 minutes by default).
- **AutoPlay:** Enables you to use AutoPlay for all media and devices (turned on by default). This enables automatic startup of programs on devices such as CDs and DVDs to install programs, play music, watch videos, and so on. You can also choose AutoPlay defaults for removable devices and memory cards.
- **PC info:** Provides summary information on your computer, its operating system, and installed hardware. You can also rename your computer and change the Windows product key.

Accounts

Using the utility shown in Figure 1-15, you can create and modify user accounts and account properties, including the following tasks:

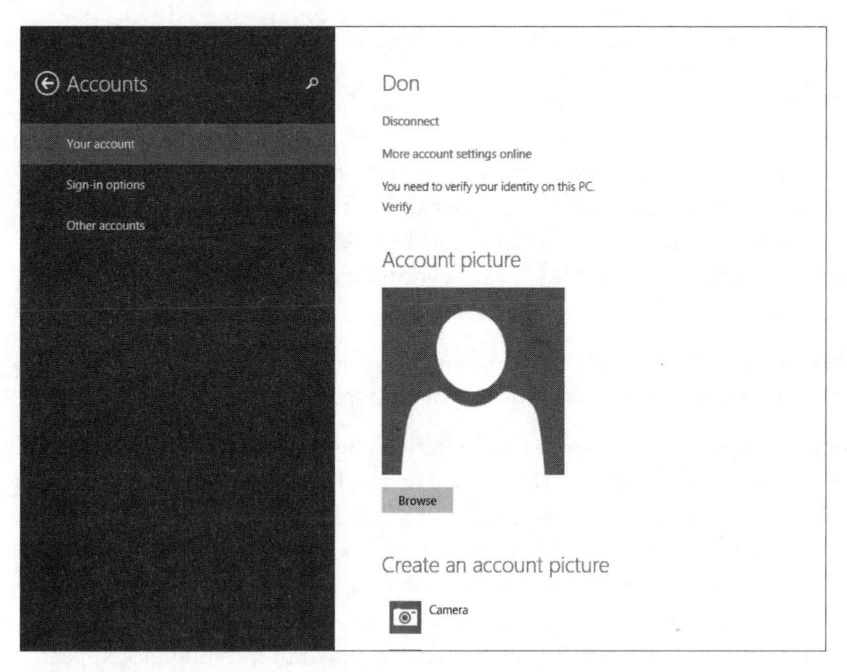

Figure 1-15 The Accounts utility enables you to modify user account properties or create new user accounts.

- **Your account:** Enables you to view and configure options related to the account with which you are currently signed in. Click **Disconnect** to sign out and sign in as a different user. You can choose to set up a Microsoft account such as Hotmail, Messenger, or Xbox Live as your user account. Doing so enables you to perform actions such as downloading apps from the Windows Store, obtaining online content in Microsoft apps, and syncing settings online to make different computers act in the same fashion, including settings such as browser favorites and history. Follow the instructions presented in the wizard that is displayed. From this option, you can also select a picture to be associated with the account. If you have a camera attached to your computer, you can click **Camera** to photograph yourself and create a personalized account picture.
- **Sign-in options:** Enables you to specify the following options related to your user account password:
  - **Password:** Click **Change** to change the password on the account currently in use.
  - **Picture password:** This option enables you to use a picture password, as described earlier in this chapter. Follow the instructions provided to select any picture from your Pictures folder and create your three desired gestures. You are asked to confirm these gestures.

TIP Use a fairly simple image and easily repeatable gestures when creating a picture password.

- **PIN:** Enables you to create a PIN for logging on to your computer. This is a four-digit code used in place of a password. This is most useful when using a tablet where a virtual keyboard will be displayed on the screen during the logon process. Confirm your password; then enter and confirm your PIN.
- **Password policy:** Enables you to modify the policy that governs the strength and usage of passwords on your computer.

- **Other accounts:** Enables you to add additional user accounts. Click **Add a user** and follow the instructions provided on the How will this person sign in? page to add an additional user by means of an email address. If you want to add a user without an email address, select the **Sign in without a Microsoft account** option on the How will this person sign in? page and then select **Local account**. You can also use the User accounts applet in Control Panel, described later in this chapter. Any user accounts added to the computer appear beneath the Add a user option. Note that the local user account cannot download apps from the Microsoft store and is not shared with other computers.

We discuss user accounts, picture passwords, PINs, password policies, and other account properties in more detail in Chapter 13, "Configuring Authentication and Authorization."

OneDrive

Originally called SkyDrive, OneDrive is Microsoft's new cloud-based storage option. Everyone who sets up a Microsoft account is entitled to 7 GB of free storage, from which you can store files such as images, music, and data so that you can access them from a remote location or to provide a secure backup. You have the following options:

- **File storage:** Displays the amount of available and used storage space. Click **Buy more storage** to access a page that displays several options for purchasing additional storage space.

- **Files:** Displays the options shown in Figure 1-16 for managing data stored on OneDrive. Click **See my files on OneDrive** to open a page that enables you to list files under Documents, Favorites, Public, Shared favorites, and Test album categories.
- **Sync settings:** Enables you to synchronize most of the PC settings for accessing different computers and OneDrive when you are using a Microsoft account. Settings on this screen are available only when you have configured the Users section to use a Microsoft account as your user account. You have the following options:
  - **Sync settings with OneDrive:** Enables you to sync PC settings across all devices that will access SkyDrive, including backup settings.
  - **Personalization settings:** Enables you to specify synchronization of the Start screen tiles and their layout, the display colors, backgrounds, themes, taskbar, high contrast settings, lock screen, account picture, and so on.
  - **App settings:** Enables you to synchronize installed Windows Store apps and associated data between your devices.
  - **Other settings:** Enables you to specify several additional synchronization options, including web browser favorites, open tabs, home pages, history, and settings; passwords for accessing apps, websites, and so on; language preferences; accessibility settings such as narrator, magnifier, and so on; and other Windows settings, such as Control Panel settings for items such as File Explorer, mouse, printers, and so on.
  - **Back up settings:** Enables you to determine whether you want to back up your settings to SkyDrive. If you choose On (the default), you can restore your settings to your PC at any time in the future.
- **Metered connections:** Enables you to determine whether synchronization occurs when using a connection where you are charged according to the length of connect time.

Search and Apps

As shown in Figure 1-17, the Search and Apps utility enables you to modify the behavior of the Search charm.

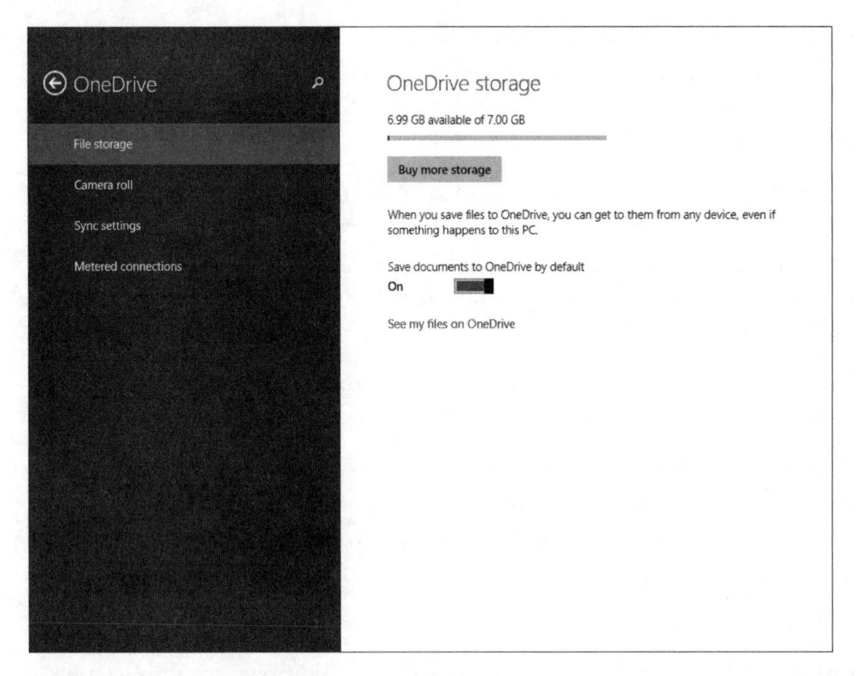

Figure 1-16 The OneDrive utility enables you to manage data stored on your account in OneDrive.

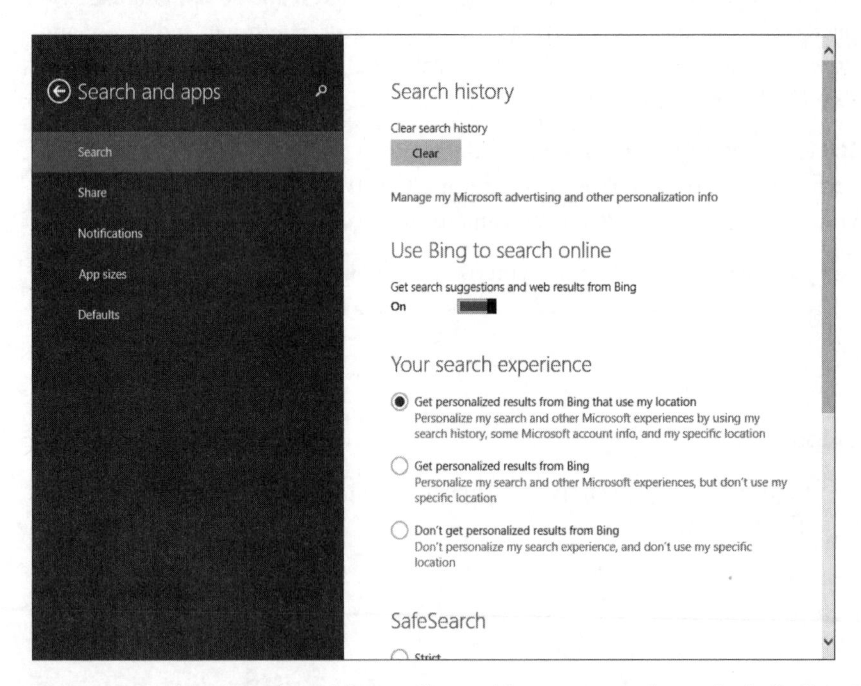

Figure 1-17 The Search and Apps utility enables you to configure the behavior of the Search app, together with several other apps in Windows 8.1.

Search and Apps includes the following subtopics:

- **Search:** As shown in Figure 1-17, this utility enables you to specify several actions related to your search experience, including the use of Bing for searching online. Click **Clear** to delete your search history. The SafeSearch option provides several options for including adult-related content in your search results.
- **Share:** The Share utility displays several settings that relate to the behavior of the Share charm. Options are similar to those provided for Search, enabling you to show apps used most often at the top of the app list and the apps used for sharing. Note that only certain apps are able to share; for the default apps included with Windows 8.1, this includes Mail, People, and Reading List only.
- **Notifications:** The Notifications utility enables you to specify whether various Start screen apps display notifications on the Start screen and/or lock screen, and you can choose which apps can show notifications. You can also decide whether notifications play sounds. You can specify quiet hours during which app notifications will be suppressed, such as during the night. Note that setting the **Show app notifications** option at the top to **Off** disables all other toggles on this page.
- **App sizes:** This utility lists all Windows 8.1 and Windows Store apps installed on your computer, together with the quantity of space used by each and the amount of available space. To uninstall any app, click it and click **Uninstall**; then confirm your intention in the message box that appears.
- **Defaults:** This utility enables you to choose the default apps used for web browser, email, music player, video player, photo viewer, calendar provider, and map address. You can also modify the default apps associated with file types and protocols.

Privacy

The Privacy utility enables you to modify privacy settings associated with the following subtopics:

- **General:** As shown in Figure 1-18, this utility lets you modify your privacy settings associated with Internet browsing (all are set to On by default). Click **Manage my Microsoft advertising and other personalization info** to display a web page from Microsoft that provides several choices for receiving personalized advertising from Microsoft and other companies. Click **Privacy statement** to display a web page that describes privacy information for users of Windows 8.1 and Windows Server 2012 R2, including options for usage of your personal information and contact options. Links provided in this document enable you to address additional privacy details.

- **Location:** Enables you to determine whether Windows and installed apps can use your geographic location.
- **Webcam:** Enables you to determine whether several installed apps can use your webcam if one is installed on your computer.
- **Microphone:** Enables you to determine whether several installed apps can use your microphone if one is installed on your computer.
- **Other devices:** If your computer is equipped with other devices that enable you to control app access, these devices would be displayed on this page.

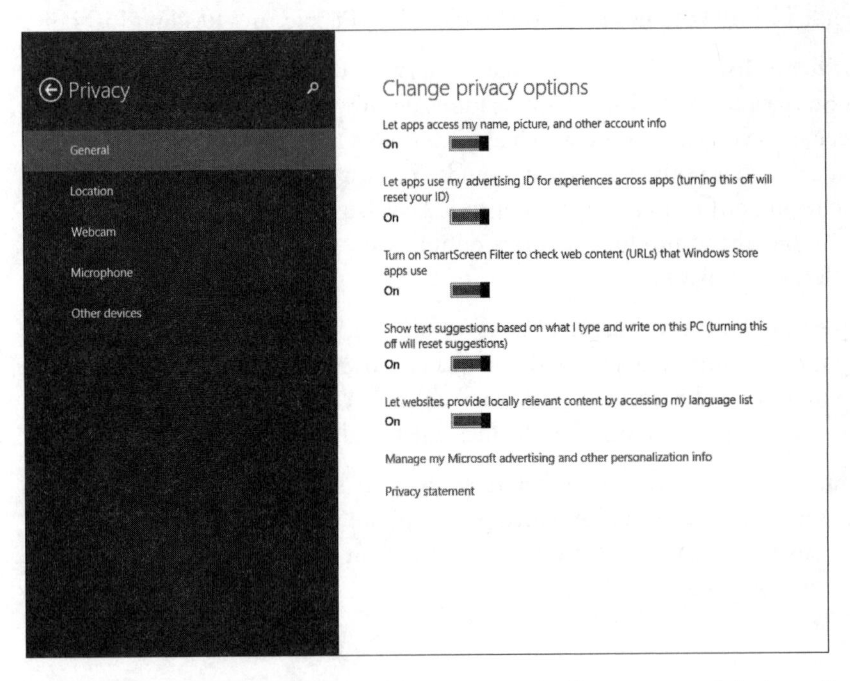

Figure 1-18 The Privacy utility enables you to control how apps and devices attached to your computer use your personal information.

Network

As shown in Figure 1-19, the Network utility enables you to configure several network settings as described in the list that follows. We discuss network configuration in more detail in Chapter 8, "Configuring TCP/IP Settings," and Chapter 9, "Configuring Networking Settings."

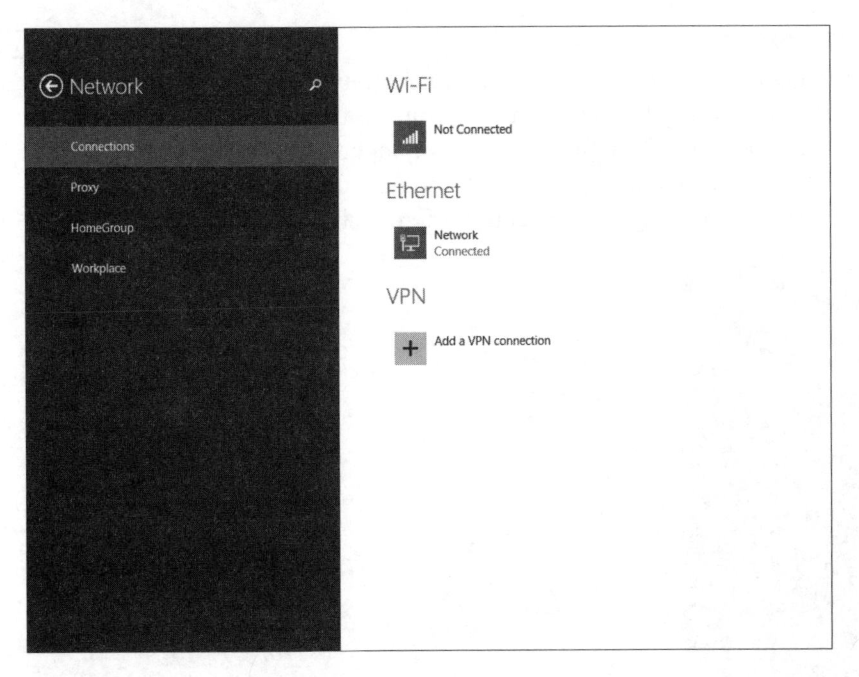

Figure 1-19 The Network utility enables you to configure several networking properties.

- **Connections:** Enables you to view the properties of your Wi-Fi and Ethernet connections. Click **Add a VPN connection** to set up a VPN connection to a corporate network utilizing this service.
- **Proxy:** Enables you to specify automatic or manual setup for use of a proxy server for Ethernet or Wi-Fi connections.
- **HomeGroup:** Enables you to specify what files and devices you want to share with the rest of your HomeGroup, which can consist of other computers running Windows 7/8/8.1 that are configured as such. It also provides the ability to leave an existing HomeGroup or create a new one. You can choose which types of content are shared among other computers in the HomeGroup. More information on HomeGroup networking is provided in Chapter 9.
- **Workplace:** Enables you to enter a domain-based user ID that you can use for joining your workplace network. You also have an option for turning on apps and services provided by network administrators at your company.

Time and Language

As shown in Figure 1-20, the Time and Language utility enables you to specify options related to the display format of dates and times and the time zone in which your computer is located. Click **Region and language** to specify the country or region used by Windows and apps to provide local content, or add an additional language if you need to work with documents written in different languages.

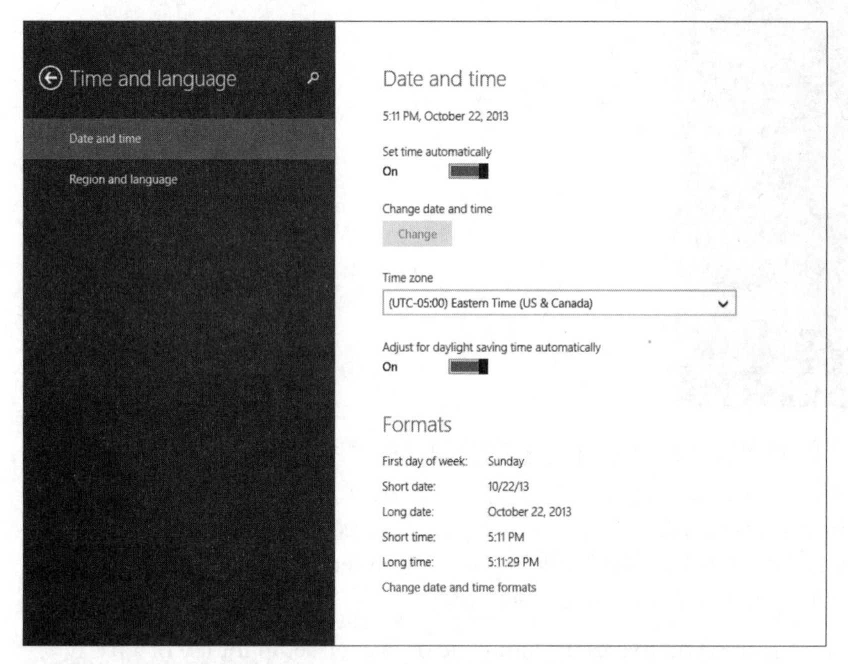

Figure 1-20 The Time and Language utility enables you to modify options related to display of dates and times, as well as languages used on your computer.

Ease of Access

As shown in Figure 1-21, Ease of Access enables you to configure accessibility options for visibility and hearing-challenged users.

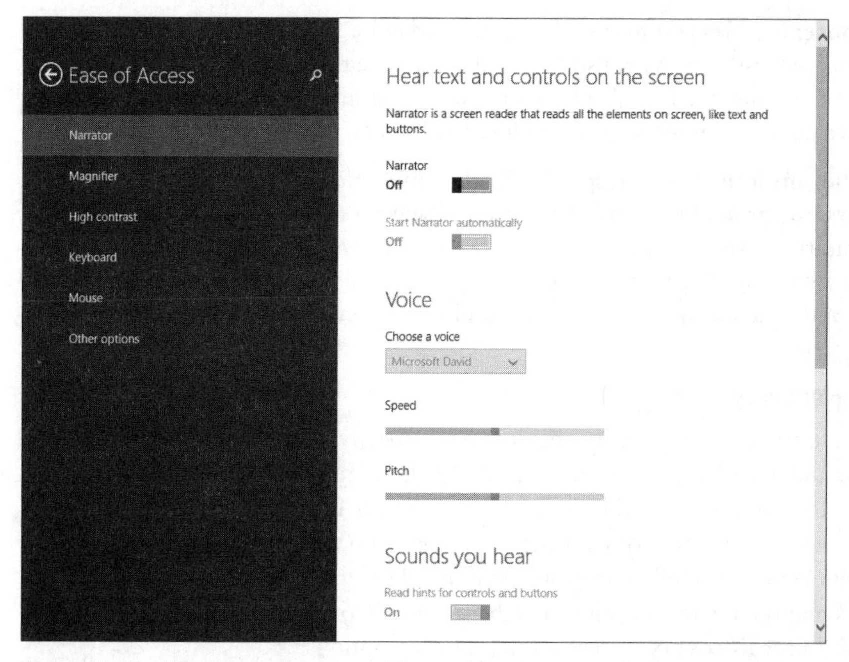

Figure 1-21 The Ease of Access utility enables you to configure several accessibility options.

You have the following options:

- **Narrator:** Enables you to have a computerized voice read the options displayed on the screen for sight-impaired users. Set the Narrator option at the top to **On** to enable the other options, including the voice used and the types of information read back to you. You can also have the cursor highlighted and the insertion point follow the information read by the narrator.
- **Magnifier:** Magnifies information on the display to aid sight-impaired users. You can also have Windows track the keyboard focus and follow the mouse cursor.
- **High contrast:** Enables you to select from one of several preconfigured high-contrast themes. You can also customize the appearance of text, hyperlinks, disabled text, selected text, button text, and the background.
- **Keyboard:** Enables you to display an onscreen keyboard, which you can use by clicking with your mouse or tapping on a touch screen. You can turn on the additional keyboard options:
  - **Sticky keys:** Enables you to press one key at a time for keyboard shortcuts.
  - **Toggle keys:** Sounds a tone when you press the Caps Lock, Num Lock, and Scroll Lock keys.
  - **Filter keys:** Ignores brief or repeated keystrokes.

- **Mouse:** Enables you to specify the size and color of the mouse pointer, for improved visibility. You also have options to use the numeric keypad to move the mouse, use Ctrl to speed up the mouse pointer motion or Shift to slow it down, and determine whether mouse keys can be used when Num Lock is on.
- **Other options:** You can specify whether animations are played or the Windows background is shown. You can also select a time interval (5 seconds by default) for which notifications are shown (it provides several durations of up to 5 minutes). The Cursor thickness option enables you to increase the visibility of the cursor by specifying the number of pixels (up to 20) used.

Update and Recovery

The Update and Recovery utility enables you to specify whether your computer will search for and install updates automatically. Click **Check now** to connect to the Windows Update website and look for updates. Select **File History** to enable the automatic backup of copies of your personal files in libraries to an external drive. We discuss Windows Update in more detail in Chapter 16, "Configuring Windows Updates," and the recovery options in Chapter 19, "Configuring System Recovery Options." Select **Recovery** to access the following options:

- **Refresh your PC without affecting your files:** Reinstalls Windows 8.1 without losing any personal files such as documents, photos, music, videos, and so on.
- **Remove everything and reinstall Windows:** Reformats your system drive and reinstalls Windows 8.1. You must back up anything on the system partition that you want to keep because all application and personal files on this partition will be deleted.
- **Advanced startup:** Select **Restart now** to reconfigure Windows startup settings or restore Windows from a system image.

NOTE For additional introductory information on Windows 8.1 apps, utilities, and settings, refer to any introductory text on Windows 8.1 such as Katherine Murray's *My Windows 8.1* (Que, 2013).

TIP If you really don't like the new look of Windows 8.1, you can make the interface look more like the familiar Windows 7 interface. To do so, perform actions such as the following:

Uninstall all the built-in Metro apps that you have no desire to use.

Change the background of the Start screen to an appearance similar to that of the desktop. To do so, access the **Settings** charm and choose **Personalize**.

Adjust the Start screen navigation properties—for example, to go directly to the desktop at logon and to show the Apps view when you click **Start**. Refer to Figure 1-7 for more information.

Pin your favorite desktop apps to the taskbar. Right-click their icons and choose **Pin to taskbar**.

Set default apps to desktop programs rather than Metro apps. By default, several file types open in Metro apps (such as image files opening with Photos). Right-click the desired file, choose **Open with**, and then select the desired desktop app (such as **Windows Photo Viewer** for image files).

Set your default browser to another option such as Firefox or Google Chrome. Any web link will open automatically in the desktop version of the browser you've set.

Administrative Tools

You can now add tiles for the various tools found in the Administrative Tools folder to the Start screen. Open the Charms bar and select **Settings**. From the Settings bar, select **Tiles** and then toggle the switch under **Administrative Tools** to **Yes**. To remove the Administrative Tools tiles, repeat this action and choose the **No** option. You might need to close and re-open the Start screen to view the Administrative Tools tiles (see Figure 1-22). We discuss the functionality of most of these tools in various chapters of this Cert Guide.

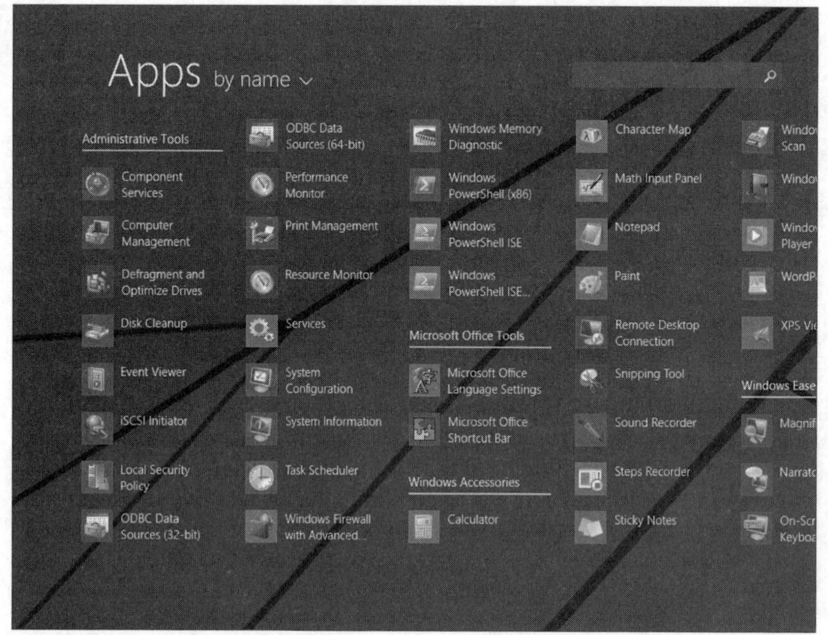

Figure 1-22 Windows 8.1 enables you to add tiles for Administrative Tools to the Start screen.

> **TIP** You can also bring up a quick access menu that links to many of the more frequently used Administrative Tools by right-clicking the lower-left corner of the screen from either the desktop or Start screen. New to Windows 8.1, you can also press the **Windows key + X** key combination to open a menu of Administrative Tools.

Control Panel

Microsoft has continued the idea of categories that first appeared in Windows XP and was enhanced in Windows Vista and 7, and has included links that assist you in performing many common tasks. From the desktop, right-click **Start** and choose **Control Panel**, or open the **Settings** charm and click **Control Panel** to obtain the window shown in Figure 1-23. You can also open the **Search** charm, type `control` in the Search field, and then click the **Control Panel** tile that appears.

This section provides a quick introduction to the Control Panel features. You learn about many of these features in detail in subsequent chapters of this book.

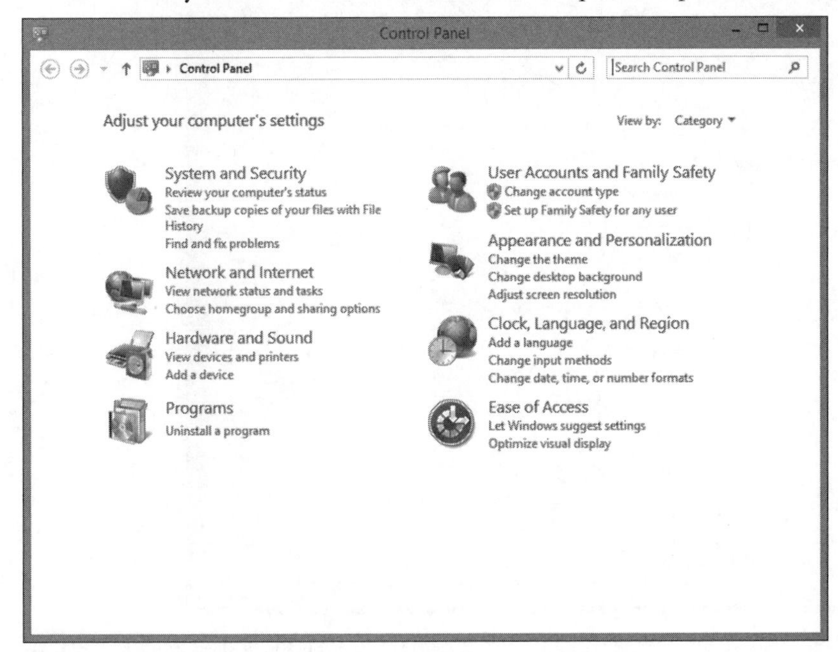

Figure 1-23 The Windows 8.1 Control Panel offers links to frequently used applets.

System and Security

Shown in Figure 1-24, the System and Security category includes several tasks that enable you to configure performance options and obtain information about your computer. Note that the left side of the window includes links to other Control Panel categories. This feature assists you in navigating among categories and is displayed for all Control Panel categories.

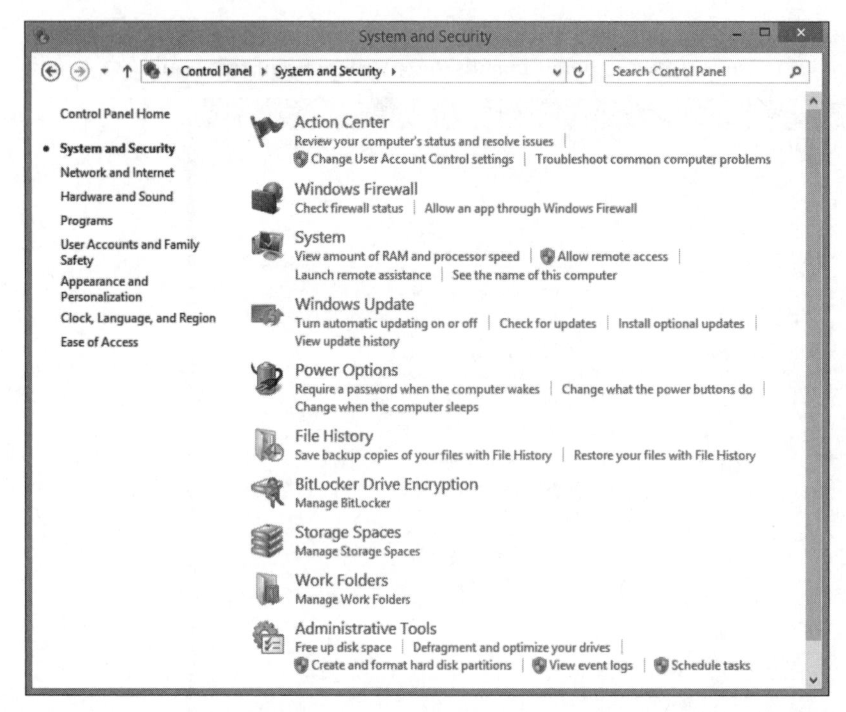

Figure 1-24 The System and Security category includes basic system- and security-related configuration tasks.

The task options available through the System and Security category include the following:

- **Action Center:** This new applet provides a one-stop connection to many security- and maintenance-related tasks.
- **Windows Firewall:** Builds on the firewall first introduced in Windows XP SP2 that protects your computer against both incoming and outgoing threats. You can configure which programs are permitted to send or receive data through the firewall.
- **System:** Provides a summary of information related to your computer, including the hardware configuration, computer name, workgroup or domain information, and activation status.
- **Windows Update:** Enables your computer to download various updates, including patches and hotfixes, from the Microsoft Windows Update website. You can view and download available updates and add features to Windows 8.1 from this location, and you can also configure settings that control the downloading and installation of updates.

- **Power Options:** Enables you to select a power plan to conserve energy by turning off items such as your display or hard disks after a period of inactivity or maximize performance of your computer. You can also customize a power plan to suit your needs.
- **File History:** Enables you to save copies of your files to a backup location in the event of loss or corruption, or to restore files to a previous point in time. We discuss backup and restore in detail in Chapter 19.
- **BitLocker Drive Encryption:** Enables you to encrypt the contents of your hard drive so that intruders or thieves are unable to access your data. You can also enable BitLocker To Go, which protects the contents of removable drives from unauthorized access.
- **Storage Spaces:** Enables you to save files to additional drives to help protect you against a drive failure.
- **Work Folders:** New to Windows 8.1, this applet enables you to set up Work Folders to keep your work files separate from your personal files and keep them in sync with data stored on a file server and on all your devices. You can use your work email address to retrieve corporate settings.
- **Administrative Tools:** Links to a large number of administrative tools, many of which we discuss in subsequent chapters of this book.

NOTE For more information on the new Work Folders feature, refer to "Work Folders Overview" at http://technet.microsoft.com/en-us/library/dn265974.aspx.

Network and Internet

Shown in Figure 1-25, the Network and Internet category includes several tasks that enable you to configure connections to your local area network (LAN) or the Internet, as well as several other network-related tasks. If you've installed connections to other Internet-based resources such as iCloud, these will appear.

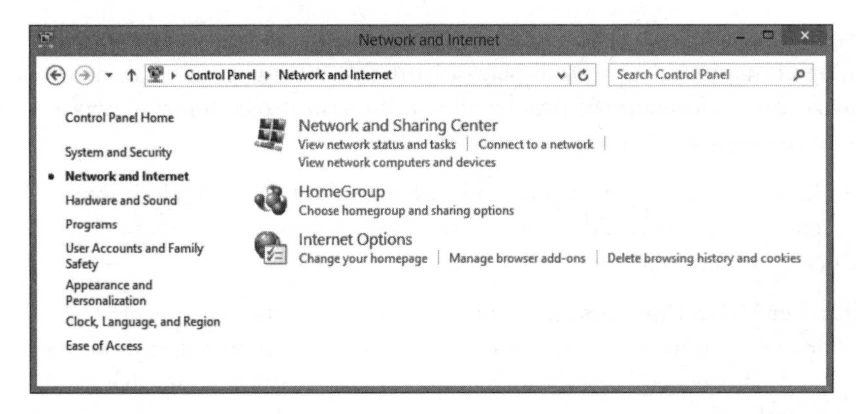

Figure 1-25 The Network and Internet category enables you to perform network-related tasks.

The task options provided by the Network and Internet category include the following:

- **Network and Sharing Center:** Enables you to establish and configure options related to networks accessible to your computer. It provides a local view of the network to which your computer is attached, and enables you to perform several tasks related to sharing of items such as files, folders, printers, and media. You can view the current status of your network connections, enable or disable network connections, and diagnose connectivity problems.
- **HomeGroup:** Enables you to modify sharing options for libraries and printers. You can also stream pictures, music, and videos to other networked devices, and modify HomeGroup security options.
- **Internet Options:** Enables you to configure the properties of Internet Explorer 10 or 11. You can specify your home page, delete your browsing history, modify tabbed browsing, configure security and privacy options, and perform many more actions. We look at these options in Chapter 6, "Configuring Internet Explorer."

Hardware and Sound

Shown in Figure 1-26, the Hardware and Sound category includes applets that enable you to configure all your computer's hardware components. Note that the applets that appear in this category depend on the hardware present on your computer; third-party manufacturers might add additional applets to the category.

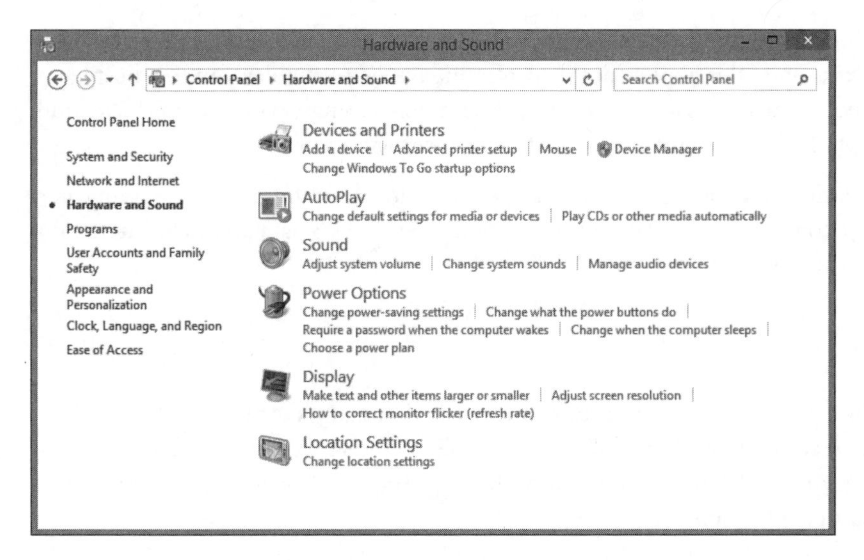

Figure 1-26 The Hardware and Sound category enables you to manage a diverse range of hardware components.

The Hardware and Sound category includes the following applets:

- **Devices and Printers:** Enables you to add printers and fax devices and configure properties of these devices. You can view and manage print queues, configure printer permissions, modify settings related to a specific printer type, and troubleshoot problems related to printers and faxes. You can configure mouse properties such as button settings, pointer appearance, scroll wheel actions, and so on. You can also access the Device Manager, which enables you to view information on hardware devices on your computer. Device Manager enables you to enable or disable devices; identify resources used by each device; identify, update, and roll back device drivers; and so on.
- **AutoPlay:** Enables you to configure default actions that take place when you insert media of a given type such as audio CDs, DVDs, blank discs, and so on.
- **Sound:** Enables you to configure the settings associated with audio recording and playback devices. You can create and modify sound schemes that include the sounds that are associated with Windows and program events.
- **Power Options:** Enables you to choose and configure a power plan, the same as accessed through the System and Security category.
- **Display:** Enables you to specify the size of text and other items on the screen. Links from this applet enable you to adjust screen resolution and the use of Clear Type text, and access the Magnifier tool, which can temporarily enlarge a portion of your screen.

- **Windows Mobility Center:** Available on laptops, tablets, and other mobile devices only, this applet (not shown in Figure 1-26) enables you to adjust parameters such as display settings, presentation settings, connected devices, and so on. It also includes a display of battery charge status.
- **Location Settings:** Enables you to control how location-aware programs on your computer use location information such as GPS data and help Microsoft improve its location services.

Programs

Shown in Figure 1-27, the Programs category includes applets that enable you to configure features related to applications installed on your computer, including programs that run by default at startup as well as locating, downloading, installing, and removing of applications.

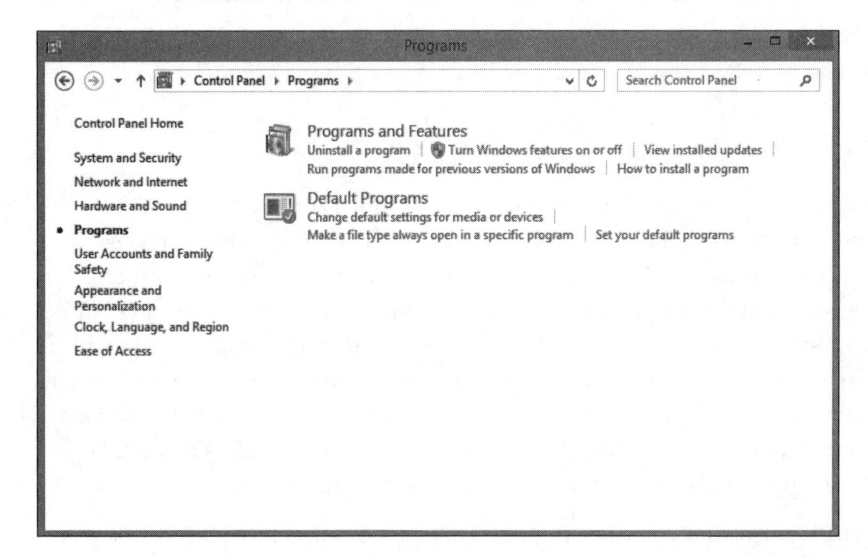

Figure 1-27 The Programs category lets you manage applications on your computer.

Applets provided by the Programs category include the following:

- **Programs and Features:** This applet is a complete reworking of the Add or Remove Programs applet in Windows versions prior to Vista; it enables you to uninstall, change, or repair applications installed on your computer. You can also view installed updates or run programs created for previous Windows versions.

- **Default Programs:** This applet enables you to configure which applications Windows uses by default for opening files of specific type. You can also control access to various types of applications and configure AutoPlay settings.

User Accounts and Family Safety

Shown in Figure 1-28, the User Accounts and Family Safety category enables you to configure several options related to user accounts and logon credentials.

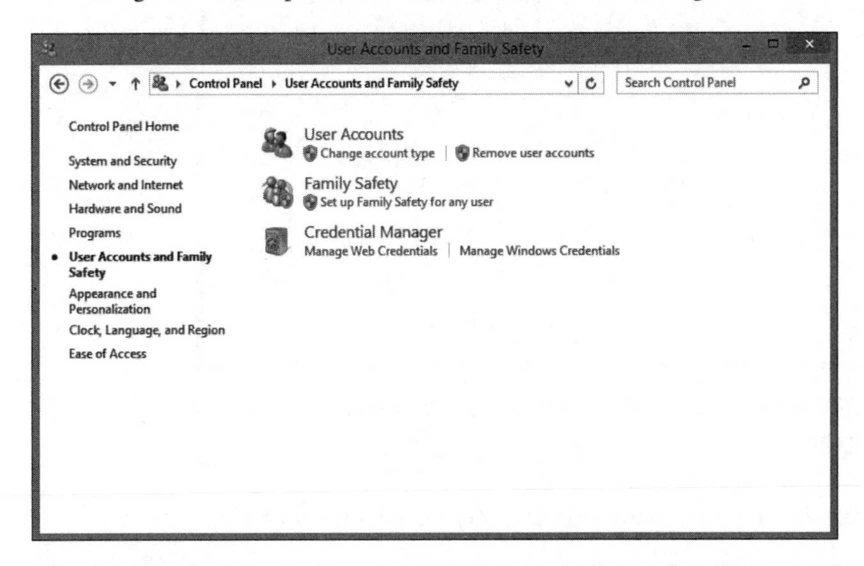

Figure 1-28 The User Accounts and Family Safety category enables you to configure user account properties.

Applets provided by the User Accounts and Family Safety category include the following:

- **User Accounts:** Enables you to create or remove user accounts and modify use account properties.
- **Family Safety:** Previously known as Parental Controls, this option enables you to set limits on actions performed by other users of your computer such as children by blocking access to specific types of websites or folders, blocking specific content categories such as pornography, blocking file downloads, setting time limits, restricting games, and so on.
- **Credential Manager:** Enables you to configure the Windows Vault, which stores credentials used for logging on to other computers or websites.

Appearance and Personalization

As shown in Figure 1-29, the Appearance and Personalization category enables you to configure properties of your computer related to how items appear on the display.

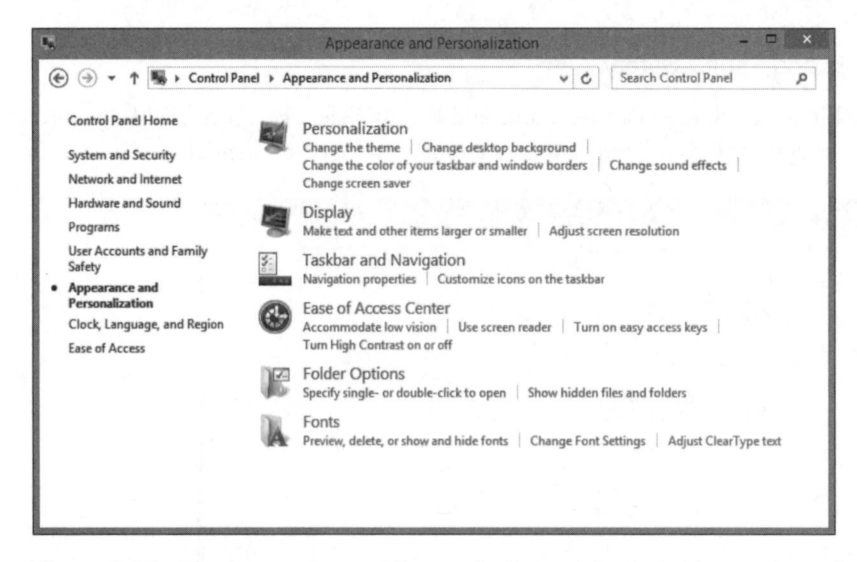

Figure 1-29 The Appearance and Personalization category enables you to configure appearance-related options.

The Appearance and Personalization category includes the following:

- **Personalization:** Enables you to configure a large range of mostly display-related options such as color and appearance of windows, desktop background, screen saver, Windows themes, display resolution and refresh, and so on. You can go online to get additional themes.
- **Display:** Enables you to configure display properties, the same as in the Hardware and Sound category.
- **Taskbar and Navigation:** Same as accessed by right-clicking the taskbar and choosing **Properties**, as already discussed.
- **Ease of Access Center:** Contains several accessibility options that enable vision- and mobility-challenged users to use the computer. You can access a wizard that helps you select the appropriate options for individuals with different requirements.
- **Folder Options:** Enables you to modify how folder windows display their contents. You can configure whether files open with a single- or double-click, show hidden files and folders, and so on.
- **Fonts:** Enables you to manage fonts stored on your computer. You can add or remove fonts and display samples of fonts installed on your computer.

NOTE Desktop gadgets previously included in Windows Vista and Windows 7 have been discontinued in Windows 8/8.1 because serious vulnerabilities have been found. Consequently, Microsoft has discontinued this feature.

Displaying File Extensions

As in previous Windows versions, Windows 8.1 does not display extensions for common file types by default. To display file extensions, access the Folder Options applet, click the **View** tab, and clear the check box labeled **Hide Extensions for Known File Types**. This helps you distinguish between files with otherwise similar names. It also helps guard against undesirable files with double extensions; for example, `data.txt.exe` would appear as `data.txt` and could hide a malicious executable if you have not cleared this check box.

Clock, Language, and Region

The Clock, Language, and Region category contains three applets that enable you to configure the time and date displayed on your computers; configure your time zone; add additional display languages (so that you can view windows and dialog boxes in another language); and select how your computer displays items such as dates, times, numbers, and currency according to the country in which you live. You can also add or remove display languages, set which language is displayed by default, and adapt your keyboard for specific languages.

Ease of Access

The Ease of Access category provides access to the Ease of Access Center, which is also included in the Appearance and Personalization category. It also includes the Speech Recognition applet, which enables you to configure microphones and train your computer to understand your voice. You can take a tutorial that shows you how to use speech on your computer and view or print a list of speech-related commands.

The Computer Management Snap-in

First introduced in Windows 2000 and improved since then with each successive Windows version, the Computer Management snap-in enables you to perform a series of management actions on Windows 8.1 computers. As shown in Figure 1-30, this snap-in includes the following management tools:

- **Task Scheduler:** Used for configuring programs and utilities to run at predetermined times and repeated schedules.

- **Event Viewer:** Used for troubleshooting errors.
- **Shared Folders:** Used for managing shares and connections to your computer.
- **Local Users and Groups:** Used for managing local users and groups on the computer.
- **Performance:** Used for troubleshooting errors as well as optimizing performance.
- **Device Manager:** Used for configuring devices, updating or uninstalling device drivers, rolling back device drivers, enabling and disabling devices, and troubleshooting.
- **Disk Management:** Used for viewing and managing volume and disk configuration.
- **Services:** Used for starting and stopping services related to a device.
- **WMI Control:** Used for turning error logging on or off or backing up the Windows Management Instrumentation (WMI) repository (in most cases, you will not use this tool).

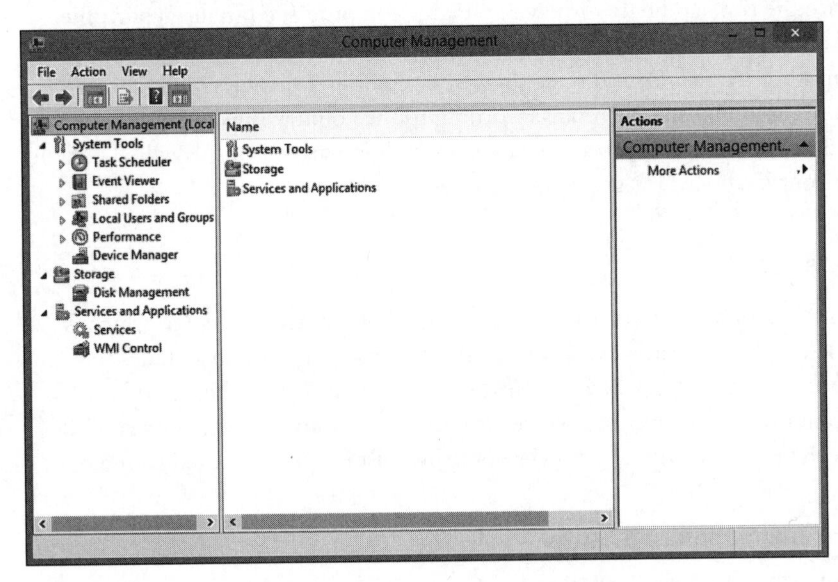

Figure 1-30 The Computer Management snap-in includes several important Windows 8.1 management utilities.

Evaluating Hardware Readiness and Compatibility

As a network support technician, you will be faced with the task of deciding whether to upgrade existing computers to Windows 8.1, purchase new hardware to run Windows 8.1 on, or leave the current operating system on your company's computers. For the 70-687 exam, Microsoft expects you to know how to evaluate existing hardware for its capability to run Windows 8.1.

Windows 8.1 Hardware Requirements (Including Screen Resolution)

Microsoft has defined the minimum level of hardware requirements for computers running Windows 8.1. These requirements represent the bare minimum required to run the core features of Windows 8.1 and provide a basic user experience.

Table 1-3 lists the base hardware requirements for Windows 8.1. Although these are the minimum hardware requirements for supporting the operating system, they are not necessarily adequate to support additional applications or for reasonable performance. When designing the hardware requirements for installation, you should allow for extra RAM and hard disk space and probably a faster processor for applications.

Table 1-3 Hardware Requirements for Windows 8.1

Device	Minimum Supported Hardware
Processor	1 GHz or higher with support for Physical Address Extension (PAE), NX processor bit (NX), and Streaming SIMD Extensions 2 (SSE2).
RAM	1 GB RAM (32-bit) or 2 GB RAM (64-bit)
Graphics processor	DirectX 9-capable with WDDM 1.0 or higher driver
Hard disk	At least 16 GB (32-bit) or 20 GB (64-bit)

NOTE For more information on processor characteristics required in Windows 8.1, refer to "What is PAE, NX, and SSE2?" at http://windows.microsoft.com/en-US/windows-8/what-is-pae-nx-sse2.

If you want to access a network (including accessing the Windows Store to download and run apps), you should have a network adapter installed that is compatible with the network infrastructure. For Internet access, at a minimum, you need a dial-up modem or broadband connection to connect to an Internet service provider (ISP). Video conferencing, voice, fax, and other multimedia applications generally require a high-speed connection, microphone, sound card, and speakers or headset. Video conferencing itself requires a video conferencing camera. Other required hardware depends on purposes you might use Windows 8.1 for, such as the following:

- To use touch, you must have a tablet or monitor that is touch-compatible.
- To run Windows Store apps, you need a screen resolution of at least 1024 × 768. To snap apps, you need a screen resolution of at least 1366 × 768.
- Complete Media Center functionality requires a TV tuner.
- BitLocker requires the TPM 1.2.

Hardware Compatibility

Microsoft makes it easy to check your hardware's compatibility by providing a list of supported hardware. Microsoft designed the Windows Hardware Certification Program with the aim of assisting users to identify hardware components that are compatible with Windows 8.1 and Windows Server 2012 R2. Microsoft states that the "Windows Certification Program (previously known as the Windows Logo Program) provides you the tools, guidance, and support to help ensure your product is reliable and compatible with Windows." Microsoft's Windows Hardware Certification Kit (HCK) extends the functionality of the previous Logo program to provide benefits such as updated certification requirements and needs for products and drivers used with Windows 8.1, automation of much of the hardware test processes, improvement in diagnostics logged by the Event Viewer utility, and an enhanced test management console, among other improvements.

NOTE For more information on the Windows Hardware Certification program, refer to "Windows Hardware Certification" at http://msdn.microsoft.com/en-us/library/windows/hardware/gg463010.aspx and additional documents referenced in this article.

An issue that can interrupt the installation process is the use of incompatible critical device drivers. If a compatible driver is not available, Setup stops until updated drivers are found. Operating system upgrades will not migrate incompatible drivers based on older Windows operating systems. The only way to ensure a smooth installation is to make certain you have all the drivers available at the start of the installation process. Do not be concerned about unattended installations because there is a folder in which you can place any additional or updated drivers for hardware that is not included in the base Windows 8.1 files.

Before you deploy Windows 8.1 on any system, you should ensure that the hardware and Basic Input/Output System (BIOS) are compatible with the operating system. Older hardware may not have a compatible BIOS even though the devices within the PC itself are all listed in the Windows Hardware Certification Program. The original equipment manufacturer (OEM) should have an updated BIOS available that can be downloaded from the OEM's website.

If you have an Internet connection, you can use the Windows Update feature to connect to the Windows Update website during setup. Windows 8.1 automatically downloads and installs updated drivers during the setup process from the Windows Update website. More information on Windows Update is provided in Chapter 16.

Using 32-Bit or 64-Bit Windows

You can have either 32-bit or 64-bit Windows operating systems, but you cannot have both simultaneously. Consequently, you should know which bit level is most appropriate for your situation. In general, a 32-bit operating system runs on hardware equipped with a 32-bit processor, and a 64-bit operating system runs on hardware equipped with a 64-bit processor. Windows 8.1 and Windows Server 2012 R2 support the Unified Extensible Firmware Interface (UEFI)-based hardware platforms. You need to match the architecture version of UEFI to that of the operating system. For example, a 32-bit UEFI platform can boot only 32-bit Windows, whereas a 64-bit UEFI platform can boot only 64-bit Windows.

The benefit of running 64-bit Windows is that it can handle large amounts of memory more efficiently than 32-bit Windows; this is most apparent for a computer equipped with 4 GB of RAM or more. Such a computer is more responsive when the user is running several programs at the same time and switching among them frequently.

Hardware platforms must meet one of the following requirements:

- A machine shipping with 32-bit Windows must be certified for 32-bit UEFI and Windows 8.1 x86.
- A machine shipping with 64-bit Windows must be certified for 64-bit UEFI and Windows 8.1 x64.
- A machine shipping with both 32-bit and 64-bit configurations must be certified for both configurations.
- A machine that is capable of both 32-bit and 64-bit support but shipping with one of these configurations must be certified for the configuration in which it ships.
- A machine that ships with Windows 7 installed must be certified for both Windows 7 with compatibility support module (CSM) and Windows 8.1 x64 with 64-bit UEFI.

NOTE For more information on UEFI, refer to "What is UEFI?" at http://windows.microsoft.com/en-ID/windows-8/what-uefi.

You should also be aware of the following considerations when selecting 32-bit or 64-bit Windows 8.1:

- Most 32-bit programs can run efficiently on a 64-bit platform, with the exception of some antivirus programs.
- Programs specifically designed to run on a 64-bit platform won't work on 32-bit Windows. But some programs such as Microsoft Office 2010 and later are available in both 32-bit and 64-bit versions.
- You need 64-bit device drivers to use all your hardware devices with 64-bit Windows. Drivers designed for 32-bit Windows won't work on a machine running 64-bit Windows. Check the hardware device's website to locate and download 64-bit drivers.

Choosing Between an Upgrade and a Clean Installation

If you have a computer that is currently running Windows XP, Vista, 7, or 8, and it meets the hardware requirements for running Windows 8.1, you might be able to either upgrade the existing Windows installation to Windows 8.1 or perform a clean installation. Refer to the following considerations when deciding whether to upgrade your current installation:

- If you upgrade your current installation of Windows to Windows 8.1, all your applications, data, and settings such as usernames and passwords are retained and will work with Windows 8.1. However, if a program is not compatible with Windows 8.1, it will not work unless you are able to configure it in a compatibility mode. Refer to the program manufacturer's website for further information; in many cases, you will be able to purchase an upgrade for the program.
- You must ensure that all drivers used with hardware devices attached to your computer are compatible with Windows 8.1. Refer to the device's website for information on available drivers and to download updated drivers.
- If you perform a clean installation of Windows 8.1, you must reinstall all programs that you used with the previous version of Windows. Further, you must re-create all settings such as usernames and passwords. If you use the same disk partition as the previous installation of Windows, all data stored on that partition will be lost; consequently, you must back up data to another location before starting your installation.

- If you perform a clean installation of Windows 8.1 to a different partition than your previous Windows installation, you will create a dual-boot system in which you can boot either Windows 8.1 or the previous installation of Windows. You can access any data stored on the previous Windows partition; however, you must reinstall all programs that you intend to use on Windows 8.1 (accessing programs on the previous Windows partition and double-clicking executable files will generally not work).

Microsoft provides the Windows Upgrade Assistant, which helps you decide whether your computer can be upgraded to Windows 8.1 or if it requires a clean installation to run Windows 8.1. Use the following procedure to run Windows Upgrade Assistant:

Step 1. Navigate to http://windows.microsoft.com/en-US/windows-8/upgrade-to-windows-8 and click the **Windows 8.1 Upgrade Assistant** link.

Step 2. Click **Run** to start downloading the program. After a few seconds, the program will be downloaded and will start automatically.

Step 3. If you receive a User Account Control prompt, click **Yes**.

Step 4. The program starts with a Let's see what's compatible dialog box. Wait while the upgrade assistant checks your apps and devices.

Step 5. After several minutes, you receive a message similar to the one shown in Figure 1-31, informing you of the number of items you should review. To review these items, click **See compatibility details**.

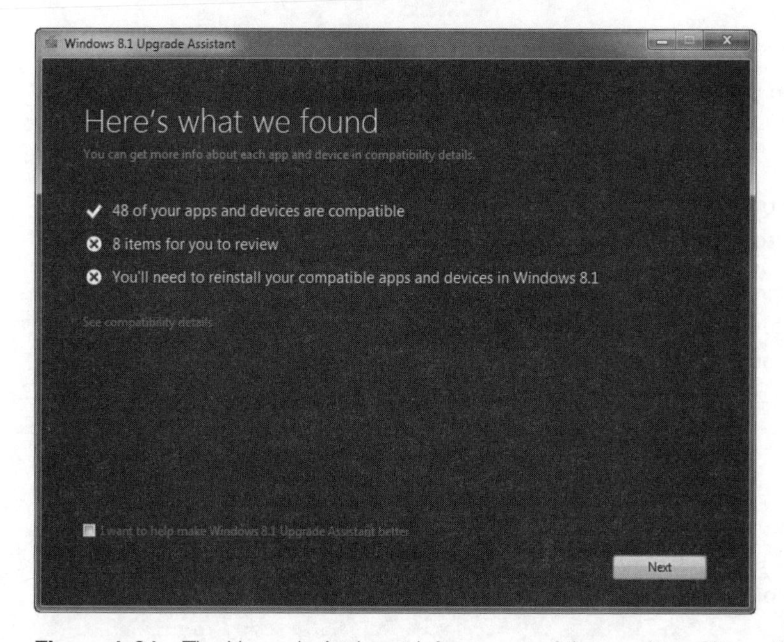

Figure 1-31 The Upgrade Assistant informs you of the number of items that you should review.

Step 6. Windows Upgrade Assistant provides information on the issues you should check, as shown in Figure 1-32. Click **Print** to print this list or **Save** to save it as an HTML-based web page. When finished, click **Close** to close this dialog box and then click **Next** to continue.

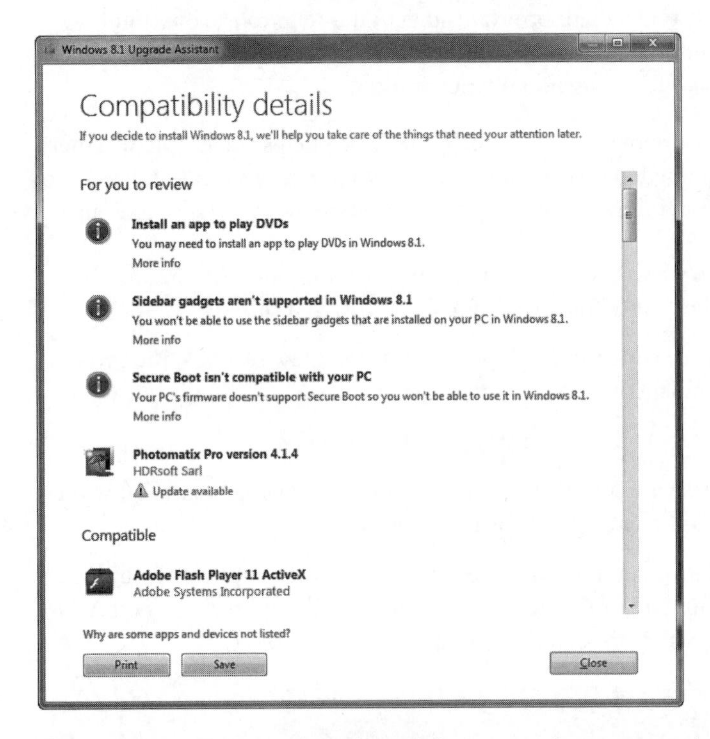

Figure 1-32 The Upgrade Assistant informs you of programs or hardware settings you should check before upgrading to Windows 8.1.

Step 7. Select one of the options shown in Figure 1-33 according to what items you would like to keep from your current Windows installation, and then click **Next**.

Step 8. You are informed which installation of Windows 8.1 is appropriate. If your computer cannot run Windows 8.1, you are informed of the hardware upgrades required to run Windows 8.1. Click **Close** to exit the Upgrade Assistant.

NOTE For more information on preparing for Windows 8 and 8.1, refer to links provided in the document "Install, Deploy, and Migrate to Windows 8" at http://technet.microsoft.com/library/hh832022.aspx.

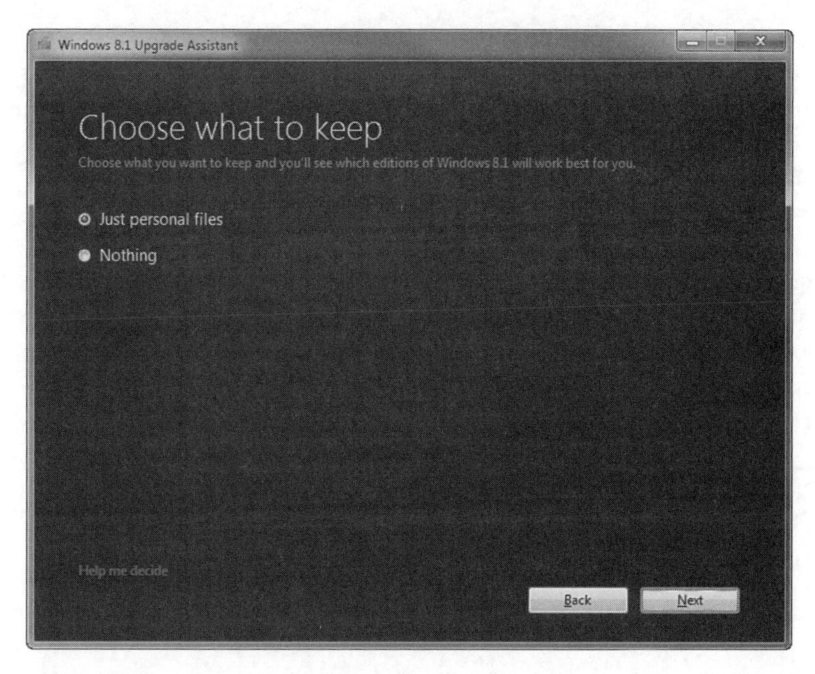

Figure 1-33 The Upgrade Assistant provides options that determine what items will be kept from your current Windows installation.

Software Compatibility

As you have noted when running the Windows 8.1 Upgrade Assistant, current software on your computer might not be compatible with the new operating system. This need to ensure software compatibility is frequently one of the more difficult parts of the development and testing phase of any operating system deployment project. The operating system that you deploy is important because it provides the basic functionality for the computer, but productivity usually depends on business applications that are installed, which makes applications more important to the organization. If an application is not compatible with the operating system, you have the following options:

- Upgrade the application to a compatible version.
- Replace the application with a similar type of application that is compatible with Windows 8.1.
- Retire the application.

Before you are faced with these decisions, your first task in determining software compatibility is to identify all the applications that are used and that will be installed in your deployment project. You should develop a matrix of applications that is organized according to priority of business productivity and by number of users that use the application. For example, if you determine that 100% of all your users use APP A, but that it does not directly contribute to business productivity (such as an antivirus application), you would place it in the high use, low productivity quadrant. If you determine that 10% of your users use APP B, and it contributes highly to business productivity, you would place it in the low use, high productivity quadrant. If 5% of users use APP C, and it has no impact on business productivity, you would place that in the low use, low productivity quadrant. The applications in that low use, low productivity quadrant are the ones that you should analyze for potentially retiring. If you find that 90% of all users use APP D, and it is considered business-critical, you would put APP D in the high use, high productivity quadrant. All applications in this quadrant should receive priority during the project. Figure 1-34 attempts to place these applications into this perspective.

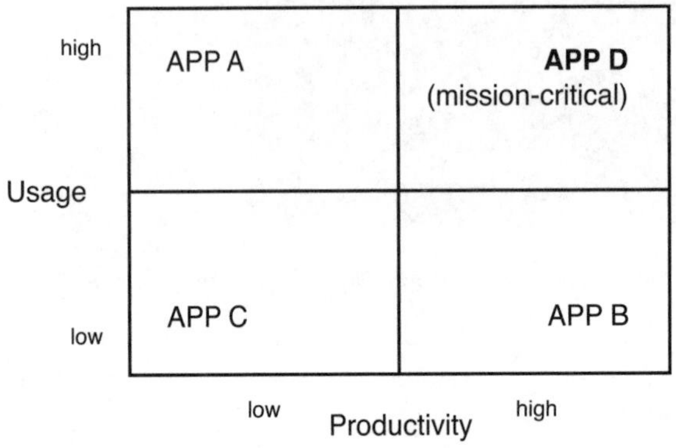

Figure 1-34 You should prioritize all applications used in your company according to their usage and productivity.

You might decide to include additional criteria to your matrix to better pinpoint the applications that will require more of your time during the project. For example, you could identify which applications are developed for Windows 8.1 and which are developed specifically for older Windows operating systems, as well as which have been developed in-house. Applications that have been developed for Windows XP, Windows Vista, or Windows 7 might not run properly on Windows 8.1. Antivirus applications are typically incompatible if they were developed for older Windows versions. In nearly all cases, applications that worked properly on Windows 7 should work with Windows 8.1; if problems do occur, you should be able to run these applications in compatibility mode.

After you have an inventory of your current software, you should then build a test lab and test the applications with Windows 8.1. With each application that has compatibility problems, you should decide whether the application is important enough to fix. If it is important, you should then determine the fixes you need to undertake to make it compatible. You can then package the fixes using the Microsoft Application

Compatibility Toolkit. This toolkit assists software developers and corporate IT professionals in determining whether their applications are compatible with Windows 8.1; it also enables these individuals to determine how applications are affected by the update to Windows 8.1. Finally, you should test the deployment and perform a quality assurance check on the test PCs to see whether the applications install and run properly.

NOTE For more information on the Microsoft Application Compatibility Toolkit, refer to "Application Compatibility Toolkit (ACT) Technical Reference" at http://technet.microsoft.com/en-us/library/hh825181.

Determining Which SKU to Install

Microsoft provides two versions (SKUs) of each Windows 8.1 edition: an upgrade SKU and a full SKU. The upgrade SKU sells for a lower price than the full SKU but is otherwise identical in its features. After running the Upgrade Assistant as described earlier in this section, you are informed of which edition you should buy. Simply put, the upgrade version will check for evidence of an older Windows operating system somewhere in the computer (XP, Vista, or 7); if it is unable to find this information, you will be unable to activate and use Windows 8.1. In such cases, you must purchase the full version of Windows 8.1.

NOTE For more information on upgrading to Windows 8.1, including the use of the Upgrade Assistant and use of upgrade versus full SKU editions, refer to "Update to Windows 8.1: FAQ" at http://windows.microsoft.com/en-US/windows-8/upgrade-to-windows-8.

Determining Requirements for Windows Features

Windows 8.1 introduces several new features that you can use according to the hardware configuration of your computer. They include the following:

- Client Hyper-V
- Miracast Display
- Pervasive Device Encryption
- Virtual smart cards
- Secure Boot

Table 1-4 introduces the hardware requirements for each of these features.

Table 1-4 Hardware Requirements for New Windows Features

Feature	Minimum Supported Hardware
Client Hyper-V	A 64-bit computer with at least 4 GB RAM and running Windows 8.1 Pro or Enterprise, as well as a processor that supports virtualization. Additional RAM as needed to support the virtual machines being installed on your computer.
Miracast Display	A display device that is compatible with the wireless Miracast format (such as a compatible HDTV) to allow wireless streaming of the computer display image to the external device. A Miracast-compatible adapter that wirelessly connects to your computer and uses HDMI to transmit the display to the Miracast-enabled device.
Pervasive Device Encryption	A Windows 8.1 laptop that supports connected standby and meets the Windows Hardware Certification Kit (HCK) requirements for TPM and Secure Boot. A Microsoft account configured with administrative privileges so that a recovery key can be backed up to Microsoft servers. You can alternately join your laptop to an Active Directory Domain Services (AD DS) domain, in which the domain will receive the recovery key.
Virtual smart cards	A Windows 8.1 Pro or Enterprise computer equipped with a TPM. You will also need access to an AD DS domain with a domain server running a fully installed certification authority (CA).
Secure Boot	A Windows 8.1 computer that meets the UEFI specifications version 2.3.1, Errata C, or higher. Note that a TPM is not required.

We take a look at installation and configuration of these features in Chapter 2, "Installing Windows 8.1."

Exam Preparation Tasks

Review All the Key Topics

Review the most important topics in the chapter, noted with the key topics icon in the outer margin of the page. Table 1-5 lists a reference of these key topics and the page numbers on which each is found.

Table 1-5 Key Topics for Chapter 1

Key Topic Element	Description	Page Number(s)
List	Describes available Windows 8.1 editions	9
Figure 1-1	Displays the Windows 8.1 Start screen as it appears after you install Windows 8.1 for the first time	18
List	Describes new actions that you can perform from the Windows 8.1 Start screen	19-20
Figure 1-11	Displays the PC settings screen, which enables you to configure a large number of settings that affect the behavior of your computer	31
Figure 1-22	Shows how to add tiles for Administrative Tools to the Windows 8.1 Start screen	46
Table 1-3	Describes the minimum hardware requirements for running Windows 8.1	57
List	Describes considerations you should think of when deciding between 32-bit and 64-bit editions of Windows 8.1	60
Step List	Shows you how to run the Windows 8.1 Upgrade Assistant	61
Table 1-4	Describes the hardware requirements for several new Windows 8.1 features	66

Complete the Tables and Lists from Memory

Print a copy of Appendix B, "Memory Tables," (found on the CD), or at least the section for this chapter, and complete the tables and lists from memory. Appendix C, "Memory Tables Answer Key," also on the CD, includes completed tables and lists to check your work.

Definitions of Key Terms

Define the following key terms from this chapter and check your answers in the glossary.

Apps, Application Compatibility Toolkit, Charms, Computer Management snap-in, File Explorer, Metro, Windows 8.1 Upgrade Assistant, Windows Hardware Certification Program, Windows RT 8.1

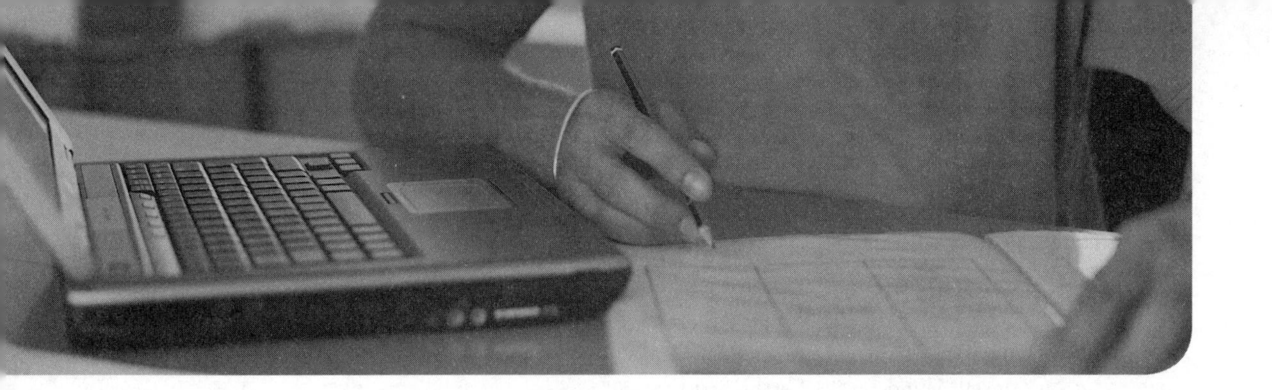

This chapter covers the following subjects:

- **Performing a Clean Installation:** This section describes the procedure for performing a basic installation of Windows 8.1 from the DVD-ROM media.
- **Upgrading to Windows 8.1 from a Previous Version of Windows:** Microsoft provides several upgrade paths for users with older computers wanting to upgrade to Windows 8.1. Depending on the upgrade path chosen, users might be able to keep personal files, applications, and Windows settings.
- **Upgrading from One Edition of Windows 8.1 to Another:** It is possible to upgrade the base version of Windows 8.1 to Windows 8.1 Pro by purchasing and entering the appropriate product key.
- **Installing as Windows To Go:** New in Windows 8 and 8.1, Microsoft provides the ability to install a completely functional version of Windows 8.1 together with applications and settings on a supported USB drive. You can use this drive to boot a computer with supported hardware into the USB copy of Windows 8.1, bypassing the operating system installed on the computer you're using.
- **Using a VHD:** You can host a complete copy of Windows 8.1 on a virtual hard disk (VHD) that can be copied and deployed to a large number of computers in an enterprise situation. This section introduces VHDs and discusses the procedures you need to be familiar with to create, mount, deploy, and boot a computer from a VHD.

CHAPTER 2

Installing Windows 8.1

The Microsoft 70-687 exam assesses your ability to install, configure, and administer Windows 8 and 8.1 and focuses on how to do so in a business environment. Basic to any installation type is the manual, clean installation of Windows 8.1 on a new computer.

As an adjunct to Murphy's Law, what can go wrong during an operating system installation does go wrong, and then the situation needs troubleshooting. Windows 8.1 is no exception. Knowing how to handle unexpected errors makes all the difference to a network support technician or administrator.

"Do I Know This Already?" Quiz

The "Do I Know This Already?" quiz allows you to assess whether you should read this entire chapter or simply jump to the "Exam Preparation Tasks" section for review. If you are in doubt, read the entire chapter. Table 2-1 outlines the major headings in this chapter and the corresponding "Do I Know This Already?" quiz questions. You can find the answers in Appendix A, "Answers to the 'Do I Know This Already?' Quizzes."

Table 2-1 "Do I Know This Already?" Foundation Topics Section-to-Question Mapping

Foundations Topics Section	Questions Covered in This Section
Performing a Clean Installation	1–5
Upgrading to Windows 8.1 from a Previous Version of Windows	6–9
Upgrading from One Edition of Windows 8.1 to Another	10
Installing as Windows To Go	11–14
Using a VHD	15–16

1. Which of the following are items you should have on hand before beginning a Windows 8.1 installation? (Choose all that apply.)
   a. Windows 8.1 drivers from the manufacturer for any hardware not appearing in the Windows Hardware Certification Program
   b. BIOS that meets the minimum requirements for Windows 8.1 compatibility
   c. Windows 8.1 product code
   d. Internet connection
   e. A CD-ROM drive
   f. Backup of all your existing data and the drivers for your backup device

2. Which of the following settings can you configure during an installation of Windows 8.1 from a DVD-ROM? (Choose all that apply.)
   a. Username and password
   b. Domain membership
   c. Computer name and background color
   d. Language, time, and currency format
   e. Charms bar

3. What tool would you use to create or edit answer files used for unattended installations of Windows 8.1?
   a. Windows SIM
   b. Windows AIK
   c. Windows ADK
   d. `Sysprep`

4. You want to set up your computer to triple-boot Windows 8.1, Windows XP, and Windows 7. What should you do first?
   a. Install Windows 7
   b. Install Windows 8.1
   c. Install Windows XP
   d. Install MS-DOS

5. Which Setup log records modifications performed on the system during Setup?
   a. `netsetup.log`
   b. `setuperr.log`
   c. `setupapi.log`
   d. `setupact.log`

6. You are preparing to upgrade your Windows 7 computer to Windows 8.1. Which of the following tasks should you perform before beginning the upgrade? (Choose all that apply.)
   a. Run the Windows Upgrade Assistant.
   b. Run the Windows Anytime Upgrade.
   c. Ensure that all hardware in use is listed in the Windows Certification Program.
   d. Check for any available upgrades for your computer's BIOS.
   e. Scan your computer for viruses.
   f. Remove or disable your antivirus program.
   g. Install the latest service pack for Windows 7.

7. Your computer is running Windows XP Professional. You want to upgrade to Windows 8.1 Pro. Which of the following is the cheapest and simplest way to perform the upgrade?
   a. Insert the Windows 8.1 DVD and upgrade directly to Windows 8.1 Pro.
   b. Insert the Windows Vista DVD and upgrade to Windows Vista Ultimate. Then insert the Windows 8.1 DVD and upgrade to Windows 8.1 Pro.
   c. Insert the Windows 7 DVD and upgrade to Windows 7 Ultimate. Then insert the Windows 8.1 DVD and upgrade to Windows 8.1 Pro.
   d. Insert the Windows 8.1 DVD and install a clean copy of Windows 8.1 Pro.

8. Your computer is running Windows XP Professional. You insert the Windows 8.1 DVD and choose the option to perform a clean installation of Windows 8.1. You then select the same partition on which the Windows XP system files are located and proceed with the upgrade without formatting this partition. Which of the following best describes what happens to your Windows XP system files?

   a. The Windows XP system files are overwritten with the Windows 8.1 system files.

   b. The Windows XP system files are placed in a new folder named `Windows.old`.

   c. The Windows XP system files remain in the same location in an unaltered state, and you create a dual-boot system.

   d. The Windows XP system files are moved to a new partition and you create a dual-boot system.

9. Fred has saved a large number of Word documents on his computer running Windows XP Home Edition. He installs Windows 8.1 on his computer, using the same partition on which Windows XP was installed. He does not reformat this partition. What happens to these documents?

   a. They are placed in the Windows.old\Documents and Settings\Fred\My Documents folder.

   b. They remain in the Documents and Settings\Fred\My Documents folder.

   c. They are placed in the Users\Fred\My Documents folder.

   d. They are lost; Fred must restore them from backup.

10. Your computer runs the base version of Windows 8.1, and you want to upgrade to Windows 8.1 Pro. You have gone online and purchased a Windows 8.1 Pro upgrade license. What should you do?

   a. From the Charms bar, click **Search**, type **`add features`** in the search box, and then click **Add features to Windows 8.1**. Then click **I already have a product key**, enter your product key, and then click **Next**. Select the check box to accept the license terms and then click **Add features**. Then wait while Windows is upgraded and the computer is restarted.

   b. From the Charms bar, click **Settings** and then click **Add features**. Then click **I already have a product key**, enter your product key, and then click **Next**. Select the check box to accept the license terms and then click **Add features**. Then wait while Windows is upgraded and the computer is restarted.

c. Insert the Windows 8.1 DVD, select the option to install Windows, enter the key code for the Pro edition, and run the upgrade.

d. Insert the Windows 8.1 DVD, select the option to perform a clean install of Windows, enter the key code for the Pro edition. Then wait while Windows is upgraded and the computer is restarted.

11. Which of the following best describes Windows To Go?

    a. A portable computer on which Windows 8.1 is installed and booted with user credentials obtained from a USB device.

    b. A copy of Windows 8.1 located on a network drive that you access from any computer using a USB device that contains user credentials and a path to the network drive.

    c. A copy of Windows RT 8.1 imaged onto a USB device that enables a user to boot any computer with compatible hardware into the operating system on the USB device.

    d. A copy of Windows 8.1 imaged onto a USB device that enables a user to boot any computer with compatible hardware into the operating system on the USB device.

12. Windows To Go works on which editions of Windows 8.1?

    a. Windows 8.1 Pro and Enterprise

    b. Windows 8.1 Enterprise only

    c. All except Windows RT

    d. Windows To Go can run any edition

13. What Windows feature is not available and cannot be used on a Windows To Go workspace?

    a. BitLocker drive encryption

    b. Hibernate

    c. Microsoft App store

    d. Windows Recovery Environment

14. Which of the following hardware requirements are NOT necessary for running Windows To Go?

    a. A USB drive that supports USB 3.0

    b. A USB 3.0 port

    c. A computer cable of USB boot

    d. 2 GB or greater of RAM

15. Which of the following are valid types of VHDs in Windows 8.1? (Choose three.)

- **a.** Basic
- **b.** Fixed
- **c.** Dynamic
- **d.** Updating
- **e.** Differencing

16. Which of the following tools could you use to create a new VHD?

- **a.** Disk Management MMC
- **b.** DiskPart command-line utility
- **c.** DISM
- **d.** `Sysprep`
- **e.** Windows PE

Foundation Topics

Performing a Clean Installation

As an IT professional, you should run through at least one or two attended installations even if you are planning to deploy only unattended installations of Windows 8.1 throughout your organization. By going through the process, you can see each stage of installation and relate it to sections within the answer files and with the unattended process later. If you need to troubleshoot an unattended installation, you will be better able to identify the point at which the installation failed if you have already become familiar with the attended installation process.

Performing an Attended Installation

You can run an attended installation process for either an upgrade or a clean installation of Windows 8.1. Upgrading to Windows 8.1 is covered later in this chapter, so we walk through a clean installation process in this section.

Before you begin, check to make certain that you have gathered all the information you need and are prepared to install. You should have the following:

- A computer that meets the minimum hardware requirements previously given in Table 1-3 in Chapter 1, "Introducing Windows 8.1."
- Windows 8.1 drivers from the manufacturer for any hardware that does not appear in the Windows Hardware Certification Program. It's imperative that you have the hard disk drivers, especially if they are RAID or SCSI devices.
- Windows 8.1 DVD or installation files available across a network.
- Basic Input/Output System (BIOS) that meets the minimum requirements for Windows 8.1 compatibility.
- Product code, which should be listed on the DVD package or provided to you from the network administrator.
- If across a network, a boot disk that can access network shares and appropriate network adapters.
- Internet connection for Automatic Updates and access to updated drivers and Windows Product Activation (WPA).
- A backup of all your existing data and the drivers for the backup device so that you can restore the data.

When you have all the preceding items in hand, you're ready to install Windows 8.1. Your first step in the installation is to boot up the computer into the setup process. This process involves running `Setup.exe`, which is the application that installs Windows 8.1 on a new computer or updates an older Windows computer to Windows 8.1. Use the following procedure to install Windows 8.1 using a bootable DVD-ROM rather than a network installation:

Step 1. Insert the Windows 8.1 installation DVD and boot the computer. If you receive a message that the DVD has been autodetected and the prompt `Press any key to boot from CD or DVD`, press the spacebar or any other key within five seconds or the computer will attempt to boot from the hard disk.

Step 2. The screen displays a Windows logo as initial files are loaded. After a minute or so, the Windows Setup dialog box shown in Figure 2-1 appears. If you need to change the language, time, and currency format, or keyboard or input method settings, do so. Otherwise, click **Next** to proceed.

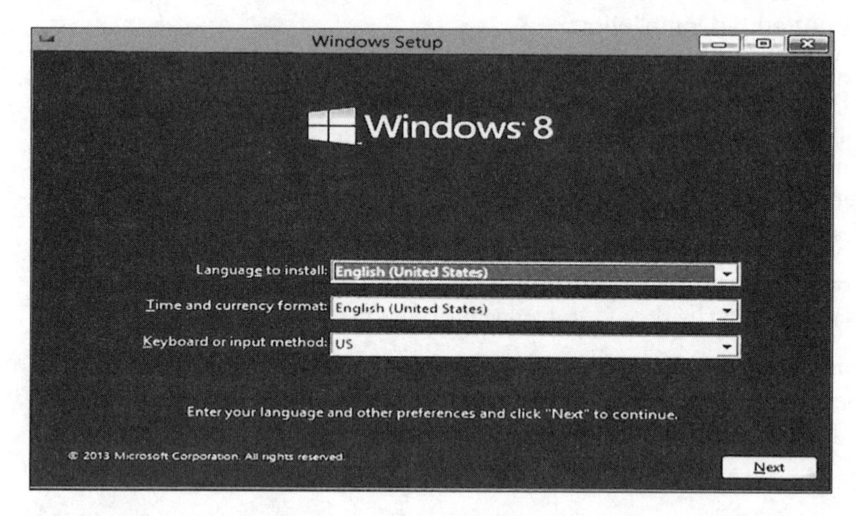

Figure 2-1 The Windows Setup dialog box offers options for language, time and currency, and keyboard or input method.

Step 3. Click **Install now** to begin installation.

Step 4. If you receive a dialog box prompting you to enter the product key to activate Windows, type the product key supplied (it should be on the box containing the DVD or provided with the download) and then click **Next**.

Step 5. You are informed that Setup is starting, and then another Windows Setup dialog box (see Figure 2-2) asks you to read the license terms. You must select the **I accept the license terms** check box to accept the licensing agreement as indicated at the bottom of the screen. Then click **Next**.

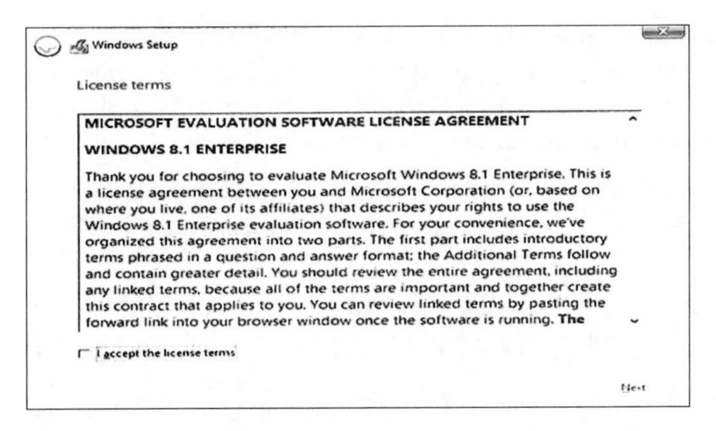

Figure 2-2 You must accept the license terms to install Windows 8.1.

Step 6. The Which type of installation do you want? screen shown in Figure 2-3 offers you a choice of upgrade or custom installation. The Upgrade option is disabled (grayed out) unless you are running the installation on a computer running a compatible copy of Windows Vista/7 with sufficient free disk space to accommodate the upgrade. Select the **Custom: Install Windows only (advanced)** option to continue.

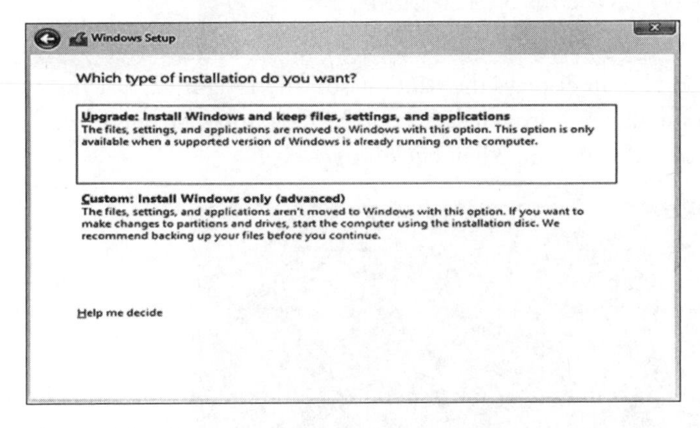

Figure 2-3 Choosing between an upgrade and a custom installation.

Step 7. The next screen shows the available partitions and unpartitioned disk space where you can install Windows 8.1. Make certain you select a partition that has enough available disk space, preferably 40 GB but at least 16 GB for an x86 installation or 20 GB for an x64 installation. If unpartitioned space is available, you can select the unpartitioned space and create a new partition for the operating system at this point. Click **Next**.

Step 8. If the selected partition contains files from a previous Windows installation, you receive a message box informing you of this fact and that these files will be moved to a folder named `Windows.old`. Click **OK** to proceed or **Cancel** to go back and select a different partition.

Step 9. The next window tracks the progress of installing Windows 8.1 and informs you that your computer will restart several times, as shown in Figure 2-4. Take a coffee break.

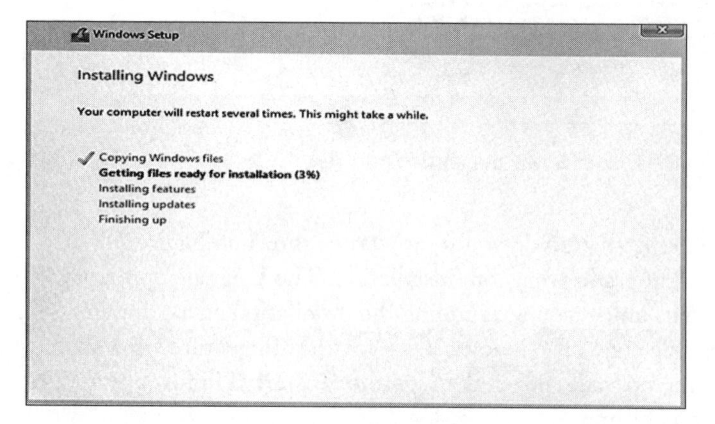

Figure 2-4 Tracking progress of the Windows 8.1 installation.

Step 10. After the final reboot, Setup displays the window shown in Figure 2-5. Type a computer name in the text box provided. Accept the default background color or select another color if you wish. Then click **Next**.

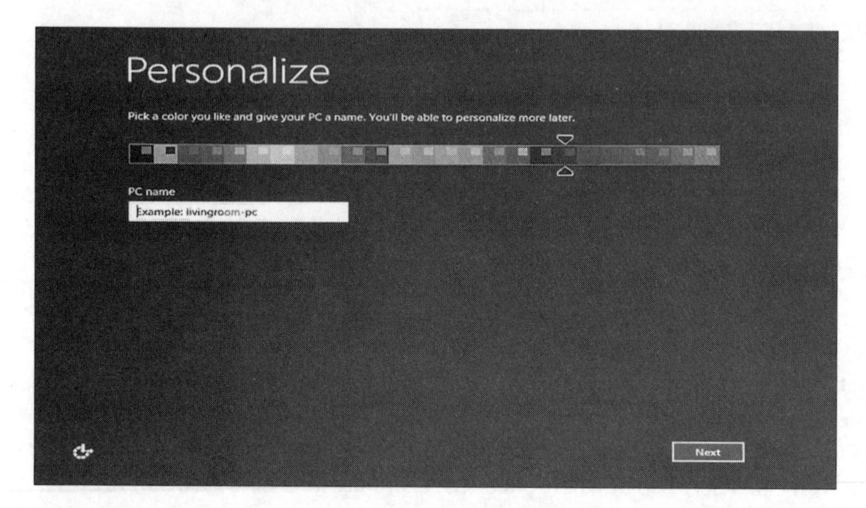

Figure 2-5 Setup asks you to provide a computer name and background color.

Step 11. Setup asks you to sign in to your Microsoft account, as shown in Figure 2-6. This is an email account in the `@hotmail.com` or `@outlook.com` domain, which enables you to access the Windows Store as well as your email using the built-in Mail app. Type the email address and its associated password in the spaces provided, and then click **Next**. If you don't have a Microsoft account, click **Create a new account** to create a Microsoft account or **Don't have an account** to proceed without creating a Microsoft account.

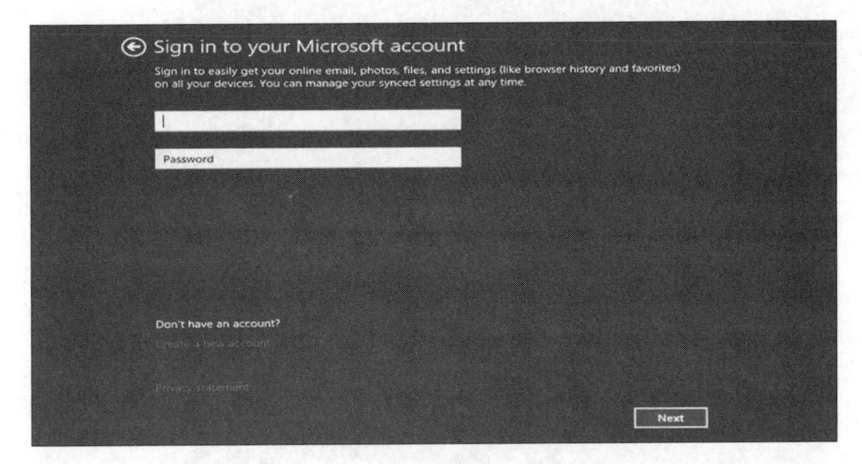

Figure 2-6 Setup asks you to sign in to your Microsoft account.

Step 12. Setup asks you if you want to specify customized settings for several options regarding updates, security, and so on. If you want to modify the default settings, click **Customize** and follow the instructions provided. Otherwise, click **Use express settings**.

Step 13. The Help us protect your info page, shown in Figure 2-7, asks you if you want to use a security code to verify your identity. To receive this code by email, select the default provided. If you are currently unable to access the email account indicated, click **I can't do this right now**. Then click **Next**.

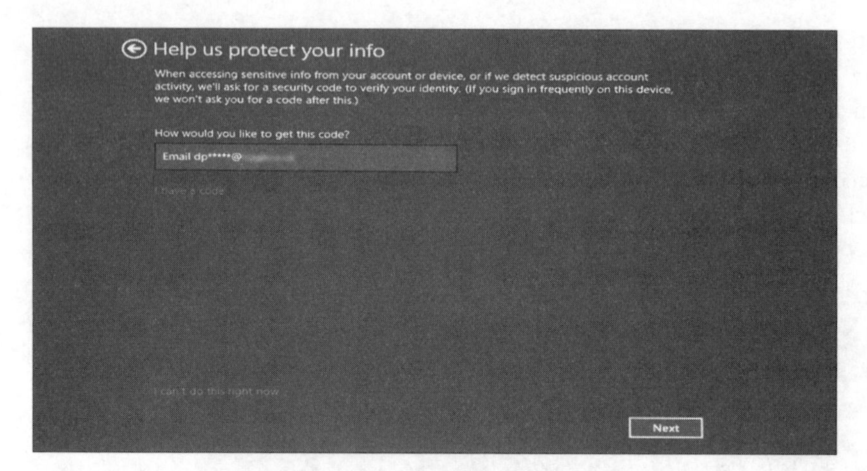

Figure 2-7 Setup asks you if you want to receive a security code.

Step 14. The How should we set up your PC? page, shown in Figure 2-8, enables you to copy settings and Windows Store apps from another computer, or set up your computer as a new PC. Make a selection and then click **Next**.

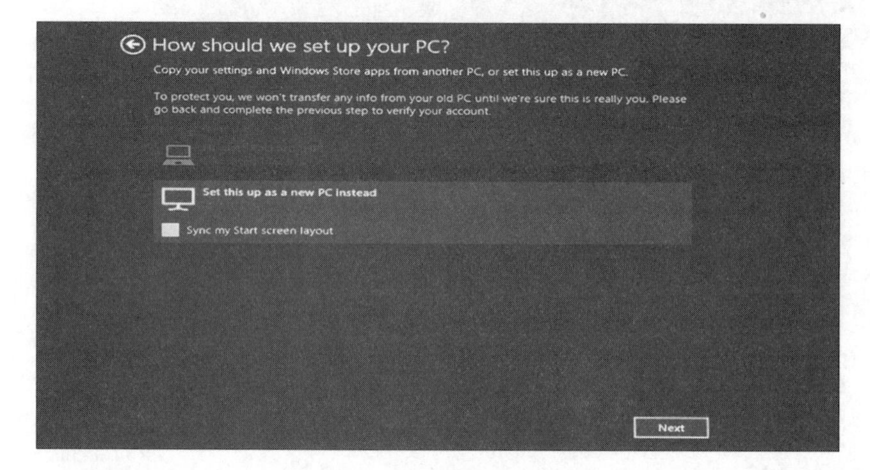

Figure 2-8 You can copy settings and Windows Store apps from another computer if you wish.

Step 15. The SkyDrive (now called OneDrive) is your cloud storage page, shown in Figure 2-9. It asks you if you want to back up data to the cloud so that you can get your files from any device. If you do not want to use SkyDrive, click **Turn off these SkyDrive settings (not recommended)**. Click **Next** to continue.

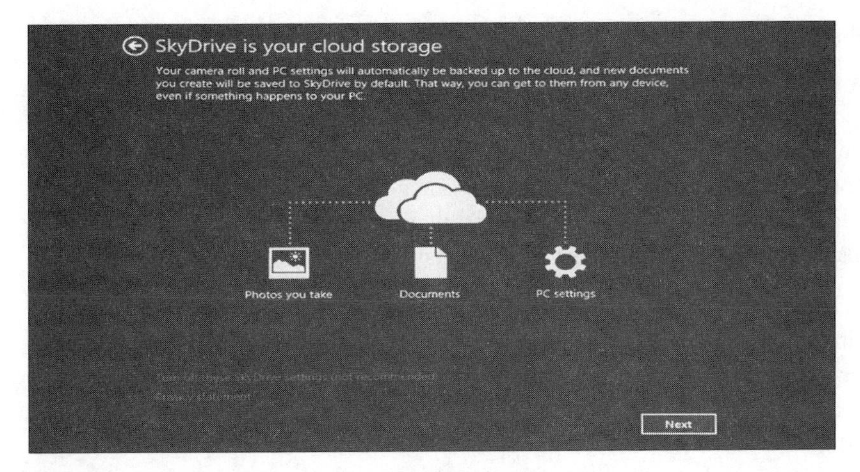

Figure 2-9 Setup asks you if you want to use SkyDrive.

Step 16. Setup sets up your account and then restarts your computer. You receive several additional messages as your apps are installed, informing you that you can get new apps from the Windows Store.

Step 17. After a minute or two, the Windows 8.1 Start screen appears. The computer attempts to access the Internet to download and install updates from the Microsoft website, and a message at the bottom of the desktop informs you of the update progress. You are now ready to work with Windows 8.1.

You have just completed a full, manual installation of Windows 8.1 from scratch. In a typical installation, you would next confirm the date, time, and time zone settings; specify networking settings; join a workgroup or domain; install additional applications; restore data from backup; and customize the desktop to meet your needs.

Performing an Unattended Installation of Windows 8.1

A typical installation of Windows 8.1, as explained in the previous section, is fine if you have only one or two computers to be installed. But what if you have a large number of computers on which you want to install Windows 8.1? Entering the same information repeatedly becomes tedious and error-prone, so Microsoft has developed methods for automating the installation of Windows 8.1 on a series of computers. Unattended installations typically utilize an answer file that contains answers to questions asked by `Setup.exe`, so the installation proceeds smoothly without operator intervention.

Understanding Answer Files

Typically called `Unattend.xml` or `Autounattend.xml`, the answer file was first used with Windows Vista and replaces the `Unattend.txt` file that was formerly used with older Windows operating systems. You can include setup options (such as partitioning and formatting of disks), which Windows image to install, and the product key that should be used. You can also include installation-specific items (such as usernames, display settings, and Internet Explorer favorites).

Windows System Image Manager (SIM) enables you to create answer files from information included in a Windows image (`.wim`) file and a catalog (`.clg`) file. You can also include component settings and software packages to be installed on the computers with Windows 8.1. The following are several actions you can accomplish using SIM:

- Create new answer files and edit existing ones
- Validate the information in an answer file against a `.wim` file
- View and modify the component configurations in a `.wim` file
- Include additional drivers, applications, updates, or component packages in the answer file

You can use SIM to create unattended answer files. You should have two computers, as follows:

- A computer from which you install SIM and create the answer files. Microsoft refers to this computer as the technician computer.
- A computer without an operating system but equipped with a DVD-ROM drive, network card, and a floppy drive (or USB support). Microsoft refers to this computer as the reference computer.

Understanding Configuration Passes

When you use an unattended installation answer file for installing Windows, settings are applied at various stages of the setup process that Microsoft calls configuration passes. Table 2-2 describes the different configuration passes used in setting up Windows 8.1 and Windows Server 2012 R2.

Table 2-2 Configuration Passes

Configuration Pass	Description
1 Windows PE	Configures Windows PE options and basic Windows Setup options. Use this configuration pass to add any drivers required for Windows PE to access the local or network hard drive. Also use this configuration pass to add any basic information such as a product key.
2 offlineServicing	Applies updates including packages, software fixes, language packs, and security updates to the Windows image.
3 generalize	Used only when running the sysprep /generalize command; enables you to configure this command for removing system-specific settings such as the security identifier (SID).
4 specialize	Creates and applies system-specific information such as network, domain, and international settings.
5 auditSystem	Used only when booting to Audit mode after running Sysprep; processes unattended Setup settings before a user logs on.
6 auditUser	Used only when booting to Audit mode after running Sysprep; processes unattended Setup settings after a user logs on.
7 oobeSystem	Applies Windows settings before Windows Welcome starts.

NOTE For more information on configuration passes and their usage, refer to "How Configuration Passes Work" at http://technet.microsoft.com/en-us/library/cc749307(WS.10).aspx.

Creating an Answer File

Windows SIM is a component of the Windows Assessment and Deployment Kit (ADK) for Windows 8 or 8.1, which replaces the Windows Automated Installation Kit (AIK) previously used with Windows Vista and 7. To use SIM to create the files required for performing unattended installations, you first need to download and install the ADK from Microsoft and copy the appropriate files from the Windows 8.1 DVD-ROM. You should perform these steps on a computer running Windows Vista, Windows 7, Windows 8, or Windows 8.1. Use the following steps to download and install the ADK:

Step 1. Open Internet Explorer, navigate to http://www.microsoft.com/en-US/download/details.aspx?id=39982, and follow the instructions provided to download the Windows ADK.

Step 2. You should receive a User Account Control (UAC) dialog box. Click **Yes** to display the Specify Location screen shown in Figure 2-10.

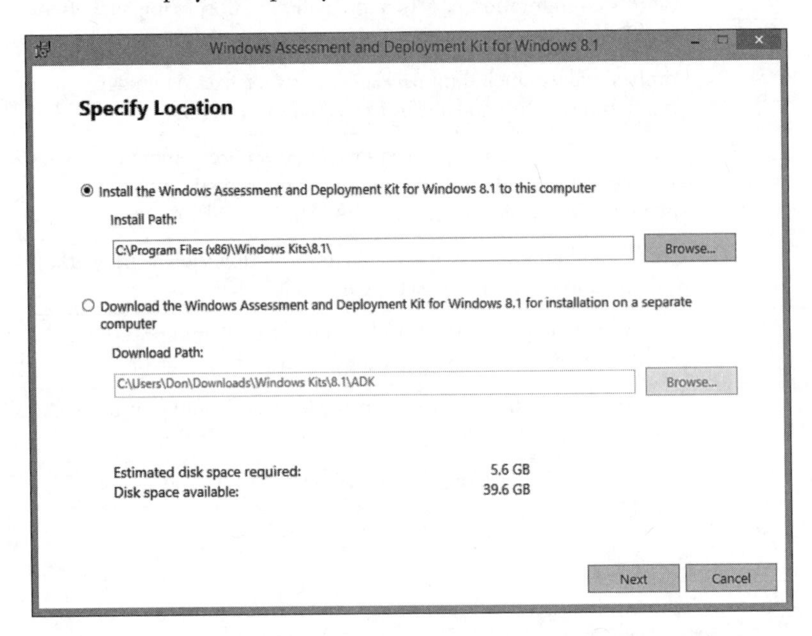

Figure 2-10 Installing the Windows Assessment and Deployment Kit.

Step 3. Accept the default installation path or click **Browse** to specify an alternate location, and then click **Next**.

Step 4. If you receive the Join the Customer Experience Improvement Program screen, click **Next**.

Step 5. Click **Accept** to accept the license agreement.

Step 6. On the Select the features you want to install page shown in Figure 2-11, accept the defaults and then click **Install**.

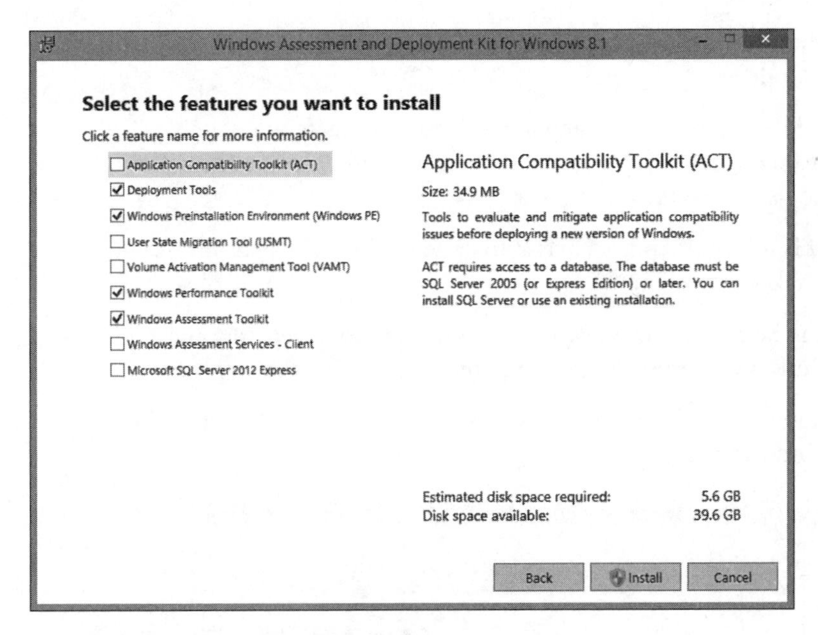

Figure 2-11 Selecting the ADK features to be installed.

TIP You might want to select **User State Migration Tool (USMT)** for use when you study Chapter 3, "Migrating Users and Applications to Windows 8.1," and **Application Compatibility Toolkit (ACT)** for use when you study Chapter 5, "Installing, Configuring, and Securing Applications in Windows 8.1."

Step 7. If you receive an additional UAC dialog box, click **Yes**.

Step 8. An Installing features page appears as the ADK tools are installed. This process can take up to an hour. When installation finishes, click **Close**.

After you have installed the ADK, a folder is present on the technician computer, from which you can create answer files. To create an answer file based on the default Windows image found on the Windows 8.1 DVD, use the following procedure:

Step 1. Insert the Windows 8.1 DVD-ROM. If you receive an Install Windows screen, click **Cancel**.

Step 2. If you receive an AutoPlay window, click the **Open folder to view files** option. If not, open a File Explorer (Computer on Windows 7 or Vista) window, navigate to the Windows 8.1 DVD-ROM, right-click, and select **Open**.

Step 3. Open the Sources folder, navigate to the `boot.wim` file, right-click, and then choose **Copy**.

Step 4. Open a File Explorer (or Computer) window, navigate to a suitable location, and create a folder to hold the installation files, for example, `C:\Windows_Install`.

Step 5. Open this folder and press **Ctrl+V** to paste the `install.wim` file into it. This process takes several minutes.

Step 6. Open the Search charm and type **`Windows System Image Manager`**. Then select **Windows System Image Manager** from the list that appears.

Step 7. In Windows System Image Manager, shown in Figure 2-13, click **File > Select Windows Image**.

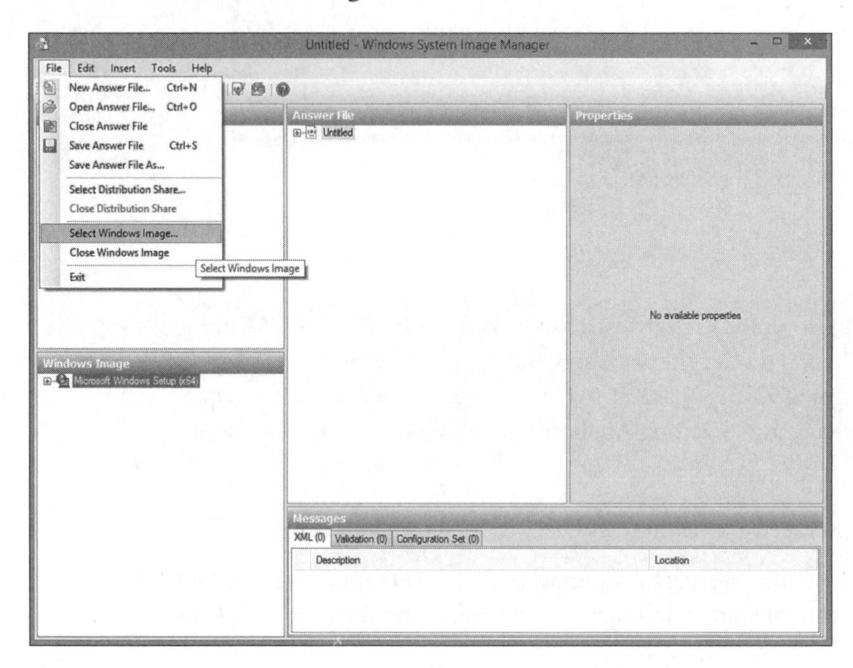

Figure 2-12 You need to select a Windows image file to create an answer file.

Step 8. In the Select a Windows Image dialog box shown in Figure 2-13, navigate to the folder you copied the `boot.wim` file to, select this file, and then click **Open**.

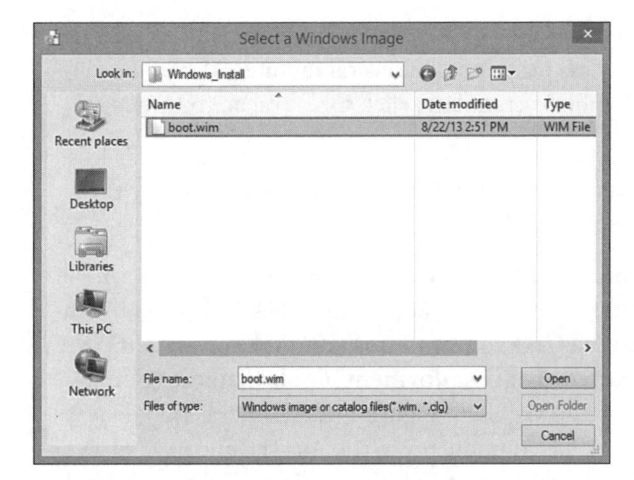

Figure 2-13 Selecting the `boot.wim` file.

Step 9. In the Select an Image dialog box shown in Figure 2-14, select **Microsoft Windows Setup (x64)**, and then click **OK**.

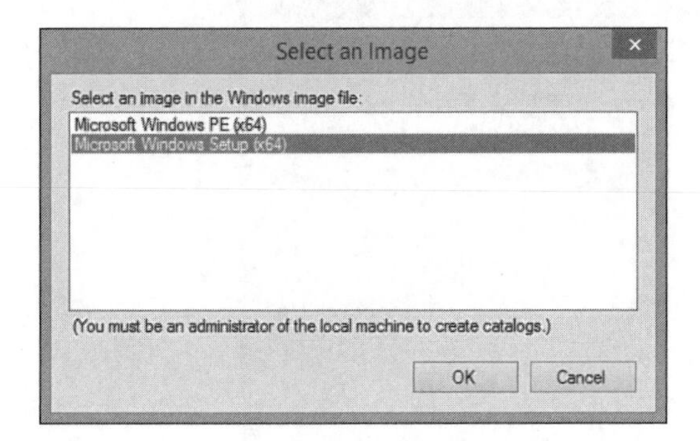

Figure 2-14 Selecting a Windows 8.1 image.

Step 10. SIM displays the message shown in Figure 2-15, asking you to create a catalog file. Click **Yes** and then click **Yes** in the UAC dialog box that appears.

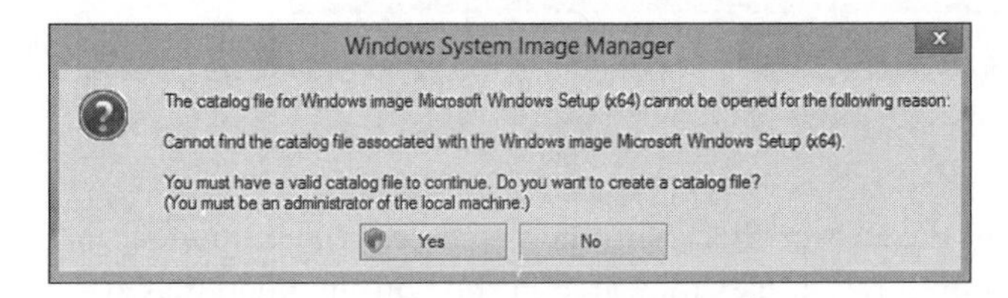

Figure 2-15 You are asked to create a catalog file.

Step 11. A Generating Catalog File message box appears as the files are processed and the catalog file is created. This process takes several minutes. When the process of generating a catalog file is complete, click **OK**. You are returned to Windows SIM.

Step 12. In the Windows Image pane, expand the Components node to display the available components.

Step 13. To create a new answer file, click **File > New Answer File**. To use a sample answer file as a template for creating your answer file, click **File > Open Answer File** and navigate to the **C:\Program Files (x86)\Windows Kits\8.1\Assessment and Deployment Kit\Deployment Tools\Samples\Unattend** folder. (These options are visible in Figure 2-12.) Either action displays a hierarchical tree of answer file components in the Answer File pane of Windows SIM as shown in Figure 2-16, including the configuration passes previously described in Table 2-2 and placed in the Components node.

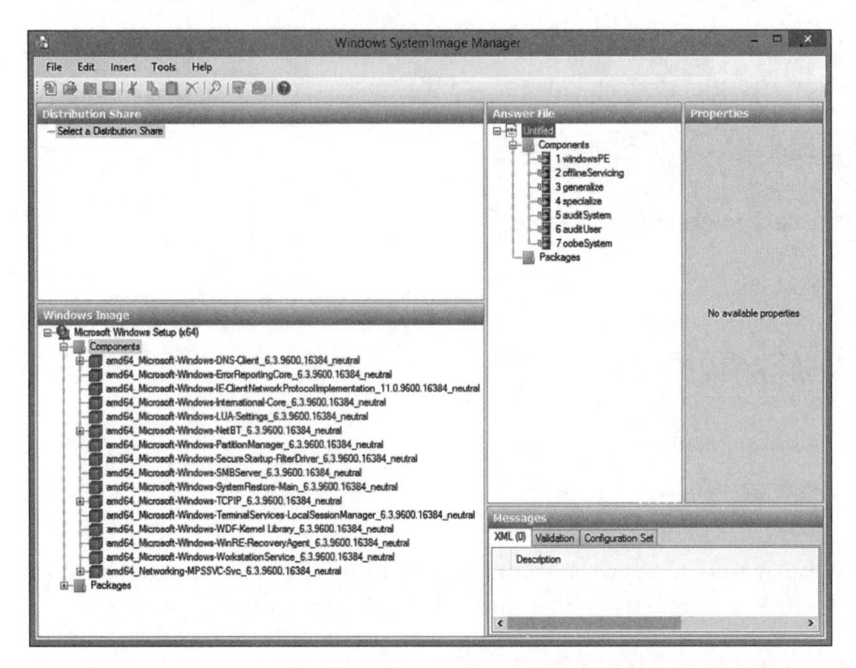

Figure 2-16 Windows SIM displays the available components in the Windows Image pane and the raw answer file with its configuration passes in the Answer File pane.

Step 14. To add components to the answer file, right-click each desired component in turn and add to the configuration pass indicated in the pop-up menu that appears. Repeat this step as needed until you've added all needed components.

Step 15. To add packages to the answer file, expand the Packages node in the Windows Image section of Windows SIM, right-click each desired package in turn, and choose **Add to Answer File**. Note that a package is used for adding software updates, service packs, language packs, and new Windows features to the Windows image.

Step 16. The Answer File pane should display all the settings you have added. To complete the creation of an answer file for a basic Windows 8.1 installation, select and configure any settings required for components you've added. To do this, expand the configuration path containing the component to be configured, select the required component, and then add or modify the desired setting displayed in the Properties pane of Windows SIM.

Step 17. Validate the settings you have configured by selecting **Validate Answer File** from the Tools menu.

Step 18. If you receive an error message, double-click the message in the Messages pane, correct the error, and then repeat step 16.

Step 19. After all errors have been corrected, click **File > Save Answer File**. Save the answer file as `Autounattend.xml` and then copy this file to removable media such as a flash drive.

CAUTION Be aware that you cannot create catalog files for 32-bit computers when using the 64-bit version of Windows SIM. However, the 32-bit version is capable of creating catalog files for either 32- or 64-bit Windows installations.

NOTE For more information on answer files in Windows 8.1 and Windows Server 2012 R2, refer to "Answer Files Overview" at http://technet.microsoft.com/en-us/library/hh825121.aspx. For more information on using Windows SIM, refer to the topics listed in "Windows SIM How-to Topics" at http://technet.microsoft.com/en-us/library/hh824845.aspx. Also refer to the Help files that come with Windows SIM (from the Help menu, select **Image Manager Help**). For more information on the Windows ADK, refer to "Windows Deployment with the Windows ADK" at http://technet.microsoft.com/library/hh824947.aspx?ocid=wc-nl-insider and "Step-by-Step: Windows 8 Deployment for IT Professionals" at http://technet.microsoft.com/en-us/library/hh825212.aspx, together with links included in these two documents.

CAUTION It is possible to edit an answer file by using a text editor, such as Notepad. However, you must take care when editing answer files. When using Notepad to edit the answer file or UDF file, you must ensure that you follow the rules of syntax exactly; otherwise, unattended installations will either fail or prompt the user for additional information.

Using the Answer Files to Perform an Unattended Installation

Having created the answer files as described in the previous procedure, you can easily run the automated installation of Windows 8.1 on a new computer (often called the target computer) without an operating system, as shown in the following steps:

Step 1. Start the target computer and insert the Windows 8.1 DVD-ROM and the flash drive you created in the previous procedure.

Step 2. To run `Setup.exe`, press **Ctrl+Alt+Delete**. The computer restarts and searches the flash drive for the `Autounattend.xml` file.

Step 3. Setup should proceed automatically and install Windows 8.1 with all customizations you have previously configured.

Dual-Booting Windows 8.1

As in previous versions of Windows, you can install Windows 8.1 alongside a different version of Windows in a dual-boot configuration. This refers to installing two operating systems (for example, Windows 7 and Windows 8.1) side by side on the same computer so that you can boot the computer to one operating system or the other. By specifying a partition that does not have an operating system installed in step 7 of the procedure outlined in the section titled "Performing an Attended Installation," you can select a different partition on which to install Windows 8.1. This retains all applications and settings you have configured in the previous version of Windows and creates a clean installation of Windows 8.1 on the partition you have specified. You can even create multiboot systems with more than two different operating systems, including different editions of Windows 8.1, on the same computer. Dual-booting or multibooting has the following advantages:

- You can test various editions of Windows 8.1 without destroying your current operating system.
- If you are running applications that are not compatible with Windows 8.1, you can boot into an older operating system to run these applications.
- Developers can test their work on different Windows versions without needing more than one computer.

Boot Management Programs Used by Windows 8.1

Windows 8.1 includes several new boot management programs, which were first introduced in Windows Vista and Windows Server 2008, and replaces the older programs used with previous Windows versions. They include the following:

- **`Bootcfg.exe`:** This program enables you to edit, modify, or delete boot entry settings in the `boot.ini` file used in older Windows operating systems.
- **`Bcdedit.exe`:** This editing application enables you to edit boot configuration data on Windows Vista/7/8/8.1 or Windows Server 2008/2012 R2. This is the only program that offers boot management editing capabilities for Windows 8.1.
- **`Winload.exe`:** The operating system loader is included with each instance of Windows Vista, Windows 7, Windows 8/8.1, Windows Server 2008, or Windows Server 2012 R2 installed on any one computer. `Winload.exe` loads the operating system, its kernel, hardware abstraction layer (HAL), and drivers on startup.
- **`Winresume.exe`:** Included with each instance of Windows Vista, Windows 7, Windows 8/8.1, Windows Server 2008, or Windows Server 2012 R2 installed on any one computer, this program resumes the operating system from hibernation.

NOTE For more information on using `Bootcfg.exe` and `Bcdedit.exe`, refer to "Adding Boot Entries" at http://msdn.microsoft.com/en-us/library/windows/hardware/ff541231(v=vs.85).aspx.

Setting Up a Dual-Boot System

The procedure for setting up a dual-boot operating system can vary, but you should generally proceed along the following lines:

Step 1. If you haven't already installed the oldest operating system, install and configure it first. For example, you would install Windows XP, then Windows 7, and then Windows 8.1 in that order if you wanted a triple-boot configuration with these three operating systems.

Step 2. While running the older operating system, insert the Windows 8.1 DVD-ROM.

Step 3. When you receive the option with a choice of upgrade or clean installation (step 6 of the procedure outlined in the section "Performing an Attended Installation"; refer back to Figure 2-3), select the **Custom: Install Windows only (advanced)** option to continue.

Step 4. The next screen displays the list of available partitions, which include the partition or partitions on which you have installed the older operating system(s). Select a different partition or create a new partition from unpartitioned space, and then click **Next**.

Step 5. Follow the remaining steps in the procedure for performing an attended installation to complete the installation of Windows 8.1.

Refreshing Windows 8.1

If you are encountering problems with an existing installation of Windows 8.1, you can reinstall Windows 8.1 on top of your current installation, also known as a reset and refresh. Refreshing your installation deletes all Windows settings and applications, but retains all data files and folders. Use the following procedure to refresh Windows 8.1:

Step 1. From the Charms bar, click **Settings**.

Step 2. At the bottom of the Settings utility, click **Change PC settings**.

Step 3. In the left column, click **Update and recovery** and then click **Recovery**.

Step 4. Under Refresh your PC without affecting your files, click **Get started**.

Step 5. Follow the instructions presented, which are similar to those described for a clean installation of Windows 8.1 earlier in this chapter.

You can also remove all applications, files, and settings, resetting Windows to its original installation settings. Ensure that you have backed up any data on the Windows partition that you want to retain before performing this action. Use the same steps as in the preceding procedure, except in step 4, click **Get started** under the Remove everything and reinstall Windows section.

Troubleshooting Failed Installations

A network administrator's best friend in a crisis is an Error log file. This is also true for Windows 8.1 installation failures. While installing, Windows 8.1 Setup generates log files that point you in the right direction when you need to troubleshoot.

The Action log (`Setupact.log`) reports which actions Setup performed in chronological order. This log indicates which files were copied and which were deleted. It records whether any external programs are run and shows where errors have occurred.

Setup creates an Error log (`Setuperr.log`) to record only the errors. Given that the Action log is extremely large, this log makes it easier to review errors and their severity levels. Although you might see some errors in the Action log, you probably won't see them in the Error log unless they are fairly severe. For example, the Action log reports an error if Setup cannot delete a file because the file was already moved or deleted, but that error does not appear in the Error log.

Table 2-3 describes some of the more important logs created during installation:

Table 2-3 Windows 8.1 Setup Logs

Log Filename	Description
`%systemroot%\panther\miglog.xml`	Records information about the user directory structure, including SIDs.
`%systemroot%\panther\setupact.log`	Records modifications performed on the system during Setup.
`%systemroot%\inf\setupapi.dev.log`	Records data about Plug-and-Play devices and drivers. Check this file for device driver installation information.
`%systemroot%\inf\setupapi.setup.log`	Records data about Windows and application installation.
`%systemroot%\setuperr.log`	Records errors generated by hardware or driver issues during Windows installation.
`%systemroot%\security\logs\scesetup.log`	Logs the security settings for the computer.

Stop Errors or Blue Screen of Death (BSOD)

If you receive a Stop error that appears on the Microsoft blue screen (commonly known as the Blue Screen of Death [BSOD]), you have encountered a serious error with the installation. Stop errors have some instructions to follow on the screen. Not only should you follow the instructions, but also you should check the compatibility of the hardware before attempting to install again. Use the following steps to resolve a Stop error:

Step 1. Shut down the computer.

Step 2. Remove all new hardware devices.

Step 3. Start up the computer and remove the associated drivers. Shut down.

Step 4. Install one of the removed hardware devices. Boot the computer and install the appropriate driver. Reboot. If no BSOD occurs, continue adding devices, one at a time.

Step 5. Open **Device Manager** and look for devices with a black exclamation point on a yellow background, or a red X. Run hardware diagnostic software.

Step 6. Check for hardware compatibility and BIOS compatibility. Check to see whether you have the latest available version of the BIOS.

Step 7. Check the System log in Event Viewer for error messages. These may lead to a driver that is causing the Stop error.

Step 8. Visit http://search.microsoft.com and perform a search on the Microsoft Knowledge Base for the Stop error number (for example, Stop: 0x0000000A). Follow the instructions given in the Knowledge Base article(s) for diagnosing and repairing the error.

Step 9. Disable BIOS options such as caching or shadowing memory.

Step 10. If the Stop error specifies a particular driver, disable the driver and then download and update the driver to the latest version available from the manufacturer.

Step 11. Video drivers are commonly the cause of a BSOD. Therefore, switch to the Windows Low-Resolution video (640 × 480) driver (available from the Advanced Startup Options menu) and then contact the manufacturer for updated video drivers.

Step 12. If using a small computer system interface (SCSI) adapter and device, ensure that the SCSI chain is properly terminated and that there are no conflicts with the SCSI IDs.

TIP The code and text associated with a Stop error are a great help in troubleshooting. For example, an error could be STOP 0x00000001 (DRIVER IRQL NOT LESS OR EQUAL). You can search for this code number and text on Microsoft's website for an explanation of the cause and possible ways to fix the problem.

Stopped Installation

Windows 8.1 might stop in the middle of an installation. This can happen because of a hardware conflict, incompatibility, or unsuitable configuration. To resolve the conflict, you should follow the usual procedure of removing all unnecessary devices from the computer and attempting installation again. After Windows 8.1 is installed, you can add one device at a time back to the computer, load the latest manufacturer's drivers, and boot to see whether the computer functions properly. It is important that you add only one device at a time so that you can discover which device (or devices) might have been the cause of the problem.

NOTE For more information on various aspects of installing and deploying Windows 8 and 8.1, refer to links provided in the document "Install, Deploy, and Migrate to Windows 8" at http://technet.microsoft.com/library/hh832022.aspx. For information on enterprise-level Windows 8.1 deployment strategies, refer to "Windows 8 Deployment Strategies" at http://technet.microsoft.com/en-us/windows/dn282135.aspx?ocid=wc-nl-insider.

Upgrading to Windows 8.1 from a Previous Version of Windows

Many individuals who have purchased Windows 7 computers since its rollout in 2009 are attracted to the new Windows Start screen and its easy-to-use Windows Store apps and other features discussed in Chapter 1. Microsoft has provided paths for upgrading these computers to Windows 8.1. Further, some users of Windows XP computers would like to take advantage of the latest and greatest of Microsoft operating systems. In this section, you look at which computers can be upgraded directly to Windows 8.1 and which computers require a complete reinstall of the operating system.

Other users might have purchased a computer running the base edition of Windows 8.1, but later want to utilize features available only in a higher edition such as Windows 8.1 Pro. Consequently, Microsoft has made upgrade paths available that enable these users to move to a higher version of Windows 8.1. As with the upgrade of an earlier version of Windows, these paths enable users to retain Registry settings and account information from the lower version of Windows 8.1.

Upgrade paths from previous Windows versions depend on the operating system version currently installed. Table 2-4 lists the available upgrade paths for older operating systems.

Table 2-4 Upgrading Older Operating Systems to Windows 8.1

Operating System	Upgrade Path
Windows 8 (any edition)	Can be upgraded to the same or higher version of Windows 8.1.
Windows 7 Starter, Home Basic, or Home Premium	Can be upgraded directly to Windows 8.1 or Windows 8.1 Pro.
Windows 7 Professional or Ultimate	Can be upgraded directly to Windows 8.1 Pro.
Windows 7 Professional (Volume license) or Enterprise (Volume license)	Can be upgraded directly to Windows 8.1 Enterprise.
Windows Vista Home Basic or Home Premium	Can be upgraded directly to Windows 8.1 or Windows 8.1 Pro.

Operating System	Upgrade Path
Windows Vista Business or Ultimate	Can be upgraded directly to Windows 8.1 Pro.
Windows Vista Enterprise	Can be upgraded directly to Windows 8.1 Enterprise.
Cross-architecture (32-bit to 64-bit) Windows Vista/7/8	Cannot be upgraded.
Non-Windows operating systems (Unix, Linux, OS X)	Cannot be upgraded. You need to perform a clean installation of Windows 8.1.

Furthermore, the type of data you can keep during upgrade depends on the installation path to Windows 8.1. It is possible that you can keep Windows data and system settings, personal files, applications, or nothing at all according to the upgrade path. Table 2-5 summarizes your options.

Table 2-5 Supported Upgrade Paths to Windows 8.1

Operating System	Keep Windows Settings, Personal Files, and Applications	Keep Windows Settings and Personal Files	Keep Personal Files Only	Keep Nothing
Windows 8 (any edition)	Yes	Yes	Yes	Yes
Windows 7 (any edition)	Yes	No	Yes	Yes
Windows Vista	No	No	Yes	Yes
Windows Vista SP1	No	Yes	Yes	Yes
Windows Vista or 7 (cross-language)	No	No	Yes	Yes
Windows Vista or 7 (cross-architecture (32-bit to 64-bit)	No	No	No	No
Windows XP (SP3)	No	No	Yes	Yes

NOTE For more information on supported upgrade paths to Windows 8 and Windows 8.1, refer to "Windows 8 and Windows 8.1 Upgrade Paths" at http://technet.microsoft.com/en-us/library/jj203353.aspx.

Preparing a Computer to Meet Upgrade Requirements

In addition to running one of the supported versions of Windows mentioned here, a computer to be upgraded to Windows 8.1 must meet the hardware requirements previously described in Chapter 1. Note that this should always be true because the hardware requirements for Windows 8.1 are the same as those for Windows 7. Furthermore, all hardware components should be found in the Windows Certification Program. As described in Chapter 1, you should download and run the Windows Upgrade Assistant and then follow any recommendations provided for actions such as upgrading or uninstalling incompatible software programs. Older software applications may not be compatible with Windows 8.1. Such applications might need to be upgraded or replaced to work properly after you have upgraded your operating system.

Before you upgrade a Windows 7 computer to Windows 8.1, you should perform several additional tasks, as follows:

- Check the BIOS manufacturer's website for any available BIOS upgrades and upgrade the computer's BIOS to the latest available functional version if necessary. You should perform this step before a clean install or an upgrade to Windows 8.1.
- Scan and eliminate any viruses from the computer, using an antivirus program that has been updated with the latest antivirus signatures. You should then remove or disable the antivirus program because it may interfere with the upgrade process. In addition, you should use a third-party program to scan for and remove malicious software (malware).
- Install any upgrade packs that may be required to render older software applications compatible with Windows 8.1. Consult software manufacturers for details.
- Install the latest service pack for Windows 7 (SP1 at the time of writing), plus any other updates that Microsoft has published. At the very minimum, you must have SP1 installed.

Upgrading the Computer to Windows 8.1

After you have checked system compatibility and performed all tasks required to prepare your computer for upgrading, you are ready to proceed. The upgrade takes place in a similar fashion to a new installation, except that answers to some questions asked by the setup wizard are taken from the current installation. Perform the following procedure to upgrade a Windows Vista or 7 computer to Windows 8.1:

Step 1. Insert the Windows 8.1 DVD-ROM.

Step 2. If you receive a UAC prompt, click **Yes**. (If running Vista, click **Continue**.)

Step 3. Setup copies temporary files, and then the Get the latest page appears. If you are connected to the Internet, select the **Go online to install updates now (recommended)** option. Otherwise, select the **No, thanks** option. Then click **Next**.

Step 4. Type your product key and then click **Next**.

Step 5. On the License terms page, select the check box labeled **I accept the license terms** and then click **Accept**.

Step 6. You receive the Choose what to keep page, shown in Figure 2-17. Note that the options appearing on this page depend on the upgrade path chosen, as described previously in Table 2-5. Select an option and then click **Next**.

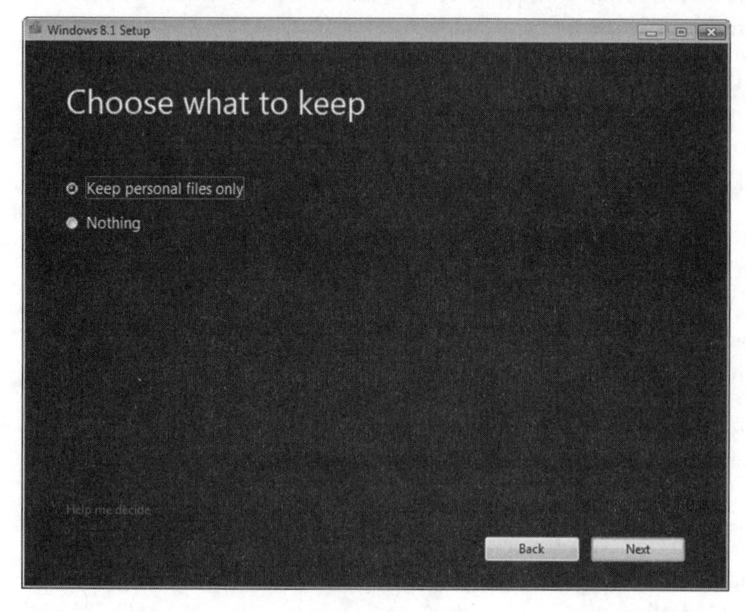

Figure 2-17 You can choose which items are to be kept from the previous Windows installation.

Step 7. Setup checks for anything that might need your attention and displays the Compatibility details page with information about any applications or drivers that are not supported in Windows 8.1 (similar to that shown in Figure 1-31 in Chapter 1). Note the information provided and then click **Next**. If the compatibility check does not find any issues, this page might not appear.

Step 8. Setup presents a Ready to install page as shown in Figure 2-18, which summarizes the settings you've chosen. Click **Back** if you need to make any changes. When finished, click **Install**.

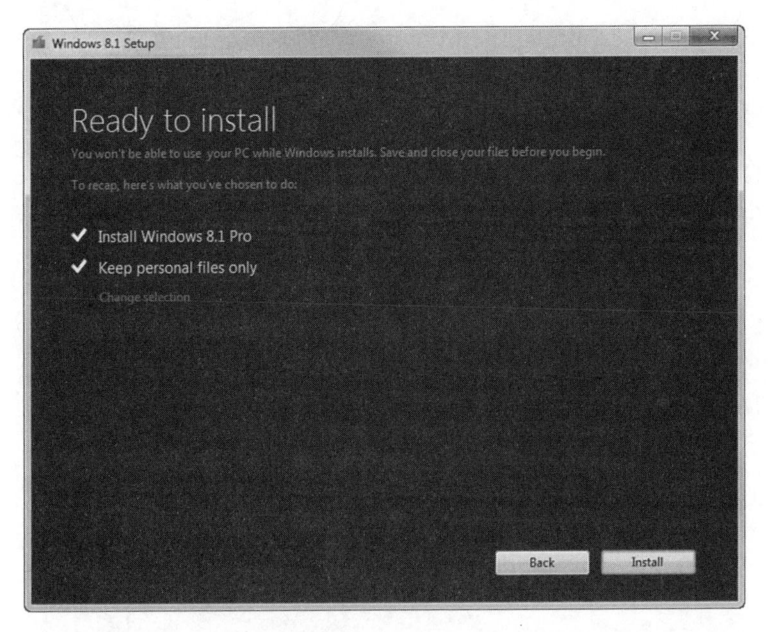

Figure 2-18 The Ready to install page provides a summary of the selections you've made.

Step 9. Setup displays an Installing Windows 8.1 screen as it proceeds with the upgrade. This proceeds in a fashion similar to that of a clean installation. It asks only for any information it cannot retrieve from the previous Windows installation.

Step 10. After installation has completed and the computer has rebooted, you receive the sign-on screen, which displays the username obtained from the previous Windows version. Type the same password that you used in Windows Vista or 7. Windows 8.1 should accept these and, after a minute or two, the Start screen will appear.

Upgrading from Windows 8 to Windows 8.1

Upgrading from any edition of Windows 8 except the Enterprise edition is very simple; you simply need to access the Windows Store, download, and follow the instructions provided to download and install the upgrade in much the same fashion as you would for installing or upgrading a Windows Store app. Note that this process may take an hour or more, depending on the bandwidth of the Internet connection used. The computer will restart several times during the upgrade. At the end of the upgrade, you will be asked to accept the license terms; you will then receive an opportunity to accept express settings or configure customized settings.

You cannot upgrade Windows 8 Enterprise from the Windows Store in this fashion; you need to download Windows 8.1 Enterprise from the Microsoft Volume Licensing Service Center. The media available from this location enable you to either perform an in-place update or use Microsoft Deployment Tool (MDT) 2013 or System Center 2012 R2 Configuration Manager to refresh an existing computer. You can also burn the media to a DVD or copy to a USB key for installing on a different machine.

NOTE For more information on upgrading Windows 8 to 8.1, refer to "Windows 8.1 General Availability: The IT Pro Perspective" at http://blogs.windows.com/windows/b/springboard/archive/2013/10/18/windows-8-1-general-availability-the-it-pro-perspective.aspx and "Upgrade to Windows 8.1 from Windows 8" at http://windows.microsoft.com/en-us/windows-8/update-from-windows-8-tutorial.

NOTE If you have not chosen the option to include your files and later decide you want to recover files from the earlier Windows installation, this might be possible if you did not reformat your hard disk. During an upgrade, Windows places operating system and data files from the earlier installation into a folder named `Windows.old`. In the File Explorer, access the drive where Windows is installed to locate the `Windows.old` folder. Double-click this folder, double-click the `Users` folder within it, double-click your username, and then access the library in which the files or folders to be retrieved is located. Then copy and paste the desired files into another folder on your computer. For more information on recovering personal files after an upgrade, refer to "Retrieve Files from the Windows.old Folder" at http://windows.microsoft.com/en-US/windows-8/restore-files-upgrade-windows-old.

Upgrading from One Edition of Windows 8.1 to Another

Chapter 1 introduced you to the editions Microsoft has produced for Windows 8.1. Just as you can upgrade Vista or 7 to Windows 8.1, you can also upgrade a lower edition of Windows 8.1 to a higher one. Table 2-6 summarizes the available upgrade paths.

Table 2-6 Upgrading One Edition of Windows 8.1 to a Higher One

Windows Edition You Are Upgrading	You Can Upgrade to This Edition
Windows RT 8.1	Cannot be upgraded (this is a special edition designed specifically for ARM devices only)
Windows 8.1 (base version)	Windows 8.1 Pro
Windows 8.1 Pro	Cannot be upgraded further

Microsoft makes available the Windows 8.1 Pro Pack or Windows 8.1 Media Center Pack for upgrading the base version of Windows 8.1. Use the following procedure to upgrade from the base version of Windows 8.1 to Windows 8.1 Pro:

Step 1. Access the Charms bar and click **Search**.

Step 2. Type `add features` in the search box and then click **Settings**.

Step 3. Click **Add features to Windows 8.1** and then do one of the following:

- To purchase a product key, select **I want to buy a product key online**. You then are guided through the required steps and, after you purchase it, the product key is entered for you.
- If you already have a product key, click **I already have a product key**.

Step 4. Enter your product key and then click **Next**.

Step 5. You receive the license page. Select the check box to accept the license terms and then click **Add features**.

Step 6. Wait while Windows is upgraded. The computer will restart automatically and Windows 8.1 Pro with Media Center will be ready for use.

NOTE Unlike it does for Windows 7, Microsoft does not offer an official path for uninstalling Windows 8.1 and returning your computer to the previous Windows installation. However, if a `Windows.old` folder exists on your computer, you might be able to uninstall Windows 8.1 and revert to the previous version of Windows. If you have the original Windows 7 DVD, you might be able to insert the DVD and install Windows 7 on the Windows 8 partition. You will need to reinstall all applications and restore data from backup after you've finished installing Windows 7. Refer to http://answers.microsoft.com/en-us/windows/forum/windows_8-windows_install/uninstall-windows-8-reinstallwindows-7-on-pc/8ddc787d-e9cb-46f6-9561-a918f3b4ab3a for more information.

Installing as Windows To Go

New to Windows 8.1 Enterprise, Windows To Go enables you to create a workspace on a USB device that you can boot on any computer that meets the Windows 7 or Windows 8.1 hardware requirements. Using Windows To Go, technicians can prepare standardized corporate Windows 8.1 images from which users can access their desktop on any machine in alternative work locations such as home, hotel, or client computer location. All necessary files, applications, and the Windows 8.1 operating system are hosted on a portable USB drive such as a thumb drive or portable hard drive. Windows To Go is designed for medium to large businesses and is available only for Windows 8.1 Enterprise.

Windows To Go can also be useful for staff or consultants who use their own non-domain-joined computers or laptops, tablets, or similar devices. You can provide them with a Windows To Go workspace to use in your environment. In this way, you can enforce organizational network and domain policies without needing to provision a separate physical computer.

When you first insert a Windows To Go drive to a given host computer, Windows To Go detects all hardware on the computer and installs any required drivers. On subsequent boots of Windows To Go on the same computer, Windows To Go identifies the host computer and automatically enables all required drivers.

Windows To Go operates in much the same manner as any other Windows 8.1 installations, with the following exceptions:

- **Internal disks are offline:** Internal hard disks on the host computer are offline by default when the computer is booted into a Windows To Go workspace. The purpose is to ensure that data security on the host computer is not compromised in any way.
- **Trusted Platform Module (TPM) is not used:** If BitLocker Drive Encryption is used, a preboot password is used for security rather than the TPM because the TPM is linked to a specific computer and Windows To Go drives can move among different computers. We discuss BitLocker in Chapter 15, "Configuring and Securing Mobile Devices."
- **Hibernation is disabled by default:** The purpose is to ensure complete portability of Windows To Go workspaces between computers. However, you can re-enable hibernation using Group Policy.
- **Windows Recovery Environment isn't available:** If you need to recover your Windows To Go workspace, simple re-image it with a new Windows image.
- **Refreshing or resetting a Windows To Go workspace is not supported.**

- **Windows Store is disabled by default:** The reason is that apps licensed from Windows Store are linked to specific hardware. It is possible to enable the store if Windows To Go workspaces won't be roaming among multiple host machines.

Preparing USB Drives for Windows To Go

Windows To Go requires Windows 8.1 Enterprise edition, as well has a USB drive with specific characteristics. Most commodity flash drives cannot support Windows To Go; however, Microsoft has provided a Windows 8.1 certification program for hardware manufacturers that want to support the Windows To Go workspace functionality. These devices have been specially optimized for Windows To Go and meet several specific requirements for running a full version of Windows 8.1.

Drives certified for Windows To Go have certain specific characteristics:

- The drive must be a USB 3.0 drive and have read/write performance specifications that will support the demands of the Windows 8.1 operating system. Windows To Go will not run on USB 2.0 drives.
- The drive is tuned to ensure it will boot and run on any computer that has been certified for use with Windows 7 or Windows 8.1.
- The drive has been manufactured to quality standards that ensure endurance under the typical demand for Windows To Go. This includes a manufacturer warranty for operation and reliability under normal use with a Windows To Go workspace.

NOTE You can find information about the USB drives Microsoft has certified for use with Windows To Go at http://technet.microsoft.com/library/hh831833.aspx#wtg_hardware.

Provisioning a Windows To Go Workspace

To create a Windows To Go workspace, you need an installation image file for your environment (a `.wim` file), or a Windows 8.1 Enterprise installation image file (`.iso`) in DVD format. Typically, the `.wim` file is stored on a network share that you can access from your Windows 8.1 Enterprise computer. The `.iso` file with the Windows 8.1 installation needs to be downloaded to your local computer. We cover more details for creating and managing Windows images in Chapter 7, "Configuring Hyper-V."

If you are using an `.iso` file for the Windows 8.1 installation image, copy the `.iso` file to your computer's `Downloads` folder and then open the Downloads folder, right-click the Windows 8.1 installation image `.iso` file, and then select **Mount**. Windows mounts the ISO file as a new drive letter and opens the drive in Explorer.

You are then ready to create a Windows To Go workspace:

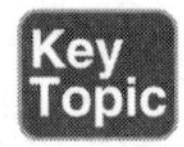

Step 1. Point your mouse to the upper-right corner of the screen, click the **Settings** charm, and then open the Control Panel by clicking on the **Control Panel** app.

Step 2. In the Control Panel search box, type **`windows to go`** and then click on the **Windows To Go** Control Panel link to open the Windows To Go provisioning tool, as shown in Figure 2-19.

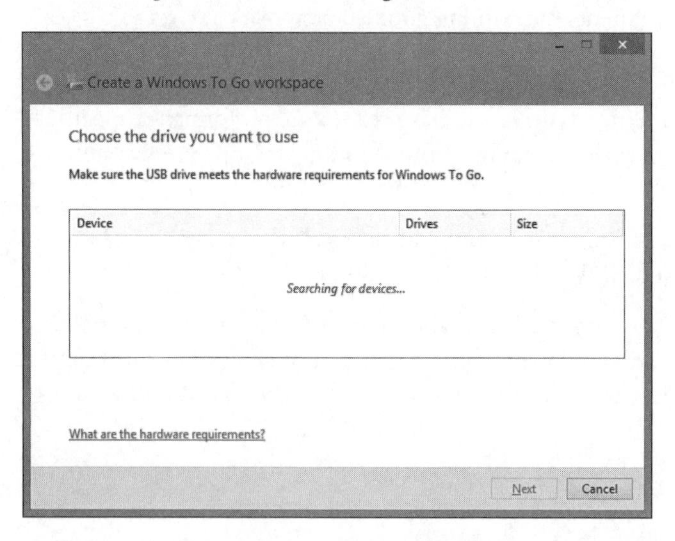

Figure 2-19 The Windows To Go provisioning tool searches the computer for compatible USB drives to install the Windows To Go workspace.

Step 3. Select your USB drive from the list. If your drive is not compatible with Windows To Go, Windows will not allow you to install Windows To Go on it. Also, if the drive is a slower device, Windows may present a warning. After selecting the USB device to use, click **Next** to proceed.

Step 4. Windows searches for installation images to use. If the image file you want is not listed, click the **Search Options** button and select the folder where your `.wim` file is located. If you mounted an `.iso` image, select the drive where the image was mounted, as shown in Figure 2-20. When you have found the image you want to use, select it from the list and click **Next**.

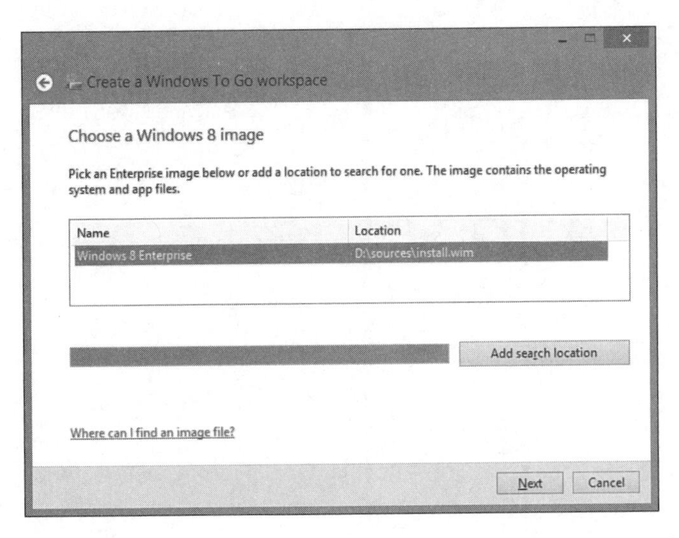

Figure 2-20 Select the image file to use for your Windows To Go workspace.

Step 5. Windows To Go provides an option to encrypt the workspace using BitLocker. Encrypting your portable drive is recommended because these drives are small and can be easily lost. Encrypting the drive ensures that no one will be able to load your workspace or open your files if the drive is lost or stolen.

To encrypt the drive with BitLocker, select the **Use BitLocker with my Windows To Go workspace** check box and type your password in the boxes supplied, and click **Next**.

If you do not want to use BitLocker, click the **Skip** button.

Step 6. The last dialog box is displayed, describing the drive that will be used to create the Windows To Go workspace. When you are ready, click **Create**.

Step 7. The provisioning tool takes some time to create your Windows To Go workspace on your USB drive, displaying progress, as shown in Figure 2-21.

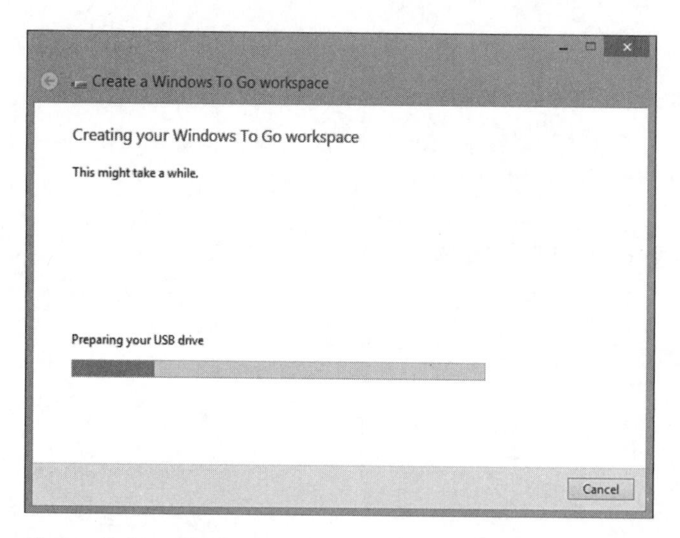

Figure 2-21 Windows To Go workspace provisioning installs the bootable image on the USB drive.

Step 8. After the workspace is installed, Windows asks you to choose a boot option, as shown in Figure 2-22. This changes the computer's firmware to automatically boot from any plugged-in USB device. If you will be using this computer to boot Windows To Go, select **Yes** to allow Windows to change this setting. You can then select either **Save and restart** to boot Windows To Go or select **Save and close** if you want to continue working.

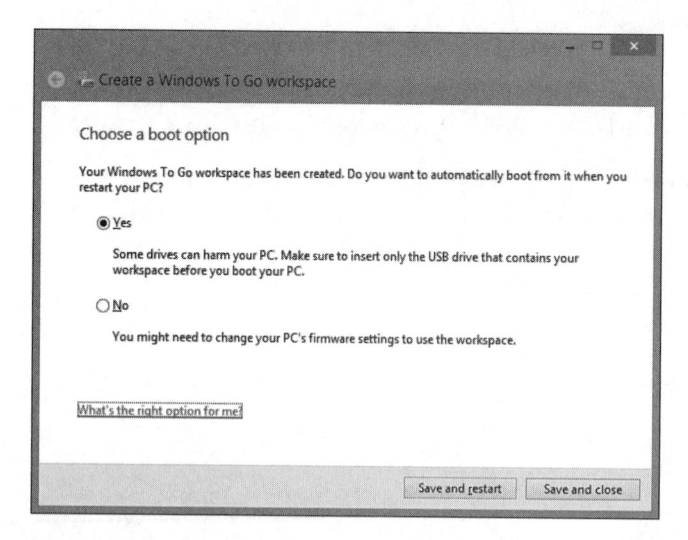

Figure 2-22 Choose a boot option in the Windows To Go provisioning tool.

CAUTION When Windows creates the Windows To Go workspace on your USB drive, it completely reformats and deletes all contents on the drive. Be sure that you select the correct drive and that any files on the drive are removed or backed up.

NOTE For more information on using Windows To Go, refer to "Windows To Go: Feature Overview" at http://technet.microsoft.com/en-us/library/hh831833.aspx and "Deploy Windows To Go in Your Organization" at http://technet.microsoft.com/en-us/library/jj721578.aspx.

Using Windows To Go on a Host Computer

The Windows To Go USB drive works on any desktop computer or laptop or tablet that is certified to run Windows 7 or Windows 8.1. You might need to access the computer BIOS or firmware settings to enable the computer to boot from a removable device.

For instance, on many Dell computers, you can press the F12 button when the computer first posts to access the boot menu, and select the boot drive or device. This technique provides a one-time option for booting the computer from an alternate device. If you will be using the computer frequently, it is more convenient to change the BIOS settings so that the computer will attempt to boot from a USB device whenever one is available. Typically, the BIOS allows you to set a "boot order," so the computer checks each device in turn until it finds a bootable partition. If the first hard disk is set as the first boot device, it will never find the USB device to run the Windows To Go workspace.

The first time you load the Windows To Go workspace by booting a computer from the USB drive, Windows takes some time finding and loading device drivers and displays `Getting devices ready` as it loads. If you used the Windows installation `.iso` to create the workspace, Windows will then walk you through a few setup tasks just as it would for a new computer:

Step 1. Windows displays a dialog box displaying the EULA ID. You must select the **I accept the license terms** check box and click **Next** to proceed.

Step 2. The next screen asks you to pick a color and a PC name to personalize your Windows To Go workspace. You must enter a name in the box provided. Click **Next** to continue.

Step 3. At this point, Windows displays the Settings dialog box, where you have an opportunity to customize a number of settings such as for security, location, updates, and more. This is the same Settings customization screen displayed during the attended installation described earlier in this chapter. You may want to adjust some of these settings for your Windows To Go workspace, which you can do by selecting the **Customize** option. If not, select **Use express settings** to proceed.

Step 4. Windows To Go then asks you to sign in to your PC. You have the same options as you normally do for a Windows 8.1 workstation, using a Microsoft account or a local account. Refer to Figure 2-7.

Step 5. After a few minutes, your new Windows To Go workspace will be ready to use.

Like all Windows operating systems starting with Windows XP, your Windows To Go workspace requires activation, so it needs to be connected to a corporate network that supports volume activation. This can be implemented using either Key Management Service (KMS) or Active Directory–based volume activation. KMS activation is good for 180 days, so mobile workers using Windows To Go can stay offline for an extended period of time. They need to renew the activation within the 180-day period (by connecting to the corporate network), or the workspace activation will lose validity.

You can carry your Windows To Go USB drive from computer to computer and boot to a familiar environment everywhere you go. This capability is very convenient for workers who travel from place to place, where equipment is already available, and it can save costs over supplying each mobile worker with a separate laptop or tablet computer.

Using a VHD

A virtual hard disk (VHD) is a special type of image file that contains all the operating system files, applications, and data that might be found on a typical hard disk partition, encapsulated in a single file. Using VHD technology, Microsoft has expanded the field of client virtualization (also known as desktop virtualization) to provide powerful new means of management for desktops in a corporate environment. It is even now possible to utilize servers with lots of RAM and several powerful processors with a series of virtual machines installed on these servers and accessed by users from their own desktop. Users can communicate with these virtual desktops by means of a client device that supports protocols such as Remote Desktop Protocol (RDP).

Understanding VHDs

The virtual hard disk specification consists of a single file that includes all the files and folders that would be found on a hard disk partition—hence the term virtual hard disk. This file is capable of hosting native file systems and supporting all regular disk operations. Although it was first supported in Windows 7 and Windows Server 2008 R2, Microsoft has continued the support and use of VHDs in Windows 8.1 Enterprise and Windows Server 2012 R2 (all editions except the Foundation edition) without the need for a hypervisor (an additional layer of software below the operating system for running virtual computers). These operating systems enable you to create, configure, and boot physical computers directly from VHDs, and they provide administrators and developers with the following capabilities:

- You can standardize image formats and toolsets used within the company.
- You can reduce the quantity of images that must be cataloged and supported.
- Developers can test applications on multiple operating systems on different virtual drives; if applications break operating systems, developers can restore the operating system with minimal lost time and cost.
- You can have a common image format that runs on both physical and virtual machines.
- VHDs enable you to improve server utilization, with consequent energy savings.
- You can use disk-management tools to attach a VHD and perform offline image management.
- You or your clients can run Windows 7, Windows 8.1, and Windows Server 2012 R2, or any combination needed, all on the same computer in different virtual spaces.

Windows operating systems prior to Windows 7 require you to install the Windows Server 2008 or 2012 Hyper-V role, Microsoft Virtual Server, or Windows Virtual PC.

Types of Virtual Hard Disks

Windows 8.1 and Windows Server 2012 R2 offer three types of VHDs: fixed, dynamic, and differencing. Table 2-7 explains how these types differ.

Table 2-7 Types of VHDs

Tool	Description
Fixed	This VHD has a fixed size. For example, if you create a fixed VHD of 30 GB size, the file size is always about 30 GB (some space is used for the internal VHD structure), regardless of how much data is contained in it.
Dynamic	This VHD is only as large as the data contained in it. You can specify the maximum size. For example, if you create a dynamic VHD of 30 GB size, it starts out at around 8.10 MB but expands as you write data to it. It cannot exceed the specified maximum size. Fixed VHDs are recommended over dynamic because they offer the highest I/O performance; also, as a dynamic disk expands, the host volume could run out of space, causing write operations to fail.
Differencing	Also known as a child VHD, this VHD contains only the modified disk blocks of the parent VHD with which it is associated. The parent VHD is read-only, and all modifications are written to the differencing VHD. The parent VHD can be any of these three VHD types, and multiple differencing VHDs are referred to as a differencing chain. A differencing VHD is useful in a test environment; when a developer performs tests, all updates are made on the differencing VHD. To revert to the clean state of the parent VHD, you just need to delete the differencing VHD and create a new one.

CAUTION If you are using differencing VHDs, you should not modify the parent VHD. If you do so, the block structure between the parent and differencing VHD will no longer match, resulting in corruption of the differencing VHD. Furthermore, you must keep both the parent and differencing VHDs within the same folder on a local volume for native-boot scenarios. Otherwise, the differencing VHD will not boot. If the differencing VHD is not used for native-boot, the VHDs can be on different folders or volumes.

Tools Used with Virtual Hard Disks

Microsoft provides several tools that you can use for configuring and managing VHDs, available either as part of the Windows 8.1 operating system or included with the Windows ADK. Table 2-8 introduces these VHD management tools. We discuss the use of these tools in Chapter 7.

Table 2-8 Tools Used with VHDs

Tool	Description
Disk Management	A Microsoft Management Console (MMC) snap-in that enables you to manage VHDs, including creating, attaching, detaching, expanding, and merging VHDs.
DiskPart	A command-line tool that enables you to perform VHD management activities similar to those available with Disk Management. You can script these actions using DiskPart.
BCDEdit	A command-line tool that enables you to manage boot configuration data (BCD) stores.
BCDBoot	A command-line tool that enables you to manage and create new BCD stores and BCD boot entries. You can use this tool to create new boot entries when configuring a system to boot from a new VHD.
Deployment Image Servicing and Management (DISM)	A command-line tool that enables you to apply updates, applications, drivers, and language packs to a Windows image, including a VHD.
Sysprep	A utility that enables you to prepare an operating system for imaging and deployment by removing user and computer-specific data.
Windows PE	Windows Preinstallation Environment (Windows PE) is included with the ADK and is used to prepare a computer for installation and servicing of Windows.

All these tools are included with Windows 8.1 and Windows Server 2012 R2, except Windows PE, which is included with the Windows ADK. Also included with Windows Server 2012 R2 and Windows 8.1 Pro, but not with Windows 8.1 (basic) or Windows RT 8.1, is the Windows Hyper-V Manager, which is an MMC snap-in that enables you to create VHD images, including the ability to install Windows from installation media or an ISO image file.

Configuring a VHD for Native Boot

For the 70-687 exam, you need to know how to work with VHDs, including how to install Windows 8.1 on the VHD; deploy a Windows 8.1 VHD to other machines; and use methods for booting from the VHD. For installing Windows 8.1, you need to use a VHD with native-boot capabilities, which enables the VHD to run on a computer without a hypervisor such as Hyper-V.

Like Windows 7 and Windows Server 2008 R2, Windows 8.1 and Windows Server 2012 enable you to manage virtual disks directly in the disk management tools, without the need to install the Hyper-V Server role or the Hyper-V Manager console. You can use either the Disk Management MMC snap-in or the command-line–based DiskPart tool to create and configure VHDs. You use Disk Management here and learn about the DiskPart tool in Chapter 7.

Native VHD boot requires at least two partitions—a system partition with the Windows 8.1 boot environment and boot configuration data (BCD) store—and a partition to store the VHD file. In addition, the partition containing the VHD must have enough free disk space for expanding a dynamic VHD and for the page file created when booting the VHD. When you are using native boot VHDs, the page file is created outside the VHD.

You also should be aware of a few limitations when working with native VHDs:

- Native VHD does not support hibernation (sleep mode is supported, however).
- You cannot place a VHD inside a VHD (nesting).
- BitLocker encryption cannot be used on a host volume that contains a native boot VHD or on the volumes in the VHD.
- VHDs do not work with dynamic disks, so a VHD cannot be configured as a dynamic disk, and the parent volume of a VHD cannot be configured as a dynamic disk.

Using Disk Management

The Disk Management snap-in contains all the utilities necessary to create and configure disks and partitions. We look at this snap-in in detail in Chapter 17, "Disk Management." Use the following procedure to create a VHD:

Step 1. Open File Explorer, right-click **Computer**, and choose **Manage**. This opens the Computer Management snap-in, which contains Disk Management as a component snap-in.

Step 2. In the console tree, click **Disk Management** to make its contents visible in the details pane.

Step 3. Right-click **Disk Management** and choose **Create VHD**. This displays the Create and Attach Virtual Hard Disk dialog box, as shown in Figure 2-23.

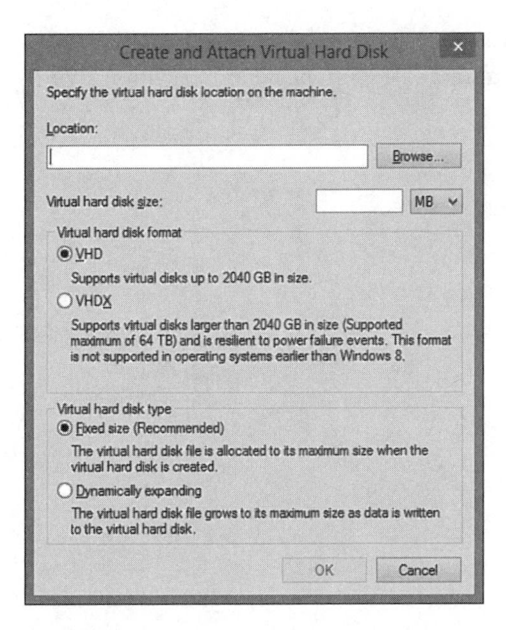

Figure 2-23 The Create and Attach Virtual Hard Disk dialog box enables you to create a new VHD.

Step 4. Type a path and filename for the VHD in the Location text box, or use the **Browse** button to browse to a suitable location.

Step 5. Specify a size in the Virtual hard disk size text box, and for Virtual hard disk format, choose **VHD**.

Fixed size (Recommended): Creates a fixed VHD.

Dynamically expanding: Creates a dynamic VHD, as described earlier in Table 2-7.

Step 6. Select from the choices available under Virtual hard disk type (**Fixed** is recommended) and then click **OK**.

NOTE The VHDX format is new for Windows 8.1 and Windows Server 2012. It is used only for virtualization inside a hypervisor, and not for native boot. Virtualization and Hyper-V are covered in Chapter 7.

Step 7. The disk is created and attached and appears as an unknown disk in Disk Management. This process might take several minutes, particularly for a VHD large enough to hold a Windows 8.1 installation.

Step 8. Right-click the unknown disk in Disk Management and choose **Initialize Disk**. In the dialog box shown in Figure 2-24, keep the default partition style and then click **OK**.

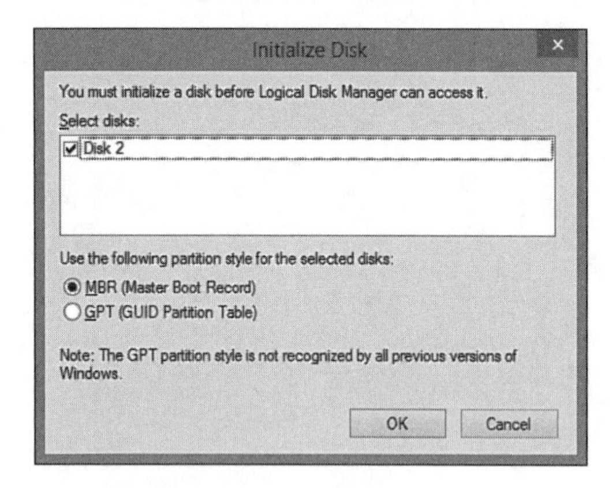

Figure 2-24 Initializing the VHD.

Step 9. You don't need to format the VHD; this will be done when you install Windows 8.1 to the disk.

Installing Windows 8.1 to a VHD

Now that you have a VHD prepared, you can use a number of techniques to apply an image to it and make it bootable. You cannot install Windows 7 or Windows Server 2008 R2 directly from the installation DVD to a VHD file, but you can now do this for Windows 8.1. This makes creating your initial image much simpler, and you can customize it within the VHD. When the image is ready, you only need to run `Sysprep` to generalize the image and it is ready to deploy to multiple computers.

After you have created a VHD, write down the drive, folder, and filename of the VHD file; then insert the Windows 8.1 DVD and reboot the computer to the Windows 8.1 Setup program:

Step 1. Start by following the initial steps 1–5 in the "Performing an Attended Installation" earlier in this chapter. At the end of step 5, you should see the Which type of installation do you want? screen from Figure 2-3. You need a way to access the VHD on this computer, so you can install Windows there instead of on the physical disks. In Windows 8.1 Setup, you can now invoke an administrative command prompt using Shift+F10.

Step 2. Press **Shift+F10** to open the administrative command prompt. As shown in Figure 2-25, Windows PE displays the prompt, defaulting to the X:\ drive (the Windows PE RAM disk).

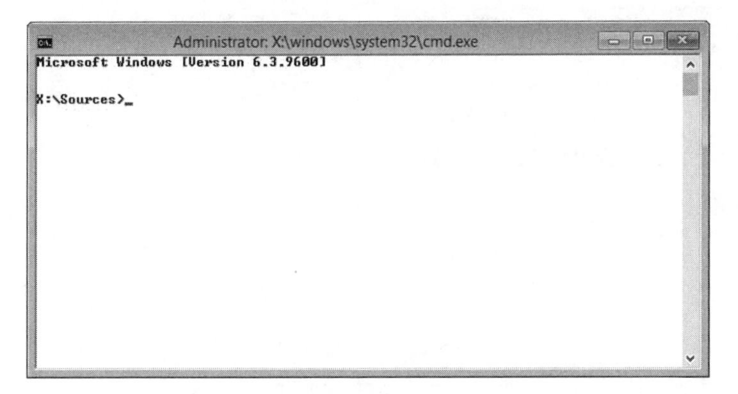

Figure 2-25 Press **Shift+F10** during setup to display an administrative command prompt.

Step 3. Type the **`diskpart`** command to open the `diskpart` prompt; then select and attach the VHD using the following commands:

```
Select vdisk file=<letter>:\<filename>
Attach vdisk
```

where *<letter>* is the drive letter where the VHD file was created, and *<filename>* is the name of the VHD file.

NOTE The Windows PE environment may not have the same drive letters as the installed Windows 8.1 operating system. For instance, if you have a C: drive, a DVD drive, and an E: drive in Windows 8.1, Windows PE will assign a different letter to the DVD drive, and your E: drive will likely now be drive D:.

Step 4. Type **`exit`** to close `diskpart`; then type **`exit`** again to close the administrative command prompt.

Step 5. Back at the Windows Setup screen, select **Custom: Install Windows only (advanced)**.

Step 6. When the Where do you want to install Windows? screen shown in Figure 2-26 is displayed, it shows all the available disks and partitions, including the VHD just attached using `diskpart`. Select the VHD partition as the installation partition.

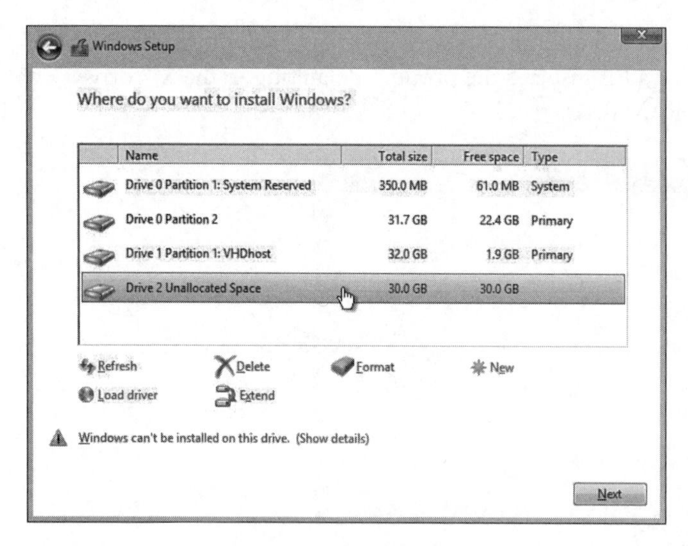

Figure 2-26 Selecting a VHD for Windows Setup.

NOTE Windows displays a warning saying that Windows can't be installed on this drive when you select the VHD. You can ignore this warning.

Step 7. Click **Next** and Windows begins copying files and installing Windows 8.1. The installation proceeds as illustrated in Figure 2-5, and the computer reboots several times.

Step 8. The last time that Windows boots, it presents two boot options, as shown in Figure 2-27. The volume numbers depend on the drives and partitions on the computer during Setup. You can change the description of the selections using **BCDEdit** to make it less confusing.

You need to run `Sysprep /generalize` on this VHD file before deploying it to multiple computers.

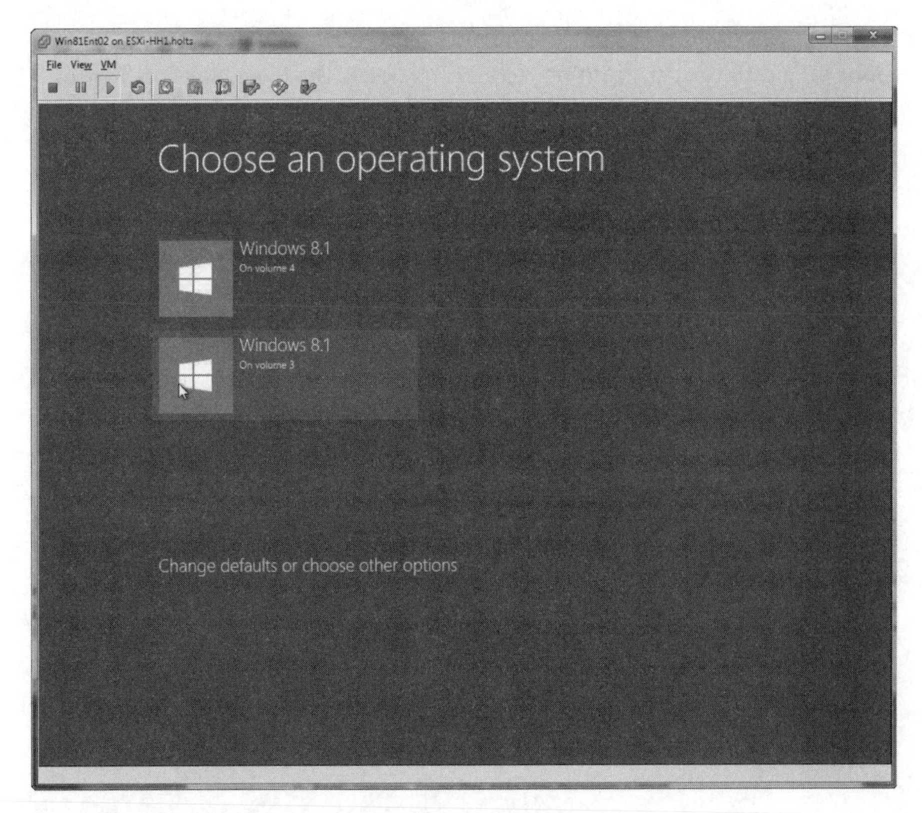

Figure 2-27 Windows dual-boot options with VHD.

Best Practices for Using Native-Boot VHDs

Microsoft recommends the following best practices for using native-boot VHDs:

- **Store mission-critical data outside the native-boot VHDs.** This facilitates recovery of the data if the VHD becomes corrupted.
- **Use fixed VHDs in production environments.** It is possible to use any of the three VHD types; however, it is recommended you use fixed VHDs in production environments for reasons mentioned earlier. You can use dynamic or differencing VHDs in development and test scenarios.
- **Use a maximum size that is larger than the minimum disk requirements for Windows.** The VHD holds additional information about the virtual disk; furthermore, Windows updates take up disk space as they are added.
- **Ensure that sufficient space is available on the host volume for the page file (pagefile.sys).** The page file is created on the host volume outside the VHD. You can use another physical volume for optimum performance.

- **Use `Sysprep` to generalize the image before using the VHD for native boot on a different computer.** `Sysprep` prepares the image for copying to additional computers. When you do so, Windows detects hardware devices and initializes properly for running on another computer.

> **TIP** You can use Windows Deployment Services (WDS) to deploy the VHD image to large numbers of computers. WDS in Windows Server 2012 R2 includes the capability to add VHD image files to its image catalog, making them available to target computers using PXE boot. These computers copy the VHD file locally and configure booting from the VHD. On first boot, the computer configures Windows for the physical devices and performs the usual mini-setup. Using WDS in this manner facilitates rapid deployment of Windows to many computers. You can also script the use of WDS by using the command-line tool `WDSUTIL`.

> **TIP** Another way to create the VHD file is to use an open source tool called `WIM2VHD`, available from the MSDN code gallery at http://gallery.technet.microsoft.com/scriptcenter/Convert-WindowsImageps1-0fe23a8f. This scriptable command-line tool converts the `.wim` file to a VHD that can be booted.

Booting VHDs

Windows 7 introduced the ability to boot from a VHD, and this capability exists in Windows 7, Windows 8.1, and Windows Server 2012 R2. You must configure the boot loader from the default Windows installation, using the `BCDEdit` command-line utility. This tool manages BCD stores, which replace the `Boot.ini` file used in Windows versions prior to Vista. You can use `BCDEdit` for several purposes, including creating new stores, modifying existing stores, adding or removing boot menu options, and so on. Use the following procedure:

Step 1. Open an administrative command prompt.

Step 2. Type **`bcdedit`**. This starts the Windows boot loader utility and displays the default Windows boot information, as shown in Figure 2-28.

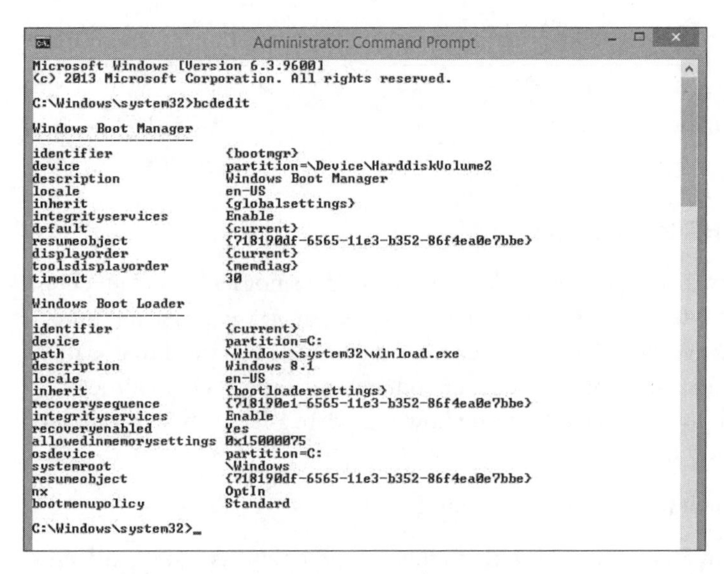

Figure 2-28 The Windows boot loader program provides default Windows boot information.

Step 3. Type **`bcdedit /copy {current} /d "Boot from VHD"`**. This command copies the current Windows boot loader information, creating a new entry that you can modify for booting from the VHD.

Step 4. Type **`bcdedit`** again. You will notice a duplicate entry, identified by the globally unique identifier (GUID) in the `identifier` line. Make careful note of this GUID.

Step 5. Type **`bcdedit /set {`*`guid`*`} device vhd=[`*`drive`*`:]\`*`<path_to_vhd_file>`***, where *`guid`* is as noted in step 4, *`drive`* is the drive on which the VHD file is located, and *`<path_to_vhd_file>`* is the location of the VHD file on its drive. For example:

```
bcdedit /set {35bbc226-7920-11de-b6f7-a0288f236347} device
VHD="[C:]\users\don\documents\my virtual machines\w7vhd.vhd"
```

Step 6. Set the OS device by typing **`bcdedit /set {`*`guid`*`} osdevice vhd=[`*`drive`*`:]\`*`<path_to_vhd_file>`***. The syntax of this command is identical to the previous one, except that `device` is replaced by `osdevice`.

Step 7. Set the Detect Hal command by typing **`bcdedit /set {`*`guid`*`} detecthal on`**.

Step 8. Provide a description for this boot by typing **`bcdedit /set {`*`guid`*`} description`** ***`<description>`***, where *`description`* is a description of the boot that will appear at startup. Enclose the description in double quotation marks if it contains spaces.

Step 9. Verify your output by typing **`bcdedit`** again. You should see a screen similar to Figure 2-27, allowing you to boot either into the full, previously configured operating system or to the VHD file.

If you want to delete the entry, take note of the GUID listed in `BCDEdit` and use the following command:

```
bcdedit /delete {GUID} /cleanup
```

Adding a Native-Boot VHD to an Older Computer

An older computer, such as one running Windows XP, does not have the same boot loader file; it has the older `Boot.ini` file, which is loaded by `Ntldr` at startup time. If you are adding a native-boot VHD to such a computer, you will need to update the system partition first by using the `BCDBoot` tool before editing the boot menu with `BCDEdit`. The following steps show you how to update a BIOS-based computer to include a Windows 7 boot menu:

Step 1. Open an administrative command prompt.

Step 2. Use **`diskpart`** to attach the VHD file to this computer and assign it a driver letter, as already described.

Step 3. Use BCDBoot to copy the boot environment files and BCD configuration from the `\Windows\System32` folder of the VHD to the system partition. For example, type

```
cd <letter>:windows\system32
bcdboot <letter>:\windows /s c:
```

In these commands, *`<letter>`* is the drive letter you assigned to the mounted VHD file, and it is assumed that the system partition is on drive C:. After you perform these steps, you can use `BCDEdit` as already described to edit the boot loader files to enable booting from the VHD.

Installing Additional Windows Features

As introduced in Chapter 1, Windows 8.1 includes the following additional Windows features, the installation and configuration of which we discuss in this section:

- Client Hyper-V
- Miracast Display
- Pervasive Device Encryption
- Virtual smart cards
- Secure Boot

Client Hyper-V

Installation of Client Hyper-V is a simple task, as the following procedure shows:

Step 1. Right-click **Start**, choose **Control Panel**, and select the **Programs** category.

Step 2. From the list of applets in this category, select **Programs and Features**.

Step 3. From the task list, select **Turn Windows features on or off**.

Step 4. You receive the Windows Features dialog box shown in Figure 2-29. Select **Hyper-V** and then click **OK**.

Figure 2-29 Installing Client Hyper-V.

Step 5. A Windows Features dialog box appears as the required files are located and the changes are applied. When informed that Windows has completed the requested changes, click **Close**.

Use the following procedure to create a virtual machine:

Step 1. From the Search charm, type `hyper` and then select **Hyper-V Manager**.

Step 2. From the Action menu of the Hyper-V Manager snap-in that appears, select **Connect to Server**.

Step 3. On the Select Computer dialog box, select **Local computer** to create a virtual machine on the local computer. To create a remote virtual machine, select **Another computer** and then type the name of or browse for the name of the required computer, and then click **OK**.

Step 4. From the Action menu, click **New > Virtual Machine**.

Step 5. Follow the steps of the New Virtual Machine Wizard that appears. You are asked to provide a name and location, memory and networking requirements, and operating system installation options.

Step 6. Review your selections as provided on the Summary page of the wizard and then click **Finish** to create the virtual machine.

After you created the virtual machine, you can access it from the Hyper-V Virtual Machine Connection tool, which is accessible from the Search charm. This tool operates in a similar fashion to the Remote Desktop Connection tool, which is discussed in Chapter 14, "Configuring Remote Management and Remote Connections."

NOTE For more information on Client Hyper-V in Windows 8.1, refer to "Run Virtual Machines on Windows 8.1 with Client Hyper-V" at http://windows.microsoft.com/en-us/windows-8/hyper-v-run-virtual-machines and "Client Hyper-V" at http://technet.microsoft.com/en-us/library/hh857623.aspx.

Miracast Display

To enable a Miracast display, connect the Miracast adapter to the HDTV or other compatible Miracast display, and then perform the following steps:

Step 1. From the Devices charm, click **Project**.

Step 2. Click **Add a wireless display**.

Step 3. Windows displays the Devices panel as it searches for the Miracast display device.

Step 4. When it locates the desired device, select it and enter a PIN (found on information provided with your device). Then click **Next**.

Step 5. On the Project screen that appears, click **Duplicate** to duplicate the display on your local monitor on the HDTC or **Extend** to extend your display on the HDTV. You can also select **Second screen only** to blank out your local monitor and transfer its display to the HDTV.

NOTE For more information on using a Miracast display, refer to "Windows 8.1 + Miracast" at http://winsupersite.com/windows-8/windows-81-miracast and "Projecting to Wireless Displays with Miracast in Windows 8.1" at http://blogs.windows.com/windows/b/springboard/archive/2013/11/12/projecting-to-wireless-displays-with-miracast-in-windows-8-1.aspx.

Pervasive Device Encryption

A laptop or tablet that meets the hardware requirements for Pervasive Device Encryption should enable this feature automatically. An older laptop that has been upgraded from an earlier version of Windows to Windows 8.1 does not enable encryption by default. In this case, use the following procedure:

Step 1. From the Settings charm, click **Change PC settings**.

Step 2. Click **PC info.**

Step 3. Under Device Encryption, select **Turn On**. This option then changes to **Turn Off**, which you can select to disable Pervasive Device Encryption if desired.

NOTE For more information on Pervasive Device Encryption, refer to "Will Windows 8.1 Laptop Encryption Work on Your Laptop?" at http://www.geeksuper.com/will-windows-8-1-laptop-encryption-work-laptop/ and "Windows 8.1 Will Start Encrypting Hard Drives By Default: Everything You Need to Know" at http://www.howtogeek.com/173592/windows-8.1-will-start-encrypting-hard-drives-by-default-everything-you-need-to-know/.

Virtual Smart Cards

Enabling virtual smart cards (VSCs) is a complex procedure that involves the following steps:

- Creating and enabling a certificate template on the certificate server for a certificate capable of supporting VSCs
- Creating the TPM VSC on the domain-joined client computer using the `tpmvscmgr.exe` command-line utility in Windows 8.1
- Enrolling for the certificate on the TPM VSC manager software utility

NOTE For more information on VSCs including details for performing each step, refer to "Understanding and Evaluating Virtual Smart Cards" at http://www.microsoft.com/en-us/download/details.aspx?id=29076.

Secure Boot

Secure Boot is enabled automatically on computers that meet its hardware requirements. If it has not been enabled, or if you see a `Secure Boot isn't configured properly` message, you need to access the BIOS menu by pressing the required key during startup. Then you need to find the Secure Boot setting and set it to **Enabled**. The location of this setting depends on the BIOS manufacturer, and is usually in the Security tab, the Boot tab, or the Authentication tab. Save your change and then reboot.

TIP You can determine whether the computer can enable Secure Boot by accessing the System Information utility. Right-click **Start**, choose **Run**, and then type **`msinfo32`**. If the BIOS mode reads `Legacy`, the computer cannot enable Secure Boot. If the BIOS mode reads `UEFI`, check the Secure Boot State, which will read `On` if Secure Boot is enabled. If it reads `Off`, access the BIOS as already described to turn it on.

NOTE For more information on Secure Boot, refer to "Secure Boot Overview" at http://technet.microsoft.com/library/hh824987.aspx.

Configuring Windows for Additional Languages

Windows 8.1 includes support for hundreds of languages, including native letters and scripts. The Control Panel Language applet enables you to add or change available languages. Use the following procedure:

Step 1. From the Settings charm, click **Change PC settings**.

Step 2. From the PC settings panel, click **Time and language**, click **Region and language**, and then click **Add a language**.

Step 3. You receive the screen shown in Figure 2-30. Scroll to select the desired language. If regional versions are available, a list is provided; select the desired version.

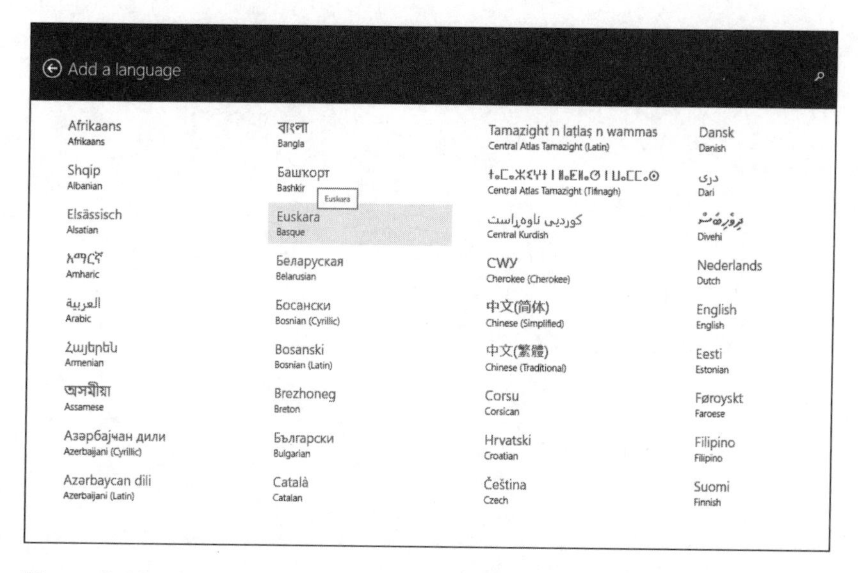

Figure 2-30 Adding an additional language from PC Settings.

Step 4. You return to the Time and language page. To make the selected language your primary one, click it and then click the **Set as primary** button. To complete this procedure, log off and then log back on.

Step 5. To configure additional language properties, click **Options**. This allows you to configure options such as freehand handwriting and available keyboards.

Step 6. To remove a language, select it and click **Remove**.

You can also modify your language settings from the Control Panel Language applet, as follows:

Step 1. Right-click **Start**, choose **Control Panel**, and select **Add a language** under the Clock, Language, and Region category. The Language applet appears, showing the language or languages available on the computer.

Step 2. Click **Add a language**.

Step 3. You receive the Add a language applet, as shown in Figure 2-31. Scroll this applet to locate the desired language, select it, and then click **Add**. If the selected language includes different regional versions, click **Open**, select the desired version, and then click **Add**. The language is added to the list of available languages in the Language applet.

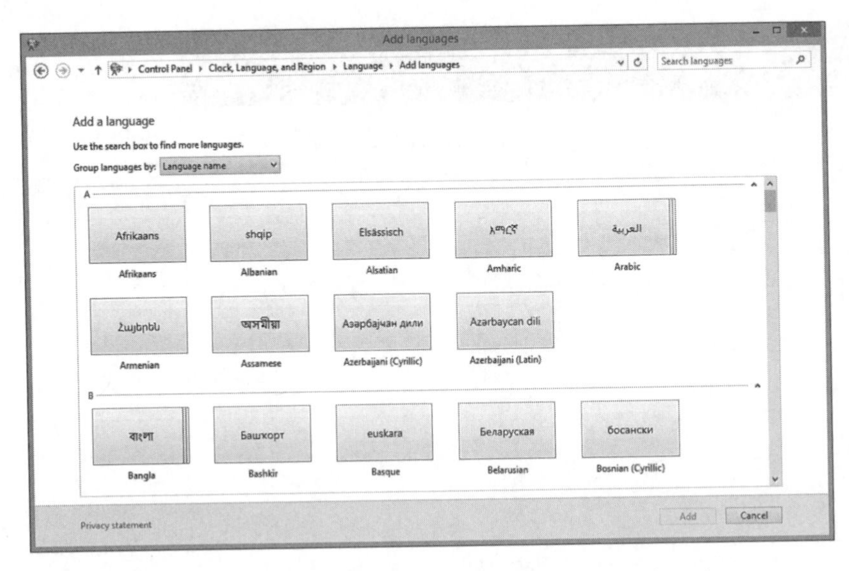

Figure 2-31 Adding an additional language from the Control Panel.

Step 4. Languages on this applet are listed in order of preferences. To modify this list, select a language and click **Move up** or **Move down** as required.

Step 5. To remove a language, select it and click **Remove**.

Exam Preparation Tasks

Review All the Key Topics

Review the most important topics in the chapter, noted with the key topics icon in the outer margin of the page. Table 2-9 lists a reference of these key topics and the page numbers on which each is found.

Table 2-9 Key Topics for Chapter 2

Key Topic Element	Description	Page Number
List	Lists items you should have on hand before starting a Windows 8.1 installation	75
Step List	Shows how to install Windows 8.1 from an installation DVD	76
Step List	Describes how to use Windows ADK to create an answer file	85

Key Topic Element	Description	Page Number
Step List	Describes how to use an answer file to perform an unattended installation of Windows 8.1	90
List	Describes advantages of setting up a dual-boot system	90
Table 2-3	Describes important Windows 8.1 setup log files	93
Table 2-4	Describes available paths for upgrading older Windows operating systems to Windows 8.1	95
Table 2-5	Describes the types of information that can be kept when upgrading older Windows operating systems to Windows 8.1	96
List	Describes tasks you should perform before upgrading to Windows 8.1	97
Table 2-6	Describes available paths for upgrading to a higher edition of Windows 8.1	101
List	Describes how Windows To Go operates similar to a regular installation of Windows 8.1 with several exceptions	102
List	Provides characteristics of Windows To Go USB drives	103
Step List	Shows how to provision a Windows To Go workspace	104
Table 2-7	Lists types of VHDs	110
Table 2-8	Lists tools used for configuring VHDs	111
List	Lists limitations when working with native VHDs	112
Step List	Shows how to create a VHD using Disk Management	112
Step List	Shows how to install Windows 8.1 to a VHD	114
Step List	Shows how to edit the boot loader for booting a VHD	118
Step List	Shows how to edit the boot loader on older Windows XP	120

Complete the Tables and Lists from Memory

Print a copy of Appendix B, "Memory Tables," (found on the CD), or at least the section for this chapter, and complete the tables and lists from memory. Appendix C, "Memory Tables Answer Key," also on the CD, includes completed tables and lists to check your work.

Definitions of Key Terms

Define the following key terms from this chapter and check your answers in the glossary.

Basic Input/Output System (BIOS), `BCDBoot`, `BCDEdit`, Differencing VHD, Dynamic VHD, Fixed VHD, Hypervisor, `setup.exe`, Miracast Display, Pervasive Device Encryption, virtual hard disk (VHD), `Windows.old`, Windows To Go

This chapter covers the following subjects:

- **Migrating Users and Their Profiles:** Microsoft provides methods you can use for migrating user files plus desktop and application settings from one computer to another: the User State Migration Tool (USMT) and the Windows Easy Transfer Wizard. This section shows you how to use these tools and provides guidelines as to when you should use each one.
- **Configuring Folder Redirection:** You can redirect library folders such as documents, music, pictures, and videos to common locations such as shared folders on a server. This enables you to keep track of users' documents and ensure that they are properly and regularly backed up. Group Policy provides policy settings that can be used to enforce folder redirection.
- **Configuring Profiles:** Windows provides user profiles that are composed of desktop settings, files, application data, and the specific environment established by the user. You can configure roaming user profiles that are stored on a server so that they are available to users regardless of the computer they access, or mandatory profiles that users are not able to modify.

CHAPTER 3

Migrating Users and Applications to Windows 8.1

Many companies can purchase new computers with Windows 8.1 already loaded or upgrade certain computers from Windows XP, Vista, or 7. Users who will be working with these computers may have been using older Windows computers for several years, and these computers will have applications with user- or company-specific settings as well as important data on them. Microsoft provides tools to assist you in migrating users and applications to new Windows 8.1 computers, and it expects you to know how to perform these migrations in an efficient manner as part of the 70-687 exam.

"Do I Know This Already?" Quiz

The "Do I Know This Already?" quiz allows you to assess whether you should read this entire chapter or simply jump to the "Exam Preparation Tasks" section for review. If you are in doubt, read the entire chapter. Table 3-1 outlines the major headings in this chapter and the corresponding "Do I Know This Already?" quiz questions. You can find the answers in Appendix A, "Answers to the 'Do I Know This Already?' Quizzes."

Table 3-1 "Do I Know This Already?" Foundation Topics Section-to-Question Mapping

Foundations Topics Section	Questions Covered in This Section
Migrating Users and Their Profiles	1–5
Configuring Folder Redirection	6–7
Configuring Profiles	8–9

1. You have been called to help a home user who has bought a Windows 8.1 computer move her documents and settings from her old computer running Windows XP Home Edition to the new computer. What tool should you use?
   a. Files and Settings Transfer Wizard
   b. User State Migration Tool (USMT)
   c. Windows Easy Transfer
   d. Windows Assessment and Deployment Kit (ADK)

2. Your company is migrating 50 users in one department from old computers running Windows XP Professional to new computers running Windows 8.1 Pro. What tool should you use?
   a. Files and Settings Transfer Wizard
   b. User State Migration Tool (USMT)
   c. Windows Easy Transfer
   d. Windows Assessment and Deployment Kit (ADK)

3. Which of the following items are components included with USMT 5.0? (Choose all that apply.)
   a. `ScanState.exe`
   b. `LoadState.exe`
   c. `Migwiz.exe`
   d. `MigApp.xml`
   e. `Migapp.exe`
   f. `Usmtutils.exe`

4. You are charged with the responsibility of migrating 100 users in the same department to new Windows 8.1 Pro computers. What program should you use to collect user settings and data from their old computers?
   a. `ScanState.exe`
   b. `LoadState.exe`
   c. `Migwiz.exe`
   d. `Fastwiz.exe`

5. You have stored user settings and data from all the employees in your company's Marketing department on a file server. You have also set up new Windows 8.1 computers for these employees and installed all required applications. What program should you use now to transfer the user settings and data to these new computers?

   a. `ScanState.exe`

   b. `LoadState.exe`

   c. `Migwiz.exe`

   d. `Xcopy.exe`

6. Which of the following folders can you redirect to a shared folder on a server so that they can be easily backed up? (Choose all that apply.)

   a. Documents

   b. Music

   c. Pictures

   d. Videos

7. Which of the following are components of a domain-based folder redirection implementation? (Choose all that apply.)

   a. A Windows Server 2012 R2 computer configured as a router

   b. A Windows Server 2012 R2 computer configured as a domain controller

   c. A group policy object (GPO) that specifies folder redirection settings

   d. A Windows Server 2012 R2 computer configured as a global catalog server

   e. A Windows Server 2012 R2 computer configured with a shared folder accessible to network users

8. You want to ensure that all users on your company's network are provided with common settings that appear on any computer on the network, regardless of the computer they log on to. Further, you want to ensure that these settings cannot be modified by users and kept after logging off. What profile type do you configure?

   a. Roaming profile

   b. Mandatory profile

   c. Local profile

   d. Permanent profile

9. You want to copy a user profile so that another user of the same computer can use the same settings specified in the first profile. What do you do?

  a. From the System dialog box, click **Advanced system settings**. In the System Properties dialog box that appears, select the **Profiles** tab, select the default profile, and then click **Copy To**. Then type or browse to the desired location and click **OK**.

  b. From the System dialog box, click **Advanced system settings**. In the System Properties dialog box that appears, select the **Profiles** tab and then click **Settings.** Select the default profile and click **Copy To**. Then type or browse to the desired location and click **OK**.

  c. From the System dialog box, click **Advanced system settings**. In the System Properties dialog box that appears, select the **Advanced** tab and then click **Settings** under User Profiles. Then, in the User Profiles dialog box, select the default profile and click **Copy To**. Then type or browse to the desired location and click **OK**.

  d. In File Explorer, browse to **%systemdrive%\Users\Default User\Profiles**. Right-click this folder, choose **Copy**, browse to the desired user in the Users subfolder, access the **\Profiles** subfolder of this user, right-click it, and choose **Paste**.

Foundation Topics

Migrating Users and Their Profiles

Windows 8.1 provides two tools that assist you in migrating users from old computers to new ones. Windows Easy Transfer is a wizard-based tool that replaces the Files and Settings Transfer Wizard used in Windows XP; it is designed to facilitate the migration of one user or a small number of users, including their data and profiles. If you have a large number of users to migrate in a corporate environment, the User State Migration Tool (USMT) 5.0 is designed for this purpose. Running it from the command line, you can customize USMT to suit the needs of your migration requirements.

User State Migration Tool

Intuitively, you might first think that migrating a large number of users to new Windows 8.1 computers could be as simple as using the `xcopy` command or a tool such as Robocopy to move files from their old computers to a network share, and then moving them back to the new computers at a later time. However, users like to store data on various locations on their local hard drives; they have customized application settings and specific files (such as Microsoft Outlook PST files) that might be hard to locate after such a move is finished. Users also like to set up individual desktop preferences, such as wallpapers and screen savers. Using USMT enables you to move all these items and more in a seamless manner to their appropriate locations on the new computer so that the users can resume working on this computer with minimal delay.

You can use USMT 5.0 to quickly and easily transfer any number of user files and settings as a part of operating system deployment or computer replacement. This tool is included with the Windows Assessment and Deployment Kit (Windows ADK) for Windows 8.1. It includes migration of the following items:

- Local user accounts.
- Personalized settings from these accounts, such as desktop backgrounds, sounds, screen savers, mouse pointer settings, Internet Explorer settings, and email settings including signature files and contact lists.
- Personal files belonging to these accounts including user profiles, the Desktop folder, the My Documents folder, and any other folder locations users might have utilized. USMT 5.0 includes the capability to capture files even when they are in use, by means of Volume Shadow Copy technology.
- Operating system and application settings, including the Applications folder within Program Files, user profile folders, or storage folders on the local disk defined within specific application settings.

- Information contained in previous Windows installations and included in `Windows.old` folders.

This tool reduces the costs of operating system deployment by addressing the following items:

- Technician time associated with migration
- Employee learning and familiarization time on the new operating system
- Employee downtime and help desk calls related to repersonalizing the desktop
- Employee downtime locating missing files
- Employee satisfaction with the migration experience

USMT consists of three executable files, `ScanState.exe`, `LoadState.exe`, and `UsmtUtils.exe`, and three migration rule files, `MigApp.xml`, `MigUser.xml`, and `MigDocs.xml`. You can modify these migration rules files as necessary. They contain the following settings:

- **`MigApp.xml`:** Rules for migrating application settings
- **`MigDocs.xml`:** Rules that locate user documents automatically without the need to create custom migration files
- **`MigUser.xml`:** Rules for migrating user profiles and user data

NOTE You should not use `MigDocs.xml` and `MigUser.xml` together in the same migration. Otherwise, some migrated files might be duplicated if these files include conflicting instructions regarding target locations.

You can also create customized `.xml` files according to your migration requirements, as well as a `Config.xml` file that specifies files and settings to be excluded from migration (such as a user's large folder full of images and music). `ScanState.exe` collects user information from the old (source) computer based on settings contained in the various `.xml` files, and `LoadState.exe` places this information on a newly installed Windows 8.1 (destination) computer. The source computer can be running Windows XP, Vista, 7, 8, or 8.1.

New to USMT 5.0 is the `Usmtutils.exe` tool, which provides the following capabilities:

- Improved capability to determine cryptographic options for your migration

- Removal of hard-link stores that cannot otherwise be deleted due to a sharing lock
- Determination of corruption in any files in the compressed migration store
- Extraction of files from the compressed migration store when migrating data to the destination computer

NOTE For more information about `Usmtutils.exe`, refer to "UsmtUtils Syntax" at http://technet.microsoft.com/en-us/library/hh825264.aspx.

CAUTION USMT is designed specifically for large-scale, automated transfers. If your migrations require end-user interaction or customization on a computer-by-computer basis, USMT is not recommended. In these cases, use Windows Easy Transfer instead.

Using the USMT involves running `ScanState.exe` at the source computer to collect the user state data to be migrated and transferring it to a shared folder on a server. Then you must run `LoadState.exe` on the destination computer to load the user state data there, as shown in Figure 3-1. Microsoft refers to the server used for this purpose as the technician computer. When migrating multiple users, you can create a script to automate this process.

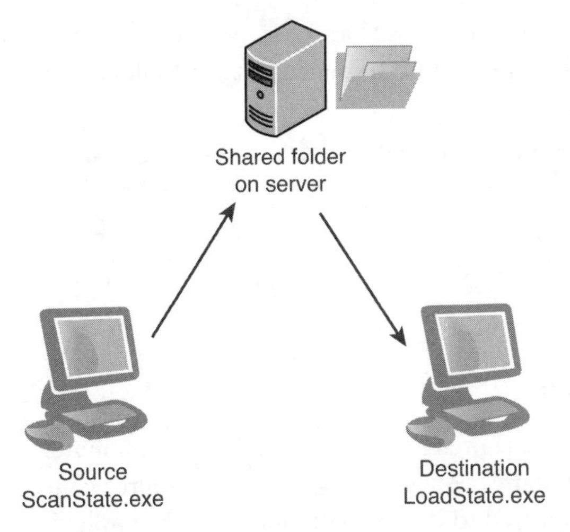

Figure 3-1 To use USMT, run `ScanState.exe` at the source computer to transfer the files to a shared folder on a server and then run `LoadState.exe` at the destination computer to load the data there.

NOTE You can use a server running Windows Server 2008 R2 or 2012 R2 as the technician computer. You can also use a computer running Windows Vista, Windows 7, or Windows 8 or 8.1.

Preparing the Server to Run USMT

You need to create and share the appropriate folders on the technician computer before running USMT. This procedure requires the Windows ADK for Windows 8.1, which you can download as an `.iso` file from http://www.microsoft.com/en-US/download/details.aspx?id=39982 and burn to a blank DVD. Use the following procedure:

Step 1. Create and share a folder named `USMT` on the technician computer. The migrating user should have Read permission to this folder, and the local administrator on the destination computer should have at least Modify permission to this folder. Ensure that this folder has enough storage space available to meet the needs of all computers to be migrated.

Step 2. Create and share a folder named `MigStore` on the technician computer. Both the migrating user and the local administrator on the destination computer should have at least Modify permission to this folder.

Step 3. In the `USMT` folder, create two subfolders named `Scan` and `Load`.

Step 4. Insert the Windows ADK disc and follow the instructions in the Setup program that automatically starts to install Windows ADK.

Step 5. Copy all files from the `C:\Program Files(x86)\Windows Kits\8.1` folder created during the Windows ADK installation to the `USMT` shared folder. For example, use the following syntax:

```
xcopy " C:\Program Files (x86)\Windows Kits\8.1\Assessment and
Deployment Kit\User State Migration Tool\x86" \\server\share\USMT
```

Step 6. Make any required modifications to the `.xml` files included in this folder, or create any additional `.xml` files as needed.

Collecting Files from the Source Computer

After you have created and shared the appropriate files on the technician computer, including the USMT folder and its contents, you are ready to scan the source computer and collect information to be exported to the new computer. Use the following procedure:

Step 1. Log on to the source computer with an account that has administrative privileges. This user should have permissions to the shares on the server as described in the previous procedure.

Step 2. Map a drive to the `USMT` share on the server.

Step 3. Open a command prompt and set its path to the `Scan` folder on the mapped `USMT` share.

Step 4. To run `ScanState`, type the following command:

```
scanstate \\servername\migration\mystore /config:config.xml
/i:miguser.xml /i:migapp.xml /v:13 /l:scan.log
```

In this command:

`/i:` is the include parameter, which specifies an XML file that defines the user, application, or system state that is being migrated.

`/config`: specifies the `config.xml` file used by `scanstate.exe` to create the store.

`servername` is the name of the server on which you installed the Windows ADK tools.

`l:` is a parameter that specifies the location of `Scan.log`, which is the name of a log file that will be created in the USMT share and will hold any error information from problems that might arise during the migration. If any problems occur, check the contents of this file.

The `v:13` parameter specifies verbose, status, and debugger output to the log file.

NOTE Both `ScanState` and `LoadState` support a large range of command-line options. Refer to the `USMT.chm` help file in the Windows ADK for a complete list and description of the available options. Also refer to "ScanState Syntax" at http://technet.microsoft.com/en-us/library/hh825093.aspx.

Loading Collected Files on the Destination Computer

Before loading files to the destination computer, you should install Windows 8.1 and all required applications on this computer. However, do not create a local user account for the migrating user (this account is created automatically when you run `LoadState`). Join the computer to the domain if in a domain environment. Then perform the following procedure:

Step 1. Log on to the destination computer as the local administrator (not the migrating account).

Step 2. Map a drive to the `USMT` share on the server.

Step 3. Open an administrative command prompt and set its path to the `Load` folder on the mapped `USMT` share.

Step 4. To run `LoadState`, type the following command: (The set of `.xml` files should be the same as used when running `ScanState`.)

```
loadstate \\servername\migration\mystore /config:config.xml
/i:miguser.xml /i:migapp.xml /lac /lae /v:13 /l:load.log
```

Step 5. Log off and log on as the migrating user and verify that all required files and settings have been transferred.

In this command, `/lac` and `/lae` specify that local accounts from the source computer will be created and enabled on the destination computer. The other parameters are the same as defined previously for the `ScanState` tool. Note that passwords are not migrated (they are blank by default).

> **NOTE** For more information on `LoadState`, refer to "LoadState Syntax" at http://technet.microsoft.com/en-us/library/hh825190.aspx. For more details on all three USMT procedures, refer to "Step-by-Step: Basic Windows Migration Using USMT for IT Professionals" at http://technet.microsoft.com/en-us/library/hh824873.aspx.

Using the User State Migration Tool

As already discussed, USMT 5.0 is designed for use when large numbers of users must be migrated from older computers to new computers running Windows 8.1. You can also use this tool when you have upgraded these computers from Windows Vista/7 to Windows 8.1. After performing the upgrade, you can use a USB drive to hold the required commands for migrating user data from the `Windows.old` folder. Use the following procedure:

Step 1. Download and install the Windows ADK as discussed earlier in this chapter.

Step 2. Prepare an external USB drive by creating a `USMT` folder in the root directory. This folder should have `x86` and `amd64` subfolders for migrating 32-bit and 64-bit installations, respectively.

Step 3. Copy the `Program Files\Windows ADK\Tools\USMT` folder from the computer on which you installed Windows ADK to the `USMT` folder in the USB drive.

Step 4. Use Notepad to create a batch file for `x86` file migrations. Microsoft suggests the following batch file:

```
@ECHO OFF
If exist D:\USMT\*.* xcopy D:\USMT\*.* /e /v /y C:\Windows\USMT\
If exist E:\USMT\*.* xcopy E:\USMT\*.* /e /v /y C:\Windows\USMT\
If exist F:\USMT\*.* xcopy F:\USMT\*.* /e /v /y C:\Windows\USMT\
If exist G:\USMT\*.* xcopy G:\USMT\*.* /e /v /y C:\Windows\USMT\
If exist H:\USMT\*.* xcopy H:\USMT\*.* /e /v /y C:\Windows\USMT\
If exist I:\USMT\*.* xcopy I:\USMT\*.* /e /v /y C:\Windows\USMT\
If exist J:\USMT\*.* xcopy J:\USMT\*.* /e /v /y C:\Windows\USMT\
If exist K:\USMT\*.* xcopy K:\USMT\*.* /e /v /y C:\Windows\USMT\
Cd c:\windows\usmt\x86
ScanState.exe c:\store /v:5 /o /c /hardlink /nocompress /efs:hardlink
/i:MigApp.xml /i:MigDocs.xml /offlineWinOld:c:\windows.old\windows
LoadState.exe c:\store /v:5 /c /lac /lae /i:migapp.xml /i:migdocs.xml
/sf /hardlink /nocompress
:EOF
```

Step 5. Save this file to the USB drive as `Migrate.bat`.

Step 6. Log on to the computer that has been upgraded using an administrative account.

Step 7. Insert the USB drive and copy the `Migrate.bat` file to the desktop.

Step 8. Right-click this file and choose **Run as administrator**. If you receive a User Account Control (UAC) prompt, click **Yes**.

Step 9. When the batch file finishes, access the `C:\ Users` folder and confirm that all user files have been migrated to the appropriate file libraries.

This batch file locates USMT files and copies them to the `C:\Windows` folder so that the `ScanState.exe` command can create a hard-link migration store at `C:\Store` from the `Windows\old` folder. This hard-link migration process creates a catalog of hard links to files that are to be migrated. The `LoadState.exe` command then remaps the catalog of hard-links to their appropriate locations in the Windows 8.1 installation. For AMD 64-bit machines, modify the batch file by changing the `x86` subfolder references to `amd64`.

NOTE For more information on this process, refer to "Step-by-Step: Offline Migration with USMT" at http://technet.microsoft.com/en-us/library/hh824880.aspx.

Windows Easy Transfer

Windows Easy Transfer enables you to transfer files and settings from an old computer to a new one across a network or by means of an external hard drive, a USB flash drive, or the Easy Transfer cable. You can purchase the Easy Transfer cable from a computer store or on the Web. This cable uses USB to link to cables and transfers data at about 20 GB/hour.

Windows Easy Transfer includes a wizard that helps you transfer your files, folders, and settings to a new computer or to a clean installation of Windows 8.1 on an existing computer, by collecting them at the old (source) computer and then transferring them to a new computer running Windows 8.1 (called the destination computer). This is the simplest method when only a few computers are affected or when users are individually responsible for migrating the user states on their own computers.

Using Windows Easy Transfer to Collect Files at the Source Computer

You can use the following procedure to collect files from any computer running Windows 7, Windows 8, or Windows 8.1. The steps shown here are as they occur for a USB drive on a computer running Windows 7; they are somewhat different if you are using the Windows Easy Transfer Cable or a network connection. Note that Windows Easy Transfer in Windows 8.1 no longer supports the transfer of data from a computer running Windows XP or Vista.

Step 1. On a Windows 7 computer, click **Start > Run**, type `migwiz`, and press **Enter**. On a Windows 8/8.1 computer, access the Search charm, type `migwiz`, and select **Windows Easy Transfer** from the list that appears. If you receive a UAC prompt, click **Yes**. This starts the Windows Easy Transfer Wizard, as shown in Figure 3-2.

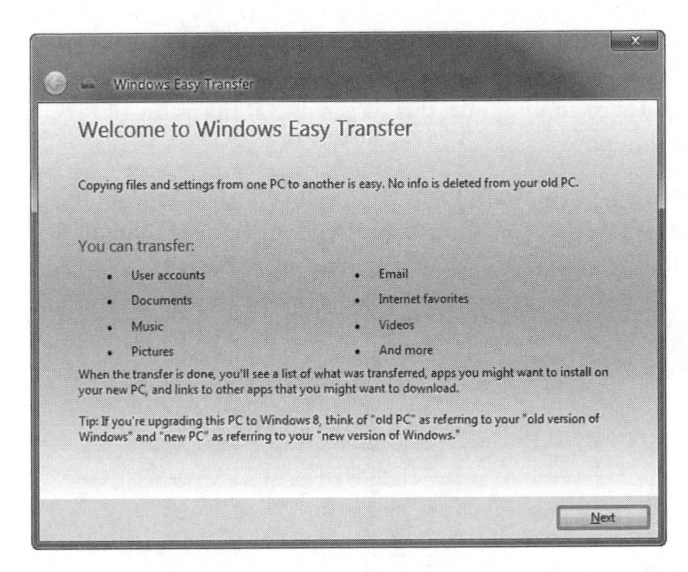

Figure 3-2 Windows Easy Transfer presents a wizard that facilitates transferring files from an old computer running Windows XP or later.

Step 2. Click **Next**. The wizard provides the three choices shown in Figure 3-3 for storing the collected data. Click the desired choice.

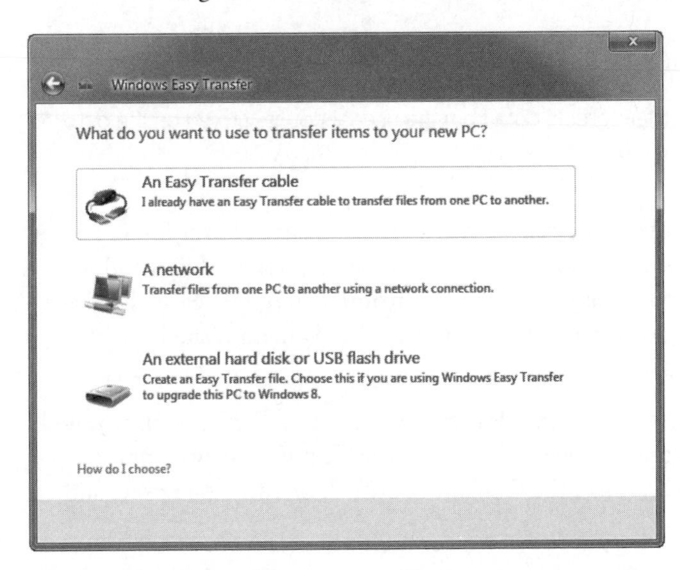

Figure 3-3 Windows Easy Transfer provides three choices for storing the collected data.

Step 3. On the next page, confirm that you are at the old computer (if you are transferring from a Windows 7 or 8 computer to a Windows 8.1 computer or from a Windows 8.1 computer to another one, this screen asks if this is the old computer or the new one).

Step 4. The wizard displays the page shown in Figure 3-4 as it collects data from this computer. This process takes several minutes or even longer, depending on the amount of data to be transferred. When it is done, click **Next**.

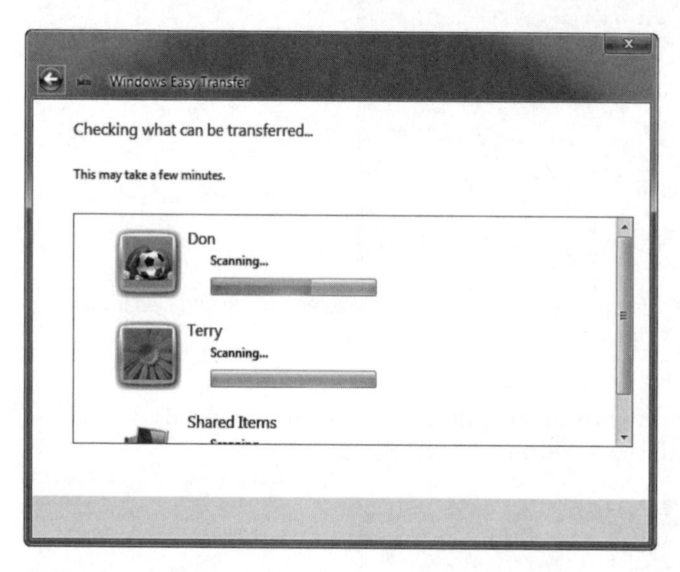

Figure 3-4 Windows Easy Transfer collects data from the user accounts stored on the old computer.

Step 5. On the Choose what you can transfer page, clear the check boxes for any users whose data you do not want to transfer. To modify the types of files and settings to be transferred for any user, click **Customize** and then clear the check boxes for any file types you do not want to transfer. When finished, click **Next**.

Step 6. On the Save your files and settings for transfer page (see Figure 3-5), type and confirm a password that you will need to enter later at your new computer. Then click **Save** and confirm the filename provided, or enter a new one and click **Save** again.

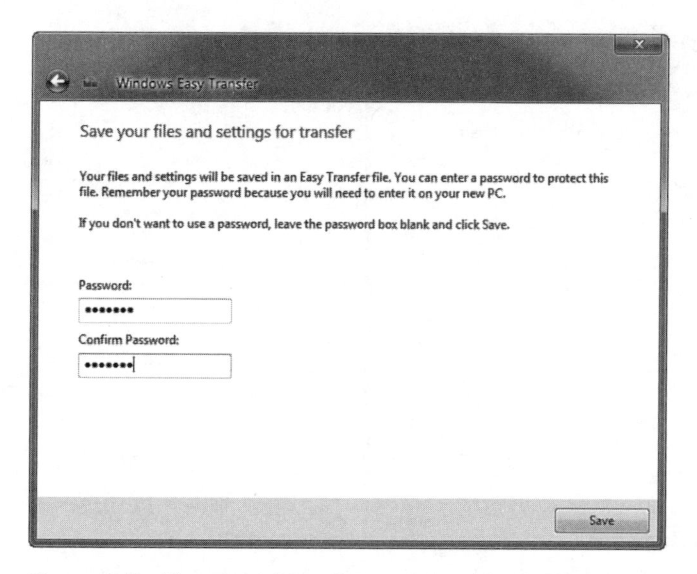

Figure 3-5 You should specify a password for the transfer to take place.

Step 7. The save process takes several minutes or longer, depending on the amount of data to be transferred. When informed that the files have been saved, click **Next**.

Step 8. Click **Next** again and then click **Close** to finish the wizard.

Using Windows Easy Transfer to Save Files at the Destination Computer

After you have installed Windows 8.1 plus any required applications on the destination computer, you can save the collected files by performing the following procedure:

Step 1. At the destination computer, connect the USB drive and double-click the file containing the migrated information.

Step 2. Windows Easy Transfer starts and displays the page shown in Figure 3-6 asking you for the password you specified when you collected your files. Type this password and then click **Next**.

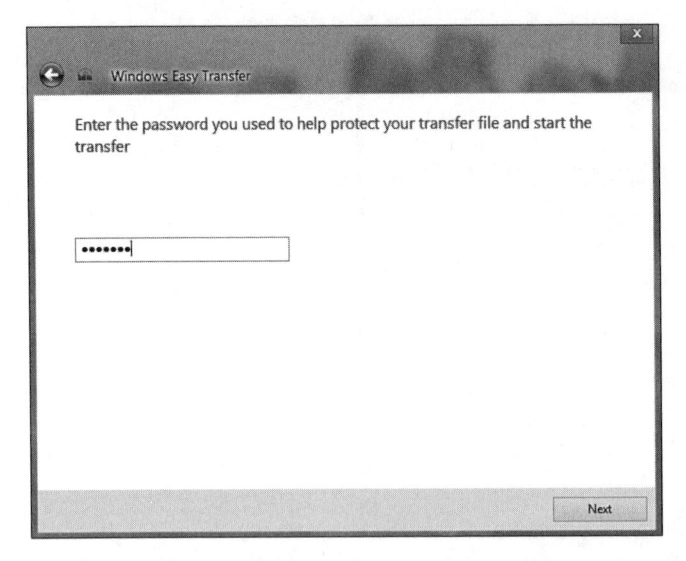

Figure 3-6 Type the password you specified at the old computer.

Step 3. On the Choose what to transfer to this PC page shown in Figure 3-7, deselect any users whose files and settings you do not want to transfer. If you want to map your user account to a different account on the new computer, or select a drive on the new computer to which you want to transfer files, click **Advanced options** and make the appropriate choices.

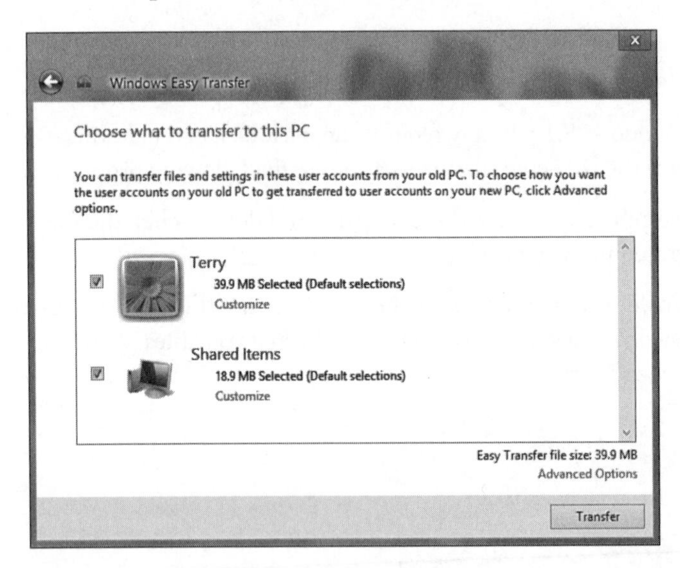

Figure 3-7 Windows Easy Transfer enables you to choose what is transferred to the new computer.

Step 4. To begin the transfer, click **Transfer**.

Step 5. The wizard transfers the files and, when finished, displays a `Your files have been transferred` message. Click **Close**.

NOTE For more information on using Windows Easy Transfer in Windows 8.1, refer to "How to Use Windows Easy Transfer to Transfer Files and Settings in Windows 8" at http://support.microsoft.com/kb/2735227.

Configuring Folder Redirection

Microsoft includes the technologies of folder redirection and offline files for redirection of the paths of local folders to a network location while caching their contents locally for increased speed and availability. In this section, we take a look at folder redirection. Offline files are covered in Chapter 15, "Configuring and Securing Mobile Devices." Using folder redirection, you can redirect the path of a known folder to a local or network location either manually or by using Group Policy. The process is transparent to the user, who works with data in the folder as if it were located in its default place.

NOTE For more information on folder redirection, see the links found at "Deploy Folder Redirection, Offline Files, and Roaming User Profiles" at http://technet.microsoft.com/en-us/library/jj649074.aspx.

Benefits of Folder Redirection

Users and administrators benefit from using folder redirection in the following ways:

- Users' documents are always accessible to them, regardless of which computer they log on to.
- When roaming user profiles are used, only the network path to a folder such as the Documents folder is actually part of the profile. This eliminates the need for copying the contents of this folder back and forth at each logon and logoff, thereby speeding up the logon/logoff process.

- You can configure the Offline File technology so that users' files are always available to them even when they are not connected to the network. Their files are automatically cached and are in the same logical location (for example, the U: drive) on the laptop as they are when they are connected to the network, facilitating their working on the files when they are away from the office.
- It is easy to back up all users' files from a central server without interaction by the user. The administrator or backup operator can accomplish this task as part of the routine backup task.
- Administrators can use Group Policy to configure disk quotas, thereby controlling and monitoring the amount of disk space taken up by users' folders. We discuss disk quotas in Chapter 11, "Configuring and Securing Access to Files and Folders."
- You can standardize users' working environments by redirecting the Desktop folder to a common shared location. This standardization can help with remote support problems because the support staff will know the desktop layout of the users' computers.

Redirecting Library Folders

First introduced with Windows 7 and continued in Windows 8.1 is the concept of virtualized folders. In Windows 8.1, a *library* is a set of virtual folders that is shared by default with other users of the computer. By default, Windows 8.1 includes four libraries (Documents, Pictures, Music, and Videos), which you can access from the Start menu, or from the task list on the left side of any File Explorer window. From the taskbar, click the folder icon to view the libraries on your computer, as shown in Figure 3-8. You can also see them when you open a File Explorer window and navigate to `C:\Users\Public`. The subfolders you see here are actually pointers to the folder locations on the computer. You can also think of them as the results of search queries. From the Libraries folder, you can create a new library by clicking **New library** in the toolbar and providing a name for your new library.

Right-click any library and choose **Properties** to view its contents. You will notice that each library contains a user-based subfolder, located by default at `C:\Users\%username%`,. You can add additional folders by clicking the **Add** button shown in Figure 3-9 and navigating to the desired folder in the Include Folder in Documents dialog box, as shown in Figure 3-10; this can even include shared folders located on other computers on the network. You can also add folders to a library from any File Explorer window by selecting the folder and clicking the **Add to Library** option in the Explorer toolbar.

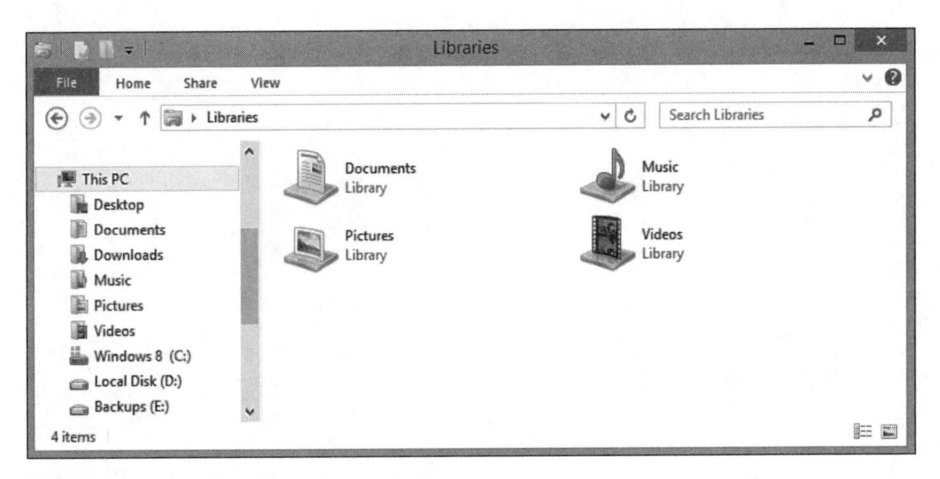

Figure 3-8 Windows 8.1 creates these four default libraries.

Key Topic

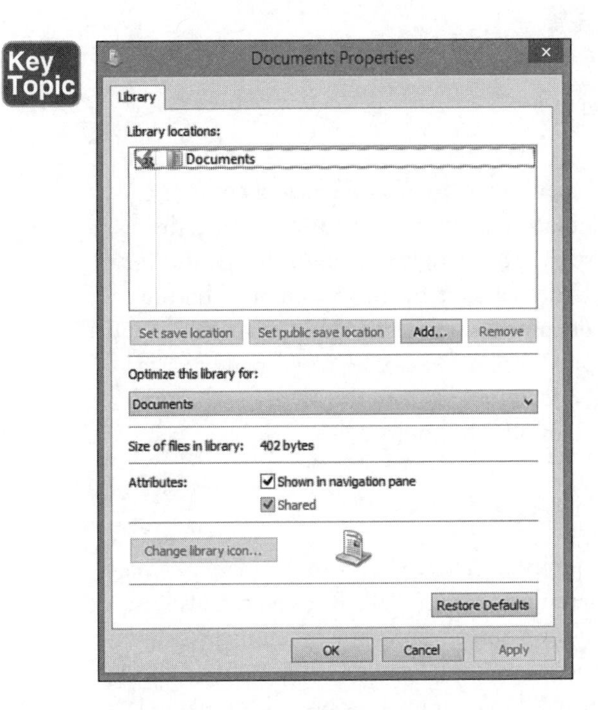

Figure 3-9 Each library by default contains a user subfolder.

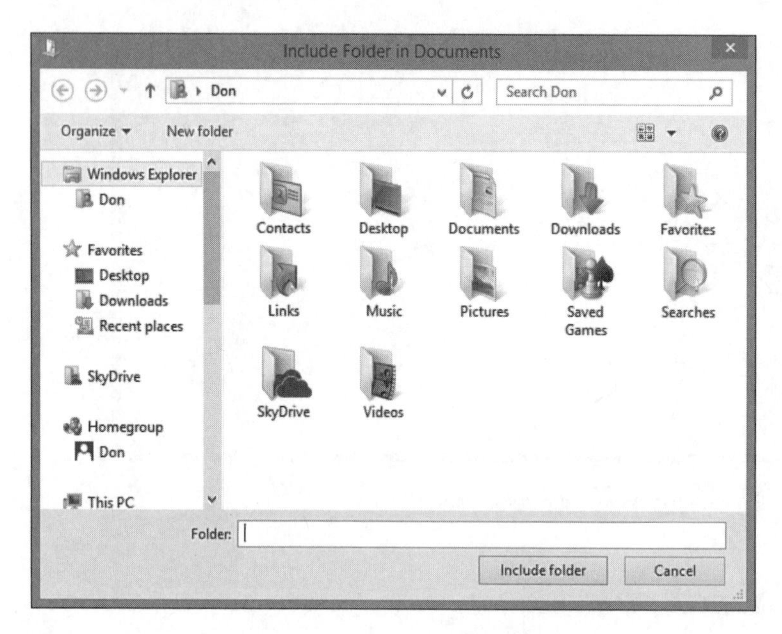

Figure 3-10 Adding a folder to the Documents library.

The library's Properties dialog box also enables you to add folders and configure several additional properties. The check mark shown in Figure 3-9 indicates the default save location used by programs such as Microsoft Office; to change this location, select the desired location and click the **Set save location** command button. To change the location of public saved documents, select the appropriate folder and click the **Set public save location** button. To remove a folder from the library, select it and click **Remove**. To remove all added folders from the library and reset it to its default settings, click the **Restore Defaults** button.

Implementing Domain-Based Folder Redirection

Implementation of folder redirection requires an Active Directory Domain Services (AD DS) domain and a server running Windows Server 2012 R2. You can also use a server running an older version of Windows Server, but some functionality might not be available. Use the following procedure to implement a Group Policy Object (GPO) that enables folder redirection in an AD DS domain or organizational unit (OU):

Step 1. Open Server Manager on a computer with the Group Policy Management console installed.

Step 2. Click **Tools > Group Policy Management** to display the Group Policy Management Console.

Step 3. Right-click the domain or OU where you want to configure Folder Redirection and choose **Create a GPO in this domain, and Link it here**.

Step 4. In the New GPO dialog box, type a name for the GPO and then click **OK**.

Step 5. Right-click this GPO and choose **Edit** to open the Group Policy Management Editor console.

Step 6. Navigate to **User Configuration\Policies\Windows Settings\Folder Redirection**. You receive the options shown in Figure 3-11.

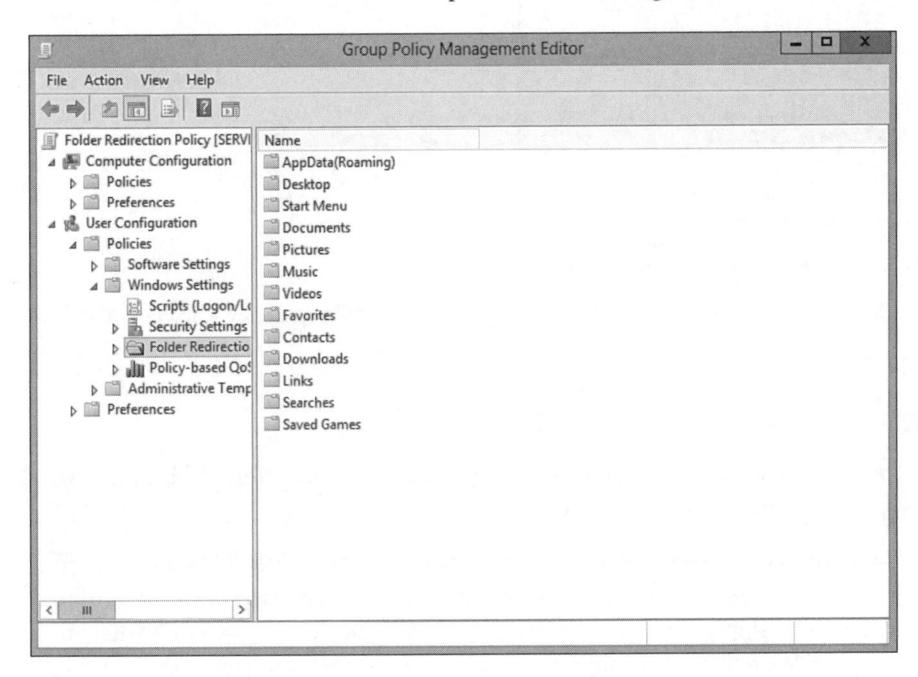

Figure 3-11 Implementing folder redirection in Windows Server 2012 R2.

Step 7. Right-click the folder to be redirected from the details pane in Figure 3-11 and choose **Properties**. This action displays the Properties dialog box for the selected folder, as shown in Figure 3-12.

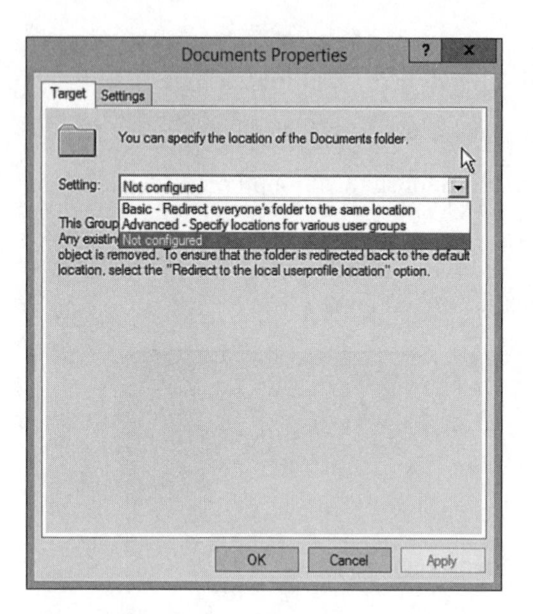

Figure 3-12 You have three choices for implementing folder redirection in Windows Server 2012 R2.

Step 8. Under Setting, select from the following choices:

- **Basic–Redirect everyone's folder to the same location:** This option redirects all folders to this location.
- **Advanced–Specify locations for various user groups:** This option redirects folders to different locations depending on the users' security group memberships. The bottom part of the dialog box changes so that you can specify a universal naming convention (UNC) path for each security group.
- **Not configured:** Folder redirection is not applied.

Step 9. Choose an option from those shown in Figure 3-13 and described here. To create a folder for each user, choose **Create a folder for each user under the root path**. Type or browse to the desired path (in general, you will want to use a UNC path such as `\\server1\docoments`), and then click **OK** or **Apply**.

- **Redirect to the user's home directory:** This option redirects users' folders to the home directory as specified in the user account's Properties dialog box in the Active Directory Administrative Center. This option works only for client computers running Windows XP Professional, Windows Server 2003, or later, and is available only for the Documents folder.

- **Create a folder for each user under the root path:** This option enables you to specify a root path in the form of a UNC path to a shared location. A subfolder is automatically created for each user in this location, and the folder path appears at the bottom of the dialog box.
- **Redirect to the following location:** This option enables you to specify a UNC path to the specific folder for each user. The username is automatically appended to the path you provided to create a unique folder name.
- **Redirect to the local userprofile location:** This option redirects users' folders to the local user profile location specified in the user account's Properties dialog boxes in Active Directory Administrative Center. This option is useful for returning redirected folders to their original default location.

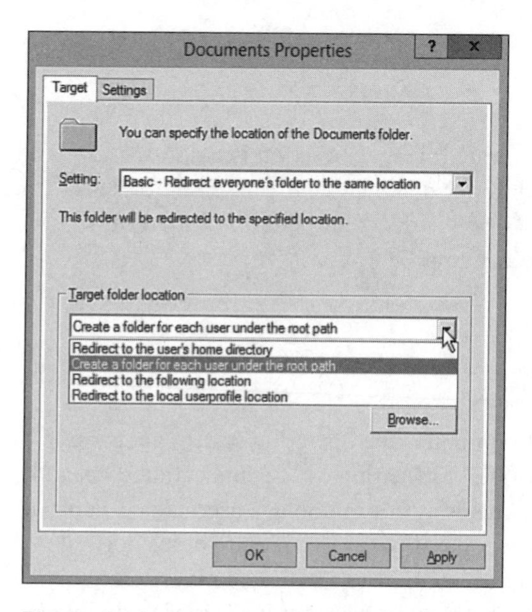

Figure 3-13 Specifying a location for folder redirection.

Step 10. You receive the message box shown in Figure 3-14 regarding Group Policy settings in Windows Server 2003 or older operating systems. Click **Yes** to accept this message and implement folder redirection.

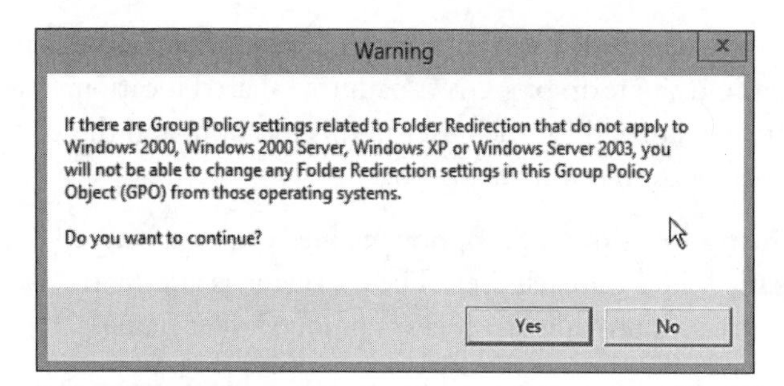

Figure 3-14 You receive this warning message about older Group Policy settings.

Step 11. You are returned to the Group Policy Management Console. Ensure that the GPO you created displays a GPO status of `Enabled` and that the Link Enabled column reads `Yes`.

NOTE For more information on implementing folder redirection in a domain environment, including a complete procedure for deploying domain-based folder redirection, refer to "Deploy Folder Redirection with Offline Files" at http://technet.microsoft.com/en-us/library/jj649078.aspx.

Configuring Profiles

When a user logs on to a Windows 8.1 computer, the operating system generates a user profile. This profile is composed of desktop settings, files, application data, and the specific environment established by the user. For example, a user named Peter logs on to Windows 8.1, changes his desktop wallpaper to a picture of his dog, edits the user information in Microsoft Word, configures a dial-up connection to his Internet service provider (ISP), and adjusts the mouse so that it is easier to double-click. When Sharon logs on to the same computer using her own account, she sees the default settings for Windows 8.1, not Peter's settings. When Peter logs on next, Windows finds Peter's existing profile and loads his settings—the wallpaper, the Word data, the dial-up connection, and the mouse click settings.

Windows 8.1 provides the following profile versions:

- **Local:** A profile that is available only on the computer and for the user for which it is configured.
- **Roaming:** A profile that has been placed on a server so that it is available to a given user no matter which computer she is logged on to. A user is free to make changes to this profile version at any time.

- **Mandatory:** A profile that has been placed on a server but is configured as read-only, such that the user is unable to make any changes to it.

In addition to these profile types, it is possible to set up a temporary profile, which is loaded by default if the user is unable to load her normal profile.

When Windows 8.1 is connected to a Windows network, you can configure a user profile to roam the network with the user. Because the profile is stored in a subfolder in the Users folder on the `%systemdrive%` volume, you can configure the profile to be placed on a network drive rather than a local hard disk, thereby making it accessible to the user regardless of which computer she is using.

User profiles allow users to customize their own settings without impairing another user's configuration. User profiles were developed in response to organizations that routinely provided shared desktop computers. In cases where a user absolutely requires certain settings to use the computer comfortably, having to share a computer with another person who then removes the needed configuration can be frustrating; plus it causes a loss of productivity. Another advantage to user profiles is that, when used in conjunction with network storage of data, the desktop computer is easily replaceable; users can use any computer on the network without having to perform extra tasks to customize the computer to suit their needs.

To use profiles, each user must have a separate user account. The user account can be a domain account or a local account. There are four different types of profiles, which are detailed in Table 3-2.

Table 3-2 Profile Types

Profile	Created For	How It Works
Local	Every user at first logon	When the user logs on to a computer, whether or not it is connected to a network, a local profile is created and saved in the local Users folder for that user. All changes are saved when the user logs off.
Roaming	Users who log on to different computers on the network	The profile is stored on a server. When a user logs on to a network computer, the profile is copied locally to the computer. When the user logs off the network, changes to the profile are copied back to the server.
Mandatory	Administrative enforcement of settings (this is applied to user accounts that are shared by two or more users)	The profile is stored on a server. When a user logs on to a network computer, the profile is copied locally to the computer. No changes are saved when the user logs off the server. Only an administrator can make changes to the profile.
Temporary	Users who were unable to load their profile	When an error condition exists that prevents a user from loading his normal profile, a temporary profile is loaded. When the user logs off, all changes are deleted.

User profiles consist of a registry hive that incorporates the data typically found in `NTuser.dat`, saved as a file that is mapped to the HKEY_CURRENT_USER Registry node and a set of profile folders.

You can change the location that Windows looks for a user's profile. When you do so, you must be logged on to the computer as a member of the Administrators group. Use the following procedure:

Step 1. Right-click **Start** and choose **Computer Management**.

Step 2. Expand the Local Users and Groups folder and select **Users**. Information about all users configured on the computer appears in the details pane, as shown in Figure 3-15.

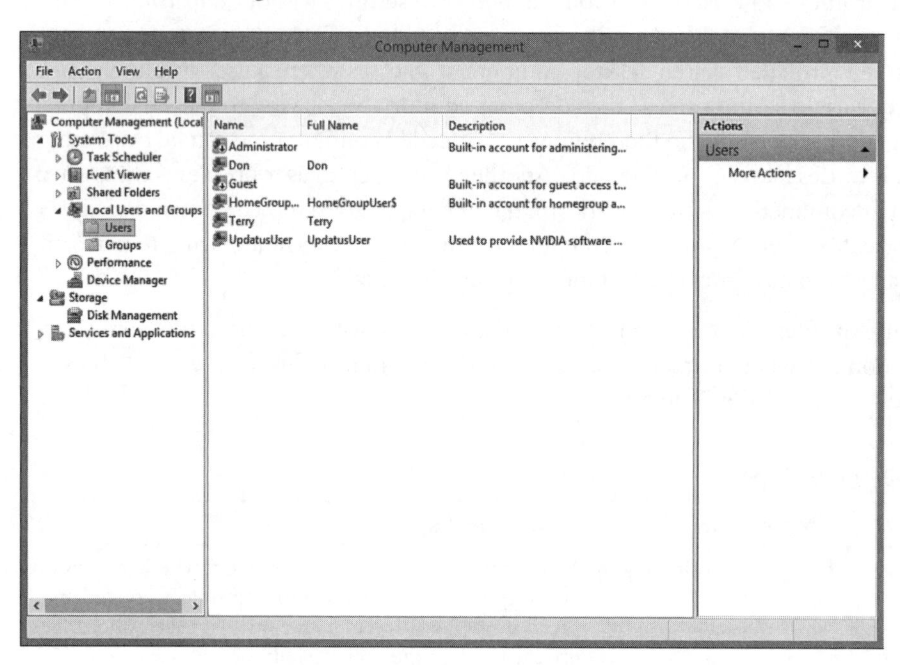

Figure 3-15 Profile information can be found in the Computer Management console.

Step 3. Right-click a user account and select **Properties** from the shortcut menu.

Step 4. Click the **Profile** tab.

Step 5. Type the location of the profile in the Profile Path text box. For example, type the UNC path as shown in Figure 3-16. Then click **OK**.

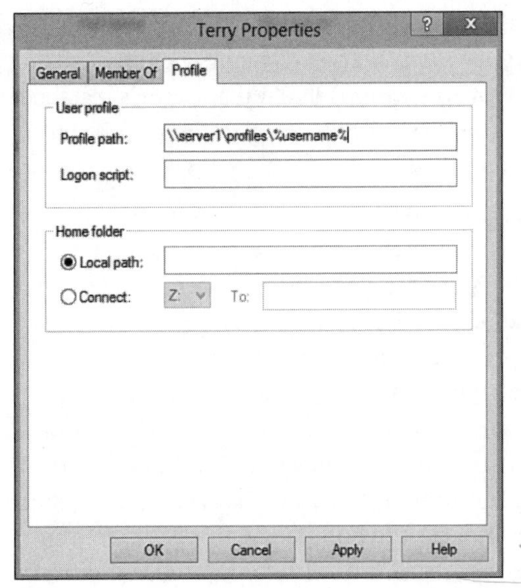

Figure 3-16 Configuring a user's profile path.

Step 6. From this dialog box, you can perform the following actions:

- Click **Default Profile** and then click **Copy To** in order to copy an existing profile to another computer. This is useful in a nondomain situation where you want to standardize profiles between computers.
- Click **Delete** to delete a profile for a user. This is useful when you are moving a computer to a different user.
- Click **Change Type** to change the profile from a local profile to a roaming profile or vice versa.

Step 7. When finished, click **OK**.

Using Roaming and Mandatory Profiles with Active Directory

Roaming and mandatory profiles require a network server for implementation. Although it is recommended that you have an AD DS network for this, you can implement these profiles on other network servers. An AD DS network is recommended for use with roaming and mandatory profiles because of the additional management features that are provided by Group Policy. For example, you can specify additional folders to include in the profile, as well as mark certain folders to exclude from the profile.

An additional advantage to using Group Policy in conjunction with roaming profiles is that you can prevent users from running applications that you deem to be unacceptable, or to allow a user to run only a short list of applications. Even if a user has installed the application and incorporated its data into the user's profile prior to the restriction policy, the GPO will prevent the user from running it.

When you use Group Policy together with roaming profiles, you can ensure that a user's Windows 8.1 settings are exactly what you wish the user to have. You can create a default user profile that includes the desktop icons, startup applications, documents, Start menu items, and other settings. Then you can use Group Policy to manage the way that the user interacts with the network, such as preventing access to Control Panel. You can even use Group Policy to publish certain applications that the user is allowed to install, and you can redirect users' Documents and Desktop folders to a network location. When a user logs on to the network the first time, the desktop will be configured with the settings that are appropriate for your organization. If the user makes changes to the profile, those changes will be saved. The user can then log on to an entirely different computer the next day and automatically see the environment he configured for himself, plus have immediate access to his personal files, folders, and applications.

NOTE For more information on using roaming profiles in AD DS, including a detailed procedure for setting up a sample implementation, refer to "Deploy Roaming User Profiles" at http://technet.microsoft.com/en-us/library/jj649079.aspx.

Implementing Roaming Profiles

Local profiles cause an administrative headache when users roam around the network and when computers are routinely exchanged throughout the network. For example, if Joe logs on at PC1 and saves a file that holds key information for his job on his desktop, and later Joe logs on at PC2 because PC1 was replaced with new hardware, he is likely to have a panic attack to discover that his file is missing. Roaming profiles overcome this problem.

When a user with a roaming profile logs on for the first time, the following process takes place:

Step 1. Windows 8.1 checks for the path to the user's roaming profile.

Step 2. Windows 8.1 accesses the path and looks for the profile. If no profile exists, Windows 8.1 generates a folder for the profile.

Step 3. Windows 8.1 checks for a cached copy of the profile listed in `HKLM\SOFTWARE\Microsoft\Windows NT\CurrentVersion\ProfileList`. If a local profile is found, and the computer is a member of a domain, Windows 8.1 looks in the domain controller's NETLOGON share for a default profile for the domain. The default domain profile is copied to the local computer folder `%systemdrive%\Users\%username%`. If there is no domain default, Windows 8.1 copies the default local profile to the same location.

Step 4. The `NTuser.dat` file is mapped to the Registry's HKEY_CURRENT_USER key.

Step 5. Windows 8.1 updates the user's `%userprofile%` environment variable with the new location of the profile.

Step 6. When the user logs off, the local profile is copied to the network path configured in Windows 8.1.

Step 7. The next time the user logs on to the same computer, Windows 8.1 opens the locally cached copy of the user's profile and compares it with the copy on the domain server. Windows 8.1 merges the contents of the two profiles.

You can make changes to whether a computer uses local or roaming profiles in the Control Panel. Use the following procedure:

Step 1. From the System and Security category of Control Panel, click **System**. You can also right-click **Start** and choose **System** from the programs list that appears.

Step 2. From the System dialog box that appears, click **Advanced system settings**.

Step 3. Click the **Advanced** tab to display the dialog box shown in Figure 3-17.

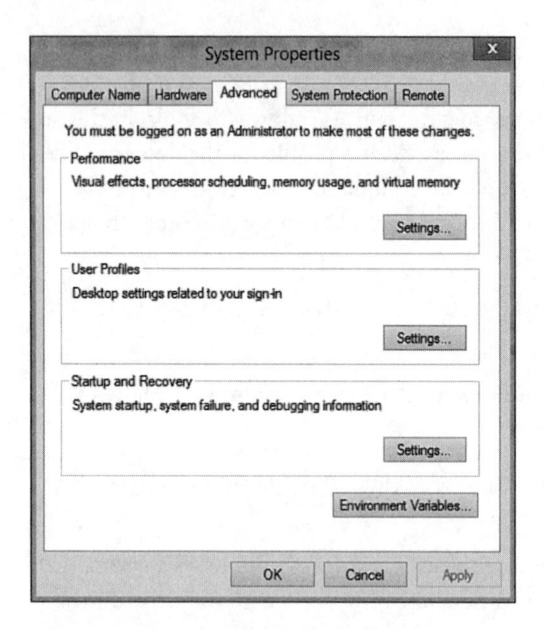

Figure 3-17 You can access user profile settings in the System Properties dialog box.

Step 4. In the User Profiles section, click **Settings** to display the dialog box shown in Figure 3-18.

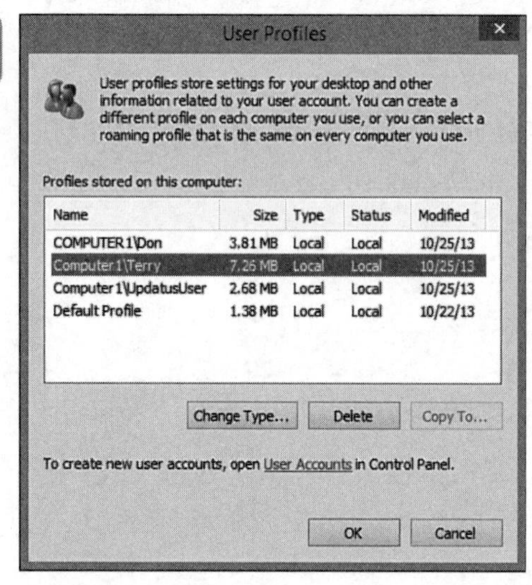

Figure 3-18 Some profile management options are to copy, delete, or change the type of user profile for specific users.

Step 5. From this dialog box, you can perform the following actions:

- **Change profile type:** Select a profile and click **Change Type** to change the profile from a local profile to a roaming profile or vice versa.
- **Delete a profile:** Select a profile and click **Delete** to delete an existing profile. This is useful when you are moving the computer to a different user.
- **Copy a profile:** Select a profile and click **Copy To** in order to use the same settings for another user on the same computer.

Step 6. When finished, click **OK**.

Establishing Mandatory Profiles

A mandatory profile is a roaming profile that can't be changed by the user. You configure the profile identically to the roaming profile. After the profile has been configured and saved as the `NTuser.dat` file in the user's profile path on the network, you simply need to rename the file to `NTuser.man`.

When the `NTuser.dat` file is renamed with the `.man` extension, it is treated as though it is a read-only file. At user logon, the file is read the same way as a roaming profile. However, if a user makes any changes to the environment, the changes are discarded when the user logs off. A mandatory profile is helpful in managing the desktop environment for users who unpredictably and accidentally delete items from their desktop and Start menu, or make other unintended changes. A mandatory profile is not useful for users who need a dynamic environment for running a variety of applications.

New to Windows 8.1 and Windows Server 2012 R2, mandatory profiles become super-mandatory profiles when stored in a profile path ending in `.man`; for example, `\\server\share\mandatoryprofile.man\`. When a super-mandatory profile is in use, users who use these profiles cannot log on if the server on which the profile is stored becomes unavailable. With ordinary mandatory profiles, a user can log on with the locally cached copy of the mandatory profile.

When you configure a mandatory profile to be used in an organization to be shared by a variety of users or computers, and when a single user moves around a network to use different computers, the profile's graphical presentation should be made to run at a level that all the computers can support. For example, if you have some computers that support a maximum 1680 × 1050 resolution, you should not create a profile with a 1920 × 1080 resolution setting because it will not display correctly on some of the computers.

If you need to make changes to a mandatory profile, rename the profile back to `NTuser.dat`, log on as the user, and configure the computer. After you complete the changes, you should log off so that the changes are saved to the profile. Then, after logging on as an administrator, you can rename the file as `NTuser.man`. If this is a profile that should be used by multiple people, you can replace the other users' `NTuser.man` files with the new version.

NOTE For more information on mandatory user profiles, refer to "Mandatory User Profiles" at http://msdn.microsoft.com/en-us/library/windows/desktop/bb776895(v=vs.85).aspx.

User Profiles and Operating System Versions

Most networks include computers running different Windows versions, such as Windows 7, Windows 8, and Windows 8.1, as well as servers running either the original or R2 versions of Windows Server 2008 or 2012. Each newer operating system version has introduced modifications to roaming and mandatory user profiles. Consequently, if a user moves between computers running different Windows versions, the user profiles are not compatible with each other. Profile versions include the following:

- Version 1 profiles used by Windows Vista, Windows Server 2008, and older Windows versions
- Version 2 profiles used by Windows 7 and Windows Server 2008 R2
- Version 3 profiles used by Windows 8 and Windows Server 2012
- Version 4 profiles used by Windows 8.1 and Windows Server 2012 R2

When a user logs on to a Windows 8.1 computer for the first time after using an older computer, Windows 8.1 automatically updates the profile to version 4. If the user then logs on to an older computer, the available profile is incompatible and is not loaded; further, the profile might become corrupted.

Microsoft recommends that you keep roaming, mandatory, super-mandatory, and domain default profiles created in one Windows version separate from those that were created in a different Windows version. Microsoft also makes available an update rollup that fixes this issue in Windows 8.1, and a hotfix that performs the same task in Windows 8. For more information, including the Registry entry that must be created, refer to "Incompatibility Between Windows 8.1 Roaming User Profiles and Those in Earlier Versions of Windows" at http://support.microsoft.com/kb/2890783.

Exam Preparation Tasks

Review All the Key Topics

Review the most important topics in the chapter, noted with the key topics icon in the outer margin of the page. Table 3-3 lists a reference of these key topics and the page numbers on which each is found.

Table 3-3 Key Topics for Chapter 3

Key Topic Element	Description	Page Number
Paragraph	Describes the USMT	136
Paragraph	Describes the Windows Easy Transfer	142
Bulleted List	Describes benefits achieved with folder redirection	147
Paragraph	Shows you how to redirect library folders	148
Figure 3-9	Describes library folder properties	149
Step List	Shows you how to implement domain-based folder redirection	150
Figure 3-16	Shows you how to configure local profile paths	157
Figure 3-18	Shows how to manage user profiles on a Windows 8.1 computer	160

Definitions of Key Terms

Define the following key terms from this chapter and check your answers in the glossary.

Destination computer, Folder redirection, `LoadState.exe`, Local user profile, Mandatory profile, Roaming profile, `ScanState.exe`, Source computer, User profile, User State Migration Tool (USMT), Windows Easy Transfer

This chapter covers the following subjects:

- **Installing and Configuring Device Drivers:** This section teaches you how to install device drivers and use Device Manager for configuring and Windows Update for updating drivers.
- **Maintaining Device Drivers:** This section introduces the concept of driver signing and checking for valid driver signatures. It also discusses permissions for installing drivers and settings that you can configure from a driver's Properties dialog box; it also covers managing driver packages.
- **Resolving Driver Issues:** This section discusses the use of Device Manager to resolve driver problems including conflicts and to roll back problematic drivers.
- **Configuring Driver Settings:** This section covers methods for configuring settings for device drivers.

CHAPTER 4

Configuring Devices and Device Drivers

When you first install Windows 8.1, it performs an inventory of all devices it finds on the computer and records information about them in the Registry under HKEY_LOCAL_MACHINE\Hardware. Each device is associated with a software program called a driver. This program enables the device to communicate properly with the operating system. Typically, a driver is in the form of an `.inf` file (for example, `Mydevice.inf`). These files are typically located in the hidden subfolder, `%systemroot%\inf`. Device manufacturers frequently issue driver updates that improve device functionality or solve problems that users have reported. In addition, Microsoft issues updates at least once a month. For the 70-687 exam, Microsoft expects you to know how to use Device Manager to ensure that your devices are installed, updated, and working properly, and to be able to troubleshoot problems with drivers and ensure that drivers are configured with the proper settings.

"Do I Know This Already?" Quiz

The "Do I Know This Already?" quiz allows you to assess whether you should read this entire chapter or simply jump to the "Exam Preparation Tasks" section for review. If you are in doubt, read the entire chapter. Table 4-1 outlines the major headings in this chapter and the corresponding "Do I Know This Already?" quiz questions. You can find the answers in Appendix A, "Answers to the 'Do I Know This Already?' Quizzes."

Table 4-1 "Do I Know This Already?" Foundation Topics Section-to-Question Mapping

Foundations Topics Section	Questions Covered in This Section
Installing and Configuring Device Drivers	1–4
Maintaining Device Drivers	5–7
Resolving Driver Issues	8–11
Configuring Driver Settings	12–13

1. From which of the following locations can you access Device Manager in Windows 8.1? (Choose all that apply).
   a. Right-click **Start** and choose **Computer Management**. Then select **Device Manager** from the console tree of the Computer Management console.
   b. Right-click **Start** and choose **Device Manager**.
   c. From a File Explorer window, right-click **This PC** and choose **Properties**. Click **Advanced system settings**, select the **Hardware** tab of the System Properties dialog box, and click **Device Manager**.
   d. From the Search charm, type **`device manager`** in the search box. Then click **Device Manager**.
   e. When on the desktop, select the **Settings** charm, select **Control Panel**, select the **Hardware and Sound** category, and then select **Device Manager**.
   f. From the Hardware tab of the System Properties dialog box, click **Device Manager**.

2. You are looking in Device Manager to determine whether any hardware devices are disabled. What icon should you look for?
   a. A black exclamation point icon on a yellow triangle background appearing next to the device icon indicates that a device is functioning but experiencing problems.
   b. A red X appearing over the device icon.
   c. A yellow question mark.
   d. A blue "i" on a white field.

3. You are removing an old device from your computer and are not planning on replacing it in the immediate future. You want to ensure that its drivers are permanently removed. What should you do?
   a. Use Device Manager to disable the driver.
   b. Use Device Manager to uninstall the driver.
   c. Use Device Manager to roll back the driver.
   d. Use Windows Update to update all drivers on your computer.

4. You would like to review the actions taken by Windows in the past few months with regard to the drivers used by your computer's network adapter card, so you open Device Manager and select the Properties dialog box for the network adapter. Which tab provides you with this information?
   a. General
   b. Driver

c. Details

d. Events

5. What program would you use to determine whether any unsigned drivers are present on your computer?

   a. `sfc.exe`

   b. `sigverif.exe`

   c. `msinfo32.exe`

   d. `gpedit.exe`

6. You install an updated driver for your network adapter card, and now the card does not work. What should you do to get the card working again?

   a. Update the driver.

   b. Roll back the driver.

   c. Uninstall the driver.

   d. Disable the driver.

7. You want to configure Device Manager so that it displays all devices present according to their IRQ, DMA, and memory addresses. What view should you use?

   a. Devices by type

   b. Devices by connection

   c. Resources by type

   d. Resources by connection

8. You install a new Blu-ray disc writer on your computer. When you restart your computer, you discover not only that this device does not work, but also that you are unable to access the Internet. What should you be looking for?

   a. A resource conflict

   b. Insufficient power from your computer's power supply

   c. Outdated device drivers

   d. Unsigned device drivers

9. You want to obtain information on the IRQ lines, DMA channels, and I/O ports being used by a device. Where should you look? (Choose two.)

   a. Access the Search charm, type **`msinfo32`**, and then select the **Hardware Resources** node from the System Information dialog box.

b. Access the Search charm, type `msinfo32`, and then select the **Components** node from the System Information dialog box.

c. Access the General tab of the device's Properties dialog box.

d. Access the Details tab of the device's Properties dialog box.

e. Access the Resources tab of the device's Properties dialog box.

10. Which of the following tools enables you to view device-related problems but does not provide any tools to correct these problems?

a. Device Manager

b. `sigverif.exe`

c. Action Center

d. System Information

11. What task should you perform before installing or upgrading device drivers?

a. Create a System Image.

b. Back up user files.

c. Run Driver Verifier.

d. Create a Restore Point.

12. You are troubleshooting an issue with a computer that is displaying STOP messages and restarting. Which tools will help you identify a driver that may be causing the issue?

a. `sigverif.exe`

b. Device Manager

c. Action Center

d. Driver Verifier

e. Advanced Startup options

13. You need to change the speed of a network adapter. Which tab of the driver's Properties dialog box will allow you to change this setting?

a. Details

b. Properties

c. Advanced

d. Power Management

Foundation Topics

Installing and Configuring Device Drivers

Device drivers are software utilities that enable hardware components to communicate with the operating system. All components that you see in Device Manager, including disk drives, display adapters, network interface cards, removable media (floppy, CD-ROM, DVD-ROM, and so on) drives, keyboards, mice, sound cards, USB controllers, and so on, utilize drivers for this purpose. External components such as printers, scanners, and so on also use drivers. With each new version of the operating system, it becomes necessary for hardware manufacturers to produce new drivers. Drivers written for older operating systems such as Windows XP, Vista, and Windows 7 might work with Windows 8 or 8.1 but can result in reduced device functionality, or they might not work at all. You need to be able to install, configure, and troubleshoot drivers for various components for the 70-687 exam and for real-world computer support tasks.

When you first install or upgrade your computer to Windows 8 or 8.1, the operating system searches for hardware devices attached to your system and loads drivers required for these devices to function. In most cases, this process occurs automatically without the user even knowing that it's taking place. It is only when the operating system is unable to locate the proper drivers for a device that you really become aware that a problem might exist.

Windows 7 brought about several improvements in the location and installation of updated drivers. Windows 8 and 8.1 continue to add support for new hardware and features, as follows:

- **Support for USB 3.0:** Windows 8 adds a new driver stack in support of USB 3.0 devices. Included is support for new capabilities of USB 3.0, including static streams support and remote suspend and wake-up features according to the USB 3.0 specification.
- **Support for the USB Attached SCSI Protocol (UASP):** Windows 8 includes a new USB storage driver that uses static streams for bulk endpoints, according to the implementation of UASP.
- **Support for Windows To Go:** As introduced in Chapter 1, "Introducing Windows 8.1," Windows To Go enables booting Windows from a flash drive or external drive. Support for the required drivers is included.
- **New device driver interfaces:** New interfaces are included that support the new features and improvements in Windows 8 and USB 3.0.

- **Enhanced diagnostic and debugging capabilities:** Windows 8 provides new utilities that facilitate the rapid diagnosis of USB 3.0 problems. Included are new USB 3.0 kernel debugger extensions that examine USB 3.0 host controller and device statuses.
- **New diagnostic failure messages in Device Manager:** Provided are USB 3.0-specific error messages that describe the reason for failure to enumerate an attached USB device.

In addition to driver installation, Windows Update offers updates to software applications installed on your computer as well as the operating system itself. Also available from time to time are optional updates that improve the functionality of your computer and its devices or add additional features. We look at Windows Update in Chapter 16, "Configuring Windows Update."

Device Setup

When you connect a Plug-and-Play (PnP) device to a Windows 8.1 computer, Windows automatically makes the device ready to use by automatically locating and installing all required software so that the device will function as intended. Included in the setup process is the distribution of device drivers, metadata, and Windows Store apps. The device metadata contains information about the device. Windows Store device apps are provided by device manufacturers to enhance device functionality in Windows 8.1; such apps are automatically distributed to users from the Windows Store according to instructions contained in the device metadata.

You can initiate device setup either manually or automatically in several fashions, by performing such actions as plugging in a USB device, using the Add a Device Wizard to recognize a Bluetooth device or Windows phone, setting up a network printer, adding the device to the network to which the computer is connected, connecting the computer to a new network (thereby initiating the setup of network devices accessed by the computer), and so on. Installing hardware devices typically takes three steps:

Step 1. Adding the device: For internal devices like hard drives or network adapters, you need to shut down your computer and, for some devices, open the case and insert it in the appropriate expansion slot or bay. For a USB or FireWire device, you simply plug it into a connector located somewhere on the computer. For network devices, you simply plug them into the network or plug the computer into a new network.

Step 2. Locating appropriate device drivers for the device: Windows detects the device at startup and displays a message on the taskbar that it is installing device driver software. In most cases, this message goes away within a few seconds and your device is ready for use.

Step 3. Configuring device settings: For PnP devices, this generally happens automatically. If Windows is unable to locate the driver, it requests any needed information, including any manufacturer-supplied media. You might also be able to locate hardware drivers from the Microsoft Windows Update website.

When device setup is complete, a sound is played. If a Windows Store device app is associated with the device, a tile for the device app appears on the Start screen.

Device Stage

Device Stage is a Windows 8.1 application that acts as a home page for hardware devices, providing a single location from which you can manage all devices that have been properly installed on your computer, as shown in Figure 4-1. You can access Device Stage by using any of the following methods:

- Starting from the Desktop, select **Control Panel** from the Settings charm or from the Start right-click menu and then select **View devices and printers** under the Hardware and Sound category.
- Right-click **Start** and choose **Control Panel**. Then select **View devices and printers** under the Hardware and Sound category. Either of these first two methods opens a Control Panel applet that shows all devices and printers attached to your computer, as shown in Figure 4-1.
- From the Search charm, type `devices` in the search field, and then select **Device settings**. This option displays a vertical list of devices on the PC & devices screen, as shown in Figure 4-2.

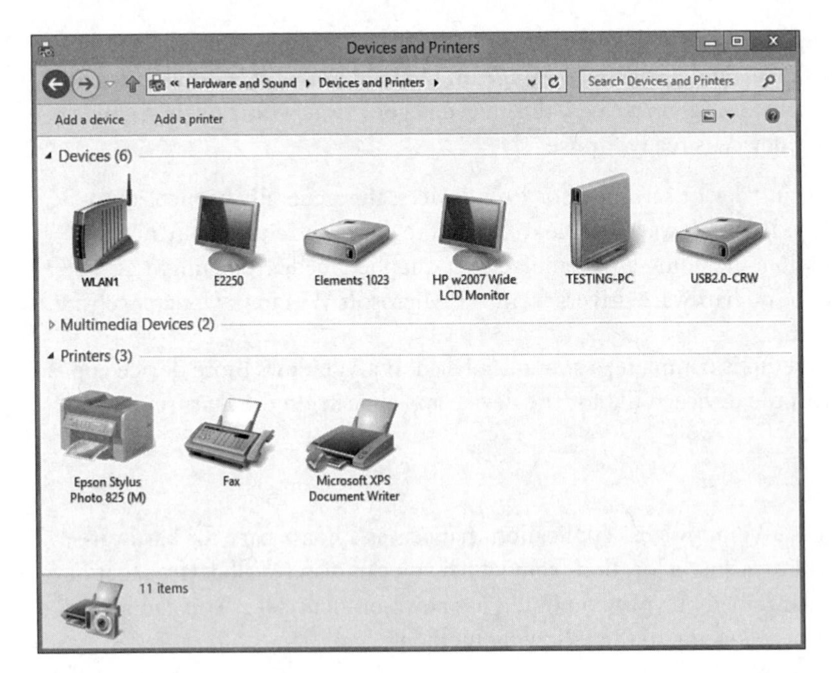

Figure 4-1 The Devices and Printers applet in Control Panel displays all devices connected to the computer.

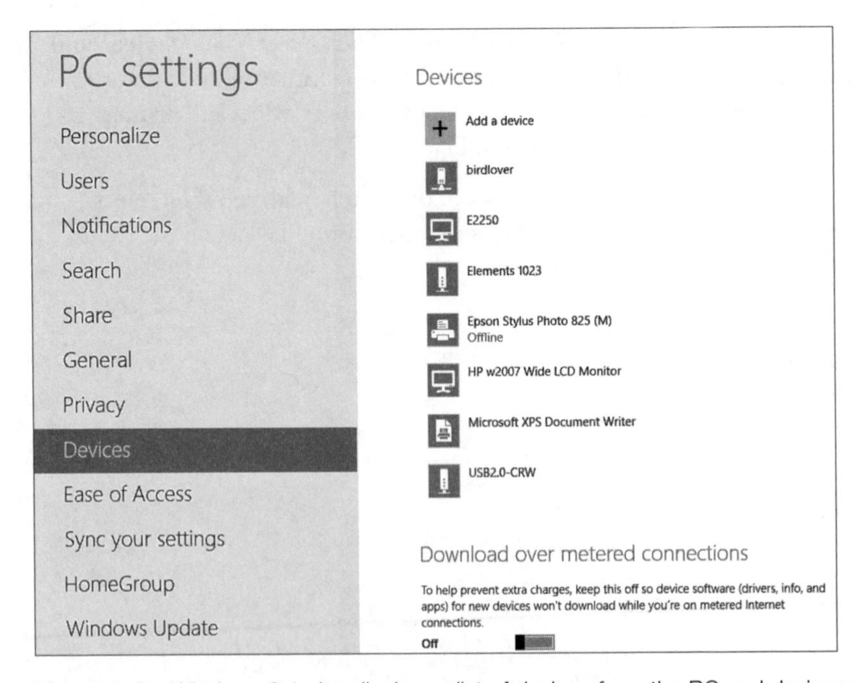

Figure 4-2 Windows 8.1 also displays a list of devices from the PC and devices screen.

When you connect a device, Device Stage attempts to add it automatically with the aid of an XML-based definition file provided by the manufacturer. If the device is not automatically detected, you can click **Add a device** to start the Add a Device wizard that searches for devices that might be attached to your computer. Ensure that your device is properly plugged in and turned on. The wizard should display a selection of device types, from which you can select the appropriate device. Click **Next** and follow the remaining steps presented to install your device. When the process is complete, the device is added to the Devices list shown in Figure 4-1 or 4-2.

TIP If you do not want Windows to automatically download drivers for new hardware devices, you can modify this behavior. Access the Hardware tab of the System Properties dialog box and click the **Device Installation Settings** command button. On the dialog box that appears, click **No, let me choose what to do**. Select the desired option from those displayed in Figure 4-3, and then click **Save Changes**.

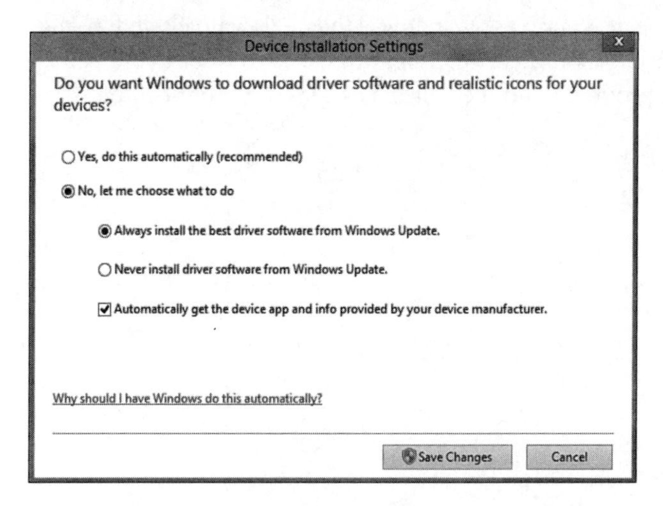

Figure 4-3 You can modify the default driver installation behavior if you wish.

NOTE For more information on setting up and configuring devices, including network-based devices, in Windows 8.1, refer to "Device setup user experience in Windows 8" at http://msdn.microsoft.com/en-US/library/windows/hardware/jj159306.

Updating Drivers

Windows Update provides a seamless, automatic means of updating all the device drivers on your computer. From the Control Panel, select the **System and Security** category and then click **Windows Update** (or type `Windows Update` into the search box in the Search charm). From here, you can check the Windows Update website for updates, from which ActiveX controls compare the drivers on the computer with the latest updates and display a list of available updates. This method works by comparing the hardware IDs of installed devices with drivers made available on the Microsoft website. Only if an exact match is found is the driver downloaded and installed.

Windows Update does not display driver updates initially. It considers driver updates to be optional in nature and informs you that optional updates are available, as shown in Figure 4-4. If critical or important updates are available, click the link provided to display the list of optional updates, as shown in Figure 4-5. Scroll this list to search for any driver updates that you might want to install. To install any desired updates, select them from the list in Figure 4-5 and click **Install**. If a User Account Control (UAC) prompt appears, click **Yes**. Windows Update downloads and installs the update(s). After installation is finished, you might be asked to restart your computer; if so, close any open programs and then click **Yes** to restart your computer.

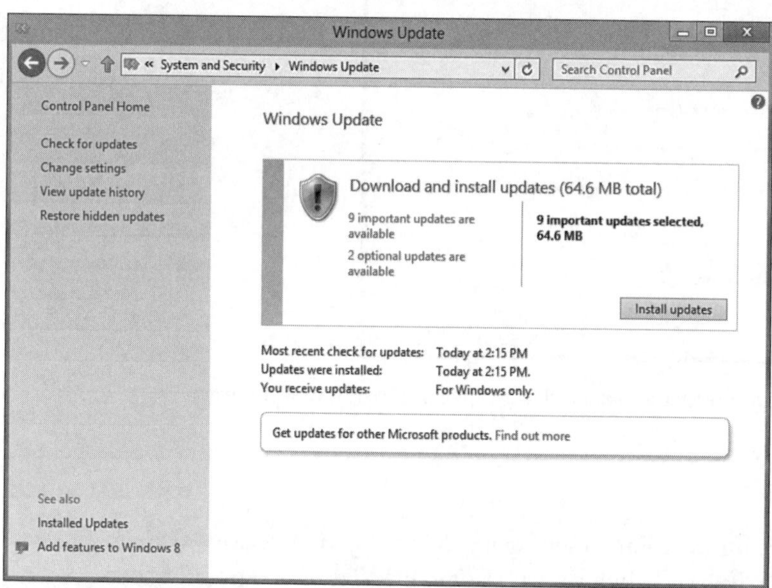

Figure 4-4 Windows Update informs you whether any updates are available for your computer.

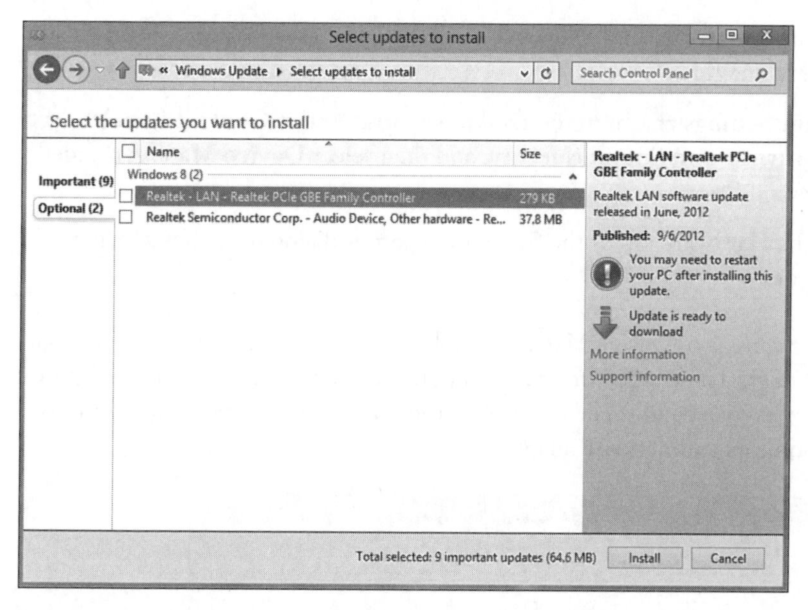

Figure 4-5 Windows Update enables you to select optional updates from this list.

Microsoft places these drivers on the Update site only if they are digitally signed, meet certain Web publishing standards, and have passed the testing requirements for the Windows Certification Program. These procedures verify that drivers included on the site are certified to do what they are supposed to do.

Using Device Manager

The majority of the work involving device implementation, management, and troubleshooting for many types of hardware devices is found in the Device Manager utility. You can run Device Manager either as a standalone Microsoft Management Console (MMC) snap-in or as a component of the Computer Management snap-in.

You can access Device Manager in any of the following ways:

- Right-click **Start** and choose **Computer Management**. This opens the Computer Management console, from which you can open Device Manager by clicking its icon in the console tree.
- Right-click **Start** and choose **Device Manager**. This opens Device Manager in its own console.
- From a File Explorer window, right-click **This PC** and choose **Properties**. Click **Advanced system settings** and select the **Hardware** tab of the System Properties dialog box and click **Device Manager**.

- From the Search charm, type `device manager` in the search box. Then click **Device Manager**.
- From the Settings charm in the Desktop context, select **Control Panel**, select the **Hardware and Sound** category, and then select **Device Manager** under Devices and Printers.
- From the Hardware tab of the System Properties dialog box, click **Device Manager.**

As shown in Figure 4-6, Device Manager displays a list of all types of hardware components that might be installed on your computer. Click the triangles on the various device categories to expand them and display the actual devices that are present (as shown for monitors and network adapters).

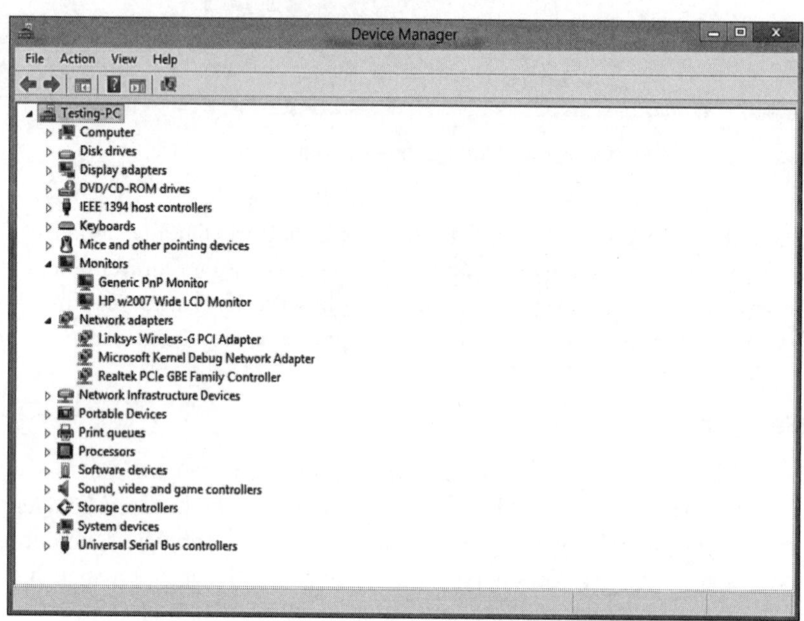

Figure 4-6 Device Manager enables you to configure and troubleshoot all hardware devices on your computer.

After you determine that a hardware device is installed correctly and is listed in the Windows Certification Program, you should check to see whether the device is detected by Windows 8.1 and is functioning by checking Device Manager for its listing. Devices shown in Device Manager might display icons that indicate their status. These include the following:

- If a device is disabled, an icon with a black downward-pointing arrow appears over the device icon. A disabled device is a device that is physically present in the computer and is consuming resources but does not have a protected-mode driver loaded.

- A red X appearing over the device icon indicates that the device is disabled.
- A black exclamation point icon on a yellow triangle background appearing next to the device icon indicates that a device is functioning but experiencing problems.
- A yellow question mark icon in place of the device's icon indicates a hardware device that is not properly installed or is in conflict with another device in the system.
- A blue "i" on a white field (for Information) indicates that the device has been configured manually with resource configurations.

When you right-click a device, a shortcut menu similar to the one displayed in Figure 4-7 appears. You can select to update the driver, or uninstall or disable the device. You may also scan the device for hardware changes or access the device's properties. When you open the device's Properties dialog box, you can put a variety of configurations into effect, as well as disable or enable the device.

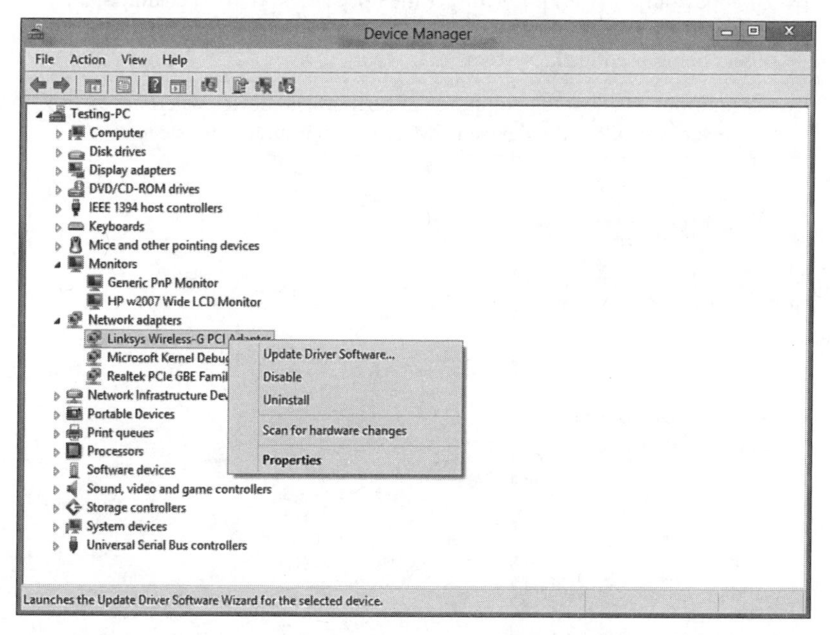

Figure 4-7 The right-click menu in Device Manager provides several configuration options.

Every device has its own Properties dialog box (see Figure 4-8), specific to its device type and sometimes specific to the manufacturer and model (depending on the installed driver). Table 4-2 describes the standard tabs found in any device's Properties dialog box (not all these tabs are found for every device, and manufacturers might add additional tabs not included here).

Table 4-2 Tabs Found in a Device's Properties Dialog Box

Tool	Description
General	Displays the device's description and status.
Advanced	Provides additional configurable properties.
Driver	Displays the current device driver's information, and enables you to perform several configuration options. We discuss these options later in this chapter.
Details	Displays the device's specifications. You can choose from a long list of device properties.
Events	Displays a time-based list of actions that have occurred with regard to the device. Actions include such things as installing and configuring drivers, adding services, and so on.
Resources	Displays the system resources being consumed, including interrupt requests (IRQs), input/output (I/O) ports, direct memory access (DMA) channels, and physical memory range. Displays whether these resources are in conflict with any others being used in the system.
Power Management	Provides options to allow the computer to turn off the device when not in use to save power, and allow the device to wake the computer from sleep mode.

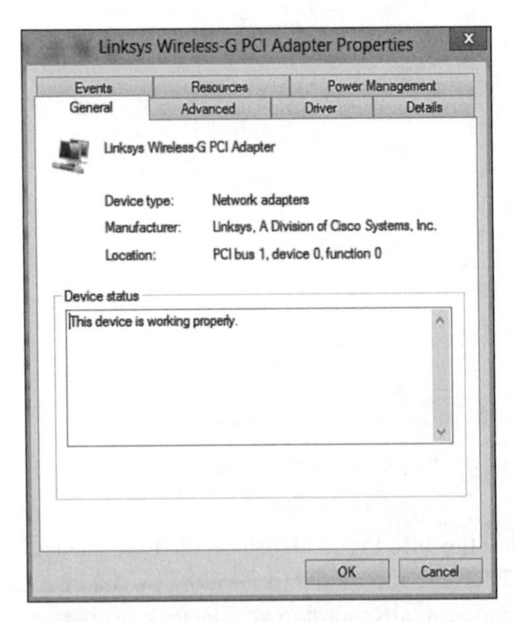

Figure 4-8 Each device in Device Manager has a Properties dialog box that enables you to configure a wide range of device properties.

Using Device Manager to Uninstall Drivers

When you uninstall a device driver, the driver is completely removed from the computer. To uninstall a driver, right-click the device in Device Manager and choose **Uninstall**. In the Confirm Device Uninstall dialog box shown in Figure 4-9, select the **Delete the driver software for this device** check box if desired and then click **OK**. Note that Windows will redetect the device at the next restart (if the device is still attached to the computer) and attempt to reinstall it.

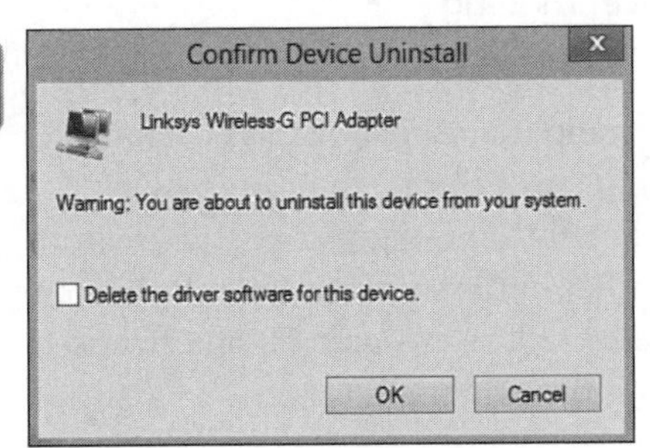

Figure 4-9 Uninstalling a driver.

Using Device Manager to Disable Drivers

Rather than uninstalling the device completely, you can disable the driver. The hardware configuration is not changed. Right-click the device in Device Manager and choose **Disable**. You receive a message box similar to that shown in Figure 4-10. Click **Yes** to disable the driver. The device appears in Device Manager with a small black arrow indicating that it is disabled. To re-enable the device, right-click it again and choose **Enable**. The device is re-enabled without any further prompts.

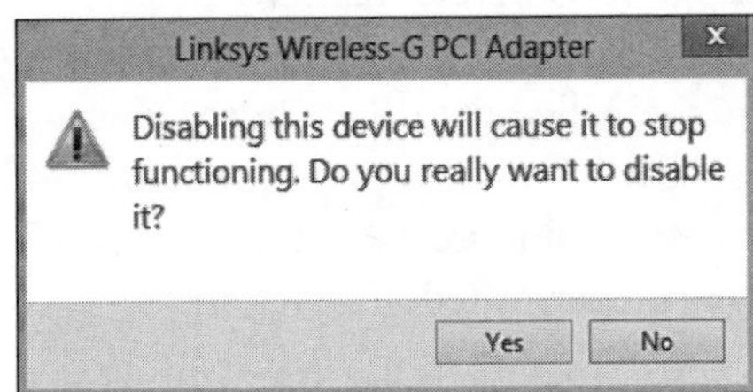

Figure 4-10 Disabling a driver.

Maintaining Device Drivers

Manufacturers often release updated drivers for their devices, which provide new features or improve the functionality of their device. Occasionally an updated driver will not function properly on a particular machine. At times, you might need to download an updated driver from Microsoft or the manufacturer's website to fix problems with device functionality caused by poorly written drivers or by changing technology. You need to know how to maintain device drivers to ensure that all the computers in your responsibility function properly and individuals using these computers can get their work done.

Managing and Troubleshooting Drivers and Driver Signing

Driver signing is a process that Microsoft follows to validate files that a third-party manufacturer creates for use in a Windows 8.1 computer. A manufacturer submits its drivers to Microsoft, and after Microsoft completes a thorough quality assurance testing process, Microsoft signs the files digitally. This digital signature is an electronic security mark that indicates the publisher of the software and information that can determine whether a driver has been altered. Driver signing is an extra assurance of the quality of the software installed on the computer.

Device drivers that are included on the Windows 8.1 installation DVD or downloaded from the Microsoft Update website include a Microsoft digital signature. If you have problems installing a driver or a device is not working properly, you should access Windows Update as described earlier in this chapter to look for optional driver updates. You should also visit the device manufacturer's support website to obtain an up-to-date digitally signed driver for your device.

Driver Signing Requirements in Windows 8.1

The following driver signing requirements were initiated in Windows 7 and continued in Windows 8.1:

- Standard (nonadministrative) users can install only drivers that have been signed by either a Windows publisher or trusted publisher. These drivers are placed in a protected location on the computer called the driver store. Microsoft implemented this requirement because drivers run as a part of the operating system with unrestricted access to the entire computer. Therefore, it is critical that only properly authorized drivers be permitted.
- Standard users cannot install unsigned drivers or drivers that have been signed by an untrusted publisher; you cannot modify this policy in Windows 8.1.
- Administrators can install drivers that have been signed by an untrusted publisher, and they can also add the publisher's certificate to the trusted certificates store, thereby enabling standard users to install drivers signed by this publisher. This is known as staging driver packages.

- If drivers are unsigned or have been altered, administrators are warned. They can proceed in a manner similar to how they would if the drivers were from an untrusted publisher.

NOTE You cannot install a driver that lacks a valid digital signature, or one that was altered after it was signed, on x64-based versions of Windows.

If you install a device, Windows 8.1 looks for the driver signature as a part of System File Protection, which is a feature that prevents applications from replacing critical Windows files by creating and maintaining backups of many critical program files. When it fails to find one, Windows notifies you that the drivers are not signed and prompts you to continue or stop the installation, provided you have administrative privileges. Otherwise, the installation attempt fails. If you continue with the installation, Windows 8.1 automatically creates a restore point, which facilitates returning to the previous configuration. Restore points are discussed in more depth in Chapter 19, "Configuring System Recovery Options."

NOTE For more details on signing and staging device drivers, refer to "Device Management and Installation Step-by-Step Guide: Signing and Staging Device Drivers in Windows 7 and Windows Server 2008 R2" at http://technet.microsoft.com/en-us/library/dd919230(WS.10).aspx. Information in this guide should be applicable to Windows 8.1 and Windows Server 2012 R2 with only the new methods described in this chapter for accessing programs such as Device Manager.

Checking Drivers for Digital Signatures

Dynamic link libraries (DLLs) and other files are often shared by programs. Sometimes a program overwrites files that were originally installed by a digitally signed driver. If a device behaves oddly, you might want to verify that its driver still has the signature. You can check to validate the driver by looking in Device Manager. Double-click the device and click the **Driver** tab of its Properties dialog box. You should see the statement: `Digital Signer: Microsoft Windows Hardware Compatibility Publisher.`

You can check individual files further by clicking the **Driver Details** button. Files that are signed have an icon of a sealed certificate, which appears to the left of the name (see Figure 4-11). Files that have not been digitally signed do not have a certificate icon next to the filename.

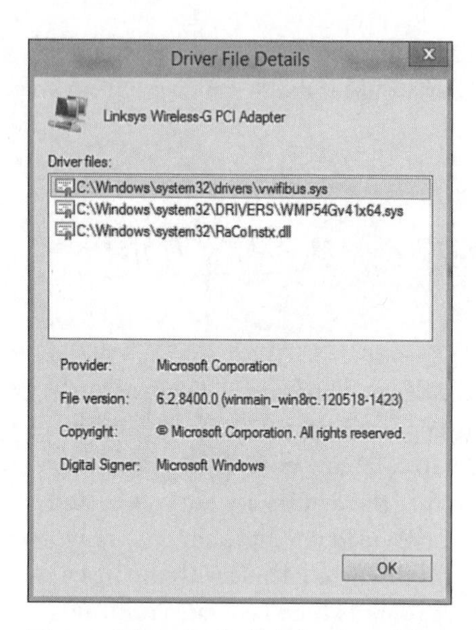

Figure 4-11 Each digitally signed file is displayed with an icon for easy identification.

If you want to verify device drivers throughout the system, you can run the `sigverif` application. To do so, access the Search charm and type **`sigverif`** in the search box. Then click **`Sigverif.exe`**. The File Signature Verification program starts, as shown in Figure 4-12. Click the **Advanced** button and verify that `sigverif` will log the results and save them to a file. Click **OK** and then click **Start**. After the program has completed its check, the program displays any files that were not signed in a window; plus, you can see the results in the `Sigverif.txt` file. If the program does not detect any unsigned files, it displays a message box with the message `Your files have been scanned and verified as digitally signed.` Otherwise, it displays a list of files that have not been digitally signed.

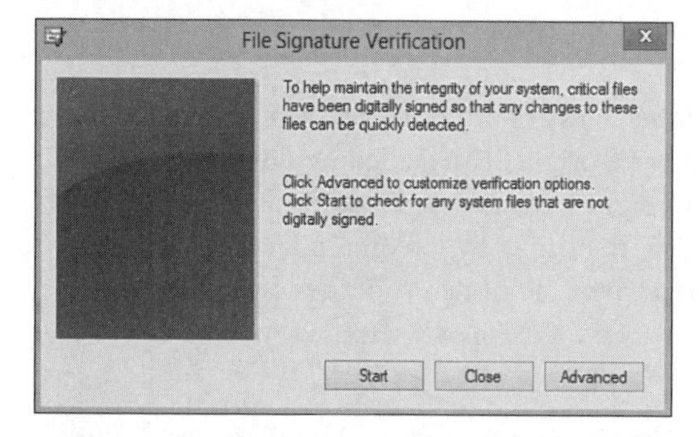

Figure 4-12 The File Signature Verification program checks all drivers for digital signatures.

Unsigned drivers might not cause a problem. If you are having problems with a device that has an unsigned driver, you should disable the driver. If you are having unspecified problems, such as the computer does not go into Sleep mode, you should determine which devices have unsigned drivers, disable them one at a time, and then test to see whether the problem is resolved. To disable an unsigned driver that has already been installed, you should disable the device that uses the driver, uninstall the driver, or rename the driver files.

TIP When in doubt, check the system files. The System File Checker, which you can execute from the command line with `sfc.exe`, can check the digital signature of system protected files. With other uses, such as repopulating the DLLCACHE folder and replacing system files that are missing or incorrect, you can execute `sfc.exe` from a batch program or script. This program has several options; the `/scannow` option is one of the most useful, scanning the integrity of all protected system files and performing repairs where possible. This process takes several minutes. To view information on all available options, run `sfc.exe /?`. Note that in Windows 8.1, as was the case in Windows Vista and 7, you must run this command as an administrator; right-click the **Command Prompt** option, select **Run as Administrator** from the list of options displayed at the bottom of the screen, and then click **Yes** in the UAC dialog box.

Driver Installation Permissions in Windows 8.1

In versions of Windows prior to Windows 7, only users with administrative privileges could install drivers. Consequently, many enterprises provided their users with local administrative rights; this enables users to perform these tasks, but they also allowed users to undertake actions that could compromise security or configure the computer such that it would not run properly. These actions resulted in increased support costs and demands on the help desk.

In Windows 8 and 8.1, as was the case in Windows 7, an administrator can implement a policy that prevents the installation of a driver according to its device ID or device setup class. If such a policy is present, Windows will not install devices that are forbidden by these policies. An administrator can also permit standard users to install device drivers that are members of specified device setup classes.

Managing Driver Packages

A *driver package*, in essence, is the full set of files installed as part of a device driver. When you select the **Driver Details** button on the driver properties Driver tab, a list of the files associated with the driver are displayed. For many drivers, these files make up the entirety of the driver package. All files that make up the driver are considered critical to installation of the device.

Some manufacturers may deliver a driver package with a richer set of functionality than a simple interface to the operating system. Instead, some driver packages include a custom user interface (UI), utilities, administration tools, and other software. These packages are usually deployed as installable files, such as executables or Microsoft Software Installer (MSI) files, and provide the user with additional features for controlling the device.

The following are examples of devices that often include a richer driver package:

- Printer drivers often include diagnostic software, custom color adjustments, or calibration tools.
- Digital cameras and camcorders often include customized UI screens to allow the user to copy pictures and videos to the computer or its own photo sharing software.
- Scanners nearly always include additional software and control packages for use in previewing scans, adjusting the scan image, performing file conversion, or producing searchable documents using Optical Character Recognition (OCR).

These are just a few examples; other devices may also include rich driver packages, and not all printers, cameras, and scanners require custom user interfaces. But you should have an idea of the potential varied functionality that could be included in a driver package.

When you install a device driver in Windows 8.1, it adds the driver to the driver store for the system. Administrators can install signed and unsigned drivers to the store, which will make them available for any user who plugs in a matching device. In this way, standard images can be deployed with drivers for all the devices typically used in a business, and they will be available for any user.

You can add drivers to the store using a setup program provided by Microsoft or the device manufacturer, by including the drivers in an Windows Setup answer file during an automated deployment or by using the `PnPUtil` program.

A Windows 8.1 computer may end up with more than one driver that qualifies for a specific device. When this happens, Windows uses `PnPUtil`, a command-line utility for installing and staging device drivers using an `.inf` file. It requires an administrative command prompt and the name of the driver `.inf` file. You can use several parameters with the `PnPUtil` command to manage drivers:

- `-e` is used to enumerate (or list) all third-party driver packages.
- `-a` is used to add the driver to the driver store.
- `-i` is used to install the driver package.
- `-d` is used to delete the package associated with the `.inf` file.

NOTE For more details on `PnPUtil`, reference "To install a device driver by using `PnPUtil` at a command line" at http://technet.microsoft.com/en-us/library/cc732408.aspx#BKMK_Anchor2.

Resolving Driver Issues

Even with all the improvements Microsoft has made in device and driver management in recent Windows versions, problems still do occur. Drivers use system resources, including IRQ lines, I/O ports, DMA channels, and physical memory addresses. If two hardware components attempt to use the same location of any of these resources, a conflict results, and these components will not work. For example, you install a new scanner and discover that your network adapter does not work. Such a situation happens more often when using a non-PnP device. In such a situation, you should check resource assignments for conflicts. It is frequently necessary to modify settings on the non-PnP device, for example, with the aid of jumpers or DIP switches. Some devices may have configuration settings available in the computer BIOS, such as built-in devices. Reconfigure the device with the aid of manufacturer instructions, which may be located on a label placed on the device or manufacturer's documentation.

In this section, we take a look at troubleshooting driver resource conflicts and resolving other driver issues.

Using Device Manager to Resolve Driver Conflicts

You can use Device Manager to determine whether a resource conflict exists by changing the view. Device Manager offers several view types that assist in monitoring, as described in Table 4-3.

Table 4-3 Device Manager Views

View	What It Displays
Devices by type	Displays devices by the type of installed device, such as monitor or mouse. This is the default view. If you have multiple monitors, for example, you see each of the monitors displayed below the Monitor node.
Devices by connection	Displays devices according to the type of connection. For example, all the disk drives and CD or DVD drives connected to the IDE controller are displayed under the IDE connection node.
Resources by type	Displays devices according to resource type. Resources DMA, I/O, IRQ, and memory. For example, Figure 4-13 shows devices listed in the order of the I/O resources it uses.
Resources by connection	Displays resources according to their type of connection. This also serves to indicate which resources are currently available.

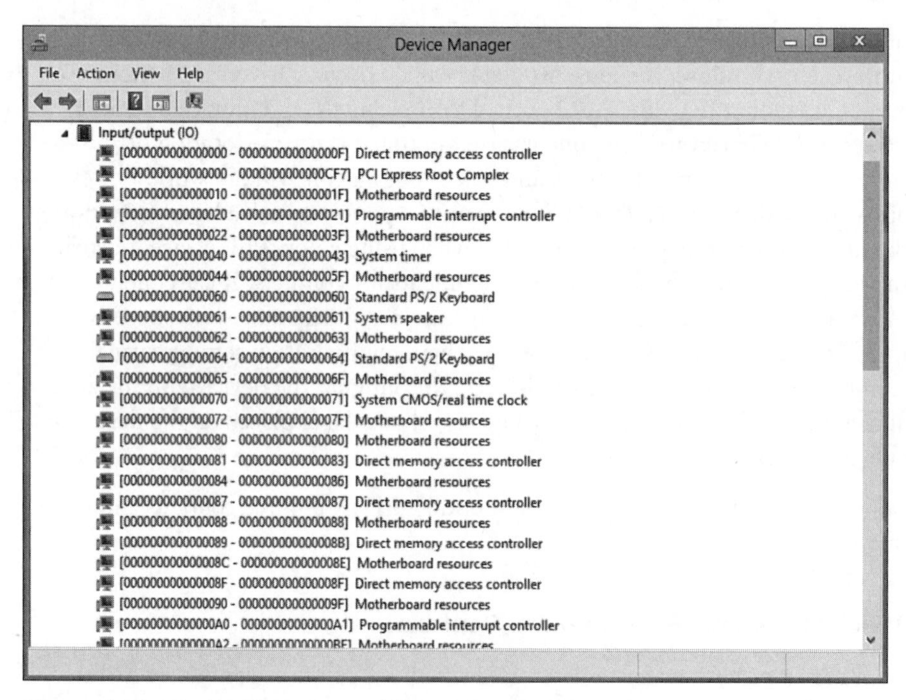

Figure 4-13 Device Manager provides an organized view of devices by the I/O resources they consume.

The View menu also offers two customization options that affect what you see. To expand the views to show non-PnP devices, select **Show hidden devices**. To modify what items Device Manager shows, select **Customize**. This displays the Customize View dialog box shown in Figure 4-14, which enables you to select what items are shown by Device Manager.

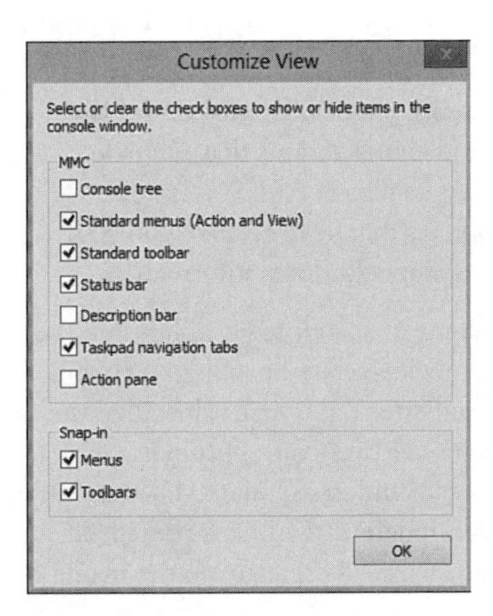

Figure 4-14 You can select which items are displayed in the Device Manager window.

To view resources being used by a specific device, access the Resources tab of the device's Properties dialog box. As shown in Figure 4-15, this tab displays a list of all resources in use and reports conflicts that might be occurring. To change resource settings, clear the **Use automatic settings** check box and then click **Change Setting**. In the dialog box that appears, select a setting that does not conflict with other settings. Device Manager will inform you if these settings conflict with any other devices; if so, modify the settings so that no conflicts occur and then click **OK**.

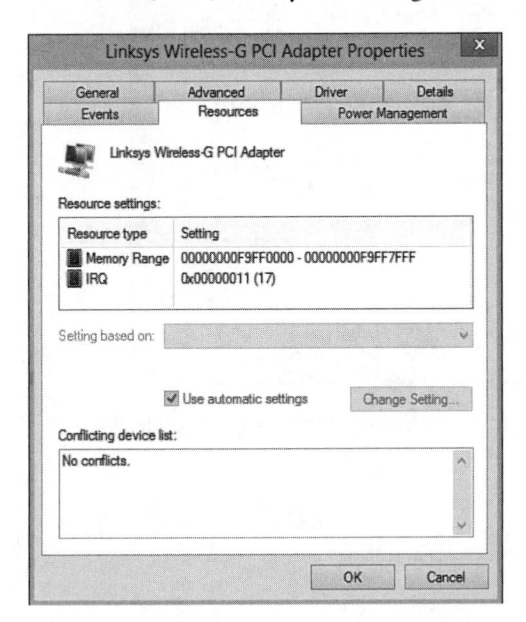

Figure 4-15 The Resources tab of a device's Properties dialog box displays all resources in use and informs you of any conflicts that might be occurring.

Use of the Action Center to View Device-Related Problems

The Windows 8.1 Action Center also offers information on device-related problems. Action Center is a central place for viewing alerts and taking actions that can help resolve issues and keep Windows running reliably. As shown in Figure 4-16, the Maintenance section of Action Center reports problems that have occurred on your computer; you can click the problems displayed to obtain additional information.

When a problem occurs, you can allow Action Center to search for problems on the Internet. The user is notified when a solution to a device-related problem is found. A web link is supplied, and notification is suppressed after the user has installed the application. Action Center can also display messages alerting you to problems and solutions related to devices that don't post drivers at Windows Update. The user is alerted to the need to download and install a driver update and a link is provided, specifying the device and providing links to the latest signed driver from the manufacturer's site.

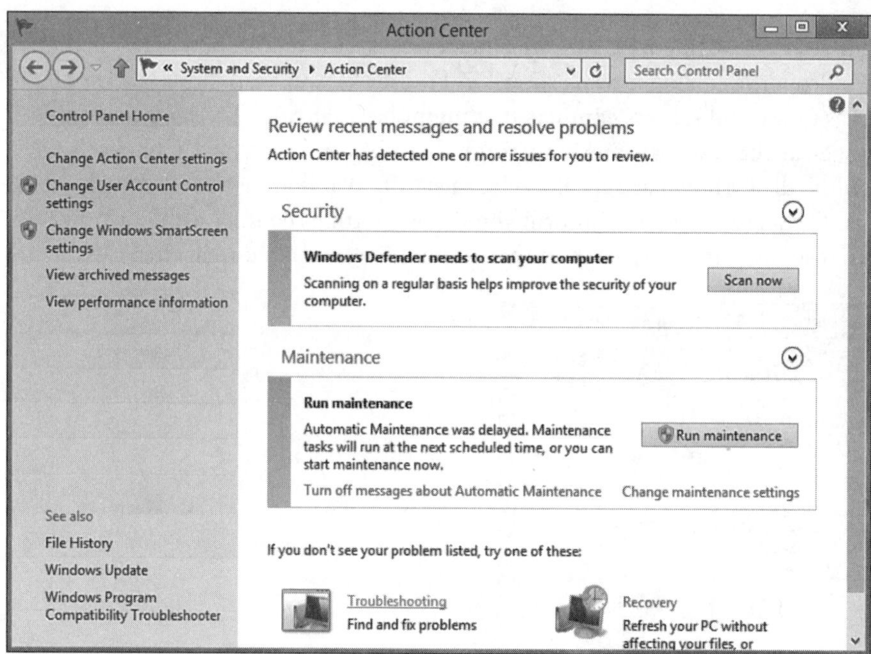

Figure 4-16 The Windows 8.1 Action Center includes a Maintenance section that displays device-related problems.

Use of System Information to View Device-Related Problems

The System Information utility is another place you can check devices and locate potential problems. In the Search charm, type `msinfo32` in the Search field, and then click `msinfo32.exe`. Expand the Hardware Resources category to obtain information, as shown in Figure 4-17. Note that the information displayed in the Conflicts/Sharing subnode does not necessarily indicate problems because some resources can be shared without creating a problem. Also note the Forced Hardware node, which displays information about devices whose default configuration has been modified by the user. Information in this node can be useful when troubleshooting resource conflicts.

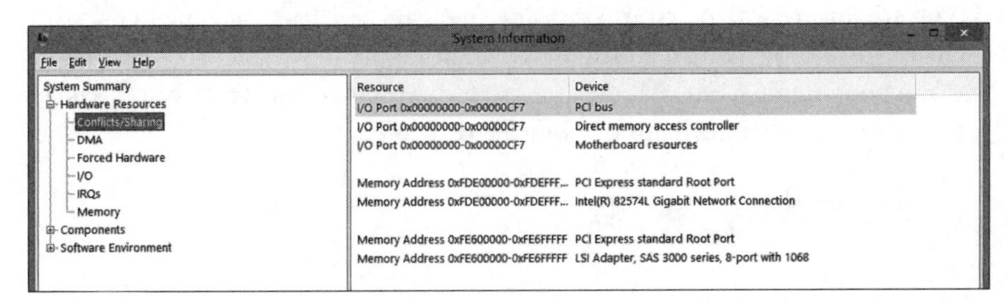

Figure 4-17 System Information displays details about Hardware Resources, including resource conflicts and sharing.

Using Windows 8.1 Rollback to Resolve a Problem Driver

If you update an existing driver to a new version and then you experience system problems, you should roll back the driver to the previous version. In versions of Windows prior to Windows XP, this was almost impossible to do. As was the case in Windows XP, Vista, and Windows 7, Windows 8.1 maintains a copy of the previous driver each time a new one is updated. If, at any time, you want to restore the previous version, simply roll back the driver. (We cover rolling back a driver in the following section, "Configuring Driver Settings.")

TIP It is usually helpful to create a restore point before installing the new driver. This enables you to restore your computer to its status as of before the driver installation, using the System Restore feature. Use of System Restore for performing these actions is covered in Chapter 19.

You can roll back all device drivers except for printers. You might receive a UAC prompt before either updating a driver or rolling it back to a previous version.

In some cases, your computer might not even start after installing a problem driver and rebooting. You can try the following options:

- **System Restore** will reset the PC to a recent restore point. This capability is especially helpful if you have created a restore point in advance.
- **Automatic Repair** will look for common issues, including recent device changes, and attempt to resolve the issue automatically.
- You can also use **System Image Recovery** if you have a recent image available.
- If you are unsure which driver is causing the issue, you can use your PC's Startup and Recovery dialog box, as shown in Figure 4-18, to enable options such as boot logging, Safe Mode, and disable automatic restart on system failure to gather more information about the problem.

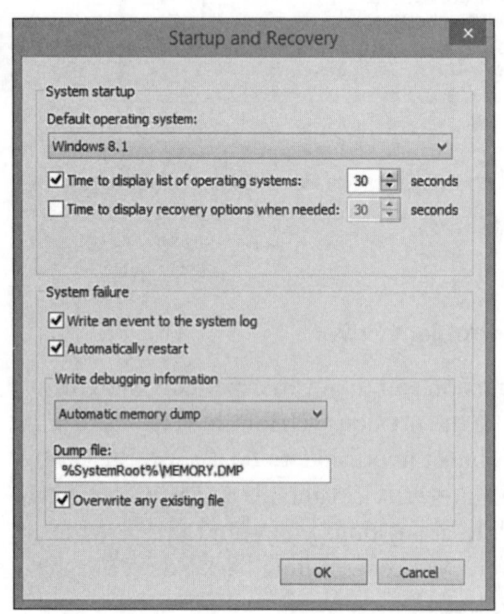

Figure 4-18 Advanced options in Windows 8.1 Startup provide several alternate troubleshooting tools for resolving driver issues.

We discuss these and other startup options in Chapter 19.

Configuring Driver Settings

Like Windows 7, Windows 8.1 provides access to a comprehensive list of device driver settings for each device. Ordinarily you would not need to change these settings from their installation defaults, but you should understand some of the more common settings and how to modify them if needed, for the 70-687 exam and when working as a Windows support professional.

In previous sections, we covered some of the basic driver settings such as resource drivers and how to modify them. This section covers some of the more advanced settings, when they might be needed, and how to adjust the settings when necessary.

Driver Verifier

Windows Driver Verifier is included in all versions of Windows since Windows 2000 and in versions of Windows Server 2003 and later. You can use this tool to troubleshoot issues with a driver or to help identify any driver or driver setting that may be causing an issue.

Use Driver Verifier by starting Verifier, selecting the options you want, and restarting the computer. Verifier will check the drivers based on your options and collect the information for you to review.

Step 1. To start Driver Verifier, click on the **Search** charm, type `verifier` in the search box, and select `verifier.exe` from the results that appear. The Driver Verifier Manager dialog box shown in Figure 4-19 appears, allowing you to select from a list of settings for how to run the Verifier.

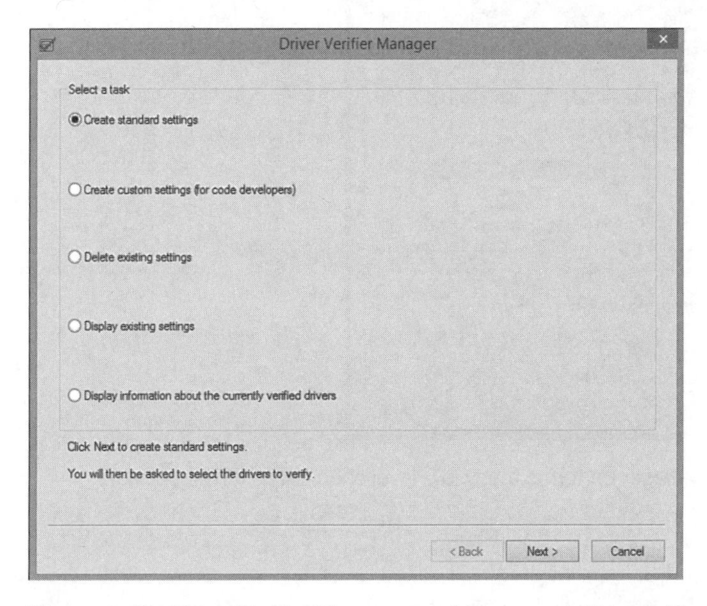

Figure 4-19 Driver Verifier Manager provides several driver verification options.

Step 2. From the Select a task screen of the Driver Verifier Manager, select **Create standard settings** and then click **Next**. This is the option to start with the first time you verify your drivers. After Verifier has run, you can choose from other Verifier Manager options:

- Create custom settings (for code developers)
- Delete existing settings
- Display existing settings
- Display information about the currently verified drivers

Step 3. The Select what drivers to verify screen appears. From here, you can select a subset of drivers to verify based on the issue you are working to resolve. For instance, you may suspect a driver that was developed for an older Windows version or that an unsigned driver may be causing the problem. Otherwise, select the **Automatically select all drivers** option and click **Next**.

Step 4. Click the **Finish** button and then restart Windows.

Step 5. When Windows restarts, run Verifier again to see the results of the verifications you selected.

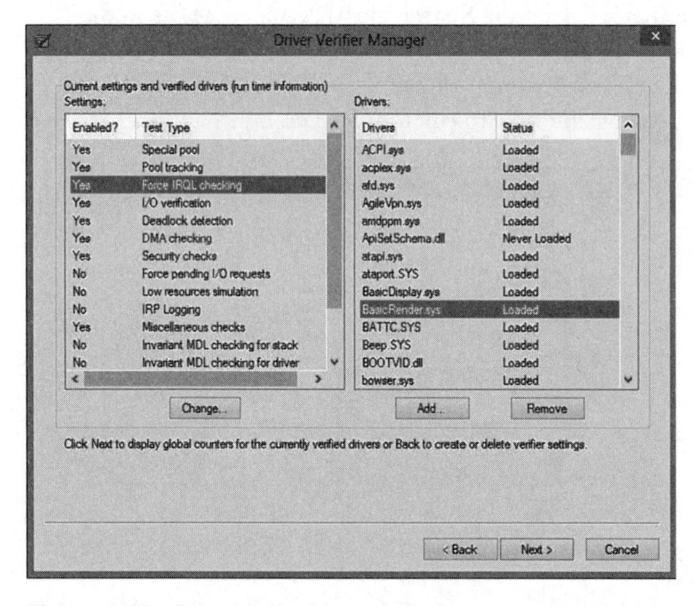

Figure 4-20 Driver Verifier Manager performs many low-level checks on driver behavior.

As you can see from Figure 4-20, Driver Verifier Manager is an advanced tool for troubleshooting drivers and issues. Typically, you would use this tool if you have a computer displaying bug checks or blue screens, and you need to identify which driver or device is behaving poorly.

NOTE After you finish working with Verifier, run the Verifier Manager again and select **Delete existing settings**. Verifier injects code into each driver and can affect performance of Windows if it is left running.

NOTE For more information on using Driver Verifier, refer to "Using Driver Verifier to identify issues with Windows drivers for advanced users" at http://support.microsoft.com/kb/244617.

Configuring Driver Settings

The Driver tab of a device's Properties dialog box enables you to configure the options shown in Figure 4-21:

- **Driver Details:** Provides details about the driver in use, including the certificate icon already mentioned.
- **Update Driver:** Starts the Update Driver Software Wizard, which enables you to search automatically for updated drivers (including those located on the Internet) or to browse your computer for drivers. The latter option enables you to insert a CD or floppy disk containing drivers, if you have one.
- **Roll Back Driver:** Enables you to remove an updated driver and return the last functioning driver, should you experience problems after updating your driver, as shown in Figure 4-22. This option is available only if you have updated your driver previously.
- **Disable:** Disables the driver, as available from the right-click menu previously shown in Figure 4-7.
- **Uninstall:** Uninstalls the driver, as available from the right-click menu previously shown in Figure 4-7.

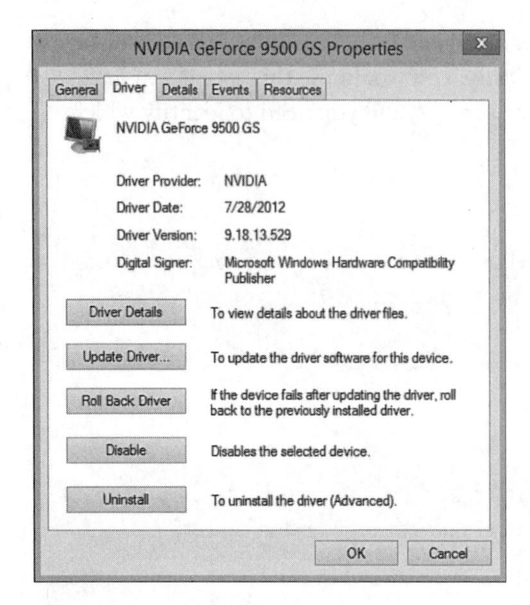

Figure 4-21 The Driver tab of a device's Properties dialog box enables you to configure several driver settings.

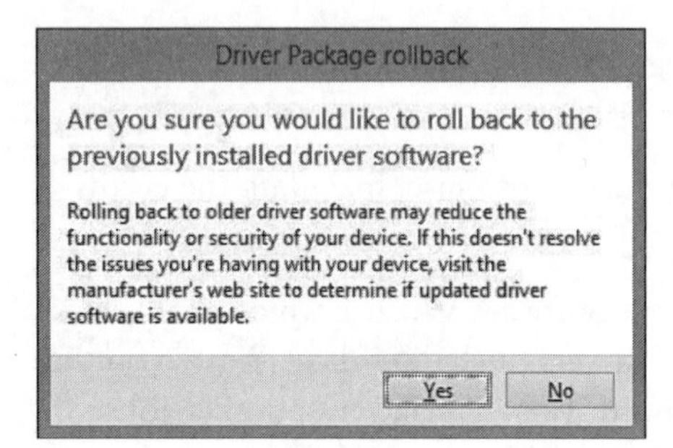

Figure 4-22 If you choose to roll back a driver, you are warned that such an action might reduce the functionality or security of the device.

Advanced Driver Settings

Windows drivers typically install with the best or most compatible settings available, based on the operating system and the underlying hardware. Situations may arise, however, when these settings need intervention for a specific use case or requirement. For instance, a network driver may fail to negotiate properly with a hub or switch, and run at a slower speed than it is capable of, impacting overall performance.

Depending on the driver and manufacturer, advanced settings may be displayed on an Advanced tab in the driver Properties. Note the tabs available as described in Table 4-2 in the "Using Device Manager" section. Not all drivers provide the Advanced tab. These drivers may have not options for modifying advanced settings, or they may come with additional software for managing them. For instance, many video driver settings include an integrated application for setting options the manufacturer has made available.

As shown in Figure 4-23, there may be many advanced settings for a driver, and network adapters typically have the most. To modify a setting on this tab, select the setting you want to change from the Property box on the left and select the setting you want from the Value selection on the right. You can modify several properties in this manner. Clicking the **OK** button applies the changes.

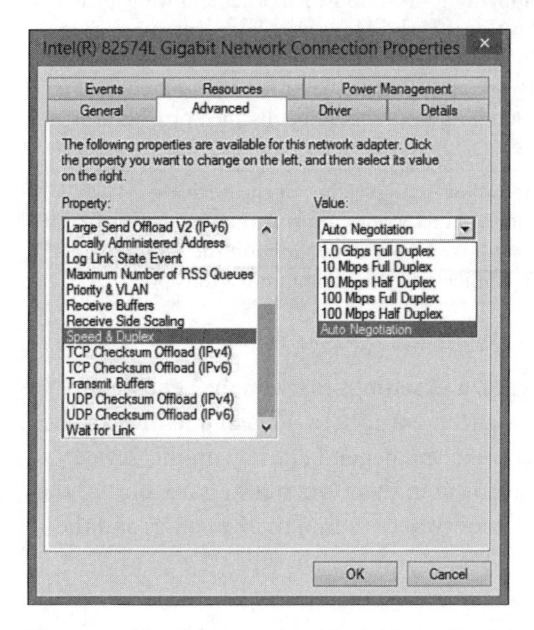

Figure 4-23 Driver settings available on the Advanced tab of the network interface card.

You occasionally need to modify driver settings. Table 4-4 lists some of the most common advanced driver settings that you will encounter.

Table 4-4 Common Advanced Driver Settings

Setting	Device Type	How It Is Used
Enable DMA	ATA bus or Optical Drive	Direct memory access, or DMA, allows disks and optical drives to perform faster. This setting may need to be adjusted if a device is malfunctioning or DMA capability was not detected properly.
Speed & Duplex	Network Adapter	The default "Auto Negotiation" may fail due to issues with the switch or hub, leaving the network running too slow or failing to connect. Ensure that the value for this setting matches the capabilities of the switch or hub, and select the value from the list.
Jumbo Packet	Network Adapter	This setting is typically disabled on network adapters to maintain compatibility with most Ethernet and wide area network (WAN) networks. However, in a corporate setting with Gigabit Ethernet, enabling this setting can significantly improve network performance. Your network administrator will know if jumbo frames should be disabled or what size should be used.
Port Settings	Serial, LPT, or USB Serial Converter	These settings allow configuration of the device's communication characteristics, such as the speed, parity, and number of data bits. This is dependent on the requirements of the device connected to the communications port.

There are many other devices, device types, and settings that you may encounter managing Windows computers, far too many to cover here. Which ones need to be manually configured and the settings required will depend entirely on the device and operating characteristics. You will learn about them when necessary, but for the exam and as a starting point, you should know where to find these settings and the steps to modify them.

Exam Preparation Tasks

Review All the Key Topics

Review the most important topics in the chapter, noted with the key topics icon in the outer margin of the page. Table 4-5 lists a reference of these key topics and the page numbers on which each is found.

Table 4-5 Key Topics for Chapter 4

Key Topic Element	Description	Page Number
Step List	Shows procedure for installing hardware devices	170
Figure 4-4	Shows available updates in Windows Update	174
Figure 4-6	Shows all hardware devices in Device Manager	176
Table 4-2	Describes tabs on a device's Properties dialog box	178
Figure 4-9	Shows how to uninstall a device driver	179
Figure 4-10	Shows how to disable a device driver	179
Section	Explains how to manage driver packages	183
Table 4-3	Describes available view options in Device Manager	186
Figure 4-16	Shows how to use Action Center to view suggested maintenance actions	188
Figure 4-18	Shows Windows 8.1 startup options for troubleshooting driver issues	190
Table 4-4	Shows common advanced driver settings	196

Complete the Tables and Lists from Memory

Print a copy of Appendix C, "Memory Tables," (found on the CD), or at least the section for this chapter, and complete the tables and lists from memory. Appendix D, "Memory Tables Answer Key," also on the CD, includes completed tables and lists to check your work.

Definitions of Key Terms

Define the following key terms from this chapter and check your answers in the glossary.

Action Center, Device driver, Device Manager, Device Stage, Direct Memory Access (DMA), Driver package, Driver signing, FireWire, Input/Output (I/O) port address, Interrupt Request (IRQ), `msinfo32`, Plug and Play (PnP), `Sigverif.exe`, `Verify.exe`

This chapter covers the following subjects:

- **Installing and Configuring Desktop Applications:** Many applications currently in use today were originally written for Windows XP or older versions of Windows. Some of these might not work properly with Windows 8.1. This section describes methods you can use to make these applications work properly. It also discusses Windows Installer, default program settings, and App-V applications.
- **Using Windows Store Applications:** Windows Store applications, or apps, were first introduced in Windows 8. The Store offers many apps, and they make use of the new start screen display and are touch enabled. In this section, you learn about the Windows Store, how to download and install new apps, and how to maintain control of store apps in an Enterprise.
- **Configuring Application and Hardware Restrictions:** In larger organizations with many computers, it is important for security and productivity reasons to be able to enforce organizational policies on the user desktop. Essential to controlling the systems is the ability to restrict applications to prevent inappropriate software from being used or installed on organization computers. Also important is ensuring that the use of certain hardware can be disabled to prevent possible unauthorized access to organizational data. In this section, you learn how to control these restrictions.

CHAPTER 5

Installing, Configuring, and Securing Applications in Windows 8.1

You have finished looking at configuration and troubleshooting of hardware devices attached to or included with your computer. Now that you have done so, it is time to turn to the software applications installed on the computer. With each new version of Windows comes updated applications including Internet Explorer, now in version number 11. However, organizations and individuals have invested big money in applications that were run on older computers running operating systems such as Windows XP, Vista, and 7. A new operating system brings with it the potential for compatibility issues, in which software written for older operating systems might not run properly, might stop responding (hang), or might not even begin to start. For the 70-687 exam, it is important that you know how to configure applications so that they work properly on Windows 8.1.

Windows 8.1 brings an entirely new suite of small-scale applications, simply called apps, that users can purchase and download from the new Windows Store. Although some of these apps can enhance productivity in a corporate environment, downloading and using many of them can become a major distraction for users during the work day. Further, such practices can consume bandwidth and create security risks. Consequently, administrators and desktop support specialists need to know how to limit or even prevent access to the Windows Store in the corporate environment. You also need to know how to place limits on traditional executable files, scripts, Windows Installer files, and other similar files; Microsoft provides AppLocker to deal with performing these tasks, as well as the older Software Restriction Policies, which you still need to be aware of if your network contains Windows XP or older computers.

"Do I Know This Already?" Quiz

The "Do I Know This Already?" quiz allows you to assess whether you should read this entire chapter or simply jump to the "Exam Preparation Tasks" section for review. If you are in doubt, read the entire chapter. Table 5-1 outlines the major headings in this chapter and the corresponding "Do I Know This Already?" quiz questions. You can find the answers in Appendix A, "Answers to the 'Do I Know This Already?' Quizzes."

Table 5-1 "Do I Know This Already?" Foundation Topics Section-to-Question Mapping

Foundations Topics Section	Questions Covered in This Section
Installing and Configuring Desktop Applications	1–4
Using Windows Store Applications	5–8
Configuring Application and Hardware Restrictions	9–12

1. You are working with a financial application your company has used successfully on Windows XP computers for more than eight years. The application does not respond when accessed on a Windows 8.1 Pro computer. What compatibility option should you try to get this program working?
   a. Run this program in compatibility mode for (and select Windows XP).
   b. Use reduced color mode.
   c. Disable display scaling on high DPI settings.
   d. Run this program as an administrator.

2. You are responsible for deploying applications to users in an Active Directory Domain Services (AD DS) environment. Which of the following methods can you use in Group Policy to accomplish this task? (Choose three.)
   a. Publish a package to users.
   b. Publish a package to computers.
   c. Assign a package to users.
   d. Assign a package to computers.

3. You want to advertise a Windows Installer package named `Program.msi` to all users of the computer. Which of the following commands should you type?
   a. `msiexec /am Program.msi`
   b. `msiexec /au Program.msi`
   c. `msiexec /jm Program.msi`
   d. `msiexec /ju Program.msi`

4. You would like all file types that currently open in Internet Explorer to open with Firefox instead. What should you do? (Each correct answer represents a complete solution. Choose two.)
   a. From the Programs applet in Control Panel, select **Set your default programs** and then select **Associate a file type or protocol with a program.** From the list that appears, select the extensions that currently

open in Internet Explorer and click **Change program**. In the Open with dialog box that appears, select **Firefox**.

b. From the Programs applet in Control Panel, select **Default Programs** and then select **Set your default programs**. From the list that appears, select **Firefox** and then click **Set this program as default**.

c. From the Programs applet in Control Panel, select **Set program access and computer defaults**. In the dialog box that appears, select **Custom** and then select **Mozilla Firefox**.

d. From a File Explorer list, right-click any file with an `.htm` or `.html` extension and choose **Open with > Choose default program**. Then select **Firefox** from the list that appears.

5. Which of the following techniques can you use to install Windows Store Packaged apps? (Choose all that apply.)

   a. Download and install from the Windows Store.

   b. Use the Control Panel Programs and Features applet.

   c. Appload using Group Policies.

   d. Sideload using Group Policies.

6. Which of the following is **not** a distinguishing characteristic of Windows Store apps?

   a. Runs full screen with multiple views

   b. Uses active icons to display content

   c. Enables touch screen and pen input

   d. Shares content with other apps

7. How does Windows notify you that updates are available for your Windows Store apps currently installed?

   a. Notification icon in the system tray

   b. Pop-up balloon from the notification area

   c. A number is displayed on the Windows Store tile

   d. Notice in the Windows Action Center

8. Your organization has several hundred Windows 8.1 Enterprise clients deployed in your Active Directory domain, and management would like to control which Windows Store apps users are allowed to run. What is the best tool to use?

a. Local Security Policy
b. Group Policies
c. Software Restriction policies
d. AppLocker rules
e. Windows firewall

9. Which of the following are types of rules you might configure in Software Restriction Policies? (Choose all that apply.)
   a. Certificate Rule
   b. Operating System Version Rule
   c. Hash Rule
   d. Internet Zone Rule
   e. Path Rule

10. Which of the following represent improvements that can be obtained through use of AppLocker rather than Software Restriction Policies? (Choose two.)
    a. You can specify any of Disallowed, Basic User, and Unrestricted rule settings.
    b. You can gather advanced data on software usage by implementing audit-only mode.
    c. You can lock down applications on a domain basis using Group Policy.
    d. You can create multiple rules at the same time with the help of a wizard.

11. With which editions of Windows 8.1 can you use AppLocker to specify the applications users are permitted to run? (Choose all that apply.)
    a. Windows 8.1
    b. Windows 8.1 Pro
    c. Windows RT 8.1
    d. Windows 8.1 Enterprise

12. You are using AppLocker to set restrictions on the Windows Store apps that users are allowed to install and use. What type of rule will you create?
    a. Publisher rule
    b. Path rule
    c. File Hash rule
    d. Registry rule

Foundation Topics

Installing and Configuring Desktop Applications

As noted in Chapter 1, "Introducing Windows 8.1," when you move to a new operating system, you should look at software compatibility while you are in the planning, development, and testing phases of the new operating system. Windows 8.1 is no different in this matter. Many applications that were originally developed for Windows XP, Vista, or 7 might not run properly on Windows 8.1; antivirus applications developed for older Windows operating systems in particular are often incompatible.

Configuring Application Compatibility Mode

As in previous Windows versions, Windows 8.1 provides the Application Compatibility mode that assists you in troubleshooting applications that do not run properly in Windows 8.1. In general, applications originally written for Windows Vista or Windows 7 should work in Windows 8.1. Applications written for Windows XP or older might not run properly, stop responding (hang), or refuse to start at all. If these applications worked properly in previous Windows versions, this might indicate a compatibility issue with Windows 8.1. Application Compatibility mode emulates the environment found on versions of Windows as far back as Windows 95 and Windows XP. This mode also provides several other options that might enable a program to run. Use the following procedure to configure Application Compatibility mode:

Step 1. Right-click the desktop shortcut to the program and choose **Properties**.

Step 2. Select the **Compatibility** tab to display the options listed in Table 5-2 and shown in Figure 5-1.

Table 5-2 Application Compatibility Options

Option	Description
Run compatibility troubleshooter	Starts a troubleshooting routine that attempts to discern the cause of compatibility problems. You will be presented with options to try a set of recommended compatibility settings or troubleshoot the program further based on problems suggested in Figure 5-2.
Run this program in compatibility mode for	Enables you to select the Windows version from the drop-down list that you know the program works properly on.
Reduced color mode	Uses a limited set of colors to run the program. Some older programs are designed to run in this color space.

Option	Description
Run in 640 × 480 screen resolution	Runs this program in a smaller window. Try this option if the graphical user interface (GUI) appears jagged or is rendered poorly.
Disable display scaling on high DPI settings	Shuts off automatic font resizing if you are using large-scale font sizes. Try this option if large-scale fonts interfere with the program's appearance.
Enable this program to work with OneDrive files	Select this option if the program is unable to open files on OneDrive. Note that a delay might occur if you are working with large files.
Run this program as an administrator	Indicates that some programs require administrator mode to execute properly. You will receive a User Account Control (UAC) prompt when this option is selected. This option is not available to nonadministrative users.
Change settings for all users	Enables you to choose settings that will apply to all users on the computer.

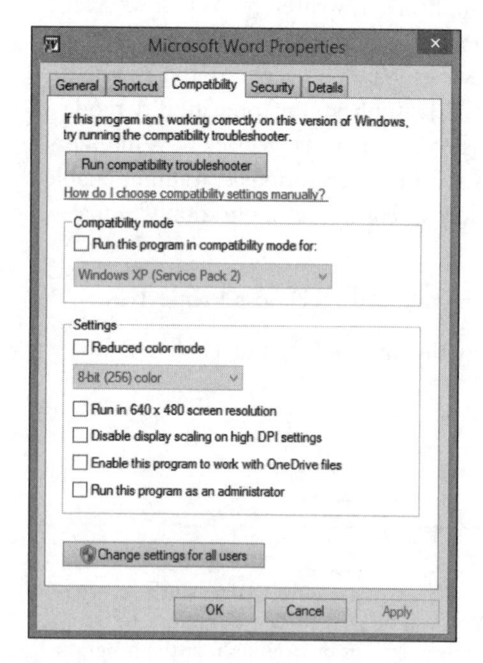

Figure 5-1 The Compatibility tab of an application's Properties dialog box.

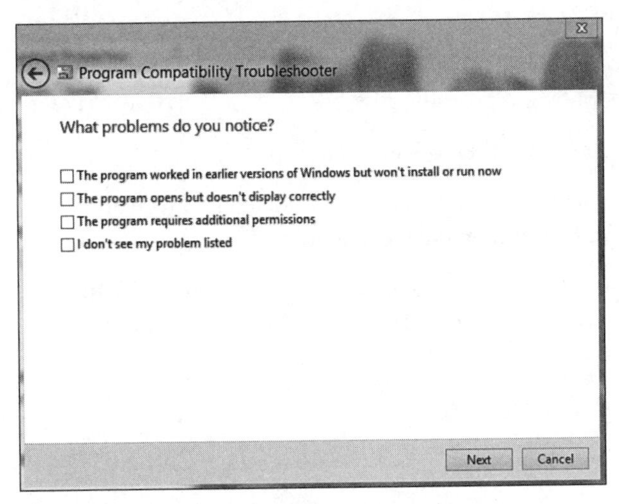

Figure 5-2 The Program Compatibility Troubleshooter enables you to choose from several possible compatibility problems.

Step 3. Select one or more of these options and then click **Apply**.

Step 4. Test the program to see if it works properly. If necessary, repeat steps 3 and 4 until the program does work properly.

> **CAUTION** You should not use the Program Compatibility options with older antivirus programs, disk utilities, or system programs. Such programs might cause data loss or create a security risk.

Using the Application Compatibility Toolkit (ACT)

ACT is a Microsoft resource that helps administrators identify the compatibility of their applications with Windows 8.1, thereby helping organizations to produce a comprehensive software inventory. It also identifies which applications might require additional testing or the use of a shim, which is a minor system compatibility fix that assists in enabling older applications to work properly with Windows 8.1. You can also test the compatibility of Web applications and websites with new releases and security updates to Internet Explorer. ACT 6.0 is included with the Windows Assessment and Deployment Kit (ADK), which you can download from http://www.microsoft.com/en-us/download/details.aspx?id=39982. If you installed the ADK as described in

Chapter 2, "Installing Windows 8.1," using the defaults as previously shown in Figure 2-11, you will need to return to the installation wizard to complete the installation and configuration of ACT. Use the following procedure:

Step 1. In the Search charm, type `adk` and then select `adksetup.exe`.

Step 2. You are informed that the features installed are up-to-date and given additional options. Click **Change** and then click **Continue**.

Step 3. From the Select the features you want to change dialog box, select **Application Compatibility Toolkit (ACT)** and **Microsoft SQL Server 2012 Express**; then click **Change**.

Step 4. If you receive a UAC prompt, click **Yes**.

Step 5. Wait while installation of ACT takes place. Click **Close** when finished.

After you install the ACT, you can access the Compatibility Administrator by typing `compatibility administrator` into the Search charm and selecting this item from the list that appears. As shown in Figure 5-3, the Compatibility Administrator comes loaded with fixes and settings for hundreds of applications that Microsoft has tested. You can apply compatibility fixes and compatibility modes to any application and then save the information you've configured to an SQL database, either on a computer running SQL server or by using SQL Express on a Windows 7, 8, or 8.1 machine. You can set up this database by using the ACT Configuration Wizard (see Figure 5-4), which is a component of the Application Compatibility Manager included with ACT.

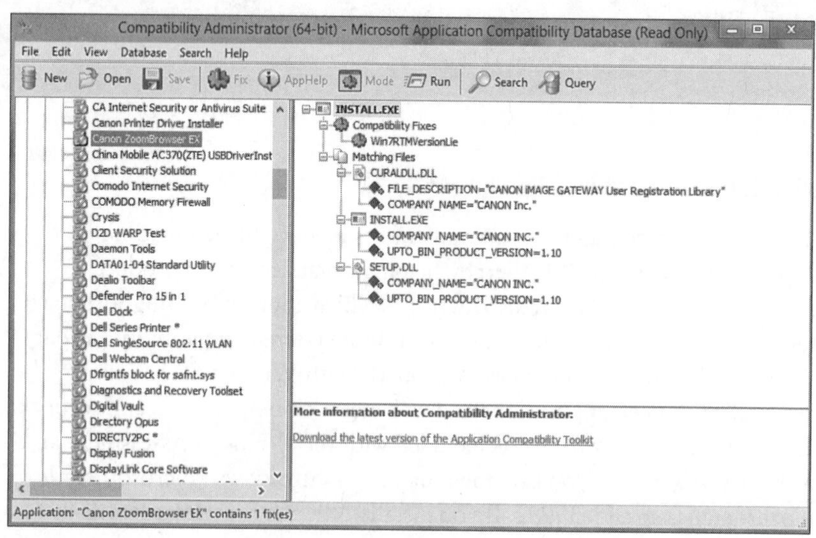

Figure 5-3 The Compatibility Administrator helps you to configure the compatibility of hundreds of applications originally written for older Windows versions.

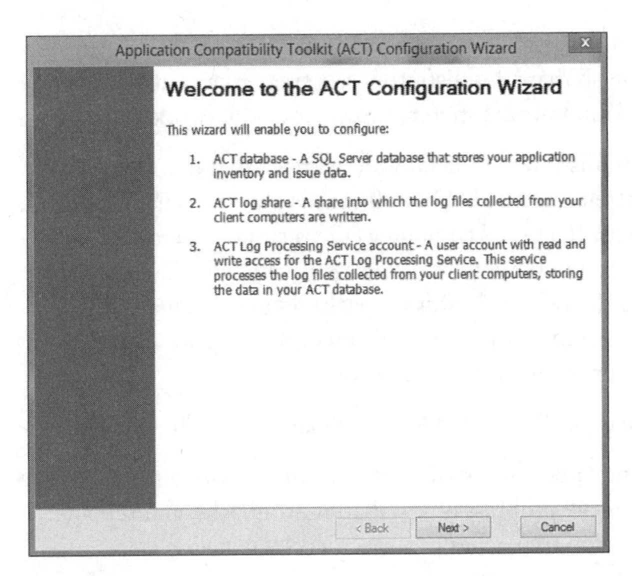

Figure 5-4 You can use the ACT Configuration Wizard to set up an SQL database and share for holding the compatibility data you've obtained.

Details in the usage and configuration of ACT are beyond the scope of the 70-687 exam and are not included here. You can obtain comprehensive information on use of the ACT from the ACT Deployment Guide, which you can download from the same page from which you download ACT itself.

NOTE You can also obtain information on ACT from "Application Compatibility Toolkit (ACT) Technical Reference" at http://technet.microsoft.com/en-us/library/hh825181.aspx and "Windows Assessment and Deployment Kit (Windows ADK)" at http://msdn.microsoft.com/en-us/library/hh825420.aspx, and links contained within these documents. For more information on installing ADK, refer to "Installing the Windows ADK" at http://msdn.microsoft.com/en-us/library/hh825494.aspx.

Using Windows Installer

Windows Installer is an application installer and configuration service that Microsoft has provided with Windows versions dating back to Windows XP and Windows Server 2003. It enables you to install, configure, update, and patch applications efficiently, thereby reducing total cost of ownership (TCO). Currently in version 5.0, Windows Installer running on a Windows 8.1 or Windows Server 2012 R2 computer supports the installation of applications on all versions of Windows, including approved apps on Windows RT 8.1. Windows Installer offers a method of installing applications in a consistent manner. Using this method, a manufacturer can provide a way to package an application so that administrators can create scripted packages and deploy the application to Windows computers throughout a network.

Windows Installer enables administrators to deploy software so that it is always available to users and repairs itself if needed. The software is always available to a user, regardless of what happens. If a user's computer fails, a support person needs only to provide a replacement computer with Windows 8.1 installed. The user starts the computer and logs on, and the required software packages are automatically installed. Should necessary files become corrupted or deleted, they are automatically reinstalled the next time the user requires the application.

Recent improvements in the functionality of Windows Installer include the following:

- Windows Installer 3.0 and later can install multiple patches with a single transaction that integrates the progress of installation, rollbacks, and reboots. This includes that application of patches in a specified sequence.
- Windows Installer 4.5 and later can use transaction processing in installing multiple packages. In other words, if the entire installation cannot complete successfully or is canceled by the user, Windows Installer rolls back changes and restores the computer to its original status. This ensures that all packages in a multipackage transaction are installed or none of them are installed.
- Windows Installer 5.0 can enumerate all components installed on the computer. In addition, packages can be used to customize the services on a computer. Developers can modify packages for installing an application according to per-user or per-computer scenarios.
- Windows Installer 5.0 enables administrators to author packages to secure new accounts, Windows services, files, folders, and Registry keys. You can use a security descriptor that specifies permissions denial or inheritance from a parent source, or specifies permissions of a new account.

Windows Installer uses the following file types:

- Application installation files use the `.msi` file extension. These are the basic files that install all programs.
- Transform files use the `.mst` extension. These files are created to "transform," or script, the way the installation takes place.
- Patch files use the `.msp` extension. These files apply hotfixes or other patches that correct bugs or security problems with the associated application.

In an Active Directory Domain Services (AD DS) environment, Windows Installer takes advantage of Group Policy Objects (GPOs) for deployment purposes. You can use a GPO to deploy applications in any of the following ways:

- **Publish a package to users:** Provides users who receive this GPO the ability to install the application through the Control Panel Programs applet. The application will also be installed when the user attempts to open a file whose extension is associated with the application.
- **Assign a package to users:** Automatically provides the application within the Start screen of any computer that the user logs on to. The application installs on the activation of the icon in the Start screen or when the user attempts to open a file whose extension is associated with the application.
- **Assign a package to computers:** Installs the application automatically upon startup.

> **CAUTION** Never assign a Windows Installer Application to both a user and a computer. If you do so, and the two GPOs use different transforms, the operating system will install and uninstall the application every time it is accessed.

When you right-click any `.msi` file, you receive the options shown in Figure 5-5 pertaining to file installation actions:

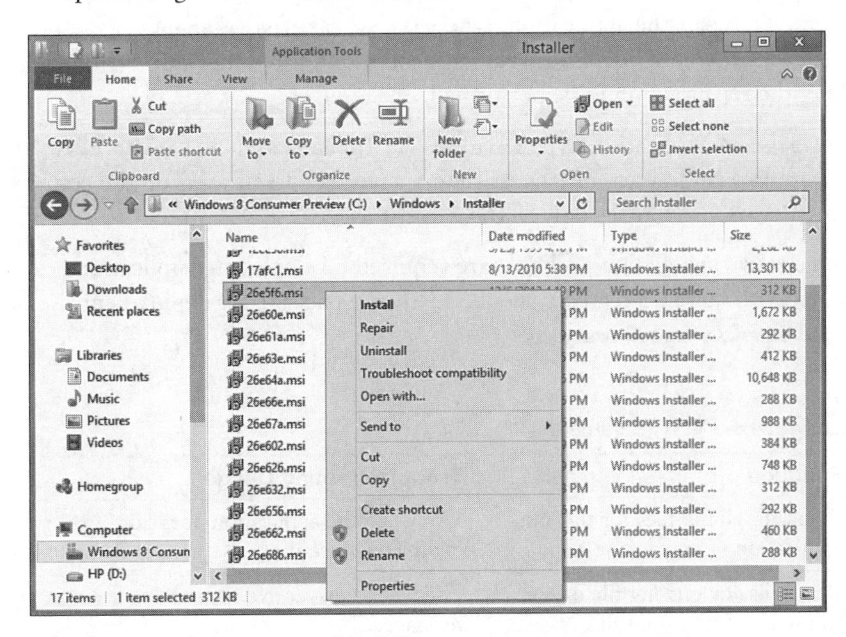

Figure 5-5 Besides the usual Windows context menu options, Windows Installer files include several options pertaining to application installation actions.

- **Install:** The default; installs the application using default parameters.
- **Repair:** Attempts to repair an unsuccessful installation. Use this option when you've had a problem.
- **Uninstall:** Enables you to remove the application, especially when the application installs improperly.
- **Troubleshoot Compatibility:** Starts a wizard that enables you to test program compatibility settings before installing the program.

From the command line, you can use the `Msiexec.exe` file along with the `.msi` package name to install, uninstall, or repair the package, as well as to advertise or create an installation package. (Advertising a program does not install it on a computer; it makes the application available for the user to install.) You can use any of the following actions with `Msiexec.exe` from a command prompt:

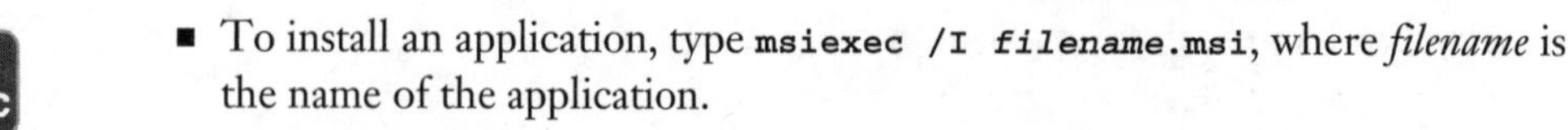

- To install an application, type **`msiexec /I`** ***`filename.msi`***, where *filename* is the name of the application.
- To remove an application, type **`msiexec /X`** ***`filename.msi`***.
- The repair parameters can assist when troubleshooting a Windows Installer problem. To repair the application, type **`msiexec /F`** ***`[parameter]`*** ***`filename.msi`***, where [*parameter*] refers to an option listed in Table 5-3 describing the repair action to be performed.
- To advertise an application, type **`msiexec /J`** ***`[parameter]`*** ***`filename.msi`***. There are two parameters for advertising: `m` advertises to all users on the computer, whereas `u` advertises only to the current user.
- Administrative installation packages are required for deploying applications from network shares. To create an administrative package for deployment, type **`msiexec /A`** ***`filename.msi`***.

Table 5-3 `Msiexec.exe` Repair Parameters

Parameter	Function	Troubleshooting Usage
`a`	Reinstalls all the files for the application	Use when the application does not completely install.
`c`	Reinstalls any missing file or one whose checksum is invalid	Use when you receive file missing error messages.
`d`	Reinstalls any missing file or an invalid version of a file	Use after installing a different application that overwrites shared files and you receive errors or experience problems.

Parameter	Function	Troubleshooting Usage
e	Reinstalls any missing file, or an equal or older version of a file	Use when you have rolled back another application's installation and then you receive error messages.
m	Rewrites the Registry entries of the applications that are attached to the computer (HKEY_LOCAL_MACHINE)	Use when the application displays the same error for all users who use the computer.
o	Reinstalls any missing file or an older version of a file	Use when you have rolled back another application's installation and then you receive error messages.
p	Reinstalls any missing file	Use when the application does not finish copying files.
s	Re-creates application shortcuts	Use when you use a Start screen or desktop icon and the application does not open, but you can run the application from the command line or Run dialog box.
u	Rewrites the Registry entries of the applications that are attached to the user (HKEY_USERS or HKEY_CURRENT_USER)	Use when the application works for one user but does not work for another, even though they are using the same computer.
v	Caches a package locally (overwriting any existing cached package) and then runs the application from the source	Use when you install from a network location that is connected by a slow or unpredictable network link, or when the application has failed during the file copy process.

NOTE For additional parameters used with `Msiexec.exe`, open a command prompt and type **`msiexec /?`**. Also refer to "Msiexec" at http://technet.microsoft.com/en-us/library/bb490936.aspx.

The Windows Installer service runs on each computer, and depends on the Remote Procedure Call (RPC) service. The Windows Installer service, by default, does not start up automatically when you boot up Windows 8.1. Instead, it starts up whenever an `.msi` package is run. The service works in conjunction with the `Msiexec.exe` executable file, which interprets the information in the `.msi` file.

NOTE You can use `Msiexec.exe` to repair `.msi` packages. If you have trouble with an `.msi` package, you can run the `Msiexec.exe` file from the command line to repair the package. You can also use `Msiexec.exe` to control the installation process through its optional command-line switches, whether you run it from the command line or use it in a script.

Before Windows Installer standards were published for use by third-party manufacturers, each manufacturer developed a proprietary method of installation. These methods used different installation executables and assorted parameters, and had varying degrees of scripting capabilities. A few companies developed software that could create a standard installation package, but they did not manage problems with files overwriting newer versions of the same file (the old DLL nightmare), and most had no method for rolling back versions and did not provide a granular deployment method.

Windows Installer uses a standard set of installation rules. Compliant applications must handle versioning rules to prevent overwriting newer files, maintain a record of any changes made to Windows—both file changes and Registry keys—and be capable of functioning with the `Msiexec.exe` file and Windows Installer service.

The `.msi` file acts as a relational database in which the fields in the file contain the instructions that can effectively deploy an application. When an installation begins, the Windows Installer service and `Msiexec.exe` cooperatively convert the `.msi` data into an installation/uninstallation script.

A management application programming interface (API) is part of Windows Installer. This API tracks the installed applications, noting which features and components are selected and the path chosen by the installer. The API is able to determine which component is not functioning properly and is able to selectively reinstall the component, which avoids having to reinstall the entire application.

You can customize how an application is installed by creating a transform file, which has the extension `.mst`. The transform file answers the questions that the installation process asks, such as the path for the application, the component selection, and other configuration options.

NOTE For more information on Windows Installer, refer to "Windows Installer" at http://msdn.microsoft.com/en-us/library/cc185688%28v=VS.85%29.aspx and links found in this document.

Configuring File Associations and Default Program Settings

By default, when you open a file with a known extension, Windows opens this file with an application known as the default program. For example, Windows opens image files with the new Windows 8.1 Photos app by default. If you have more than one image viewer program installed on your computer such as Irfan View, Breeze Browser, Adobe Bridge, or others, you can choose which program opens the image by default when you double-click an image file with a given extension such as `.jpg` or `.tif`. Windows stores information in the Registry for all file types for which a default association has been defined or for which you have created a default program setting.

Modifying Default Program Settings

To modify default program settings or create new settings, use the following steps:

Step 1. Open Control Panel from the Settings charm or from the Start button right-click menu and choose the **Programs** category.

Step 2. Click **Default Programs** to obtain the options shown in Figure 5-6.

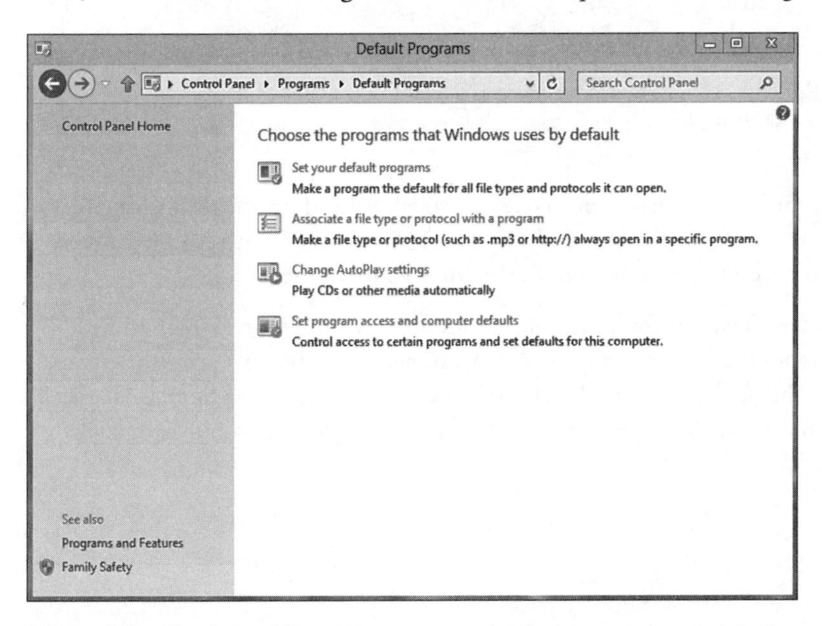

Figure 5-6 The Control Panel Programs applet enables you to set default programs or associate file types with the desired program.

Step 3. Click **Set your default programs**, and in the Set your default programs window, select the program whose options you want to configure. You receive the options shown in Figure 5-7.

Key Topic

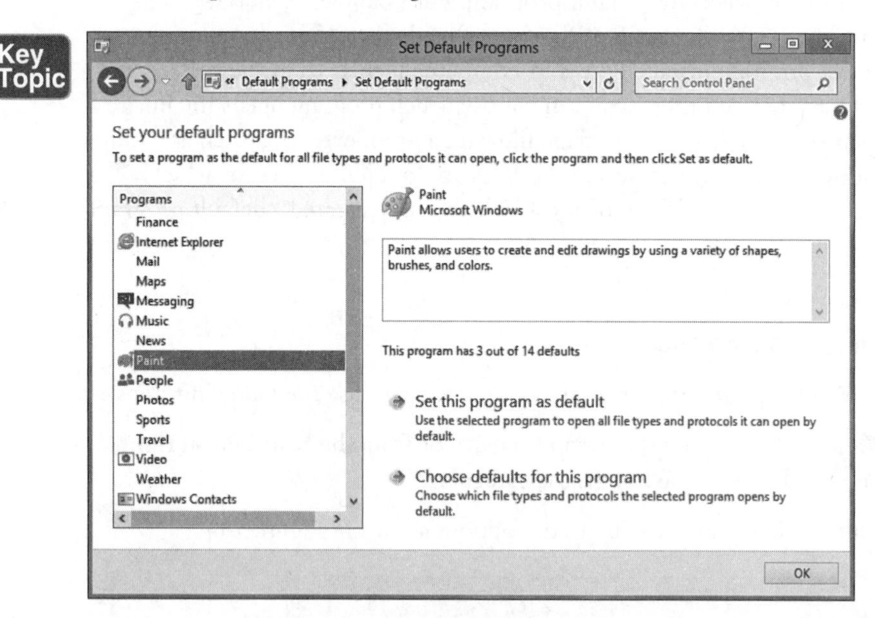

Figure 5-7 The Set your default programs window enables you to select a program that will act as the default for all file types and protocols that it can open.

Step 4. To use the selected program to open all file types and protocols it is capable of opening, click **Set this program as default**. To select from a list of file types and protocols, click **Choose defaults for this program**.

Step 5. The Set associations for a program window shown in Figure 5-8 provides a list of file types the chosen program can open. Select the file extensions you want to have the program open. To choose all file types, select the **Select All** check box. To remove file types, deselect their check boxes. When finished, click **Save**.

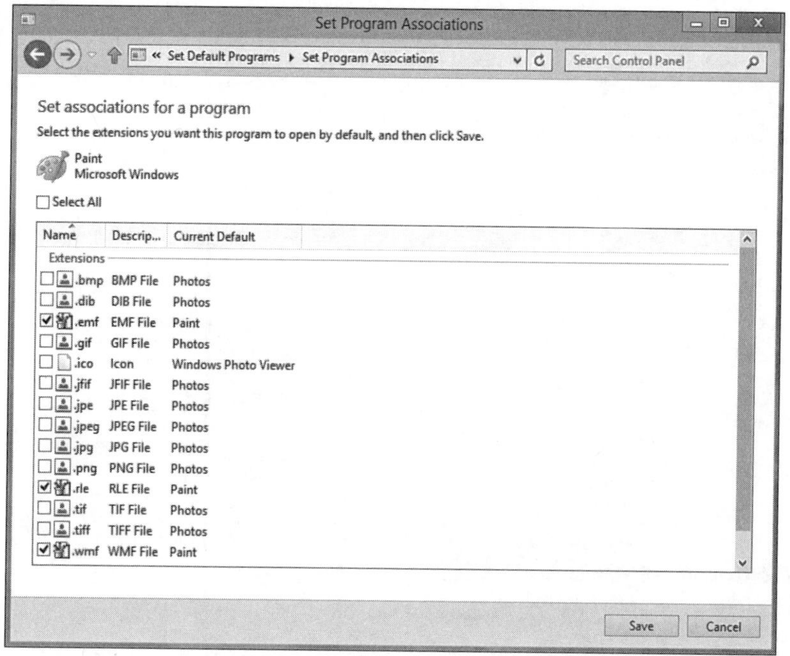

Figure 5-8 Selecting a program as the default for its file types.

Step 6. You are returned the Set your default programs window. If desired, select another program to modify its file associations. When finished, click **OK** to return to the Default Programs applet.

Associating File Extensions with Specific Programs

The Default Programs applet also lets you associate a file extension with a program. Use the following steps:

Step 1. From the Default Programs applet, click **Associate a file type or protocol with a program**. You receive the Associate a file type or protocol with a specific program window shown in Figure 5-9.

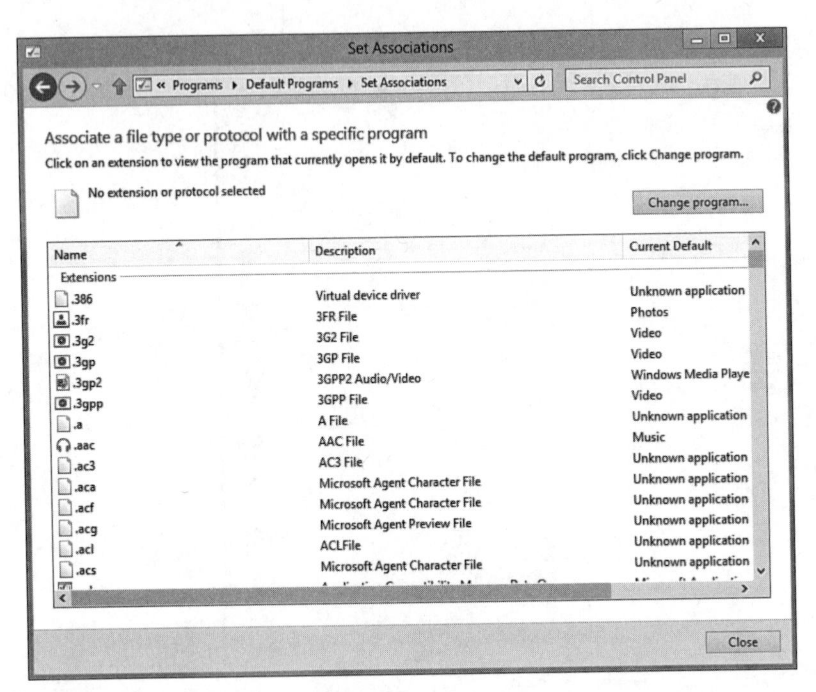

Figure 5-9 The Associate a file type or protocol with a specific program window enables you to choose the default program to be used with a file using a given extension.

Step 2. Scroll this list and select the extension whose default program you want to modify, for example, `.xls`. Then click **Change program**. You receive the option shown in Figure 5-10.

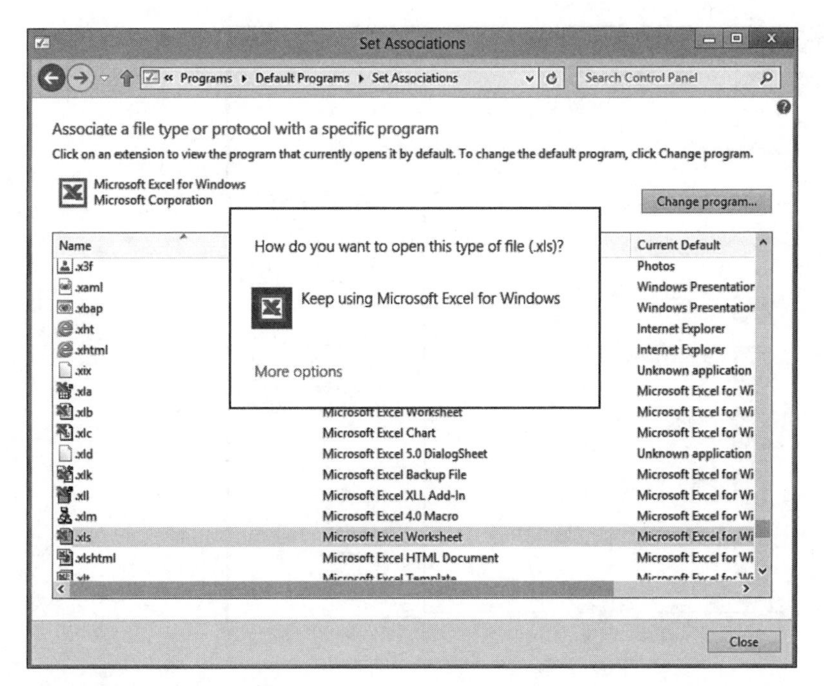

Figure 5-10 You are informed what the current default program is and given the option to change this default.

Step 3. If you want to change the default program, click **More options** to expand the list of available programs, as shown in Figure 5-11.

Key Topic

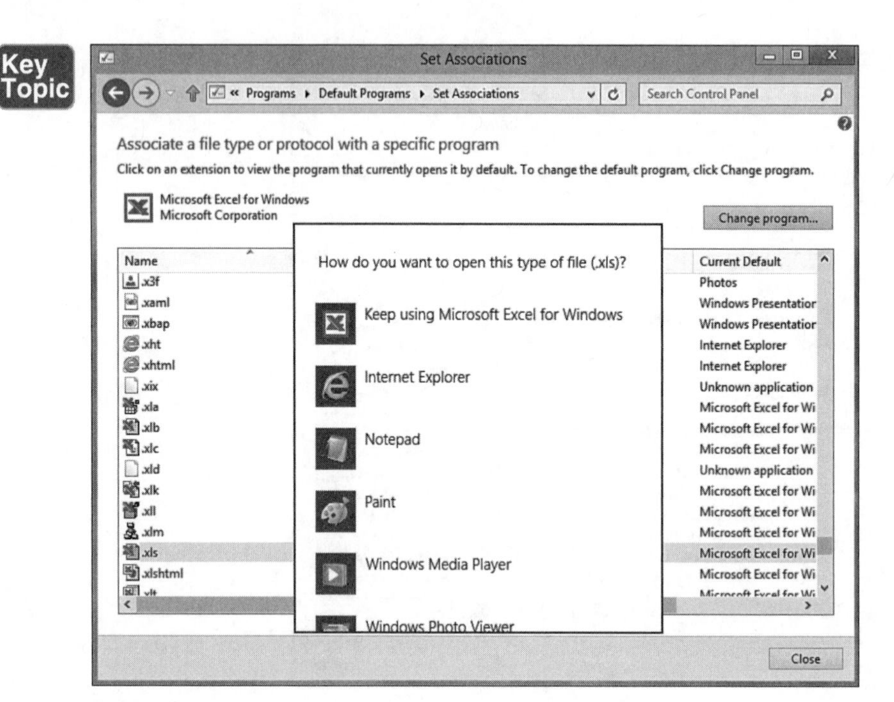

Figure 5-11 You are provided with a list of programs that are capable of opening a file with the given extension.

Step 4. Select the desired program. The list updates to reflect the change you've made.

Step 5. Repeat for any other extensions you want to modify. When finished, click **Close** to return to the Default Programs applet.

If Windows cannot associate the selected file extension with a program, you are given the option of trying an app on the computer or locating one from the Windows Store. Selecting an app on the computer brings up a list similar to that shown in Figure 5-11. Select a program you think might be able to open the file extension.

NOTE You can also modify a file association from any File Explorer window. Right-click a file with the extension you want to modify and choose **Open with**. You receive a dialog box similar to that shown in Figure 5-11, which enables you to accept the current default or choose a new one.

CAUTION It is possible that the selected application will be unable to open a file with the extension you have selected. If you receive an error message when attempting to open such a file, return to the Set Associations window, click **Change program** again, and either select another program on the computer or attempt to locate one online.

Setting Default Program Access Options

From the Default Programs applet, select **Set program access and computer defaults** to display the Set Program Access and Computer Defaults dialog box, which offers a choice between Microsoft Windows, Non-Microsoft, or Custom. Choose one of these configurations and expand it by clicking the double V at the right end of the chosen configuration; for example, if you select **Custom**, you receive the following options shown in Figure 5-12. For each option, this dialog box displays all applications of each type that it finds on your computer, enabling you to select which program should be used by default. Note that the options you see in Figure 5-12 depend on what programs are available on the computer; for example, in the Web browser section, you see only the browsers that are actually installed (Firefox appears only if installed on the computer; any other browsers such as Google Chrome might appear if you've installed them).

- Choose a default Web browser
- Choose a default e-mail program
- Choose a default media player
- Choose a default instant messaging program
- Choose a default virtual machine for Java

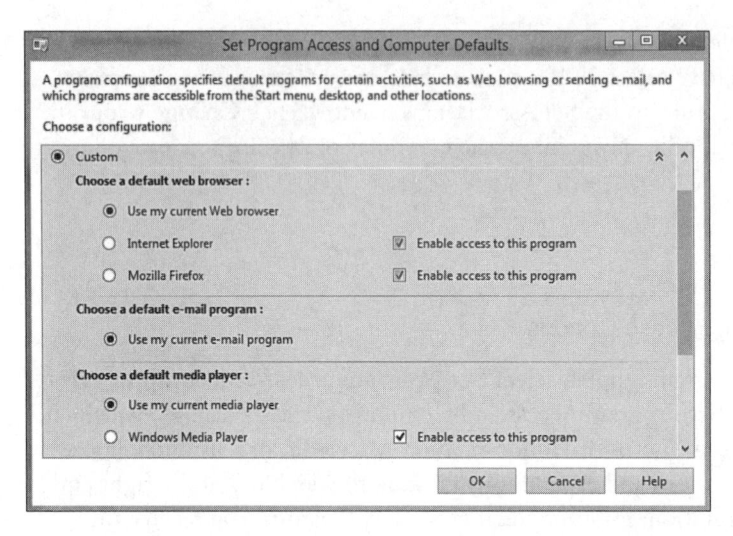

Figure 5-12 The Set Program Access and Computer Defaults dialog box enables you to set up a configuration of default programs for certain activities.

Managing App-V Applications

In recent years, as workers have become more mobile and require access to their files and applications anywhere at any time, Microsoft has developed technologies to help make mobility easier for workers and the IT professionals who support them. Virtualization technologies and cloud computing are part of this mobility evolution. Microsoft Application Virtualization (App-V) is Microsoft's application virtualization and streaming solution.

App-V enables centralized management of application management and deployment. User applications and their application settings are maintained centrally and managed using Active Directory and Group Policies. Only the App-V client is required on local Windows platforms, allowing users to access their applications from any organization client over the network, or when offline if the application has been run previously from that client computer. The application is never installed locally.

Overview of App-V

With App-V 5.0, virtual applications work more like traditional, locally installed applications. Applications are isolated as in older versions, but now separate App-V applications can be enabled to communicate with each other, allowing integrations between them when required.

To take advantage of centralized management and distribution of App-V applications, Windows Configuration Manager 2012 or App-V v5.0 server is required. The App-V client is configured to connect to the server to stream the content or, optionally, download to a local drive. Note that App-V applications can run without a centrally managed infrastructure. The applications still run in isolation and are not installed locally, but applications cannot be updated and per-user authorization is not possible.

Application Virtualization, and virtualization in general, is a complex and involved topic, with its own field of study. For the 70-687 exam, you need not be an expert in virtualization technologies, but you should be able to identify App-V as a concept and know some basics of working with the App-V client on Windows 8.1.

The App-V client is distributed as part of the Microsoft Desktop Optimization Pack (MDOP). To install the App-V 5.0 client, you need the following required software:

- Microsoft Windows .NET Framework 4 (full package)
- Windows PowerShell 3.0 or later
- Microsoft Visual C++ 2010 Redistributable (included with App-V 5.0 installer)
- The App-V Sequencer client (may be needed to manage App-V packages)

NOTE For more information on deploying the App-V client, refer to "Planning for the App-V 5.0 Sequencer and Client Deployment" at http://technet.microsoft.com/en-us/library/jj713431.aspx and links found in the document.

NOTE Managing and maintaining an enterprise App-V infrastructure is out of the scope of exam 70-687 and this book. The material is covered in depth in exam 70-243, "Administering and Deploying System Center 2012 Configuration Manager," and in the Virtualization Administrator courses.

You can manage the App-V client and configuration from the client computer using the client management console, using PowerShell, or using Group Policy.

The App-V Management Console

The App-V client provides a management application that can be used to perform some basic tasks for the App-V applications published for the user. Start the App-V client by clicking on the **Search** charm, typing `App-V` in the search box, and then clicking on the **Microsoft Application Virtualization Client** link in the Apps tile. From this screen (see Figure 5-13), you can work with the available App-V applications and App Connection Groups.

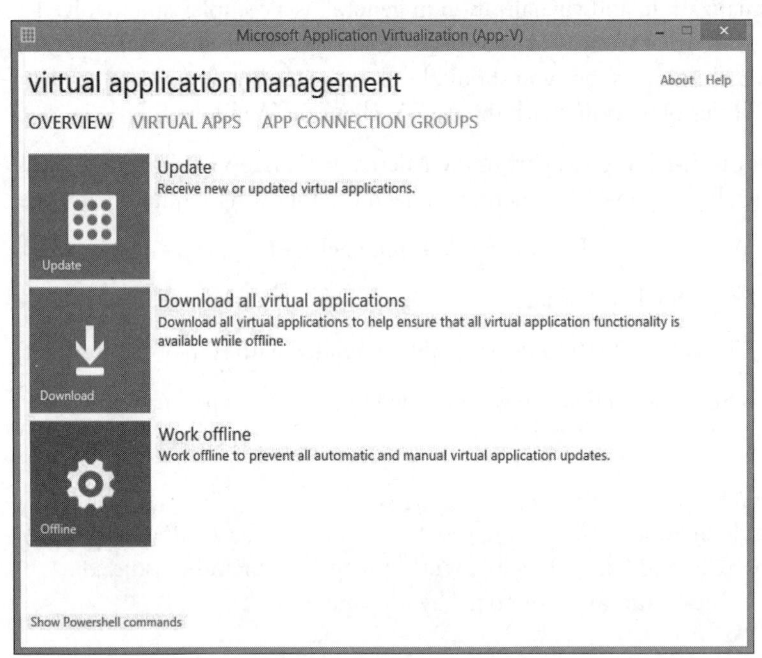

Figure 5-13 Manage App-V applications from the App-V client management console.

The App-V client management console has the features described next.

Overview Tab

The Update tile is used to refresh a App-V application or receive a new package.

Use the Download tile to download all the packages published to the user.

Offline is used to disable all automatic and manual updates of App-V applications.

Virtual Apps Tab

The Virtual Apps tab displays all the packages published to the user. You can select a package from the list to view the included applications and display information about package use and how much of the package that has been downloaded to the computer. You can also use the Repair function to repair a misbehaving App-V package, but note that this will delete any user settings for that package.

App Connection Groups

Clicking on the App Connection Groups tab displays all the connection groups available. Recall that a Connection Group is used to allow communication and integration between virtual applications. Select a group to view which packages are included.

App-V Command-Line Utilities

With App-V 5.0, Microsoft has provided a suite of PowerShell scripts for managing applications, packaging updates, and performing other tasks. These scripts require PowerShell version 3.0 or later. PowerShell version 3.0 was included with Windows 8, and PowerShell version 4.0 was included with Windows 8.1. Note the link at the bottom of the App-V management console screen from Figure 5-13 called Show Powershell commands. Clicking on the link displays the available commands available for managing App-V applications on the client. Table 5-4 describes each command and how it is used.

The `[path]` parameter in these commands refers to the location of the App-V package. Typically, this is an HTTP URL such as http://appv-server/apps/MyApplication.appv. However, the path could also be the name of a file on a file share or even the local computer.

Table 5-4 PowerShell commands for managing App-V clients

Command	Purpose
`Get-AppvClientPackage`	Returns a list of all App-V packages currently on the system. The following switch parameters are available to filter the results: `-Name`, `-Version`, `-PackageId`, and `-VersionId`.
`Mount-AppvClientPackage`	Downloads all packages published for the user.
`Set-AppvPublishServer`	Allows you to enable or disable automatic and manual updates of App-V applications.
`Mount-AppvClientConnectionGroup`	Enables you to download and/or repair Application Connection Groups available to the user.

Command	Purpose
`Get-AppvPublishingServer`	Displays the current path(s) or URL(s) used for locating and downloading App-V applications. Returns the descriptive location name and a numeric `ServerId` for each publishing server.
`Add-AppvPublishingServer`	Adds a new publishing location for App-V applications. The following parameters are required: `-Name LocationName -URL` path or url.
`Sync-AppvPublishingServer`	Checks the server and adds or removes packages and connection groups based on entitlements for the user. The parameter `-ServerId` can be used to select a specific server to sync.

NOTE For more details about these commands, open a PowerShell version 3.0 prompt from a Windows computer with App-V 5.0 client installed, and type **`Get-Help`** followed by the name of the command. See Figure 5-14 for an example.

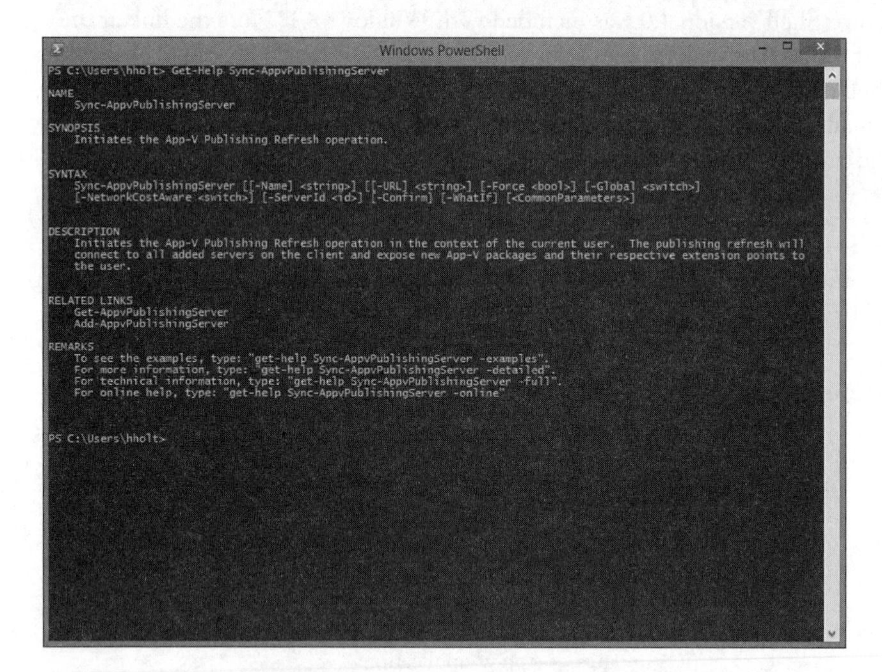

Figure 5-14 Windows PowerShell has a comprehensive help system for all commands invoked using the `Get-Help` cmdlet.

Using Windows Store Applications

The new Windows Store is an online app store integrated with Windows 8.1 that enables users to quickly and easily buy and download small applications that may be developed by Microsoft, software vendors, or even independent developers. After users create an account in the Windows Store, they can easily shop and click to add functionality to their Windows computer.

This capability can be fun and convenient for users, but in a large organization with limited IT resources, it can quickly cause problems for management, network administrators, and support personnel. Windows provides some tools for assisting IT administrators take control of the use of Windows Store, the ability to download and run applications, and the management of applications that are authorized by the organization.

Introduction to Windows Store Apps

Windows Store apps are not like typical Windows desktop applications. They are a new type of app designed for ease of use, new interfaces, and a focus on content. Apps can be designed for consumer use or for line of business (LOB) functionality. Typically, apps have certain unique characteristics:

- Apps display in one full-screen window and enable multiple views.
- They are designed for touch screens and pen input.
- Apps share and expose personalized content, allowing users to search for content across all their Windows Store apps.
- Apps implement new user interface (UI) controls, including the apps bar and charms.
- Apps use tiles instead of icons, and content can be delivered through a tile even when the app is not running.

The main delivery channel for apps is the Windows Store, and apps are available only by downloading them through the Windows Store app. These apps meet certain Microsoft requirements and must be certified and signed by Microsoft before they are available. However, Microsoft has provided enterprises a way to sideload unsigned apps on Windows 8.1 Enterprise edition computers that are joined to the organization's AD domain. You can also enable sideloading on other computers using a sideloading product activation key, which can be obtained with a volume license.

Installing and Updating Windows Store Apps

Working with apps from the Windows Store is designed to be easy and user-friendly. Users simply need to sign up with a Microsoft account (or use an existing account), scroll through or search for the app they want, and click on it to install. By default, users do not need any administrative or special privileges to install Windows Store apps. The following steps outline a typical process:

Step 1. From the Start screen, click on the **Store** tile.

Step 2. Scroll through the categories to look for an app, or use the Search for apps box in the upper right. For this example, scroll to the Top Free section on the far right and click the **Top free** category.

Step 3. Look for Adobe Reader Touch. You install the Windows Store Adobe Reader Touch app in this example. Click the tile when you have located it.

Step 4. The next screen displays user ratings, a description, and list of features. There are tabs for selecting the overview, details, and user reviews. Click the **Install** button to install the app.

Step 5. If you are not logged in to a Microsoft account, you are prompted to enter your Microsoft account credentials. You can also sign up for a new one by clicking on the link.

Step 6. In the upper-right corner, installation progress is displayed. You receive a notification when the installation is complete.

Step 7. Return to the Start screen to access the new app. If it is not displayed, you can use the Search charm to locate it.

> **NOTE** When you run Adobe Reader, you will notice how different it is from the Adobe Reader desktop application used in older versions of Windows. It implements all the app characteristics from the introduction section.

Updating Windows Store apps is a similar process, but even easier because you do not have to scroll or search through a large list of options and apps; only installed apps with updates are available for selection.

Step 1. Click the **Start** charm or **Start** button to access the Start screen.

Step 2. Click the **Windows Store** tile or the **Windows Store app** button in the Apps view.

NOTE You can tell if updates are available for Windows Store apps by just glancing at the Start screen. If updates are available, a number displayed in the lower-right corner of the tile indicates how many apps have available updates.

If updates are available, a link appears in the upper-right corner of the Windows Store screen, indicating updates are available and the number of updates in parentheses, similar to Figure 5-15 (note the `Updates (10)` indicator in the upper right). Click the link to see the updates available.

Figure 5-15 Indicator on the Windows Store screen notifying that updates are available for 10 Windows Store apps.

On the App updates screen, the app updates are listed, and all apps are selected by default. You can select or unselect apps by clicking on them. When you finish selecting apps, click the **Install** charm to being installing the updates.

The Installing apps screen is displayed. You can watch the installation progress or continue working on something else while they install.

Managing Windows Store Content

Windows Store makes installing apps easy and quick for end users. If you have browsed through the apps available, you may have noticed all the games and entertainment apps available. Managers in many organizations would prefer that their staff members do not have access to these kinds of distractions during the workday and often turn to IT for a solution.

We can be thankful that Microsoft has considered this issue and provided Windows system administrators with a number of ways to control access to the Windows Store and the apps available. The tools you use depend on your environment.

As noted in Table 5-5, the ability to control access to specific apps, using AppLocker policies, is available only for domain-joined computers running Windows 8.1 Enterprise. AppLocker is covered in detail later in this chapter.

Table 5-5 Options for Controlling Access to Windows Store

Requirement	Tool to Use
Turn off Windows Store to all Windows 8.1 computers	Group policies
Control which apps can be installed on Windows 8.1 Enterprise computers	AppLocker
Control which apps can be installed on Windows 8.1 Pro computers	N/A
Control which users can access the Windows Store	Group policies
Control which computers can access the Windows Store	Group policies

Controlling Windows Store Access

If you need to block access to the Windows Store, you can use Local Policies. You can lock down these policies either by disallowing users to modify Local Policies or by enforcing them with Group Policy Objects. To turn off access to the Store, you can simply block users from using Microsoft accounts (see Figure 5-16).

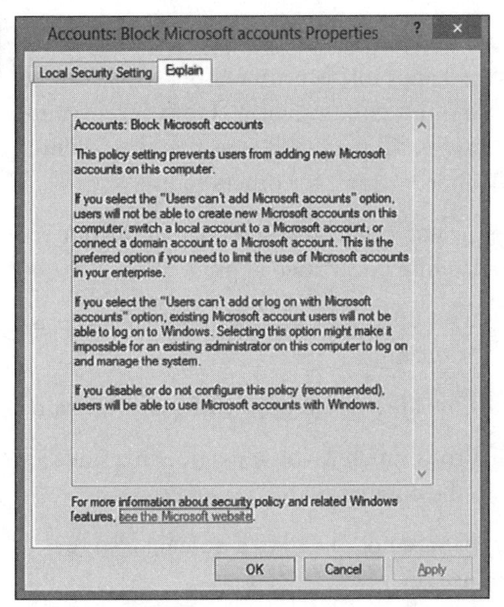

Figure 5-16 Disable access to Windows Store using the Local Security Policy to block Microsoft accounts.

Table 5-6 lists the Group Policies available for controlling access to the Windows Store.

Table 5-6 Group Policies for Windows Store

Policy Setting	Applies To	Help Text
Turn off the Store application	User or Machine	Denies or allows access to the Store application. If you enable this setting, access to the Store application is denied. Access to the Store is required for installing app updates. If you disable or do not configure this setting, access to the Store application is allowed.
Allow Store to install apps on Windows To Go workspaces	Machine	Allows or denies access to the Store application on Windows To Go workspaces. If you enable this setting, access to the Store application is allowed on the Windows To Go workspace. Enable this policy only when the Windows To Go workspace will be used only with a single PC. Using it with multiple PCs is not supported. If you disable or do not configure this setting, access to the Store application is denied on the Windows To Go workspace.
Turn off Automatic Download of updates	Machine	Enables or disables the automatic download of updates. If you enable this setting, automatic download of updates is turned off. If you disable or do not configure this setting, automatic download of updates is turned on.

Sideloading Apps

Microsoft has restricted the ability to sideload apps for security reasons. Apps can be installed only through the Windows Store in most circumstances. However, organizations may find it useful to develop their own LOB packaged apps that they do not want to have certified and loaded on the Windows Store for others to use.

If your organization has LOB apps to deploy, you can enable sideloading in your enterprise. The following is required for sideloading uncertified apps:

- Clients must be running Windows Server 2012 R2 or Windows 8.1 Enterprise and must be joined to a Windows AD domain.
- You must enable the Group Policy **Allow all trusted applications to install**.
- To sideload apps for a Windows 8.1 Pro computer, you must obtain a sideloading product key and activate it on the computer.
- Windows 8.1 Enterprise computers that are not joined to a domain also require activation of a sideloading product key.

NOTE For more information on sideloading packaged apps, refer to "Sideload Apps with DISM" at http://technet.microsoft.com/en-us/library/hh852635.aspx.

Configuring Application and Hardware Restrictions

Application restrictions enable you to limit the types of software that run on computers to which the policy applies. For individual computers running Windows 8.1 Pro or Enterprise, or those that belong to a homegroup or workgroup, you can set these policies by using the Local Security Policy tool. On an AD DS domain, you can use Group Policy to configure these policies at a site, domain, or organizational unit (OU) level.

Windows 8.1 and Windows Server 2012 R2 include two types of application restrictions: software restriction policies and application control policies.

- Software restriction policies are the same policies that were included in Windows XP/Vista/Server 2003/2008/2012/R2, and can be used to limit application installation and use on these computers, as well as Windows 7, 8, and 8.1 computers.

- Application control policies are new to Windows 7 and continued in Windows 8 and Windows 8.1 and enable you to create separate rules for Windows Installer files, executable files, and script files. The AppLocker feature, introduced with Windows 7, enables you to restrict applications according to publisher rules, which limit application execution according to the application's digital signature. This even allows you to specify which versions are permitted; for example, you could allow Microsoft Office 2007 or later, while preventing use of older versions of Office.

Configuring application restrictions provides you with the following benefits:

- **Control which programs can run on computers on your network:** You can allow only those programs that users require to do their jobs properly, and you can restrict the use of other programs such as games. You can also limit the downloading of ActiveX controls and ensure that only digitally signed scripts can be run. This also helps to prevent viruses, Trojan horses, and other malware programs from executing.
- **Control which programs users on multiuser computers can run:** When more than one user can access a computer, you can set user-specific policies that prevent users from accessing programs only needed by other users of the same computer.
- **Control whether software restriction policies apply to all users:** You can specify whether or not software restriction policies apply to administrators.
- **Prevent email attachments from executing:** If you are concerned about users receiving viruses through email, you can apply policies that restrict files with certain extensions from executing.

Setting Software Restriction Policies

Local Security Policy and Group Policy both enable you to set software restriction policies and application control policies. You can choose to set policies according to security levels, and you can also configure additional rules. Security Level rules enable you to set a default policy and create exceptions. You can choose from the following security levels:

- **Disallowed:** Does not allow any software to run, regardless of a user's access rights. Four Registry path rules that allow system software to run are specified in the Additional Rules folder, preventing users from being completely locked out of the computer.

- **Basic User:** Enables the user to run applications as a normal user only. This privilege level was introduced in Windows Vista and is no longer supported on newer versions of Windows or Windows Server computers.
- **Unrestricted:** Allows software to run according to a user's access rights. This is the default policy level.

Use the following steps to configure software restriction policies at the local computer level:

Step 1. Use one of the following methods to open the Local Security Policy snap-in:

- If you have placed a tile for Administrative Tools on the Start screen as described in Chapter 1 (refer back to Figure 1-22), click this tile and then double-click **Local Security Policy** from the Administrative Tools dialog box that appears.
- Right-click **Start**, choose **Control Panel** (or select this item from the Settings charm), and then choose **Administrative Tools**. Then double-click **Local Security Policy** from the Administrative Tools dialog box that appears.
- In the Search charm, type `local security policy` and then select this option from the list that appears.

Step 2. Right-click the **Software Restriction Policies** node and choose **New Software Restriction Policies**. This creates a default set of software restriction policies, which are displayed in the details pane as shown in Figure 5-17.

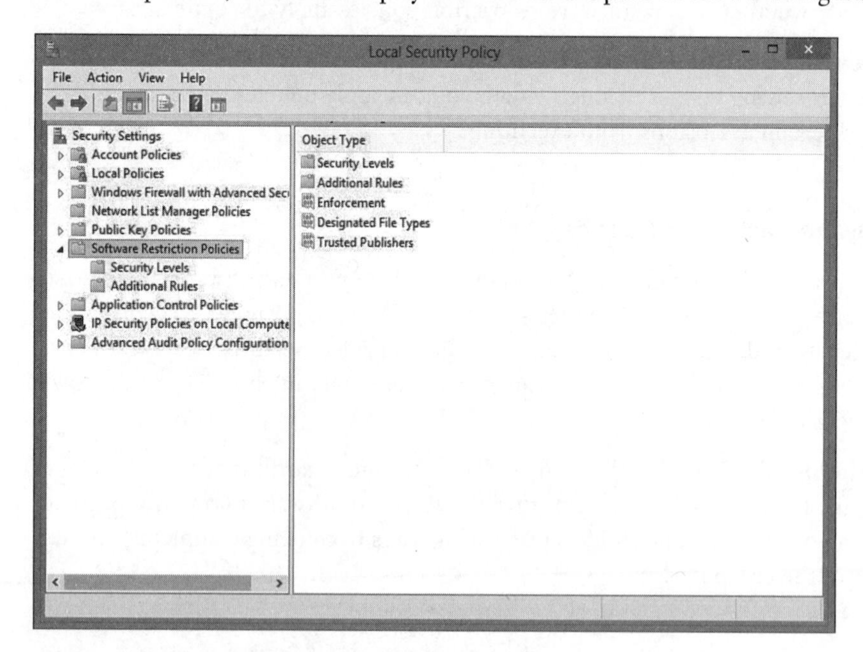

Figure 5-17 Enabling software restriction policies.

Step 3. To specify either the Basic User or Disallowed security level, right-click the desired level and choose **Set As Default**. You are warned that the default level you selected is more restricted than the current security level (see Figure 5-18). Click **Yes** to continue.

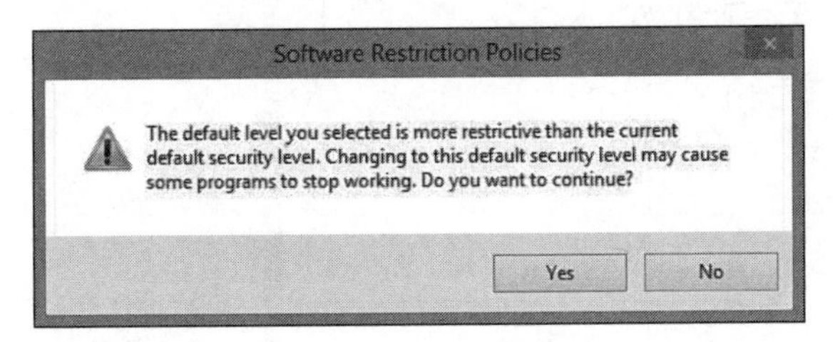

Figure 5-18 This message warns you that the chosen security level is more restricted than the current security level.

Step 4. To specify rules that govern exceptions to the security level you specified, right-click **Additional Rules** and choose one of the following four rules, as shown in Figure 5-19.

- **New Certificate Rule:** This type of rule identifies software according to its signing certificate. You can use a certificate rule to specify the source of trusted software that should be allowed to run without prompting a user.
- **New Hash Rule:** A hash is a fixed-length series of bytes that uniquely identifies an application or file. The policy uses a hash algorithm to calculate the hash of a specified program and compares this to the hash of a program that a user attempts to run, to determine whether the application or file should run.
- **New Network Zone Rule:** This type of rule identifies software according to an Internet Explorer network zone. We discuss the available zones later in this chapter. You can specify zone rules only for Windows Installer software packages.
- **New Path Rule:** This type of rule identifies software according to its local or Universal Naming Convention (UNC) file path. This rule enables you to grant access to software located in a specific folder for each user.

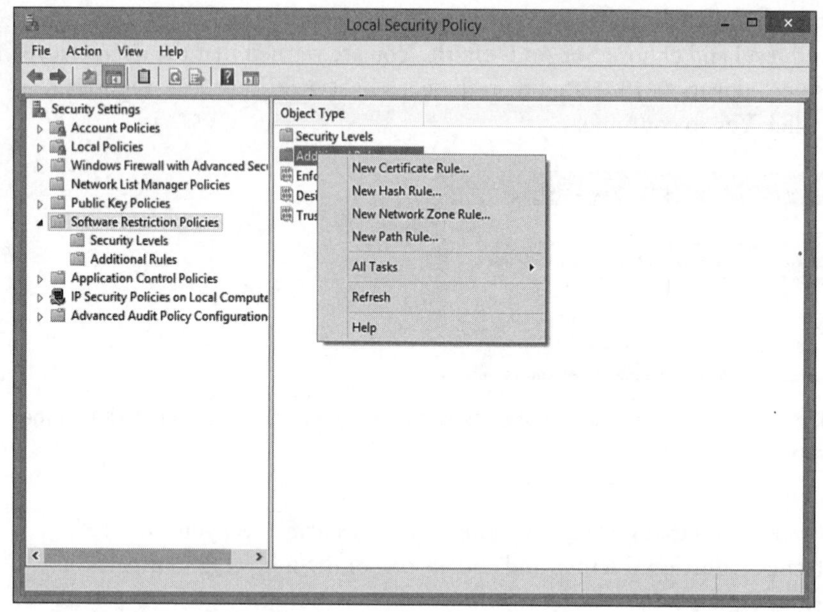

Figure 5-19 You can configure four types of new rules in the Additional Rules folder.

Step 5. For example, to specify a path rule, select **New Path Rule** to display the New Path Rule dialog box, as shown in Figure 5-20. To create an exception to the Disallowed security level, type the path to the applications that are allowed, choose **Basic User** or **Unrestricted** from the drop-down list, and then click **OK**. If you have retained the default Unrestricted security level, choose **Disallowed** from the drop-down list to disallow the specified software. You may also type an optional description. You can follow a similar procedure to designate any of the other rule types.

Figure 5-20 The New Path Rule dialog box enables you to specify the path to software defined by an additional rule.

Step 6. If required, specify rules for enforcement, designated file types, and trusted publishers by clicking **Software Restriction Policies** in the console tree to display these items in the details pane, as shown previously in Figure 5-17. The following describes the functions of these items:

- **Enforcement:** You can determine the scope of software restriction policies, as shown in Figure 5-21. This capability is useful for exempting local administrators from software restriction policies or for ignoring certificate rules.
- **Designated File Types:** This option determines what file types, in addition to standard file types such as `.exe`, are considered as executable code and subject to software restriction policies.
- **Trusted Publishers:** This option enables you to determine which users can select trusted publishers and to check for revoked certificates.

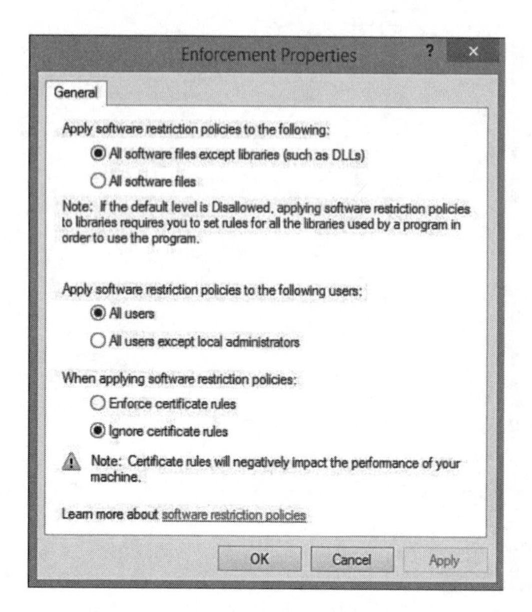

Figure 5-21 You can modify the scope of software restriction policies from the Enforcement Properties dialog box.

CAUTION Use caution when selecting the **Disallowed** security level. This security level prevents all applications from running except those you have specified using additional rules.

Application Control Policies

Introduced in Windows 7 and updated for Windows 8.1, AppLocker improves on the older Software Restriction Policies by using Application Control Policies, which include the AppLocker feature. AppLocker provides enhancements that enable you to specify exactly what users are permitted to run on their desktops according to unique file identities. You can also specify the users or groups permitted to execute these applications. Users are allowed to run the applications and scripts required for them to be productive while still providing the operational, security, and compliance benefits provided by application standardization.

Starting with Windows 8 and Windows Server 2012, and included in Windows 8.1 and Windows Server 2012 R2, AppLocker is the Packaged app Rules control policy. These policies can be used to control Windows Store apps, setting restrictions on users and apps that can be installed, and to implement application controls to enforce organization policies.

NOTE You can use AppLocker on computers running Windows 8 or 8.1 Enterprise, or any edition of Windows Server 2008 R2 or Windows Server 2012 R2 Standard or Datacenter. You can also use a computer running Windows 7 Professional to create AppLocker rules, but you cannot enforce these rules on Windows 7 Professional or Windows 8.1 Pro or RT 8.1.

NOTE For detailed information on using AppLocker for managing Windows Store apps, refer to "Manage Packaged Apps with AppLocker" and links cited therein at http://technet.microsoft.com/en-us/library/jj161142.aspx.

Capabilities of AppLocker

AppLocker provides enhanced options for managing the configuration of desktop computers. It enables you to perform actions such as the following:

- Specify the types of applications that users can run, including executables, scripts, Windows Installer files, and DLL files.
- Define rules according to file attributes specified in the digital signature, such as the publisher, product name, filename, and file version. For example, you can allow Adobe Acrobat Reader 9.0 and later to run, while forbidding the use of an older version.
- Prevent the execution of unlicensed, unapproved applications or those that destabilize machines and increase help desk support calls.
- Prevent unauthorized applications such as malware from executing.
- Prevent users from running programs that needlessly affect the corporate computing environment by consuming network bandwidth.
- Enable users to run approved applications and software updates while maintaining the requirement that only administrative users are permitted to install applications and software updates.
- Specify rules that apply to a given user or security group.
- Ensure that your computers are in compliance with licensing and corporate requirements.
- Create Publisher rules for packaged apps.
- Monitor your environment to verify rules are effective, and update rules as new packaged apps are introduced in the environment.

Table 5-7 provides a comparison of AppLocker with Software Restriction Policies.

Table 5-7 Comparing AppLocker to Software Restriction Policies

Feature	AppLocker	Software Restriction Policies
Rule scope	Specific users or groups	All users
Rule conditions	File hash, path, and publisher	File hash, path, certificate, Registry path, and Internet zone
Rule types	Allow and deny	Disallowed, Basic User, and Unrestricted
Default rule action	Implicit denial	Unrestricted
Audit-only mode	Yes	No
Wizard for creating multiple rules at the same time	Yes	No
Policy import or export	Yes	No
Rule collection	Yes	No
Support for PowerShell	Yes	No
Custom error messages	Yes	No

Basic Configuration of AppLocker Policies

As with Software Restriction Policies, you can configure AppLocker policies for the local computer in the Local Group Policy or Local Security Policy snap-in. You can also configure policies for an AD DS domain from the Group Policy Object Editor. Use the following procedure to configure default AppLocker rules on a local computer:

Step 1. In the Local Security Policy snap-in, expand Application Control Policies to reveal AppLocker. AppLocker displays information and configurable links in the details pane as shown in Figure 5-22.

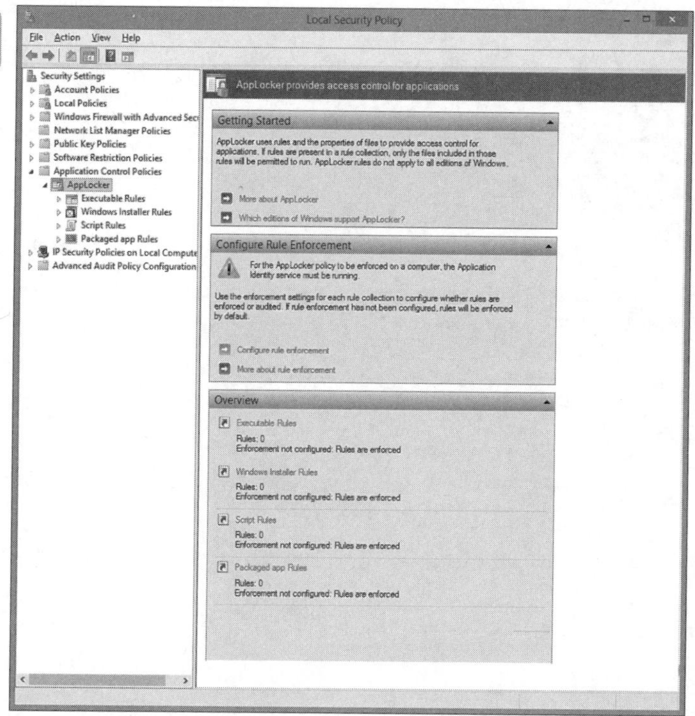

Figure 5-22 You can configure AppLocker from the Application Control Policies node of Local Security Policy.

Step 2. Click **Configure Rule Enforcement**. In the AppLocker Properties dialog box shown in Figure 5-23, select the check boxes against the three rule types that you want to configure. From the drop-down lists, select **Enforce rules** to create rules you want to enforce or **Audit only** to test rules for future use. Then click **OK**.

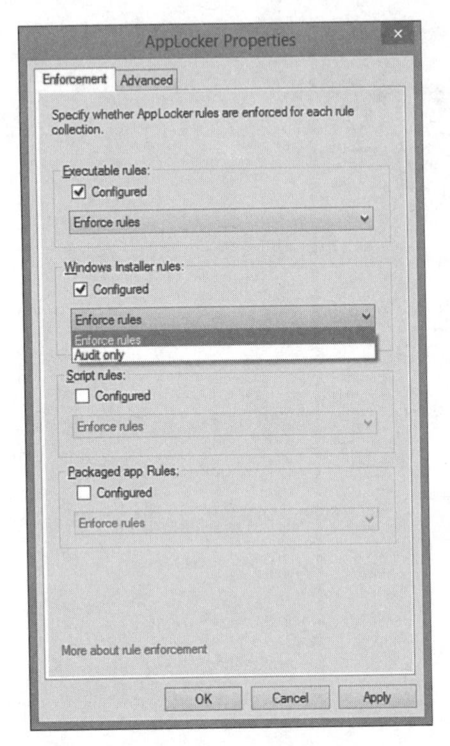

Figure 5-23 You can choose to enforce AppLocker rules or select Audit only to gather information.

TIP The Audit only option enables you to determine who is using which applications in your company, without enforcing the rules you have specified. When a user executes an application specified in the rule, information about that use is written into the AppLocker event log.

Step 3. In the console tree, expand AppLocker to reveal subnodes for each of these three rule types.

Step 4. For each of the rule types you want to configure, create a default set of rules by right-clicking the rule type and choosing **Create Default Rules**. This adds the three rules (all set to Allow) indicated in Table 5-8 to each specified rule type.

Table 5-8 Default AppLocker Rules

Default Group	Executable Rule	Windows Installer Rule	Script Rule
Everyone	All files located in the Program Files folder	All digitally signed Windows Installer files	All scripts located in the Program Files folder

Default Group	Executable Rule	Windows Installer Rule	Script Rule
Everyone	All files located in the Windows folder	All Windows Installer files in `%systemdrive%\Windows\Installer`	All scripts located in the Windows folder
BUILTIN\Administrators	All files	All Windows Installer files	All scripts

Step 5. If you want to delete any of these default rules, right-click the desired rule and choose **Delete**. Then click **Yes** in the confirmation dialog box that appears.

Creating Additional AppLocker Rules

AppLocker provides wizards that assist you in creating application-specific rules and policies. Before you begin creating these rules, ensure that you have installed the required applications or scripts and created any required security groups. You can automatically generate AppLocker rules for executables, Windows Installer, or scripts; the procedure is similar for each of these items. The following example describes a procedure that applies to creating a rule for the Windows Media Player executable:

Step 1. In the Local Security Policy snap-in, right-click the desired subnode of AppLocker and choose **Automatically Generate Rules**. This starts a wizard with the Folder and Permissions page, as shown in Figure 5-24.

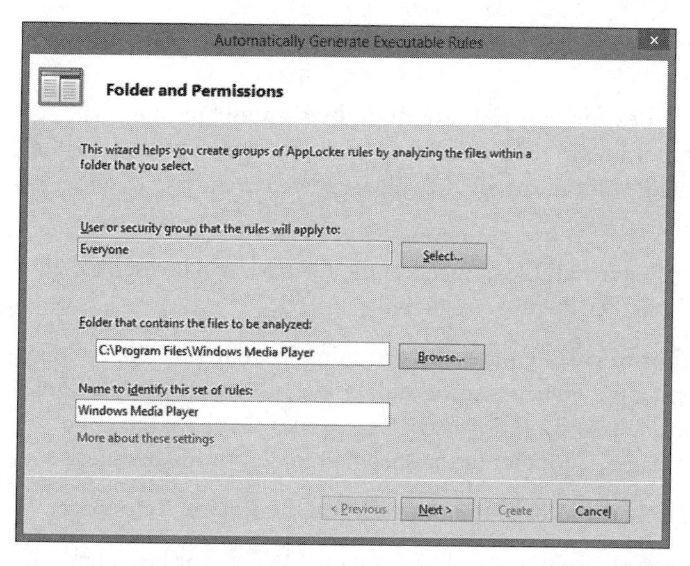

Figure 5-24 Creating AppLocker rules to be applied to Windows Media Player.

Step 2. Type or browse to the folder containing the executable files.

Step 3. Specify the user or security group to which the rule will apply. Click **Select** to display the Select User or Group dialog box, from which you can select the desired user or group. The wizard supplies a name based on the folder containing the executable. If you want to change this name, do so.

Step 4. Click **Next** to display the Rule Preferences page shown in Figure 5-25, and then specify the following options:

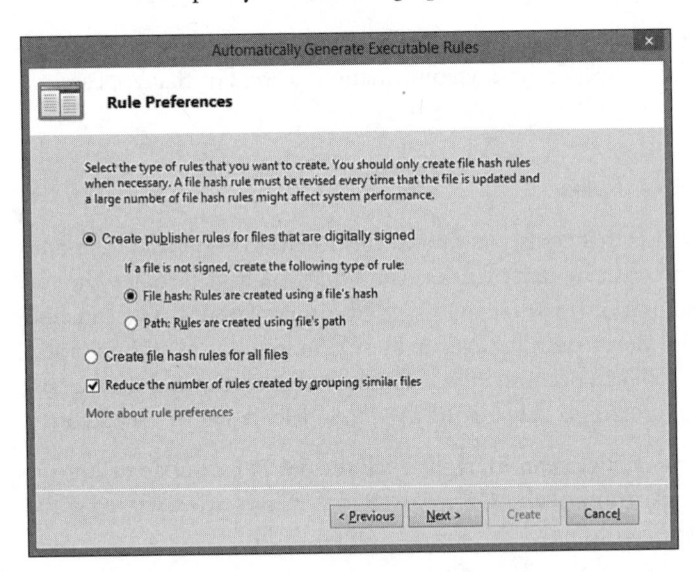

Figure 5-25 Specifying the types of rules to be created.

- **Create publisher rules for files that are digitally signed:** Specifies that rules are created according to the publisher for digitally signed files. If the file is not digitally signed, you can specify the rule is created according to either a file hash or a path.
- **Create file hash rules for all files:** Specifies the file hash will be used for all files, regardless of whether the files are digitally signed.
- **Reduce the number of rules created by grouping similar files:** Selected by default, this option helps you to organize AppLocker rules by creating a single publisher, path, or file hash condition according to files that have the same publisher, product name, subfolder of the specified folder, or file hash.

Step 5. Click **Next** and review the information provided on the Review Rules page.

Step 6. If you need to change any rule types, click **Previous**. When finished, click **Create** to create the rules and close the wizard.

AppLocker also includes a wizard that you can use to create granular rules according to any of the available options. To use this wizard, proceed as follows:

Step 1. In the Local Security Policy snap-in, right-click the desired subnode of AppLocker and choose **Create New Rule**. This starts the wizard with a Before You Begin page that describes preliminary steps you should take.

Step 2. Click **Next** to display the Permissions page. On this page, specify the **Allow** or **Deny** action and then click the **Select** button to display the Select User or Group dialog box, which enables you to select the desired user or group.

Step 3. Click **Next** to display the Conditions page, from which you can select **Publisher**, **Path**, or **File Hash**.

NOTE If you are configuring policies for Windows Store (Packaged) apps, you must create a Publisher rule. This is the only type of rule that can be applied to packaged apps because updates can change the hash, and the installation location is not predictable.

Step 4. If you select **Publisher**, you receive the page shown in Figure 5-26. Click **Browse** to browse to the desired publisher, as shown (for example) for Skype. This page also enables you to choose how specific you want the rule to become, by moving the slider provided. For example, to create a rule that applies to all Skype Technologies products, you would move the slider up to the Publisher line.

Step 5. Click **Create** to create your rule or click **Next** to specify exceptions. These include any publisher or path you want to exclude from the rule.

Step 6. The wizard creates a name for the rule automatically. Click **Next** to modify this name and add an optional description. When finished, click **Create** to create the rule. This creates the rule and adds it to the list in the details pane of the Local Security Policy or Group Policy Object Editor snap-in.

At step 3 of this procedure, you can also choose **Path** and then browse to or type a local or UNC path to the executable file(s) the rule is to cover. Or you can select **File Hash** and then browse to the folder or file containing the file hash. You can specify any number of folders containing hashes to be covered by this rule.

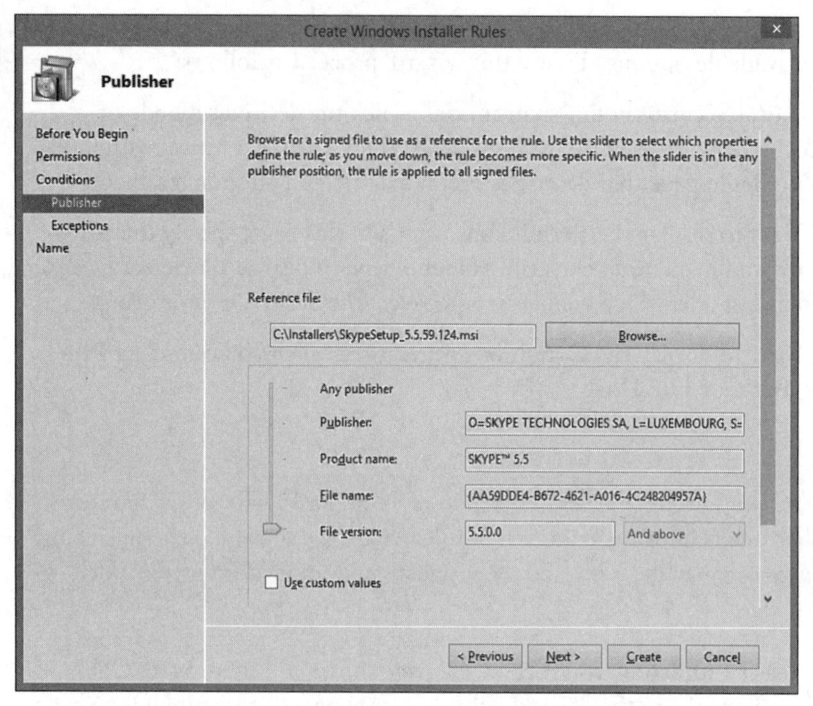

Figure 5-26 Creating a publisher-based executable file rule.

You can also edit the properties of any rule you've created by any of the methods described here. To do so, right-click the rule in the details pane and click **Properties**. This displays the dialog box shown in Figure 5-27, which enables you to modify the properties described in Table 5-9: Note that not all tabs listed will appear; the type of rule being configured determines whether you see the Path, Publisher, or File Hash tab.

Table 5-9 Configurable AppLocker properties

Tab	Description
General	Enables you to modify the action (allow or deny) and select a different group to apply the rule to.
Path	Enables you to change the path to the files or folders to which the rule should apply. This tab appears only for rules that have path conditions. (It is not shown in Figure 5-27.)
Publisher	Enables you to change the publisher, product name, filename, and file version. This tab appears only for rules that have publisher conditions.
File Hash	Enables you to add or remove files to be included in a file hash rule. This tab appears only for this type of rule. (It is not shown in Figure 5-27.)
Exceptions	Enables you to add, edit, or remove exceptions to the rule, according to publisher, file path, or hash.

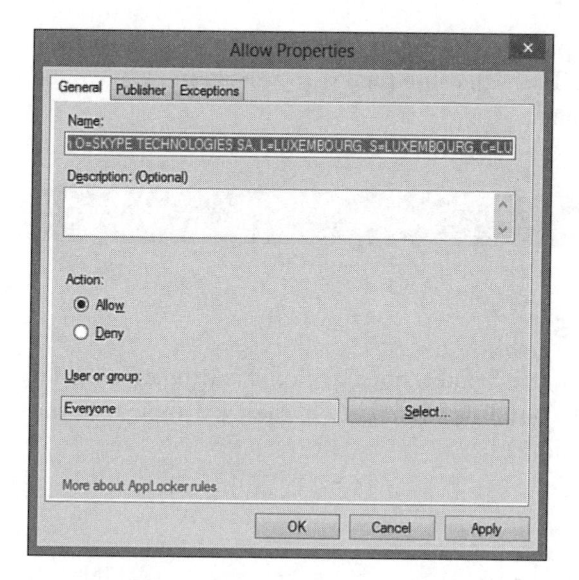

Figure 5-27 You can modify the properties of any AppLocker rule from the rule's Allow Properties dialog box.

Configuring Assigned Access

New for Windows 8.1 is the ability to use assigned access, which allows you to create a basic Windows account and allow the account to run only one specific Windows Store app. This capability is useful, for instance, for using Windows to run a kiosk, an office check-in system, or other public access system.

When the configured account is used, it can run only the assigned app. The user is unable to close the app, switch to any other app, and no app notifications appear.

To configure assigned access, first make sure you have created a standard account on the Windows PC you want to configure and then follow these steps:

Step 1. Access the Settings charm and then select **Change PC settings**.

Step 2. Click **Accounts**, select **Other accounts**, and then select **Set up an account for assigned access**.

Step 3. On the Assigned access screen, select **Choose an account** and select the standard account to use. If only there are no standard accounts, no accounts will be presented. It is not possible to use assigned access for an administrator account.

Step 4. Click **Choose an app** and then select the app from the list that you want to allow the selected account to use.

Step 5. Restart the PC and sign in with the assigned access account.

To exit from the assigned access app, you need to rapidly press the Windows logo key on the PC keyboard five times. This will cause the PC to restart, and you will be able to sign in with a different account.

Exam Preparation Tasks

Review All the Key Topics

Review the most important topics in the chapter, noted with the key topics icon in the outer margin of the page. Table 5-10 lists a reference of these key topics and the page numbers on which each is found.

Table 5-10 Key Topics for Chapter 5

Key Topic Element	Description	Page Number
Table 5-2	Describes available application compatibility options	203
Figure 5-3	Shows how the Compatibility Administrator helps you to configure compatibility settings for older programs	206
List	Lists file types used with Windows Installer	208
List	Describes available methods of software deployment using Group Policy	209
List	Describes types of actions you can perform using `Msiexec.exe`	210
Figure 5-7	Shows how to set up default file types and protocols to be opened by a program	214
Figure 5-8	Shows how to select file extensions to be opened by a program by default	215
Figure 5-11	Shows you how to select a default program to be used with a specific file extension	218
Figure 5-13	Shows how to manage App-V applications from the App-V client management console	222
Table 5-4	Describes PowerShell commands for managing App-V clients	223
Step List	Describes how to install apps from the Windows Store	226
Step List	Describes how to update apps from the Windows Store	226
Figure 5-15	Shows an indicator on the Windows Store screen notifying that updates are available	227

Key Topic Element	Description	Page Number
Figure 5-16	Shows how to disable access to Windows Store using Local Security Policy to block Microsoft accounts	229
List	Lists requirements for sideloading packaged apps	230
List	Lists software restriction policies and application control policies	230
Figure 5-19	Shows how to configure four types of Software Restriction rules in the Additional Rules folder	234
List	Lists capabilities of AppLocker	237
Step List	Describes how to do a basic configuration of AppLocker Policies	238
Figure 5-22	Shows how to configure AppLocker from the Application Control Policies node of Local Security policy	239
Table 5-8	Lists default AppLocker rules	240
Figure 5-26	Shows how to create a publisher-based AppLocker rule, the type of rule used to control packaged apps	244
Table 5-9	Lists configurable AppLocker properties	244

Complete the Tables and Lists from Memory

Print a copy of Appendix B, "Memory Tables," (found on the CD), or at least the section for this chapter, and complete the tables and lists from memory. Appendix C, "Memory Tables Answer Key," also on the CD, includes completed tables and lists to check your work.

Definitions of Key Terms

Define the following key terms from this chapter and check your answers in the glossary:

Application compatibility, Application Compatibility Manager, Application Compatibility Toolkit (ACT), AppLocker, App-V, default program, `.msi` file, `.msp` file, `.mst` file, packaged app, Software Restriction Policies

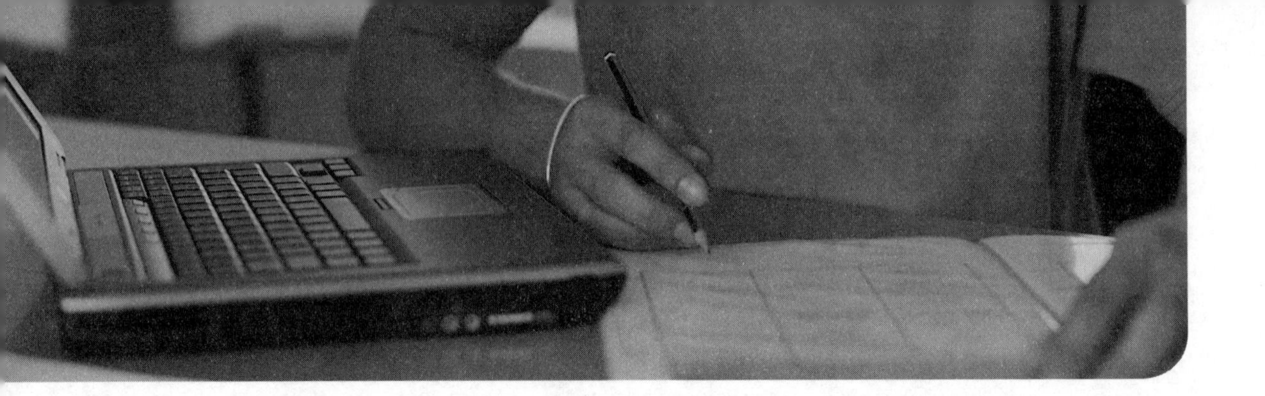

This chapter covers the following subjects:

- **Configuring Internet Explorer 11 and Internet Explorer for the Desktop:** Windows 8.1 introduces two new versions of Internet Explorer: Internet Explorer 11 (as accessed from the Start screen) and Internet Explorer for the Desktop. This section compares and contrasts these versions of Internet Explorer and introduces their new features.
- **Configuring Compatibility View:** The Compatibility View feature enables websites designed for earlier versions of Internet Explorer to display properly in Internet Explorer 11. This section shows you how to specify which websites are displayed in Compatibility View; it also introduces Group Policy settings you can use to configure compatibility settings in a domain environment.
- **Configuring Security Settings:** A lot of time can be lost over users running inappropriate applications or malicious websites downloading and installing inappropriate software. This section looks at methods you can use to limit what software can run.
- **Managing Add-ons:** Add-ons are optional additional features that you can install in Internet Explorer to provide additional functionality. This section shows you how to work with add-ons and avoid possible security pitfalls.
- **Configuring WebSockets:** WebSockets refers to a new protocol and API that are part of the HTML version 5 standards, introduced in IE 11. It enables a more interactive experience for web applications and can be used for Windows Store apps as well.
- **Configuring Download Manager:** Download Manager is a tool included with Internet Explorer 9, 10, and 11 that makes managing file downloads more intuitive for IE users.

CHAPTER 6

Configuring Internet Explorer

Internet Explorer 11 (IE 11), introduced with Windows 8.1, brings new and improved browsing and security features that enhance the user experience and help to protect users from malicious websites and the software they might place on their machines. For the 70-687 exam, you are expected to have the skills to configure and troubleshoot various aspects of IE 11, including tabbed browsing, pop-ups, add-ons, WebSockets, and Download Manager.

"Do I Know This Already?" Quiz

The "Do I Know This Already?" quiz allows you to assess whether you should read this entire chapter or simply jump to the "Exam Preparation Tasks" section for review. If you are in doubt, read the entire chapter. Table 6-1 outlines the major headings in this chapter and the corresponding "Do I Know This Already?" quiz questions. You can find the answers in Appendix A, "Answers to the 'Do I Know This Already?' Quizzes."

Table 6-1 "Do I Know This Already?" Foundation Topics Section-to-Question Mapping

Foundations Topics Section	Questions Covered in This Section
Configuring Internet Explorer 11 and Internet Explorer for the Desktop	1
Configuring Compatibility View	2
Configuring Security Settings	3–5
Managing Add-ons	6–7
Configuring WebSockets	8–9
Configuring Download Manager	10

1. Which of the following are not included in the new Start screen version of Internet Explorer 11 in Windows 8.1 but are included in the desktop version? (Choose all that apply.)
   a. Integration with Adobe Flash
   b. Really Simple Syndication (RSS) feeds
   c. The ability to pin websites to the taskbar
   d. Tabbed browsing
   e. Compatibility view
   f. The ability to directly access the Internet Options dialog box (as opposed to accessing this dialog box from the Control Panel).

2. You are responsible for configuring Group Policy to regulate the use of Compatibility View in your company's domain. Which of the following can you specify when doing so? (Choose all that apply.)
   a. Turn on Internet Explorer 7 Standards Mode.
   b. Turn off Compatibility View.
   c. Turn off Compatibility View button.
   d. Use Policy List of Internet Explorer 7 sites.
   e. Use Policy List of Quirks Mode sites.

3. Into what security zone are all websites placed by default in Internet Explorer 11?
   a. Trusted Sites
   b. Internet
   c. Local Intranet
   d. Restricted

4. You receive an email from your bank asking you to confirm your account data, so you access the linked website. You are afraid you might be duped into supplying information to an unauthorized website and want Internet Explorer 11 to display a warning if this is so. Which feature should you ensure is turned on?
   a. Protected Mode
   b. Pop-up Blocker
   c. InPrivate Browsing
   d. SmartScreen Filter

5. You want to configure the Pop-up Blocker settings in Internet Explorer, so you open the Internet Options dialog box. On which tab do you find the option to configure these settings?
   a. Security
   b. Privacy
   c. Content
   d. Advanced

6. Which of the following are items that the Manage Add-ons dialog box lets you configure in Internet Explorer 11? (Choose two.)
   a. InPrivate Browsing
   b. Search Providers
   c. Accelerators
   d. SmartScreen Filter

7. Your Internet connection has failed and it will take several days before a repair can be completed. You must submit a report by tomorrow morning, so you drive to an Internet café on the other side of town. You want to ensure that no traces of your activities are left behind on this computer. Which feature should you ensure is activated?
   a. Protected Mode
   b. Pop-up Blocker
   c. InPrivate Browsing
   d. SmartScreen Filter

8. You are trying to use a WebSockets application over the Internet, and the page loads fine, but the application does not work. What is the first thing you should check that could cause the application to fail to run?
   a. Protected Mode
   b. ActiveX Controls
   c. Active Scripting
   d. Windows Firewall

9. You are a desktop support technician in a large company, and the security manager is concerned about new technologies being accessed by users. Despite your assurances, he has asked you to help disable any access to WebSockets applications by users in the company. What technique do you recommend to accomplish this?
   a. Turn off WebSockets access using Windows Firewall settings.
   b. Disable Active Scripting in Internet Explorer using Group Policy settings.
   c. Use Group Policy settings to disable WebSocket access.
   d. Use IE Enhanced Security Configuration.

10. Your job requires you to maintain a significant number of PDF documents from courts and legislative offices. You are concerned about making sure that when you download the documents from those agency websites they are saved to a network share so they do not get lost if your workstation becomes unavailable. What is the best way to ensure the documents are kept in a safe location?
    a. Configure Download Manager to use the network share.
    b. Create a sync folder.
    c. Copy all the files downloaded to the network each day.
    d. Use SmartScreen Filter to check the files.

Foundation Topics

Configuring Internet Explorer 11 and Internet Explorer for the Desktop

Windows 8.1 includes Internet Explorer 11, which provides new management and usability features that enhance the Internet browsing experience while providing the latest security enhancements that help to maintain a safe environment while accessing websites and other Internet resources.

As with recent versions of Internet Explorer, Microsoft has continued to improve the reliability and security of its flagship Internet browser. Windows 8.1 enables you to run Internet Explorer 11 in two different versions:

- **From the Start screen:** Run as a default app from the Start screen, Internet Explorer provides a touch-first, immersive experience when used on a touch-screen monitor or tablet. Note that most of the configuration options discussed in this chapter are not available when you run Internet Explorer from the Start screen; we mention the options available with this version of Internet Explorer as they are encountered.
- **From the desktop:** Run from the desktop, Internet Explorer provides a more traditional window and tab management experience. You can access this version by clicking the icon for Internet Explorer that appears by default on the taskbar. Use this option for configuring Internet Explorer as discussed in the sections to follow.

TIP If you need to switch from the Start screen version of Internet Explorer to the desktop version, click the wrench icon that appears near the bottom-right corner and select **View on the desktop** from the list of options that appears. This opens the currently viewed website in the desktop version. This capability can be useful if the website does not appear properly in the Start screen version or if you need to configure an option not found in the Start screen version. Note, however, that only the current tab in a multitab session is moved to the desktop version.

The initial version of Windows 8 included Internet Explorer 10, which upgraded the experience of previous Internet Explorer versions in Windows 7 by introducing enhanced memory protection and the HTML5 sandbox attribute, which enable security restrictions for HTML components that contain untrusted content that might perform malicious actions against the user or browser. Enhanced Protected

Mode provides additional security by limiting an attacker's ability to install malicious code or modify or destroy a user's data. ActiveX Filtering limits the effect that ActiveX controls can interact with your browsing session. You can enable or disable ActiveX Filtering for a specific website or all websites in Internet Explorer 11.

Internet Explorer 11 includes an extensive series of new improvements, the most significant of which are as follows:

- **Improved web browsing and navigation:** Enables users to access information more rapidly, with improved browsing efficiency even across slow networks. Smarter web page caching that includes prefetch and prerender help to enhance the rate of access to information.
- **Compatibility with many device types:** Supports orientation-based viewing on tablets and other portable devices. On touch-based screens, Internet Explorer 11 supports actions such as touch-based drag-and-drop, hover, and highlighting of active links. On large monitor systems, Internet Explorer supports multimonitor support and high-pixel scaling for optimal viewing experience. You can also sync your browsing history and favorites across multiple devices.
- **Phone capability:** Provides clickable links when used with phone-based apps such as Skype or Windows Phone devices.
- **Integration with Adobe Flash:** Included out-of-the box, Adobe Flash can run on both the desktop and Start screen versions of Internet Explorer 11.
- **New Group Policy settings:** Enable you to control actions such as use of the swiping motion, automatic phone number detection, the provision of personalized search results, and many more.
- **Do Not Track (DNT) exceptions:** By default, websites are not allowed to track users. Websites can ask for exceptions from users based on DNT. If a user grants this exception, headers can be sent from the user to the website that enable tracking, allowing the user to develop a trusted privacy relationship with desired websites.
- **Improved developer features:** Supports an enhanced set of web standards, as well as new debugging utilities and application programming interfaces (APIs) for actions such as animated scrolling effects and enhanced video capabilities.

NOTE For more information on new features in Internet Explorer 11, refer to "What's New in Internet Explorer 11" at http://technet.microsoft.com/en-us/ie/dn269977.

Internet Explorer Interfaces

As introduced at the beginning of this section, Internet Explorer in Windows 8 or Windows 8.1 can be accessed from either the Start screen or the desktop view. Each presents a slightly different experience. The major differences in the two browser interfaces are as follows:

- The Start screen version is a streamlined mobile-friendly version that behaves in a manner similar to that of other Windows 8.1 Start screen apps, whereas the desktop version behaves in a similar fashion to Internet Explorer in Windows 7 and older Windows versions.
- The Start screen version enables you to know whether an associated Windows Store app is available from the website you're viewing. You can also download the app from the Windows Store if you haven't installed it or switch to the app if you already have it.
- The Start screen version of Internet Explorer 11 provides new Search and Share options for selected text. Search launches a query using the selected text in the default search provider. Share displays available Windows Store apps registered as share targets. These options are not available on the desktop version.
- The address bar appears by default at the bottom of the Start screen version, whereas it appears at its customary top location in the desktop version. If the address bar does not appear in the Start screen version, you can bring it back by pressing **F4**.
- Both versions of Internet Explorer 11 support tabbed browsing, but to open a new tab in the Start screen version, right-click an empty space in the current website and then click the **+** icon that appears in the top-right corner. When multiple tabs are open, they are represented by thumbnail images across the top of the browser window.
- If you access a website from a Windows Store app, the website opens in the Start screen version of Internet Explorer; if you access a website from a desktop program, the website opens in the desktop view. You can modify these settings from the Programs tab of the Internet Options dialog box.
- Only the desktop version of Internet Explorer supports Really Simple Syndication (RSS) feeds. However, both versions share your favorites, frequent sites, history, and typed URLs. Note that if you are using a Microsoft account, these items are synced across all Windows 8/8.1 machines that you use with Internet Explorer.

- The Start screen version of Internet Explorer enables you to pin websites to the Start screen. Click the pin icon in the toolbar to do so. On the desktop version, you can pin sites to the Windows taskbar by dragging and dropping the tab, as in previous Internet Explorer versions.
- The Start screen version provides a reading view that enables a streamlined, book-like reading view of web pages, suppressing secondary content on the page. You can enable or disable reading view from a book icon on the address bar that contains Switch to reading view/Leave reading view options. You can also select several styles for reading view by accessing **Options** from the Settings charm when running Internet Explorer in the Start screen version. The desktop version does not support reading view.
- On the desktop version, the toolbar appears at the top, as in previous versions. If hidden, you can display the toolbar by pressing **Alt**. On the Start screen version, the toolbar appears at the bottom. Although it is normally hidden, you can display it by pressing **Esc**.

NOTE For more information on comparing the two versions of Internet Explorer, refer to "Internet Explorer on Windows 8.1: One Browser, Two Experiences" at http://msdn.microsoft.com/en-us/library/ie/hh771832(v=vs.85).aspx.

Configuring Compatibility View

The Compatibility View feature enables websites designed for earlier versions of Internet Explorer to display properly in Internet Explorer 11. Internet Explorer 11 displays the Compatibility View button in the address bar when it recognizes a noncompatible website. Simply click this button to turn on Compatibility View. You can also click **Compatibility View** from the Tools menu button. Doing so causes the website to be displayed as if you were using an older version of Internet Explorer.

To configure the desktop version of Internet Explorer to add or remove websites displayed in Compatibility View, press **Alt** to view the menu bar and then click **Tools > Compatibility View Settings**. This displays the Compatibility View Settings dialog box shown in Figure 6-1, with the current website displayed in the Add this website text box. Click **Add** to specify that this website will be displayed in Compatibility View. This adds the website to the list under Websites you've added to Compatibility View, thereby enabling the website to always be displayed in Compatibility View on future visits to the same website. To remove a website from this list, select it and click **Remove**. To clear the list of websites to be viewed in Compatibility View, press **Alt** to view the menu bar and then click **Tools > Delete browsing history**. You can also modify Compatibility View settings by configuring the following two options available at the bottom of the Compatibility View Settings dialog box:

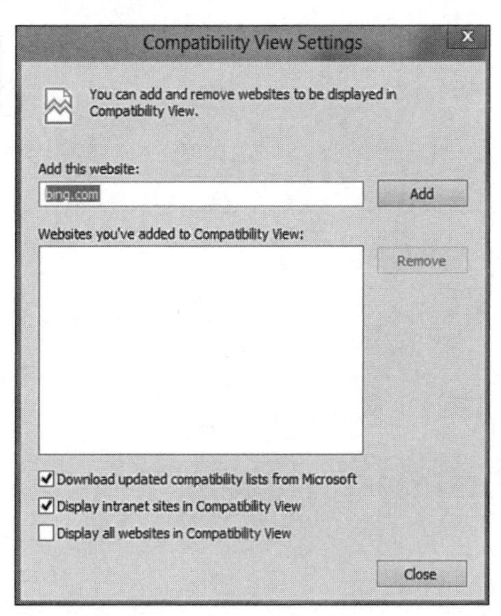

Figure 6-1 The Compatibility View Settings dialog box enables you to specify which websites are displayed in Compatibility View.

- **Display intranet sites in Compatibility View:** Select this check box if your company's intranet websites were designed for older versions of Internet Explorer. This check box is selected by default.
- **Use Microsoft compatibility lists:** Microsoft provides lists of websites that function better in Compatibility View. These lists also include lists of hardware devices such as graphics devices that have known compatibility issues. Selecting this check box enables these lists to be downloaded and used. This check box is selected by default.

Deleting Browsing History

Internet Explorer 11 keeps a record of several types of information that a user has downloaded from the Internet or that websites have provided to the user. This includes a history of websites that you've visited; this component includes those websites that have been viewed in Compatibility View. You can clear the list of websites viewed in Compatibility View as well as other types of information by clicking the small gear wheel near the top-right corner of the Internet Explorer window and selecting **Safety > Delete browsing history**. This brings up the dialog box shown in Figure 6-2. Select the types of history items to be deleted and then click **Delete**.

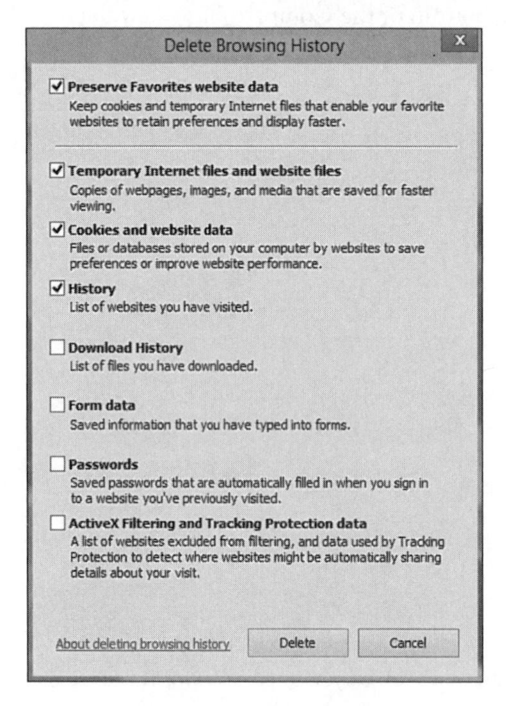

Figure 6-2 The Delete Browsing History dialog box enables you to selectively delete several components of your browsing history.

TIP You can also delete the browsing history when running the Start screen version of Internet Explorer. Open the **Settings** charm and click **Options**. In the History section of the Options window that appears, click **Select**. You receive options similar to those shown in Figure 6-2 that enable you to select which history items are deleted.

Using Group Policy to Configure Compatibility View

You can also use Group Policy to configure Compatibility View in an Active Directory Domain Services (AD DS) domain. From either the Computer Configuration or User Configuration section of the Group Policy Object Editor, access the **Administrative Templates\Windows Components\Internet Explorer\Compatibility View** node. This provides the following policies shown in Figure 6-3:

- **Turn on Internet Explorer 7 Standards Mode:** Forces all websites to display in a mode compatible with Internet Explorer 7.
- **Turn off Compatibility View:** Prevents users from using the Compatibility View feature or the Compatibility View Settings dialog box.
- **Turn on Internet Explorer Standards Mode for Local Intranet:** Controls the display of local intranet websites so that they appear in a mode compatible with Internet Explorer 7. Enable this setting if your company's intranet websites do not display properly in Internet Explorer 11.
- **Turn off Compatibility View button:** Prevents users from using the Compatibility View button on the toolbar.
- **Include updated website lists from Microsoft:** Enables the browser to use the compatible website lists provided by Microsoft. These websites are automatically displayed in Compatibility View.
- **Use Policy List of Internet Explorer 7 sites:** Enables users to add specific sites that are displayed in Compatibility View.
- **Use Policy List of Quirks Mode sites:** Enables Internet Explorer to use an Internet Explorer 7 user agent string of websites, which are displayed in Quirks Mode. This mode enables Internet Explorer to match the behavior of other leading browsers while retaining the compatibility support generally expected by users.

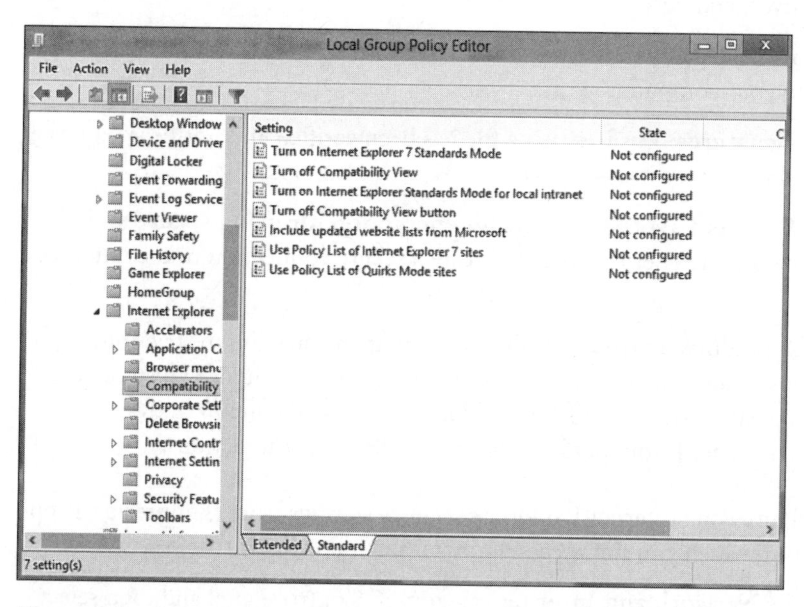

Figure 6-3 Group Policy in Windows 8.1 contains a series of settings that control the use of Compatibility View.

Configuring Security Settings

Each iteration of Internet Explorer has added additional security features that help protect your security and privacy when browsing online. Security features in Internet Explorer 11 include the following:

- **Information bar:** Internet Explorer displays an information bar at the top of the page under certain circumstances to alert you of possible security problems. They include attempts by a website to install an ActiveX control, open a pop-up window, download a file, or run active content. You will also see an information bar if your security settings are below recommended levels, if you access an intranet web page without turning on intranet address checking, or if you access a website whose address contains native language letters or symbols. You can obtain additional information or take action by clicking the information bar message.
- **SmartScreen Filter:** Helps protect you from fraudulent websites that masquerade as legitimate sites (such as banks) and attempt to hijack your password and account information.
- **Enhanced Protected Mode:** Helps protect you from websites that attempt to install malicious software or data files on your computer.
- **Pop-up blocker:** Blocks most pop-up windows that display advertising or attempt to entice you to visit malicious websites.
- **Add-on Manager:** Enables you to disable or allow browser add-ons or undesired ActiveX controls.
- **Notification:** Displays a message if a website attempts to download software or files to your computer.
- **Digital signatures:** Ensures that a file has been verified and notifies you if the file was altered since it was signed.
- **Secure Sockets Layer (SSL) 128-bit encryption for using secure websites:** Enables Internet Explorer to create a secure connection to e-commerce websites.
- **HTML5 sandbox attribute:** Enhances security by enabling restrictions for web pages containing iframe elements with untrusted content. This is a new object type supported by HTML version 5. Untrusted content in iframe elements is prevented from performing potentially malicious actions.

You can configure your Internet Explorer's security settings from the Internet Properties dialog box, which you can access by any of the following methods:

- Access the **Network and Internet** category in Control Panel and then select **Internet Options**.

- Access the Search charm and type `Internet options`. Then select **Internet options** from the list that appears.
- In the desktop version of Internet Explorer, click the small gear wheel near the top-right corner of the Internet Explorer window and then choose **Internet options** from the menu list that appears.
- In the desktop version of Internet Explorer, press **Alt** and then select **Tools > Internet options**.

Configuring Internet Explorer Security Zones

The Security tab of the Internet Options dialog box displays a list of website types called Internet zones, as shown in Figure 6-4.

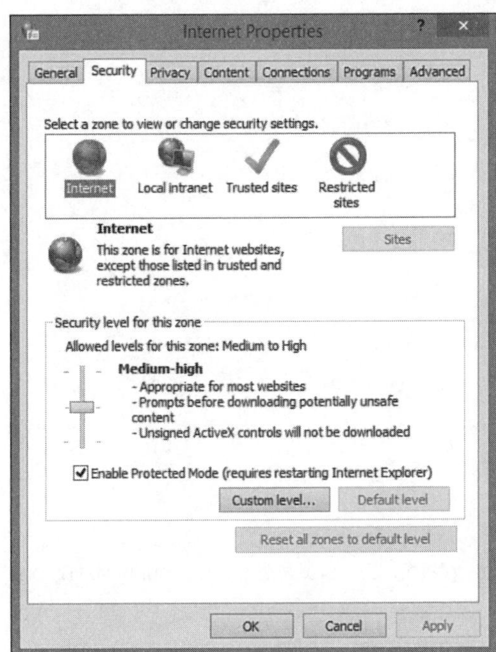

Figure 6-4 You can establish security settings separately to each type of website location.

By default, all websites are included in the Internet zone. To move a website to another zone, select the desired zone and click **Sites**. On the dialog box that appears, type or copy the URL to the text box provided (if it is not already present), click **Add**, and then click **Close**. You can return a site to the Internet zone by selecting it and clicking **Remove**. You can also limit the Local intranet and Trusted sites zones to secured sites whose URL starts with https: by selecting the check box labeled **Require server verification (https:) for all sites in this zone**.

CAUTION The default security for the Trusted sites zone is considerably lower than that for any of the other zones. Be absolutely certain that you trust a website implicitly before adding the site to this zone. If you are uncertain, you should leave the site in the Internet zone until you have investigated it thoroughly.

To configure the security settings for a zone, click the desired zone to select it and then click the **Custom level** command button. The Security Settings dialog box opens, as shown in Figure 6-5, where you can select each individual security setting or set an Internet zone to a predefined group of security settings, including Low, Medium-low, Medium, Medium-high (default), and High. Note that the default Internet zone does not include the Low and Medium-low options.

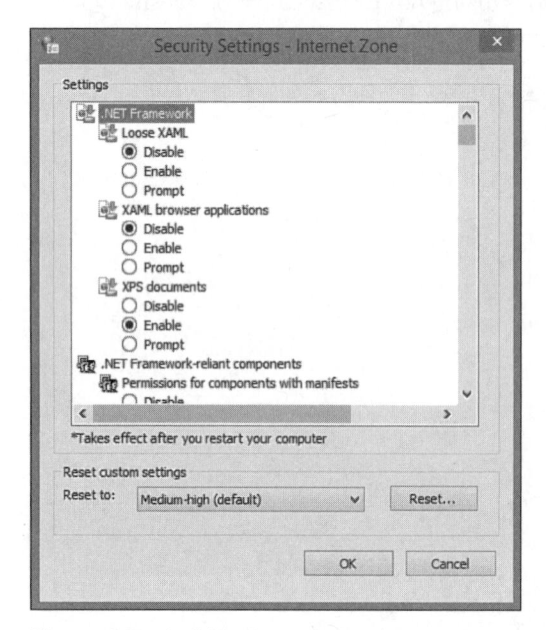

Figure 6-5 Individual security settings apply to an Internet zone for a custom security definition.

To establish the privacy settings, click the **Privacy** tab. Here, you can select a preset level for handling cookies. If you click the **Sites** button, you can block or allow privacy information to be exchanged with specific websites. To establish a different method for handling cookies in the Internet zone, click the **Advanced** button and select your preferred settings.

For security settings that govern specific behaviors in Internet Explorer, click the **Advanced** tab and scroll down the window to the **Security** category. Here, you can set options such as reducing problems caused by software downloaded and installed from the Internet. (Do this by clearing the **Allow software to run or install even if the signature is invalid** check box; this check box is cleared by default.)

TIP Another way that you can secure Internet Explorer is to ensure that it is updated with the latest patches and service packs available. Access Windows Update as described in Chapter 16, "Configuring Windows Updates," and ensure that security and optional updates to Internet Explorer are downloaded.

Configuring Protected Mode in Internet Explorer

First introduced with Internet Explorer 7 in Windows Vista and continued with all more recent versions of Internet Explorer, Protected Mode provides enhanced levels of security and protection from malware. Protected Mode prevents websites from modifying user or system files and settings or downloading unwanted software unless you provide your consent. It displays a prompt similar to those available with User Account Control (UAC), asking you to confirm any action that attempts to download something to your computer or launch a program. The user can ensure that these actions are desired and that they prevent any harmful action that might otherwise occur. You can stop any such type of action and confirm the trustworthiness of the website before proceeding. Protected Mode also prevents Internet Explorer from writing data to any location except the Temporary Internet Files folder unless you provide consent (such as during a desired download).

Protected Mode is enabled by default on all Internet zones except the Trusted Sites zone, and Internet Explorer confirms this fact by displaying a message `Protected Mode: On` in the status bar. If this message does not appear, you can turn on Protected Mode by selecting the check box labeled **Enable Protected Mode** on the Security tab (shown previously in Figure 6-4) and then restarting Internet Explorer. Internet Explorer may also display an information bar informing you that Protected Mode is turned off in this instance.

TIP Internet Explorer runs in protected mode by default and informs you of this fact with a message in the status bar at the bottom of the browser window. You should not turn off this mode; if it is turned off by mistake, you can re-enable it by resetting Internet Explorer to default settings.

Configuring the SmartScreen Filter

The SmartScreen Filer first introduced in Internet Explorer 8 and continued in versions 9, 10, and 11 enhances the capabilities of the phishing filter first introduced with Internet Explorer 7. Besides checking websites against a list of reported phishing sites, this filter checks software downloads against a list of reported malware websites. The practice of phishing refers to the creation of a fake website that closely mimics a real website and contains a similar-looking URL, intending to scam users into sending confidential personal information such as credit card or bank account numbers, birthdates, Social Security numbers, and so on. The attacker sends email messages that appear to originate from the company whose website was spoofed so that users connect to the fake website and provide this type of information. The attacker can use this information for identity theft and other nefarious purposes.

Microsoft built the SmartScreen Filter into Internet Explorer 11 to check websites for phishing activity using the following methods:

- Comparing website addresses visited by users with dynamically updated lists of reported legitimate sites saved on your computer.
- Comparing website addresses against lists of dynamically updated lists of sites reported as downloading malicious software to your computer.
- Analyzing website addresses against characteristics (such as misspelled words) used by phishing sites.
- Comparing website addresses with those in an online service that Microsoft operates for immediate checking against a list of reported phishing sites. This list is updated several times each hour using material gathered by Microsoft or other industries or reported by users. Other global databases of known phishing sites are also used.

If the SmartScreen Filter detects a known phishing or malware site, Internet Explorer displays the address bar in red and replaces the website with a message informing you of the risks. You receive options to close the website or continue to it. If the site is not a known phishing or malware site but behaves in a similar manner to such a site, the address bar appears in yellow and a warning message appears. The user can report the site to the Microsoft SmartScreen Filter list or gather further information to report a false positive if the site turns out to be legitimate.

If you suspect that a website you are visiting is a phishing site (whether the address bar has turned yellow or not), you can check the following items:

- **The URL appearing in the address bar:** A spoofed domain name will appear similar to the authentic one but contain misspelled or additional words. Internet Explorer 11 makes this easier to check by displaying all domain names in bold.
- **URLs associated with page links:** Although some of these may point to the authentic site, others might point to the phisher's site. Check the address that appears in the bottom-left corner of the status bar when you hover your mouse pointer over the link.
- **Advertisements or other content not associated with the legitimate site:** Many phishers use free Web-hosting services that might add advertising or other content to the fake site.
- **Failure to use a secure (https) connection:** Legitimate sites use secure connections for transmitting all sensitive data. Internet Explorer displays a gold lock icon in the address bar for all https connections. If this icon does not appear, you are most likely dealing with a phishing site.
- **Addresses used for submitting forms:** In general, the phisher site will contain a form that you are asked to fill out with your personal information and include a button that says **Submit** or something similar. To check this address, select **View > Source** and then locate the value of the `<form>` tag's `Action` attribute. If this is a nonlegitimate address, you know you are on a phishing site.

Use the following procedure to configure the SmartScreen Filter:

Step 1. Open **Internet Explorer** to a website that you suspect might be a phishing site.

Step 2. On the Safety menu, select one of the following options:

- **Check this website:** Checks the current website. Click **OK** in the SmartScreen Filter message box that appears to receive a message informing you of the result.
- **Turn on SmartScreen Filter:** Displays the dialog box shown in Figure 6-6, which enables you to turn the filter on or off as desired. This menu item appears as Turn off SmartScreen Filter when the filter is already on.
- **Report unsafe website:** Enables you to report a phishing website or remove an authentic site that has been flagged as a phishing one.

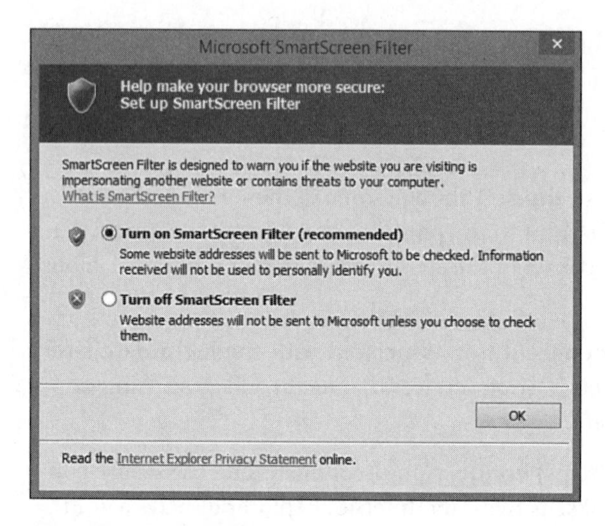

Figure 6-6 The Microsoft SmartScreen Filter dialog box enables you to turn the automatic phishing filter on or off.

Privacy Tab Settings

The Privacy tab of the Internet Properties dialog box, shown in Figure 6-7, enables you to configure cookie handling, location services, the pop-up blocker, and InPrivate browser settings. We discuss the InPrivate browser mode later in this chapter.

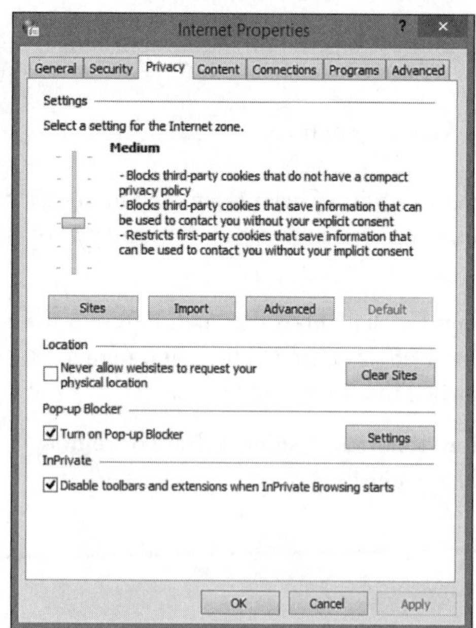

Figure 6-7 The Privacy tab enables you to configure cookie settings and the pop-up blocker.

Handling Cookies

Cookies are small files that websites place on your computer to facilitate improved browsing or advertisement display on future visits to the same website. Information you provide on a form displayed by the website is placed in the cookie to be sent to the web server when you next visit the website, which then customizes the page sent to you with items such as your name and interests. You can choose from the following options:

- **Block All Cookies:** Prevents all websites from storing cookies on your computer and from reading existing cookies.
- **High:** Prevents websites that do not have a compact privacy policy from storing cookies on your computer. This is a condensed computer-readable privacy statement. Websites are also prevented from storing cookies that use personally identifiable information without your consent.
- **Medium High:** Prevents websites that do not have a compact privacy policy from storing cookies on your computer. Also blocks third-party cookies that use personally identifiable information without your explicit consent or first-party cookies that use personally identifiable information without implicit consent.
- **Medium:** Prevents websites that do not have a compact privacy policy from storing cookies on your computer. Limits websites that place first-party cookies that save information but use identifiable information without your implicit consent.
- **Low:** Allows websites to place cookies on your computer, including those that do not have a compact privacy policy or that use personally identifiable information without your explicit consent.
- **Accept All Cookies:** Allows all websites to place cookies on your computer and allows websites that create cookies to read them.

Using Location Services

New to Internet Explorer 11, Location Services enables websites to request your physical location in order to improve their services. For example, a mapping website can open its map to your physical location. Location Services attempts to determine your location according to your computer's IP address and data from nearby Wi-Fi access points when using a wireless connection. If you do not want websites to determine your physical location, from the Location section of the Privacy tab, select the check box labeled **Never allow websites to request your physical location**. To remove any websites that have previously been allowed to request your location, click the **Clear Sites** command button. To enable location requests on a per-site basis when requested, click **Allow once**. Or to provide your location every time you visit the same website, click **More options for this site** and then click **Always allow**.

Blocking Pop-ups

Initially included with Internet Explorer 6 on Windows XP with SP2, the Pop-up Blocker eases the frustrations of many Internet users. Pop-ups are additional windows that appear while browsing the Internet. Advertisers often use them to display ads to Internet users. Some pop-ups even deploy malware and are displayed in such a way that the only possible way to close the pop-up without installing the malware is to use the Task Manager to force the window to close. Users who do not know how to do this often end up with huge amounts of pop-up traffic, viruses, spy software, and other problems.

You can configure how the Pop-up Blocker feature functions by opening the **Tools** menu, selecting the **Pop-up Blocker** submenu, and then clicking **Pop-up Blocker settings**. The Pop-up Blocker Settings dialog box opens, as shown in Figure 6-8. (This option is not available if the Pop-up Blocker is currently off.) The other options in the Pop-up Blocker submenu are **Turn Off Pop-up Blocker** (if it is turned on) or **Turn On Pop-up Blocker** (if it is turned off).

Key Topic

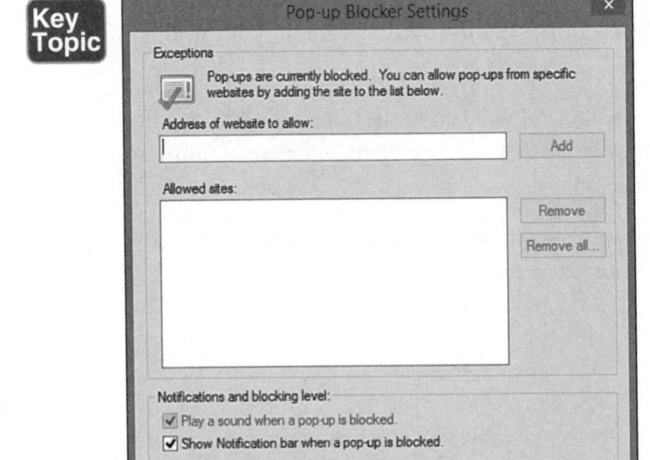

Figure 6-8 You can allow pop-ups from certain websites by editing the Pop-up Blocker Settings.

To allow pop-ups from a certain website, type the URL in the Address of website to allow text box and then click the **Add** button. You can select whether to display the information bar and whether to play a sound when a website's pop-up is blocked. The Blocking level list box enables you to select whether to block all pop-ups (High: Block all pop-ups [Ctrl+Alt to override]), most pop-ups (Medium: Block most automatic pop-ups), or just the pop-ups that are from nonsecure sites (Low: Allow pop-ups from secure sites).

When Internet Explorer blocks a pop-up, it displays an information bar beneath the line of tabs. You can click this bar to temporarily allow pop-ups, always allow pop-ups from this site, or configure additional pop-up settings including suppressing the information bar.

Content Tab Settings

The Content tab includes the following security-related options:

- **Family Safety:** Links to the Family Safety applet in Control Panel that enables you to control the types of content your children are permitted to access, as well as time limits, app restrictions, and other limits.
- **Certificates:** Controls the behavior of certificates used for encrypted connections and identification. We discuss the use of certificates later in this chapter.
- **Auto Complete:** Stores information from previously visited web pages and tries to complete entries you make on Web addresses, forms, usernames, passwords, and so on. Click **Settings** to specify the types of entries that Auto Complete is used for. You can delete Auto Complete history from the General tab of the Internet Properties dialog box.
- **Feeds and Web Slices:** Enables you to configure settings for RSS feeds and Web slices, which enable you to receive up-to-date information on the Internet at times that are convenient for you.

Advanced Tab Settings

The Advanced tab of the Internet Properties dialog box contains a large range of settings that you can configure in the subjects of accessibility, browsing, HTTP 1.1, international, multimedia, printing, searching, and security. Figure 6-9 shows most of the security settings available from this tab.

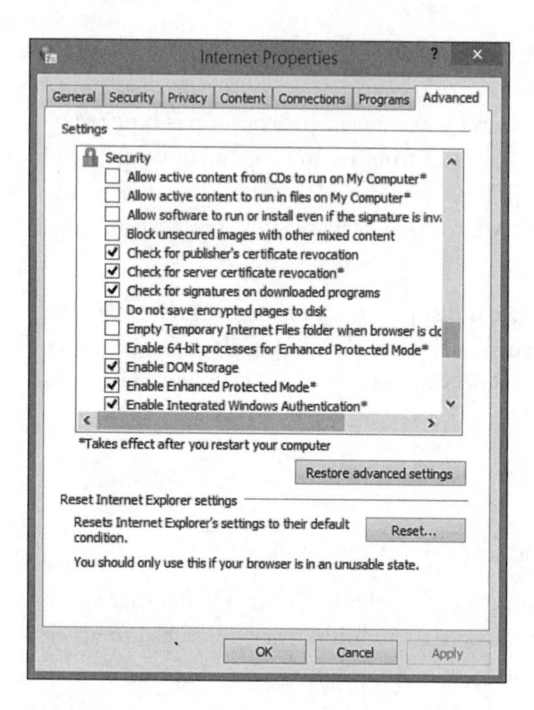

Figure 6-9 The Advanced tab contains a series of settings that affect the security of Internet Explorer 11.

The following types of settings are included in the Advanced tab:

- **Accelerated graphics:** Enables you to use software rendering instead of GPU rendering on computers with supported hardware.
- **Accessibility:** Provides several options to enhance accessibility for visually or hearing-challenged users.
- **Browsing:** Provides a series of options for displaying error or debugging messages, enabling crash recovery, suggested sites, visual styles, notification of downloads, display of hyperlinks, use of Auto Complete, and other visual enhancements.
- **HTTP settings:** Enables the use of HTTP 1.1 either directly or through proxy connections. Added in Internet Explorer 11 is an option to use Google's new SPDY web protocol.
- **International:** Provides several options governing display of websites from international locations.
- **Multimedia:** Provides several options for animations, sounds, images, and so on.

- **Security:** Provides security-related options as shown in Figure 6-9, as well as options for using the SmartScreen filter and different versions of Secure Sockets Layer (SSL) and Transport Layer Security (TLS).

From this tab, you can click **Restore advanced settings** to reset all settings to their defaults, or you can click **Reset** to reset all Internet Explorer settings to their defaults.

Managing Add-ons

Add-ons are optional additional features that you can install in Internet Explorer to provide additional functionality. They generally come from sources on the Internet and are sometimes installed without your knowledge. At other times, the Internet source will ask you for permission to install an add-on before proceeding. However, if you deny this permission, the web page may not display as intended by its creators.

Internet Explorer enables you to manage add-ons in several ways. Use the following procedure to manage add-ons:

Step 1. In Internet Explorer 11, click the gear wheel and then click **Manage add-ons** from the list that appears (or select **Manage add-ons** from the Tools menu). The Manage Add-ons dialog box shown in Figure 6-10 opens.

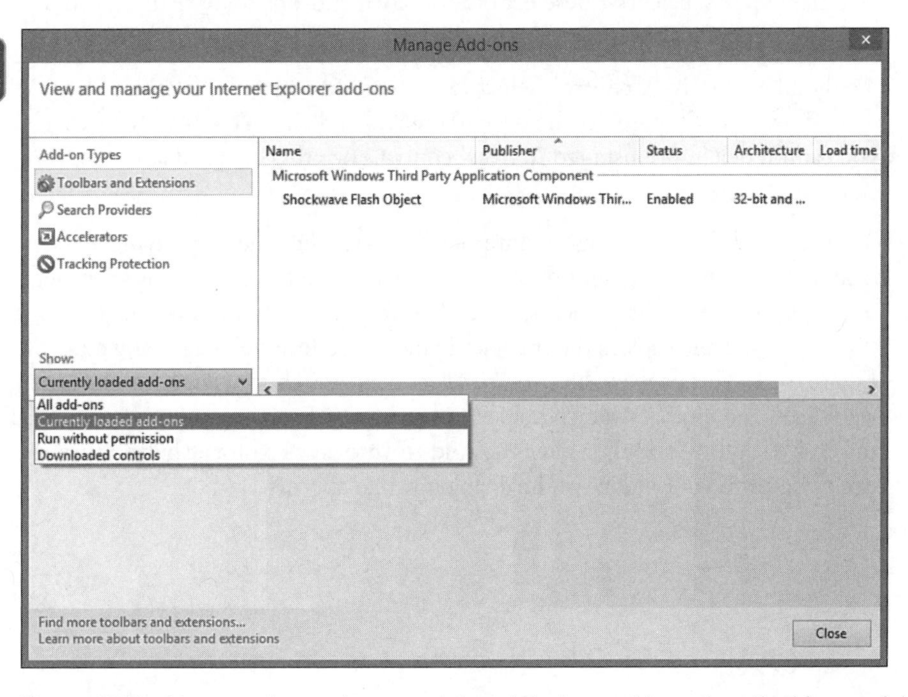

Figure 6-10 You can view and manage Internet Explorer add-ons from the Manage Add-ons dialog box.

Step 2. Select one of the following options from the Show drop-down list:

- **All add-ons:** Lists all add-ons that have been downloaded to Internet Explorer at any time since you installed Windows plus those that were pre-approved by Microsoft or your computer manufacturer.
- **Currently loaded add-ons:** Displays only those add-ons used by a currently or recently viewed web page. This list appears by default when you first open the Manage Add-ons dialog box.
- **Run without permission:** Displays all add-ons that were pre-approved by Microsoft, your computer manufacturer, or your Internet service provider (ISP). These add-ons have generally been digitally signed and run without displaying any permissions message box. Any unsigned add-ons carry the message `(Not verified)` in the Publisher column.
- **Downloaded controls:** Displays 32-bit ActiveX controls only. Although these controls add functionality to Internet Explorer, malicious software writers often use them for undesirable purposes.

Step 3. If an add-on appears to be causing problems or preventing a web page from displaying properly, select it and click **Disable**. In the Disable Add-on dialog box that appears, select or deselect other related add-ons that are displayed and then click **Disable** to disable the chosen add-on.

Step 4. To disable an ActiveX control, select **Downloaded controls** from the Show drop-down list. Then select the desired control and click **Disable**. Note that you cannot delete preinstalled ActiveX controls or other types of add-ons; you can only disable them.

Step 5. To locate additional add-ons for Internet Explorer, click the magnifying glass icon immediately to the right of the address bar. From the bottom-right corner of the pop-up menu that appears, select **Add** from the bottom of the history list that appears. This displays the Internet Explorer Gallery web page shown in Figure 6-11. This page enables you to select from search providers, accelerators, web slices, and toolbars, which help to enhance your browsing experience. Select the desired add-on and then click the **Add to Internet Explorer** button that appears. Confirm your choice in the dialog box that appears.

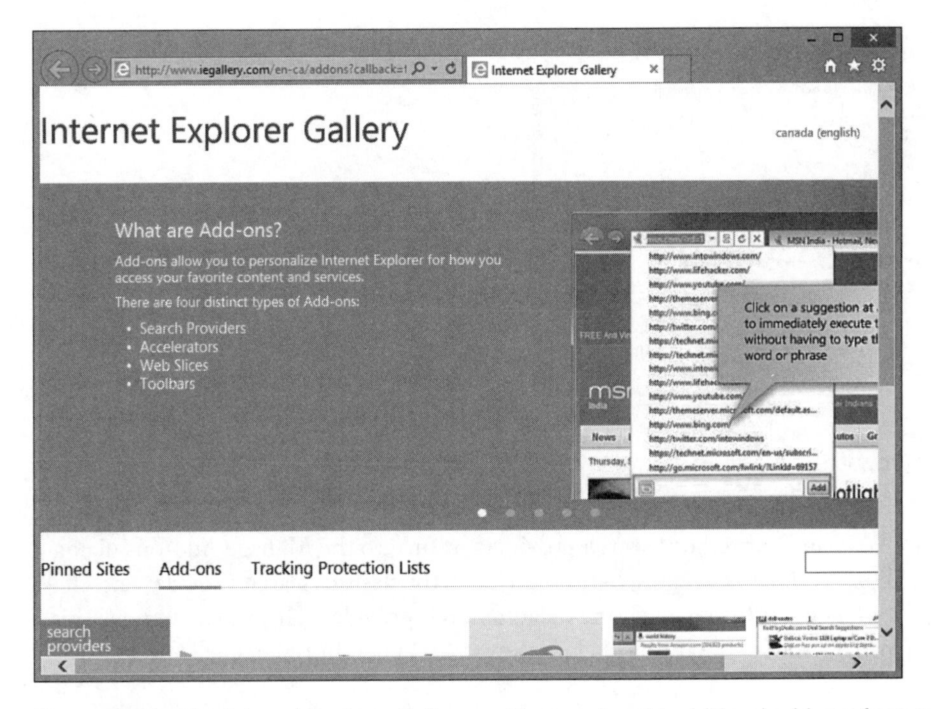

Figure 6-11 The Internet Explorer Gallery enables you to add additional add-ons from many categories.

Configuring Providers

By default, Internet Explorer uses Bing as its search provider when you first open it. Use the following procedure to change the default search provider or add additional search providers to this box.

Step 1. From the Manage Add-ons dialog box, select **Search Providers** under Add-on Types, and then click **Find more search providers**.

Step 2. Internet Explorer opens a new page displaying the Internet Explorer Gallery web page. Scroll to select the desired search provider and then click the **Add to Internet Explorer** command button.

Step 3. The Add Search Provider dialog box shown in Figure 6-12 appears. If you want to use this provider as your default, select the check box provided. Then click **Add**.

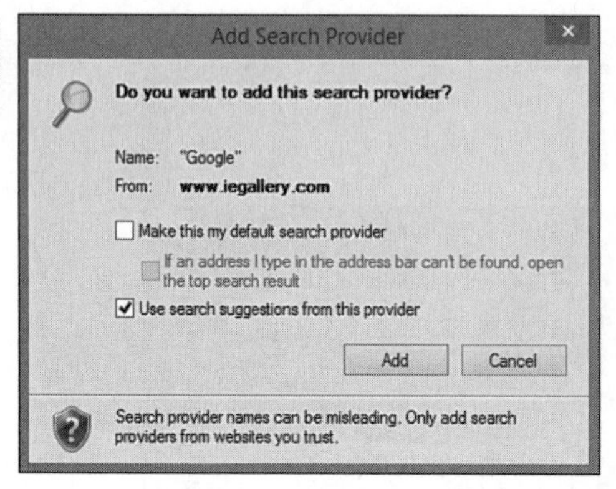

Figure 6-12 The Add Search Provider dialog box enables you to add search providers and set a default provider.

Step 4. To change or remove search providers, return to the Manage Add-ons dialog box. As shown in Figure 6-13, right-click the desired search provider and click **Set as default** to make it the default search provider. Or you can remove this provider from the list by clicking **Remove**. When finished, click **Close**.

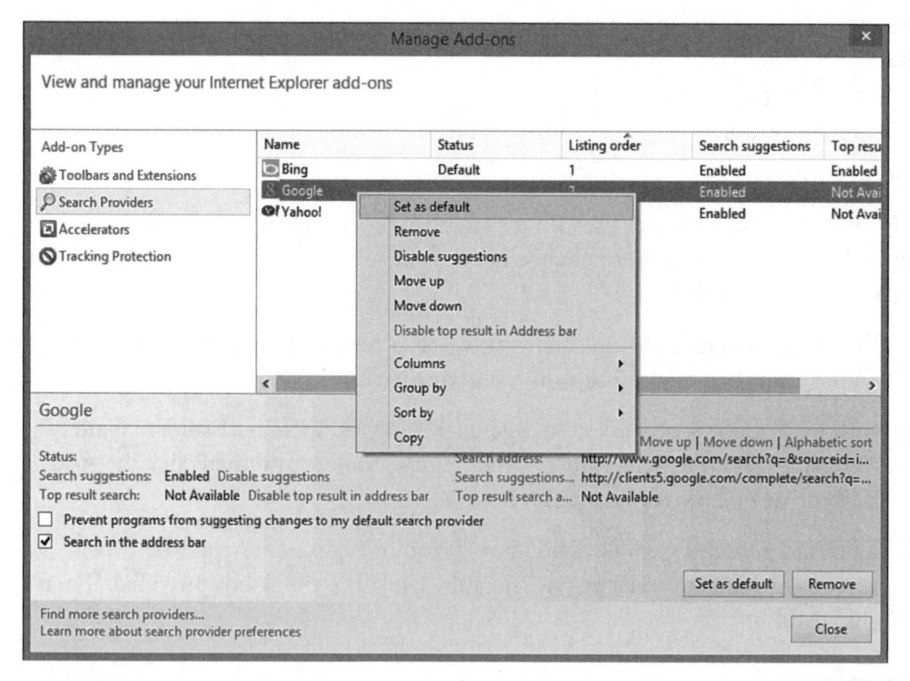

Figure 6-13 You can specify your default search provider or remove search providers from the Manage Add-ons dialog box.

After you have added search providers, it is simple to perform a search with an alternate provider. Simply click the same small magnifier that was shown in Figure 6-11 and select the icon for the desired search provider. This procedure enables you to change the search provider temporarily without changing the default provider.

Using Accelerators

An accelerator is a special type of add-on that enables users to perform actions against text they have selected from a website without leaving the website. Internet Explorer provides a default selection of accelerators. You can choose additional accelerators from an online list that is frequently updated.

Microsoft offers the following default types of accelerators:

- **Blog:** Enables you to post the selected text directly to your blog.
- **Email:** Pastes the selected text into a new email message, which you can then send to a recipient.
- **Map:** Uses an online mapping service to locate an address included in the selected text.
- **Search:** Uses your default search engine to locate additional information about the selected text.
- **Translate:** Enables you to use an online translation service to translate the selected text into another language.

Proceed as follows to use accelerators:

Step 1. Open **Internet Explorer 11** to the desired website.

Step 2. Select the text that you want to use with an accelerator.

Step 3. Right-click the text, select **All Accelerators**, and then choose the desired accelerator from the fly-out list. You can also click the small blue button that appears next to the selected text.

Step 4. To find additional accelerators that might work with the selected text, right-click the text and choose **All Accelerators > Find more Accelerators**. You are taken to the Add-ons Gallery: Accelerators website that includes accelerators specific to the selected text.

Using InPrivate Browsing Mode

First introduced in Internet Explorer 8 and continued in more recent versions of Internet Explorer is the InPrivate Browsing mode, which opens a new browser window that is isolated from items such as browser history and temporary Internet files.

This improves your privacy, especially when using a computer that is shared among several users (for example, when at an Internet café or library kiosk machine). All tabs that you open within this browser window are protected, but any additional windows you might open are not protected by InPrivate browsing.

To start a session in InPrivate Browsing mode, select **InPrivate Browsing** from the Safety menu. This opens a new browser window labeled InPrivate at the address bar. The home page that is displayed provides information about this browsing mode, as shown in Figure 6-14. The following types of information are discarded after you end your InPrivate browsing session by closing the browser window:

- Cookies and temporary Internet files (stored in memory during the browsing session only so that pages work properly)
- Website browsing history
- Information you supply on form pages including passwords
- AutoComplete and address bar information
- Automatic Crash Restore information that would normally restore browser tabs if Internet Explorer should crash

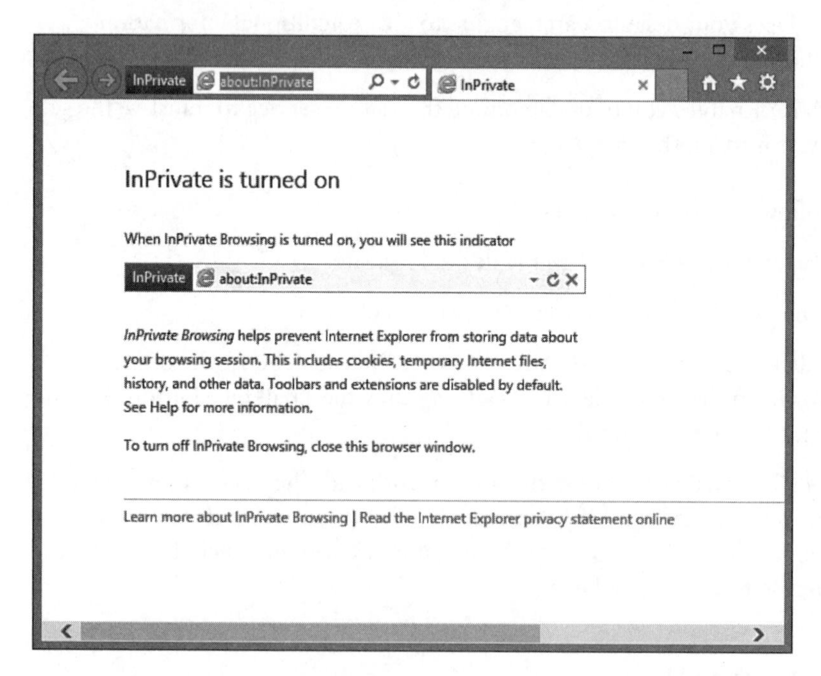

Figure 6-14 Enabling InPrivate Browsing.

TIP You can also start an InPrivate session from the Start screen version of Internet Explorer. To do so, right-click a blank area of any browser window to display open tabs and click the ellipsis icon that appears near the top-right corner. From the drop-down list that appears, select **New InPrivate tab**. This starts a new tab within the Start screen version that displays the same message as shown in Figure 6-14.

NOTE The InPrivate Filtering feature of the InPrivate Browsing mode, which was previously included in Internet Explorer 8 on Windows 7, is no longer supported in Internet Explorer 10 or 11.

Configuring WebSockets

HTML version 5.1 is the most current web standard, defined by the World Wide Web Consortium (W3C). This draft of version 5 is already being implemented by web technology vendors, including Microsoft, in IIS and Internet Explorer. Following the standards guarantees interoperability between, say, Firefox and IIS, or Internet Explorer and Apache web servers. And the early implementations help inform the members of the W3C consortium on which features are useful to technology vendors and which specifications need clarification or revision.

Most of the HTML specification deals with documents and the document elements, defined in the Document Object Model (DOM). WebSockets is composed of some interacting standards, including the Internet Engineering Task Force (IETF) WebSocket protocol that defines the communication between clients and servers, and the WebSocket API defined by the W3C. The WebSocket API specification defines how web pages can use the WebSocket protocol for bidirectional communication with a remote host.

In practice, WebSockets functionality is similar to AJAX (Asynchronous JavaScript and XML), which can update an item or small portion of a web page without refreshing the entire page. WebSockets, like the older AJAX technologies, enables very fast interaction between web pages and a remote server. Both technologies can be used to create highly responsive web-based applications, but using WebSockets is much more efficient because it was designed specifically for fast communication and displaying results in a preloaded web page.

NOTE For more information on the W3C WebSocket API specification, see "The WebSocket API" at http://www.w3.org/TR/websockets/. For more information on HTML version 5, refer to "HTML 5.1 Nightly: A vocabulary and associated APIs for HTML and XHTML" at http://www.w3.org/html/wg/drafts/html/master/.

To use a WebSockets application, you must be using a browser that supports it. Microsoft introduced WebSockets support in Internet Explorer starting with version 10 and continued this support with Internet Explorer 11 (included with Windows 8.1 and Windows Server 2012 R2).

You should know that WebSockets does not use the HTTP or HTTPS protocols typically used for requesting web pages (you see these protocols at the start of any URL in your browser's address bar). Instead, WebSockets uses WS (for unsecured communications) and WSS (for encrypted communication using SSL). Table 6-2 lists the common protocols used when accessing Internet resources.

Table 6-2 Accessing Resources Via a Browser

Command	Sample URL	Usage
`http://`	`http://www.microsoft.com`	Downloads HTML files from Internet web servers and displays the file within the browser
`https://`	`https://www.microsoft.com`	Downloads HTML files using SSL so that the information exchanged is secured
`ftp://`	`ftp://ftp.microsoft.com`	Downloads a file from an FTP server
`file://`	`file://server/share/folder/file`	Opens the file specified from a network server
`http://`	`http://printserver/printers`	Displays a list of the printers that are being shared by a computer configured with IIS for sharing printers
`http://`	`http://printserver/printer`	Opens the printer page for the printer
`ws://`	`ws://echo.websocket.org`	Opens a two-way WebSocket connection to a server
`wss://`	`wss://echo.websocket.org`	Opens a two-way WebSocket connection to a server, secured by SSL encryption

TIP Handling passwords when using FTP can be tricky. When you open a file using FTP, for example, you may need a password. Because Internet Explorer doesn't support password prompting, you need to supply that password within your URL. In this example, the correct syntax is ftp://user:password@ftpserver/url-path.

Configuring WebSockets in Windows 8.1

Like AJAX, WebSockets API clients rely on JavaScript support in the browser and may require some additional support. Strict security and other settings may affect the ability of Internet Explorer 11 to make use of WebSockets applications.

NOTE Do not confuse browser-based JavaScript with the Java language (and Java plug-in). JavaScript, based on the standard ECMAScript, is an interpreted language built into every browser that supports it. It does not require a plug-in or Java client to be installed on the computer. IE 10 introduced "ECMAScript 5 Strict Mode," described at http://msdn.microsoft.com/en-us/library/ie/hh673540(v=vs.85).aspx, and IE 11 now supports some of the commonly used and well-defined features proposed for the next official version of ECMAScript 6. Learn more about the ECMAScript standard at http://www.ecma-international.org/publications/standards/Ecma-262.htm.

The default IE 11 configuration on Windows 8.1 will work with WebSockets without any additional configuration; it requires only JavaScript and a network connection to the server. There are a few ways to disable WebSockets functionality in IE 11, but note that you cannot disable network access to a website specifically to block WebSockets. The reason is that WebSockets works on the same network protocol (TCP) and ports (80 and 443) as HTTP and HTTPS.

You can disable scripting in IE, as shown in Figure 6-15, which will disable any access to WebSockets API applications. If you set the security level to **High** for any zone, it will disable scripting from any site in that zone, and WebSockets will not work. Most modern websites use JavaScript to enhance the user experience, so disabling scripting altogether will have a significant impact on how pages are rendered and how they function.

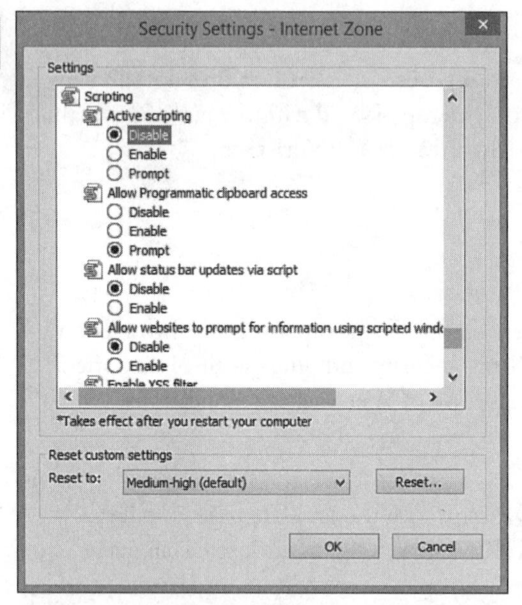

Figure 6-15 Disabling scripting support in IE 11.

Using Group Policy to Configure WebSockets

Several new Group Policy settings available for IE 11 can be used to control the new HTML 5 features, including WebSockets. If you need to restrict access to WebSockets in your enterprise, this is the recommended method for doing so.

The new Group Policy settings available for managing WebSockets setting in IE 11 are as follows:.

- **Set the maximum number of WebSocket connections per server:** Allows you to change the default limit of WebSocket connections per server. The default is 6. You can change this setting to any value from 2 to 128.
- **Turn off the WebSocket Object:** Allows you to enable or disable the WebSocket object, affecting Internet Explorer's ability to request data using WebSockets.

Configuring Download Manager

Internet Explorer includes a tool for managing the files downloaded from the Internet, intranet, and other locations. Over the course of days or weeks, some users may download many files such as spreadsheets, documents, tools, and installation files.

The Download Manager, included since Internet Explorer version 9, provides a handy location for tracking the history of file downloads, and managing the files and locations.

Download Manager integrates with users' Downloads library folder, and allows them to interact with file downloads in a central location. It can also be used to control current downloads, such as pausing or canceling downloads that are in progress.

IE's SmartScreen Filter works with Download Manager to identify risky programs and files and block any potentially harmful content. Users can interact with Download Manager to decide what to do with any downloads that SmartScreen Filter has identified as higher risk, or you can use Group Policy settings to prevent users from accessing these files.

Working with Download Manager

Download Manager is automatically started by Internet Explorer whenever you attempt to access certain files. Generally, this includes anything that IE does not recognize as a document that can be rendered in the browser. Initially, a small box appears at the bottom of the browser asking how Download Manager should handle the file, as shown in Figure 6-16:

- **Open:** Enables you to download the file to a temporary location and then open it with the associated program or application.
- **Save:** Includes a drop-down list:
    - **Save:** Enables you to download the file to the default location.
    - **Save As:** Enables you to specify a location and name for the download.
    - **Save and Open:** Enables you to download the file to the default location and then open it with the associated program or application.
- **Cancel:** Abandons the download and closes Download Manager. Clicking the small "X" on the right edge of the Download Manager box also cancels the download.

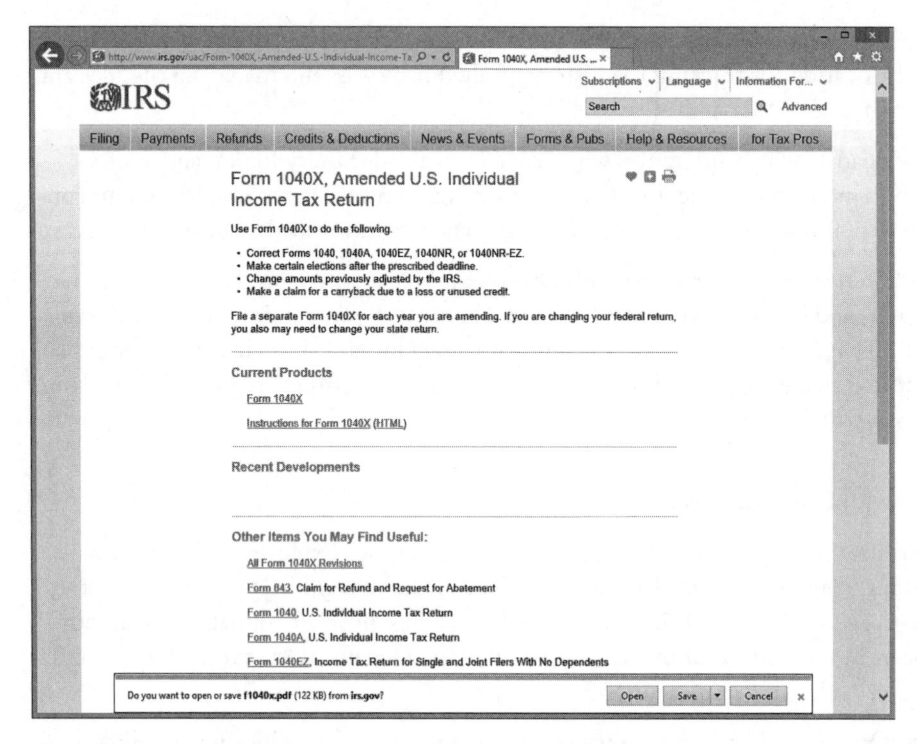

Figure 6-16 Download Manager dialog box in Internet Explorer 11.

Download Manager keeps track of the location and disposition of all files downloaded through IE. When you click on the **View downloads** button on the Download Manager bar after downloading a file, or from the **Settings** button on the IE toolbar, Download Manager opens to display the list of files it knows about, as shown in Figure 6-17.

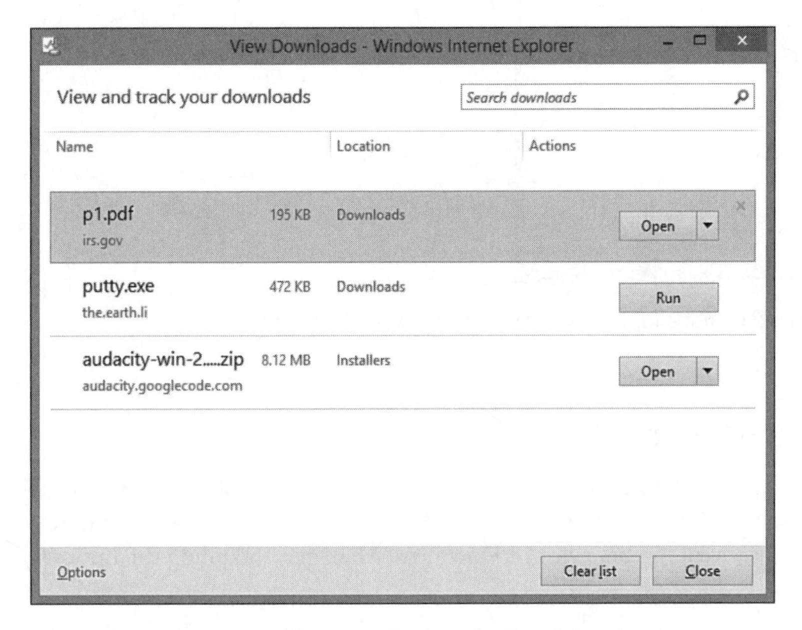

Figure 6-17 Download Manager displays the list of downloads.

Each entry in the list provides the file's name, which includes the original source of the file, the file size, the location, and any actions you can take. The Location column is actually a link to the location folder, and clicking on the link opens the folder location and highlights the file for you.

The buttons in the Actions column are sensitive to the type of file. So, for example, the Run action is displayed for an executable file. Other files display the Open button, including an Open As drop-down option to specify the application you want to use to open the file. To remove a file from the list, click the **Remove** ("X") button.

TIP When you open the Download Manager window, if any downloads are currently in progress, you can hover your mouse pointer over the file to display the transfer speed.

In the lower-left corner of the Download Manager window is the Options button. This link displays the Download Options dialog box as shown in Figure 6-18. From this window, you can configure the default location for saving your downloads and whether to display a notification when the downloads are complete.

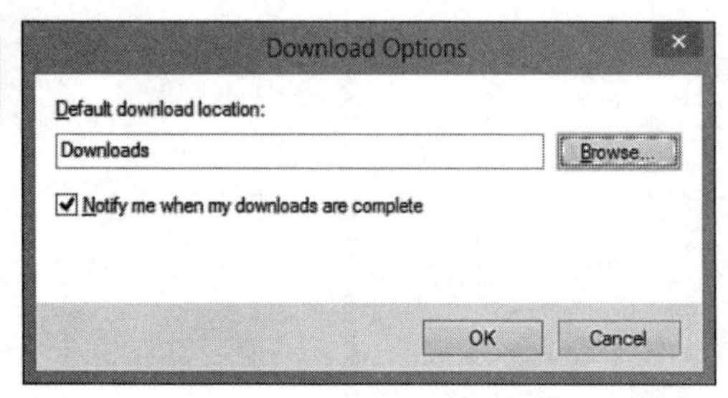

Figure 6-18 Download Options for Internet Explorer Download Manager.

Using Group Policy to Configure Download Manager

Download Manager configuration provides only a few options, as shown in Figure 6-18. Starting with IE9, there are some Group Policy settings that network administrators can use to control the behavior of Download Manager, including the options available to users.

The following Group Policy settings can be used to control Download Manager in IE 9 and IE 10:

- **Prevent Deleting Download History:** Enabling this option disables users' access to the Clear List button and Remove button in Download Manager.
- **Prevent users from bypassing SmartScreen Filter's application reputation warnings about files that are not commonly downloaded from the Internet:** If you enable this setting, users are blocked by SmartScreen Filter warnings displayed in the Download Manager and cannot override the SmartScreen Filter.

Exam Preparation Tasks

Review All the Key Topics

Review the most important topics in the chapter, noted with the key topics icon in the outer margin of the page. Table 6-3 lists a reference of these key topics and the page numbers on which each is found.

Table 6-3 Key Topics for Chapter 6

Key Topic Element	Description	Page Number
Figure 6-1	Shows how to configure Compatibility View settings	257
Figure 6-4	Shows the available Security zones in Internet Explorer	261
Figure 6-7	Shows available cookie and pop-up blocker settings in Internet Explorer	266
Figure 6-8	Shows how to configure the pop-up blocker	268
Figure 6-10	Shows how to manage add-ons	271
Figure 6-12	Shows how to add search providers	274
List	Describes items that are discarded when an InPrivate browsing session ends	276
Table 6-2	Describes the common protocols used when accessing Internet resources	278
Figure 6-15	Shows how to disable scripting support in IE 11	280
List	Lists Group Policy settings to control WebSockets	280
Figure 6-18	Shows Download Options for Internet Explorer Download Manager	284
List	Lists Group Policy settings for Download Manager	284

Complete the Tables and Lists from Memory

Print a copy of Appendix B, "Memory Tables," (found on the CD), or at least the section for this chapter, and complete the tables and lists from memory. Appendix C, "Memory Tables Answer Key," also on the CD, includes completed tables and lists to check your work.

Definitions of Key Terms

Define the following key terms from this chapter and check your answers in the glossary:

Add-on Manager, Add-ons, Compatibility View, Download Manager, HTML5 sandbox attribute, Information bar, InPrivate browsing, Phishing, Pop-up windows, Protected Mode, Secure Sockets Layer (SSL), SmartScreen Filter, WebSockets

This chapter covers the following subjects:

- **Understanding VHDs:** In Chapter 2, "Installing Windows 8.1," you learned about virtual hard disks (VHDs) and native boot VHDs; you also learned how to install Windows 8.1 on them. This section covers VHDs in more detail, and you learn about the new VHDX format optimized for Hyper-V and how to create, configure, and use VHDs in the virtual environment.
- **Creating Virtual Machines:** Hyper-V, Microsoft's virtualization technology used in Windows Server 2008 and later, was made available for Windows 8 and Windows 8.1. This section introduces Client Hyper-V, the virtualization technology used in Windows 8.1. You learn how to deploy VHDs and virtual machines in Client Hyper-V and how to configure virtual machines.
- **Creating and Configuring Virtual Switches:** When using Hyper-V, you work with not only virtual machines and hard disks, but also virtual networks. Virtual networks utilize software representations of network switches, and this section discusses the types of virtual switches used with Hyper-V, how to create and configure them, and how the virtual networks interact with the host computer and the outside world.

Configuring Hyper-V

Virtualization is a technique for carving up physical computer resources into multiple pseudo machines, allowing multiple operating systems to run on a single hardware platform. The virtual machine (VM) appears to be a complete physical computer to the operating system running inside it. A special underlying operating system known as a hypervisor is responsible for controlling access to the physical hardware and presenting the virtualized resources to the operating system guests.

This technology is not new. IBM came out with the first system capable of virtualization in 1972 with the release of VM/CMS for its mainframe systems. Microcomputers, using smaller, cheaper commodity hardware, slowly started replacing mainframes in the datacenter, and as the Intel and AMD platforms became more powerful, eventually virtualization also was introduced in these platforms. Initially, virtualization for large servers and datacenters was a way to make use of all the idle cycles on the servers, which became even more efficient when manufacturers began producing microprocessors with multiple cores on a single chip. For companies with requirements for lots of servers to run their businesses, virtualization was a way to save money on hardware, power, and rack space by running more servers on fewer machines.

Microsoft introduced the final production version of its virtualization product, now called Hyper-V, in June of 2008. Hyper-V is now available without additional license fees for all versions of Windows Server 2008 and later.

Client Hyper-V is now built into Windows 8.1, and is the same virtualization technology as previously used in Windows Server 2008 and later. It allows you to run more than one operating system at the same time on the same workstation computer. Guest operating systems run in a VM, and you can quickly switch between the Windows 8.1 host operating system and any VM.

For the 70-687 exam, you are expected to understand some basics of how virtualization works, know the hardware and operating system requirements for running Client Hyper-V, and have the skills to install the Hyper-V hypervisor in Windows 8.1. You should also know how to create and manage virtual hard disks (VHDs), deploy VMs using VHDs, and configure and manage virtual switches, which are virtual representations of physical hardware that run right inside the host machine's virtualized environment.

"Do I Know This Already?" Quiz

The "Do I Know This Already?" quiz allows you to assess whether you should read this entire chapter or simply jump to the "Exam Preparation Tasks" section for review. If you are in doubt, read the entire chapter. Table 7-1 outlines the major headings in this chapter and the corresponding "Do I Know This Already?" quiz questions. You can find the answers in Appendix A, "Answers to the 'Do I Know This Already?' Quizzes."

Table 7-1 "Do I Know This Already?" Foundation Topics Section-to-Question Mapping

Foundations Topics Section	Questions Covered in This Section
Understanding VHDs	1–3
Creating Virtual Machines	4–9
Creating and Configuring Virtual Switches	10–11

1. Virtual hard disks are used for deploying Windows operating systems in a number of ways, including in a Hyper-V virtual environment. What type of VHD is optimized for use in Hyper-V?
   a. Native-boot VHDs
   b. VHDX-formatted VHDs
   c. Hyper-VHDs
   d. VHDs in `.AVHD` format

2. The new VHD format optimized for Hyper-V supports which of the following features? (Select all that apply.)
   a. Storage capacity up to 2 TB
   b. Metadata logging to prevent file system corruption
   c. Larger block sizes for dynamic and differencing disks
   d. User-defined custom metadata

3. Which of the following tools can be used to create a VHD? (Select all that apply.)
   a. DiskPart
   b. Hyper-V Manager
   c. BCDEdit
   d. Disk Management

4. You are a desktop support technician for a large corporation, and one of the developers in your organization has asked you to install Hyper-V on his corporate workstation for use in testing some new application software. You have obtained the detailed order slip for the computer and realize that you will not be able to install Hyper-V on it. Which item did you discover on the order specifications that led to that conclusion?

   a. Dell Computer with Intel Core i-7 processor

   b. Windows 8.1 Enterprise 32-bit

   c. 6 GB of system RAM

   d. 250 GB Internal IDE Hard Drive

   e. BIOS version 2012.23a with VT and XD enabled

5. You are a desktop support technician for a large corporation, and one of the developers in your organization has asked you to install Hyper-V on her corporate workstation for use in testing some new application software. She has ordered a new workstation that meets all the necessary requirements, and now you need to install the Hyper-V software. How do you obtain the necessary installation files?

   a. The software is already available on the computer.

   b. Download from the Microsoft website.

   c. Obtain a disk from your Enterprise License administrator.

   d. Order it from your software reseller.

6. You are modifying the configuration of a virtual machine in Client Hyper-V from the Hyper-V Manager. The computer has 12 GB of system RAM. What is the maximum amount of RAM you can select in the virtual machine's configuration settings?

   a. 12 GB

   b. 10 GB

   c. 120 GB

   d. 1 TB

7. You have a test computer with several Hyper-V virtual machines configured. One of the VMs is hosting an application that you want to test in various operating systems and configurations, so you have several VMs to use for testing access to the application. You have now run into problems when several of the VMs are running, and the host processors are running high utilization, which causes the application host to perform too slowly to test properly. What should you do to ensure that the VM hosting the application can respond properly?

- **a.** Enable Dynamic Memory
- **b.** Increase the Memory weight of the application VM
- **c.** Assign a higher relative weight to the application VM's processor
- **d.** Add more processors to the test VMs

8. You are running Client Hyper-V on a large workstation equipped with 16 GB of system RAM and two processors with four cores each. If you are running four VMs on this computer, what is the maximum number of virtual processors you can assign to each one?

- **a.** 2 virtual processors
- **b.** 4 virtual processors
- **c.** 8 virtual processors
- **d.** 16 virtual processors

9. You are performing testing on a Client Hyper-V virtual machine and have created checkpoints every day for the past five days. You select the first checkpoint from the list in the Hyper-V Manager and delete the first checkpoint. What happens to the virtual machine?

- **a.** All changes since the first checkpoint are lost.
- **b.** The VM is reverted to its condition before the first checkpoint.
- **c.** Changes made since the checkpoint are merged into the running state.
- **d.** The VM is restarted, and the checkpoint changes are lost.

10. You are creating virtual switches for use with your VMs and would like to ensure that they can access the Internet and Windows Update. What type of virtual switch would you create for these VMs?

- **a.** Internal virtual switch
- **b.** External virtual switch
- **c.** Public virtual switch
- **d.** Private virtual switch

11. You have used the Hyper-V Manager to create a new internal virtual switch and connected all of your VMs to the new switch, but the VMs' network configurations are still using private autoconfiguration addresses and you cannot ping any of the VMs from the host. What should you do to allow the host to communicate with the VMs?

    a. Manually configure the IP settings of the host and VMs

    b. Use connection sharing on the Hyper-V host

    c. Use an external virtual switch instead

    d. Turn off the firewall

Foundation Topics

Understanding VHDs

In Chapter 2, we covered how to use a virtual hard disk (VHD) in Windows 8.1 and how to install Windows 8.1 on an existing VHD. Some of this material is a review of the "Using a VHD" section of Chapter 2, but it goes further in depth into the types of VHDs and how they are created, managed, and deployed in Hyper-V.

Recall from Chapter 2 that the VHD was used to create a new bootable Windows 8.1 installation, which was then added to the computer's boot menu. This technique was a convenient way to create a Windows 8.1 image that could then be copied to other computers and booted from the boot menu. It makes deploying Windows 8.1 to multiple machines very convenient, but VHDs are useful in many other ways, especially when combined with Hyper-V.

A VHD can be used not just for Windows 8.1 or Windows 7; it could alternatively contain Windows XP, a Linux or Unix distribution, or a custom, bootable appliance. And with Hyper-V, you do not need to add this image to the boot menu and restart the computer. Instead, the alternative operating system (OS) can run in a VM as a guest while the Windows 8.1 OS is running as a host. Some vendors, including Microsoft, offer fully functional operating systems for download over the Internet, ready to boot from Windows 8.1 Hyper-V, on a preconfigured VHD.

NOTE You can explore some of the VHD downloads offered by Microsoft on the Virtual Hard Disk Test Drive Program at http://technet.microsoft.com/en-us/bb738372.aspx.

Creating and Configuring VHDs

Before creating and running operating system guests under Client Hyper-V, you need to create a virtual disk for the guest OS to use. Client Hyper-V can run guests installed on VHD files or the new VHDX format, designed specifically for VMs running under Hyper-V.

The new VHDX format provides several advantages over the VHD format, but note that VHDX formatted disks cannot be used as native-boot VHDs; only guests running in Hyper-V or Client Hyper-V can make use of VHDX files. The VHDX format supports the following features:

- Support for storage capacity up to 64 TB (compared to 2 TB for VHD format)
- Support for VHDX metadata logging, to protect against file system corruption during power failures and improper shutdown
- Improved alignment for greater efficiency on large sector disks
- Large block sizes for dynamic and differencing disk
- Support for 4 KB logical sector VHDs
- Support for user-editable custom metadata for the VHDX file
- Support for smaller file sizes using trim, when using trim-compatible hardware

In Chapter 2, you created a VHD using the Disk Management snap-in. You also used BCDBoot to set up a boot environment, and used BCDEdit to manage the boot configuration for a native boot VHD. This is probably the most common method of creating a VHD in Windows 8.1, but you should understand and know how to use other tools and procedures. You should review Table 2-8 and be familiar with the available tools.

You can also create a VHD using the Hyper-V Manager in Windows 8.1. This utility can be run on any Windows 8.1 machine even if the computer cannot support the Hyper-V platform. Installing and using the Hyper-V Manager is covered in the next section.

This section covers the process for creating a VHD using the DiskPart command-line tool. It is included with Windows 8.1 as part of the default installation, and no further installation is needed to start using it.

Using DiskPart to Create a VHD

The DiskPart utility enables you to create a VHD from the command line. You can script this action to create multiple VHDs if necessary. The DiskPart command-line tool is available in all Windows desktop editions starting with Windows Vista and all Windows Server versions starting with Windows Server 2003. It is used to manage storage objects including disks, partitions, and volumes by using scripts, or you can use it directly from the command prompt.

Using DiskPart requires that you use commands to focus on an object using DiskPart commands to list and select a particular storage object and then use commands that act on that object. In the following example, the `create` commands act to focus on the objects created, and subsequent DiskPart commands act on that object.

NOTE For more information on the DiskPart utility, syntax, and the commands available, see the topic "DiskPart Command-Line Options" at http://technet.microsoft.com/en-us/library/cc766465%28v=ws.10%29.aspx.

Step 1. Open a command prompt by clicking on the **Search** charm, typing **`cmd`** in the search box, right-clicking the **Command Prompt** link, and then selecting the **Run as administrator** option from the pop-up menu. Click **Yes** in the User Account Control prompt that appears.

Step 2. Type **`diskpart`** in the administrative command prompt. You receive the `diskpart` command prompt.

Step 3. To create a 20 GB dynamic VHD using the VHDX format and named `win01.vhdx`, type **`create vdisk file="c:\win01.vhdx" maximum=20000 type=expandable`**. The format is taken from the extension used (`.vhd` or `.vhdx`).

Step 4. When you are informed that DiskPart has successfully created the file, type **`attach vdisk`**.

Step 5. When DiskPart informs you that the disk was attached, type **`list disk`** to show that the disk is present and online. This command also provides the disk number that you must enter in the next step of the procedure.

Step 6. To create a partition on the VHD, type **`select disk`** *n*, press **Enter**. Then type **`create partition primary`** and press **Enter** again. In this command, *n* is the disk number you obtained from the previous step.

Step 7. To perform a quick format on the partition using the NTFS file system, type **`format fs=ntfs quick`**.

Step 8. To assign the drive letter `f:` to the new partition, type **`assign letter=f`**.

Step 9. To mark the partition as active, type **`active`**.

These steps complete the creation of a VHD on drive `f:` that is suitable for installing a virtual copy of Windows. Figure 7-1 shows how these steps appear at the console. Table 7-2 outlines the parameters of the `vdisk` command that are most useful for creating and working with VHDs.

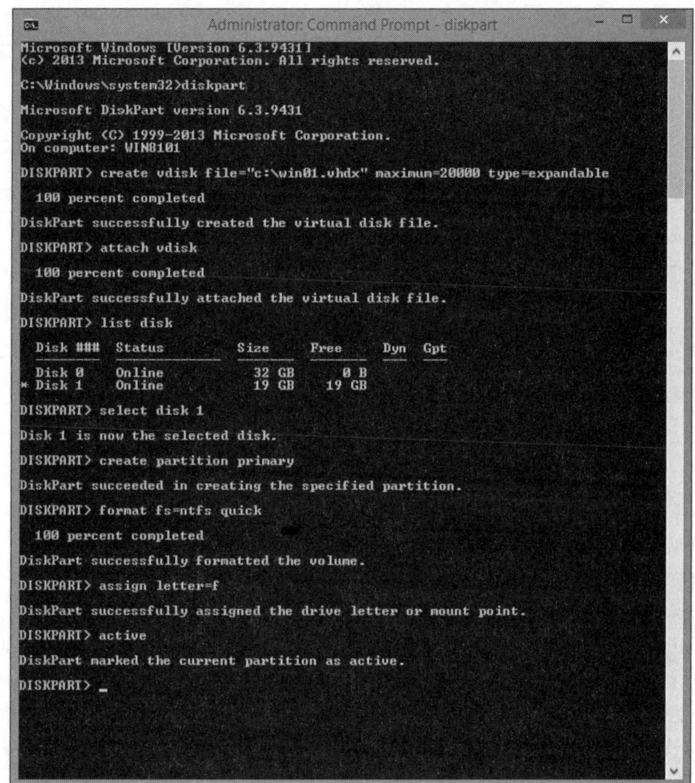

Figure 7-1 Using DiskPart to create, format, and assign a VHD.

Refer to Table 7-2 for some common DiskPart command parameters and how they are used.

Table 7-2 DiskPart Commands Used in Creating VHDs

Command	Purpose
`create vdisk file="filename" maximum=size type=type`	Creates a VHD named *filename*, with maximum size stated in megabytes, and *type* = *fixed*, *expandable*, or *differencing*. The extension used for the filename determines whether the format used is VHD or VHDX.
`attach`	Attaches (mounts) the VHD.
`list disk`	Shows all disks (physical and virtual) attached to the system, together with their size and identifying number.
`Select disk=n`	Selects the VHD so that it can be partitioned and formatted, where *n* is the number of the disk as shown by the list disk command.

Command	Purpose
`create partition primary`	Creates a primary partition on the VHD, using the maximum available space. If you want to use only a portion of the VHD, include the keyword `size=`*nnnn*, where *nnnn* is the partition size in megabytes.
`format fs=`*`filesystem`*	Formats the partition using the file system named *`filesystem`* (which can be `fat`, `fat32`, or `ntfs`). Add the keyword `quick` to perform a quick format.
`assign letter=`*`letter`*	Assigns a drive letter to the partition.
`active`	Marks the selected partition as active.

Mounting VHDs

The act of creating a VHD, described in the preceding section, also mounts the VHD automatically so that it is accessible to the physical machine as a distinct drive with its own drive letter. It is also possible to create a VHD on one computer, make copies of it, and use these copies on other computers. To do so, you must mount the VHD on each new computer. Simply put, this is the virtual analogy of opening the computer, installing and connecting a new hard disk, closing the computer, and rebooting it. Recall from Chapter 2 that you can perform these tasks using Disk Management by using the Attach VHD command, as shown in Figure 7-2.

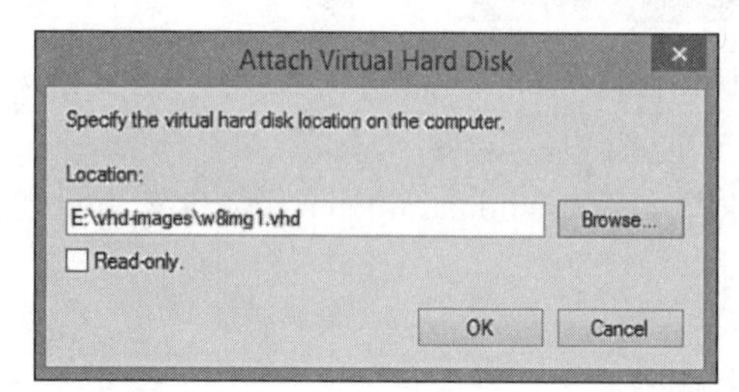

Figure 7-2 Attaching a VHD using the Disk Management snap-in.

You can also dismount a VHD from either of these two utilities. In Disk Management, right-click the VHD in the details pane and choose **Detach VHD**. In DiskPart, select the VHD and then type **`detach vdisk`**.

TIP You can even mount a VHD located on another computer across the network, provided you have proper access permissions to its location. In Disk Management, click **Browse**, click **Network**, and browse to the proper network location. In DiskPart, type the universal naming convention (UNC) path to the shared location for path in step 3 of the preceding procedure.

TIP You can use Windows Deployment Services (WDS) to deploy the VHD image to large numbers of computers. WDS in Windows Server 2012 R2 includes the capability to add VHD image files to its image catalog, making them available to target computers using PXE boot. Mass deployment and management of Windows 8.1 computers and virtual environments are beyond the scope of the 70-687 exam. These topics are covered in detail in 70-688, "Managing and Maintaining Windows 8."

Creating Virtual Machines

After you create a VHD in Windows 8.1, you can create a VM guest using the VHD as the VM's drive. You can then load and run the VM in Client Hyper-V on your Windows 8.1 Pro or Windows 8.1 Enterprise workstation.

This is the easiest method for supporting a VM, but note that a VHD is not strictly a requirement. Virtual machines can also be run using actual disks, passed directly to the VM. It is also possible to run a VM from a VHD on a remote file server.

To support Client Hyper-V, you need to be aware of a few requirements:

- A 64-bit version of Windows 8.1 Pro or Windows 8.1 Enterprise. Client Hyper-V does not run on Windows 8.1 or any 32-bit edition.
- A CPU that supports Second Level Address Translation (SLAT). All current versions of AMD 64-bit processors support SLAT, as do many 64-bit processors from Intel. Some budget and mobile editions of Intel processors do not support SLAT.
- A BIOS with virtualization support—either VT for Intel platforms or AMD-V for AMD-based systems.
- Hardware Data Execution Prevention (DEP). This is called Execute Disable, or XD, on Intel processors; and No Execute, or NX, on AMD processors. The option must be enabled in the BIOS.
- At least 4 GB of system RAM.

The number of VMs you can run and the performance of each depend on the amount of RAM you have available. You can create VMs that use up to 512 GB of RAM, and each VM will require some overhead memory, in addition to the memory required by the host operating system and the hypervisor.

NOTE For more details on hardware and software requirements for Client Hyper-V, see the Microsoft TechNet article "Client Hyper-V" at http://technet.microsoft.com/library/hh857623.aspx.

Enabling Client Hyper-V in Windows 8.1

Windows 8.1 Pro and Enterprise editions come with Client Hyper-V available out of the box, but it must be installed using the Windows Features installer from the Control Panel's Programs snap-in. The feature installer provides a convenient way to make sure that your Windows 8.1 computer can support the Hyper-V hypervisor because it can detect many of the requirements and disable the option if any requirements are missing.

Use the following steps to enable Hyper-V:

Step 1. Right-click the **Start** button and select **Control Panel** from the menu.

Step 2. In the Control Panel window, select **Programs**.

Step 3. From the list of Programs and Features functions, click **Turn Windows features on** or **off**.

Step 4. Expand the Hyper-V folder, displaying the selections Hyper-V Management Tools and Hyper-V Platform.

NOTE If Client Hyper-V is not supported due to any missing requirements, the Hyper-V Platform option will be disabled. Hover your mouse pointer over the disabled option, and Windows will display a ToolTip to explain why you cannot install the Hyper-V Platform. In Figure 7-3, Hyper-V is disabled because the processor does not support all the necessary features.

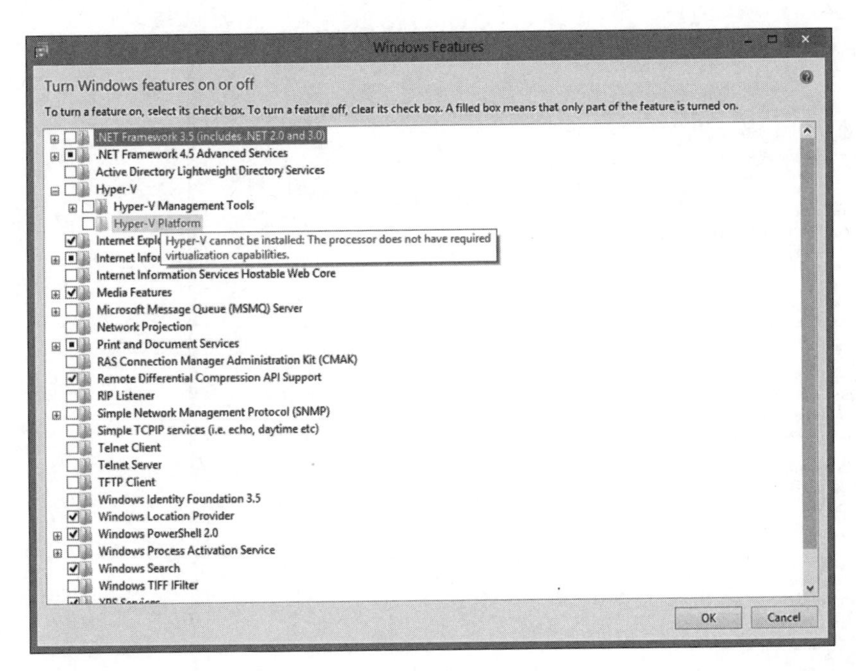

Figure 7-3 Hyper-V cannot be installed because the processor does not support the necessary virtualization features.

Step 5. Select all Hyper-V options to include Management Tools and the Hyper-V Platform, as shown in Figure 7-4.

Step 6. Click **OK** to install the Hyper-V features. Windows takes a few minutes to perform the installation and then requests a reboot to complete the changes.

Step 7. Click **Reboot Now** to complete the installation.

Step 8. After Windows 8.1 restarts, Hyper-V is installed and ready to use.

Figure 7-4 Selecting all Hyper-V Windows Features for installation.

Creating a Hyper-V Virtual Machine

Many scenarios make the use of virtual machines in a client environment a compelling solution for efficient use of resources and time. Server virtualization provides many advantages for making the best use of costly hardware resources. Client Hyper-V offers some of the same efficiencies, but that is less of a consideration than other use cases:

- Developers and systems engineers can maintain multiple test environments.
- You can run older versions of Windows for applications that will not run on current versions.
- You can build a test lab infrastructure on a computer or laptop. Workstations or server VMs tested in the virtual lab can be migrated to a virtualized production environment.
- Developers or quality assurance (QA) professionals can test applications or changes on multiple operating systems, using a single Client Hyper-V computer.

- You can export a VM from the production environment to a Client Hyper-V test machine. From there, you can troubleshoot, apply and test fixes, and restart the system multiple times without impacting the current production systems.
- You can use VM checkpoints while a machine is running to test invasive changes. You can test changes and revert to the point-in-time before the checkpoint if things go wrong or apply the checkpoint back to the running VM if the testing is successful.
- Using a workstation that has a fast processor and enough RAM, you can deploy an entire working environment as VMs on Client Hyper-V, to include all networking configurations and virtual switches. You can use it for testing, software development, or even demonstration of a proof-of-concept.

Designing a virtual environment for some of these scenarios may require some planning. Alternatively, it can serve as a proof-of-concept environment as a preliminary step to planning an environment. Because you are not deploying expensive hardware and all your changes can be easily reversed, changed, or simply deleted, a virtual environment provides the freedom to experiment with options without much risk. You can document the changes you make and systems you design as you go, and you can perform planning when technical challenges are overcome. Deciding when to take a checkpoint of a VM or a set of VMs may be the most difficult planning decision to make during the testing. The only disruption any of your changes will cause is to a single workstation.

Note one of the scenarios listed here was based on a use case for running older applications that do not work in current versions of Windows. This scenario may be rare, but it does happen. Applications can become obsolete and unsupported but are still required for business needs that cannot easily be replaced. In Windows Vista and Windows 7, this type of issue was addressed with Windows XP Mode, which allowed users to run a virtualized version of Windows XP on top of their Windows Vista or Windows 7 computer. In Windows 8.1, this trimmed-down virtualization feature has been replaced with Hyper-V.

Using the Hyper-V Manager

After you install Hyper-V and the Hyper-V management tools, the Hyper-V Manager is ready to run. You can start the Hyper-V Manager from the Start screen. If you cannot find the link, click on the **Search** charm and type `hyper` in the search box. The link for the Hyper-V Manager appears in the Apps section. Click on it to start the management interface, which starts in desktop mode. When you click on the host computer name, it looks similar to the screen in Figure 7-5.

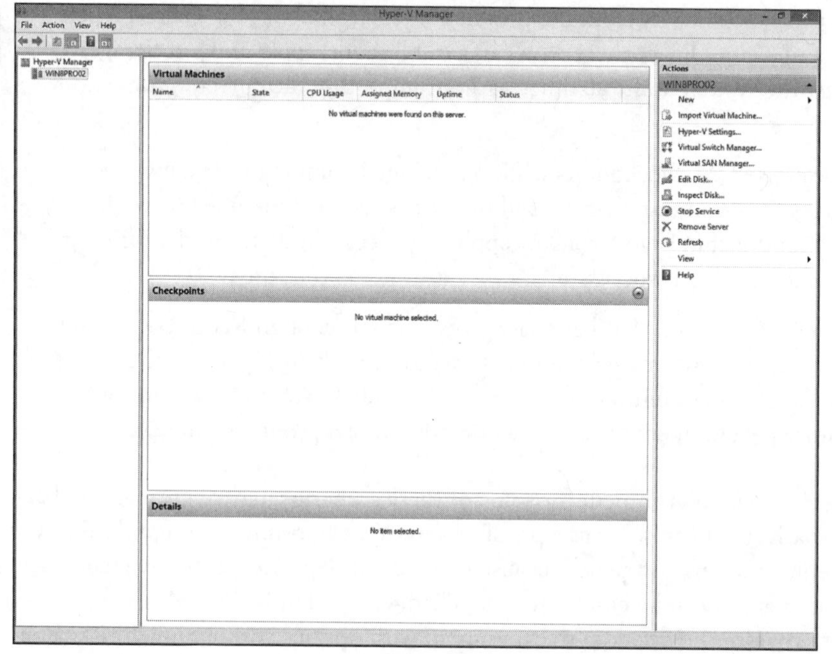

Figure 7-5 The Hyper-V Manager screen before any virtual machines are added.

The Hyper-V Manager is a central location for managing your Hyper-V virtual hosts and the VMs running on those hosts. Similar to the way you use other Microsoft Management Console snap-ins, you can connect to other computers and servers running the Hyper-V Platform and perform the same tasks on those hosts and VMs.

The manager interface is composed of three sections. The left navigation pane shows the Hyper-V host machines and allows you to focus on a specific host and add new ones to the inventory.

The central pane displays the VMs for the current host, an area to display checkpoints for a selected VM, and finally a Details list for displaying configuration specifics of the VM you are working with. When a running VM is selected, the Details section displays a miniature image of the virtual console and tabs for checking the current memory and networking usage.

The right pane is the Actions section, where you can create new virtual machines, manage the host configuration settings, manage VHDs and storage area network (SAN) storage locations, and perform other functions. Each of these actions is also available from the right-click menu of each host name in the navigation pane.

Creating Virtual Machines

You can create a new VM in Hyper-V Manager by following a simple wizard-like interface. The following steps create a basic virtual machine ready to run:

Step 1. In Hyper-V Manager's Actions pane, click **New > Virtual Machine**. The New Virtual Machine Wizard screen is displayed.

Step 2. Read the information on the Before You Begin page and then click the **Next** button.

Step 3. When the **Specify Name and Location** screen depicted in Figure 7-6 is displayed, enter a descriptive name for the new VM in the box provided. Optionally, you can change the folder location for the VM. This location refers only to the configuration files for the VM itself, not the virtual disk that the VM guest will use for storage. Click the **Next** button to proceed.

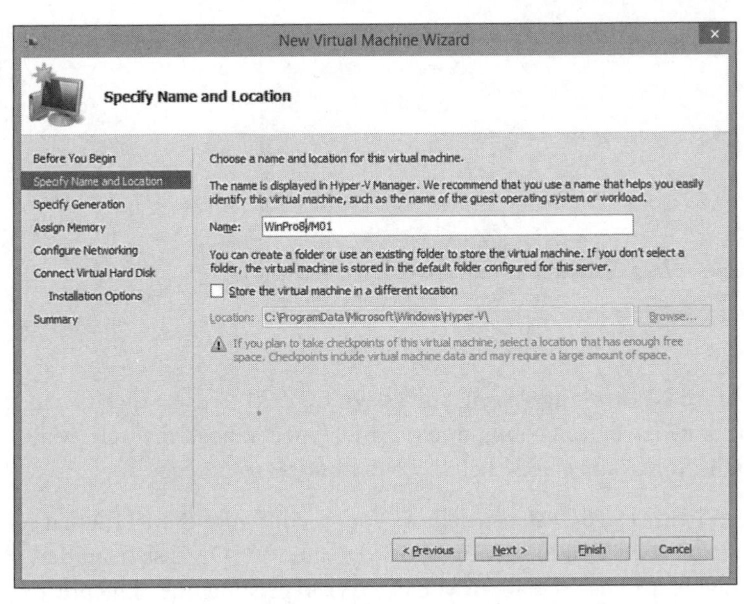

Figure 7-6 Creating a new virtual machine.

Step 4. On the Specify Generation screen, you can select whether to use the Generation 1 or Generation 2 virtual machine. The Generation 2 option, new for Windows 8.1 and Windows Server 2012 R2, supports features available in newer hardware such as Unified Extensible Firmware Interface (UEFI) and secure boot. If you are installing Windows Server 2012 or a 64-bit edition of Windows 8 as the guest, you can use Generation 2. Otherwise, you must select Generation 1.

Step 5. On the Assign Memory screen (see Figure 7-7), decide how much memory the VM will use. The minimum is 8 MB, and the maximum depends on the amount of RAM available on the physical host. The default is 512 MB of RAM. When you have assigned the memory you want the VM to use, click the **Next** button.

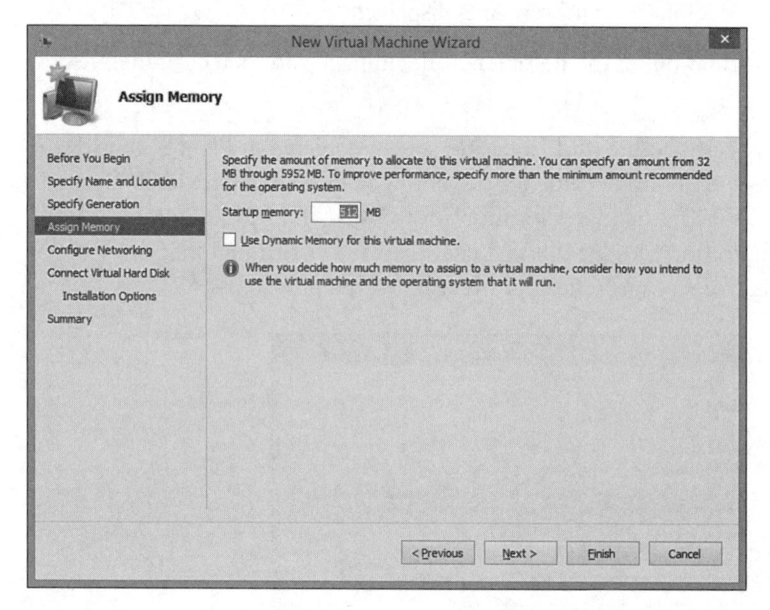

Figure 7-7 Assigning memory for a new virtual machine.

Step 6. On the Configure Networking screen, you assign the VM to use a specific virtual switch. If none have been configured on the Hyper-V host, the only available selection is Not Connected. Click the **Next** button to proceed.

Step 7. The Connect Virtual Hard Disk page allows you to configure the VHD that will be used by the VM. You can create a new dynamic VHDX disk from the Connect Virtual Hard Disk screen, or you can use an existing one. The previous section covered creating a VHDX using DiskPart, and in Figure 7-8, this disk is assigned to the new VM. Click **Next** to proceed.

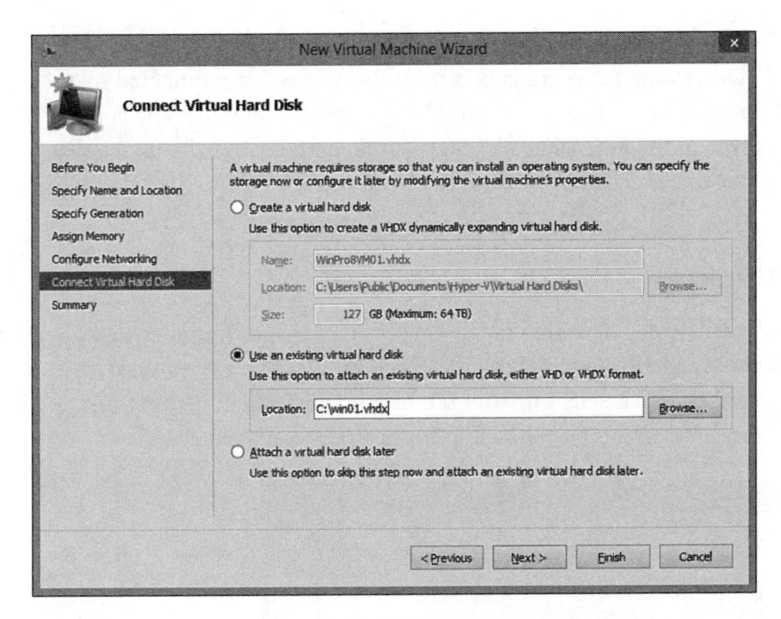

Figure 7-8 Assigning an existing VHD to a new virtual machine.

Step 8. The Completing the New Virtual Machine Wizard page shown in Figure 7-9 displays a description of your selections. When you click the **Finish** button, the wizard creates the new VM.

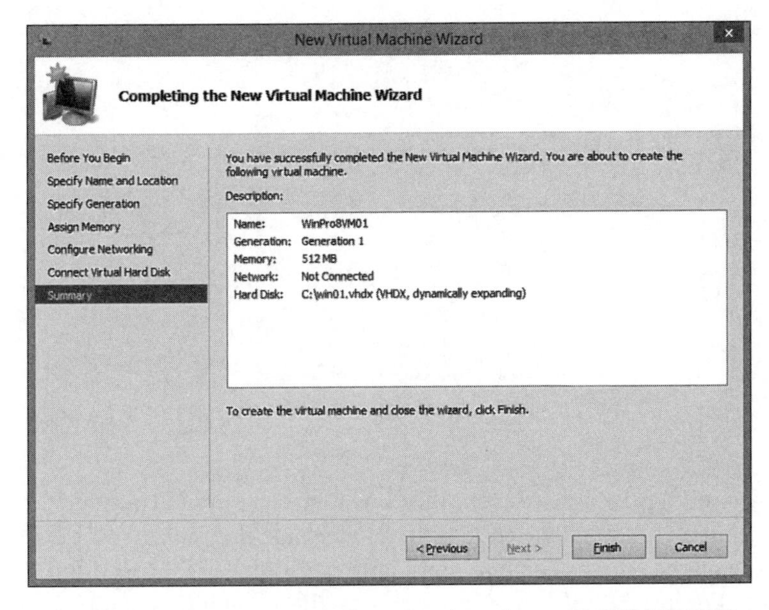

Figure 7-9 Ready to create a new virtual machine with 512 MB RAM and no networking.

The VM created with this method is a pretty basic machine. Unless you use a VHD with an existing Windows image, there is no OS. If the VM is not connected to a virtual switch, it has no networking. There are many ways to make the VM actually useful, which we cover in the following sections. But first we look at the many VM configuration options that were not available from the wizard.

Configuring Virtual Machines

When you first create a VM, it is added to the Hyper-V Manager but is turned off. Some settings can be changed only while the VM is powered off. To configure the settings for a powered-off VM, select it from the list and then click the **Settings** action for the machine. The dialog box shown in Figure 7-10 is displayed.

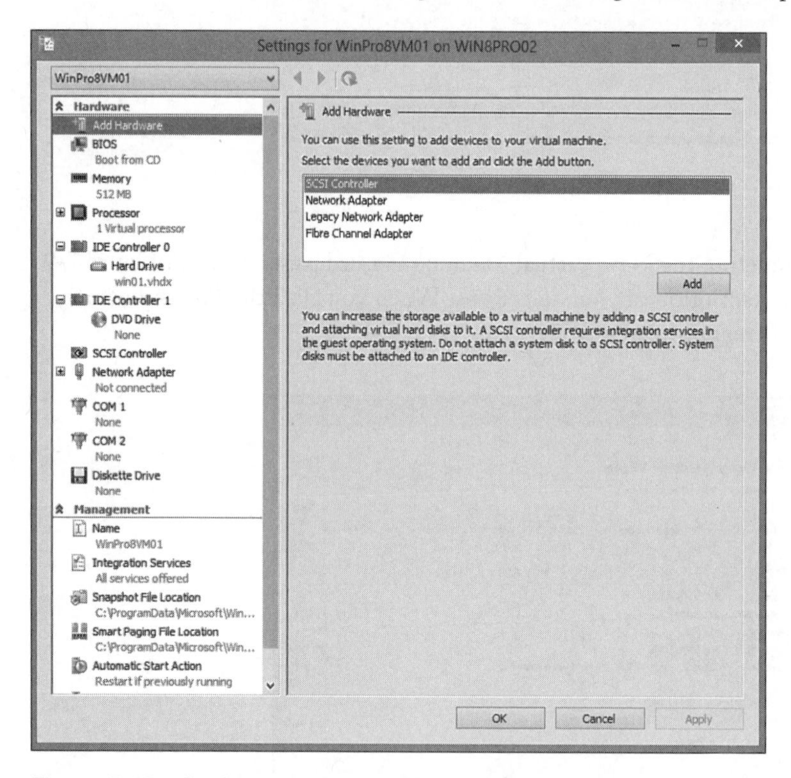

Figure 7-10 Configuring virtual machine settings.

The virtual machine settings include many of the same items you would consider when purchasing a physical computer, but in a virtual machine, they either make use of existing hardware on the host machine or are simply carved out of thin air using software emulation. For instance, if you want to increase the amount of memory or disk space, the resources used by the VM would consume some memory or disk space on the host or storage attached to the host. You also can simulate items such as SCSI controllers, network adapters, COM ports, and other hardware inside the hypervisor even if these items do not exist on the host computer.

The VM settings include the following configurable items, which are grouped as VM Hardware settings and Management settings:

- **Add Hardware:** Add new hardware to the virtual machine. The following items are available:
  - **SCSI Controller:** One controller is created for the virtual machine by default, but you can add additional controllers here. This way, you can simulate complex RAID configurations using VHDs that could all reside on a single disk drive.
  - **Network Adapter:** You can add a virtual network interface card to the VM. If you want to enable a connection for the network adapter, a virtual switch must be available in the Hyper-V host environment.
  - **Legacy Network Adapter:** The legacy adapter is available for performing network-based installation of the guest OS or when integration services are not available on the guest. Guest VM integration services are covered later in this section.
  - **Fibre Channel Adapter:** This adapter is used for connecting the guest to an existing, physical Fibre Channel storage. It acts as a pass-through adapter so that a VM can access physical storage over Fibre Channel.
- **BIOS:** Some basic BIOS settings are available, most importantly the ability to select startup order for boot devices. This capability is convenient for installation of operating systems on the VM.
- **Memory:** The amount of memory available to a VM affects performance more than any other setting. The latest version of Hyper-V (included with Windows 8.1) includes support for Dynamic Memory. You should understand how these settings are used. Dynamic Memory is examined in detail in Table 7-3.
- **Processor:** You can specify the number of virtual processors assigned to the VM. From this page, you can also reserve or limit a percentage of resources the VM should use. Refer to Table 7-4 for details on the Processor configuration settings and how they are used.
- **IDE Controller:** By default, the New Virtual Machine wizard adds two IDE controllers (0 and 1) to the VM and assigns the first VHD to IDE Controller 0. You can add new hard drives or DVD drives to either IDE controller:
  - **New Hard Drive:** When you add a new hard drive to the VM's IDE con-

troller, it either can be VHDs or it can be attached to a physical hard disk available on the host computer. If you want to add a physical hard disk, it must be offline in the host before you can add it. That drive is unavailable to the host OS.

  - **New DVD Drive:** If you want to add a DVD drive to the VM, you must add it to the IDE controller. The guest SCSI controller does not support DVD drives. Similar to an IDE hard disk, the DVD drive can be either a physical drive from the host or a DVD image file in ISO format (an `.iso` file).

- **SCSI Controller:** This is a virtual SCSI controller that the VM operating system will treat as an actual SCSI controller. You can add VHDs and physical disks to the VM's SCSI controller. Physical disks that you add to this simulated controller do not need to be attached to a physical SCSI device; they can be IDE disks or even USB disk drives.

- **Network Adapter:** You can modify a number of settings for the VM's network adapter, including changing the virtual switch it is using. This is analogous to moving the network cable from one switch to another on a physical computer. You can find more details about the network adapter configuration in the section "Creating and Configuring Virtual Switches."

- **COM 1 and COM 2:** You can attach the virtual COM ports to named pipes on the local host or a remote computer to simulate serial communications on the VM.

- **Diskette Drive:** You can attach a simulated floppy disk drive to the VM. You cannot use a physical device for the VM, however; it must be a virtual floppy disk (`.vfd`) file.

- **Name:** You can set the descriptive name for this VM used by Hyper-V. This section also allows you to add descriptions and notes for the VM, which is convenient for keeping track of how you are using the VM.

- **Integration Services:** You can configure which hypervisor services will be available for the VM. These services require installation of Integration Services on the guest VM.

- **Checkpoint File Location:** You also can specify where Hyper-V should store snapshot images for the VM.

- **Smart Paging File Location:** Smart Paging allows the hypervisor to deal with excessive demands of memory from virtual machines, typically during startup. In this setting, you can specify the folder that Hyper-V should use to store the Smart Paging files for this VM.

- **Automatic Start Action:** You can tell Hyper-V whether to automatically start this VM when the hypervisor is started. If you enable automatic start, you can also specify a number of seconds to delay the startup.
- **Automatic Stop Action:** You can configure how Hyper-V will manage the VM state when the host is shut down. By default, Hyper-V saves the current state of the VM.

CAUTION If you select **Turn off the virtual machine** for the VM's Automatic Stop Action, be aware that doing so is like immediately pulling the power on a physical machine. If the operating system is loaded and running when this happens, it can cause file system corruption, loss of data, and potentially disk errors that prevent the operating system from loading the next time the VM is started.

When configuring your Hyper-V virtual environment, you should be aware of the memory and processor settings available for the VMs (see Table 7-3). This configuration helps manage the physical resources and balance the requirements for the virtual machines between each other and the resources needed by the host operating system itself.

Table 7-3 Virtual Machine Dynamic Memory

Option	Description
Startup RAM	Startup RAM tells the hypervisor how much memory to assign the VM when it first loads. If Dynamic Memory is not enabled, this setting specifies the total amount of memory the VM will use at all times.
Enable Dynamic Memory	When Dynamic Memory is enabled, Hyper-V adjusts the amount of RAM assigned to the VM based on the demand from the guest operating system.
Minimum RAM	This option sets the minimum amount of memory to assign to the VM. If there is not enough physical memory on the host to satisfy this requirement, the VM does not load.
Maximum RAM	This option sets the maximum amount of memory that can be assigned to the VM by the hypervisor. The actual amount assigned will not exceed the amount of physical memory available on the host, regardless of this setting. In Windows 8.1 Hyper-V, a VM can be assigned as much as 1 TB of RAM, but the amount is also limited by the amount of physical memory in the host and the amount of RAM the guest operating system is capable of addressing.

Option	Description
Memory buffer	Hyper-V uses this setting to provide an amount of memory above the demands of the VM's operating system. Performance counters are used to determine the memory the VM is requesting for use. The buffer percentage is used to add some amount to that demand when allocating memory. For instance, if the operating system requests 1000 MB for its use, and the buffer is 20%, the hypervisor actually assigns 1200 MB of RAM to the VM.
Memory weight	The weighting set here, from Low to High, is used when multiple VMs are running under the hypervisor requesting memory. You can adjust this setting so that VMs that have a higher priority for performance are provided a higher weight. VMs with a lower rating perform slower when there is a high demand for memory resources on the hypervisor as a whole.

The processor options that can be specified or used for a VM depend heavily on the physical processor characteristics available on the host machine (see Table 7-4). You should understand the basics of how these settings are used by Hyper-V.

Table 7-4 Virtual Machine Processor Configuration Options

Option	Description
Number of virtual processors	You can set the number of processors the guest OS will see when it starts. You can assign as many processors as the number of cores in the host computer.
Resource control	Resource control is important when a number of VMs are running at the same time on a single host. Note that these settings are specific to the number of virtual processors assigned. Reserve a percentage of the resources available to the VM to ensure that the VM always has that amount of processor available to use. Set a limit to ensure the VM never uses more resources on the processor(s) than that percentage amount. Finally, you can assign a relative weight for this VM. The weight is an arbitrary number and is relevant only when compared to the weight of other VMs running on the host.
Processor compatibility	Generally, Hyper-V maximizes performance by using all the features and instruction sets available on the physical processor. If you are planning a VM architecture that may be deployed to a server environment or other hosts, you can select the compatibility setting to ensure that the virtual machines can be migrated to hosts with different types of processors. Hyper-V uses a basic set of features and instructions available on all supported processor architectures.

Option	Description
NUMA configuration	Nonuniform memory architecture, or NUMA, is a memory allocation technology that groups memory locations and processors into nodes, to avoid performance issues caused by multiple processors attempting to access the same memory location, or accessing memory in a location slower to access for the processor that requests it. The physical NUMA configuration can have an effect on VM performance, and in some high-performance applications, it may be useful to simulate a NUMA topology different than the physical host. For best performance on the VMs, use the physical topology.

Deploying Virtual Machines

The Hyper-V virtual machine created using the steps in the preceding section can be configured, started, and run, but if you used a new VHDX or the one created using DiskPart in the first section, it does not have an operating system.

From the Hyper-V Manager, you can access a virtual console for any VM either by right-clicking the VM and selecting **Connect**, or by double-clicking the icon in the Summary tab at the bottom of the central pane. The result is similar to the illustration in Figure 7-11.

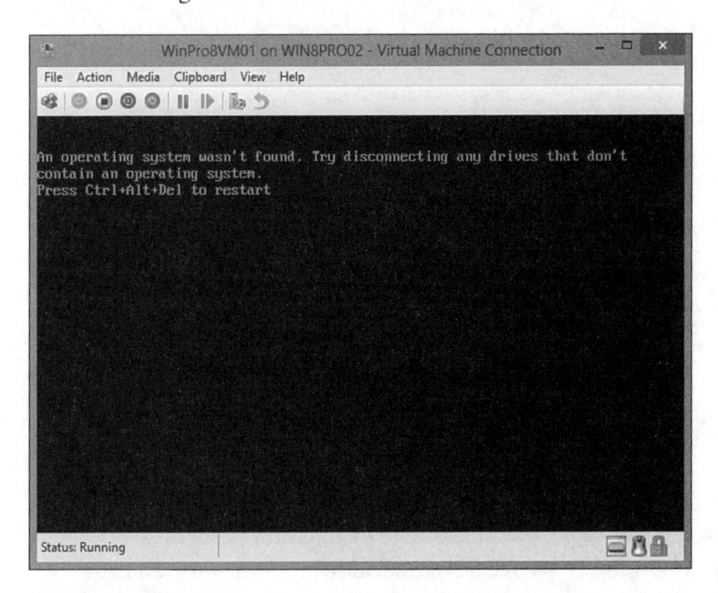

Figure 7-11 New virtual machine started with an empty virtual hard disk.

The obvious fix for this is to insert a boot DVD and install a new operating system. You cannot add a DVD drive to the VM while it is running, so you need to turn it off to add it. In Figure 7-12, a DVD drive is being added to the IDE Controller using an `.iso` file as the DVD media. Recall that you can use an `.iso` file as a DVD drive, and you can change the BIOS setting to boot from the DVD drive first.

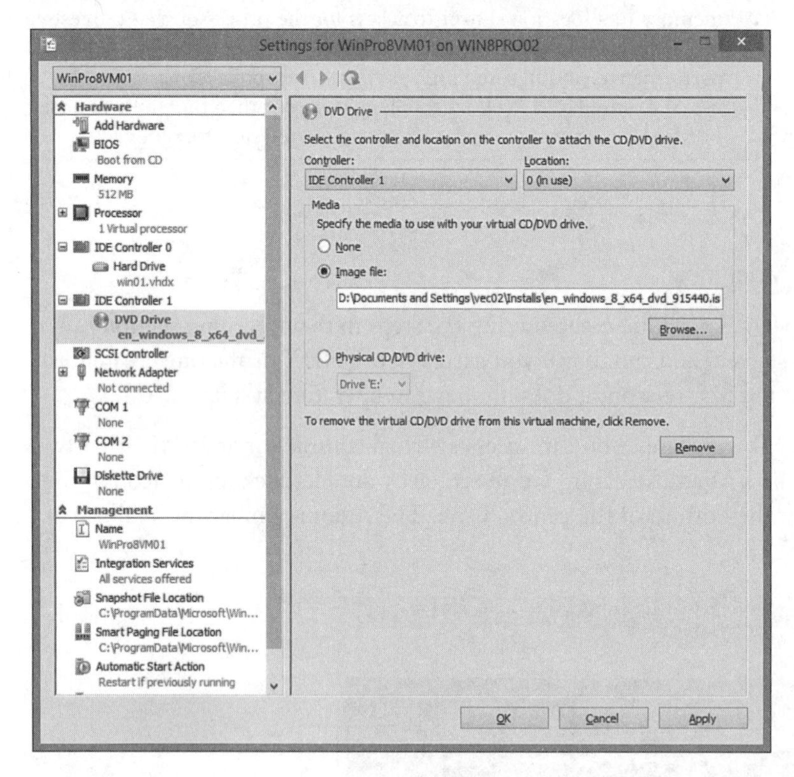

Figure 7-12 Adding a DVD drive from an `.iso` image file.

From there, you can connect to the console, start the VM by clicking the **Start** button on the console window's toolbar, and install Windows using the procedures described in Chapter 2. After the operating system is loaded, you can use it as you would a physical machine, either through the Hyper-V console connection or using Remote Desktop Services if the networking is configured.

To take full advantage of Hyper-V enhancements for your virtual machines, you should install Integration Services on the guest. The installation procedure is designed to work on most operating systems. Use the following procedure to install Integration Services:

Step 1. Connect to the virtual machine, start it running if it is turned off, and then log in to the operating system.

Step 2. From the virtual console window, click the **Action** menu and select **Insert Integration Services Setup Disk**. Hyper-V uses the DVD drive on the computer to insert an image of the appropriate Integration Services setup files. When Windows detects the DVD has been inserted, it displays a notice similar to the one in Figure 7-13.

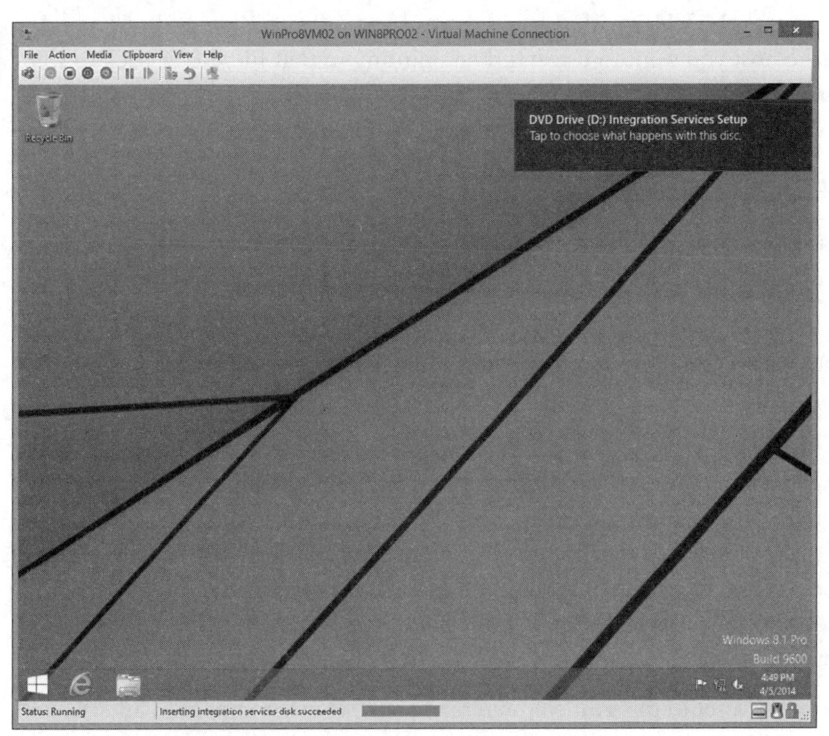

Figure 7-13 Windows Hyper-V attaches the Integration Services DVD to the guest operating system's DVD drive.

Step 3. Open the Integration Services drive and run the installation program.

NOTE On a Windows 8.1 or Windows 2012 R2 guest, you may receive a prompt stating that a previous installation of the Hyper-V Integration Services is detected. If so, click **OK** to proceed with the upgrade.

Step 4. After the installation program is complete, you need to restart the guest to complete the setup of Integration Services.

Recall from Chapter 2 that the process of deploying Windows 8.1 to multiple computers can be streamlined by creating a VHD with an existing, configured Windows 8.1 image, which can be used on many machines. The same technique can be used to deploy multiple virtual machines using preconfigured VHD images.

The procedure for this is exactly the same as the steps laid out previously; the only change is copying the VHD with the image to a location accessible to the Hyper-V service on the host you want to use and then pointing to that file. Refer back to step 6 and Figure 7-8 in the "Creating Virtual Machines" section.

Converting a Physical Machine

In some cases, you may need to convert a physical machine to a Hyper-V virtual machine. You may need to do so in several different scenarios, such as the following:

- To test some invasive changes on a production computer—for instance, an operating system upgrade, a major application change, or any other risky modification. You can reduce the risk by first testing the changes in a virtual copy of the system.
- To support an older PC with unsupported applications when rolling out a hardware or operating system upgrade. For instance, a business requirement may necessitate the use of an out-of-date application that does not run under Windows 8.1. Rather than leaving the users of this application on old hardware running Windows XP, you can convert the system to a VM and run it under Hyper-V when the users need to use the application.
- To convert a set of physical computers to a virtual environment. This scenario takes a lot of careful planning, but due to the savings available using virtual hosts, you might find exploring this option worthwhile when planning for hardware upgrades or replacements.

NOTE Techniques and procedures for converting physical machines to VMs is beyond the scope of this text and the 70-687 exam. There are several methods for converting physical machines, including Microsoft's Virtual Machine Manager and the Sysinternal's Disk2VHD tool. For more information, see "Virtual Machine Manager" at http://technet.microsoft.com/en-us/library/gg610610.aspx and "Disk2vhd v2.01" at http://technet.microsoft.com/en-us/sysinternals/ee656415.aspx.

Using Virtual Machine Checkpoints

A virtual machine *checkpoint* (called a snapshot in Windows 8) works exactly as it sounds. It saves a point-in-time state of the virtual machine. Checkpoints save not only the state of the hard disk files, but also the state of the running machine and hardware configuration, by creating a copy of the machine's memory at the time the checkpoint is taken.

Checkpoints work well for testing various software changes or applications that can significantly modify the computer. If things go wrong, you can quickly and easily return the machine to its previous state. They also are handy in a production environment if virtual machines are being used. Potentially risky operations such as applying software updates or service packs can be rolled out after taking a checkpoint of the machine. If testing shows issues with the update, you can quickly restore the machine to its previous state until the issue can be resolved.

A VM checkpoint is stored as an `.avhd` file, in the location specified in the virtual machine's settings. It is important not to keep checkpoints around for an extended period of time because they can grow large very quickly. Perform the changes that you planned and apply or revert the checkpoint when you are satisfied.

CAUTION Do not expand a virtual hard disk used by a virtual machine while the VM has checkpoints associated with it. Doing so makes the checkpoints unusable, the hard disk is reverted to the previous state, and you are unable to apply the checkpoint changes.

You can create a checkpoint from the Hyper-V Manager interface in several ways:

- Right-click the VM and select **Checkpoint** from the pop-up menu.
- With the VM selected in the Virtual Machines list box, select **Checkpoint** from the Actions menu in the right pane.
- When connected to the virtual machine connection, click the **Checkpoint** button from the toolbar.
- Select **Checkpoint** from the Action menu of the virtual machine connection screen.

When you create a checkpoint, it is listed in the Checkpoints section of the Hyper-V Manager whenever the VM is selected in the list, as shown in Figure 7-14. Each checkpoint appears in a hierarchy from the original state to the currently running state, and the VM can be reverted to any version in the list. Each checkpoint lists the date and time it was taken, and the current state of the VM is simply listed as `Now`.

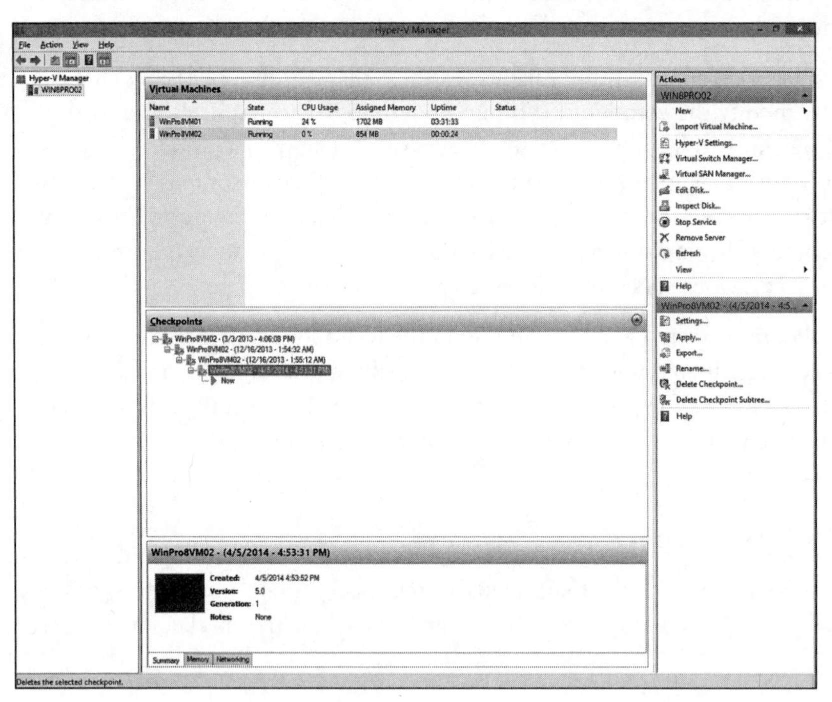

Figure 7-14 Virtual machine checkpoints are displayed in a hierarchy with the oldest version at the top.

The hypervisor takes a few seconds to a few minutes to create the checkpoint, depending on the state of the computer, amount of memory in use, size of the disk drives, and so on. While the checkpoint is created, the status column displays the current progress, as shown in Figure 7-15.

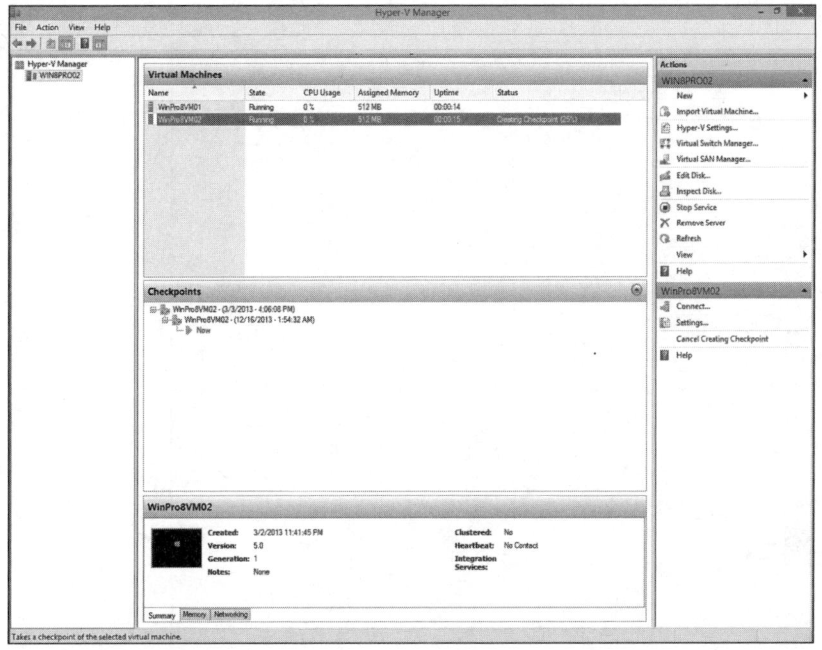

Figure 7-15 Checkpoint progress is displayed on the Status column of the virtual machine in Hyper-V Manager.

Working with checkpoints is a little counterintuitive. The reason is that when you select **Delete Checkpoint** from the right-click or Actions menu, the checkpoint is actually merged into the VM's current state. In other words, to delete the checkpoint means that you want to keep all the changes made to the VM and abandon the old, saved state. When you delete a checkpoint, the VM's status changes to `Merge in Progress` and displays the percentage complete as the changes are merged.

Alternatively, if you select a checkpoint and choose the **Apply** action, your changes since the checkpoint was created are actually removed, and the state of the running VM is reverted to the state of the checkpoint. Subsequent checkpoints, if any, remain available, so it is possible to return the state of the machine to the point in time of any of those checkpoints.

To illustrate, Figure 7-16 shows that the VM's current state (indicated by the Now icon in the list) is after the third checkpoint, but all the changes included in the last two checkpoints are not included. You can roll the VM state forward to one of the other checkpoints taken. Note that if you do this, any changes you make to the VM since applying the current checkpoint are lost.

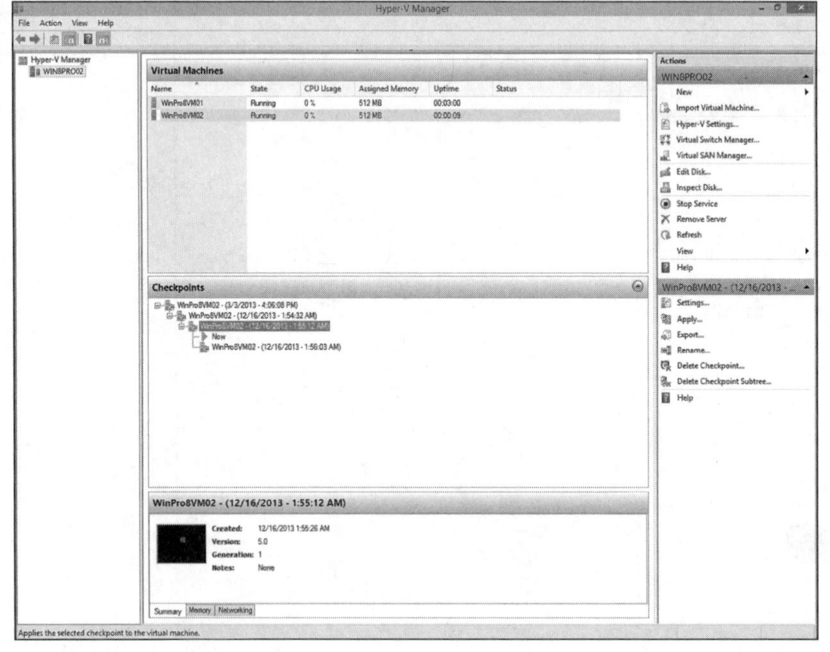

Figure 7-16 Virtual machine checkpoints and current state of the virtual machine.

Another way to abandon the changes made since the checkpoint was created is to right-click the virtual machine and select the **Revert** option. You are prompted to confirm that you want to revert the virtual machine to the previous state. Again, in this case, you are deleting all the changes made to the VM since the checkpoint was created.

If you have created several checkpoints and want to merge all your changes, you can select the first checkpoint and apply the **Delete Checkpoint Subtree** action. This merges all the changes at and below the checkpoint you select and merges all the changes into the current state of the VM.

Creating and Configuring Virtual Switches

In the previous sections, you learned about virtual hard disks and virtual machines. They are both very useful for testing, experimenting, and running legacy applications and other tasks. This section introduces virtual switches, which are needed if any of the Hyper-V virtual machines need to communicate with each other, your host machine, or the outside world.

Client Hyper-V's virtual machine connection is useful for interacting directly with the virtual machines, similar to using a physical monitor. This is the only way to utilize the VMs unless they are connected to a virtual switch. There are three basic types of virtual switches that you can create in the Client Hyper-V environment:

- **External:** You can create a virtual switch merged with the host network adapter. The VMs have full access to the host computer network.
- **Internal:** You can create a virtual switch with connectivity for the VMs and the host computer. The VMs are unable to access the host computer network, but the host and VMs can communicate with each other.
- **Private:** A virtual switch created using private network is completely isolated from the physical network and the host computer. Only the VMs can connect to the private virtual switch.

To enable basic networking for your Client Hyper-V guests and allow them to use the network just like the Windows 8.1 host, you would typically add an external virtual switch and connect the VMs to it. Note that this process actually modifies the host's network configuration. This allows the guests to connect through the existing physical network interface card (NIC) in the host, although in a roundabout way.

We discuss the mechanics of how the different virtual switches work later in this section. First, we cover the basic steps for creating a virtual switch:

Step 1. From the Hyper-V Manager's Actions menu, select **Virtual Switch Manager**. The Virtual Switch Manager screen is displayed.

Step 2. From the left pane, select **New virtual network switch**.

Step 3. In the right pane, a list box is displayed. Select the type of virtual switch you want and then click the **Create Virtual Switch** button.

Step 4. On the next screen, as shown in Figure 7-17, you enter the properties for the new switch. The following properties are available:

- **Name:** Choose a descriptive name for your virtual switch. You may want to include the type of switch (External, Internal, or Private) as part of the name to quickly identify your switches.
- **Connection type:** Choose the type of connection you want, as just described. The type you selected on the previous screen is filled in for you, but you can change your selection here. Note that if you select **External** network, you also need to select the host computer's physical connection. That physical network is connected to your external virtual switch.

- **VLAN ID:** If you want to use virtual local area network (VLAN) identification numbers, check the box here and choose a unique ID to associate with the VLAN. Typically, you do not use this in a Client Hyper-V environment; it is used to create separate VLANs within a large virtual environment and "tag" all packets with the ID for more efficient routing and network filtering.

NOTE For more information on VLAN IDs and tagging, refer to the "Hyper-V 2008 R2: Virtual Networking Survival Guide" at http://social.technet.microsoft.com/wiki/contents/articles/151.hyper-v-virtual-networking-survival-guide.aspx.

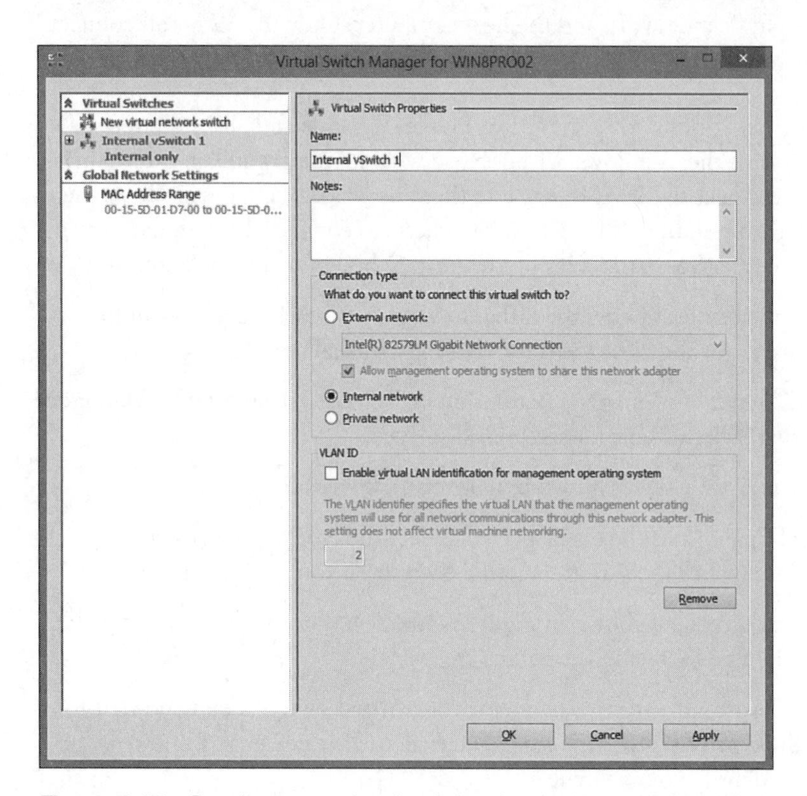

Figure 7-17 Creating a new virtual switch using the Hyper-V Virtual Switch Manager.

Step 5. Click **OK** to create the new virtual switch. Hyper-V displays a dialog box while it applies your changes.

Using an External Virtual Switch

Before adding switches to Hyper-V, examine the network configuration for the host. When Hyper-V services is installed, Windows adds the Hyper-V Extensible Virtual Switch protocol adapter to the network. As shown in Figure 7-18, the adapter is initially not bound to any of the host's NIC connections when there are no Hyper-V external virtual switches.

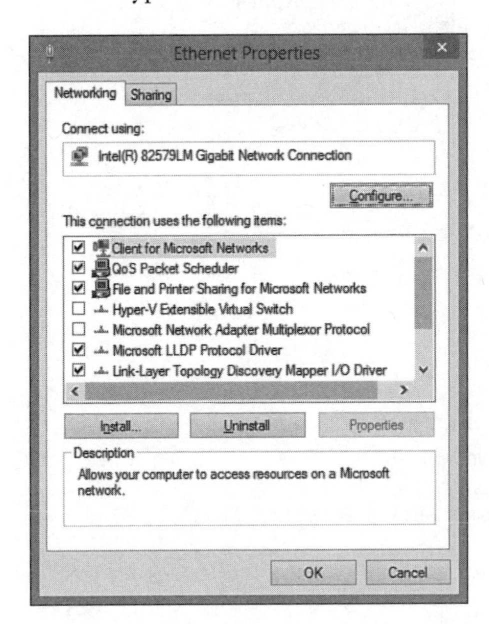

Figure 7-18 Ethernet Properties and the Hyper-V extensible virtual switch.

Note that there is one physical NIC in the computer, connected to the physical switch using an Ethernet cable. When you create an external virtual switch, Hyper-V creates a virtual switch, but it also creates a new virtual NIC for your host.

Note the network depicted in Figure 7-19. This is how Hyper-V configures your host computer when it creates an external virtual switch. The physical NIC no longer communicates directly with the applications on your host. Instead, all traffic from the external network that flows through the host's network adapter is routed first to the virtual switch. From there, it is routed either to one of the guest computers or to the new virtual NIC used by all network applications on the host.

Key Topic

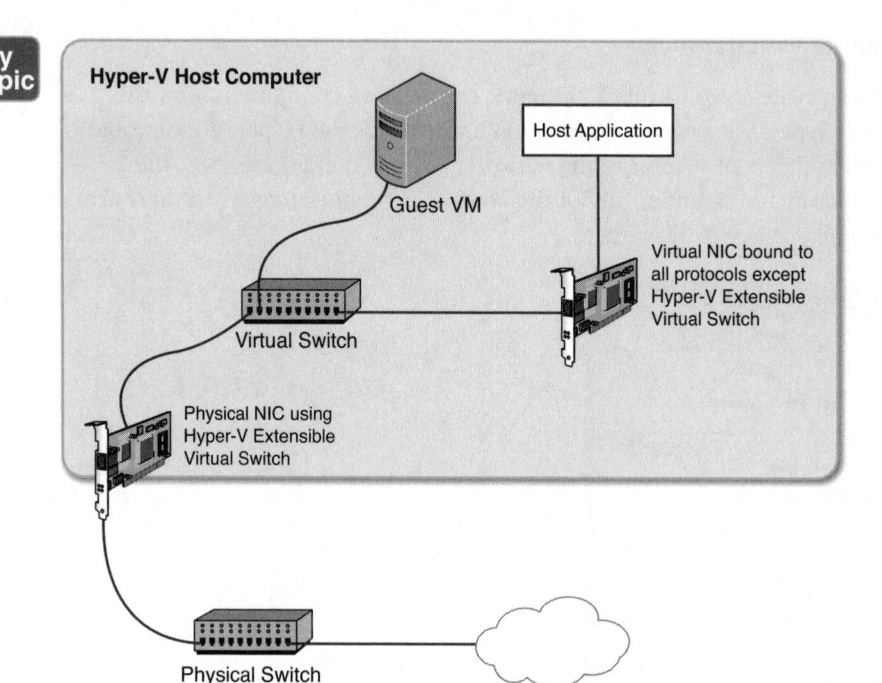

Figure 7-19 Network routing in a Hyper-V host using an external virtual switch.

Using Internal Virtual Switches

As described earlier, the Hyper-V internal virtual switch is a connection for your guest VMs that cannot access the host's physical network but can communicate with the host OS. This switch provides better security for your VMs and avoids the routing modifications to the host network depicted in Figure 7-19. However, because the VMs cannot access the external network, they do not have access to the same network services that the host enjoys, such as DHCP automatic network addressing and Domain Name System (DNS) for host name lookup.

Configuring network settings is discussed in detail in Chapter 8, "Configuring TCP/IP Settings," and Chapter 9, "Configuring Networking Settings." Refer to those chapters for specifics on configuring your virtual network.

For your host to communicate with your VMs, Hyper-V creates a new Ethernet adapter connected to the new virtual switch (see Figure 7-20). You can modify the settings for this adapter based on the network configuration of your VMs. By default, the new adapter, and the VMs networks that you attach to it, use Autoconfiguration IPv4 addresses and are able to communicate over the network.

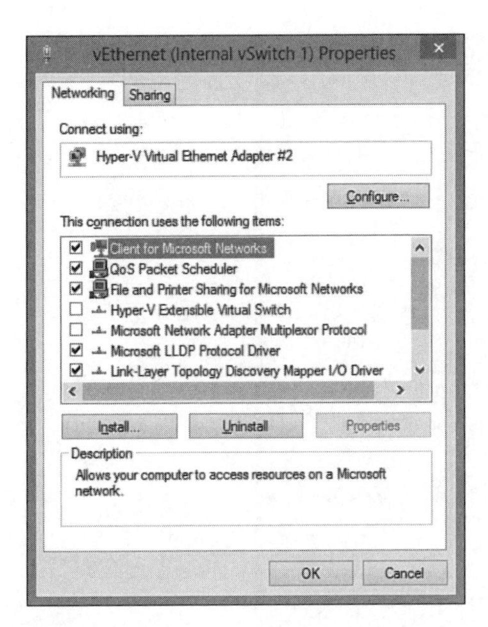

Figure 7-20 A virtual Ethernet adapter is created for the Hyper-V host to use when communicating with hosted VMs.

Using Private Virtual Switches

A private virtual switch works exactly like an internal virtual switch, but without the connection to the host computer. When Hyper-V creates a private virtual switch, it does not create the virtual Ethernet adapter illustrated in Figure 7-20.

Private virtual networks are useful for test environments, especially if you want to simulate an existing environment including the network configurations. You can copy the hosts as they are and create multiple private virtual switches to match the physical switches in the environment you are simulating.

Connecting Virtual Machines

After you have created at least one virtual switch, you can connect your virtual machines to it. This is similar to connecting a network cable from a physical computer to a physical hub or switch. The VM operating system detects the connection and attempts to set up the network configuration.

We covered modifying virtual machine settings in the previous section. To connect a VM to a switch, simply select the VM from the list in Hyper-V Manager, invoke the Settings function, and select the Network Adapter, as shown in Figure 7-21.

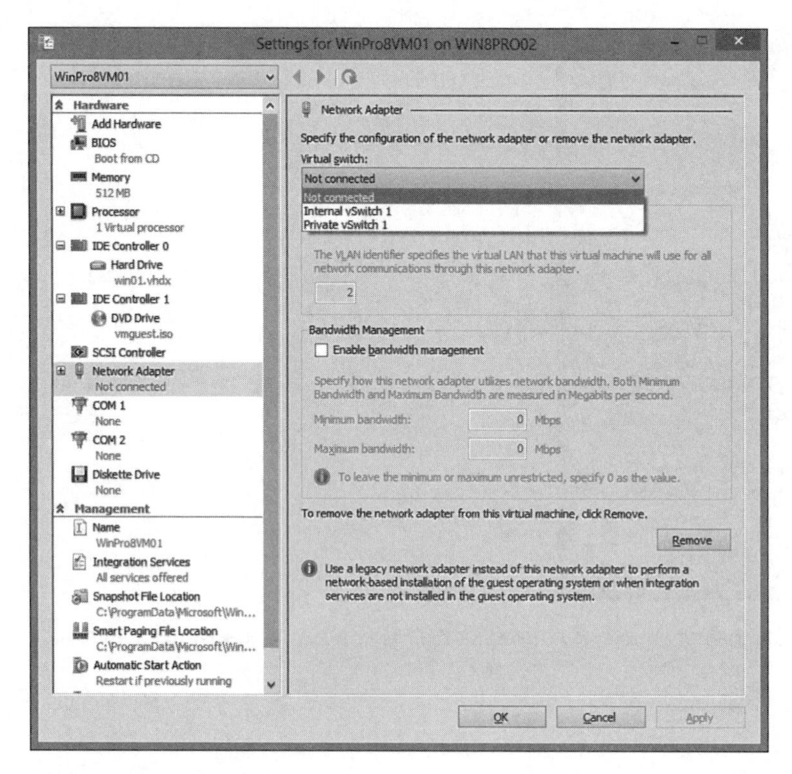

Figure 7-21 Virtual machine network adapter configuration.

The following Network Adapter configuration settings are available:

- **Virtual Switch:** Select the previously created virtual switch you want to connect. If you named your switches according to type, they are easier to identify from the list.
- **VLAN ID:** If VLAN identifiers are needed for your network, you can enable VLAN IDs and enter the ID here.
- **Bandwidth Management:** If you want to limit or reserve the amount of total network resources the VM can use, select the **Enable bandwidth management** check box. To limit the bandwidth for the VM, enter the Megabits per second (Mbps) in the Maximum bandwidth box. Alternatively, you may want to ensure that the VM always has some amount of network bandwidth available. If so, enter an amount in the Minimum bandwidth box, and Hyper-V will reserve that much bandwidth to the VM, regardless of the network demands from other VMs.

Exam Preparation Tasks

Review All the Key Topics

Review the most important topics in the chapter, noted with the key topics icon in the outer margin of the page. Table 7-5 lists a reference of these key topics and the page numbers on which each is found.

Table 7-5 Key Topics for Chapter 7

Key Topic Element	Description	Page Number(s)
Step List	Describes how to use DiskPart to create a VHD	294
Figure 7-1	Shows how to use DiskPart to create, format, and assign a VHD	295
List	Lists client Hyper-V hardware and software requirements	297
Figure 7-5	Shows the Hyper-V Manager	302
Figure 7-6	Shows how to create a new VM	303
List	Lists virtual machine hardware and management settings	307
Table 7-3	Describes Virtual Machine Dynamic Memory	309
Table 7-4	Describes Virtual Machine Processor configuration options	310-311
Figure 7-13	Shows Hyper-V Integration Services	313
Figure 7-14	Shows how to manage virtual machine checkpoints	316
Figure 7-15	Shows how to create a virtual machine checkpoint	317
Figure 7-16	Shows virtual machine checkpoints and current state of the virtual machine	318
List	Lists types of virtual switches in Client Hyper-V	319
Step List	Shows how to create a virtual switch using Hyper-V Manager	319
Figure 7-19	Shows network routing in a Hyper-V host using an external virtual switch	322

Definitions of Key Terms

Define the following key terms from this chapter and check your answers in the Glossary:

Checkpoint, Client Hyper-V, DEP, DiskPart, Fibre Channel, Guest, Hypervisor, Integration Services, ISO, NIC, NUMA, SLAT, Smart Paging, VFD, VHD, VHDX, virtual switch, virtual machine, virtualization, VLAN, VT, WDS, Windows XP Mode

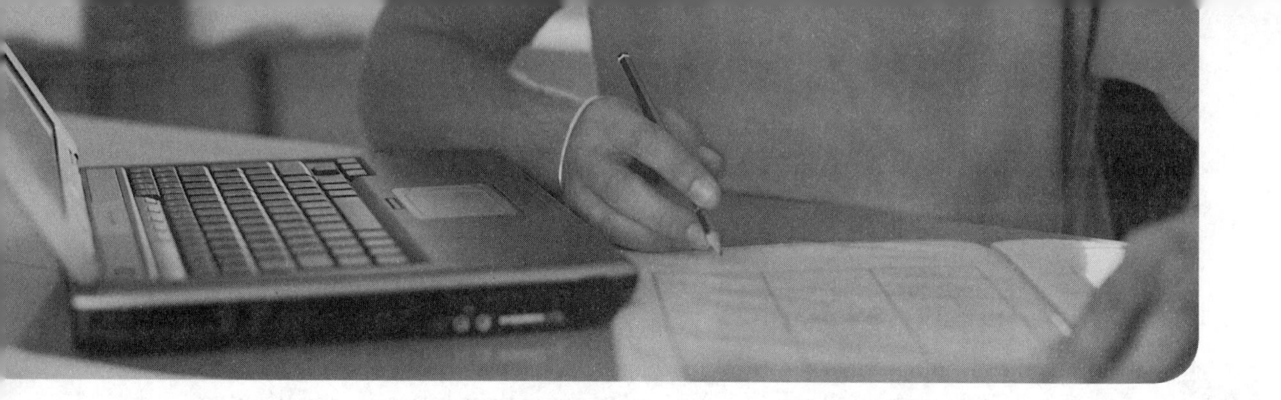

This chapter covers the following subjects:

- **Understanding the TCP/IP Protocol Suite:** TCP/IP is the primary protocol suite used by computers connecting with each other and the Internet. This section introduces you to the important components of versions 4 and 6 of the TCP/IP protocol suite that you must be familiar with for the 70-687 exam. In this section, you are introduced to the various types of IPv4 and IPv6 addresses that are used on Windows-based networks.
- **Connecting to Wired Networks:** This section shows you how to connect your computer to IPv4- and IPv6-based networks.
- **Configuring Name Resolution:** This section shows you how to configure your computer to use DNS for name resolution on IPv4- and IPv6-based networks.
- **Configuring Network Locations:** Windows uses the concept of network locations to set several network properties pertaining to such items as network security and the ability to share resources such as files and printers on the network. This section shows you how to select network locations and configure sharing of network connections.
- **Resolving Connectivity Issues:** Many factors can result in an inability to access other computers on the network or can result in intermittent connectivity. This section introduces common troubleshooting techniques you should be aware of when your computer cannot connect to others.

CHAPTER 8

Configuring TCP/IP Settings

Connectivity between Windows 8 and 8.1 computers and other networks (inclusive of the Internet and other computers) is provided in a variety of ways, all based on the older version 4 or the newer version 6 of the Transmission Control Protocol/Internet Protocol (TCP/IP) networking protocol stack. Windows 8 and 8.1 improve on the Network and Sharing Center that was first introduced with Windows Vista and continued in Windows 7. This tool consolidates many applications and utilities into one convenient location from which you can create and manage different types of network connections as well as file and print sharing. In this chapter, you study versions 4 and 6 of the TCP/IP protocol suite. You then look at the Network and Sharing Center and its use for configuring and troubleshooting network connections.

You not only explore each of these components in this chapter, but also look at their features and dependencies as they exist within the Windows 8.1 operating system.

"Do I Know This Already?" Quiz

The "Do I Know This Already?" quiz allows you to assess whether you should read this entire chapter or simply jump to the "Exam Preparation Tasks" section for review. If you are in doubt, read the entire chapter. Table 8-1 outlines the major headings in this chapter and the corresponding "Do I Know This Already?" quiz questions. You can find the answers in Appendix A, "Answers to the 'Do I Know This Already?' Quizzes."

Table 8-1 "Do I Know This Already?" Foundation Topics Section-to-Question Mapping

Foundations Topics Section	Questions Covered in This Section
Understanding the TCP/IP Protocol Suite	1–7
Connecting to Wired Networks	8–9
Configuring Name Resolution	10
Configuring Network Locations	11
Resolving Connectivity Issues	12–15

1. Which of the following are component protocols contained within TCP/IP? (Choose three.)
   a. User Datagram Protocol (UDP)
   b. Internet Control Message Protocol (ICMP)
   c. Dynamic Host Configuration Protocol (DHCP)
   d. Address Resolution Protocol (ARP)

2. You need to ensure that your IPv4-enabled computer can access other subnets on your company's network, as well as the Internet. Which addressing component should you ensure is specified properly?
   a. IP address
   b. Subnet mask
   c. Default gateway
   d. DNS server address
   e. WINS address

3. Your computer is configured with the IP address 131.107.24.5. To which class does this IP address belong?
   a. A
   b. B
   c. C
   d. D
   e. E

4. Your company is making use of the 192.168.21.0/24 network. This network address is an example of what type of address notation?
   a. Windows Internet Naming Service (WINS)
   b. Unicast
   c. Multicast
   d. Classless Inter-Domain Routing (CIDR)

5. Your company has transitioned to using the IPv6 protocol, and you are responsible for configuring Internet servers that need direct access to the Internet. Which of the following types of IPv6 addresses should you use for this purpose?
   a. Global unicast
   b. Link-local unicast
   c. Site-local unicast
   d. Multicast
   e. Anycast

6. Your computer is using an IPv6 address on the fe80::/64 network. What type of IPv6 address is this?
   a. Global unicast
   b. Link-local unicast
   c. Site-local unicast
   d. Teredo

7. Your computer is using an IPv6 address that includes the 32-bit prefix of 2001::/32. What type of IPv6 address prefix is this?
   a. Global unicast
   b. Link-local unicast
   c. Site-local unicast
   d. Teredo

8. Your network is configured to use DHCP for assignment of IP addresses and DNS servers. Which of the following options should you ensure are selected in the Internet Protocol Version 4 (TCP/IPv4) Properties dialog box? (Choose two.)
   a. Obtain an IP address automatically
   b. Use the following IP address
   c. Obtain DNS server address automatically
   d. Use the following DNS Server Addresses

9. Your computer is configured to use the IPv4 address 169.254.183.32. What system is being used by your computer?

   a. Dynamic Host Configuration Protocol (DHCP)

   b. Automatic Private Internet Protocol Addressing (APIPA)

   c. Private IPv4 network addressing

   d. Alternate IP configuration

10. You need to configure a client computer running Windows 8.1 Pro to respond to three different DNS servers in order to resolve all names on the network. What should you do?

   a. From the General tab of the Internet Properties dialog box, select the **Use the following DNS server addresses** option and type the IP addresses of the three DNS servers in the text boxes provided.

   b. From the General tab of the Internet Properties dialog box, select the **Use the following DNS server addresses** option and type the IP addresses of the two most used DNS servers in the text boxes provided. Then select the **Alternate Configuration** tab and type the IP address of the third DNS server at this tab.

   c. From the General tab of the Internet Properties dialog box, select the **Use the following DNS server addresses** option and click the **Advanced** button. On the Advanced TCP/IP Settings dialog box that appears, click **Add** and type the three DNS server IP addresses, one at a time. Then ensure that they are sequenced in the order they will most likely need to be accessed.

   d. You cannot specify more than two DNS servers at the client computer; you must configure the DHCP server to supply the required DNS server IP addresses.

11. You are using a Windows 8.1 laptop and have gone on the road to a hotel with free Wi-Fi access. You are afraid that an unauthorized individual might access confidential company information on your computer without your knowledge. What setting should you enable to minimize this risk with the least amount of effort?

   a. Public network profile

   b. Private network profile

   c. Turn off file and printer sharing

   d. HomeGroup connections

12. Your computer is configured to use DHCP on the IPv4 network 192.168.4.0 but is unable to connect to other computers. You run **ipconfig /all** and notice that the computer is using the address 169.254.231.98. You must try again immediately to connect to other network computers. Which parameter of the `ipconfig` command should you use?

    a. `/release`

    b. `/renew`

    c. `/flushdns`

    d. `/displaydns`

13. Which two TCP/IP utilities provide information on the route taken by packets from your computer when connecting to a remote host? (Choose two.)

    a. `Route`

    b. `Netstat`

    c. `Ping`

    d. `Tracert`

    e. `Pathping`

14. You are troubleshooting the inability of your computer to connect to others on the network, so you are planning to run several TCP/IP utilities. Arrange the following in the sequence in which you should perform them:

    a. Ping the computer's own IP address.

    b. Ping a host that is on another subnet.

    c. Ping 127.0.0.1 or ::1.

    d. Run **ipconfig /all**.

    e. Ping the default gateway.

15. Computers on your network are configured to use static IP addresses. Your computer has been able to connect to the network most mornings when you start up, but one morning when you do not arrive until 9:30 a.m., your computer is unable to connect. Which of the following is the most likely reason for this problem?

    a. Your computer is using APIPA.

    b. Your computer is configured with an incorrect subnet mask.

    c. Your computer is configured with an IP address that is a duplicate of another one that has started up first.

    d. Your computer is configured with an alternate IP address and is using the alternate.

Foundation Topics

Understanding the TCP/IP Protocol Suite

From its earliest days, the Internet has made use of the Transmission Control Protocol/Internet Protocol (TCP/IP) suite to facilitate connections among computers across the world. To favor seamless integration with the Internet, Microsoft has standardized on the use of TCP/IP and no longer uses older, proprietary network protocol suites that were once common. Since its introduction of Active Directory (AD) in Windows 2000, Microsoft has made TCP/IP the protocol suite required for Windows networks that use AD. The reason is largely due to the AD's dependence on Domain Name System (DNS) to provide the name and address resolution for all AD resources.

TCP/IP is a suite of protocols that govern the transmission of data across computer networks and the Internet. The following is a brief description of the major protocols that you should be aware of:

- **Transmission Control Protocol (TCP):** Provides connection-oriented, reliable communication between two hosts, typically involving large amounts of data. Note that a host includes any device on the network (such as a computer or router) that is configured for TCP/IP. This kind of communication also involves acknowledgments that data has been correctly received.
- **User Datagram Protocol (UDP):** Used for fast, non-connection-oriented communications with no guarantee of delivery, typically small short bursts of data. Applications using UDP data transmission are responsible for checking their data's integrity.
- **Internet Protocol (IP):** Handles, addresses, and routes packets between hosts on a network. It performs this service for all other protocols in the TCP/IP protocol suite.
- **Internet Control Message Protocol (ICMP):** Enables hosts on a TCP/IP network to share status and error information. It is specifically responsible for reporting errors and messages regarding the delivery of IP datagrams. It is not responsible for error correction. Higher layer protocols use information provided by ICMP to recover from transmission problems. The `ping` command uses ICMP to check connectivity to remote computers.
- **Address Resolution Protocol (ARP):** Used to resolve the IP address of the destination computer to the physical or Media Access Control (MAC) address, which is a unique 12-digit hexadecimal number that is burned into ROM on every network adapter card.

These are only a few of the many protocols that make up the TCP/IP protocol suite. If you need additional information on these protocols and details on the other protocols that make up TCP/IP, refer to any book that specializes in computer internetworking.

By default, the earliest versions of Windows used version 4 of the IP protocol, simply known as IPv4. With its 32-bit address space, this version has performed admirably well in the more than 30 years since its initial introduction. However, with the rapid growth of the Internet in recent years, its address space has approached exhaustion, and security concerns have increased. Consequently, the Internet Engineering Task Force (IETF) introduced version 6 of the IP protocol with Request for Comment (RFC) 1883 in 1995 and updated with RFCs 2460, 3513, and 4193 in more recent years. Simply known as IPv6, this protocol provides for 128-bit addressing, which allows for a practically infinite number of possible addresses, as well as the following benefits:

- **An efficient hierarchical addressing scheme:** IPv6 addresses are designed to enable an efficient, hierarchical, and summarizable routing scheme, making way for multiple levels of Internet service providers (ISPs), which is becoming more common nowadays.
- **Simpler routing tables:** Backbone routers on the Internet are more easily configured for routing packets to their destinations.
- **Stateful and stateless address configuration:** IPv6 simplifies host configuration with the use of stateful address configuration (configuring IP addresses in the presence of a Dynamic Host Configuration Protocol [DHCP] server) or the use of stateless address configuration (configuring IP addresses in the absence of a DHCP server). Stateless address configuration enables the automatic configuration of hosts on a subnetwork according to the addresses displayed by available routers.
- **Improved security:** IPv6 includes standards-based support for IP Security (IPSec). In fact, IPv6 requires IPSec support. You can configure IPSec connection security rules for IPv6 in the same fashion as with IPv4. IPSec is discussed further in Chapter 10, “Configuring and Maintaining Network Security.”
- **Support for Link-Local Multicast Name Resolution (LLMNR):** This enables IPv6 clients on a single subnet to resolve each other’s names without the need for a DNS server or using NetBIOS over TCP/IP.
- **Improved support for Quality of Service (QoS):** IPv6 header fields improve the identification and handling of network traffic from its source to destination, even when IPSec encryption is in use.

- **Extensibility:** You can add extension headers after the IPv6 packet header, which enable the inclusion of new features as they are developed in years to come.

By using a TCP/IP implementation known as the Next Generation TCP/IP stack (first included with Windows Vista), Windows 8 and 8.1 enable a dual IP layer architecture enabling the operation of both IPv4 and IPv6 at the same time. Unlike with Windows XP and older Windows versions, Windows 8 and 8.1 do not require you to install a separate IPv6 component; IPv6 is installed and enabled by default.

NOTE For more introductory information on IPv6, refer to "Microsoft's Objectives for IP Version 6" at http://technet.microsoft.com/en-us/library/bb726949.aspx.

Configuring TCP/IP Version 4

Much of TCP/IPv4 is transparent to users and to administrators. The administrator may need to configure the address information applied to the network interface. Table 8-2 describes this address information.

Table 8-2 IPv4 Addressing Components

Addressing Component	Description
IP address	The unique, logical 32-bit address that identifies the computer (called a host or node) and the subnet on which it is located. The IP address is displayed in dotted decimal notation (each decimal represents an octet of binary ones and zeros). For example, the binary notation of an address may be 10000000.00000001.00000001.00000011, which in dotted decimal notation is written as 128.1.1.3.
Subnet mask	The subnet mask is applied to an IP address to determine the subnetwork address and the host address on that subnet. All hosts on the same subnet must have the same subnet mask for them to be correctly identified. If a mask is incorrect, both the subnet and the host address will be wrong. (For example, if you have an IP address of 128.1.1.3, and an incorrect mask of 255.255.128.0, the subnet address would be 128.1.0 and the host address would be 1.3. If the correct subnet mask is 255.255.255.0, then the subnet address would be 128.1.1 and the host address would be 3.)
Default gateway	The address listed as the default gateway is the location on the local subnet to which the local computer will send all data meant for other subnets. In other words, this is the IP address for a router that is capable of transmitting the data to other networks.

Addressing Component	Description
DNS server address	The place where names of IP hosts are sent so that the DNS server will respond with an IP address. This process is called *name resolution*. DNS is a distributed database of records that maps names to IP addresses, and vice versa. A HOSTS file that maps names to IP addresses can be placed on the local computer and used instead of DNS, which renders this an optional setting, although it is rare that a network is small enough to make a HOSTS file more efficient than a DNS server. When a user types in a DNS name such as **`BlakePC.mydomain.local`**, the computer sends the name to the DNS server. If the name is one that the DNS server knows, it sends back the IP address. Otherwise, the DNS server sends the name request to a higher-level DNS server, and this recursive process continues until either the IP address is found and returned to the original requestor, or until all avenues have been exhausted and the original requestor is notified that the name cannot be found.
Windows Internet Naming Service (WINS) address	The WINS server address is the location where network computers send requests to resolve NetBIOS names to IP addresses. WINS is used on Microsoft Windows networks where older Windows computers or applications require NetBIOS naming. When a user types in a NetBIOS name, such as **`BLAKEPC`**, the computer sends the name to the WINS server. Because WINS is a flat-file database, it returns an IP address or a Name not found message. WINS server addresses, like DNS server addresses, are optional. A computer can use a local LMHOSTS file to map the NetBIOS names to IP addresses rather than use WINS.

Static IPv4 Addressing

IP addresses indicate the same type of location information as a street address. A building on a street has a number, and when you add that number to the street name, you can find it fairly easily because the number and the street are unique within a city. This type of address scheme—an individual address plus a location address—allows every computer on the Internet to be uniquely identified.

A static IP address is one that is permanently assigned to a computer on the network. Certain computers (such as routers or servers) require static IP addresses because of their functions. Client computers are more often assigned dynamic addresses because they are more likely to be moved around the network or retired and replaced. DSL and cable modem users are usually given a static IP address, whereas dial-up users are provided with dynamic addresses.

As discussed earlier, IP addresses consist of two parts: one that specifies the network and one part that specifies the computer. These addresses are further categorized with classes, as described in Table 8-3.

Table 8-3 IPv4 Address Classes

Class	Dotted Decimal Hosts per Range	First Octet Binary	Usage	Number of Networks	Number of Hosts per Network
A	1.0.0.0–126.255.255.255	0xxxxxxx	Large networks/ISPs	126	16,777,214
B	128.0.0.0–191.255.255.255	10xxxxxx	Large or mid-size ISPs	16,384	65,534
C	192.0.0.0–223.255.255.255	110xxxxx	Small networks	2,097,152	254
D	224.0.0.0–239.255.255.255	1110xxxx	Multicasting	N/A	N/A
E	240.0.0.0–254.255.255.255	1111xxxx	Reserved for future use	N/A	N/A
Loopback	127.0.0.1–127.255.255.255	01111111	Loopback testing	N/A	N/A

NOTE The concept of loopback testing is the use of a predefined IP address that a computer can dial up itself to see whether the TCP/IP stack is properly set up. If TCP/IP is configured, you should be able to run the ping 127.0.0.1 command when troubleshooting a connectivity problem.

The portion of the address that decides on which network the host resides varies based on the class, and, as you will see later, the subnet mask. In the following list, the uppercase Ns represent the part of the IP address that specifies the network, and the lowercase Cs represent the part of the address that specifies the computer. This explains why there are differing numbers of networks per class and different numbers of hosts per network, as listed in Table 8-3.

- **Class A:** NNNNNNNN.cccccccc.cccccccc.cccccccc
- **Class B:** NNNNNNNN.NNNNNNNN.cccccccc.cccccccc
- **Class C:** NNNNNNNN.NNNNNNNN.NNNNNNNN.cccccccc

These address portions coincide with the default subnet masks for each address class. A Class A subnet mask is 255.0.0.0, a Class B subnet mask is 255.255.0.0, and a Class C subnet mask is 255.255.255.0.

Subnet masks enable you to reconfigure what constitutes the network portion and what constitutes the computer portion. When you apply the subnet mask to the IP address by using a "bitwise logical AND" operation, the result is a network number. A bitwise logical AND operation adds the bit, whether 1 or 0, to the corresponding bit in the subnet mask. If the subnet mask bit is a 1, the corresponding IP address bit is passed through as a result. If the subnet mask bit is a 0, a zero bit is passed through. For example, if the IP address is 141.25.240.201, you have the following:

- **IP address:** 10001101.00011001.11110000.11001001
- **Subnet mask:** 11111111.11111111.00000000.00000000
- Result from bitwise logical AND
- **Network:** 10001101.00011001.00000000.00000000

This example shows the network address as 141.25.0.0 and the host address as 0.0.240.201. If you add bits to the mask, you will be able to have additional subnetworks when you perform a bitwise logical AND, and each subnetwork will have fewer hosts because fewer bits are available for the host portion of the address. If you use the same address and add five bits to the subnet mask, you receive the following:

- **IP address:** 10001101.00011001.11110000.11001001
- **Subnet mask:** 11111111.11111111.11111000.00000000
- Result from bitwise logical AND
- **Network:** 10001101.00011001.11110000.00000000

In this case, the subnet mask changes the network address to 141.25.240.0. The host address changes to 0.0.0.201. Other IP addresses that are under the default Class B subnet mask that would otherwise be part of the same network (such as 140.25.192.15 and 140.25.63.12) are now on different subnets.

For an organization with a large number of physical networks where each requires a different subnet address, you can use the subnet mask to segment a single address to fit the network. You can easily calculate how many subnets and hosts you will receive when you subnet a network. The formula is $2^n - 2$, where n is the number of bits. The number 2^n is 2 raised to the power of the number of bits, and that result minus 2 (the addresses represented by all 1s and all 0s) equals the available subnets or hosts. Therefore, if you have a subnet of 5 bits (as previously shown), you are able to achieve $2^5 -2 = 32 - 2 = 30$ subnets. Because there are 11 bits left for host addresses, each subnet will have $2^{11} - 2 = 2048 - 2 = 2{,}046$ hosts.

Classless Inter-Domain Routing

When you multiply 2,046 by 30, you see that you have 61,380 addresses available for network hosts and that you "lost" 4,154 addresses. This is the problem that Classless Inter-Domain Routing (CIDR) solves.

When you consider that a Class A address has more than 16 million host addresses and that no organization with a Class A address has managed to utilize each of those addresses, you realize the use of classful addressing (an IP addressing system that does not segment the network into smaller subnetworks) is extremely wasteful. CIDR was developed to prevent the Internet from running out of IP addresses by reusing some of the unused addresses and expanding the addresses available when subnetting.

With CIDR, a subnet mask is not considered separate from the network portion of the mask. Instead, whatever portion of the mask is used for the network determines how many networks there are. This means that a company can "supernet" two (or more) Class C addresses to put more than 254 hosts on a single physical network. Supernetting is the process of subtracting bits from the default subnet mask. This adds bits to the host portion, increasing the number of hosts available.

CIDR notation allows you to simply specify the number of bits that are used for a mask after the IP address. For example, 192.168.1.0 with a subnet mask of 255.255.255.0 is written as 192.168.1.0/24. If the address were supernetted, it could be 192.168.1.0/22.

Private IPv4 Networks

IPv4 specifications define sets of networks that are specified as *private IPv4 networks*. The private IP address classes are used on private networks that utilize Network Address Translation (NAT) or proxy services to communicate on the Internet. Internet routers are preconfigured not to forward data that contains these IP addresses. Table 8-4 describes these networks.

Table 8-4 Private IPv4 Network Addresses

Class	Dotted Decimal Hosts per Range	First Octet Binary	Number of Networks	Number of Hosts per Network
A	10.0.0.0–10.255.255.254	00001010	1	16,777,214
B	172.16.0.0–172.31.255.254	10101100	1	65,534
C	192.168.0.0–192.168.255.254	11000000	254	254

NOTE For more information on TCP/IP version 4, refer to "IPv4 Addressing" at http://technet.microsoft.com/en-us/library/dd379547%28v=ws.10%29.aspx and "Fundamentals of Classful IPv4 addressing" at https://learningnetwork.cisco.com/docs/DOC-12872.

Configuring TCP/IP Version 6

The 128-bit addressing scheme used by IPv6 enables an unimaginably high number of 3.4×10^{38} addresses, which equates to a total of 6.5×10^{23} addresses for every square meter of the Earth's surface. Consequently, this is a complicated addressing scheme, as described in the following sections.

IPv6 Address Syntax

Whereas IPv4 addresses use dotted-decimal format, as explained earlier in this chapter, IPv6 addresses are subdivided into 16-bit blocks. Each 16-bit block is portrayed as a 4-digit hexadecimal number and is separated from other blocks by colons. This addressing scheme is referred to as *colon-hexadecimal*.

For example, a 128-bit IPv6 address written in binary could appear as follows:

0011111111111110 1111111111111111 0010000111000101
0000000000000000 0000001010101010 0000000011111111
1111111000100001 0011101000111110

The same address written in colon-hexadecimal becomes 3ffe:ffff:21a5:0000:00ff:fe21:5a3e.

You can remove any leading zeros, converting this address to 3ffe:ffff:21a5::ff:fe21:5a3e.

In this notation, note that the block that contained all zeros appears as ::, which is called *double-colon*.

IPv6 Prefixes

Corresponding to the network portion of an IPv4 address is the prefix, which is the part of the address containing the bits of the subnet prefix. IPv6 addresses do not employ subnet masks; they use the same CIDR notation used with IPv4. For example, an IPv6 address prefix could be 3ffe:ffff:21a5::/64, where 64 is the number of bits employed by the address prefix.

Types of IPv6 Addresses

IPv6 uses the following three types of addresses:

- **Unicast:** Represents a single interface within the typical scope of unicast addresses. In other words, packets addressed to this type of address are to be delivered to a single network interface. Unicast IPv6 addresses include global unicast, link-local, site-local, and unique local addresses. Two special addresses are also included: unspecified addresses (all zeros, equivalent to the IPv4 address of 0.0.0.0) and the loopback address, which is 0:0:0:0:0:0:0:1 or ::1, which is equivalent to the IPv4 address of 127.0.0.1.
- **Multicast:** Represents multiple interfaces to which packets are delivered to all network interfaces identified by the address. Multicast addresses have the first eight bits set to ones, so begin with ff.
- **Anycast:** Also represents multiple interfaces. Anycast packets are delivered to a single network interface that represents the nearest (in terms of routing hops) interface identified by the address.

Table 8-5 provides additional details on the IPv6 classes and subclasses.

Table 8-5 IPv6 Address Classes and Subclasses

Class	Address Prefix	Additional Features	First Binary Bits	Usage
Global unicast	2000::/3	Use a global routing prefix of 45 bits (beyond the initial 001 bits), which identifies a specific organization's network; a 16-bit subnet ID, which identifies up to 54,536 subnets within an organization's network; and a 64-bit interface ID, which indicates a specific network interface within the subnet.	001	Provides globally routable Internet addresses that are equivalent to the public IPv4 addresses
Link-local unicast	fe80::/64	Equivalent to APIPA-configured IPv4 addresses in the 169.254.0.0/16 network prefix.	111111101000	Used for communication between neighboring nodes on the same link. These addresses are assigned automatically when you configure automatic addressing in the absence of a DHCP server.

Class	Address Prefix	Additional Features	First Binary Bits	Usage
Site-local unicast	fec0::/10	Equivalent to the private IPv4 address spaces mentioned previously in Table 8-4. Prefix followed by a 54-bit subnet ID field within which you can establish a hierarchical routing structure within your site.	111111101100	Used for communication between nodes located in the same site.
Unique local IPv6 unicast	fc00::/7	Prefix followed by a local (L) flag, a 40-bit global ID, a 16-bit subnet ID, and a 64-bit interface ID.	11111100	Provides addresses that are private to an organization but unique across all the organization's sites.
Multicast	ff	Use the next 4 bits for flags (Transient [T], Prefix [P], and Rendezvous Point Address [R]), the following 4 bits for scope (determines where multicast traffic is forwarded), and the remaining 112 bits for a group ID.	11111111	Provides multiple interfaces to which packets are delivered to all network interfaces identified by the address.
Anycast	(from unicast addresses)	Assigned from the unicast address space with the same scope as the type of unicast address within which the anycast address is assigned.	(varies)	Utilized only as destination addresses assigned to routers.

NOTE Site-local IPv6 addresses are equivalent to the private IPv4 addresses mentioned in Table 8-4. You can access site-local addresses only from the network in which they are located; they are not accessible from external networks such as the Internet.

NOTE For more information on IPv6 and its latest enhancements as it relates to Windows 8.1, refer to "Internet Protocol Version 6 (IPv6) Overview" at http://technet.microsoft.com/en-us/library/hh831730.

Compatibility Between IPv4 and IPv6 Addresses

To assist in the migration from IPv4 to IPv6 and their coexistence, several additional address types are used, as follows:

- **IPv4-comaptible addresses:** Nodes communicating between IPv4 and IPv6 networks can use an address represented by 0:0:0:0:0:0:w.x.y.z, where w.x.y.z is the IPv4 address in dotted-decimal.
- **IPv4-mapped address:** An IPv4-only node is represented as ::ffff:.w.x.y.z to an IPv6 node. This address type is used only for internal representation and is never specified as a source or destination address of an IPv6 packet.
- **Teredo address:** Teredo is a tunneling communication protocol that enables IPv6 connectivity between IPv6/IPv4 nodes across NAT interfaces, thereby improving connectivity for newer IPv6-enabled applications on IPv4 networks. Teredo is described in RFC 4380. Teredo makes use of a special IPv6 address that includes the following components in the sequence given:
  - A 32-bit Teredo prefix, which is 2001::/32 in Windows Vista/7/8 and Windows Server 2008/2012.
  - The 32-bit IPv4 address of the Teredo server involved in creating this address.
  - A 16-bit Teredo flag field and an obscured 16-bit UDP port interface definition.
  - An obscured external IPv4 address corresponding to all Teredo traffic across the Teredo client interface.
- **6-to-4 address:** Two nodes running both IPv4 and IPv6 across an IPv4 routing infrastructure use this address type when communicating with each other. You can form the 6-to-4 address by combining the prefix 2002::/16 with the 32-bit public IPv4 address to form a 48-bit prefix. This tunneling technique is described in RFC 3056.

NOTE More information on compatibility addresses and technologies used for transition to IPv6 is available in "Internet Protocol Version 6, Teredo, and Related Technologies in Windows 7 and Windows Server 2008 R2" at http://technet.microsoft.com/en-us/library/ee126159(WS.10).aspx. Although this paper was written for Windows 7 and Windows Server 2008 R2, the technologies involved are largely unchanged for Windows 8/8.1 and Windows Server 2012 R2.

Dynamic IP Addressing

Dynamic IP addresses are provided to a computer when it needs to be connected to the network. The provider is the DHCP server. When the computer is disconnected, the IP address becomes available for use by another computer. The address does not become available immediately, however. It is leased for a specified period of time (the administrator specifies this time period when configuring the DHCP server), and when the lease is up, the IP address is placed back in an IP address pool and can be delivered to another computer.

Before DHCP was developed, network administrators were forced to manually assign a separate IP address to each computer on the network. If a user left for a two-month vacation and the computer was off the entire time, the IP address was unusable by anyone else. If the administrator (yes, to err is human) forgot to reuse an IP address for a computer that was retired, then the number of IP addresses available was also reduced. Other administrative errors included assigning duplicate IP addresses to computers on the network and misconfiguring the subnet mask, default gateway, and DNS server addresses. DHCP resolves these problems.

NOTE DHCP has a set communication process that is used to lease an IP address to a DHCP client. This process occurs each time a client starts up or when it requires a new IP address lease (typically after 50% of the lease period has expired or when a user issues the `ipconfig /renew` command).

1. Client boots up and broadcasts a DHCPDiscover packet.
2. Server responds with a DHCPOffer packet containing an IP address, subnet mask, and often including the default gateway and DNS server addresses.
3. Client replies with a DHCPRequest packet as a broadcast, requesting verification that it is okay to use the address. This notifies any other DHCP servers that they do not need to hold a reservation of an IP address for the client if they also responded to the original DHCPDiscover packet.
4. Server responds with a DHCPACK acknowledgment packet and the client begins using the address.

On a Windows 8.1 computer, you can configure any network connection to be a DHCP client by selecting the option **Obtain an IP Address automatically**, which is configured in the Internet Protocol (TCP/IP) Properties dialog box. If you change from a manual address to a dynamic one, you need to clear out the manual IP addressing information first.

Connecting to Wired Networks

Windows 8.1 simplifies the process of connecting to diverse types of networks, including wired and wireless networks. In this section, you learn about connecting your computer to wired networks. Chapter 9, "Configuring Networking Settings," extends this discussion to include methods used for connecting to and securing wireless networks. In Windows 8 and 8.1, you can quickly obtain a view of available network devices by accessing the Search charm and typing `network`. The Control Panel Network applet displays this information, as shown in Figure 8-1.

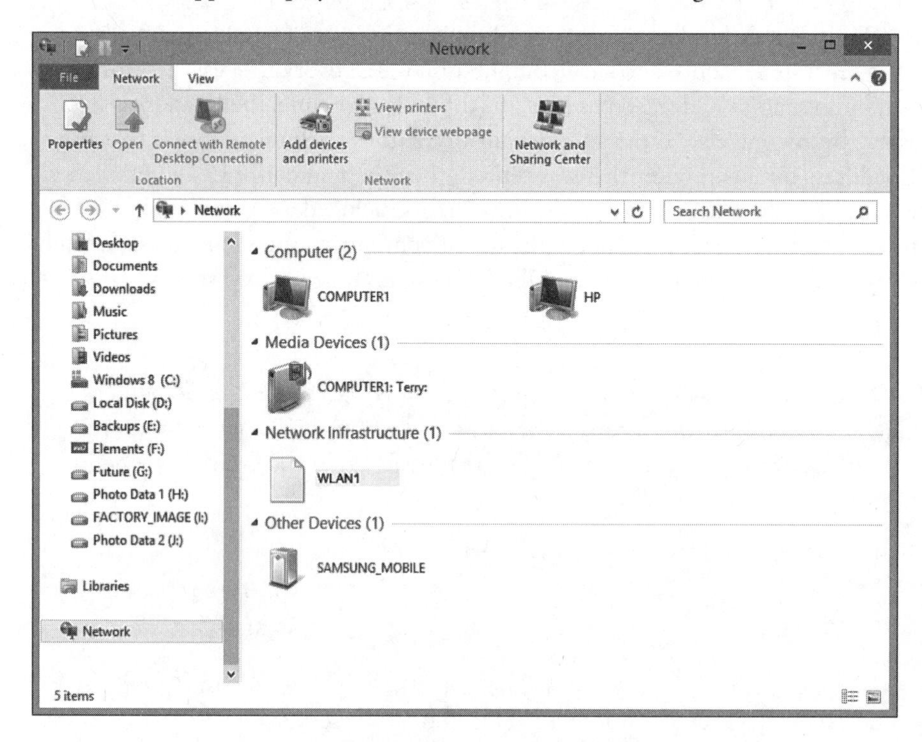

Figure 8-1 The Network app in Windows 8.1 displays several types of networked devices.

The Network and Sharing Center

First introduced in Windows Vista and continued in Windows 7, Windows 8, and Windows 8.1, the Network and Sharing Center, shown in Figure 8-2, brings all networking tasks together in a single convenient location. You can configure connections to other computers and networks, share folders, printers, and media, view devices on your network, set up and manage network connections, and troubleshoot problems from this location.

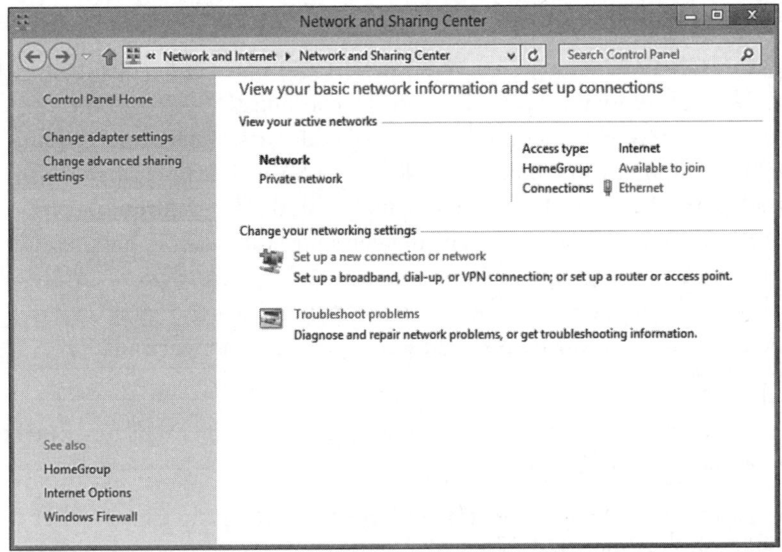

Figure 8-2 The Network and Sharing Center provides a centralized location for configuring network properties.

You can open the Network and Sharing Center by using any of the following methods:

- If you have the Network window open as previously shown in Figure 8-1, simply click the icon for the **Network and Sharing Center** on the menu bar.
- Open the **Search** charm and type `network and sharing`. From the icons displayed, click **Network and Sharing Center**.
- Open the **Settings** charm and select **Control Panel**. On the Control Panel home page, click **Network and Internet** and then click **Network and Sharing Center** or **View network status and tasks**.

The Network and Sharing Center enables you to configure connections to other computers and networks, share folders, printers, and media, view devices on your network, set up and manage network connections, and troubleshoot connectivity problems.

Using the Network and Sharing Center to Set Up a TCP/IPv4 Connection

You can configure TCP/IP version 4 on a Windows 8.1 computer either manually or dynamically. The default method is to dynamically configure TCP/IP. If the infrastructure includes DHCP services that deliver IP addresses to network computers, a Windows 8.1 computer can connect after logon with the default configuration of the network adapter. However, if you need to apply a static IPv4 address and other parameters, your only option is to manually configure the network adapter. Manually configuring a single computer is time-consuming and error-prone. Multiply that by hundreds of computers and you can see why dynamic configuration has become so popular. Use the following procedure to configure a network adapter with a static IPv4 Address:

Step 1. Open the Network and Sharing Center by using any of the methods described in the preceding section.

Step 2. From the Tasks list on the left side of the Network and Sharing Center, click **Change adapter settings**. This opens the Network Connections dialog box, as shown in Figure 8-3.

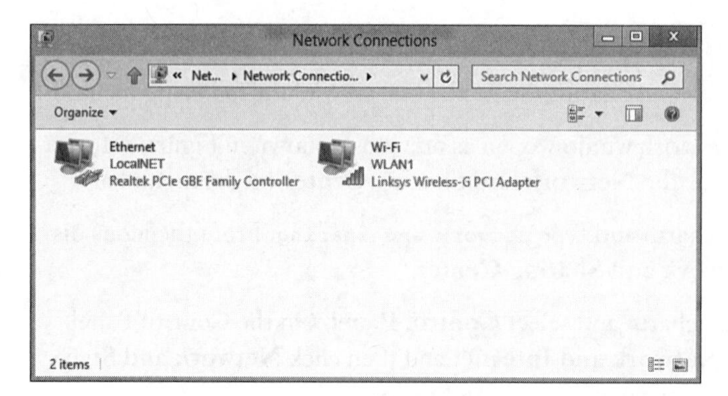

Figure 8-3 The Network Connections dialog box displays the network connections configured for your computer.

Step 3. Right-click the connection that represents the adapter you are going to configure and select **Properties**. If you receive a User Account Control (UAC) prompt, click **Yes**. The Ethernet Properties dialog box opens, as shown in Figure 8-4.

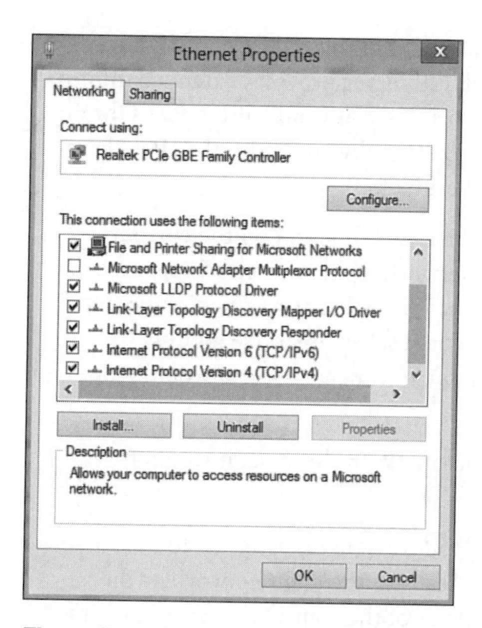

Figure 8-4 The network adapter is considered a network connection.

Step 4. Click to select **Internet Protocol Version 4 (TCP/IPv4)**. (You might need to scroll through other services to reach this item.) Click **Properties**. The Internet Protocol Version 4 (TCP/IPv4) Properties dialog opens, as shown in Figure 8-5.

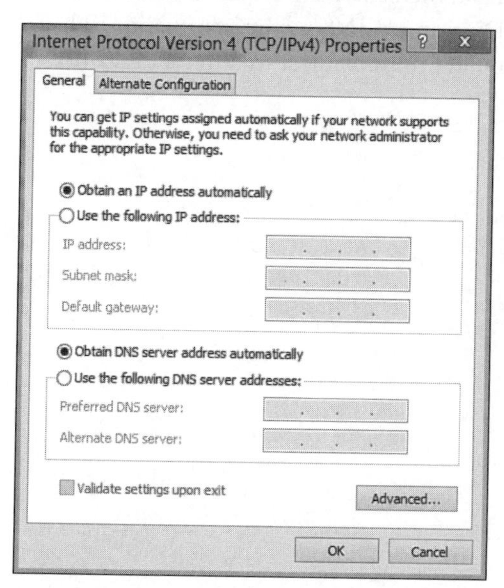

Figure 8-5 The Internet Protocol Version 4 (TCP/IPv4) Properties dialog box enables you to define manual or dynamic IPv4 address information.

Step 5. To use DHCP services, you should make certain that **Obtain an IP address automatically** is selected, and if the DHCP server provides extended information—including the DNS server information—you would also select **Obtain DNS server address automatically**. To manually configure the IP address, you should click **Use the following IP address**.

Step 6. In the IP address box, type the address that will function on the current network segment. For example, if the network segment uses a Class C address 192.168.1.0 with a subnet mask of 255.255.255.0, and you've already used 192.168.1.1 and 192.168.1.2, you could select any node address from 3 through 254 (255 is used for broadcasts), in which case, you would type `192.168.1.3`.

Step 7. In the Subnet Mask box, type the subnet mask. In this case, it would be `255.255.255.0`.

Step 8. In the Default gateway box, type the IP address that is assigned to the router interface on your current segment that leads to the main network or the public network. In this case, the IP address of the router on your segment is 192.168.1.1 and the IP address of the router's other interface is 12.88.54.179. In the Default Gateway box, you would type `192.168.1.1`.

Step 9. To configure an alternate IP address on a computer configured to use DHCP, click the **Alternate Configuration** tab to display the dialog box shown in Figure 8-6. Click **User configured** and then enter the required IP address, subnet mask, default gateway, and DNS and WINS server information. Then click **OK**. This is useful if your computer must connect to different networks such as work and home.

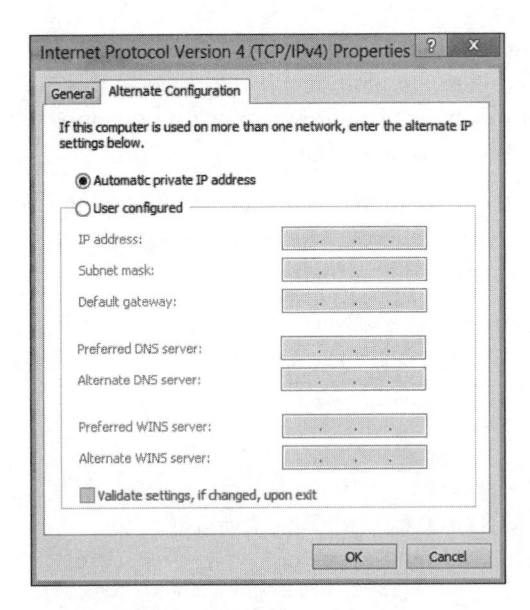

Figure 8-6 The Alternate Configuration tab enables you to enter an additional set of IP settings for use on a different network.

Step 10. Click the **Advanced** button. The Advanced TCP/IP Settings dialog box opens, as shown in Figure 8-7.

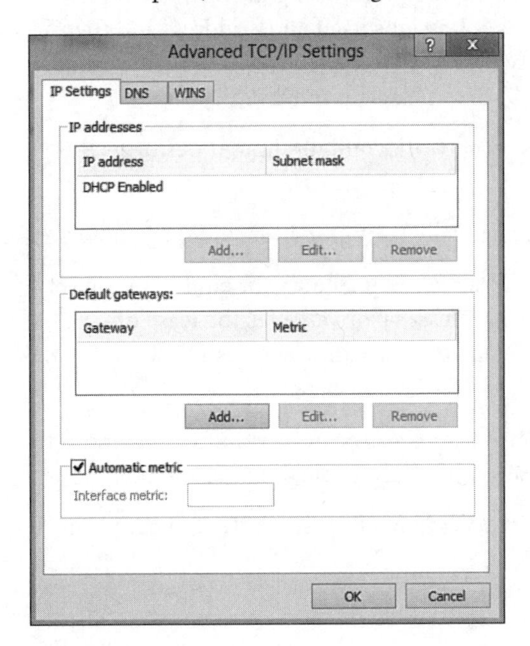

Figure 8-7 The Advanced TCP/IP Settings dialog box allows you to control granular IP addressing options.

Step 11. If you require more than one IP address for a computer, such as for hosting two different websites, you can configure the additional IP addresses in this dialog box by clicking the **Add** button under IP addresses. You cannot configure any additional IP addresses if you are using DHCP.

Step 12. If your network segment is connected to more than one router leading to the main or outside networks, you can configure these gateway addresses in the Default Gateways section by clicking the **Add** button.

Step 13. When finished, click **OK** until you return to the Network Connections dialog box.

TIP Many hardware routers, including those used when connecting home networks to high-speed Internet connections, include DHCP functionality. If you are using one of these, simply leave the defaults selected in step 5 of the preceding procedure.

Implementing APIPA

The Automatic Private Internet Protocol Addressing (APIPA) system provides an alternate configuration to DHCP for automatic IP addressing in small networks. When a computer uses APIPA, Windows 8.1 assigns itself an IP address and then verifies that it is unique on the local network. To work effectively, APIPA is useful only on a small local area network (LAN) or as a backup to DHCP.

When a Windows 8.1 computer begins its network configuration, it performs the following procedures:

1. It checks to see whether there is a manually configured (or static) IP address.
2. If there is none, it contacts a DHCP server with a query for configuration settings. A response from a DHCP server leases—or validates the lease of—an IP address, subnet mask, and extended IP information such as DNS server, default gateway, and so on.
3. If there is no DHCP server response within six seconds, Windows 8.1 looks to see whether an alternate configuration has been applied by the administrator.
4. If there is no alternate configuration, Windows 8.1 uses APIPA to define an IP address unique on the LAN.

APIPA defines its IP addresses in the range of 169.254.0.1 to 169.254.255.254. The subnet mask on these addresses is configured as 255.255.0.0. You do have administrative control over APIPA. When Windows 8.1 selects an address from this range, it then performs a duplicate address detection process to ensure that the IP address it has selected is not already being used, while continuing to query for a DHCP server in the background. If the address is found to be in use, Windows 8.1 selects another address. The random IP selection occurs recursively until an unused IP address is selected, a DHCP server is discovered, or the process has taken place 10 times.

Connecting to a TCP/IP Version 6 Network

You can let IPv6 configure itself automatically with a link-local address described previously in Table 8-5. You can also configure IPv6 to use an existing DHCP server or manually configure an IPv6 address as required. Configuration of IPv6 addresses is similar to the procedure used with configuration of IPv4 addresses, as the following procedure shows:

Step 1. Open the Network and Sharing Center by using any of the methods previously described.

Step 2. From the Tasks list on the left side of the Network and Sharing Center, click **Change adapter settings**. This opens the Network Connections dialog box, as previously shown in Figure 8-3.

Step 3. Right-click the connection that represents the adapter you are going to configure and select **Properties**. If you receive a UAC prompt, click **Yes**.

Step 4. Click to select **Internet Protocol Version 6 (TCP/IPv6)**. (You might need to scroll through other services to reach this item.) Click **Properties**. The Internet Protocol Version 6 (TCP/IPv6) Properties dialog opens, as shown in Figure 8-8.

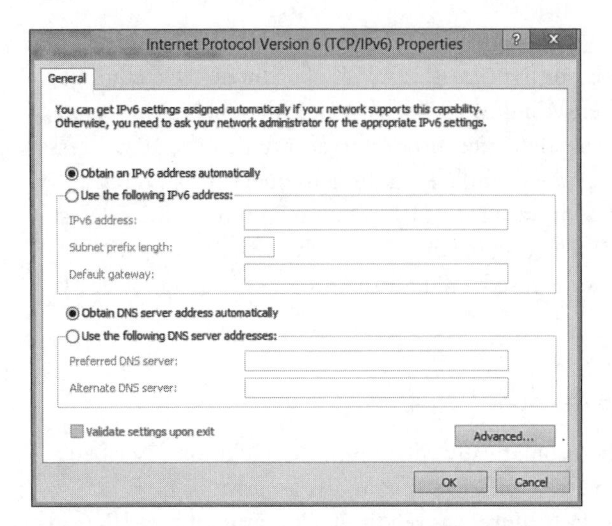

Figure 8-8 The Internet Protocol Version 6 (TCP/IPv6) Properties dialog box enables you to define manual or dynamic IPv6 address information.

Step 5. To use DHCP, ensure that the **Obtain an IPv6 address automatically** radio button is selected. If the DHCP server provides DNS server information, ensure that the **Obtain DNS server address automatically** radio button is also selected. You can also select these options to configure IPv6 automatically with a link-local address using the address prefix fe80::/64 previously described in Table 8-5.

Step 6. To manually configure an IPv6 address, select **Use the following IPv6 address**. Then type the IPv6 address, subnet prefix length, and default gateway in the text boxes provided. For unicast IPv6 addresses, you should set the prefix length to its default value of 64.

Step 7. To manually configure DNS server addresses, select **Use the following DNS server addresses**. Then type the IPv6 addresses of the preferred and alternate DNS server in the text boxes provided.

Step 8. Click **Advanced** to display the Advanced TCP/IP Settings dialog box shown in Figure 8-9.

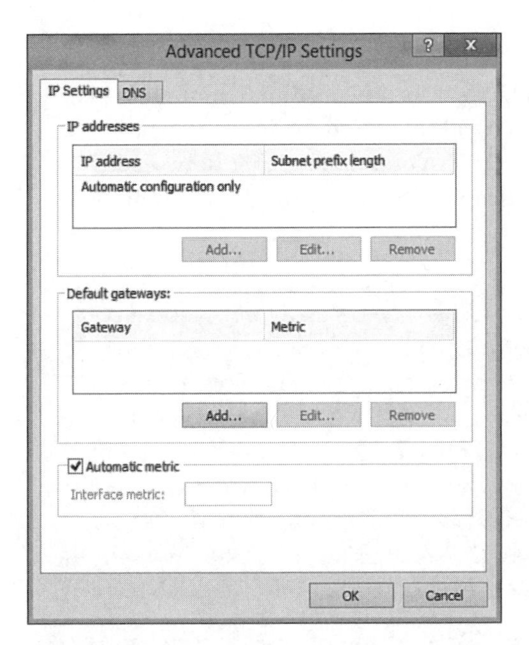

Figure 8-9 The Advanced TCP/IP Settings dialog allows you to control granular IPv6 addressing options.

Step 9. As with IPv4, you can configure additional IP addresses if you are not using DHCP. Click **Add** and type the required IP address in the dialog box that appears.

Step 10. As with IPv4, if your network segment is connected to more than one router, configure additional gateway addresses in the Default Gateways section by clicking the **Add** button.

Step 11. When finished, click **OK** until you return to the Network Connections dialog box.

TIP You can also use the `netsh.exe` tool with the interface IPv6 subcommand to configure IPv6 from the command line. For example, the command `netsh interface IPv6 set address "local area connection 2" fec0:0:0:ffee::3` sets the IPv6 address of the second local area connection to the specified address. For more information, refer to "IPv6 Configuration Information with the Netsh.exe Tool" at http://technet.microsoft.com/en-us/library/bb726952.aspx#EBAA.

Configuring Name Resolution

As previously noted, Windows 8.1 uses DNS as its primary name resolution service. DNS is the name resolution service used by all servers on the Internet; when you type a URL into the address box in Internet Explorer or any other browser, DNS resolves this URL into an IP address so that you can obtain the desired website.

NOTE If your network includes a DNS server, this server is used directly for any name resolution requirements within the network. When a client requests an Internet resource such as www.microsoft.com, an iterative name resolution process occurs in which the local DNS server accesses a series of Internet DNS servers to obtain the IP address of the requested resource. Each server that is accessed knows the locations of one level of servers within the hierarchical DNS namespace (in other words, is authoritative for this level by possessing in its database what is known as an A [address] resource record, which holds the hostname to IPv4 address mapping). For example, the following happens when you type `http://www.Microsoft.com` into your web browser:

1. The local DNS server checks with a root server on the Internet to locate the IP address of a server that is authoritative for .com addresses.
2. The .com server on the Internet locates the IP address of a server that is authoritative for Microsoft.com addresses.
3. The Microsoft.com server on the Internet locates the IP address of the www.Microsoft.com web server.
4. These servers return the required IP address to the client, whose browser then displays the home page of the requested website.

The Local Area Connection Properties dialog box enables you to configure your computer to access a DNS server, as outlined in the following procedure:

Step 1. Use the procedure outlined earlier in this chapter to access the Internet Protocol Version 4 (TCP/IPv4) Properties dialog box.

Step 2. If your network is configured to use DHCP to automatically configure client computers with the address of the DNS server, you need only ensure that the **Obtain DNS server address automatically** option is selected.

Step 3. If your network is not configured with DHCP, click the **Use the following DNS server addresses** option and type the IP address for at least one DNS server.

Step 4. Click **Advanced** to bring up the Advanced TCP/IP Settings dialog box previously shown in Figure 8-7.

Step 5. Click the **DNS** tab to display the settings shown in Figure 8-10.

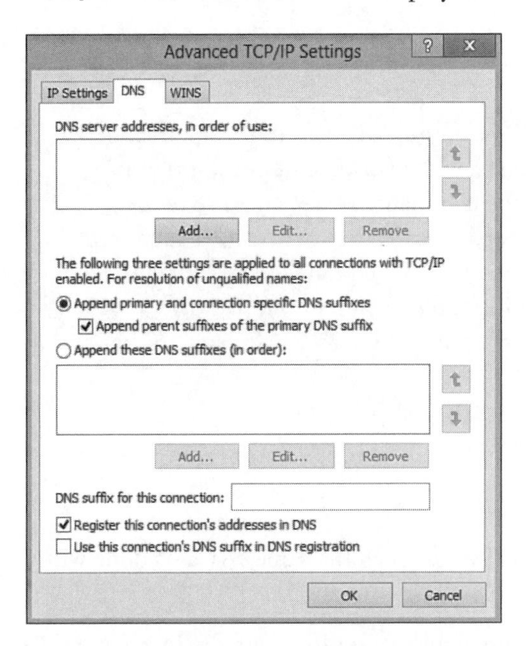

Figure 8-10 The DNS tab of the Advanced TCP/IP Settings dialog box enables you to configure additional DNS settings to be used by your network connection.

Step 6. To specify additional DNS servers, click the **Add** button under the DNS server addresses section, type the IP address to the additional DNS server, and then click **Add**.

Step 7. The lower section of the DNS tab applies to the fully qualified domain name (FQDN) of resources. Users sometimes use a simple name for a computer or printer. This section enables you to configure the last portion of the domain name that will be appended to the simple name to create an FQDN. For example, if you configure `mydomain.local` and `jubilee.local` in this box, and the user types in **`server`**, the computer automatically attempts to contact `server.mydomain.local`. If that fails, the computer then attempts to contact `server.jubilee.local`. Click the **Append these DNS suffixes (in order)** option. Then click the **Add** button to configure the DNS suffixes.

Step 8. For a DNS server that provides Dynamic DNS, and when you want to share files or printers from your computer, you should register your computer's DNS name and IP address in the DNS database. To do so, select the **Register this connection's addresses in DNS** check box.

Step 9. Click the **WINS** tab. WINS provides resolution for NetBIOS names to IP addresses on Windows networks. If you use legacy networks or have applications that require NetBIOS names, you should configure the address for a WINS server on the network.

> **TIP** You can also use the `netsh.exe` tool to configure IPv4 from the command line. This tool enables you to perform almost any network configuration action from the command prompt. For example, the command `netsh interface ip set address "Local Area connection" static 192.168.0.2 255.255.255.0 192.168.0.1` configures the computer's local area connection with the static IP address 192.168.0.2, subnet mask 255.255.255.0, and default gateway 192.168.0.1. For more information, refer to "Netsh Overview" at http://technet.microsoft.com/en-us/library/cc732279(WS.10).aspx.

Configuring TCP/IPv6 Name Resolution

You can configure name resolution with IPv6 in much the same way as is done with IPv4, as the following steps demonstrate:

Step 1. Use the procedure outlined in the previous section to access the Internet Protocol Version 6 (TCP/IPv6) Properties dialog box.

Step 2. If your network is configured to use DHCP to automatically configure client computers with the address of the DNS server, you need only ensure that the **Obtain DNS server address automatically** option is selected.

Step 3. If your network is not configured with DHCP, click the **Use the following DNS server addresses** option and type the IPv6 address for at least one DNS server.

Step 4. Click **Advanced** to bring up the Advanced TCP/IP Settings dialog box previously shown in Figure 8-9.

Step 5. Click the **DNS** tab to display the available DNS settings, which are identical to those found in the DNS tab for IPv4 described previously and shown in Figure 8-10. Click **Add** under the DNS server addresses section to add the IPv6 addresses of additional DNS servers, as required.

Step 6. To specify additional DNS servers, click the **Add** button under the DNS server addresses section, type the IPv6 address to the additional DNS server, and then click **Add**.

Step 7. As was the case with IPv4, if you need additional DNS suffixes to specify the FQDN of resources, click the **Append these DNS suffixes (in order)** option. Then click the **Add** button to configure the DNS suffixes.

Step 8. For a DNS server that provides Dynamic DNS, and when you want to share files or printers from your computer, you should register your computer's DNS name and IP address in the DNS database. To do so, select the **Register this connection's addresses in DNS** check box.

Step 9. Click **OK** until you're returned to the Local Area Connection Properties dialog box.

NOTE DNS name resolution in IPv6 operates in a manner similar to that previously mentioned for IPv4, except that DNS servers use AAAA resource records to hold the hostname to IPv6 address mapping, as opposed to A records used for IPv4 mapping.

Disabling IPv6

You cannot remove IPv6 from a Windows 8.1 computer. However, you can disable IPv6 on a specific connection. From the Ethernet Properties dialog box shown previously in Figure 8-4, clear the check box beside **Internet Protocol Version 6 (TCP/IPv6)** and then click **OK**. You can do this selectively for each network connection on your computer.

NOTE You can also selectively disable IPv6 components. This more complex procedure involves editing the Registry and is beyond the scope of this book. For more details, refer to "How to Disable IPv6 or Its Components in Windows" at http://support.microsoft.com/kb/929852.

Configuring Network Locations

When you first install Windows 8.1 (as covered in Chapter 2, "Installing Windows 8.1"), you receive the option to set your network location. A network location defines a set of conditions contained within a network profile that govern whether computers on the network can view your computer and resources such as files, folders, and printers to which it is connected. Microsoft makes available network profiles corresponding to private and public network locations that are configured by default to enhance the security of your computer when connected to a public network such as a Wi-Fi hotspot.

Setting Up New Network Connections

The Network and Sharing Center enables you to set up new networking connections. Click **Set up a new connection or network** (refer to Figure 8-2) to display the Set Up a Connection or Network Wizard shown in Figure 8-11 (note that this dialog box may not display all these options; the options vary according to the networking hardware attached to your computer). Select from the following options and then click **Next**:

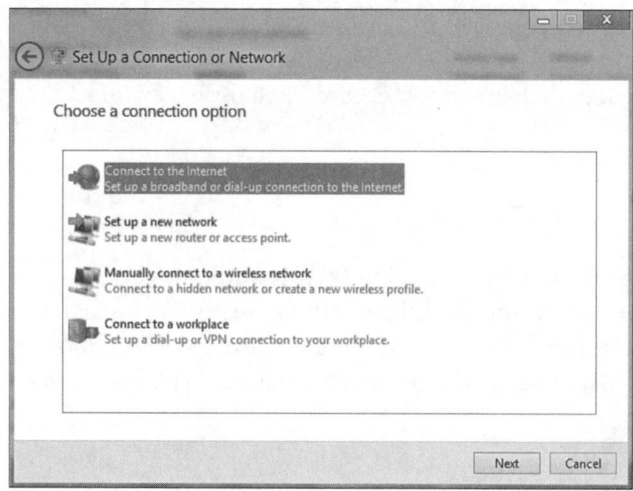

Figure 8-11 The Set Up a Connection or Network Wizard offers several options for connecting your computer to networks.

- **Connect to the Internet:** Detects any type of device (such as a cable or DSL broadband connection) and enables you to enter the username and password provided by your ISP, as shown in Figure 8-12. You can also enter a connection name that helps you to identify this connection later. If you want to enable other users on the computer to connect, select **Allow other people to use this connection**.
- **Set up a new network:** Searches for the wireless router or access point you want to configure and then attempts to configure this device for you. Although the wizard states that it might take up to 90 seconds to display unconfigured devices, this process can take considerably longer.

- **Manually connect to a wireless network:** Enables you to enter the wireless network information required for connecting to the network. We discuss wireless networking in Chapter 9.
- **Connect to a workplace:** Enables you to connect by means of a virtual private network (VPN) connection across the Internet or to dial directly to the workplace network using a phone line without using the Internet. We discuss VPN connections in Chapter 14, "Configuring Remote Management and Remote Connections."

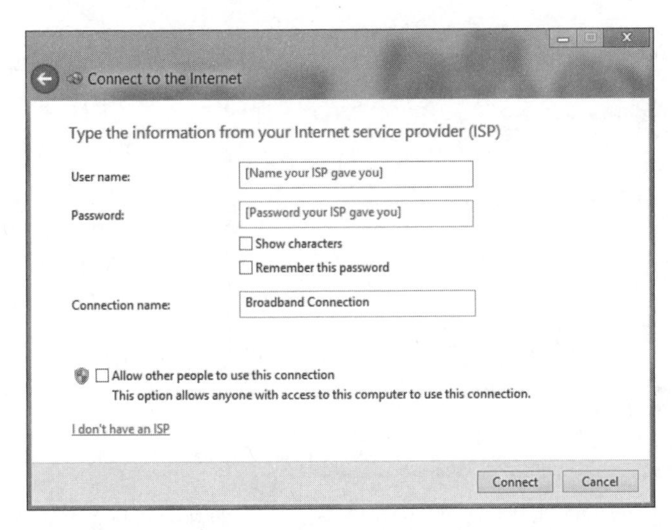

Figure 8-12 Enter your username and password to connect to the Internet.

Connecting to Existing Networks

The Network applet previously shown in Figure 8-1 enables you to manage connections to networks you have previously set up. When you open this applet, you are informed which network you are connected to and which networks are available. Select a desired network and then click **Connect**. To disconnect from a network, select it and then click **Disconnect**.

Setting Up Network Sharing and Discovery

You can access additional sharing and network discovery options from the Network and Sharing Center. Click **Change advanced sharing settings**, found in the left side of the Network and Sharing Center. As shown in Figure 8-13, the Advanced

Sharing Settings dialog box enables you to configure the following additional networking options (available options depend on the profile you're using, either Private or All Networks):

Key Topic

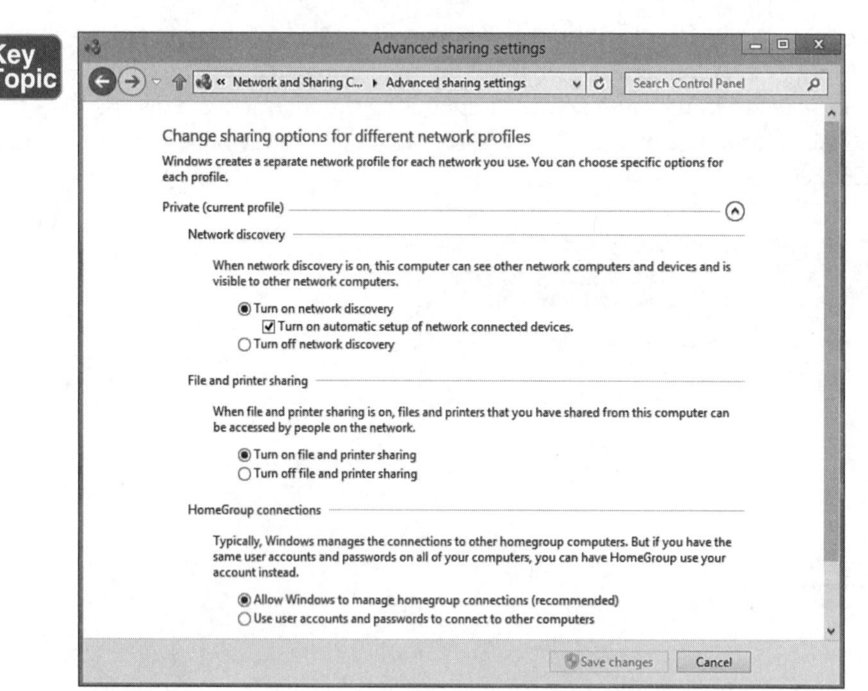

Figure 8-13 The Advanced Sharing Settings dialog box enables you to configure sharing options for different network profiles.

- **Network Discovery:** Enables your computers to see other network computers and devices, and enables these machines to access your computer. To ensure that all network devices are detected and configured, ensure that the **Turn on automatic setup of network connected devices** option is selected (this option is selected by default).
- **File and printer sharing** and **Public folder sharing:** Enable you to share files and printers on your computer that will be visible to other computers on the network. We discuss these options in Chapter 11, "Configuring and Securing Access to Files and Folders."
- **Media streaming:** Enables machines on the network to access shared photos, videos, and music stored on your computer. Enables your computer to locate these types of shared information on other network computers.

- **File sharing connections:** Enables you to select the strength of encryption used for protecting file sharing connections with other machines on the network. By default, file sharing is enabled for machines that use 40- or 56-bit encryption, but you can choose to increase security by selecting 128-bit encryption. However, devices that do not support 128-bit encryption will be unable to access resources on your computer.
- **Password protected sharing:** Requires users attempting to access shared resources on your computer to have a user account with a password. Turn off this option if you want to enable users without a password to have access.
- **HomeGroup connections:** Enables you to determine whether Windows will utilize simple homegroup-based sharing or use the classic type of file sharing model employed by Windows versions prior to Windows 7. More information is provided in Chapter 11.

TIP You can configure sharing options for two network profiles:

1. Private
2. All Networks

This enables you to maintain these network profiles when switching between different network types so that when you connect to a public network, you can select the **All Networks** option to apply more restrictive sharing options automatically.

Using Internet Connection Sharing to Share Your Internet Connection

Quite often, it is not feasible for a small office or a home user to install a high-speed dedicated link to the Internet (such as a T1 line) or have each computer dial up to an ISP. Nowadays, home users can utilize a dedicated broadband link such as a reasonably priced cable or DSL link.

One of the growing trends for small office or home networks is to share an Internet connection with all the members of the network. Windows 8.1 contains a feature called Internet Connection Sharing (ICS), which enables a small office or home network to use one computer on the network as the router to the Internet.

Windows 8.1's ICS components consist of the following:

- **Auto-dial:** A method of establishing the Internet connection when attempting to access Internet resources on a computer that does not host the Internet connection.

- **DHCP Allocator:** A simplified DHCP service that assigns IP addresses from the address range of 192.168.0.2–192.168.0.254, with a mask of 255.255.255.0 and default gateway of 192.168.0.1.
- **DNS Proxy:** Forwards DNS requests to the DNS server and forwards the DNS replies back to the clients.
- **Network Address Translation (NAT):** Maps the range of private Class C IPv4 addresses (192.168.0.1–192.168.0.254) to the public IP address, which is assigned by the ISP. NAT is a specification in TCP/IP that tracks the source private IP addresses and outbound public IP address(es), reformatting the IP address data in the header dynamically so that the source requests reach the public resources and the public servers can reply to the correct source-requesting clients.

NOTE NAT runs on a server or router and is capable of translating multiple external IP addresses to internal private IP addresses used on client computers. The NAT server/router can also be configured to provide DHCP services to the client computers. For more information on NAT, refer to "Design TechNotes" at http://www.cisco.com/en/US/tech/tk648/tk361/technologies_tech_note09186a0080094831.shtml.

You can use ICS to share any type of Internet connection, although it must be a connection that is enabled for all users on the PC dial-up for sharing to be effective. To enable ICS, you need to make sure that the Internet-connected computer has been configured with connections for a modem and a network adapter. If you are using broadband, you need two network adapters: one to connect to the broadband device for the Internet and the other to connect to the network. Use the following procedure at the computer that is connected to the Internet to set up ICS:

Step 1. From the Network and Sharing Center, click **Change adapter settings**, found on the left side. This opens the Network Connections dialog box previously shown in Figure 8-3.

Step 2. Right-click the connection you want to share and choose **Properties**. If you receive a UAC prompt, click **Yes**.

Step 3. Select the **Sharing** tab to open the dialog box shown in Figure 8-14.

Step 4. Select the check box labeled **Allow other network users to connect through this computer's Internet connection**.

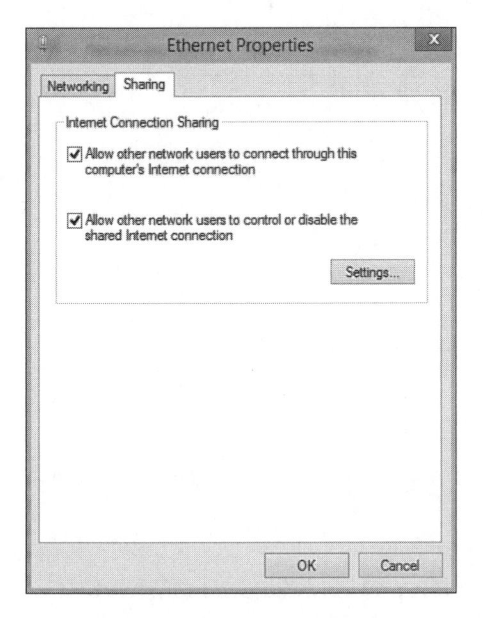

Figure 8-14 The Sharing tab of the Ethernet Properties dialog box enables you to share your computer's Internet connection with other computers on the network.

Step 5. If desired, select the check box labeled **Allow other network users to control or disable the shared Internet connection**.

CAUTION Before you configure ICS, you should ensure that no computers are currently assigned an IP address of 192.168.0.1 because the network adapter on the ICS computer is automatically assigned that address when ICS is configured.

After you share your connection, you need to configure the other computers to use this connection, as follows:

Step 1. In the bottom-left corner of the Network and Sharing Center, click **Internet Options** to display the Internet Properties dialog box.

Step 2. Select the **Connections** tab.

Step 3. Click the **LAN Settings** command button.

Step 4. On the Local Area Network (LAN) Settings dialog box shown in Figure 8-15, clear the check boxes for **Automatically detect settings**, **Use automatic configuration script**, and **Use a proxy server for your LAN**. Then click **OK**.

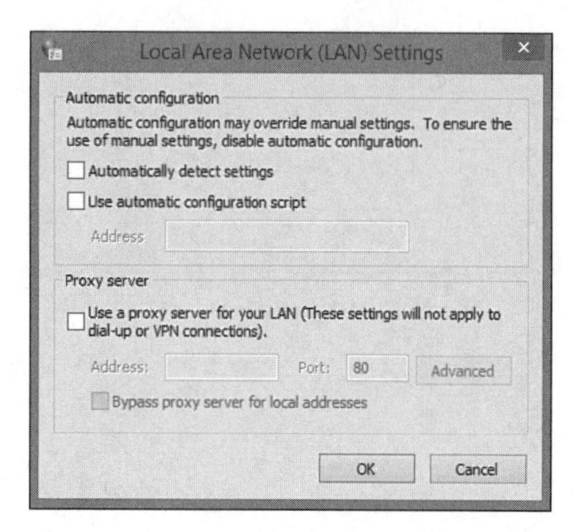

Figure 8-15 On an ICS client computer, you should clear the three check boxes in the Local Area Network (LAN) Settings dialog box.

Step 5. From the Network Connections dialog box previously shown in Figure 8-3, right-click the shared connection and choose **Properties**.

Step 6. Click **Internet Protocol Version 4 (TCP/IPv4)** or **Internet Protocol Version 6 (TCP/IPv6)** and then click **Properties**.

Step 7. On the Properties dialog box, select **Obtain an IP address automatically** or **Obtain an IPv6 address automatically**.

If you have problems with ICS, you should open Event Viewer and check out the System log for any errors related to ICS. In addition, you can view the `nsw.log` file to look for errors. The following are several additional suggestions in case users are unable to access the Internet from the client computers:

- Check the configuration of the client Internet browser. We mentioned client configuration earlier in this section.
- Ensure that the client can connect to the host computer. Check the connection by typing **`ping 192.168.0.1`**. If this ping is unsuccessful, check the physical network connections.
- Use `ipconfig` to check the client computer's IP configuration. Ensure that the client has an IP address on the proper subnet and that the default gateway is set to 192.168.0.1.

NOTE For more information on ICS, including its use with IPv6, refer to "Using Wireless Hosted Network and Internet Connection Sharing" at http://msdn.microsoft.com/en-us/library/dd815252(VS.85).aspx.

NOTE Windows enables you to disable the Network Location Wizard for all users on a computer or for a specific user. The procedure involves editing the Registry. For more information, refer to "Turn Off the Network Location Wizard" at http://technet.microsoft.com/en-us/library/gg252535(WS.10).aspx. Always keep in mind the caution that improper editing of the Registry can seriously affect the performance of the computer and might even prevent Windows from starting.

Resolving Connectivity Issues

With any type of computer network, connectivity problems can and do occur whether you have configured your network to use IPv4, IPv6, or both. You should be aware of the types of problems that you might encounter and the steps to use for determining the source of the problem and the means to correct it.

Windows 8.1 Network Diagnostics Tools

Windows 8.1 provides several tools that are often useful in troubleshooting network and Internet connectivity failures. These tools provide wizards that ask questions as to what problems might exist and suggest solutions or open additional troubleshooters.

The Network and Sharing Center provides a comprehensive networking problem troubleshooter. Click **Troubleshoot Problems** from the Change your networking settings list to obtain the Troubleshoot problems–Network and Internet dialog box shown in Figure 8-16. Clicking any of the options on this dialog box takes you to a wizard that attempts to detect a problem associated with the selected option. If the wizard is unable to identify a problem, it suggests additional options that you might explore.

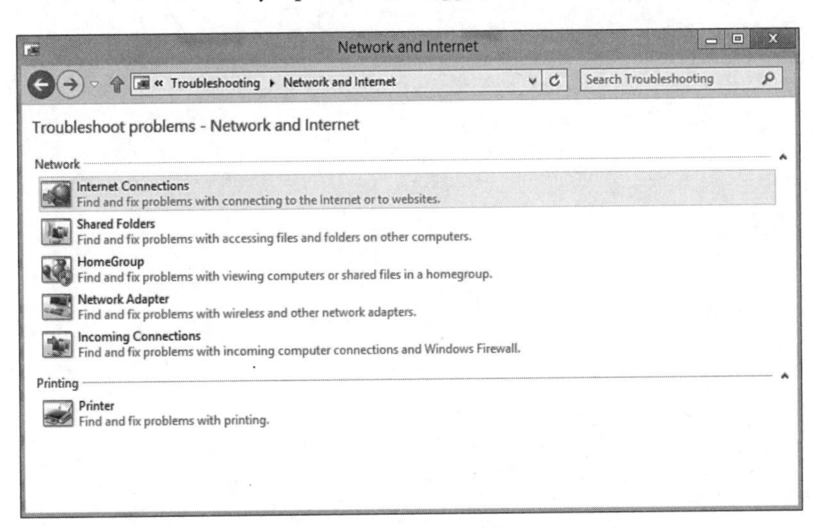

Figure 8-16 You can open a wizard that attempts to troubleshoot problems with any of these network and printing categories.

You can also check the status of a LAN connection from the Network Connections dialog box previously shown in Figure 8-3. Right-click your connection icon and choose **Status** to display the Ethernet Status dialog box shown in Figure 8-17. This dialog box provides information on your LAN connectivity. To obtain details on your LAN connection, click **Details**. The Network Connection Details dialog box shown in Figure 8-18 provides a subset of the information also provided by the `ipconfig` command discussed in the next section. To view or configure the properties of the connection, click the **Properties** button shown in Figure 8-17. This takes you to the same Ethernet Properties dialog box discussed earlier in this chapter and shown in Figure 8-4.

Figure 8-17 The Ethernet Status dialog box provides information on the connectivity of your LAN connection.

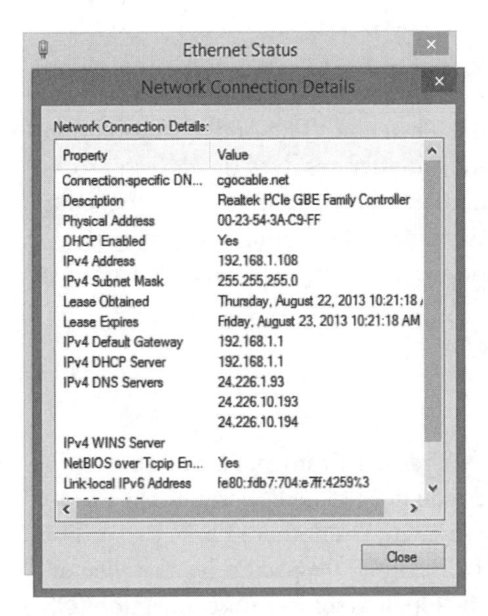

Figure 8-18 The Network Connection Details dialog box provides IPv4 and IPv6 configuration information.

If you suspect a problem, click the **Diagnose** button shown in Figure 8-17 to open a troubleshooter. You are then informed of any problem that exists, such as a disconnected network cable or malfunctioning network adapter card.

Using TCP/IP Utilities to Troubleshoot TCP/IP

The TCP/IP protocol suite includes a number of tools that can help you isolate the source of connectivity problems. As with previous Windows versions, Windows 8.1 incorporates these tools as command-line executables. Each tool is different in what information it provides and when you might want to use it.

When you are troubleshooting a connectivity problem, remember that sometimes the problem is the hardware—a failed network adapter, a failed port on the hub, a failed switch, and so on. If the communication is between two different physical segments, it could be a problem with the router between them. And if you were able to communicate in the past but now cannot, the most likely suspect is a configuration change on one of the computers, and the second most likely is that a piece of equipment has failed. To check whether there is an adapter failure, look at Device Manager.

`Arp`

After data reaches the segment on which the IP address resides, it needs to discover the Media Access Control (MAC) address of the machine. The Address Resolution Protocol (ARP) is the protocol in the TCP/IP suite that resolves IP addresses to MAC addresses by creating an Address Resolution table in each host that transmits data on the network segment. The TCP/IP suite provides a utility called `Arp` that can check the table for errors. You should use the `Arp` utility when data is sent to an incorrect computer unexpectedly.

FTP and TFTP

File Transfer Protocol (FTP) and Trivial File Transfer Protocol (TFTP) are not considered troubleshooting tools. Sometimes you need to make certain that a protocol is able to move data from one network segment to another. These two utilities can help out in a pinch because they verify TCP and UDP specifically as well as all the protocols down to the Physical layer of the Open Systems Interconnection (OSI) networking stack.

If you want to verify whether TCP is functioning across a router, you can use FTP to download a file from an FTP server on another subnet. If you want to verify whether UDP is functioning across a router, you can use TFTP to download a file from a TFTP server on another subnet.

`Ipconfig`

Windows 8.1 uses the `Ipconfig` utility without any additional parameters to display summary information about the IP address configuration of its network adapters. When you are experiencing a problem with connectivity, this is the first thing you should check (besides the link lights on the network adapter). If you are using DHCP, you can see whether the adapter was able to obtain an IP address lease. If you are using a static IP address, you can verify and validate whether it has been configured correctly. You can use `Ipconfig` with the following switches:

- **`Ipconfig /all`:** Displays a comprehensive set of IPv4 and IPv6 address data for all network adapters including IPv6 Teredo interfaces, as shown in Figure 8-19. Use this command to see whether an adapter has been misconfigured, or if the adapter did not receive a DHCP lease. You can also determine whether the IP address the computer is using has been provided by APIPA; check the `Autoconfiguration Enabled` line of this output. If this line states `Yes` and the IP address is 169.254.0.1 through 169.254.255.254, you are using an APIPA address.

```
Command Prompt
Microsoft Windows [Version 6.3.9431]
(c) 2013 Microsoft Corporation. All rights reserved.

C:\Users\Don>ipconfig /all

Windows IP Configuration

   Host Name . . . . . . . . . . . . : Computer1
   Primary Dns Suffix  . . . . . . . :
   Node Type . . . . . . . . . . . . : Hybrid
   IP Routing Enabled. . . . . . . . : No
   WINS Proxy Enabled. . . . . . . . : No
   DNS Suffix Search List. . . . . . : cgocable.net

Wireless LAN adapter Wi-Fi:

   Media State . . . . . . . . . . . : Media disconnected
   Connection-specific DNS Suffix  . :
   Description . . . . . . . . . . . : Linksys Wireless-G PCI Adapter
   Physical Address. . . . . . . . . : 00-22-6B-A5-F5-C8
   DHCP Enabled. . . . . . . . . . . : Yes
   Autoconfiguration Enabled . . . . : Yes

Ethernet adapter Ethernet:

   Connection-specific DNS Suffix  . : cgocable.net
   Description . . . . . . . . . . . : Realtek PCIe GBE Family Controller
   Physical Address. . . . . . . . . : 00-23-54-3A-C9-FF
   DHCP Enabled. . . . . . . . . . . : Yes
   Autoconfiguration Enabled . . . . : Yes
   Link-local IPv6 Address . . . . . : fe80::fdb7:704:e7ff:4259%3(Preferred)
   IPv4 Address. . . . . . . . . . . : 192.168.1.108(Preferred)
   Subnet Mask . . . . . . . . . . . : 255.255.255.0
   Lease Obtained. . . . . . . . . . : Thursday, August 22, 2013 10:21:18 AM
   Lease Expires . . . . . . . . . . : Friday, August 23, 2013 10:21:17 AM
   Default Gateway . . . . . . . . . : 192.168.1.1
   DHCP Server . . . . . . . . . . . : 192.168.1.1
   DHCPv6 IAID . . . . . . . . . . . : 50340692
   DHCPv6 Client DUID. . . . . . . . : 00-01-00-01-19-7B-8F-29-00-23-54-3A-C9-FF

   DNS Servers . . . . . . . . . . . : 24.226.1.93
                                       24.226.10.193
                                       24.226.10.194
   NetBIOS over Tcpip. . . . . . . . : Enabled

Tunnel adapter isatap.cgocable.net:

   Media State . . . . . . . . . . . : Media disconnected
   Connection-specific DNS Suffix  . : cgocable.net
   Description . . . . . . . . . . . : Microsoft ISATAP Adapter
```

Figure 8-19 The `ipconfig /all` command provides a comprehensive set of TCP/IP configuration information.

- **`Ipconfig /release`:** Releases the current DHCP lease. Use this command to remove an IP address that is misconfigured or when you have moved from one network to another and the wrong IP address is still leased to the adapter.
- **`Ipconfig /release6`:** Same as the `/release` switch used by IPv4.
- **`Ipconfig /renew`:** Renews (or tries to renew) the current DHCP lease. Use this command to see whether the computer can contact the DHCP server.
- **`Ipconfig /renew6`:** Same as the `/renew` switch used by IPv4.
- **`Ipconfig /displaydns`:** Displays the contents of the DNS cache. Use this command when the computer connects to the wrong network.
- **`Ipconfig /flushdns`:** Flushes the contents of the DNS cache. Use this command when the computer connects to the wrong network and you see incorrect entries after using the `ipconfig /displaydns` command.
- **`Ipconfig /registerdns`:** Renews (or tries to renew) all adapters' DHCP leases and refreshes the DNS configuration. Use this command when the network has temporarily disconnected and you have not rebooted the PC.

- **`Ipconfig /showclassid`** adapter: Shows the DHCP class ID. If you use the asterisk (*) in place of adapter, you see the DHCP class ID for all adapters.
- **`Ipconfig /setclassid`** adapter: Changes the DHCP class ID for an adapter. If you use the asterisk (*) in the place of adapter, you see the DHCP class ID of all adapters.

Nbtstat

The `Nbtstat` utility is used on networks that run NetBIOS over TCP/IP. This utility checks to see the status of NetBIOS name resolution to IP addresses. You can check current NetBIOS sessions, add entries to the NetBIOS name cache, and check the NetBIOS name and scope assigned to the computer.

Netstat

The `Netstat` command-line tool enables you to check the current status of the computer's IP connections. If you do not use switches, the results are port and protocol statistics and current TCP/IP connections. You should use `Netstat` to look for the services that are listening for incoming connections, if you have already checked the IP configuration and, though it is correct, the computer still displays a connectivity problem.

NSLookup

Name Server Lookup, or `NSLookup`, is a command-line utility that communicates with a DNS server. There are two modes to `NSLookup`: interactive and noninteractive. The interactive mode opens a session with a DNS server and views various records. The noninteractive mode asks for one piece of information and receives it. If more information is needed, a new query must be made.

Ping

Packet InterNet Groper (`ping`) is a valuable tool for determining whether there is a problem with connectivity. The `ping` command uses an Echo packet at the Network layer—the default is to send a series of four echoes in a row—transmitting the packets to the IP address specified. The Echo returns an acknowledgment if the IP address is found. The results are displayed in the command window. If an IP address is not found, you see only the response `Request timed out` or `Destination host unreachable`. You see similar results to those shown in Figure 8-20, where the first address that was pinged was found and the second address was not found. The `ping` command indicates how long each packet took for the response. You can use the `ping` command to determine whether a host is reachable and to determine whether you are losing packets when sending/receiving data to a particular host.

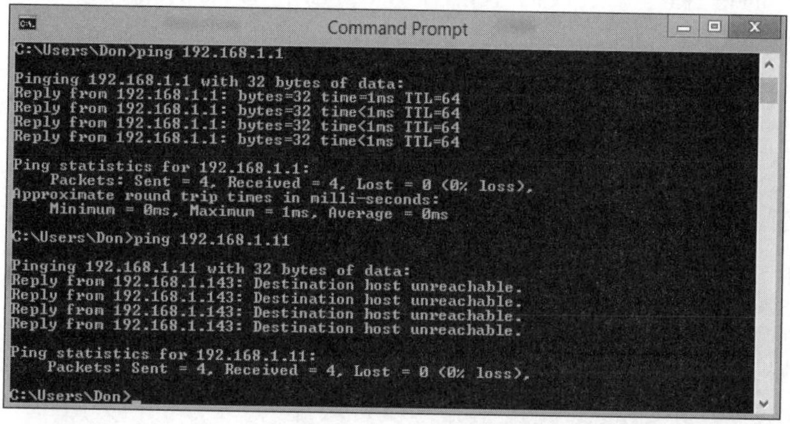

```
Command Prompt
C:\Users\Don>ping 192.168.1.1

Pinging 192.168.1.1 with 32 bytes of data:
Reply from 192.168.1.1: bytes=32 time=1ms TTL=64
Reply from 192.168.1.1: bytes=32 time<1ms TTL=64
Reply from 192.168.1.1: bytes=32 time<1ms TTL=64
Reply from 192.168.1.1: bytes=32 time<1ms TTL=64

Ping statistics for 192.168.1.1:
    Packets: Sent = 4, Received = 4, Lost = 0 (0% loss),
Approximate round trip times in milli-seconds:
    Minimum = 0ms, Maximum = 1ms, Average = 0ms

C:\Users\Don>ping 192.168.1.11

Pinging 192.168.1.11 with 32 bytes of data:
Reply from 192.168.1.143: Destination host unreachable.
Reply from 192.168.1.143: Destination host unreachable.
Reply from 192.168.1.143: Destination host unreachable.
Reply from 192.168.1.143: Destination host unreachable.

Ping statistics for 192.168.1.11:
    Packets: Sent = 4, Received = 4, Lost = 0 (0% loss),

C:\Users\Don>_
```

Figure 8-20 The ping command displays its results in a command window.

You can use the `ping` command to determine whether the internal TCP/IP protocol stack is functioning properly by pinging the loopback testing address. The command for IPv4 is

```
ping 127.0.0.1
```

For IPv6, the command is

```
ping ::1
```

> **NOTE** Firewall settings can prevent you from receiving responses from pinged hosts. In Windows 8.1, by default, you cannot ping other computers on your network. We take a look at configuring firewall settings and policies in Chapter 10.

`Tracert`

When you have a problem communicating with a particular host, yet you have determined that your computer is functioning well, you can use the `Tracert` (Trace Route) utility to tell you how the data is moving across the network between your computer and the one that you are having difficulty reaching. The `tracert` command offers a somewhat higher level of information than `ping`. Rather than simply tell you that the data was transmitted and returned effectively, as `ping` does, `tracert` logs each hop through which the data was transmitted. Figure 8-21 shows the results of a `tracert` command. Keep in mind that some network routers strip out or refuse to reply to `tracert` requests. When this happens, you see `Request timed out` messages.

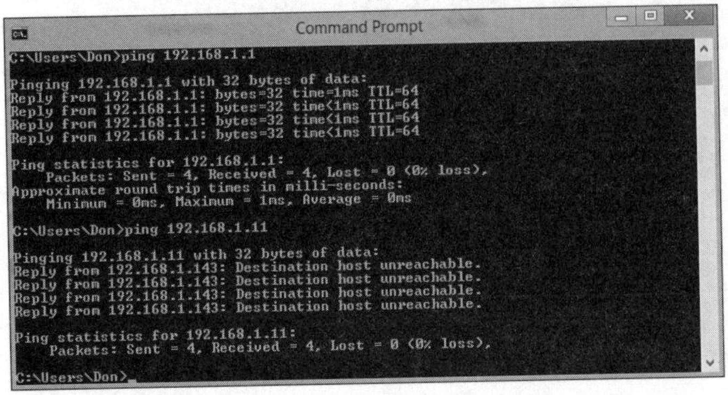

```
Command Prompt
C:\Users\Don>ping 192.168.1.1

Pinging 192.168.1.1 with 32 bytes of data:
Reply from 192.168.1.1: bytes=32 time=1ms TTL=64
Reply from 192.168.1.1: bytes=32 time<1ms TTL=64
Reply from 192.168.1.1: bytes=32 time<1ms TTL=64
Reply from 192.168.1.1: bytes=32 time<1ms TTL=64

Ping statistics for 192.168.1.1:
    Packets: Sent = 4, Received = 4, Lost = 0 (0% loss),
Approximate round trip times in milli-seconds:
    Minimum = 0ms, Maximum = 1ms, Average = 0ms

C:\Users\Don>ping 192.168.1.11

Pinging 192.168.1.11 with 32 bytes of data:
Reply from 192.168.1.143: Destination host unreachable.
Reply from 192.168.1.143: Destination host unreachable.
Reply from 192.168.1.143: Destination host unreachable.
Reply from 192.168.1.143: Destination host unreachable.

Ping statistics for 192.168.1.11:
    Packets: Sent = 4, Received = 4, Lost = 0 (0% loss),

C:\Users\Don>
```

Figure 8-21 The `tracert` command provides detailed information about the path that data travels between two IP hosts.

`Pathping`

The `pathping` command combines the actions of the `ping` and `tracert` utilities into a single command that tests connectivity to a remote host and maps the route taken by packets transmitted from your computer to the remote host. It also provides data on packet loss across multiple hops, thereby providing an estimate of the reliability of the communication links being used.

> **NOTE** Also available for network connectivity testing is the new IP Address app produced by Jujuba Software. This app tracks IP address and network connectivity in real time. As with other third-party applications, it is not covered on any Microsoft exam. For more information, refer to "IP Address" at http://apps.microsoft.com/windows/en-us/app/ip-address/ce78edd3-5d91-4db8-bc10-b1c11fcdfb1d.

Troubleshooting IPv4 and IPv6 Problems

Many problems can result in your inability to reach other hosts on your local subnet, other subnets on your local network, or the Internet. The 70-687 exam presents you with scenarios in which you must figure out the cause of and solution to problems with IPv4 and IPv6 connectivity failures. We cover the use of the TCP/IP troubleshooting tools already presented to test connectivity and follow this up with additional suggestions you can use for troubleshooting connectivity problems, both on the 70-687 exam and in the real world.

A Suggested Response to a Connectivity Problem

Microsoft recommends a troubleshooting procedure for TCP/IP connectivity problems similar to the following:

Step 1. Verify the hardware is functioning.

Step 2. Run `Ipconfig /all` to validate the IP address, subnet mask, default gateway, and DNS server, and whether you are receiving a DHCP leased address.

Step 3. Ping 127.0.0.1 or ::1, the loopback address, to validate that TCP/IP is functioning.

Step 4. Ping the computer's own IP address to eliminate a duplicate IP address as the problem.

Step 5. Ping the default gateway address, which tells you whether data can travel on the current network segment.

Step 6. Ping a host that is not on your network segment, which shows whether the router will be able to route your data.

Additional possible troubleshooting steps you can use include the following:

- Use FTP on a file from an FTP server not on your network, which tells you whether higher-level protocols are functioning. Use TFTP on a file from a TFTP server on a different network to determine whether UDP packets are able to cross the router.
- Check the configuration of routers on a network with multiple subnets. You can use the `tracert` and `pathping` commands to verify connectivity across routers to remote subnets. Also use the `route print` command to check the configuration of routing tables in use.
- Clear the ARP cache by opening a command prompt and typing **`netsh interface ip delete arpcache`**.
- Check the computer's DNS configuration. You can also clear the DNS client resolver cache by using the `ipconfig /flushdns` command.

Many LAN connection problems can be traced to improper TCP/IP configuration. Before looking at the use of TCP/IP utilities for troubleshooting these problems, this section reviews briefly some of the problems you might encounter.

Network Discovery

Network Discovery is a tool that is enabled by default on Windows 8.1 computers. For computers to be able to connect to one another, ensure that Network Discovery has not been turned off at either the source or destination computer. To check this setting, access the Network and Sharing Center and click **Change advanced sharing settings**, found in the list on the left side. As you can see in Figure 8-22, you can configure a series of sharing options for different network profiles. Ensure that the **Turn on network discovery** option is selected and then click **Save changes**.

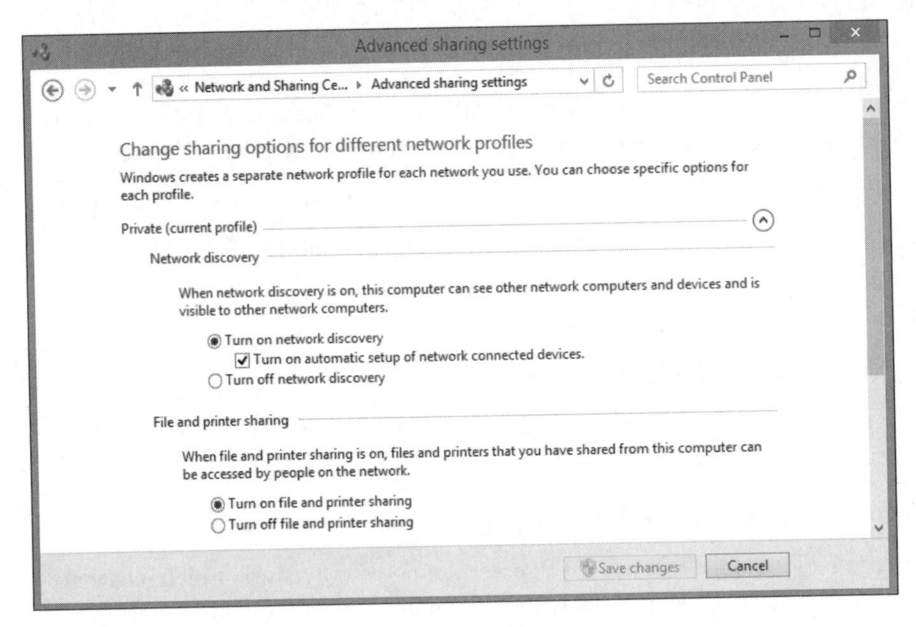

Figure 8-22 Checking the Network Discovery setting.

Incorrect IPv4 Address or Subnet Mask

Recall from earlier in this chapter that the subnet mask determines the number of bits assigned to the network portion of the IP address and the number of bits assigned to the host portion. Be aware of the fact that the network portion of the IP address must match properly on all computers within a network segment and that the subnet mask must be configured appropriately to ensure that the computer is able to determine whether the computer to which it is attempting to connect is on the same or different subnet.

For example, suppose you are at a computer configured with an IP address of 192.168.1.2 with a subnet mask of 255.255.255.0. If you want to reach a computer with the IP address of 192.168.2.1, the subnet mask indicates that this computer is located on a different subnet. Connection will take place across a router. Should the computer where you are working be configured with the same IP address but a subnet mask of 255.255.248.0, this would indicate that the destination computer with the IP address of 192.168.2.1 is on the same subnet. If, in fact, this computer is located across a router on another subnet, you will fail to connect to it.

Router problems could also cause a failure to access a computer on another subnet. These problems are beyond the scope of the 70-687 exam. For further information, consult any reference on computer networking.

Unable to Connect to a DHCP Server

If you configure your computer to automatically receive an IPv4 address and the DHCP server is down, the computer assigns itself an APIPA address as already described. If you notice this when using `ipconfig /all`, check the connectivity to the DHCP server or contact an administrator responsible for this server.

Duplicate IP Address

If your computer is using an IP address that duplicates another computer on the network, you will be unable to connect to any computer on the network. When this happens, the first computer on the network performs properly but receives a message when the second computer joins the network. Ping your computer's IP address to check for this problem. This problem cannot occur if you are using DHCP to obtain an IP address automatically or if your computer is configured for an IP address using APIPA.

Unable to Configure an Alternate TCP/IPv4 Configuration

The Alternate Configuration tab of the TCP/IPv4 Properties dialog box (refer back to Figure 8-6) enables you to configure an alternate IPv4 address, which is useful in situations in which you need to connect to a second network (for example, when you are using a portable computer and traveling to a branch office of your company). However, to use the alternate configuration, your primary connection must be set to obtain an IP address automatically. If this is not the case, this tab does not appear.

Using Event Viewer to Check Network Problems

One of Windows 8.1's standard troubleshooting tools is Event Viewer, which is incorporated into the Computer Management console. You can rely on this utility to be able to see errors and system messages. The ones that would be of most concern for a network problem are in the System Event log. You learn about Event Viewer in more detail in Chapter 18, "Managing and Monitoring System Performance."

Additional Troubleshooting Hints When Using IPv6

When verifying IPv6 network connectivity, you may need to specify a zone ID for the sending interface by using the `ping` command. The zone ID is a locally defined parameter that you can obtain from the `ipconfig /all` command or the `netsh interface ipv6 show interface` command. Using this zone ID, to verify connectivity with a machine whose IPv6 address is fe80::b3:00ff:4765:6db7, you would type **`ping fe80::b3:00ff:4765:6db7%12`** at a command prompt (if the zone ID is 12).

Before using `ping` to check IPv6 network connectivity, clear the neighbor cache on your computer. This cache contains recently resolved link-layer IPv6 addresses. To view this cache, open an administrative command prompt and type **`netsh interface ipv6 show neighbors`**; to clear it, type **`netsh interface ipv6 delete neighbors`**.

NOTE For further suggestions with regard to troubleshooting IPv6 network connectivity, refer to "Troubleshooting IPv6" at http://technet.microsoft.com/en-us/library/bb878005.aspx.

Exam Preparation Tasks

Review All the Key Topics

Review the most important topics in the chapter, noted with the key topics icon in the outer margin of the page. Table 8-6 lists a reference of these key topics and the page numbers on which each is found.

Table 8-6 Key Topics for Chapter 8

Key Topic Element	Description	Page Number(s)
Table 8-2	Describes important addressing components of TCP/IP version 4	334-335
Table 8-3	Describes the various IPv4 address classes	336
Paragraph	Explains how to use subnet masks to separate the network and machine portions of an IPv4 address	337
Table 8-4	Describes private IPv4 networks	338
Table 8-5	Explains IPv6 address classes and subclasses	340-341
List	Describes the network address types used for interoperability between IPv4 and IPv6	342

Key Topic Element	Description	Page Number(s)
Figure 8-2	Shows how to use the Network and Sharing Center to configure networking settings	345
Step List	Explains how to configure a network adapter with a static IPv4 address	346
Step List	Shows how to configure your computer to connect to an IPv6 network	351
Step List	Explains how to configure your computer to access a DNS server on IPv4	354
Step List	Explains how to configure your computer for IPv6 name resolution	356
Figure 8-11	Shows several options for setting up new network connections	358
Figure 8-13	Displays options available for different network profiles	360
Step List	Shows you how to set up Internet Connection Sharing	362
Figure 8-17	Shows how to use the Ethernet Status dialog box to check LAN connection status	366
Figure 8-19	Shows how to use the `ipconfig /all` command	369
Step List	Describes a procedure that tests your computer's IP connectivity	373

Complete the Tables and Lists from Memory

Print a copy of Appendix B, "Memory Tables," (found on the CD), or at least the section for this chapter, and complete the tables and lists from memory. Appendix C, "Memory Tables Answer Key," also on the CD, includes completed tables and lists to check your work.

Definitions of Key Terms

Define the following key terms from this chapter, and check your answers in the Glossary:

Address Resolution Protocol (ARP), Anycast IPv6 address, Automatic Private IP Addressing (APIPA), Classless Inter-Domain Routing (CIDR), Default gateway, Domain Name System (DNS), Dynamic Host Configuration Protocol (DHCP), Global unicast IPv6 address, host, Internet Connection Sharing (ICS), Internet Control Message Protocol (ICMP), IP address, `Ipconfig`, IP version 4 (IPv4), IP version 6 (IPv6), Link-local IPv6 address, Link-Local Multicast Name Resolution (LLMNR), Multicast IPv6 address, Network Address Translation (NAT), Network and Sharing Center, Site-local IPv6 address, Subnet mask, Teredo

This chapter covers the following subjects:

- **Connecting to Wireless Networks:** In this section, you learn about the various settings in Windows that enable you to connect to wired or wireless networks, including the Internet. You are also introduced to the wireless networking protocols used by Windows 8.1 and the available security settings that help protect your connection.
- **Managing Preferred Wireless Networks:** When you are connecting to wireless networks, manually and automatically, it is important to make sure that the network access points that Windows finds and accesses are the intended networks. This section discusses ways for managing preferred wireless networks and how each connection should be handled.
- **Configuring Network Adapters:** Network adapters available in Windows 8.1 include wired Ethernet connections, wireless adapters, Bluetooth PAN adapters, as well as virtual adapters used for tunneling, VPN, and dial-up connectivity. This section shows you how to configure your network adapter settings, networking configurations, and other options specific to adapters and adapter types.
- **Configuring Location Aware Printing:** A recent feature of Windows is the capability to automatically associate configured printers with the network where the printer is available. This section discusses Location Aware Printing technology, the benefits it provides, and how to configure and manage printer settings.

Configuring Networking Settings

Connectivity between Windows 8.1 computers and other networks (inclusive of the Internet and other computers) is provided in a variety of ways. Windows 8.1 computers utilize a variety of tools, applications, and protocols for connecting to networks. Chapter 8, "Configuring TCP/IP Settings," introduced you to the Network and Sharing Center, which consolidates many of these applications and utilities into one convenient location from which you can create and manage different types of network connections as well as file and printer sharing. This chapter continues our discussion of networking by introducing additional networking components, including how to install, configure, or manage them:

- Dial-up networking
- Wireless networking
- Network adapter configuration
- Location Aware Printing

You not only explore each of these components in this chapter, but also look at their features and dependencies as they exist within the Windows 8.1 operating system.

"Do I Know This Already?" Quiz

The "Do I Know This Already?" quiz allows you to assess whether you should read this entire chapter or simply jump to the "Exam Preparation Tasks" section for review. If you are in doubt, read the entire chapter. Table 9-1 outlines the major headings in this chapter and the corresponding "Do I Know This Already?" quiz questions. You can find the answers in Appendix A, "Answers to the 'Do I Know This Already?' Quizzes."

Table 9-1 "Do I Know This Already?" Foundation Topics Section-to-Question Mapping

Foundations Topics Section	Questions Covered in This Section
Connecting to Wireless Networks	1–7
Managing Preferred Wireless Networks	8–9
Configuring Network Adapters	10–11
Configuring Location Aware Printing	12

1. When you are connecting to a new wireless network on a Windows 8.1 computer, which of the following wireless security protocols are available? (Choose all that apply.)
   a. WPA
   b. WEP
   c. Private
   d. PEAP
   e. Open

2. When you connect to an ad hoc wireless network, which security profile will Windows 8.1 use by default?
   a. WEP
   b. WPA
   c. WPA2-Personal
   d. WPA2-Enterprise

3. Which of the following wireless networking protocols uses 5 GHz frequency for communication between the computer and the access point? (Select all that apply.)
   a. 802.11a
   b. 802.11b
   c. 802.11g
   d. 802.11n

4. Which of the following are wireless security options that you can configure for protecting data sent from a Windows 8.1 computer? (Choose all that apply.)
   a. Temporal Key Integrity Protocol (TKIP)
   b. Advanced Encryption Standard (AES)
   c. Wired Equivalent Privacy (WEP)
   d. Wi-Fi Protected Access (WPA and WPA2)
   e. Service Set Identifier (SSID)

5. You want to select a wireless networking protocol that will enable you to transmit data at a rate of up to 150 Mbps while offering high resistance to interference from other electronic devices. Which of the following should you choose?
   a. 802.11a
   b. 802.11b
   c. 802.11g
   d. 802.11n

6. You are configuring security for your company's wireless network. You want to enable a security protocol that uses Advanced Encryption Service (AES) encryption by default; users should be required to type a security key or passphrase to access the network. What protocol should you choose?
   a. WPA-Personal
   b. WPA2-Personal
   c. WPA-Enterprise
   d. WPA2-Enterprise

7. Your network provider charges for all of your bandwidth based on the amount of data transferred over the connection. You want to set up a wireless connection to ensure that the amount of data transferred while connected is minimized. What setting should you use?
   a. Estimated data usage
   b. Turn sharing on or off
   c. Metered connection
   d. Dial-up connection speed

8. You have been traveling a great deal with your Windows 8.1 laptop and want to clean up the leftover wireless network profiles that you will probably not use again in the near future. How can you delete the wireless profiles?

   a. Select each from the Network list, right-click, and select **Forget this network.**

   b. Use the `netsh` command `netsh wlan delete` for each profile.

   c. Use the Network and Sharing center to delete the network connections.

   d. You cannot delete the profiles.

9. You currently have several wireless networks that you connect to frequently. Your home network uses WPA, the engineering department near your office uses WPA2-Personal, the coffee shop around the corner uses Open Wi-Fi, and the conference room near your office uses WEP. You hosted a demonstration in the conference room before you left the office yesterday, and then you used your home AP to VPN to the company network last night. When you arrive at the office in the morning and turn on your laptop, which network will your Windows 8.1 computer attempt to connect with first?

   a. Your home network AP

   b. The conference room

   c. The engineering department

   d. The coffee shop

10. You need to make changes to the Advanced properties of a network adapter device. To access the properties, you open the Change adapter settings from the Network and Sharing Center, access the adapter properties from the right-click menu, and then the NIC properties using the **Configure** button. This is similar to the properties from the Device Manager device properties, but some settings are unavailable. What can you not configure from this dialog box that is available when using Device Manager?

   a. Advanced properties

   b. Driver details

   c. Power Management

   d. Resources

11. Which of the following Advanced properties of a network adapter are available for a wireless connection? (Choose all that apply.)

    a. 802.11n Mode

    b. Speed and Duplex

    c. Transmit Buffers

    d. Preferred Band

    e. Receive Buffers

12. Your laptop now automatically uses the Richardson office printer when you are visiting the Richardson office and the color laser printer near your office when you are at headquarters. Recently, the color printer was moved to another floor and a newer printer installed in its place. You have installed the new printer drivers and tested it, but whenever you return to headquarters, it prints to the printer that is now on another floor. How can you use Location Aware Printing features of Windows 8.1 to fix this issue?

    a. Delete the original color printer.

    b. Turn off Location Aware Printing.

    c. Use the Printer Troubleshooting tool.

    d. Change the printer associated with the HQ network.

Foundation Topics

Connecting to Wireless Networks

The recent advances in wireless networking technology have enabled individuals to connect to networks from virtually any place a wireless access point (WAP) is available. Many offices are taking advantage of the ease of setup of wireless local area networks (WLANs), which allow for mobility and portability of computers and other devices located within the office. And public access points in locations such as restaurants and airports permit users to send and receive data from many places that would have been unthought of not too many years ago. Along with this convenience comes an increased chance of unauthorized access to the networks and the data they contain.

Wireless networks are easy to install and use, and they have gained tremendous popularity for small home and office networks. Security is still not perfected for wireless networks, so large corporations have been slower to implement large wireless networks. Windows 8.1 supports the 802.11 protocols for WLANs and is capable of transparently moving between multiple WAPs, changing to a new Internet protocol (IP) subnet, and remaining connected to the network. Each time the IP subnet changes, the user is re-authenticated. In Windows 8.1, you can configure wireless networking in the Network and Sharing Center. This enables you to connect to wireless networks, configure an ad hoc connection or the use of a WAP, and manage your wireless networks.

Windows 8.1 provides similar wireless technologies to those of Windows Vista and 7, improving on the wireless support included with Windows XP so that wireless networking is as well integrated with the operating system as normal networking. Consequently, wireless network reliability, stability, and security are considerably enhanced over that of Windows XP. The following are some of the more important security improvements in wireless networking available in recent Windows versions:

- Windows 8.1 minimizes the amount of private information, such as the Service Set Identifier (SSID), that is broadcast before connecting to a wireless network.
- When users connect to an unencrypted public network (such as an airport or restaurant Wi-Fi hotspot), users are warned of the risks so that they can limit their activities accordingly.
- Windows 8.1 supports a complete range of wireless security protocols, from Wired Equivalent Privacy (WEP) to Wi-Fi Protected Access (WPA and WPA2), Protected Extensible Authentication Protocol (PEAP), and its combination with Microsoft Challenge Handshake Authentication Protocol version 2 (MS-CHAP v2) and Extensible Authentication Protocol Transport Layer Security (EAP-TLS).

- Windows 8.1 uses WPA2-Personal for maximum security when communicating by means of an ad hoc wireless network (direct communication with another wireless computer without use of an access point [AP]). This helps to protect against common vulnerabilities associated with such unprotected networks.
- On an Active Directory Domain Services (AD DS) network, administrators can use Group Policy settings to configure Single Sign On (SSO) profiles that facilitate wireless domain logon. IEEE 802.1x authentication precedes the domain logon, and users are prompted for wireless credentials only if absolutely necessary. The wireless connection is therefore in place before the domain logon proceeds.

Wireless Networking Protocols

Table 9-2 describes four wireless networking protocols available to Windows 8.1.

Table 9-2 Characteristics of Wireless Networking Protocols

Protocol	Transmission Speed	Frequency Used	Comments
802.11b	11 Mbps	2.4 GHz	The 2.4 GHz frequency is the same as that which is used by many appliances such as cordless phones and microwave ovens; this can cause interference. This technology also is limited in that it supports fewer simultaneous users than the other protocols.
802.11a	54 Mbps	5 GHz	While reducing interference from other appliances, this technology has a shorter signal range and is not compatible with network adapters, routers, and WAPs using the 802.11b protocol. However, some devices are equipped to support either 802.11a or 802.11b.
802.11g	54 Mbps	2.4 GHz	You can have 802.11b and 802.11g devices operating together on the same network. This standard was created specifically for backward compatibility with the 802.11b standard. The signal range is better than that of 802.11a, but this technology suffers from the same interference problems as 802.11a.
802.11n	Up to 150–600 Mbps, depending on the number of data streams	2.4 or 5 GHz	This technology is compatible with devices using the older protocols at the same frequency. It also has the best signal range and is most resistant to interference, although it can have the same problems as 802.11b if using the 2.4 GHz frequency.
802.11ac	Up to 1.3 Gbps	5 GHz	New technology approved as a standard in January 2014, it improves on 802.11n by offering faster speeds and improved scalability. Computer and device manufacturers are beginning to produce compatible units, with devices expected to be widely available by 2015.

NOTE For more information on 802.11ac and the improvements it offers, refer to "802.11ac: The Fifth Generation of Wi-Fi Technical White Paper" at http://www.cisco.com/en/US/prod/collateral/wireless/ps5678/ps11983/white_paper_c11-713103.html.

Setting Up a Wireless Network Connection

Windows 8.1 provides a wizard that simplifies the process of setting up various types of network connections and connecting to wireless and other networks. Use the following procedure to set up a wireless network connection:

Step 1. Use one of the methods outlined in Chapter 8 to access the Network and Sharing Center.

Step 2. Click **Set up a new connection or network** (refer back to Figure 8-2) to start the wizard.

Step 3. Click **Set up a new network** and then click **Next**. You are informed that detecting unconfigured network devices might take up to 90 seconds.

Step 4. When the wizard detects the required wireless router or WAP, select it and click **Next**.

Step 5. On the Give Your Network a Name page, type the network name and security key used by the required router or WAP. Choose the required security level and encryption type (more about these later in this chapter) and then click **Next**.

Step 6. The wizard configures your network. When done, click **Finish**.

You can connect to a network that you have previously set up by following these steps:

Step 1. From the Network and Sharing Center, click **Set up a new connection or network**.

Step 2. Click **Manually connect to a wireless network** and then click **Next**.

Step 3. The wizard displays the Manually connect to a wireless network page shown in Figure 9-1. Enter the following information and then click **Next**.

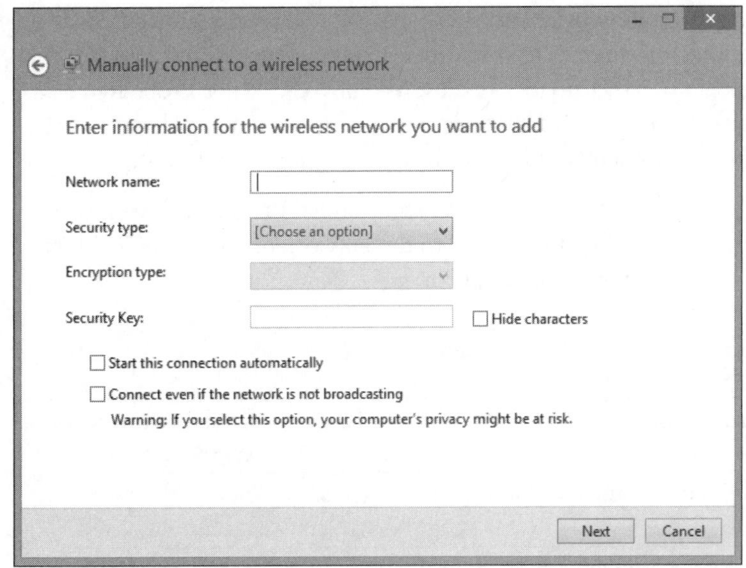

Figure 9-1 The Manually connect to a wireless network page enables you to enter the information required for connecting to a wireless network.

- **Network name:** Set the name (SSID) of the wireless network you are connecting to.
- **Security type:** Select the authentication method to be used in connecting to the wireless network. Table 9-3 lists the available security types.
- **Encryption type:** Select the method to be used for encryption of data sent across the wireless network. You can choose from 128-bit WEP, 128-bit Temporal Key Integrity Protocol (TKIP), or 128-bit Advanced Encryption Standard (AES) according to the security type chosen (see Table 9-3).
- **Security Key:** Enter the security key required by the security type selected (the WEP key for the WEP security type), the WPA preshared key (for the WPA-Personal security type), or the WPA2 preshared key (for the WPA2-Personal security type). Clear the Hide characters check box to view the information typed here.
- **Start this connection automatically:** When this option is selected, Windows 8.1 automatically connects to the network when you log in. When it is cleared, you must use the **Connect to a network** option from the Network and Sharing Center to connect to the network.

- **Connect even if the network is not broadcasting:** This option specifies whether Windows will attempt to connect even if the network is not broadcasting its name. This can be a security risk because Windows 8.1 sends Probe Request frames to locate the network, which unauthorized users can use to determine the network name. Consequently, this check box is not selected by default.

Step 4. The wizard informs you that it has successfully added the network you specified. Click the link specified to connect to the network or click the **Close** button to finish the wizard without connecting.

Table 9-3 Available Wireless Security Types

Security Type	Description	Available Encryption Types
No authentication (open)	Open system authentication with no encryption	None
WEP	Open system authentication using WEP	WEP
WPA-Personal	Wi-Fi Protected Access (WPA) using a preshared passphrase or key	TKIP (default) or AES
WPA2-Personal	Version 2 of WPA using a preshared passphrase or key	TKIP or AES (default)
WPA-Enterprise	WPA using IEEE 802.1x authentication	TKIP (default) or AES
WPA2-Enterprise	Version 2 of WPA using IEEE 802.1x authentication	TKIP or AES (default)
802.1x	IEEE 802.1x authentication using WEP (also known as dynamic WEP)	WEP

NOTE WPA2-Enterprise security provides the highest level of wireless networking authentication security. It requires authentication in two phases: first, an open system authentication; second, authentication using EAP. It is suitable for domain-based authentication and on networks using a Remote Authentication Dial-In User Service (RADIUS) authentication server. In environments without the RADIUS server, you should use WPA2-Personal security.

The wireless network you configured is visible in the Network and Sharing Center, from which you can connect later if you have not chosen the **Start this connection automatically** option.

TIP On the 70-687 exam, you may be asked to choose between the four available types of WPA wireless security. You should select **WPA** (either Personal or Enterprise) to use TKIP encryption by default or **WPA2** (either Personal or Enterprise) to use AES encryption by default. In addition, if you are required to type a security key or passphrase, you should select one of the **Personal** options. If you are not required to type a security key or passphrase, you should select one of the **Enterprise** options.

Managing Wireless Network Connections

After you have configured one or more wireless network connections, you can manage them from the Settings charm, as shown in Figure 9-2.

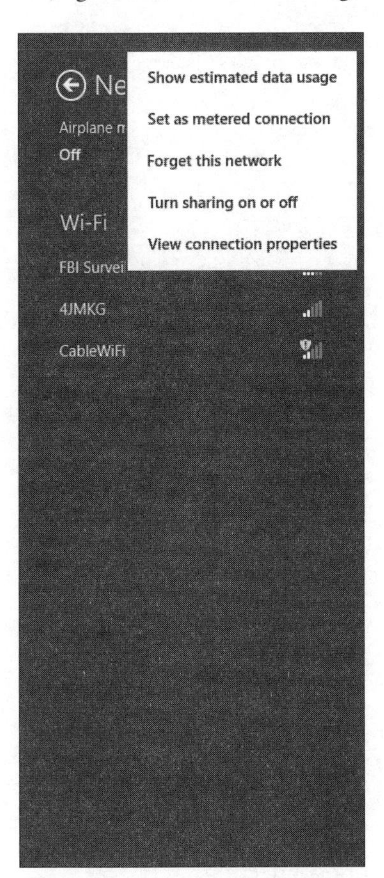

Figure 9-2 Connecting to wireless networks and context menu options for connected network.

To access the settings, select the **Settings** charm and then click on the wireless network icon. All currently available wireless networks are displayed. Left-click a network to connect to it, and select or deselect the **Connect automatically** option, as shown in Figure 9-3.

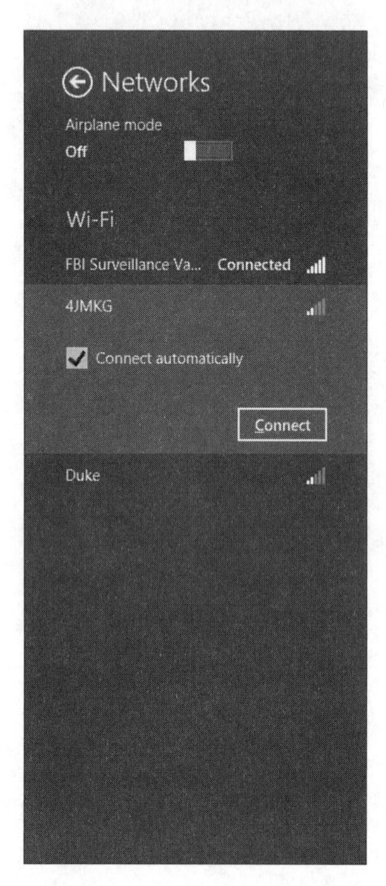

Figure 9-3 Wireless networks and connection options.

Several options are available for network connections. To access the network settings, select the **Settings** charm, choose **Change PC settings**, select **Network** and then **Connections**. Each network connection is categorized as either Wi-Fi or Ethernet. Click the device to view the connection menu as depicted in Figure 9-4. The following options are typically available for any network connection:

- **Find devices and content:** This setting determines whether Windows will search for and advertise network services on this network connection. Turning on this option enables file and printer sharing and allows others on the network to see your PC. Keep this option turned off when connecting to public networks.

- **Show my estimated data use in the Networks list:** When this option is turned on, the network connection displays the amount of data transferred over the connection when selected from the Networks charm. The last 60 days is displayed by default, or the time since the last reset or initial use of the connection.
- **Set as a metered connection:** This setting configures Windows to limit data usage on the connection. When you are using a metered connection, Windows attempts to use less bandwidth by requesting low-resolution images and videos, pause updates to Start screen tiles, defer downloading of nonpriority Windows updates, and stop automatic synchronization of offline files.
- **Properties:** This option sets the network properties for the connection. Several configuration items are listed for each network connection. Note that none of the properties listed here can be modified, but you can use the **Copy** button to copy the settings to the Clipboard, for pasting into Notepad or other applications.

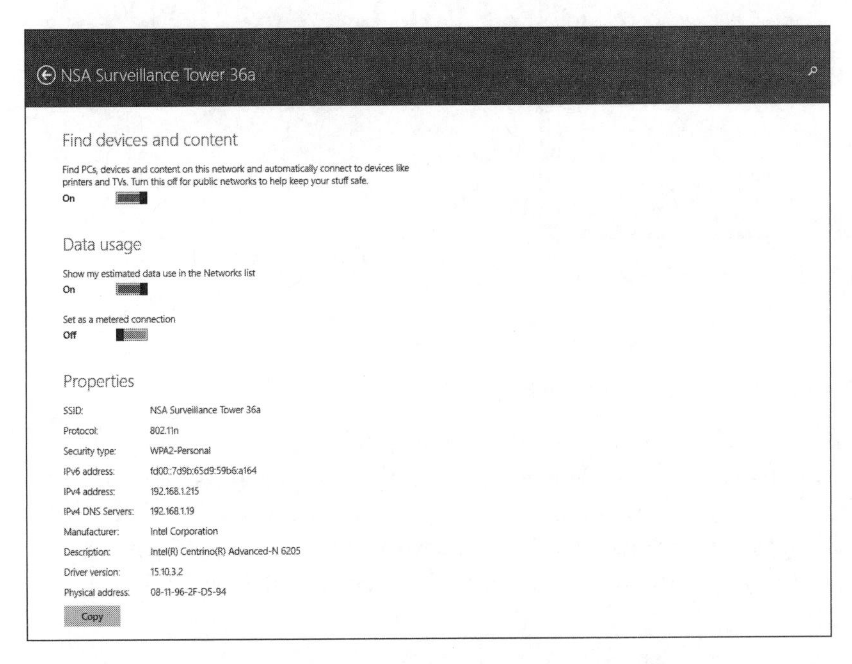

Figure 9-4 Wireless connection properties view in the Modern UI.

Some settings for wireless network connections are available only from the Network and Sharing Center on the desktop. To access these settings, open the **Control Panel** and enter `Network` in the search box and then click on **Network and Sharing Center**. Click the link for your wireless network, and the Network Properties dialog box is displayed.

Several configuration options are available from this dialog box, as shown in Figure 9-5. From here, you can access the properties described earlier when manually connecting to a wireless network, including the security settings, accessible from the Security tab.

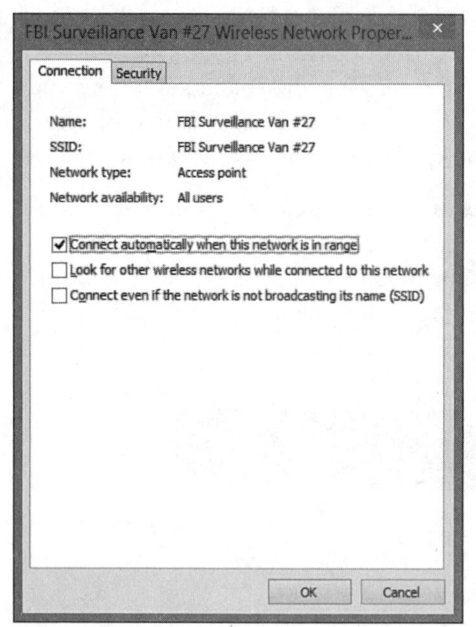

Figure 9-5 Wireless Network Properties dialog box.

Managing Preferred Wireless Networks

For Windows 8.1, Microsoft has simplified the user experience for working with wireless connections. Normally, Windows detects the type of wireless network, sets security options, and manages profiles behind the scenes. Untrusted networks are set as public and sharing is disabled. Private networks with security available are preferred, and Windows uses these networks before unsecured networks when available.

Note from Figure 9-2 the shield icon on some network connections. This indicates to the user that the network is not secured, and Windows will treat the network as public. As described earlier, users can override the automated sharing selected and turn sharing on or off when connected to the network.

Whenever you connect to a new network and enable the **Connect automatically** option, Windows places that network at the top of the priority list of preferred wireless networks.

Windows adjusts the priority of your list of preferred wireless networks based on the following criteria:

1. On connection to a new (undefined) wireless network, with **Connect automatically** enabled, that network is added to the list, and Windows connects to that network while it's in range.
2. If you connect to another wireless network while in range of the first network, also setting the **Connect automatically** option, Windows prefers the second network over the first one.
3. For mobile broadband networks, manually connecting to a mobile broadband network when there is a Wi-Fi network in range sets the mobile broadband network as preferred only for that session. The next time the computer is in range of both networks, the wireless network will be preferred. Mobile broadband networks are typically metered, but this behavior persists even if the mobile broadband network is not specifically marked as metered.
4. To force Windows to prefer a mobile broadband network over Wi-Fi, click the Wi-Fi network in the list of networks and then click **Disconnect**. Windows does not automatically connect to that Wi-Fi network.

Wireless Network Profiles

When you need to delete or make changes to the settings, you can usually do so from the right-click menu of the connection as described in the previous section. However, some tasks require the use of the command prompt. For instance, managing the automatically created wireless profiles Windows 8.1 maintains for your wireless connections requires the use of the `netsh` command-line utility.

A wireless network profile is a set of wireless networks available to a given user on a Windows 8.1 computer. The profile contains information such as the SSID, the security settings as configured earlier in this chapter, and whether the network is an infrastructure or ad hoc network. There are two types of wireless network profiles:

- **Per-user profiles:** These profiles apply to specific users of the computer and are connected when that user logs on to the computer. Note that these profiles can cause a loss of network connectivity when logging off or switching between users.
- **All-user profiles:** These profiles apply to all users of the computer and are connected regardless of which user is logged on to the computer.

To view the list of wireless profiles for the current user, open a command prompt, and type **`netsh wlan show profiles`**. To view the All User profiles, run the same command from an administrative command prompt. The result should be similar to Figure 9-6.

```
Administrator: Command Prompt
Microsoft Windows [Version 6.2.9200]
(c) 2012 Microsoft Corporation. All rights reserved.

C:\Windows\system32>netsh wlan show profiles

Profiles on interface Wi-Fi:

Group policy profiles (read only)
---------------------------------
    <None>

User profiles
-------------
    All User Profile     : YellowPine-guest
    All User Profile     : HTC Vivid F5DC
    All User Profile     : taZa
    All User Profile     : FBI Surveillance Van #27

C:\Windows\system32>
```

Figure 9-6 The `netsh wlan` commands are used to manage wireless profiles.

The `netsh` command lists all wireless network profiles, even if not in range, while the network list, as is shown in Figure 9-2, includes only networks that are currently in range. You can delete a network profile using `netsh` commands, which is the same function as the **Forget this network** option accessible from the Options menu.

Other important `netsh` commands for managing wireless networks and profiles are listed in Table 9-4. You should be aware that these commands return profiles based on the user context. To manage all user profiles, use an administrative command prompt.

Table 9-4 Important `netsh` Wireless Networking Commands

Command	Description
`netsh wlan show profiles`	Displays all wireless profiles on the computer
`netsh wlan show profile name="`*<profilename>*`" key=clear`	Displays security key information for a profile named *<profilename>* that's out of range

Command	Description
netsh wlan delete profile name="<*profilename*>"	Deletes a profile that's out of range
netsh wlan set profileparametername= "<*profilename*>" connectionmode=manual	Stops automatically connecting to a network that's out of range

NOTE Many other netsh commands are available for managing networks. For more information, download the "Network Shell (Netsh) Overview" from http://technet.microsoft.com/en-us/library/jj129394.aspx.

In addition to using the netsh command to manage wireless network profiles, you can also use Group Policy to deploy or maintain wireless network profiles. Whenever you connect to a wireless network, Windows creates a wireless profile entry in the Group Policies for the local computer. You will find the profiles under Computer Configuration\Policies\Windows Settings\Security Settings\Network List Manager Policies. You can set various policies for each network, as shown in Figure 9-7. Note that both wired and wireless networks are included.

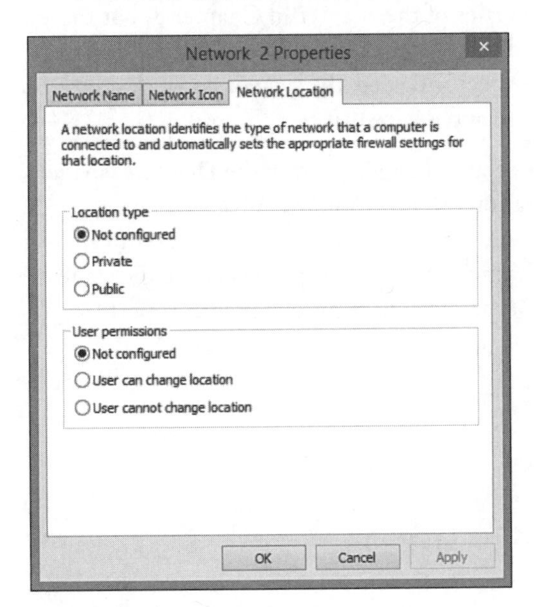

Figure 9-7 Local Group Policy settings for configured networks.

You also can deploy wireless network profiles from Windows Server using domain-based group policies.

NOTE For more information on deploying wireless network profiles in a Windows domain, see "Managing the Wireless Network (IEEE 802.11) Policies" at http://technet.microsoft.com/en-us/library/hh994695.aspx.

Configuring Network Adapters

In Chapter 4, "Configuring Devices and Device Drivers," you learned how to use Device Manager to install, configure, and troubleshoot various types of hardware devices. In this section, we take a further look at the use of Device Manager and the network adapter dialogs and options that can be used for configuring wired and wireless network adapters.

The majority of the work involving device implementation, management, and troubleshooting for many types of hardware devices is found in the Device Manager utility. From this utility, you can access many of the hardware properties of network adapters. We covered the network properties of the adapter in Chapter 8, but there are more network interface card (NIC)-level properties you can set for the device. The available properties depend on the specific device, the type of network it enables, and the capabilities of the hardware and device driver.

When you open a network device's Properties dialog box from the Device Manager, you have access to a variety of configuration options from the Advanced tab, as shown in Figure 9-8. As you select an item in the Properties list, the current value is displayed in the section on the right, which may be a drop-down, a spinner, a text box, or other control type based on the type of value required for the property.

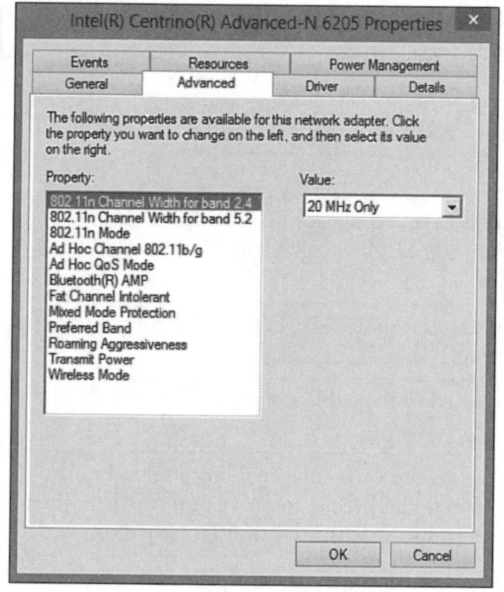

Figure 9-8 The Advanced tab of a network adapter device provides several configuration options.

NOTE You can also access this dialog box from the Network and Sharing Center. To do so, select the **Change adapter settings** link, right-click the adapter from the network connections list, and then select **Properties**. From the Network Properties dialog box, click the **Configure** button. Note also that when you open the device properties this way, the Resources tab is not displayed.

The configuration settings available for the network adapter can vary widely. Wireless adapters have different options than wired connections, and different devices from manufacturers expose different options through the driver interface. Typically, you would not need to adjust any of these settings, but you should be aware of a few, and that may need to be changed for specific environments or application and network requirements.

Table 9-5 lists many of the more common options you may encounter and need to adjust.

Table 9-5 Important Network Adapter Advanced Properties

Property	Adapter Type	Description
Preferred Band	Wireless	Some wireless networks can use 2.4 GHz or 5.2 GHz to communicate with the AP. You can adjust the preferred band to use.
Wireless Mode	Wireless	You can specify whether to use 802.11a, 802.11b, 802.11g, or some combination.
802.11n Mode	Wireless	You can specify whether to enable the capability to use 802.11n mode.
Jumbo Packet/Jumbo Frames	Wired	For fast networks (gigabit or faster), enabling Jumbo Frames (also known as Jumbo Packet) can improve performance when all devices on a network path can transmit larger packets.
Speed and Duplex	Wired	Typically, the network adapter negotiates with the switch to determine the speed and full or half duplex operation. If the autonegotiation is not working correctly, you can manually tell the adapter the speed and duplex mode to use.
Transmit Buffers / Receive Buffers	Wired	These properties allow you to set the number of buffers used when moving data between memory and the network. Increasing the number of buffers consumes more system memory.

Troubleshooting Network Adapter Issues

Recall from Chapter 8 that we covered some network troubleshooting techniques. If an issue occurs at the computer's hardware layer, it can often be resolved by resetting the network adapter. You can perform this task from the device's Properties dialog box, as described in Chapter 4. You can also do this from the Network and Sharing Center, by selecting the **Change adapter settings** link and right-clicking the connection, as shown in Figure 9-9. You can reset the adapter by selecting **Disable** from the pop-up box, waiting for the adapter to shut down, and then selecting **Enable** from the right-click menu.

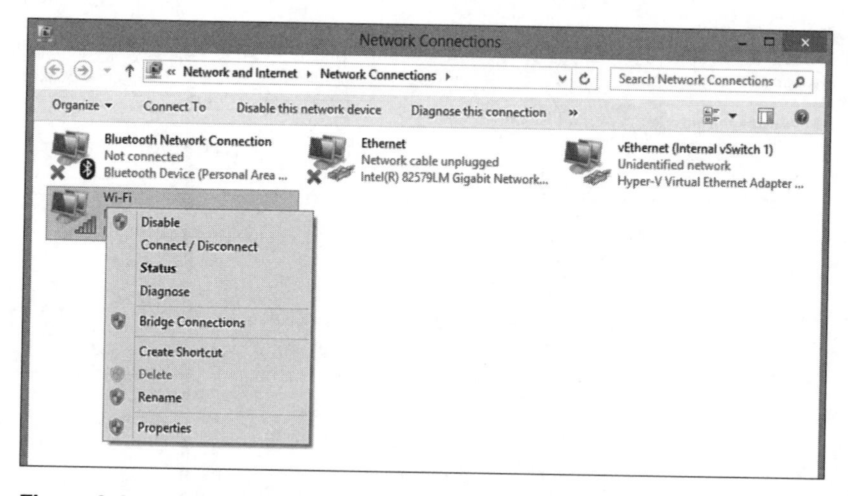

Figure 9-9 Enabling and disabling a network adapter from the Network Connections dialog box.

You can troubleshoot problems specific to the network adapter using the Windows 8.1 troubleshooting tool, described previously. To troubleshoot problems with the network adapter, follow these steps:

Step 1. Open the Control Panel by clicking the **Control Panel** link from the Settings charm.

Step 2. In the search box, type `troubleshooting` and then click on the **Troubleshooting** link.

Step 3. From the Troubleshooting screen, click on the **Network and Troubleshooting** link. This opens the dialog box displayed in Figure 9-10.

Step 4. Select the **Network Adapter** option to start the adapter troubleshooting wizard shown in Figure 9-11.

Step 5. To be most effective, the wizard can be run in Administrator mode. To do so, click the **Advanced** link and then click **Run as Administrator**. Click the **Next** button to proceed.

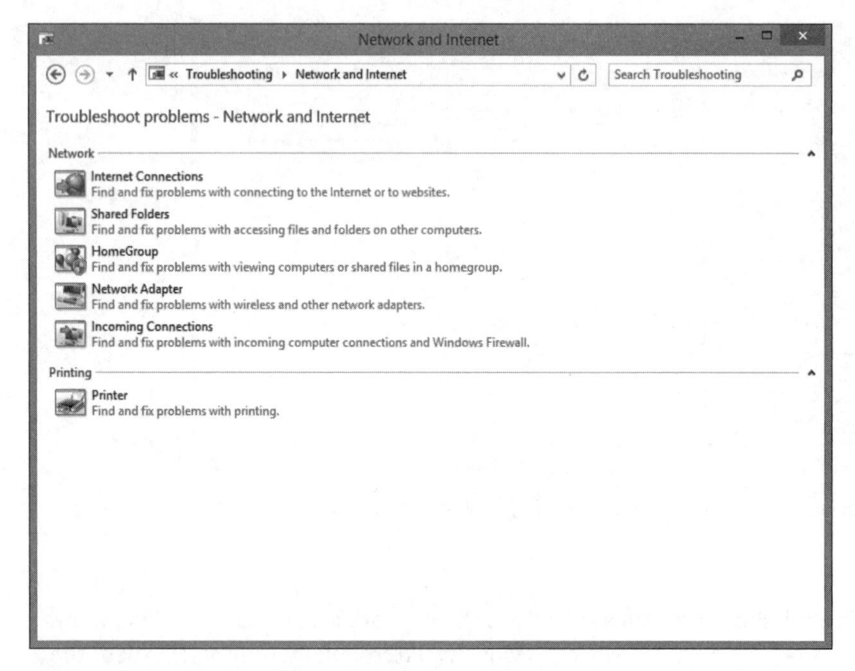

Figure 9-10 The Network and Internet Troubleshooting options.

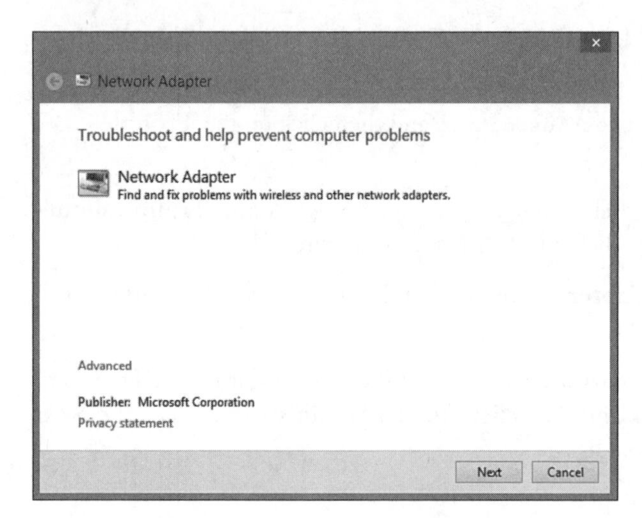

Figure 9-11 The Network Adapter Troubleshooting Wizard.

Step 6. The wizard will run, starting diagnostics. If you have more than one network adapter, the wizard then prompts you to select the adapter to troubleshoot, as shown in Figure 9-12. You can select a specific adapter or **All network adapters**. Click the **Next** button.

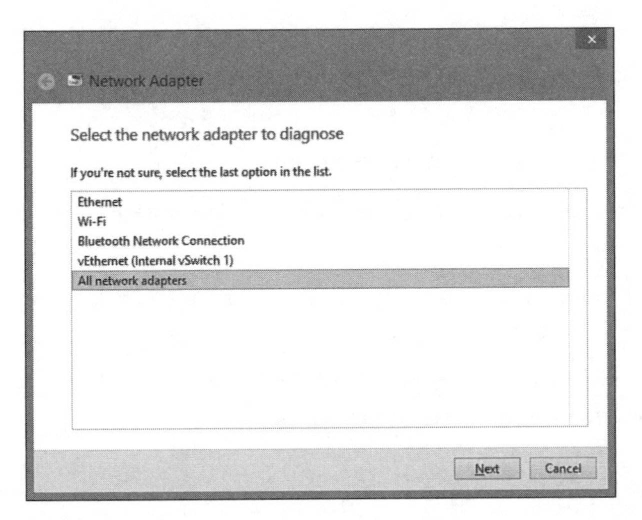

Figure 9-12 Select the adapter to use with the Network Adapter Troubleshooting Wizard.

Step 7. The wizard diagnoses the adapter or adapters and attempts to fix any issues that are found.

When the wizard completes, it indicates whether any issues were found and whether the troubleshooter was able to fix them. You can click on the **View detailed information** link to access a set of reports on the network adapter issues and the detection details. The report contains a lot of detailed information, and if the issue was not fixed, you can print the report for a hardware technician or vendor to help determine where the problem lies.

Configuring Location Aware Printing

Location Aware Printing, first introduced in Windows 7, enables you to automatically print to a printer on the network your computer is currently connected to. For example, if you have a portable computer that you use both at home and in the office, you can print to the office computer when you are at work. Returning home in the evening, you print a document, and this print job automatically goes to the home printer without your having to change the default printer, thereby simplifying this task and reducing problems from attempting to print to the wrong printer.

Location Aware Printing in Windows 8.1 obtains network names from several sources, including the Active Directory Domain Services (AD DS) domain name at work and the SSID of your home wireless network. The Manage Default Printers dialog box then enables you to associate a default printer with each network to which you connect, and Windows 8.1 automatically specifies the assigned printer as the default when you connect to its network.

To use Location Aware Printing, you need to be running Windows 8.1 Pro or Enterprise edition. The feature is not available in Windows RT or the basic edition of Windows 8.1.

Use the following procedure to set up Location Aware Printing:

Step 1. Open the Devices and Printers dialog box, either from the Control Panel or by using the Search charm.

Step 2. From the Devices and Printers dialog box, select a printer and then click **Manage default printers** from the Ribbon.

Step 3. From the Manage Default Printers dialog box shown in Figure 9-13, select **Change my default printer when I change networks**.

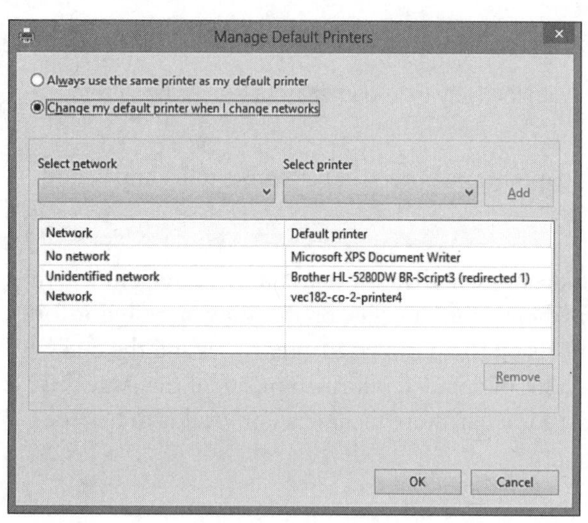

Figure 9-13 The Manage Default Printers dialog box enables you to select a default printer that will be used at each network location.

Step 4. For each network shown in the Select network drop-down list, select a printer from the Select printer drop-down list and then click **Add**.

Step 5. When finished, click **OK**.

If you want to change the default printer for a network, you can use the Select network and Select printer drop-down boxes to select the network and printer, and click the **Update** button to change to the new setting. You can also remove a network-printer association by selecting it from the list and clicking the **Remove** button at the bottom of the dialog box.

Exam Preparation Tasks

Review All the Key Topics

Review the most important topics in the chapter, noted with the key topics icon in the outer margin of the page. Table 9-6 lists a reference of these key topics and the page numbers on which each is found.

Table 9-6 Key Topics for Chapter 9

Key Topic Element	Description	Page Number
Table 9-2	Lists characteristics of wireless networking protocols	385
Step List	Shows how to set up a wireless network connection	386
Figure 9-1	Shows you how to manually connect to a wireless network	387
Table 9-3	Describes wireless security types	388
Figure 9-5	Shows wireless network properties	392
List	Lists criteria of preferred wireless networks	393
Figure 9-6	Shows how to manage wireless network profiles with `netsh`	394
Figure 9-8	Shows network adapter advanced properties	397
Figure 9-13	Shows how to configure Location Aware Printing	402

Complete the Tables and Lists from Memory

Print a copy of Appendix B, "Memory Tables," (found on the CD), or at least the section for this chapter, and complete the tables and lists from memory. Appendix C, "Memory Tables Answer Key," also on the CD, includes completed tables and lists to check your work.

Definitions of Key Terms

Define the following key terms from this chapter, and check your answers in the Glossary:

> 802.11, AES, Duplex, Jumbo Frames, Location Aware, Metered connection, NIC, PEAP, RADIUS, Service Set Identifier (SSID), TKIP, WAP, Wired Equivalent Privacy (WEP), Wi-Fi Protected Access (WPA), Wireless network profile, WLAN

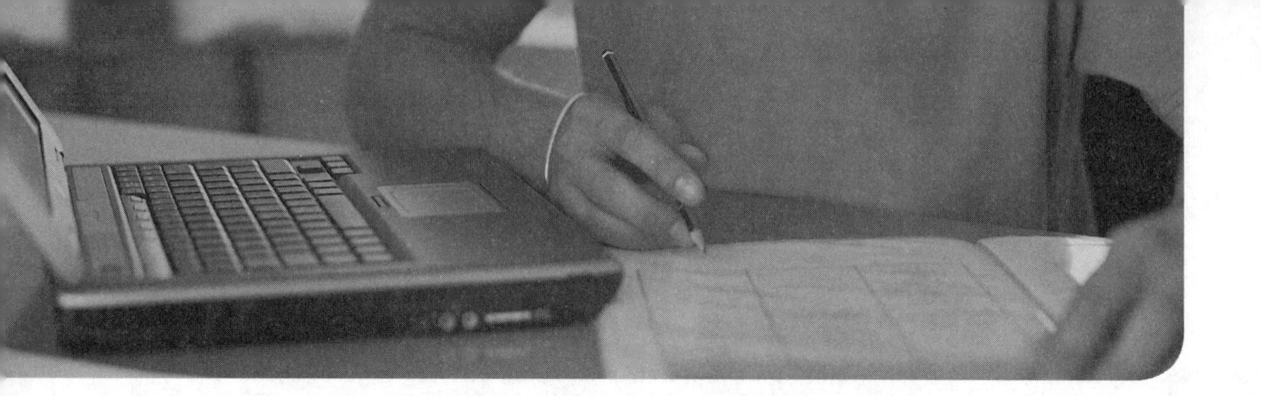

This chapter covers the following subjects:

- **Configuring Windows Firewall:** Windows Firewall is a comprehensive stateful packet-filtering application that is enabled by default in Windows 8.1. This section introduces you to the Windows Firewall Control Panel applet and shows you how to create exceptions that allow specified programs or ports to communicate through the firewall.
- **Configuring Windows Firewall with Advanced Security:** The Windows Firewall with Advanced Security Microsoft Management Console snap-in provides a comprehensive interface for configuring all types of inbound, outbound, and connection security rules. This section shows you how to create and modify the various types of rules available with this tool.
- **Configuring Authenticated Exceptions:** When creating connection rules for Windows Firewall, you might need to allow connections only for specific users or computers on the network. This section discusses the methods for creating rules designed to allow or block specific local users, remote users, and remote computers.
- **Configuring Network Discovery:** Windows Network Discovery is a technology that enables computers to locate and connect to other computers, devices, and services on the network. This is convenient for users, but may present a security risk on untrusted networks. In this section, you learn about Network Discovery, network profiles, and how to configure discovery for a Windows 8.1 computer.
- **Managing Wireless Security:** Windows 8.1 has made connecting to Wi-Fi networks easy, and wireless networks are available in many locations. But this ease of use comes with risks. This section looks at technologies used to ensure that private information remains private even when it is transmitted over the air where it can be picked up by anyone.

CHAPTER 10

Configuring and Maintaining Network Security

In Chapter 9, "Configuring Network Settings," you learned how to set up and maintain wireless networks. The explosion of wireless networks with many hotels and restaurants offering free Wi-Fi connections has made it easy for cybercriminals to go about the business of intercepting and stealing information for financial gain, political purposes, and many other nefarious endeavors. In fact, the year 2013 started out with a report that the Japanese Ministry of Agriculture, Forestry, and Fishery was hacked with the theft of more than 3,000 documents, including some of their negotiating strategies, and late in 2013, the Target department store chain was hacked, compromising of as many as 40 million customers in the United States and Canada. Many experts predict an increase in the frequency and complexity of cyber attacks as the year progresses. Anyone who works with or supports a modern computer network must be able to ensure that the network maintains an adequate level of security, so Microsoft expects you to know basic security practices as a component of the 70-687 exam.

"Do I Know This Already?" Quiz

The "Do I Know This Already?" quiz allows you to assess whether you should read this entire chapter or simply jump to the "Exam Preparation Tasks" section for review. If you are in doubt, read the entire chapter. Table 10-1 outlines the major headings in this chapter and the corresponding "Do I Know This Already?" quiz questions. You can find the answers in Appendix A, "Answers to the 'Do I Know This Already?' Quizzes."

Table 10-1 "Do I Know This Already?" Foundation Topics Section-to-Question Mapping

Foundations Topics Section	Questions Covered in This Section
Configuring Windows Firewall	1–2
Configuring Windows Firewall with Advanced Security	3–6
Configuring Authenticated Exceptions	7
Configuring Network Discovery	8–9
Managing Wireless Security	10–11

1. You want to configure Windows Firewall settings on your notebook computer so that others are unable to access anything on your computer. Which type of network location should you enable?
   a. Wireless
   b. Ethernet
   c. Public or Guest
   d. Private

2. Which of the following actions can you perform from the Windows Firewall Control Panel applet on your Windows 8.1 computer? (Choose three.)
   a. Specify ports that are allowed to communicate across the Windows Firewall.
   b. Specify programs that are allowed to communicate across the Windows Firewall.
   c. Set the firewall to block all incoming connections, including those in the list of allowed programs.
   d. Configure logging settings for programs that are blocked by the firewall.
   e. Specify a series of firewall settings according to the type of network to which you are connected.

3. You open the Windows Firewall with Advanced Security snap-in and notice that a large number of firewall rules have already been preconfigured. Which of the following rule settings types does not include any preconfigured firewall rules?
   a. Inbound rules
   b. Outbound rules
   c. Connection security rules
   d. Monitoring rules

4. You want to configure Windows Firewall so that Windows Media Player can receive data only from connections that have been authenticated by IPSec. What setting should you configure?
   a. Run the New Inbound Rule Wizard, specify the path to Windows Media Player on the program page, and then specify the **Allow the connection if it is secure** option.

b. Run the New Outbound Rule Wizard, specify the path to Windows Media Player on the program page, and then specify the **Allow the connection if it is secure** option.

c. Run the New Connection Security Rule Wizard, specify the path to Windows Media Player on the program page, and then specify the **Allow the connection if it is secure** option.

d. Merely select **Windows Media Player** from the Allowed Programs and Features list in the Windows Firewall Control Panel applet.

5. You have configured a new inbound rule that limits connections by a specific application on your computer to only those connections that have been authenticated using IPSec. The next day when you start your application, you realize that you should have configured this rule as an outbound rule. What should you do to correct this error with the least amount of effort?

   a. Access the Scope tab of the Properties dialog box for your rule and change the scope from Inbound to Outbound.

   b. Access the Advanced tab of the Properties dialog box for your rule and change the interface type from Inbound to Outbound.

   c. Select the rule from the list of inbound rules in the details pane of Windows Firewall with Advanced Security and drag the rule to the Outbound Rules node in the console tree.

   d. You must deactivate or delete the inbound rule you configured and then use the New Outbound Rule Wizard to set up a new rule that is specific to your application.

6. You want Windows Firewall with Advanced Security to display a notification when a program is blocked from receiving inbound connections. What should you do?

   a. Right-click **Windows Firewall with Advanced Security** at the top of the console tree and choose **Properties**. From the tab corresponding to the required profile, click **Customize** under Settings. Then ensure that the Display a Notification drop-down list is set to **Yes**.

   b. Right-click the **Inbound Rules** node in the console tree and choose **Properties**. From the tab corresponding to the required profile, click **Customize** under Settings. Then ensure that the Display a Notification drop-down list is set to **Yes**.

c. Right-click the **Monitoring** node in the console tree and choose **Properties**. From the tab corresponding to the required profile, click **Customize** under Settings. Then ensure that the Display a Notification drop-down list is set to **Yes**.

d. Right-click the **Firewall** subnode below the Monitoring node in the console tree and choose **Properties**. From the tab corresponding to the required profile, click **Customize** under Settings. Then ensure that the Display a Notification drop-down list is set to **Yes**.

7. You are configuring a firewall rule to allow only the Accounting group to connect to network shares on a computer. What Action in General settings should you select before specifying the group in the Remote Users setting?

   a. Allow the connection

   b. Allow the connection if it is secure

   c. Block the connection

   d. Block edge traversal

8. In which Network Profiles can you turn off Network Discovery? (Select all that apply.)

   a. Private

   b. Guest or Public

   c. Domain

   d. All Networks

9. You are configuring Network discovery, turning it on for a network. You have also configured network discovery to perform automatic setup of network-connected devices. Which network profile are you configuring?

   a. Private

   b. Guest or Public

   c. Domain

   d. All Networks

10. You are configuring a wireless router for use in your company's conference room. A variety of users will be connecting to the access point, and you want to make sure that the encryption is as strong as possible to prevent users outside the building from collecting information from the network traffic. The access point supports WPA2 security. Which encryption type should you enforce?

    a. WEP

    b. AES

    c. TKIP

    d. 802.1x

11. You are offsite with a coworker and want to collaborate by creating an ad hoc network to connect your individual Windows 8.1 laptops to each other. Which wireless security type will be used when the two computers establish a connection?

    a. WEP

    b. WPA-Enterprise

    c. WPA2-Enterprise

    d. WPA-Personal

    e. WPA2-Personal

Foundation Topics

Configuring Windows Firewall

Originally called the Internet Connection Firewall (ICF) in Windows XP prior to SP2, Windows Firewall is a personal firewall, stopping undesirable traffic from being accepted by the computer. Using a firewall can avoid security breaches as well as viruses that utilize port-based TCP or UDP traffic to enter the computer's operating system. For computers that use broadband Internet connections with dedicated IP addresses, the Windows Firewall can help avoid attacks aimed at disrupting a home computer. When you take your laptop to a Wi-Fi–enabled public location such as an airport, hotel, or restaurant, the firewall protects you from individuals who might be probing the network to see what they can steal or infect. Even people with dial-up Internet connections can benefit from added protection. The Windows Firewall is enabled by default when you install Windows 8 or 8.1, as it was in Windows Vista and 7.

Windows Firewall is a stateful host-based firewall that you can configure to allow or block specific network traffic. It includes a packet filter that uses an access control list (ACL) specifying parameters (such as IP address, port number, and protocol) that are allowed to pass through. When a user communicates with an external computer, the stateful firewall remembers this conversation and allows the appropriate reply packets to reach the user. Packets from an outside computer that attempts to communicate with a computer on which a stateful firewall is running are dropped unless the ACL contains rules permitting them.

Windows Vista introduced considerable improvements to its original implementation in Windows XP SP2, including outbound traffic protection, support for IP Security (IPSec) and IP version 6 (IPv6), improved configuration of exceptions, and support for command-line configuration. In Windows 7 and again in Windows 8 and 8.1, Microsoft has improved Windows Firewall even further. The following are some of the important new features in the Windows 8.1 and Windows Server 2012 R2 implementation:

- **Support for Internet Key Exchange version 2 (IKEv2) for IPSec transport mode:** Additional scenarios have been supported including IPSec end-to-end transport mode connections. Included is expanded support for interoperability with other operating systems using IKEv2 for end-to-end security, and the support for Suite B requirements described in Request for Comment (RFC) 4869.
- **Windows Store app network isolation:** You can fine-tune network access in Windows Firewall to provide added control of Windows Store apps. You can enforce network boundaries that allow compromised apps to access only networks to which they have been explicitly granted. Doing so significantly reduces the scope of their impact on other networks, the system, and the network. You can also isolate apps and protect them for malicious access across the network.

- **New Windows PowerShell cmdlets for Windows Firewall:** You can use PowerShell for configuration and management of Windows Firewall, IPSec, and related features. Full configuration capabilities are now available.

You can perform basic configuration of Windows Firewall from a Control Panel applet; you can also perform more advanced configuration of Windows Firewall, including the use of security policies from a Microsoft Management Console (MMC) snap-in. We look at each of these in turn.

Basic Windows Firewall Configuration

The Windows Firewall Control Panel applet, found in the System and Security category and shown in Figure 10-1, enables you to set up firewall rules for each of the same network types introduced earlier in this chapter for configuring network settings.

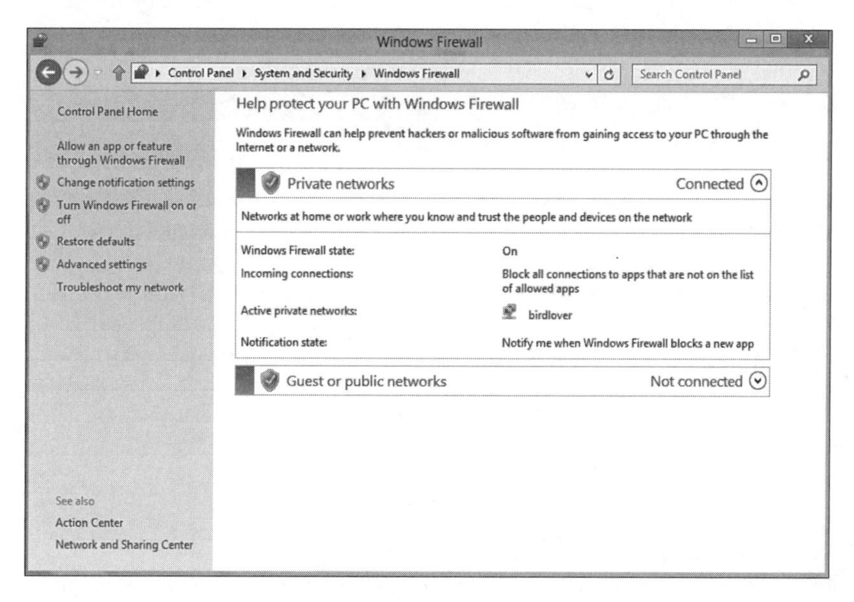

Figure 10-1 You can configure basic firewall settings for different network locations from the Windows Firewall Control Panel applet.

> **NOTE** If your computer is joined to an Active Directory Domain Services (AD DS) domain, an additional location called Domain Networks is added in Figure 10-1. Settings in this location are configured through domain-based Group Policy and cannot be modified here.

You can enable or disable the Windows Firewall separately for each connection. In doing so, you are able to use Windows Firewall to protect a computer connected to the Internet via one adapter, and not use Windows Firewall for the adapter connected to the private network. Use the following instructions to perform basic firewall configuration:

Step 1. Open the Windows Firewall applet by using any of the following methods:

- In the Settings charm, select **Control Panel**. Or right-click **Start** and choose **Control Panel**. Then click **System and Security > Windows Firewall**.
- In the Search charm, type `firewall` in the Search field. From the list of programs displayed, click **Windows Firewall**.
- Open the Network and Sharing Center and select **Windows Firewall** from the list in the bottom-left corner.

Step 2. From the left pane, select **Turn Windows Firewall on or off**. If you receive a UAC prompt, click **Continue**. This displays the Customize settings for each type of network dialog box, shown in Figure 10-2.

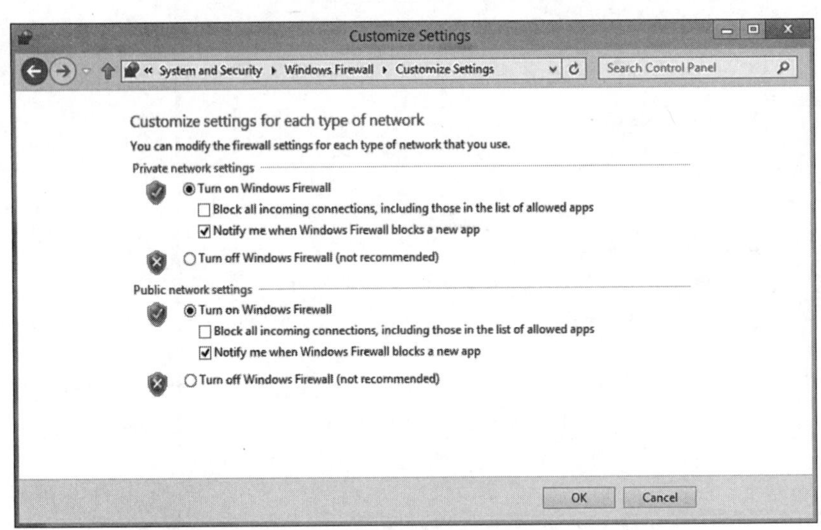

Figure 10-2 The Customize settings for each type of network dialog box enables you to turn the firewall on or off and to block incoming connections.

Step 3. If you are connected to a corporate network with a comprehensive hardware firewall, select **Turn off Windows Firewall (not recommended)** under the Private Network Location Settings section. If you connect at any time to an insecure network, such as an airport or restaurant Wi-Fi hot spot, select the **Block all incoming connections, including those in the list of allowed programs** option under Public network location settings. This option disables all exceptions you've configured on the Exceptions tab.

WARNING Don't disable the firewall unless absolutely necessary, even on the Private Network Location Settings section. Never select the **Turn off Windows Firewall** option shown in Figure 10-2 unless you're absolutely certain that your network is well protected with a good firewall. The only exception should be temporarily to troubleshoot a connectivity problem; after you've solved the problem, be sure to re-enable the firewall immediately.

Step 4. To configure program exceptions, return to the Windows Firewall applet and click **Allow an app or feature through Windows Firewall**.

Step 5. From the list shown in Figure 10-3, select the programs or ports you want to have access to your computer on either of the Private or Public profiles. Table 10-2 describes the more important items in this list. Clear the check boxes next to any programs or ports to be denied access, or select the check boxes next to programs or ports to be granted access.

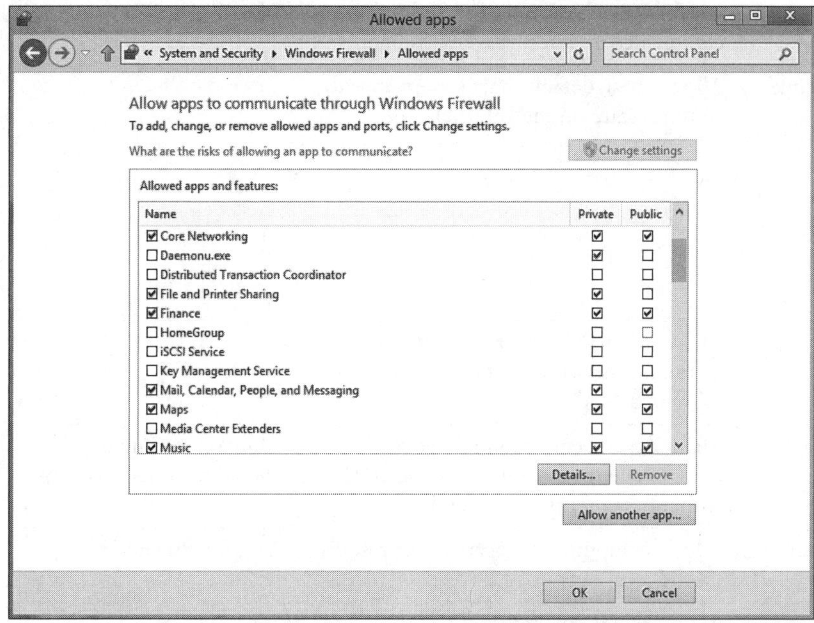

Figure 10-3 The Allow apps to communicate through Windows Firewall dialog box enables you to specify which programs are allowed to communicate through the firewall.

Table 10-2 Windows Firewall Configurable Exceptions

Exception	Description	Enabled by Default?
Core Networking Network Discovery	Each option works with the other to enable your computer to connect to other network computers or the Internet	Yes; network discovery for home or work only
Distributed Transaction Coordinator	Coordinates the update of transaction-protected resources such as databases, message queues, and file systems	No
File and Printer Sharing	Enables your computer to share resources such as files and printers with other computers on your network	Yes
HomeGroup	Allows communication to other computers in the homegroup	Yes, for Private only when joined to a homegroup
iSCSI Service	Enables you to connect to iSCSI target servers and devices	No
Key Management Service	Used for machine counting and license compliance in enterprise environments	No
Bing Food & Drink Bing Health & Fitness Mail, Calendar, People and Messaging Maps Photos	Allows these default Start screen apps to communicate on the Internet	Yes
Media Center Extenders	Allows Media Center Extenders to communicate with a computer running Windows Media Center	No
Netlogon Service	Maintains a secure channel between domain clients and a domain controller for authenticating users and services	Only on a computer joined to an AD domain
Network Discovery	Allows computers to locate other resources on the local network	Yes, for Private only
Performance Logs and Alerts	Allows remote management of the Performance Logs and Alerts service	No
Remote Assistance	Enables an expert user to connect to the desktop of a user requiring assistance in a Windows Feature	Yes, for Private only
Remote Desktop	Enables a user to connect with and work on a remote computer	No

Exception	Description	Enabled by Default?
Remote (item) Management	Enables an administrator to manage items on a remote computer, including event logs, scheduled tasks, services, and disk volumes	No, for all these tasks
Routing and Remote Access (RRAS)	Enables remote users to connect to a server to access the corporate network (used on RRAS server computers only)	No
Windows Easy Transfer	Enables a user to copy files, folders, and settings from an old computer running Windows 2000 or later to a new Windows 8.1 computer	Yes
Windows Remote Management	Enables you to manage a remote Windows computer	No

Step 6. To add a program not shown in the list, click **Allow another app**. From the Add an app dialog box shown in Figure 10-4, select the program to be added and then click **Add**. If necessary, click **Browse** to locate the desired program. You can also click **Network types** to choose which network type is allowed by the selected program.

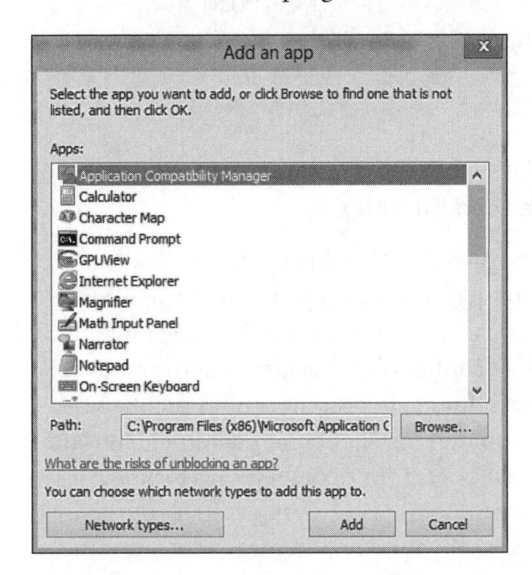

Figure 10-4 The Add an app dialog box enables you to allow specific programs access through the Windows Firewall.

Step 7. Use the Allow apps to communicate through Windows Firewall dialog box (refer to Figure 10-3), to view the properties of any program or port on the list, select it, and click **Details**.

Step 8. To remove a program from the list, select it and click **Remove**. You can do this only for programs you added using step 6.

Step 9. If you need to restore default settings, return to the Windows Firewall applet previously shown in Figure 10-1 and click **Restore defaults**. Then confirm your intention in the Restore Default Settings dialog box that appears.

Step 10. If you are experiencing networking problems, click **Troubleshoot my network** to access the troubleshooter previously shown in Figure 8-16 in Chapter 8, "Configuring TCP/IP Settings."

Step 11. When you are finished, click **OK**.

TIP When allowing additional programs to communicate through the Windows Firewall, by default these programs are allowed to communicate through the Home/Work network profile only. You should retain this default unless you need a program to communicate through the Internet from a public location. From the Public column of the dialog box shown in Figure 10-3, you should select the boxes next to any connections that link to the Internet; you should clear the boxes next to any connections to a private network.

Configuring Windows Firewall with Advanced Security

First introduced in Windows Vista and enhanced in Windows 7, 8, and 8.1, the Windows Firewall with Advanced Security snap-in enables you to perform a comprehensive set of configuration actions. You can configure rules that affect inbound and outbound communication, and you can configure connection security rules and the monitoring of firewall actions. Inbound rules help prevent actions such as unknown access or configuration of your computer, installation of undesired software, and so on. Outbound rules help prevent utilities on your computer performing certain actions, such as accessing network resources or software without your knowledge. They can also help prevent other users of your computer from downloading software or inappropriate files without your knowledge.

Use any of the following methods to access the Windows Firewall with Advanced Security snap-in:

- Access the Search charm, type `firewall` in the Search field of the Start menu and then select **Windows Firewall with Advanced Security** from the Programs list.
- From the task list on the left side of the Windows Firewall applet (refer back to Figure 10-1), select **Advanced settings.**
- If you have enabled the Administrative Tools option from the Settings charm as described in Chapter 1, "Introducing Windows 8.1," click the **Windows Firewall with Advanced Security** tile on the Start screen.

After accepting the UAC prompt (if you receive one), the snap-in shown in Figure 10-5 is displayed.

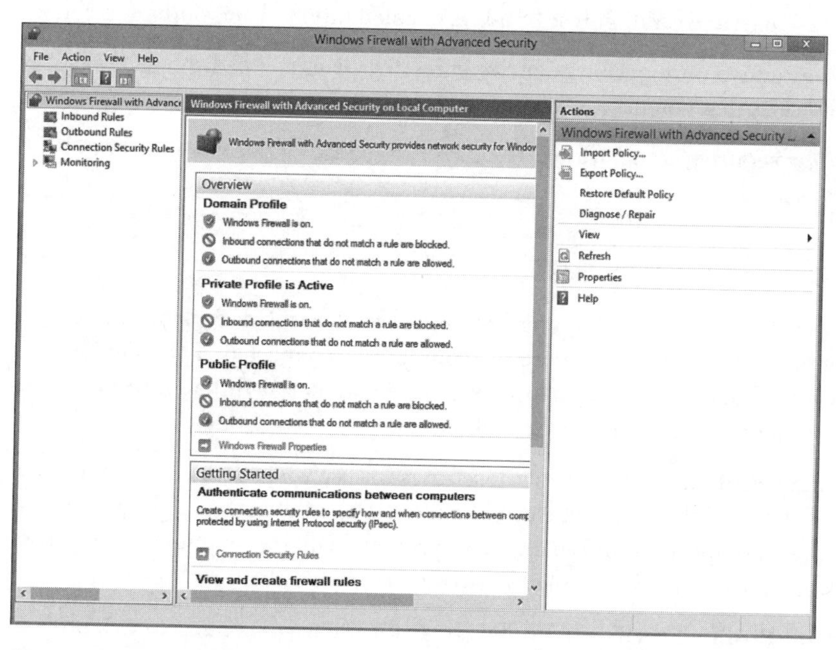

Figure 10-5 The Windows Firewall with Advanced Security snap-in enables you to perform advanced configuration options.

When the snap-in first opens, it displays a summary of configured firewall settings. From the left pane, you can configure any of the following types of properties:

- **Inbound Rules:** Displays a series of defined inbound rules. Enabled rules are shown with a green check mark icon. If the icon is dark in appearance, the rule is not enabled. To enable a rule, right-click it and select **Enable Rule**; to disable an enabled rule, right-click it and select **Disable Rule**. You can also create a new rule by right-clicking **Inbound Rules** and selecting **New Rule**. We discuss creation of new rules later in this section.

- **Outbound Rules:** Displays a series of defined outbound rules, also with a green check mark icon for enabled rules. You can enable or disable rules, and create new rules in the same manner as with inbound rules.
- **Connection Security Rules:** By default, this branch does not contain any rules. Right-click it and choose **New Rule** to create rules that are used to determine limits applied to connections with remote computers.
- **Monitoring:** Displays a summary of enabled firewall settings and provides links to active rules and security associations. This includes a domain profile for computers that are members of an AD DS domain. The following three links are available from the bottom of the details pane:
  - **View active firewall rules:** Displays enabled inbound and outbound rules.
  - **View active connection security rules:** Displays enabled connection security rules that you have created.
  - **View security associations:** Displays IPSec main mode and quick mode associations.

Configuring Multiple Firewall Profiles

A *profile* is simply a means of grouping firewall rules so that they apply to the affected computers dependent on where the computer is connected. The Windows Firewall with Advanced Security snap-in enables you to define different firewall behavior for each of the following three profiles:

- **Domain Profile:** Specifies firewall settings for use when connected directly to an AD DS domain. If the network is protected from unauthorized external access, you can specify additional exceptions that facilitate communication across the local area network (LAN) to network servers and client computers.
- **Private Profile:** Specifies firewall settings for use when connected to a private network location, such as a home or small office. You can open up connections to network computers and lock down external communications as required.
- **Public Profile:** Specifies firewall settings for use when connected to an insecure public network, such as a Wi-Fi access point at a hotel, restaurant, airport, or other location where unknown individuals might attempt to connect to your computer. By default, network discovery and file and printer sharing are turned off, inbound connections are blocked, and outbound connections are allowed.

To configure settings for these profiles from the Windows Firewall with Advanced Security snap-in, right-click **Windows Firewall with Advanced Security** at the top-left corner and choose **Properties**. This opens the dialog box shown in Figure 10-6.

Figure 10-6 The Windows Firewall with Advanced Security on Local Computer Properties dialog box enables you to configure profiles that are specific for domain, private, and public networks.

You can configure the following properties for each of the three profiles individually from this dialog box:

- **State:** Enables you to turn the firewall on or off for the selected profile and block or allow inbound and outbound connections. For inbound connections, you can either block connections with the configured exceptions or block all connections. Click **Customize** to specify which connections you want Windows Firewall to help protect.
- **Settings:** Enables you to customize firewall settings for the selected profile. Click **Customize** to specify whether to display notifications to users when programs are blocked from receiving inbound connections or allow unicast responses. You can also view but not modify how rules created by local administrators are merged with Group Policy-based rules.
- **Logging:** Enables you to configure logging settings. Click **Customize** to specify the location and size of the log file and whether dropped packets or successful connections are logged (see Figure 10-7).

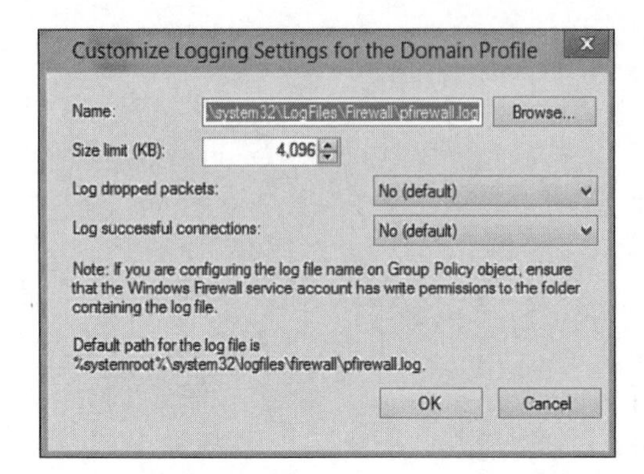

Figure 10-7 You can customize logging settings for each of the Windows Firewall profiles.

In addition, you can configure IPSec settings from the IPSec Settings tab (refer to Figure 10-6), including defaults and exemptions. IPSec authentication rules enable you to configure bypass rules for specific computers that enable these computers to bypass other Windows Firewall rules. Doing so enables you to block certain types of traffic while enabling authenticated computers to receive these types of traffic. Configuring IPSec settings is beyond the scope of the 70-687 exam and is not discussed further here.

Configuring New Firewall Rules

By clicking **New Rule** under Inbound Rules or Outbound Rules in the Windows Firewall with Advanced Security snap-in (refer to Figure 10-5), you can create rules that determine programs or ports that are allowed to pass through the firewall. Use the following procedure to create a new rule:

Step 1. Right-click the desired rule type in the Windows Firewall with Advanced Security snap-in and choose **New Rule**. This starts the New (Inbound or Outbound) Rule Wizard, as shown in Figure 10-8. (We chose a new inbound rule, so our example shows the New Inbound Rule Wizard.)

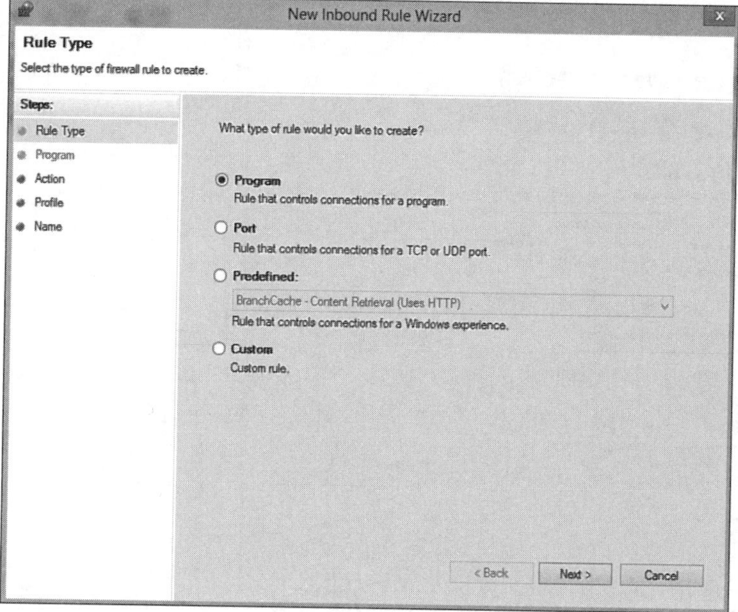

Figure 10-8 The New (Inbound or Outbound) Rule Wizard starts with a Rule Type page, which enables you to define the type of rule you want to create.

Step 2. Select the type of rule you want to create:

- **Program:** Enables you to define a rule that includes all programs or a specified program path.
- **Port:** Enables you to define rules for specific remote ports using either the TCP or UDP protocol.
- **Predefined:** Enables you to select from a large quantity of predefined rules covering the same exceptions described previously in Table 10-2 and shown in Figure 10-3. Select the desired exception from the drop-down list.
- **Custom:** Enables you to create rules that apply to combinations of programs and ports. This option combines settings provided by the other rule-type options.

Step 3. Once you've selected your rule type, click **Next**.

Step 4. The content of the next page of the wizard varies according to which option you've selected. On this page, define the program path, port number and protocol, or predefined rule that you want to create, and then click **Next**.

Step 5. On the Action page, specify the action to be taken when a connection matches the specified conditions, as shown in Figure 10-9.

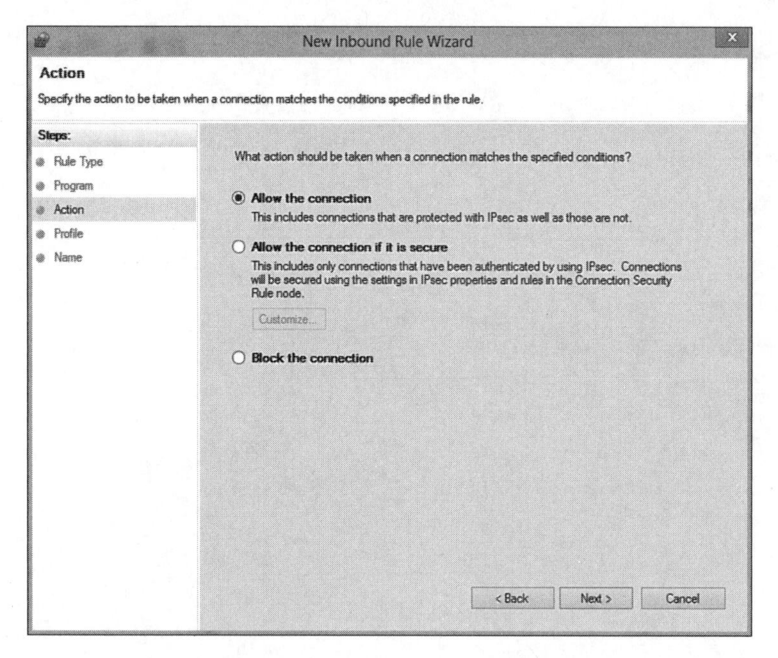

Figure 10-9 The Action page enables you to specify the required action type.

Step 6. If you choose the **Allow the Connection if it is secure** option, click **Customize** to display the dialog box shown in Figure 10-10. From this dialog box, select the required option as explained on the dialog box and click **OK**. If you desire that encryption be enforced in addition to authentication and integrity protection, select the **Require the connections to be encrypted** option and also select the check box provided if you want to allow unencrypted data to be sent while encryption is being negotiated.

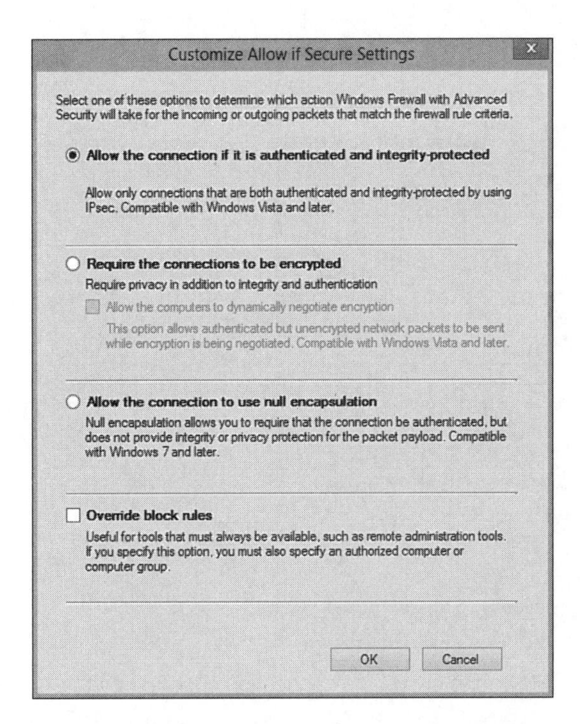

Figure 10-10 The Customize Allow if Secure Settings dialog box enables you to select additional actions to be taken for packets that match the rule conditions being configured.

Step 7. Click **Next** to display the Users page, shown in Figure 10-11. This page enables you to limit the users who are allowed to connect using this rule. By default, all users are authorized to connect. To limit authorized users, select the check box labeled **Only allow connections from these users** and click **Add** to display the Select Users or Groups dialog box, which enables you to select one or more users to be allowed access. To prevent users who are otherwise authorized to use the connection, select the check box labeled **Skip this rule for connections from these users** and click **Add** to display the Select Users or Groups dialog box and specify the desired users. The latter option is useful if you want to prevent access by a specific user while allowing access by other users of the group to which the first user belongs.

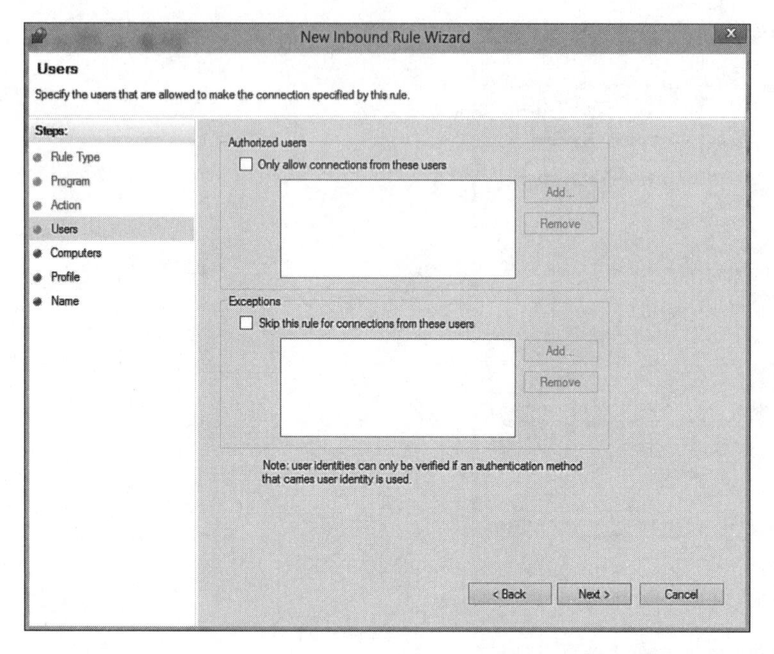

Figure 10-11 Specifying the users that are allowed to create the connection specified by the rule.

Step 8. Click **Next** to display the Computers page. Options on this page are similar to those for users in Figure 10-11, and enable you to limit the computers that are allowed to use the rule you're creating.

Step 9. Click **Next** to display the Profile page. On this page, select the profiles (**Domain**, **Private**, and **Public**) to which the rule is to be applied. Then click **Next**.

Step 10. On the Name page, specify a name and optional description for your new rule. Click **Finish** to create the rule, which will then appear in the details pane of the Windows Firewall with Advanced Security snap-in.

Configuring New Connection Security Rules

Creating a new connection security rule is similar to that for inbound or outbound rules, but the options are slightly different. From the Windows Firewall with Advanced Security snap-in previously shown in Figure 10-5, right-click **Connection Security Rules** and choose **New Rule** to display the New Connection Security Rule Wizard, as shown in Figure 10-12. Connection security rules manage authentication of two machines on the network and the encryption of network traffic sent between them using IPSec. Security is also achieved with the use of key exchange and data integrity checks. As shown in Figure 10-12, you can create the following types of connection security rules:

- **Isolation:** Enables you to limit connections according to authentication criteria that you define. For example, you can use this rule to isolate domain-based computers from external computers such as those located across the Internet. You can request or require authentication and specify the authentication method that must be used.
- **Authentication exemption:** Enables specified computers, such as DHCP and DNS servers, to be exempted from the need for authentication. You can specify computers by IP address ranges or subnets, or you can include a predefined set of computers.
- **Server-to-server:** Enables you to create a secured connection between computers in two endpoints that are defined according to IP address ranges.
- **Tunnel:** Enables you to secure communications between two computers by means of IPSec tunnel mode. This encapsulates network packets that are routed between the tunnel endpoints. You can choose from several types of tunnels; you can also exempt IPSec-protected computers from the defined tunnel.
- **Custom:** Enables you to create a rule that requires special settings not covered explicitly in the other options. All wizard pages except those used to create only tunnel rules are available.

Key Topic

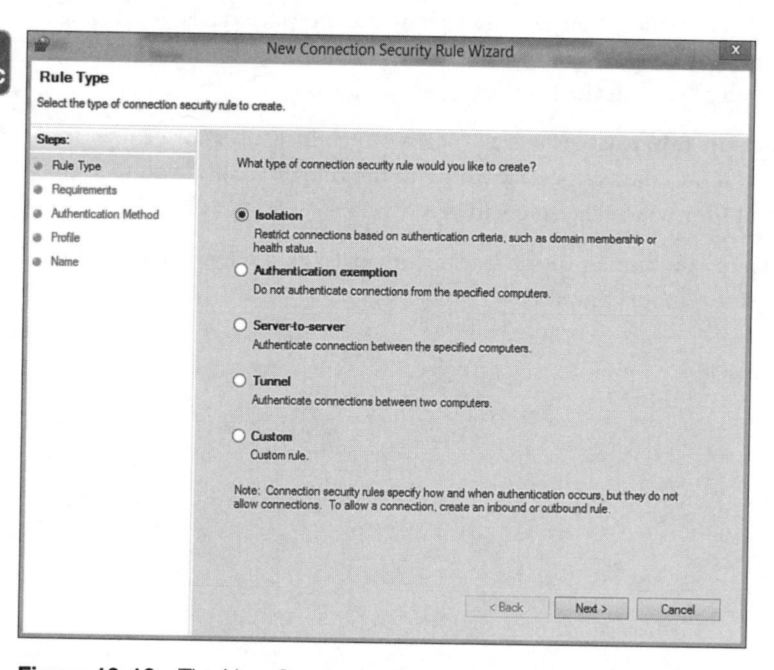

Figure 10-12 The New Connection Security Rule Wizard enables you to create five types of connection security rules.

Modifying Rule Properties

You can modify any Windows Firewall rule from its Properties dialog box, accessed by right-clicking the rule in the details pane of the Windows Firewall with Advanced Security snap-in and choosing **Properties**. From the dialog box shown in Figure 10-13, you can configure the following properties:

- **General tab:** Enables you to edit the name and description of the rule or change the action.
- **Programs and Services tab:** Enables you to define which programs and services are affected by the rule.
- **Remote Computers tab:** Enables you to specify which computers are authorized to allow connections according to the rule or enables you to specify computers for which the rule will be skipped.
- **Protocols and Ports tab:** Enables you to specify the protocol type and the local and remote ports covered by the rule.
- **Scope tab:** Enables you to specify the local and remote IP addresses of connections covered by the rule. You can specify Any Address or select a subnet or IP address range.
- **Advanced tab:** Enables you to specify the profiles (domain, private, or public) to which the rule applies. You can also specify the interface types (local area network, remote access, and/or wireless) and whether edge traversal (traffic routed through a NAT device) is allowed or blocked.
- **Local Principals tab:** Enables you to specify which local users or groups are authorized to allow connections according to the rule or enables you to specify users or groups for which the rule will be skipped.
- **Remote Users tab:** Similar to the Local Principals tab, except works with users or groups at remote computers.

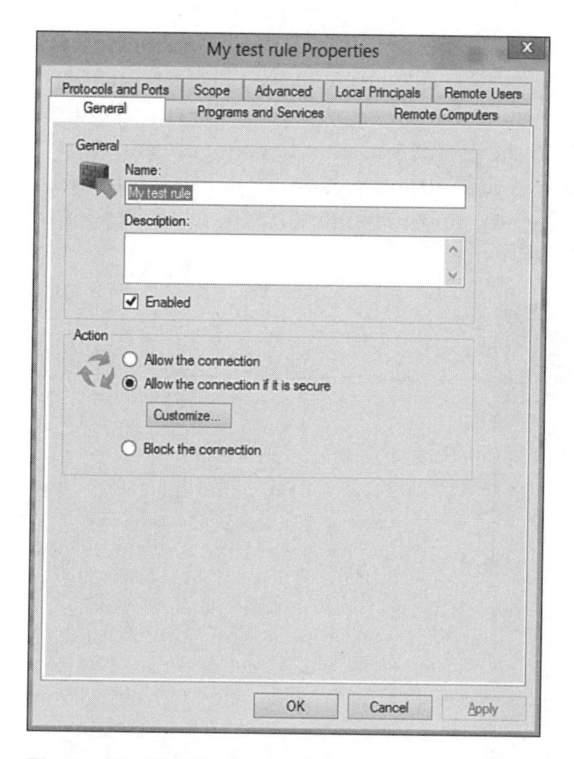

Figure 10-13 The Properties dialog box for a firewall rule enables you to modify rules criteria for rules you have created or default rules supplied in Windows Firewall with Advanced Security.

NOTE For additional information on all aspects of using the Windows Firewall with Advanced Security snap-in, refer to "Windows Firewall with Advanced Security" at http://msdn.microsoft.com/en-us/library/windows/desktop/ff956124%28v=vs.85%29.aspx, "Windows Firewall with Advanced Security Overview" at http://technet.microsoft.com/en-us/library/hh831365.aspx, and "What's New in Windows Firewall with Advanced Security" at http://technet.microsoft.com/en-us/library/cc755158(WS.10).aspx.

Configuring Notifications

You can configure Windows Firewall with Advanced Security to display notifications when a program is blocked from receiving inbound connections according to the default behavior of Windows Firewall. When you have selected this option and no existing block or allow rule applies to this program, a user is notified when a program is blocked from receiving inbound connections.

To configure this option, right-click **Windows Firewall with Advanced Security** at the top of the left pane in the Windows Firewall with Advanced Security snap-in and then choose **Properties**. This opens the dialog box previously shown in Figure 10-6. Select the tab that corresponds to the profile you want to configure and then click the **Customize** command button in the Settings section. From the Customize Settings for the (selected) Profile dialog box shown in Figure 10-14, select **Yes** for Display a notification and then click **OK** twice.

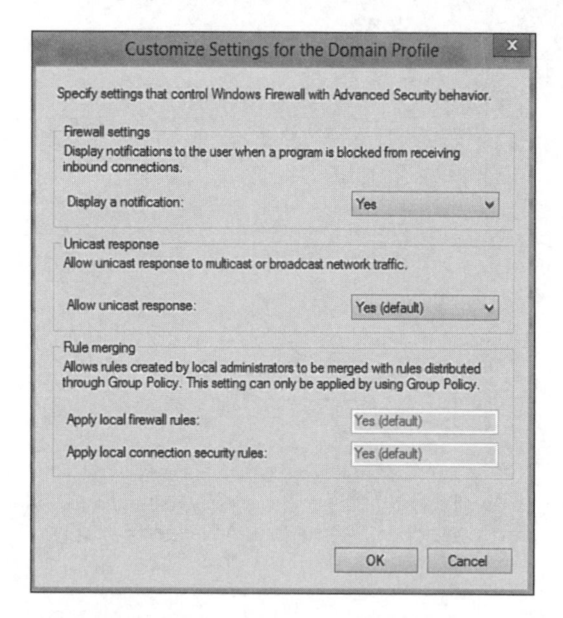

Figure 10-14 Configuring Windows Firewall to display notifications.

Group Policy and Windows Firewall

Group Policy in Windows Firewall enables you to configure similar policies to those configured with the Windows Firewall with Advanced Security snap-in. Use the following procedure to configure Group Policy for Windows Firewall:

Step 1. From the Search charm, type `gpedit.msc`, and then click **gpedit.msc** in the Programs list. If you receive a UAC prompt, click **Continue**.

Step 2. Navigate to the **Computer Configuration\Windows Settings\Security Settings\Windows Firewall with Advanced Security\Windows Firewall with Advanced Security – Local Group Policy Object** node. The right pane displays the Windows Firewall with Advanced Security settings, as shown in Figure 10-15.

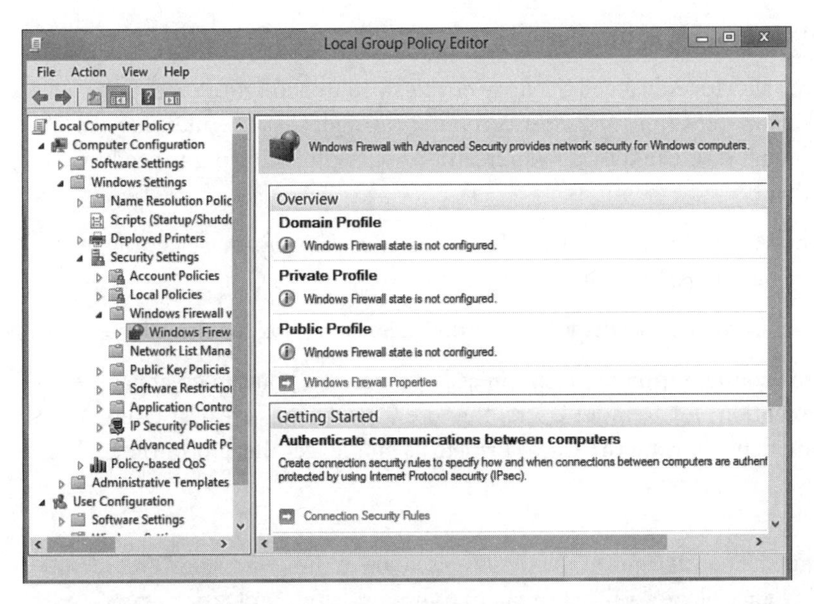

Figure 10-15 You can use Group Policy to configure Windows Firewall with Advanced Security options.

Step 3. Scroll the details pane to select links for inbound rules, outbound rules, and connection security rules. These links open subnodes in the console tree.

Step 4. Unlike the Group Policy with Windows Firewall snap-in, no default rules are present. To add rules, right-click in the details pane and select **New Rule**. This starts the New Rule Wizard, which enables you to create rules using the same options already discussed in this section.

After you add firewall rules in Group Policy, you can filter the view according to profile (domain, private, or public) or by state (enabled or disabled).

TIP A Group Policy feature first introduced in Windows Vista and continued in Windows 7, 8, and 8.1 enables you to configure common policy settings for all user accounts on a computer used by more than one user. This includes Windows Firewall, as discussed here, as well as UAC and all other policy settings. In addition, you can configure separate policies for administrators or nonadministrators. If necessary, you can even configure local group policies on a per-user basis.

Configuring Authenticated Exceptions

Windows Firewall with Advanced Security enables you to configure exceptions for users and computers accessing your computer through firewall rules that are included by default or created by an administrator. Use the following procedure to configure authenticated exceptions:

Step 1. From the Windows Firewall with Advanced Security snap-in, select the inbound or outbound rule you want to configure.

Step 2. Double-click the rule to display the Properties dialog box for the selected rule.

Step 3. Select the configuration tab from the rule properties. You can create authenticated exceptions for Remote Users, Remote Computers, or Local Users. Local Users are defined using the Local Principals tab. Select the appropriate tab.

NOTE You cannot set an exception for remote users on an inbound rule. The reason for this should be fairly obvious: Because the outbound rules are only for network connections initiated on the local computer, a remote user would never apply. You can set exceptions for a remote computer because a local user might initiate a connection to that remote computer. Inbound rules do not have a Remote Users tab on their properties dialog box.

Step 4. To create an exception for a remote computer or remote user account, set the Action for the rule to **Allow the connection if it is secure**. Windows enforces this restriction so that a rule does not request authentication credentials if they would be transferred over an unsecure network connection. If you attempt to do so, you encounter an error such as the one displayed in Figure 10-16.

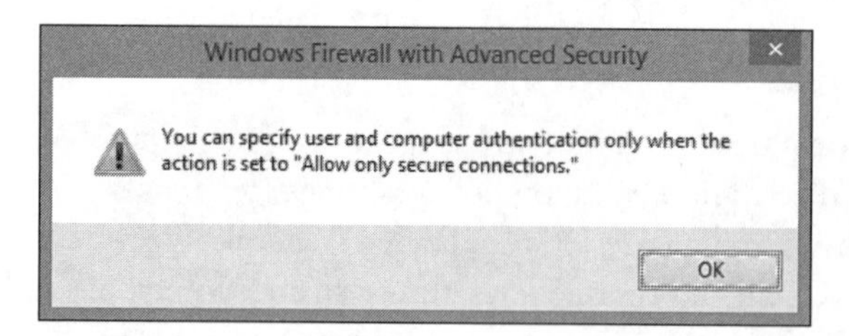

Figure 10-16 Windows does not allow authentication exceptions for a rule over an unsecure connection.

Step 5. For authenticated users, select the check box labeled **Only allow connections from these users**. After the box is checked, the Add button is enabled. The tab for Remote Computers is similar, but the check box refers to computers instead of users.

Step 6. Click the **Add** button and specify the user or group accounts in the Select Users or Groups dialog box. When you are finished selecting user and group objects, click **OK** to add them to the Authorized users list, as shown in Figure 10-17. If you are working with the Remote Computers tab, the process is the same, but you can select only from **Groups** and **Built-in security principals**.

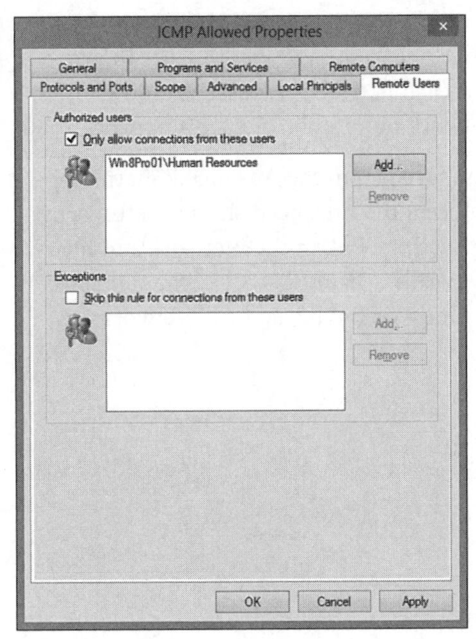

Figure 10-17 Selecting authenticated users allowed to use a network connection.

Step 7. The Exceptions section is used to exclude any Authorized users or computers that may be selected from a group. For example, if you include the group Human Resources in the Authorized users list, all members of the group are allowed to use the connection. However, you might want to exclude the Human Resources receptionist, who is also a member of the group. In this case, you would check the **Skip this rule for connections from these users** box and add the receptionist to the Exceptions list.

Configuring Network Discovery

Network Discovery was introduced in Windows Vista to improve the security of the operating system by enabling better control over how Windows computers communicate and find each other over a network. Network Discovery is enabled by default on Windows 8.1 when it is connected to a private network, and turned off when it detects that it is connected to a public or unidentified network. You can configure settings for each network profile that is created.

Windows Vista and Windows 7 included three types of network profiles called Public, Home, and Work. This naming system was a little confusing for users because the Home and Work profiles essentially worked the same. Network Discovery was enabled for both and turned off for the Public network. Windows 8.1 has improved the profiles by creating a separate profile for each network you use. Windows 8.1 now describes your network as a Private network or a Public or Guest network.

In Windows 8.1, Network Discovery is configured from the Advanced Sharing options of the Network and Sharing Center. Access the Advanced sharing settings by clicking on the **Change advanced sharing settings** link in the Network and Sharing Center, as illustrated in Figure 8-14. Typically a Windows 8.1 computer starts with three network profiles, called Private, Guest or Public, and All Networks, as shown in Figure 10-18.

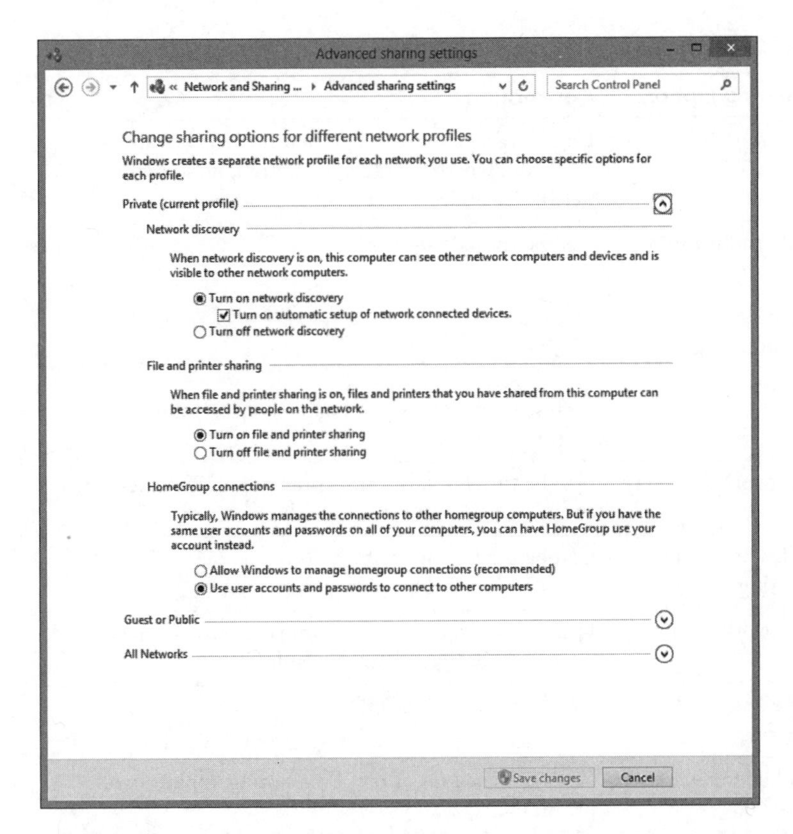

Figure 10-18 Typical network profiles in the Advanced sharing settings dialog box.

If you join the Windows 8.1 computer to an Active Directory domain, a Domain profile is added, as shown in Figure 10-19. The configuration options differ slightly for each profile type created by Windows. The individual options were covered in Chapter 8. Table 10-3 lists the options that are available for each type of network profile.

Table 10-3 Network Discovery and Sharing Options for Windows 8.1 Network Profiles

Network Profile	Sharing Option	Description
Private	Network discovery	Can be turned on or off. When turned on, can also configure whether to turn on automatic setup of network-connected devices.
Private	File and printer sharing	Can be turned on or off.
Private	Homegroup connections	Options: Allow Windows to manage homegroup connections Use user accounts and passwords to connect to other computers.
Guest or Public	Network discovery	Can be turned on or off. Automatic setup of network-connected devices is not available.
Guest or Public	File and printer sharing	Can be turned on or off.
Domain	Network discovery	Can be turned on or off. Automatic setup of network-connected devices is not available.
Domain	File and printer sharing	Can be turned on or off.
All Networks	Public folder sharing	Can be turned on or off. This setting applies to all profiles.
All Networks	Media streaming	Media streaming options available for music, pictures, and videos. This setting applies to all profiles.
All Networks	File sharing connections	Select between strong (128-bit) encryption and weaker (40- or 56-bit) encryption. Strong encryption is recommended but may not work for some devices or older computers. This setting applies to all profiles.
All Networks	Password-protected sharing	Can be turned on or off. This setting applies to all profiles. Not available on Domain-joined computers. If the computer is joined to a Domain, password-protected sharing is always enabled.

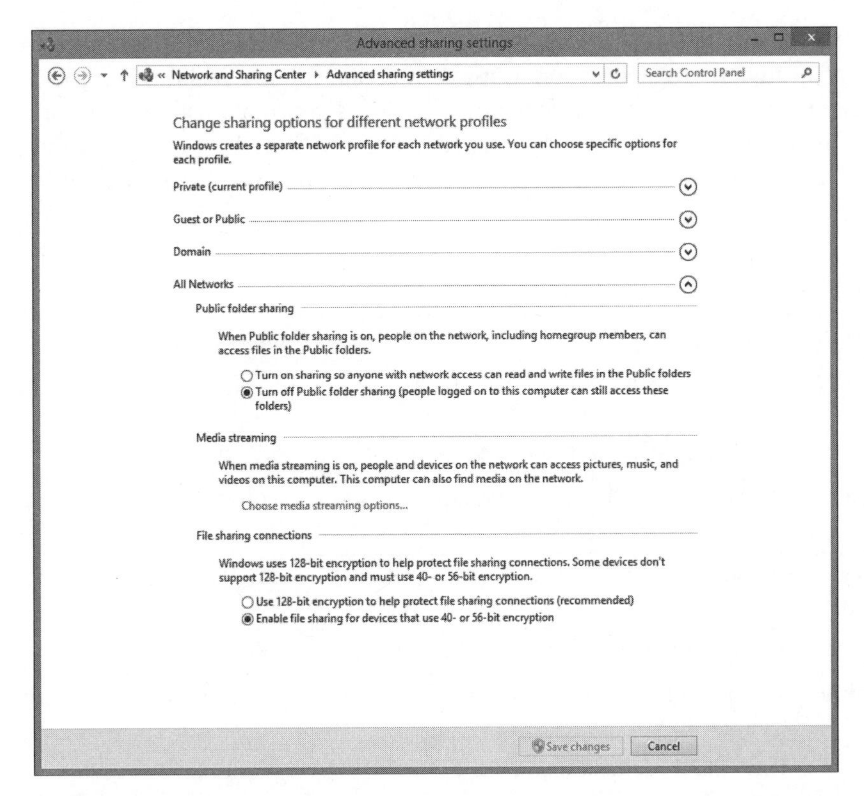

Figure 10-19 All networks settings available on a domain-joined Windows 8.1 computer.

Managing Wireless Security

Wireless connectivity creates a tempting attack vector for criminals looking for access to valuable private information. Wireless networks are ubiquitous today, and corporations are rolling out wireless infrastructure in their offices to provide convenience for employees and to save costs. It is important to ensure not only that the information moving through the network is secure, but also that unauthorized outside entities stay off your network and cannot access any resources for their own purposes.

Windows 8.1 supports the complete range of wireless security protocols, supported in Windows 7, from Wired Equivalent Privacy (WEP) to Wi-Fi Protected Access (WPA and WPA2), Protected Extensible Authentication Protocol (PEAP), and its combination with Microsoft Challenge Handshake Authentication Protocol version 2 (MS-CHAP v2) and Extensible Authentication Protocol Transport Layer Security (EAP-TLS).

Windows 8.1 will use WPA2-Personal for maximum security when communicating by means of an ad hoc wireless network (direct communication with another wireless computer without use of an access point). This helps to protect against common vulnerabilities associated with such unprotected networks. Table 10-4 lists the types of wireless security available in Windows 8.1 and the encryption (of each) that can be used.

Table 10-4 Wireless Security Types in Windows 8.1

Security Type	Description	Available Encryption
Open (anonymous connections)	Open network without authentication or encryption	None
WEP	Open network using Wireless Equivalent Privacy	WEP
WPA-Personal	Wi-Fi Protected Access (WPA) using a preshared key or password	TKIP or AES
WPA2-Personal	Version 2 of WPA using a preshared key or password	TKIP or AES
WPA-Enterprise	WPA using IEEE 802.1x authentication	TKIP or AES
WPA2-Enterprise	Version 2 of WPA using IEEE 802.1x authentication	TKIP or AES
802.1x	IEEE 802.1x authentication using WEP	WEP

NOTE WPA2-Enterprise security provides the highest level of wireless networking authentication security. It requires authentication in two phases: first, an open system authentication and, second, authentication using EAP. It is suitable for domain-based authentication and on networks using a Remote Authentication Dial-In User Service (RADIUS) authentication server. In environments without the RADIUS server, you should use WPA2-Personal security

The WPA and WPA2 protocols can use either TKIP or AES for encryption. These are strong encryption protocols, and AES is considered especially secure. WPA2 still supports TKIP but uses AES by default instead of TKIP.

WARNING Microsoft, and most network security professionals, recommend against using WEP. Because of the limitations of WEP's encryption, a hacker can capture enough frames in a fairly short amount of time to determine the shared keys or shared secret key used between access point and stations, and decrypt the packets. WPA and WPA2 are more secure and not as vulnerable to sniffing and intrusion.

TIP On the 70-687 exam, you might be asked to choose between the four available types of WPA wireless security. You should select **WPA** (either Personal or Enterprise) to use TKIP encryption by default or **WPA2** (either Personal or Enterprise) to use AES encryption by default. In addition, if you are required to type a security key or passphrase, you should select one of the Personal options. If you are not required to type a security key or passphrase, you should select one of the Enterprise options.

When Windows 8.1 connects to a new wireless network, it prompts you to decide whether or not you want to turn on sharing for that network. Selecting **No, don't turn on sharing or connect to devices** tells Windows 8.1 to configure the connection as a Public network. As covered in the previous section, Network discovery is disabled by default on Public networks, so your computer will not advertise its presence to other computers on the network.

You can examine the connection properties, including the security and encryption types, for any wireless network your computer is connected to. To do so, right-click the **Start** button and select **Network Connections**. When the window is displayed, right-click the wireless network connection, select **Status**, and then click **Wireless Properties**. Select the **Security** tab to view the security settings.

The result is similar to Figure 10-20. If you know the security types available on the network, you can change the current setting from the **Security type** drop-down. Similarly, if you want to select a different encryption type, choose from the options available in the **Encryption type** drop-down. When you click **OK**, Windows temporarily disconnects from the access point and attempts to reconnect using the settings you selected.

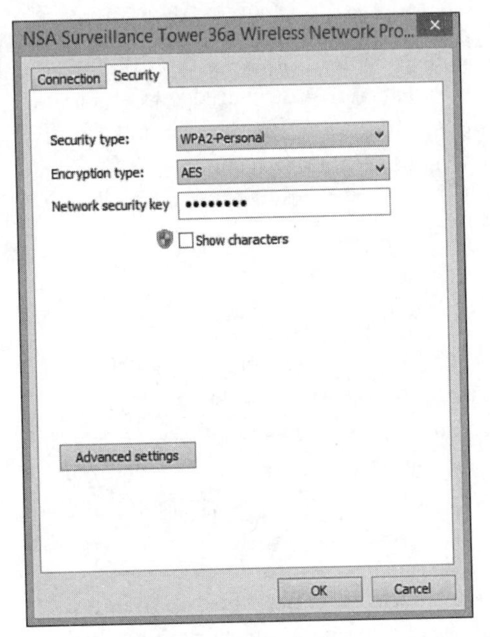

Figure 10-20 Configuring security settings for a wireless network connection.

Exam Preparation Tasks

Review All the Key Topics

Review the most important topics in the chapter, noted with the key topics icon in the outer margin of the page. Table 10-5 lists a reference of these key topics and the page numbers on which each is found.

Table 10-5 Key Topics for Chapter 10

Key Topic Element	Description	Page Number
Step List	Shows how to perform basic Windows Firewall configuration	412
Figure 10-2	Shows how to customize Windows Firewall settings for each network type	412
Figure 10-3	Shows how to allow apps to communicate through Windows Firewall	413
List	Describes available Windows Firewall with Advanced Security rule types	417
List	Describes types of available Windows Firewall with Advanced Security profiles	418
Figure 10-8	Shows how to create new firewall rules of different types	421
Figure 10-12	Shows different types of firewall connection security rules	425
Step List	Shows how to configure authenticated exceptions	430
Figure 10-17	Shows how to select authenticated users allowed to use a network connection	431
Table 10-3	Describes network discovery settings and sharing options for Windows 8.1 network profiles	434
Table 10-4	Provides wireless security types	436
Figure 10-20	Shows how to configure security settings for a wireless network connection	438

Complete the Tables and Lists from Memory

Print a copy of Appendix B, "Memory Tables," (found on the CD), or at least the section for this chapter, and complete the tables and lists from memory. Appendix C, "Memory Tables Answer Key," also on the CD, includes completed tables and lists to check your work.

Definitions of Key Terms

Define the following key terms from this chapter, and check your answers in the Glossary:

AES, Authenticated exceptions, Firewall profile, Firewall rule, Internet Protocol Security (IPSec), Network discovery, TKIP, WEP, WPA, WPA-2, Windows Firewall, Windows Firewall with Advanced Security

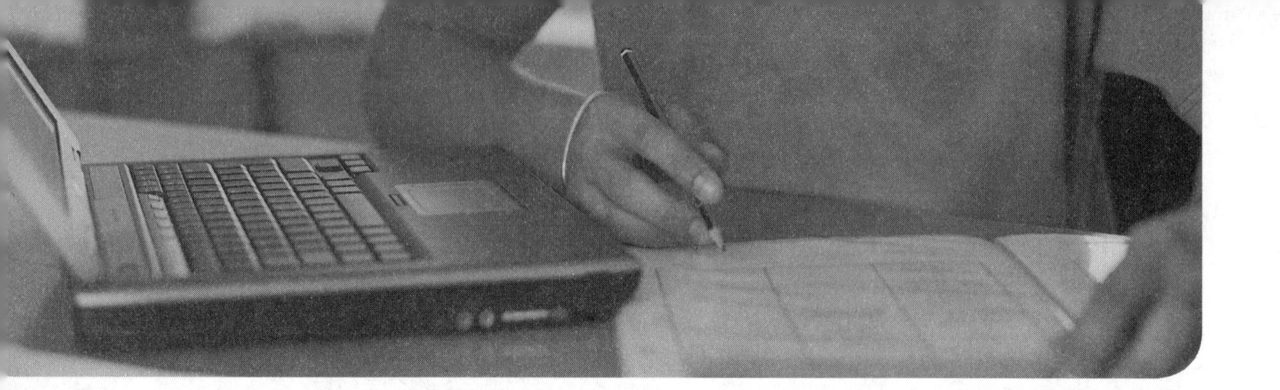

This chapter covers the following subjects:

- **Configuring Shared Folder Permissions:** Windows 8.1 provides two ways of sharing resources such as folders and printers on your computer so that users on other computers can access them. This section shows you how to configure your computer to share the public folder and how to set up a standard set of permissions and enable the sharing of individual folders and printers.
- **Configuring NTFS Permissions:** Windows 8.1 enables you to secure files and folders on your computer so that you can determine who can access them and what level of access they are granted or denied. This section shows you how to configure these permissions and how they interact with shared folder permissions.
- **Configuring Data Encryption:** Windows 8.1 provides the Encrypting File System (EFS), which provides an additional layer of protection for sensitive data. This section shows you how to use EFS and explains the need for backing up encryption keys and using data recovery agents to ensure that encrypted data can always be decrypted if users move or lose their encryption certificates and keys.
- **Configuring File Libraries:** Windows 8.1 provides four default file libraries, which act as pointers to user-specific and shared folders for documents, pictures, music, and videos. This section shows you how to configure these libraries and add or remove folders from them.
- **Configuring Shared Printers:** You can share printers so that users at other computers on the network can print to a printer on your computer. This section shows how you can control access to your printer.
- **Configuring OneDrive (formerly SkyDrive):** OneDrive provides cloud storage for Windows systems, enabling sharing across devices, with other users, and synchronized on-demand file storage.
- **Configuring Near Field Communication:** Near Field Communication (NFC) enables proximity-enabled devices and apps to share data within a small area. Also called "Tap and Go," NFC is used for sharing on an ad hoc basis or connecting NFC-enabled devices.
- **Configuring Object Access Auditing:** Auditing lets you record actions that take place on your computer, including attempts to access files, folders, and printers. This section shows you how to use Group Policy to set up a policy that effectively tracks these types of activities.

CHAPTER 11

Configuring and Securing Access to Files and Folders

One of the major reasons for connecting computers in a network is to share resources such as folders, files, and printers among them. Resources can exist on computers that are not connected to a network; and these resources may need to be secured, protected, and accessed by different users as well. Windows 8.1 comes with a host of tools designed to secure and manage resources wherever they may be found. Nowadays, resources can even exist remotely on the cloud; Windows 8.1 introduces the OneDrive feature (initially called SkyDrive) that enables you to share images, documents, and so on among computers, smartphones, and other devices in different physical locations. Microsoft expects you to be knowledgeable about all these new features when taking the 70-687 exam.

In a modern workplace, workers require access to information created by others in the company, and work they produce must be made available to their coworkers and superiors. Therefore, such resources must be shared so that others can access them. But lots of confidential information is also out there, and it must be protected from access by those who are not entitled to view it. At home, family members need to share things such as photos, videos, and music. But parents have sensitive information, such as family finances, that must be protected as well.

From the earliest version of Windows NT right up to the present, Windows has had a system of access permissions in place that determine who has access to what and what can they do to it. More recent versions of Windows have enabled users to protect data even further with encryption methods that can help to prevent those who might have circumvented other access controls from viewing or modifying confidential information. Included also is a system of auditing access attempts to files and folders so that individuals in charge of security are able to track all types of access on the network and take appropriate measures to protect sensitive information. This chapter looks at these and other methods of sharing and protecting resources on computers and their networks.

"Do I Know This Already?" Quiz

The "Do I Know This Already?" quiz allows you to assess whether you should read this entire chapter or simply jump to the "Exam Preparation Tasks" section for review. If you are in doubt, read the entire chapter. Table 11-1 outlines the major headings in this chapter and the corresponding "Do I Know This Already?" quiz questions. You can find the answers in Appendix A, "Answers to the 'Do I Know This Already?' Quizzes."

Table 11-1 "Do I Know This Already?" Foundation Topics Section-to-Question Mapping

Foundations Topics Section	Questions Covered in This Section
Configuring Shared Folder Permissions	1–4
Configuring NTFS Permissions	5–10
Configuring Data Encryption	11–12
Configuring File Libraries	13
Configuring Shared Printers	14
Configuring OneDrive (formerly SkyDrive)	15–16
Configuring Near Field Communication	17
Configuring Disk Quotas	18
Configuring Object Access Auditing	19

1. You want users at other computers on your network to be able to access folders located in the libraries of your Windows 8.1 computer without the need to perform additional sharing tasks, so you open the Advanced sharing settings dialog box. Which option should you enable?
   a. File and printer sharing
   b. Public folder sharing
   c. Password-protected sharing
   d. Media streaming

2. Which of the following are true about hidden administrative shares? (Choose three.)
   a. These shares are suffixed with the $ symbol and are visible in any Explorer window.
   b. These shares are suffixed with the $ symbol and are visible only in the Shares node of the Computer Management snap-in.

c. These shares are suffixed with the $ symbol and can be accessed from the Network and Sharing Center.

d. You can access these shares by entering the UNC path to the share in the Run command.

e. These shares are created by default when Windows 8.1 is first installed and cannot be removed.

3. Which of the following are valid permissions you can set for shared folders? (Choose three.)

   a. Full Control

   b. Modify

   c. Change

   d. Read & Execute

   e. Read

4. You attempt to join your Windows 8.1 Pro computer to a homegroup, but the option for joining the homegroup is not available. Which of the following is a valid reason for the inability to join a homegroup?

   a. Your computer is joined to an Active Directory Domain Services (AD DS) domain.

   b. Your computer should be running the basic (home) version of Windows 8.1.

   c. The homegroup you want to join has no password configured.

   d. Your network location is set to Public.

5. You have granted a user named Bob the Read NTFS permission on a folder named Documents. Bob is also a member of the Managers group, which has Full Control NTFS permission on the Documents folder. What is Bob's effective permission on this folder?

   a. Full Control

   b. Modify

   c. Read

   d. Bob does not have access to the folder.

6. You have granted a user named Jim the Read NTFS permission on a folder named Documents. Jim is also a member of the Interns group, which has been explicitly denied the Full Control NTFS permission on the Documents folder. What is Jim's effective permission on this folder?
   a. Full Control
   b. Modify
   c. Read
   d. Jim does not have access to the folder.

7. You have granted a user named Carol the Full Control NTFS permission on a shared folder named Documents on your Windows 8.1 computer, which also has the Read shared folder permission granted to Everyone. Carol will be accessing this folder across the network on her computer. What is Carol's effective permission on this folder?
   a. Full Control
   b. Modify
   c. Read
   d. Carol does not have access to the folder.

8. You have granted a user named Sharon the Full Control NTFS permission on a shared folder named Documents on your Windows 8.1 computer, which also has the Read shared folder permission granted to Everyone. Sharon will be accessing this folder on your computer. What is Sharon's effective permission on this folder?
   a. Full Control
   b. Modify
   c. Read
   d. Sharon does not have access to the folder.

9. You have granted the Managers group Full Control NTFS permission on a folder named Accounts, which is located within the `C:\Documents` folder, which has the Modify NTFS permission applied to it. You copy the Accounts folder into the `D:\Confidential` folder, to which the Managers group has been granted the Read permission. A user named Ryan accesses the `D:\Confidential\Accounts` folder. What effective permission does Ryan have to this folder?

a. Full Control
b. Modify
c. Read
d. Ryan does not have access to the folder.

10. You have granted the Managers group Full Control NTFS permission on the `C:\Documents\Projects.doc` file. You move this file to the `C:\Confidential` folder, to which the Managers group has been granted the Read permission. A user named Jennifer, who is a member of the Managers group, accesses the `C:\Confidential\Projects.doc` file. What effective permission does Jennifer have to this file?
    a. Full Control
    b. Modify
    c. Read
    d. Jennifer does not have access to the folder.

11. You want to encrypt the Confidential folder. This folder is located on the `D:\` volume, which is formatted with the FAT32 file system. You access the folder's Properties dialog box and click the **Advanced** button. But the option to encrypt the folder is not available. What do you need to do to encrypt this folder? (Each correct answer presents a complete solution to the problem. Choose two.)
    a. Format the `D:\` volume with the NTFS file system.
    b. Use the `Convert.exe` utility to convert the `D:\` volume with the NTFS file system.
    c. Move the Confidential folder to the `C:\` volume, which is formatted with the NTFS file system.
    d. Decompress the Confidential folder.

12. You are the desktop support specialist for your company. A user named Peter has left the company, and you have deleted his user account. Later you realize that he had encrypted his Work folder on his Windows 8.1 computer, and you must regain access to this folder. What should you do?
    a. Log on to Peter's computer with your user account and decrypt the file.
    b. Log on to Peter's computer with the default administrator account and decrypt the file.
    c. Re-create Peter's user account, log on with this account, and decrypt the file.
    d. You cannot access this folder; it is permanently lost.

13. Which of the following is not true about file libraries in Windows 8.1?

  a. Libraries are virtual folders that are actually pointers to the Documents, Pictures, Music, and Videos folder locations on the computer.

  b. Each library consists of a user-specific folder and a public folder.

  c. You can add additional folders to any library at any time in Windows 8.1.

  d. You are limited to the four default libraries; it is not possible to designate additional libraries in Windows 8.1.

14. You have shared your printer so that others can access it on the network. You want Kristin, who works at another computer on the network, to be able to pause, resume, restart, and cancel all documents, but you do not want her to be able to modify printer properties or permissions. What printer permission should you grant her user account?

  a. Print

  b. Manage This Printer

  c. Manage Documents

  d. Full Control

15. You have a folder connected to your OneDrive storage on your Windows 8.1 PC but would like to use a new corporate OneDrive account with more storage. How can you change your OneDrive folder?

  a. Go to OneDrive.com and configure the account to use a different computer and folder name.

  b. Open Control Panel, find the OneDrive applet, and change the credentials in OneDrive settings.

  c. Add the corporate account to the computer and log on to the system with the new corporate account.

  d. Open PC Settings, access the OneDrive settings, and change the OneDrive account credentials under Sync settings.

16. You are using a Windows 8.1 PC and have a number of files on your OneDrive storage that you want to keep in sync on your local computer automatically. What would you use to enable this feature?

  a. Configure the OneDrive Windows app to copy the files.

  b. Open the OneDrive app, select the folders and files you want to keep in sync, and select the **Make offline** app command to make the files available offline.

c. Log into OneDrive.com and select the computer and synchronization settings you want to use.

d. Use the OneDrive mobile app to copy your files.

17. Management at your company has learned that some sensitive information was leaked from the network shares by mobile phone using NFC-based Tap and Go with an employee's laptop while it was connected to the corporate VPN at a coffee shop. The management staff absolutely want to prevent any further breaches of this kind but without interfering with the mobile workers' ability to access files from the VPN. How would you lock down the Windows 8.1 workstations to prevent this type of breach?

    a. Disable Wi-Fi on all the Windows 8.1 laptops.

    b. Enable encryption on all the Windows 8.1 laptops.

    c. Create a new firewall rule to prevent any Windows app from communicating with any network interfaces.

    d. Disable the Windows Firewall rule for Proximity sharing.

18. Your company has hired several college students for the summer as interns. They will be storing files on the `D:` drive of a Windows 8.1 computer. You have created user accounts for each student and added these accounts to a group named Interns. You want to ensure that these students do not store a large amount of data on the `D:` drive, so you decide to limit each user to 500 MB space on the `D:` drive. What should you do? (Each correct answer presents part of the solution. Choose two.)

    a. Ensure that the `D:\` drive is formatted with the NTFS file system.

    b. Ensure that the `D:\` drive is formatted with the FAT32 file system.

    c. In the Add New Quota Entry dialog box, select the **Do not limit disk usage** option and specify the 500 MB limit and the Interns group.

    d. In the Add New Quota Entry dialog box, select the **Limit disk space to** option and specify the 500 MB limit and the Interns group.

    e. In the Add New Quota Entry dialog box, create a separate disk quota for each user in the Interns group that specifies the **Do not limit disk usage** option and the 500 MB limit.

    f. In the Add New Quota Entry dialog box, create a separate disk quota for each user in the Interns group that specifies the **Limit disk space to** option and the 500 MB limit.

19. You are responsible for maintaining data security on a Windows 8.1 Pro computer used by your boss. He has stored a large number of documents containing sensitive corporate information that only a limited number of individuals are permitted to access. He would like to know when others attempt to access this information. To this extent, you have enabled object access auditing on his computer.

A couple of weeks later, your boss informs you that he has noticed a couple of files have been altered in an inappropriate fashion. He has checked the Security log on his computer, but no information is available to suggest who is accessing these files, so he asks you to rectify this problem. What should you do?

  a. You also need to enable auditing of logon events in the Local Security Policy snap-in on your boss's computer.

  b. You also need to access File Explorer on your boss's computer. From this location, ensure that the appropriate auditing entries have been enabled for the folder in which the sensitive documents are located.

  c. You need to ask your boss to check events recorded in the System log of his computer.

  d. You should move the folder containing the sensitive documents to a server located in a secured room and on which auditing has been enabled.

Foundation Topics

Configuring Shared Folder Permissions

Sharing is a basic concept of networking in any computer environment. Simply put, sharing means making resources available on a network. Typically, this means a folder on one computer is made accessible to other computers that are connected to the first computer by a network. The purpose of sharing folders is to give users access to network applications, data, and user home folders in one central location. You can use network application folders for configuring and upgrading software. This serves to centralize administration because applications are not maintained on client computers. Data folders allow users to store and access common files, and user home folders provide a place for users to store their own personal information. You can also share other resources such as printers so that users can print to a printer not directly attached to their computer.

You can share folders according to either or both of two file-sharing models:

- **Public Folder Sharing:** The simplest means of sharing folders, this model involves the use of a shared folder located within each of the Windows libraries. However, you cannot limit access to items in these public folders; you can only enable or disable public folder sharing for all libraries from the Advanced Sharing Settings dialog box in the Network and Sharing Center, previously introduced in Chapter 8, "Configuring TCP/IP Settings."
- **Standard Folder Sharing:** This model enables you to utilize a standard set of permissions that determine user access to files and folders across the network, in a similar fashion to that used in previous Windows versions. Because it is more secure than public folder sharing, you can enable or disable standard folder sharing on a per-computer basis.

Using the Network and Sharing Center to Configure File Sharing

As introduced in Chapter 8, the Network and Sharing Center enables you to perform actions related to sharing of resources on your computer with others on the network. Click **Change advanced sharing settings** to open the Advanced sharing settings dialog box shown in Figure 11-1. Among other networking options, you can specify the following file-sharing options:

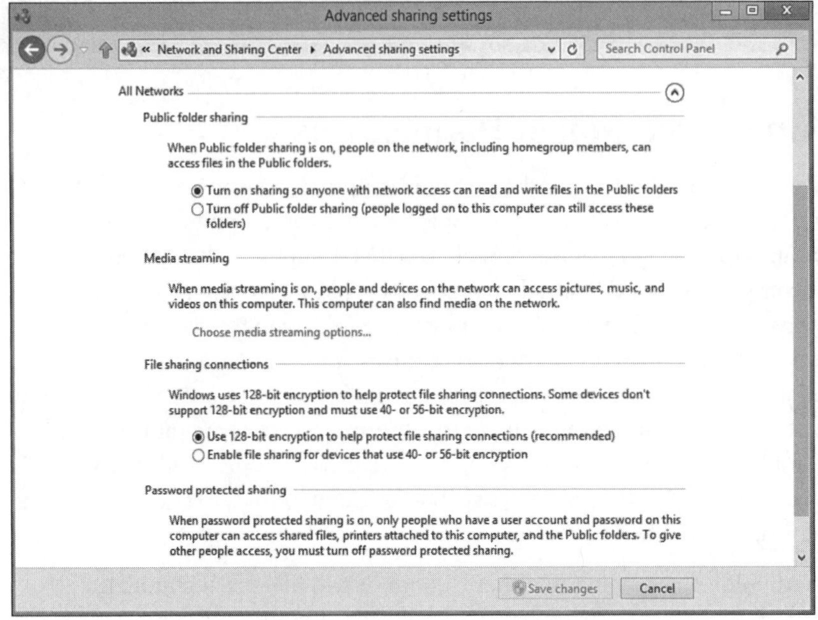

Figure 11-1 The Advanced sharing settings dialog box enables you to configure several global file and folder sharing settings.

- **Public folder sharing:** Enables the Public Folder sharing model, thereby allowing others on the network to access files in your Public folders of each Windows library (Documents, Pictures, Videos, and Music).
- **Media streaming:** Enables others on the network to access shared music, pictures, and videos on the computer and enables your computer to access these types of shared information on the network.
- **File sharing connections:** Enables you to select the level of encryption used to protect file-sharing connections. You should keep the default of 128-bit encryption selected unless you need to share files with devices that understand a lower level of encryption only.
- **Password protected sharing:** Increases security by limiting access of shared files and printers to only those who have a user account and password on your computer.

Sharing Files, Folders, and Printers

Shared folders are folders on the local hard drive that other users on a network can connect to. For the exam, it is critical that you understand how to manage and troubleshoot connections to shared resources, how to create new shared resources, and how to set permissions on shared resources. The process that Windows 8.1 uses to share folders is that an administrator selects a folder, regardless of its location in the local folder hierarchy, and shares it through the Sharing tab of the folder's Properties dialog box.

Administrators may find that the Computer Management snap-in is helpful in file and folder security management. To open this snap-in in Windows 8.1, right-click **Start** and choose **Computer Management** from the menu that appears. You can also open Computer Management from within Administrative Tools, which is found in the System and Security category of Control Panel. If you have enabled the Administrative Tools feature on the Start screen, simply click the tile for **Computer Management** from this location. To manage file and folder security, expand the Shared Folders node in the left pane. Select the **Shares** subnode to see the shared folders, as shown in Figure 11-2. The hidden administrative shares are followed by a dollar sign ($) and cannot be modified. From the remaining shared folders, select one to double-click and view the security settings on the folder.

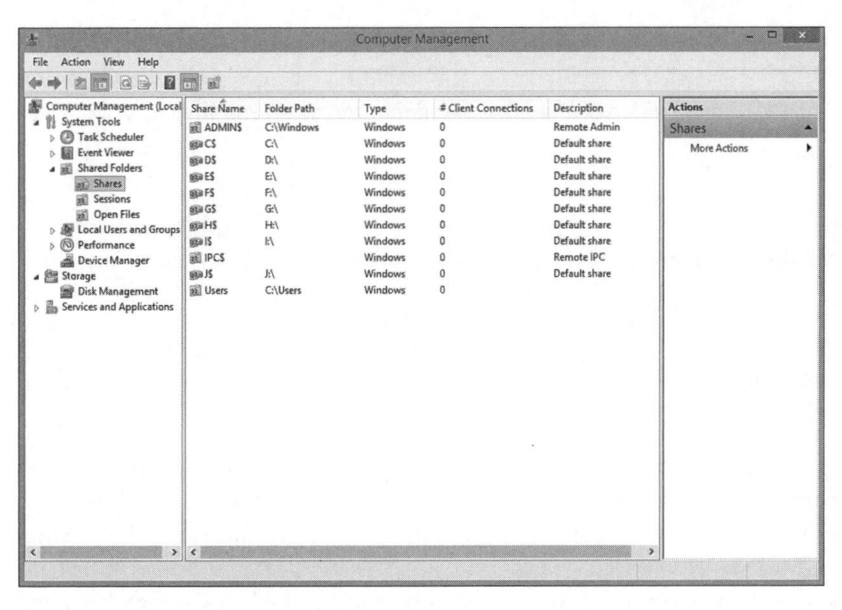

Figure 11-2 You can view the shares on your computer from the Shared Folders node of the Computer Management snap-in.

Aside from the Public folder (`C:\Users\Public`) and the default administrative shares, no folders are automatically shared with the network. To share files with other users across the network, you must manually do so for each folder containing the files that you want to share. To share a folder with other network users, you can open any File Explorer window and then use the following procedure:

Step 1. In a File Explorer window, navigate to the folder, right-click it, and select **Share With,** and then click **Specific people**. The File Sharing dialog box opens, as shown in Figure 11-3.

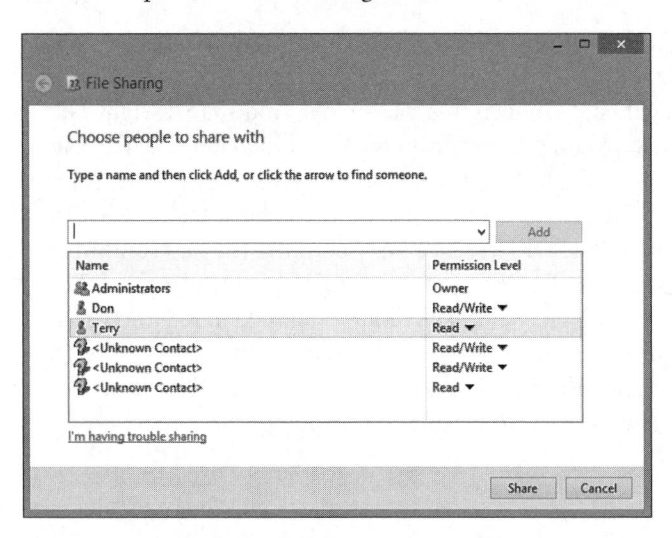

Figure 11-3 The File Sharing dialog box enables you to choose those you want to share a file with.

Step 2. Type the name of a user with whom you want to share the folder and then click **Add**. The name appears in the Name list with a default permission level of Read (for example, Terry in Figure 11-3).

Step 3. To share with another user, repeat step 2 as many times as required. When finished, click **Share**. If you receive a User Account Control (UAC) prompt, click **Yes**.

Step 4. When the file is shared, you receive a message informing you that your folder is shared. This message enables you to email the link to the users with whom you shared the folder or copy it to other programs or documents. Click **Done**.

To add people to the sharing list, repeat this procedure and select **Change Sharing Permissions** from the File Sharing dialog box. Then type the name of the required user and click **Add**. To remove a shared folder, right-click the folder and select **Share with > Stop sharing**.

Modifying Shared Folder Properties

Windows 8.1 shares folders to others as Read, which means that the users you specify can view but not modify available files. The Advanced Sharing feature in Windows 8.1 enables you to modify these properties when necessary.

When you grant full access to your local files to other users across a network, your computer becomes vulnerable to both unintentional and intentional attacks. Not only can the data simply be viewed for malicious purposes, such as corporate spying, but it also can be altered or destroyed on purpose or accidentally. For this reason alone, you should always grant the most restrictive permissions necessary for a network user to conduct work on those files. Granting just enough permission without being too lenient requires careful consideration. If you are too stringent, users can't get their jobs done. If you are too lenient, the data is at risk.

Use the following procedure to modify shared folder properties:

Step 1. In a File Explorer window, right-click the shared folder and choose **Properties**.

Step 2. Click the **Sharing** tab (see Figure 11-4).

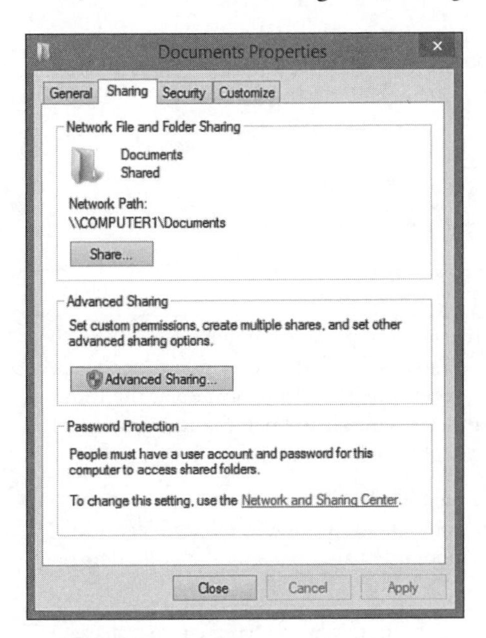

Figure 11-4 The Sharing tab of a folder's Properties dialog box enables you to modify shared folder properties.

Step 3. Click **Advanced Sharing.** If you receive a UAC prompt, click **Yes**. The Advanced Sharing dialog box shown in Figure 11-5 appears. This dialog box provides you with the shared folder options introduced in Table 11-2.

Figure 11-5 The Advanced Sharing dialog box enables you to configure several properties of shared folders.

Table 11-2 Shared Folder Options in Windows 8.1

Option	Description
Share this folder	Click to start sharing the folder.
Share name	This is the folder name that remote users will employ to connect to the share. It will appear in a user's File Explorer window, or the user can access it by typing `\\computername\sharename` at the Run command. (Press the **Windows key +R** to open the Run command, or select it from the **Start** right-click menu.)
Comment	This information is optional and identifies the purpose or contents of the shared folder. The comment appears in the Map Network Drive dialog box when remote users are browsing shared folders on a server.
User limit	This sets the number of remote users who can connect to a shared resource simultaneously, reducing network traffic. For Windows 8.1, the limit is 20 (it was 10 on Windows Vista and older client versions of Windows).
Permissions	Permissions can be assigned to individual users, groups, or both. When a folder is shared, you can grant each user and each group one of the three types of permissions for the share and all its subdirectories and files or choose to specifically deny them those permissions.
Caching	This option enables offline access to a shared folder.

Step 4. To add an additional share name, click **Add** under the Share name section. (If this command button is dimmed, ensure that the **Share this folder** option is selected and click **Apply**.) An additional share name enables users to access the shared folder under this name.

Step 5. To change the maximum number of simultaneous users, type the required number or use the arrows to select a number. This number cannot be higher than 20 on a Windows 8.1 computer.

Step 6. To change shared folder permissions, click **Permissions**. This displays the Permissions for (folder name) dialog box shown in Figure 11-6. By default, the creator of the share receives Full Control permission, and other users receive the Read permission. Click **Add** to add an additional user or group and then modify this user's permissions as desired. Click **OK** when finished. The available shared folder permissions are as follows:

- **Read:** Users are allowed to view but not modify files.
- **Change:** Users are allowed to view and modify files but not change the attributes of the shared folder itself.
- **Full Control:** Users are allowed to perform any task on the folder or its constituent files, including modifying their individual attributes and permissions used by others accessing them.

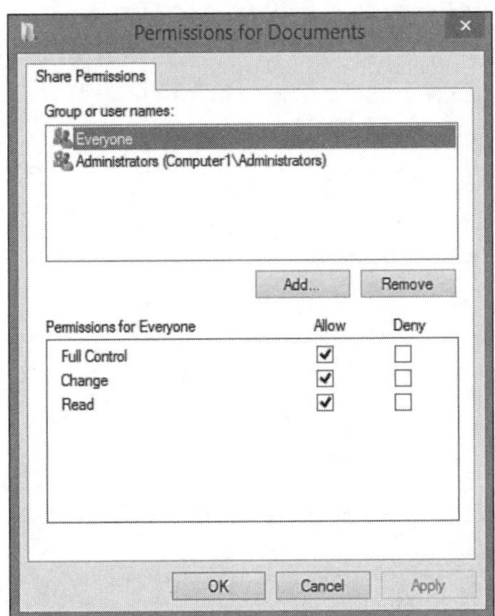

Figure 11-6 The Permissions for (folder name) dialog box enables you to configure permissions that apply to users accessing the folder across the network.

TIP If you select permissions from the Deny column, you are explicitly denying access to that user or group. Such an explicit denial overrides any other permissions allowed to this group. Remember this fact if users experience problems accessing any shared resources across the network.

Step 7. To modify settings that affect how users view and access shared folder contents, click **Caching** (as shown earlier in Figure 11-5) and configure the settings in the Offline Settings dialog box as required. We discuss these settings in Chapter 15, "Configuring and Securing Mobile Devices."

Step 8. To set granular security permissions on the folder, click the **Security** tab and modify the settings in the dialog box shown in Figure 11-7 as required. These permissions apply to everyone accessing the folder either locally or across the network; more restrictive permissions configured here override those configured from the Sharing tab. We discuss these settings in detail later in this chapter.

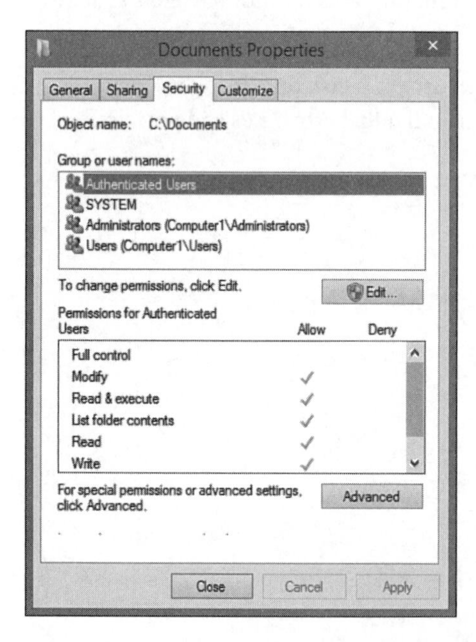

Figure 11-7 The Security tab of a folder's Properties dialog box enables you to configure granular permissions for users and groups accessing the folder.

Step 9. When you are finished, click **OK** to close the folder's Properties dialog box. You can also click **Apply** to apply your changes and continue making modifications.

Use of the Public Folder for Sharing Files

Windows 8.1 provides the Public folder as a location for sharing files as a default. By default, Public folder sharing is turned off. To use this folder for sharing files, access the Advanced sharing settings dialog box shown previously in Figure 11-1 and specify the desired option in the Public Folder Sharing section. You have the following options at `C:\Users\Public`:

- **Turn on sharing so anyone with network access can read and write files in the Public folders:** Shares the folder with Full Control shared folder permission. If password-protected sharing is turned on, a password is required.
- **Turn off Public folder sharing (people logged on to this computer can still access these folders):** Disables sharing of the Public folder.

By default, this folder is located at `C:\Users\Public` and becomes visible when you select the **Turn on sharing** option. You can configure additional security options on this folder by accessing the Sharing tab of its Properties dialog box from this location and following the procedure outlined earlier in this section.

Mapping a Drive

Mapping a network drive means associating a shared folder on another computer with a drive letter available on your computer. This facilitates access to the shared folder. Proceed as follows to map a drive on a Windows 8.1 computer:

Step 1. Right-click **Start** and choose **File Explorer**.

Step 2. From the menu bar, click **Computer > Map Network Drive**.

Step 3. In the Map Network Drive Wizard, select the drive letter to be assigned to the network connection for the shared resource. Drive letters being used by local devices are not displayed in the Drive list. You can assign up to 24 drive letters.

Step 4. Enter a universal naming convention (UNC) path to specify the network path to the computer and the shared folder. For example, to connect to the shared folder Documents on a computer named Computer2, type **`\\computer2\documents`**, as shown in Figure 11-8. You can also click **Browse** to find the shared folder and then select the desired path.

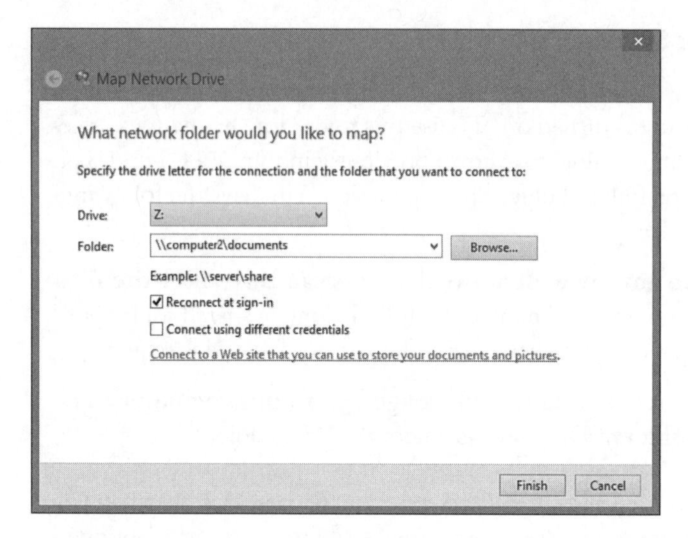

Figure 11-8 Mapping a network drive.

Step 5. Select a connection option, as follows:

- **Reconnect at sign-in:** This option is enabled by default and creates permanent connections. It reconnects the user to the shared folder each time the user logs on unless the user manually disconnects from the resource.
- **Connect using different credentials:** This option enables you to connect to a shared folder using a different user account. It is useful if you are at another user's computer and need to connect to a resource to which the currently logged in user does not have the appropriate access.

Step 6. Click **Finish**.

Command-Line Administration of Shared Folders

Windows 8.1 provides the `net share` command that you can use to manage shared resources. This is useful if you need to use scripts for automating administrative tasks. The syntax is as follows:

```
net share [sharename] [/parameters]
```

In this command, *`sharename`* is the name of the shared resource, and *`/parameters`* refers to any of a series of parameters that you can use with this command. Table 11-3 describes several of the more common parameters used with this command.

Table 11-3 Several Common Parameters Used with the `net share` Command

Parameter	Description
`/users:`*`number`*	Specifies the maximum number of users who can access the shared resource at the same time. Specify unlimited to allow the licensed limit of users.
`/cache:`*`option`*	Enables offline caching, according to the value of *option*: **Documents:** Specifies automatic reintegration of documents **Programs:** Specifies automatic reintegration of programs **Manual:** Specifies manual reintegration **None:** Advises the client that caching is inappropriate
`/delete`	Stops sharing the specified resource.
`/remark:"`*`text`*`"`	Adds a descriptive comment. Enclose the comment (*text*) in quotation marks.

Note that you can also use this command without any parameters to display information about all the shared resources on the local computer.

Password-Protected Sharing

When password-protected sharing is turned on, only users with a local user account and password on your computer can access shared files and printers, including the Public shared folder. To enable others to access shared resources, access the **Password protected sharing** section of the Advanced sharing settings dialog box and select the **Turn off password protected sharing** radio button. Then click **Save changes**.

Media Streaming

Turning on media streaming enables users and devices on the network to access music, pictures, and videos in Windows Media Player and from devices attached to the computer, such as digital cameras, portable digital assistants (PDAs), smartphones, and so on. In addition, the computer can locate these types of shared files on the network. To turn on media sharing, access the **Media streaming** section of the Advanced sharing settings dialog box and click **Choose media streaming options**. In the Choose Media Streaming Options for Computers and Devices dialog box that appears, click **Turn on media streaming**. You can then customize media streaming options including selecting a media library and choosing what types of media will be accessible according to star ratings and parental control settings.

NOTE For further information on media streaming, consult the Windows 8.1 Help and Support Center.

Configuring Homegroup Settings

First introduced in Windows 7 and continued in Windows 8 and 8.1 is the concept of a HomeGroup, which is a small group of Windows 7, 8, or 8.1 computers connected together in a home or small office network that you have designated in the Network and Sharing Center as a home network. Computers running any edition of Windows 7, 8, or 8.1 can join a homegroup, but you must have the Pro or Enterprise edition of Windows 8 or 8.1 to create a homegroup. Computers running Windows Vista or earlier cannot join a homegroup. To create or join a homegroup, you must set your computer's network location profile setting (discussed in Chapter 8) to **Private**. In Chapter 8, refer to the section "Setting Up Network Sharing and Discovery" and Figure 8-13 for more information.

Creating a Homegroup

You can create a homegroup from the HomeGroup applet, which you access from the Network and Internet category of Control Panel by clicking **HomeGroup**. You can also access this applet by accessing the **Search** charm and typing `homegroup` in the Search field or by clicking **HomeGroup** from the Network and Sharing Center. From the Share with other home computers dialog box shown in Figure 11-9, click **Create a homegroup** and then click **Next**. As shown in Figure 11-10, the Create a Homegroup Wizard enables you to select the types of resources you want to share with other computers. For each resource listed here, select Shared or Not shared as required. After you make your selections and click **Next**, the wizard provides you with a password that you can use to add other computers to the homegroup (see Figure 11-11). Make note of this password so that you can join other computers to the homegroup and then click **Finish**.

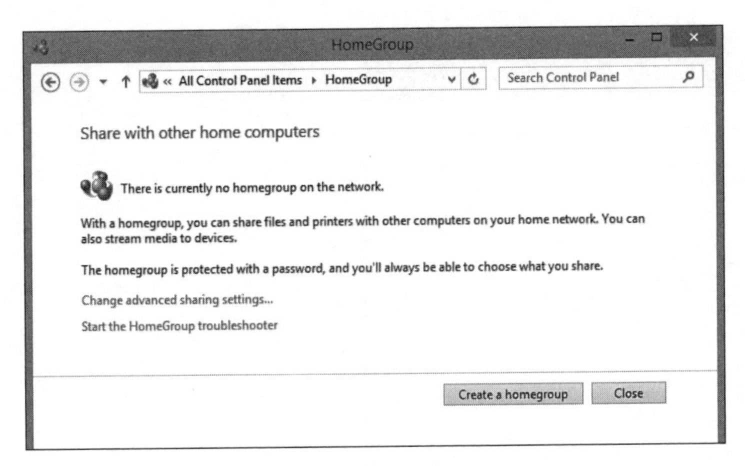

Figure 11-9 If your computer does not belong to a homegroup, you are provided with the option to create one.

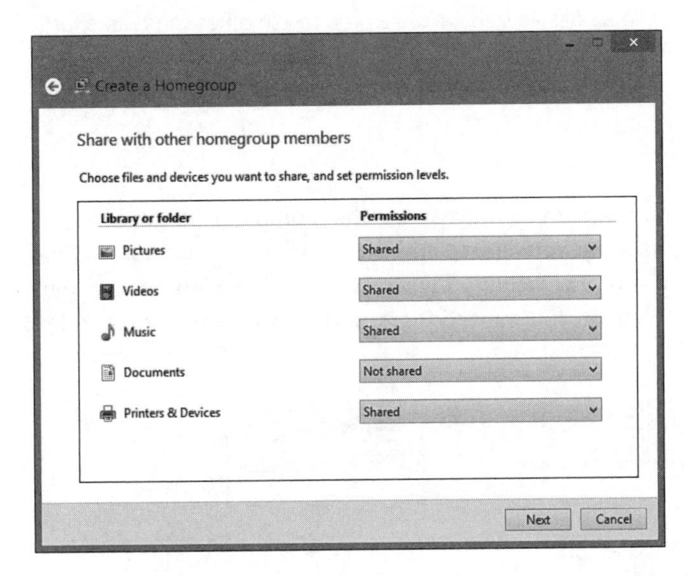

Figure 11-10 Determining the types of resources you want to share on the homegroup.

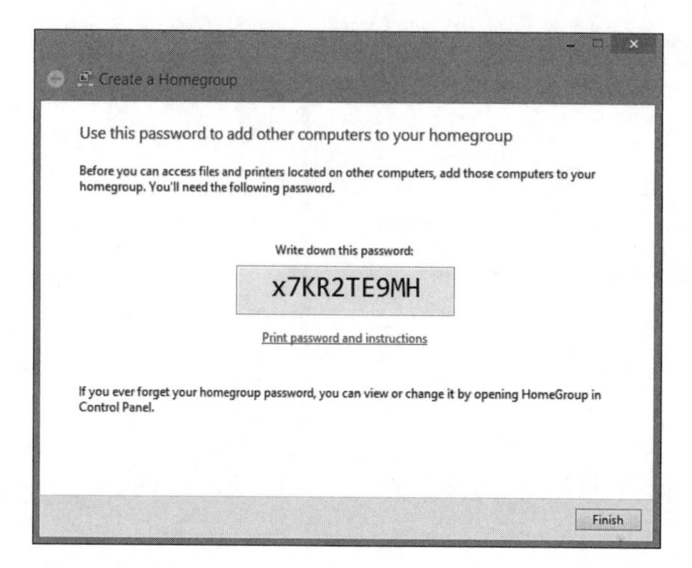

Figure 11-11 You are provided with a password that enables you to join other computers to the homegroup.

Joining a Homegroup

After you create a homegroup, when you move to another computer on the network, the computer recognizes the homegroup and the Share with other home computers dialog box informs you of this fact (see Figure 11-12). Click **Join now** to join the homegroup, select the libraries you want to share, and then type the homegroup password when requested.

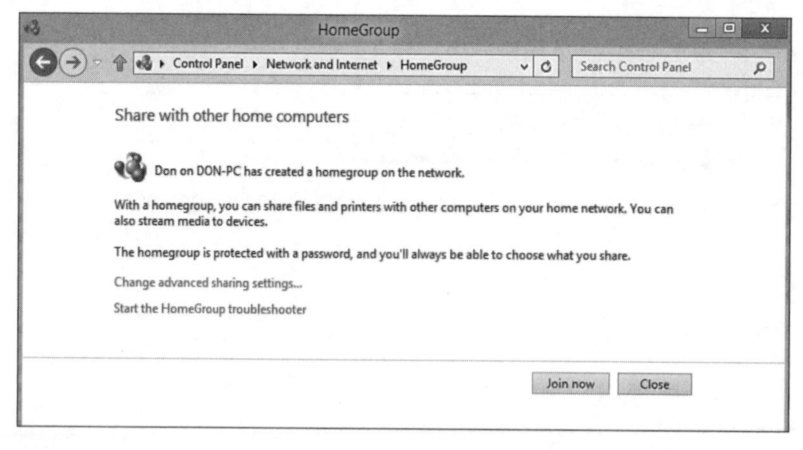

Figure 11-12 If a homegroup exists on the network, you are prompted to join it.

NOTE If your computer is joined to a domain, you can still join a homegroup. However, you cannot share libraries or printers to the homegroup. This feature enables you to bring a portable computer home from work and access shared resources on your home network. Furthermore, it is possible to use Group Policy to prevent domain computers from being joined to a homegroup.

Modifying Homegroup Settings

After you've joined a homegroup, you receive the Change homegroup settings dialog box shown in Figure 11-13 when you access the HomeGroup option in the Control Panel Network and Internet category. From here, you can change the types of libraries and printers that are shared with other homegroup computers. You can also perform any of the other self-explanatory actions shown in Figure 11-13 under Other homegroup actions. Selecting the **Change advanced sharing settings** option takes you to the Advanced sharing setting dialog box previously shown in Figure 11-1.

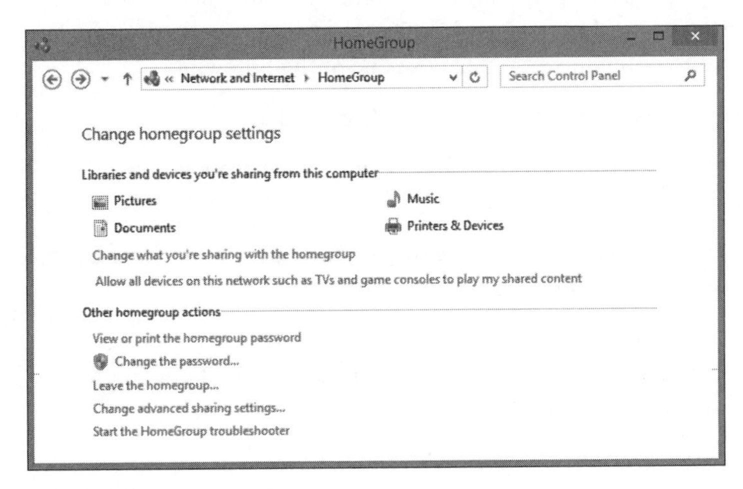

Figure 11-13 The Change homegroup settings dialog box enables you to change which items you share on the homegroup or perform other configuration actions.

Selecting the **Allow all devices on this network such as TVs and game consoles to play my shared content** option displays the dialog box shown in Figure 11-14. The list includes all computers and other media devices found on the network including media players, electronic picture frames, and others. You can allow or block media access to each device individually by selecting the drop-down lists provided, or you can allow or block all devices by choosing from the appropriate command buttons provided.

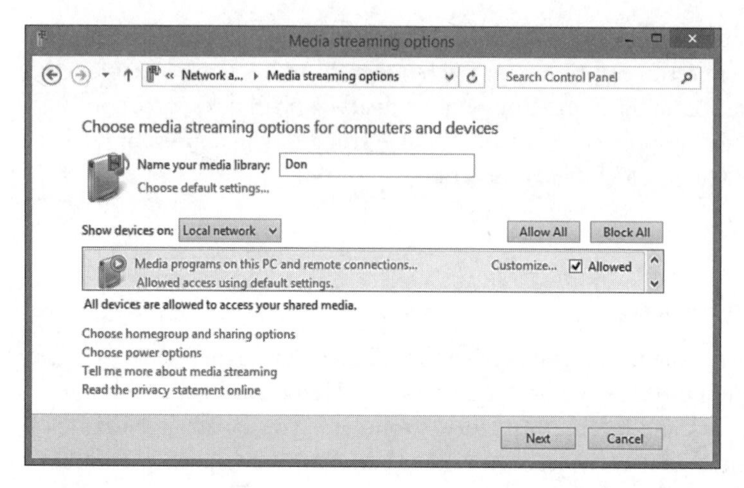

Figure 11-14 The Choose media streaming options for computers and devices dialog box enables you to choose which devices are allowed to access shared media.

You can also modify the file-sharing options for subfolders located within any of your shared libraries. To do this, navigate to the desired library and select the folder. From the Share With menu option, choose one of the following:

- **Nobody:** Prevents all sharing of the selected file or folder.
- **Homegroup (view):** Shares the file or folder with Read permission to all users in the homegroup.
- **Homegroup (view and edit):** Shares the file or folder with Full Control permission to all users in the homegroup.
- **Specific people:** Displays the Choose people to share with dialog box previously shown in Figure 11-3. Type the name of the user with whom you want to share the folder and then click **Add**.

Configuring NTFS Permissions

The preceding section introduced you to sharing folders and the permissions you can attach to shared folders. These permissions apply only when you access the folders across the network. Windows 8.1 provides another means to secure files and folders on the local computer. The New Technology File System (NTFS) that has existed since the early days of Windows NT enables you to secure and manage access to resources on both a network level and on a local level. These NTFS file and folder permissions are also known as security permissions; they can apply to both files and folders, and they apply on your computer to files and folders whether a folder is shared or not shared at all. Keep in mind, however, that although Windows 8.1

supports FAT and FAT32 partitions, NTFS permissions apply only on partitions that are formatted using NTFS. Because you are already familiar with shared folder permissions, we use that as a jumping-off point to describe NTFS permissions.

NTFS File and Folder Permissions

Like the shared permissions, which you can assign to users and groups, NTFS permissions for a folder control how users access a folder. Windows stores an access control list (ACL) with every file and folder on an NTFS partition. The ACL is a list of users and groups that have been granted access for a particular file or folder, as well as the types of access that the users and groups have been granted. Collectively, these kinds of entries in the ACL are called access control entries (ACEs). If you think of the ACL as a list, it isn't hard to conceive that a list contains entries of various kinds. Windows uses the ACL to determine the level of access a user should be granted when he attempts to access a file or folder.

NTFS file permissions control what users can do with files within a folder. More specifically, the permissions control how users can alter or access the data that files contain. Table 11-4 describes the standard NTFS file permissions in detail.

Table 11-4 NTFS File and Folder Permissions

Permission	What a User Can Do on a Folder	What a User Can Do on a File
Full Control	Change permissions, take ownership, and delete subfolders and files. All other actions allowed by the permissions listed in this table are also possible.	Change permissions, take ownership, and perform all other actions allowed by the permissions listed in this table.
Modify	Delete the folder as well as grant that user the Read permission and the List Folder Contents permission.	Modify a file's contents and delete the file as well as perform all actions allowed by the Write permission and the Read and Execute permission.
Read & Execute	Run files and display file attributes, owner, and permissions.	Run application files and display file attributes, owner, and permissions.
List Folder Contents	List a folder's contents, that is, its files and subfolders.	(n/a)
Read	Display filenames, subfolder names, owner, permissions, and file attributes (Read Only, Hidden, Archive, and System).	Display data, file attributes, owner, and permissions.
Write	Create new folders and files, change a folder's attributes, and display owner and permissions.	Write changes to the file, change its attributes, and display owner and permissions.

Applying NTFS Permissions

It is simple to apply NTFS permissions, as the following procedure shows:

Step 1. Right-click a folder or file and choose **Properties**.

Step 2. Select the **Security** tab of the Properties dialog box. Also known as the ACL Editor, the Security tab enables you to edit the NTFS permissions for a folder or file. See Figure 11-15.

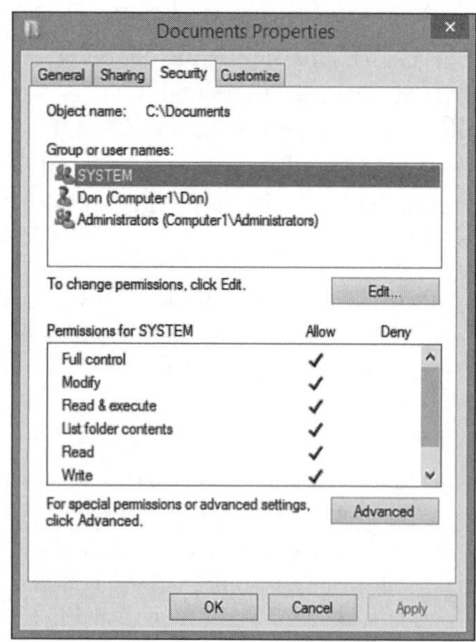

Figure 11-15 The Security tab of a file or folder's Properties dialog box displays its security permissions.

Step 3. Click **Edit** to display the dialog box shown in Figure 11-16. You can configure the options described in Table 11-5 and either allow or deny the permissions already described in Table 11-4.

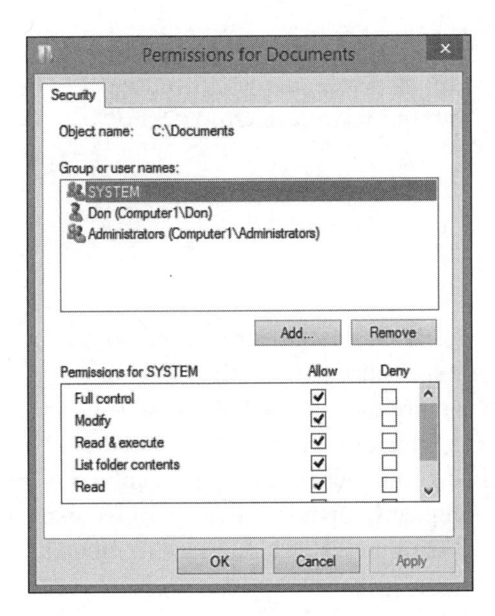

Figure 11-16 The Permissions for (file/folder name) dialog box enables you to configure security permissions.

Table 11-5 Security Tab Options

Option	Description
Group or user names	Start by selecting the user account or group for which you want to change permissions or that you want to remove from the permissions list.
Permissions for (user or group name as specified)	Select the Allow check box to allow a permission. Select the Deny check box to deny a permission.
Add	Click Add to open the Select User or Group dialog box to select user accounts and groups to add to the Name list.
Remove	Click Remove to remove the selected user account or group and the associated permissions for the file or folder.

Step 4. When finished, click **OK** to return to the Security tab shown in Figure 11-15.

Step 5. If you need to configure special permissions or access advanced settings, click **Advanced**. The next section discusses these permissions.

NOTE You can also configure NTFS permissions from the command line by using the `icacls.exe` utility. This utility is useful for scripting permissions configuration. For more information on this utility, refer to "Icacls" at http://technet.microsoft.com/en-us/library/cc753525.aspx.

Specifying Advanced Permissions

For the most part, the standard NTFS permissions are suitable for managing user access to resources. On some occasions, a more specialized application of security and permissions is appropriate. To configure a more specific level of access, you can use NTFS special access permissions. It isn't a secret, but it is not obvious in the Windows 8.1 interface that the NTFS standard permissions are actually combinations of the special access permissions. For example, the standard Read permission is composed of the List Folder/Read Data, Read Attributes, Read Extended Attributes, and Read Permissions special access permissions.

In general, you will use only the standard NTFS permissions already described. In exceptional cases, you might need to fine-tune the permissions further, and this is the point at which the special access NTFS permissions come in. To configure special access permissions, use the following steps:

Step 1. From the Security tab of the appropriate file or folder, click **Advanced** to access the Advanced Security Settings dialog box shown in Figure 11-17.

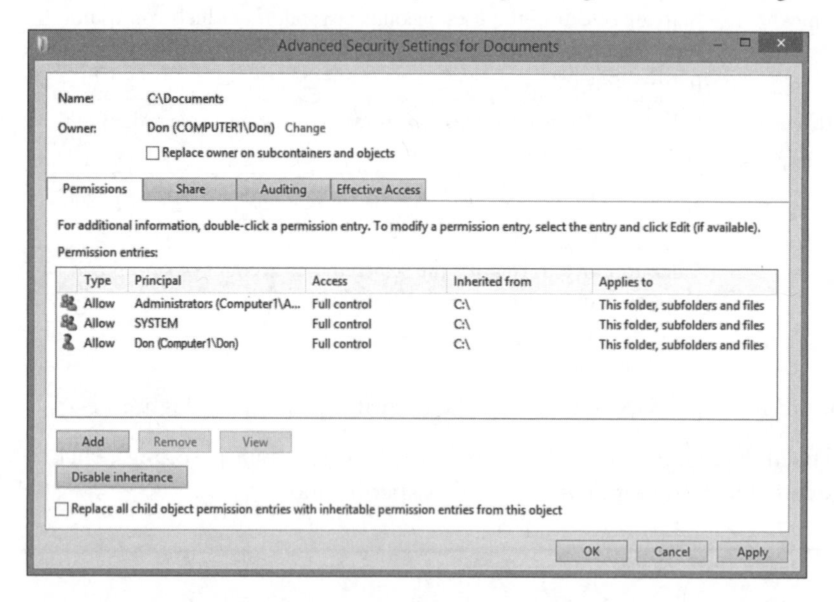

Figure 11-17 The Advanced Security Settings dialog box displays information about the permissions currently assigned to the file or folder, and enables you to add or edit permissions.

Step 2. To add a user with special access permissions, click **Add** to display the Permission Entry for (folder name) dialog box.

Step 3. Click **Select a principal** to display the Select User or Group dialog box shown in Figure 11-18.

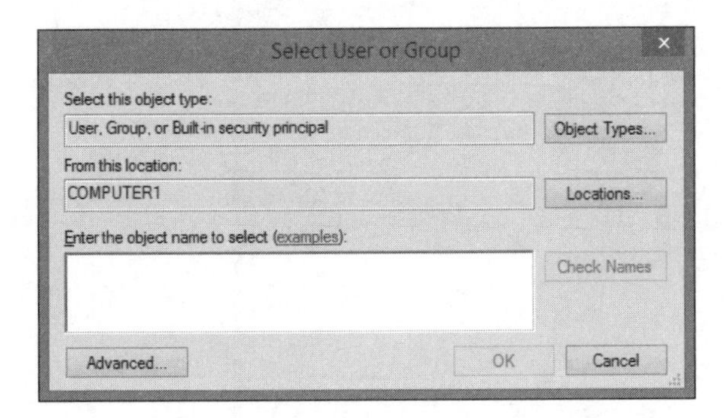

Figure 11-18 The Select User or Group dialog box enables you to select a user or group to which the permission being configured will apply.

Step 4. Type the required user or group name and click **OK**. The user or group is added to the Permission Entry dialog box, as shown in Figure 11-19.

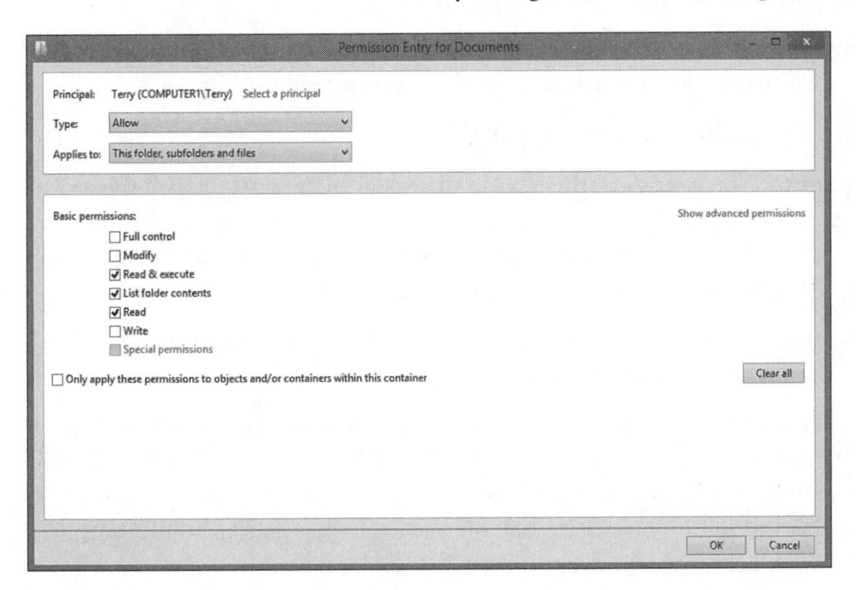

Figure 11-19 The Permission Entry dialog box first displays basic permissions.

Step 5. Click **Show advanced permissions**. The dialog box displays the advanced permissions, as shown in Figure 11-20.

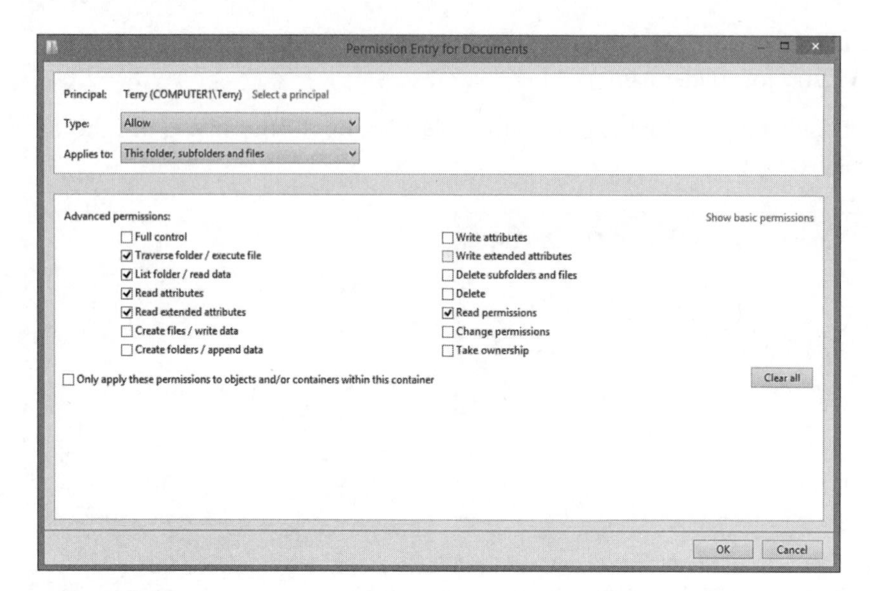

Figure 11-20 The Permission Entry dialog box enables you to configure advanced permissions.

Step 6. Configure the following options as required:

- **Principal:** The user account or group name appears on this line, but you can select a different one by clicking the **Select a principal** link.
- **Type:** Select **Allow** or **Deny** as required.
- **Applies to:** You can adjust the level in the folder hierarchy at which the special permissions apply and are inherited. When permissions are not being inherited from a parent folder, you can choose between this folder, subfolders and files or any one or two of these components.
- **Advanced Permissions:** You can configure any one or more of the special access permissions by selecting their corresponding check boxes.
- **Only apply these permissions to objects and/or containers within this container:** Here, you can adjust a particular folder's properties so that files and subfolders inherit their permissions from the folder you are working on. Selecting this option propagates the special access permissions to files within and folders below your current location in a folder hierarchy.
- **Clear All:** You can clear all selected permissions.

Step 7. When finished, click **OK**.

Table 11-6 describes the special access file and folder permissions that you can configure from this location.

Table 11-6 NTFS Special Access Permissions

Folder Permission	What a User Is Allowed to Do	File Permission	What a User Is Allowed to Do
Full control	Includes all special access permissions.	Full control	Includes all special access permissions.
Traverse folder	Navigate through folders that a user normally can't access to reach files or folders that the user does have permission to access.	Execute file	Run executable files.
List folder	View files or subfolders.	Read data	View data in a particular file.
Read attributes	View folder attributes. These attributes are defined by NTFS.	Read attributes	View file attributes. These attributes are defined by NTFS.
Read extended attributes	View extended folder attributes. Extended attributes are defined by software and may vary.	Read extended attributes	View extended file attributes. Extended attributes are defined by software and may vary.
Create files	Create files within a folder.	Write data	Write changes to or overwrite a file.
Create folders	Create subfolders.	Append data	Make changes to the end of a file by appending data. Does not allow changing, deleting, or overwriting existing data.
Write attributes	Change the attributes of a folder, such as read-only or hidden. Attributes are defined by NTFS.	Write attributes	Change the attributes of a file, such as read-only or hidden. Attributes are defined by NTFS.
Write extended attributes	Change the extended attributes of a folder. Extended attributes are defined by programs and may vary.	Write extended attributes	Change the extended attributes of a file. Extended attributes are defined by programs and may vary.

Folder Permission	What a User Is Allowed to Do	File Permission	What a User Is Allowed to Do
Delete subfolders and files	Delete subfolders, even if the Delete permission has not been granted on the subfolder.	Delete subfolders and files	Delete files, even if the Delete permission has not been granted on the file.
Delete	Delete a folder or subfolder.	Delete	Delete a file.
Read permissions	Read permissions for a folder, such as Full Control, Read, and Write.	Read permissions	Read permissions for a file, such as Full Control, Read, and Write.
Change permissions	Change permissions for a folder, such as Full Control, Read, and Write.	Change permissions	Change permissions for a file, such as Full Control, Read, and Write.
Take ownership	Take ownership of a folder.	Take ownership	Take ownership of a file.

Taking ownership is a very special type of access permission. In Windows 8.1, each NTFS folder and file has an owner. Whoever creates a file or folder automatically becomes the owner and, by default, has Full Control permissions on that file or folder. If that person is a member of the Administrators group, then the Administrators group becomes the owner. The owner possesses the ability to apply and change permissions on a folder or file that she owns, even if the ACL does not explicitly grant her that ability. This does make it possible for the owner of a particular file or folder to deny Administrators access to a resource. But an administrator can exercise the optional right to take ownership of any resource to gain access to it, if this becomes necessary.

In Table 11-4, which describes the standard access permissions, you may have noticed that a standard permission like Modify enables a user to do more than one thing to a file or folder. A special access permission typically enables a user to do one thing only. All special permissions are encompassed within the standard permissions.

NTFS Permissions Inheritance

All NTFS permissions are inherited; that is, they pass down through the folder hierarchy from parent to child. Permissions assigned to a parent folder are inherited by all the files in that folder and also by the subfolders contained in the parent folder. Unless you specifically stop the process of files and folders inheriting permissions from their parent folder, any existing files and subfolders and any new files and subfolders created within this tree of folders will inherit their permissions from the original parent folder. To use the fancy term, permissions are propagated all the way down the tree.

Windows 8.1 lets you modify this permissions inheritance sequence if necessary. To check whether permissions are being inherited and to remove permissions inheritance, use the following procedure:

Step 1. From the Advanced Security Settings dialog box previously shown in Figure 11-17, click the **Disable inheritance** command button.

Step 2. The Block Inheritance dialog box opens, as shown in Figure 11-21, which prompts you to specify one of the following permissions inheritance options:

- **Convert inherited permissions into explicit permissions on this object:** Select this option to add existing inherited permissions assigned for the parent folder to the subfolder or file. This action also prevents subsequent permissions inheritance from the parent folder.
- **Remove all inherited permissions from this object:** Select this option to remove existing inherited permissions assigned for the parent folder to the subfolder or file. Only permissions that you explicitly assign to the file or folder will apply.
- **Cancel:** Select **Cancel** to abort the operation and retain the default permissions inheritance.

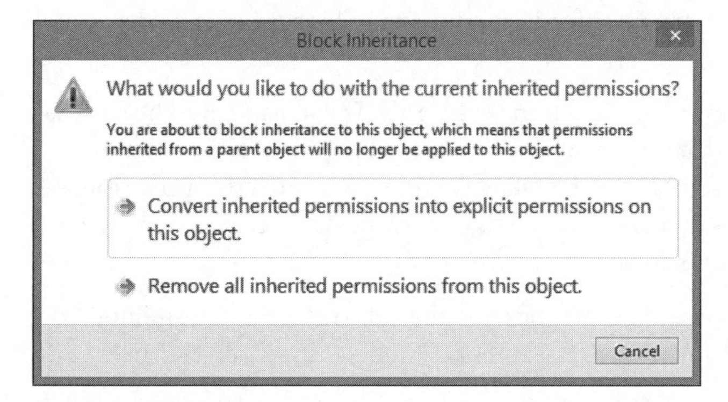

Figure 11-21 The Block Inheritance dialog box enables you to decide how inherited permissions are going to be applied.

Step 3. You return to the Advanced Security Settings dialog box. Click **OK** or **Apply** to apply your changes.

Taking Ownership of Files and Folders

In certain cases, you might need to grant the special Take Ownership permission to a user account. This can be valuable if a user is taking over responsibilities and resources from another individual. A user with the Full Control NTFS permission or the Take Ownership special permission can take ownership of a file or folder from the folder's Properties dialog box, as follows:

Step 1. From the Advanced Security Settings dialog box previously shown in Figure 11-17, click the **Change** link under Owner near the top of the dialog box.

Step 2. In the Select User or Group dialog box that appears (refer to Figure 11-18), type the name of the desired user or group, and then click **OK**.

Step 3. You return the Advanced Security Settings dialog box, and the Owner line reflects the new owner. Click **OK**.

Effective Permissions

Users who belong to more than one group may receive different levels of permission. Both shared folder and NTFS permissions are cumulative. Your effective permissions are a combination of all permissions configured for your user account and for the groups of which you are a member. In other words, the effective permission is the least restrictive of all permissions that you have. For example, if you have Read permissions for a given file, but you are also a member of a group that has Modify permissions for the same file, your effective permissions for that file or folder would be Modify.

However, there is one important exception to this rule. If you happen to be a member of yet another group that has been explicitly denied permissions to a resource (the permission has been selected in the Deny column), your effective permissions do not allow you to access that resource at all. Explicit denial of permission always overrides any allowed permissions.

When you put the two types of permissions together, the rules for determining effective permissions are simple:

- At either the shared folder or NTFS permissions level by itself, if a user receives permissions by virtue of membership in one or more groups, the *least restrictive* permission is the effective permission. For example, if a user has Read permission assigned to his user account and Full Control permission by virtue of membership in a group, he receives Full Control permission on this item.
- If the user is accessing a shared folder over the network and has both shared folder and NTFS permissions applied to it, the *most restrictive* permission is

the effective permission. For example, if a user has Full Control NTFS permission on a folder but accesses it across the network where she has Read shared folder permission, her effective permission is Read.

- If the user is accessing a shared folder on the computer where it exists, shared folder permissions do not apply. In the previous example, this user would receive Full Control permission when accessing the shared folder locally.
- If the user has an explicit denial of permission at either the shared folder or NTFS level, he is denied access to the object, regardless of any other permissions he might have to this object.

TIP It is important to remember that specifically denying permission to a file within a folder overrides all other file and folder permissions configured for a user or for a group that may contain that user's account. There is no real top-down or bottom-up factor to consider when it comes to denying permissions. If a user is a member of a group that has been denied a permission to a file or folder, or if a user's individual account has been denied a permission to a particular resource, that is what counts. If you are denied access to a folder, it does not matter what permissions are attached to a file inside the folder because you cannot get to it.

Viewing a User's Effective Permissions

Windows 8.1 enables you to view a user or group's effective permissions. This is most useful in untangling a complicated web of permissions received by a user who is a member of several groups. Use the following procedure:

Step 1. From the Security tab of the folder's Properties dialog box previously shown in Figure 11-15, click **Advanced** to display the Advanced Security Settings dialog box previously shown in Figure 11-17, and then click the **Effective Access** tab.

Step 2. To view effective permissions for a user or group, click **Select a user** to display the Select User or Group dialog box previously shown in Figure 11-18.

Step 3. Type the name of the desired user or group, click **OK**, and then click the **View effective access** command button.

Step 4. You return to the Effective Access tab, which now displays the effective permissions for the user or group, as shown in Figure 11-22. In the case illustrated here, the user's access was limited by a denial of access specified in a group to which the user belonged; this limitation is indicated by the red X entries and the `File Permissions` entry appearing in the Access limited by column of the dialog box.

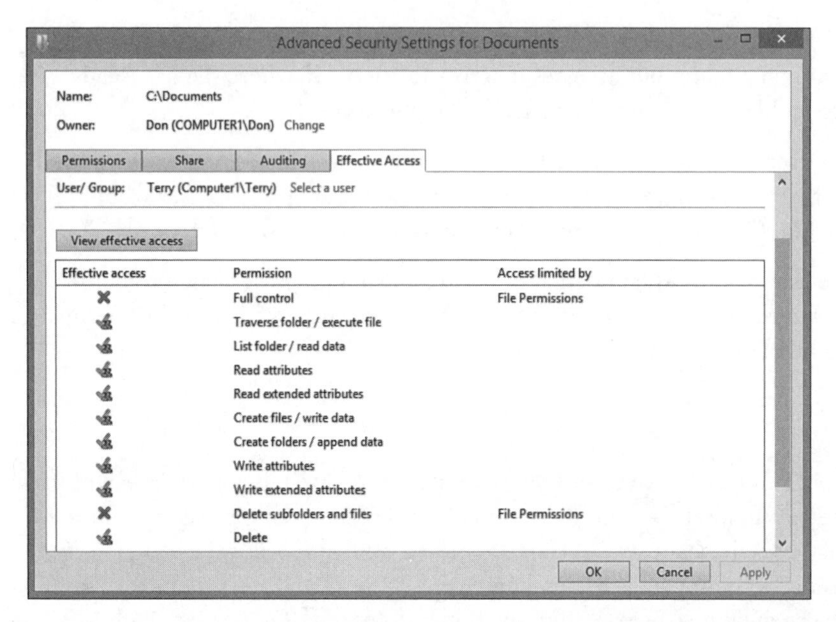

Figure 11-22 You can view a user's or group's effective permissions to a resource from the Effective Access tab of the Advanced Security Settings dialog box.

Copying and Moving Files and Folders

When you copy or move a file or folder that is configured with NTFS permissions, those NTFS permissions can change. The action that occurs depends on whether you are copying the file or folder or whether you are moving the file or folder.

Copying Files and Folders with NTFS Permissions

When you copy a file or folder that is configured with NTFS permissions, those NTFS permissions can change. If you are copying files and folders to a place where the NTFS permissions match exactly, the permissions stay the same. The potential for change is always there, however, when you copy files and folders with NTFS permissions. There are no exceptions to this rule. To ensure that NTFS permissions are applied effectively on your computer, you need to keep in mind how copying can change NTFS permissions. There are essentially three possible outcomes, as outlined in Table 11-7.

Table 11-7 The Effect of Copying Files or Folders on Their NTFS Permissions

Action	Result
Copy a file or folder within the same partition	The copy inherits the NTFS permissions of the destination folder.
Copy a file or folder from one NTFS partition to another NTFS partition	The copy inherits the NTFS permissions of the destination folder.
Copy a file or folder from an NTFS partition to a FAT or FAT32 partition	The copy of a file or folder loses its NTFS permissions completely. NTFS permissions cannot apply anywhere else but on an NTFS partition.

To copy files from an NTFS partition, you need to have at least the Read permission for the originating folder. To complete the copy operation so that the copied versions are written to disk, you need to have at least the Write permission for the destination folder.

CAUTION A close look at Table 11-7 should alert you to the fact that copying a file or folder from an NTFS partition to a FAT or FAT32 partition will strip the file or folder of its NTFS permissions and make it fully available to all users at the local computer.

Moving Files and Folders with NTFS Permissions

Moving files with NTFS permissions may change those permissions. Depending on the circumstances, especially the destination of the move, the permissions may change or they may stay the same. As outlined in Table 11-8, there are also three possible outcomes.

Table 11-8 The Effect of Moving Files or Folders on Their NTFS Permissions

Action	Result
Move a file or folder within the same partition	The file or folder retains its NTFS permissions, regardless of the permissions that exist for the destination folder.
Move a file or folder from one NTFS partition to another NTFS partition	The file or folder inherits the NTFS permissions of the destination folder.
Move a file or folder from an NTFS partition to a FAT or FAT32 partition	The file or folder loses its NTFS permissions completely. NTFS permissions cannot apply anywhere else but on an NTFS partition.

To move files within an NTFS partition or between two NTFS partitions, you need to have at least the Modify permission for the originating folder. To complete the move operation so that the moved versions are written to disk, you need to have at least the Write permission for the destination folder. The Modify permission is required at the source so that source files and folders can be deleted after the files or folders are safely relocated to their new home.

NOTE After you have had time to think about how copying and moving files and folders affects NTFS permissions, there is an easy way to remember how all these possible outcomes will work. One simple sentence can serve to summarize what is going on: "Moving within retains." The only sure way to retain existing NTFS permissions during a copy or move operation is to move files within a single NTFS partition. All the other options hold a very real potential for altering NTFS permissions.

Using the Mouse to Copy or Move Objects from One Location to Another

Keep in mind the following facts about dragging objects between locations:

- When you use the mouse to drag an object from one folder to another on the same partition, you are moving that object.
- If you drag the object to a folder on another partition, you are copying that object.
- If you hold down the **Ctrl** key while dragging, you are copying the object, whether it is to the same or another partition.
- You can also right-drag the object. In this case, when you release the mouse button, you receive choices of copying the object, moving it, or creating a shortcut to the object in its original location.

Practical Guidelines on Sharing and Securing Folders

When you share folders, it is important to control how they are used. To control the use of shared folders, you should be aware of how shares are applied in Windows 8.1. Be sure to keep the following facts in mind.

- **Denying permissions overrides all other shared permissions that may be applied to a folder:** If a user is part of a group that is denied permission to access a particular resource, that user will not be able to access that resource, even if you grant her user account access to the share.

- **Multiple permissions accumulate:** You may be a member of multiple groups, each with a different level of permissions for a particular shared resource. Your effective permissions are a combination of all permissions configured for your user account and the groups of which you are a member. As a user, you may have Read permissions for a folder. You may be a member of a group with Change permissions for the same folder. Your effective permissions for that folder would be Change. If you happen to be made a member of yet another group that has been denied permissions to a folder, your effective permissions will not allow you to access that folder at all. That is the one important exception to this rule.
- **Copying or moving a folder alters the shared permissions associated with that folder:** When you copy a shared folder, the original shared folder is still shared, but the copied folder is not. When you move a shared folder to a new location anywhere, that folder is no longer shared by anyone.
- **When you share a folder that is located on an NTFS volume, you still need to consider the NTFS permissions that apply to that folder:** There may already be NTFS permissions in place on a folder that you are in the process of sharing. You need to consider how your NTFS and shared folder permissions combine. (See the next item.) If that folder doesn't have any NTFS permissions, you may need to configure NTFS permissions for your shared folder, or it is possible that no one will be able to access it.
- **When shared folder and NTFS file and folder permissions combine, the most restrictive permissions apply:** When both NTFS and shared folder permissions apply to the same folder, the more restrictive permission is the effective permission for that folder. Do not lose sight of the fact, however, that shared folder permissions have no effect on users who are logged in to the computer locally.
- **When a folder resides on an NTFS volume:** In this case, you need at least the NTFS Read permission to be able to share that folder at all.

Configuring Data Encryption

You often hear news reports that mention thefts of laptop computers containing valuable data. In one such case, a computer stolen from a doctor's car in Toronto contained the records of thousands of patients, exposing them to misuse and potential identity theft. The computer was protected with a password, but the data was not encrypted. Windows 8.1 includes the following two systems of data encryption, designed to protect data not only on your laptop when you are in a place such as an airport or hotel where a thief can grab it when you're momentarily distracted, but also at any other place where an unauthorized individual might attempt to either connect to it across the network or physically access it.

- First introduced with Windows Vista, BitLocker Drive Encryption encrypts a computer's entire system partition. We look at BitLocker in Chapter 15.
- First introduced with Windows 2000 and refined with each successive iteration of Windows, the Encrypting File System (EFS) can be used to encrypt files and folders on any partition that is formatted with the NTFS file system. We discuss EFS in this section.

EFS enables users to encrypt files and folders on any partition that is formatted with the NTFS file system. The encryption attribute on a file or folder can be toggled the same as any other file attribute. When you set the encryption attribute on a folder, all its contents—whether subfolders or files—are also encrypted.

The encryption attribute, when assigned to a folder, affects files the same way that the compression attribute does when a file is moved or copied. Files that are copied into the encrypted folder become encrypted. Files that are moved into the encrypted folder retain their former encryption attribute, whether or not they were encrypted. When you move or copy a file to a file system that does not support EFS, such as FAT16 or FAT32, the file is automatically decrypted.

TIP Remember that the file system must be set to NTFS if you want to use EFS, and no file can be both encrypted and compressed at the same time. On the exam, you may be presented with a scenario where a user is unable to use EFS or file compression on a FAT32 volume; the correct answer to such a problem is to convert the file system to NTFS, as described in the section "Preparing a Disk for EFS" later in this chapter.

Encrypting File System Basics

EFS uses a form of public key cryptography, which utilizes a public and private key pair. The public key or digital certificate is freely available to anyone, while the private key is retained and guarded by the user to which the key pair is issued. The public key is used to encrypt data, whereas the private key decrypts the data that was encrypted with the corresponding public key. The key pair is created the first time a user encrypts a file or folder using EFS. When another user attempts to open the file, that user is unable to do so. Therefore, EFS is suitable for data that a user wants to maintain as private, but not for files that are shared.

Windows 8.1 has the capability to encrypt files directly on any NTFS volume. This ensures that no other user can use the encrypted data. Encryption and decryption of a file or folder are performed in the object's Properties dialog box. Administrators should be aware of the rules to put into practice to manage EFS on a network:

- Use only NTFS as the file system for all workstation and server volumes.
- Keep a copy of each user's certificate and private key on a USB flash drive or other removable media.
- Remove the user's private key from the computer except when the user is actually using it.
- When users routinely save documents only to their Documents folder, make certain their documents are encrypted by having each user encrypt his own Documents folder.
- Use two recovery agent user accounts that are reserved solely for that purpose for each Active Directory Domain Services (AD DS) organizational unit (OU) if computers participate in a domain. Assign the recovery agent certificates to these accounts.
- Archive all recovery agent user account information, recovery certificates, and private keys, even if obsolete.
- When planning a network installation, keep in mind that EFS does take up additional processing overhead; plan to incorporate additional CPU processing power in your plans.

A unique encryption key is assigned to each encrypted file. You can share an encrypted file with other users in Windows 8.1, but you are restricted from sharing an entire encrypted folder with multiple users or sharing a single file with a security group. This is related to the way that EFS uses certificates, which are applicable individually to users; and how EFS uses encryption keys, which are applicable individually to files. Windows 8.1 continues the ability introduced with Windows Vista to store keys on smart cards. If you are using smart cards for user logon, EFS automatically locates the encryption key without issuing further prompts. EFS also provides wizards that assist users in creating and selecting smart card keys.

You can use different types of certificates with EFS: third-party–issued certificates; certificates issued by certification authorities (CAs), including those on your own network; and self-signed certificates. If you have developed a security system on your network that utilizes mutual authentication based on certificates issued by your own CA, you can extend the system to EFS to further secure encrypted files. For more information on using certificates with EFS, refer to the Windows 8.1 Help and Support Center.

NOTE For more information on the technology behind EFS, refer to "How EFS Works" at http://technet.microsoft.com/en-us/library/cc962103.aspx.

Preparing a Disk for EFS

Unlike in versions of Windows prior to Vista, the system and boot partition in Windows 8.1 must be formatted with NTFS before you can install Windows 8.1, as you learned in Chapter 2, "Installing Windows 8.1." However, a data partition can be formatted with the FAT or FAT32 file systems. But you must ensure that such a partition is formatted with NTFS before you can encrypt data using EFS. If it is not, you can convert the hard disk format from FAT to NTFS or format the partition as NTFS. There are two ways to go about this:

- Use the command-line `Convert.exe` utility to change an existing FAT16 or FAT32 partition that contains data to NTFS without losing the data.
- Use the graphical Disk Management utility to format a new partition, or an empty FAT partition, to NTFS. If the volume contains data, you will lose it. (You can also use the command-line `Format.exe` utility to format a partition as NTFS.)

The `Convert.exe` utility is simple to use and typically problem-free, although you should make certain to back up the data on the partition before you convert it as a precaution. Perform the following steps to use this utility:

Step 1. Log on to the computer as an administrator. Know which drive letter represents the partition that you plan to convert because only the partition that contains the encrypted files needs to be formatted with NTFS. For example, if users store all their data on drive D: and want to encrypt those files, you convert drive `D:` to NTFS.

Step 2. From the Search charm, type **`cmd`** in the search box and press **Enter**.

Step 3. The command prompt window opens. At the prompt, type **`convert d: /fs:ntfs`**.

Step 4. The conversion process begins. If you are running the `Convert.exe` utility from the same drive letter prompt as the partition you are converting, or a file is open on the partition, you are prompted with the message `Convert cannot gain exclusive access to D:, so it cannot convert it now. Would you like to schedule it to be converted the next time the system restarts (Y/N)?` Press **Y** at the message.

Step 5. Restart the computer. The disk converts its format to NTFS. This process takes considerable time to complete, but at completion, you can access the Properties dialog box for the disk you've converted and note that it is formatted with the NTFS file system.

Encrypting Files

You can use either the `cipher` command-line utility or the advanced attributes of the file or folder to encrypt a file. To use the `cipher` utility for encrypting a file named `Myfile.txt` located in the `C:\mydir` folder, the full command to use is as follows:

```
cipher /e /s:c:\mydir\myfile.txt
```

To change the Advanced encryption attribute of a file, open File Explorer and navigate to the file. Right-click the file and select **Properties**. On the General tab, click the **Advanced** button in the Attributes section. The Advanced Attributes dialog box opens, as shown in Figure 11-23.

Figure 11-23 The Advanced Attributes dialog box enables you to either compress or encrypt a file.

Select the **Encrypt contents to secure data** check box and click **OK**. Then click **OK** again to close the file's Properties dialog box. A warning dialog box enables you to choose between encrypting just the file that you had selected or both the file and its parent folder. Select one of the options and click **OK**.

NOTE Note that the compression and encryption attributes are mutually exclusive. In the Advanced Attributes dialog box, if you select the **Compress contents to save disk space** check box, the check mark disappears from the Encrypt contents to secure data check box. These two attributes are mutually exclusive; you can select only one.

After a file has been encrypted, you can view its encryption attribute details by again right-clicking the file, selecting **Properties**, and then clicking the **Advanced** button on the General tab. In the Advanced Attributes dialog box, click the **Details** button. The User Access To (file) dialog box opens, as shown in Figure 11-24.

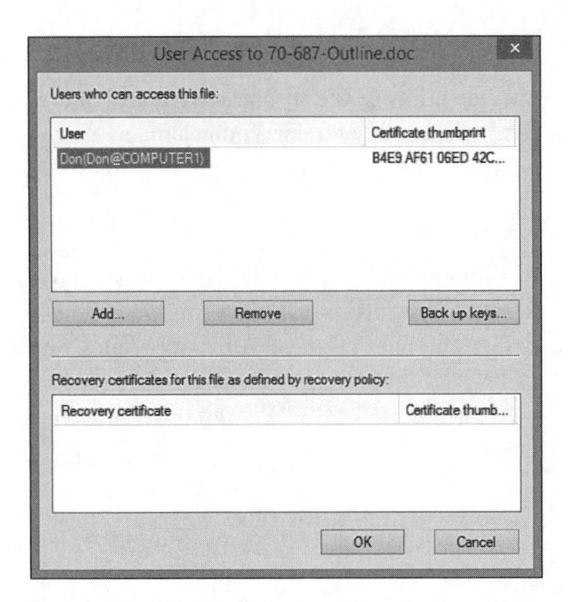

Figure 11-24 After a file has been encrypted, you can add other users to access the file.

You can see who is able to open the encrypted file, and you can add other user accounts to share the encrypted file and view the designated data recovery agent, if any. Click the **Add** button to share the encrypted file. A dialog box listing all the EFS-capable certificates for users opens. If a user has never been issued a certificate, the user's account does not appear in this dialog box.

TIP If the desired user has not been issued an EFS certificate, she needs only to log on to the computer and encrypt a different file. This automatically creates a certificate that will be visible the next time you attempt to share an encrypted file.

After a file is encrypted, an unauthorized user attempting to open the file is given an error message that says the user does not have access privileges. If an unauthorized user tries to move or copy an encrypted file, the user receives an `Access is denied` error message.

Backing Up EFS Keys

What if a user were to encrypt a file using EFS and then the user's account were to become corrupted or be deleted for any reason? Or what if the user's private key were to become corrupted or lost? You would be unable to decrypt the file, and it would be permanently inaccessible. Windows 8.1 offers the capability for backing up EFS certificates and keys to reduce the likelihood of this occurring. Use the following procedure to back up EFS keys:

Step 1. From the User Access dialog box previously shown in Figure 11-24, click **Back up keys**.

Step 2. The Certificate Export Wizard starts. Click **Next**.

Step 3. On the Export File Format page, the Personal Information Exchange–PKCS #12 (.PFX) format is selected by default. If desired, select the **Include all certificates in the certification path if possible** and **Export All extended properties** options and then click **Next**.

Step 4. On the Password page, type and confirm a password. This is mandatory, and you should choose a hard-to-guess password that follows the usual complexity guidelines. Then click **Next**.

Step 5. On the File to Export page, type the name of the file to be exported and then click **Next**. By default, this file is created in the user's Documents library with the `.pfx` extension.

Step 6. Review the information on the completion page and then click **Finish**.

Step 7. You are informed the export was successful. Click **OK**.

Step 8. You should move this file to a location separate from the computer, such as a floppy disk or USB key that you store securely (such as in a locked cabinet).

Decrypting Files

The process of decryption is the opposite of encryption. You can either use the `cipher` command or change the Advanced attribute for encryption on the file.

To use the `cipher` command to decrypt the file, access the Search charm, type **`cmd`** in the search box, and then press **Enter**. At the command prompt, type **`cipher /d /s:c:\myfolder\myfile.txt`** and press **Enter**. The file is then decrypted.

To use the Advanced Attributes method, open File Explorer and navigate to the file. Right-click the file and select **Properties**. On the General tab, click the **Advanced** button. In the ensuing Advanced Attributes dialog box, clear the **Encrypt contents to secure data** check box. Click **OK** and then click **OK** again.

If you are not the person who originally encrypted the file, or if you are not the designated recovery agent, you receive an error for applying attributes that says the access is denied.

EFS Recovery Agents

What if the user's keys, even though backed up, were to become lost or corrupted? Without some type of recovery capability, such a file would become permanently inaccessible. EFS in Windows 8.1 uses the concept of recovery agents as a means to recover encrypted data in such a situation.

Designated recovery agents are user accounts authorized to decrypt encrypted files. When a user account is designated as a recovery agent, you essentially are granting it a copy of the key pair. If you lose the key pair, or if they become damaged, and if there is no designated recovery agent, there is no way to decrypt the file and the data is permanently lost. By designating a recovery agent before a user first uses EFS, you can ensure that encrypted files and folders remain accessible by someone responsible for their maintenance.

Windows 8.1 can include two levels of EFS recovery agents:

- **Local computer:** By default, the local administrator account created when you first install Windows 8.1 is the recovery agent. Note that this account is not the account whose name you specify during Windows 8.1 installation; it is a built-in account that can be accessed from the Local Users and Groups node of the Computer Management snap-in. The account is disabled by default, but you can enable it from its Properties dialog box by clearing the **Account is disabled** check box.

- **Domain:** When you create an AD DS domain, the first domain administrator account is the designated recovery agent. You can use Group Policy to designate additional recovery agents, and you can delegate the responsibility of EFS recovery to other users if desired.

You can use Group Policy to designate additional recovery agents. A user must have an appropriate certificate before he can be designated as a recovery agent. To designate a recovery agent, use the following procedure:

Step 1. Open Group Policy and navigate to the **Computer Configuration\Windows Settings\Security Settings\Public Key Policies\Encrypting File System** node.

Step 2. Right-click this node and choose **Add Data Recovery Agent**.

Step 3. The Add Recovery Agent Wizard starts with a Welcome page. Click **Next**.

Step 4. On the Select Recovery Agents page shown in Figure 11-25, select a user from the Recovery agents list and then click **Next**. (If necessary, click **Browse Folders** to locate a certificate for the desired user.)

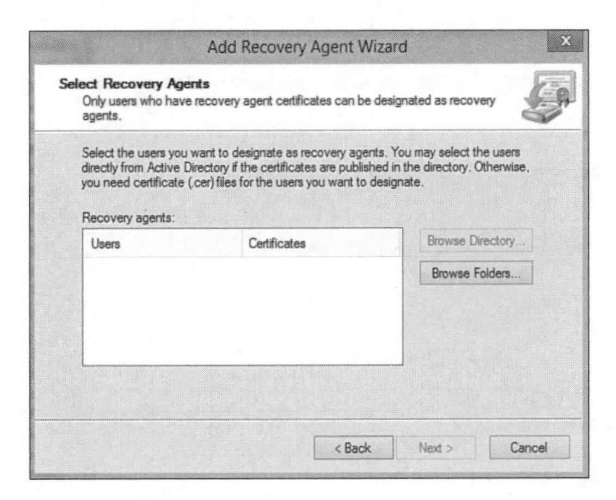

Figure 11-25 The Add Recovery Agent Wizard enables you to designate additional users as EFS recovery agents.

Step 5. You are informed that you have successfully completed the wizard. Review the information about the designated recovery agents, and then click **Finish**.

NOTE For more information on backing up keys and designating recovery agents in EFS, refer to "How to back up the recovery agent Encrypting File System (EFS) private key in Windows" at http://support.microsoft.com/kb/241201 and "Create a recovery certificate for encrypted files" at http://windows.microsoft.com/en-US/windows7/Create-a-recovery-certificate-for-encrypted-files. Although written for Windows 7, the information in these references is for the most part applicable for Windows 8.1.

Configuring File Libraries

First introduced in Windows 7 and continued in Windows 8.1, a library is a set of virtual folders that is shared by default with other users of the computer. By default, Windows 8.1 includes four libraries (Documents, Pictures, Music, and Videos), which you can access by clicking the folder icon on the taskbar when you don't have any other File Explorer windows open. You can also access the libraries by clicking **View** on the File Explorer toolbar, and then on the expanded toolbar that appears, click **Navigation Pane > Show Libraries.** This adds a Libraries entry to the folder list of the File Explorer window. Click this entry to view the libraries, as shown in Figure 11-26. The subfolders you see here are actually pointers to the folder locations on the computer. You can also think of them as the results of search queries.

From the Libraries folder, you can create a new library by right-clicking **Libraries** in the folder list and choosing **New > Library** in the toolbar and providing a name for your new library.

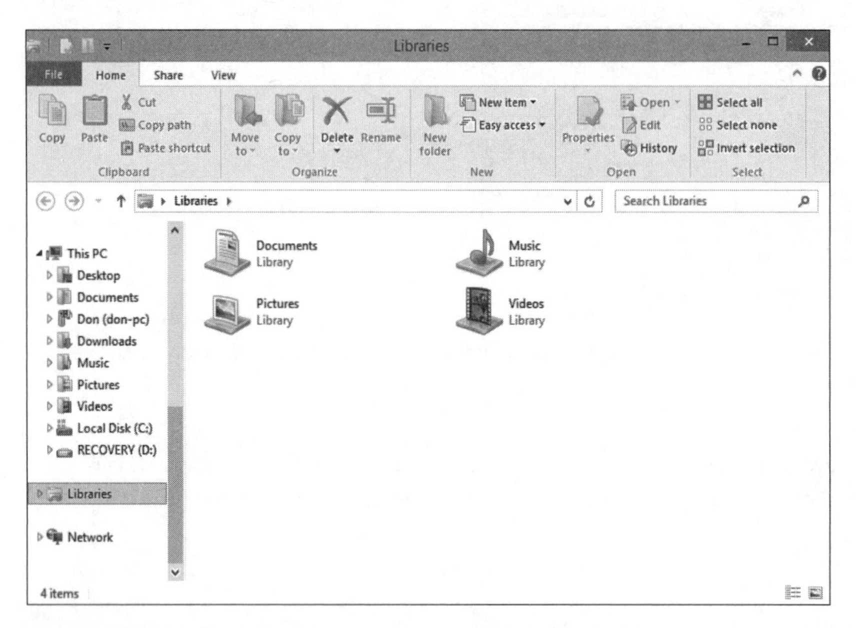

Figure 11-26 Windows 8.1 creates these four default libraries.

Each library contains a user-based subfolder, located by default at `C:\Users\%username%`, as well as a public subfolder from `C:\Users\Public`, which you can view by right-clicking the library and choosing **Properties**. In addition, if you have configured OneDrive, a OneDrive folder is included in the libraries (see Figure 11-27). You can add additional folders by clicking the **Add** button and navigating to the desired folder; this can even include shared folders located on other computers on the network. You can also add folders to a library from any explorer window by right-clicking the folder and choosing the **Include in Library** option from the pop-up window.

The Properties dialog box shown in Figure 11-27 enables you to change several other properties of the selected library. The check mark indicates the default save location used by programs such as Microsoft Office; to change this location, select the desired location and click the **Set save location** button. You can add additional folders to the library by clicking **Add** and selecting the desired folder, similar to that discussed in the previous paragraph. To remove a folder from the library, select it and click **Remove**. To remove all added folders from the library and reset it to its default settings, click the **Restore Defaults** button.

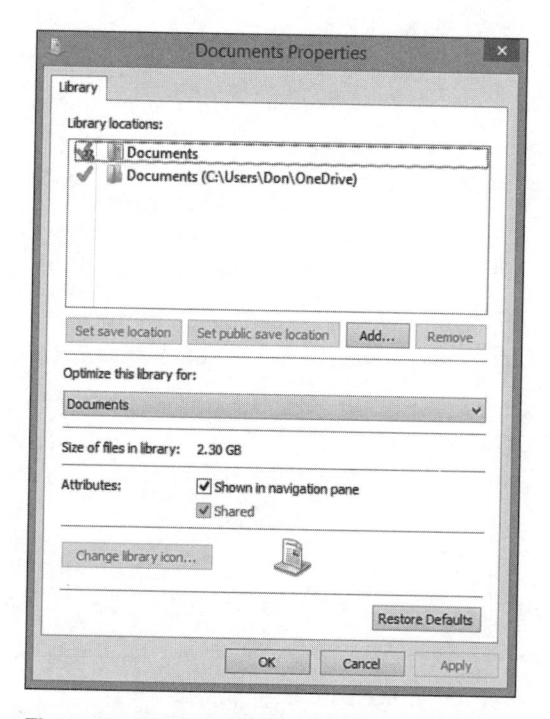

Figure 11-27 Each library, by default, contains a user subfolder and a public subfolder. A One-Drive folder is included when configured in Windows 8.1.

Configuring Shared Printers

If you have turned on file and printer sharing from the Advanced Sharing Settings dialog box, you can share any printer attached to your computer so that others on the network can print documents to it. Use the following steps to share a printer:

Step 1. From the Search charm, type `printers`, and then select **Devices and Printers**. You can also access the Hardware and Sound category in Control Panel and select **Devices and Printers**.

Step 2. In the Devices and Printers Control Panel applet, right-click your printer and choose **Printer properties**.

Step 3. Click the **Sharing** tab to display the dialog box shown in Figure 11-28.

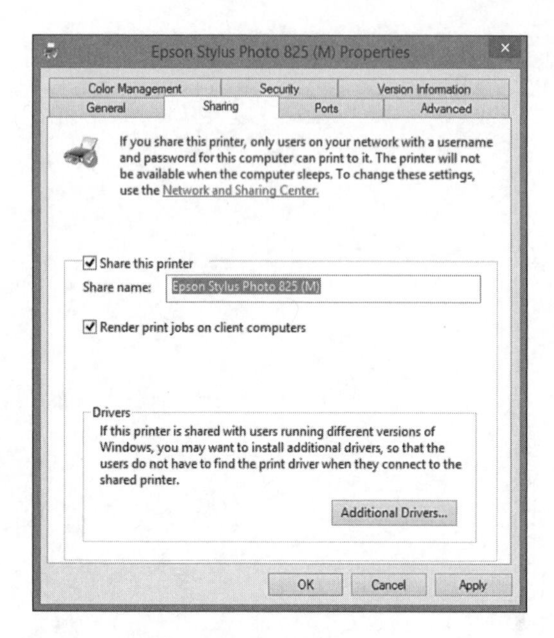

Figure 11-28 Sharing a printer.

Step 4. Click **Share this printer** and either accept the share name provided or type a different name. This name identifies the printer to users on other computers.

Step 5. If users are running older Windows versions, click **Additional Drivers** to install drivers for these Windows versions. Select the required drivers from the Additional Drivers dialog box that appears and then click **OK**.

As with shared folders, you can assign share permissions for printers. Select the **Security** tab of the printer's Properties dialog box to configure the options shown in Figure 11-29. By default, the Everyone group receives the Print permission, and the Administrators group receives the Print, Manage this printer, and Manage documents permissions. Table 11-9 describes the printer permissions, including Special permissions.

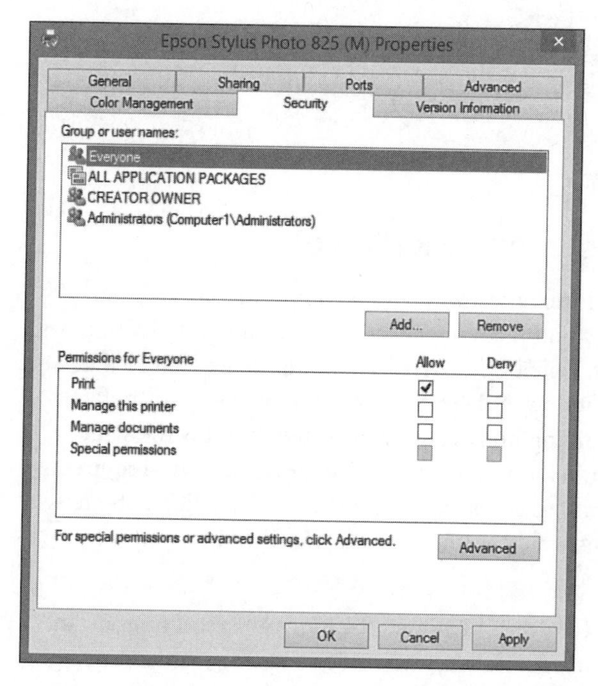

Figure 11-29 Configuring permissions for shared printers.

Table 11-9 Printer Permissions in Windows 8.1

Parameter	Description
Print	Users can connect to a given printer to print documents and control print job settings for their own documents only. This can include pausing, deleting, and restarting only their own documents in the print queue as needed.
Manage this printer	Users can assign forms to paper trays and set a separator page. In addition, they can change the printing order of documents in the queue, pause, resume, and purge the printer, change printer properties, and actually delete the printer itself or change printer permissions. Users with this permission can also perform all tasks related to the Manage documents permission.
Manage documents	Users can pause, resume, restart, and cancel all documents. They can also set the notification level for finished print jobs and set priority levels and specific printing times for documents to print.
Special permissions	This parameter enables the assignment of granular permissions, including Read Permissions, Change Permissions, and Take Ownership. To configure special permissions, click the Advanced button.

NOTE For more information on configuring printer permissions, refer to "Assigning printer permissions" at http://technet.microsoft.com/en-us/library/cc773372(WS.10).aspx.

Configuring OneDrive (formerly SkyDrive)

As a companion to Windows 8.1 integration with cloud computing using cloud apps, cloud communication, and cloud accounts, Microsoft has integrated Windows 8.1 with its cloud storage solution called OneDrive. This is the same feature that was formerly called SkyDrive. Windows 8.1 features and Explorer will still refer to it as SkyDrive until all the renaming updates are completed, but it is the same feature with a new name. As with Windows Store Apps, use of OneDrive requires a Microsoft account. Each account has access to 7 GB for free, and Microsoft announced that in July of 2014. This would be increased to 15 GB. Microsoft offers upgraded storage for an annual fee.

OneDrive enables a single cloud for every Windows 8.1 user. A person's important files are centrally available, instantly accessible, and ready to share, enabled by single sign-on with a Windows account. OneDrive is the Windows 8.1 user's solution to the problem of keeping files in sync across multiple devices; instead, all devices connect to the OneDrive, and users can easily share files by providing permission for others Windows account users to access their files.

Windows account holders can access their OneDrive storage in four ways:

- The Windows 8.1 OneDrive app, available only on Windows 8.1 computers.
- The OneDrive desktop application, which is available for Windows 7, Windows Vista, and Mac OS X 10.7 ("Lion") and later versions. The features of the desktop application are built into Windows 8.1.
- Using OneDrive.com from a web browser. From OneDrive.com or SkyDrive.com, users can also share files with others by enabling permissions, and access to their files from any computer.
- Using the OneDrive mobile app for tablets and mobile phones.

Reference the following sections for information about the OneDrive app, the OneDrive desktop application, and the configuration options for OneDrive.

OneDrive app

Open the OneDrive app by clicking on the **OneDrive** tile on the Start screen. If you are not logged in to your Windows account, you are prompted to log in or sign up for an account when you click on the tile. The first time you open the OneDrive app, you see a screen similar to Figure 11-30.

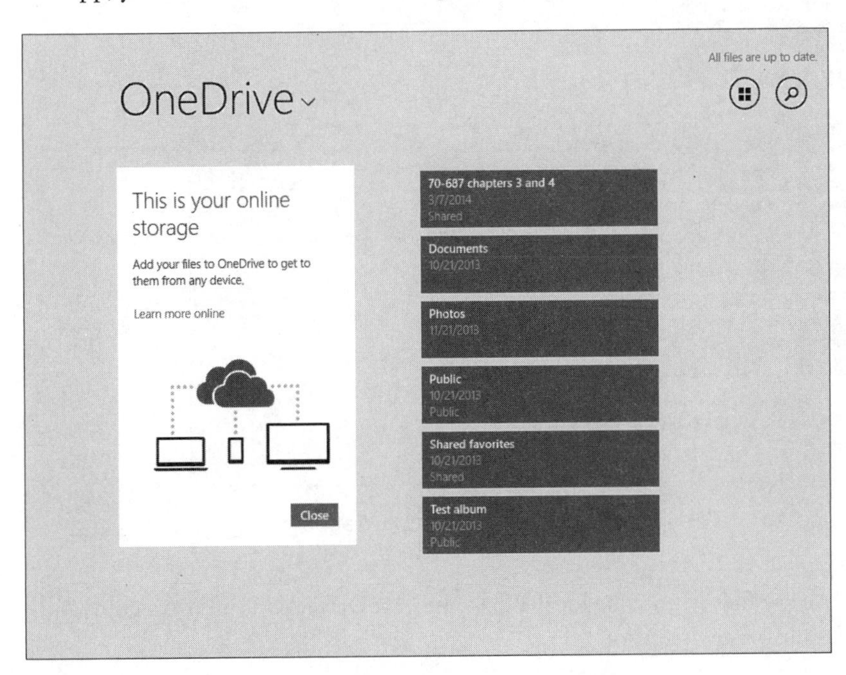

Figure 11-30 The OneDrive app opened for the first time.

Initially, OneDrive has three folders for storing files: Documents, Pictures, and Public. Files uploaded to the Public folder are shared publicly by default. Use the right-click menu in the OneDrive app to upload files, create new folders, and perform other tasks.

You can also access local files from the OneDrive app. Notice the down-pointing arrow next to OneDrive in Figure 11-30. Clicking this arrow and selecting **This PC** displays a screen similar to Figure 11-31. From here, you can access library folders, drives, and any network-attached folders.

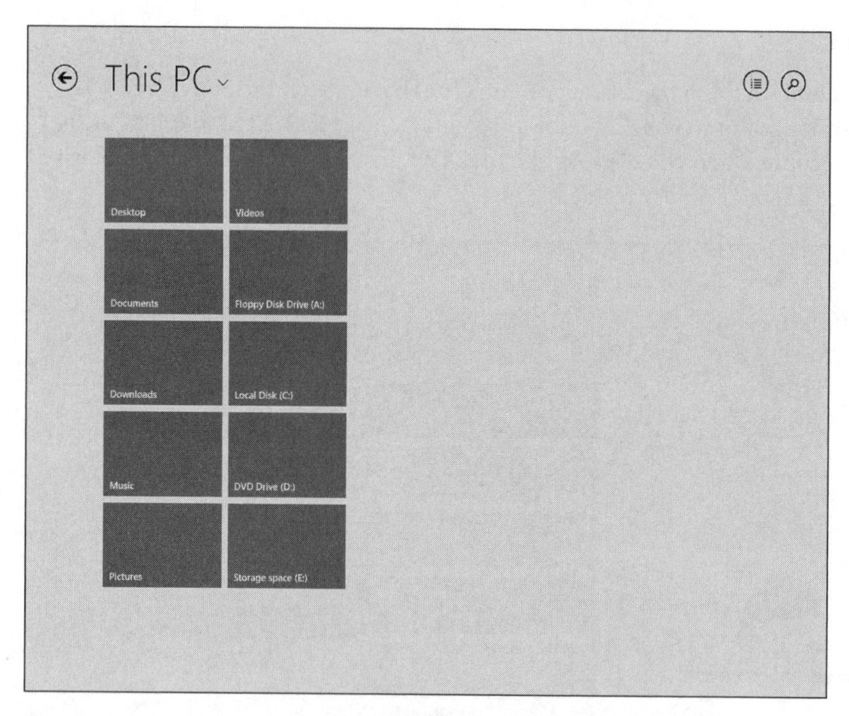

Figure 11-31 Access local files and folders from the OneDrive app.

To move or copy files from your local PC to the OneDrive, you can use a copy-and-paste or cut-and-paste operation:

Step 1. Browse the folders in **This PC** to the file you want to move or copy.

Step 2. Right-click the file or files to select them.

Step 3. Click **Cut** from the app commands to move the files or **Copy** to copy them.

Step 4. Click the arrow next to This PC and select **OneDrive**.

Step 5. Right-click to open the app commands and then click **Paste**.

You can also use Add files app command on a OneDrive folder to copy files. When you select the **Add files** command, you can browse the folders from the local computer and select the files to copy. The selected files are uploaded to the OneDrive folder.

During the move or copy operation, you can keep track of the progress by watching the status in the upper-right corner of the OneDrive app screen, as shown in Figure 11-32, where OneDrive tells you it is `Uploading 4 items...`.

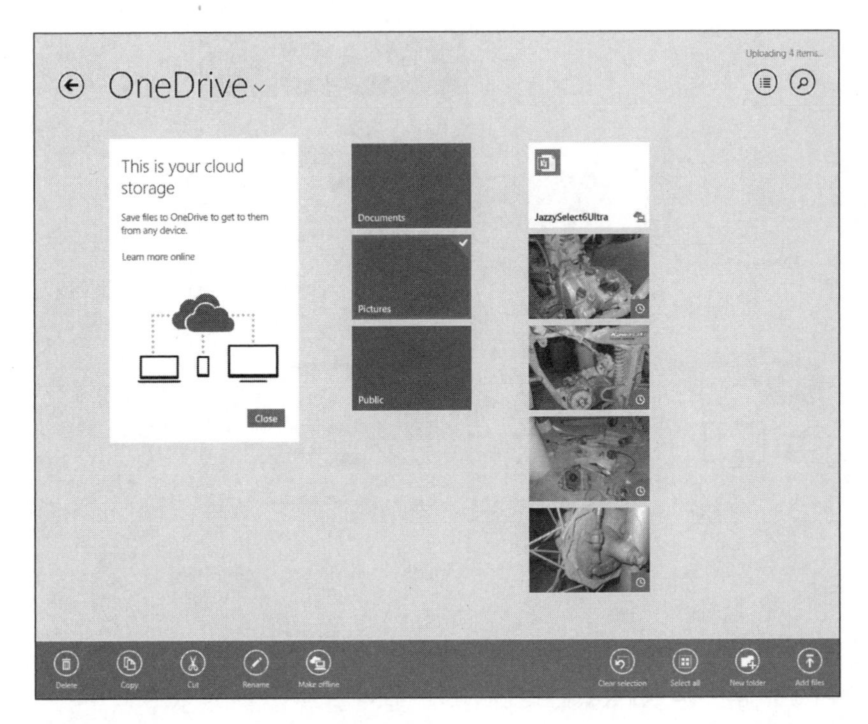

Figure 11-32 Uploading files to OneDrive.

By default, you can always browse all the files and folders in the OneDrive, but you can open or edit them only when you are online. You can change this to make some folders available offline or to make the entire OneDrive storage available offline.

To select specific folders, open the OneDrive app and then right-click the folder. Select the **Make offline** app command. When the dialog box is displayed, select the **Make offline** button.

If you have plenty of space on your PC, you might want to make the entire OneDrive available offline. This setting also ensures that any new folders that you create will also be available offline the next time you want to access them. To change this setting, open the OneDrive app, swipe or point to the right side of the screen, click on the **Settings** charm, and then click **Options** to view the OneDrive Options bar. To make the files and folders in your OneDrive available offline, toggle the Access all files offline setting to **On**, as shown in Figure 11-33.

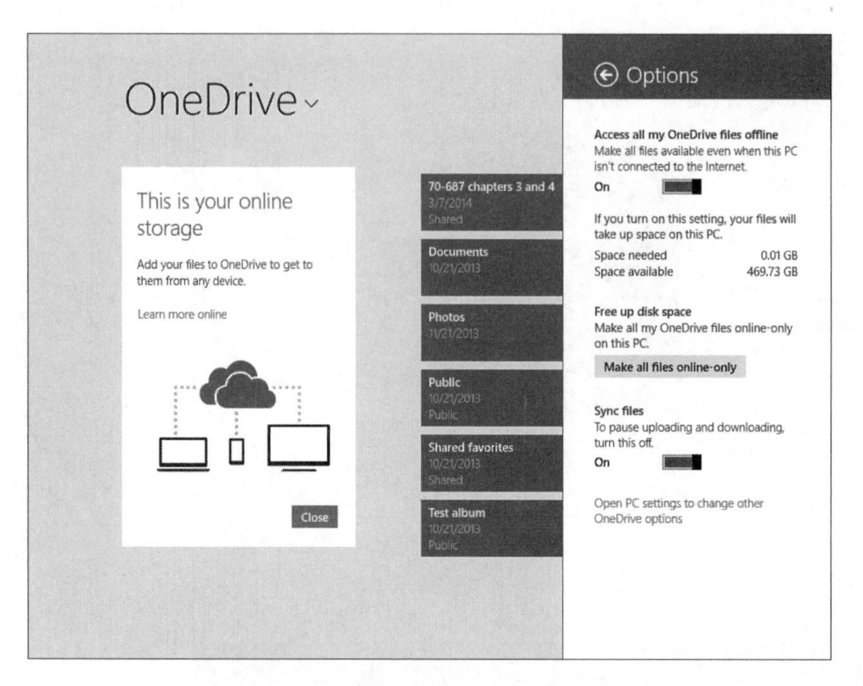

Figure 11-33 Make a OneDrive folder available offline.

OneDrive Desktop

When you are logged in to a Windows account on your PC, OneDrive storage is integrated with File Explorer and desktop applications. You can use the OneDrive and the files and folders in it just like any other drive. Remember, however, that files in the OneDrive Public folder are shared publicly on the Internet by default.

You can save files directly from many desktop applications to the OneDrive folders just as you would to any other location. For many desktop applications, such as Microsoft Office, you will notice that OneDrive is the recommended location that appears when you save documents.

NOTE For computers running older version of Windows or other Mac OS X versions, the OneDrive desktop app must be downloaded from the Microsoft website before integration with the File Explorer will work. See http://windows.microsoft.com/en-us/skydrive/download for the download location. The download link does not appear on computers running Windows 8.1.

OneDrive Settings

All OneDrive settings in Windows 8.1 are now configured in the PC settings screen. In Figure 11-33, notice the link Open PC settings to change other SkyDrive options. You can use that link to open the settings dialogs, or you can click the **Settings** charm, select **Change PC settings**, and then select **OneDrive** from the list of PC settings.

From this app screen, shown in Figure 11-34, you can access all the OneDrive configuration settings.

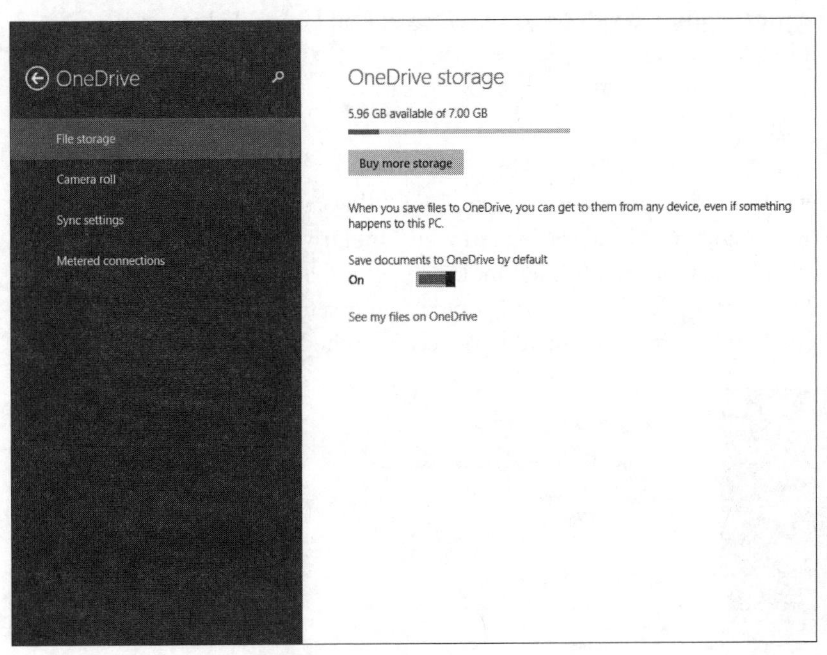

Figure 11-34 OneDrive configuration settings.

File Storage

By default, all Windows account users are provided 7 GB of storage at no charge. Additional storage can be purchased from Microsoft. From this screen, you can buy additional storage.

This section also allows you to modify the default location for saving documents. When the Save documents to SkyDrive by default toggle is on, most document types default to the SkyDrive when the save dialog is displayed. Toggle this to off to have the application present local drives for the default save location.

Camera Roll

If your PC or other device has a camera, you can choose to automatically upload photos and videos to the OneDrive's Camera roll folder. The options available include:

- **Don't upload photos:** Turns off automatic photo uploading.
- **Upload photos at good quality:** Is the default setting.
- **Upload photos at best quality:** Uploads the photos at the highest available quality setting for your camera.
- **Automatically upload videos to OneDrive:** Can be toggled on or off. The default is off.

Sync Settings

The Sync settings section, shown in Figure 11-35, allows you to configure your PC to synchronize a number of local settings to your OneDrive storage. By default, all your local settings are uploaded to the OneDrive. This feature provides a convenient way to move from device to device and take your settings along, as long as you log in with your Microsoft account and have access to the Internet.

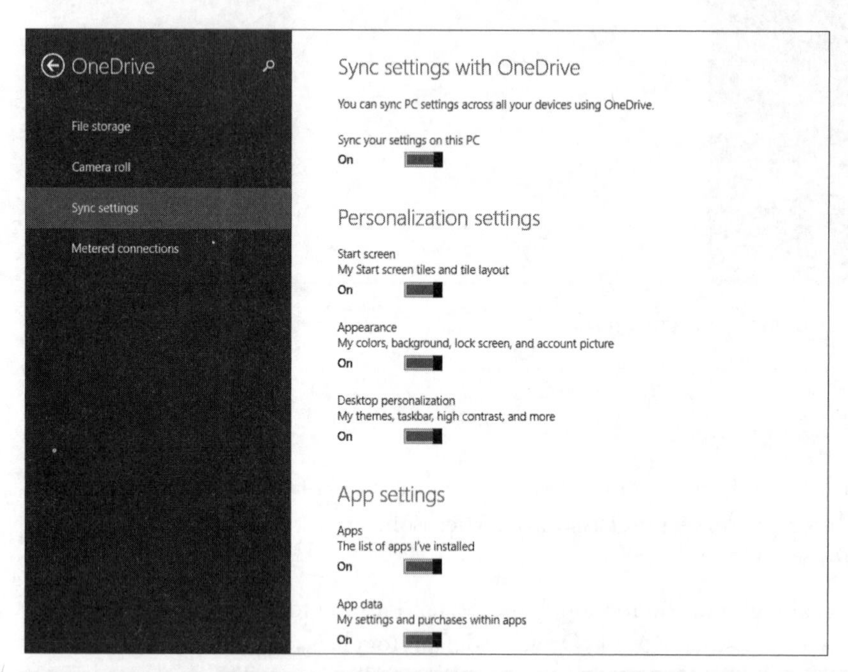

Figure 11-35 OneDrive sync settings.

The following settings can be toggled on or off for OneDrive sync:

- **Sync settings with SkyDrive:** Automatically syncs your PC settings across all your devices when it is toggled on.
- **Personalization settings:**
  - Start screen
  - Appearance
  - Desktop personalization
- **App settings:**
  - Apps
  - App data
- **Other settings:**
  - Web Browser
  - Passwords
  - Language preferences
  - Ease of Access
  - Other Windows settings
- **Back up settings:** Allows you to restore your settings to your PC.

Metered Connections

If your device typically uses a network connection from a provider that charges for the amount of data that you consume, you can modify the way OneDrive synchronizes files. By default, the settings try to make sure OneDrive does not use your connection when you are roaming, which typically incurs higher charges. You can also turn off uploading and all syncing settings when you are on a metered connection.

The following settings are available. Each one can be toggled on or off.

- Upload and download files over metered connections
- Upload and download files over metered connections even when I'm roaming
- Sync and back up settings over metered connections
- Sync and back up settings over metered connections even when I'm roaming

Configuring Near Field Communication

With Windows 8.1, Microsoft has consolidated its latest operating system for PCs, tables, smartphones, and major portability. Data sharing across devices in a simple and intuitive way is important for this ecosystem, and one of the enabling technologies now employed is Near Field Communication, or Near Field Proximity as Microsoft often refers to its supporting application interfaces. On Windows Phone, it's often referred to as App to App Communication.

Near Field Communication (NFC) takes place only in very close proximity, within a few inches. It works within and even smaller range than personal area networks (PANs), using technologies such as Bluetooth. NFC is a set of standards that has been used in smartphones for a few years, allowing users to transfer files, perform payment transactions, and share contact information by touching phones or holding them very close together. Windows 8.1 now brings this capability to laptops, tablets, smartphones, and PCs.

As more devices and third-party apps and software become available with NFC capability, Windows 8.1 will be able to leverage more capabilities. Some of the ways that Windows 8.1 can take advantage of NFC-tagged devices include:

- **NFC tap-to-pair printing:** Allows you to simply tap your Windows device against an NFC-enabled printer to enable printing to the device. Existing printers can be updated by attaching an NFC tag.
- **Native Miracast wireless display:** Allows you to project your presentation through a Miracast-enabled display device by pairing your Windows device using NFC.
- **Auto-triggered VPN:** Enables one-click sign-in to your company when you select an app or resource that needs access through a VPN client.

Windows Store apps can make use of NFC capabilities in a number of ways, including enabling devices such as keyboards and headsets. Generally, these apps configure themselves and work automatically. However, you should be aware of the options for configuring NFC in Windows 8.1, working with configuration options, and understanding how to lock down NFC when required for securing a business environment.

Typically, Windows 8.1 uses NFC to work with devices. When you click on the Devices charm, a list of devices you can interact with is displayed (see Figure 11-36). That includes printers or USB-connected cameras, for instance, but if there are any NFC-enabled devices in range, they also appear in the Devices charm.

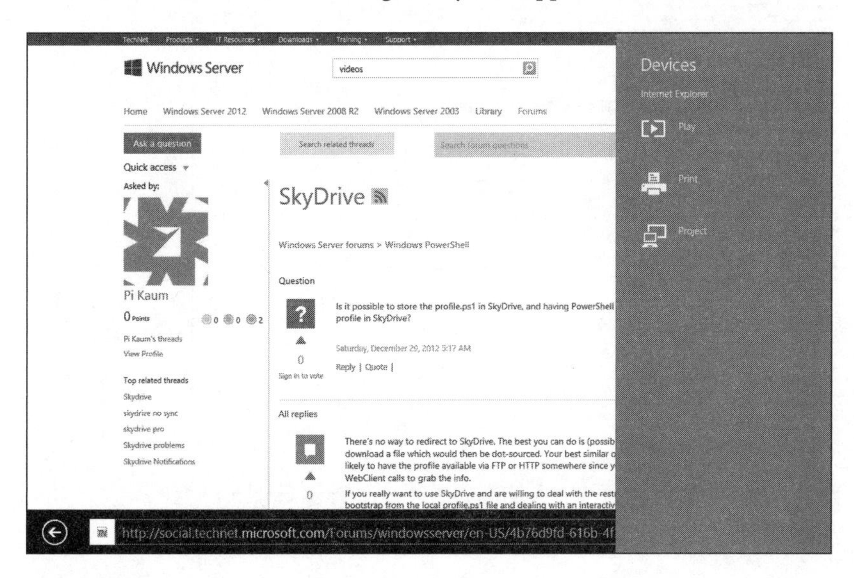

Figure 11-36 Devices available for interaction.

There is currently no UI in Windows 8.1 for enabling or disabling NFC (or Proximity services). To disable apps from sending or receiving data through NFC, you must disable the firewall rule on Windows Firewall or using Group Policies. Use the following steps to disable Proximity sharing:

Step 1. Open **Windows Firewall with Advanced Security**, using either the Administrative Tools shortcut or though the Windows Firewall Control Panel applet.

Step 2. Select **Inbound Rules** and then locate the rule called **Proximity sharing over TCP** (this is a built-in rule included with the Windows 8.1 default firewall rules).

Step 3. Right-click the rule and select **Disable** from the right-click menu, as shown in Figure 11-37.

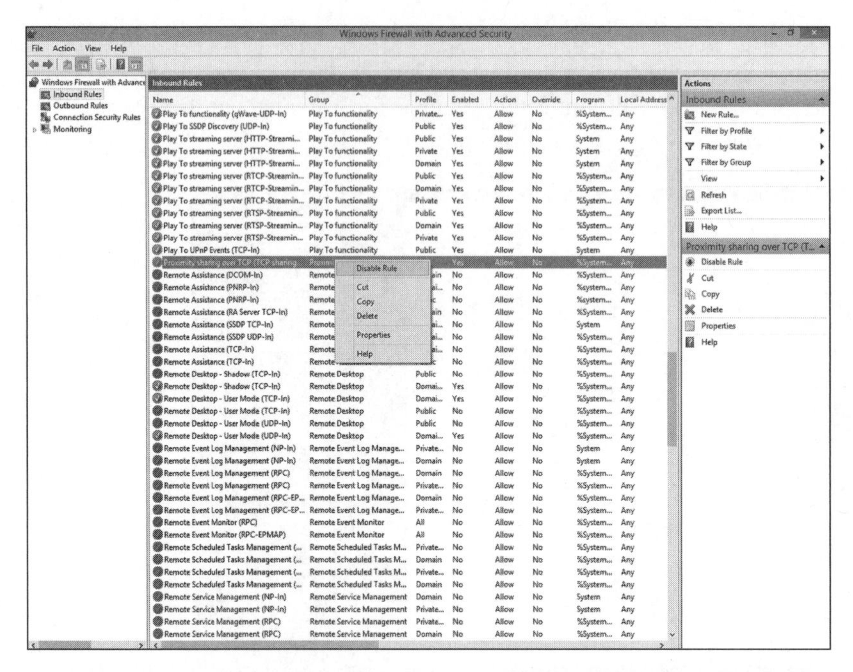

Figure 11-37 Disable Proximity sharing to lock down NFC communications.

Configuring Disk Quotas

First introduced in Windows 2000 and improved with each successive version of Windows is the concept of disk quotas. This feature allows an administrator to set a limit on the amount of disk space used by an individual user. You can send a warning to users when they reach a certain level of disk usage, and you can write an event to the event log if a user attempts to exceed his quota. When you have enabled disk quotas, Windows 8.1 also collects disk usage statistics for all users enabled on the volume, thus allowing the administrator to keep track of disk usage. Thereby, the administrator can manage disks more efficiently and prevent users from "hogging" disk space.

File Explorer enables you to enable quotas on a per-volume, per-user basis. Use the following procedure to enable disk quotas:

Step 1. In File Explorer, right-click the volume (partition) on which you want to enable disk quotas and then select **Properties**.

Step 2. In the Properties dialog box, click the **Quota** tab and then click the **Show Quota Settings** command button to display disk quota information.

Step 3. On the Quota Properties dialog box, select the **Enable quota management** check box. Then specify values for the quota parameters described in Table 11-10 and shown in Figure 11-38.

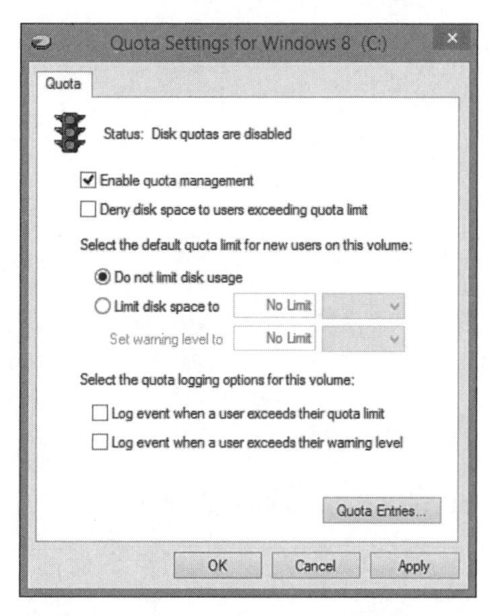

Figure 11-38 You can enable disk quotas for individual users on given disks.

Step 4. To configure quota entries for specific users, click the **Quota Entries** command button. From the Quota Entries dialog box, you can view the status of all quotas configured on the volume, including the username, amount of space used, quota limit, warning level, and percent used.

Step 5. To add a quota entry, click **Quota > New Quota Entry**, type the username to whom the quota will apply in the Select Users dialog box, and then click **OK**. Then in the Add New Quota Entry dialog box (see Figure 11-39), select **Limit disk space to**, specify the desired limit and warning levels, and then click **OK**. Repeat as needed to add quotas for other users.

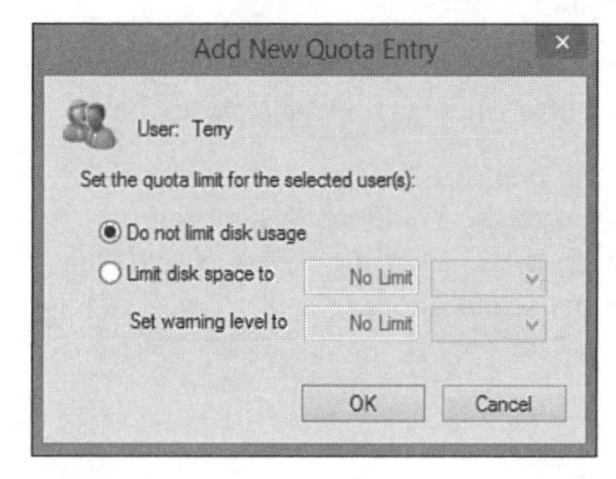

Figure 11-39 The Add New Quota Entry dialog box enables you to add a disk quota for a single user.

Step 6. After making any changes and closing the Quota Entries dialog box, click **OK** or **Apply**. A Disk Quota message box (see Figure 11-40) warns you that the disk will be rescanned and that this process may take several minutes.

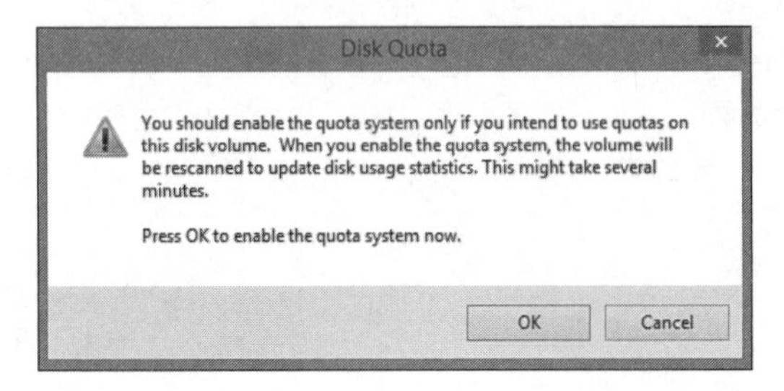

Figure 11-40 You are warned that the disk volume will be rescanned to update disk usage statistics.

Step 7. Click **OK** to close this message box and start the scan.

Table 11-10 describes the options that are available on the Quota tab of the disk's Properties dialog box.

Table 11-10 Disk Quota Configuration Options

Option	Description
Enable quota management	This option enables quota management and enables the other options so that you can configure them.
Deny disk space to users exceeding quota limit	When users exceed their quota, they receive an Out of disk space message, and they cannot write further data.
Do not limit disk usage	Select this option when you do not want to limit the amount of disk space used.
Limit disk space to	This option configures the disk space limit per user.
Set warning level to	This option configures the amount of disk space that a user can write before receiving a warning.
Log event when a user exceeds their quota limit	This option writes an event to the Windows system log on the computer running disk quotas whenever a user exceeds her quota limit.
Log event when a user exceeds their warning level	This option writes an event to the Windows system log on the computer running disk quotas any time a user exceeds his quota warning level, not his actual quota.

When the disk quota system is active, a user checking the properties of the volume where it is enabled sees only the amount of space permitted on the quota; the available space is the permitted space minus the space already used. If a user tries to copy a file that is larger than the allowed space, he receives a message that the file cannot be copied. In addition, an event is written to the Event log if you have selected the appropriate check box described in Table 11-10. You can view usage statistics by clicking the **Quota Entries** button.

NOTE You can enable quotas only on volumes formatted with the NTFS file system. Only administrators can enable quotas, but they can permit users to view quota settings.

Some Guidelines for Using Quotas

The following are a few guidelines for using disk quotas:

- When installing applications, use the default Administrator account rather than your own user account. That way, the space used by the applications will not be charged against your quota if you have one.
- If you want to use disk quotas only to monitor disk space usage, specify a soft quota by clearing the **Deny disk space to users exceeding quota limit** check box in File Explorer. That way, users are not prevented from saving important data.
- Set appropriate quotas on all volumes that a user can access. Provide warnings to the users, and log events when they exceed their quota limit and/or warning level.
- Be aware that use of hard quotas might cause applications to fail.
- Monitor space used and increase the limits for those users who need larger amounts of space.
- Set quotas on all shared volumes, including public folders and network servers, to ensure appropriate use of space by users.
- If a user no longer stores files on a certain volume, delete her disk quota entries. You can do this only after her files have been moved or deleted, or after someone has taken ownership of them.

NOTE You should be aware that NTFS file compression actually has no particular effect on the amount of quota space available to such a user. Disk quotas are calculated based on the amount of space occupied by uncompressed folders and files, regardless of whether files are compressed or not compressed.

Configuring Object Access Auditing

Users on a network are naturally curious about the myriad of volumes, folders, and files that they find. They like to "poke around" to see what's there. And some can have malicious thoughts. So sensitive information might be accessed, modified, or even deleted. Corporate security policies generally stipulate that records of who attempts to access or modify such sensitive information must be kept. For this purpose, Microsoft has included object access auditing in its operating systems ever since the early days of Windows NT.

Object access is just one kind of a large list of events that Windows enables you to audit. Windows enables you to audit user access to files, folders, and printers by configuring the Audit policy for the local computer. If you need to audit computers that are members of an AD DS domain, you can configure the Group Policy in the domain or OU that contains these computers. Otherwise, you can configure the Local Group Policy setting for object access auditing. We discuss auditing in more detail in Chapter 12, "Configuring Local Security Settings."

To configure object access auditing, you must configure two pieces of information:

- Enable success or failure auditing for object access.
- Specify the folders, files, or printers for which access is to be audited.

Enabling Object Access Auditing

Use the following procedure to enable object access auditing on a Windows 8.1 computer:

Step 1. From the Search charm, type `gpedit.msc` in the text box and select **gpedit.msc**. This opens the Local Group Policy Editor MMC snap-in.

Step 2. Navigate to the **Computer Configuration\Windows Settings\Security Settings\Local Policies\Audit Policy** node. You receive the series of policy options shown in Figure 11-41.

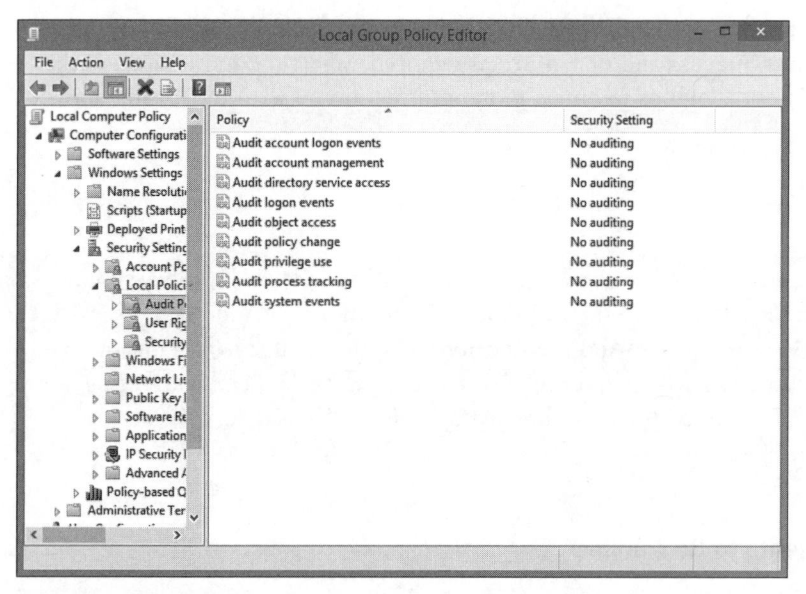

Figure 11-41 The Audit Policy subnode in the Local Group Policy Editor enables you to audit several types of actions on your Windows 8.1 computer.

Step 3. Double-click **Audit object access**. You receive the Audit object access Properties dialog box shown in Figure 11-42.

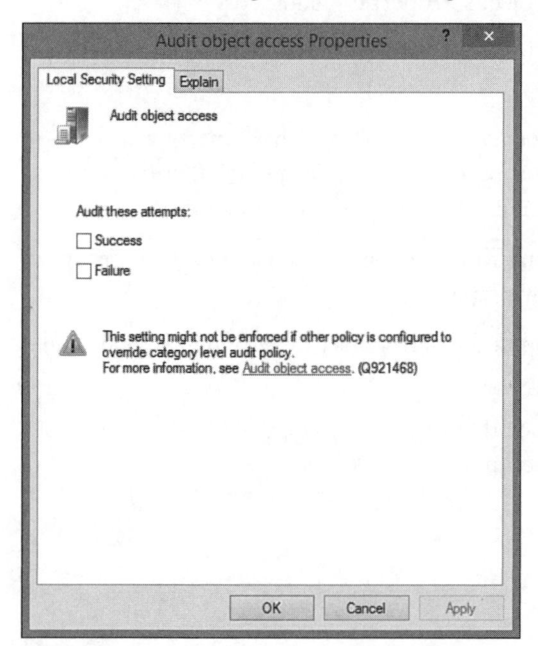

Figure 11-42 You can enable auditing to trigger an event log entry when an action has completed successfully, has failed, or both.

Step 4. To audit successful and/or failed attempts at accessing files, folders, or printers, select **Success** and/or **Failure** as required. Select the **Explain** tab of the Properties dialog box to obtain more information on what the setting does.

Step 5. Click **OK** or **Apply**.

NOTE Additional audit policies are available in the Advanced Audit Policy subnode of Group Policy, available from the Computer Configuration\Windows Settings\Security Settings\Local Policies\Audit Policy node. For more information on advanced audit policy settings as a whole, refer to "Advanced Security Audit Policy Settings" at http://technet.microsoft.com/en-us/library/dd772712(WS.10).aspx.

Specifying Objects to Be Audited

To track object access or directory service access, you must configure the system access control list (SACL) for each required object. Use the following procedure:

Step 1. In File Explorer, right-click the required file, folder, or printer and choose **Properties**.

Step 2. Select the **Security** tab of the object's Properties dialog box.

Step 3. Click **Advanced** to open the Advanced Security Settings dialog box and then select the **Auditing** tab.

Step 4. You are warned that you must be an administrator or have the appropriate privileges to view the auditing properties of the object. Click **Continue** to proceed and then click **Yes** in the UAC prompt if you receive one.

Step 5. Click **Add** to display the Auditing Entry dialog box. To add users or groups to this dialog box, click **Select a principal**.

Step 6. Type the required user or group in the Select User or Group dialog box and then click **OK**.

Step 7. On the Auditing Entry dialog box that appears (see Figure 11-43), select the types of actions you want to track and then click **OK**.

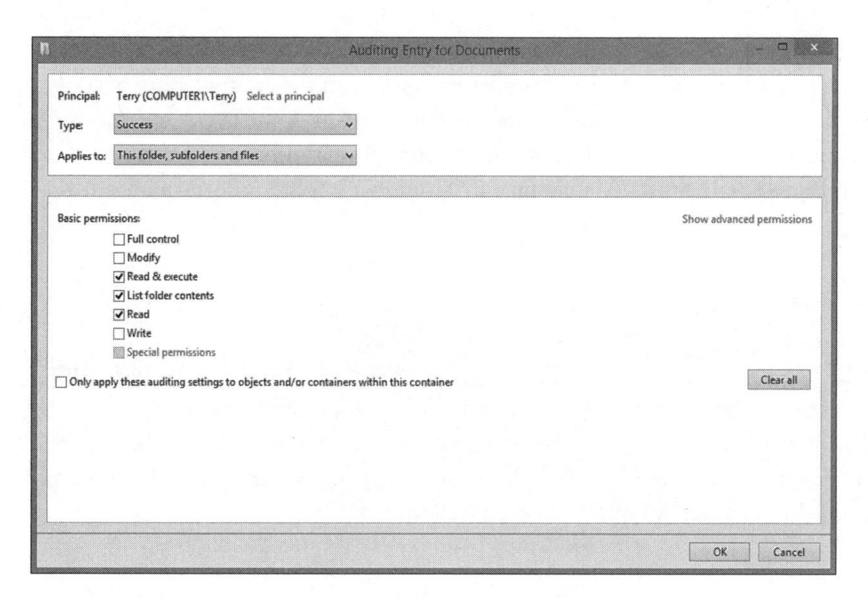

Figure 11-43 Configuring the SACL for a user or group.

Step 8. The completed auditing entries appear in the Advanced Security Settings dialog box, as shown in Figure 11-44. Click **OK** twice to close these dialog boxes.

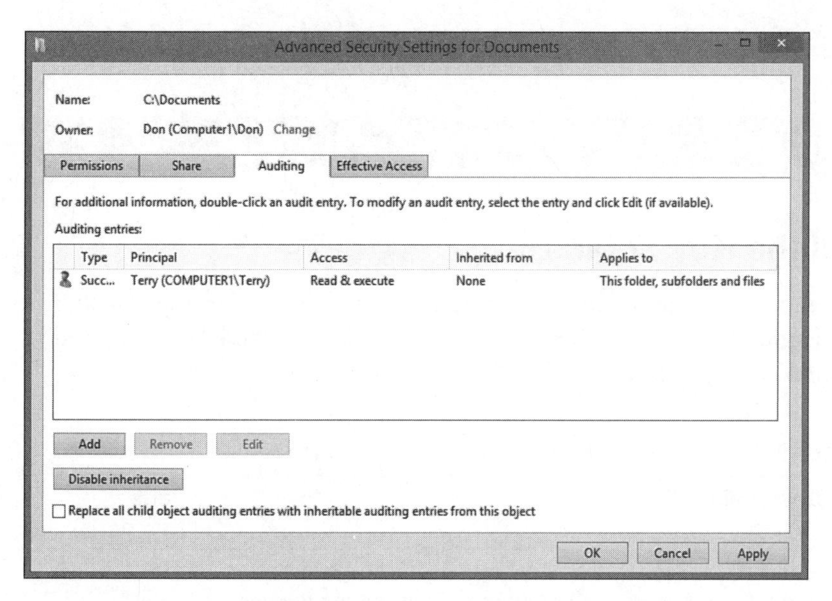

Figure 11-44 The Advanced Security Settings dialog box displays information on the types of object auditing actions that have been specified.

After you configure object access auditing, attempts to access audited objects appear in the Security log, which you can view from Event Viewer in the Administrative Tools folder. For more information on any audited event, right-click the event and choose **Event Properties**. For more information on Event Viewer and viewing the logs it contains, refer to Chapter 18, "Managing and Monitoring System Performance."

TIP Ensure that the Security log has adequate space to audit the events that you configure for auditing because the log can fill rapidly. The recommended size is at least 128 MB. You should also periodically save the existing log to a file and clear all past events. If the log becomes full, the default behavior is that the oldest events are overwritten (and therefore lost). You can also configure the log to archive when full and not to overwrite events, but new events are not recorded. Loss of recorded events could be serious in the case of high-security installations.

NOTE You can also use the `Auditpol.exe` command-line tool to perform audit policy configuration actions. For information on the subcommands available for this command, open a command prompt and type **`auditpol /?`**. For additional information on this command, refer to "Auditpol" at http://technet.microsoft.com/en-us/library/cc731451.aspx.

Exam Preparation Tasks

Review All the Key Topics

Review the most important topics in the chapter, noted with the key topics icon in the outer margin of the page. Table 11-11 lists a reference of these key topics and the page numbers on which each is found.

Table 11-11 Key Topics for Chapter 11

Key Topic Element	Description	Page Number(s)
Figure 11-1	Shows the Advanced sharing settings dialog box, which enables you to configure several global file-sharing options	450
Figure 11-5	Shows how to share a folder	454
Table 11-2	Describes available folder-sharing options	454
Figure 11-6	Shows how to specify shared folder permissions	455

Key Topic Element	Description	Page Number(s)
Paragraph	Describes how to create a homegroup	460
Table 11-4	Describes NTFS file and folder security permissions	465
Figure 11-15	Shows how to configure security permissions	466
Bulleted List	Describes how shared folder and security permissions interact with each other	474
Figure 11-23	Shows how to use EFS to encrypt files or folders	483
Step List	Shows how to back up EFS keys	485
Paragraph	Describes the concept of libraries	487
Table 11-9	Describes available printer permissions	491
Figure 11-34	Shows the OneDrive settings options	497
Step List	Shows how to configure Windows Firewall for Near Field Communications	501
Step List	Shows how to configure disk quotas	502-504
Table 11-10	Describes available disk quota configuration options	504
Step List	Shows how to enable object access auditing	506-508
Step List	Shows how to specify objects to be audited	508-509

Complete the Tables and Lists from Memory

Print a copy of Appendix B, "Memory Tables," (found on the CD), or at least the section for this chapter, and complete the tables and lists from memory. Appendix C, "Memory Tables Answer Key," also on the CD, includes completed tables and lists to check your work.

Definitions of Key Terms

Define the following key terms from this chapter, and check your answers in the Glossary:

Access control list (ACL), Administrative shares, Auditing, Certificate, Cloud, Decryption, Disk quotas, Encryption, Encrypting File System (EFS), Hidden shares, HomeGroup, Library, NFC, NTFS permissions, Private key, Public key, Public folder sharing, Recovery agent, Shared folder permissions, Shared folders, OneDrive, Special Access permissions, System access control list (SACL)

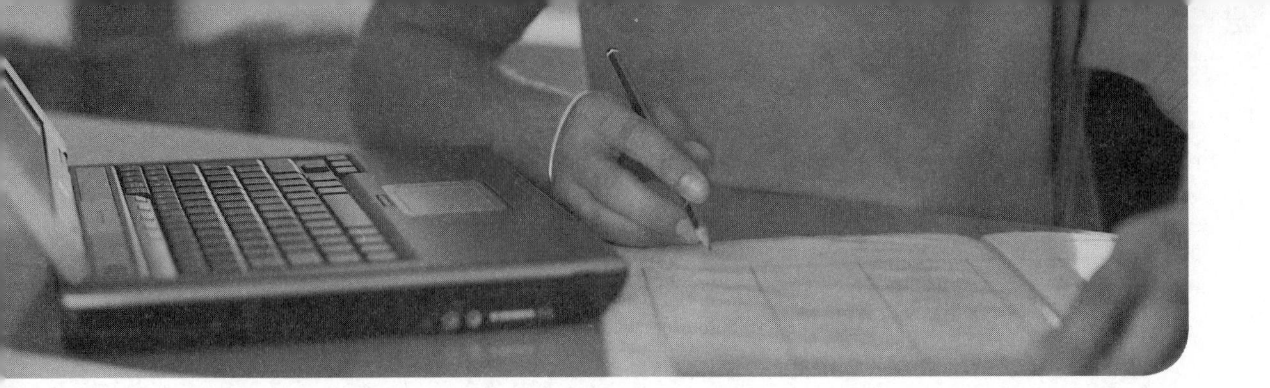

This chapter covers the following subjects:

- **Configuring Local Security Policy:** Local Security Policy presents a subset of Group Policy with settings designed to enhance the security of a local Windows 8.1 computer. This section shows you how to configure policies affecting users logging on to the computer, as well as auditing of actions that users might perform on the computer and several other security-related settings.
- **Configuring User Account Control:** UAC is designed to enable all users, even administrators, to run with a standard access token. When a user requires administrative privileges for a task that can affect system properties, such as installing a program, the user receives a prompt that requests administrative credentials. UAC helps prevent unauthorized program installation and system modification. In Windows 8.1, you can modify the settings that determine when these prompts appear; you learn how to work with these settings in this section.
- **Configuring Secure Boot:** Secure boot is a new feature of Windows, introduced with Windows 8 and Windows Server 2012 R2, that enhances security of computers by preventing unauthorized software and operating systems from running on the system. Secure Boot takes advantage of advances in computer hardware available on newer computers. This section introduces Secure Boot, requirements to use it, and how to configure Secure Boot startup.
- **Using SmartScreen Filters:** Another recent security enhancement in Windows, SmartScreen Filters can be used to automatically block software accessed over the Internet or remote locations that could damage or compromise the computer. SmartScreen features for Internet Explorer were covered previously in Chapter 6, "Configuring Internet Explorer." In this section, you learn about other Windows SmartScreen features.

Configuring Local Security Settings

In Chapter 10, "Configuring and Maintaining Network Security," we covered use of Windows Firewall on the local computer as well as network security tools such as IP Security (IPSec), network discovery, and wireless security. We continued security topics in Chapter 11, "Configuring and Securing Access to Files and Folders," with a discussion of shared folder and security permissions as well as topics such as disk quotas and object access auditing. In that chapter, you learned how resources are shared across the network and how you can control access to files, folders, and printers. You learned how to specify who can do what with these items.

Now, we take these steps further by showing you how to configure Local Security Policy, User Account Control (UAC), Secure Boot, and SmartScreen Filters. Local Security Policy is a subset of Group Policy settings available on Windows Servers that enables you to specify what users are allowed to do on the local computer and across the network. UAC provides additional security by requesting administrative permission before performing tasks such as installing applications or modifying the Registry. Secure Boot helps to prevent access to the computer by unauthorized firmware, operating systems, or drivers during system startup. SmartScreen Filter is an Internet Explorer filter that protects browsing sessions by detecting phishing websites and preventing the download or installation of malicious software.

"Do I Know This Already?" Quiz

The "Do I Know This Already?" quiz allows you to assess whether you should read this entire chapter or simply jump to the "Exam Preparation Tasks" section for review. If you are in doubt, read the entire chapter. Table 12-1 outlines the major headings in this chapter and the corresponding "Do I Know This Already?" quiz questions. You can find the answers in Appendix A, "Answers to the 'Do I Know This Already?' Quizzes."

Table 12-1 "Do I Know This Already?" Foundation Topics Section-to-Question Mapping

Foundations Topics Section	Questions Covered in This Section
Configuring Local Security Policy	1–3
Configuring User Account Control	4–8
Configuring Secure Boot	9–11
Using SmartScreen Filters	12–13

1. What password policy actually weakens password security and is therefore not recommended for use by Microsoft?
    a. Enforce password history
    b. Minimum password age
    c. Maximum password age
    d. Complexity requirements
    e. Store passwords using reversible encryption

2. You want to ensure that users cannot cycle rapidly through a series of passwords and then reuse their old password immediately. Which password policy should you enable to prevent this action from occurring?
    a. Enforce password history
    b. Minimum password age
    c. Maximum password age
    d. Password must meet complexity requirements
    e. Store passwords using reversible encryption

3. One day after logging on to your Windows 8.1 computer, which you have shared with several others in your department, you notice that the time zone has been changed to an improper setting. You would like to discover who is making improper modifications to your computer's settings. Which of the following audit policies should you enable?
    a. Account management
    b. Policy change
    c. Privilege use
    d. System events

4. You have just migrated to a brand new Windows 8.1 Pro computer after having worked on a Windows XP Professional computer for the past eight years. You are using an administrative user account, but when you start to install Microsoft Office 2010, your screen dims and you are asked to confirm your intent. What happened and why?
   a. The media containing your Microsoft Office program has been compromised by an unknown entity, and Windows has discovered this problem.
   b. You need to check the Microsoft Office installation media for viruses or spyware before proceeding to install Office 2010.
   c. You have not configured your user account with the ability to install programs older than Windows 8.1, and you are being asked to configure the program for compatibility with Windows XP.
   d. This is normal behavior in Windows 8.1; UAC is asking you to provide administrative consent to install Microsoft Office 2010.

5. You right-click **Computer** and choose **Properties** to obtain system settings and perform some basic configuration activities on your Windows 8.1 computer. You notice a shield icon against several actions that you can access from here. What does this mean for a default configuration?
   a. When you select one of these actions, you always receive a UAC prompt regardless of your user credentials.
   b. When you select one of these actions while running as a standard (nonadministrative) user, you receive a UAC prompt.
   c. When you select one of these actions while running as a standard (nonadministrative) user, you have to log off and log back on as an administrator.
   d. These icons merely warn you to be careful with the actions you're intending to perform, but you are able to do them regardless of your user credentials.

6. You have downloaded an executable file from the Internet. When you attempt to run this program, you receive a UAC message box with a red title bar and red shield informing you that the program has been blocked. What does this mean and what should you do to run this program?
   a. This program is an unsigned program from a verified publisher. Simply click **Yes** to run it.
   b. This program is an unsigned program from a nonverified publisher. Click **Yes** and re-enter your password to run it.
   c. This program is a high-risk program from a nonverified publisher. Click **Yes** and re-enter your password to run it.
   d. This program is a high-risk program that Windows has blocked completely. You cannot run it in its present form, and you should check the program's publisher on the Internet and locate a certified version that will run.

7. You sometimes use the built-in Administrator account on your Windows 8.1 computer, so you have configured this account with a strong username and password. You want to have this account display UAC prompts in the same fashion as other administrative accounts. What should you do?
   a. From the User Account Settings Control Panel applet, select the **Always notify** option.
   b. From the User Account Settings Control Panel applet, select the **Notify me only when programs try to make changes to my computer** option.
   c. In Group Policy, you should enable the **Admin Approval Mode for the Built-In Administrator account** policy.
   d. Do nothing. By default, this account works just like any other user account that belongs to the Administrators group.

8. You have had problems with users installing unapproved software on the Windows 8.1 computers in your small office. These users all have standard user accounts. You would like to configure UAC to block any programs that require elevated privileges in order to run the programs. So you access the Group Policy editor. What policy should you enable?
   a. You should enable the Behavior of the elevation prompt for standard users policy and then select the **Prompt for credentials** option.
   b. You should enable the Behavior of the elevation prompt for standard users policy and then select the **Prompt for credentials on the secure desktop** option.
   c. You should enable the Behavior of the elevation prompt for standard users policy and then select the **Automatically deny elevation requests** option.
   d. You should enable the Only Elevate executables that are signed and validated policy.

9. What Windows 8.1 and Windows Server 2012 R2 operating system feature can protect computers from rootkits and boot sector viruses?
   a. Microsoft Secure Boot
   b. UEFI Boot
   c. DiskPart
   d. BitLocker

10. You are a support technician in a company, and a user has ordered a new laptop with Windows 8.1 preinstalled. While she is learning the new operating system, she would like to be able to dual-boot to Windows 7 and has called you because she cannot get Windows 7 set up to run on the new computer. The user has a free partition on the hard drive to install it on. You arrive to assist with the computer and discover that Secure Boot is enabled. How can you install Windows 7?

    a. Start Windows 7 setup from the DVD drive.

    b. Copy a Windows 7 image to a USB drive and boot to the USB drive.

    c. Disable Secure Boot, if possible.

    d. Change the computer's setup to startup in legacy BIOS-compatibility mode.

11. You have performed a default installation of Windows 8.1 on a new computer using the UEFI startup. After the installation is completed, how many partitions are on the computer's boot drive?

    a. 3

    b. 4

    c. 1

    d. 2

12. When running a new application for testing that your company's developers have delivered, you receive a warning from Windows SmartScreen indicating that it is an unrecognized app. You know the developer, and he has recently compiled the program, so you know that it is safe. What should you do?

    a. Inform the developer so that he can update his SmartScreen signature for the application.

    b. Change the SmartScreen settings to turn off Windows SmartScreen.

    c. Add the application to the SmartScreen database.

    d. Click the **More Info** link on the SmartScreen warning message and select **Run anyway**.

13. In which of the following ways does Windows SmartScreen protect your computer? (Select all that apply.)

    a. Analyzes web pages for suspicious characteristics

    b. Scans your hard drive files for malicious software signatures

    c. Examines downloaded files and blocks any downloads from compromised or malicious software sites

    d. Compares application files against a database of files and blocks applications that are not recognized or that are known to be malware

Foundation Topics

Configuring Local Security Policy

You can access the Local Security Policy snap-in through Administrative Tools under Control Panel's System and Security category or by accessing the Search charm, typing `local security`, and then clicking **Local Security Policy**. The policies defined in this utility affect all users on the computer, unless the policies allow you to configure them on a per-user or per-group basis. This snap-in is shown in Figure 12-1.

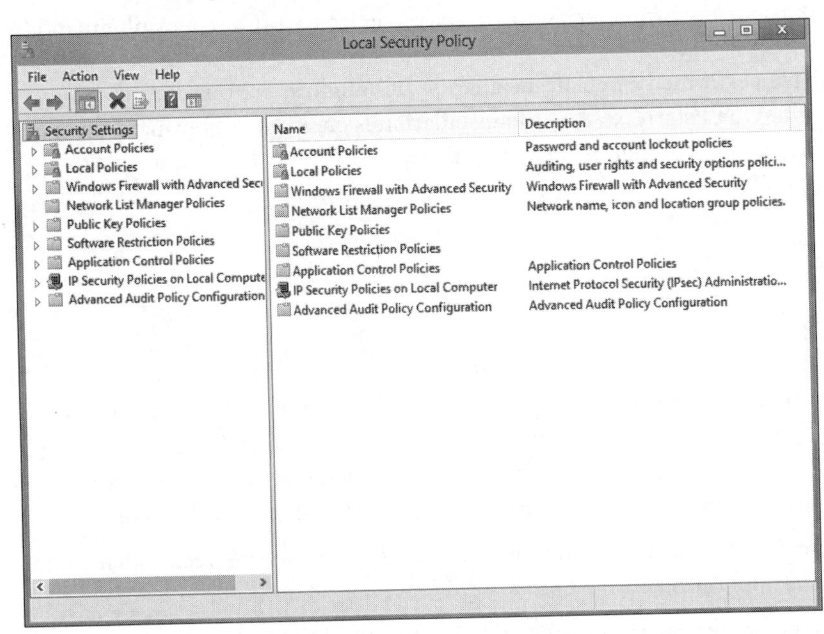

Figure 12-1 You can configure numerous local security policy settings with the Local Security Policy snap-in in Windows 8.1.

The Local Security Policy snap-in enables you to configure a large range of security-related policy settings. These settings are summarized here:

- **Account Policies:** Includes password policies and account lockout policies. We discuss account policies later in this section.
- **Local Policies:** Includes audit policies, user rights assignment, and security options. We discuss these policies later in this chapter.
- **Windows Firewall with Advanced Security:** Enables you to configure properties of Windows Firewall for domain, private, and public profiles. You can specify inbound and outbound connection rules as well as monitoring settings.

- **Network List Manager Policies:** Enables you to control the networks that computers can access and their location types such as public and private (which automatically specifies the appropriate firewall settings according to location type). You can also specify which networks a user is allowed to connect to.
- **Public Key Policies:** Enables you to configure public key infrastructure (PKI) settings. Included are policies governing the use of Encrypting File System (EFS), Data Protection, and BitLocker Drive Encryption.
- **Software Restriction Policies:** Enables you to specify which software programs users can run on network computers, which programs users on multiuser computers can run, and the execution of email attachments. You can also specify whether software restriction policies apply to certain groups such as administrators.
- **Application Control Policies:** These are a set of software control policies first introduced with Windows 7 that include the AppLocker feature. AppLocker provides new enhancements that enable you to specify exactly what users are permitted to run on their desktops according to unique file identities. We covered software restriction policies and application control policies in Chapter 5, "Installing, Configuring, and Securing Applications in Windows 8.1."
- **IP Security Policies on Local Computer:** Controls the implementation of IP Security (IPSec) as used by the computer for encrypting communications over the network.
- **Advanced Audit Policy Configuration:** First introduced in Windows 7, this node contains 53 new policy settings that enable you to select explicitly the actions that you want to monitor and exclude actions that are of less concern.

NOTE Be aware that in an Active Directory Domain Services (AD DS) domain environment, all these policies can be configured at the site, domain, or organizational unit (OU) level, and that any policies configured at these levels override conflicting local policies. If a local policy does not apply as configured, consult your domain administrator for assistance.

Configuring Account Policies

The Windows 8.1 Local Security Policy tool includes the Account Policies node, which contains settings related to user accounts, including the password policy and account lockout policy.

Password Policies

You can configure password policy settings that help to protect users of Windows 8.1 client computers. The options available in Windows 8.1 are similar to those found in previous Windows versions. Password policies are generally intended to make passwords more difficult for intruders to discover. Figure 12-2 shows the available password policies and their default settings.

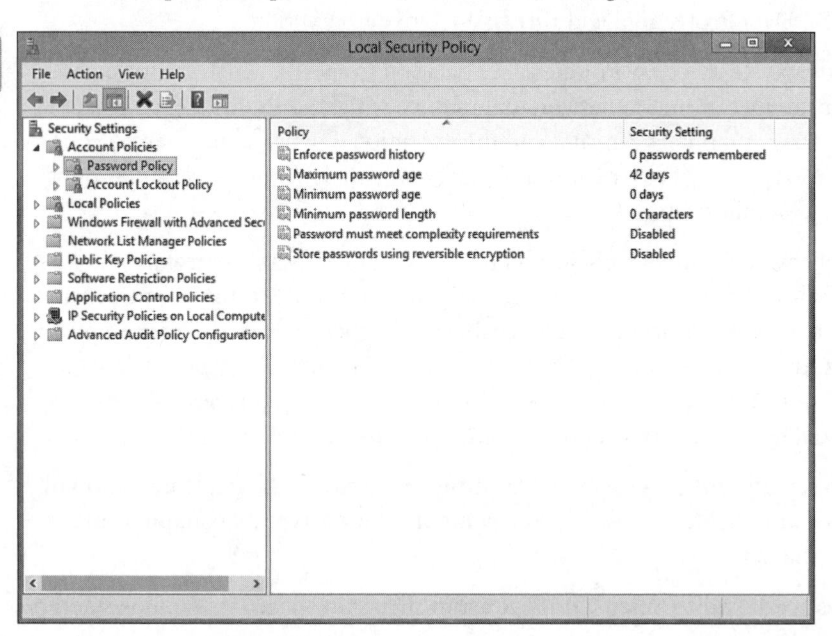

Figure 12-2 Windows 8.1 provides default values for the available password policies.

The following password policy settings are available:

- **Enforce password history:** Determines the number of passwords remembered by Windows for each user. Values range from 0 to 24. A user cannot reuse a password retained in the history list. A value of 0 means that no password history is retained and a user can reuse passwords at will.

- **Maximum password age:** Determines the number of days that a user can use a password before being required to specify a new one. Values range from 0 to 999. A value of 0 means that a user is never required to change his password. The default is 42 days.

- **Minimum password age:** Determines the minimum number of days a password must be used before it can be changed. Values range from 0 to 999 days and must be less than the maximum password age. The default value of 0 allows the user to immediately change a new password. This value allows a user to cycle through an entire history list of passwords in a short time; in other words, a user can repeatedly change a password in order to reuse his old password. This obviously defeats the purpose of enforcing password history, so you should configure this value to be at least one day.

- **Minimum password length:** Determines the minimum number of characters that can make up a password. Values range from 0 to 14. A value of 0 permits a blank password. Use a setting of 10 or higher for increased security.
- **Password must meet complexity requirements:** Stipulates that a password must meet complexity criteria, as follows: The password cannot contain the user account name or full name or parts of the name that exceed two consecutive characters. It must contain at least three of the following four items:
  - English lowercase letters
  - English uppercase letters
  - Numerals
  - Nonalphanumeric characters such as $; [ ] { } ! .
- **Store passwords using reversible encryption:** Determines the level of encryption used by Windows 8.1 for storing passwords. Enabling this option reduces security because it stores passwords in a format that is essentially the same as plain text. This option is disabled by default. You should enable this policy only if needed for clients who cannot use normal encryption, such as those using Challenge Handshake Authentication Protocol (CHAP) authentication or Internet Information Services (IIS) Digest Authentication.

To configure these policies, expand the **Account Policies\Password Policy** node of the Security Settings tool as shown in Figure 12-2. Right-click the desired policy and choose **Properties**. Then configure the appropriate value and click **OK**. Each policy setting also has an Explain tab that provides additional information on the policy setting and its purpose.

Account Lockout

A cracked user account password jeopardizes the security of the entire network. The account lockout policy is designed to lock an account out of the computer if a user (or intruder attempting to crack the network) enters an incorrect password a specified number of times, thereby limiting the effectiveness of dictionary-based password crackers. The account lockout policy contains the following settings:

- **Account lockout duration:** Specifies the number of minutes that an account remains locked out. Every account except for the default Administrator account can be locked out in this manner. You can set this value from 0 to 99999 minutes (or about 69.4 days). A value of 0 means that accounts that have exceeded the specified number of failed logon attempts are locked out indefinitely until an administrator unlocks the account.
- **Account lockout threshold:** Specifies the number of failed logon attempts that can occur before the account is locked out. You can set this value from 0 to 999 failed attempts. A value of 0 means that the account will never be locked out. Best practices recommend that you should never configure a setting of 0 here.
- **Reset account lockout counter after:** Specifies the number of minutes to wait after which the account lockout counter is reset to 0. You can set this value from 1 to 99999.

When you configure this policy, Windows 8.1 sets default values for the account lockout settings. To configure an account lockout policy, right-click **Account lockout threshold**, choose **Properties**, and then specify a value of your choice. As shown in Figure 12-3, Windows suggests default values for the other two policy settings. Click **OK** to define the policy settings and set these defaults. If you want to change the other settings, right-click the appropriate settings, choose **Properties**, and then enter the desired value.

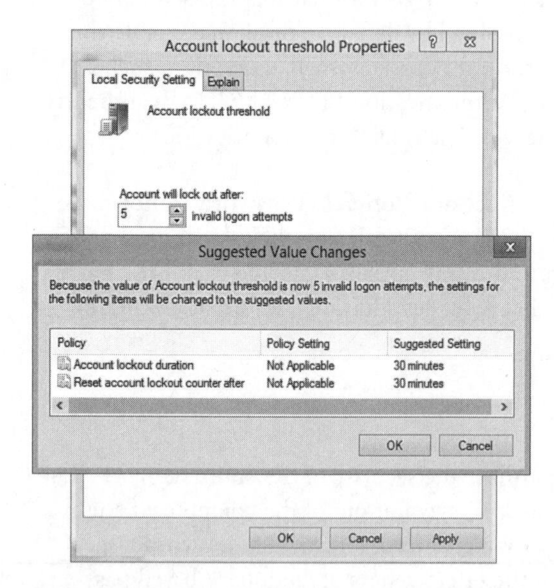

Figure 12-3 When you define an account lockout policy, Windows suggests defaults for the other two lockout policy settings.

Unlocking an Account

When a user account is locked out because of too many incorrect attempts at entering a password, it is simple for an administrator or a user who is delegated the task to unlock it. Right-click the user account in the Local Users and Groups node of the Computer Management snap-in and choose **Properties**. On the General tab of the user's Properties dialog box, clear the **Account is locked out** check box and then click **OK** or **Apply**.

NOTE You cannot lock out a user account by selecting this check box; it is provided for unlocking the account only. An account is locked out only by the user entering an incorrect password the specified number of times.

Configuring Local Policies

The Local Policies subnode of Security Settings enables you to configure audit policies, user rights assignment, and security options. We discuss user rights assignment in Chapter 13, "Configuring Authentication and Authorization."

Audit Policies

You have the ability to audit user access to files, folders, and printers by configuring the Audit policy for the local computer. If you need to audit computers that are members of a domain, you can configure the Group Policy in the organizational unit (OU) that contains these computers. Otherwise, you can configure the Audit Policy node, which is under Local Policies, as shown in Figure 12-4.

Using the audit policy settings, you can identify undesirable activities on the computer. For example, if you have a computer whose local user and group configuration was inexplicably changed, you can enable the Audit account management policy and select **Success** to determine who has made these changes. This policy configuration is depicted in Figure 12-5.

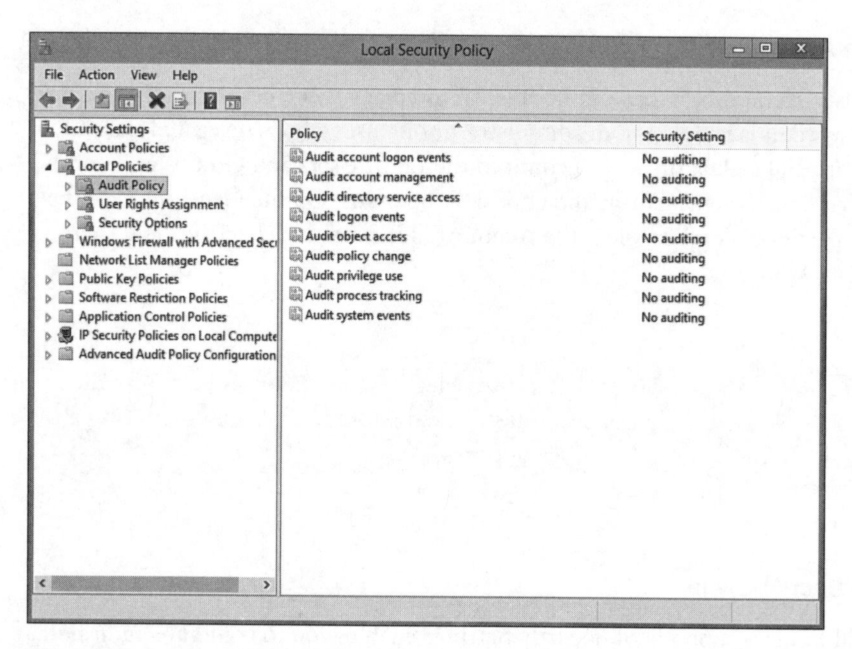

Figure 12-4 You can enable auditing in the Local Policies section of the Local Security Policy snap-in.

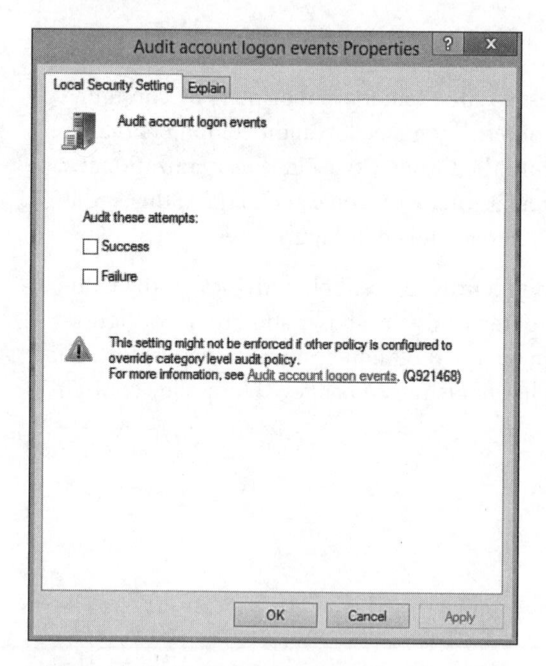

Figure 12-5 You can enable auditing to trigger an event log entry when an action has completed successfully, or has failed, or both.

Windows 8.1 enables you to audit the following types of events:

- **Account logon:** Logon or logoff by a domain user account at a domain controller. You should track both success and failure.
- **Account management:** Creation, modification, or deletion of computer, user, or group accounts. Also included are enabling and disabling of accounts and changing or resetting passwords. You should track both success and failure.
- **Directory service access:** Access to an AD DS object as specified by the object's system access control list (SACL). This category includes the four subcategories mentioned earlier in this section; enabling directory service access from the Group Policy Management Editor enables all four subcategories. Enable this category for failures (if you record success, a large number of events will be logged).
- **Logon events:** Logon or logoff by a user at a member server or client computer. You should track both success and failure (success logging can record an unauthorized access that succeeded).
- **Object access:** Access by a user to an object such as a file, folder, or printer. You need to configure auditing in each object's SACL to track access to that object. Track success and failure to access important resources on your network.
- **Policy change:** Modification of policies including user rights assignment, trust, and audit policies. This category is not normally needed unless unusual events are occurring.
- **Privilege use:** Use of a user right, such as changing the system time. Track failure events for this category.
- **Process tracking:** Actions performed by an application. This category is primarily for application developers and does not need to be enabled in most cases.
- **System events:** Events taking place on a computer such as an improper shutdown or a disk with very little free space remaining. Track success and failure events.

Group Policy or Local Security Policy enables you to configure success or failure for these types of actions. In other words, you can choose to record successful actions, failed attempts at performing these actions, or both. For example, if you are concerned about intruders that might be attempting to access your network, you can log failed logon events. You can also track successful logon events, which is useful in case the intruders succeed in accessing your network. For purposes of auditing files, folders, or printers, you need to enable object access auditing.

There is an additional policy that is more applicable to domain controllers than it is for Windows 8.1 client computers—that is, the Audit Account Logon Events. This, although similar to Audit Logon Events, triggers an event log entry only when a user logs on to a computer but has been authenticated by another computer. You might want to use this and the Audit Logon Event policies together on your domain controllers to get an idea of how your AD DS site configuration is affecting your logon traffic, but it does not give you much to go on for a Windows 8.1 computer that is not part of a domain.

NOTE For more information on auditing and new features in Windows 8.1 and Windows Server 2012 R2, refer to "Security Auditing Overview" at http://technet.microsoft.com/en-us/library/hh849642.aspx.

Security Options

The Security Options subnode within this node includes a large set of policy options as shown in Figure 12-6 that are important in controlling security aspects of the local computer. Several of the more important options that you should be familiar with are as follows:

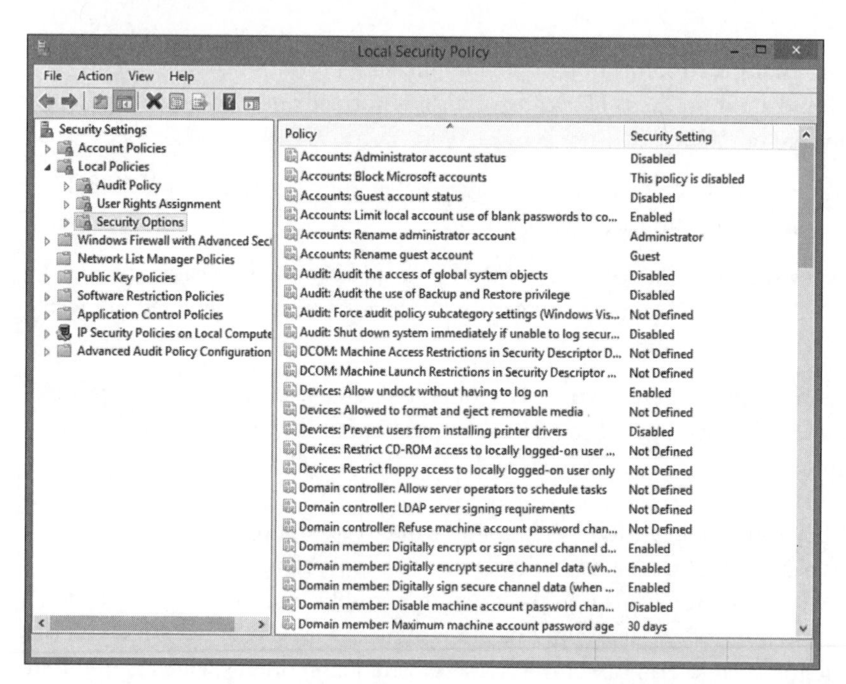

Figure 12-6 The Security Options subnode contains a comprehensive set of policy settings that help enhance the security of a Windows 8.1 computer.

- **Accounts: Block Microsoft accounts:** New to Windows 8 and Windows 8.1, this setting enables you to prevent users from adding Microsoft accounts. By selecting **Users can't add Microsoft accounts**, you can prevent users from adding Microsoft accounts, switching local accounts to a Microsoft account, or connect a domain account to a Microsoft account. By selecting **Users can't add or log on with Microsoft accounts**, you can prevent existing Microsoft account users from logging on. Be aware that this option might make it impossible for an existing administrator to log on if the administrator is using a Microsoft account. Microsoft recommends that you keep this policy disabled or not configured.
- **Accounts: Rename administrator account:** This option renames the default administrator account to a value you specify. Intruders cannot simply look for "Administrator" when attempting to crack your network.
- **Interactive logon: Do not display last user name:** Enabling this option prevents the username of the last logged-on user from appearing in the logon dialog box, thus preventing another individual from seeing a username. This can also help to reduce lockouts.
- **Interactive logon: Do not require CTRL+ALT+DEL:** When this option is enabled, a user is not required to press **Ctrl+Alt+Delete** to obtain the logon dialog box. Disable this policy in a secure environment to require the use of this key combination. Its use prevents rogue programs such as Trojan horses from capturing usernames and passwords.
- **Interactive logon: Require smart card:** When this option is enabled, users must employ a smart card to log on to the computer.
- **User Account Control:** Several policy settings determine the behavior of the UAC prompt for administrative and nonadministrative users, including behavior by applications that are located in secure locations on the computer such as `%ProgramFiles%` or `%Windir%`. We discuss UAC in the next section.

NOTE For more information on the policy settings in the Security Options subnode, refer to "Security Options" at http://technet.microsoft.com/en-us/library/cc749096(WS.10).aspx.

You can obtain additional information on many of these policy settings in the Windows 8.1 Help and Support Center.

Configuring User Account Control

In versions of Windows prior to Vista, many users became frustrated with the inability to perform many common tasks and therefore ran their computers with an administrative user account, often the default Administrator account created when Windows was installed. These users received total system privileges as required for installing and configuring applications, modifying system configuration, running background system tasks, installing device drivers, and performing other system configuration actions. Such a practice left the computers open to many types of attacks by malware programs such as viruses, worms, rootkits, and others.

Administrators and technical support personnel in a corporate environment were often left in a dilemma. They could grant users administrative privileges, which can result in users changing settings, either accidentally or deliberately, that disrupted computer or network performance or compromised security. Or they could limit user privileges, which often limited productivity because users were unable to perform basic tasks such as connecting to a wireless network or installing a printer driver.

Beginning with Windows Vista, Microsoft addressed this problem by introducing a new feature called User Account Control (UAC). Simply put, UAC requires users performing high-level tasks to confirm that they actually initiated the task. Members of the Administrators group are logged on with only normal user privileges and must approve administrative actions before such actions will run. Nonadministrative users must provide an administrative password. Providing administrative approval to run such tasks places the computer into Admin Approval Mode.

However, the implementation of UAC in Windows Vista generated large numbers of system prompts, even for such tasks as moving, renaming, or deleting files created or modified by a different user. One of the authors of this book frequently experienced this problem in working with his extensive collection of photographic images, many of which had been originally copied onto an older computer running Windows XP. These annoying prompts contributed to the overall low consumer satisfaction of Vista and led many people to disable UAC completely, thereby negating its advantages. Microsoft improved UAC when Windows 7 was introduced, making it more user-friendly and less annoying while still providing protection against undesirable activities (such as installing unwanted software, unwittingly installing malware, and so on). UAC in Windows 8.1 behaves much the same as it did in Windows 7. You can now configure UAC to manage the extent of prompts provided, as discussed in the sections to come.

NOTE For additional introductory information on UAC in Windows 8.1 and Windows Server 2012 R2, refer to "User Account Control Overview" at http://technet.microsoft.com/en-us/library/jj574089.aspx.

Features of User Account Control

UAC requests approval before running administrative tasks on the computer. UAC redefines what a standard user is permitted to do. Such a user can perform many basic functions that pose no security risk; these functions previously required a user to have administrative privileges. In addition, UAC facilitates the act of providing administrative credentials when users need to perform higher-level tasks, such as installing an application or configuring system settings. Furthermore, UAC makes administrative accounts safer by limiting the types of tasks that can be performed without users providing additional consent. UAC still requests consent before allowing users to perform tasks that require higher privileges, such as system tasks.

Under UAC, all users (administrative or not) can perform the following tasks without supplying administrative credentials:

- Viewing the system clock and calendar and configuring the time zone (but users cannot change the system time)
- Modifying power management settings
- Installing printers and hardware devices that an administrator has allowed using Group Policy
- Interfacing portable devices (such as Bluetooth) with the computer
- Using Wired Equivalent Privacy (WEP) to connect to approved wireless networks
- Creating and configuring approved virtual private network (VPN) connections
- Installing ActiveX controls from sites that an administrator has approved
- Installing critical updates from Windows Update

TIP The tasks summarized here are similar to those granted to members of the Power Users group in Windows versions prior to Vista. Windows 8.1 includes the Power Users group solely for backward-compatibility purposes. You do not need to add users to this group to perform these functions. Add users to this group only if required for running noncertified or legacy applications. To grant this group all the privileges provided in Windows XP, you must apply a default security template that modifies default permissions on system folders and the Registry.

When authenticating a member of the Administrators group, Windows 8.1 issues two access tokens:

- **A full administrator token:** The administrator token is used only when administrative privileges are required.
- **A standard user token:** The standard token is used for all actions that do not require administrative privileges.

Windows 8.1 also marks tasks and programs as belonging to one of two integrity levels, which are implied levels of trust in these actions:

- **Low integrity:** A task or application (such as a web browser, email, or word processing program) that is less likely to compromise the operating system.
- **High integrity:** An action that performs tasks (such as installing applications) that have a higher potential for compromising the system. Applications running at low integrity levels cannot modify data in applications using a higher integrity level.

Windows 8.1 informs you when a task requires elevated (administrative) privileges by displaying shield icons such as those that appear in the left column of the System applet shown in Figure 12-7. On selecting one of these tasks, you receive a UAC prompt as shown in Figure 12-8. Click **Yes** to proceed with the task or **No** to cancel it. When you selected one of these tasks on a Windows Vista computer, the screen dimmed and a UAC prompt (also known as an elevation prompt) was displayed. When you accepted the prompt, the administrative access token granted you elevated privileges, enabling you to perform the task you selected. In Windows 8.1, as was the case with Windows 7, this behavior depends on the UAC setting you've specified (as you learn later in this section). The default setting enables administrators to perform most of the actions marked with shield icons without receiving UAC prompts; they receive prompts for performing tasks such as installing programs or running the Registry Editor or other programs that have a high potential for producing damaging effects.

The dimmed screen indicates that the UAC prompt is running in secure desktop mode (such as when the Ctrl+Alt+Delete prompt appears when logging on to a domain-based computer). This means that you must either approve or cancel the UAC prompt before you can continue performing any other task on the computer.

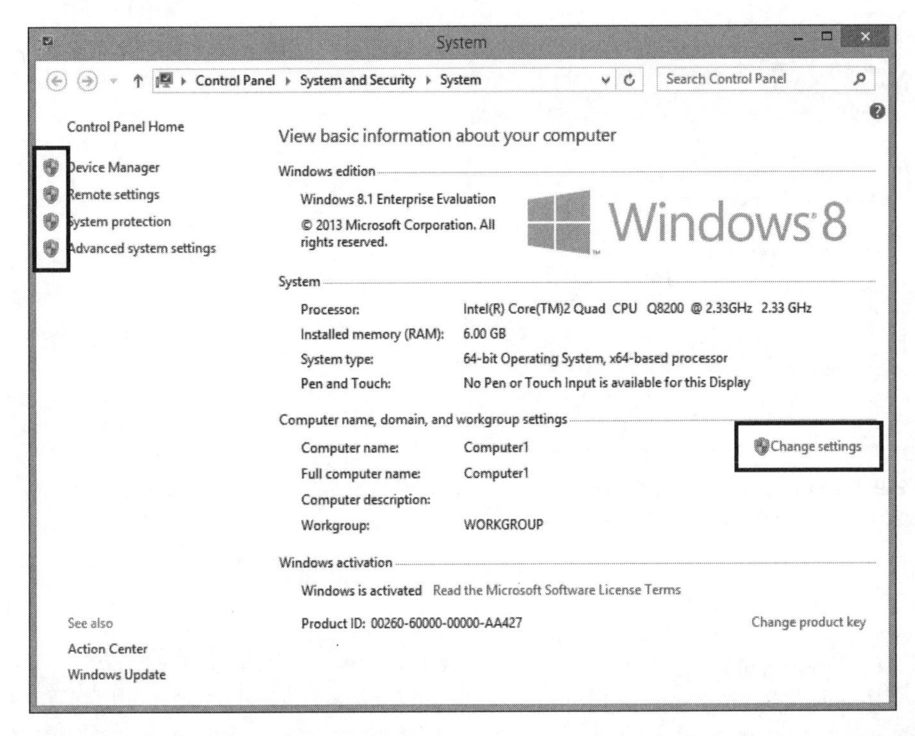

Figure 12-7 Windows 8.1 uses a shield icon to inform you when a task requires administrative privileges.

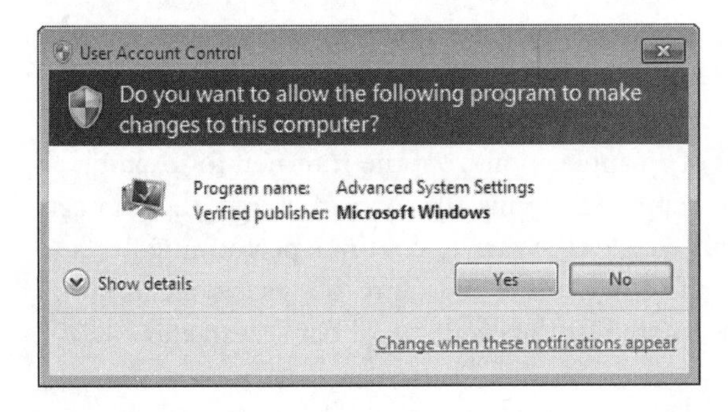

Figure 12-8 User Account Control displays this prompt to ask for approval of an administrative task.

A user who is not a member of the Administrators group receives only the standard user token when access is authenticated. Such a user receives the UAC prompt shown in Figure 12-9, which requires that a password for an Administrator user account be entered. By default in Windows 8.1, a nonadministrative user receives this prompt for any action marked by a shield icon.

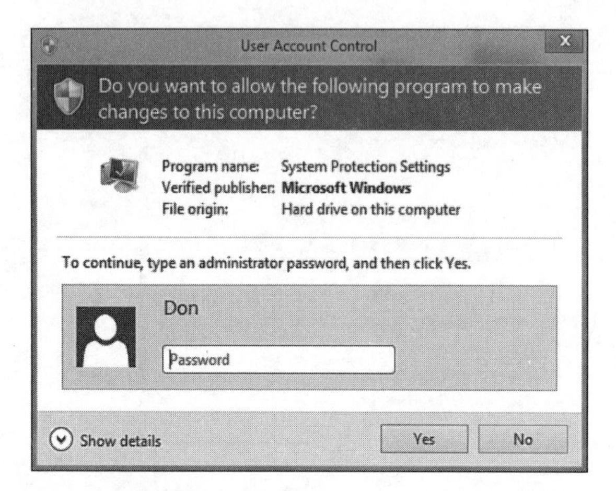

Figure 12-9 User Account Control requests that an administrative user password be entered when displayed from a nonadministrative user account.

CAUTION When you receive a UAC prompt, always ensure that the action that launches the prompt is the one you want to perform. This is especially true if a UAC prompt appears unexpectedly, which could indicate a malware program attempting to run. Should this happen, click **No** and the program cannot run. You should then scan your computer with one or more malware detection programs.

If a background application that is minimized to the taskbar requires elevated privileges, the UAC prompt appears on the taskbar and blinks to draw attention. This might happen in the downloading of an application from the Internet, for example. When the download completes and approval for installation is required, the user can click the prompt to approve it. This enables the user to continue performing other tasks, such as reading email, while the download is underway; the user can continue with these tasks without being interrupted by the dimming of her screen and a UAC prompt displaying onscreen.

Application Prompts

UAC causes some third-party applications to display prompts when you attempt to run them. This helps to secure your computer because the prompt informs you of the program that is attempting to run so that you can verify that this is a program you really want to run. Click **Yes** to run the program or **No** to exit. The type of shield icon depends on the security risk involved in running the program:

- **High-risk blocked program:** Windows displays a message box with a red title bar and red shield stating `This program has been blocked for your protection`. Such a program comes from a blocked publisher and cannot be run under any circumstances.
- **Program signed by Windows:** The UAC prompt includes a blue title bar and blue and yellow shield similar to that of Figure 12-8 for an administrative user. Click **Yes** to run the program. For a nonadministrative user, the prompt is similar to that shown in Figure 12-9. Provide an administrative password to run the program.
- **Unsigned program from a verified publisher:** When running with an administrative account, a program with a legitimate digital signature that includes its name and publisher displays a prompt similar to that shown in Figure 12-10. Click **Yes** to run the program. A nonadministrative user receives a prompt that asks for an administrative password.
- **Unsigned program from a non-verified publisher:** If the third-party program does not have a digital signature that includes its name and publisher, the prompt that appears is a stronger caution. It uses a yellow title bar and yellow shield, as shown in Figure 12-11. Click **Yes** to run the program. Again, a nonadministrative user receives a prompt that asks for an administrative password.

Figure 12-10 User Account Control displays a prompt similar to this when an administrative user starts a third-party program with a legitimate digital signature.

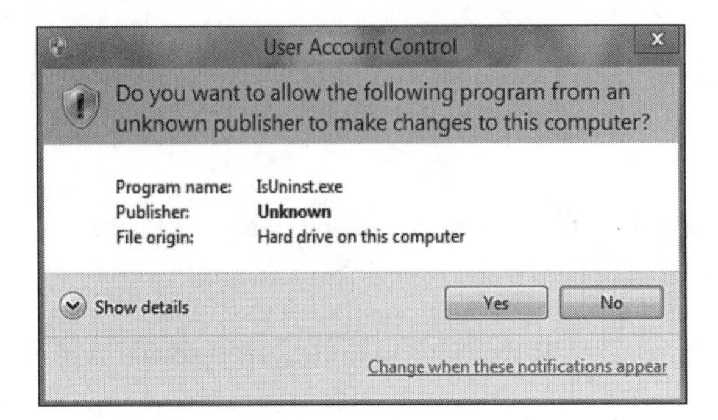

Figure 12-11 When a program that does not have a digital signature attempts to run, UAC displays this prompt to an administrative user.

NOTE For additional information on UAC in Windows 8.1 and Windows Server 2012 R2 including the various prompts that UAC can issue, refer to "How User Account Control Works" at http://technet.microsoft.com/en-us/library/jj574202.aspx.

Running Programs with Elevated Privileges

Microsoft has provided several means of configuring applications and tasks to run with elevated privileges. Use the following procedure to perform a task with elevated privileges:

Step 1. Start the program or task that is displayed with a shield icon. The display dims and the UAC prompt appears, as previously shown in Figure 12-8.

Step 2. Verify that the UAC prompt is requesting privileges for the task you're attempting to run (remember, some malware can deceive you here, so make certain the correct program or task is described in this prompt). If desired, click **Show details** for more information on the task.

Step 3. If this is indeed the correct program or task, click **Yes** to start the task or application.

You can also mark an application to always run with elevated privileges. This situation may occur if the application developer has coded the program to access protected folders such as the `%ProgramFiles%` or `%Systemroot%` folders, or requires access to the Registry. You can also configure a program to request administrative privileges from its shortcut properties. When you do this, the program always displays a UAC prompt when started from its shortcut. Use the following procedure to mark an application to always run with elevated privileges:

Step 1. Ensure that you are logged on to the computer as a member of the local Administrators group.

Step 2. If necessary, drag a shortcut to the desktop.

Step 3. Right-click the shortcut and choose **Properties**.

Step 4. On the Shortcut tab, click the **Advanced** button.

Step 5. On the Advanced Properties dialog box, select the **Run as administrator** check box as shown in Figure 12-12 and then click **OK**.

Step 6. Click **OK** to close the shortcut Properties dialog box.

Figure 12-12 The Advanced Properties dialog box for a shortcut enables you to specify that the program always runs as an administrator.

CAUTION If you are logged on using the default Administrator account created when you installed Windows 8.1, you do not receive any UAC prompts. Do not use this account except under emergency conditions. Best practices recommend that this account remain disabled; it is disabled by default in Windows 8.1.

User Account Control Options

In Windows 8.1, as already mentioned, you can configure several levels of UAC that determine whether prompts are displayed and how they appear on the screen. Open **Control Panel** from the Settings charm, select **System and Security,** and then select **Change User Account Control settings** under Action Center. Alternatively, you can type `User Account Control` into the Search charm and then select this option from the search list. This opens the dialog box shown in Figure 12-13.

Select from the following options, click **OK**, and then accept the UAC prompt that appears:

- **Always notify me when:** Windows displays a UAC prompt whenever you make changes to Windows settings or programs try to install software or make changes to your computer. This behavior is similar to that of Vista.
- **Notify me only when apps try to make changes to my computer (default):** The default setting in Windows 8.1, this setting does not prompt you when you make changes to Windows settings. You are prompted on the secure desktop (that is, the desktop dims) when you perform higher-level actions, such as installing programs or accessing the Registry Editor.
- **Notify me only when programs try to make changes to my computer (do not dim my desktop):** Similar to the default setting, except that the desktop does not dim when a UAC prompt appears. With this setting, you can ignore the UAC prompt and continue performing tasks other than the task that is requesting approval.
- **Never notify me when:** Disables UAC completely. You are not notified if apps try to install software or make changes to your computer, or when you make changes to Windows settings. This setting is not recommended; you should use it only when absolutely necessary to run a program that displays the red shield icon mentioned earlier in this section.

Key Topic

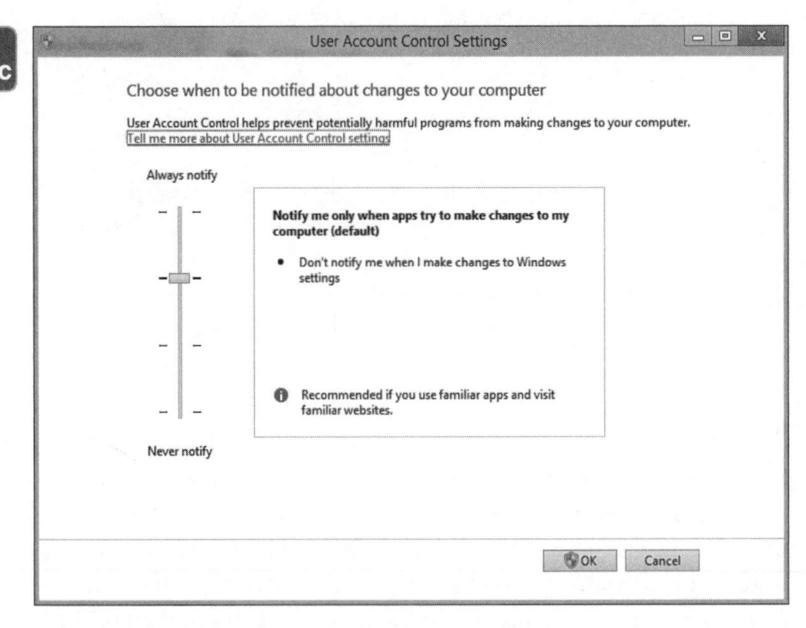

Figure 12-13 The User Account Control Settings dialog box provides four settings for governing the behavior of UAC on your computer.

CAUTION If you select the **Never notify me** when option in Figure 12-13, Windows 8.1 does not let you run any Windows Store apps.

User Account Control Policies

Microsoft has provided a series of policies in Windows 8.1 Group Policy that govern the behavior of UAC. These policies are available from the Group Policy Management Editor snap-in (`gpedit.msc`) or from the Local Security Policy snap-in discussed earlier in this chapter. Use the following procedure to configure UAC policies:

Step 1. From the Search charm, type **`gpedit.msc`** in the Search field, and then press **Enter**.

Step 2. Navigate to the **Computer Configuration\Windows Settings\Security Settings\Local Policies\Security Options** node.

Step 3. Scroll to the bottom of the policy list to view and configure the available policies, as shown in Figure 12-14.

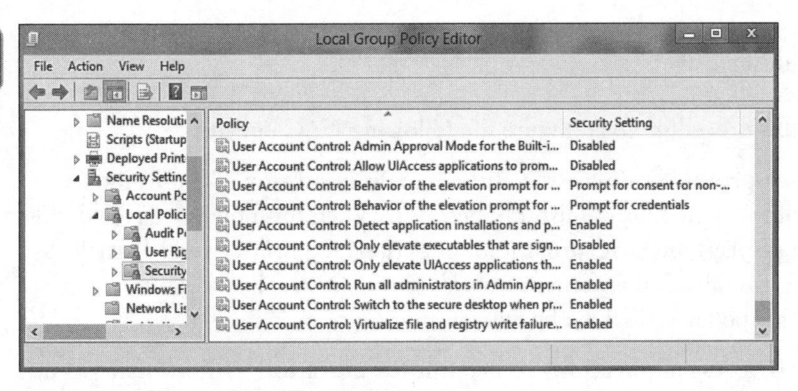

Figure 12-14 Group Policy provides a series of policies that govern UAC behavior.

Step 4. To configure a policy, right-click it and choose **Properties**. Choose **Enabled** or **Disabled** as required and click **OK**. Two of the policies offer options from a drop-down list, as shown in Figure 12-15. You can also click the **Explain** tab for further information on each policy.

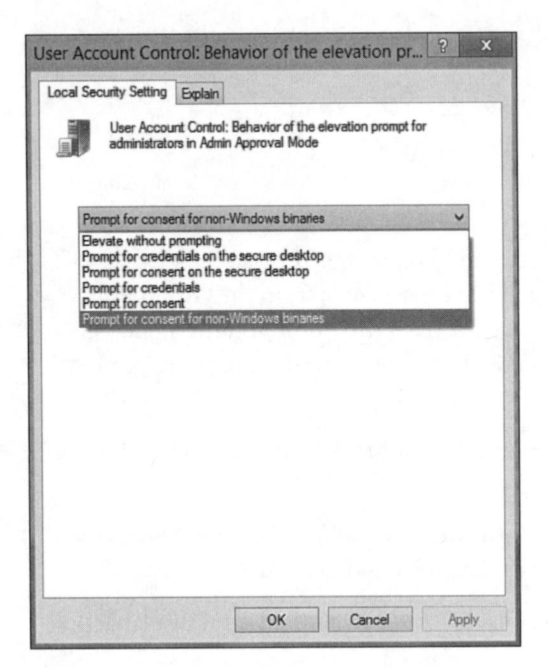

Figure 12-15 You can configure each policy or obtain more information from its Properties dialog box.

Step 5. When finished, click **OK**.

You can use this procedure to configure the following UAC policies:

- **Admin Approval Mode for the Built-in Administrator:** Governs the behavior of the built-in Administrator account. When this policy is enabled, this account displays the UAC prompt for all actions requiring elevated privileges. When it is disabled, this account runs all actions with full administrative privileges. This policy is disabled by default.
- **Allow UIAccess applications to prompt for elevation without using the secure desktop:** Determines whether User Interface Accessibility (UIAccess) programs can automatically disable the secure desktop with a standard user. When this policy is enabled, these programs (such as Remote Assistance) automatically disable the secure desktop for elevation prompts. When it is disabled, the application runs with UIAccess integrity regardless of its location in the file system. Note that UI (User Interface) Access-application programs and accessibility tools are used by developers to push input to higher desktop windows that require the uiAccess flag to be equal to true (that is, `uiAccess=true`). Also, the application program that wants to receive the `uiAccess` privilege must reside on the hard drive in a trusted location and be digitally signed. This policy is disabled by default.

- **Behavior of the elevation prompt for administrators in Admin Approval Mode:** Determines the behavior of the UAC prompt for administrative users. This policy has the following options:
  - **Prompt for consent for non-Windows binaries:** Prompts a user on the secure desktop to select either **Permit** or **Deny** when a non-Microsoft program needs elevated privileges. Select **Permit** to run the action with the highest possible privileges. This option is the default setting.
  - **Prompt for consent:** Prompts a user to select either **Permit** or **Deny** when an action runs that requires elevated privileges. Select **Permit** to run the action with the highest possible privileges.
  - **Prompt for credentials:** Prompts for an administrative username and password when an action requires administrative privileges but does not display the secure desktop. When this option is selected, administrative users receive the prompt previously shown in Figure 12-9 for nonadministrative users.
  - **Prompt for consent on the secure desktop:** Prompts a user to select either **Permit** or **Deny** on the secure desktop when an action runs that requires elevated privileges. Select **Permit** to run the action with the highest possible privileges.
  - **Prompt for credentials on the secure desktop:** Prompts for an administrative username and password on the secure desktop when an action requires administrative privileges. When this option is selected, administrative users receive the prompt previously shown in Figure 12-9 for nonadministrative users.
  - **Elevate without prompting:** Enables the administrator to perform the action without consent or credentials. In other words, the administrator receives Admin Approval Mode automatically. This setting is not recommended for normal environments.
- **Behavior of the elevation prompt for standard users:** Determines the behavior of the UAC prompt for nonadministrative users. This policy has the following options:
  - **Prompt for credentials:** Displays a prompt to enter an administrative username and password when a standard user attempts to run an action that requires elevated privileges. This option is the default setting.
  - **Prompt for credentials on the secure desktop:** Displays a prompt on the secure desktop to enter an administrative username and password when a standard user attempts to run an action that requires elevated privileges.

- **Automatically deny elevation requests:** Displays an `Access is Denied` message similar to that shown in Figure 12-16 when a standard user attempts to run an action that requires elevated privileges.

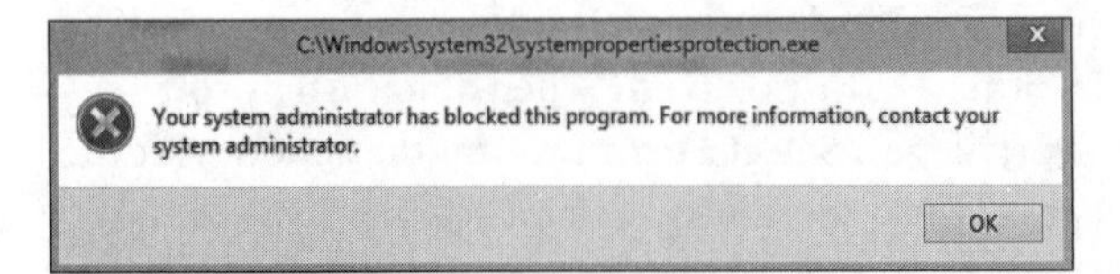

Figure 12-16 When you have configured the policy to automatically deny elevation requests, nonadministrative users receive an error when they attempt to run a program requiring administrative credentials.

- **Detect application installations and prompt for elevation:** When this option is enabled, displays a UAC prompt when a user installs an application package that requires elevated privileges. When it is disabled, domain-based Group Policy or other enterprise-level technologies govern application installation behavior. This option is enabled by default in an enterprise setting and disabled by default in a home setting.
- **Only elevate executables that are signed and validated:** When this option is enabled, performs public key infrastructure (PKI) signature checks on executable programs that require elevated privileges before they are permitted to run. When it is disabled, no PKI checks are performed. This option is disabled by default.
- **Only elevate UIAccess applications that are installed in Secure locations:** When this option is enabled, runs applications only with UIAccess integrity if situated in a secure location within the file system such as `%ProgramFiles%` or `%Windir%`. When it is disabled, the application runs with UIAccess integrity regardless of its location in the file system. This option is disabled by default.
- **Run all administrators in Admin Approval Mode:** When this option is enabled, enforces Admin Approval Mode and other UAC policies. When it is disabled, all UAC policies are disabled and no UAC prompts are displayed. In addition, the Windows Security Center notifies the user when it is disabled and offers the option to enable UAC. This option is enabled by default.
- **Switch to the secure desktop when prompting for elevation:** When this option is enabled, displays the secure desktop when a UAC prompt appears. When it is disabled, the UAC prompt remains on the interactive user's desktop. This option is enabled by default.
- **Virtualize file and registry write failures to per user locations:** When this option is enabled, redirects application write failures for pre-Windows 8.1

applications to defined locations in the Registry and the file system, such as `%ProgramFiles%`, `%Windir%`, or `%Systemroot%`. When it is disabled, applications that write to protected locations fail, as was the case in previous Windows versions. This option is enabled by default.

WARNING If you disable the Run all administrators in Admin Approval Mode policy setting, you disable UAC completely and no prompts appear for actions requiring elevated privileges. This leaves your computer wide open for attack by malicious software. Do *not* disable this setting at any time! If you do disable this setting, note that the Windows Action Center displays a message from the notification area.

NOTE For information on problems you might encounter with UAC in Windows 8.1, consult the links referenced in "User Account Control Troubleshooting Guide" at http://technet.microsoft.com/en-ca/library/ee844169(WS.10).aspx?ITPID=insider. Though written for Windows Server 2008 R2, most of the information presented in these links applies to Windows 8.1 and Windows Server 2012 R2.

Configuring Secure Boot

Malicious software (also known as malware) is a major security issue in almost every computing environment. Antivirus software helps stop many forms of malware from infecting Windows computers, but one way that malware authors have attempted to subvert security measures is to develop what is known as boot-sector viruses. These programs infect the startup environment of computers at the very lowest level, before antivirus or even the operating system is loaded. They can then run their payload "under the radar" of most antimalware software solutions.

Secure Boot is designed to thwart these types of attacks using the hardware and firmware of the computer to ensure that only authorized firmware, operating systems, or Unified Extensible Firmware Interface (UEFI) drivers are allowed to run at boot time. It does this by maintaining a list of software signatures that are preapproved to run on a specific computer.

Signatures are maintained by the computer in two databases: the signature database and the revoked signatures database. The signature database contains an image hash of each authorized driver and operating system, and the revoked signature database lists any image hashes that are no longer allowed and may not be loaded.

On a Secure Boot–enabled computer, the Microsoft signature for the Windows 8.1 Boot Manager must be included in the signature database of the computer when it is built at the factory. The manufacturer loads the signatures into the computers' firmware, allowing the computer to load the Windows 8.1 Boot Manager using Secure Boot. The firmware is then locked from editing before shipping.

UEFI replaced the older BIOS firmware interface used in many computers today. If you want to use Secure Boot, the computer must meet the UEFI 2.3.1 specifications.

NOTE The UEFI specification is an open standard managed by the Unified EFI Forum, an industry standards working group. For more information about the standard and specifications, check the UEFI website at http://www.uefi.org/specsandtesttools. Membership in the UEFI Forum is required to download the full specification.

Enabling UEFI Secure Boot

Before installing Windows 8.1 on a system that supports UEFI 2.3.1, you should first ensure that you will be installing Windows in UEFI mode, and not legacy BIOS-compatibility mode, which may be an option depending on the computer and the original equipment manufacturer (OEM).

Step 1. Ensure the computer is starting up in UEFI mode, and not BIOS-Compatibility mode. To switch from BIOS-Compatibility mode to UEFI mode on the computer's startup settings, press the required key during power-on. This key varies on each computer but is typically the **ESC** key, **DEL** key, or **F1**.

Step 2. When the computer's boot device menu loads, you need to locate the UEFI boot setting. The menus can vary widely from one manufacturer to another, but it should have a selection for Boot Mode and UEFI Boot Device. For example, Figure 12-17 shows an HP computer's boot menu configuration, with a selection to enable UEFI Boot Mode and the UEFI Boot Order.

Step 3. Note from Figure 12-17 that the menu does not include an option to boot from a specific device or file. If there is a startup option such as Boot from UEFI File, you can use that option to load the EFI file. If not, you need to use the UEFI internal shell.

File
Security
System Configuration
Floppy boot
PXE Internal NIC boot
USB device boot
Upgrade Bay Hard Drive boot
eSATA boot
UEFI Boot Mode
UEFI Boot Order
OS Boot Manager
Notebook Upgrade Bay (UEFI)
Notebook Ethernet (UEFI)
Legacy Boot Order
USB CD-ROM
Notebook Upgrade Bay
Notebook Hard Drive
eSATA Drive
USB Floppy
USB Hard Drive
Notebook Ethernet
SD Card
Dock Upgrade Bay
Save
Help
Exit

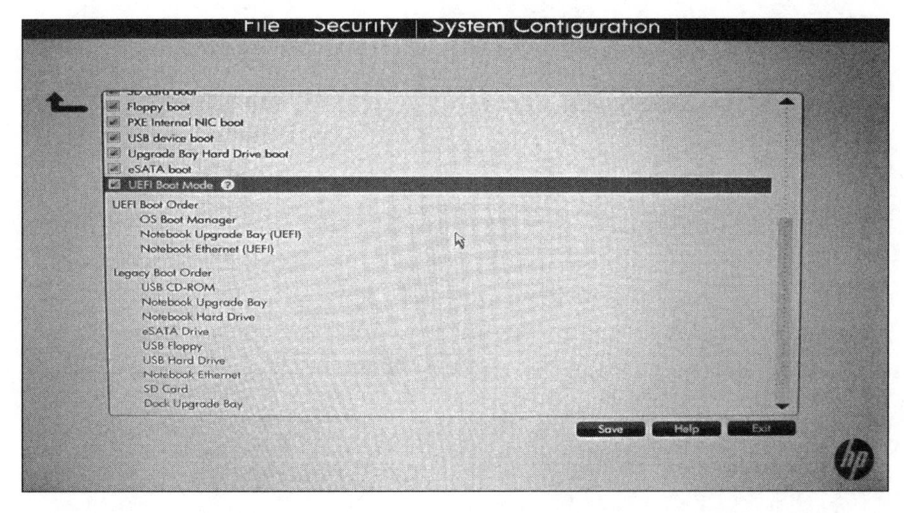

Figure 12-17 Locating the UEFI Boot Mode in the HP startup settings menu.

Step 4. The UEFI Shell in Figure 12-18 displays the block devices that have been detected and enabled by the UEFI configuration, showing that the Windows 8.1 DVD is mapped to `fs0`. Using the **`dir`** command for `fs0:` displays the EFI directory. The file you need should be `\EFI\BOOT\BOOTX64.EFI`. To do that, switch to `fs0:` and then type **`\EFI\BOOT\BOOTX64.EFI`** and press **Enter**.

Key Topic

Device mapping table
fs0 :CDRom - Alias cd10c1 blk0
PciRoot(0x0)/Pci(0x7,0x1)/Ata(Secondary,Master,0x0)/CDROM(0x1,0x86E,0x
1AA76A)
blk0 :CDRom - Alias cd10c1 fs0
PciRoot(0x0)/Pci(0x7,0x1)/Ata(Secondary,Master,0x0)/CDROM(0x1,0x86E,0x
1AA76A)
blk1 :CDRom - Alias (null)
PciRoot(0x0)/Pci(0x7,0x1)/Ata(Secondary,Master,0x0)/CDROM(0x0,0x86C,0x
8)
blk2 :BlockDevice - Alias (null)
PciRoot(0x0)/Pci(0x7,0x1)/Ata(Secondary,Master,0x0)
blk3 :Removable BlockDevice - Alias (null)
PciRoot(0x0)/Pci(0x15,0x0)/Pci(0x0,0x0)/Scsi(0x0,0x0)
Press ESC in 1 seconds to skip startup.nsh, any other key to continue.
Shell> dir fs0:
Directory of: fs0:\
07/25/12 03:00p <DIR> 512 EFI
0 File(s) 0 bytes
1 Dir(s)
Shell> _

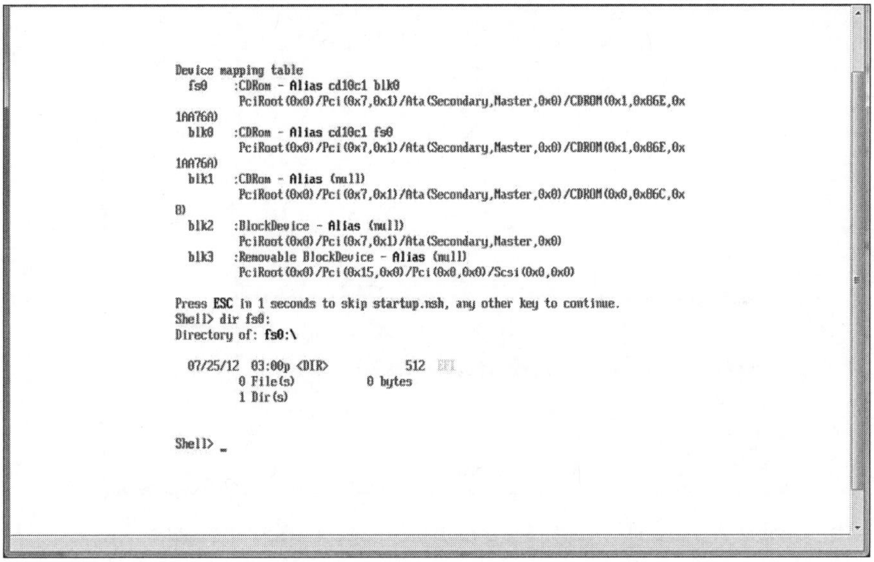

Figure 12-18 Working with the UEFI Shell interface.

Step 5. When the loader loads the EFI file, the Windows Boot Manager is started. Proceed to install Windows normally as covered in Chapter 2, "Installing Windows 8.1."

NOTE When installing Windows in UEFI Secure Boot mode, you must configure the hard disk used for boot using the globally unique identifier (GUID) partition table (GPT) instead of the master boot record (MBR) partition structure used in legacy BIOS mode. Windows Setup detects the startup and configures disk partitions accordingly, but you manually configure partitions. Therefore, be sure to use GPT partitions; otherwise, Windows will not boot.

UEFI Partition Requirements

As mentioned in the previous section, Windows 8.1 requires GPT partitioning to boot under a UEFI startup using Secure Boot. Windows Setup configures the partitions by default if it has a new drive (by creating a GPT partitioning scheme) and creates the default partitions it needs, as shown in Figure 12-19. If you are using answer files or custom images, you should know about the partitions required.

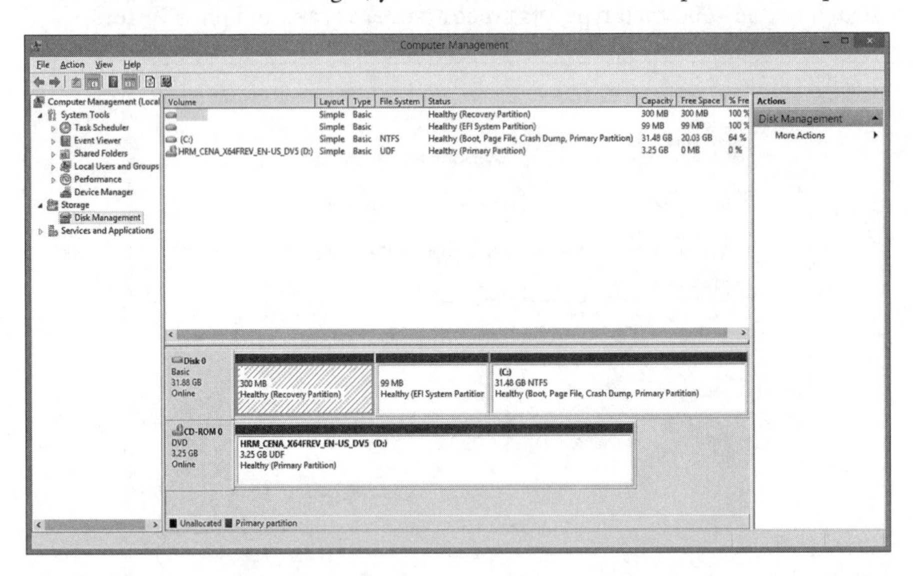

Figure 12-19 Default Windows 8.1 partitioning for a UEFI Secure Boot installation.

A GPT drive can have up to 128 partitions. The partitions required for Windows 8.1 are as follows:

- The Windows RE Tools partition, which must be at least 300 MB. The partition needs a specific Type ID, which is DE94BBA4-06D1-4D40-A16A-BFD50179D6AC.
- The System Partition, which on a UEFI computer is also called the EFI System Partition or the ESP. Windows uses this partition to boot the Windows PE environment. It must be at least 100 MB and formatted using FAT32.
- The Microsoft Reserved Partition (MSR). The MSR should be 128 MB. This partition is used for drive management and does not have a partition ID. No user data can be stored on this partition.
- The Windows partition, which is the main data drive for the Windows operating system, programs, and user files. It must be at least 20 GB (16 GB for 32-bit versions of Windows). It must use the NTFS format.

Procedures and details for creating these partitions and preparing images for mass deployment are beyond the scope of the 70-687 exam. You should be aware that you need the DiskPart tool to create the partitions if you are not using the default Windows Setup because the Disk Management tool cannot create the required partition types.

NOTE For more information on partition requirements and configuring partitions required for Secure Boot, see the topic and links referenced in "Configure UEFI/GPT-Based Hard Drive Partitions" at http://technet.microsoft.com/en-us/library/hh824839.aspx.

Using SmartScreen Filters

The SmartScreen Filter first introduced in Internet Explorer 8 and continued in versions 9, 10, and 11 enhances the capabilities of the phishing filter first introduced with Internet Explorer 7. Besides checking websites against a list of reported phishing sites, this filter checks software downloads against a list of reported malware websites.

We covered the SmartScreen filter and how to configure the Internet Explorer SmartScreen settings in Chapter 6. Recall that SmartScreen helps protect your computer in the following ways:

- Works in the background as you browse the Web, analyzing web pages for suspicious characteristics, and displaying messages and warnings when it detects potentially harmful content.

- Checks sites you visit against a database of phishing sites and compromised sites distributing malware, and blocks sites that match the list, displaying a red warning that the site has been blocked.
- Examines downloaded files against the online database of malicious software sites, blocking downloads that match the list and displaying a warning that the download has been blocked.

In Windows 8.1, these features are available not just for Internet Explorer, but are built into the operating system itself, so that the same protections can be applied for Windows apps that access websites and other third-party web browsers that you may have installed.

The built-in feature is referred to as Windows SmartScreen, and you can access its settings from the Start screen and from the Action Center dialog box. You can open Action Center from the desktop by clicking on the **Action Center** flag in the notification area and then clicking **Open Action Center**.

From Action Center, click on **Change Windows SmartScreen** settings to display the dialog box shown in Figure 12-20. Windows SmartScreen offers the following options:

- **Get administrator approval before running an unrecognized app from the Internet (recommended)**
- **Warn before running an unrecognized app, but don't require administrator approval**
- **Don't do anything (turn off Windows SmartScreen)**

Figure 12-20 Windows SmartScreen configuration settings.

As noted, the first option is the recommended setting, and it requires a local administrator to run an app that Windows does not recognize. The second option may be useful if you trust your users to be careful with the apps they run, but they typically are not given administrator rights on their workstations.

When you attempt to download or run an application, Windows SmartScreen checks to see whether the application is recognized or could be a malicious software file. If it detects an application with a suspicious signature, it displays the SmartScreen block message, as shown in Figure 12-21, and stops the application from loading.

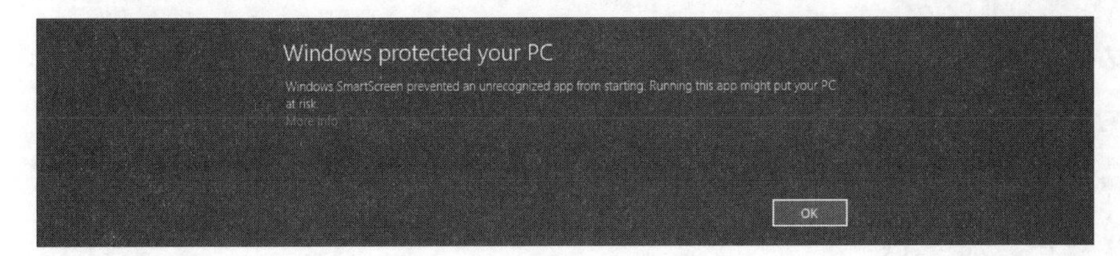

Figure 12-21 Windows SmartScreen blocks a suspicious application.

You can click on the **More info** link to display information about the file such as the publisher and filename. When you do, you have the opportunity to choose **Run anyway** or **Don't run**, as illustrated in Figure 12-22. Click the **Run anyway** button if you decide you trust the application and want to bypass the SmartScreen warning.

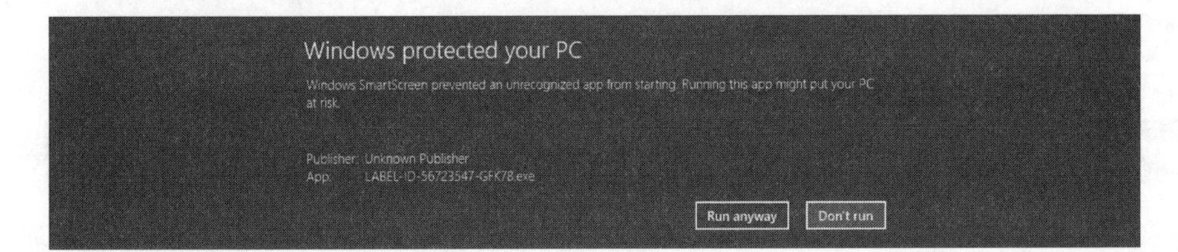

Figure 12-22 SmartScreen offers the option to bypass the application block.

The option in Figure 12-22 is available only because the user is a local administrator on the computer. If SmartScreen is configured as recommended (see Figure 12-20), only an administrator is allowed to bypass the SmartScreen block. The second option in the SmartScreen configuration enables the Run anyway button for all users.

SmartScreen filter is also available for Windows apps, to check Internet locations that Windows apps may try to access. By default, SmartScreen filter is enabled for Windows apps, and this is the recommended setting. To turn off SmartScreen (or to ensure that it is on), access **PC Settings** from the **Settings** charm and then select **Privacy**. The toggle for SmartScreen filter is the third option on the list, as shown in Figure 12-23.

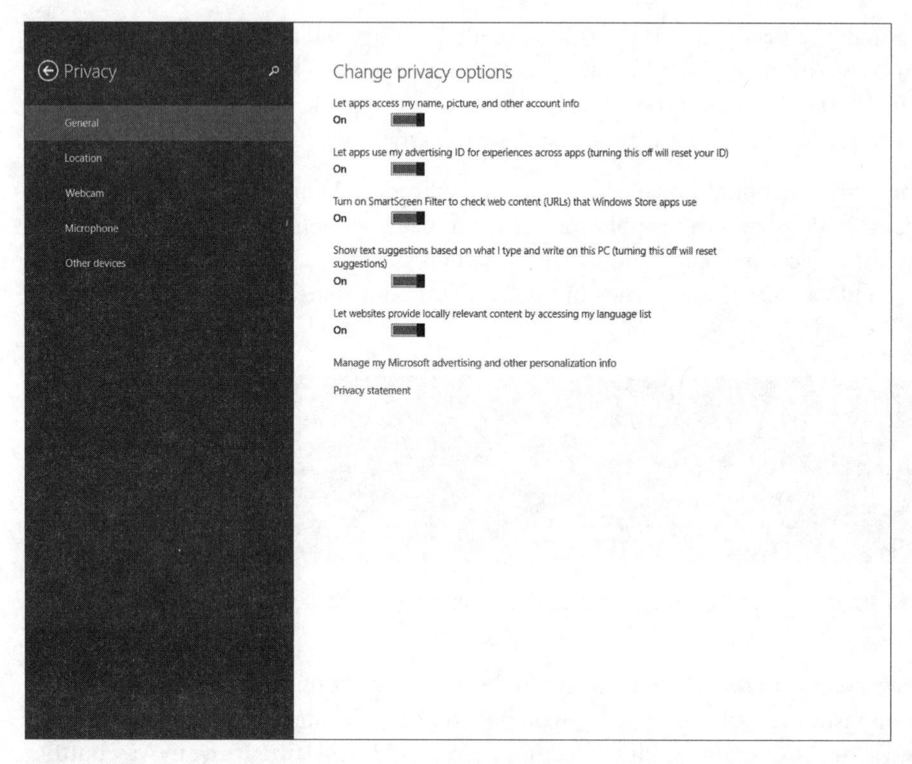

Figure 12-23 Privacy settings include the option to turn SmartScreen Filter on or off for Windows Store apps.

Exam Preparation Tasks

Review All the Key Topics

Review the most important topics in the chapter, noted with the key topics icon in the outer margin of the page. Table 12-2 lists a reference of these key topics and the page numbers on which each is found.

Table 12-2 Key Topics for Chapter 12

Key Topic Element	Description	Page Number(s)
List	Describes setting categories available from the Local Security Policy snap-in	518
Figure 12-2	Shows available password policies	520
List	Describes available auditing policies	525
Paragraph	Describes the workings of UAC	530
List	Describes the types of prompts issued by UAC	533
Step List	Explains how to configure a program to always require elevated privileges	535
Figure 12-13	Shows how to specify the levels of prompts that UAC can issue	536
Figure 12-14	Shows available UAC Group Policy settings	537
Step List	Describes how to enable UEFI Secure Boot	542-544
Figure 12-18	Shows how to work with UEFI	543
Figure 12-20	Shows how to configure Windows SmartScreen	546

Definitions of Key Terms

Define the following key terms from this chapter and check your answers in the Glossary:

Account lockout policy, Admin Approval mode, Local Security Policy, Password policy, Secure Boot, SmartScreen, UEFI, User Account Control (UAC)

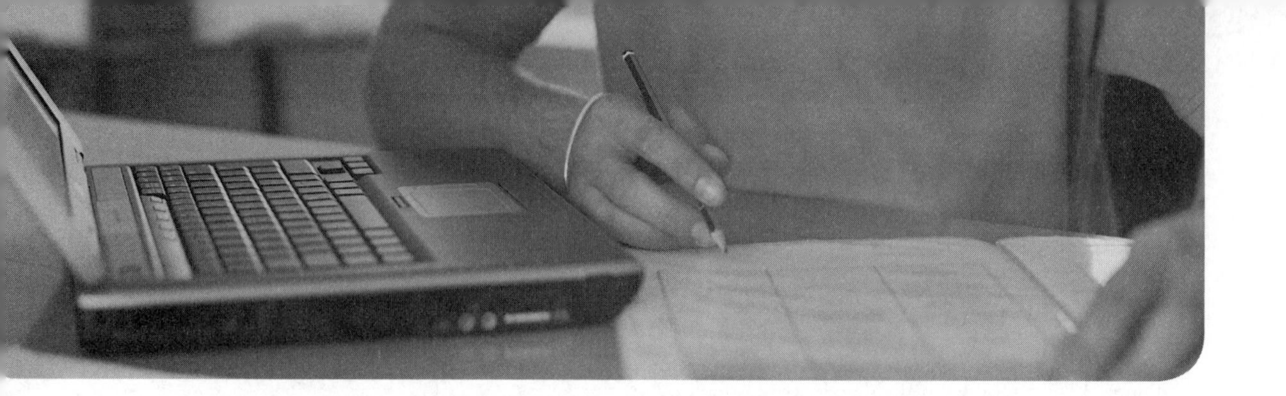

This chapter covers the following subjects:

- **Controlling Windows Logon:** Managing Windows 8.1 effectively means understanding the authentication and logon technologies available and selecting the right level or combination of processes for the given environment. In this section, you learn about the processes for verifying the identity of objects, services, and users in Windows 8.1, and the techniques available for ensuring only proven identities are recognized and allowed access to resources.

- **Managing Credentials:** Credentials in Windows (and most computers systems) are the account name and authentication details that provide access to systems and resources. This section details how to manage users' and administrators' credentials on Windows 8.1; describes how they are configured; provides some information on creating, disabling, modifying, and resetting credentials; and details how to perform these tasks on groups of credentials simultaneously.

- **Managing Certificates:** Windows 8.1, as in earlier versions of Windows, makes extensive use of X.509 certificates for enabling identification and confidentiality in a secure environment. We discuss the methods and tools for managing certificates in this section and touch on the management of certificates for domain-joined Windows 8.1 computers.

- **Configuring Smart Cards and PINs:** When security is vital for protecting corporate information or Personal Information (PI) data sources, smart cards and PINs can play a role in designing dual-factor authentication methods. This section discusses the principles behind dual-factor and multifactor authentication and how you can implement them in a Windows 8.1 environment. This section also covers PIN-based logon.

- **Configuring User Rights:** Users on a Windows 8.1 system are granted rights to local and network resources based on a number of factors. Group membership, security policies, Group Policies, and object ACLs all play a role. This section covers the tools and procedures for configuring these user rights on Windows 8.1.

- **Setting Up and Configuring a Microsoft Account:** New in Windows 8.1 from previous versions of Windows is the ability to use a cloud account, specifically a Microsoft account for Windows 8.1, to log on to the PC and perform tasks. In this section, you learn how to use a Microsoft account in Windows 8.1, manage Microsoft account access, and handle other details related to the use of a cloud account.

CHAPTER 13

Configuring Authentication and Authorization

All users on a Windows 8.1 computer must be known to the operating system; in other words, they must be authenticated to Windows and authorized to use resources on the local computer and located on the network. In Chapter 11, "Configuring and Securing Access to Files and Folders," you learned how to configure and provide access to files, folders, shared printers, and other local and network resources. This chapter covers other authorizations that you need to configure and delves into the many ways of authenticating users in Windows 8.1, including cloud-based Microsoft account authentication. Microsoft expects you to be knowledgeable about all these topics and the new features when taking the 70-687 exam.

In a modern Internet-connected workplace with a growing number of users joining the always-available mobile workforce, it becomes increasingly important that users of our systems can positively identify themselves when accessing systems from anywhere in the world. Being able to trust that users are who they say they are when accessing sensitive data and using expensive networked resources is a matter of ensuring that system authentication methods are robust, easy to use, and hardened against impersonation. Lots of confidential information is out there, and it must be protected from access by those who are not entitled to view it.

At home, family members need to share things like photos, videos, and music. But parents have sensitive information, such as family finances, that must be protected as well.

From the earliest version of Windows NT right up to the present, Windows has had a system of access permissions in place that determine who has access to what and what can they do to it. More recent versions of Windows have enabled users to protect data even further with encryption methods that can help to prevent those who might have circumvented other access controls from viewing or modifying confidential information. Included also is a system of auditing access attempts to files and folders so that individuals in charge of security are able to track all types of access on the network and take appropriate measures to protect sensitive information. This chapter looks at these and other methods of sharing and protecting resources on computers and their networks.

"Do I Know This Already?" Quiz

The "Do I Know This Already?" quiz allows you to assess whether you should read this entire chapter or simply jump to the "Exam Preparation Tasks" section for review. If you are in doubt, read the entire chapter. Table 13-1 outlines the major headings in this chapter and the corresponding "Do I Know This Already?" quiz questions. You can find the answers in Appendix A, "Answers to the 'Do I Know This Already?' Quizzes."

Table 13-1 "Do I Know This Already?" Foundation Topics Section-to-Question Mapping

Foundations Topics Section	Questions Covered in This Section
Controlling Windows Logon	1–3
Managing Credentials	4–7
Managing Certificates	8–9
Configuring Smart Cards and PINs	10–12
Configuring User Rights	13
Setting Up and Configuring Microsoft Account	14–15

1. Which of the following is an example of authentication?
   a. User access to a shared folder
   b. Membership in the Administrator account
   c. User signing in with a password
   d. User rights assignment

2. Which of the following are true about the Windows 8.1 Logon screen? (Choose three.)
   a. When a Windows 8.1 computer is joined to a domain, users must press **Ctrl+Alt+Delete** to log on by default.
   b. To sign in with a domain account for the first time, select the **Other User** option on the logon screen and enter the domain and username.
   c. By default, a domain-joined Windows 8.1 computer allows users the options to sign on using a Microsoft account, a Local account, or a domain account.
   d. Users cannot use a four-digit PIN to log on to a domain-joined computer.
   e. You change any user's password using the Users section of PC settings.

3. Configuring a picture password requires how many gestures over the picture?
    a. One
    b. Two
    c. Three
    d. Six
    e. Eight

4. Which of the following types of credentials can be backed up to a remote location using Credential Manager? (Select three.)
    a. Web Credentials
    b. Windows Credentials
    c. Certificate-based Credentials
    d. Generic Credentials
    e. Windows app Credentials

5. Your network administrator has provided a certificate for you to use when signing in to the secure server. You would like to add the credential to the Credential Manager so it is available when you try to access the server. Which certificate store should you use when installing the certificate?
    a. Trusted Publishers
    b. Enterprise Trust
    c. Personal
    d. Trusted People

6. You use a Microsoft account for your home computer and a Windows RT tablet, and your Web Credentials are available on these computers when you are browsing the Web. You have a domain-joined Windows 8.1 computer at work, and you have added your Microsoft account, but your credentials are not working. What could be wrong?
    a. You used the wrong Microsoft account.
    b. You must restore your Web Credentials to the work computer.
    c. Credential roaming is disabled on domain-joined computers.
    d. Your administrator has deleted the credentials.

7. You have backed up your Windows Credentials on a USB thumb drive, and you now have a new computer. You want to restore the credentials to the new computer but have forgotten the password you used when creating the backup. How can you restore the credentials?
   a. Without the password, the credentials cannot be restored.
   b. Have your network administrator reset the password.
   c. Use a PIN.
   d. Copy the file locally and use your Windows password.

8. What are the three types of certificate stores available on a Windows 8.1 computer?
   a. Personal, Trusted, Enterprise
   b. User, Computer, Network
   c. Local computer, User, Services
   d. Personal, Trusted Enterprise, Service Trust

9. Which Windows 8.1 tool do you use to manage certificates?
   a. The Certificates Control Panel applet
   b. The Certificates MMC snap-in
   c. The Certificates Windows app
   d. The Certificates Manager on the PC settings screen

10. Your network administrator has issued a smart card for your use when logging in to the corporate network when you are on the road or other remote locations. You have configured the card and used it before, but now it does not recognize your PIN. What should you do?
    a. Reset the smart card from Windows.
    b. Keep guessing the PIN until you hit the right one.
    c. Ask your network administrator to reset the card.
    d. The card will need to be replaced.

11. You have been asked to implement virtual cards for all the mobile workers at your organization. They will be required when logging in to the AD domain from any remote location. What are the requirements for implementing virtual smart cards? (Choose all that apply.)
    a. Windows 8.1 Pro or Enterprise
    b. A computer with a TPM built-in
    c. A smart card that supports PIV
    d. Certificate services in the AD domain

12. You are the desktop support specialist for your company. Management has rolled out fingerprint scanners for all computers in the agency to improve authentication throughout the organization. The hardware and drivers seem to be working, but users cannot access the domain when they log on with the fingerprint readers. What needs to be done to fix the issue?
    a. Disable UAC on the Windows 8.1 computers.
    b. Modify the Group Policy to **Allow domain users to log on using biometrics**.
    c. Add the biometric provisioning data to the domain account credentials.
    d. Domain users must continue to use their passwords to access domain resources.

13. A new support technician has been hired at your organization and has asked to be able to access all event logs on the user's workstations for troubleshooting purposes. What would you do to provide the technician this access without exceeding the minimum privileges he needs?
    a. Add his account to the Administrators built-in group.
    b. Use Group Policy to provide his user account access through User Rights Assignment.
    c. Add his account to the Event Log Readers built-in group.
    d. Give him the password for the local Administrator account on all the workstations.

14. What are the benefits to users when using a Microsoft account for Windows sign on? (Select all that apply.)

a. Integration of contacts with Internet accounts like Facebook, Twitter, and Hotmail

b. Access and sharing of Internet-based storage like OneDrive, Facebook, and Flickr

c. Using and synchronizing Windows Store apps

d. Personal settings kept in sync among all Windows devices

15. Management at your organization has decided to set up corporate Microsoft accounts for all users but does not want users to use their own Microsoft accounts on the company computers. How do you enforce this policy?

a. Set the Group Policy Block Microsoft Accounts to **Disabled**.

b. Set the Group Policy Disallow Microsoft Accounts to **Enabled**.

c. Set the Group Policy Block Microsoft Accounts to **Users can't add Microsoft accounts**.

d. Set the Group Policy Block Microsoft Accounts to **Users can't add or log on with Microsoft accounts**.

Foundation Topics

Controlling Windows Logon

To use a Windows 8.1 computer, whether the computer belongs to a workgroup or HomeGroup or to an Active Directory Domain Services (AD DS) domain, a user must prove that she is who she says she is. This is what authentication is all about. Simply put, authentication is the process of a user or computer proving its identity to the operating system. Ensuring that credentials are authentic is an important factor in any computer system, but becomes even more important when applied to remote access communications through telephone lines or through the Internet. You learn about remote access authentication in Chapter 14, "Configuring Remote Management and Remote Connections." Here, we discuss authentication on the local network and Windows 8.1 local logon.

For years, most companies have generally employed the simple means of usernames and passwords for authenticating users to their networks. In recent years with increased prevalence of password-guessing schemes and hacking software, companies have moved to multifactor authentication systems employing technology such as smart cards and biometric devices to improve the reliability of authentication. A smart card is a credit-card–sized device that includes information about the user and his rights and privileges; the user inserts the card in a reader attached to his computer and enters a personal identification number (PIN) to log on. Windows 8.1 supports the new Personal Identity Verification (PIV) smart card standards and policies that improve the security of this authentication method.

Windows 8.1 Lock Screen and Logon Prompts

By default, a Windows 8.1 computer that is not part of a domain displays the lock screen at startup and after a user has logged off. Touching or clicking the lock screen displays the Windows 8.1 logon screen, which is also displayed when a user selects the **Switch account** option from the Start screen. The logon screen displays all enabled user accounts, allowing a user to select the appropriate account and enter the password if one has been specified.

New in Windows 8.1 is the ability to use a Microsoft account to logon to the local computer. In Chapter 2, "Installing Windows 8.1," we covered how to create an account for a newly installed Windows 8.1 computer using either a Microsoft account or a local account. When you create new accounts for Windows 8.1, they can either use a local logon or a Microsoft account. The process is covered later in this section.

Although the default logon screen is convenient, especially in a home environment, it does pose a security risk in a corporate environment, even in a small office. In an AD DS environment, the Classic Logon screen is no longer enabled by default in Windows 8.1. Instead, an option called Other User selection is made available to allow the user to enter domain credentials previously unknown by the local machine.

You can change the way that a domain-joined Windows 8.1 computer displays the logon screen using the User Accounts applet from Control Panel. From the Advanced tab, just click the check box in the Secure sign-in section labeled **Require users to press Ctrl+Alt+Delete**, as shown in Figure 13-1.

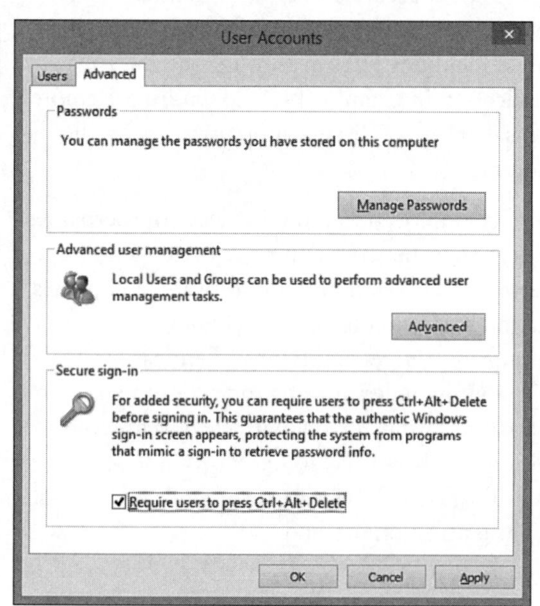

Figure 13-1 Enabling Secure sign-in using the User Accounts Control Panel applet.

You can use Group Policy to require the use of the Logon screen on domain-joined as well as non–domain-joined Windows 8.1 computers.

For a workgroup or non–domain-joined computer, open the **Local Group Policy Editor**, which you can find by searching for Group Policy from the Search charm. Navigate to the **Computer Configuration\Administrative Templates\System\Logon** node and then enable the **Always use classic logon policy** (see Figure 13-2).

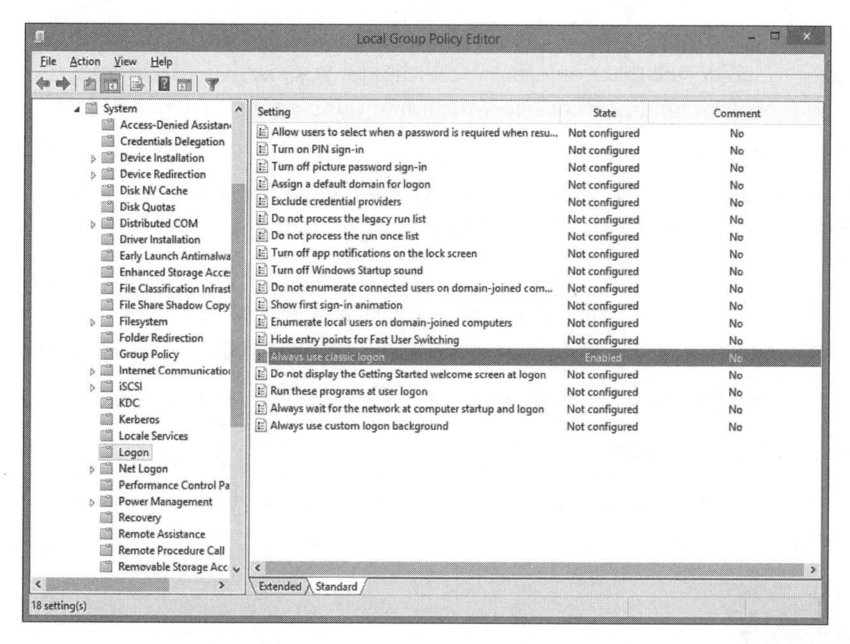

Figure 13-2 Enabling classic logon using Local Group Policy Editor.

Note that the Always use classic logon policy Group Policy Object (GPO) setting works when the computer is not in a domain. For domain-joined Windows 8.1 computers, you must use the GPO setting **Interactive logon: Do not require Ctrl+Alt+Delete**. The policy is found in under Computer Configuration\Windows Settings\Security Settings\Local Policies\Security Options.

NOTE The behavior of this setting has changed for Windows 8.1. On previous editions, a domain-joined computer disabled this policy by default (disabled means users were required to press Ctrl+Alt+Delete). For Windows 8.1 computers, the policy is enabled by default, so users are not required to press Ctrl+Alt+Delete.

To remove the display of the last username, navigate to the **Computer Configuration\Windows Settings\Security Settings\Local Policies\Security Options** node and enable the Interactive logon: Do not display last user name policy.

Configure Picture Password

The traditional logon previously described works on any Windows 8.1 computer. But a new feature first introduced for Windows 8 is the *picture password*. You can enable this security feature if your computer has a touch-enabled device or screen. On a tablet or touch device that you often use without a keyboard at all, this can provide a more convenient and secure password than using a touch-based soft keyboard.

A picture password is probably better termed a gesture password. You select a picture as the basis; then your gestures across the picture become the basis of your logon authentication.

Before enabling picture password, make sure you have a picture saved to the local Windows 8.1 machine that you want to use. Then follow this procedure to set it up:

Step 1. Select the **Settings** charm and then click the **Change PC settings** link.

Step 2. Select or click **Accounts**.

Step 3. From the Sign-in options section, shown in Figure 13-3, select **Add** under Picture password.

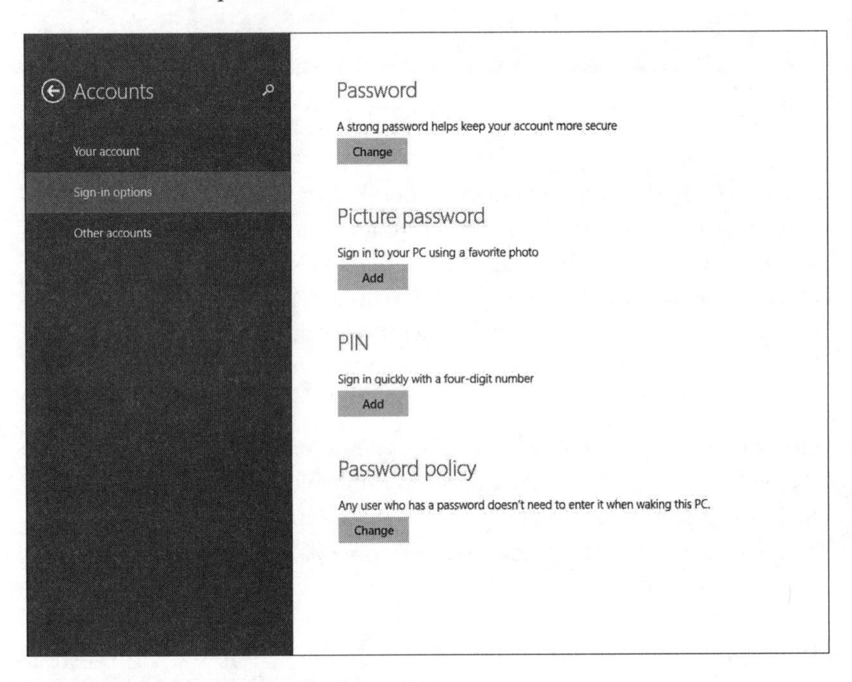

Figure 13-3 PC settings Sign-in options.

Step 4. Windows prompts you for your current password. Enter the password and click **OK**.

Step 5. On the Welcome to picture password screen, click the **Choose picture** button to browse for the picture you want to use.

Step 6. On the How's this look? screen, shown in Figure 13-4, you have the opportunity to reposition the picture or use **Choose new picture**. When you are satisfied, select the **Use this picture** option.

Figure 13-4 Selecting a picture for picture password.

Step 7. Start drawing your gestures. You draw three gestures as the wizard walks you through the steps. Three types of gestures are available:

- Circles
- Straight lines
- Taps

Your three gestures can be any combination of these types. Remember that when you enter your picture password, you must repeat the gestures in the same place on the picture and in the same order. See Figure 13-5 for an example of a Straight line gesture.

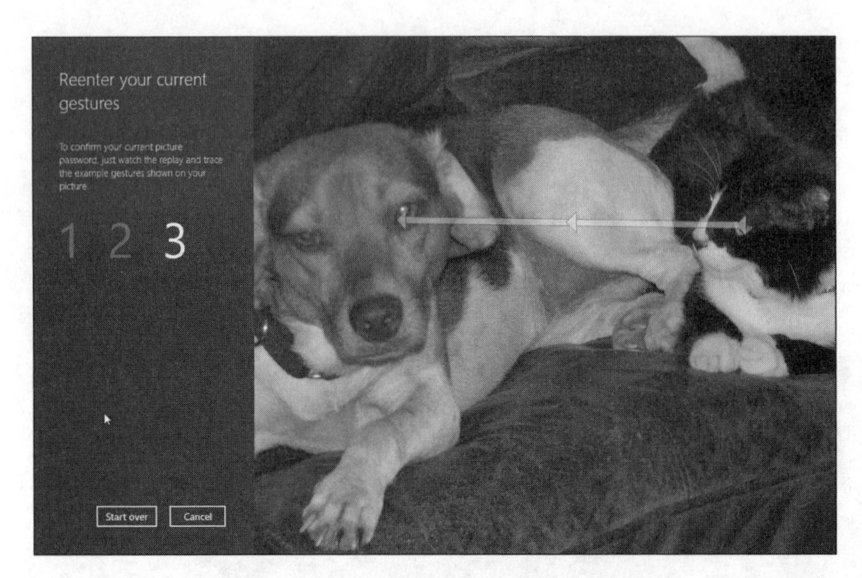

Figure 13-5 Using gesture replay to confirm picture password.

Step 8. Enter your three gestures a second time to confirm your password. After you enter the gestures the same way twice, click the **Finish** button to confirm your new password.

Step 9. If you forget your picture password but remember your plain-text password, you can return to the Picture password screen and use **Replay** to practice your original gestures again.

After you have set up a picture password, the system prompts for the password using the picture selected. You also have the option of using the text password; just select **Switch to text password** at the Picture password screen. When you do so, the text password prompt is used until you switch back to picture passwords. By default, if you perform the wrong gesture 5 times in a row, Windows automatically switches back to text passwords.

In a business or corporate environment, you might want to disable the use of picture passwords by users. You can accomplish this using Local Group Policies. Navigate to **Computer Configuration\Administrative Templates\System\Logon** and select **Turn off picture password sign-in**. Enabling this policy, as shown in Figure 13-6, disables the use of the picture password, and users are unable to use or configure them for their account.

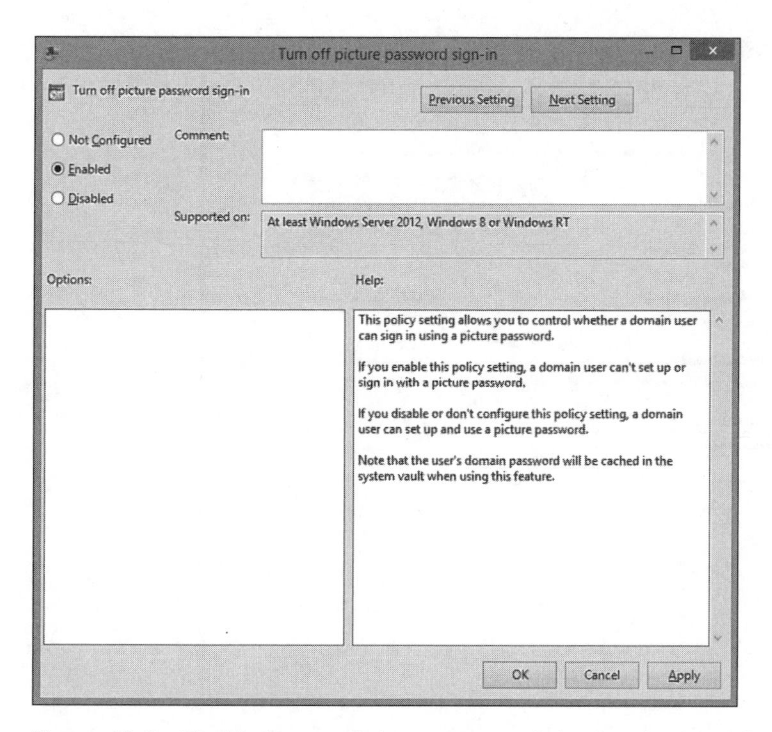

Figure 13-6 Disable the use of picture password sign-in using Local Group Policy Editor.

Managing Credentials

The preceding section covered user logon and authentication to the Windows 8.1 computer. Users also need access to other network resources not controlled by Windows or the local AD domain. This can include websites, terminal servers, applications, and other resources that require credentials to use.

Windows 8.1 provides the Credential Manager for storing credentials in an electronic Windows vault, facilitating logon to these other resources. You can use Credential Manager to create stored credentials for each resource a user needs to work with.

You can start Credential Manager from the Control Panel under User Accounts and Family Safety, or by searching for **credential** using the Search charm. Credential Manager organizes credentials as either Web Credentials or Windows Credentials, presenting these broad categories as shown in Figure 13-7.

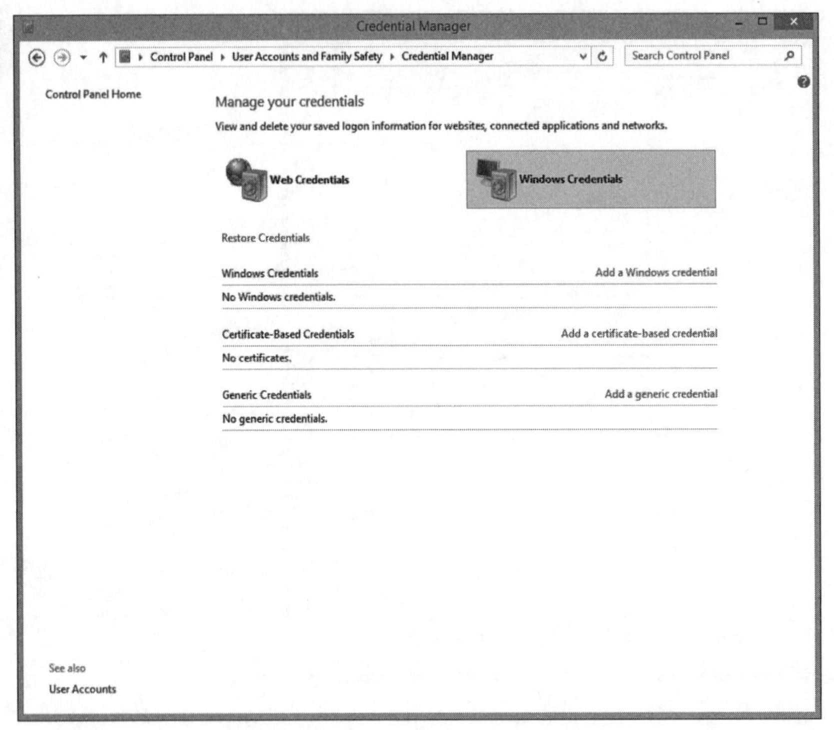

Figure 13-7 Credential Manager and Windows Credentials.

Windows Credentials includes the following credential types:

- **Windows Credentials** are used to store authorization accounts for other Windows servers and computers.
- **Certificate-based Credentials** are used to associate Internet or network addresses with user-based certificates. The certificates used for these credentials must be stored in the user's Personal store in Certificate Manager. Managing Certificates is covered in the next section.
- **Generic Credentials** include things like OneDrive and other cloud accounts, Microsoft accounts, and other integrated services credentials.

Adding, Editing, and Removing Credentials in Credential Manager

To add a credential, start by opening Credential Manager, as previously described, and then select the desired type of credential. For a Windows or generic credential, you receive a screen similar to that shown in Figure 13-8. Enter the required server or network name, username, and password, and then click **OK**. You return to the Credential Manager where the added credential appears under the appropriate category. You can now add additional credentials if needed.

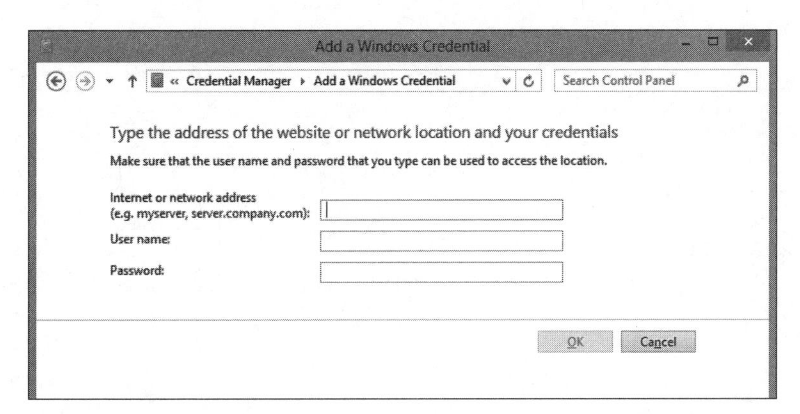

Figure 13-8 Entering a new Windows Credential into Credential Manager.

Entering a certificate-based credential is slightly different. Enter the required server or network name, and then click **Select certificate** to locate a certificate that should be stored in the Personal store of Certificate Manager or on a smart card. When done, click **OK**.

Credential Manager also enables you to modify or remove existing credentials. Click the arrow next to the stored credential to expand its entry, as shown in Figure 13-9. Clicking **Edit** takes you to the Edit Windows Credential screen, on which you can change the username and password or certificate. To delete a credential, click **Remove** and then click **Yes** to confirm your intentions.

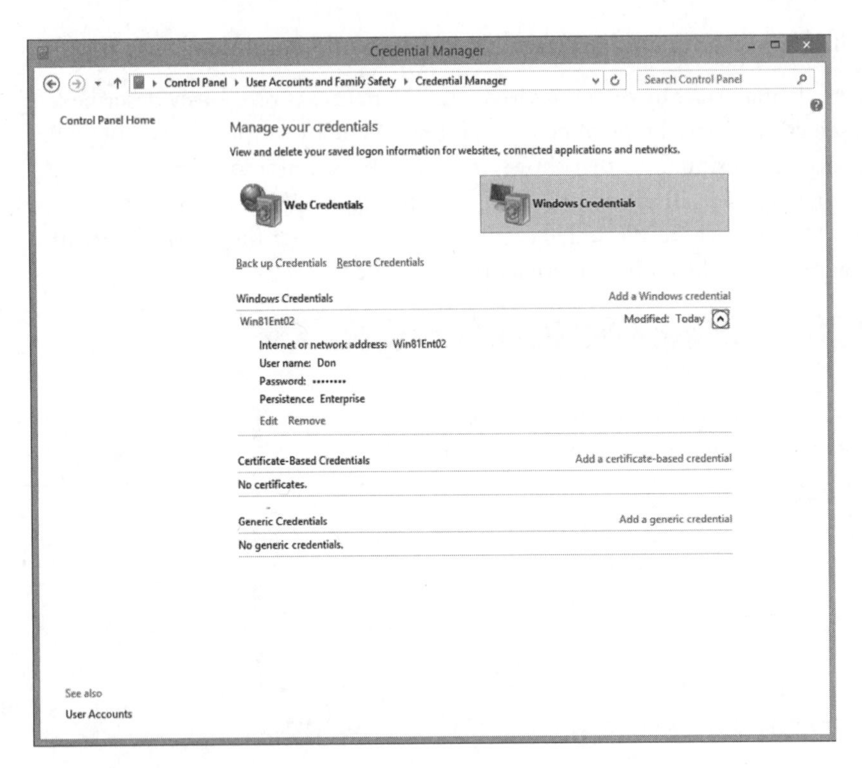

Figure 13-9 Edit or remove a credential in Credential Manager.

Credential Manager can also be leveraged by Windows 8.1 apps, so if you have an online identity associated with a Windows app, it can place your credentials into the Credential Manager. If you use a Microsoft account for your PC, your credentials follow you to each device you use with your Microsoft account. This type of credential roaming is enabled by default on non–domain-joined computers and disabled on domain-joined computers.

TIP Windows automatically adds credentials to Credential Manager for you when you are working and saves a logon that you have entered. For instance, selecting the **Remember my credentials** check box when logging in to a Remote Desktop Connection or checking the box when connecting to a remove file share tells Windows to save the credential in Credential Manager.

Windows Credentials Backup and Restore

You can back up your Windows Credentials using Credential Manager, store them in a separate location, and restore your credentials if your computer or hard drive is replaced. To do so, use the following procedure:

Step 1. In Credential Manager, select **Windows Credentials** and then click on **Back up Credentials** to display the dialog box shown in Figure 13-10.

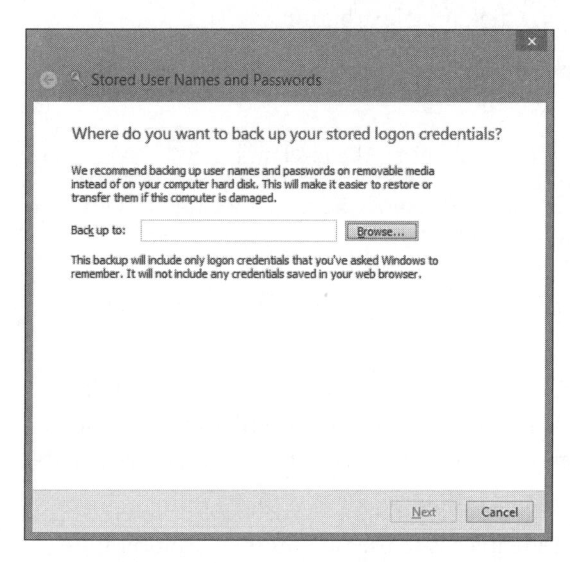

Figure 13-10 Select a location to store your Windows Credentials backup.

Step 2. Type the path to the desired location or click **Browse** to locate the appropriate folder. It is recommended that you use removable media or a trusted network location. Click **Next**.

Step 3. On the next screen, press **Ctrl+Alt+Delete** to continue the backup on the Secure Desktop.

Step 4. The next screen asks you to secure the backup with a password. Enter and confirm your password in the text boxes provided and then click **Next**. Be sure to use a good password that you will remember. You will need this password if you need to restore your credentials.

Step 5. The next screen indicates that the backup was successful. Click the **Finish** button to exit the wizard.

Restoring your credentials follows a similar process. You can use this if your computer or hard drive is replaced, or you want to transfer your credentials from one computer to another. Use the following procedure to restore credentials:

Step 1. In Credential Manager, select **Windows Credentials** and then click on **Restore Credentials**.

Step 2. On the resulting dialog box, type the path to the backup file or click the **Browse** button to navigate to it. Click the **Next** button.

Step 3. On the next screen, press **Ctrl+Alt+Delete** to continue the restore on the Secure Desktop.

Step 4. Enter the password you used when backing up the credentials.

Step 5. The credentials are restored. If you used removable media for the backup location, you can remove it and then click **Finish**.

Web Credentials

The Web Credentials store was a new feature in Windows 8 and is also included in Windows 8.1. This Credentials store is integrated with Internet Explorer and used to store any saved passwords for websites, FTP sites, and other Internet services accessed through the web browser.

The alternate way to access Web Credentials is to use the Internet Explorer Options:

Step 1. From the Internet Explorer settings menu, select **Internet options**.

Step 2. Click the **Content** tab from the Internet Options dialog.

Step 3. Under the **AutoComplete** section, click the **Settings** button.

Step 4. From the resulting AutoComplete Settings dialog box, click the **Manage Passwords** button.

The Credential Manager is displayed with the **Web Credentials** section selected, similar to Figure 13-11. From here, you can display the credential details, remove credentials, and display the password by clicking on the **Show** link.

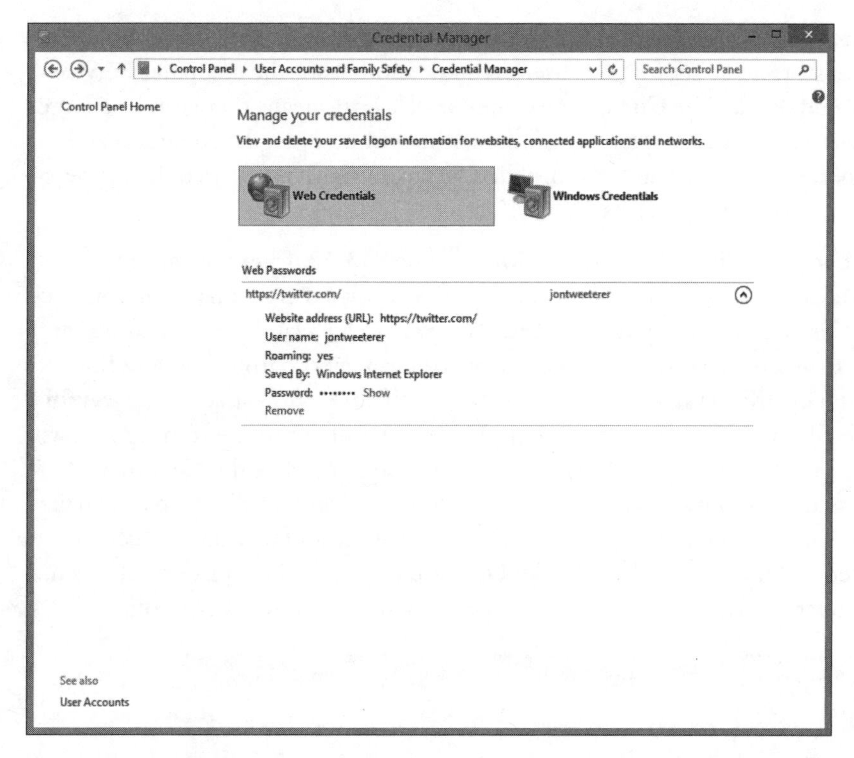

Figure 13-11 Web Credentials displays the accounts and information saved from websites using Internet Explorer.

Note that unlike Windows Credentials, there is no interface for adding credentials or for backing up and restoring Web Credentials. Because Web Credentials can display the original plain-text password used, backing up these credentials to another location can cause a security risk.

Managing Certificates

When you use Credential Manager to store a certificate-based credential as discussed in the previous section, it looks for the certificate in the Personal store of Certificate Manager. When you log on using a smart card, the smart card contains a certificate with information that verifies your identity. When you use Encrypting File System (EFS) to encrypt a file, as discussed in Chapter 11, you create a certificate that is stored in the same certificate store. Windows 8.1 provides the Certificate Manager Microsoft Management Console (MMC) snap-in to manage stored certificates.

Certificates are managed in several stores, and Windows 8.1 maintains three separate sets of stores: one set for your user account, another for the computer Service accounts, and one for the Computer account itself. That means there can be a large number of separate sets, depending on the number of users on the computer and the number of service accounts for installed services. There is always only one set of stores for the local computer itself.

You can open Certificate Manager, shown in Figure 13-12, from the page in Credential Manager that enables you to add a certificate-based credential. You can also load Certificate Manager by typing `certificates` in the Search charm text box and selecting the mode of certificates to manage. You can choose from **Manage file encryption certificates**, **Manage computer certificates**, or **Manage user certificates**. Certificate Manager opens and displays a series of certificate stores, as shown in Figure 13-12. Expand any of these certificate stores and click the **Certificates** subnode to display any available certificates. Double-click a certificate to display its details, as shown in Figure 13-13. You can see the purposes for which the certificate is intended and the validity period. The Details tab includes information such as the serial number, signature hash algorithm, issuer, public key value, and so on.

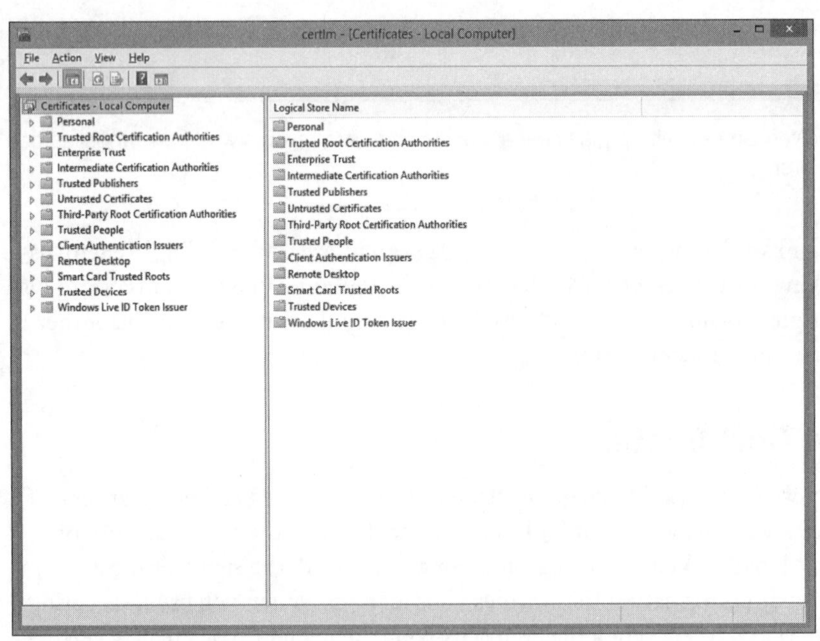

Figure 13-12 Certificate Manager is used to view and manage different types of certificates in different certificate stores.

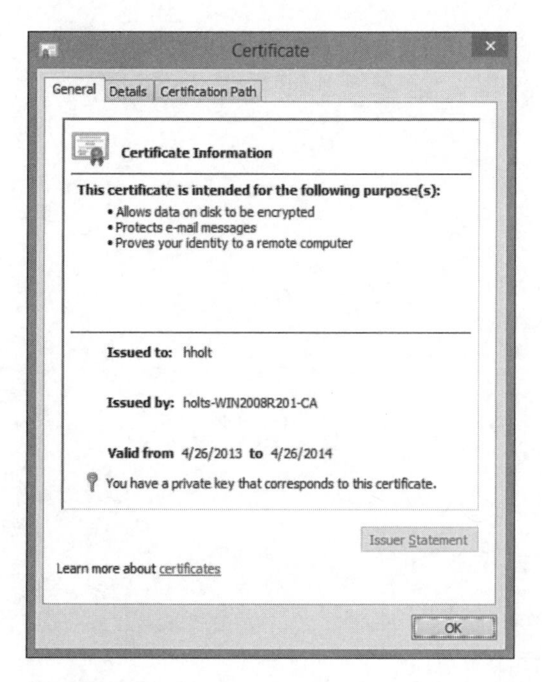

Figure 13-13 Viewing the properties of a certificate.

You can also view additional information and configure certificate properties by selecting the Details tab and clicking the Edit Properties button. From the Certificate Properties dialog box shown in Figure 13-14, you can modify the certificate purposes, specify cross-certificate download URLs, specify Online Certificate Status Protocol (OCSP), download URLs, and extend validation parameters.

Using the Friendly name field and the Description field in the General tab can help to differentiate among similar certificates. Cross-certificates are used to establish trust between separate certification authority (CA) hierarchies, such as those used on diverse networks. OCSP responders are used to verify certificate validity and check against certificate revocation lists issued by CAs. For more information about these certificate properties, click the **Learn more about certificate properties** link at the bottom of the Properties dialog box shown in Figure 13-14.

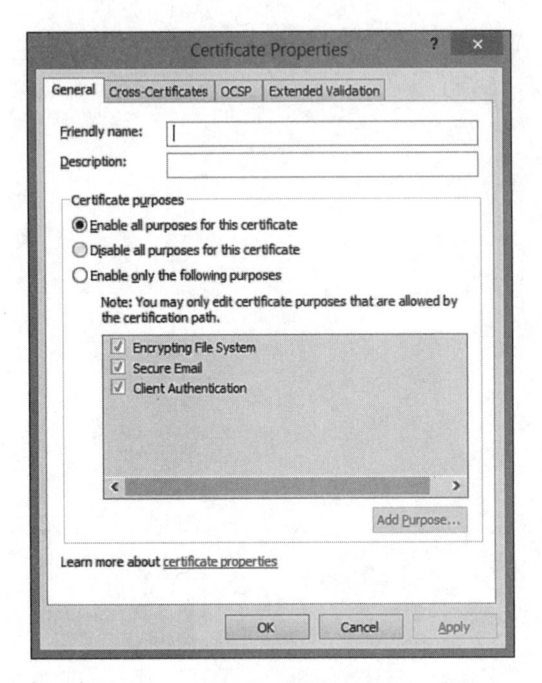

Figure 13-14 Dialog box for editing certificate properties.

Requesting Certificates

There are a number of ways to request a personal or computer certificate for use in encryption and authentication. You may be provided a certificate by your company, or it may be loaded on a smart card or installed on your workstation. Companies often implement their own Public Key Infrastructure (PKI), with an internal certificate authority (CA) to issue certificates.

A common way to implement certificate distribution in a large company is to provide users with a web interface to request certificates using their Active Directory account. Using this technique, users need only the URL of the CA to request a personal certificate. They can then use it for VPN, email, and other purposes. The procedure is as follows:

Step 1. Open Internet Explorer and type in the URL for the CA. A screen is displayed similar to Figure 13-15.

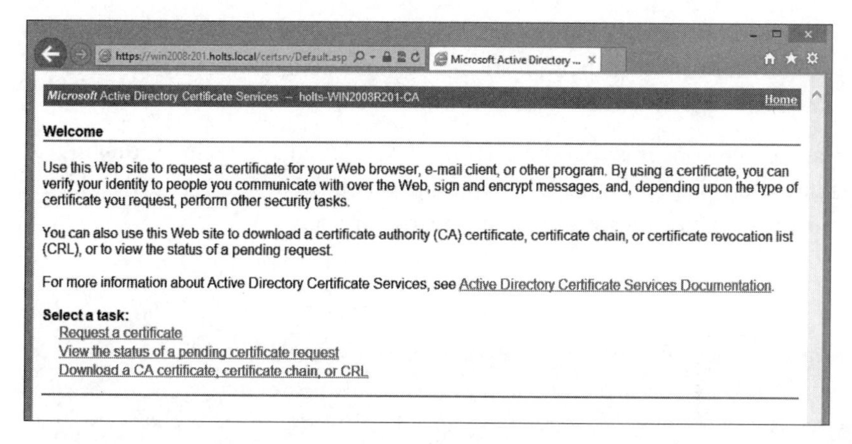

Figure 13-15 Accessing a company Certificate Authority server to request a certificate.

Step 2. Click the **Request a certificate** link on the web page.

Step 3. The next page gives you the opportunity to select a certificate type or submit an advanced certificate request.

Step 4. To request a personal certificate, click the **User Certificate** link. You are prompted with a Web Access Confirmation dialog box. Click **Yes** to confirm.

Step 5. If you are prompted for credentials, enter your username and password in the fields provided. The CA uses your credentials for the request.

Step 6. On the next screen, the server confirms your request and provides a Submit button to submit the request. Click the **Advanced** link to display details about the certificate and modify the provider type, private key protection, and certificate format, as shown in Figure 13-16. Typically, you would accept the defaults presented by the CA.

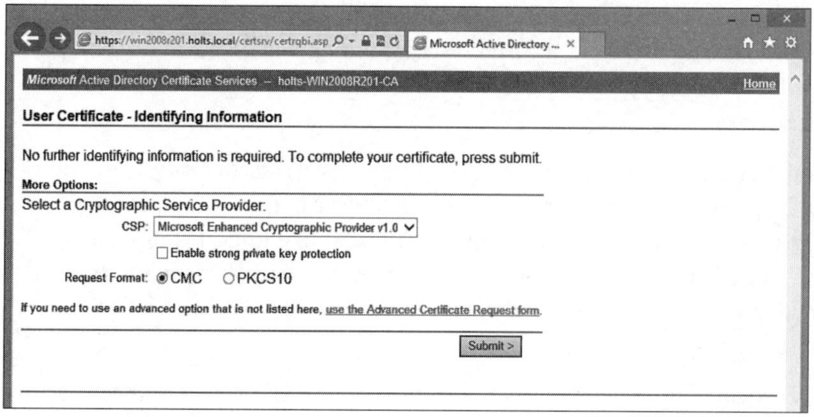

https://win2008r201.holts.local/certsrv/certrqbi.asp
Microsoft Active Directory ...
Microsoft Active Directory Certificate Services -- holts-WIN2008R201-CA
Home
User Certificate - Identifying Information
No further identifying information is required. To complete your certificate, press submit.
More Options:
Select a Cryptographic Service Provider:
CSP: Microsoft Enhanced Cryptographic Provider v1.0
Enable strong private key protection
Request Format: CMC PKCS10
If you need to use an advanced option that is not listed here, use the Advanced Certificate Request form.
Submit >

Figure 13-16 Ready to submit certificate request.

Step 7. Click the **Submit** button. You are prompted again with the Web Access Confirmation to confirm that the website can perform a digital certificate operation, just as in step 4. Click **Yes** to confirm.

Step 8. The last screen confirms that the certificate was issued and includes the link Install this certificate. Click the link and the certificate is automatically added to your Personal certificate store and is ready for use.

NOTE Enterprise Certificate Services is beyond the scope of the 70-687 exam and this text. If you would like to learn more about implementing and managing a PKI in a Windows environment, refer to "Active Directory Certificate Services Overview" at http://technet.microsoft.com/library/hh831740.

Configuring Smart Cards and PINs

To improve the security of user logons and avoid the hassle of password problems, organizations are implementing advanced authentication techniques, commonly referred to as multifactor, two-factor, or strong authentication. Smart card or chip card technology is becoming commonplace in companies, businesses, and government organizations. These multifactor authentication mechanisms help to provide secure, tamper-proof identification and authentication of users. You can use them for secure authentication of clients logging in to an AD DS domain as well as for those logging in remotely.

A *smart card*, typically a type of chip card, is a plastic card with an embedded computer chip that stores and transacts data. Smart cards used with PINs provide a cost-effective form of two-factor authentication. In this scenario, often referred to as "something you have and something you know," the user must have the smart card and know the PIN to access secured systems and network resources. This significantly reduces the risk of unauthorized access to sensitive organization data and expensive resources.

Many manufacturers produce Plug-and-Play smart card readers certified by Microsoft for use on Windows computers. Many of the newer portable computers even feature built-in smart card readers or biometric devices like fingerprint scanners. You can use Active Directory Certificate Services (AD CS) in Windows Server (2008 R2 and later) for enrolling certificates for smart cards that can be used for Windows 8.1 logons.

Smart cards provide improved security for authentication by providing three key properties that maintain trusted security:

- **Nonexportability:** The private data, keys, and other information stored on the card cannot be extracted and used on another card or media.
- **Isolated cryptography:** Any encryption and decryption performed related to the card functionality occur solely on the card processor itself, and the hosting computer does not have access to those operations or transactions.
- **Antihammering:** The card includes features to prevent brute-force attacks attempting to guess the PIN, so too many consecutive attempts will cause the card to disable itself.

NOTE On Windows RT, smart cards must support either the PIV standard from the National Institute of Standards and Technology (NIST), or the Generic Identity Device Specification (GIDS). Smart card readers that connect to USB ports must use the Chip/Smart Card Interface Devices (CCID) specification.

Virtual Smart Cards

New for Windows 8 is the ability to use *virtual smart cards*. This technology eliminates the need for a separate hardware device that can be easily lost or damaged, and instead uses the increasingly available Trusted Platform Module (TPM) chip built into the computer or laptop device. The TPM chip is a hardware-level security device that provides all the security and encryption capabilities of a separate smart card device.

To configure a TPM on a Windows 8.1 computer to act as a virtual smart card, you need the following prerequisites:

- You must have a Windows 8.1 computer with a TPM built in.
- Windows 8.1 must be joined to a Windows Active Directory domain.
- The domain must have Certificate Services implemented.
- Certificate Services must be implemented with a Certificate template for Smart Card Logon.

When your computer and environment meet the listed requirements, you can enable the TPM as a virtual smart card. Use the following procedure:

Step 1. Open an administrative command prompt. You can do so by searching for **cmd** in the Search charm, right-clicking on **Command Prompt**, and selecting **Run as administrator**. In Windows 8.1, you can also right-click **Start** and choose **Command Prompt (Admin)**.

Step 2. Use the `tpmvscmgr.exe` command-line tool to create the virtual smart card. A typical command is:

```
tpmvscmgr.exe create /name MyVSC /pin default /adminkey random
/generate
```

This command creates the smart card on the TPM with the name MyVSC. The default PIN is 12345678, and an administrative key is randomly generated. The administrative key is used to reset the smart card in case the user forgets her PIN. See Figure 13-17 for an example.

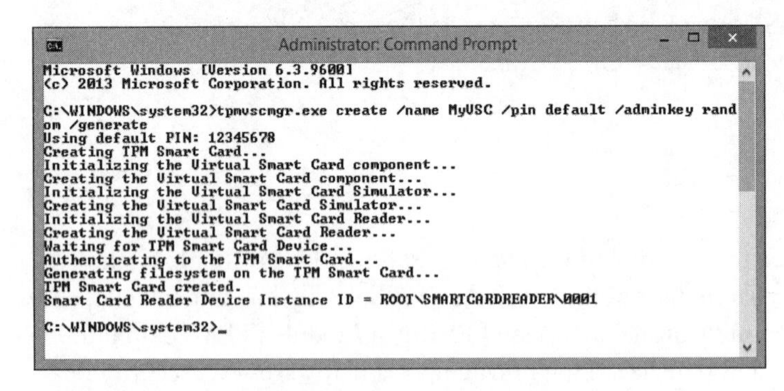

Figure 13-17 Creating a virtual smart card using the TPM.

Step 3. Open Certificate Manager as described in the previous section.

Step 4. Right-click the **Personal** folder and then select **All Tasks > Request New Certificate**.

Step 5. Follow the prompts on the Certificate Enrollment wizard, and when prompted to select a template, locate the **Smart Card logon** template and select it, as shown in Figure 13-18.

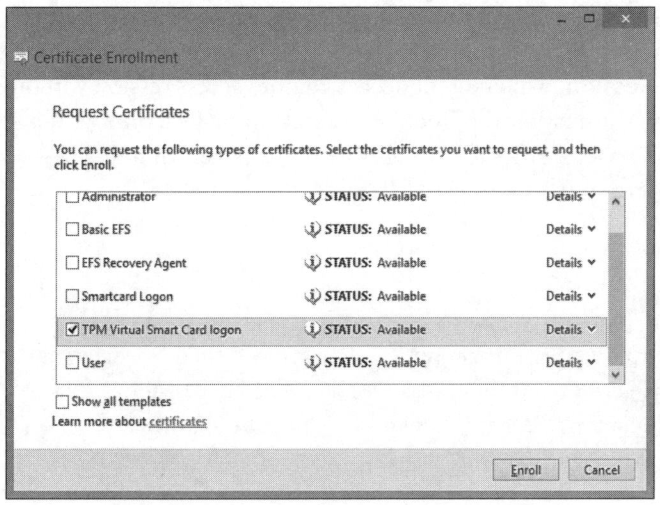

Figure 13-18 Enrolling a smart card certificate from the domain CA.

Step 6. Enter the PIN for the smart card. From the example in step 2, the default PIN 12345678 is used. Click **OK**.

Step 7. When the enrollment is completed, click the **Finish** button.

With these steps completed, the user can now use the TPM virtual smart card as an alternative to log on to the domain. With the correct Group Policies in place for the domain, you can require users to use their TPM (or other smart card) when logging in remotely or from a VPN connection.

Smart Card Group Policies

You can use Windows 8.1 Local Group Policies to control the use of smart cards. Under the Computer Configuration\Windows Settings\Security Settings\Local Policies\Security Options node, the following policies are available:

- **Interactive logon: Require smart card:** When this policy is enabled, users must employ a smart card to log on.
- **Interactive logon: Smart card removal behavior:** This policy governs the action that occurs if a logged-on user removes her smart card. By default, no action takes place. You can also specify **Lock Workstation**, which locks the

computer but retains the active session when the smart card is removed; **Force Logoff**, which automatically logs off the user; and **Disconnect if a Remote Desktop Services Session**, which disconnects a remote access session without logging off the user. With either the **Lock Workstation** or **Disconnect if a Remote Desktop Services Session** settings, the user can return to her session simply by reinserting the smart card.

NOTE You should be aware of some changes to smart card behavior for Windows 8.1. For instance, in Windows 8.1, if a transaction is held for more than five seconds between operations, the card is reset and the transaction is canceled. For more information, see the Microsoft document "What's New in Smart Cards" at http://technet.microsoft.com/en-us/library/hh849637.aspx.

Configuring Biometrics

Another form of multifactor authentication used increasingly in secure organization environments is *biometrics*. Biometric authentication includes devices such as retina scanners, fingerprint readers, and other peripherals that confirm your identity using unique biological characteristics of a person that cannot be easily duplicated. Even people born as twins have different and unique fingerprints distinguishable by computer and forensic specialists.

Windows supports these devices through the Windows Biometric Framework (WBF), first introduced in Windows 7 and Windows Server 2008 R2. Beginning with Windows 8 and Windows Server 2012, and continuing with Windows 8.1 and Windows Server 2012 R2, the WBF has been improved in a number of ways, including improving the reliability of the services and compatibility with biometric devices through hardware drivers and interfaces. WBF includes services that provide client applications with the ability to capture, compare, and store biometric information and does so in a secure fashion through the Local System context.

Biometric Devices

Configuring biometrics starts with configuration of the device used. Often newer computers and laptops come equipped with fingerprint readers or other devices, or they can be add-ons connected through USB ports.

Your device needs to be compatible with the WBF framework in order to work with Windows logon. When your compatible device is installed, the new Biometric Devices applet is available in the Control Panel. The following settings are available under Change settings on the Biometric Devices applet:

- **Biometrics on:** Enables the biometric device. With this option enabled, the following selections are also enabled for selection:
  - Allow users to log on to Windows using their fingerprints
  - Allow users to log on to a domain using their fingerprints (only available for domain-joined computers)
- **Biometrics off:** Disables the biometric device.

Group Policies for Biometrics

The Group Policy settings shown in Table 13-2 are available for controlling the use of biometric devices in Windows 8.1. All are available in the Local Group Policy under Computer Configuration\Administrative Templates\Windows Components\Biometrics.

Table 13-2 Group Policies for Biometric Devices in Windows 8.1

Policy Name	Description
Allow automatic logon using boot-time biometric authentication	Determines whether a user will be automatically logged on after providing a biometric sample at boot time.
Specify timeout for preboot auto-logon authentication	Specifies the time after system startup that a preboot biometric authentication will be used for auto-logon before being discarded.
Allow the use of biometrics	Allows or prevents the Windows Biometric Service to run.
Allow users to log on using biometrics	Determines whether users can log on (or elevate User Account Control [UAC] permissions) using biometrics.
Allow domain users to log on using biometrics	Determines whether users with a domain account can log on (or elevate UAC permissions) using biometrics. By default, domain users cannot use biometrics to log on. Enabling this policy allows users to log on to a domain-joined computer with a biometric identity.

Configuring PINs

At the other end of security from using multifactor authentication with smart cards and biometrics, Windows 8.1 now provides the option to log on to the computer using a four-digit PIN. Note that smart cards require a minimum of eight digits for a PIN, as previously described, which provides better security. This functionality was provided to make it easier for users of tablets and Windows RT devices to sign on to their devices without the frustration of using a soft keyboard to type in a complex password.

To set up a PIN for an account, follow these steps:

Step 1. Access the **PC settings**, select **Accounts**, and then select the **Sign-in options** section, as shown earlier in Figure 13-3. Note the **Add** button under PIN. Click the button to create a PIN.

Step 2. When prompted for your current password, enter it in the space provided and then click **OK**.

Step 3. The next screen allows you to enter your four-digit pin, as shown in Figure 13-19. Enter the PIN twice to confirm it and then click the **Finish** button.

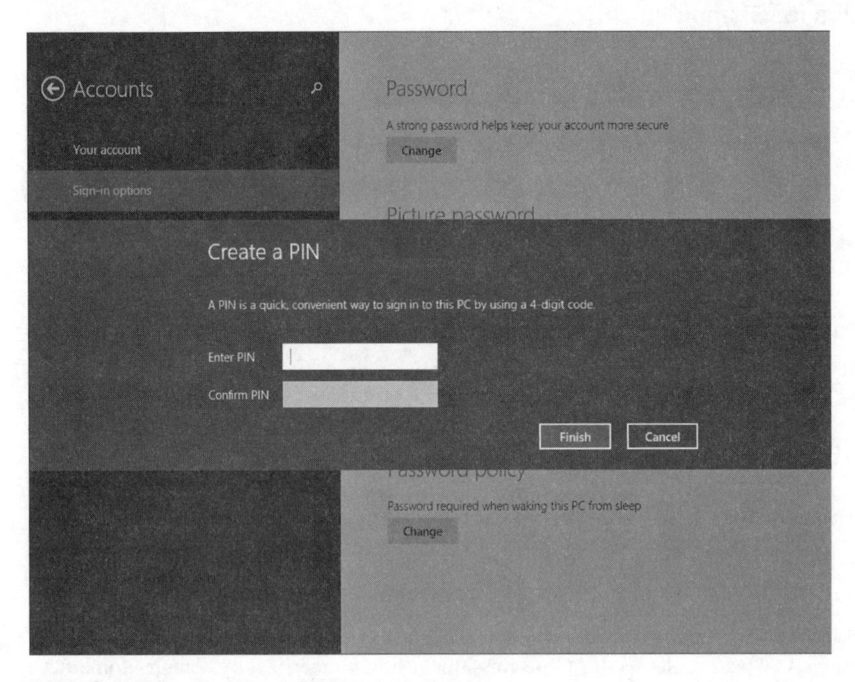

Figure 13-19 Creating a PIN for user sign on.

Step 4. Sign out from the computer and confirm you can log on using your new PIN.

The PIN must be four digits. The user doesn't need to press **Enter** when signing on with a PIN because it is always four digits. Windows confirms the correct PIN and logs on the user as soon as it has all four correct digits.

When a PIN is first configured, it is the default option for logon. You can change the logon method at the logon screen by clicking the **Sign-in options** link. Depending on the sign-in options you have configured, you can then select between password, picture password, or PIN.

Managing the Use of PINs

Because of the simple nature of a four-digit numeric PIN, which is much easier to guess than a longer, complex password, it is considered insecure. By default, PIN sign-on is disabled on Windows 8.1 when it is joined to a domain.

You can manage the use of PINs for Windows 8.1 logon using Group Policies. The Turn on PIN sign-on policy is found under Computer Configuration\Administrative Templates\System\Logon. Enable this policy to allow users to sign in using a PIN. By default, users on domain-joined computers cannot use a PIN. Enabling this setting allows PIN sign-on even on a domain-joined computer. The user's domain password is cached in the Credential Manager when enabling this policy and using PINs.

CAUTION It is not recommended that you enable PIN logons for domain-joined computers. You should use care when enabling them for other Windows 8.1 computers. As previously noted, four-digit numeric PINs are trivial to guess, and unauthorized access can occur. A user guessing the PIN to sign on to a domain-joined computer means he also has access to the user's domain credentials and all the network resources the user is authorized to use.

Configuring User Rights

User rights are defined as a default set of capabilities assigned to built-in local groups that define what members of these groups can and cannot do on the network. They consist of privileges and logon rights.

Managing Local Accounts and Groups

To create new Local accounts in Windows 8.1, you use the PC settings screen. Click the **Add an account** link in the Other accounts section, select **Sign in without a Microsoft account**, and then select **Local account**, as shown in Figure 13-20. This is similar to the process for creating the first account for a new Windows 8.1 install, as covered in Chapter 2.

You can manage existing accounts using the User Accounts Control Panel applet or the Local Users and Groups section of the Computer Management snap-in. The snap-in provides greater control of local accounts and allows you to use specific groups to provide authorization for each account. You can add users to groups from the Local Users and Groups node of the Computer Management snap-in. Right-click the desired group in the Groups folder and choose **Properties** as shown in

Figure 13-21. In the Properties dialog box that appears, click **Add**, type the desired username, and then click **OK**. Click **OK** again in the group's Properties dialog box to close it and add the user to the group.

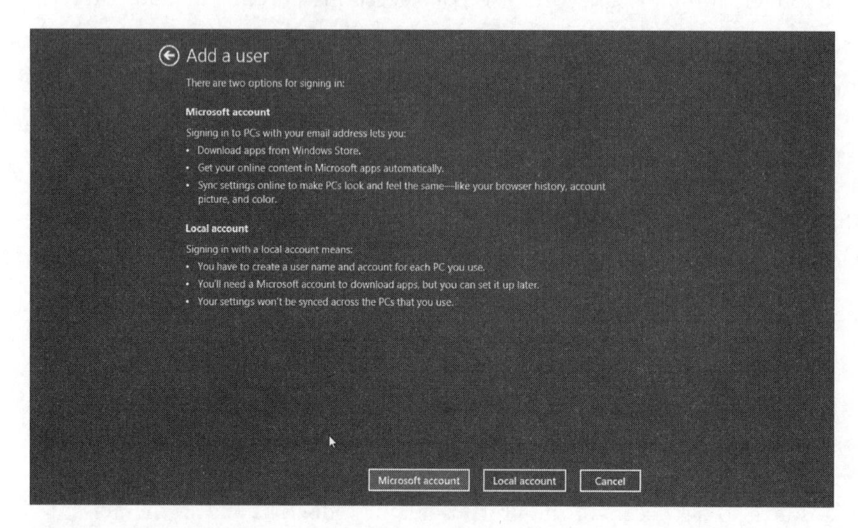

Figure 13-20 Adding a new user in Windows 8.1.

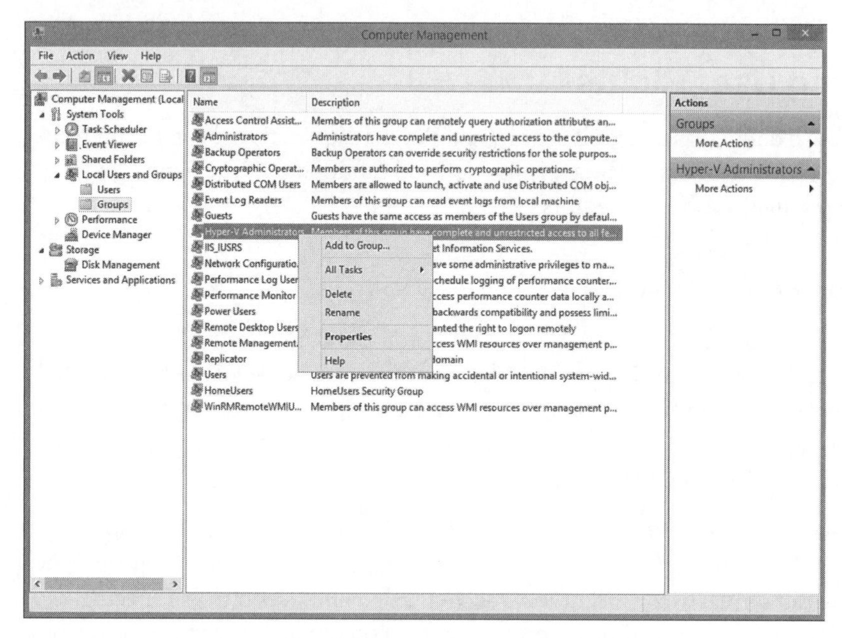

Figure 13-21 Windows 8.1 Built-in Groups in Local Users and Groups snap-in.

When you change the Account Type using the Control Panel, you can select either a Standard account or an Administrator account. This simply adds or removes the user from the local Administrators group. There are several additional built-in groups you can use for better control of authorization. Table 13-3 summarizes the available built-in local groups.

Table 13-3 Built-in Local Groups in Windows 8.1

Group Name	Default Rights	Default Local Membership
Access Control Assistance Operators	Access to remotely query authorization attributes and permissions for resources	N/A
Administrators	Unrestricted access and all privileges	Administrator
Backup Operators	Access to run Windows Backup and sufficient access rights that override other rights when performing a backup or restore	N/A
Cryptographic Operators	Authorization to perform cryptographic operations	N/A
Distributed COM users	Able to launch, activate, and use Distributed COM objects on the local computer	N/A
Event Log Readers	Read access to event logs	N/A
Guest	Limited to explicitly granted rights and restricted usage of the computer	Guest (disabled by default)
Hyper-V Administrators	Members of this group have complete and unrestricted access to all features of Hyper-V	N/A
Network Configuration Operators	Some administrative privileges to manage network configuration and features	N/A
Performance Log Users	Able to schedule logging of performance counters, enable trace providers, and collect event traces both locally and remotely	N/A
Performance Monitor Users	Access to performance counter data locally and remotely	N/A
Power Users	Used only for backward compatibility with Windows XP and earlier, limited administrative privileges	N/A
Remote Desktop Users	Access to the computer using Remote Desktop	N/A

Group Name	Default Rights	Default Local Membership
Remote Management Users	Access to WMI resources over management protocols such as the Windows Remote Management service; limited by WMI namespace access granted to the user	N/A
Replicator	Able to support file replication in a domain	N/A
Users	Able to prevent users from making accidental or intentional systemwide changes and can run most applications	All local accounts and authenticated users in a domain-joined environment

Controlling User Rights

You can manage the default predefined user rights from the Computer Configuration\Policies\Windows Settings\Security Settings\Local Policies\User Rights Assignment node in the Local Group Policy Editor. From this node, you can view the default rights assignments, as shown in Figure 13-22. To modify the assignment of any right, right-click it and choose **Properties**. In the Properties dialog box, click **Add User or Group**, and in the Select Users or Groups dialog box, type or browse to the required user or group. Then click **OK**.

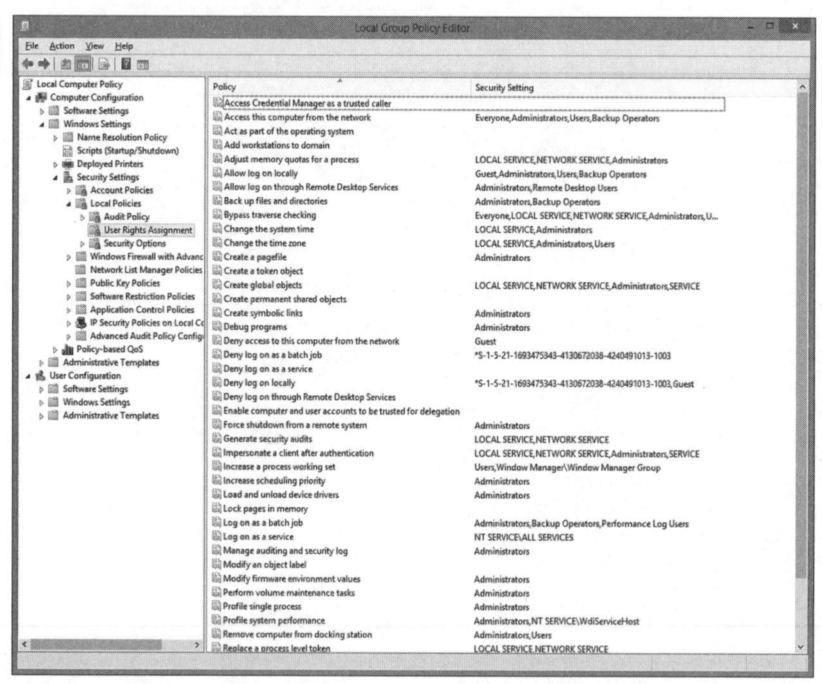

Figure 13-22 User Rights Assignment policies available in Windows 8.1 Local Group Policy Editor.

In total, Windows 8.1 includes 44 user rights. For the purposes of the 70-687 exam, it is unlikely that you would need to know what these user rights actually involve. Although you can grant users these rights directly from the Local Group Policy Editor, as explained here, the typical method is to add the desired user to the appropriate default built-in local group, as previously described. User Rights Assignment settings can provide more fine-grained control over the rights granted to users and groups when it is needed.

Setting Up and Configuring a Microsoft Account

With Windows 8, Microsoft consolidated its latest operating system for PCs, tablets, smartphones, and major portability. Users may have a work computer, a home PC, a smartphone, and a tablet all running Windows 8.1 or Windows RT, and they expect their settings, Windows apps, and services to work the same across all of these devices. The way to enable the consistency across all these devices is to use a Microsoft account.

When the same Microsoft account is used on all of a user's devices, he has automatic access to many resources, apps, files stored in the cloud and on remote computers, and consistent settings that roam from device to device.

Signing In Using a Microsoft Account

Recall from Chapter 2 that the default method for creating the first account at the end of the setup process was to use a Microsoft account. You can use any email address for the Microsoft account. Users only need to provide their email address and create a password for the Microsoft account, and they can use the account on any Windows 8.1 or Windows RT computer.

Using a Microsoft account provides several advantages, especially for home users:

- Contacts and friend status can be integrated from Outlook.com, Facebook, Twitter, and LinkedIn.
- Photos, documents, and other files can be accessed from OneDrive, Facebook, and Flickr.
- Using Windows Store apps is easier and requires a Microsoft account. You can use purchased apps that are installed on one computer on up to five devices using Windows 8.1 or Windows RT.
- Personal settings are automatically kept in sync online and among all the devices using the same Microsoft account. They include themes, browser favorites and history, and content and settings for Microsoft apps and services.

Creating a Microsoft account for use with Windows 8.1 is a simple process. Assuming you are already using a local account, you can switch to using a Microsoft account using this procedure:

Step 1. Swipe or point to the right edge of the screen, select **Settings**, and then select **Change PC settings**.

Step 2. Select **Accounts**. Then in the Your account section, select **Connect to a Microsoft account**.

Step 3. When prompted, enter your current password or PIN and then click **Next**.

Step 4. Enter the email address to use for the new Microsoft account. If you do not have an email address you want to use, or you want to create a new one, click on the **Create a new account** link. You then have the option of creating an email address on Outlook.com, Hotmail.com, or Live.com.

Step 5. Fill out the Create a Microsoft account form, as shown in Figure 13-23. Note that passwords must have a minimum of eight characters and contain at least two out of this list: uppercase letters, lowercase letters, numbers, and symbols.

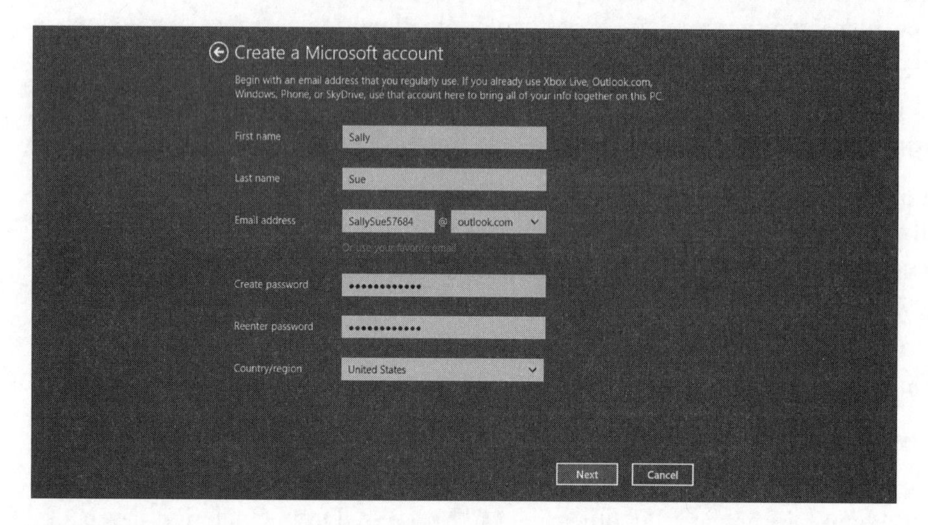

Figure 13-23 Set up a Microsoft account.

Step 6. When the form is complete, click **Next**.

Step 7. On the **Add security info** screen, you can enter some additional information in case you lose your password. Fill out the fields as desired and then click **Next**. The birth date and at least two types of security info are required.

Step 8. On the Finish up screen, sign up for the advertising and promotional material you want to receive and then click **Next**.

Step 9. The next screen asks you to confirm you are a real person. Enter the scrambled letters that appear on the screen and click **Next** when done.

Step 10. Windows takes a few moments creating your account. When it is done, click **Finish** to sign on to Windows with your new Microsoft account.

Like many online accounts that you create, you are asked to confirm your email address for your Microsoft account by clicking a link in an email from Microsoft's servers. The Windows Action Center displays a warning in Windows until you have confirmed your account.

Like other methods of signing on to Windows 8.1, when you set up a Microsoft account the first time, it becomes the default Sign-on method. To sign on using a different method, select the **Sign-on options** link on the logon screen.

Domain Accounts

Users on domain-joined Windows 8.1 computers can connect their domain account to their Microsoft account. This provides the ability to sync their settings, favorites, and Microsoft apps from their home PC or tablet with their domain-joined computer without signing into services separately.

The process is similar to that listed for a nondomain account, but domain users are presented with a Connect your Microsoft account option on the Accounts screen. When that option is selected, users can choose what settings to synchronize, as shown in Figure 13-24. Choose the desired sync settings and click **Next**, and the rest of the process is the same.

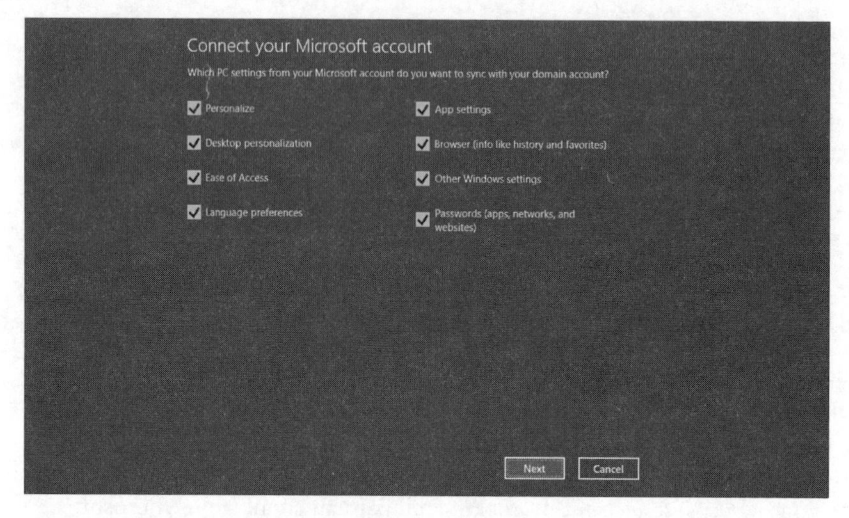

Figure 13-24 Select the PC settings to sync with your domain account.

Managing the Use of a Microsoft Account

In many organizations, it may be inappropriate to allow users to sign on to their PCs using a Microsoft account. As described in the previous section, using a Microsoft account on a business PC means that a lot of personal information is synced and made available on the local PC. This may cause disruption and possible security risks.

To block the use of Microsoft accounts, you can configure the Group Policy Accounts: Block Microsoft Accounts, which is found under Computer Configuration\Windows Settings\Security Settings\Local Policies\Security Options. Three options are available:

- **This policy is disabled:** Users can create and log on with Microsoft accounts and connect their domain account to their Microsoft account.
- **Users can't add Microsoft accounts:** Users are not able to create new Microsoft accounts, switch a local account to a Microsoft account, or connect a domain account to a Microsoft account.
- **Users can't add or log on with Microsoft accounts:** Existing Microsoft account users are not able to log on to Windows.

> **NOTE** The Block Microsoft Accounts setting applies only to using Microsoft accounts for local system logon and syncing with a domain account. Users can still use their Microsoft account for tasks such as accessing email over the Internet and using OneDrive to access cloud-based storage.

Exam Preparation Tasks

Review All the Key Topics

Review the most important topics in the chapter, noted with the key topics icon in the outer margin of the page. Table 13-4 lists a reference of these key topics and the page numbers on which each is found.

Table 13-4 Key Topics for Chapter 13

Key Topic Element	Description	Page Number(s)
Figure 13-1	Shows how to enable secure sign-in using the User Accounts Control Panel applet	558
Step List	Describes how to configure a picture password	560-562
Figure 13-7	Shows the Credential Manager	564
Figure 13-12	Shows the Certificate Manager	570
Figure 13-18	Shows how to enroll a smart card certificate	577
Paragraph	Describes configuration of biometrics	578
Step List	Explains how to configure Windows 8.1 PIN sign-on	580
Table 13-3	Lists built-in local groups in Windows 8.1	583-584
Figure 13-22	Shows User Rights Assignment policies	584
Step List	Describes how to set up a Microsoft account	586-587
List	Details how to configure the use of Microsoft account	588

Definitions of Key Terms

Define the following key terms from this chapter, and check your answers in the Glossary:

Authentication, Authorization, Biometrics, CA, Certificate, Cloud, Credentials, Decryption, Dual-factor authentication, Encryption, Gesture, GIDS, Microsoft account, MMC, OCSP, PIN, PIV, PKI, Smart card, TPM

This chapter covers the following subjects:

- **Configuring Remote Authentication:** To secure sensitive and valuable organizational resources, you must ensure that users connecting from remote locations using the Internet or dial-up connections are positively authenticated. In this section, you learn about processes and technologies available for securely authenticating the users requesting access to your network and computers.
- **Configuring Remote Desktop and Remote Management Settings:** This section describes new and improved methods of connecting to and managing computers remotely. You learn about time-saving management options that enable you to perform a large range of management tasks on remotely located computers directly from your Windows 8.1 computer.
- **Using Windows PowerShell and MMCs for Remote Management:** This section covers some basics of Windows PowerShell, configuring PowerShell Remoting, and using MMC snap-ins for managing remote computers and enabling remote access for these tools.
- **Configuring VPN Authentication and Settings:** In this section, you learn how to set up dial-up and VPN connections for access to organization resources from the Internet and other remote locations.
- **Managing Broadband Connections:** Windows 8.1 enables you to make connections to remote computers in a variety of ways. This section covers the use of Remote Desktop Gateway and some basics of DirectAccess for accessing organizational resources using specially configured Windows Server 2008 R2 and Windows Server 2012 R2 computers.

Configuring Remote Management and Remote Connections

Chapter 13, "Configuring Authentication and Authorization," introduced you to the various tools and technologies available in Windows 8.1 for ensuring that only authenticated users gain access to computers and the resources they contain. In this chapter, we continue the discussion of computer management by looking at the methods available for accessing and managing computers across the network, and in particular the methodologies used for managing computers in remote locations. We take a look at accessing and managing computers through a virtual private network (VPN), using new technologies like Remote Desktop Gateway and DirectAccess, and addressing the authentication techniques you need to be aware of.

You also learn about technology that enables you to manage computers from afar and make connections to these computers from diverse locations. You will see that you can be in a distant location such as home or hotel and perform almost anything that you could do directly from the computer console. When that emergency occurs late at night, you can diagnose many problems and perform fixes without the need to travel to the office.

"Do I Know This Already?" Quiz

The "Do I Know This Already?" quiz allows you to assess whether you should read this entire chapter or simply jump to the "Exam Preparation Tasks" section for review. If you are in doubt, read the entire chapter. Table 14-1 outlines the major headings in this chapter and the corresponding "Do I Know This Already?" quiz questions. You can find the answers in Appendix A, "Answers to the 'Do I Know This Already?' Quizzes."

Table 14-1 "Do I Know This Already?" Foundation Topics Section-to-Question Mapping

Foundations Topics Section	Questions Covered in This Section
Configuring Remote Authentication	1–2
Configuring Remote Desktop and Remote Management Settings	3–5
Using Windows PowerShell and MMCs for Remote Management	6–8
Configuring VPN Authentication and Settings	9–11
Managing Broadband Connections	12–13

1. Which of the following remote access authentication protocols should you avoid because it sends credentials in unencrypted form?
   a. PAP
   b. CHAP
   c. EAP-TTLS
   d. MS-CHAPv2

2. Which of the following remote authentication protocols uses a secure tunnel and can be used with 802.1X authentication as well as RADIUS servers?
   a. CHAP
   b. PAP
   c. Smart Cards
   d. EAP-TTLS

3. You are working from home on your Windows 8.1 Pro computer and need to access your work computer, which is also running Windows 8.1 Pro by means of your cable Internet connection. What tool should you use to make this connection?
   a. Hyper-V
   b. Remote Assistance
   c. Remote Desktop
   d. Virtual Private Network

4. You are working from home on your Windows 8.1 computer and experience a problem that you cannot fix. You want to contact a user on another Windows 8.1 computer that you believe can help you correct your problem. What tool should you use?

   a. Hyper-V

   b. Remote Assistance

   c. Remote Desktop

   d. Virtual Private Network

5. Yesterday evening, you worked on an important project from home on your wife's home computer, which runs the base version of Windows 8.1. Your children interrupted you and you forgot to upload your work to your work computer. The work computer runs Windows 7 Professional. Needing the upgraded project files, you attempt to connect to your home computer but are unable to do so. What do you need to do to make this connection?

   a. Download the Remote Desktop Connection Software application from Microsoft and install it on your home computer.

   b. Upgrade your work computer to Windows 8.1 Pro or Enterprise.

   c. Upgrade your home computer to Windows 8.1 Pro.

   d. Use Remote Assistance to make the connection.

6. Which of the following are valid commands that you can enter at a PowerShell interface? (Choose all that apply.)

   a. `Get-process`

   b. `Value-output`

   c. `Select-object`

   d. `Format-data`

   e. `Folder-create`

7. You are helping a worker in your organization with a configuration issue and decide to run some PowerShell cmdlets you have to check some items on the remote computer. When you run the command, specifying the remote computer name, the command fails to connect to the remote computer and dies with the error `WinRMOperationTimeout`. What is the most likely cause of failure?

   a. You do not have administrative access to the remote computer.

   b. The Remote computer is not in the PowerShell list of Trusted Computers.

   c. PowerShell Remote is not enabled.

   d. The command syntax was incorrect.

8. You want to be able to use all the tools in the Computer Management administrative tool to manage a remote computer. Which of the following firewall application settings do you need to enable? (Select all that apply.)

   a. Remote Event Log

   b. Remote Scheduled Tasks Management

   c. Windows Firewall with Advanced Security

   d. Remote Service Management

9. Which of the following remote access protocols does not provide data encryption on its own?

   a. PPTP

   b. L2TP

   c. SSTP

   d. IKEv2

10. You have created a VPN connection but now need to enable the use of File and Printer Sharing for Microsoft Networks so that you can print a report on the office network that your manager needs to have by 8:00 tomorrow morning. You right-click the connection and choose **View Connection Properties**. Which tab contains the option that you must configure?

    a. General

    b. Options

    c. Security

    d. Networking

    e. Sharing

11. You are downloading a large file to your laptop at the airport Wi-Fi connection while waiting for your flight to be called. You are concerned that you might need to interrupt the download and want to be able to resume the download at your destination hotel room, so you have enabled VPN Reconnect. What protocol does this feature use?

    a. PPTP

    b. L2TP/IPSec

    c. SSTP

    d. IKEv2

12. You have set up a new Windows Server 2012 R2 computer on which you want to enable users to connect remotely for Remote Desktop sessions. What role will you be configuring?

    a. VPN Reconnect

    b. DirectAccess

    c. RD Gateway

    d. Internet Connection Sharing

13. You have decided to configure a DirectAccess server for your mobile workforce to use when they need files from the servers, access to the network printers, and other needs. You are ready to start rolling out a pilot and need to order the laptops for the mobile staff. What is the best client operating system to use?

    a. Windows RT 8.1

    b. Windows 8.1

    c. Windows 8.1 Pro

    d. Windows 8.1 Enterprise

Foundation Topics

Configuring Remote Authentication

Microsoft has built several remote management tools into Windows 8.1 and Windows Server 2012 R2 that allow you to connect to computers located across the hall or across the continent. You can use these tools to save precious minutes out of a busy day or an entire trip lasting days to manage and troubleshoot resources located on these computers. Users in other locations can connect to your computer, and you can offer suggestions or train them in procedures that correct problems or make their day's work go more smoothly.

Whenever you connect a computer or network to the public Internet, it becomes a target for a vast array of criminals and nefarious actors hoping to exploit resources that do not belong to them. Authenticating over a remote connection is necessary for a wide range of functionality, but it is also a potential attack vector for malicious activity. It is important that users and administrators, as well as business process services, are able to use remote connections for access to resources. But those connections must be secure, authentication must be robust, and unauthorized access must be detected and stopped.

Remote Authentication Planning

The methods of authentication used for remote workers and administrators depend entirely on the infrastructure of the network, the services available, the type of remote access required, and the sensitivity of the data being exposed over the remote connection. This chapter covers some details on configuring different types of remote connections, include Remote Desktop (RD), Remote Management, virtual private networks (VPNs), and Broadband connections. You should be aware of the authentication types, and variations, used for these different types of services.

You should also be familiar with the authentication methods previously discussed in Chapter 13, which can also come into play when managing remote authentication, and often configured through group policies to enforce more stringent requirements on top of the specific protocol connections. For instance, in a domain environment, you can require dual-factor authentication for all connections or only for remote connections. Or you may require that any computers connecting to your network remotely have their own certificate previously issued by the domain certification authority (CA), and disallow any connections that do not present recognized certificates.

Throughout this text, including this chapter and others, you learn about various types of remote connection technologies and ways of authenticating users and computers. It would be impractical to list every combination available for use in a Windows environment and especially in a mixed computing environment with Windows servers and workstations playing various roles. Table 14-2 lists some of the connection types and the most common authentication technologies that can play a role. Details of each are found throughout the text, referenced in the last column.

Table 14-2 Remote Connection Types and Common Remote Authentication Technologies

Connection Type	Authentication Technologies	Chapter References
Remote Desktop	Network Level Authentication, Smart Cards, Certificates, NTLM, Kerberos	Chapter 13, Chapter 14
VPN	Smart Cards, Machine Certificate, CHAP, EAP, PEAP, PAP, PSK	Chapter 13, Chapter 14 (see Table 14-3)
DirectAccess	Smart Cards, Kerberos, NTLM	Chapter 13
Remote Management	Kerberos, NTLM, Certificates	Chapter 13, Chapter 14

Be sure that you can distinguish between connection security and remote authentication. Table 14-2 lists authentication methods, including certificates; it should be noted that certificates play a part in authentication as well as connection security (certificates can be used both to authenticate the certificate owner and negotiate end-to-end encryption between trusted certificate owners).

Remote Access Authentication Protocols

Authentication is the first perimeter of defense that a network administrator can define in a remote access system. The process of authenticating a user is meant to verify and validate a user's identification. If the user provides invalid input, the authentication process should deny the user access to the network. An ill-defined authentication system, or lack of one altogether, can open the door to mischief and disruption because the two most common methods for remote access are publicly available: the Internet and the public services telephone network.

Remote authentication protocols fall into two main categories: Extensible Authentication Protocol (EAP) methods and non-EAP methods. Non-EAP methods are not considered secure, and Microsoft recommends those with TLS-based confidentiality such as PEAP or EAP-TTLS. Table 14-3 discusses the authentication protocols supported by in Windows 8.1 and Windows Server 2012 R2.

Table 14-3 Authentication Protocols for Remote Access

Acronym	Name	Usage	Security
CHAP	Challenge Handshake Authentication Protocol	Client requests access. Server sends a challenge to client. Client responds using MD5 hash value. Values must match for authentication.	Non-EAP. One-way authentication. Server authenticates client.
MS-CHAPv2	Microsoft Challenge Handshake Authentication Protocol version 2	Requires both the client and the server to be Microsoft Windows based. Does not work with local area network (LAN) Manager. Client requests access, server challenges, client responds with an MD5 hash value and piggybacks a challenge to server. If a match is found, server responds with a success packet granting access to client, which includes an MD5 hash response to the client's challenge. Client logs on if the server's response matches what client expects. Note that the older MS-CHAP authentication protocol is no longer supported as of Windows 7.	Non-EAP. Mutual (two-way) authentication.
EAP-TTLS	Extensible Authentication Protocol Tunneled Transport Layer Security	Developed for Point-to-Point Protocol (PPP) and can be used with IEEE 802.1X. Is capable of heading other authentication protocols, so improves interoperability between remote access server (RAS) systems, Remote Authentication Dial-In User Service (RADIUS) servers, and RAS clients. First supported natively in Windows 8.1 and Windows Server 2012.	EAP method. Provides additional authentication types based on plug-in modules; enables enhanced interoperability and efficiency of authentication process.
PEAP	Protected Extensible Authentication Protocol with Transport Layer Security	A highly secure password-based authentication protocol combination that utilizes certificate-based authentication.	EAP method. Uses certificate-based encryption.
PAP	Password Authentication Protocol	Client submits a clear-text user identification and password to server. Server compares to information in its user database. If a match, client is authenticated.	Non-EAP. Clear-text, one-way authentication. Least secure method.

Acronym	Name	Usage	Security
Smart cards	Certificates	User must have knowledge of PIN and possession of smart card. Client swipes card, which submits smart card certificate, and inputs PIN. Results are reviewed by server, which responds with its own certificate. If both client and server match, access is granted. Otherwise, error that credentials cannot be verified.	Certificate-based, two-way authentication.

NOTE When using certificate authentication, the client computer must have a way of validating the server's certificate. To ensure absolutely that this validation will work, you can import the server's certificate into the client's Trusted Publishers list. If there is no way for a client to validate the server's certificate, an error is displayed stating that the server is not a trusted resource.

NTLM and Kerberos Authentication

As noted in Table 14-2, both Kerberos and NTLM authentication are used in many scenarios. These are the default authentication technologies used to authenticate a user, using a username and password, to a Windows computer. Kerberos is available only in Active Directory domains, whereas NTLM is generally always used between computers that are not domain-joined.

NTLM authentication actually includes several discrete authentication protocols, namely LAN Manager, NTLM version 1 (NTLMv1), and NTLM version 2 (NTLMv2). When NTLM is used, the resource computer either contacts a domain authentication service for the user's account or looks up the user in the local account database. NTLM credentials consist of a domain name or server name, a username, and information that can be used to confirm the user's password (typically a password hash). Older LAN Manager and NTLMv1 protocols are more vulnerable than newer protocols used in Windows XP and Windows Server 2003 and later versions.

Kerberos authentication works with an Active Directory Domain Services (AD DS) domain by the use of *tickets* issued by domain controllers based on the credentials passed from a client. The ticket is then used to authenticate the user to other domain-managed computers and resources. In this way, both the computer requesting authentication and the computer granting access first check in with the server to confirm authentication.

Kerberos provides several advantages over NTLM authentication:

- Always includes server authentication
- Provides stronger cryptography
- Performs faster on repeated connections, using a single ticket
- Can fall back to NTLM authentication when Kerberos authentication is not available

Generally, the use of Kerberos or NTLM is decided by the Windows security providers available, the domain controllers when they are available, and the policies put in place at the domain level.

Keep in mind that when using remote connections, especially when directly connecting to Remote Desktop computers over the Internet or an untrusted network, Kerberos cannot be used because there will be no connection between the remote computer and the domain controllers on the remote network. So in those scenarios, NTLM authentication is used.

NOTE For more information about NTLM Authentication, refer to "NTLM Authentication" at http://technet.microsoft.com/en-us/library/jj865680(v=ws.10).aspx, and the links provided in that document. You can learn more about Kerberos authentication by referring to "Kerberos Authentication Overview" at http://technet.microsoft.com/en-us/library/hh831553.aspx.

Remote Authentication Group Policies

Several group policies can be utilized to control remote authentication protocols in Windows 8.1. You find these policies in the Local Group Policy Editor under Computer Configuration\Windows Settings\Security Settings\Local Policies\Security Options, as shown in Figure 14-1. The following are several of the more important policy settings that you should be familiar with:

- **Network security: Configure encryption types allowed for Kerberos:** This setting allows you to specify which encryption types can be used for domain-based Kerberos authentication. By default, all supported encryption types are allowed.
- **Network security: Minimum session security for NTLM SSP based (including secure RPC) clients:** This setting ensures that NTLM authentication can occur only over strong (128-bit) encryption. This is the recommended setting and is the default policy for Windows 7, Windows 8, Windows 8.1, Windows Server 2008 R2, and Windows Server 2012 R2.

- **Network security: Restrict NTLM: Audit Incoming NTLM traffic:** If enabled, the server logs events for NTLM pass-through authentication requests that would be blocked when the Network Security: Restrict NTLM: Incoming NTLM traffic policy is set to Deny all domain accounts. Events are logged to the Operational log under the Applications and Services Log/Microsoft/Windows/NTLM.
- **Network security: Restrict NTLM: Incoming NTLM traffic:** You can block NTLM authentication for all accounts or for domain accounts. Note that blocking NTLM authentication on a computer that is not domain-joined will disable authentication entirely because only domain accounts can use Kerberos authentication.
- **Network security: LAN Manager authentication level:** This security setting determines which challenge/response authentication protocol is used for network logons. Reducing or eliminating the use of LAN Manager (LM) authentication and NTLM version 1 (NTLMv1) removes vulnerable password hashes from the network, and therefore increases network security.

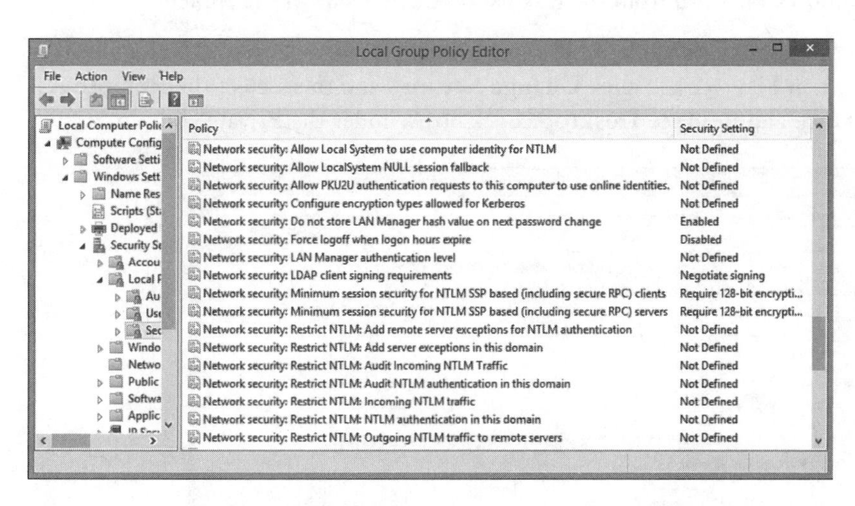

Figure 14-1 Network Security Group Policy settings in Windows 8.1.

Configuring Remote Assistance and Easy Connect

First introduced with Windows XP, Remote Assistance allows a user running a Windows 8 or 8.1 computer on a network to request assistance online; it also allows for an expert to offer assistance remotely. Regardless of how the session is initiated, the result is that the expert can remotely view the user's console and provide assistance to the user by taking control of the session, or can simply view the session and give the user specific directions on how to fix the problem the user is experiencing. Introduced with Windows 7 and continued in Windows 8 and 8.1 is the Easy Connect option, which uses the Peer Name Resolution Protocol (PNRP) to send the Remote Assistance invitation across the Internet. Easy Connect provides a password that you must provide separately to the other individual (for example, by making a phone call).

Configuring Remote Assistance

The requirements for Remote Assistance are that both computers must be configured to use it. If an AD DS domain is used, Group Policy for Remote Assistance must also allow the user to accept Remote Assistance offers and must list from which experts the users can accept offers. An Active Directory network also requires both users to be members of the same or trusted domains.

Windows Firewall can affect whether a user can receive Remote Assistance offers or use Remote Desktop. To configure Windows Firewall to use either or both of these features, follow these steps:

Step 1. Use any of the methods previously described in Chapter 10, "Configuring and Maintaining Network Security," to open Windows Firewall.

Step 2. In the Windows Firewall applet, select **Allow an app or feature through Windows Firewall** from the task list on the left side of the applet.

Step 3. On the Allow apps to communicate through Windows Firewall dialog box shown in Figure 14-2, click **Change Settings** and then select the **Remote Assistance** and **Remote Desktop** check boxes under the Private column.

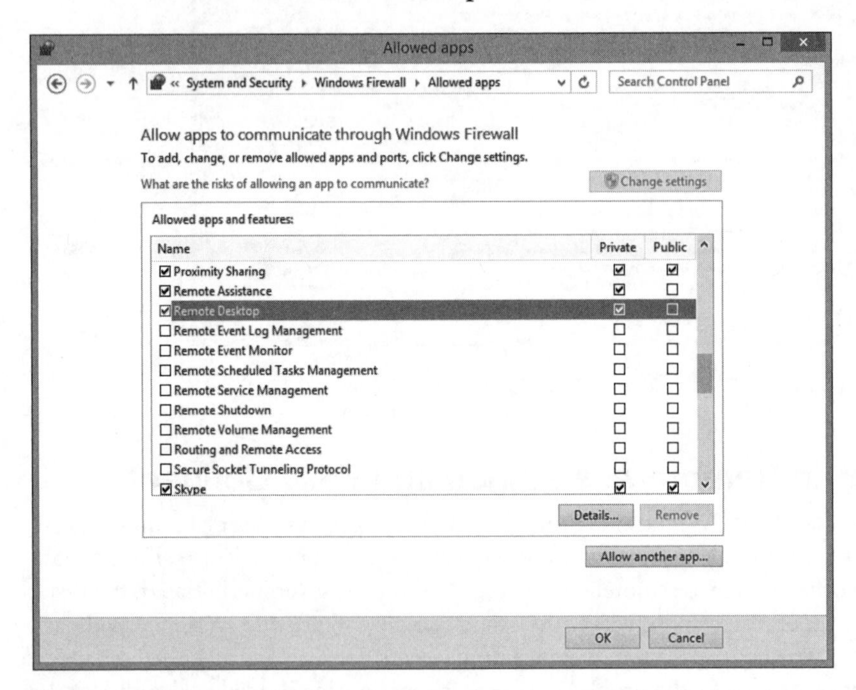

Figure 14-2 You need to allow Remote Assistance and Remote Desktop to communicate through Windows Firewall.

Step 4. Click **OK** to close the applet.

CAUTION Select these options under the Public column only if you need to accept requests from individuals on public networks; deselect these options after you complete the action. (If you have made changes to the port number of any service, you need to use Windows Firewall with Advanced Security to enable a firewall rule allowing that port to pass. You learned how to do this in Chapter 10.

Use the following steps to configure Windows 8.1 to accept Remote Assistance Offers:

Step 1. Right-click **Start** and choose **System**. You can also open the **Search** charm, type `system` in the search box, and then select **System** from the list of settings that appears. This opens the Control Panel System applet. You can also access the **Settings** charm, select **Control Panel**, and then select the **System** applet from the System and Security category.

Step 2. Click **Advanced system settings**. If you receive a User Account Control (UAC) prompt, click **Yes** to proceed.

Step 3. Select the **Remote** tab of the System Properties dialog box, as shown in Figure 14-3.

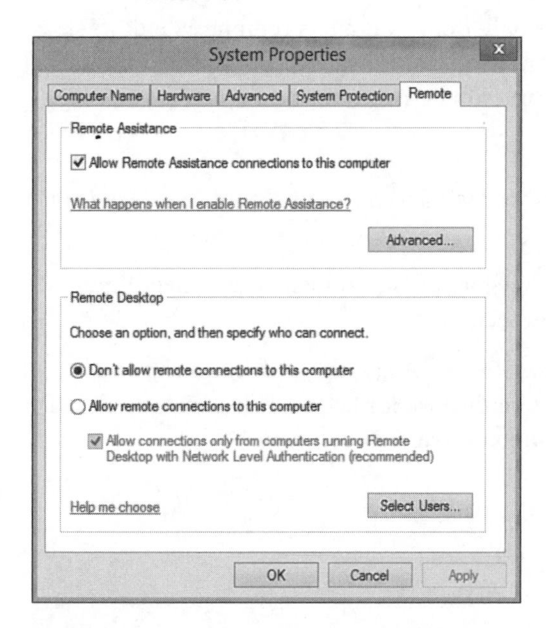

Figure 14-3 The Remote tab of the System Properties dialog box enables you to configure Remote Assistance and Remote Desktop settings.

Step 4. Select the **Allow Remote Assistance connections to this computer** option in the Remote Assistance section.

Step 5. Click the **Advanced** button to display the Remote Assistance Settings dialog box shown in Figure 14-4 and select the **Allow this computer to be controlled remotely** check box.

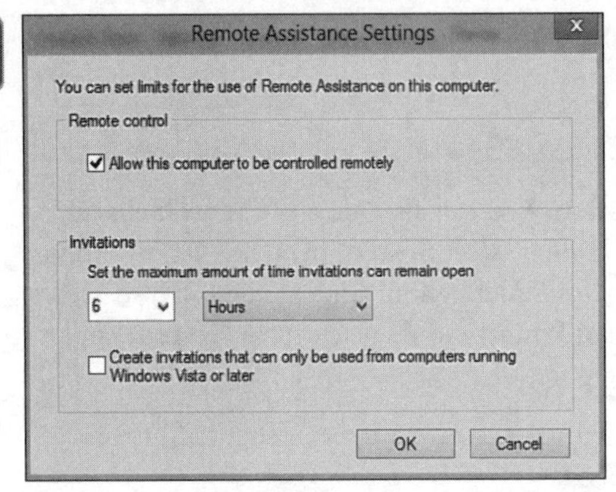

Figure 14-4 Configuring Remote Assistance Settings.

Step 6. If you want to allow connections only from computers running Windows Vista/7/8/8.1 or Windows Server 2008 R2/2012 R2, select the check box labeled **Create invitations that can only be used from computers running Windows Vista or later**.

Use the following steps to send a Remote Assistance invitation to receive help from an expert user:

Step 1. Access the System and Security category of Control Panel and select **Launch remote assistance** in the System section.

Step 2. This action displays the Windows Remote Assistance dialog box shown in Figure 14-5, which enables you to either ask for help or help someone else. To ask for help, click **Invite someone you trust to help you**.

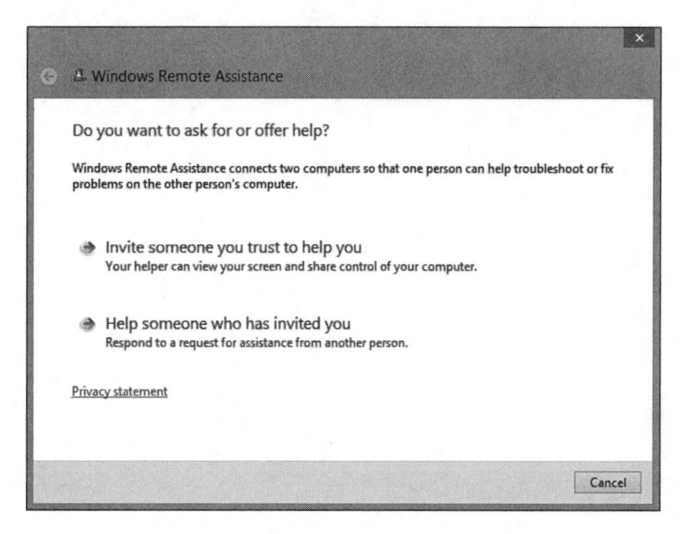

Figure 14-5 Windows Remote Assistance enables you to either ask for help or help someone else.

Step 3. Select one of the three options on the following page, shown in Figure 14-6:

- **Save the invitation as a file:** Creates an invitation file in the Microsoft Remote Control Incident (MsRcIncident) format. You can use this method with Web-based email programs by sending it as an attachment.
- **Use e-mail to send an invitation:** Available only if you have configured an email account in the Mail app or installed another email client.
- **Use Easy Connect:** Uses the Peer Name Resolution Protocol to send the invitation across the Internet. The other person must also be using a Windows 7 or 8.1 computer.

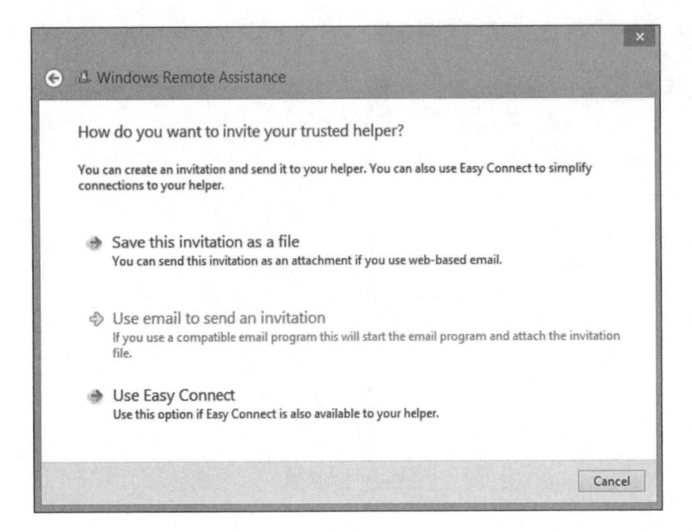

Figure 14-6 Remote Assistance allows you to send invitations three ways.

Step 4. The next step depends on the option you've selected from Figure 14-6:

- If you save the invitation as a file, you are prompted for a name and location to save the file.
- If you use email, your email program opens and provides a prepared message including an invitation attachment. Supply the email address of the expert who will be helping, and then send the message.
- If you use Easy Connect, you receive a password as shown in Figure 14-7, that you need to provide to the expert by another means such as by phone. You can also click **Chat** to start an online chat session. See the next section for more information on Easy Connect.

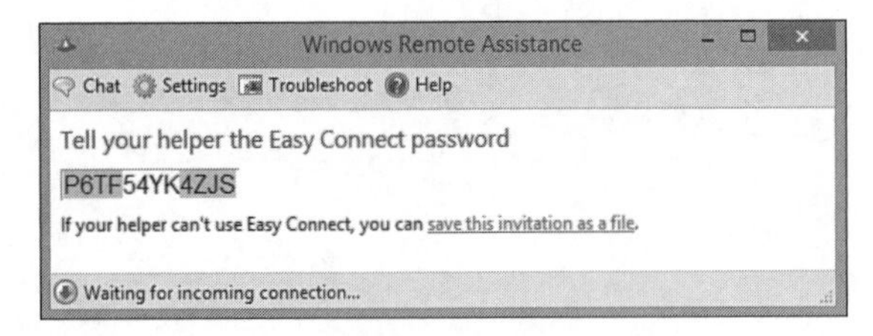

Figure 14-7 Easy Connect provides a password that you need to provide to the expert.

Depending on the person from whom you are requesting information and how you are requesting it, you should make a selection that will best reach the expert user. Whichever method you select for use, you can password-protect the session; the

Easy Connect option has already done that for you. If you have created an invitation for assistance and want to cancel it before it expires, you can use the View Invitation Status option and cancel the invitation.

After the expert receives the email or the invitation file, he can open Remote Assistance on his computer and select the **Help someone who has invited you** option previously shown in Figure 14-5. He can then open the invitation file that the other person has sent and begin offering assistance to the user. He sees a Remote Assistance Expert console that provides a real-time view of the user's session. This is called a *shadow session*. If remote control has been enabled, the expert can click the **Take Control** button, notifying the user that the expert is asking to share control of the keyboard and mouse. The user can prevent a remote control session by pressing the **Esc** key, pressing **Ctrl+C**, or clicking the **Stop Control** button in the chat window.

NOTE For more information about using Remote Assistance including a detailed step-by-step procedure, refer to "Remote Assistance in Windows 8" at http://blogs.msdn.com/b/hyperyash/archive/2013/01/18/remote-assistance-in-windows-8.aspx. This reference also provides information on running Remote Assistance without first having received an invitation from the remote user.

TIP You can ask a user who is experiencing problems to make a recording of the steps she has taken. To do so, ask her to type `psr` into the Search charm in Windows 8 or 8.1 or the Start Menu Search text box in Windows Vista or 7. Then select **Steps Recorder** or **psr.exe**. This opens the Steps Recorder shown in Figure 14-8. She can click **Start Record**, perform the steps that are creating the problem, and then click **Stop Record** when she's finished. At that time she can click **Add Comment** and then save the recording as a zip file that she can attach to the email Remote Assistance request email message.

Figure 14-8 The Steps Recorder enables a user to record the steps that created a problem.

Configuring and Using Easy Connect

As already introduced, Easy Connect provides a simple way to create a Remote Assistance session between two computers running Windows 7/8/8.1 without the need for sending an invitation file. As already shown in Figure 14-7, the user receives a password that she needs to provide to the expert by another means such as by phone.

Once the user has selected the **Use Easy Connect** option, the expert will receive the Remote Assistance dialog box shown in Figure 14-9, asking him to type the password that Remote Assistance provided to the other person. Using the supplied password, the expert can initiate the session and the user's computer validates the password and invitation before the user is prompted to start the session.

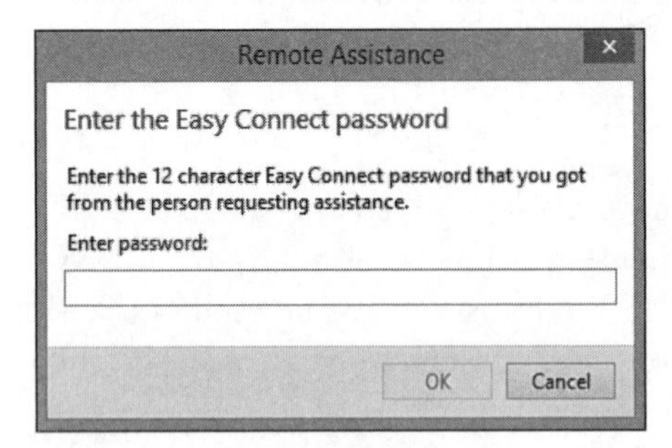

Figure 14-9 Provide the password to open the Remote Assistance session.

The following are several problems that might be encountered when attempting to use Easy Connect:

- **The user's computer is running an older Windows version:** For Easy Connect to be available, both computers must be running Windows 7, Windows 8, or Windows 8.1.
- **Limited access to the Internet:** If access to the Internet is limited on either computer, Easy Connect is disabled. Some corporate networks might limit Internet access.
- **A router in the network doesn't support Easy Connect:** Easy Connect uses the PNRP when transferring the assistance request over the Internet. Microsoft provides a utility for determining whether routers are configured for PNRP. You should install PNRP on any router running a version of Windows Server 2008/2012/R2.

Configuring Remote Desktop and Remote Management Settings

Windows 8.1 continues to improve on the Remote Desktop and Remote Assistance tools first introduced with Windows XP and upgraded with each iteration of the Windows operating system. The Remote Server Administration Tools (RSAT) for Windows 8.1 download enables you to manage roles and features installed on servers running Windows Server 2003 or later from your Windows 8.1 desktop. Also offered are the new Windows Remote Management service and (introduced with Vista) the Windows PowerShell command-line interface.

CAUTION Only limited management of servers running older versions of Windows Server is possible when using RSAT for Windows 8.1. In the original and R2 versions of Windows Server 2008, you can perform most administrative actions but you cannot install or remove server roles or features. Support for Windows Server 2003 is generally limited to most Active Directory and network management tools.For more information on server components that can be managed using RSAT in Windows 8.1, refer to "Description of Remote Server Administration Tools for Windows 8.1 and Remote Server Administration Tools for Windows 8" at http://support.microsoft.com/kb/2693643.

Remote Desktop

Windows 8.1 incorporates the Remote Desktop Protocol (RDP), which was originally introduced with Terminal Services and included with Windows XP Professional. The protocol allows any user to use the Remote Desktop application to run a remote control session on a Windows Terminal Server or of a Windows 7 or 8.1 computer that has been configured to provide Remote Desktop services. RDP is also used when a Remote Assistance session is conducted, as described in the previous section.

When Windows 8.1 is configured to be a Remote Desktop host, there is a restriction for usage that does not apply to a Terminal Services computer. This restriction is that only one user can ever execute an interactive session on the computer at any one time. So if you run a Remote Desktop session, and a user is already logged on to the Remote Desktop server, that user will be logged off (at your request) for your own session to run. However, that users' session will be saved so that he can resume it later.

Establishing a Remote Desktop Connection with Another Computer

Any version of Windows 8.1 can be a Remote Desktop client. However, only the Pro or Enterprise edition of Windows 8.1 can be a Remote Desktop host (server). You can run a Remote Desktop session with another computer running Windows 8.1 or any older Windows version back to Windows XP. Use the following instructions to make a Remote Desktop connection:

Step 1. Open the **Search** charm, type `remote` in the Search field, and then select **Remote Desktop Connection** from the program list. This opens the Remote Desktop Connection dialog box, as shown in Figure 14-10.

Figure 14-10 The Remote Desktop Connection dialog box requires you to know the name and/or IP address of the target computer.

The Computer list shows only Windows Terminal Servers. Windows 8.1 computers do not advertise the Remote Desktop service, so you are required to know the full name or IP address of the computer.

Step 2. Type the name or IP address of the Windows XP, Vista, Windows 7, Windows 8, or 8.1 computer and click **Connect**. You should see a message box informing you that you are connecting, followed by a remote session with a logon screen prompting you for a user ID and password.

Step 3. Click the **Show Options** button. The General tab for the connection's Properties dialog box opens. You can save the current logon settings or open a file containing previously saved settings, as well as change the computer name in this dialog box.

Step 4. Click the **Display** tab. If your session is running slowly, you can increase performance by reducing the number of colors and size of the screen.

Step 5. Click the **Local Resources** tab. You can choose whether to map sounds, disk drives, printers, clipboard, and serial ports. You can also select how the key combination Alt+Tab works when executing that key combination while in the remote session. By clicking the **More** button, you can choose to use smart cards and specified ports on this computer to be used within the remote session.

Step 6. Click the **Programs** tab. If you would like to configure a connection that starts a single application, rather than all the applications, you can type the command line in this screen so that it executes automatically.

Step 7. Click the **Experience** tab. This tab enables you to enable or disable various display behaviors shown in Figure 14-11 to enhance the computer's performance according to the connection speed as selected from the drop-down list provided.

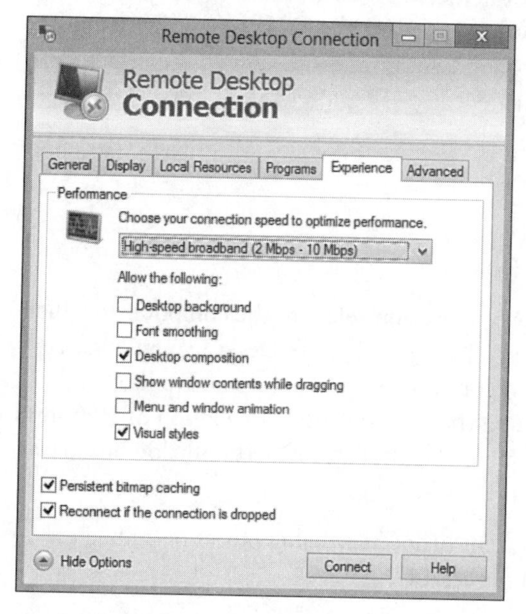

Figure 14-11 The Experience tab of the Remote Desktop Connection dialog box enables you to select the performance options applicable to the remote session.

Step 8. Click the **Advanced** tab. You can choose from three options that describe the behavior if authentication fails: **Warn me** (the default), **Connect and don't warn me**, or **Do not connect**. You can also configure Remote Desktop Gateway settings that apply for connections to remote computers located behind firewalls.

Step 9. Click the **Hide Options** button to return to the original logon screen. Type the information for your username and password and click **OK** to start the session.

Step 10. If someone else is already logged on to the computer, you are asked whether you should log off the existing user. Click **Yes**. The session begins.

NOTE A Start screen version of Remote Desktop is also available for Windows 8.1. This is a free app that you can download by accessing Windows Store from the Start screen. After you download and install this app, you can connect to a remote computer by accessing the app from the Start screen and typing the name or IP address of the desired computer in the text box provided and clicking the **Connect** button. To connect to other computers on your corporate network without setting up a VPN, select the **Use a Remote Desktop Gateway server** option. You receive the Connection settings window, which enables you to configure the devices on your computer to be used in the connection and specify the name or IP address of the server to which you want to connect.

Configuring the Server Side of Remote Desktop

The Server side of the Remote Desktop connection refers to the computer to which you are making the connection. Before you can use Remote Desktop, you must enable the computer to which you want to connect to receive Remote Desktop connections. This computer must be running the Pro or Enterprise edition of Windows 8.1. You can do this from the Remote tab of the System Properties dialog box, as follows:

Step 1. Access the **Remote** tab of the System Properties dialog box as described earlier in this chapter and shown in Figure 14-3.

Step 2. Select the **Allow Remote connections to this computer** option.

Step 3. You receive the message box shown in Figure 14-12 warning you that users cannot connect if the computer is in sleep or hibernation mode. If you want to change this behavior, select the **Power Options** link provided. When finished, click **OK**.

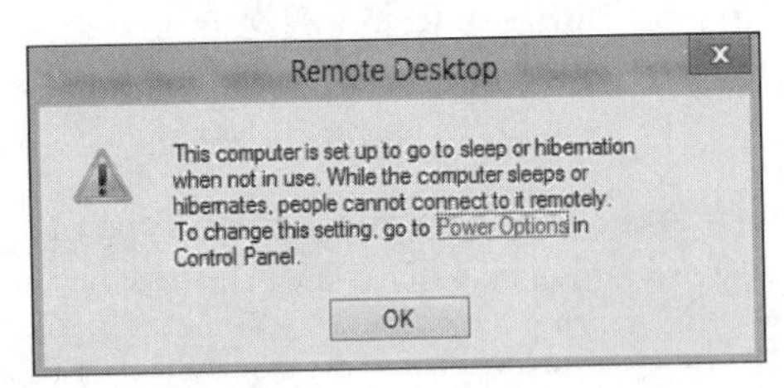

Figure 14-12 Remote Desktop warns you that users will be unable to connect to your computer if it enters sleep or hibernation mode.

Step 4. If desired, select the check box labeled **Allow connections only from computers running Remote Desktop with Network Level Authentication (recommended)**. This option enables users with computers running Remote Desktop with Network Level Authentication to connect to your computer. This is the most secure option if people connecting to your computer are running Windows 7, 8, or 8.1. If you do not select this option, users with any version of Remote Desktop can connect to your computer, regardless of Windows version in use.

Step 5. Click **OK** or **Apply**.

You also need to specify the users who are entitled to make a remote connection to your computer. By default, members of the Administrators and Remote Desktop Users groups are allowed to connect to your computer. To add a nonadministrative user to the Remote Desktop Users group, click the **Select Users** button in the Remote tab previously shown in Figure 14-3. This opens the Remote Desktop Users dialog box shown in Figure 14-13. Click **Add**, and in the Select Users dialog box that appears, type the name of the user to be granted access, and then click **OK**. The Select Users dialog box also enables you to add users from an AD DS domain if your computer is a domain member.

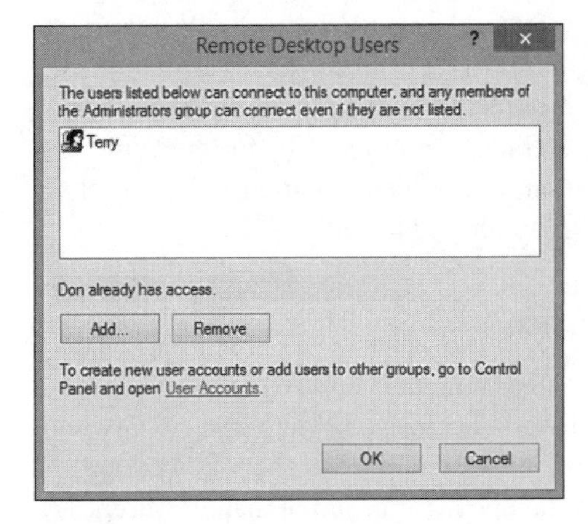

Figure 14-13 The Remote Desktop Users dialog box enables you to grant Remote Desktop access to nonadministrative users.

Selecting a Nondefault Port

You can configure the listening port, from the default TCP 3389, to another port of your choice. When you do so, only the people who specify the port can connect and then run a remote session. In Windows 8.1, you are able to adjust the port only by editing the Registry:

Step 1. Open the Registry Editor, supply your UAC credentials, and navigate to the **HKEY_LOCAL_MACHINE\System\CurrentControlSet\Control\TerminalServer\WinStations\RDP-Tcp** key.

Step 2. Select the **PortNumber** value, click the **Edit** menu, and then select **Modify**.

Step 3. Click **Decimal** and type in the new port number.

Step 4. Click **OK** and close the Registry Editor.

On the client computer, you then make a connection by opening the Remote Desktop Connection dialog box as previously described and shown in Figure 14-10. In the Computer text box, type the name or IP address of the Remote Desktop host computer, concatenated with a colon and the port number. For example, if you edited the Registry of the host computer named NANC511 with an IP address of 192.168.0.8 and changed the port number to 4233, you would type either `NANC511:4233` or `192.168.0.8:4233` in the Computer text box of the Remote Desktop Connection dialog box.

Keep in mind that a Remote Desktop connection functions across any TCP/IP link, whether dial-up, local, or otherwise. You can link to a host computer with older Windows versions such as Windows XP, but you need to have the client software to do so. You can download the client software to connect Windows XP computers from Microsoft at http://www.microsoft.com/en-us/download/details.aspx?id=856. When you configure a host computer, be sure to add users to the Remote Desktop users group and to create an exception for Remote Desktop traffic for the Windows Firewall. You should also create the exception on the client computer. Refer back to Chapter 10 for information on configuring Windows Firewall.

Using Windows Remote Management Service

Microsoft has provided Windows Remote Management (WinRM) to assist you in managing hardware on a network that includes machines that run a diverse mix of operating systems. WinRM is the Microsoft implementation of the WS-Management Protocol, which was developed by an independent group of manufacturers as a public standard for remote computer management. You can use WinRM to monitor and manage remote computers.

WinRM is a series of command-line tools that operate from an administrative command prompt. Use the following procedure to set up the Remote Management Service:

Step 1. Right-click **Start** and choose **Command Prompt (Admin)**.

Step 2. Accept the UAC prompt, type `winrm quickconfig` and then press **Enter.**

Step 3. You receive the output shown in Figure 14-14. Type `y` twice as shown in the figure to enable the granting of remote administrative rights to local users, create a WinRM listener on HTTP, and enable a firewall exception that allows WinRM packets to pass.

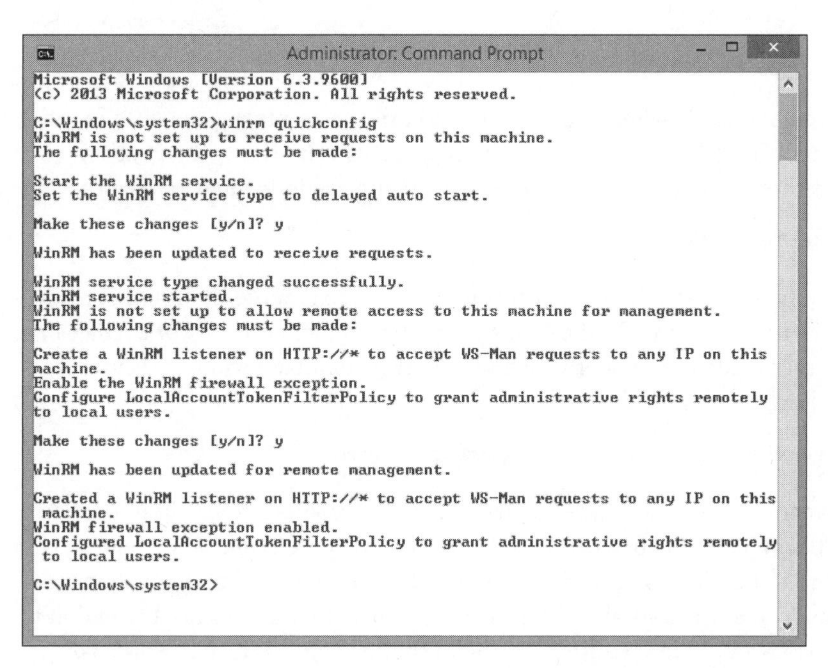

Figure 14-14 You can enable WinRM from an administrative command prompt or an administrator Windows PowerShell session.

You can also configure WinRM by means of Group Policy. This enables you to enable WinRM for all computers in the same AD DS site, domain, or organizational unit (OU). Access the **Computer Configuration\Administrative Templates\Windows Components\Windows Remote Management** node. This node contains two subnodes: WinRM Client and WinRM Service. The WinRM Client policies deal with permitted authentication methods and available trusted hosts, whereas the WinRM Service policies deal with how the service listens on the network for requests, as well as client authentication methods that it will accept and whether unencrypted messages are permitted. You can also enable or disable an HTTP listener. For more information on the available policies in each of these subnodes, double-click any policy and consult the Help text provided.

After you set up WinRM, you are able to use either of two tools included in the Remote Management Service: Windows Remote Shell and Windows PowerShell. We take a quick look at each of these tools in turn. See the next section for use of Windows PowerShell.

NOTE For more information about Windows Remote Management, refer to "About Windows Remote Management" at http://msdn.microsoft.com/en-us/library/aa384291(VS.85).aspx.

Using Windows Remote Shell

Windows Remote Shell (WinRS) enables you to execute command-line utilities or scripts against a remote computer. For example, you can run the `ipconfig` command on a remote computer named Server1 by typing the following command:

```
winrs -r:Server1 ipconfig
```

You can specify the NetBIOS name of a computer located on the local subnet or the fully qualified domain name (FQDN) of a computer on a remote network. You can also specify user credentials under which the WinRS command will be executed, by using the following command:

```
Winrs -r:Server1 -u:user_name -p:password command
```

In this command, *user_name* is the username in whose context you want to run the command, *password* is the password associated with this username, and *command* is the command to be run. You can use this syntax to remotely execute any command that you can normally run locally using the `cmd.exe` command prompt. If you don't specify the password, Windows Remote Shell prompts you for the password. You can also use `http://` or `https://` against the computer name in the `-r` parameter to specify an HTTP or Secure HTTP connection to a remote computer specified by its URL or IP address.

NOTE For more information on using WinRS, open a command prompt and type **winrs /?**.

Using Windows PowerShell and MMCs for Remote Management

Windows PowerShell, currently in version 4.0 for Windows 8.1, is a task-based command-line scripting interface that enables you to perform a large number of tasks, and is particularly useful for remote management. PowerShell includes the Integrated Scripting Environment (ISE), which assists you in the task of writing, testing, and executing scripts. You can control and automate the administration of remote Windows computers and their applications. Installed by default in Windows 7, Windows 8/8.1, Windows Server 2008 R2, and Windows Server 2012 R2, PowerShell also enables you to perform automated troubleshooting of remote computers. You can even read from and write to the Registry as though its hives were regular drives; for example, HKLM for HKEY_LOCAL_MACHINE and HKCU for HKEY_CURRENT_USER.

Windows PowerShell 4.0 makes using Windows PowerShell easier, especially for managing remote computers. Windows PowerShell Desired State Configuration, new for this release, lets you manage configuration data for software services, and the environments in which those services run. You can debug remote scripts, and you can now debug Windows PowerShell workflows by using the Windows PowerShell debugger, in both Windows PowerShell ISE ("graphical PowerShell") and the Windows PowerShell console. The Save-Help cmdlet now lets you save updatable help for modules that are installed on remote computers, but not necessarily installed on a local client.

NOTE For more information on all aspects of Windows PowerShell, refer to "Windows PowerShell" at http://msdn.microsoft.com/en-us/library/dd835506(VS.85).aspx and "What's New in Windows PowerShell" at http://technet.microsoft.com/en-us/library/hh857339.aspx.

You can also use PowerShell on computers running older versions of Windows, and upgrade the PowerShell version in many cases. Any scripts you write using PowerShell 4.0 or 3.0 can then be run on computers using any of these older operating systems that support it. To install PowerShell 4.0, download the Windows Management Framework 4.0, which includes PowerShell, Windows Management Instrumentation (WMI), WinRM, and other tools. For information on the operating system requirements for the newer PowerShell versions, see "Windows PowerShell System Requirements" at http://technet.microsoft.com/en-us/library/hh847769.aspx.

TIP To determine the current version of PowerShell running on any Windows operating system, use the `$host` command in a PowerShell prompt. The result will display the version number and a few details about the PowerShell host environment.

PowerShell and PowerShell ISE

Windows PowerShell borrows from the functionality of the object-oriented Microsoft .NET programming model. Objects used by this mode have well-defined properties and methods; for example, a file object has properties such as its size, modification date and time, and so on. All commands issued to PowerShell are in the form of a command-let, or *cmdlet*, which is an expression of the form *verb-object*, for example, `Get-process`. You can run a cmdlet on its own or build these tools into complex scripts that enable you to perform almost unlimited tasks against any computer on the network. The following verbs are used in many cmdlets:

- **`Get:`** Retrieves data
- **`Set:`** Modifies or establishes output data
- **`Format:`** Formats data
- **`Select:`** Selects specific properties of an object or set of objects. Also finds text in strings, files, or XML documents
- **`Out:`** Outputs data to a specific location

You can start a PowerShell session from the command line by typing **`powershell`**, or from the PowerShell ISE in Administrative Tools, or by searching for **`power-shell`** in the **Search** charm. Starting PowerShell from the Start screen icon starts a PowerShell command session, similar to that shown in Figure 14-15.

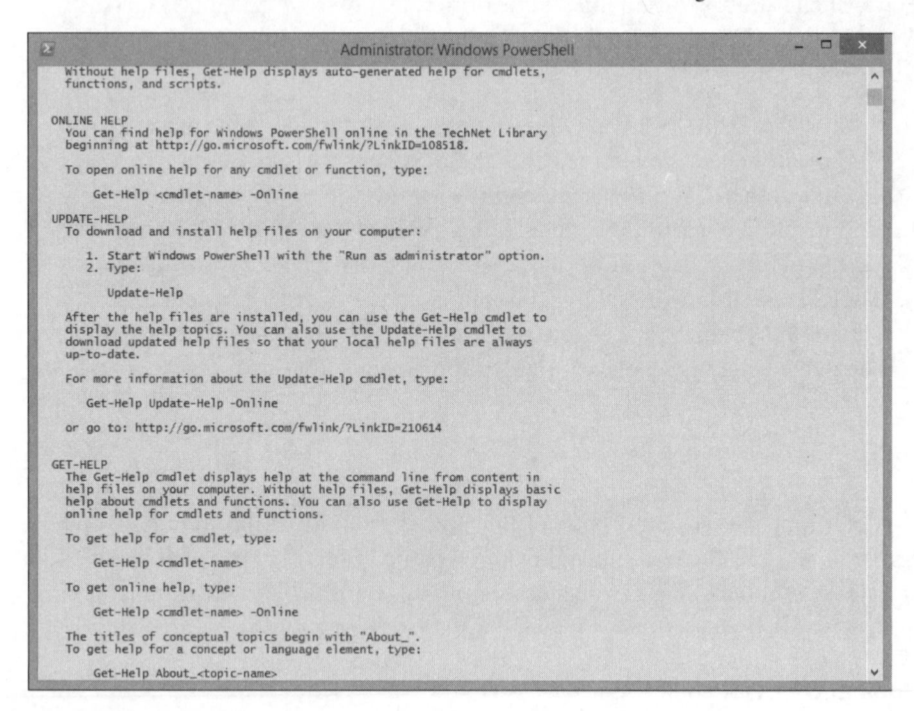

Figure 14-15 You can execute a large number of cmdlets from a PowerShell session.

Help functions are provided for all available cmdlets, but as described in the figure, you must run the `Update-Help` command as an administrator to download the help files and install them for use on the PowerShell command line. After you have the help files loaded, you can type **`help`** ***`verb-*`***, where *`verb`* is an available PowerShell verb, including (but not restricted to) those mentioned in the previous paragraph.

You can also get help on PowerShell objects by typing **`help`** ***`*-object`***, where *`object`* is a PowerShell object. See the next paragraph for an example of obtaining help for the `content` object.

A new feature introduced with PowerShell 3.0 is the `-Online` option of the `help` command. It is useful if the help files are not installed, or when you do not want to install the help files on the local computer. The `Get-Help -Online` feature opens the online version of the help topic directly in the default web browser. For instance, running the PowerShell command `Get-Help Get-Process -Online` will display the help in Internet Explorer, as shown in Figure 14-16.

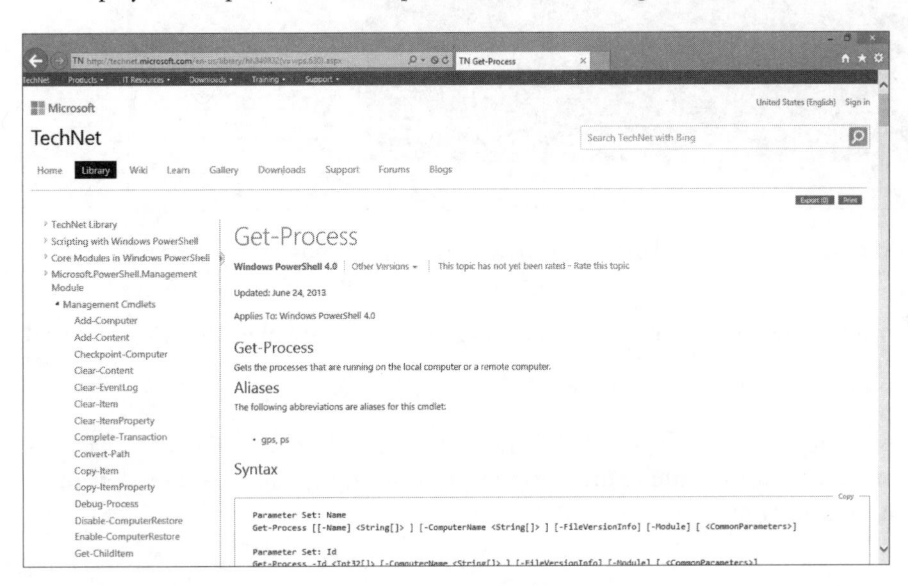

Figure 14-16 Viewing online help for PowerShell cmdlets.

When you write a cmdlet, you can populate the `HelpUri` property of your cmdlet class so that others using the script can obtain help information from the Internet or the local intranet on the organization's servers.

PowerShell 3.0 and later also includes the PowerShell ISE, which is a PowerShell graphical user interface (GUI) that enables you to run commands and write, edit, run, test, and debug scripts in the same window. Access this tool from either from the Administrative Tools menu, or the PowerShell ISE link when searching for

PowerShell in the Search charm. PowerShell ISE also includes debugging, multiline editing capabilities, selective execution, and many other components that aid you in writing and debugging complex scripts. An example of PowerShell ISE is shown in Figure 14-17.

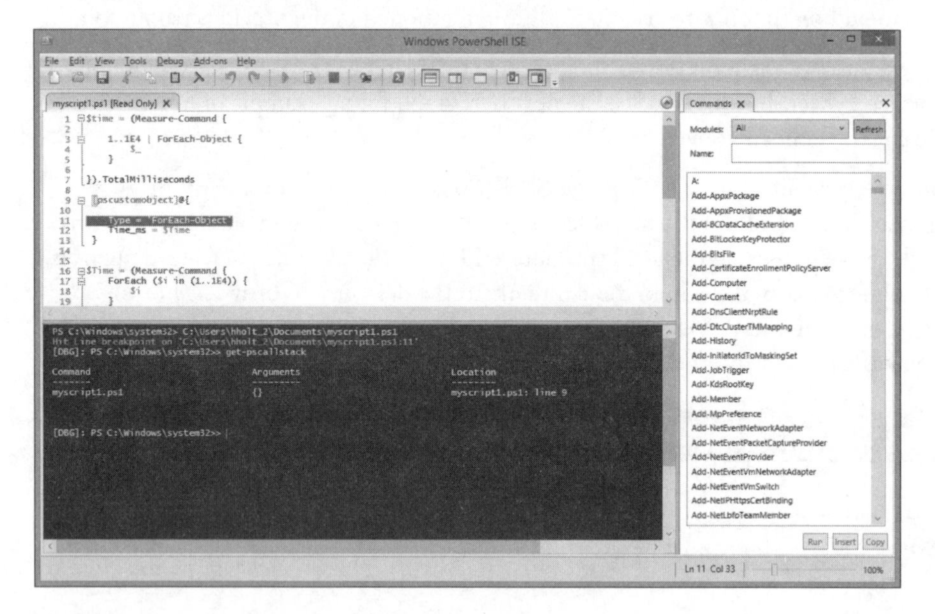

Figure 14-17 You can write and debug complex scripts using Windows PowerShell ISE.

To run a PowerShell command against a remote computer, use the following command:

```
Icm computername {powershell-cmd}
```

In this command, `Icm` is the Invoke-Command cmdlet, *`computername`* is the name of the computer you are running the command against, and *`{powershell-cmd}`* is the command being run.

PowerShell Remoting

You can use PowerShell to automate management tasks on any computer in your network or with connectivity. PowerShell Remoting works with WinRM to enable scripting support for a remote management tasks.

You can enable PowerShell Remoting on any Windows computer with PowerShell 3.0 or later version installed using the `Enable-PSRemoting` command from an Administrative PowerShell command prompt (see Figure 14-18). Because PowerShell Remoting relies on WinRM, the cmdlet also performs the WinRM autoconfiguration tasks and enables other features required. The cmdlet performs all the following setup tasks:

- Starts the WS-Management service and sets the startup type to **Automatic**
- Creates a listener to accept remote requests for PowerShell Remoting commands
- Enables firewall exceptions for WS-Management
- Registers and enables the PowerShell session configurations
- Modifies the security descriptor for all session configurations to enable remote access
- Restarts the WS-Management service

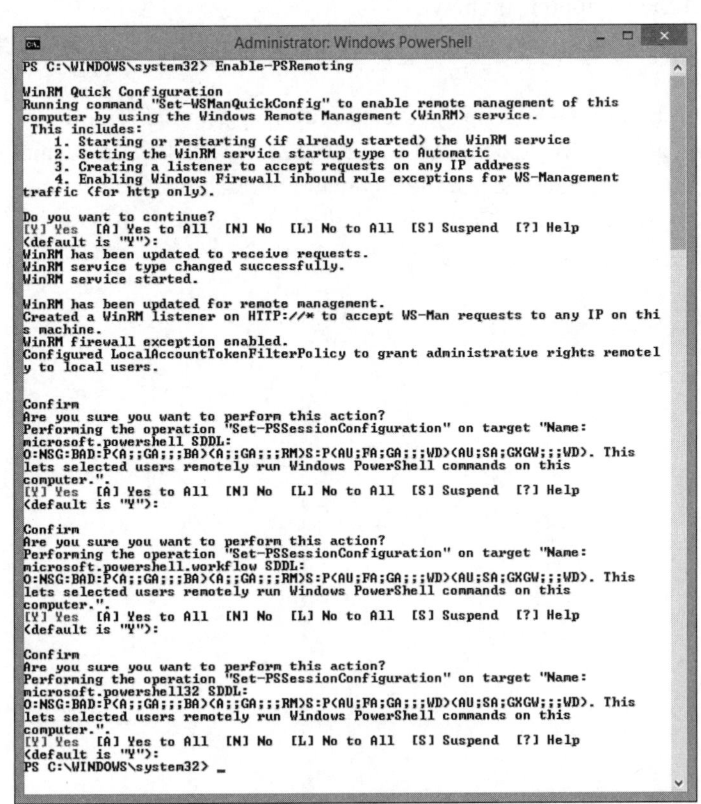

Figure 14-18 Enabling PowerShell Remoting using the `Enable-PSRemoting` cmdlet.

After configuring PowerShell Remoting, you can use PowerShell Remoting commands to manage remote computers in a trusted domain. If you want to manage remote computers in other domains, or computers that are not domain-joined, you also need to add the remote computer to the list of trusted hosts. To do so, you use the `winrm` command. For example, to add a remote computer named `Win8Pro01` to the list of trusted hosts on the local computer, open an administrative command prompt and type

```
winrm set winrm/config/client @{TrustedHosts="Win8Pro01"}.
```

You can then use PowerShell Remoting commands on `Win8Pro01`. You need to repeat the command for any remote computers that are not part of the local domain.

This is a very powerful remote management tool. For instance, suppose you want to check the free disk space on a remote computer. You can query the status of any WMI object using the PowerShell `Get-WMIObject` cmdlet. You can enter the following command to get free space on all the logical disks, replacing *`computername`* with the actual name of the computer to query:

```
Invoke-Command computername {Get-WMIObject win32_logicaldisk}.
```

The output, as shown in Figure 14-19, displays the disks available on the remote computer, the total size, and the free space. You could write a PowerShell command script to read a list of remote computers, run the command on each one, and create a file you can check each week to check for potential storage issues on all the computers you manage.

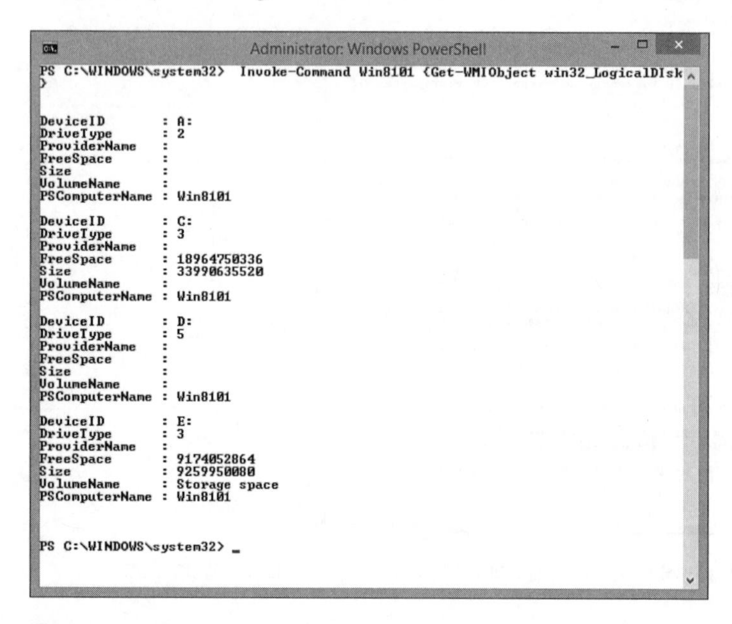

Figure 14-19 Query information about logical disks on remote computers using PowerShell Remoting.

You can perform this type of query on any WMI object, and there are many related to hardware devices, operating system parameters, Windows objects, and Registry settings. You can get a complete list by entering `Get-WMIObject -List`. As you can see, using PowerShell with its Remoting capabilities provides a wealth of administration tools for managing Windows computers.

Using MMC Snap-ins for Remote Management

Microsoft's Windows Remote Management framework is also used to enable many of the Microsoft Management Console snap-ins to work remotely for many administrative tasks. For instance, the Computer Management snap-in works well for managing Windows services, for scheduling tasks, and for performing Disk Management tasks on any remote computer where WinRM has been enabled.

Recall from the previous section that enabling WinRM, using either PowerShell or the `WinRM quickconfig` command, enables the firewall rules for WinRS and PowerShell Remoting. Many of the Microsoft Management Console (MMC) snap-ins use different protocols and ports, and they need their own firewall rules before they will work remotely. The rules for these tools need to be enabled using the following procedure:

Step 1. Swipe your pointer to the right side of the screen, or gesture with your finger, and select the **Settings** charm; then select **Control Panel**.

Step 2. In the Search Control Panel box, type **`firewall`**, and then click **Allow an app through Windows firewall**.

Step 3. Click the **Change settings** button.

Step 4. Make sure the check box is selected next to the apps with the following names, as desired for the remote management tasks you want to enable:

- **Performance Logs and Alerts:** Allows you to view performance information from the Performance Monitor snap-in.
- **Remote Event Log:** Allows you to view and manage Windows logs using the Event Viewer snap-in.
- **Remote Scheduled Tasks Management:** Allows you to view, manage, and run scheduled tasks using the Scheduled Tasks snap-in.
- **Remote Service Management:** Allows you to view, start, stop, and change startup configuration of Windows services using the Services snap-in.
- **Remote Volume Management:** Allows you to use the Disk Management snap-in to manage disks and volumes on remote computers.
- **Windows Firewall Remote Management:** Allows you to use the Windows Firewall with Advanced Security snap-in to manage firewall rules and settings.

Step 5. Click the **OK** button to save your settings.

The computer is now ready to allow MMC snap-ins to connect from remote computers. To connect to a remote computer from a network-enabled MMC snap-in, simply right-click the snap-in name in the left pane, and then select **Connect to another computer**. In the resulting dialog box, type the name of the remote computer in the Another computer box and then click **OK**.

Some snap-ins, such as the Event Viewer, allow you to specify an account name to use when authenticating to the remote computer, as shown in Figure 14-20. This may be needed in a workgroup environment or when connecting to a computer joined to a different domain.

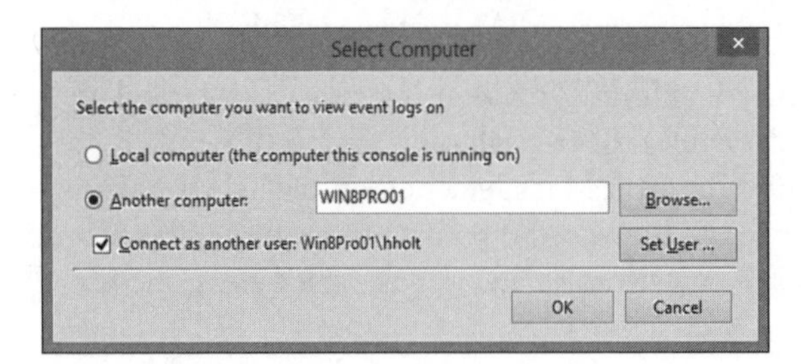

Figure 14-20 Connecting to a remote computer from the Event Viewer MMC snap-in.

Configuring VPN Authentication and Settings

Connectivity is the single most valuable capability in a computer. By connecting to other computers, a computer is able to access other information, applications, and peripheral equipment. Businesses have long since discovered that their employees will work longer hours and greatly increase their productivity when they are able to connect to the company's network from remote sites. For this reason, they provide Remote Access Service (RAS) servers with VPN servers and Internet connections, and may offer dial-up networking with modems when needed. When connecting to a corporate network using VPN (or dialing up with a modem), the user can open files and folders, use applications, print to printers, and pretty much use the network just as if she were connected to the network through its network adapter.

When you configure a VPN connection in Windows 8.1, it typically negotiates protocols with the server automatically. You can configure which protocols to use manually. Organizations need to protect the entire connection for remote users on VPN connections, including routing information for the internal network. The encryption, therefore, is performed at the network level between the two endpoints, namely the Windows 8.1 client and the device or server at the other end.

The following are standard protocols used to create a VPN connection:

- **Point-to-Point (PPP) VPN protocol:** The oldest of the protocols, it uses Microsoft Point-to-Point Encryption (MPPE) to secure the connection data. It uses 128-bit keys and is considered to have weaker security than others.
- **Point-to-Point Tunneling Protocol (PPTP):** A protocol used to transmit private network data across a public network in a secure fashion. PPTP supports multiple networking protocols and creates a secure VPN connection.
- **Layer 2 Tunneling Protocol (L2TP):** Very similar to PPTP, it improves security by including support for IPSec. Used with IP Security (IPSec), it creates a secure VPN connection encrypted with either 3DES or AES, which can use up to 256 bit keys.
- **Secure Socket Tunneling Protocol (SSTP):** A newer tunneling protocol that uses Secure Hypertext Transfer Protocol (HTTPS) over TCP port 443, and is able to transmit traffic across firewalls and proxy servers that might block PPTP and L2TP traffic. SSTP uses Secure Sockets Layer (SSL) for transport-level security that includes enhanced key negotiation, encryption, and integrity checking.
- **Internet Key Exchange version 2 (IKEv2):** A tunneling protocol that uses IPSec Tunnel Mode over UDP port 500. This combination of protocols also supports strong authentication and encryption methods.

NOTE Windows 8.1 supports a wide variety of VPN protocols and works with a number of industry standard VPN solutions. To learn more about Windows 8.1 and Windows Server 2012 R2 VPN protocols, download the document "VPN Compatibility and Interoperability in Windows 8 and Windows Server 2012" at http://technet.microsoft.com/library/jj613765.aspx.

Understanding Remote Access

When you set up a new connection or network in Windows 8.1, the Connect to a workplace option allows you to set up dial-up networking connections using a modem or any other type of connection—between two different computers, between a computer and a private network, between a computer and the Internet, and from a computer through the Internet to a private network using a tunneling protocol. You can share both dial-up connections and connections configured as VPN connections using Internet Connection Sharing (ICS). All these functions and features offer different ways of connecting computers across large geographical distances.

When a computer connects to a remote access server, it performs functions nearly identical to logging on locally while connected to the network. The major difference is the method of data transport at the physical level because the data is likely to travel across a rather slow telephone line for dial-up and some Internet connections. Another difference between a local network user and a remote access user is the way that the user's identification is authenticated. If using Remote Authentication Dial-In User Service (RADIUS), the RADIUS server takes on the task of authenticating users and passing along their data to the directory service(s) in which the users' accounts are listed.

Don't confuse remote access with remote control. Remote access is the capability to connect across a dial-up or VPN link, and from that point forward, to be able to gain access to and use network files, folders, printers, and other resources identically to the way a user could do on a local network computer. Remote control, on the other hand, is the capability to connect to a computer remotely, and then, through the use of features such as Remote Desktop or Remote Assistance discussed earlier in this chapter, control the computer as if you were at the console.

Establishing VPN Connections and Authentication

We've already touched on VPN connections. The way a VPN works is rather interesting. The private network is connected to the Internet. One method for establishing a VPN or DirectAccess services is for an administrator to set up a VPN server or appliance that sits basically between the private network and the Internet (also known as dual-homed). When a remote computer connects to the Internet, whether via dial-up or other means, the remote computer can connect to the VPN server by using TCP/IP. Then the tunneling protocols encapsulate the data inside the TCP/IP packets that are sent to the VPN server. After the data is received at the VPN server, it strips off the encapsulating headers and footers and then transmits the packets to the appropriate network servers and resources.

The tunneling protocols, although similar and all supported by Windows 8.1 and Windows Server 2012 R2, act somewhat differently. PPTP incorporates security for encryption and authentication in the protocol by using MPPE. SSTP encrypts data by encapsulating PPP traffic over the SSL channel of the HTTPS protocol. IKEv2 encapsulates datagrams by using IPSec ESP or AH headers. L2TP does not provide encryption on its own. Instead, you must use IPSec to secure the data.

To establish the VPN client connection on Windows 8.1, use the following procedure. To follow along with this exercise and to test it, you should have a client computer and a VPN server that can both connect to the Internet. These two computers should not be connected in any other way than through the Internet.

Step 1. Open the Network and Sharing Center by searching for it in the **Search** charm under **Settings**, or by right-clicking on the network icon in the notification area and selecting **Open Network and Sharing Center**.

Step 2. Click **Set up a new connection or network**.

Step 3. The Set Up a Connection or Network page shown in Figure 14-21 offers several connection options. Select **Connect to a workplace** and then click **Next**.

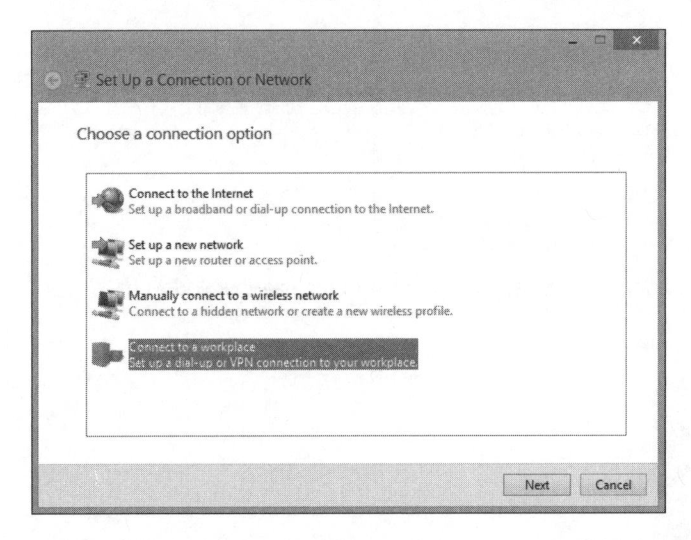

Figure 14-21 The Set Up a Connection or Network dialog box enables you to connect to several types of networks.

Step 4. You are given the option for selecting a dial-up or a VPN connection. Click **Use my Internet connection (VPN)**.

Step 5. On the Connect to a Workplace page (see Figure 14-22), type the name of the organization and the Internet address (FQDN, IPv4 address, or IPv6 address). You can select to use a smart card if it is required, and if you check the **Remember my credentials** box, your authentication information for the connection will be saved by Credential Manager. Selecting the **Allow other people to use this connection** check box configures the connection for use with ICS. After you finish with the options, click **Create**.

Step 6. Windows displays the Networks settings pane after it creates the connection. Click the new connection and then click the **Connect** button that appears to start the connection.

Step 7. On the **Network Authentication** prompt, type the username and password you will use to access the network. If this is a domain-based network, type the domain name with the username in the box, as depicted in Figure 14-23. Click **OK** to connect.

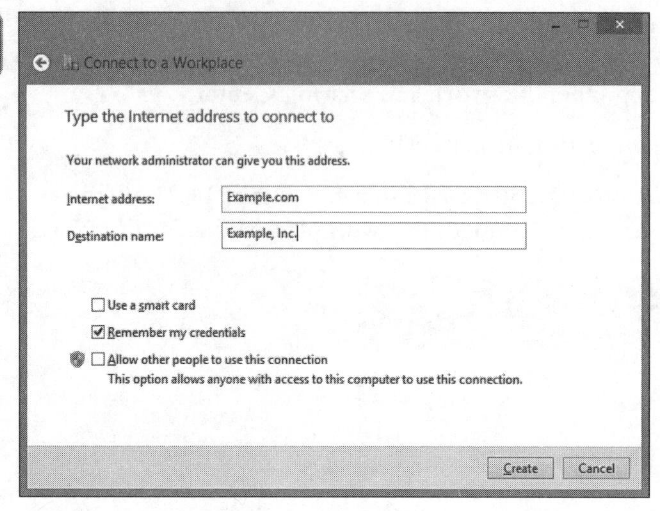

Figure 14-22 Type the Internet address and destination name of the network you want to access.

Figure 14-23 Enter authentication credentials for connecting to the VPN network.

Step 8. To connect later to your connection, access the charms, click the **Settings** charm, and then select **Network**. The available networks appear. You can tell whether a network is connected by the icon it displays, as in Figure 14-24.

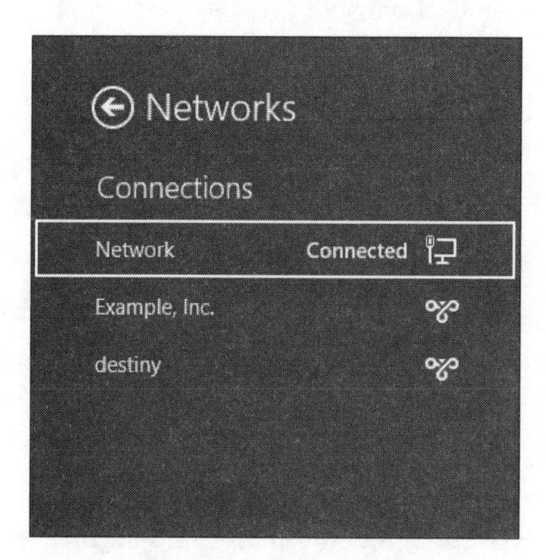

Figure 14-24 Available network connections, connected and ready to use.

After you set up a VPN connection, you can modify its properties if required. From the Network Settings pane, right-click the connection and choose **View connection properties**. The connection's Properties dialog box consists of the following tabs, each with different types of configurations:

- **General:** This tab enables you to specify the hostname or IP address of the destination and the need to connect to a public network such as the Internet before attempting to set up the VPN connection.
- **Options:** This tab provides access to disable credential saving and a setting to determine how long to allow an idle connection before closing the network (or hanging up). The PPP Settings button enables you to use link control protocol (LCP) extensions and software compression, or to negotiate multilink (use of multiple dial-up lines for increased transmission speed) for single-link connections.
- **Security:** As you can guess, the Security tab lets you select the type of VPN (automatic, PPTP, L2TP/IPSec, SSTP, or IKEv2), the authentication protocols to use, including EAP (for smart cards, certificates already on this computer, or trusted root certification authorities), CHAP, MS-CHAPv2, PAP, and so on. You can also configure encryption to be optional, required, or required at maximum strength.

- **Networking:** This tab enables you to specify the use of TCP/IPv4 and TCP/IPv6, as well as File and Printer Sharing for Microsoft Networks, and the Client for Microsoft Networks. Click **Install** to install additional features, including network clients, services, and protocols. To install these features, you should have an installation disc.
- **Sharing:** This tab lets you configure ICS in order to share the connection with other computers on your local network. You can also select options to establish dial-up connections when other computers attempt to access the Internet or allow other users on the network to control or disable a shared connection. Click **Settings** to configure ICS.

VPN Connection Security

As already mentioned, any of PPTP, L2TP, SSTP, or IKEv2 enable you to set up a tunneled connection from a remote location across the Internet to servers in your office network and access shared resources as though you were located on the network itself. Recall that PPTP, SSTP, and IKEv2 include built-in security for encryption and authentication, whereas L2TP does not. You must use IPSec to secure data being sent across an L2TP connection.

An issue that you should be aware of concerns the encryption levels used by client and server computers when establishing a VPN connection. If these encryption levels fail to match, you might receive an error code 741 accompanied by the message `The local computer does not support the required encryption type` or an error code 742 with the message `The remote server does not support the required encryption type`. This problem occurs if the server is using an encryption level different from that of your mobile computer. Servers running Windows 2000 Server or Windows Server 2003 use Rivest Cipher 4 (RC4) encryption at a level of either 40-bits or 56-bits. By default, Windows Vista, Windows 7, and Windows 8.1 use 128-bit encryption. You can try modifying the encryption level on the client to resolve this:

Step 1. From the Network and Sharing Center, click **Change adapter settings** to access the Network Connections dialog box.

Step 2. Right-click the desired VPN connection and select **Properties**.

Step 3. On the Security tab of the VPN Connection Properties dialog box shown in Figure 14-25, select **Maximum strength encryption (disconnect if server declines)** and then click **OK**.

Step 4. Attempt your connection again.

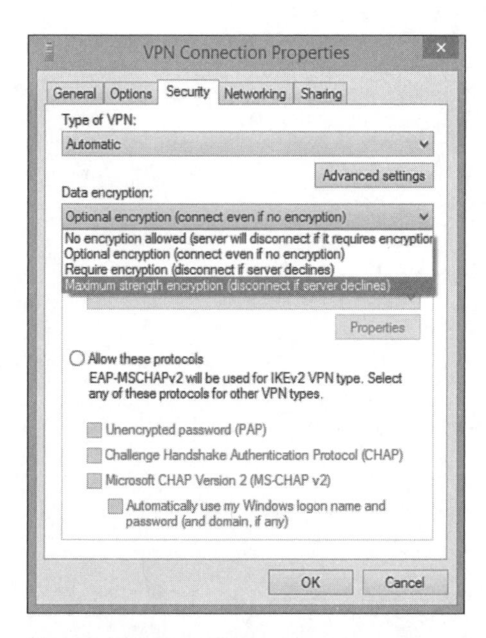

Figure 14-25 The Security tab of the connection's Properties dialog box enables you to specify the level of encryption used in a VPN connection.

Enabling VPN Reconnect

First introduced in Windows 7 is the VPN Reconnect feature, which utilizes IKEv2 technology to automatically reestablish a VPN connection when a user has temporarily lost her Internet connection. This avoids the need to manually reconnect to the VPN and possibly having to restart a download. VPN Reconnect can reestablish a connection as long as eight hours after the connection was lost. A user could be connected to an airport Wi-Fi connection when his flight is called for boarding; when he lands at his destination, he can reconnect and finish his download.

Use the following procedure to set up VPN Reconnect:

Step 1. Access the Security tab of the connection's Properties dialog box as previously shown in Figure 14-25.

Step 2. Click the **Advanced settings** button.

Step 3. In the Advanced Properties dialog box shown in Figure 14-26, click the **IKEv2** tab and ensure that **Mobility** is selected and then select a value (30 minutes by default) in the Network outage time dialog box.

Step 4. Click **OK** and then click **OK** again to close the connection's Properties dialog box.

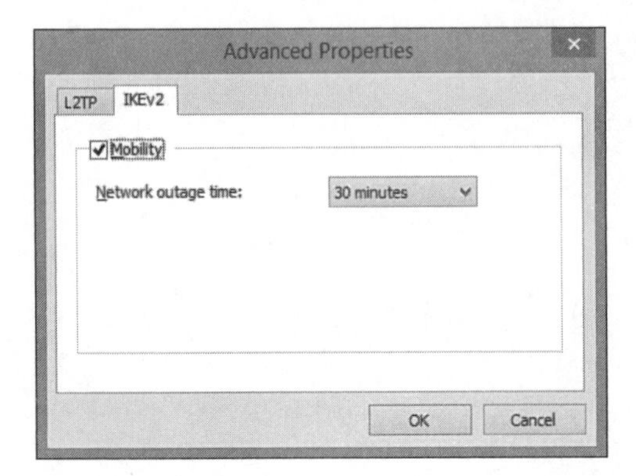

Figure 14-26 You can choose a reconnection time of up to eight hours from the Advanced Properties dialog box.

NOTE For further information and a sample detailed procedure, refer to "Set Up and Edit VPN Connections in Windows 8" at http://technet.microsoft.com/en-us/library/jj613767.aspx.

Managing Broadband Connections

By now you should have a good understanding of setting up and managing Internet connections, dial-up, VPN, and other broadband connection technologies in Windows 8.1. This section covers managing and planning for other types of remote access technologies recently introduced in Windows Enterprise networking, namely the RD Gateway and DirectAccess technologies.

RD Gateway and DirectAccess

Microsoft has introduced some new technologies to enable remote access requirements that make it easier for administrators and the mobile workforce to configure and manage. Introduced in Windows Server 2008 R2 and supported in Windows 7 and Windows 8.1 are the RD Gateway and DirectAccess. You do not need to know the details of server-side configuration of these technologies for the 70-687 exam, but you should be familiar with how they work and when they should be used in an organization.

RD Gateway

RD Gateway, which replaces the Terminal Services feature included with older versions of Windows Server, enables you to connect to remote servers on the corporate network from any computer that is connected to the Internet. RD Gateway utilizes the RDP together with HTTPS to enable a secure, encrypted connection to the internal servers through TCP port 443.

When using RD Gateway, you connect directly to a specially configured RD Gateway server on the internal network, which in turn allows connections to any computer that has been granted access. This server is a Windows Server 2008 R2 or Windows Server 2012 R2 computer on which you have installed the RD Gateway server role through Server Manager. Advantages of using an RD Gateway server for accessing published applications include the following:

- Connections to remote computers across firewalls are facilitated.
- You do not need to set up a VPN connection to enable the RD Gateway connection.
- You can share the network connection with other applications running on your computer, thereby enabling you to use your ISP connection to transmit data across the remote connection.

You learned how to set up a Remote Desktop connection earlier in this chapter. To use RD Gateway, proceed as follows:

Step 1. Access the Remote Desktop Connection dialog box as previously described and shown in Figure 14-10.

Step 2. Click **Show Options** to expand this dialog box and select the **Advanced** tab.

Step 3. Click **Settings** to open the RD Gateway Server Settings dialog box, as shown in Figure 14-27.

Figure 14-27 The RD Gateway Server Settings dialog box enables you to specify server settings.

Step 4. Select **Use these RD Gateway server settings** and type the FQDN or IP address of the server to which you want to connect.

Step 5. Select one of the following available logon methods:

- **Allow me to select later:** Enables you to select a logon method when you connect.
- **Ask for password (NTLM):** Uses NT LAN Manager (NTLM) and prompts you for a password when you connect.
- **Smart card:** Prompts you to insert your smart card when you connect.

Step 6. If you need to prevent traffic to and from local network addresses from going through the RD Gateway server, select the **Bypass RD Gateway server for local addresses** check box (selected by default).

Step 7. You can also specify in Logon settings to use the same credentials for the remote computer as you will specify for the RD Gateway connection.

Step 8. When finished, click **OK**. You can now connect to the RD Gateway server through the Remote Desktop Connection dialog box.

NOTE Windows Server 2012 R2 includes several changes and improvements for RD Gateway. For details of the changes, see "What's New in Windows Server 2012 Remote Desktop Gateway" at http://blogs.msdn.com/b/rds/archive/2013/03/14/what-s-new-in-windows-server-2012-remote-desktop-gateway.aspx. Note that you will need an MSDN account to access this.

RD Gateway Policies

You can use Group Policy to specify RD Gateway configuration. This enables you to set up uniform policy settings for all client computers that belong to an AD DS domain. Navigate to the **User Configuration\Administrative Templates\Windows Components\Remote Desktop Services\RD Gateway** node to access the configuration for the following policies:

- **Set RD Gateway authentication method:** Enable this policy to specify the authentication method to be used. You can allow users to change this setting, or you can specify that users will be asked for credentials using the Basic or NTLM method, locally logged-on credentials, or smart card.
- **Enable connection through RD Gateway:** When this policy is enabled, clients attempt to connect to the remote computer through an RD Gateway server whose IP address is specified in the next policy.
- **Set RD Gateway server address:** This policy specifies the IP address of the RD Gateway server to which clients will connect.

More information on each of these policies is available on the Help text of each policy setting's Properties dialog box.

DirectAccess

DirectAccess, first introduced as a feature with Windows 7 and Windows Server 2008 R2, enables users to directly connect to corporate networks from any Internet connection. When it is enabled, a user can access network resources as though he were actually at the office. DirectAccess uses IPv6 over IPSec to create a seamless, bidirectional, secured tunnel between the user's computer and the office network, without the need for a VPN connection.

The benefits of DirectAccess include the following:

- **Improved mobile workforce productivity:** Users have the same connectivity to network resources whether they are in or out of the office. Users can be connected through any Internet connection, such as a client's office, home, hotel, airport Wi-Fi connection, and so on.

- **Improved management of remote users:** You can apply Group Policy updates and software updates to remote computers whenever they are connected by means of DirectAccess.
- **Improved network security:** DirectAccess uses IPv6 over IPSec to enable encrypted communications and secured authentication of the computer to the corporate network even before the user has logged on. IPv6 also provides globally routable IP addresses for remote access clients. Encryption is provided using Data Encryption Standard (DES), which uses a 56-bit key, and Triple DES (3DES), which uses three 56-bit keys.
- **Access control capabilities:** You can choose to allow only specific applications or subnets of the corporate network or to allow unlimited network access by DirectAccess users.
- **Simplified network traffic:** Unnecessary traffic on the corporate network is reduced because DirectAccess separates its traffic from other Internet traffic. You can specify that DirectAccess clients send all traffic through the DirectAccess server.

Windows Server 2008 R2 and later includes the required server functionality to operate DirectAccess. Optionally, you can also include Microsoft Forefront Unified Access Gateway (UAG). This option provides enhanced security within and outside the corporate network, enabling DirectAccess for IPv4-only applications and resources on the network. Security is improved on the DirectAccess server, and built-in wizards and tools simplify deployment and reduce configuration errors.

Windows 8.1 DirectAccess client computers must be running Windows Enterprise. It is not available in Windows 8.1, Windows 8.1 Pro, or Windows RT 8.1. DirectAccess also requires an AD DS domain with one or more DirectAccess servers that meet the following requirements:

- The server must be running Windows Server 2008 R2 or Windows Server 2012 R2 and be a domain member server. This server needs to have the Web Server (IIS) server role installed.
- You need to install the DirectAccess Management Console server feature from the Server Manager Add Features Wizard to enable the server to act as a DirectAccess server.
- The server must be equipped with two network adapters: one connected directly to the network and one connected to the corporate intranet.
- The network adapter connected to the Internet must be configured with two consecutive IPv4 public addresses.

- The server requires digital certificates obtained from an Active Directory Certificate Services (AD CS) server configured as an Enterprise Certification Authority (CA). DirectAccess clients use certificates from the same CA; doing so enables both client and server to trust each other's certificates.

In addition, the domain must have at least one domain controller and Domain Name System (DNS) server that runs Windows Server 2008 SP2 or later Windows Server version. If UAG is not in use and connection to IPv4-only resources is required, you must have a Network Address Translation 64 (NAT64) device.

Exam Preparation Tasks

Review All the Key Topics

Review the most important topics in the chapter, noted with the key topics icon in the outer margin of the page. Table 14-4 lists a reference of these key topics and the page numbers on which each is found.

Table 14-4 Key Topics for Chapter 14

Key Topic Element	Description	Page Number(s)
Table 14-3	Describes authentication protocols for Remote Access	598-599
List	Lists Remote Authentication Group Policies	600
Figure 14-4	Shows how to enable Remote Assistance	604
Step List	Describes how to send a Remote Assistance invitation	604-606
Figure 14-10	Shows how to specify incoming Remote Desktop Connection options	610
Figure 14-18	Shows how to enable PowerShell Remoting	621
List	Lists connection protocols for VPN connections	625
Figure 14-22	Shows how to create a VPN connection	628
Figure 14-27	Shows RD Gateway Server Settings	634

Complete the Tables and Lists from Memory

Print a copy of Appendix B, "Memory Tables," (found on the CD), or at least the section for this chapter, and complete the tables and lists from memory. Appendix C, "Memory Tables Answer Key," also on the CD, includes completed tables and lists to check your work.

Definitions of Key Terms

Define the following key terms from this chapter, and check your answers in the Glossary:

Challenge Handshake Authentication Protocol (CHAP), DirectAccess, EAP-TTLS, Internet Key Exchange version 2 (IKEv2), Layer 2 Tunneling Protocol (L2TP), Microsoft Challenge Handshake Authentication Protocol version 2 (MS-CHAPv2), Password Authentication Protocol (PAP), Point-to-Point Protocol (PPP), Point-to-Point Tunneling Protocol (PPTP), PowerShell Remoting, Protected Extensible Authentication Protocol-Transport Layer Security (PEAP-TLS), RemoteApp, Remote Assistance, Remote Desktop, Remote Desktop Gateway (RD Gateway), Secure Socket Tunneling Protocol (SSTP), Virtual Private Network (VPN), Windows PowerShell, Windows Remote Management (WinRM) Service

This chapter covers the following subjects:

- **Configuring Offline File Policies:** The Offline Files feature enables users to work with files stored on a network share when they are disconnected from that share. You can specify how files are synchronized with the copies on the offline computer and how to deal with synchronization conflicts.
- **Configuring Power Policies:** Microsoft provides several options for configuring power management on Windows 8.1 computers. This section introduces you to these options as well as configuring Group Policy for power management settings.
- **Configuring Wi-Fi Direct:** Wi-Fi Direct is a new technology that enables users on portable computers to create ad hoc wireless connections with devices such as smartphones and TVs, and share data with these devices without the need for an access point.
- **Configuring BitLocker and BitLocker To Go:** Microsoft has enhanced the BitLocker whole drive encryption scheme, first introduced in Windows Vista, by allowing you to encrypt data partitions. BitLocker To Go extends the BitLocker drive encryption to USB drives and portable hard drives.
- **Configuring Startup Key Storage:** This section covers the use of removable disks and devices for storing startup keys for BitLocker and other purposes, and how to enable and manage BitLocker without a built-in TPM.
- **Configuring Remote Wipe:** Remote Wipe is an important security tool for ensuring that when mobile devices are lost or stolen the device can be reset and personal information cleared. In this section you learn about the state of Remote Wipe for Windows devices.
- **Configuring Location Settings:** New for Windows 8.1 is the Windows Location services, now enabled with GPS for devices equipped with GPS hardware. In this section, you learn how to configure location information settings for Windows 8.1 systems and Windows apps.

Configuring and Securing Mobile Devices

Mobile computing has entered the mainstream of everyday business activity, with portable devices of all kinds, including laptops, tablets, and smartphones presenting an unprecedented level of computing power. You can do almost as much on a notebook or laptop computer or tablet as on a desktop with the added convenience of portability to any workplace, client, hotel, or home situation as the demand requires. Along with the convenience of portability comes the risk of exposing valuable data to unauthorized access as a result of loss or theft of the computer. Microsoft has enhanced the BitLocker full drive encryption feature and added the new BitLocker To Go portable drive encryption feature.

New to Windows 8 and continued in Windows 8.1 are several useful mobile computing features, such as the ability to obtain a geographic location based on data collected by a GPS sensor, storage of startup keys, and the ability to remotely wipe information stored on a lost or stolen computer. Microsoft has continued and enhanced features introduced with older Windows versions, including the Windows Mobility Center, offline file access, power management, and presentation settings. This chapter introduces you to these portable computer features.

"Do I Know This Already?" Quiz

The "Do I Know This Already?" quiz allows you to assess whether you should read this entire chapter or simply jump to the "Exam Preparation Tasks" section for review. If you are in doubt, read the entire chapter. Table 15-1 outlines the major headings in this chapter and the corresponding "Do I Know This Already?" quiz questions. You can find the answers in Appendix A, "Answers to the 'Do I Know This Already?' Quizzes."

Table 15-1 "Do I Know This Already?" Foundation Topics Section-to-Question Mapping

Foundations Topics Section	Questions Covered in This Section
Configuring Offline File Policies	1–3
Configuring Power Policies	4–5
Configuring Wi-Fi Direct	6
Configuring BitLocker and BitLocker To Go	7–9
Configuring Startup Key Storage	10–12
Configuring Remote Wipe	13
Configuring Location Settings	14

1. You have configured the Offline Files option on your Windows 8.1 computer and want to ensure that all available files on a network share are automatically cached to your computer. Which option should you enable?
   a. Open Sync Center
   b. Disk Usage
   c. Sync Selected Offline Files
   d. Always Available Offline

2. You are configuring server options for offline files and want to ensure that users can always run cached files locally so that performance as experienced by the users is always optimized. Which settings should you configure? (Each answer represents part of the solution. Choose two.)
   a. **Only the files and programs that users specify are available offline.**
   b. **No files or programs from the shared folder are available offline.**
   c. **All files and programs that users open from the shared folder are automatically available offline.**
   d. **Optimized for performance.**

3. You want to enable client computers to temporarily cache all files obtained across a slow WAN link. What Group Policy setting should you enable?
   a. Configure Background Sync
   b. Enable Transparent Caching
   c. Administratively assigned offline files
   d. Configure Slow link mode

4. You want to reduce the processor power being used so that you can watch a movie on your laptop computer while on a long flight without running out of battery power. What setting should you configure? (Choose two; each is a complete solution to this problem.)

   a. Balanced power plan

   b. Power saver power plan

   c. Processor power management advanced setting

   d. Sleep advanced setting

   e. Multimedia advanced setting

5. Which of the following tasks can you configure directly from the battery meter on a Windows 8.1 portable computer? (Choose all that apply.)

   a. Choose a power plan.

   b. Use presentation mode.

   c. Adjust screen brightness.

   d. Specify hard disk settings.

   e. Open the Power Options dialog box.

6. You are planning to implement Wi-Fi Direct on your wireless network. Which of the following are advantages that you will gain from the Wi-Fi implementation? (Choose all that apply.)

   a. Computers will be able to connect seamlessly with any wireless devices without the need for additional hardware.

   b. You can create an ad hoc connection among five computers running any version of Windows 8.1.

   c. Computers can connect concurrently to the Internet and to devices such as smartphones.

   d. You can stream media between devices over a high bandwidth connection.

   e. Windows 8.1 Start screen apps can communicate over Wi-Fi Direct without the need for additional setup and configuration.

   f. Devices requiring IP address assignment can automatically receive an IP address from a DHCP server or from a built-in DHCP allocator in Windows 8.1.

7. You are sure your Windows 8.1 Enterprise computer is equipped with a Trusted Platform Module (TPM), but when you try to enable BitLocker from the System and Security category of Control Panel, the BitLocker Drive Encryption option is not available. What do you need to do first?
   a. Enable TPM in the BIOS.
   b. Configure TPM to use a startup key.
   c. Use Group Policy to enable TPM.
   d. Contact your hardware manufacturer for a firmware update.

8. Which of the following is something you should not do when enabling BitLocker and BitLocker To Go on your Windows 8.1 computer?
   a. Use BitLocker To Go to encrypt your USB flash drive containing the BitLocker recovery key.
   b. Use AD DS to save backup copies of your recovery keys.
   c. Use BitLocker without additional keys on a computer that is equipped with a TPM.
   d. Use Group Policy to enable BitLocker on a computer that is not equipped with a TPM.

9. You are using BitLocker To Go to protect portable hard drives in your organization. Users on Windows XP computers need access to data on these hard drives. What do you need to do to ensure these users have access? (Choose two; each answer is part of the solution.)
   a. Copy the BitLocker To Go reader to the Windows XP computers.
   b. Select the **Require a startup key at every startup** option.
   c. Enable the **Configure Use of Passwords for Fixed Data Drives** policy.
   d. Enable the **Allow Access to BitLocker-Protected Fixed Data Drives from Earlier Versions of Windows** policy.
   e. Enable the **Allow Data Recovery Agent** policy.

10. Which of the following are possible ways you can use to back up BitLocker recovery keys and passwords? (Choose all that apply.)
    - a. Save the key to a USB flash drive.
    - b. Save the key to a file on a portable drive.
    - c. Save the key to Active Directory Domain Services (AD DS).
    - d. Save the key to a Microsoft account.
    - e. Print the key.

11. You would like to use BitLocker on a computer without TPM, but when you try to enable it, an error is displayed indicating you must contact an administrator to enable it. What must you do to use BitLocker on this computer?
    - a. Enable BitLocker from the Control Panel.
    - b. Enable the **Require additional authentication at startup** Group Policy.
    - c. Disable the **BitLocker TPM** Group Policy.
    - d. Update the signature of the operating system drive in Disk Management.

12. You are configuring BitLocker on a computer without a built-in TPM. Which of the following is not an option for saving your recovery key?
    - a. Floppy disk
    - b. Microsoft account
    - c. To the domain on a domain-joined computer
    - d. From a printed hard copy of the recovery password

13. You can use ActiveSync to remote wipe all data on which Windows devices? (Select all that apply.)
    - a. Windows RT 8.1
    - b. Windows Phone
    - c. Windows 8.1 laptops
    - d. Android phones

14. What sources of information does Windows Location Platform use for determining the current location of a Windows 8.1 computer? (Select all that apply.)
    - a. GPS
    - b. IP Address
    - c. Wi-Fi access points
    - d. Time zone

Foundation Topics

Configuring Offline File Policies

The Offline Files feature in Windows 8 and 8.1 enables a user to access and work with files and folders stored on a network share when the user is disconnected from that share. For example, such a situation could occur when the user is working from a laptop, tablet, or smartphone on the road or at home. This feature ensures that users are always working with the most recent version of their files.

When you enable Offline Files, the feature makes anything you have cached from the network available to you. It also preserves the normal view of network drives, and so on, as well as shared folder and NTFS permissions. When you reconnect to the network, the feature automatically synchronizes any changes with the versions on the network. Also, changes made to your files while online are saved to both the network share and your local cache. New to Windows 8.1 is the Always Offline feature, which keeps the computer operating in offline mode even when the server is available. This mode can enhance the performance of the computer because it always retrieves data from the local hard disk rather than going across the network to the server (which can limit performance if the network or server happens to be slow).

Offline files are stored on the local computer in a special area of the hard drive called a cache. More specifically, this is located at `%systemroot%\CSC`, where CSC stands for client-side caching. By default, this cache takes up 10% of the disk volume space.

You need to configure both the client computer and the server to use the Offline Files feature. Keep in mind that, in this sense, the "server" refers to any computer that holds a shared folder available to users of other computers. This may be a computer running Windows XP Professional, Vista Business, Enterprise, or Ultimate; Windows 7 Professional, Enterprise, or Ultimate; or Windows 8.1 Pro or Enterprise; as well as a server running Windows Server 2008 R2 or Windows Server 2012 R2.

NOTE For more information on new features of Offline Files in Windows 8, 8.1, and Windows Server 2012 R2, refer to "Folder Redirection, Offline Files, and Roaming User Profiles Overview" at http://technet.microsoft.com/en-us/library/hh848267.aspx.

Client Computer Configuration

By default, the Offline Files feature is enabled on the client computer. The following procedure shows you how to configure the available client options:

Step 1. Access the Search charm, type `offline files` in the search box, and then select **Manage offline files** from the list that appears.

Step 2. The Offline Files dialog box appears. By default, Offline Files should be enabled, as shown in Figure 15-1. If it informs you that Offline Files is currently disabled, you will see an **Enable offline files** command button in place of the **Disable offline files** button shown in Figure 15-1. Click this button to enable Offline Files. You are asked to restart your computer. After restarting, you will be able to access the available options shown in Figure 15-1.

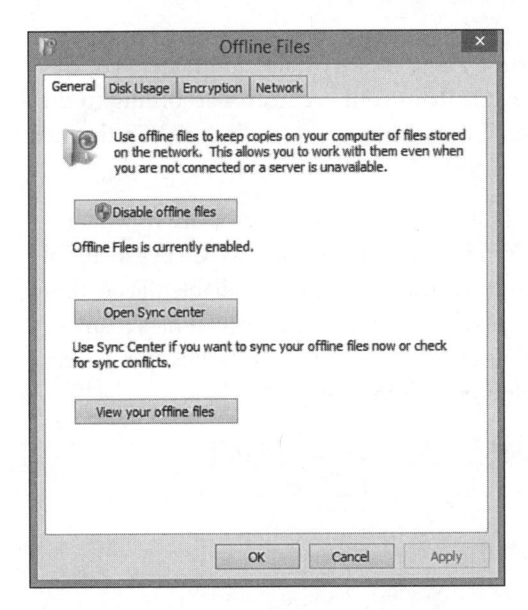

Figure 15-1 You can configure offline files at the client computer from the Offline Files dialog box.

Step 3. From the General tab, select the following options as required:

- **Disable offline files:** Select this command button if you do not want to use Offline Files. You must restart your computer to disable offline files. If Offline Files are disabled, this command button enables you to enable Offline Files.
- **Open Sync Center:** Select this command button to open the Sync Center.
- **View your offline files:** Select this command button to open a File Explorer window displaying the contents of the Offline Files folder.

Step 4. Select the **Disk Usage** tab to configure the amount of disk space currently used for storing offline files. Click **Change limits** to modify this setting. Click **Delete temporary files** to delete locally stored files.

Step 5. Select the **Encryption** tab and then click **Encrypt** to encrypt offline files. This feature uses the Encrypting File System (EFS) to encrypt offline files, keeping them secure from unauthorized users. By default, offline files are not encrypted.

Step 6. Select the **Network** tab to check for slow network connections. You can specify the number of minutes (five by default) at which Windows 8.1 checks for a slow connection.

Step 7. When finished, click **OK** or **Apply**.

After you enable your computer for Offline Files, copies of files and folders you access across the network are stored automatically in your cache area according to the server configuration parameters in effect. These parameters are discussed in the next section.

You can also automatically cache all available files from a network share to which you have connected. Right-click the shared folder icon and choose **Always available offline**, as shown in Figure 15-2. This automatically caches all available files without your having to open them first. You can also synchronize your cached files manually when you are connected to the network share. To do so, right-click the shared folder icon and choose **Sync > Sync Selected Offline Files**.

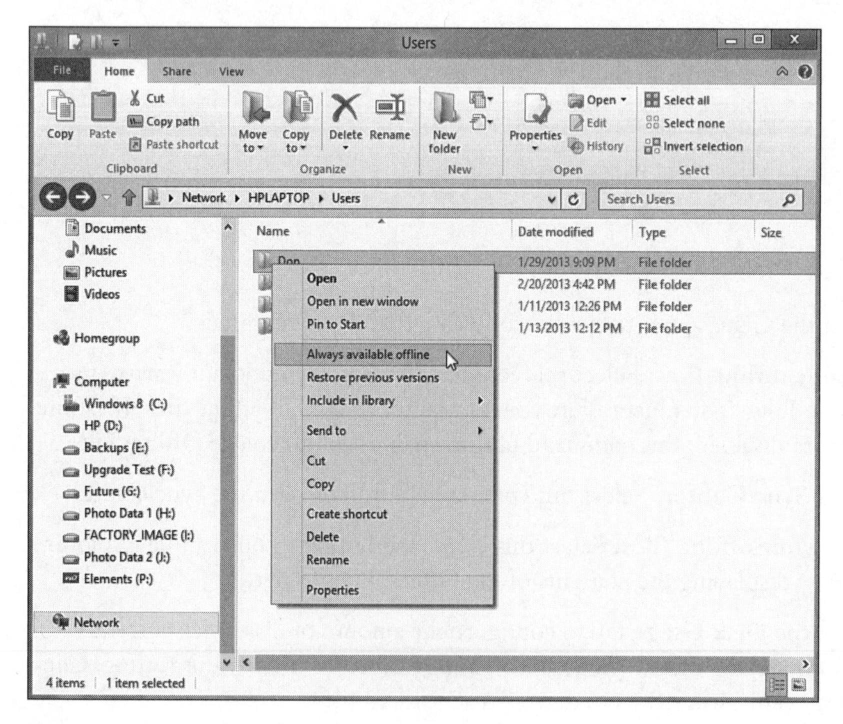

Figure 15-2 Caching files from a network share.

Server Configuration

To enable the caching of files stored on a shared folder, you need to configure the shared folder on the server and specify the type of caching available. The following procedure shows you how to perform these tasks on a Windows 8.1 computer:

Step 1. Right-click the shared folder and choose **Properties**.

Step 2. On the Sharing tab of the folder's Properties dialog box, click **Advanced Sharing**. If you receive a User Account Control (UAC) prompt, click **Yes**.

Step 3. On the Advanced Sharing dialog box, click **Caching** to open the Offline Settings dialog box shown in Figure 15-3.

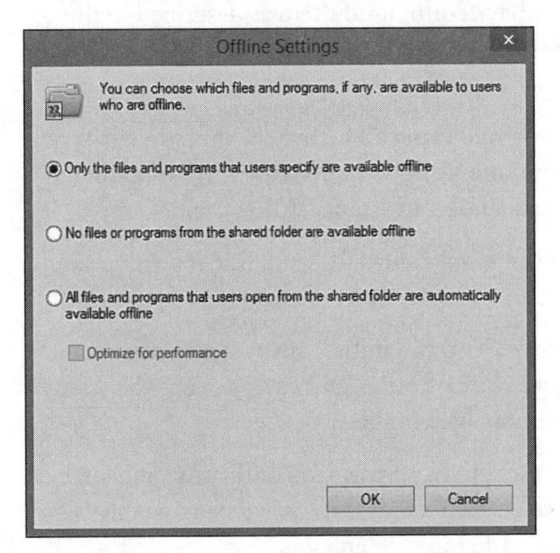

Figure 15-3 The Offline Settings dialog box provides several options for enabling offline caching in Windows 8.1.

Step 4. Select from the following options and then click **OK**:

- **Only the files and programs that users specify are available offline:** Requires that a user connecting to the share specifically indicate the files to be made available for caching. This is the default setting.
- **No files or programs from the shared folder are available offline:** Effectively disables the Offline Files feature.
- **All files and programs that users open from the shared folder are automatically available offline:** Makes every file in the share available for caching by a remote user. When a user opens a file from the share, the file is downloaded to the client's cache and replaces any older versions of the file.

- **Optimize for performance:** Enables expanded caching of shared programs so that users can run them locally, thereby improving performance. Available only if you have selected the **All files and programs that users open from the shared folder are automatically available offline** option.

Step 5. Click **OK** to close the Advanced Sharing dialog box and then click **Close** to close the Properties dialog box for the shared folder.

Use of the Sync Center

The Sync Center was first included in Windows Vista; it enables you to manage cached offline files and folders after you have configured them as described in the previous sections. Shown in Figure 15-4, the Sync Center enables you to perform the following actions:

- **Synchronization with different device types:** The Sync Center enables you to synchronize data with other computers and with devices such as smartphones, digital media devices, personal data assistants (PDAs), and so on.
- **Multiple synchronization:** You can synchronize files and folders with a single device or all available devices.
- **Manage synchronization activities:** You can initiate manual synchronization, stop actions in progress, check device connectivity status, view the status of activities, and be notified about possible conflicts.
- **Conflict resolution:** If different users have performed conflicting edits on a file (such as a Word document), the Sync Center informs you and enables you to save multiple copies of the edited file for later analysis.
- **Sync partnerships:** Sync Center establishes sync partnerships for all shared folders that you have cached locally. You can configure these partnerships to specify how and when the folders are synced.

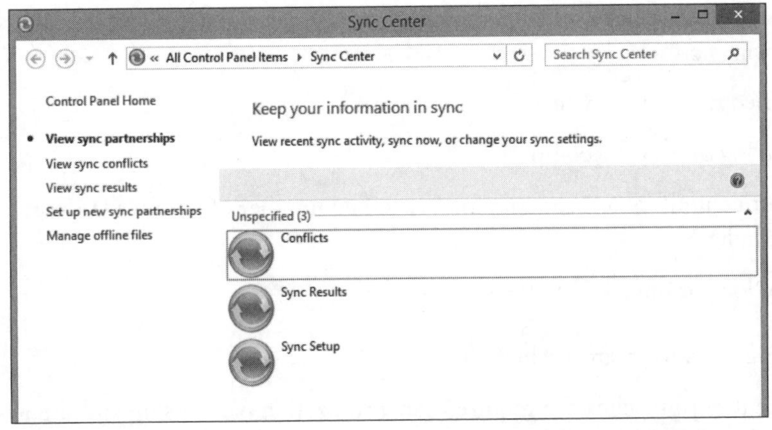

Figure 15-4 The Sync Center enables you to view and manage file and folder synchronization.

Use the following procedure to view sync partnerships and synchronize files:

Step 1. Use one of the following methods to open the Sync Center:

- From the Windows Mobility Center, click **Sync Settings**.
- Access the Search charm, and type `sync center` in the search box. Click **Sync Center** in the Programs list.
- From the Offline Files dialog box previously shown in Figure 15-1, click **Open Sync Center**.

Step 2. In the task list on the left side of the Sync Center, click **View sync partnerships** to display configured partnerships.

Step 3. To set up a new sync partnership, click **Set up new sync partnerships**.

Step 4. To synchronize a specific network share, right-click its partnership and then click **Sync offline files**.

Sync Center also enables you to schedule synchronization activities to take place at any of the following actions:

- At a specified time and synchronization interval
- When you log on to your computer
- When your computer has been idle for a specified number of minutes (15 minutes by default)
- When you lock or unlock Windows

Use the following steps to create a schedule:

Step 1. In Sync Center, right-click the required synchronization partnership and then click **Schedule for Offline Files**.

Step 2. In the Offline Files Sync Schedule dialog box that appears, select the items to be synced on this schedule and then click **Next**.

Step 3. To specify a time for the sync to begin, select **At a scheduled time**. To initiate synchronization when an event occurs, select **When an event occurs** and then select the desired action or actions. Available events include when I log on to my computer, My computer is idle for a specified number of minutes, I lock Windows, and I unlock Windows.

Step 4. If you select **At a scheduled time**, Sync Center automatically provides the current date and time as a start time and a one-day repeat interval (see Figure 15-5). Accept these or specify a different date, time, and interval as required, and then click **Next**.

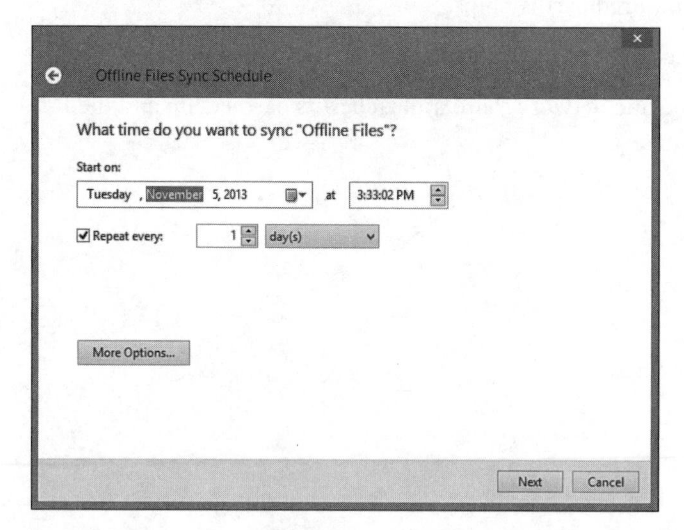

Figure 15-5 You can specify the date, time, and synchronization interval for your sync schedule.

Step 5. Specify a descriptive name for the scheduled synchronization and then click **Save schedule**.

After you create a synchronization schedule, the Offline Files Sync Schedule dialog box provides additional options for viewing or editing an existing sync schedule or deleting the schedule.

If different users modify a synchronized file while working on different computers, a synchronization conflict occurs. Sync Center informs you when conflicts have occurred. To view information about sync conflicts, click **View sync conflicts** in the Tasks pane. As shown in Figure 15-6, Sync Center informs you about the file or files that are in conflict.

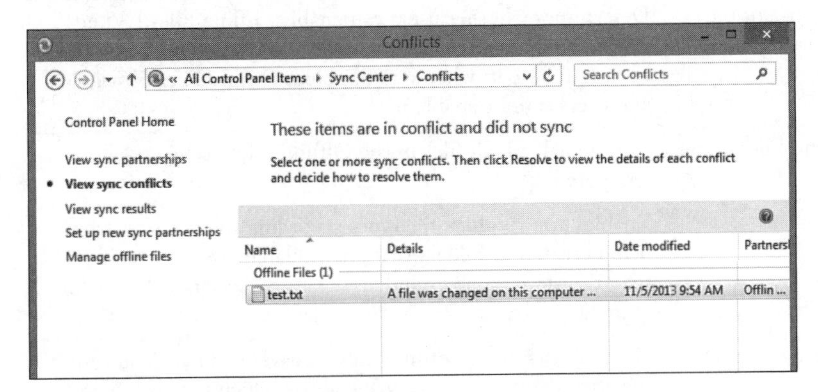

Figure 15-6 Sync Center informs you when synchronization conflicts occur.

To resolve a conflict, select it and click **Resolve**. Sync Center enables you to keep either or both versions by using an altered filename, thereby allowing you to compare them and resolve differences at a later time.

Offline File Policies

Group Policy makes available a series of policy settings. In Local Group Policy Editor or Group Policy Management Editor, navigate to **Computer Configuration\Administrative Templates\Network\Offline Files** to display the policy settings shown in Figure 15-7. Note that some of the policy settings available here are applicable to computers running older Windows versions only and are provided for backward-compatibility purposes. Table 15-2 describes the more important policy settings relevant to Windows 8, 8.1, and Windows Server 2012 R2 computers that you should be aware of.

Table 15-2 Offline File Policies

Policy	Description
Specify administratively assigned offline files	Specifies network files and folders that are always available offline. Type the universal naming convention (UNC) path to the required files.
Configure Background Sync	Enables you to control synchronization of files across slow links. You can configure sync interval and variance parameters, as well as blackout periods when sync should not occur.
Limit disk space used by Offline Files	When enabled, limits the amount of disk space in megabytes used to store offline files.
Allow or Disallow use of the Offline Files feature	Determines whether users can enable Offline Files. When this policy is enabled, Offline Files is enabled and users cannot disable it; when it is disabled, Offline Files is disabled and users cannot enable it.
Encrypt the Offline Files cache	When enabled, all files in the Offline Files cache are encrypted.
Enable file screens	Enables you to block file types according to extension from being created in folders that are available offline. Specify the extensions to be excluded, separated by semicolons—for example, *.jpg; *.mp3.
Enable Transparent Caching	Controls caching of offline files across slow links. You can specify a network latency value above which network files are temporarily cached. More about this policy in the next section.
Configure slow-link mode	Controls background synchronization across slow links and determines how network file requests are handled across slow links.
Configure Slow link speed	Specifies the threshold link speed value below which Offline Files considers a network connection to be slow. Specify the value in bits per second divided by 100; for example, specify 1280 for a threshold of 128,000 bps.
Enable file synchronization on costed networks	Determines whether offline files are synchronized in the background when extra charges on cell phone or broadband networks could be incurred.
Remove "Work offline" command	Prevents users from manually changing whether Offline Files is in online mode or offline mode by removing the Work offline command from File Explorer.

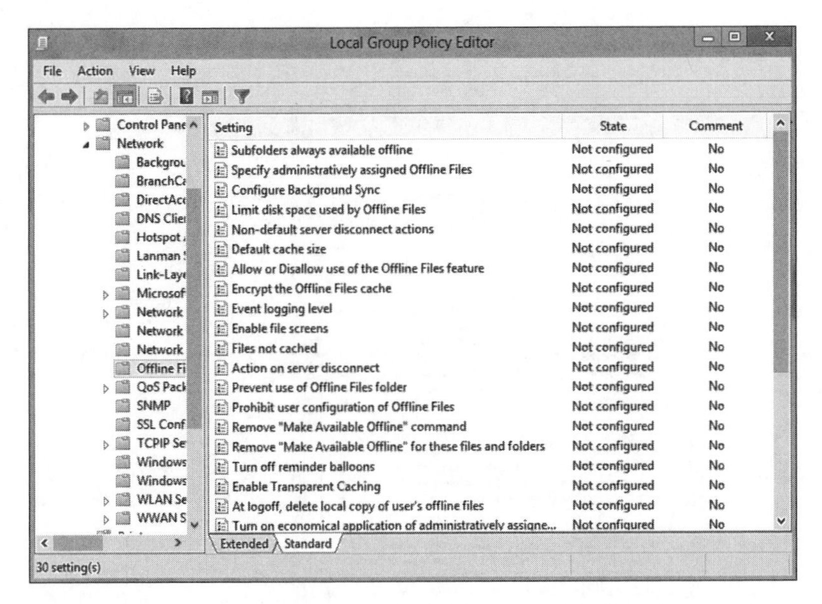

Figure 15-7 You can configure a large number of policy settings related to the use of Offline Files.

Using the Always Offline Mode

New to Windows 8 and continued in Windows 8.1 is the Always Offline mode that enables faster access to cached files and redirected folders in an Active Directory Domain Services (AD DS) environment. Enabling this mode reduces bandwidth usage because users are always working offline even when connected to the network.

Use the following steps to enable the Always Offline mode:

Step 1. At a server running Windows Server 2012 or a computer running the Remote Server Administration Tools, access the Group Policy Management Editor focused on a Group Policy Object (GPO) focused on the desired domain, site, or organizational unit (OU).

Step 2. Navigate to the **Computer Configuration\Policies\Administrative Templates\Network\Offline Files** node.

Step 3. Right-click the **Configure slow-link mode** policy and choose **Edit** to display the Configure slow-link mode dialog box shown in Figure 15-8.

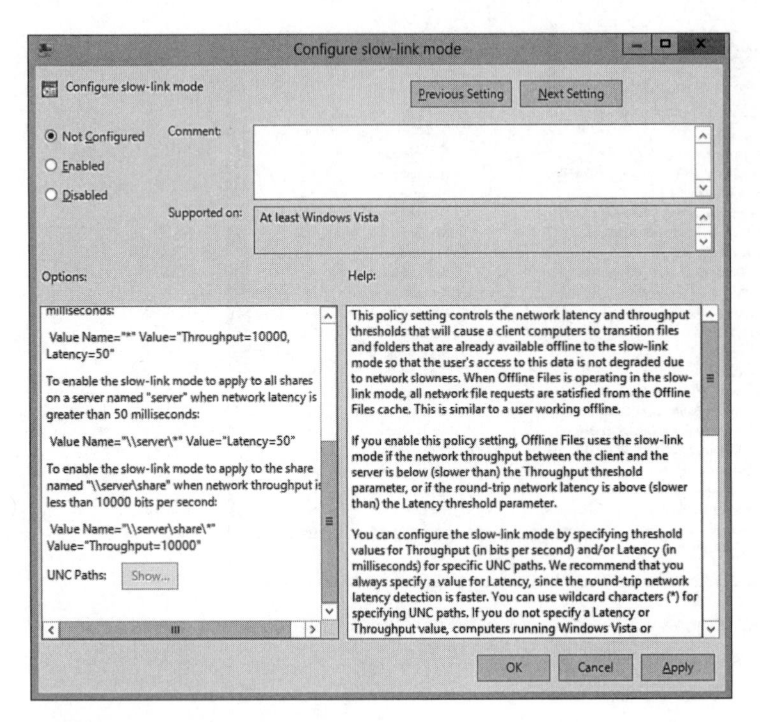

Figure 15-8 Configuring slow-link mode.

Step 4. Select **Enabled**.

Step 5. Scroll the Options section of this dialog box to click **Show** at the bottom of this section.

Step 6. From the Show Contents dialog box, specify the file share for which the Always Offline mode should be enabled, as shown for `\\server1\documents` in Figure 15-9.

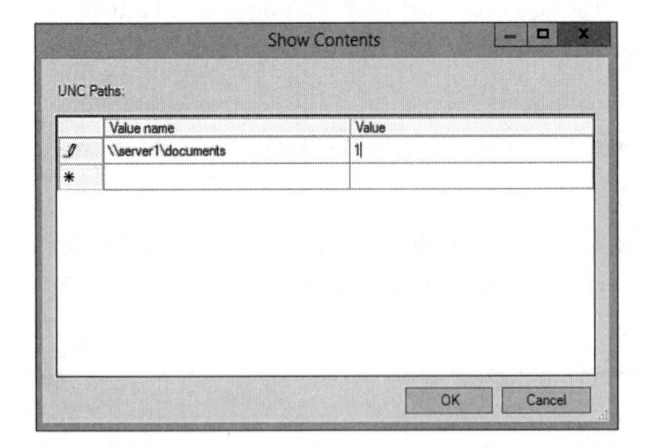

Figure 15-9 Specifying a shared folder that should always be available offline.

Step 7. In the Value column, specify a latency value in milliseconds (as shown for 1 millisecond in Figure 15-9) and then click **OK**.

Step 8. Click **OK** to close the Configure slow-link mode dialog box.

NOTE For more information on the Always Offline mode, refer to "Enable the Always Offline Mode to Provide Faster Access to Files" at http://technet.microsoft.com/en-us/library/hh968298.aspx.

Configuring Transparent Caching of Offline Files

Introduced with Windows 7 and continued in Windows 8 and 8.1 is the concept of transparent file caching, which enables client computers to temporarily cache files obtained across a slow wireless area network (WAN) link more aggressively, thereby reducing the number of times the client might have to retrieve the file across the slow link. Use of transparent caching also serves to reduce bandwidth consumption across the WAN link. Prior to Windows 7, client computers always retrieved such a file across the slow link.

The first time a user accesses a file across the WAN, Windows 8.1 retrieves it from the remote computer; this file is then cached to the local computer. Subsequently, the local computer checks with the remote server to ensure that the file has not changed and then accesses it from the local cache if its copy is up-to-date. Note that this type of file caching is temporary; clients cannot access these files when they go offline.

You can configure the Enable Transparent Caching policy shown in Figure 15-10 so that clients can perform transparent caching. Enable this policy and set the network latency value, which is the number of milliseconds beyond which the client will temporarily cache files obtained across the WAN.

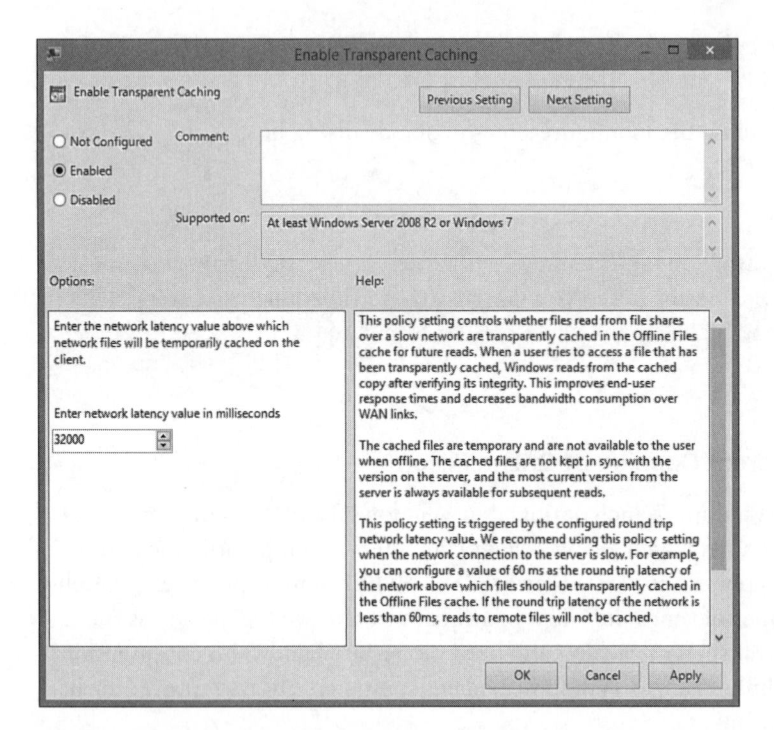

Figure 15-10 Enable the Enable Transparent Caching policy setting so that clients can temporarily cache files obtained across a slow WAN link.

Configuring Power Policies

The Hardware and Sound category of Control Panel contains two applets of particular interest to mobile users. Open the Control Panel and select **Hardware and Sound** to display the window shown in Figure 15-11, which features the following applets among others:

- **Power Options:** Enables you to configure power use for specific conditions, including connecting your computer to an AC outlet or running it on battery power.
- **Windows Mobility Center:** Enables you to configure common mobile computer settings, such as display settings, speaker volume, and battery status. We introduce the Windows Mobility Center later in this chapter.

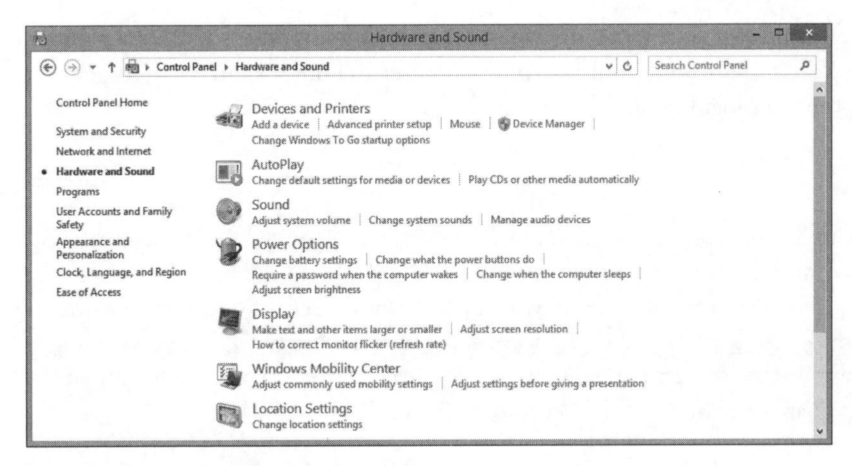

Figure 15-11 The Hardware and Sound category of Control Panel features two applets of particular interest to mobile computer users.

Configuring Power Options

The chief issue with system performance for mobile users is that of managing power consumption on mobile computers when running on battery power. Microsoft provides the Control Panel Power Options applet for configuring several power management options that enable you to configure energy-saving schemes appropriate to your hardware.

> **NOTE** While designed with mobile users in mind, the power options discussed in this section are available to all users of Windows 8.1. Users of desktop computers can utilize these options to decrease electricity consumption in these days of ever-increasing electric utility bills.

Windows 8.1 uses sleep mode, which replaces the standby mode used in Windows versions prior to Vista and offers the following advantages compared to shutting down your computer:

- Windows 8.1 automatically saves your work and configuration information in RAM and turns off the computer's monitor, hard disk, and other system components. Should your battery run low, Windows 8.1 saves your work to the hard disk and turns off your mobile computer.
- Entering the sleep state is rapid: it takes only a few seconds.

- When you wake your computer, Windows 8.1 restores your work session rapidly. You don't need to wait for your computer to boot up and restore your desktop after logging on.

NOTE Hibernation is available in Windows 8.1 as an advanced power management setting. This option saves configuration information and data to the hard disk and turns off all computer components. You need an amount of free hard disk space equal to the amount of RAM on the computer to save the entire contents of RAM. Waking from hibernation takes more time than waking from sleep mode. You learn about advanced power management settings later in this section.

You can access the Power Options applet from the Hardware and Sound section or the System and Security section of Control Panel. You can also access this applet by accessing the Search charm and typing `power options`. This opens the applet shown in Figure 15-12, from which you can configure the options described in the following section.

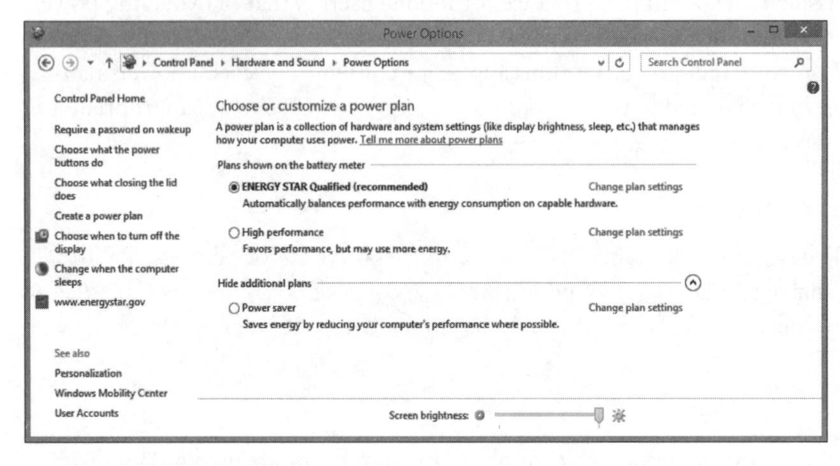

Figure 15-12 The Power Options applet provides several options for configuring power management.

Power Plans

Microsoft has supplied three preconfigured power plans that help to strike a balance between usability and power conservation. The High-performance power plan optimizes the computer for performance at the expense of battery life and is suitable for individuals who run graphics-intensive or multimedia applications frequently.

The Power saver plan optimizes battery life by slowing down the processor, and is suitable for those who use the computer primarily for purposes such as email, web browsing, and word processing. The Balanced plan strikes a balance between these extremes. You can edit one of these power schemes or create a new one if the preconfigured power schemes do not fulfill your needs. Table 15-3 compares the three preconfigured power plans.

Table 15-3 Windows 8.1 Power Plans

Power Plan	When on Battery Power	When Plugged into AC Outlet
Balanced	Turns off display after 5 minutes Sleeps after 10 minutes	Turns off display after 10 minutes Sleeps after 20 minutes
Power saver	Turns off display after 2 minutes Sleeps after 10 minutes	Turns off display after 5 minutes Sleeps after 15 minutes
High performance	Turns off display after 10 minutes Does not sleep	Turns off display after 15 minutes Does not sleep

NOTE Some computers might label the Balanced power plan as ENERGY STAR Qualified.

CAUTION Do not use sleep mode when on a commercial airplane. Airline regulations forbid the use of electronic devices during takeoff and landing. Because a computer can wake to perform a scheduled task or other action, you should turn off your computer completely at these times.

Additional Power Plan Options

Windows 8.1 enables you to perform additional power management actions that you can use to tailor your computer's power scheme to your needs.

Selecting any of the top three options on the task list in the Power Options applet previously shown in Figure 15-12 brings up the System Settings screen shown in Figure 15-13, which includes the following sections:

- **Power and sleep buttons and lid settings:** You can choose from Do nothing, Sleep mode, Hibernation, and Shut down for each of these actions on battery or AC power. The Shut down option is not available for the sleep button.
- **Password protection on wakeup:** You can choose whether or not to require a password when the computer wakes from sleep mode.
- **Shutdown settings:** You can enable fast startup, sleep mode, or hibernate mode. You can also enable display of the Lock screen.

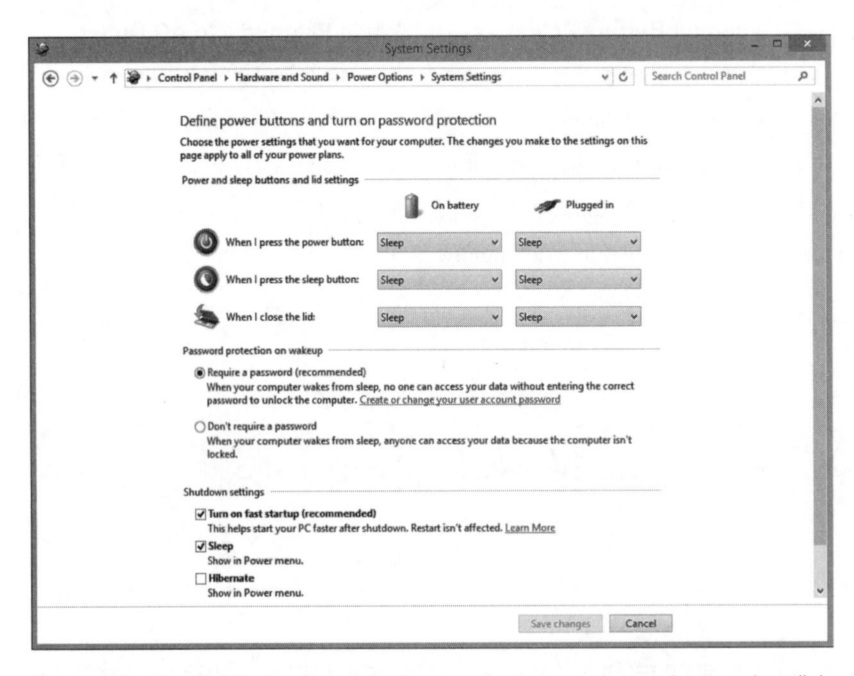

Figure 15-13 The Define power buttons and turn on password protection dialog box enables you to define power lid actions, configure password protection, and enable several shutdown settings.

You can also modify any of the existing power plans or create your own custom power plan. To do so, select the **Change plan settings** link under the desired power plan or any of the last three links on the left side of the Power Options applet previously shown in Figure 15-12. You open the Edit Plan Settings dialog box shown in Figure 15-14, focused on the power plan currently in use or the plan whose link you selected.

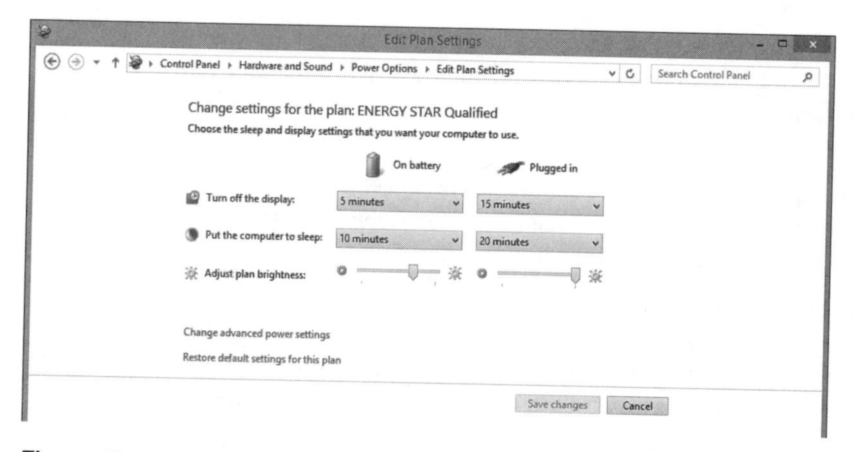

Figure 15-14 You can modify the settings for any of the predefined power plans.

Advanced Power Settings

Click **Change advanced power settings** to bring up the dialog box shown in Figure 15-15 for the following additional options, each of which you can define separately for operation on battery power or AC connection:

- **Require a password on wakeup:** You can choose to require a password on waking from either battery power or AC connection.
- **Hard disk:** You can specify the number of minutes of inactivity after which the hard disk is turned off.
- **Internet Explorer:** You can configure the JavaScript Timer frequency for either maximum performance (the default when plugged in) or maximum power savings (the default when operating on battery power).
- **Desktop background settings:** You can choose whether to make the background slide show available or to pause it.
- **Wireless adapter settings:** You can specify a maximum performance, or low, medium, or maximum power savings for the adapter. The more power savings you specify, the poorer the signal throughput might become.
- **Sleep:** You can specify the number of minutes after which your computer enters sleep or hibernation mode. You can also turn on hybrid sleep, which saves all open documents to both memory and the hard disk. Should a power failure occur when in hybrid sleep, Windows can restore your data from the hard disk. If hybrid sleep is not enabled and a power failure occurs, your data is lost.
- **USB Settings:** You can enable the USB selective suspend setting, which enables Windows 8.1 to turn off the USB root hub when not in use.

- **Power buttons and lid:** You can define the action that occurs when you close the lid or press the power or sleep buttons, in a manner similar to that described previously. You can also define the action (sleep, hibernate, or shut down) that occurs when you select the power off button from the Start menu.
- **PCI Express:** You can define the level of power savings for link state power management, which controls the power management state for devices connected to the PCI Express bus if present in the computer.
- **Processor power management:** You can control the minimum and maximum power status of the processor, also known as throttling the processor. Reducing the processor power levels saves battery power at the expense of lengthening the time required to respond to keyboard and mouse actions.
- **Display:** You can control the display brightness and the length of time before it is turned off. You can also enable adaptive display, which increases the waiting time before turning off the display if you wake the computer frequently.
- **Multimedia settings:** You can control whether the computer enters sleep mode when sharing multimedia with other users. If you set this option to **Prevent idling to sleep**, the computer does not go to sleep if media is being shared with other computers or devices.
- **Battery:** You can specify actions to take place when the battery power reaches a low or critical level, as well as the battery level at which these events occur. By default, low battery level is at 10% and produces a notification but takes no action. The critical level is at 5%; in this case, you are notified and the computer is put into hibernation when running on battery power.

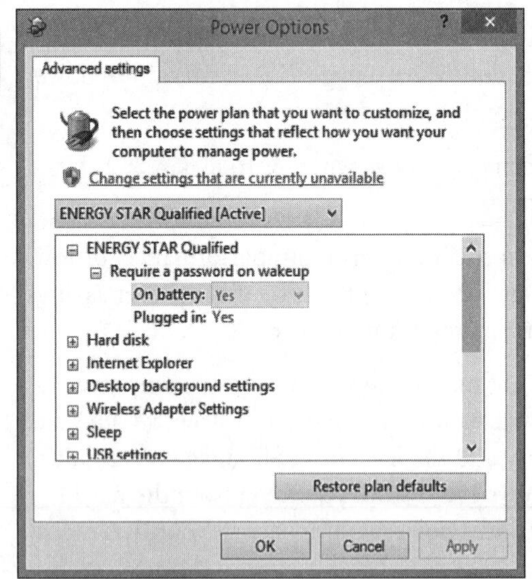

Figure 15-15 The Power Options dialog box provides several options for configuring power management.

TIP Configure power plans to turn off components after a period of inactivity. If you set up a power plan to turn off components separately after an interval of nonuse, the computer progressively moves toward sleep mode. This should happen if a user is away from his laptop for 20 or 30 minutes. At the same time, a user doing presentations should not have her computer go into sleep mode. Remember that the user can enable presentation settings so that this and other actions do not occur.

You can customize a power plan to suit your needs if required. Use these steps to create a custom power plan:

Step 1. From the left pane of the Power Options applet previously shown in Figure 15-12, click **Create a power plan**.

Step 2. On the Create a power plan dialog box that appears, select the default plan (balanced, power saver, or high performance) that is closest to your desired plan.

Step 3. Provide a descriptive name for the plan and then click **Next**.

Step 4. On the Change settings window, select the time interval after which the display is turned off and put to sleep, select the display brightness, and then click **Create**.

Step 5. You are returned to the main Power Options window. If you want to configure additional settings for the plan you just created, click **Change advanced power settings** to display the dialog box previously shown in Figure 15-15.

Battery Meter

Windows 8.1 and RT 8.1 uses the battery meter to help you keep track of remaining battery life. This is represented by a battery icon in the notification area, which also contains a plug icon when the mobile device is plugged into AC power. Hover your mouse pointer over this icon to view the percent battery power left and the power plan in use. To view the battery meter in full, as shown in Figure 15-16, click the battery icon.

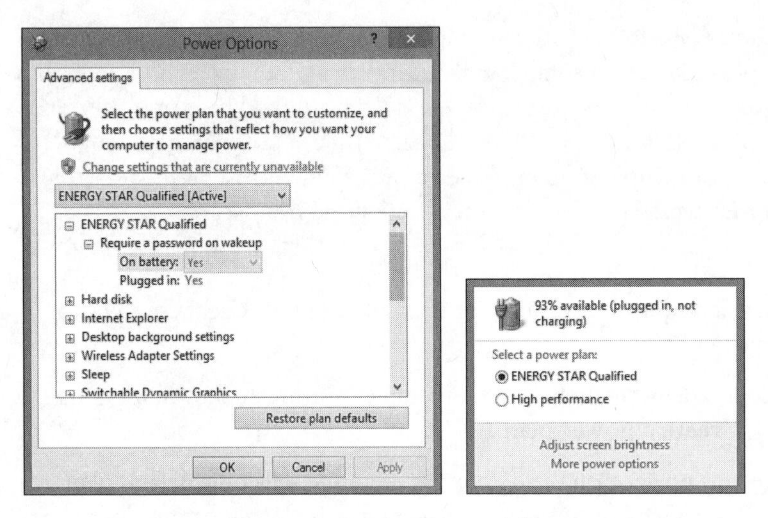

Figure 15-16 The battery meter informs you of the current battery charge level.

From the battery meter, you can also perform the following tasks:

- **Select a power plan:** Enables you to choose any of the default or custom power plans configured on your computer.
- **Adjust screen brightness:** Opens the Power Options applet as previously described and shown in Figure 15-12, where you can adjust the Screen brightness slider.
- **More power options:** Opens the Power Options applet as previously described and shown in Figure 15-12.

When the battery power drops below 25%, the notification area icon and the full battery meter display a yellow exclamation point triangle. When the power drops below 10% (or any other value configured in the Power Options dialog box), you receive a warning message informing you to either plug in your computer or shut it down and change the battery; the battery meter and icon display a red X icon. Some computers can sound an audible notification. You should plug your computer into a power outlet when this message appears.

NOTE For more information on battery properties in mobile devices, refer to "Battery: Frequently Asked Questions" at http://windows.microsoft.com/en-us/windows-8/battery-meter-frequently-asked-questions.

Power Management and Group Policy

Windows 8.1 includes the capability for configuring power management settings in Group Policy. When you configure policies for power management, a nonadministrative user cannot modify the power settings.

Use the following procedure to use Group Policy to configure power management settings:

Step 1. Access the Search charm and type `gpedit.msc` in the search box. Then select **gpedit.msc** from the list that is displayed.

Step 2. Navigate to the **Computer Configuration\Administrative Templates\System\Power Management** node. You receive the policy settings shown in Figure 15-17.

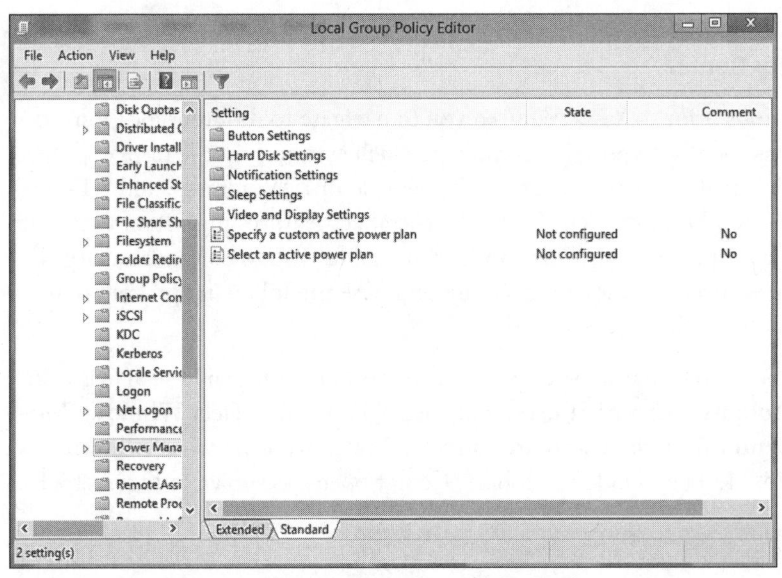

Figure 15-17 Group Policy enables you to configure a large range of power management settings.

Step 3. Configure the following groups of settings as required:

- **Button Settings:** Enables you to define the actions that occur when the power button, sleep button, or Start menu power button is pressed or the lid closed. You can define these separately for battery and AC power conditions.
- **Hard Disk Settings:** Enables you to specify when the hard disk will be turned off when the computer is plugged in and when the computer is running on battery.

- **Notification Settings:** Enables you to define the battery levels at which low and critical alarm notifications take place and the actions that will occur.
- **Sleep Settings:** Includes settings for controlling when and how the computer enters sleep mode and when and how it reawakens.
- **Video and Display Settings:** Enables you to specify how long the computer must be inactive before the display is turned off and whether the time interval is adjusted according to the user's keyboard and mouse usage.
- **Power plans:** Enables you to select either an active power plan or specify a custom power plan to be active on all computers controlled by the Group Policy object.

Step 4. When finished, close the Group Policy Object Editor.

Windows Mobility Center

Windows versions prior to Vista required you to navigate to different locations to perform actions specific to portable computers (such as adjusting the display properties, power conservation, wireless networking, and so on). Windows 8 and 8.1 continue the Windows Mobility Center, which centralizes features important to mobile computing in a single location. This application enables you to configure a large range of features specific to notebook computers. Use the following procedure to access the Windows Mobility Center:

Step 1. Access the Search charm, type `mobility` in the search box, and then click **Windows Mobility Center** in the program list. You can also select **Windows Mobility Center** from the Hardware and Sound category as previously shown in Figure 15-11. The Windows Mobility Center opens, as shown in Figure 15-18.

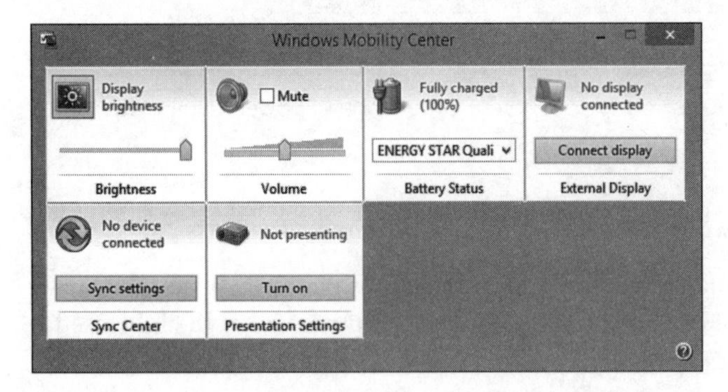

Figure 15-18 Windows Mobility Center enables you to control several features related to portable computers.

Step 2. Select the control provided by the appropriate applet. The following may be available, depending on the edition of Windows 8.1 and the capabilities of your computer:

- **Brightness:** Enables you to control the brightness of your portable computer display by adjusting the slider provided.
- **Volume:** Enables you to control your computer's speaker volume by adjusting the slider or select the **Mute** check box to turn it off.
- **Battery Status:** Displays the current charge level of your computer's battery. You can also select a power scheme from the drop-down list provided, which might include custom settings set up by the computer manufacturer if available. We discuss power options later in this chapter.
- **Wireless Network:** Provides the current connection status and signal strength. Select the command button provided to toggle the wireless network on or off. You learned about configuring wireless network settings in Chapter 9, "Configuring Networking Settings."
- **Screen Orientation:** Available on Tablet PC devices only, enables you to toggle the display orientation between horizontal (landscape) and vertical (portrait) modes.
- **External Display:** Enables you to connect an external monitor to your mobile computer or its docking station and configure its properties.
- **Sync Center:** Displays your current synchronization settings. Select the command button provided to view synchronization activities or modify the settings.
- **Presentation Settings:** Enables you to turn on and modify settings for giving presentations by selecting the command button provided.

NOTE Mobility Center controls depend on your computer's features. Windows 8.1 does not display modules associated with features not supported by your mobile computer. In addition, certain editions of Windows 8.1 do not support, and therefore do not display, certain portability features. Furthermore, computer manufacturers might add additional modules to the Mobility Center.

Configuring Wi-Fi Direct

Wi-Fi Direct is a new industry standard connectivity technology in Windows 8 and 8.1 that enables data and content sharing between devices and PCs on a peer-to-peer network without the need for separate Wi-Fi access points. It supplants the older ad hoc mode of wireless networking between two portable computers. In Windows 8.1, for example, you can sync data between a smartphone and a portable computer while sitting at the airport waiting for your flight to be called. Wi-Fi Direct supports that latest security technologies including Wi-Fi Protected Access 2 (WPA2) security, which is enabled by default, minimizing the risk of data being intercepted by unauthorized users or devices. No infrastructure devices such as wireless routers are needed for the connection.

The following are several properties of Wi-Fi Direct in Windows 8.1:

- Wi-Fi Direct is integrated into the Wi-Fi stack and is enabled by default. You can connect to any device that supports Wi-Fi Direct.
- Wi-Fi Direct builds on existing Wi-Fi hardware. You can enable Wi-Fi Direct without the need for added hardware components such as chipsets or antennas. Microsoft has worked with hardware manufacturers to ensure compatibility and support.
- Wi-Fi Direct permits concurrent connection to the Internet and to devices such as smartphones. The chipset can be used for multiple simultaneous connections.
- Wi-Fi Direct is optimized for power savings. It is turned on by demand and turns off when not in use.
- It is simple to set up devices for direct streaming of media between devices over a high bandwidth connection. For example, you can share high-definition video between computers and TVs, including video, as you download it from the Internet.
- Windows 8.1 Start screen apps can communicate over Wi-Fi Direct without the need for additional setup. The apps can talk to each other by leveraging proximity application programming interface (API).

Windows automatically detects and installs devices after Wi-Fi Direct pairing occurs; consequently, installation and configuration of Wi-Fi Direct devices is simple, as the following procedure shows:

Step 1. From the Control Panel Devices and Printers applet, select **Add a device**.

Step 2. If the device comes with a PIN, enter the PIN when requested.

Step 3. Windows installs any required drivers and the device is ready for use.

Windows 8.1 apps can communicate between devices using Wi-Fi Direct. Proximity sensors on newer PCs and devices can detect each other when the devices are placed near to each other, and the computers can communicate with each other and share information when both computers are running the same app; users need only open the app on each computer with a simple tap on touch-sensitive screens or a click of the mouse. Developers can create additional apps that automatically connect with each other when in close proximity; such a connection is managed by Windows, and the developer does not need to manage Wi-Fi Direct semantics.

Wi-Fi Direct works in Windows 8.1 by means of a simple three-step sequence:

1. **Finding the device:** This happens automatically when you click **Add a device** as already explained. Extended attributes included with devices (known as the container ID) help identify the device.
2. **Pairing with the device:** In other words, Windows 8.1 is creating a relationship to the device. This takes place after the user selects the device. Extended attributes help to provide an improved experience during the pairing process and enable the user to remain in control. These attributes include a container ID, which represents the physical device, and a vertical device ID, which represents logical devices within the physical device.
3. **Connecting to the device:** The device remains connected only when actually in use. When the user resumes use of the device, Windows initiates an on-demand reconnection. This provides advantages, for example, optimizing battery life on the device. Further, Wi-Fi Direct enables multiple devices to connect to Windows concurrently; however, only two computers can participate in a single Wi-Fi Direct session. Devices requiring IP address assignment can automatically receive an IP address from a DHCP server. A built-in lightweight DHCP allocator in Windows 8.1 can assign IP addresses in the range 192.168.173.0/24 to devices needing them.

NOTE For more information on Wi-Fi Direct, refer to "Understanding Wi-Fi Direct in Windows 8" at http://channel9.msdn.com/events/BUILD/BUILD2011/HW-329T.

Configuring BitLocker and BitLocker To Go

First introduced with Windows Vista, BitLocker is a hardware-enabled data encryption feature that serves to protect data on a computer that is exposed to unauthorized physical access. Available on the Pro and Enterprise editions of Windows 8.1,

BitLocker encrypts the entire Windows volume, thereby preventing unauthorized users from circumventing file and system permissions in Windows or attempting to access information on the protected partition from another computer or operating system. BitLocker even protects the data should an unauthorized user physically remove the hard drive from the computer and use other means to attempt access to the data.

BitLocker uses startup keys to allow users to access the encrypted drive when the boot drive is encrypted. Typically, the startup keys are stored on the hardware-based TPM module, as discussed in previous chapters. BitLocker can also be used on computers without TPM using removable media such as a USB drive. Storing startup keys is discussed next.

Introduced with Windows 7 and continued with Windows 8 and 8.1 is BitLocker To Go, which offers similar data encryption features to USB portable drives and external hard drives. BitLocker To Go creates a virtual volume on the USB drive, which is encrypted by means of an encryption key stored on the flash drive. BitLocker To Go also includes a Data Recovery Agent (DRA) feature, which is modeled on the Encrypting File System (EFS) recovery agent that you learned about in Chapter 11, "Configuring and Securing Access to Files and Folders."

BitLocker Drive Encryption

Available on selected editions of Windows 8 and 8.1 and all editions of Windows Server 2012, BitLocker utilizes the Trusted Platform Module (TPM) version 1.2 to provide secure protection of encryption keys and checking of key components when Windows is booting. A TPM is a microchip that is built into a computer that is used to store cryptographic information such as encryption keys. Information stored on the TPM is more secure from external software attacks and physical theft. You can store keys and passwords on a USB flash drive that the user must insert to boot his computer. You can also employ an option that requires the user to supply a PIN, thereby requiring multifactor authentication before the data becomes available for use. If an unauthorized individual has tampered with or modified system files or data in any way, the computer will not boot up.

On a computer that is equipped with a compatible TPM, BitLocker uses this TPM to lock the encryption keys that protect the contents of the protected drive; this includes the operating system and Registry files when you have used BitLocker to protect the system drive. When you're starting up the computer, TPM must verify the state of the computer before the keys are accessed. Consequently, an attacker cannot access the data by mounting the hard drive in a different computer.

At startup, TPM compares a hash of the operating system configuration with an earlier snapshot, thereby verifying the integrity of the startup process and releasing the keys. If BitLocker detects any security problem (such as a disk error, change to the Basic Input/Output System (BIOS), or changes to startup files), it locks the drive and enters Recovery mode. You can store encryption keys and restoration passwords on a USB flash drive or a separate file for additional data security and recovery capability. Should a user need to recover data using BitLocker's recovery mode, she merely needs to enter a recovery password to access data and the Windows operating system.

The following are several enhancements to BitLocker in Windows 8 and 8.1:

- Nonadministrative users are able to reset the BitLocker PIN and password on protected drives.
- When you enable BitLocker, you can choose to encrypt just the used space on a drive. Additional space is encrypted as required.
- BitLocker supports pre-encrypted hard drives that meet the Windows Logo requirements.
- Administrators can unlock BitLocker-protected drives without the PIN entry when using a special network key on a trusted wired network. This enables you to perform remote maintenance on BitLocker-protected computers without physical presence at the computer.
- On an AD DS network, you can tie a BitLocker key protector to a user, computer, or group account. You can use this key protector to unlock BitLocker-protected data volumes when logged on with proper AD DS credentials.
- In Windows 8.1, BitLocker added support for encryption on computers equipped with a TPM that supports connected stand-by.

A user's computer does not need to be equipped with the TPM in order to use BitLocker. If your computer is equipped with TPM, you can use BitLocker in any of the following modes:

- **TPM only:** TPM alone validates the boot files, the operating system files, and encrypted drive volumes during system startup. This mode provides a normal startup and logon experience to the user. However, if the TPM is missing or the integrity of the system has changed, BitLocker enters recovery mode, in which you are required to provide a recovery key to access the computer.
- **TPM and PIN:** Uses both TPM and a user-supplied PIN for validation. You must enter this PIN correctly; otherwise, BitLocker enters recovery mode.
- **TPM and startup key:** Uses both TPM and a startup key for validation. The user must provide a USB flash drive containing the startup key. If the user does not have this USB flash drive, BitLocker enters recovery mode.

- **TPM and smart card certificate:** Uses both TPM and a smart card certificate for validation. The user must provide a smart card containing a valid certificate to log on. If the smart card is not available or the certificate is not valid, BitLocker enters recovery mode.

NOTE For additional introductory information on BitLocker in Windows 8.1 and Windows Server 2012 R2, refer to "BitLocker Overview" at http://technet.microsoft.com/library/hh831713.aspx and "What's New in BitLocker for Windows 8.1 and Windows Server" at http://technet.microsoft.com/en-us/library/dn306081.aspx.

NOTE Many newer computers are equipped with TPM, but TPM is not always activated. You might need to enter your BIOS setup system to enable TPM. The location of this setting depends on the BIOS in use, but it is typically in the Advanced section.

Enabling BitLocker

If your computer is equipped with a TPM, you can use the following procedure to enable BitLocker on your operating system drive:

Step 1. Access the Control Panel and click **System and Security > BitLocker Drive Encryption**. The BitLocker Drive Encryption dialog box appears, as shown in Figure 15-19. You can also access this utility by typing `bitlocker` into the Search charm and then selecting **Manage BitLocker** from the Programs list.

Step 2. Opposite the drive you want to encrypt, click the **Turn on BitLocker** link. You can also right-click the desired drive in an Explorer window and choose **Turn on BitLocker**.

Step 3. If you receive a UAC prompt, click **Yes** to proceed.

NOTE If you receive a dialog box indicating `This device can't use a Trusted Platform Module`, as shown later in Figure 15-29, it means that the computer does not have a compatible TPM module. You need to perform the procedure given in the "Configuring Startup Key Storage" section before you can enable BitLocker.

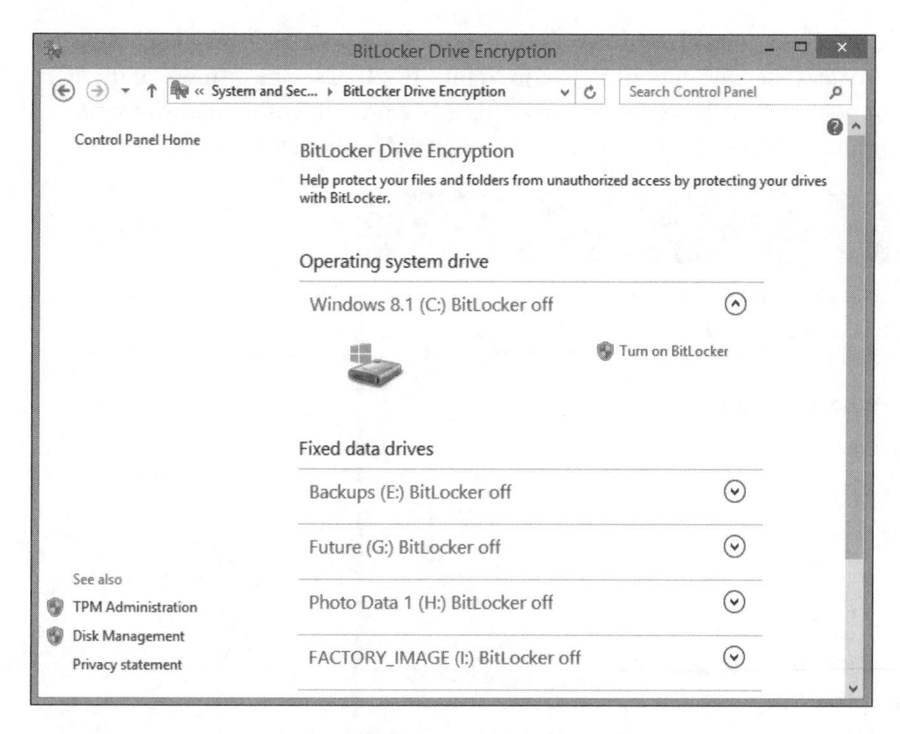

Figure 15-19 BitLocker offers to protect all available drives.

Step 4. Windows checks your computer's configuration, and after a few seconds, the BitLocker Drive Encryption setup window appears, informing you that the computer will prepare your drive for BitLocker and then encrypt the drive.

Step 5. Click **Next**. Windows prepares your drive for BitLocker and informs you that an existing drive or unallocated free space will be used to enable BitLocker.

Step 6. Click **Next**. You are informed that you will no longer be able to use Windows Recovery Environment unless it is manually enabled and moved to the system drive.

> **NOTE** If you have previously configured BitLocker drive encryption, you might not see all of steps 3 to 6 when you next perform this procedure.

Step 7. Click **Next**. The Choose how to unlock your drive at startup page provides options for inserting a USB flash drive or entering a password. Choose the desired option. If you choose the **Insert a USB flash drive** option, insert the drive and select it from the Save your startup key page that appears. Then click **Save**. If you choose the **Enter a password** option, type and confirm the password on the page that appears.

Step 8. Click **Next**. The **How do you want to back up your recovery key?** page provides the four options shown in Figure 15-20. Use one or more of these options to save the recovery password. If you print it, ensure that you save the printed document in a secure location. Click **Next** when finished.

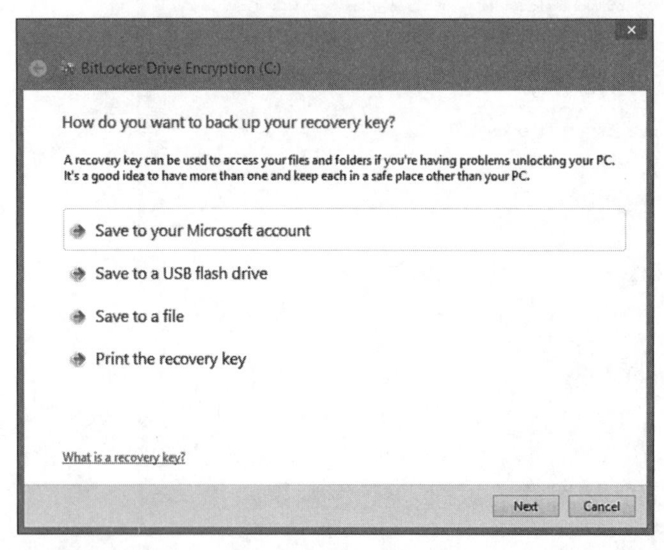

Figure 15-20 You are given four options for storing your recovery key.

Step 9. The Choose how much of your drive to encrypt page appears, as shown in Figure 15-21. Choose the appropriate option and then click **Next**.

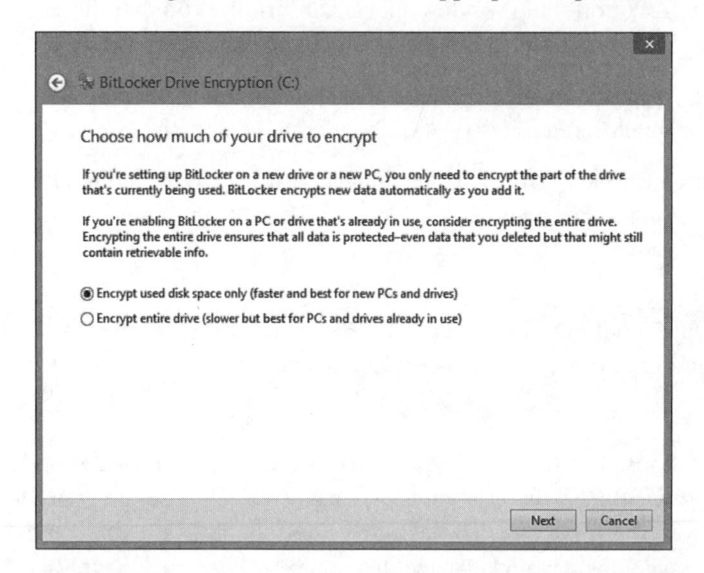

Figure 15-21 You can choose to encrypt used disk space only (the default) or encrypt the entire drive.

Step 10. The Are you ready to encrypt this drive? dialog box appears, as shown in Figure 15-22. Ensure that the check box labeled **Run BitLocker system check** is selected and then click **Continue** to proceed.

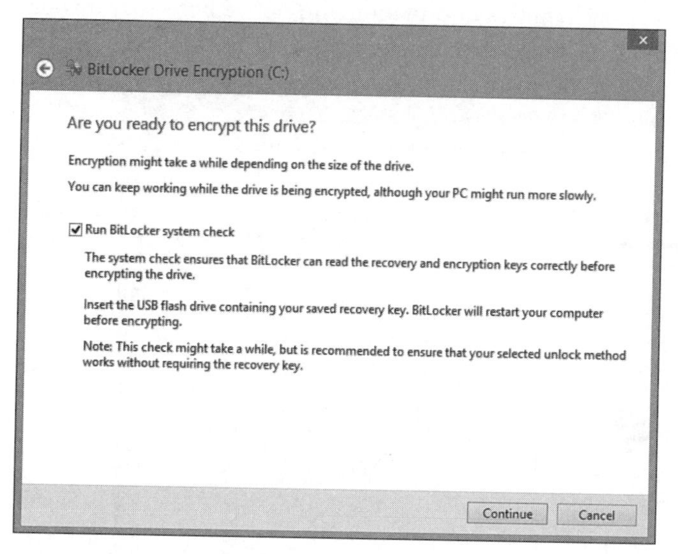

Figure 15-22 Select **Continue** to encrypt your partition.

Step 10. You need to restart your computer to proceed. Click **Restart now**.

Step 11. Encryption takes place and Windows 8.1 displays an icon in the notification area. This process can take an hour or longer, but you can use your computer while it is occurring. You can track the progress of encryption by hovering your mouse pointer over this icon. You are informed when encryption is complete. Click **Close**.

WARNING Ensure that you do not lose the recovery password. If you lose the recovery password, your Windows installation and all data stored on its partition are permanently lost. In this case, you need to repartition your hard drive and reinstall Windows. Consequently, you should create at least two copies of the password as described in the previous procedure and store them in a secure location.

Managing BitLocker

After you encrypt your drive using BitLocker, the BitLocker applet shows additional options for the protected drive, as shown in Figure 15-23. The Suspend Protection option enables you to temporarily disable BitLocker. Select this option and then click **Yes**. After doing so, this option changes to Resume Protection; click it to re-enable BitLocker. The Back up your recovery key option enables you to create an additional backup; selecting this option brings up the dialog box previously shown in Figure 15-20. You can also back up this information into Active Directory if your computer belongs to an Active Directory Domain Services (AD DS) domain.

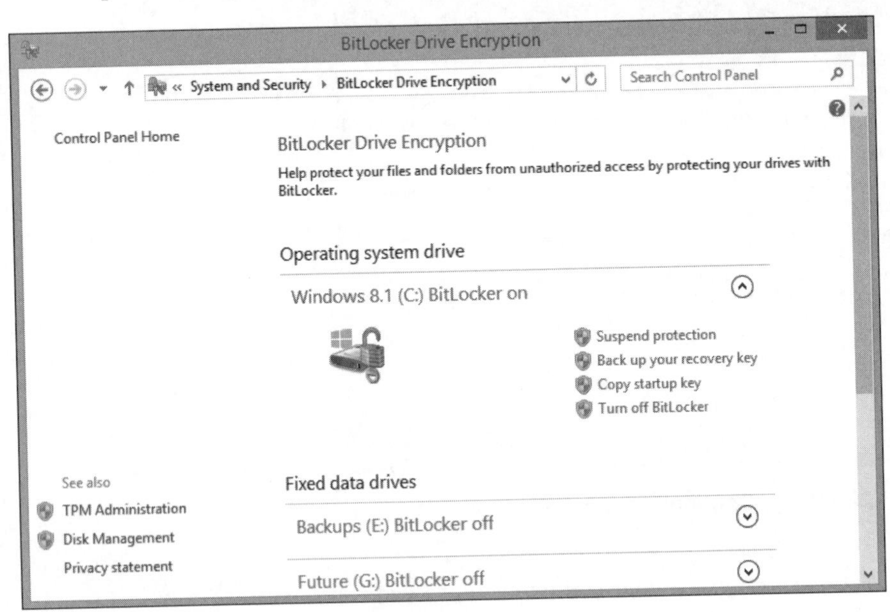

Figure 15-23 The BitLocker applet displays a distinctive icon for the protected drive and provides several options for its management.

The change password option brings up a Change startup password dialog box that is similar to the dialog box presented when you change a user account password. The Remove password option enables you to remove a password; it is only available if you have configured another unlocking mechanism such as a USB key.

The Turn off BitLocker option enables you to remove BitLocker protection. To do so, select **Turn off BitLocker**. On the BitLocker Drive Encryption dialog box that appears, select **Turn off BitLocker**. This procedure decrypts your volume and discards all encryption keys; it begins immediately without further prompts. You are able to monitor the decryption action from an icon in the notification area.

BitLocker To Go

As already mentioned, BitLocker To Go extends the full volume encryption capabilities of BitLocker to USB flash drives and portable hard drives. You can protect all portable drives regardless of whether they are formatted with the FAT, FAT32, or NTFS file systems. Microsoft engineers modified BitLocker to overlay what they called a "discovery volume" on top of the original physical volume on the portable drive. This volume includes a BitLocker To Go Reader that also enables use of the BitLocker To Go volume on computers running Windows XP and Vista. Users of these computers can download a reader from the Microsoft Download Center.

Use the following procedure to enable BitLocker To Go:

Step 1. Access the Control Panel and click **System and Security > BitLocker Drive Encryption** to display the screen previously shown in Figure 15-19.

Step 2. Insert the USB drive and click **Turn On BitLocker** beside the drive icon.

Step 3. The Choose how you want to unlock this drive dialog box appears, as shown in Figure 15-24. If using a password, select this option and then type and confirm a strong password. If using a smart card, insert the smart card in your reader. Then click **Next**.

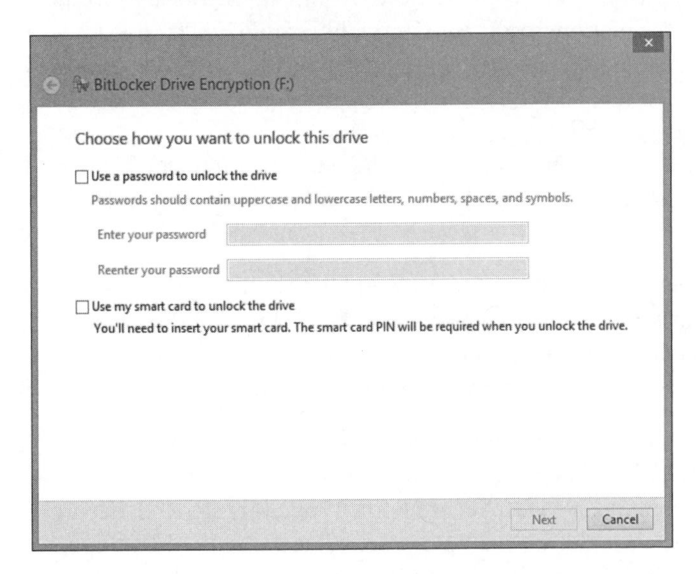

Figure 15-24 You can use either a password or smart card to secure your USB drive with BitLocker To Go.

Step 4. Select an option to save the recovery password to your Microsoft account, save it to a file, or print it. Then click **Next**.

Step 5. The Choose how much of your drive to encrypt page appears, as previously shown in Figure 15-21. Choose the appropriate option and then click **Next**.

Step 6. From the Are you ready to encrypt the Drive? page, select **Start Encrypting**.

Step 7. You return to the BitLocker Drive Encryption applet, which tracks the progress of encrypting your drive and informs you when the drive is encrypted. Do not disconnect your drive until encryption is completed.

CAUTION Do not enable BitLocker To Go on the USB drive containing your BitLocker startup key. Windows 8.1 currently does not permit this, although a future update or service pack might add this capability.

BitLocker Policies

Besides the policy already mentioned to enable BitLocker on a computer that is not equipped with a TPM, Group Policy has a series of settings that help you to manage BitLocker. You can access these polices from the Computer Configuration\Administrative Templates\Windows Components\BitLocker Drive Encryption node. This node has three subnodes: Fixed Data Drives, Operating System Drives, and Removable Data Drives, as well as several policies that affect all types of drives. Microsoft provides recommendations for many of these settings at "BitLocker Group Policy Settings" at http://technet.microsoft.com/en-us/library/jj679890.aspx.

Operating System Drives

The Local Group Policy Editor shown in Figure 15-25 enables you to configure a large number of policies that govern BitLocker as used on operating system drives, including the following:

- **Allow network unlock at startup:** New to Windows 8/8.1 and Windows Server 2012 R2, this policy controls a portion of the behavior of the Network Unlock feature. When it is enabled, clients using BitLocker are enabled to create the necessary network key protector during encryption.
- **Allow Secure Boot for integrity validation:** New to Windows 8/8.1 and Windows Server 2012 R2, this policy controls how BitLocker-enabled system volumes behave in conjunction with Secure Boot. When it is enabled, Secure Boot validation takes place during the boot process, verifying Boot Configuration Data (BCD) settings for platform integrity.
- **Require additional authentication at startup:** As mentioned in the "Configuring Startup Key Storage" section later in this chapter, this setting enables you to use BitLocker on a computer without a TPM. By enabling this policy, you can also specify whether BitLocker requires additional authentication including a startup key and/or PIN.

- **Require additional authentication at startup (Windows Server 2008 and Windows Vista):** Enables similar settings for Windows Vista and Windows Server 2008 computers, except that you cannot utilize both a startup key and PIN.
- **Allow enhanced PINs for startup:** Enables the use of a PIN that contains additional characters, including uppercase and lowercase letters, symbols, numerals, and spaces.
- **Configure minimum PIN length for startup:** Specifies a minimum length for the startup PIN. You can choose a minimum length of anywhere from 4 to 20 digits.
- **Configure use of hardware-based encryption for operating system drives:** Enables you to manage use of hardware-based encryption on fixed data drives and specify permitted encryption algorithms.
- **Enforce drive encryption type on operating system drives:** Enables you to specify the encryption type used by BitLocker. You either can choose full encryption to require that the entire drive be encrypted or used space only encryption to require only the portion of the drive in use to be encrypted.
- **Choose how BitLocker-protected operating system drives can be recovered:** Enables the use of a DRA. We discuss this policy later in this chapter.
- **Configure TPM platform validation profile for BIOS-based firmware configurations:** Enables you to specify how the TPM security hardware secures the BitLocker encryption key on computers running Windows Server 2012 R2 or Windows 8.1. The validation profile includes a set of Platform Configuration Register (PCR) indices, each of which is associated with components that run at startup. You can select from a series of indices provided in the policy's options.
- **Configure TPM platform validation profile (Windows Vista, Windows Server 2008, Windows 7, Windows Server 2008 R2):** Provides a validation profile with a similar set of PCR indices for computers running Windows Vista, Windows Server 2008, Windows 7, or Windows Server 2008 R2.
- **Configure TPM platform validation profile for native UEFI firmware configurations:** Provides a validation profile and PCR indices for Windows 8.1 or Windows Server 2012 R2 computers equipped with Unified Extensible Firmware Interface (UEFI) firmware (as opposed to BIOS-based firmware).

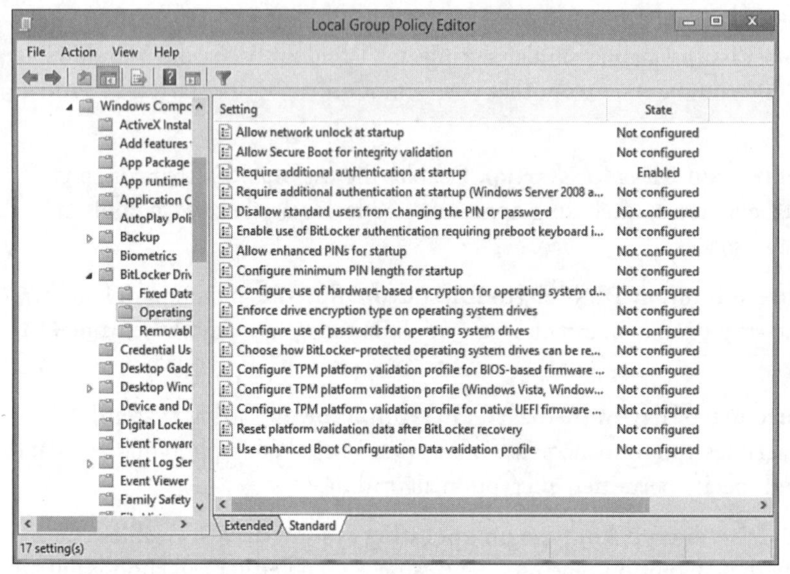

Figure 15-25 Group Policy provides these settings for BitLocker used on operating system drives.

Fixed Data Drive Policies

The Local Group Policy Editor shown in Figure 15-26 enables you to configure the following policies that govern BitLocker used on fixed data drives (in other words, internal hard drive partitions containing data but not operating system files):

- **Configure use of smart cards on fixed data drives:** Enables you to specify whether smart cards can be used to authenticate user access to drives protected by BitLocker. You can optionally require the use of smart cards.
- **Deny write access to fixed drives not protected by BitLocker:** Enables you to require BitLocker protection on writable drives. If this policy is enabled, any drives not protected by BitLocker are read-only.
- **Configure use of hardware-based encryption for fixed data drives:** Enables you to manage use of hardware-based encryption on fixed data drives and specify permitted encryption algorithms.
- **Enforce drive encryption type on fixed data drives:** Enables you to specify the encryption type used by BitLocker. You either can choose full encryption to require that the entire drive be encrypted or used space only encryption to require only the portion of the drive in use to be encrypted.

- **Allow access to BitLocker-protected fixed data drives from earlier versions of Windows:** Specifies whether or not drives formatted with the FAT or FAT32 file system can be unlocked and viewed on computers running earlier Windows versions (back to Windows XP SP2).
- **Configure use of passwords for fixed data drives:** Enables you to specify whether a password is required for unlocking BitLocker-protected fixed data drives. You can optionally specify that a password is required, and you can choose to allow or require password complexity and specify the minimum password length.
- **Choose how BitLocker-protected fixed drives can be recovered:** Similar to the corresponding operating system drives policy.

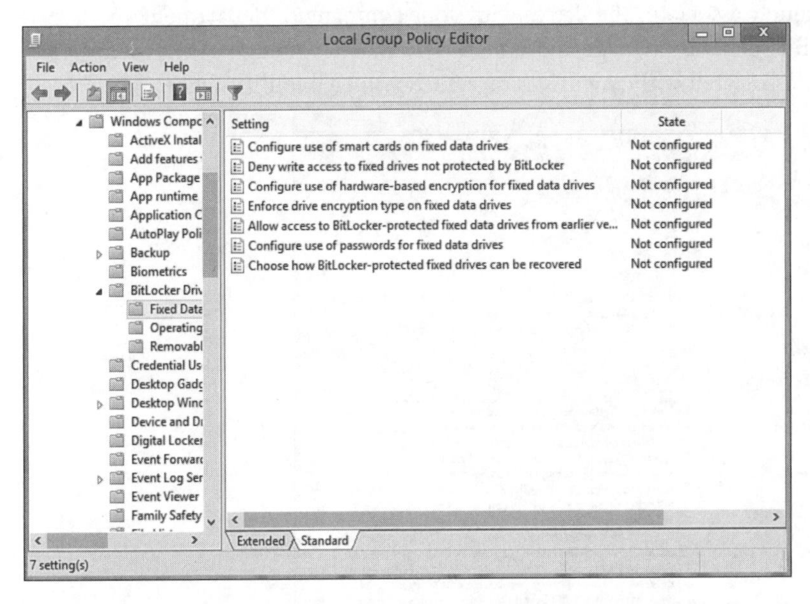

Figure 15-26 Group Policy provides these settings for BitLocker used on fixed data drives.

More information on all these policies is available from the Help field in each policy's Properties dialog box. These policies are also available for removable drives (BitLocker To Go) in the Removable Data Drives subnode of Group Policy.

Use of Data Recovery Agents

A DRA is a user account that is configured for recovering data encrypted with BitLocker in a manner analogous to the EFS recovery agent described in Chapter 11. The DRA uses his smart card certificates and public keys to accomplish this action.

To specify a DRA for a BitLocker-protected drive, you must first designate the recovery agent by opening the Local Group Policy Editor and navigating to the **Computer Configuration\Windows Settings\Security Settings\Public Key Policies\BitLocker Drive Encryption** node. Right-click this node and choose **Add Data Recovery Agent**. This starts a wizard that is similar to that used for creating EFS DRAs. You can browse for the required certificates or select them from AD DS in a domain environment.

After you specify your DRA, you need to access the **Computer Configuration\Administrative Templates\Windows Components\BitLocker Drive Encryption** node of Group Policy and enable the **Provide the unique identifiers for your organization** policy (see Figure 15-27). In the text boxes provided, specify a unique identifier that will be associated with drives that are enabled with BitLocker. This identifier uniquely associates the drives with your company or department and is required for BitLocker to manage and update DRAs. After doing so, this identifier is automatically associated with any drives on which you enable BitLocker.

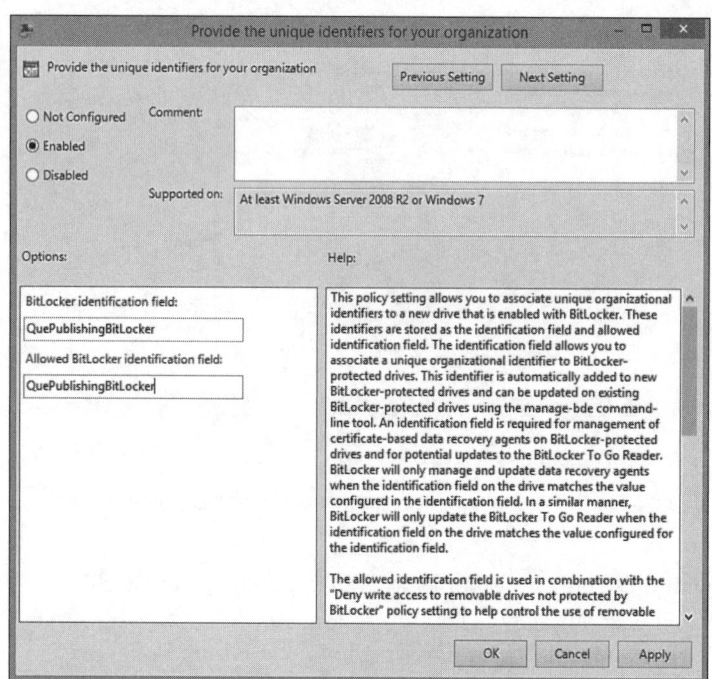

Figure 15-27 You need to provide a unique identifier to use a BitLocker DRA.

You can add this identifier to drives previously protected with BitLocker by opening an administrative command prompt and typing the following command:

```
manage-bde -SetIdentifier drive_letter
```

Where *drive_letter* is the drive letter for the BitLocker-protected drive. This utility sets the identifier to the value you've specified in Group Policy and displays a message informing you that this identifier has been set.

After you specify a DRA and the unique identifiers, you can configure policies in each subnode of the Computer Configuration\Administrative Templates\Windows Components\BitLocker Drive Encryption node of Group Policy that choose how BitLocker-protected drives can be recovered. Each of the three subnodes contains a similar policy setting that is shown for operating system drives in Figure 15-28. Enable each of these policies as required and select the **Allow data recovery agent** check box. Then configure the following options as required:

- **Allow 48-digit recovery password:** This drop-down list provides choices to allow, require, or do not allow a 48-digit recovery password. Use of a 48-digit recovery password improves DRA security.
- **Allow 256-bit recovery key:** This drop-down list provides choices to allow, require, or do not allow a 256-bit recovery key. Use of a 256-bit recovery key improves DRA security.
- **Omit recovery options from the BitLocker setup wizard:** Blocks the appearance of the recovery options previously shown in Figure 15-20; when enabled, these recovery options are determined by policy settings.
- **Save BitLocker recovery information to AD DS for operating system drives:** Enables you to choose the BitLocker recovery information that will be stored in AD DS.
- **Configure storage of BitLocker recovery information to AD DS:** Determines how much recovery information is stored in AD DS when you have selected the preceding option. You can choose to store recovery passwords and key packages or to store recovery passwords only.
- **Do not enable BitLocker until recovery information is stored to AD DS for operating system drives:** When this option is enabled, prevents users from enabling BitLocker unless the computer is attached to the domain and BitLocker recovery information can be backed up to AD DS.

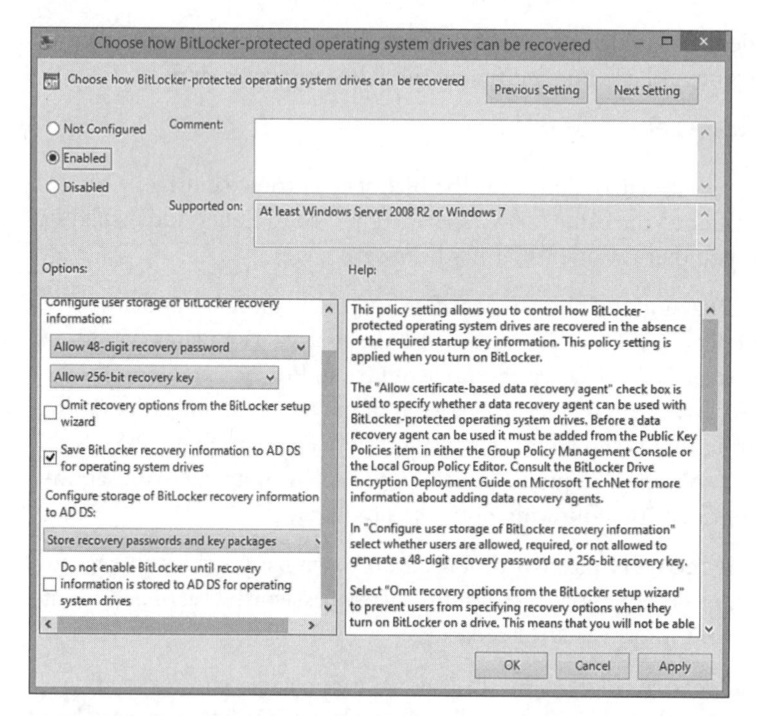

Figure 15-28 Group Policy provides these data recovery options for operating system drives.

Similar options are provided for fixed and removable data drives; the wording of the last policy setting changes to reflect the type of drive being configured.

NOTE BitLocker provides several additional DRA management options, including verification of the identification field and listing of configured DRAs. For more information, refer to “Using Data Recovery Agents with BitLocker” at http://technet.microsoft.com/en-us/library/dd875560(WS.10).aspx. For additional information on BitLocker as a whole, refer to “BitLocker Frequently Asked Questions (FAQ)” at http://technet.microsoft.com/en-us/library/hh831507.aspx.

Configuring Startup Key Storage

In the previous section, you learned about BitLocker drive encryption and using startup keys to unlock the drive for access. TPM is typically used for storing the startup key, but, as mentioned, you can use a USB flash drive or other removable disk instead. In this section, we discuss using USB drives for the storage of startup keys for BitLocker, as well as other methods for securing Windows on a mobile device, and how to protect your data from unauthorized access even when it is lost or stolen.

If the computer does not have a TPM, BitLocker uses either a USB flash drive or smart card containing a startup key. In this case, BitLocker provides encryption, but not the added security of locking keys with the TPM. When you use a USB drive to store your startup key, it is vital that you keep it secure, which means maintaining a backup. If your USB drive becomes corrupt, nonfunctional, or lost, you will permanently lose access to your Windows system.

Preparing a Computer Without a TPM to Use BitLocker

You can use a computer that does not have a TPM module if you have a USB flash drive to store the encryption keys and password. By default, Windows blocks an attempt to enable BitLocker on such a computer and displays the message shown in Figure 15-29. As mentioned in the error, you need to enable BitLocker without a TPM from Group Policy, as the following procedure describes:

Step 1. Access the Search charm and type `gpedit.msc` in the Search text box. Then select **gpedit.msc** from the list that is displayed.

Step 2. In the Local Group Policy Editor, navigate to **Computer Configuration\Administrative Templates\Windows Components\BitLocker Drive Encryption\Operating System Drives**.

Step 3. Double-click **Require additional authentication at startup**, enable this policy, select the **Allow BitLocker without a compatible TPM** option, and then click **OK**.

Step 4. Close the Local Group Policy Editor.

Step 5. In the Search charm, type `Gpupdate /force` in the search box and then press **Enter**. This forces Group Policy to apply immediately.

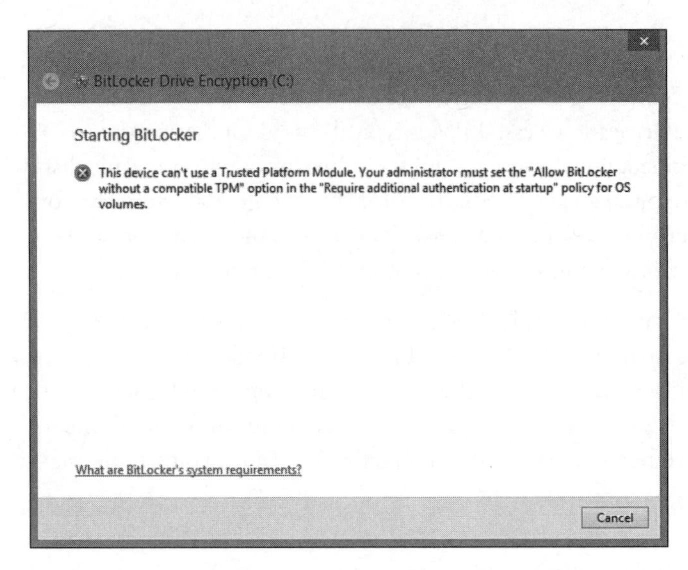

Figure 15-29 On a computer without a TPM module, Windows blocks BitLocker until the correct Group Policy is enabled to allow it.

After you complete this procedure, you are ready to enable BitLocker as described next. The procedure is similar to the procedure in the previous section, but without a TPM available, Windows presents a few different options. Begin the procedure as described in the section "Enabling BitLocker." Select **BitLocker Drive Encryption** from the Control Panel and select **Turn on BitLocker** for the drive.

Step 1. Windows checks your computer's configuration, and after a few seconds, the BitLocker Drive Encryption setup window appears, informing you that the computer will prepare your drive for BitLocker and then encrypt the drive.

Step 2. Click **Next**. Windows prepares your drive for BitLocker and informs you that an existing drive or unallocated free space will be used to enable BitLocker.

Step 3. Click **Next**. You are informed that you will no longer be able to use Windows Recovery Environment unless it is manually enabled and moved to the system drive.

Step 4. Click **Next**. The Choose how to unlock your drive at startup window appears, as shown in Figure 15-30. Choose to insert a USB flash drive or enter a password as desired.

The next step depends on the choice made here, shown in Figure 15-30. If you choose to insert a USB flash drive, insert the drive and click **Save**. If you choose to use a password, type and confirm a strong password when prompted. Then click **Next**.

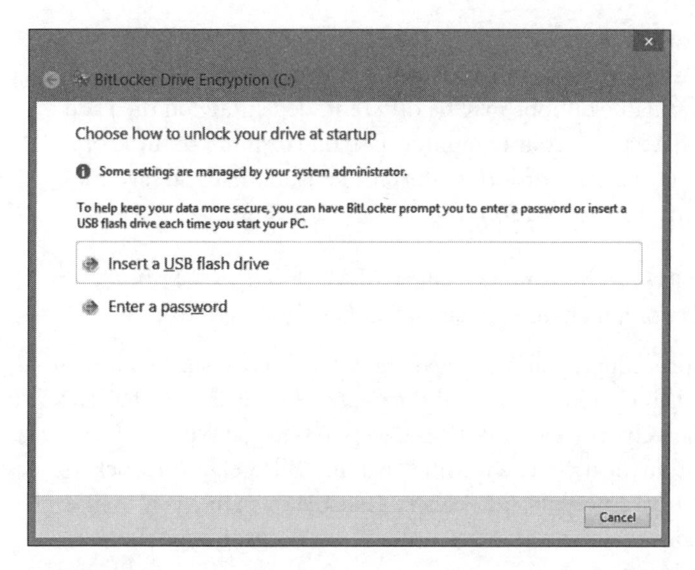

Figure 15-30 The BitLocker Drive Encryption applet in Control Panel offers two choices for unlocking your drive at startup.

Step 5. If you save it to a USB flash drive, you see the dialog box shown in Figure 15-31. Click **Save** and then click **Next**.

Key Topic

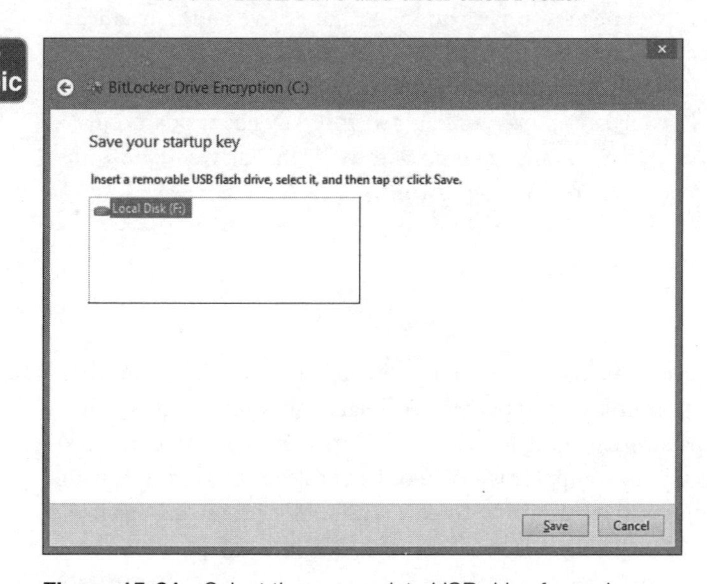

Figure 15-31 Select the appropriate USB drive for saving your password.

Step 6. The How do you want to back up your recovery key? page provides the options shown previously in Figure 15-20, as well as the additional option to use a USB drive. The available options may be different, depending on the valid location Windows detects for your computer. Use one or more of these options to save the recovery password. If you print it, ensure that you save the printed document in a secure location.

The remainder of the process is the same as using a TPM (see steps 8–11 in the "Enabling BitLocker" section), including restarting and encrypting the drive.

After you complete this procedure, you must have the USB drive to start your computer if you have chosen this option in step 4 of the previous procedure (refer back to Figure 15-30). Alternatively, you can use the recovery mode and type the recovery password that was automatically created while enabling BitLocker. BitLocker provides the BitLocker Drive Encryption Recovery Console to enable you to insert the USB drive that contains the recovery password. Or press **Enter**, type the recovery password, and press **Enter** again.

WARNING Ensure that you do not lose the recovery password. If you lose the recovery password, your Windows installation and all data stored on its partition are permanently lost. In that case, you need to repartition your hard drive and reinstall Windows. Consequently, you should create at least two copies of the password as described in the previous procedure and store them in a secure location. Do not leave the startup USB flash drive in your laptop bag; attach it to your key chain or store it elsewhere on your person. Note that you may end up with two USB drives—one with the startup key and the other with the recovery password.

Syskey Startup Keys

Another method used to protect Windows computers, included in Windows since NT 4.0 SP4, is Syskey. The Syskey utility encrypts the SAM database, which contains all the login credentials and passwords on the local system. Note that Syskey does not protect your data from access if your computer is stolen or lost because it encrypts only the SAM database, not your files or the hard drive. Syskey is useful for protecting against casual intrusion, however, by providing a layer of security to your login accounts.

If you have used EFS to encrypt files, or you have saved or cached credentials, Syskey also protects that information because your account login is used to unlock EFS files, your credentials stored in Credential Manager, and personal certificates. Syskey also protects the master key that Windows uses to unlock IPSec keys, computer keys, and Secure Sockets Layer (SSL) certificate keys.

Syskey can be used with a simple password, but the best level of security is to use a floppy disk or removable drive to store the startup key. The removable disk is then required to sign onto the computer and access any protected information. As with a BitLocker startup drive, you should take care to keep the floppy disk with your startup key secured, stored separately from the computer, and be sure to maintain a backup in case the primary one is lost or damaged. Use the following procedure to enable Syskey:

Step 1. Access the Search charm and type `syskey` in the search box. When you select it, Windows displays a UAC confirmation dialog. Select **Yes** to start the Syskey Wizard shown in Figure 15-32.

Figure 15-32 Securing the Windows Account Database.

Step 2. Select the **Update** button.

Step 3. On the Startup Key page (see Figure 15-33), you have the option of setting Password Startup or using a System Generated Password, which can be stored locally or on a floppy disk. In this case, use the most secure option, so select **Store Startup Key on Floppy Disk** and then click **OK**.

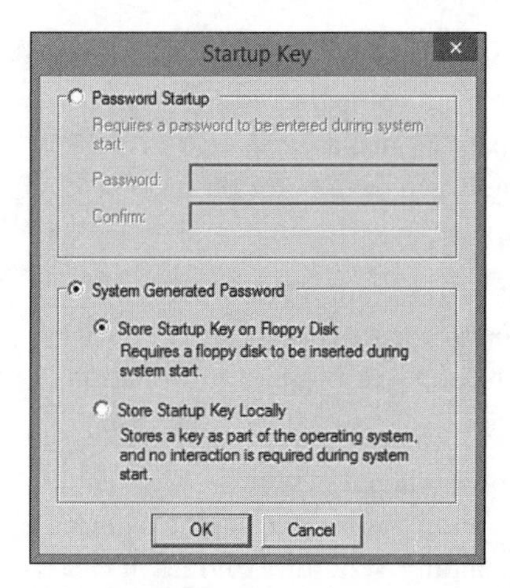

Figure 15-33 Storing the Syskey startup key on a floppy disk.

Step 4. The computer prompts you to enter the disk. Make sure the disk is in the drive and then click **OK**.

Step 5. After Windows writes the startup key to the floppy disk, you receive a message that the disk is now required to start up the computer.

Step 6. Finally, the Success dialog box is displayed, indicating that the Account Database Startup Key was changed.

The next time Windows starts, Syskey prompts you to enter the startup disk. You need to insert the disk with the startup key and click **OK** before Windows will load.

NOTE Although Syskey only stores your startup key on the A: drive, you can use a USB Flash drive if you do not have a floppy disk drive. Simply run the Disk Management tool, right-click on your USB drive, and select **Change Drive Letter and Paths.** On a computer with no floppy disk drive, you can assign the USB drive the letter A: and then run the Syskey utility to write your startup key there.

Configuring Remote Wipe

An issue with mobile devices is their portability and convenience also makes them easily lost or stolen. A lost computer in the wrong hands means not just the loss of the device, but possibly the loss of much more valuable information that the device contains. The computer could contain not only sensitive and confidential information, but also typically credentials, cached network information, and login accounts to a variety of cloud-based and business resources.

Remote Business Data Removal can remove or make corporate data inaccessible on the remote computer. It wipes only data that came from company resources, while leaving the user's personal content alone. This capability makes it easier for enterprises to allow knowledgeable workers to bring their own devices for business tasks and still maintain control over company resources.

When it becomes clear that a mobile device is lost and will not be recovered in a timely manner, the safest course of action would be to ensure that the entire device is reset to factory settings and wiped clean of any personal or business information it may contain.

Microsoft's Exchange ActiveSync system, used for mobile phones and now available for Windows 8.1 and Windows RT 8.1, has had support for remote wiping a device since its release. When used on mobile phones, including Windows Phones, it clears all data on the device. Administrators can perform a remote wipe on a managed device from the Exchange Administration Center (EAC), and users can even issue wipe commands themselves from the Outlook Web App user interface.

When used on Windows RT 8.1 and Windows 8.1, however, ActiveSync's Remote Wipe features does not delete all the data on the computer—only email, contacts, and calendar information stored in the Mail application.

Device Management with Windows Intune

Mobile devices, including devices running Windows 8.1 Pro and Windows RT 8.1, can be managed using Microsoft's Windows Intune Connector. The connector allows network administrators and even users to manage their Windows RT 8.1 and Windows 8.1 phone devices. The Intune Remote Wipe capability is not currently available for Windows 8.1 laptops, tablets, and computers, but many management and Remote Wipe capabilities are available for Windows RT 8.1.

Utilizing Exchange Active Sync extensions, Windows RT 8.1 can be managed through the System Center Configuration Manager and Intune. IT administrators can configure a policy such as

- Maximum failed password attempts
- Maximum inactivity time lock
- Minimum device password complex characters
- Minimum password length
- Password expiration
- Password history (number of passwords remembered)
- Number of failed logon attempts before device is wiped

For instance, administrators can enforce policies on Windows RT 8.1 devices that are enrolled in the Windows Intune service. Companies can then assist users who want to use their own devices to access company email and other resources. Once enrolled, administrators can configure devices to wipe themselves remotely if an invalid password is entered too many times. If the Windows RT 8.1 device is lost or stolen, the device automatically clears itself of all private data, settings, and the ability to access the organization after too many failed logon attempts.

Windows Intune can be configured to allow users to join the Intune environment from their own devices. Windows 8.1 supports this feature through the device management feature of the Workplace network.

To turn on device management, access the Settings charm, select **Change PC settings** and then **Network**. Under the Workplace option, enter the user ID assigned for the domain and then select **Turn on**, as shown in Figure 15-34. Windows confirms your credentials, contacts the Intune server, and registers the device. Users should be cautioned that the Intune administrators are granted additional control over the PC or tablet.

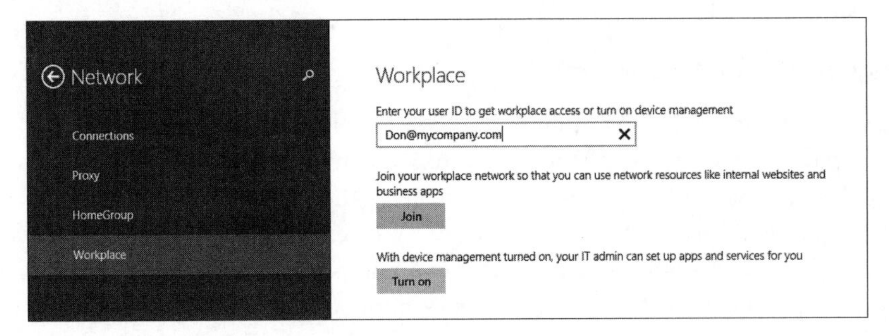

Figure 15-34 Turning on device management in Windows 8.1.

NOTE For more information about Windows Intune and managing mobile devices, see "Enabling Mobile Device Management with Windows Intune" at http://technet.microsoft.com/en-us/library/jj733654.aspx.

Configuring Location Settings

Recall from Chapter 2, "Installing Windows 8.1," that the initial installation of Windows 8.1 on a new computer does not prompt for time zone information; instead, you must select the time zone from the Date and Time dialog box. But Windows 8.1 has many other location configuration settings available, and many Windows RT 8.1 devices also include GPS devices to obtain even more specific location information for things such as mapping and searching. Windows Apps can make use of location settings to provide a more localized experience for Windows users.

The Windows Location Provider, as the subsystem is known, uses a combination of the computer's IP address, Wi-Fi network triangulation, and GPS information (when available) to calculate a current location. GPS data is generally the most accurate and reliable, but if enough Wi-Fi access points are available, very accurate location data can be obtained without GPS.

The location settings have been simplified for Windows 8.1. Users can enable or disable location for their profile, and administrators can disable location for all users on the computer. In addition to global location settings for the computer, location settings can also be applied for each Windows app that is location-aware.

Configuring System Location

The location settings for a Windows 8.1 computer control whether the Windows Location can be used for apps and enabled by users for their apps. To access the system location settings, use the Search charm and search for `location` in settings, or open the Control Panel and select **Location Settings**. Doing so opens a dialog box called Change location settings, as shown in Figure 15-35.

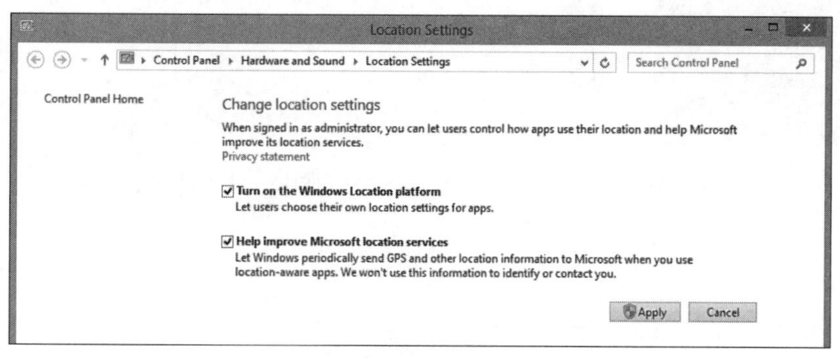

Figure 15-35 Enabling location settings.

By default, Windows Location is enabled, and users can choose location settings for their own apps and the Location Provider. Select the desired settings, click the **Apply** button, and confirm the UAC prompt when it is displayed.

With Windows 8.1, Microsoft has included global search results powered by Bing in an aggregated view of many content sources. Bing search uses Windows Location if it is enabled. Users can access location settings from the Start screen settings by selecting the **Settings** charm, clicking **Change PC settings**, selecting the **Privacy** option, and then selecting **Location**. If the **Turn on the Windows Location platform** option is disabled in the Control Panel, the Let Windows and apps use my location setting is disabled, as shown in Figure 15-36.

Figure 15-36 Location settings for apps is disabled unless the Windows Location platform is enabled in Control Panel.

Configuring Windows App Location Settings

Windows apps require permission before they can access location settings, so when a new app is installed, location for that app is disabled by default. When it tries to access location settings through the Windows Location platform, it first asks the user for permission. Desktop apps similarly do not have permission to access location information by default and prompt the user for permission before doing so.

Location permissions for each app can be modified by accessing the Settings charm from within the app, as shown in Figure 15-37.

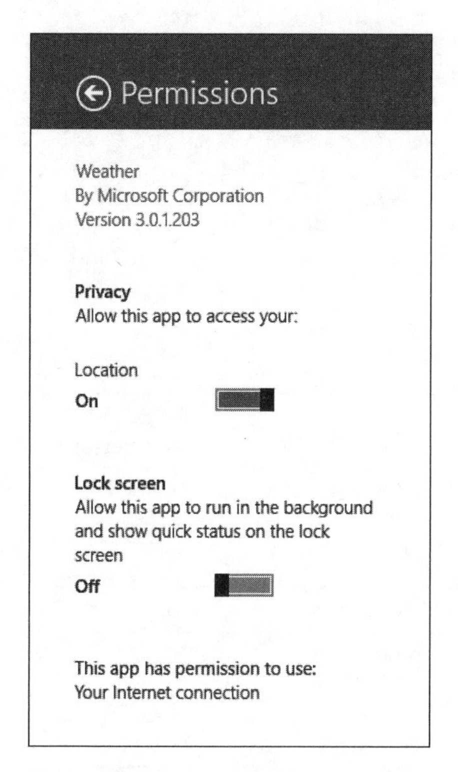

Figure 15-37 Configuring location settings permission for a Windows app. Apps that use Windows Location services can also be individually configured in the Privacy settings, as previously shown in Figure 15-36.

Location Settings Group Policies

You can control the settings for the Windows Location provider, as well as some aspects of how Windows Location information is used, by setting Group Policies.

To completely disable the use of the Windows Location provider and prevent users from enabling location settings in Control Panel or Windows apps settings, enable the policy **Turn off Windows Location Provider**. It is located in Group Policies under Computer Configuration\Administrative Templates\Windows Components\Location and Sensors\Windows Location Provider.

You can also disable scripting for location. The policy Turn off location scripting was first available in Windows 7; it blocks VBScript programs and other scripts from accessing the location information.

Exam Preparation Tasks

Review All the Key Topics

Review the most important topics in the chapter, noted with the key topics icon in the outer margin of the page. Table 15-4 lists a reference of these key topics and the page numbers on which each is found.

Table 15-4 Key Topics for Chapter 15

Key Topic Element	Description	Page Number(s)
Step List	Shows how to configure a client computer for using offline files	647-648
Figure 15-4	Shows how to use the Sync Center	651
Table 15-2	Describes Offline Files Group Policy settings	654
Table 15-3	Summarizes default Windows 8.1 power plans	661
Figure 15-15	Shows advanced power settings	664
Figure 15-17	Shows Power Options Group Policy settings	667
Paragraph	Describes how BitLocker functions	672
Step List	Shows how to enable BitLocker	674-677
Figure 15-23	BitLocker displays a distinctive icon when enabled	678
Figure 15-25	Shows management options for BitLocker-encrypted drive	682
Figure 15-27	Shows BitLocker Policy settings for providing a unique identifier to use a BitLocker DRA	684
Figure 15-31	Shows how to select the appropriate USB drive for saving your password	689
Paragraph	Describes Remote Wipe functions	692
Figure 15-35	Shows how to enable Location settings	695

Definitions of Key Terms

Define the following key terms from this chapter and check your answers in the Glossary:

Battery meter, BitLocker, BitLocker To Go, Cache, Data recovery agent (DRA), GPS, Hibernation, Offline files, Power plans, Remote Wipe, Sleep mode, Sync Center, Synchronization conflicts, Synchronizing files, Wi-Fi Direct, Wi-Fi triangulation, Windows Mobility Center

This chapter covers the following subjects:

- **Configuring Updates to Windows 8.1:** The Windows Update Control Panel applet provides a one-stop source for all types of updates available to Windows 8.1 users, by connecting to the Microsoft Windows Update website. This section shows you how to configure Windows Update, both from Control Panel and from the new Windows Update app on the Start screen.
- **Configuring Windows Update Policies:** Group Policy provides a series of settings that govern the use of Windows Update, both on the local computer and within an Active Directory domain. This section introduces the available policies, including the choices available for downloading and installing updates.
- **Reviewing Update History and Rolling Back Updates:** This section shows you how to determine what updates have been applied to your computer and how to remove problematic updates.
- **Updating Windows Store Applications:** In this section, you learn how to update Windows Store apps, keep apps up-to-date, and manage updates for apps.

CHAPTER 16

Configuring Windows Update

Whenever Microsoft releases a new version of its flagship Windows operating system, this version has already undergone many months (if not years) of testing, modifying, and updating of its source code, in an effort to optimize all facets of security, usability, and freedom from bugs and faults. But no matter how much beta testing is performed, no release is ever perfect; furthermore, as intruders discover new ways of cracking the code base, Microsoft must respond with fixes that overcome all these faults that mitigate the impact of these problems, hacks, and other difficulties. So for quite a few years now, Microsoft has released updates to Windows every second Tuesday of each month, popularly known as "Patch Tuesday." Occasional critical problems force Microsoft to issue updates at other times of the month. Further, hardware manufacturers provide driver updates from time to time; so do third-party software providers.

To facilitate release and deployment of these patches, fixes, and other updates, Microsoft operates the Windows Update website, which you can access in Windows 8 or 8.1 by typing `windows update` into the search charm. From this location, users of computers running any supported version of Windows can download and install all available updates. In addition, corporate networks can use servers running Windows Server Update Services (WSUS) as a repository for downloading, testing, and deploying updates to computers in the organization. For the 70-687 exam, Microsoft expects you to know how to use Windows Update to provide the proper updates to drivers, software programs, and operating system files.

"Do I Know This Already?" Quiz

The "Do I Know This Already?" quiz allows you to assess whether you should read this entire chapter or simply jump to the "Exam Preparation Tasks" section for review. If you are in doubt, read the entire chapter. Table 16-1 outlines the major headings in this chapter and the corresponding "Do I Know This Already?" quiz questions. You can find the answers in Appendix A, "Answers to the 'Do I Know This Already?' Quizzes."

Table 16-1 "Do I Know This Already?" Foundation Topics Section-to-Question Mapping

Foundations Topics Section	Questions Covered in This Section
Configuring Updates to Windows 8.1	1–2
Configuring Windows Update Policies	3–4
Reviewing Update History and Rolling Back Updates	5
Updating Windows Store Applications	6–7

1. Microsoft has packaged a set of updates designed to fix problems with specific Windows components or software packages such as Microsoft Office. What is this package known as?
   - **a.** A critical security update
   - **b.** An optional update
   - **c.** An update roll-up
   - **d.** A service pack

2. Your computer is connected to the Internet with a metered connection where you are charged according to the length of time you're connected. In the past, you've noticed that at peak times, Internet downloads are significantly slower and increase your connect time noticeably. You want to ensure that you receive all critical updates at a time of your choice when network usage is minimized. What option should you specify in the Windows Update settings?
   - **a.** Install updates automatically
   - **b.** Download updates but let me choose whether to install them
   - **c.** Check for updates but let me choose whether to download and install them
   - **d.** Never check for updates

3. Your Windows 8.1 Pro computer is shared among several users in your small office. Occasionally, others have informed you that the computer slows down and displays a message informing them to restart the computer to complete installing updates. This frequently occurs when they are performing important tasks that they do not want to interrupt. What should you do to ensure that all updates are installed but not until after business hours?
   - **a.** From the Windows Update Control Panel applet, click **Change settings** and then select the **Download updates but let me choose whether to install them** option.
   - **b.** From the Windows Update Control Panel applet, click **Change settings** and then select the **Check for updates but let me choose whether to download and install them** option.

c. In Group Policy, enable the Configure Automatic Updates policy and select the **2–Notify for download and for install** option.

d. In Group Policy, enable the Configure Automatic Updates policy and select the **3–Auto download and notify for install** option.

e. In Group Policy, enable the Configure Automatic Updates policy and select the **4–Auto download and schedule the install** option.

4. You have installed Windows Server Update Services on a server on your network, and you want to ensure that computers on the network do not attempt to access the Internet for downloading updates. What policy should you configure?

   a. Allow Automatic Updates immediate installation

   b. Turn on Software Notifications

   c. Specify intranet Microsoft update service location

   d. Enable client-side targeting

5. You would like to receive detailed information about an update that you think might be causing a problem on your Windows 8.1 computer. Which option should you select from the Windows Update applet?

   a. Check for updates

   b. View update history

   c. Restore hidden updates

   d. Installed updates

6. How are Windows Store apps updated?

   a. Using Windows Automatic updates

   b. Using the Store app

   c. Using either Windows Store or Automatic updates

   d. Using Group Policies

7. A user is having an issue updating an app from Windows Store. Where can you go to find more information on the error?

   a. The Store app Advanced settings dialog

   b. The Control Panel apps manager

   c. The PowerShell `Get-AppxLog` command

   d. Viewing the Windows System Event log

Foundation Topics

Configuring Updates to Windows 8.1

Chapter 2, "Installing Windows 8.1," introduced Windows Update briefly with regards to receiving the most recent installation files at the beginning of installation. Windows Update is a Control Panel applet that enables you to maintain your computer in an up-to-date condition by automatically downloading and installing critical updates as Microsoft publishes them. By default, your computer automatically checks for updates at the Windows Update website. Critical updates are automatically installed on a daily basis, and you are informed about optional updates that might be available. User input is needed only on the rare occasion for which you will receive an alert in the notification area of the taskbar. The following are several key features of Windows Update:

- Windows Update scans your computer and determines which updates are applicable to your computer. These updates include the latest security patches and usability enhancements that ensure your computer is kept as secure and functional as possible.
- Windows Update works in both the new Start screen and the classic desktop to deliver updates to all programs including the new Start screen apps.
- Updates classified by Microsoft as High Priority and Recommended can be downloaded and installed automatically in the background without interfering with your work.
- Windows Update informs you if a restart is required to apply an update. You can postpone the restart so that it does not interfere with activities in progress. Should an update apply to a software program with files in use, Windows 8.1 can save the files and close and restart the program.

In Windows 8.1, Windows Update supports the distribution and installation of the following types of updates:

- **Important updates:** Updates that Microsoft has determined are critical for a computer's security. These are typically distributed on Patch Tuesday, as already mentioned. In general, they fix problems that intruders can exploit to perform actions such as adding administrative accounts, installing rogue software, copying or deleting data on your computer, and so on.
- **Optional updates:** Potentially useful updates that are not security-related. They might include software and driver updates, language packs, and so on.

- **Update roll-ups:** Packaged sets of updates that fix problems with specific Windows components or software packages such as Microsoft Office.
- **Service packs:** Comprehensive operating system updates that package together all updates published since launch of the operating system or issuance of the previous service pack. In many cases, service packs also include new features or improvements to existing features.

Configuring Windows Update Settings

The System and Security category in Control Panel includes the Windows Update applet, which enables you to configure and work with the various options that are offered. Use the following procedure to work with Windows Update:

Step 1. From the Settings charm or the menu opened by right-clicking **Start**, access **Control Panel** and click **System and Security > Windows Update**. This opens Windows Update, as shown in Figure 16-1.

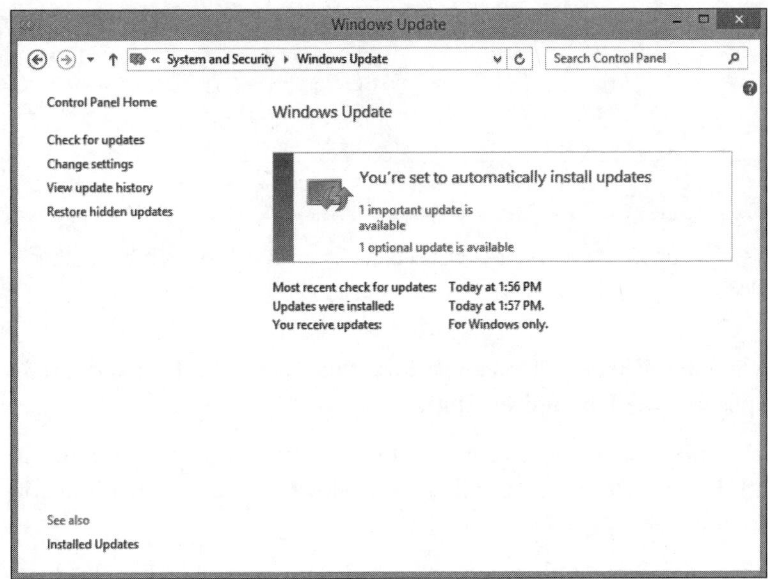

Figure 16-1 Windows Update enables you to select important and optional updates from this list.

Step 2. To perform a manual check for updates, click **Check for updates**. Windows Update checks on the Microsoft website. After a minute or two, it informs you of any available updates and offers to install them.

Step 3. To install optional updates, click the link that informs you of how many optional updates are available. You receive the Select the updates you want to install page shown in Figure 16-2. Select the check box in front of each update you want to install and then click **Install**. You return to the Windows Update applet, which tracks the progress of downloading and installing the updates.

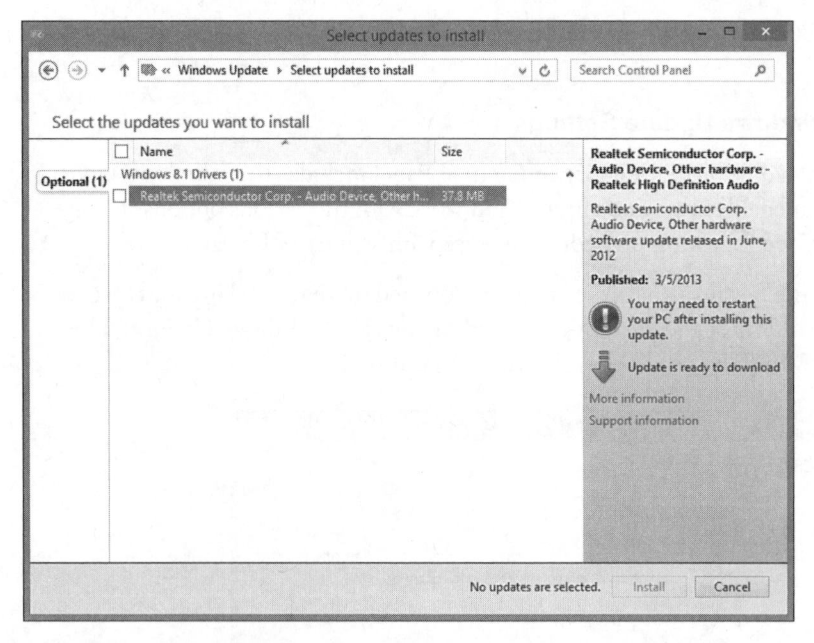

Figure 16-2 The Select the updates you want to install page enables you to choose whether to install optional updates.

Step 4. To modify the way Windows Update performs automatic checking and installation of updates, click **Change settings**.

Step 5. This action displays the Choose your Windows Update settings page shown in Figure 16-3. From the Important updates drop-down list, select one of the following options:

- **Install updates automatically (recommended):** Automatically downloads and installs updates at the day and time specified in the drop-down list boxes provided. You should ensure that your computer is on and connected to the Internet at the time you specify. This is the default setting.
- **Download updates but let me choose whether to install them:** Downloads updates when they are available and informs you by means of an icon in the notification area. You can select which updates should be installed by clicking this icon and choosing **Install**.

- **Check for updates but let me choose whether to download and install them:** Provides an icon in the notification area to inform you that updates are available from the Windows Update website. You can download these updates by clicking this icon and choosing **Start Download**. After the updates are installed, you can select **Install** to install them.
- **Never check for updates (not recommended):** You are not informed of any available updates and you must access the Windows Update website regularly to check for updates. You can do this by means of the link provided.

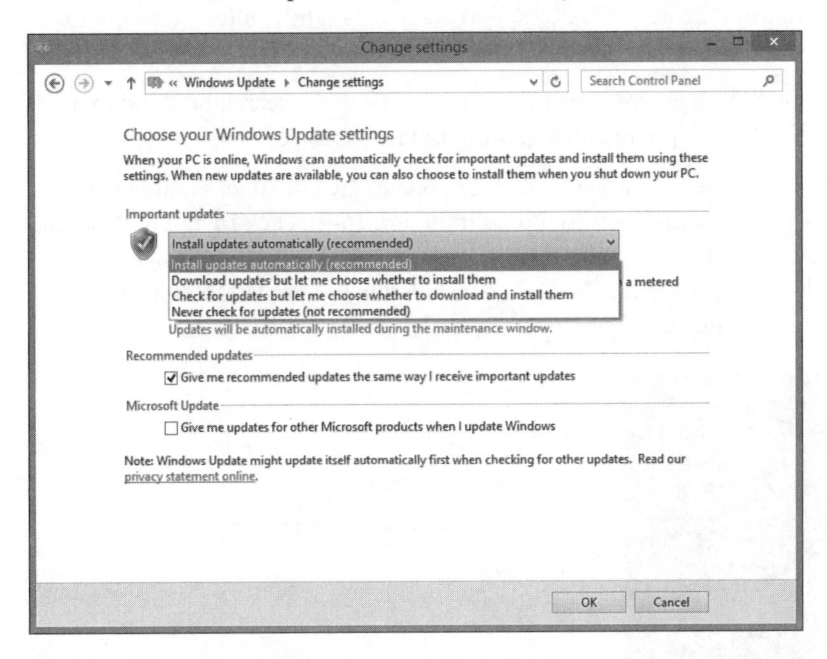

Figure 16-3 The Choose your Windows Update settings page enables you to configure options related to downloading and installation of updates.

Step 6. By default, Windows Update checks for both important and recommended updates including drivers as well as updated definition files for Windows Defender. To limit the check to critical updates only, clear the check box labeled **Give me recommended updates the same way I receive important updates.**

Step 7. If you want to receive updates for other Microsoft products such as Office or Outlook, select the check box labeled **Give me updates for other Microsoft products when I update Windows.**

Step 8. Click **OK** to return to Windows Update.

Step 9. Updates may become hidden if you have asked Windows not to notify you or install updates automatically. (You can hide updates by right-clicking an update from the page previously shown in Figure 16-2 and choosing **Hide update**.) To view and restore any hidden updates that might be available, select **Restore hidden updates**. On the page that appears, select the updates to be installed and then click **Restore**.

Step 10. When you are finished, click **OK**.

The procedure from the new Windows Start screen is slightly different, as the following steps show:

Step 1. Access the Search charm, type **`windows update`** in the search box, and then select **Windows Update settings** from the list displayed.

Step 2. Windows Update informs you whether updates are available, as shown in Figure 16-4. If an update is found (as in Figure 16-4), click **Install** to proceed. Windows Update then tracks the progress of downloading and installing the updates and displays a message when installation is complete. Restart your computer if requested.

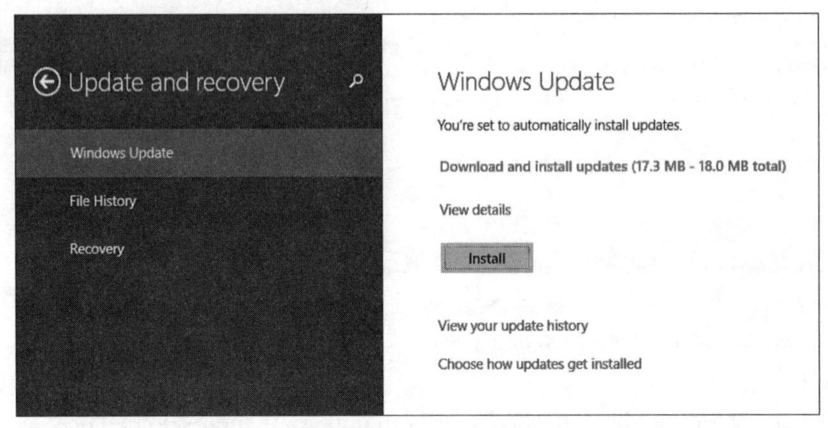

Figure 16-4 When run from the Windows Start screen, Windows Update informs you whether any updates are available.

Step 3. If you receive a `There aren't any updates to download automatically, but you can install other updates` message, other less important updates might still be available. To perform a manual check for updates, click **Check now**. Windows Update checks on the Microsoft website. After a minute or two, it informs you if any available updates are available and offers to install them.

Step 4. If you receive a message stating `There are some other updates available`, click **View details**. You are taken to the View details page shown in Figure 16-5. Select the desired updates by selecting their check boxes, or click **Select all available updates** to install all updates. Then click **Install** to install the selected updates. For more information on any available update, click **Details**.

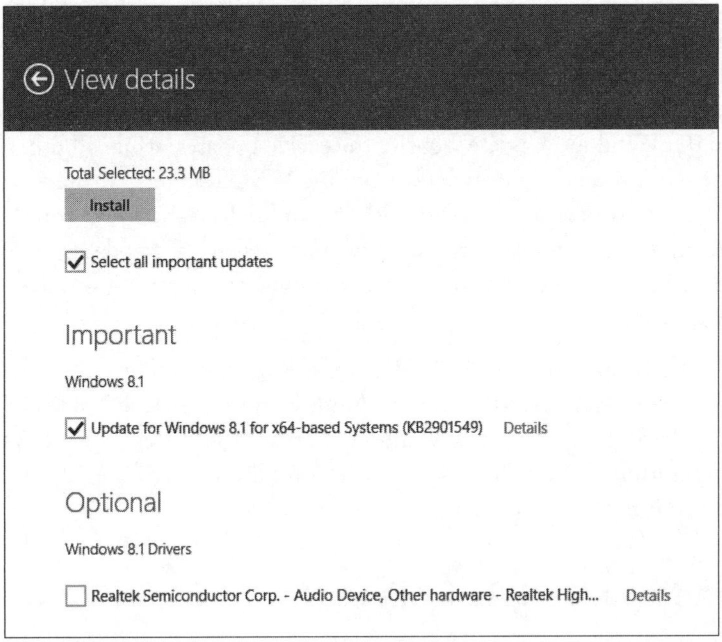

Figure 16-5 The View Details page lists the available important and optional updates, and enables you to select which updates should be installed.

> **TIP** When you type **`windows update`** in the Search charm, you also receive links to perform many of the actions discussed in this section without having to access the Windows Update Control Panel applet first.

Checking for New Updates

As already stated, Windows 8.1 checks for new updates automatically according to the settings already described that you have configured. As previously shown in Figure 16-1, the Windows Update Control Panel applet displays the time at which the most recent check for updates took place. It is easy to perform a manual check for new updates: simply click the **Check for updates** link on the left side of this applet. Windows Update accesses the Microsoft Update website and informs you whether any important or optional updates are available.

Using a WSUS Server with Windows 8.1

Windows Server Update Services (WSUS) is a server-based component that enables you to provide update services to computers on a corporate network without the need for individual computers to go online to the Microsoft Windows Update website to check for updates. It saves valuable bandwidth because only the WSUS server actually connects to the Windows Update website to receive updates, while all other computers on the network receive their updates from the WSUS server. Furthermore, WSUS provides network administrators with the ability to test updates for compatibility before enabling computers on the network to receive the updates, thereby reducing the chance of an update disrupting computer or application functionality across the network.

You can download WSUS 3.0 Service Pack 2 (SP2) from Microsoft and install it on a computer running Windows Server 2008 R2 or Windows Server 2012 R2. This most recent release of WSUS supports new Windows Server 2012 R2 and Windows 8.1 machines. Configuration of the WSUS server is beyond the scope of the 70-687 Windows 8.1 exam and is not discussed here.

Configuring Windows Update Policies

Group Policy in Windows 8.1 provides a series of policies that govern the actions performed by Windows Update. To view and configure these policies, open the Group Policy Object Editor by performing the following steps:

Step 1. Access the Search charm, type `gpedit.msc` in the search box and then select **gpedit.msc** from the list displayed.

Step 2. If you receive a User Account Control (UAC) prompt, click **Yes**.

Step 3. Navigate to the **Computer Configuration\Administrative Templates\Windows Components\Windows Update** node to obtain the policy settings shown in Figure 16-6.

Step 4. To use Group Policy to specify the behavior of automatic updates, double-click the **Configure Automatic Updates** policy setting (shown in Figure 16-6) to open the Configure Automatic Updates properties dialog box shown in Figure 16-7.

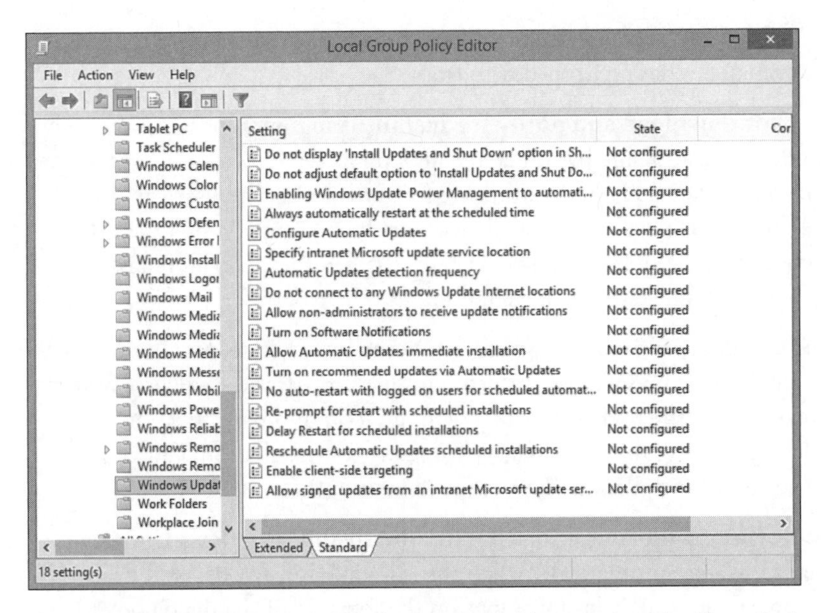

Figure 16-6 Group Policy in Windows 8.1 provides a series of settings that govern the operation of Windows Update.

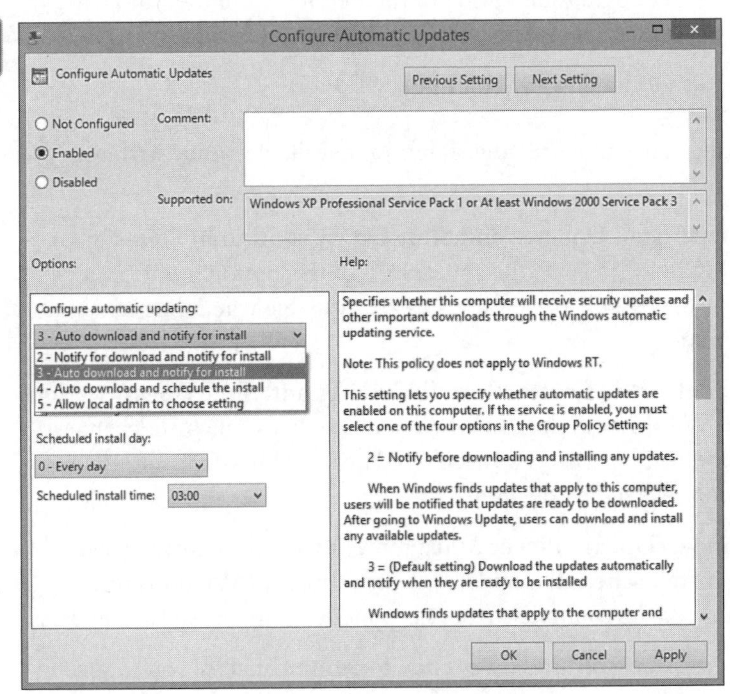

Figure 16-7 The Configure Automatic Updates dialog box offers four choices for configuring automatic updating of Windows 8.1 computers.

Step 5. Select **Enabled** and then choose one of the following settings from the Configure automatic updating drop-down list:

- **2–Notify for download and notify for install:** Windows Update notifies you when updates are available by displaying an icon in the notification area and a message stating that updates are available for download. The user can download the updates by clicking either the icon or the message. When the download is complete, the user is informed again with another icon and message; clicking one of them starts the installation.
- **3–Auto download and notify for install:** Windows Update downloads updates in the background without informing the user. After the updates have been downloaded, the user is informed with an icon in the notification area and a message stating that the updates are ready for installation. Clicking one of them starts the installation. This is the default option.
- **4–Auto download updates and schedule the install:** Windows Update downloads updates automatically when the scheduled install day and time arrive. You can use the drop-down lists on the left side of the dialog box to specify the desired days and times, which, by default, are daily at 3:00 a.m.
- **5–Allow local admin to choose setting:** This setting enables local administrators to select a configuration option of their choice from the Automatic Updates control panel, such as their own scheduled time for installations.

Step 6. Click **OK** to return to the Local Group Policy Editor.

The following describes several of the other important available policy settings shown in Figure 16-6:

- **Do not display "Install Updates and Shut Down" option in Shut Down Windows dialog box:** Prevents the appearance of this option in the Shut Down Windows dialog box, even if updates are available when the user shuts down his computer.
- **Do not adjust default option to "Install Updates and Shut Down" option in Shut Down Windows dialog box:** When this policy is enabled, changes the default shut down option from Install Updates and Shut Down to the last shut down option selected by the user.
- **Enabling Windows Update Power Management to automatically wake up the system to install scheduled updates:** Uses features of Windows Power Management to wake up computers from sleep mode to install available updates.
- **Specify intranet Microsoft update service location:** Enables you to specify a WSUS server for hosting updates from the Microsoft Windows Update website (as described in the previous section).

- **Automatic Updates detection frequency:** Specifies the length of time in hours used to determine the waiting interval before checking for updates at an intranet update server. You need to enable the Specify Intranet Microsoft Update Service Location policy to have this policy work.
- **Allow non-administrators to receive update notifications:** Enables users who are not administrators to receive update notifications according to other Automatic Updates configuration settings.
- **Turn on Software Notifications:** Enables you to determine whether users see detailed notification messages that promote the value, installation, and usage of optional software from the Microsoft Update service.
- **Allow Automatic Updates immediate installation:** Enables Automatic Updates to immediately install updates that neither interrupt Windows services nor restart Windows.
- **Turn on recommended updates via Automatic Updates:** Enables Automatic Updates to include both important and recommended updates.
- **No auto-restart with logged on users for scheduled automatic updates installations:** Prevents Automatic Updates from restarting a client computer after updates have been installed. Otherwise, Automatic Updates notifies the logged-on user that the computer will automatically restart in five minutes to complete the installation.
- **Re-prompt for restart with scheduled installations:** Specifies the number of minutes from the previous prompt to wait before displaying a second prompt for restarting the computer.
- **Delay Restart for scheduled installations:** Specifies the number of minutes to wait before a scheduled restart takes place.
- **Reschedule Automatic Updates scheduled installations:** Specifies the length of time in minutes that Automatic Updates waits after system startup before proceeding with a scheduled installation that was missed because a client computer was not turned on and connected to the network at the time of a scheduled installation, as previously specified by option 4 from the Configure Automatic Updating drop-down list.
- **Enable client-side targeting:** Enables you to specify a target group name to be used for receiving updates from an intranet server such as a WSUS server. The group name you specify is used by the server to determine which updates are to be deployed.
- **Allow signed updates from an intranet Microsoft update service location:** Enables you to manage whether Automatic Updates accepts updates signed by entities other than Microsoft when the update is found on an intranet Microsoft Update location.

For more information on these policies, consult the Help information provided on the right side of each policy's Properties dialog box.

Reviewing Update History and Rolling Back Updates

The Windows Update applet enables you to review your update history and roll back problematic updates, as described in the following procedure:

Step 1. Open the **Windows Update Control Panel** applet, as previously described.

Step 2. From the list of options on the left side of this page, select **View update history**. The Review your update history page shown in Figure 16-8 displays a list of the updates installed on your computer, including definition updates for Windows Defender. This page also indicates whether updates were successfully installed.

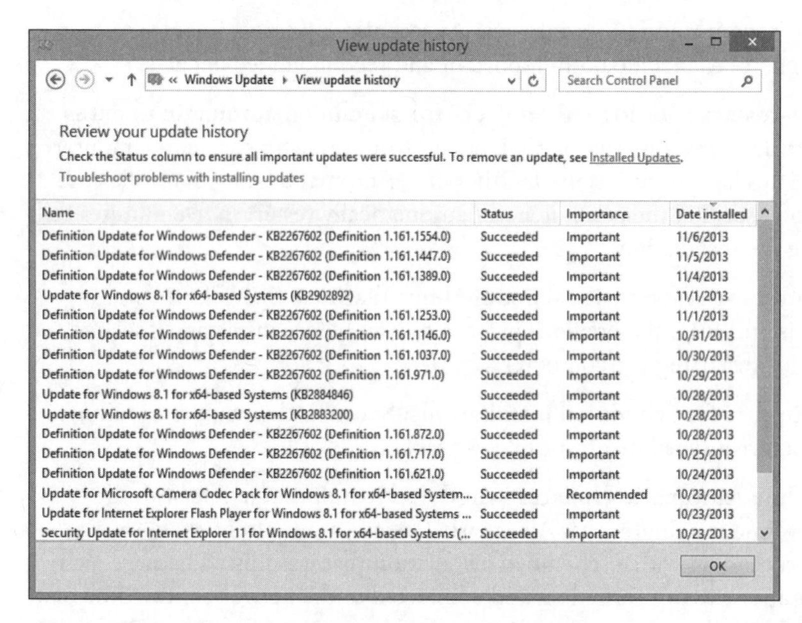

Figure 16-8 The Review your update history page displays all updates that have been installed on your computer.

Step 3. Double-click any update to provide detailed information, as shown in Figure 16-9.

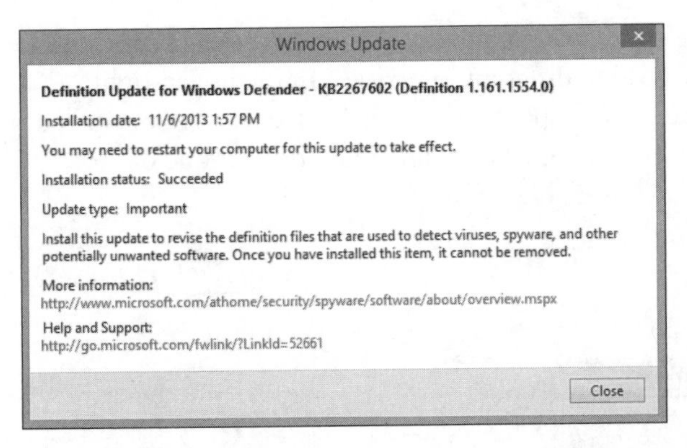

Figure 16-9 Windows Update provides information on all updates it has installed, as well as links to websites that you can refer to.

Step 4. If an update is causing problems and you want to remove it, click the **Installed Updates** link (found in the Review your update history page shown in Figure 16-8). On the Uninstall an Update page that appears, right-click the update you want to uninstall and select **Uninstall**. Confirm your intentions by clicking **Yes** in the message box that appears.

Updating Windows Store Applications

Windows 8.1 and Windows RT 8.1 give you access to apps for the first time. Thousands of apps are available from the Windows Store, and the latest version of Windows comes with several apps preloaded, such as the contacts app (People), Mail, Music, and others.

We discussed Windows Store apps in Chapter 5, "Installing, Configuring, and Securing Applications in Windows 8.1," and discussed some aspects of how the app store works and how to download apps and control access to apps in an organization. Windows apps are not updated automatically from Windows Update. Instead, app updates come from the Windows Store, and you can control when to perform updates and which apps you want updated when new versions are available.

NOTE You can tell if there are updates for Windows Store apps by just glancing at the Start screen. If updates are available, a number is displayed in the lower-right corner of the Store tile indicating how many apps have available updates.

From the Start screen, selecting the **Store** tile opens Windows Store and provides access to apps available for download in different categories. In the upper-right corner of the Store, a link appears if any updates are available for currently installed apps. For instance, in Figure 16-10, the Update (1) link tells you that one of the apps currently installed has updates available.

Figure 16-10 Windows Store and updates available count.

Click the **Update** link to display the apps that are ready for updating. Windows then presents the App Updates screen, similar to Figure 16-11, specifying the installed apps and selecting all of them for updating. From this screen, you can choose which updates to install. The check mark in the upper-right corner of the app's bar indicates that it is selected for updating. Left-click an app bar to select or deselect that app.

Figure 16-11 Windows Store app updates ready for installation.

When you are ready to install the updates, click the **Install** app command at the bottom of the screen. Windows proceeds to install updates for all the selected apps and provides progress of the installation for each app, as depicted in Figure 16-12. When all updates are installed, Windows displays `All of your apps have been updated`.

Figure 16-12 Progress of selected app updates.

Other Tools for Managing Windows App Updates

Windows 8.1 includes some command-line utilities and Group Policy options for managing Windows app updates. Recall from Chapter 5 that the Group Policy setting Turn off Automatic Download of updates stops Windows from automatically checking for app updates. Users need to manually check for updates using the Store app. Users can also adjust this setting on their own, if the Group Policy has not been set. The following procedure can be used to manage the setting:

Step 1. Open the **Store** app by clicking on its tile on the Start screen.

Step 2. Access the charms by swiping or moving your pointer to the right.

Step 3. Select the **Settings** charm and then click on **App updates**.

Step 4. From the App updates screen shown in Figure 16-13, you can select whether to automatically download updates.

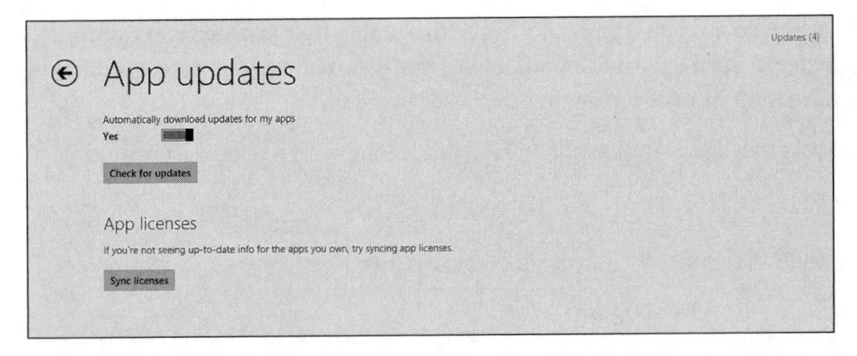

Figure 16-13 The App updates setting screen.

Step 5. If the setting is set to **No**, you can check for updates by selecting the **Check for updates** option.

You can install and remove Store apps by using PowerShell cmdlets, and you also can check the logs for app installations and updates. For instance, if an app update fails, you can enter `Get-Appxlog` to display the error messages to help troubleshoot the issue. An example is shown in Figure 16-14.

```
Windows PowerShell

C:\Users\hholt>PowerShell Get-Appxlog

Time                     ID        Message
----                     --        -------
6/6/2013 12:34:22 PM     301       The calling process is
                                   C:\Windows\system32\svchost.exe
6/6/2013 12:34:22 PM     603       Started deployment DeStage operation on a package
                                   with main parameter:
                                   Microsoft.ZuneMusic_1.3.59.0_x64__8wekyb3d8bbwe.
                                   See http://go.microsoft.com/fwlink/?LinkId=235160
                                   for help diagnosing app deployment issues.
6/6/2013 12:34:22 PM     10002     Creating Resiliency File C:\ProgramData\Microsoft\
                                   Windows\AppRepository\5afc26ed-c16f-4b48-9742-f799
                                   cd93e7a3_S-1-5-18_7.rslc for Remove Operation on
                                   Package
                                   Microsoft.ZuneMusic_1.3.59.0_x64__8wekyb3d8bbwe.
6/6/2013 12:34:22 PM     702       Windows cannot remove
                                   Microsoft.ZuneMusic_1.3.59.0_x64__8wekyb3d8bbwe
                                   because the current user does not have that
                                   package installed. Use Get-AppxPackage to see the
                                   list of packages installed.
6/6/2013 12:34:22 PM     605       The last successful state reached was De-Queued.
6/6/2013 12:34:22 PM     401       Deployment DeStage operation on Package
                                   Microsoft.ZuneMusic_1.3.59.0_x64__8wekyb3d8bbwe
                                   from:   failed with error 0x80073CF1. See
                                   http://go.microsoft.com/fwlink/?LinkId=235160 for
                                   help diagnosing app deployment issues.
6/6/2013 12:34:22 PM     404       error 0x80073CF1: AppX Deployment operation
                                   failed. The specific error text for this failure
                                   is: Windows cannot remove
                                   Microsoft.ZuneMusic_1.3.59.0_x64__8wekyb3d8bbwe
                                   because the current user does not have that
                                   package installed. Use Get-AppxPackage to see the
                                   list of packages installed.


C:\Users\hholt>_
```

Figure 16-14 Displaying the App error log using PowerShell.

These PowerShell commands generally apply to a single user profile. You can use elevated privileges, such as inside an administrative command prompt, to display additional information or take action on other user profiles.

Table 16-2 lists the set of Appx cmdlets available, along with a brief description of their use.

Table 16-2 PowerShell Cmdlets for Managing Windows Store Apps

Cmdlet Name	Description
`Add-AppxPackage`	Adds an app package to a user account
`Get-AppxLastError`	Gets the most recent error recorded from an app installation
`Get-AppxLog`	Displays the application log created during an app installation
`Get-AppxPackage`	Lists the app packages installed, or information about a specific app installed in a user profile
`Get-AppxPackageManifest`	Displays the manifest of an app package
`Remove-AppxPackage`	Removes an app package

Exam Preparation Tasks

Review All the Key Topics

Review the most important topics in the chapter, noted with the key topics icon in the outer margin of the page. Table 16-3 lists a reference of these key topics and the page numbers on which each is found.

Table 16-3 Key Topics for Chapter 16

Key Topic Element	Description	Page Number(s)
List	Describes types of updates handled by Windows Update	704
Figure 16-1	Shows available updates in Windows Update	705
List	Describes ways of configuring download and installation of updates	706-707
Figure 16-4	Shows how to install updates from the new Start screen	708
Figure 16-7	Shows how to configure Automatic Updates properties	711
List	Lists four Group Policy settings that control the downloading and installation of updates	712
Figure 16-10	Shows Windows Store app updates	716
Step List	Describes how to manage Windows app update settings	718-719

Definitions of Key Terms

Define the following key terms from this chapter and check your answers in the Glossary:

Service pack (SP), Update roll-up, Windows Server Update Services (WSUS), Windows Update

This chapter covers the following subjects:

- **Managing Disks and Volumes:** Windows 8.1 enables you to create several types of disk volumes on your computer. This section introduces you to these volume types and shows you how to create, manage, and troubleshoot problems with disks.
- **Managing File System Fragmentation:** If you edit and delete a large number of files on your computer, new files can become fragmented; in other words, they can be stored in several noncontiguous portions of your disk. This section shows you how to defragment your disks so that performance is kept optimum.
- **Managing Storage Spaces:** Storage Spaces is a recent technology innovation in Windows that helps solve the problems encountered when additional disk storage space is needed for a computer, or whenever multiple drives are needed to support space requirements. This section introduces Storage Spaces in Windows, the types of scenarios where you should consider using Storage Spaces, and how it is used and configured.

CHAPTER 17

Disk Management

Storage needs for computers have changed significantly over time. You could feed the data of hundreds of computers from just 10 years ago into a single computer today and still not fill its hard disk. Part of the reason is that today's data is much different than that of 10 years ago. It includes multimedia files, 20-plus megapixel images, extended attributes, complex formulas, and What You See Is What You Get (WYSIWYG) formatting. The result is that the size of a single file can be hundreds of megabytes (MB) or even several gigabytes (GB). So, although storage space has grown, the demand for storage space has increased along with it.

As the amount of information stored on hard disks and accessed across various types of networks has grown, information storage technology has kept pace. Windows 8, 8.1, and Windows Server 2012 R2 introduce the new Storage Spaces technology, which enables you to create cost-effective, highly available, scalable, and flexible storage systems by using virtualization technology to create pools of storage on groups of physical disks. Microsoft expects you to be up-to-date on this latest in information storage technologies.

"Do I Know This Already?" Quiz

The "Do I Know This Already?" quiz allows you to assess whether you should read this entire chapter or simply jump to the "Exam Preparation Tasks" section for review. If you are in doubt, read the entire chapter. Table 17-1 outlines the major headings in this chapter and the corresponding "Do I Know This Already?" quiz questions. You can find the answers in Appendix A, "Answers to the 'Do I Know This Already?' Quizzes."

Table 17-1 "Do I Know This Already?" Foundation Topics Section-to-Question Mapping

Foundations Topics Section	Questions Covered in This Section
Managing Disks and Volumes	1–8
Managing File System Fragmentation	9–10
Managing Storage Spaces	11–13

1. Your hard disk is configured as a basic disk, and you do not want to convert it to dynamic storage because you want to enable dual-booting. Which of the following partition types can you configure on the disk? (Choose all that apply.)
   a. Simple volume
   b. Primary partition
   c. Extended partition
   d. Spanned volume
   e. Mirrored volume
   f. Striped volume
   g. Logical drive
   h. RAID-5 volume

2. You have added a new 5 TB hard disk to your Windows 8.1 computer and initialized it. You now want to create a single volume that uses the entire space on the disk, so you start the DiskPart tool from an administrative command prompt. On attempting to create the volume, you receive an error. Which of the following commands should you execute first?
   a. `convert basic`
   b. `convert dynamic`
   c. `convert gpt`
   d. `convert mbr`

3. You want to add additional space to your D: partition so that you can store a large number of digital images. You do not want to add an additional drive letter, so you run the Extend Volume Wizard. What type of volume are you creating?
   a. Simple volume
   b. Spanned volume
   c. Mirrored volume
   d. RAID-5 volume

4. Which tab of a volume's Properties dialog box enables you to check the volume for errors?

   a. General
   b. Tools
   c. Hardware
   d. Quota
   e. Customize

5. You have moved a hard disk containing several years' worth of digital images from your old computer running Windows XP to your new Windows 8.1 computer. On starting Disk Management, you notice that the disk status is listed as Unknown. What should you do?

   a. Right-click the disk and choose **Initialize**.
   b. Right-click the disk and choose **Resynchronize**.
   c. Right-click the disk and choose **Properties**. Then check the disk for errors and perform corrective actions according to the output.
   d. Right-click the disk and choose **Format**. Then restore all the images from backup.

6. Which of the following RAID technologies are fault-tolerant? (Choose all that apply.)

   a. Spanning
   b. Striping
   c. Mirroring
   d. Striping with parity

7. You have four hard disks in your computer and want to create a RAID-5 volume. The amount of free space on the disks is as follows: Disk 0, 200 GB; disk 1, 150 GB; disk 2, 80 GB; disk 3, 100 GB. What is the maximum size of RAID-5 volume that you can create?

   a. 240 GB
   b. 320 GB
   c. 450 GB
   d. 530 GB

8. You want to ensure that your Windows 8.1 computer will always boot, so you decide that you want to implement fault tolerance on your system and boot volumes. Your computer has two hard disks. You start the **DiskPart** command and select the **system/boot** volume. What command should you use?

   a. `create volume stripe disk=0,1`

   b. `create volume mirror disk=0,1`

   c. `create volume raid disk=0,1`

   d. `add disk 1`

9. One morning, you start the Optimize Drives utility to optimize your C: drive. This drive is 250 GB in size with a free space of 22 GB. After lunch, this utility is still running, and you start to wonder what else you should do to optimize disk usage. Which of the following can you do to improve the rate of disk response? (Choose all that apply.)

   a. Run the Disk Cleanup utility.

   b. Back up old data and then delete this data from the drive.

   c. Uninstall several applications whose files are on this drive.

   d. Just let the Optimize Drives utility run overnight.

10. Your computer has three volumes: C:, D:, and E:. You want to optimize the C: and D: volumes only from the command line. What command will do this? (Choose two; each is a complete solution.)

   a. `defrag c: d:`

   b. `defrag /e:`

   c. `defrag /E e:`

   d. `defrag /E c: d:`

11. You have created a storage pool on a Windows 8.1 computer from two physical drives, each with 500 GB capacity. What is the maximum size you can specify for a storage space created from this pool?

   a. 1000 GB

   b. 500 GB

   c. 250 GB

   d. No limit

12. You are planning to use Storage Spaces in Windows and would like to use parity resiliency because it makes the most efficient use of disk capacity. How many drives must exist (minimum) in the storage pool?

    a. two

    b. three

    c. five

    d. one

13. You have two storage spaces, called "movies" and "music," created from a single storage pool. The total pool capacity is 500 GB, so you have created each storage space to use 250 GB size (maximum). You have only used 10% of the pool space, but you now need to copy a 300 GB file to the "movies" storage space. What is the easiest way to configure storage spaces to be able to copy the file?

    a. Delete the "music" storage space on one of the storage spaces and expand the "movies" storage space.

    b. Add an additional drive to the storage pool.

    c. Just copy the file because there is room in the storage pool.

    d. Increase the size of the "movies" storage space.

Foundation Topics

Managing Disks and Volumes

Windows 8.1 offers several tools and utilities that assist you in working with disks and volumes, including removable disks. We discuss configuring policies with removable disks later in this chapter. You can use the Computer Management Microsoft Management Console (MMC) snap-in or the DiskPart command-line utility to manage disks. We introduced the DiskPart utility in Chapter 7, "Configuring Hyper-V," with regard to creating virtual hard disks (VHDs); here we discuss them in detail.

We introduced the Computer Management tool in Chapter 1, "Introducing Windows 8.1," and have mentioned its use in several other chapters of this book. This tool includes the Disk Management snap-in, which enables you to manage disks and other storage devices in Windows 8.1. To open Computer Management, access the Administrative Tools Control Panel applet, which is found in the System and Security category of Control Panel. If you have enabled the Administrative Tools feature on the Start screen, simply click the tile for **Computer Management** from this location. In Windows 8.1, you can simply right-click **Start** and choose **Computer Management** from the menu that appears.

Windows 8.1 also enables you to open the Disk Management snap-in from its own console by right-clicking **Start** and choosing **Disk Management** from the menu that appears. Disk Management opens in its own console, as shown in Figure 17-1.

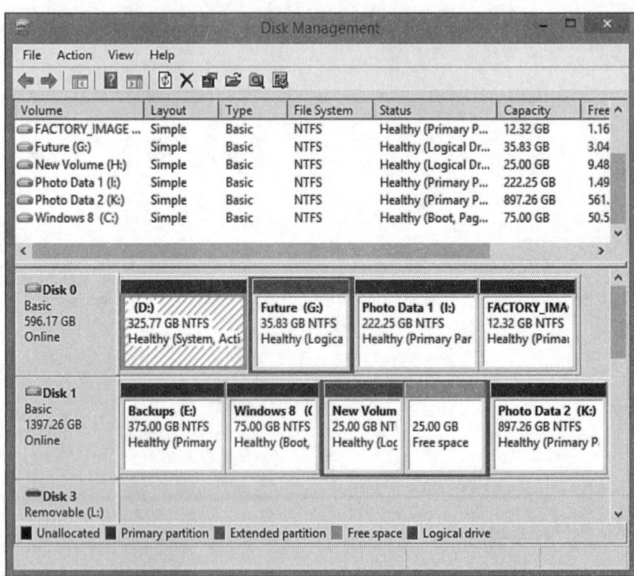

Figure 17-1 The Disk Management tool contains the main administration utilities for disk devices.

The following list summarizes the major actions you can perform from the Disk Management snap-in:

- **Create dynamic disks:** Disks can be either basic (the default) or dynamic. You can convert a basic disk to a dynamic disk but you cannot change back. Your only avenue to revert to a basic disk is to delete all volumes on the dynamic disk, lose the data, create a new basic volume, and restore the data from a backup.
- **Create volumes:** You can create several types of volumes on a dynamic disk. Microsoft provides a wizard to assist you in creating these volumes.
- **Extend volumes:** You can add additional unallocated space on a disk to an existing volume. Windows 8.1 provides the Extend Volume Wizard to assist you in this action.
- **Shrink volumes:** You can reduce the size of a volume to generate unallocated space for creating or extending a different volume.
- **Display properties of disks and volumes:** For disks, you can obtain the same information as provided by Device Manager. For volumes, you can obtain information about free space and device properties. This feature also lets you optimize (defragment) the volume, share the volume, configure an access control list (ACL), back up all files on the volume, and create shadow copies of files and folders within the volume.

Basic and Dynamic Disks

When you first install Windows 8.1, the hard disk on which you install Windows is set up as a basic disk. When you add a brand new hard disk to your computer, this disk is also recognized as a basic disk. This disk type is the one that has existed ever since the days of MS-DOS. Starting with Windows 2000, Microsoft offered a new type of disk called a dynamic disk. This disk type offers several advantages over the basic disk, including the following:

- You can create specialized disk volumes on a dynamic disk, including spanned, striped, mirrored, and RAID-5 volumes. Basic disks are limited to primary and extended partitions, and logical drives.
- You can work with and upgrade disk volumes on the fly, without the need to reboot your computer.
- You can create an almost unlimited number of volumes on a dynamic disk. A basic disk can hold a total of only four primary partitions, or three primary plus one extended partition.

Dynamic disks have their disadvantages, however:

- The disk does not contain partitions or logical drives and therefore can't be read by another operating system.
- On a multiboot computer, the disk is not readable by operating systems other than the one from which the disk was upgraded.
- Laptop computers do not support dynamic disks.

Besides a disk type, all disks have one of two partition styles:

- **Master boot record (MBR):** Uses a partition table that describes the location of the partitions on the disk. The first sector of an MBR disk contains the master boot record plus a hidden binary code file that is used for booting the system. This disk style supports volumes of up to 2 terabytes (TB) with up to four primary partitions or three primary partitions plus one extended partition that is subdivided into any number of logical drives.
- **GUID partition table (GPT):** Uses Extensible Firmware Interface (EFI) to store partition information within each partition, and includes redundant primary and backup partition tables to ensure structural integrity. This style is recommended for disks larger than 2 TB in size and for disks used on Itanium-based computers. Not all previous Windows versions can recognize this disk style, however.

When you add a new disk of less than 2 TB size, it is added as an MBR disk. You can convert an MBR disk to a GPT one using either Disk Management or the DiskPart tool, provided there are no partitions or volumes on the disk. To use Disk Management, right-click it and choose **Convert to GPT Disk**. To use DiskPart, proceed as follows:

Step 1. Open an administrative command prompt, type `DiskPart`, and accept the User Account Control (UAC) prompt. The DiskPart command window opens.

Step 2. Type `list disk` to get the disk number of the disks on your system.

Step 3. Type `select disk n` where *n* is the number of the disk you want to convert.

Step 4. Type `convert gpt`. DiskPart informs you that it has successfully converted the selected disk to GPT format.

If you want to convert a GPT disk back to MBR, the procedures are the same. You must back up all data and delete all volumes on the disk before performing the conversion. In Disk Management, right-click the disk and choose **Convert to MBR Disk**. In DiskPart, use the same steps and type `convert mbr` in the last one.

NOTE For more information on using GPT disks, refer to "Using GPT Drives" at http://msdn.microsoft.com/en-us/library/windows/hardware/gg463524.aspx.

Working with Basic Disks

When you first install Windows 8.1 on a new computer or add a new disk to an existing Windows 8.1 computer, the disk appears in Disk Management as a basic disk. Windows 8.1 enables you to create a new partition (aka a simple volume) from the free space on a new or existing disk. This partition can be a primary or extended volume or a logical volume. Keep in mind that a single basic disk can contain up to four primary partitions or three primary partitions plus an extended partition; the extended partition can contain any number of logical drives. Use the following procedure to create a partition:

Step 1. Right-click **Start > Disk Management** to open the Disk Management snap-in. Alternatively, you can open Computer Management as already discussed and then select **Disk Management** in the left pane.

Step 2. Locate the disk in the right pane that contains the unallocated space where the new volume will reside.

Step 3. Right-click the unallocated space of the disk and select **New Simple Volume** from the context menu.

Step 4. The New Simple Volume Wizard starts. Click **Next**.

Step 5. On the Specify Volume Size page, type the size of the partition in megabytes and then click **Next**.

Step 6. On the Assign Drive Letter or Path page shown in Figure 17-2, accept the drive letter provided or use the drop-down list to select a different letter. Then click **Next**.

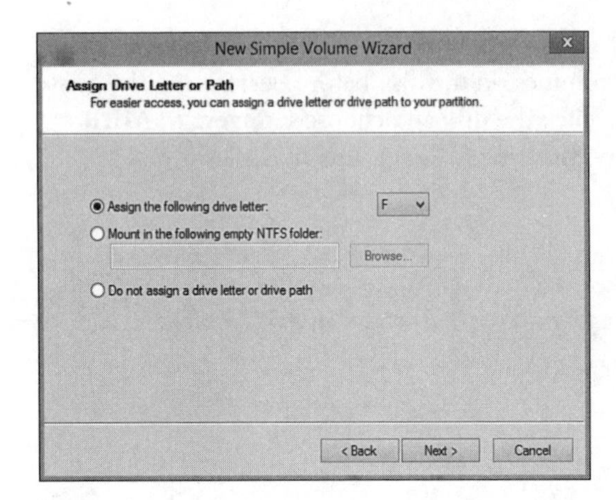

Figure 17-2 You can assign a drive letter to your partition or mount it in an empty NTFS folder.

Step 7. On the Format Partition page shown in Figure 17-3, choose the file system (FAT, FAT32, or NTFS) to format the partition. Provide a volume label name or accept the default of `New Volume` (this name will appear in the Computer window). If formatting with NTFS, you can modify the allocation unit size and/or enable file and folder compression. When done, click **Next**.

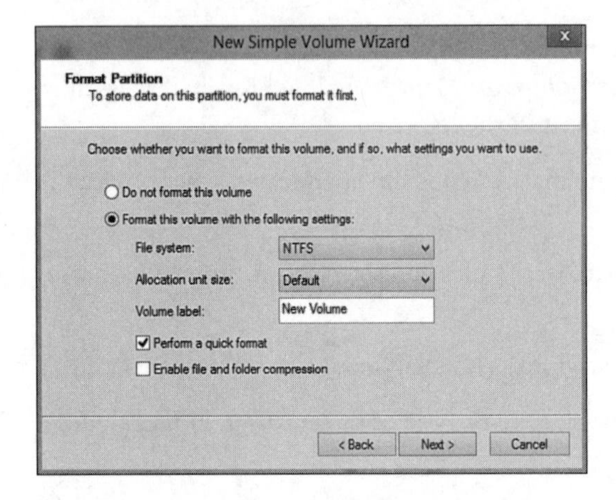

Figure 17-3 You are given several choices for formatting a new partition.

Step 8. Review the information provided on the completion page and then click **Finish**. Windows 8.1 creates and formats the partition and displays its information in the Disk Management snap-in.

On a basic disk, Disk Management also enables you to perform several other management activities. You can extend, shrink, or delete volumes as necessary. Extending a volume adds any unallocated space to the volume. Right-click the volume and choose **Extend Volume**. The Extend Volume Wizard informs you what space is available and enables you to add additional space or select a smaller amount of space, as shown in Figure 17-4. Modify the amounts in megabytes as required, click **Next**, and then click **Finish** to extend the volume.

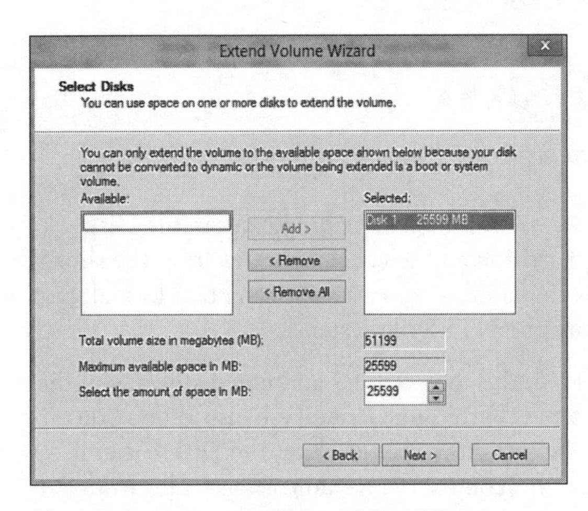

Figure 17-4 The Extend Volume Wizard helps you extend a volume on a basic or dynamic disk.

NOTE If you add additional space on another disk from the Available column in the Extend Volume Wizard, you create a spanned volume. The wizard asks you to convert the disks to dynamic storage. More about this later in this chapter.

Shrinking a partition enables you to free up space to be used on a different partition. To do so, right-click the desired partition and choose **Shrink Volume**. In the Shrink (Volume) dialog box shown in Figure 17-5, type the amount of space by which you want to shrink the volume (note the size after shrink to avoid overshrinking the volume). Then click **Shrink**.

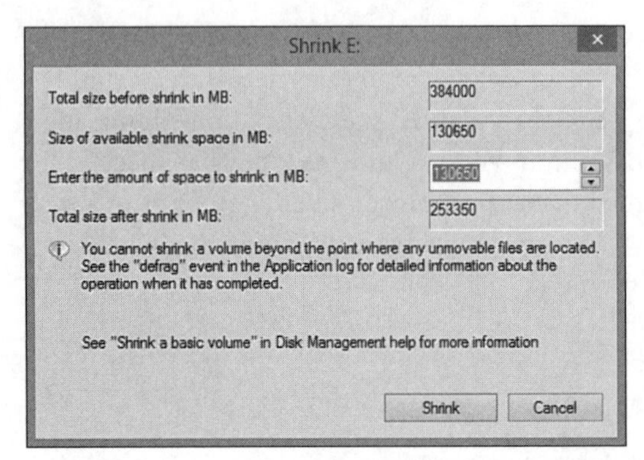

Figure 17-5 The Shrink (Volume) dialog box enables you to shrink a partition or volume.

To view how a partition is configured, you can look at its properties in the Disk Management utility. Right-click the partition and select **Properties** from the shortcut menu. The Properties dialog box that appears has the following tabs (not all tabs appear if the disk is not formatted with the NTFS file system):

- **General:** As shown in Figure 17-6, this tab provides an immediate view of the space allocation on the disk in a pie chart. The General tab also allows you to type a volume name and to click a button that executes the Disk Cleanup graphical utility. This utility enables you to remove unnecessary files from your disk such as the Temporary Internet Files folder, downloaded program install files, and the Recycle Bin.

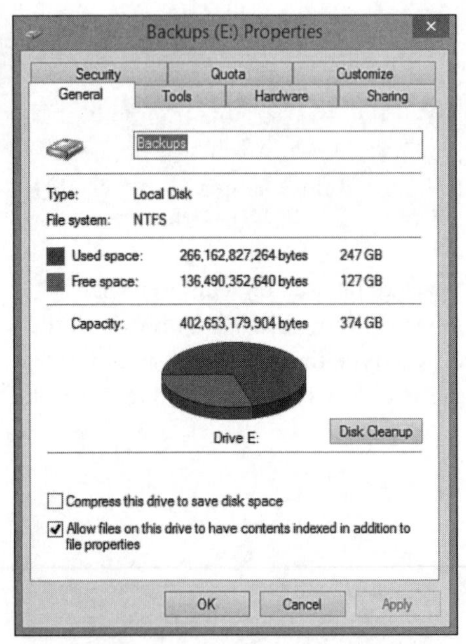

Figure 17-6 A volume's Properties dialog box displays its space allocation.

- **Tools:** This tab has the following two buttons:
  - **Check:** Displays an Error Checking dialog box that enables you to click **Scan drive**, which executes the GUI version of Chkdsk.
  - **Optimize:** Executes the GUI version of Defrag.
- **Hardware:** Displays the storage device hardware for the computer. You can obtain properties for any device, similar to that obtained from Device Manager, by selecting it and clicking **Properties**.
- **Sharing:** Enables you to share the disk so that others can access information on it, similar to that discussed for folders in Chapter 11, "Configuring and Securing Access to Files and Folders." Doing this for the entire drive is not considered a good practice. It is generally unnecessary because the computer automatically generates an administrative share for each partition when Windows starts.
- **Security:** Enables you to assign access permissions to files and folders on the disk, similar to those discussed in Chapter 11.
- **Quota:** Enables you to assign disk quotas to users on the disk, as discussed in Chapter 11. This lets you limit the amount of space used on the disk by an individual user, who will receive a `Disk Full` message if he attempts to use more space than assigned to his quota.
- **Customize:** Enables you to optimize folders on the disk for purposes such as general items, documents, pictures, music, or videos. You can also choose to display a different icon that will appear in the Computer window or restore default settings.

You can delete a logical drive or partition easily from within the Disk Management utility. Simply right-click the logical drive and select **Delete Volume** from the shortcut menu, as depicted in Figure 17-7. A prompt appears to verify that you want to delete the logical drive or partition. When you click **Yes**, Windows 8.1 deletes the drive or partition. Windows 8.1 prevents you from deleting the system partition, the boot partition, or any partition that contains an active paging file. Extended partitions can be deleted only if they are empty of data and logical drives.

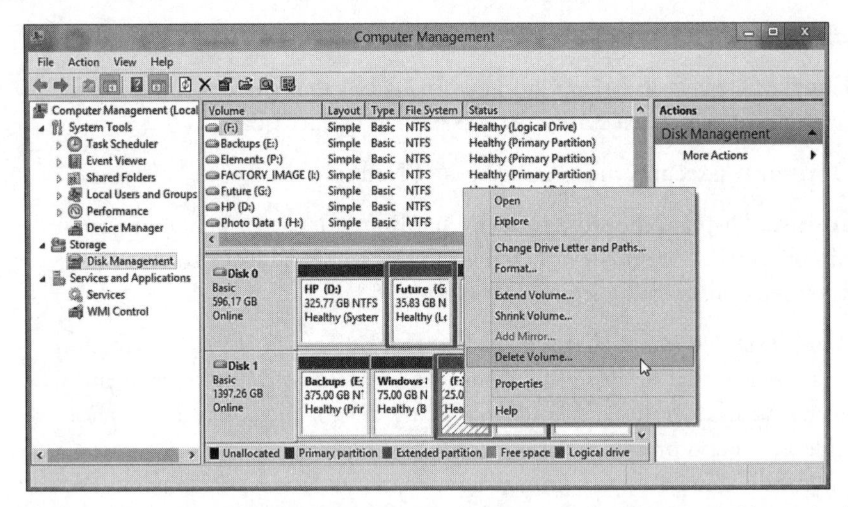

Figure 17-7 The Disk Management utility enables you to delete a partition or logical drive.

Converting Basic Disks to Dynamic

The process to convert a basic disk to a dynamic disk requires that you have a minimum of 1 MB of available space on the disk. Best practices state that when you make changes to a disk configuration, you should back up the data before starting, just in case you need to restore it after you are finished. Even so, converting a basic disk to a dynamic disk should not have any effect on your data.

You can convert a basic disk to dynamic at any time. Any partitions that are on the disk are converted to simple volumes in this process. To perform a conversion, you must be logged on as an administrator of the computer.

Step 1. In Computer Management, right-click the disk to be converted to dynamic and choose **Convert to Dynamic Disk**.

Step 2. If more than one hard disk is present, you receive the dialog box shown in Figure 17-8. Select any additional disks that you want to convert to dynamic and then click **OK**.

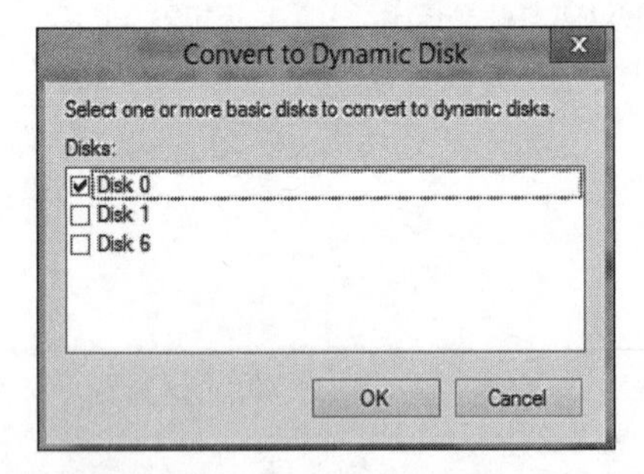

Figure 17-8 You can convert any or all of your disks to dynamic storage at the same time.

Step 3. The Disks to Convert dialog box shows you the disks that will be converted. Click **Convert** to proceed.

Step 4. Disk Management warns you (see Figure 17-9) that you will be unable to start installed operating systems except the current boot volume. Click **Yes** to proceed.

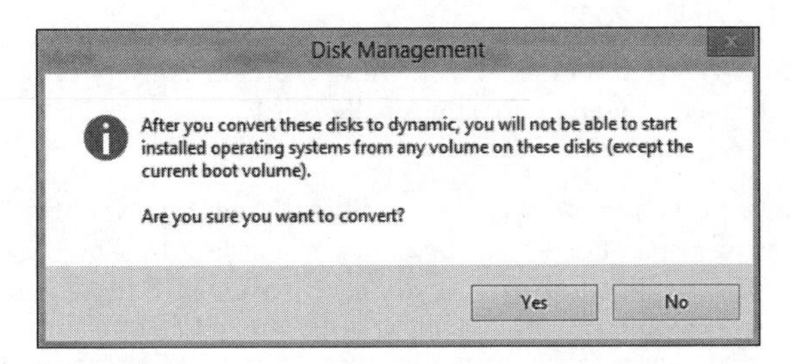

Figure 17-9 You are warned that you will be unable to start other operating systems if you convert to dynamic storage.

After the confirmation in step 4, the disk is converted to dynamic, and the display in Disk Management is updated accordingly.

To convert a dynamic disk back to basic, you must first back up all data on the disk and delete all volumes. Then right-click the disk in Computer Management and choose **Convert to Basic Disk**. The conversion proceeds and the display in Disk Management is updated within a few seconds.

Working with Dynamic Disks

When you convert a basic disk to a dynamic disk, the existing partitions are converted to simple volumes, and fault-tolerant volumes are converted into dynamic volumes. Dynamic volumes can be changed on the fly, as the name "dynamic" implies. A dynamic volume is a unit of storage initially created from the free space on one or more disks. Table 17-2 lists the volume types available on a dynamic disk.

Table 17-2 Dynamic Volume Types

Volume Type	Number of Disks	Configuration	Fault Tolerance
Simple	1	A single region or multiple concatenated regions of free space on a single disk.	None
Spanned	2 to 32	Two or more regions of free space on 2 to 32 disks linked into a single volume. Can be extended. Cannot be mirrored.	None

Volume Type	Number of Disks	Configuration	Fault Tolerance
Striped	2 to 32	Multiple regions of free space from two or more disks. Data is evenly interleaved across the disks, in stripes. Known as RAID Level 0.	None
Mirrored	2	Data on one disk is replicated on the second disk. Cannot be extended. Known as RAID Level 1.	Yes, with maximum capacity of the smallest disk
RAID-5	3 to 32	Data is interleaved equally across all disks, with a parity stripe of data also interleaved across the disks. Also known as striping with parity.	Yes, with maximum capacity of the number of disks minus one (if you have five 200 GB disks, your volume would be 800 GB)

Creating a simple volume on a dynamic disk proceeds exactly as already described for creating a partition on a basic disk. As with basic disks, you can also extend, shrink, or delete a volume. We look at the methods of creating and working with striped, mirrored, and RAID-5 volumes later in this chapter.

Dynamic volumes allow you to change their properties on an as-needed basis. If you have a computer that is running short of space, for example, you can install an extra hard drive and extend an existing simple or spanned volume so that the new space is immediately available without directing the user to use drive J: for this data, drive C: for that data, drive Y: for the network, and so on. Users find multiple drive letters confusing, so being able to keep it all under one letter is highly preferable. Unfortunately, you cannot extend a system volume or a boot volume. Because most computers are installed with a single volume, C:, which includes boot and system files, any volumes created on a new disk added to the computer must have a separate drive letter from the C: drive.

To increase the size of a simple volume, in Disk Management, right-click the existing volume and select **Extend Volume** from the shortcut menu. The Extend Volume Wizard starts, and you are prompted to select the disk or disks that contain the free space you will be adding. After you specify the size of free space to add, you need to confirm your options and click **Finish**. The volume is extended and appears in the Disk Management window with new space allocated to it.

The Disk Management utility is fairly comprehensive, but it is not the only tool available in Windows 8.1 to configure or manage disks. Some of these tools hearken back to the days of DOS and Windows 3.x, yet they are still very useful, especially if there is a problem accessing the graphical user interface (GUI):

- **`Chkdsk.exe`:** A command-line utility that verifies and repairs FAT- or NTFS-formatted volumes. (For NTFS drives, use the `CHKDSK C: /R` command to automatically check and repair disk problems.)
- **`Cleanmgr.exe`:** Also known as Disk Cleanup, a GUI utility that deletes unused files.
- **`Defrag.exe`:** Also known as Disk Defragmenter, a command-line utility that rearranges files contiguously, recapturing and reorganizing free space in the volume. Optimizes performance.
- **`DiskPart.exe`:** A command-line utility that can run a script to perform disk-related functions. DiskPart's nearest GUI counterpart is the Disk Management utility.
- **`Fsutil.exe`:** A command-line utility that displays information about the file system and can perform disk-related functions.

Troubleshooting Disk Problems

An administrator should understand how to handle the errors that can plague a hard disk. Common problems are listed in Table 17-3. We look at the Windows 8.1 Startup Repair tool in Chapter 19, "Configuring System Recovery Options."

Table 17-3 Troubleshooting Disk Errors

Error	Problem or Process	Possible Repairs
Non-System Disk or Disk Error	Basic Input/Output System (BIOS) generates this error when the MBR or boot sector is damaged, or when a different device is configured as the boot device in the BIOS.	Check the BIOS and reconfigure, if necessary. Remove any nonsystem media from the floppy, USB, or optical drives. Repair the boot volume with Windows 8.1 Startup Repair tool. Reinstall Windows 8.1. Replace the hard disk.
There is not enough memory or disk space to complete the operation	Disk is full.	Free up space on the hard disk by deleting files, removing applications, or compressing files. Add another disk and extend the volume to span both disks.

Error	Problem or Process	Possible Repairs
Missing Operating System	No active partition is defined.	Check the BIOS settings and configure if they incorrectly identify the boot disk. Boot up with a floppy or other bootable media. Use `Diskpart.exe` to mark the boot volume as active. Use Windows 8.1 Startup Repair tool. Reinstall Windows 8.1.
Invalid Media Type	Boot sector is damaged.	Repair the boot volume with Windows Startup Repair tool. Reinstall Windows 8.1. Replace the hard disk.
Hard disk controller failure	BIOS's disk controller configuration is invalid, or the hard disk controller has failed.	Check the BIOS and reconfigure the controller. Replace the hard disk controller.

The volume properties of a disk as displayed in the graphical display in the Disk Management snap-in (refer back to Figure 17-1) provide you with a status display, which can help you in troubleshooting disk problems. The following volume statuses can appear:

- **Healthy:** This status is normal and means that the volume is accessible and operating properly.
- **Active:** This status is also normal. An active partition is a partition or volume on a hard disk that has been identified as the primary partition from which the operating system is booted.
- **Failed:** This status means that the operating system could not start the volume normally. Failed usually means that the data is lost because the disk is damaged or the file system is corrupted. To repair a failed volume, physically inspect the computer to see whether the physical disk is operating. Ensure that the underlying disk(s) has an Online status in Disk Management.
- **Formatting:** This status is temporary, appearing only while the volume is being formatted.

- **Unknown:** This status means that you've installed a new disk and have not created a disk signature or that the boot sector for the volume is corrupt, possibly because of a virus. You can attempt to repair this error by initializing the underlying disk by right-clicking the disk and selecting **Initialize** from the shortcut menu.
- **Data Incomplete:** This status appears when a disk has been moved into or out of a multidisk volume. Data is destroyed unless all the disks are moved and imported on the new computer.
- **Healthy (At Risk):** This status indicates I/O errors have been detected on an underlying disk of the volume, but that data can still be accessed. The underlying disk probably shows a status of Online (Errors) and must be brought back online for the volume to be corrected.

When you see a status other than Healthy for your volumes or other than Online for your disks, you can attempt to repair by selecting the **Rescan Disks** option from the Action menu in Disk Management.

RAID Volumes

The acronym "RAID" refers to "Redundant Array of Independent (or Inexpensive) Disks"; it is a series of separate disks configured to work together as a single drive with a single drive letter. You have already seen three of the most common types of RAID arrays in Table 17-2: RAID-0 (disk striping), RAID-1 (mirroring), and RAID-5 (disk striping with parity). Other versions of RAID also exist but are generally unused; you are unlikely to see these referenced on the 70-687 exam.

When you use fault-tolerant volumes, a disk can fail and the operating system will continue to function. The failure can be repaired with no loss of data. Most Windows 8.1 computers do not have fault-tolerant volumes. An administrator should understand how to handle the errors that can plague a hard disk. Refer to Table 17-3 for common problems that can also plague fault-tolerant volumes.

CAUTION Don't confuse the RAID-5 or mirrored volumes that you can create within the Windows 8.1 operating system with RAID-5 or mirrored drives that are configured in a hardware storage array. A disk array produces a highly performing, fault-tolerant volume that appears in Windows 8.1 Disk Management as a simple volume. When you create mirrored or RAID-5 volumes in Windows 8.1, you achieve fault tolerance but lose some performance to disk management processes, especially if a disk fails.

Creating a RAID-0 Volume

A RAID-0 (striped) volume contains space on 2 to 32 separate hard disks. Data is written in 64 KB blocks (stripes) to each disk in the volume in turn. A striped volume offers considerable improvement in read/write efficiency because the read/write heads on each disk are working together during each I/O operation. A striped volume offers a maximum amount of space equal to the size of the smallest disk multiplied by the number of disks in the volume. However, the striped volume does not offer fault tolerance; if any one disk is lost, the entire volume is lost. Note that the system or boot volume cannot be housed on a striped volume.

You can create a striped volume by using 2 to 32 separate hard disks in Disk Management. To do so, use the following procedure:

Step 1. In Disk Management, right-click any one disk to be made part of the striped volume and choose **New Striped Volume**.

Step 2. The New Striped Volume Wizard starts and displays the Select Disks page shown in Figure 17-10. The disk you initially selected appears under Selected. Select the disks you want to use from the Available column and then click **Add**.

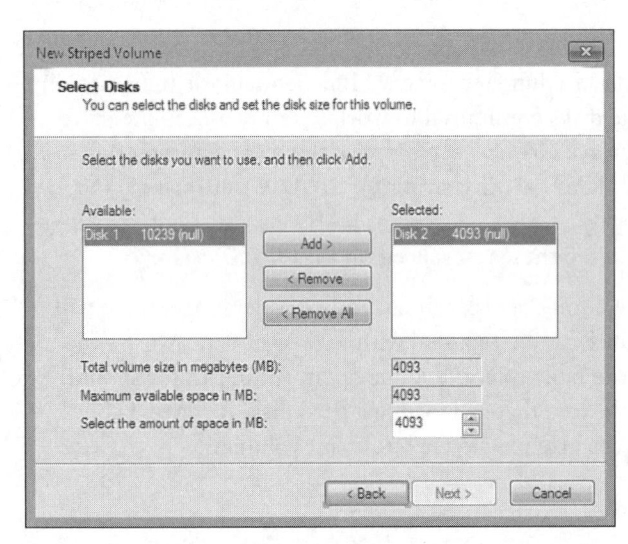

Figure 17-10 You need to select at least two disks to create a striped volume.

Step 3. Disks you add appear in the Selected column. If you want to change the amount of space to be allocated, modify the value under Select the amount of space in MB. When done, click **Next**.

Step 4. From the Assign Drive Letter or Path page shown in Figure 17-11, accept the default or choose another drive letter, or select the option to mount the volume in an empty NTFS folder if desired. Then click **Next**.

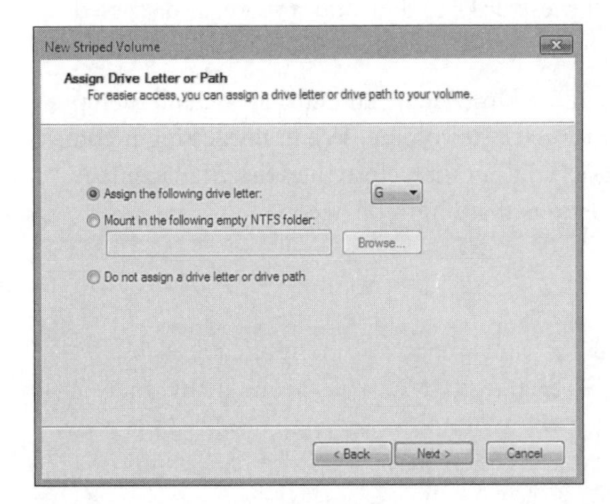

Figure 17-11 Assigning a drive letter or mount path for a striped volume.

Step 5. Choose the desired options in the Format Volume page shown in Figure 17-12 and then click **Next**.

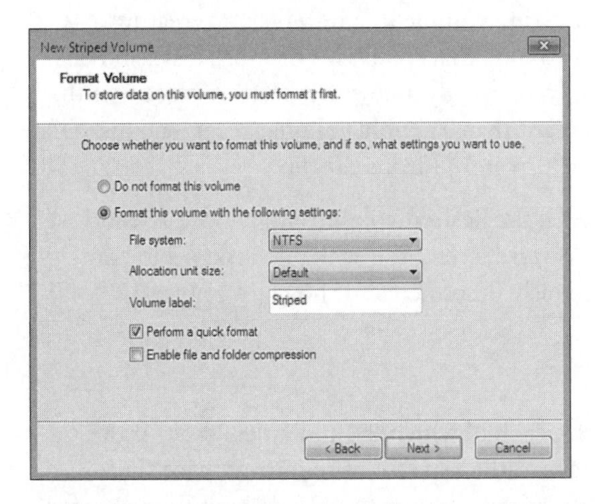

Figure 17-12 You have several options for formatting your volume.

Step 6. Review the information on the completion page and then click **Finish**.

Step 7. If any of the disks to be used in the volume are configured as basic disks, you receive the same message previously shown in Figure 17-9, warning you that you will be unable to boot other operating systems. To create your volume, you must click **Yes** and convert these disks to dynamic storage, as discussed earlier in this chapter.

Step 8. Windows displays the volume in the Disk Management snap-in, and then provides a progress indicator as it formats the volume. When formatting is complete, the volume is ready to use. You can then close the Disk Management snap-in or perform any other actions that might be needed.

WARNING Remember that RAID-0 is not fault-tolerant as mentioned in Table 17-2. RAID-0 writes data in 64 KB blocks to each disk in the array sequentially, thereby improving read/write performance. However, if you lose any one of the disks in the array, all data is lost and you must restore the data from backup after replacing the lost disk and re-creating the array.

Creating a Spanned Volume

You can extend storage space on an existing volume to a new disk by creating a spanned volume. This is essentially a volume that spans two or more disks and enables you to add space without the need to specify a new drive letter. Note that the spanned volume is even less fault-tolerant than a simple volume; if any one disk fails, all data is lost from all disks and must be restored from backup.

To create a spanned volume, right-click the desired volume and choose **Extend Volume**. From the Extend Volume Wizard, select the available disk(s) and complete the steps in this wizard, as previously described and shown in Figure 17-4.

Creating a Mirrored Volume

A mirrored volume contains two disks, each of which is an identical copy of the other, thereby providing fault tolerance at the expense of requiring twice the amount of disk space. You can use a mirrored volume to provide fault tolerance for the system and boot volumes, as well as any data volumes.

Creating a mirrored volume is similar to that of creating a striped volume. Use the following procedure:

Step 1. In Disk Management, right-click any one disk to be made part of the striped volume and choose **New Mirrored Volume**.

Step 2. Steps displayed by the New Mirrored Volume Wizard are similar to those of the New Striped Volume Wizard and outlined in the previous procedure. After you complete the procedure, the mirrored volume appears in the Disk Management display.

Creating a RAID-5 Volume

A RAID-5 volume is similar to a striped volume in that data is written in 64 KB stripes across all disks in the volume. However, this volume adds a parity stripe to one of the disks in the array, thereby providing fault tolerance. The parity stripe rotates from one disk to the next as each set of stripes is written. The RAID-5 volume offers improved read performance because data is read from each disk at the same time; however, write performance is lower because processor time is required to calculate the parity stripes. You cannot house the system or boot volumes on a RAID-5 volume.

Creating a RAID-5 volume is also similar; remember that you must have at least three disks to create this type of volume. Select **New RAID-5 Volume** from the right-click options and follow the steps presented by the New RAID-5 Volume Wizard.

NOTE For more information on how RAID-5 volumes function, refer to "RAID-5 Volumes" at http://technet.microsoft.com/en-us/library/cc938485.aspx.

Using DiskPart to Create Striped, Mirrored, and RAID-5 Volumes

You can use the DiskPart command-line utility to create striped, mirrored, and RAID-5 volumes. To perform any of these tasks, first execute the following commands from an administrative command prompt:

```
Diskpart
List disk
Select disk=n
Convert dynamic
```

The `List disk` command returns the disk numbers on your computer that you use when entering the commands to create the desired volume. The `Select disk` command selects a disk you want to work with, and the `Convert dynamic` command converts the disk to a dynamic disk; repeat these two commands for each disk that needs to be converted to dynamic storage before beginning to create your volumes.

To create a mirror, you actually add a mirror to an existing simple volume. Use the `Select volume` command to select the volume to be mirrored, and then use the following command:

```
Add disk=n [noerr]
```

In this command, *n* is the disk number of the disk to be added to the current simple volume and `noerr` enables a script containing this command to continue processing even if an error has occurred. To obtain disk numbers used in this command, use the `List disk` command.

Use the following command to create a striped volume:

```
Create volume stripe [size=size] disk=n[,n[,...]] [noerr]
```

In this command, *size* is the number of megabytes used in each disk for the striped volume and *n* is the disk number (repeat from 2 to 32 times for each disk in the striped volume). If you do not specify a size, the size is assumed to be that of the smallest disk in the array. For example, if you specify three disks with unallocated space of 300, 400, and 500 GB and do not specify a size, DiskPart uses 300 GB per disk for a total striped volume size of 900 GB.

Creating a RAID-5 volume is similar to that of creating a striped volume. Use the following command:

```
Create volume raid [size=size] disk=n[,n[,...]] [noerr]
```

The parameters have the same meaning; in this case, repeat the disk number from 3 to 32 times. For the same example with three disks with unallocated space of 300, 400, and 500 GB and that do not specify the size parameter, DiskPart uses 300 GB per disk for a total RAID-5 volume size of 600 GB.

Managing and Troubleshooting RAID Volumes

Several things can go wrong with RAID volumes. Spanned and striped volumes are particularly vulnerable; as has already been mentioned, failure of any one disk in the volume renders the entire volume useless, and data must be restored from backup. If one disk in a mirrored volume fails, you can break the mirror and use the data on the other disk as a simple volume. If one disk in a RAID-5 volume fails, the system reconstructs the missing data from the parity information and the volume is still usable, but without fault tolerance and with reduced performance until the failed disk is replaced. If more than one disk in a RAID-5 volume fails, the volume has failed and must be restored from backup after the disks have been replaced.

Besides the volume statuses already described for partitions on basic disks and simple volumes, Disk Management can display the following messages with RAID volumes:

- **Resynching:** This status indicates that a mirrored volume is being reinitialized. This status is temporary and should change to `Healthy` within a few seconds.
- **Data Not Redundant or Failed Redundancy:** For a mirrored or RAID-5 volume, this status usually means that half of a mirrored volume was imported, or that half is unavailable, or that only part of the underlying disks of a RAID-5 volume were imported. You should import the missing disk(s) to re-create the volume. You can also break the mirror and retain the half that is functioning as a simple volume. If you have all but one of the underlying disks of a RAID-5 volume, you can re-create the RAID-5 volume by adding unallocated space of a different disk.
- **Stale Data:** This status is shown when you import a disk that contains a mirrored volume half, or a portion of a RAID-5 volume, with a status other than Healthy before it was moved. You can return the disk to the original PC and rescan the disk to fix the error.

Managing File System Fragmentation

All disks, regardless of the file system in use (FAT16, FAT32, or NTFS), divide disk space into clusters, which are groups of disk sectors that are the smallest units of space available for holding files. The size of clusters depends on the file system in use and the size of the partition; for example, for NTFS-formatted volumes of more than 2 GB in size, the default cluster size is 4 KB.

A file is stored in the first available clusters on a volume or partition, and not necessarily in contiguous space. Thus, if empty space has been left on the volume as a result of moving, editing, or deleting files, these small noncontiguous clusters are used. Access to files that are fragmented in this way takes a longer time because extra read operations are required to locate and access all the pieces of the file. You can defragment your disks with either the Optimize Drives GUI tool or the command-line `defrag.exe` tool.

Optimizing Drives

Windows 8.1 provides a tool called the Optimize Drives utility (formerly called the Disk Defragmenter) to locate and consolidate these fragmented files into contiguous blocks of space. Consequently, access time is improved. You can access the Optimize

Drives utility by clicking **Optimize** from the Tools tab of any partition's Properties dialog box or by accessing the Search charm and typing `defrag` into the search box and clicking **Defragment and Optimize Drives** in the Programs list.

Any of these methods opens the newly redesigned Optimize Drives utility, as shown in Figure 17-13. This tool enables you to configure scheduled optimization or to analyze or optimize any disk volume immediately.

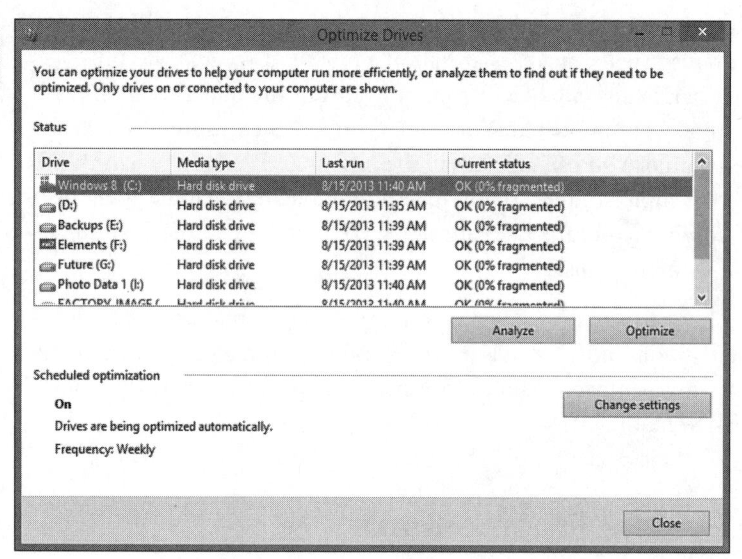

Figure 17-13 The Optimize Drives utility enables you to perform on-demand and scheduled optimization.

You can perform the following actions from the Optimize Drives GUI utility:

- **Schedule Optimization:** Click **Change settings** to set up a schedule. By default, Windows 8.1 schedules optimization to take place on all disks weekly, as shown in Figure 17-14. You can choose to optimize disks on a daily or monthly basis if desired by selecting these options from the drop-down list shown, or select disks to be optimized by clicking the **Choose** command button.
- **Analyze disk:** Select a disk and click **Analyze** to have the Optimize Drives utility check the current level of fragmentation. Although the dialog box says you need to first analyze your disks, they are first analyzed when you click **Optimize**.
- **Perform an on-demand optimization:** Select a disk and click **Optimize**. Disk optimization first analyzes the disk and then performs a multipass optimization, displaying its progress as shown in Figure 17-15. If you need to stop an optimization in progress, click **Stop operation**.

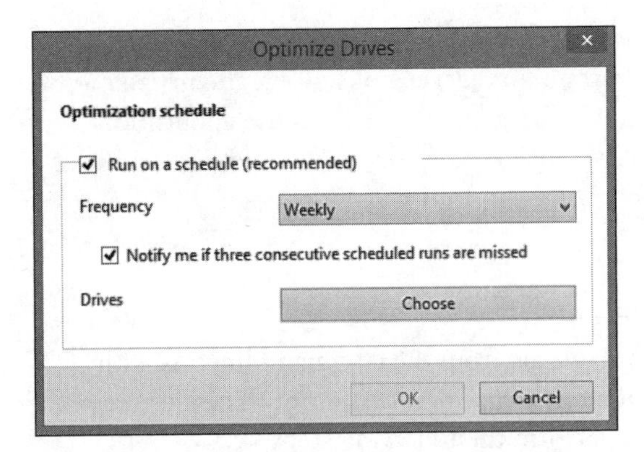

Figure 17-14 The Optimize Drives: Optimization schedule dialog box enables you to specify the schedule for optimization.

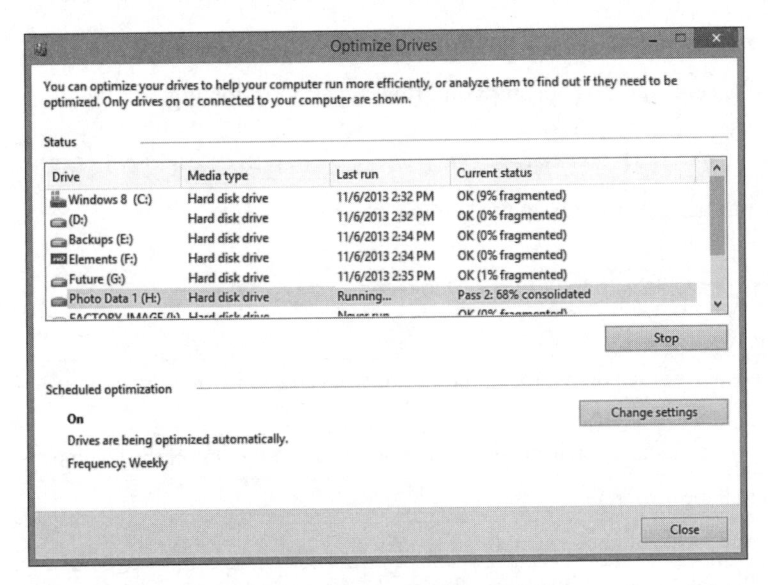

Figure 17-15 The Optimize Drives utility displays the progress of disk optimization.

NOTE It is recommended that you have at least 15% of free space on a disk volume before running the Optimize Drives utility. Otherwise, the optimization process will take much longer and may be incomplete. Use the Disk Cleanup tool first, if necessary, to optimize the amount of available free space.

> **TIP** Disks can become quite fragmented after you've uninstalled applications or deleted large files. Further, when you are installing large applications, the installation runs much better when plenty of contiguous space is available, and the application will also run better later. It is a good idea to analyze your disk after deleting large files or before installing applications and then run the optimization if necessary.

The `Defrag.exe` Command-Line Tool

You can use `Defrag.exe` to optimize a volume from the command line. As with other command-line utilities, you can include it as part of a script to be executed when the disk is not in use. To do so, perform the following steps:

Step 1. Access the Search charm, select **Settings**, and then type **`cmd`**.

Step 2. Right-click **Command Prompt** to display options at the bottom of the screen.

Step 3. From these options, select **Run as administrator**.

Step 4. Click **Yes** to accept the UAC prompt and then type the following command:

```
Defrag <volume> | /C | /E <volume> [/A | /X | /T] [/H] [/M] [/U] [/V]
```

Table 17-4 describes the parameters of the `Defrag` command:

Table 17-4 Parameters Available with the `Defrag` Command

Parameter	Meaning
volume	The drive letter of the volume to be optimized. You can specify more than one drive letter if needed.
/B	Optimizes boot files and applications but does not optimize the rest of the volume.
/C	Optimizes all local volumes.
/E	Optimizes all local volumes except those specified.
/A	Analyzes the volume and displays a report but does not optimize.
/X	Performs free space consolidation.
/T	Tracks an optimization already in progress.
/H	Runs the optimization at normal priority (by default, runs at low priority).
/M	Optimizes multiple volumes simultaneously in parallel.
/U	Prints the optimization process on the screen.
/V	Uses verbose mode, which provides additional detailed information.

For example, the command `defrag C: /X /V` would optimize the C: volume, perform free space consolidation, and provide verbose output.

Error Checking

Occasionally, a volume might not appear in the Optimize Drives dialog box. This might happen because the disk contains errors such as bad sectors. You can check a disk for errors and repair problems by accessing the Tools tab of the disk's Properties dialog box and clicking **Check**. Doing so opens the Error Checking dialog box shown in Figure 17-16. This dialog box shows any errors it finds on the drive; if none are found, it displays the `You don't need to scan this drive` message. In any case, you can perform a more thorough error checking procedure by clicking **Scan drive**. This displays an Error Checking message box and then reports any errors it happens to find.

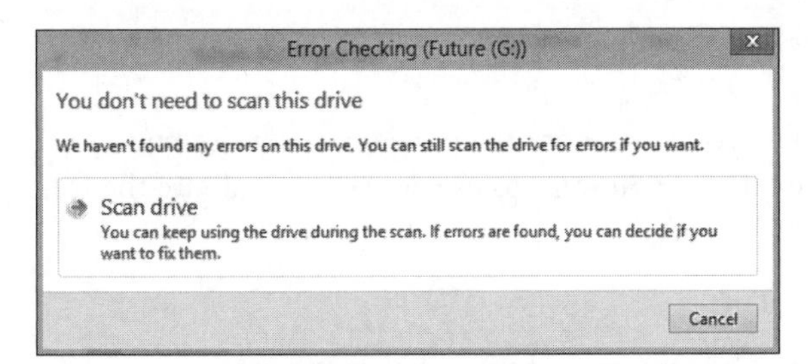

Figure 17-16 Checking a disk for errors.

Managing Storage Spaces

A new technology introduced for Windows 8.1 and Windows Server 2012 R2, Storage Spaces provides a more convenient method for adding additional storage to a computer when it is needed. Traditionally, when a Windows system becomes short on storage, adding an additional hard disk only partially solves the issue and requires some careful management of storage, requiring movement of files over multiple disks or even reinstalling software to move the installation files to the new drive, thus freeing space on the original drive.

Storage Spaces solves this problem by allowing you to add the disk to a virtual storage space, and managing the additional space for you, presenting two or more disks as a single drive. To the user, it appears as though the original drive has simply been replaced with a larger one.

With Storage Spaces, you organize physical disks together into a storage pool and use the pool capacity to create storage spaces. When a disk drive is part of a storage pool, you can add new drives to it to increase the size of the virtual drive. Note the following characteristics of Storage Spaces:

- Storage Spaces is presented as virtual drives in File Explorer. They are used like any other drive, making it easy to work with files on them.
- You can create Storage Spaces with lots of storage, adding more drives to them when you run low capacity in the pool. Drives can be attached through USB, SATA, or Serial Attached SCSI (SAS).

- Storage Spaces can provide some protection to your files. With two or more drives in the storage pool, you can create Storage Spaces with redundancy in case of a drive failure—or even failure of two drives by creating a three-way mirror storage space.
- Storage Spaces uses thin provisioning, which means that physical space is allocated only when it is actually used to store files. Thin provisioning allows you to create Storage Spaces with more virtual capacity than actually exists on the physical drives in the storage pool.

Creating a Storage Space

You can create Storage Spaces after you have more than one drive connected to the Windows computer. When all the drives you want to use are connected, use the following procedure to create a storage space:

Step 1. Access the Search charm.

Step 2. Enter `storage spaces` in the search box and then click **Settings**.

Step 3. Select the **Storage Spaces** item from the search results. The Storage Spaces Control Panel applet is displayed, as shown in Figure 17-17.

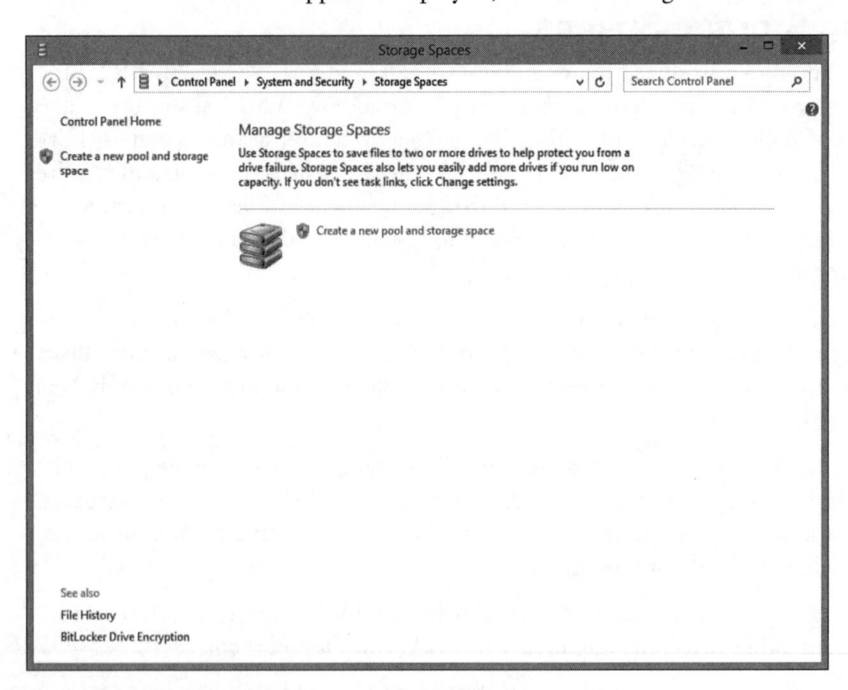

Figure 17-17 The Storage Spaces management screen.

Step 4. Click the **Create a new pool and storage space** link. If the UAC confirmation dialog box is displayed, click **Yes** to proceed.

Step 5. Select the drives you want to use for the new pool and then click **Create pool**.

Step 6. Select a drive letter and name, the Resiliency type, and the maximum size for the storage space from the screen shown in Figure 17-18.

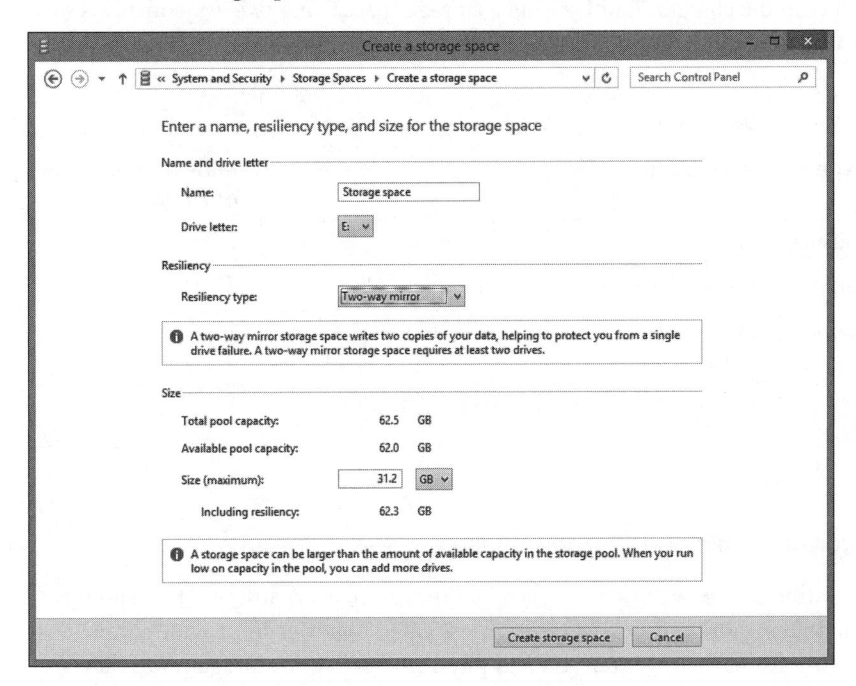

Figure 17-18 Enter a name, resiliency type, and size for a new storage space.

Step 7. Select the **Create storage space** button to complete the configuration and create the new storage space.

WARNING When adding drives for use with Storage Spaces, you don't need to format or assign letters to the new drive. If any of the drives are formatted, Windows warns you that the drive will be reformatted and any files on the drive will be permanently lost. Make sure you do not have any data that you want to keep on any of the drives you add to a storage pool because the files will be destroyed and cannot be recovered.

After the storage space is created, you can use it just as you would any other drive, with the drive letter you specified in step 6.

The Resiliency type can be used to provide protection from physical disk failure in your storage space if you use more than one drive to create it. Table 17-5 lists the resiliency options, type of hardware failure protection, and the required number of drives for each.

Note that resiliency requires more disk space, similar to using a RAID volume as discussed earlier in the chapter. Configuring a storage space using two-way mirror resiliency, for instance, allows you to use only half of the storage capacity of the two drives.

Table 17-5 Storage Space Resiliency Options

Resiliency Type	Protection	Minimum Number of Drives
Simple (no resiliency)	None	1
Two-way mirror	Protects data from failure of a single drive	2
Three-way mirror	Protects data from failure of up to two physical drives	5
Parity	Protects data from failure of a single drive	3

Managing Storage Pools and Storage Spaces

Note the distinction between *storage pools* and *storage spaces*. A storage pool simply consists of one or more physical hard drives grouped together to provide some amount of storage capacity. After you add physical drives to a storage pool, they are no longer directly usable by Windows. You can add drives to a storage pool at any time, but note that after you create storage space that makes use of the pool, drives cannot be removed from the pool without first deleting the storage space, which will destroy all the files it contains.

You can create multiple storage spaces for each storage pool. As you can see in Figure 17-18, you can specify the maximum size for a storage space when you create it. You are not limited to the amount of capacity in the storage pool; this allows you to create storage spaces with more space than is actually available. As the storage space fills up, you can simply add more drives to the storage pool. You can change the storage space size at any time, as long as it is large enough to contain the files that have been written to it.

You can manage your storage spaces and pools from the screen shown in Figure 17-19. From the links at the top, click **Create a storage space**, **Add drives**, or **Rename pool** to perform these functions. The default name of the first pool is simply Storage Pool, but as you add new storage pools to the system, you should give them meaningful names based on their use or the drives used to make up the pool. You can also add drives when you need to expand the capacity of a storage pool.

The physical drives are listed in the bottom section of the screen. You can use the **Rename** link for each drive to provide a friendlier name. In the figure, there is no **Remove** link available for the drives. The reason is that the pool is already being used by Storage Spaces. If no storage spaces existed for the pool, the **Remove** option also is available for each physical drive.

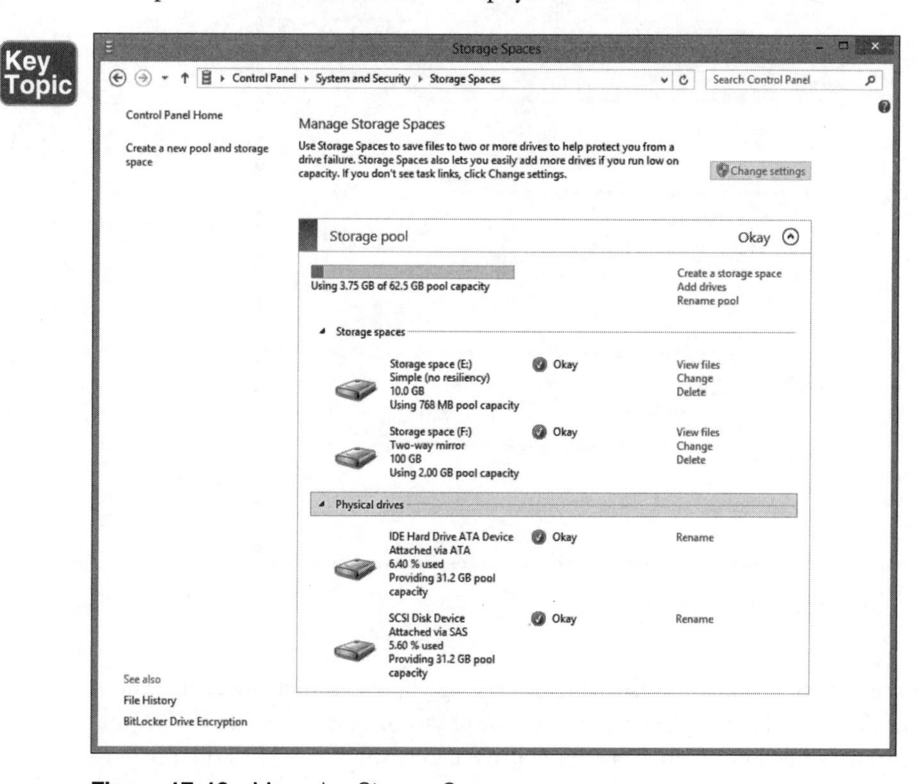

Figure 17-19 Managing Storage Spaces.

If a physical drive in a storage pool fails, you can simply replace the physical drive, add it to the storage pool, and Windows will rebuild any resiliency for you. If a Simple (no resiliency) Storage Space was using the drive, the files on that storage space will be lost. Action Center notifies you when it detects a problem with the storage pool drive, and Manage Storage Spaces displays errors or warnings, as shown in Figure 17-20.

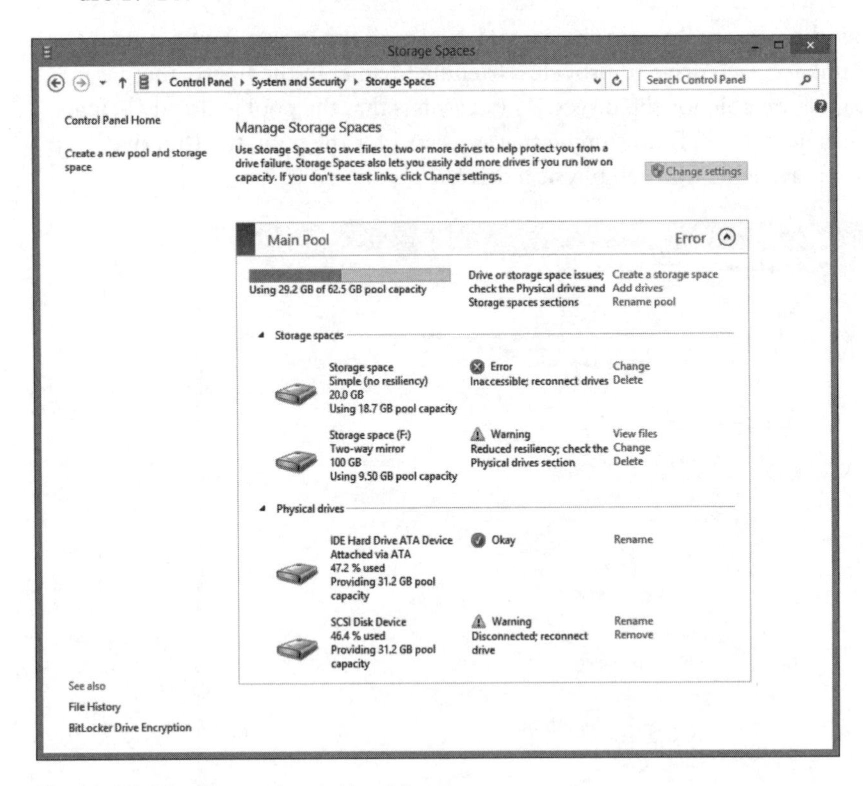

Figure 17-20 Storage pool drive failure.

After the drive is replaced, access the Manage Storage Spaces screen and select the **Add drives** link to add the replacement drive to the storage pool. Unlike RAID, the replacement drive need not match the failed drive in any way. Windows then begins repairing the resiliency on any existing storage spaces configured for resiliency in that storage pool. Figure 17-21 shows the pool with a new Physical drive attached and ready to be added to the Main Pool. It can then be used to replace the failed drive to restore the resiliency to the storage space.

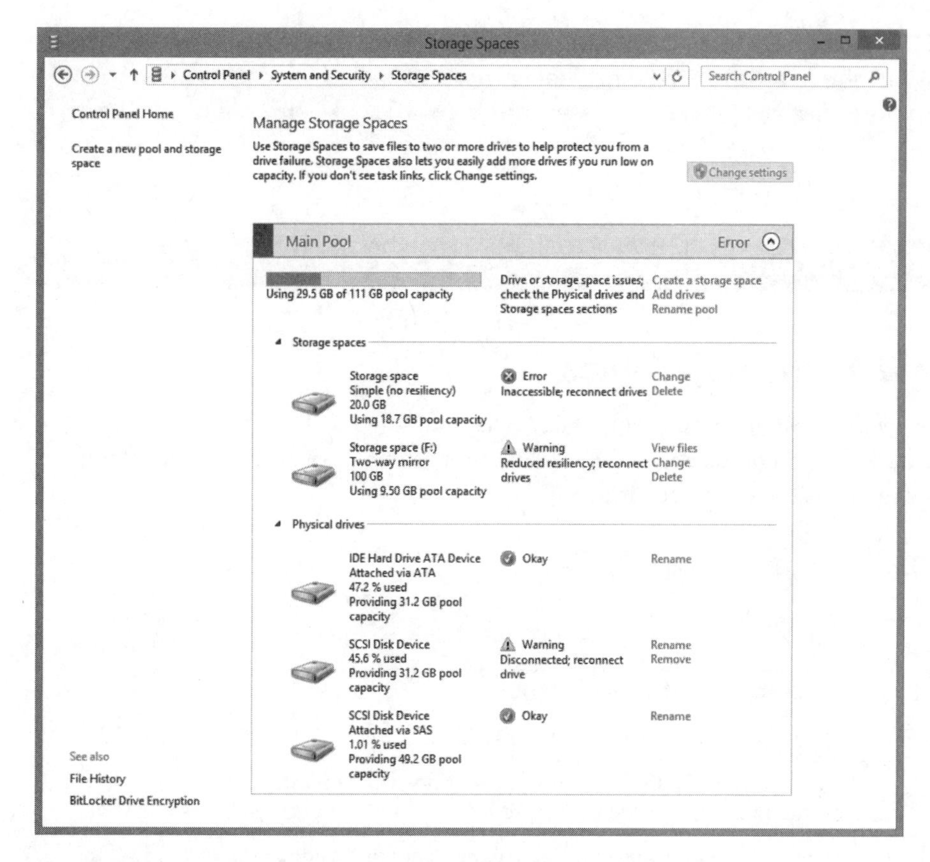

Figure 17-21 Failed and replaced drives in a storage pool.

After the new drive is added and resiliency on the storage space is rebuilt, you can then remove the failed drive from the storage pool.

Managing Storage Spaces with PowerShell

Microsoft provides several PowerShell cmdlets for managing storage pools and storage spaces. Some of the useful cmdlets available are listed here:

- **`Get-SpacesPhysicalDisk`:** Gets all physical disks that can be used to create a storage pool.
- **`New-SpacesPool`:** Creates a new storage pool. Use the `-PhysicalDisks` parameter to specify the disks to use.
- **`New-SpacesVolume`:** Creates a new storage space. This command accepts parameters including `-DriveLetterToUse`, `-ResiliencyType`, and `-Size`.
- **`Repair-SpacesConfiguration`:** Forces the rebuild of resiliency when you are replacing a failed drive or adding a new one.

NOTE For more information on PowerShell cmdlets used for managing Storage Spaces and how to use them, refer to "Storage Spaces Cmdlets in Windows PowerShell" at http://technet.microsoft.com/en-us/library/jj851254%28v=wps.620%29.aspx.

Exam Preparation Tasks

Review All the Key Topics

Review the most important topics in the chapter, noted with the key topics icon in the outer margin of the page. Table 17-6 lists a reference of these key topics and the page numbers on which each is found.

Table 17-6 Key Topics for Chapter 17

Key Topic Element	Description	Page Number(s)
Figure 17-1	Shows the Disk Management utility	728
Step List	Shows how to create a basic disk partition	731-732
Figure 17-6	Shows a volume's Properties dialog box in which you can perform a large range of management tasks	734
Table 17-2	Describes the available dynamic volume types in Windows 8.1	737-738
Table 17-3	Describes common disk errors	739-740
Step List	Shows how to create a striped volume	742-744
Figure 17-13	Shows how to use the Optimize Drives utility	748
Table 17-4	Describes parameters available with the `defrag.exe` command-line tool	750
Step List	Describes how to create a storage space	752-753
Figure 17-19	Shows how to manage Storage Spaces	755

Complete the Tables and Lists from Memory

Print a copy of Appendix B, "Memory Tables," (found on the CD), or at least the section for this chapter, and complete the tables and lists from memory. Appendix C, "Memory Tables Answer Key," also on the CD, includes completed tables and lists to check your work.

Definitions of Key Terms

Define the following key terms from this chapter and check your answers in the Glossary:

Active partition, Basic disk, Computer Management console, Disk Management snap-in, DiskPart, Dynamic disk, Extended partition, Logical drive, Mirroring, Partition, Primary partition, RAID-5, Storage pool, Storage space, Striping, Volume

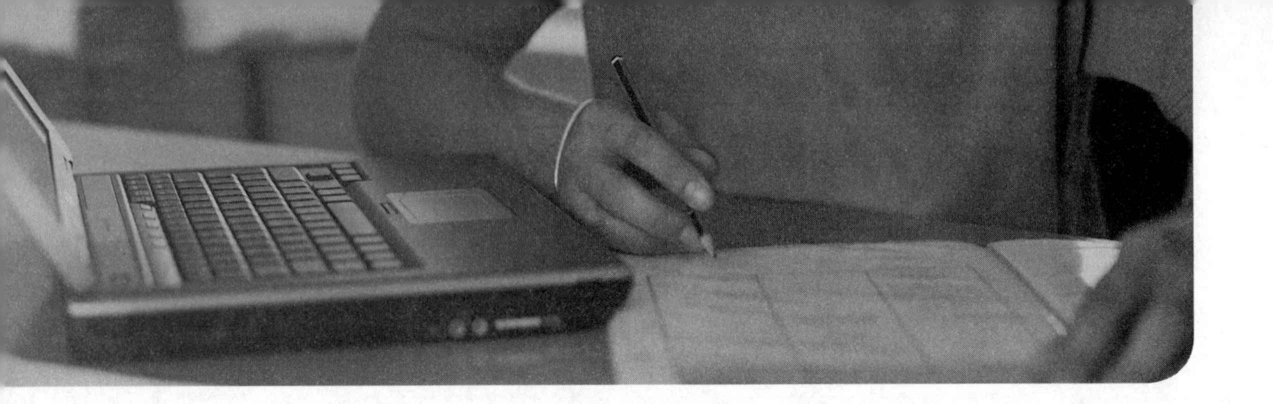

This chapter covers the following subjects:

- **Configuring and Working with Event Logs:** This section shows you how to work with Event Viewer and configure event log subscriptions that enable you to collect events from multiple computers in one place.
- **Managing and Optimizing Computer Performance:** This section describes the capabilities of Performance Monitor. It introduces the concept of performance objects and counters, and describes the more important objects and counters that you should be familiar with. It then shows you how to log information using data collector sets that can be stored for later analysis and display.
- **Configuring Task Manager:** Task Manager has been completely redesigned in Windows 8.1, providing users with an easy view of process performance information and making it easier to locate processes that consume large amounts of computer resources or are not responding. This section shows you how to configure the options presented by Task Manager.
- **Configuring Additional Performance Settings:** This section introduces several other tools that you can use to configure settings that affect your computer's performance.
- **Configuring Indexing Options:** Windows provides the Indexing service, which facilitates the locating of data on the computer. This section shows you how to optimize and troubleshoot the Indexing service so that searches for information run rapidly and locate all possible data.

CHAPTER 18

Managing and Monitoring System Performance

When you first set up a brand new Windows 8.1 computer with a baseline set of applications, you will generally find that it performs very capably. As you install additional applications, store data, and work with the computer, its performance can slow down. Factors that affect a computer's performance include memory, processor, disks, and applications. Windows 8.1 contains an extensive suite of system and performance monitoring tools that enable you to monitor system performance and diagnose problems that might be occurring, even very subtly, within your computer. Many of these tools can be found in the Computer Management console, which we introduced in Chapter 1, "Introducing Windows 8.1," and have covered in several subsequent chapters. These tools include Event Viewer, Performance Monitor, Reliability Monitor, Action Center, and Task Manager, all of which enable you to monitor and troubleshoot computer performance. This chapter looks at using these tools to troubleshoot system errors, monitor system performance, and optimize your computer to keeping it working at a level close to that observed when you first set it up.

"Do I Know This Already?" Quiz

The "Do I Know This Already?" quiz allows you to assess whether you should read this entire chapter or simply jump to the "Exam Preparation Tasks" section for review. If you are in doubt, read the entire chapter. Table 18-1 outlines the major headings in this chapter and the corresponding "Do I Know This Already?" quiz questions. You can find the answers in Appendix A, "Answers to the 'Do I Know This Already?' Quizzes."

Table 18-1 "Do I Know This Already?" Foundation Topics Section-to-Question Mapping

Foundations Topics Section	Questions Covered in This Section
Configuring and Working with Event Logs	1–4
Managing and Optimizing Computer Performance	5–7
Configuring Task Manager	8–9
Configuring Additional Performance Settings	10–11
Configuring Indexing Options	12

1. You open Event Viewer and want to access logs that store events from single components such as Distributed File Service (DFS) replication, hardware events, and Internet Explorer events. In which Event Viewer log should you look for this information?

a. Application

b. Security

c. System

d. Applications and Services Logs

2. You want to reduce the number of events viewed in the System log of Event Viewer because you've found that you waste a lot of time going through thousands of minor events when trying to locate important events that can pinpoint problems. What should you do?

a. Filter the log to display only Critical, Warning, and Error events.

b. Filter the log to display Error, Warning, and Information events.

c. Configure the log to overwrite events after 48 hours.

d. Create an event log subscription.

3. You are responsible for eight computers located in a small medical office that are configured as a workgroup. You want to collect event logs from all these computers onto a single computer so that you can spot problems more rapidly. What should you configure on this computer?

a. A source-initiated event subscription

b. A collector-initiated event subscription

c. A filter that views logs by event source

d. A filter that views logs by user and computer

4. Which of the following commands do you have to run on all computers involved in an event log subscription before setting up the subscription? (Choose two.)

   a. `Winrm`

   b. `Wdsutil`

   c. `Wecutil`

   d. `Logman`

5. You are working at your computer and a program you're using has hung; as a result, you cannot exit the program. Which utility can you use to terminate the program? (Choose two; each is a complete solution.)

   a. Reliability Monitor

   b. Resource Monitor

   c. Performance Monitor

   d. Task Manager

   e. Event Viewer

6. You want to receive a message when your computer's processor time exceeds 85%. What feature of Performance Monitor should you configure?

   a. Event Trace Data Collector Set

   b. Event log

   c. Performance Counter Alert Data Collector Set

   d. System Diagnostics Data Collector Set

7. You think your computer might need more RAM, and you're wondering how much memory is committed to either physical RAM or running processes. What counter should you check in Performance Monitor?

   a. Memory\Pages/sec

   b. Memory\Available Bytes

   c. Memory\Committed Bytes

   d. Processor\% Processor Time

   e. System\Processor Queue Length

8. Which of the following actions can you perform from the simplified interface in Task Manager? (Choose all that apply.)

  a. Close an unresponsive program.

  b. Start a new program.

  c. Open the folder in which a running executable file is located.

  d. Display summary performance statistics on a running program.

  e. Perform an Internet search on a selected program.

9. Your Windows 8.1 Pro computer has been starting slowly as of late, and you suspect that unnecessary apps are starting automatically at startup time. What should you do to locate these apps and ensure that they do not run at startup time?

  a. In the simplified interface in Task Manager, right-click the required apps and choose **Properties**. Then clear the check box labeled **Run at startup**.

  b. In the advanced interface in Task Manager, select the **Startup** tab. Then right-click the required apps and choose **Disable**.

  c. In the advanced interface in Task Manager, select the **Services** tab. Then right-click the required services and choose **Disable**.

  d. In the System Configuration utility, select the **Startup** tab. Then right-click the required apps and choose **Disable**.

10. Which of the following items can you perform by accessing the Action Center in Windows 8.1? (Choose three.)

  a. Check for possible security-related alerts.

  b. Check for solutions to possible maintenance problems.

  c. View alerts generated by data collector sets.

  d. Configure File History.

  e. Close unresponsive applications.

11. You are considering disabling some services on your Windows 8.1 computer but want to ensure that you do not disable important services that other services depend on for their functionality. Where should you check for the required information?

    a. The Dependencies tab of the service's Properties dialog box, accessed from the Services snap-in

    b. The General tab of the service's Properties dialog box, accessed from the Services snap-in

    c. The General tab of the System Configuration tool

    d. The Services subnode of the Software Environment node in the System Information tool

12. You suspect that the Indexing service on your Windows 8.1 computer is not performing properly, so you perform a search on several items you know are present on the computer. After several minutes, the computer has not located these items. What should you do?

    a. In the Indexing Options applet, click **Modify**. Then in the Indexed Locations dialog box, choose a location on a partition with lots of free space and click **OK**.

    b. In the Indexing Options applet, click **Advanced**. Then in the Advanced Options dialog box, click **Rebuild**.

    c. In the Indexing Options applet, click **Advanced**. Then in the Advanced Options dialog box, specify a location on a partition with lots of free space and click **Select new**.

    d. In the Indexing Options applet, click **Advanced**. Then in the Advanced Options dialog box, select the **File Types** tab and clear the check boxes for file extensions you're sure are not in use.

Foundation Topics

Configuring and Working with Event Logs

One of Windows 8.1's standard troubleshooting tools is Event Viewer, which has been around since the days of Windows NT but has been upgraded with each new Windows release. Event Viewer is incorporated into the Computer Management console, as well as being available from the Advanced Tools window. You can rely on this utility to be able to see errors and system messages. This tool enables you to view events from multiple event logs on the local computer or another computer to which you can connect, save event filters as custom views for future usage, schedule tasks to run in response to events, and create and manage event log subscriptions.

You can open Event Viewer by using any of the following methods:

- In Windows 8.1, right-click **Start** and choose **Event Viewer** from the menu that appears.
- If you have chosen to include tiles for administrative tools on the Start screen, simply select **Event Viewer** from this location.
- Open the Search charm and type `event` in the search box. Select **Event Viewer** from the Programs list.
- Open the Search charm and type `msconfig` in the search box. Then click **System Configuration** in the Programs list. From the Tools tab of System Configuration, select **Event Viewer** and then click **Launch**.
- While in the Desktop context, from the Settings charm, click **Control Panel**. Select the **System and Security** category and then select **View event logs** under Administrative Tools.

If you receive a User Account Control (UAC) prompt, click **Yes** or supply administrative credentials. (This depends on the UAC settings discussed in Chapter 12, "Configuring Local Security Settings.") The Event Viewer snap-in opens and displays a summary of recent administrative events in the details pane, as shown in Figure 18-1.

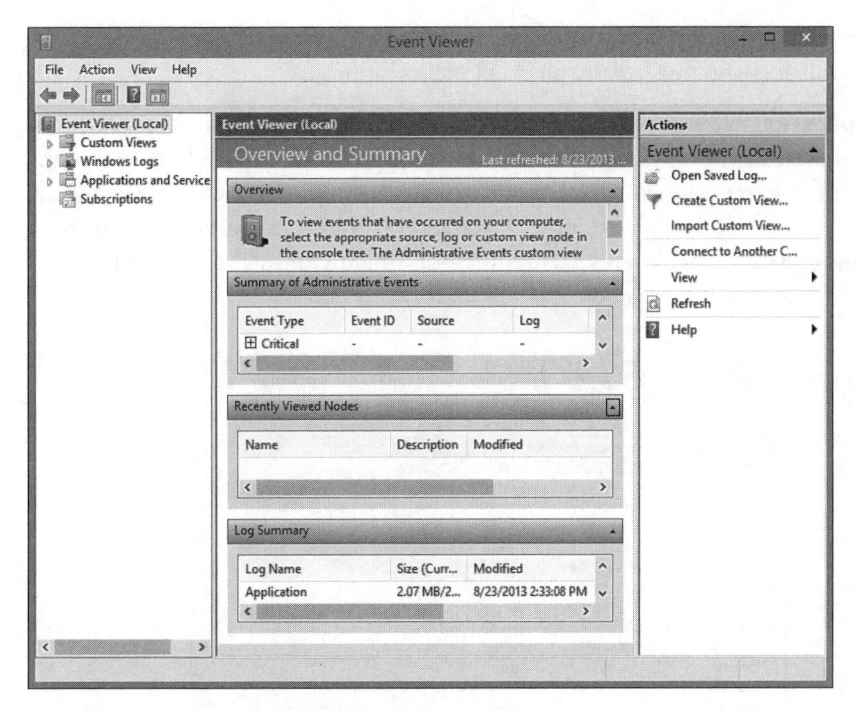

Figure 18-1 Event Viewer records events that have occurred on your computer.

The following sections provide more detail with regard to several aspects of working with Event Viewer.

Viewing Logs in Event Viewer

To view the actual event logs, expand the Event Viewer node in the console tree and then expand the Windows Logs subnode. Windows 8.1 records events in the following types of logs:

- **Application:** Logs events related to applications running on the computer, including alerts generated by data collector sets.
- **Security:** Logs events related to security-related actions performed on the computer. To enable security event logging, you must configure auditing of the types of actions to be recorded.
- **Setup:** Logs events related to setup of applications.
- **System:** Contains events related to actions taking place on the computer in general, including hardware-related events. See Figure 18-2.

- **Forwarded events:** Contains events logged from remote computers. To enable this log, you must create an event subscription.
- **Applications and Services logs:** Contained in its own subnode, these logs store events from single applications or components, as opposed to events with potential systemwide impact. Logs may include categories such as Distributed File Service (DFS) replication, hardware events, Internet Explorer events, Key Management service events, Windows Assessment Console events, and Windows PowerShell events.

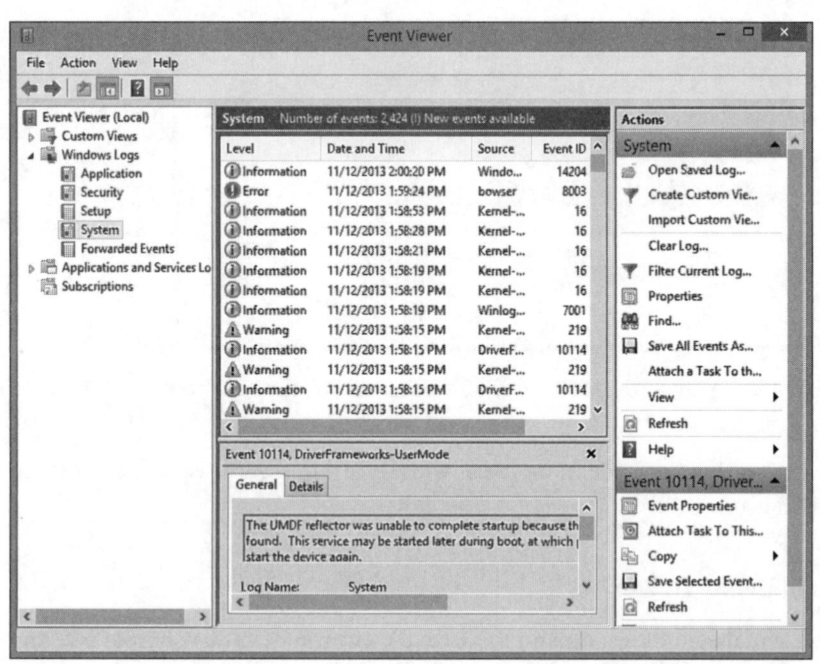

Figure 18-2 Most Event Viewer logs record errors, warning events, and informational events.

> **NOTE** If you are looking at Event Viewer on a server, you may observe additional event logs added by applications such as Active Directory and Domain Name System (DNS). Installed applications on servers and even on Windows 8.1 might add additional event logs to Event Viewer.

Most logs in Event Viewer record the three types of events—errors, warnings, and informational events—as previously seen in Figure 18-2. Error messages are represented by a red circle with a white exclamation mark in the center. Information messages are represented by a balloon with a blue “i” in the center, and warning messages are represented by a yellow triangle with a black exclamation mark in the center. Although not always true, an error is often preceded by one or more warning messages. A series of warning and error messages can describe the exact source of the problem, or at least point you in the right direction. To obtain additional information about an event, select it. The bottom of the central pane displays information related to the selected event. You can also right-click an event and select **Event Properties** to display information about the event in its own dialog box that can be viewed without scrolling.

Customizing Event Viewer

If you have selected a large number of auditable events, the Event Viewer logs can rapidly accumulate a large variety of events. Windows 8.1 provides capabilities for customizing what appears in the Event Viewer window. To customize the information displayed, right-click **Event Viewer** in the console tree and choose **Create Custom View**. This displays the Create Custom View dialog box shown in Figure 18-3.

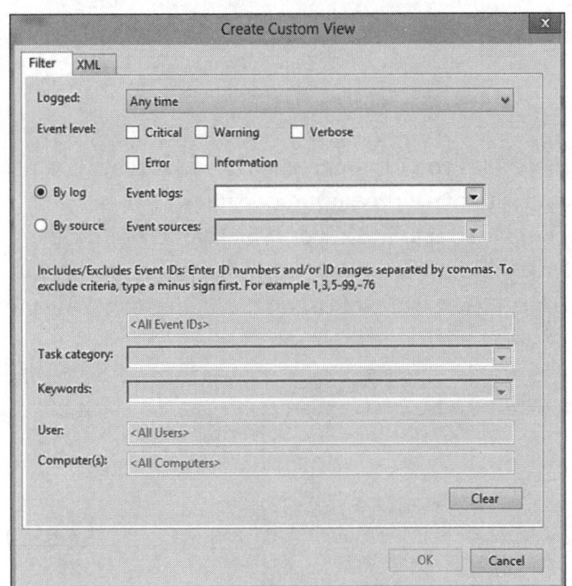

Figure 18-3 You can create custom views that filter event logs according to several categories.

Options available from this dialog box include the following:

- **Logged:** Select the time interval that you want to examine.
- **Event level:** Choose the type(s) of events you want to view. Select **Verbose** to view extra details related to the viewed events.
- **By log:** Select the Windows logs or Applications and Services logs you want to include.

- **By source:** Select from an extensive range of Windows services, utilities, and components whose logs you want to include.
- **Task category:** Expand the drop-down list and select the categories you want to view.
- **Keywords:** Select the keywords that you want to include in the customized view.
- **User** and **Computer(s):** Select the usernames of the accounts to be displayed and the names of the computers to be displayed. Separate the names in each list by commas.
- **XML tab:** Enables you to specify an event filter as an XML query.

After you make your selections, click **OK** and type a name for the custom view in the Save Filter to Custom View dialog box that appears. After you save the custom view, you can see this view by expanding the Custom Views node in the console tree to locate it by the name you provided.

Creating Tasks from Events

Event Viewer in Windows 8.1 also enables you to associate tasks with events. Event Viewer integrates with Task Scheduler to make this action possible. To do so, right-click the desired event and choose **Attach Task To This Event**. Follow the instructions in the Create Basic Task Wizard that opens, as shown in Figure 18-4. Actions that you can take include starting a specified program, sending an email, and displaying a message.

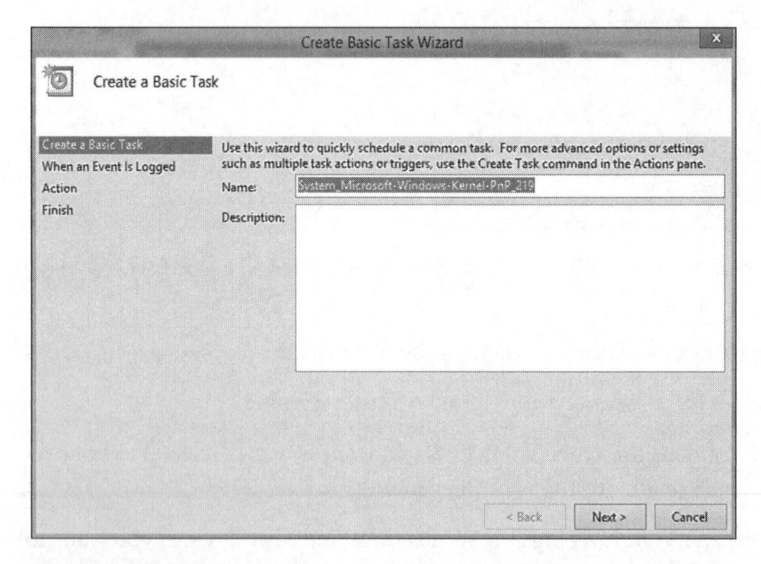

Figure 18-4 The Create Basic Task Wizard enables you to specify an action that will be taken each time a specific event takes place.

NOTE For more information on Event Viewer, refer to "Event Viewer" and links contained therein at http://technet.microsoft.com/en-us/library/cc766042.aspx.

Using Event Log Subscriptions

Event Viewer includes a Subscriptions feature that enables you to collect event logs from a number of computers (referred to as *source computers*) in a single, convenient location on a computer termed the *collector computer* that helps you keep track of events that occur on these computers. You can specify the events that will be collected and the local log in which they will be stored. After activating the subscription, you can view these event logs in the same manner as already discussed for local event logs.

The Event Subscriptions feature works by using Hypertext Transfer Protocol (HTTP) or Secure HTTP (HTTPS) to relay specified events from one or more originating (source) computers to a destination (collector) computer. It uses the Windows Remote Management (WinRM) and Windows Event Collector (Wecsvc) services to perform these actions. To configure event log subscriptions, you must configure these services on both the source and collector computers.

You can configure event subscriptions to work in either of two ways:

- **Collector-initiated:** The collector computer pulls the specified events from each of the source computers. This type is typically used where a limited number of easily identified source computers is available.
- **Source-initiated:** Each source computer pushes the specified events to the collector computer. This type is typically used where a large number of source computers is configured using Group Policy.

Configuring Computers to Forward and Collect Events

You need to run the `Winrm` and `Wecutil` commands at both the source and collector computers. To do so, log on to each source computer with an administrative user account (it is best to use a domain administrator account when configuring computers in an Active Directory Domain Services [AD DS] domain). Add the computer account of the collector computer to the local Administrators group on each source computer. In addition, type the following command at an administrative command prompt or PowerShell window:

```
Winrm quickconfig
```

Also log on to the collector computer with an administrative account, open an administrative command prompt or PowerShell window, and type the following command:

```
Wecutil qc
```

After you run these commands, the computers are now ready to forward and collect events. Note that in a workgroup environment, you can use only collector-initiated subscriptions. In addition, you need to perform the following steps:

- You must add a Windows Firewall exception for Remote Event Log Management at each source computer. We discussed configuring Windows Firewall in Chapter 10, "Configuring and Maintaining Network Security."
- You must add an account with administrative privileges to the Event Log Readers group at each source computer and specify this account in the Advanced Subscription Settings dialog box mentioned in the next section.
- At a command prompt on the collector computer, type **`winrm set winrm/config/client @{TrustedHosts="<sources>"}`**. In this command, *`<sources>`* is a list of the names of all workgroup source computers separated by commas.

NOTE For more information on the `winrm` and `wecutil` commands, refer to "Configure Advanced Subscription Settings" at http://technet.microsoft.com/en-us/library/cc749167.aspx.

Configuring Event Log Subscriptions

After you complete the preceding procedures at all source and collector computers, you are ready to configure event log subscriptions at the collector computer, by using the following procedure:

Step 1. In the console tree of Event Viewer, right-click the type of log for which you want to configure a subscription and choose **Properties**.

Step 2. Select the **Subscriptions** tab of the Properties dialog box that appears.

Step 3. If the Windows Event Collector Service is not running, Event Viewer displays the message box shown in Figure 18-5, asking you to start this service. Click **Yes** to proceed.

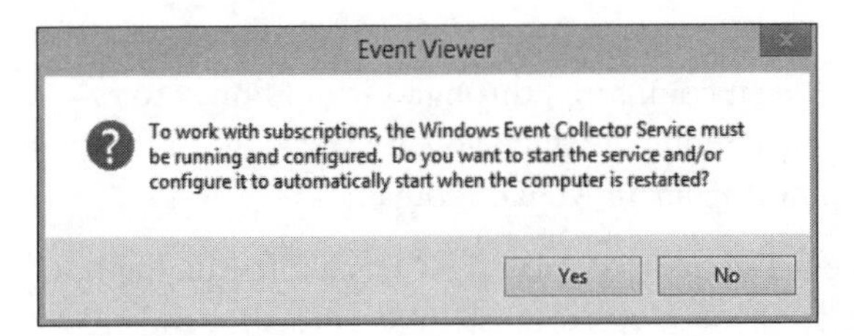

Figure 18-5 You are asked to start the Windows Event Collector Service before you can create an event log subscription.

Step 4. Click **Create** to create your first event subscription. Doing so displays the Subscription Properties dialog box shown in Figure 18-6.

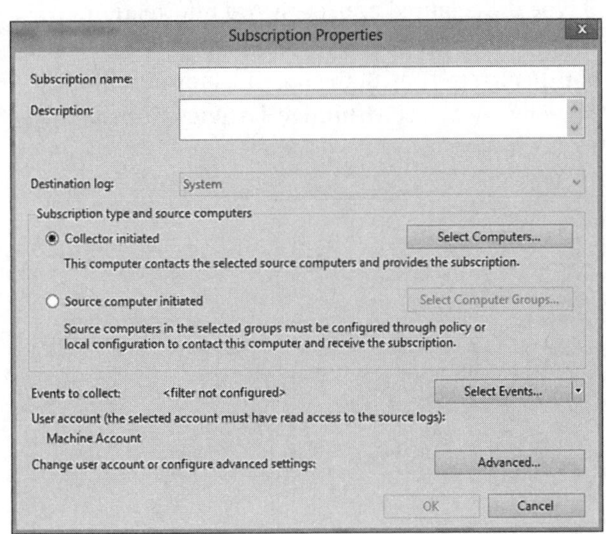

Figure 18-6 The Subscription Properties dialog box enables you to configure an event log subscription.

Step 5. Configure the following properties for your event log subscription and then click **OK** when finished.

- **Subscription name:** Provide an informative name that you will use to locate your event log subscription later. If desired, type an optional description in the field provided.
- **Destination log:** This field displays the log type, according to the Windows log you right-clicked in step 1 of this procedure.
- **Subscription type and source computers:** Select **Collector initiated** and click the **Select Computers** button to specify the computers from which you

want to collect event data. Or select **Source computer initiated** to specify groups of computers that have been configured through Group Policy to receive the subscription from the computer at which you are working. In either case, you can also select computers from an AD DS domain.

- **Events to collect:** Click **Select Events** to display the Query Filter dialog box, which provides the same options as shown previously in Figure 18-3 and enables you to select the event types that will be included in the subscription.
- **Advanced:** Click **Advanced** to display the Advanced Subscription Settings dialog box shown in Figure 18-7, which enables you to select the user account that has access to the source logs and optimize event delivery. To specify a user other than the one indicated, click **Specific User**; then click the **User and Password** button and type the required user/password information. Choose **Normal** to provide reliable event delivery without conserving bandwidth. Select **Minimize Bandwidth** to control the use of bandwidth but reduce the frequency of event delivery. Select **Minimize Latency** to ensure the most rapid delivery of events.

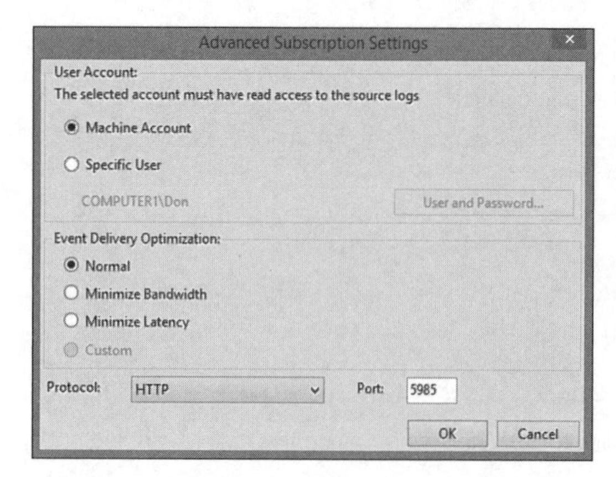

Figure 18-7 The Advanced Subscription Settings dialog box enables you to specify user account and event delivery settings.

NOTE If you select a different user account from the Advanced Subscription Settings dialog box, the account you select must be a member of the local computer's Event Log Readers group or the Administrators group.

NOTE For more information on creating and managing event log subscriptions, refer to "Event Subscriptions" at http://technet.microsoft.com/en-us/library/cc749183.aspx and "Manage Subscriptions" at http://technet.microsoft.com/en-us/library/cc749140.aspx, plus the links contained therein.

Managing and Optimizing Computer Performance

Windows 8.1 includes several tools that are used for monitoring, optimizing, and troubleshooting performance. They include Reliability Monitor, Resource Monitor, Performance Monitor, and Task Manager.

Reliability Monitor

First introduced with Windows Vista, Reliability Monitor utilizes the built-in Reliability Analysis Component (RAC) to provide a trend analysis of your computer's system stability over time. As shown in Figure 18-8, Reliability Monitor provides the System Stability Chart, which correlates the trend of your computer's stability against events that might destabilize the computer. Events tracked include Windows Updates; software installations and removals; device driver installations, updates, rollbacks, and removals, as well as driver failure to load or unload; application hangs and crashes; disk and memory failures; and Windows failures such as boot failures, crashes, and sleep failures. This chart enables you to track a reliability change directly to a given event.

Windows 8.1 enhances Reliability Monitor by integrating it with Problem Reports and Solutions to improve the correlation of system changes, events and possible problem resolutions.

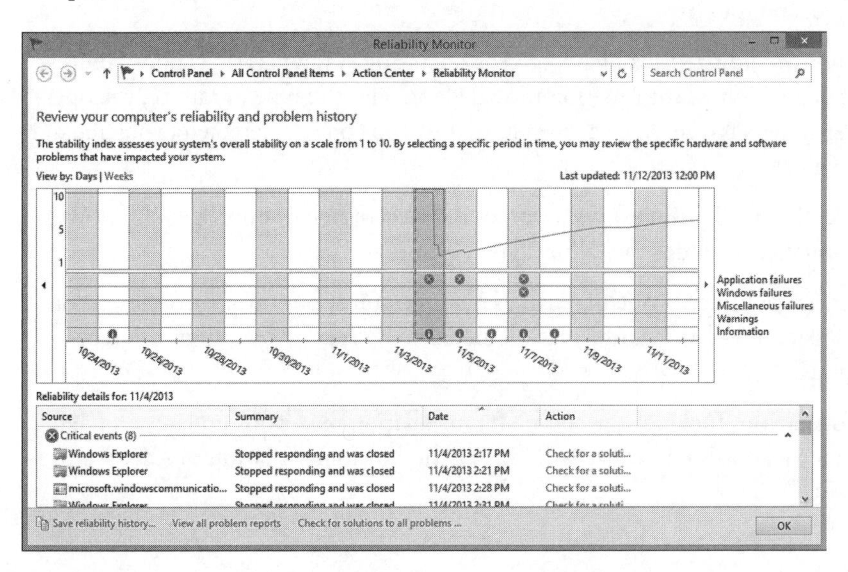

Figure 18-8 Reliability Monitor provides a trend analysis of your computer's stability.

NOTE To display data in the System Stability Chart, you must run your computer for at least 24 hours after first installation of Windows 8.1. For the first 28 days, Reliability Monitor uses a dotted line on the Stability Chart graph, indicating that the data is insufficient to establish a valid baseline for this index.

Use the following steps to run Reliability Monitor:

Step 1. Ensure that you are logged on as an administrator or have administrator credentials available.

Step 2. In the Search charm, type `reliability` in the search box. Then click **View reliability history** in the Programs list. If you receive a UAC prompt, supply administrative credentials if needed and click **Yes**.

Step 3. Wait while Reliability Monitor generates its report. As shown previously in Figure 18-8, events that cause the performance index to drop are marked in one of the event rows. Click a date containing one of these marks and then expand the appropriate section to obtain more information for the following categories:

- **Application failures:** Software programs that hang or crash. Information provided includes the name of the program, its version number, the type of failure, and the date.
- **Windows failures:** Problems such as operating system crashes, boot failures, and sleep failures. Information provided includes the type of failure, the operating system and service pack version, the Stop code or detected problem, and the failure date.
- **Miscellaneous failures:** Other types of failures such as improper shutdowns. Information includes the failure type, details, and date.
- **Warnings:** Other problems such as unsuccessful application reconfiguration or update installation. Information includes the type of reconfiguration attempted.
- **Information:** Includes the successful installation of various updates and definition packs, as well as successful installation or uninstallation of software programs.

Step 4. To view a comprehensive list of problems, click the **View all problem reports** link at the bottom of the dialog box. The list displayed includes the various types of failures noted here.

Step 5. To export an XML-based reliability report, click **Save reliability history**, specify a path and filename, and then click **Save**.

Step 6. To check for solutions to problems, click **Check for solutions to all problems.** Reliability Monitor displays a Checking for solutions message box as it goes to the Internet and attempts to locate solutions to your problems. You may need to click **Send information** to send additional information to the Microsoft Error Reporting Service.

Resource Monitor

Resource Monitor provides a summary of CPU, disk, network, and memory performance statistics including mini-graphs of recent performance of these four components. In Windows Vista, Resource Monitor was combined with Performance Monitor in a single Microsoft Management Console (MMC) snap-in; Windows 8.1 (as was the case with Windows 7 and Windows 8) separates these two applications into their own interfaces. Use any of the following procedures to open Resource Monitor:

- If you've enabled the Administrative Tools feature on the Start screen, simply click the **Resource Monitor** tile.
- From the Search charm, type `resource` in the search box. Then select **Resource Monitor** from the displayed apps.
- Open the Search charm and type `msconfig` in the search box. Then click **System Configuration** in the Programs list. From the Tools tab of System Configuration, select **Resource Monitor** and then click **Launch**.
- Open Task Manager and click **Resource Monitor** from the Performance tab.

After you open Resource Monitor, you can click the downward-pointing arrow on the right side of any of the four headings to display additional information about a component, similar to that shown for CPU in Figure 18-9.

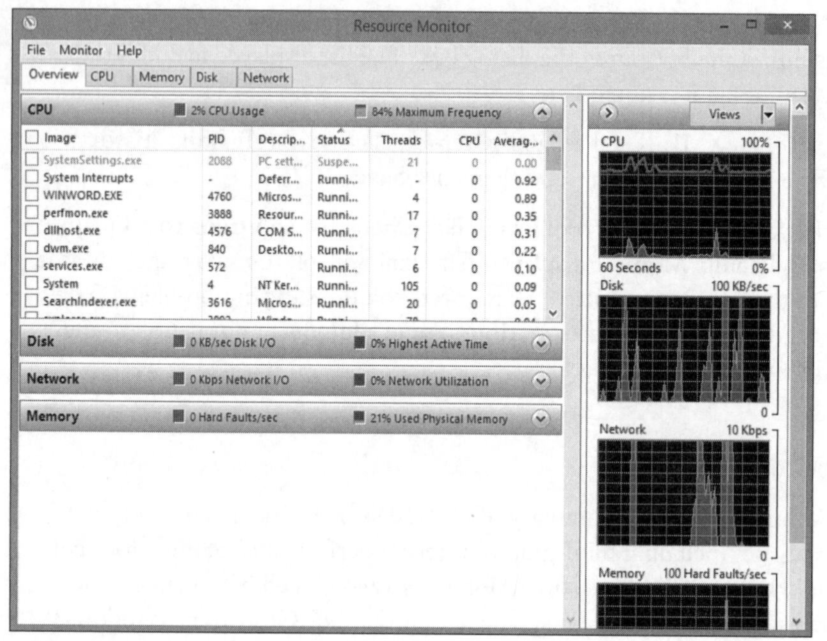

Figure 18-9 You can expand each component in Resource Monitor to obtain a summary of its performance information.

For each of the four components, the information provided on the Overview tab includes the application whose resource usage is being monitored (known as the image) and the process identifier number (PID) of the application instance. The following additional information is provided on the Overview tab for each of the four components:

- **CPU:** A brief description of the monitored application, the number of threads per application, the CPU cycles currently used by each application instance, and the average CPU resulting from each instance as a percentage of total CPU usage.
- **Disk:** The file being read or written by each application instance, the current read and write speeds in bytes/minute, the total disk input/output (I/O) in bytes/minute, the I/O priority level, and the response time in milliseconds.
- **Network:** The IP address of the network component with which the computer is exchanging data and the amount of data (bandwidth) in bytes per second (sent, received, and total) by each instance.
- **Memory:** Current hard faults per second and memory usage information in KB for committed, working set, sharable, and private memory components.

To filter the display of disk, network, and memory usage according to process, select the check box or boxes in the Image column of the CPU section, as previously shown in Figure 18-9. To change the size of the graphical displays on any tab, select **Large**, **Medium**, or **Small** from the Views drop-down list above the graphical displays on the right.

By selecting the tab associated with each component, you can view additional details about the component selected.

CPU Tab

The CPU tab provides graphical displays of the total CPU percentage utilization, as well as values for each processor or core and the Service CPU Usage. If you want to display information for certain processors or cores only, you can do so by selecting **Monitor > Select Processors** and choosing the desired processor(s) from the dialog box that appears. Tabulated information includes CPU usage by all processes and services running on the machine. You can filter the display in the information tables of any tab by selecting the check boxes for the desired processes in the Processes section, similar to the action previously described for the Overview tab. When you are filtering the results on any tab, the graphical displays include an orange line that represents the proportion of each activity type represented by the selected processes; tabulated displays show an orange information bar that informs you which processes are included.

Memory Tab

The Memory tab provides graphical displays of the Used Physical Memory, Commit Charge, and Hard Faults/sec memory counters. Besides a tabular view of memory usage by processes running on the computer, this tab includes a bar graph representation that shows the relative amount of memory apportioned to Hardware Reserved, In Use, Modified, Standby, and Free. The amount of memory that's available to programs includes the total of standby and free memory. Free memory includes zero page memory.

Disk Tab

Graphs included on the Disk tab include total disk usage over a 60-second period plus the queue length for each disk as well as the total queue length. Processes with disk activity are tabulated, along with bytes/sec values for disk reads, writes, and total access. Disk activity by process and available storage by logical disk volume are also tabulated.

Network Tab

The Network tab includes graphical display of network activity as well as the number of TCP connections and the percentage utilization of network connections across each network adapter in the computer. Tabulated information includes the processes with network activity, for which the number of bytes/sec sent, received, and total are shown. Tables of network activity, TCP connections, and listening ports are also shown; on this tab, similar to other tabs, you can filter these displays by selecting the check boxes in the top section of the tabular display.

TIP You can use Resource Monitor to end unresponsive processes in a manner similar to that of Task Manager. Such a process is displayed in red in the top section of the Overview tab. Right-click the process in the tabular display and choose **End Process**. A message box warns you that you will lose any unsaved data and that ending a system process might result in system instability. Click **End process** to end the process or **Cancel** to quit.

NOTE For more information on using Resource Monitor, refer to "Resource Availability Troubleshooting Getting Started Guide" at http://technet.microsoft.com/en-us/library/dd883276(WS.10).aspx.

Performance Monitor

The Windows 8.1 Performance console includes the following monitoring tools:

- **Performance Monitor:** Provides a real-time graph of computer performance, either in the current time or as logged historical data.
- **Data Collector Sets:** Records computer performance information into log files. Data collectors are grouped into groups that you can use for monitoring performance under different conditions.
- **Reports:** Creates a report of performance report data.

Performance Monitor, which is shown in Figure 18-10, provides a real-time graph of computer performance and enables you to perform tasks such as the following:

- Identify performance problems such as bottlenecks
- Monitor resource usage
- Track trends over time
- Measure the effects of changes in system configuration
- Generate alerts when unusual conditions occur

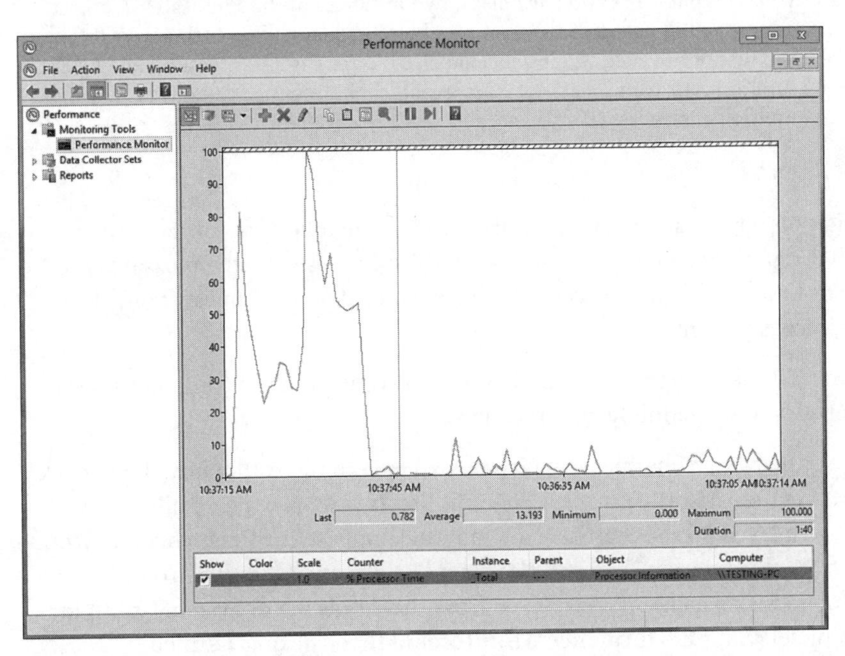

Figure 18-10 Performance Monitor displays a real-time graph of activity for selected objects and counters.

Before you learn more about the Performance Monitor tool, you need to be familiar with the terms described in Table 18-2, which are used in a specific manner when referring to performance metrics.

Table 18-2 Performance Monitor Terminology

Item	Description
Object	A specific hardware or software component that the Performance Console is capable of monitoring. It can be any component that possesses a series of measurable properties. Windows 8.1 comes with a defined set of objects; applications such as Internet Information Services (IIS) installed on Windows 8.1 may add more objects to the available set.
Counter	One of a series of statistical measurements associated with each object.
Instance	A term that refers to multiple occurrences of a given object. For example, if your computer has two hard disks, two instances of the PhysicalDisk object are present. These instances are numbered sequentially, starting with 0 for the first occurrence. An instance labeled `_Total` is also present, yielding the sum of performance data for each counter. Note that not all objects have multiple instances.

Information on objects and counters is displayed in the following format: *Object (_instance)\Counter*. For example, Processor (_0)\%Processor Time measures the %Processor time on the first processor. The instance does not appear if only a single instance is present.

Performance Monitor enables you to obtain a real-time graph of computer performance statistics. Use the following procedure:

Step 1. Access the Search charm and type **`performance`** in the search box. Then click **Performance Monitor** in the Programs list. If you have the administrative tools displayed on the Start screen, you can simply select **Performance Monitor** from this location. You can also start Performance Monitor from the Computer Management console, or from the Tools tab of System Configuration by selecting **Performance Monitor** and then clicking **Launch**.

Step 2. If you receive a UAC prompt, click **Yes** or supply administrative credentials.

Step 3. In the Performance console, click **Performance Monitor**. As previously shown in Figure 18-10, Performance Monitor displays the Processor\%Processor Time counter.

Step 4. To add objects and counters, click the green **+** icon on the toolbar.

Step 5. In the Add Counters dialog box that appears (see Figure 18-11), ensure that the Select counters from computer drop-down list reads `<Local computer>` for monitoring the local computer performance. Then select the desired object and instance from the lists directly below the Select counters list.

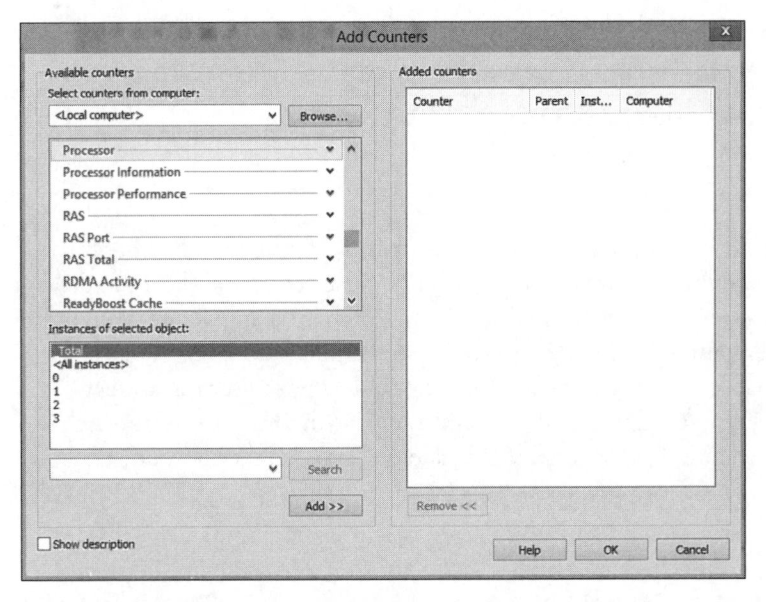

Figure 18-11 You can select from a large number of objects from the list in the Add Counters dialog box.

Step 6. Expand the desired object to display a list of available counters from which you can select one or more counters, as shown in Figure 18-12. To add counters to the graph, select the counter and click **Add**.

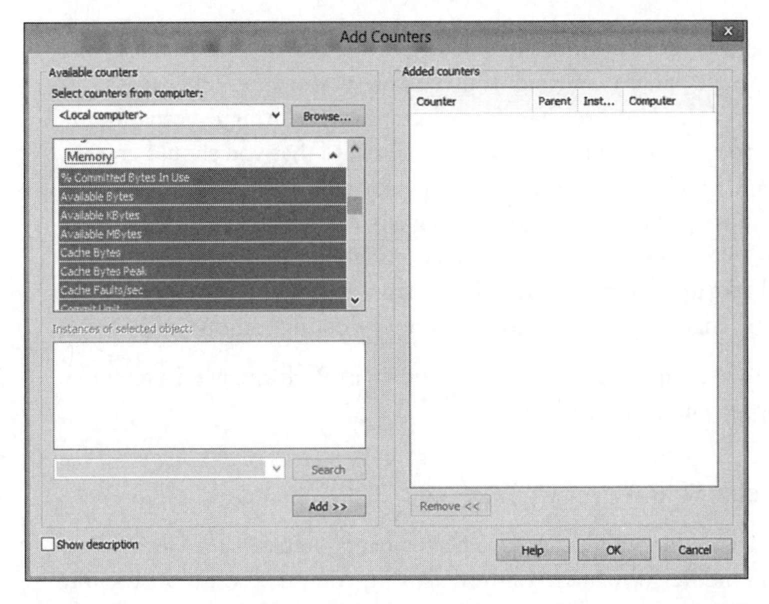

Figure 18-12 Expanding a performance object enables you to select from the available counters for that object.

Step 7. Repeat steps 5 and 6 to add more counters. You learn about suitable counters in the following sections.

Step 8. When you are finished, click **OK**.

TIP You can highlight individual counters in Performance Monitor. To highlight an individual counter in the Performance Monitor display, select it from the list at the bottom of the details pane and click the highlight icon (looks like a highlighter pen) in the taskbar. You can also press the **Backspace** key to highlight the counter. The highlighted counter appears in a heavy line. You can use the up- or down-arrow keys to toggle through the list of counters and highlight each one in turn. This feature helps you find the desired counter from a graph that includes a large number of counters.

NOTE For more information on Performance Monitor, refer to "Performance Monitoring Getting Started Guide" at http://technet.microsoft.com/en-ca/library/dd744567(WS.10).aspx.

Data Collector Sets

A data collector set is a set of performance objects and counters that enables you to log computer performance over time while you are performing other tasks. Such logging is important because changes in computer performance often occur only after an extended period of time. Best practices state that you should create a *performance baseline*, which is a log of computer performance that you can save for comparing with future performance and tracking any changes that might have occurred over time. In this way you can identify potential bottlenecks in computer performance and take any required corrective measures. You can also monitor the effectiveness of any changes you make to a computer's configuration.

The Data Collector Sets feature was formerly known as Performance Logs and Alerts in Windows versions prior to Vista.

Creating Data Collector Sets

Data collector sets are binary files that save performance statistics for later viewing and analysis in the Performance Monitor snap-in; you can also export them to spreadsheet or database programs for later analysis. Windows 8.1 creates a series of data collector sets by default. The default data collector sets enable you to log default sets of performance counters for various purposes, including system diagnostics, LAN diagnostics, system performance, wireless diagnostics, event trace sessions, and startup event trace sessions. To view these sets, expand the branches under the Data Collector Sets node of Performance Monitor. Right-click any available data collector set and choose **Properties** to view information on the selected data collector set.

You may also create your own user-defined data collector set. Use the following procedure to create a data collector set:

Step 1. In the console tree of the Performance Monitor snap-in, select and expand **Data Collector Sets**.

Step 2. Select **User Defined**.

Step 3. To create a new data collector set, right-click a blank area of the details pane and select **New > Data Collector Set**. The Create new Data Collector Set Wizard starts.

Step 4. Provide a name for the new data collector set. Select either **Create from a template (Recommended)** or **Create Manually (Advanced)**, and then click **Next**. If you select the **Create Manually (Advanced)** option, refer to the next procedure for the remainder of the steps you should perform.

Step 5. If you select the **Create from a template** option, you receive the dialog box shown in Figure 18-13, which enables you to use one of the following templates:

- **Basic:** Enables you to use performance counters to create a basic data collector set, which you can edit later if necessary.
- **System Diagnostics:** Enables you to create a report that contains details of local hardware resources, system response times, and local computer processes. System information and configuration data are also included.
- **System Performance:** Enables you to create a report that provides details on local hardware resources, system response times, and local computer processes.
- **WDAC Diagnostics:** Provides trace detailed debug information for Windows Data Access Components (WDAC) components using BidTrace.

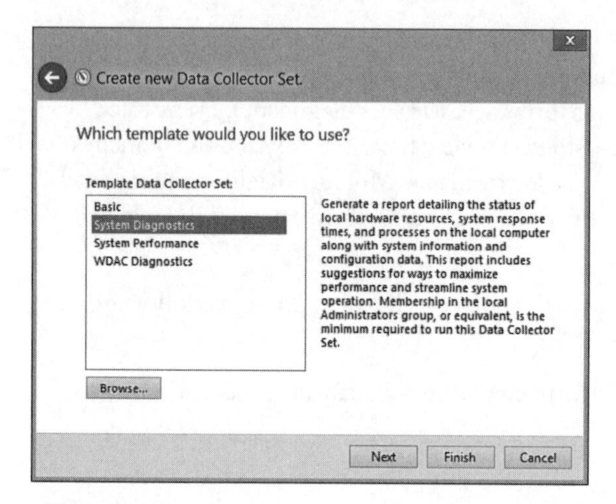

Figure 18-13 The Create new Data Collector Set wizard enables you to use several different templates.

NOTE For more information on WDAC, refer to "Data Access Tracing (Windows 8)" at http://msdn.microsoft.com/en-us/library/windows/desktop/hh829624(v=vs.85).aspx.

Step 6. Select the desired template and click **Browse** to locate a template file (XML format) if one exists. Then click **Next**.

Step 7. Select a location to which you would like the data to be saved (or accept the default location provided), and then click **Next**.

Step 8. You receive the Create the data collector set? page shown in Figure 18-14. To run the set as a different user, click **Change** and then select the desired user. To start logging now or configure additional properties, select the option provided. Then click **Finish**.

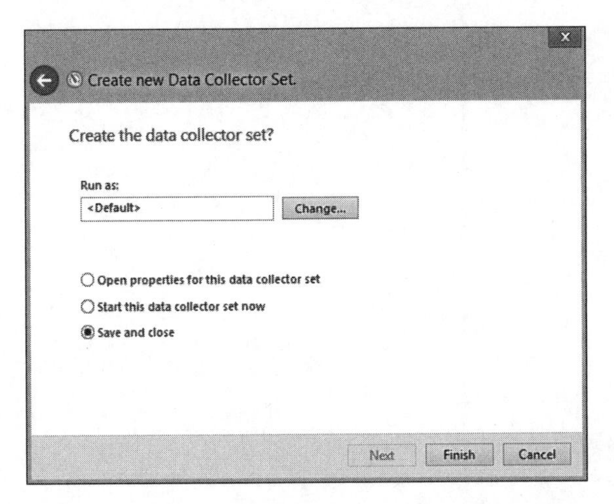

Figure 18-14 The Create the data collector set? page enables you to run the set as another user or open the properties of the data collector set.

To create a custom data collector set, use the **Create manually (Advanced)** option in step 4 of the previous procedure and then use the following steps to complete the procedure.

Step 1. After selecting the **Create manually (Advanced)** option and clicking **Next**, you receive the screen shown in Figure 18-15, which enables you to specify the following options:

- **Performance counter:** Enables you to select performance objects and counters to be logged over time. Click **Next** to specify the performance counters to be logged and the desired sampling interval.
- **Event trace data:** Enables you to create trace logs, which are similar to counter logs, but they log data only when a specific activity takes place, whereas counter logs track data continuously for a specified interval.
- **System configuration information:** Enables you to track changes in Registry keys. Click **Next** to specify the desired keys.
- **Performance Counter Alert:** Enables you to display an alert when a selected counter exceeds or drops beneath a specified value. Click **Next** to specify the counters you would like to alert and the limiting value (see Figure 18-16 for an example).

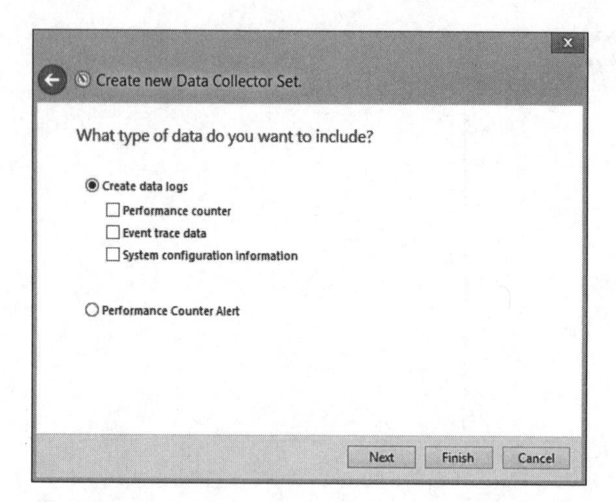

Figure 18-15 You can create several types of logs or alerts from the Create Manually option in the Create new Data Collector Set wizard.

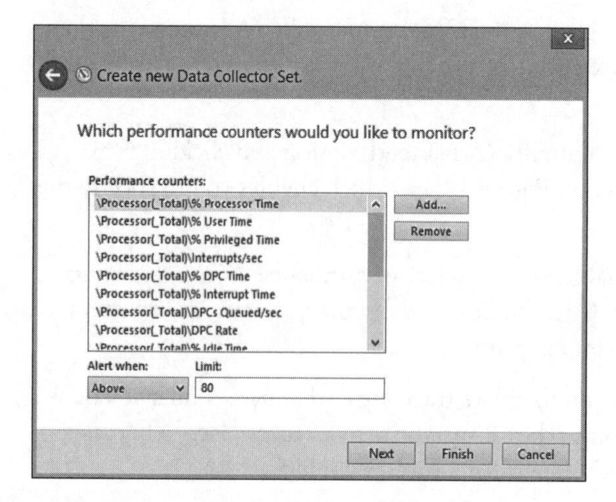

Figure 18-16 You can create an alert that informs you when the Processor\% Processor Time value exceeds 80 percent.

Step 2. After clicking **Next**, you receive the same dialog box shown previously in Figure 18-14. Make any changes needed and then click **Finish**.

Using Performance Monitor to Create a Data Collector Set

Perhaps the simplest method to create a data collector set is to use a set of counters you have already configured in Performance Monitor. The following steps shows you how:

Step 1. After creating a performance graph as described earlier in this section, right-click **Performance Monitor** in the console tree and select **New > Data Collector Set**. The Create New Data Collector Set wizard starts, as previously described.

Step 2. Provide a name for the data collector set and then click **Next**.

Step 3. Accept the location to which the data is to be saved, or type or browse to the location of your choice, and then click **Next**.

Step 4. In the Create the data collector set? page, select any required options and then click **Finish**.

The data collector set is created and placed in the User Defined section. If you select the option to start the data collector set now, logging begins immediately and continues until you right-click the data collector set and choose **Stop**.

You can view data collected by the data collector set in Performance Monitor. From the view previously shown in Figure 18-10, select the **View Log Data** icon (the second icon from the left in the toolbar immediately above the performance graph). In the Source tab of the Performance Monitor Properties dialog box that appears, select the **Log files** option and click **Add**. Select the desired log file in the Select Log File dialog box that appears, click **Open**, and then click **OK**. This displays the selected log in the performance graph.

Optimizing and Troubleshooting Memory Performance

The Memory object includes counters that monitor the computer's physical and virtual memory. Table 18-3 describes the most important counters for this object.

Table 18-3 Important Counters for the Memory Object

Counter	What It Measures	Interpretation and Remedial Tips
Pages/sec	The rate at which data is read to or written from the paging file	A value of 20 or more indicates a shortage of RAM and a possible memory bottleneck. To view the effect of paging file performance on the system, watch this counter together with LogicalDisk\% Disk Time. Add RAM to clear the problem.
Available Bytes (KBytes, MBytes)	The amount of physical memory available	A value consistently below 4 MB indicates a shortage of available memory. This might be due to memory leaks in one or more applications. Check your programs for memory leaks. You might need to add more RAM.

Counter	What It Measures	Interpretation and Remedial Tips
Committed Bytes	The amount of virtual memory that has been committed to either physical RAM or running processes	Committed memory is in use and not available to other processes. If the amount of committed bytes exceeds the amount of RAM on the computer, you might need to add RAM.
Pool Nonpaged Bytes	The amount of RAM in the nonpaged pool system memory (an area holding objects that cannot be written to disk)	If this value exhibits a steady increase in bytes without a corresponding increase in computer activity, check for an application with a memory leak.
Page Faults/sec	The number of data pages that must be read from or written to the page file per second	A high value indicates a lot of paging activity. Add RAM to alleviate this problem.

In addition to these counters, the Paging File\% Usage counter is of use when you are troubleshooting memory problems. This counter measures the percentage of the paging file currently in use. If it approaches 100%, you should either increase the size of the paging file or add more RAM.

Lack of adequate memory may also have an impact on the performance of other subsystems in the computer. In particular, a large amount of paging, or reading/writing data from/to the paging file on the hard disk, results in increased activity in both the processor and disk subsystems. You should monitor counters in these subsystems at the same time if you suspect memory-related performance problems. You learn more about monitoring counters later in the section "Optimizing and Troubleshooting Processor Utilization."

The paging file is an area on the hard disk that is used as an additional memory location for programs and data that cannot fit into RAM (in other words, virtual memory). By default, the paging file is located at `%systemdrive%\pagefile.sys` and has a default initial size of the amount of RAM in the computer plus 300 MB, and a default maximum size of three times the amount of RAM in the computer.

To improve performance on a computer equipped with more than one physical hard disk, you should locate the paging file on a different hard disk than that occupied by the operating system. You can also increase the size of the paging file or configure multiple paging files on different hard disks. Any of these configurations help to optimize performance by spreading out the activity of reading/writing data from/to the paging files. Note that you should retain a paging file on the system/boot drive to create a memory dump in case of a crash. This memory dump is useful for debugging purposes.

Use the following procedure to modify the configuration of the paging file:

Step 1. In the Search charm, type `performance` and then select **Adjust the appearance and performance of Windows** from the list of options that appears. This opens the Performance Options dialog box.

Step 2. Select the **Advanced** tab.

Step 3. In the Virtual memory section of this tab, click **Change**.

Step 4. As shown in Figure 18-17, the Virtual Memory dialog box displays the disk partitions available on the computer and the size of the paging file on each. To add a paging file to a drive, first clear the **Automatically manage paging file size for all drives** dialog box. Select the drive and choose **Custom size** to specify an initial and maximum size in megabytes or **System managed size** to obtain a default size. To remove a paging file, select the drive holding the file and click **No paging file**. Note that some programs may not work properly if you choose the **No paging file** option. Then click **Set**.

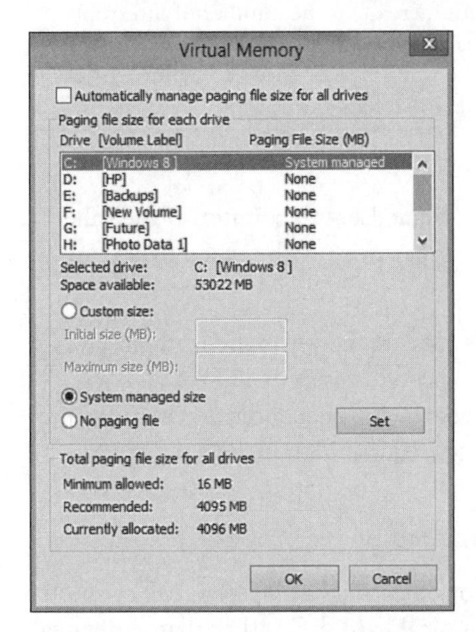

Figure 18-17 You can modify paging file properties from the Virtual Memory dialog box.

Step 5. Click **OK** three times to apply your changes and to close the Performance Options and System Properties dialog boxes.

Step 6. Click **Restart Now** to restart your computer if so prompted.

Optimizing and Troubleshooting Processor Utilization

The processor is the "heart" of the system because it executes all program instructions, whether internal to the operating system or in user-executed applications. The Processor object contains counters that monitor processor performance. Table 18-4 discusses the most important counters for this object.

Table 18-4 Important Counters for the Processor Object

Counter	What It Measures	Interpretation and Remedial Tips
% Processor Time	The percentage of time the processor is executing meaningful actions (excludes the Idle process)	If this value is consistently greater than 85%, the processor could be causing a bottleneck. You should check the memory counters discussed previously; if these are high, consider adding more RAM. Otherwise, you should consider adding a faster processor (or an additional one if supported by your motherboard).
Interrupts/sec	The rate of service requests from I/O devices that interrupt other processor activities	A significant increase in the number of interrupts without a corresponding increase in system activity may indicate some type of hardware failure. Brief spikes are acceptable.

You should also look at the System\Processor Queue Length counter. If the value of this counter exceeds 2, a processor bottleneck may exist, with several programs contending for the processor's time.

As mentioned in Table 18-4, memory shortages may frequently manifest themselves in high processor activity. It is usually much cheaper and easier to add RAM to a computer than to add a faster or additional processor. Consequently, you may want to consider this step first when you are experiencing frequent high processor activity.

Optimizing and Troubleshooting Disk Performance

Disk performance is measured by two processor objects: The PhysicalDisk counters measure the overall performance of a single physical hard disk rather than individual partitions. LogicalDisk counters measure the performance of a single partition or volume on a disk. These counters include the performance of spanned, striped, or RAID-5 volumes that cross physical disks.

PhysicalDisk counters are best suited for hardware troubleshooting. Table 18-5 describes the most important counters for this object.

Table 18-5 Important Counters for the PhysicalDisk Object

Counter	What It Measures	Interpretation and Remedial Tips
% Disk Time	The percentage of time that the disk was busy reading or writing to any partition	A value of more than 50% suggests a disk bottleneck. Consider upgrading to a faster disk or controller. Also check the memory counters to see whether more RAM is needed.
Avg. Disk Queue Length	The average number of disk read and write requests waiting to be performed	If this value is greater than 2, follow the same suggestions as for % Disk Time.
Average Disk Sec/Transfer	The length of time a disk takes to fulfill requests.	A value greater than 0.3 may indicate that the disk controller is retrying the disk continually because of write failures.

LogicalDisk counters are best suited for investigating the read/write performance of a single partition. Table 18-6 describes the most important counters for this object.

Table 18-6 Important Counters for the LogicalDisk Object

Counter	What It Measures	Interpretation and Remedial Tips
% Disk Time	The percentage of time that the disk is busy servicing disk requests	A value greater than 90% may indicate a performance problem except when using a RAID device. Compare to Processor\% Processor Time to determine whether disk requests are using too much processor time.
Average Disk Bytes/Transfer	The amount of data transferred in each I/O operation	Low values (below about 20 KB) indicate that an application may be accessing a disk inefficiently. Watch this counter as you close applications to locate an offending application.
Current Disk Queue Length	The amount of data waiting to be transferred to the disk	A value greater than 2 indicates a possible disk bottleneck, with processes being delayed because of slow disk speed. Consider adding another faster disk.
Disk Transfers/sec	The rate at which read or write operations are performed by the disk	A value greater than 50 may indicate a disk bottleneck. Consider adding another faster disk.
% Free Space	Percentage of unused disk space	A value less than about 15% indicates that insufficient disk space is available. Consider moving files, repartitioning the disk, or adding another disk.

TIP You should log disk activity to a different disk or computer. The act of recording performance logs places an extra "hit" on performance for the disk on which logs are recorded. To obtain accurate disk monitoring results, record this data to a different disk or computer.

Command-Line Utilities

You can perform several tasks associated with performance monitoring and optimization from the command line. The following are tools you can use:

- **`Logman`:** Manages data collector logs. You can start, stop, and schedule the collection of performance and trace data.
- **`Relog`:** Creates new performance logs from data in existing logs by modifying the sampling rate and/or converting the file format.
- **`Typeperf`:** Displays performance data to the command prompt window or to a log file.

You can also use the `Perfmon` command to start the Performance Monitor from a command line. For information on running these tools, type the command name followed by `/?` at a command prompt.

Configuring Task Manager

Microsoft has completely redesigned Task Manager in Windows 8 and 8.1, with the purpose of optimizing usage of Task Manager for the most common actions performed by users. Most specifically, users tend to utilize this tool to close misbehaving applications or to locate and kill processes that are using excessive quantities of computer resources. At the same time, designers wanted to ensure that no other uses of Task Manager were removed despite their not being as frequently used.

Task Manager provides data about currently running processes, including their CPU and memory usage, and enables you to modify their priority or shut down misbehaving applications. You can use any of the following methods to start Task Manager:

- In Windows 8.1, right-click **Start** and choose **Task Manager** from the menu that appears.
- Access the Search charm and type **`task manager`**. Then select **Task Manager** from the programs list.
- From the Tools tab of System Configuration, select **Task Manager** and then click **Launch**.
- Press **Ctrl+Shift+Esc**.

- Press **Ctrl+Alt+Delete** and select **Task Manager** from the Windows Security dialog box.
- Right-click a blank area on the taskbar and then select **Task Manager**.

Newly redesigned for Windows 8 and 8.1, Task Manager opens with a simplified interface that lists the apps currently running on your computer, as shown in Figure 18-18. This view displays a `Not responding` message beside any running application that has stopped functioning. Right-clicking an app enables you to perform a series of actions including the following:

- **Switch to:** Brings the focus on the desktop to the selected app.
- **End task:** Enables you to shut down an unresponsive app (the same as clicking the **End task** command button).
- **Run new task:** Brings up the Create new task dialog box (similar to the Run dialog box on previous Windows versions), which enables you to start a program or open a folder, document, or web page from the Internet. You can also create the task with administrative privileges.
- **Always on top:** Keeps the Task Manager window displayed on top of any other windows that might otherwise cover it.
- **Open file location:** Opens a File Explorer window focused on the folder in which the selected app is located.
- **Search online:** Opens Internet Explorer to your default search engine and performs an Internet search on the selected app.
- **Properties:** Displays a Properties dialog box for the selected app.

Figure 18-18 When you first start Task Manager in Windows 8.1, it provides a list of apps that are currently running on your computer.

Click **More details** to open the advanced interface of Task Manager, as shown in Figure 18-19. By default, the advanced interface displays the Processes tab, which provides information on resources (CPU, memory, disk, and network) consumed by processes running on the computer. This information is grouped according to process type (applications, background processes, and Windows processes) and is color-coded with darker colors representing resources being utilized more intensively. If an application is using an extreme amount of a given resource, the column header and the responsible application are strongly highlighted, drawing your attention to this occurrence. You can expand a process to locate multiple instances of the process, by clicking on the triangle to the left of the desired process. You can modify the properties of a running application or terminate an ill-behaved process or one that is consuming a large amount of resources (right-click the process and choose **End task**). You can also obtain information from the Internet about an unfamiliar process by right-clicking it and choosing **Search the Web**. This runs your default search engine in Internet Explorer to locate information on the selected process.

Key Topic

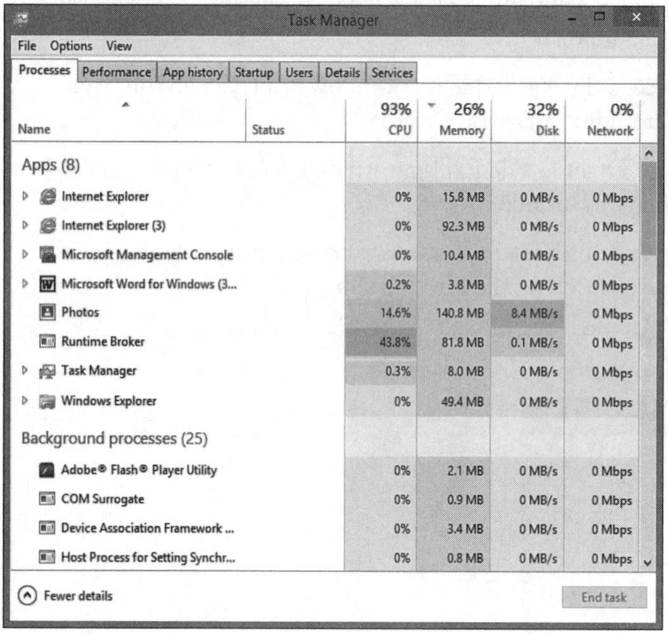

Figure 18-19 The advanced interface of Task Manager displays all the processes running on your computer and provides summary performance information on each item. Highlights draw attention to processes using the most resources.

TIP You can sort processes according to the amount of a specific resource they're consuming by clicking the title (**CPU, Memory, Disk,** or **Network**) of the desired resource. Doing so can help you to locate an ill-behaved process. For example, by clicking **Memory**, you can see which processes are using the most RAM.

The remaining six tabs perform the following tasks:

- **Performance:** Provides a limited performance monitoring function, as shown in Figure 18-20, showing processor, memory, disk, and network statistics. This tab is ideal for providing a quick snapshot of computer performance. Select any of the objects in the left column to display its statistics. You can also access the Resource Monitor application described earlier in this chapter.
- **App history:** Provides history information on CPU, network, metered network, and tile updates history, for each app on the computer since the last time usage history was deleted. Click **Delete user history** to restart collection of history data.
- **Startup:** Provides information on processes configured to start when you restart your computer. Information provided includes the publisher name, the status of the program (enabled or disabled), and the startup impact. To prevent an application from starting on the next boot, right-click it and choose **Disable**, or select it and click the **Disable** command button. On a disabled task, this button changes to **Enable**.
- **Users:** Displays the users that have sessions, active or disconnected, running on the local computer.
- **Details:** Provides detailed information on all instances of all processes running on the computer and enables you to end specific processes.
- **Services:** Provides information on services installed on the computer. You can view which services are running or stopped, the service group to which they belong, and descriptive information about each service. You can start a stopped service or stop a running service by right-clicking the service name and selecting **Start** or **Stop**. You can also determine whether a service is associated with a particular process by right-clicking the service name and selecting **Go to details**. This opens the Details tab and highlights the selected process.

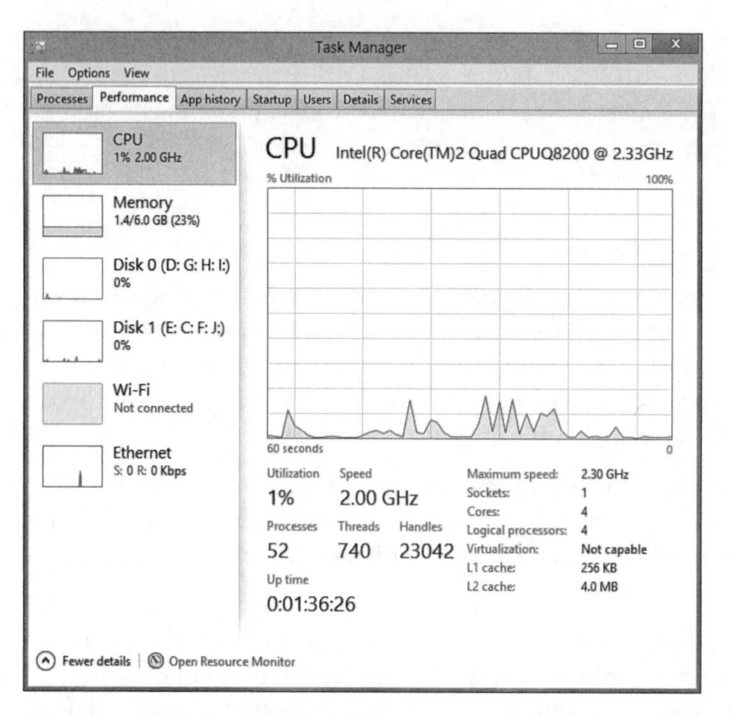

Figure 18-20 The Performance tab of Task Manager provides a simple performance graph focused on the selected performance object.

You can access additional options from the menu bar of Task Manager. In particular, you can start a new process from the File menu. Doing so is equivalent to using the Run dialog box, and is useful if the Explorer process has terminated or is misbehaving. The Options menu allows you to keep the Task Manager window always visible on the desktop. The View menu allows you to adjust the refresh rate of the graph on the Performance tab. It also allows you to modify what data is displayed on the Processes and Users tabs.

NOTE For more information on the Windows 8.1 Task Manager, including a history of Task Manager dating back to Windows 3.0, refer to "The Windows 8 Task Manager" at http://blogs.msdn.com/b/b8/archive/2011/10/13/the-windows-8-task-manager.aspx. (Note that this URL requires that you have an MSDN profile.)

Configuring Additional Performance Settings

Windows 8.1 contains several additional tools that you can use to manage your computer's performance. They include the System Configuration utility, the Action Center, and the Services console.

System Configuration Utility

The System Configuration utility enables you to disable common services and startup programs to selectively troubleshoot which items are preventing a normal startup.

To start the System Configuration utility, open the Search charm and type **`msconfig`** in the search box. Then click **System Configuration** in the Programs list. If you receive a UAC prompt, click **Yes** or supply administrative credentials. Doing so opens the dialog box shown in Figure 18-21.

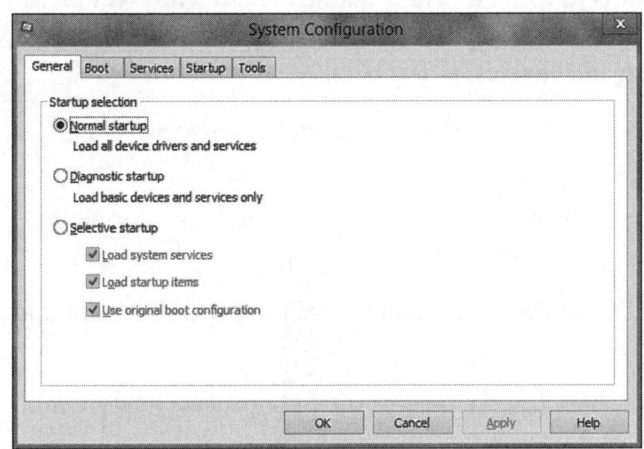

Figure 18-21 The System Configuration utility enables you to troubleshoot problems that prevent Windows from starting normally.

The following sections describe the functions available on each tab.

General Tab

The General tab allows you to choose **Normal startup**, which loads all drivers and services configured to start automatically; **Diagnostic startup**, which loads basic drivers and services; or **Selective startup**, which enables you to select the following options:

- **Load system services:** Starts all services that are configured for automatic startup.
- **Load startup items:** Starts applications that have been configured to start at boot or logon time.
- **Use original boot configuration:** Remains selected unless you modify default settings on the Boot tab.

Boot Tab

The Boot tab provides several boot options that are useful if you encounter problems starting your computer normally. You have the following boot options available:

- **Safe boot:** Provides four options for booting your computer into Safe Mode. The Minimal option brings up the Windows GUI with only critical system services loaded and networking disabled. The Alternate shell option boots to the command prompt and disables both the GUI and networking. The Active Directory repair option boots to the GUI and runs Active Directory as well as critical system services. The Network option boots to the Windows GUI with only critical services loaded and enables networking.
- **No GUI boot:** Starts Windows without displaying the Windows splash screen.
- **Boot log:** Boots according to the other options selected and logs information from the boot procedure to `%systemroot%\Ntbtlog.txt`.
- **Base video:** Uses standard VGA drivers to load the Windows GUI in minimal VGA mode.
- **OS boot information:** Displays driver names as the boot process loads them.

On a multiboot computer, the display window contains entries for the different operating systems present. To choose which operating system boots by default, select the desired entry and click **Set as default.** Use the Timeout setting to specify the number of seconds that the boot menu is displayed on a multiboot computer. In addition, the Make all boot settings permanent option disables tracking of changes made in the System Configuration utility. This option disables the ability to roll back changes when you select the **Normal startup** option from the General tab.

Services Tab

The Services tab lists all Windows services available on the computer, including those installed by other applications running on the computer. You can enable or disable individual services at boot time when you think that running services might be causing boot problems. Clear the check box for those services you want to disable for the next boot, or click the **Disable all** command button to disable all nonessential services.

To show only services installed by non-Microsoft programs, select the **Hide all Microsoft services** check box. This enables you to more rapidly locate non-Microsoft services that might be contributing to boot problems.

WARNING Ensure that you do not disable essential services. You might encounter system stability problems or other malfunctions if you disable too many services. Ensure that services you disable are not essential to your computer's operation. The Disable all option does not disable secure Microsoft services required at boot time.

Startup Tab

In previous Windows versions, the Startup tab listed all applications that are configured to start automatically when the computer starts up. This function has been removed in Windows 8.1 and replaced with a link to Task Manager; clicking this link opens the advanced version of Task Manager to the Startup tab.

Tools Tab

Shown in Figure 18-22, the Tools tab enumerates all diagnostic applications and other available tools. It provides a convenient location from which you can start a program; to do so, select the desired program and click **Launch**.

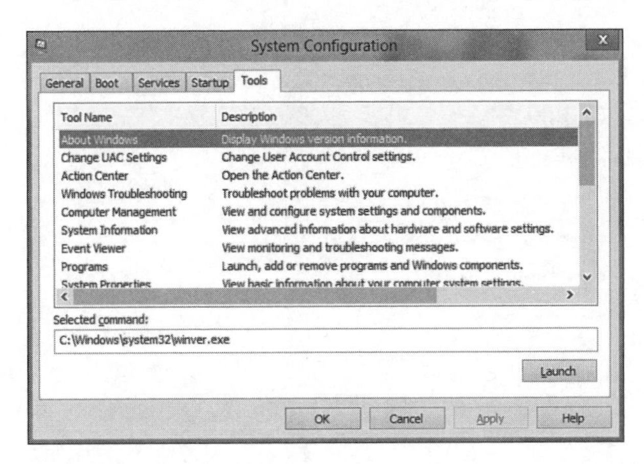

Figure 18-22 The Tools tab enables you to start a program from a comprehensive list of Windows diagnostic utilities.

NOTE For more information on using System Configuration in Windows 8.1/ Windows RT 8.1, refer to "Using System Configuration (msconfig)" at http:// windows.microsoft.com/en-us/windows/using-system-configuration.

Action Center

Introduced with Windows 7 and continued in Windows 8 and 8.1 is the Action Center, which replaces the Windows Vista Security Center and adds several maintenance and performance options. You can access Action Center by opening Control Panel to the System and Security category and selecting **Action Center**. You can open Action Center by selecting it in the Tools tab of the System Configuration utility and clicking **Launch**. You can also open the Search charm, type `action` in the search box, and then select **Action Center** from the programs list. Either of these options brings up the applet shown in Figure 18-23. Expand the Security section to configure security options that have been discussed in earlier chapters of this book. Take note of any messages appearing in the Maintenance section and click **Check for solutions** to send information to Microsoft that might provide resolution for these problems.

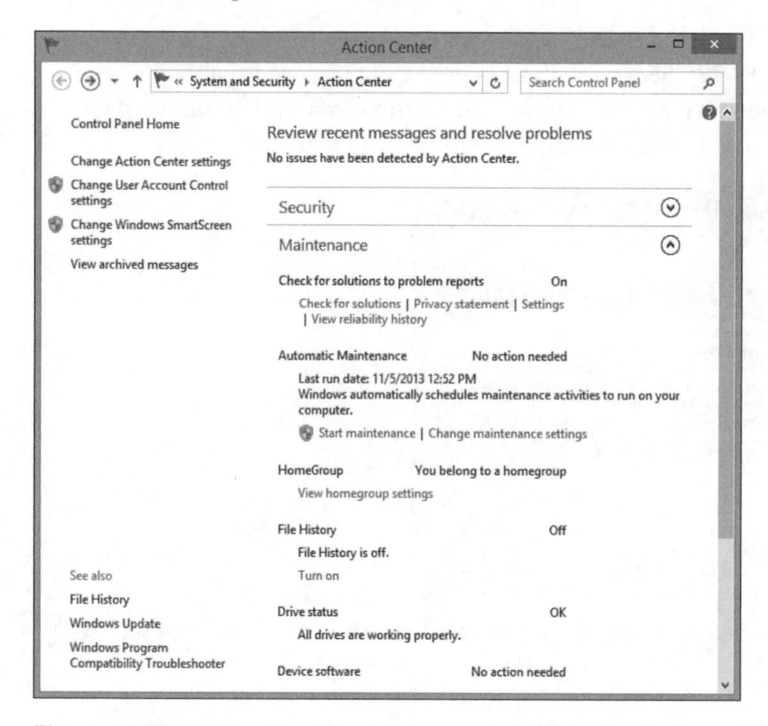

Figure 18-23 Action Center enables you to troubleshoot security, maintenance, and performance issues.

The links at the left side of the Action Center panel enable you to perform the following tasks:

- **Change Action Center settings:** Enables you to select the type of security and maintenance messages displayed by Action Center. You can also choose to participate in Microsoft's Customer Experience Improvement Program or modify problem reporting or Windows Update settings. We discussed Windows Update settings in Chapter 16, "Configuring Windows Update."
- **Change User Account Control settings:** Enables you to change the behavior of UAC, as previously discussed in Chapter 12, "Configuring Local Security Settings."
- **Change Windows SmartScreen settings:** Provides options that determine how Windows SmartScreen controls the execution of unrecognized apps. We discussed SmartScreen in Chapter 12.
- **View archived messages:** Enables you to view archived messages about computer problems that were previously reported to Microsoft.
- **File History:** Enables you to configure the new File History feature, which replaces Windows Backup in Windows 8.1. See Chapter 20, "Configuring File Recovery," for more information.
- **Windows Update:** Enables you to access the Windows Update Control Panel applet. We discussed Windows Update in Chapter 16.
- **Windows Program Compatibility Troubleshooter:** Enables you to troubleshoot application compatibility issues. We discussed program compatibility in Chapter 5, "Installing, Configuring, and Securing Applications in Windows 8.1."

Configuring Services and Programs to Resolve Performance Issues

In the preceding sections of this chapter, you have seen how to configure programs or stop them in case of performance problems. Windows services run in the background and enable significant and important functions on your computer; in fact, nearly all actions performed on the computer depend on one or more services. Many applications install their own services when you install them. Many of the services are configured to start automatically at system startup; although many of these are essential to proper computer operation, having nonessential services starting can degrade computer performance noticeably.

You have seen how you can enable or disable services from the System Configuration utility. You can also configure service startup and properties from the Services snap-in. This tool is a component of the Computer Management snap-in and can also be accessed in its own console by accessing the Search charm, and typing `services` at the search box. This brings up the console shown in Figure 18-24, which lists all services installed on the computer and indicates their status and startup type.

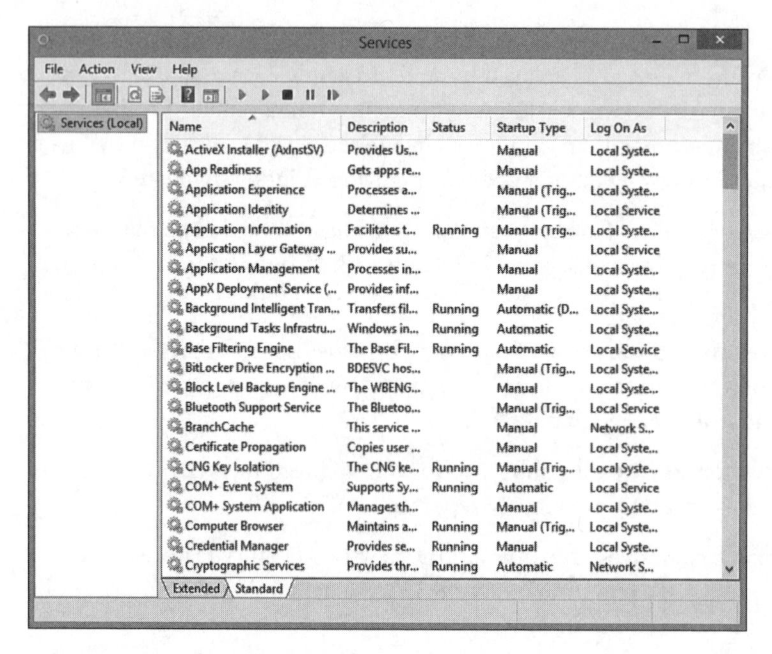

Figure 18-24 The Services console enables you to observe the status of services running on your computer.

You can modify the properties of any service, including its startup type as required. Right-click the desired service and choose **Properties** to bring up its Properties dialog box, as shown in Figure 18-25. This dialog box allows you to configure the following properties of each service:

- **General tab:** Enables you to set the startup type to Automatic, Automatic (Delayed Start), Manual, or Disabled. By disabling services that consume extra computer resources on startup, you can sometimes improve computer performance. Certain services should also be disabled for improving computer security. However, you must ensure that all essential services remain set to Automatic. Set nonessential services that perform useful tasks to Manual startup.

- **Log On tab:** Enables you to change the account used by services when logging on. In nearly all cases, you should leave this set to its default Local System Account.

- **Recovery tab:** Enables you to specify actions to be taken if the service fails, such as restarting the service, restarting the computer, running a program, or taking no action.

- **Dependencies tab:** Lists the services that this service depends on as well as the system components that depend on this service running properly. This tab has no configurable options, but the information displayed can be useful in troubleshooting failures.

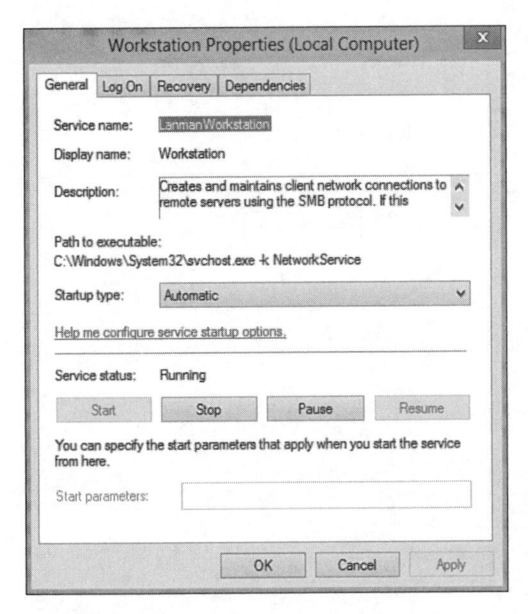

Figure 18-25 You can configure service properties from each service's Properties dialog box.

Configuring Indexing Options

Windows 8.1 helps you locate information on your computer by building an index of all the most commonly used file types on your computer. By default, Windows indexes all folders included in libraries, email, and offline files. Data that you're not likely to search, such as program files and system files, is not indexed.

Use the following procedure to configure indexing options:

Step 1. Access Control Panel, select either **Large icons** or **Small icons** under View, and then select **Indexing Options** from the list of applets displayed. You can also access the Search charm, type `indexing`, and then click **Indexing Options** from the program list. Either of these procedures opens the Indexing Options applet, as shown in Figure 18-26.

Step 2. As shown, the locations included in the index are displayed. To modify these locations, click **Modify**.

Step 3. You receive the Indexed Locations dialog box shown in Figure 18-27. To add or remove selected locations, select or clear the check boxes provided. To include or exclude folders within a location displayed, click this location to expand it, and then select or deselect the desired folders. To show additional locations (such as program files and system files), click **Show all locations**. When finished, click **OK**.

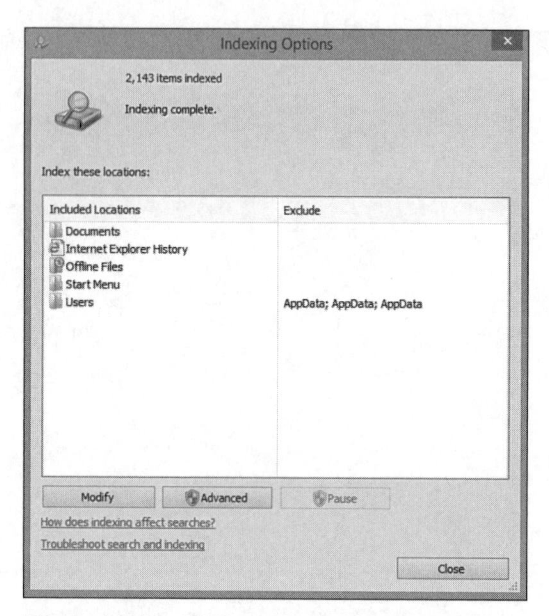

Figure 18-26 The Indexing Options applet enables you to configure how Windows indexes files on your computer.

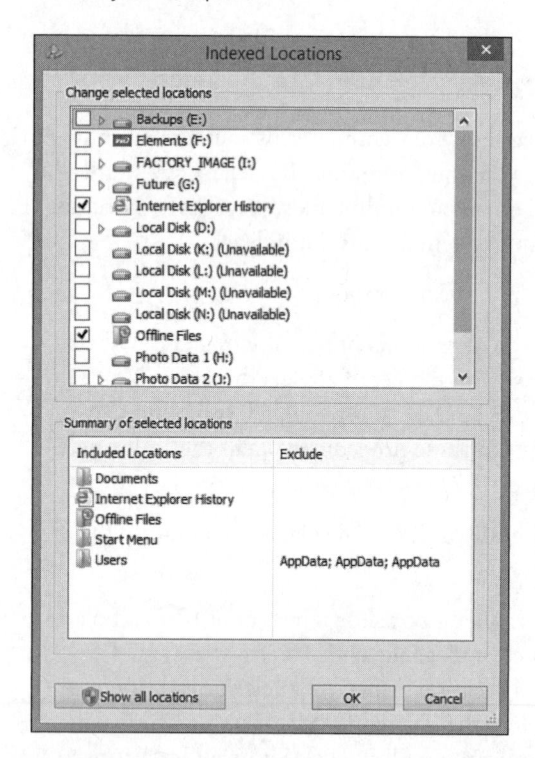

Figure 18-27 The Indexed Locations dialog box enables you to modify drives, folders, and files included in the index.

Step 4. For additional indexing options, click **Advanced** to display the Advanced Options dialog box shown in Figure 18-28. Select from the following options as desired:

- **Index encrypted files:** Includes files and folders encrypted with the Encrypting File System (EFS) or BitLocker in the index. Microsoft recommends that you enable BitLocker on the system drive if you select this option.
- **Treat similar words with diacritics as different words:** Recognizes words with accents or other diacritical marks as different (for example, resume vs. résumé).
- **Rebuild:** Enables you to re-create the index if the index is unable to find a file that you're sure is in an indexed location. This action might take several hours, during which searches might be incomplete.
- **Index location:** Enables you to change the default location of the index—for example, if you need to free up space on a given disk or partition. This action restarts the indexing service, and the change will not take place until after the service has restarted.
- **File Types tab:** Enables you to add new file types to the index according to file extension (see Figure 18-29). You can also remove existing file types by clearing their check boxes.

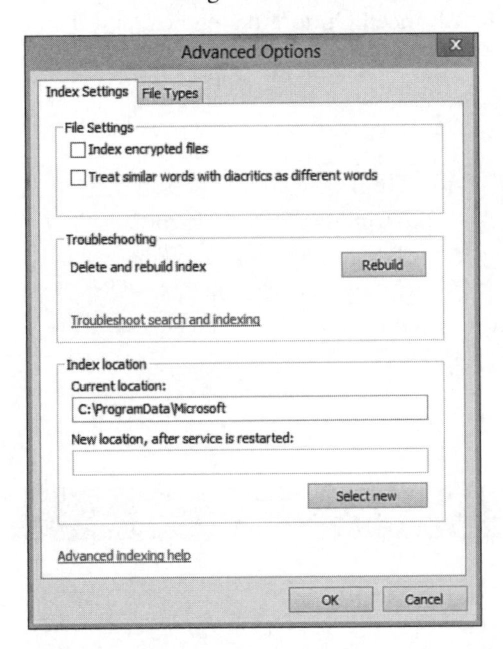

Figure 18-28 The Advanced Options dialog box enables you to configure additional indexing settings.

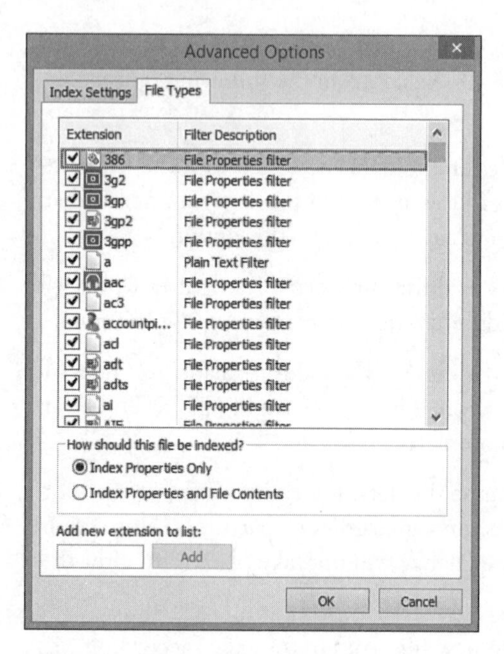

Figure 18-29 The File Types tab enables you to specify which file extensions are indexed.

Step 5. When finished, click **OK** to close the Advanced Options dialog box, and then click **Close** to close the Indexing Options applet.

NOTE For more information on indexing, refer to "Improve Windows wearches using the index: frequently asked questions" at http://windows.microsoft.com/en-US/windows7/Improve-Windows-searches-using-the-index-frequently-asked-questions and "Change advanced indexing options" at http://windows.microsoft.com/is-IS/windows7/Change-advanced-indexing-options. Although written for Windows 7, the procedures described also apply to Windows 8 and 8.1.

Exam Preparation Tasks

Review All the Key Topics

Review the most important topics in the chapter, noted with the key topics icon in the outer margin of the page. Table 18-7 lists a reference of these key topics and the page numbers on which each is found.

Table 18-7 Key Topics for Chapter 18

Key Topic Element	Description	Page Number(s)
Figure 18-2	Shows error, warning, and information messages in Event Viewer	768
Figure 18-3	Shows how to filter event logs	769
Figure 18-6	Shows how to create an event log subscription	773
Figure 18-9	Shows how to use Resource Monitor to monitor your computer's resource utilization	778
Table 18-2	Describes terminology used by Performance Monitor	782
Step List	Shows how to use Performance Monitor	782-784
Step List	Shows how to create a data collector set	785
Table 18-3	Describes the important counters for the Memory performance object	789-790
Table 18-4	Describes the important counters for the Processor performance object	792
Figure 18-18	Displays the newly redesigned Task Manager, which presents a simplified view of apps running on the computer and enables you to shut down misbehaving apps	795
Figure 18-19	Displays the advanced interface of Task Manager, which presents a color-coded view of apps, background processes, and Windows processes, highlighting those processes that are using the most resources	796
Figure 18-21	Displays the various diagnostic startup options available from System Configuration	799

Complete the Tables and Lists from Memory

Print a copy of Appendix B, "Memory Tables," (found on the CD), or at least the section for this chapter, and complete the tables and lists from memory. Appendix C, "Memory Tables Answer Key," also on the CD, includes completed tables and lists to check your work.

Definitions of Key Terms

Define the following key terms from this chapter and check your answers in the Glossary:

> Action Center, Alert, Data Collector Sets, Event log subscription, Event Viewer, Indexing, `Msconfig`, Paging file, Performance counter, Performance object, Performance Monitor, Reliability Monitor, Resource Monitor, System Configuration utility, Task Manager

This chapter covers the following subjects:

- **Creating a USB Recovery Drive:** A USB recovery drive enables you to boot your computer and perform a repair should your computer become nonfunctional. This section shows you how to create a USB recovery drive.
- **Performing System Restore:** This feature enables you to restore your computer to a previous point in time. You need to know how to recover your computer from problems caused by improper configuration, malware, or other situations.
- **Rolling Back Drivers:** When a faulty driver has been installed that results in problems with some hardware component, you can roll back the driver to a previous version. This section shows you how to perform driver rollback.
- **Performing a Push-Button Reset:** This feature makes it simple to refresh the Windows 8.1 operating system back to its factory settings. In previous version of Windows, this task often required a complete format and reinstall of the operating system. Push-Button Refresh is especially useful for Windows RT 8.1 and tablet computers.
- **Configuring Restore Points:** Windows 8.1 enables you to configure several options related to restore points, including the drives from which data is restored, the space used by restore points, and the ability to manually create or delete restore points.

CHAPTER 19

Configuring System Recovery Options

As users work with their Windows 8.1 computers, increasingly large numbers of programs, amounts of data, and other items accumulate on the hard drive. As you learned in Chapter 18, "Managing and Monitoring System Performance," the computer's performance tends to slow down for a variety of reasons. Now we go a step further: Any of a number of factors can cause a computer to become unresponsive and result in the need for system recovery actions. Windows 8.1 offers several technologies for repairing and recovering computers that are responding slowly or have stopped responding entirely. As a desktop support technician or network administrator, you need to be capable of performing system recovery, both for the real world and for the 70-687 exam.

"Do I Know This Already?" Quiz

The "Do I Know This Already?" quiz allows you to assess whether you should read this entire chapter or simply jump to the "Exam Preparation Tasks" section for review. If you are in doubt, read the entire chapter. Table 19-1 outlines the major headings in this chapter and the corresponding "Do I Know This Already?" quiz questions. You can find the answers in Appendix A, "Answers to the 'Do I Know This Already?' Quizzes."

Table 19-1 "Do I Know This Already?" Foundation Topics Section-to-Question Mapping

Foundations Topics Section	Questions Covered in This Section
Creating a USB Recovery Drive	1
Performing System Restore	2–3
Rolling Back Drivers	4
Performing a Push-Button Reset	5–9
Configuring Restore Points	10

1. You want to ensure that you can fully restore your computer to its operating system in the event of a hardware failure. Which of the following should you do to accomplish this objective with the least amount of administrative effort?
   a. Create a system recovery disc.
   b. Create a system state backup.
   c. Create a USB recovery drive.
   d. Create a Complete PC Backup.

2. Which of the following items are included in a backup created by the System Restore applet in Windows 8.1? (Choose all that apply.)
   a. Registry
   b. DLL cache folder
   c. User profiles
   d. User libraries
   e. Installed application executables
   f. COM+ and WMI information

3. You have downloaded and installed an application that you thought would improve your productivity, but you discover that this application has overwritten several drivers and other essential files. You would like to return your computer to its status as of the day before you downloaded the application. What should you do to accomplish this task with the least amount of effort?
   a. Roll back the affected drivers.
   b. Restore your user profile to that of the most recent backup created before the application was downloaded.
   c. Restore your operating system from a system image backup.
   d. Use System Restore and specify the desired date.

4. An update that you downloaded from the Internet has resulted in your sound card not working. Checking Device Manager, you discover that the sound card is using a problematic driver. What should you do to correct this problem most rapidly?
   a. Roll back the affected driver.
   b. Download and install a new driver from the sound card manufacturer's website.
   c. Use System Restore and specify a date before the download occurred.
   d. Use a system repair disc to repair your computer.

5. You want to fully restore your computer to the manufacturer's default functionality because of a virus infestation that has affected multiple locations on the hard drive. Which type of recovery should you use for this restore?

   a. Windows Complete PC Backup

   b. Push-button reset

   c. Windows Backup and Restore

   d. System Repair Disc

   e. System Restore

6. Which three of the following actions will enable you to choose Advanced Startup Options on a Windows 8.1 Pro computer that has no other operating system installed on it? (Each correct answer presents a complete solution. Choose three.)

   a. Restart your computer and press **F8** after the POST sequence has completed.

   b. From the Settings charm, select **Change PC settings**. Then from the PC settings window, click **Recovery** and then click **Restart now**.

   c. From the logon screen, click the power icon in the bottom-right corner of this screen and then hold down the **Shift** key while clicking **Restart**.

   d. Press **Ctrl+Alt+Delete** and select the **Change PC settings** option. Then from the PC settings window, click **General** and then click **Restart now**.

   e. Boot your computer from the Windows 8.1 installation DVD. When the languages preferences screen appears, click **Next** and then click **Repair your computer**.

7. You use a USB recovery drive to start your computer and choose the **Troubleshoot** option. Which of the following recovery options can you select to repair your computer? (Choose three.)

   a. Refresh your PC

   b. Reset your PC

   c. Advanced options

   d. Device Driver Rollback

   e. Recovery Console

8. You install a new video driver and reboot your computer. The display shows a large number of horizontal lines and nothing is legible, so you are unable to log on. You reboot your computer, access the Choose an option screen, and select **Troubleshoot** to select troubleshooting options. What should you do to correct this problem with the least amount of effort?
   a. From the Troubleshoot screen, select **Refresh your PC**.
   b. From the Troubleshoot screen, select **Reset your PC**.
   c. From the Troubleshoot screen, select **Advanced options**. Select **Startup settings** and then select **Enable low-resolution video**. Then perform a device driver rollback.
   d. From the Troubleshoot screen, select **Advanced options**. Select **Startup settings** and then select **Enable Safe Mode**. Then perform a device driver rollback.
   e. Use the system repair disc to reboot your computer and then select the **System Restore** option.

9. Your computer's hard disk has failed and you have installed a new 1.5 TB hard disk. You are lucky enough to have created a system image backup a week ago. What should you do to get your computer up and running again with the least amount of effort and without losing your installed applications?
   a. Start your computer with a USB recovery drive and choose the option to use a system image you created earlier to recover your computer.
   b. Start your computer with a USB recovery drive and choose the option to reinstall Windows.
   c. Start your computer with a USB recovery drive and choose the **System Restore** option.
   d. Start your computer with a Windows 8.1 DVD and perform an in-place upgrade of Windows.

10. You have downloaded an interesting application from the Internet, but are afraid that it might contain a malicious component. Some of your friends have suggested that you not install this application, but you'd really like to give it a try. What should you do before installing the application so that you can recover your computer if necessary by using the least amount of effort?
    a. Use System Restore to manually create a restore point.
    b. Boot your computer to Safe Mode and install the application; then try running the application before booting back to a regular startup.
    c. Use File History to create a backup of all your data files before installing the application.
    d. Use Windows Backup and Restore to create a system image backup.

Foundation Topics

Creating a USB Recovery Drive

You can use a USB recovery drive to boot your computer to the Windows Recovery Environment discussed later in this chapter should you need to recover from a serious error or to restore Windows on your computer. This procedure relies on a recovery image found on many computers that can be used to refresh your computer. This image is typically stored on a dedicated recovery partition and is generally 3–6 GB in size.

Use the following procedure to create a USB recovery drive:

Step 1. Right-click **Start**, choose **Control Panel > System and Security > Save backup copies of your files with File History**.

Step 2. In the File History applet, select the **Recovery** option.

Step 3. The Advanced recovery tools dialog box opens, as shown in Figure 19-1. Click **Create a recovery drive**. If you receive a UAC prompt, click **Yes**.

Key Topic

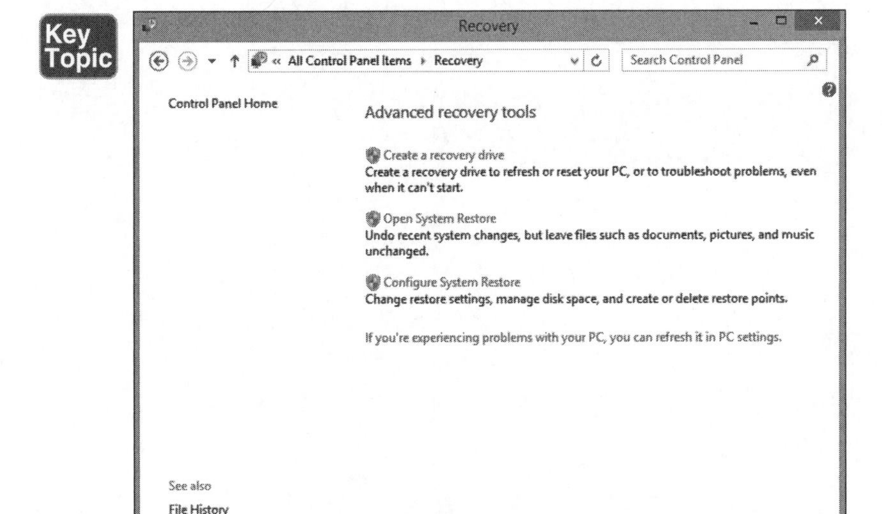

Figure 19-1 The Recovery applet includes three advanced recovery tools.

Step 4. The Recovery Drive Wizard starts with the Create a recovery drive page shown in Figure 19-2. If your computer has a recovery partition, the check box shown is available. Ensure that it is selected, and then click **Next**.

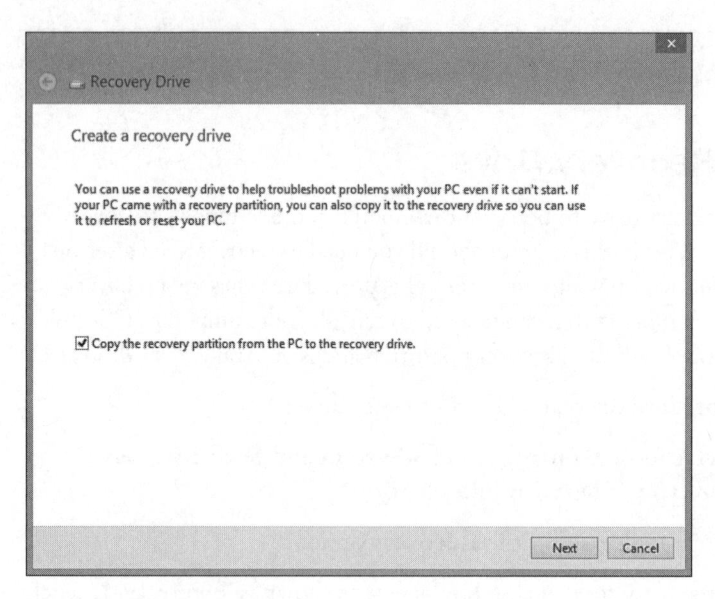

Figure 19-2 Creating a recovery drive.

Step 5. After a few seconds, the Select the USB flash drive page appears, as shown in Figure 19-3. If more than one drive is available, select the desired drive and then click **Next**.

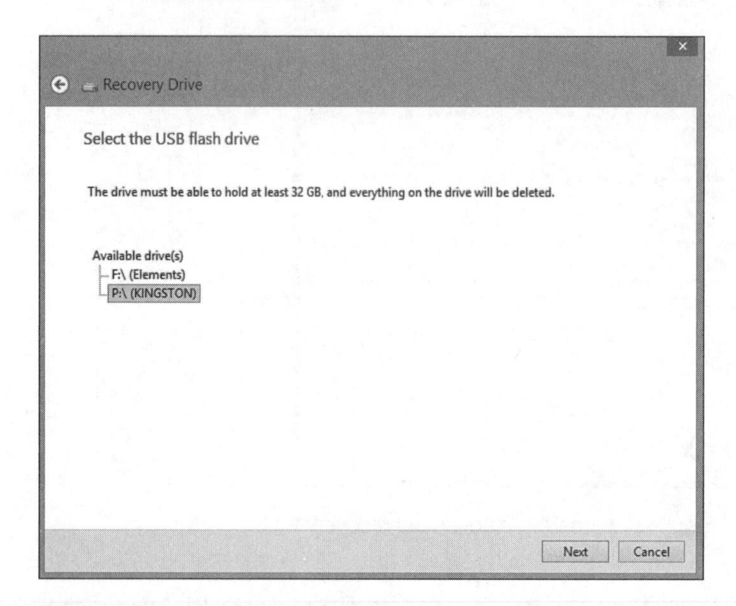

Figure 19-3 Selecting a USB drive for creating the recovery drive.

Step 6. You are warned that everything on the selected drive will be deleted. If you need to back up any files, click **Cancel** and copy these files before proceeding. When ready, click **Create** to proceed.

Step 7. The wizard tracks the process of formatting the drive and copying utilities before completing the process. When informed that the recovery drive is ready, click **Finish**.

If the check box shown in Figure 19-2 is not available (grayed out), your computer does not have a valid recovery partition. You can create a recovery partition by using the following steps:

Step 1. Right-click **Start** and choose **Command Prompt (Admin)**.

Step 2. Click **Yes** on the UAC prompt that appears.

Step 3. Type `mkdir C:\RefreshImage` and then press **Enter**.

Step 4. To create the image, type `recimg -CreateImage C:\RefreshImage` and then press **Enter**.

Step 5. The progress of creating the image is tracked in the command prompt window. This process may take a few minutes. When informed that the system image has been created, close the window.

WARNING Make sure that nothing of importance is stored on the flash drive before using it to create a recovery drive! The procedure given here erases everything stored on the USB recovery drive, so copy any important data from the drive to another location before creating the USB recovery drive.

NOTE For more information on creating a recovery drive, refer to "Create a USB Recovery Drive" at http://windows.microsoft.com/en-US/windows-8/create-usb-recovery-drive.

Performing System Restore

First introduced with Windows XP, System Restore enables you to recover from system problems such as those caused by improper system settings, faulty drivers, and incompatible applications. It restores your computer to a previous condition without damaging any data files such as documents and email. System Restore is useful when problems persist after you have uninstalled incompatible software or device drivers, or after you have downloaded problematic content from a website, or when you are having problems that you cannot diagnose but that have started recently.

During normal operation, System Restore creates snapshots of the system at each startup and before major configuration changes are started. It stores these snapshots and manages them in a special location on your hard drive. It also copies monitored files to this location before any installation program or Windows itself overwrites these files during application or device installation. These snapshots include backups of the following settings:

- Registry
- DLL cache folder
- User profiles
- COM+ and WMI information
- Certain monitored system files

System Restore points are not the same as data backup. System Restore can restore applications and settings to an earlier point in time, but it does not back up or restore any personal data files. Use the File History application to back up personal data files or recover any that have been deleted or damaged.

You can run System Restore from the System Properties dialog box. The following steps show how:

Step 1. Access the Control Panel System applet from the System and Security category. In Windows 8.1, you can also right-click **Start** and choose **System**. You can also click **Open System Restore** in the Recovery applet previously shown in Figure 19-1 (skip to step 3).

Step 2. On the left pane of the System applet, select **System protection**.

Step 3. If you receive a UAC prompt, click **Yes**. This opens the System Protection tab of the System Properties dialog box, as shown in Figure 19-4.

Step 4. Click **System Restore** to open the System Restore dialog box, as shown in Figure 19-5. You can also access this dialog box by opening the **Search** charm, typing `restore`, and clicking **Create a restore point**.

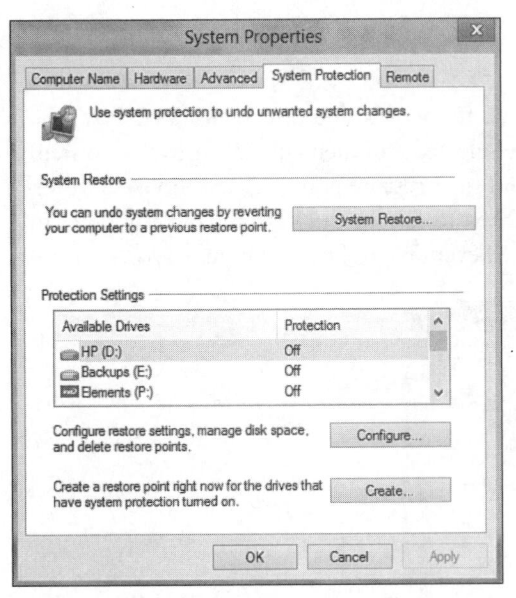

Figure 19-4 The System Protection tab of the System Properties dialog box includes a System Restore option.

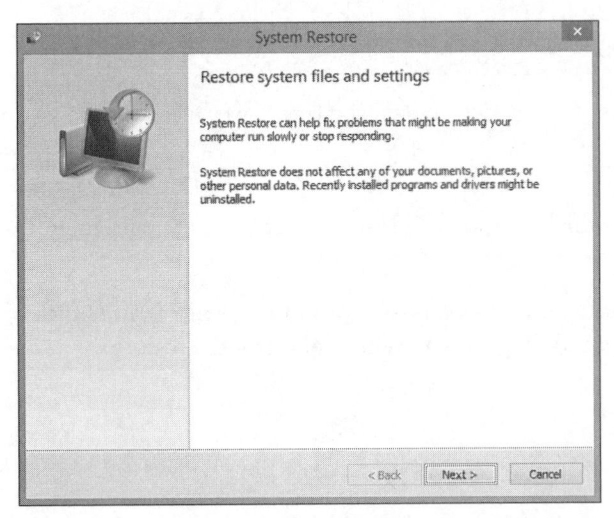

Figure 19-5 The System Restore dialog box enables you to restore system files and settings.

TIP If the System Restore dialog box informs you that no restore points have been created, click **Cancel** to return to the System Protection tab and then click **Create** to create a restore point. When informed that the restore point was created successfully, click **Close**. We discuss creating and configuring restore points later in this chapter.

Step 5. Click **Next** to display the Restore your computer to the state it was in before the selected event page.

Step 6. If you want to restore your computer to the date and time mentioned, leave the default of **Recommended restore** selected and then click **Next** to skip to step 8 of this procedure. To choose a different restore point, select **Choose a different restore point** and then click **Next** to display the Restore your computer to the state it was in before the selected event page shown in Figure 19-6.

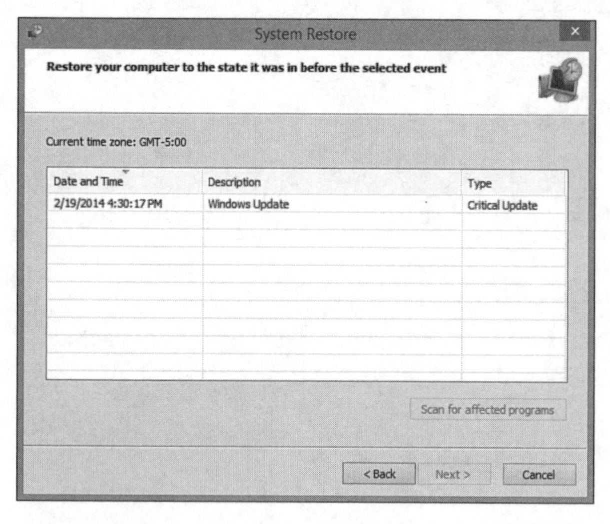

Figure 19-6 System Restore enables you to select the date and time to which you want to restore your computer.

Step 7. Select a date and time to which you want to restore your computer and then click **Next**.

Step 8. In the Confirm your restore point dialog box shown in Figure 19-7, note the warning to save open files and then click **Finish** to perform the restore.

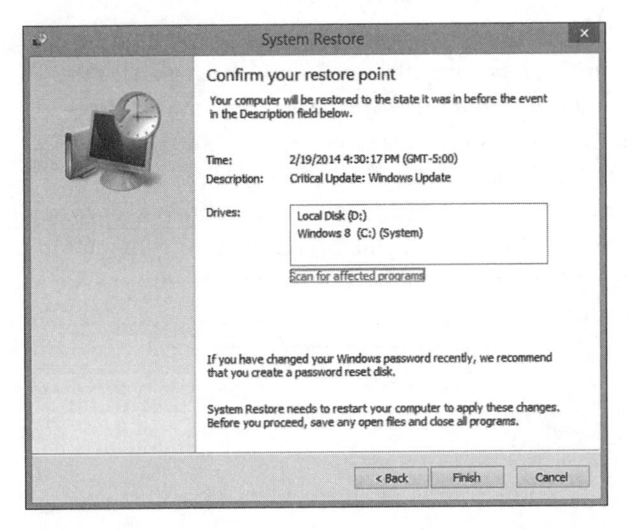

Figure 19-7 You are asked to confirm your choice of restore point.

Step 9. You receive a message box informing you that System Restore may not be interrupted and cannot be undone if being performed from Safe Mode (see Figure 19-8). Click **Yes** to proceed. The computer performs the restore and then shuts down and restarts.

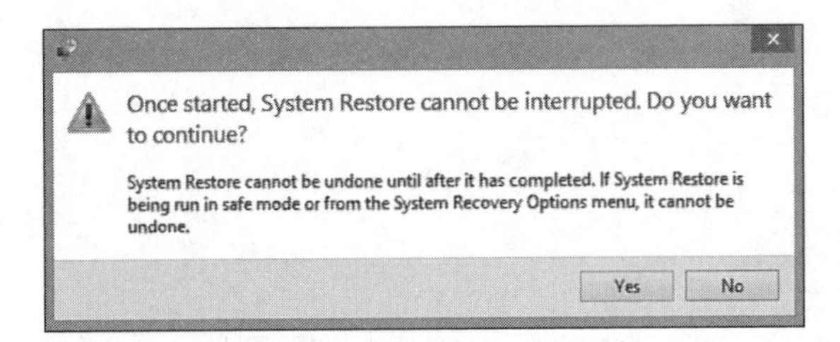

Figure 19-8 You are warned that System Restore cannot be interrupted.

Step 10. Log back on as an administrator. You receive a System Restore message box informing you that the restore completed successfully. Click **Close**.

Rolling Back Drivers

Windows 8.1 enables you to roll back a device driver to a previous version should you encounter problems with a device after updating an existing driver. Problems of this nature occasionally occur when a manufacturer releases a new driver that has not been thoroughly tested and Windows Update automatically downloads and installs the driver without your intervention.

Although you can use System Restore to restore your computer to a point prior to installation of the problematic driver, it is normally much simpler to roll back the driver. To do so, open Device Manager, right-click the device, and choose **Properties**. From the Driver tab of the device's Properties dialog box shown in Figure 19-9, click **Roll Back Driver** and then click **Yes** in the Driver Package rollback message box that appears. If this option is unavailable (dimmed), Windows does not have a previous version of the driver. If necessary, you can restart your computer in Safe Mode and then employ this procedure to roll back a troublesome driver. We discuss Safe Mode later in this chapter.

Figure 19-9 The Driver tab of a device's Properties dialog box enables you to roll back the driver.

NOTE For more information on device drivers, including updating and rollback, refer to Chapter 4, "Configuring Devices and Device Drivers."

Performing a Push-Button Reset

New to Windows 8 and continued in Windows 8.1 is the concept of the push-button reset and the push-button refresh. This new feature enables users to repair issues with their PCs in a quick and easy manner, while optionally preserving their files, data, and user settings. Added in Windows 8.1 is the capability of compressing the image to a new, highly compressed file, using the `.esd` format.

Two options are available to users for the push-button reset:

- **Refresh your PC without affecting your files:** Allows you to reinstall the original Windows 8.1 image while preserving all user accounts, files in libraries and user folders, and Windows Store apps.
- **Remove everything and reinstall Windows:** Reinstalls the original Windows 8.1 image, but also completely clears all user accounts, passwords, data, and settings. This capability is especially useful if you are selling or recycling your computer.

These push-button processes are especially useful on smaller devices such as tablets running Windows RT 8.1, which may not have traditional optical drives and removable hard drives, making it a challenge to reinstall or to ensure that user data is cleared when the device is reassigned or ready to decommission. They also often come with hardware-specific devices and drivers. With push-button refresh, the original equipment manufacturer (OEM) system image is restored, including all the device-specific hardware drivers included. You don't need to hunt down driver discs or locate them on manufacturer websites.

Refreshing Your Computer

The push-button refresh preserves data and user customizations; however, Windows Store apps and installed applications are not retained, and most settings for those applications are lost. For instance, the following system folders are reset to the original state, and any settings or data in the folders are lost:

- `ProgramData`
- `Program Files`
- `Program Files (x86)`
- `AppData` folders in User's folders
- `Windows`

All folders other than `AppData` under User profiles are preserved after the refresh, including documents and the desktop, but any files or folders users may have created outside the `\Users` folders are lost. Similar to a reinstall of Windows, the refresh creates a `Windows.old` folder in the system partition and moves many folders there, such as `ProgramData` and `Users`. All Windows Store apps are recovered after the refresh, provided that the computer was initially installed with Windows 8.1 (and not upgraded from Windows 8). These apps are returned to factory condition. However, user-installed desktop apps are lost; a list of these apps is created and stored in a file on the desktop.

NOTE For more information and details on the folders preserved and refreshed during a push-button refresh, and how to customize the refresh process, review the TechNet article "Push-Button Reset Overview" at http://technet.microsoft.com/en-us/library/jj126997.aspx.

CAUTION If you have upgraded your computer from Windows 8 to Windows 8.1, the refresh procedure restores the computer to its initial Windows 8 installation. You have to upgrade your computer again to Windows 8.1. You also have to reinstall all Windows Store apps.

Use the following procedure to perform a push-button reset to refresh a Windows 8.1 PC:

Step 1. Access the Settings charm, click **Change PC settings**, and then select the **Update and Recovery** option.

Step 2. In the Update and Recovery section, select **Recovery**. This screen displays the options shown in Figure 19-10.

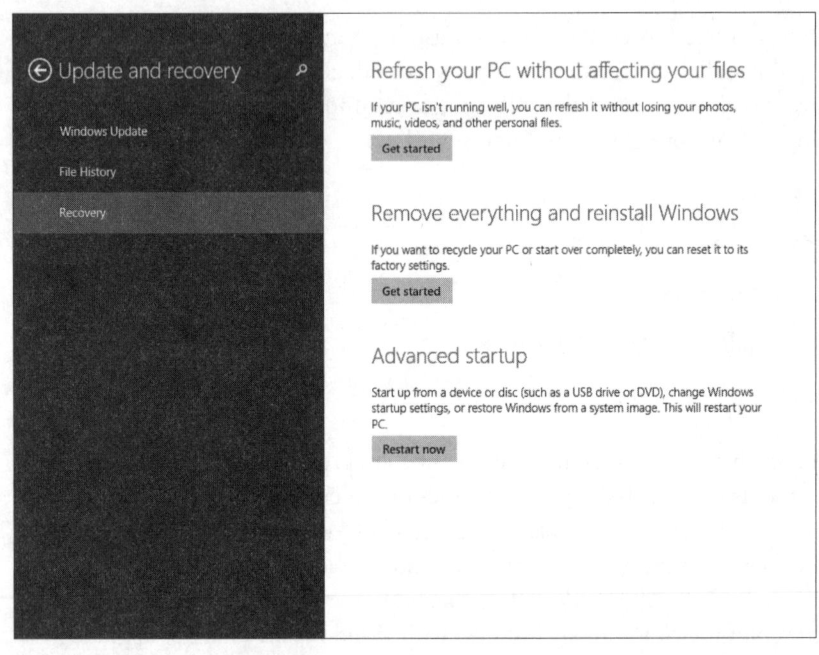

Figure 19-10 The Update and recovery screen provides three options for restoring your computer.

Step 3. Select **Get started** under Refresh your PC without affecting your files.

Step 4. The Refresh your PC screen shown in Figure 19-11 describes the refresh process and informs you of the steps you will need to perform later. Click **Next** to proceed.

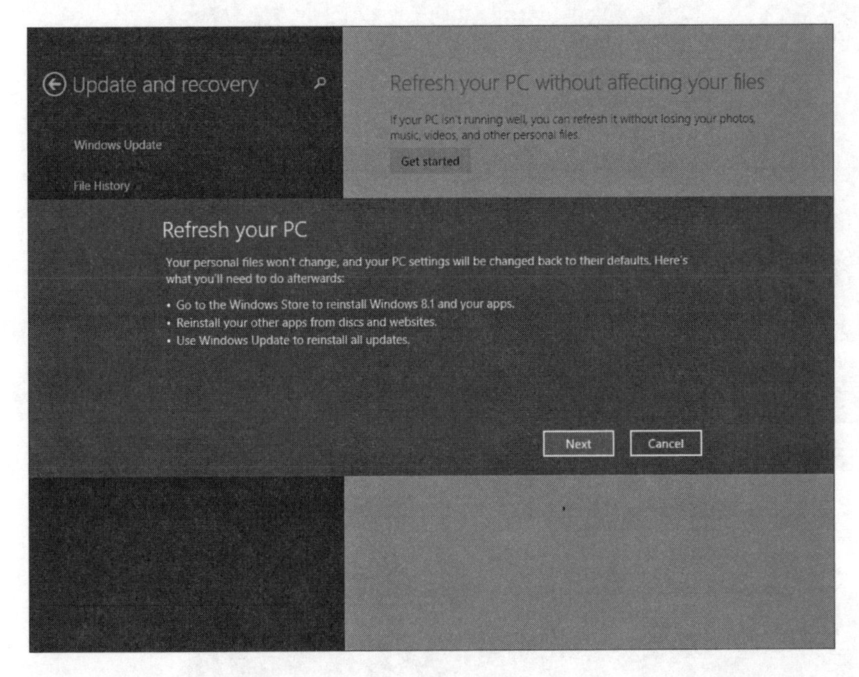

Figure 19-11 The Refresh your PC screen.

Step 5. The next screen lists the apps you'll need to reinstall. Make a note of these apps, which include desktop programs, and then click **Next** to proceed.

Step 6. The next Refresh your PC screen (see Figure 19-12) describes what will happen next. Make a note of these items and then click **Next** to proceed.

Step 7. Click **Refresh** to proceed. Windows then restarts and displays the Refreshing your PC progress screen shown in Figure 19-13 as the user files are preserved, folders are created, and the image is refreshed. After another restart, Windows 8.1 starts normally with the operating system refreshed.

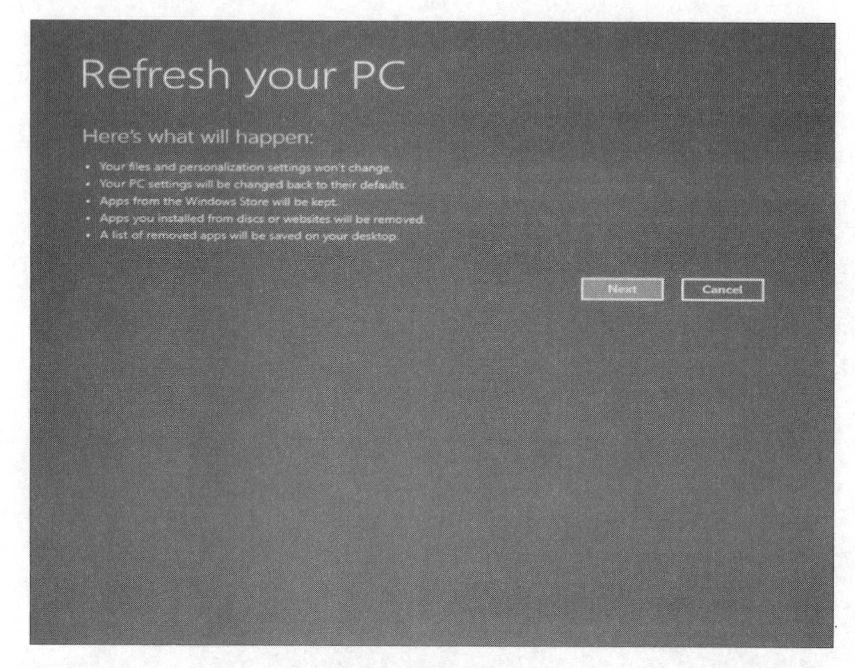

Figure 19-12 This screen describes what happens during the refresh.

Figure 19-13 Windows is refreshing your computer.

NOTE You may be prompted to insert the Windows installation DVD or media. This is typical on a computer without a recovery partition (as described in Chapter 2, "Installing Windows 8.1"). Cancel the refresh, insert the Windows 8.1 media, and restart your computer to try again.

Resetting Your Computer to Original Installation Condition

The process of resetting your computer to original installation condition is implemented by performing a complete reinstall of Windows, without preserving user accounts, data, or settings. It is otherwise similar to what is described in the preceding section. The complete reset actually takes less time to prepare because Windows does not need to save user files or create the `Windows.old` folder. Use the following procedure to perform a push-button reset to completely reset a Windows 8.1 PC:

Step 1. Use steps 1 and 2 of the preceding procedure to access the Update and recovery screen previously shown in Figure 19-10.

Step 2. Select **Get Started** under Remove everything and reinstall Windows.

Step 3. The screen shown in Figure 19-14 opens, informing you of the actions that will take place. Click **Next** to continue.

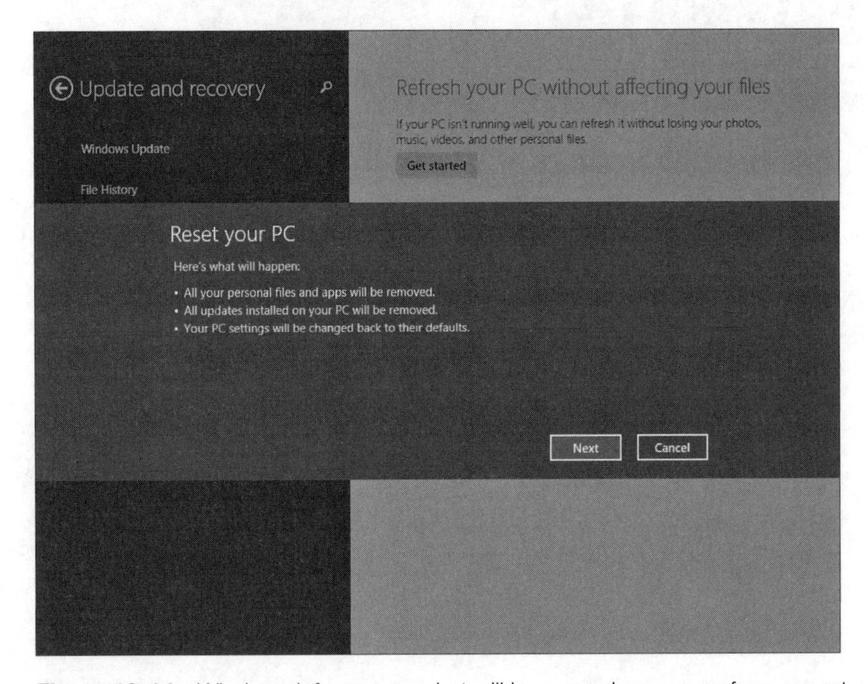

Figure 19-14 Windows informs you what will happen when you perform a reset.

Step 4. You receive the two options shown in Figure 19-15: Just remove my files or Fully clean the drive. The options are similar to the choice when formatting an NTFS volume: The quick reset simply deletes the file table, whereas a thorough reset formats the entire drive, writing zeros to every sector. Select the most appropriate option according to your needs.

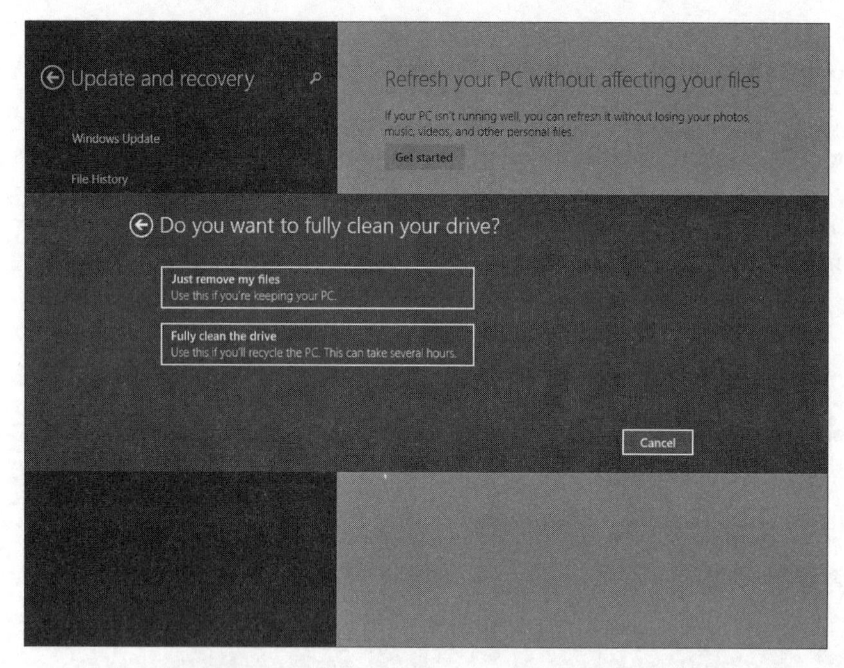

Figure 19-15 You receive two options for fully cleaning your drive.

Step 5. The Ready to reset your PC page shown in Figure 19-16 displays the actions that will take place. If you need to copy files to your File History drive, click **Cancel** and perform this task (which is described in Chapter 20, "Configuring File Recovery"). Click **Reset** to proceed.

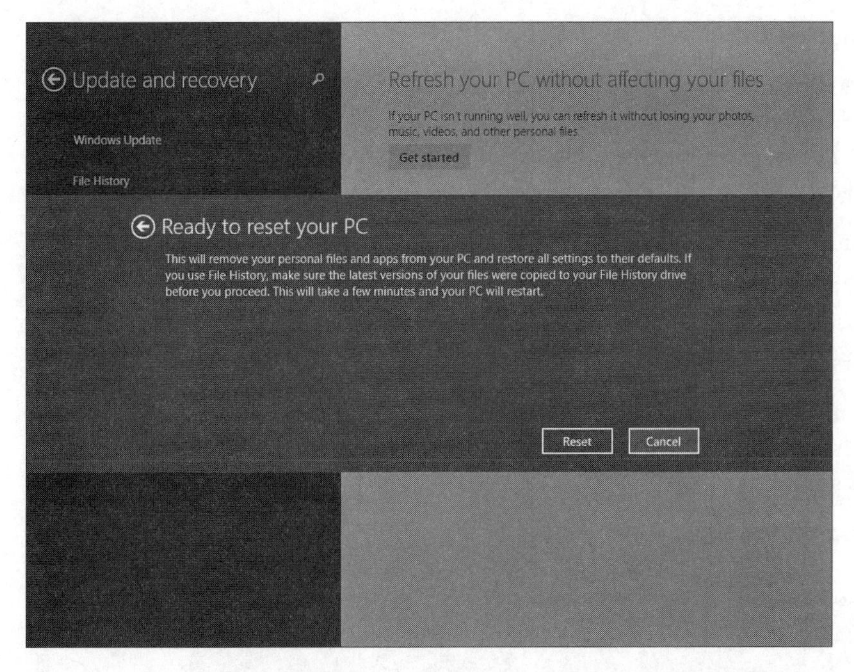

Figure 19-16 Windows is ready to reset your computer to its initially installed condition.

Step 6. The reset proceeds and the computer restarts. The time required depends on the option you selected in step 4. When finished, log back on.

NOTE Although a drive format does not perform a highly secure erase, it does make it much more difficult for the next user of the device to recover sensitive data from the drive.

NOTE For more information on the refresh and reset processes, refer to "Refresh and Reset Your PC" at http://blogs.msdn.com/b/b8/archive/2012/01/04/refresh-and-reset-your-pc.aspx.

Advanced Startup Options

The Update and recovery screen previously shown in Figure 19-10 also enables you to perform several Advanced startup actions. Click **Restart now**; after a few seconds, the Windows Recovery Environment (also known as Windows RE) starts and displays the options shown in Figure 19-17, enabling you to perform any of the following:

- **Continue:** Restarts your computer into Windows 8.1 without performing any troubleshooting actions.
- **Use a device:** Enables you to boot your computer from a USB drive, Windows recovery DVD, or network share.
- **Troubleshoot:** Enables you to refresh or reset your PC (as described earlier in this section) or boot into one of several advanced options described later in this section.
- **Turn off your PC.**

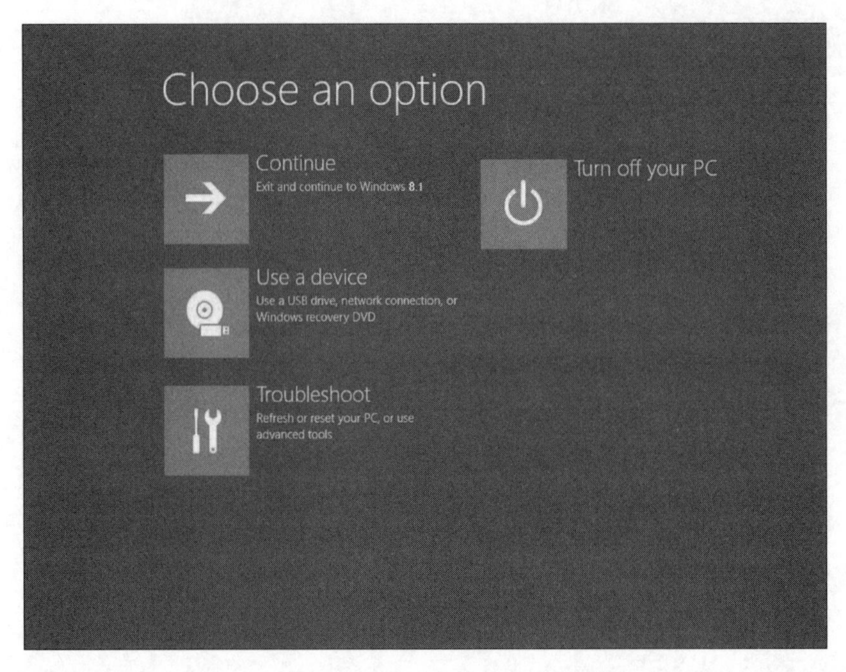

Figure 19-17 The Windows Recovery Environment provides several actions that might be useful if your computer is unable to start normally.

TIP If you are at the logon screen, you can click the power icon in the bottom-right corner of this screen and then hold down the **Shift** key while clicking **Restart**.

TIP You can also access Windows RE by booting your computer from the Windows 8.1 installation DVD. When the language preferences screen appears, click **Next** and then click **Repair your computer**.

Windows RE contains its own set of drivers and files apart from the main Windows installation; therefore, software problems within Windows do not affect starting this option, enabling you to begin troubleshooting effectively when you are unable to start your computer using any of the other options. You return to the Choose an option screen previously shown in Figure 19-17, from which you can perform tasks as outlined earlier in this section.

Selecting **Troubleshoot** from the Choose an option screen in Figure 19-17 and then **Advanced options** on the Troubleshoot screen that appears provides the options shown in Figure 19-18. From this screen, you can perform the following actions:

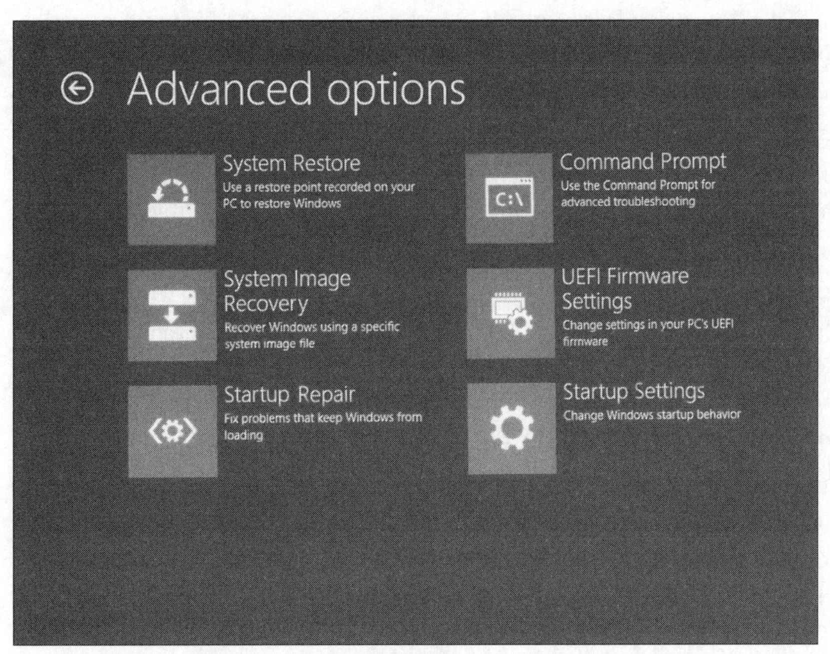

Figure 19-18 Windows provides advanced troubleshooting options.

- **System Restore:** Enables you to perform System Restore, as described earlier in this chapter and shown in Figure 19-5.
- **System Image Recovery:** Enables you to attempt recovering your computer from a system image created previously.

- **Startup Repair:** Attempts to repair problems with your computer without additional user intervention. You need to log on with an administrative account and supply your password. After a minute or so, you receive a message informing you of any changes that were made or that Startup Repair couldn't repair your PC.
- **Command Prompt:** Boots to a command prompt. This capability is useful if you cannot obtain a normal GUI.
- **UEFI Firmware Settings:** Enables you to modify United Extensible Firmware Interface (UEFI) settings.
- **Startup Settings:** Enables you to restart your computer and access additional advanced startup options, as follows:
  - **Enable low-resolution video mode:** The Enable low-resolution video option starts Windows 8.1 at the lowest video resolution of 640 × 480. This capability is useful if you have selected a display resolution and refresh rate that are not supported by your monitor and video card, or if you have installed a driver that is incompatible with your video card. You can go to the Display Properties dialog box, select an appropriate video option, and then reboot to normal mode.
  - **Enable debugging mode:** Debugging mode provides advanced troubleshooting options for experienced developers and administrators. It sends kernel debug information to another computer via a serial cable.
  - **Enable boot logging:** The Enable boot logging option starts Windows 8.1 normally while creating the `\windows\ntbtlog.txt` file, which lists all drivers that load or fail to load during startup. From the contents of this file, you can look for drivers and services that are conflicting or otherwise not functioning. After using this mode, reboot to Safe Mode to read the `ntbtlog.txt` file and identify the problematic driver.
  - **Enable Safe Mode:** Safe Mode starts your computer with a minimal set of drivers (mouse, VGA, and keyboard), so that you can start your computer when problems with drivers or other software are preventing normal startup. It is useful if your computer has stopped responding or is running very slowly or if the computer fails to respond after new hardware or software is installed. You can uninstall problematic software, disable hardware devices in Device Manager, roll back drivers, or use System Restore to roll back the computer to an earlier point in time. You can also choose **Safe Mode with Networking**, which starts network drivers as well as the other basic drivers, and **Safe Mode with Command Prompt**, which starts the computer to a command prompt. This capability can be useful if you cannot obtain a normal GUI.

- **Disable driver signature enforcement:** This option permits you to install unsigned drivers or drivers that are improperly signed. After you reboot normally, driver signatures are again enforced, but the unsigned driver is still used.
- **Disable early-launch anti-malware protection:** Select this option to prevent the startup of early launch antimalware drivers. This allows drivers that might contain malware to be installed.
- **Disable automatic restart on system failure:** This option prevents Windows 8.1 from automatically restarting if a problem is causing your computer to enter an endless loop of failure, restart attempt, and failure again.

NOTE You can use Safe Mode and System Restore together to correct problems. If you are unable to start your computer properly but are able to start in Safe Mode, you can perform a System Restore from Safe Mode to restore your computer to a functional state.

CAUTION Safe Mode has its limitations. Safe Mode does not repair problems caused by lost or corrupted system files or problems with basic drivers. In these cases, you may be able to use the Windows Recovery Environment.

NOTE For more information on Startup Repair options, refer to "Windows Startup Settings (Including Safe Mode)" at http://windows.microsoft.com/en-US/windows-8/windows-startup-settings-including-safe-mode.

Performing a System Image Recovery

Windows 8.1 enables you to perform a system image backup, which includes all files necessary to fully restore your computer in the event of a hardware failure. You have already learned how you can recover your computer using settings available from the push-button refresh feature. If you have not set up these options and are faced with a catastrophic disk failure, you can still use the system image recovery to restore your computer.

If you are using this method to restore your computer, you first need to access the Windows 8.1 startup Troubleshoot options. You can choose from three methods, depending on the current state of the system you want to repair:

- If the system is able to run Windows 8.1, access the Update and recovery option described earlier in this chapter and shown in Figure 19-10, and click the **Restart now** button. Your system restarts to the screen shown in Figure 19-17.
- If you have a USB recovery drive, insert the drive and boot the computer using the USB recovery drive. You may need to access the BIOS or EFI boot options to enable the computer to boot from the USB recovery drive.
- If the system is not running and you do not have a USB recovery drive, use a Windows 8.1 installation DVD to start the computer.

Use the following steps:

Step 1. From the startup options screen as depicted in Figure 19-17, select **Troubleshoot**. The Troubleshoot screen in Figure 19-19 is displayed.

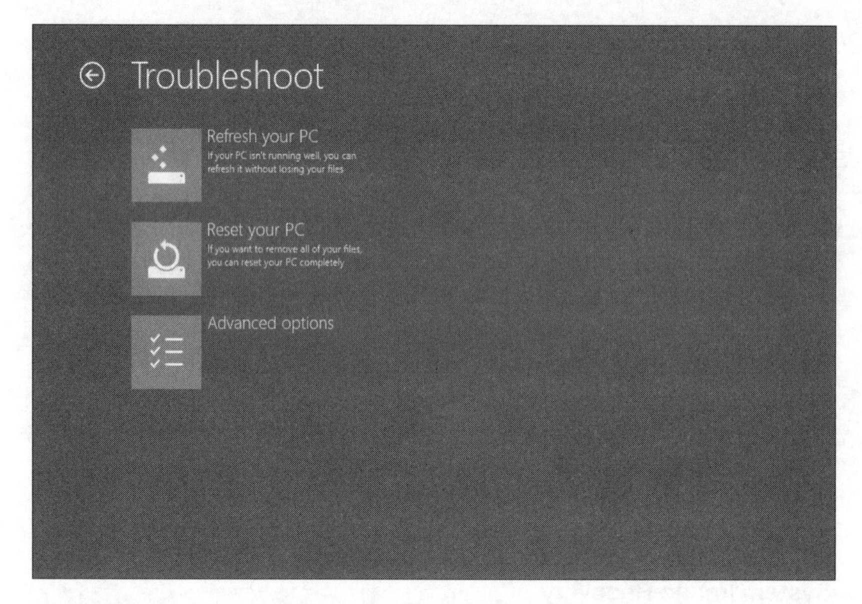

Figure 19-19 Windows 8.1 startup Troubleshoot options.

Step 2. Click **Advanced options** to display the Advanced options page previously shown in Figure 19-18.

Step 3. Select the **System Image Recovery** option.

Step 4. The computer proceeds with the recovery. If there is more than one local Administrator account, Windows may prompt you to select the one to use and to enter the password.

Step 5. The Re-image your computer options shown in Figure 19-20 enable you to select the system image to use. If the image is on an attached disk, Windows automatically locates the latest one. Otherwise, use **Select a system image** to attach or insert the disk with the system image and click **Next**.

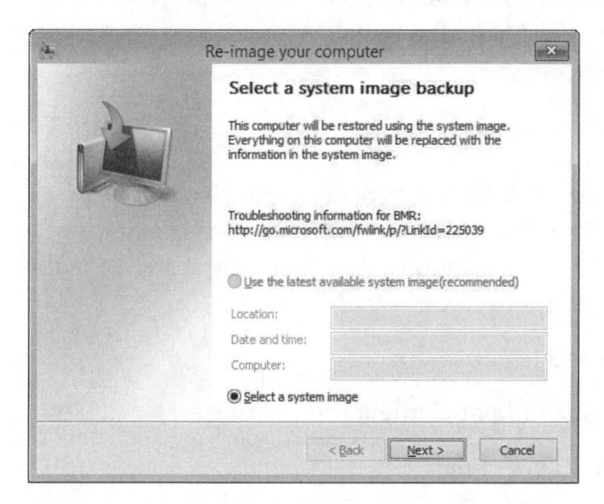

Figure 19-20 Select the system image backup to use for recovery.

Step 6. From the Re-image your computer dialog box shown in Figure 19-21, click **Install drivers** if you need to reinstall drivers for required disks or **Advanced** to specify additional options for restarting the computer and checking for disk errors. When finished, click **Next** to continue.

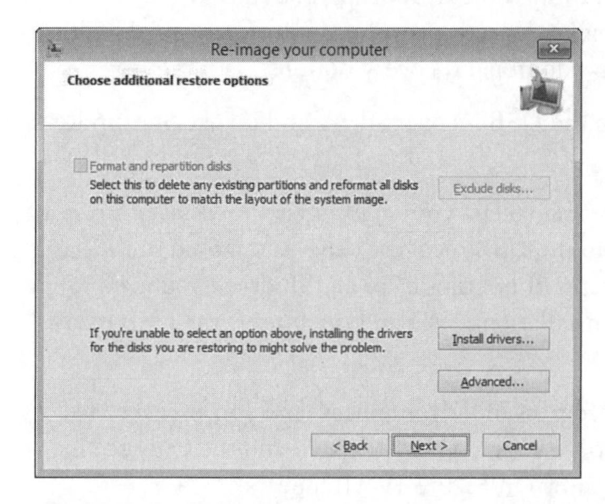

Figure 19-21 The Re-image your computer dialog box provides several additional restore options.

Step 7. Review the options provided and click **Back** if you need to make any changes. Then click **Finish** to proceed with re-imaging your computer.

Step 8. You are warned that all data on the drives to be restored will be replaced with data from the image. Click **Yes** to continue.

Step 9. A message box charts the progress of re-imaging your computer, and then the computer restarts. After you are logged back on, a Recovery message box informs you that recovery is complete and offers an option to restore user files. Click **Restore my files** to do so or **Cancel** to quit.

Using the USB Recovery Drive

Earlier in this chapter, we introduced the USB recovery drive, which attempts to automatically recover a computer that will not start normally by loading a Startup Repair routine that provides several recovery options. The following are some of the problems that Startup Repair can attempt to repair:

- Missing, corrupted, or incompatible device drivers
- Missing or corrupted system files or boot configuration settings
- Improper or corrupted Registry keys or data
- Corrupted disk metadata, such as the master boot table, boot sector, or partition table

Startup Repair provides a diagnostics-based, step-by-step troubleshooting tool that enables end users and tech support personnel to rapidly diagnose and repair problems that are preventing a computer from starting normally. When Startup Repair determines the problem that is preventing normal startup, it attempts to repair this problem automatically. If it is unable to do so, it provides support personnel with diagnostic information and suggests additional recovery options.

Use the following procedure to run the USB recovery drive and invoke Startup Repair:

Step 1. Insert the USB recovery drive and restart your computer. If necessary, press a key to boot the computer from the USB recovery drive as opposed to the hard disk. If your BIOS does not support booting from a USB drive, you need to boot from the Windows 8.1 installation DVD and then insert the USB recovery drive.

Step 2. The Windows 8.1 logo and progress indicator appear, and you are asked to select a default keyboard. Choose your keyboard layout, and the Choose an option dialog box previously shown in Figure 19-17 appears.

Step 3. Select **Troubleshoot**, and then from the Troubleshoot screen (previously shown in Figure 19-19), select **Advanced options**, and then select **Startup Repair** from the menu.

Step 4. The computer searches for Windows installations and then displays the Diagnosing your PC screen.

Step 5. If Windows finds a problem that it can fix, it then prompts you to restart the computer.

Step 6. Startup Repair searches for problems. If it does not detect any problem, it informs you and offers links to restart the computer or to bring up the **Advanced options** window, previously shown in Figure 19-18.

Step 7. If Startup Repair detects and repairs a problem, it displays a message informing you that it repaired the problem successfully.

Step 8. When you are finished, click **Finish** and then click **Restart** to restart your computer normally.

Configuring Restore Points

Earlier in this chapter, you learned how to use System Restore to restore your computer to an earlier point in time. Windows automatically creates restore points when certain actions take place. Each of these restore points contains a complete set of information required to restore the computer to that respective point in time. On computers with more than 64 GB hard disk space, restore points can occupy up to 5% of space to a maximum of 10 GB, whichever is less. With less than 64 GB hard disk space, restore points can occupy up to 3% of disk space.

Windows automatically creates restore points before certain actions take place:

- **Application installation:** Assuming that the app installer is compliant with System Restore, Windows creates a restore point that enables you to restore the computer to its previous state should problems occur during or after the application installation.
- **Automatic Windows Update installation:** After Windows Update downloads updates and before they are installed, an update is created so that you can restore the computer to its previous state should a problem occur with any update.
- **System Restore:** Windows creates a restore point before restoring the computer to a previous state. This facilitates your selecting a different restore point should you find the selected restore point to be inappropriate. When the computer restarts, you receive an option to revert to the previous condition should the restore not work properly.

In addition, Windows 8.1 automatically creates a restore point after seven days if no other restore points have been created within that time interval.

By default, System Protection is enabled for the `%systemdrive%` volume only. You can manually create a restore point for any volume at any desired time. Use the following procedure:

Step 1. Access the System Protection tab of the System Properties dialog box as described earlier in this chapter and shown in Figure 19-4.

Step 2. To configure a restore point for any volume on your computer, select it and click **Configure** to open the dialog box shown in Figure 19-22.

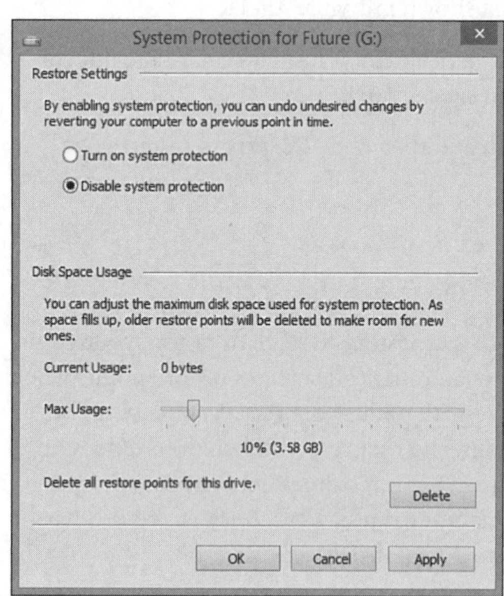

Figure 19-22 You can enable and configure system protection on any volume on your computer.

Step 3. Click **Turn on system protection** and then click **Apply**.

Step 4. Adjust the slider under Disk Space Usage to specify the maximum amount of disk space that will be used.

Step 5. If you want to delete old restore points for this drive to free up disk space, click **Delete** and then confirm your intention by clicking **Continue** in the message box that appears. Note that this cannot be undone.

Step 6. When finished, click **OK** to return to the System Protection tab.

Step 7. Repeat steps 2 to 6 as required to configure System Restore for other drive volumes on your computer.

You can also manually create a restore point from the System Protection tab previously shown in Figure 19-4. In the System Protection dialog box shown in Figure 19-23, type a descriptive name for the restore point and then click **Create**.

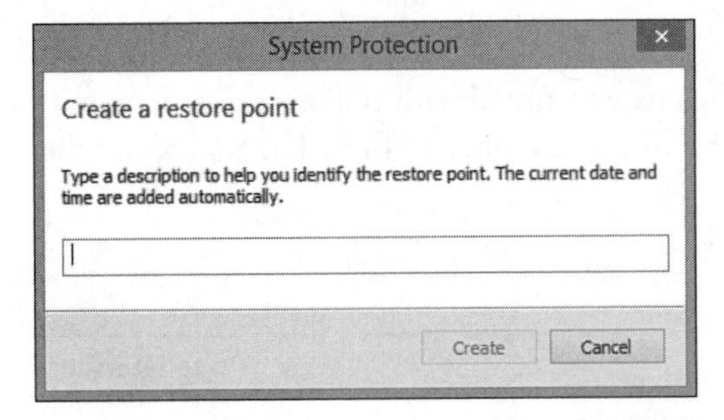

Figure 19-23 You can manually create a restore point at any time.

TIP The `Restore-Computer` PowerShell cmdlet also enables you to restore your computer to a restore point that you specify as a parameter to this cmdlet. This command restarts the computer and then performs the restore. It is supported only on client operating systems including Windows 8.1, Windows 8, Windows 7, Windows Vista, and Windows XP. For more information including available parameters and options, refer to "Restore-Computer" at http://technet.microsoft.com/en-us/library/dd347740.aspx.

NOTE For more information on restore points, refer to "Restore Points" at http://msdn.microsoft.com/en-us/library/windows/desktop/aa378910(v=vs.85).aspx.

Exam Preparation Tasks

Review All the Key Topics

Review the most important topics in the chapter, noted with the key topics icon in the outer margin of the page. Table 19-2 lists a reference of these key topics and the page numbers on which each is found.

Table 19-2 Key Topics for Chapter 19

Key Topic Element	Description	Page Number
Figure 19-1	Windows 8.1 provides advanced recovery tools	815
Figure 19-4	System Protection provides several options for restoring your operating system to a previous point in time	819
Figure 19-9	Shows you how to roll back a problematic device driver	822
Figure 19-10	Shows the Update and recovery screen, which provides three recovery options	824
Figure 19-18	Shows several advanced troubleshooting options	831
Figure 19-22	Shows how to configure options for System Protection	838

Definitions of Key Terms

Define the following key terms from this chapter and check your answers in the Glossary:

Push-button reset, Safe Mode, Startup Repair, System Protection, System Restore, USB recovery drive, Windows Recovery Environment (Windows RE)

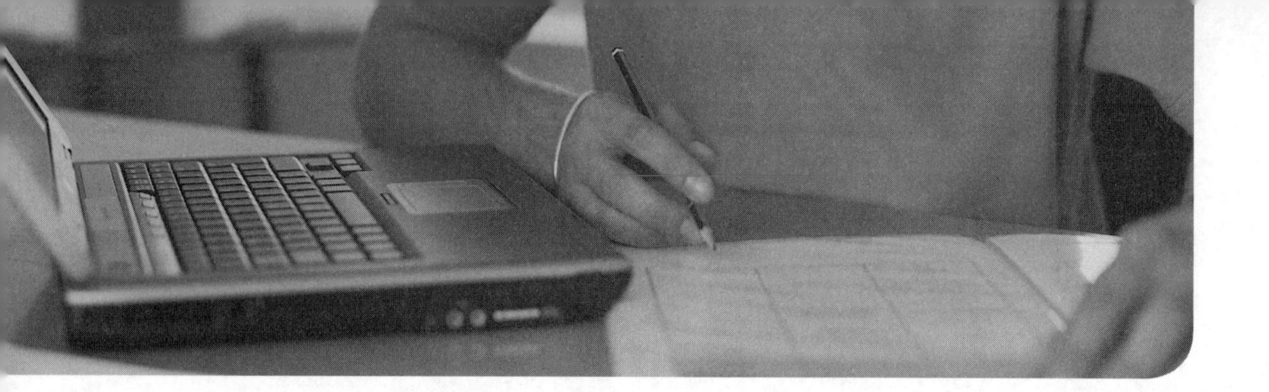

This chapter covers the following subjects:

- **Using File History to Protect Your Data:** Microsoft has created the new File History feature in Windows 8.1 as the primary application for backing up files and folders on your computer. Backups of data files are very important because you could lose valuable information should your hard disk fail. This section shows you how to configure the options available in File History.
- **Restoring Previous Versions of Files and Folders:** When a file or folder has become corrupted, improperly modified, or deleted, you can restore it from a backup to undo any harmful changes. In this section, we cover how to restore files and folders when they are lost or corrupted. Windows 8.1 provides a number of protection mechanisms for files, including File History.
- **Recovering Files from OneDrive:** OneDrive provides integrated cloud storage for Windows 8.1, as covered in Chapter 11, "Configuring and Securing Access to Files and Folders." This section shows you how to recover files and previous versions of files stored on the OneDrive service.

CHAPTER 20

Configuring File Recovery

Backing up and restoring crucial data is an important responsibility for an individual charged with this duty. Without some sort of backup strategy in place, loss of critical data could threaten the very existence of an organization. At the very least, it can make a computer unusable. Windows 8.1 offers a new backup utility called File History that simplifies the task of backing up files stored in the usual data folder locations. In this chapter, you learn about the various strategies used to back up your data and how to restore data from various locations, including your computer and Windows OneDrive.

"Do I Know This Already?" Quiz

The "Do I Know This Already?" quiz allows you to assess whether you should read this entire chapter or simply jump to the "Exam Preparation Tasks" section for review. If you are in doubt, read the entire chapter. Table 20-1 outlines the major headings in this chapter and the corresponding "Do I Know This Already?" quiz questions. You can find the answers in Appendix A, "Answers to the 'Do I Know This Already?' Quizzes."

Table 20-1 "Do I Know This Already?" Foundation Topics Section-to-Question Mapping

Foundations Topics Section	Questions Covered in This Section
Using File History to Protect Your Data	1–5
Restoring Previous Versions of Files and Folders	6
Recovering Files from OneDrive	7–8

1. Which of the following files and folders are backed up by default when using the new File History feature? (Choose all that apply.)
   a. Libraries
   b. Operating system files
   c. Contacts
   d. Application files
   e. Folders placed on the desktop

2. By default, which of the following locations can you use to hold backup copies of data created by File History? (Choose three.)
   a. Network folders
   b. CD-ROM and DVD-ROM drives
   c. Internal hard drives configured using the Storage Space feature
   d. USB thumb drives
   e. External hard drives

3. You are about to make a lot of changes to some important documents on your computer, and you want to make sure you have a good backup of the files. You know that File History is enabled, but how would you ensure that your current files are backed up?
   a. Restore the backup and watch for messages asking if you want to copy and replace files in the same location.
   b. Open File History from the Control Panel and select **Run now**.
   c. Use the Search option and specify each file that you want to check.
   d. Simply browse the backed-up files and verify that all required files are present.

4. You would like to configure File History to store only the most recent version of each file to conserve disk space. What option should you configure from the Advanced Settings dialog box?
   a. Under the Keep saved versions setting, choose the **Until space is needed** option.
   b. Under the Save copies of files setting, choose the **Most recent version only** option.
   c. Click **Clean up versions** and select the **All but the latest one** option and then click **Clean up** to proceed.
   d. Click **Clean up versions**, select a one-month interval, and then click **Clean up** to proceed.

5. You have stored your work documents in the `D:\workarea` folder on your Windows 8.1 Pro computer. You would like to ensure that File History backs up all documents in this folder. What should you do? (Each correct answer represents a complete solution. Choose two answers.)
   a. From File Explorer, add the `D:\workarea` folder to the Documents library.
   b. From the File History applet, click **Add** and add the `D:\workarea` folder.

c. From the File History applet, click **Select folder** and then select the `D:\workarea` folder in the Select folder dialog box that appears.

d. From File Explorer, create a new library named Workarea.

6. You are working on an important report that your boss needs first thing tomorrow morning and discover that an entire section that took you several days to prepare is missing. What should you do to get this section back with the least amount of effort and ensure that you do not lose your most recent changes?

   a. Access the Previous Versions tab of the report's Properties dialog box and select a version from a couple of days ago. Then click **Copy**.

   b. Access the File History and select a version from a couple of days ago. Then click **Restore**.

   c. From File History, restore a backup created a couple of days ago. When prompted, select the **Restore to** option.

   d. Restore from a backup created a couple of days ago and select the option to restore to another location.

7. You have been working on several documents on your Windows 8.1 PC's OneDrive storage and cleaning up old documents to conserve space. You also emptied the Recycle bin to recover the space. The next day you realized you had deleted two important files that you needed. How would you recover your lost files?

   a. Check the Recycle bin on your PC.

   b. Check the Recycle bin on OneDrive.com.

   c. Look in the Restore personal files dialog box in your PC's File History.

   d. Check the Volume Shadow storage for the deleted files.

8. Your OneDrive storage space is 7 GB, and you recently deleted about 4 GB of files to make room for some new files. How long will the deleted files be kept in the OneDrive Recycle bin?

   a. 30–45 days

   b. 15–30 days

   c. One week

   d. 3 days

Foundation Topics

Using File History to Protect Your Data

Chapter 19, "Configuring System Recovery Options," introduced you to the new File History backup application included with Windows 8.1. It enables you to back up files and folders located within your libraries, contacts, favorites, and desktop, and to create a USB recovery drive. You also looked at the options available in Windows 8.1 for restoring or recovering your computer when problems prevent it from starting up normally. Now you can turn your attention to ensuring that important data on your computer is backed up and that you can recover this data from any type of misadventure such as improper deletion or modification, corruption, and so on.

Recent versions of Windows have used the Backup and Restore applet in Control Panel as the central location for performing all types of backup and restore operations. Although this tool was still available in Windows 8, Microsoft has removed it in Windows 8.1 in favor of the new File History feature that enables an automatic backup of all files located in your libraries, contacts, favorites, and the desktop. Remember that libraries are collections of files and folders that hold documents, music, pictures, and videos in a centralized location that is shared across the network by default. We introduced the concept of libraries in Chapter 11, "Configuring and Securing Access to Files and Folders."

Microsoft created the File History feature with the following ideas in mind:

- File History facilitates the process of protecting data so that users can set it up and become confident that their personal information is being protected.
- File History supports backing up data to external hard drives, USB thumb drives, and network folders.
- File History reduces the complexity of configuring and running a backup program.
- File History acts as an automatic, silent service that works in the background to protect data without the need for user interaction.
- File History supports laptops and other mobile devices much better than previous backup solutions, working with situations such as changing power states and connection to and disconnection from different networks.
- File History provides an easy-to-do restore experience that facilitates the process of locating, previewing, and restoring files and folders.

Setting Up File History

Microsoft recommends that you use a portable hard drive or network location with File History. This ensures that your files and folders are protected against a catastrophic failure of some type. Use the following procedure to set up File History:

Step 1. From the Settings charm or the Start right-click menu, select **Control Panel > System and Security > File History**. You can also access the Search charm, type `backup` in the search box, and then select **Save backup copies of your files with File History** from the list that appears. As shown in Figure 20-1, the File History applet opens and informs you that File History is off. If files are encrypted with the Encrypting File System (EFS), on a network location, or on a drive that is not formatted with the NTFS file system, these files are not backed up.

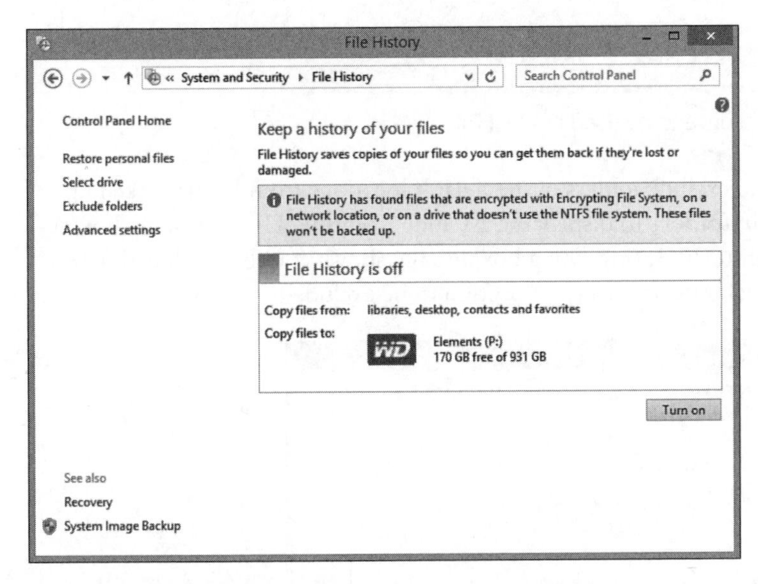

Figure 20-1 The first time you open the File History applet, it warns you that by default, File History is off.

Step 2. Click **Turn on**. File History asks whether you want to recommend the drive to other members of your homegroup. After you choose **Yes** or **No**, File History informs you that it is saving copies of your files for the first time.

Step 3. If you want to change the location where your backups are stored, click **Select drive**. You receive the Select a File History drive dialog box shown in Figure 20-2. Select the desired external hard drive or USB thumb drive or click **Add network location** to save your files to a location on the network. Then click **OK**.

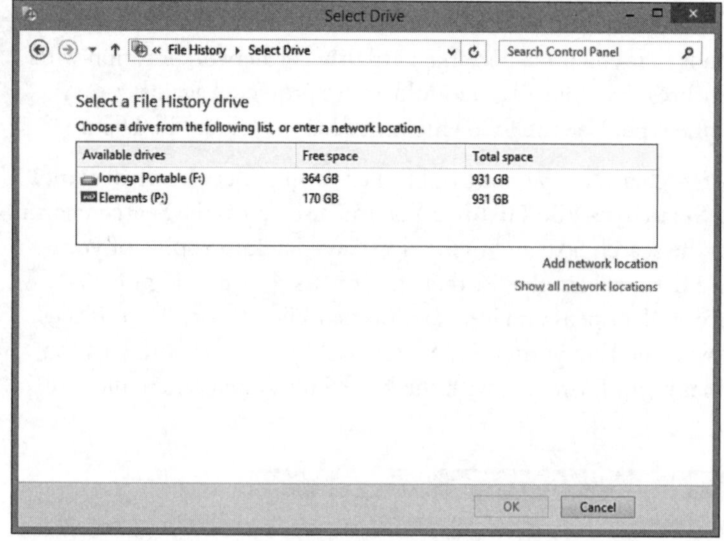

Figure 20-2 Selecting a drive to be used by File History.

Step 4. If you want to exclude folders in the default locations from being backed up, click **Exclude folders** to display the Exclude from File History dialog box. As shown in Figure 20-3, this dialog box initially shows you that no locations are excluded. Click **Add** to specify a location to be excluded.

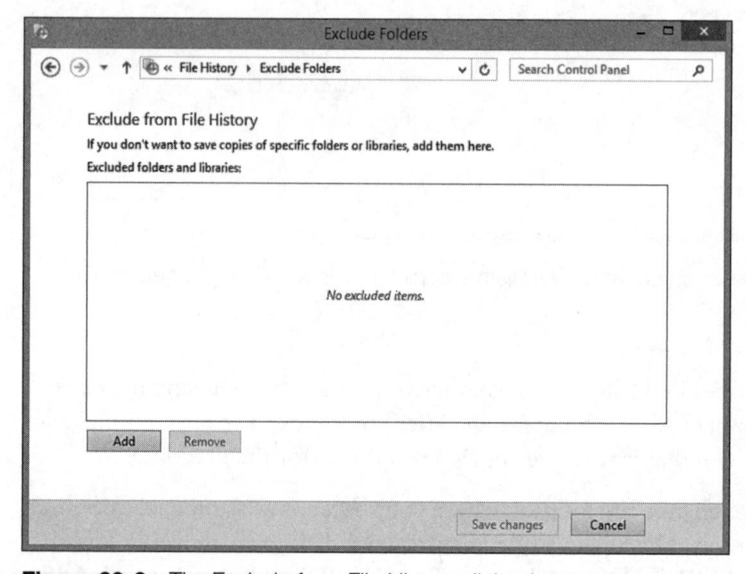

Figure 20-3 The Exclude from File History dialog box enables you to exclude specified folders from being backed up.

Step 5. In the Select Folder dialog box, double-click the library in which the folder to be excluded is located, select the desired folder as shown in Figure 20-4, and then click **Select Folder**.

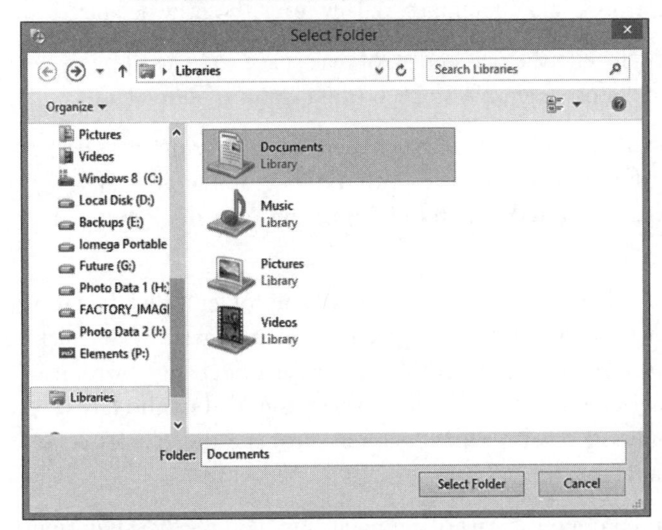

Figure 20-4 The Select Folder dialog box enables you to specify a folder that is not to be included in File History.

Step 6. Repeat as needed to exclude additional folders. When finished, click **Save changes** to return to the File History applet.

Step 7. To configure additional File History options, click **Advanced settings** to display the dialog box shown in Figure 20-5.

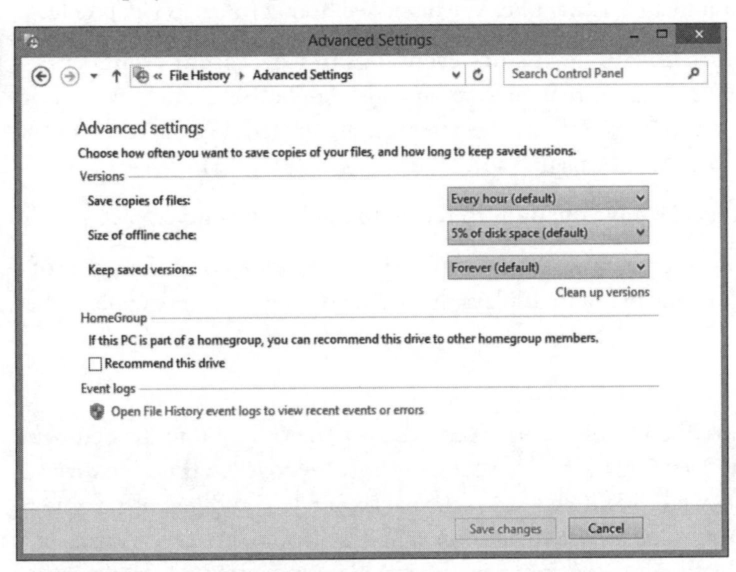

Figure 20-5 The Advanced Settings dialog box enables you to specify additional options related to how File History keeps copies of your files.

Step 8. Select from the following options as desired:

- **Save copies of files:** Specify the interval at which File History saves copies of file. You can select options from every 10 minutes to daily (every hour by default).
- **Size of offline cache:** Specify the percentage of disk space to be used by the offline cache. You can choose from 2% to 20% (the default is 5%).
- **Keep saved versions:** By default, File History keeps saved versions forever. You can choose several options from one month to two years, or you can choose the **Until space is needed** option to limit the number of older saved versions of files.
- **Clean up versions:** To delete older versions of files and folders, click **Clean up versions**. This deletes files older than a specified age (one year by default), except the most recent version of a file or folder that has not changed within the interval chosen. Select a desired interval (or select the **All but the latest one** option to keep only the most recent version of files) and then click **Clean up** to proceed or **Cancel** to exit.
- **HomeGroup:** If your computer is part of a homegroup, you receive an option to recommend the drive to other homegroup members. Select the check box provided to do so. If your computer is not part of a homegroup, you receive an option to create or join a homegroup. Click **Create or join a homegroup** to specify a homegroup that will be recommended to other computers on the homegroup. This displays the Share with other home computers dialog box previously shown in Figure 11-9 in Chapter 11 that enables you to create a new homegroup or join an existing one. We discussed homegroups in Chapter11.
- **Event logs:** Click **Open File History event logs to view recent events or errors** to open Event Viewer to a sublocation under Applications and Services Logs where errors, warnings, or informative messages are logged. We discussed Event Viewer in Chapter 18, "Managing and Monitoring System Performance."

Step 9. When finished, click **Save changes** to return to the File History applet.

Step 10. Click **Run now** to create the backup copies. File History records the status of saving copies of your files and displays the date and time files were copied when it finishes.

TIP You can also access File History from the Start screen interface. From the Settings charm, click **Change PC settings**. Then select **Update and recovery > File History**. You receive the page shown in Figure 20-6, which enables you to turn File History on or off, select a different drive to be used, and perform an initial backup. However, this app does not enable you to configure other settings mentioned in the preceding procedure.

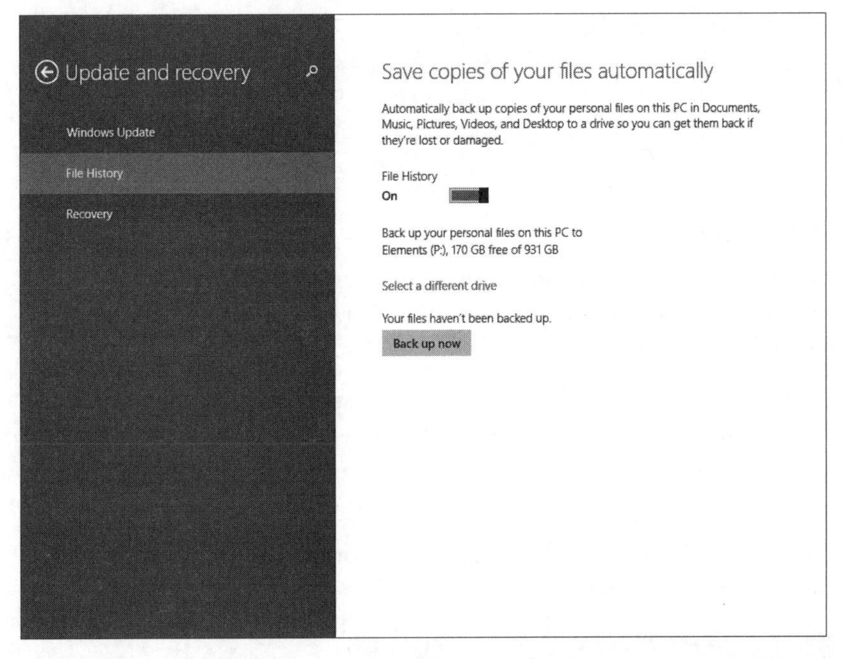

Figure 20-6 The File History Start screen app enables you to turn on File History, select a drive, and perform a backup.

Adding Additional Folders to File History

If you want to add a folder that is not located in one of the default locations used by File History, you can perform one of the following actions:

- **Add it to an existing library:** From a File Explorer window, right-click the desired folder, choose **Include in library**, and then specify the desired library.
- **Create a new library:** From the context menu displayed, choose **Create new library**. This automatically creates a new library named after the selected folder and displays this library in the list displayed on the left side of the File Explorer window.

NOTE The Windows Backup utility previously used in Windows 7 and older versions was available in Windows 8 and called Windows 7 Backup. However, this utility is no longer available in Windows 8.1. For more information, refer to "What Happened to Backup and Restore" at http://windows.microsoft.com/en-us/windows-8/what-happened-to-backup-restore.

NOTE For additional information on using the File History feature, refer to "Restore Files or Folders Using File History" at http://windows.microsoft.com/en-IN/windows-8/how-use-file-history and "Set up a drive for File History" at http://windows.microsoft.com/en-CA/windows-8/set-drive-file-history.

Creating a System Image

The File History applet provides an option to create a system image, which enables you to fully restore your computer in the event of a hardware failure. You can also use this procedure to back up your data at the same time. Use the following procedure:

Step 1. From the bottom-left corner of the File History applet (refer to Figure 20-1), click **System Image Backup**. If you receive a User Account Control (UAC) prompt, click **Yes**.

Step 2. The Where do you want to save the backup? screen shown in Figure 20-7 enables you to save the backup to a hard disk or to one or more DVDs. Make a selection and then click **Next**.

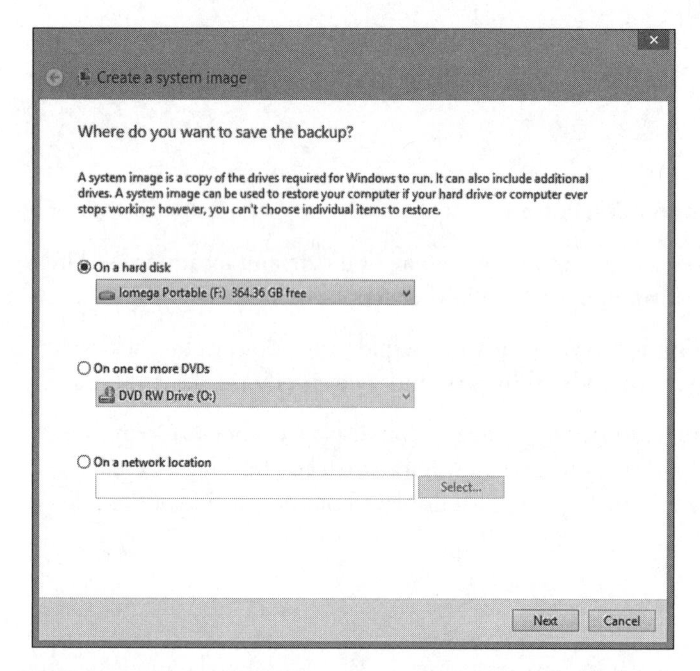

Figure 20-7 You can save a system image backup to a hard drive, a set of DVDs, or a network location.

Step 3. The Which drives do you want to include in the backup? screen shown in Figure 20-8 enables you to select the disks to be backed up. Select the required disks and then click **Next**.

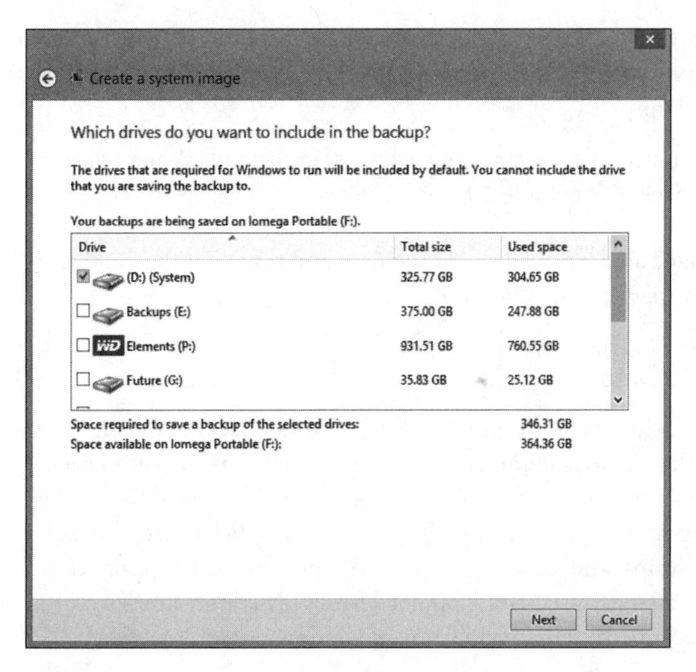

Figure 20-8 You can choose additional drives in your system image backup.

Step 4. If you selected **On a network location** to save your backup, Windows asks for the universal naming convention (UNC) path and your network credentials, as shown in Figure 20-9.

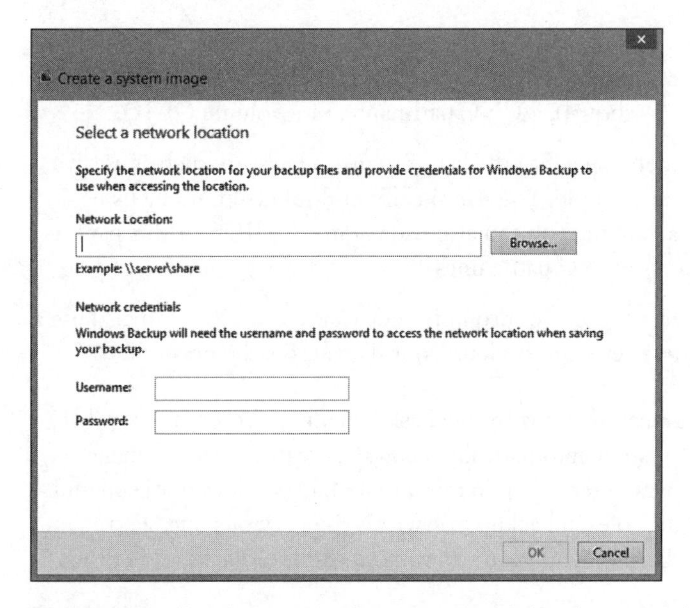

Figure 20-9 If saving your backup to a network location, enter the path of the network drive and the network credentials to use.

Step 5. The Confirm your backup settings page shows which disks will be backed up and to what location. Verify that these are correct and then click **Start backup** to perform the backup.

Step 6. Windows displays a progress chart as the backup is performed. When you are informed that the backup is completed, click **Close**.

The Create a system image applet now displays the date and time that the complete system image backup was performed.

Using `Wbadmin` to Back Up Data

Windows 8.1 no longer includes a GUI interface for Windows Backup, but you can perform backups using the `Wbadmin` command-line tool, which enables you to back up files, folders, and the system image from the command line. You need to run this tool from an administrative command prompt. To do so, right-click **Start**, choose **Command Prompt (Admin)**, and click **Yes** in the UAC prompt that appears. If you're not using an administrative account, you need to supply administrative credentials. You can also execute this command from an administrative PowerShell window.

For example, to back up the contents of the `C:\` drive to the `F:\` external hard drive, use the following:

```
wbadmin start backup -backupTarget:f: -include:c: -quiet
```

In this command:

- The `-backupTarget` parameter specifies the storage location for the backup. It can be a drive letter (as shown), a UNC pathname, or a volume GUID.
- The `-include` parameter specifies the list of items to back up, such as a drive letter, as shown in the example. You can specify multiple volumes by using a comma to delimit each item. You can also use volume GUIDs for this parameter, but you cannot use UNC pathnames.
- The `-quiet` parameter suppresses prompts back to the user. You can also use a UNC path to a remote server to back up your data across the network.

By combining the `wbadmin` command with the Task Scheduler, you can create backups of your Windows 8.1 system automatically. `Wbadmin` creates a system image using the `-allCritical` parameter. Keep in mind that `wbadmin` does not keep multiple versions of the backup, so each backup overwrites the previous one. To retain multiple versions of your backup, you need to swap out the external drive between backups.

NOTE For more information on `wbadmin` and its use for backing up and restoring data including the system image, refer to "Wbadmin" at http://technet.microsoft.com/en-us/library/cc754015.aspx, together with links to subcommands found therein.

NOTE You can also use the Microsoft Diagnostics and Recovery Toolset (DaRT) to perform system and data backup and recovery on Windows 8.1 computers. DaRT is a component of the Microsoft Desktop Optimization Pack (MDOP), which is available through Software Assurance or Microsoft Volume Licensing. As an advanced tool available only through these premium sources, DaRT is beyond the scope of the 70-687 exam. For more information, refer to "Diagnostics and Recovery Toolset" at http://technet.microsoft.com/en-us/windows/hh826071.aspx.

CAUTION Creation of shadow copies, which is required for File History to back up open files, requires that the Volume Shadow Copy service be started. By default, this service is set for Manual startup, which means that the service is started as required. If the service is set to Disabled, shadow copies are not created. If the service is not started, Windows does not create File History for any open files.

Restoring Previous Versions of Files and Folders

First introduced with Windows XP Professional and continued through Windows 8.1 is the concept of volume shadow copies, or Volume Shadow Storage (VSS), which creates shadow copies of files and folders as you work on them so that you can retrieve previous versions of files that you might have corrupted or deleted.

The shadow copy feature, first introduced with Windows XP and Windows Server 2003, has been renamed to File History in Windows 8.1 and Windows Server 2012 R2. This feature creates copies of files in real time as you work on them. Volume shadow copies enable users to work with files on the volume being backed up during the backup process, without the risk of having the backup program skip the open files. Using this technology removes the need for applications to be shut down to ensure a successful, complete backup.

Using File History to Restore Damaged or Deleted Files

In Windows 7, a front end called Previous Versions was available. It allowed you to select any file and revert to a previous version created with the Volume Shadow Copy service. The File History feature in Windows 8.1 behaves differently. Although File History still uses the Volume Shadow Copy service, it does not directly use the shadow copies, but instead copies files in the users' directory to a second drive. VSS allows File History to make backups of your files even while you are working on them.

Having backed-up files and folders with File History, you can recover previous versions of files should problems such as data corruption, deletion, or improper modification occur. Use the following procedure:

Step 1. Open File History using any of the procedures given previously.

Step 2. From the options provided on the left side of the File History applet, click **Restore personal files**. You receive the Home–File History dialog box shown in Figure 20-10.

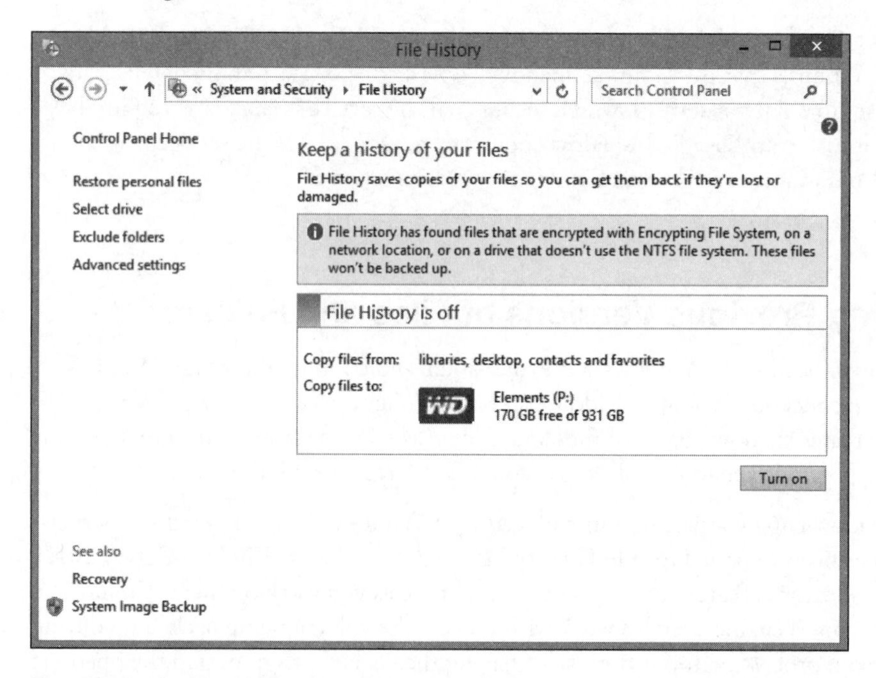

Figure 20-10 The Home–File History dialog box displays the file folders and libraries being backed up with File History.

Step 3. Double-click the desired folder and library to see its contents.

Step 4. If necessary, double-click a subfolder to access the desired file. Doing so opens a window similar to the one shown in Figure 20-11.

Figure 20-11 File History displays files available for recovery.

Step 5. Select the desired file and click the large green button to restore it.

Step 6. If the file already exists, the Replace or Skip Files dialog box shown in Figure 20-12 opens, providing options to replace, skip, or compare the files.

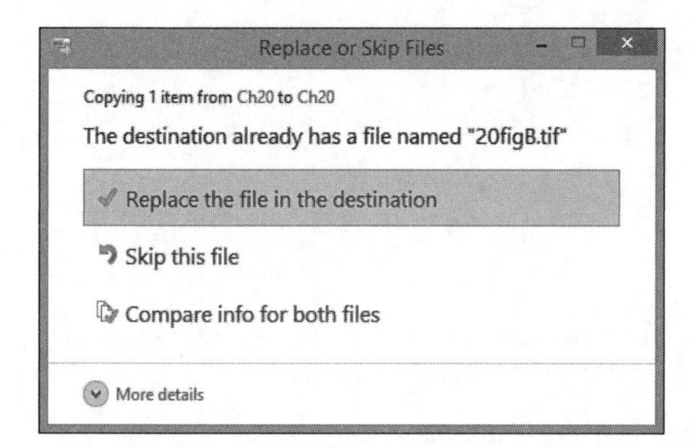

Figure 20-12 If the file already exists, you receive options for replacing or skipping it.

Step 7. Repeat these steps as needed to recover additional files if necessary.

File History does not require system protection to work; however, it does not back up files in all locations on the hard drive, but only those in the libraries, or in contacts, favorites, on the Desktop, or in your OneDrive folder.

Note that as shown in Figure 20-10, only files in certain folders are available in your File History. As described earlier in this chapter, you need to configure File History to back up files in other locations by adding folders to your libraries or creating a new library.

> **TIP** You can use the Restore function to restore multiple previous versions of a file—for example, if you need to track changes to a document that have been made by several individuals. From the File History dialog box, select a file, right-click the **Restore** button, choose the **Restore to** option, and use the File Explorer dialog box to create a folder to which you want to copy the document. Repeat this process as often as required, creating new folders with descriptive names for each previous version you want to restore. You can also rename each previous version with an appropriate descriptive name as you restore it so that you do not need to create multiple folders.

Using `Wbadmin` to Recover Data

You can use the `wbadmin` command to recover files and folders that you have previously backed up using this command, as explained earlier in this chapter. In this case, use the following syntax:

```
wbadmin start recovery -version:<VersionIdentifier> -
items:{<VolumesToRecover> | <AppsToRecover> |
<FilesOrFoldersToRecover>} -itemtype:{Volume | App | File} [-
backupTarget:{<VolumeHostingBackup> |
<NetworkShareHostingBackup>}]
```

In this command:

- The `-version:<VersionIdentifier>` parameter refers to a version identifier of the backup to recover in MM/DD/YYYY-HH:M format.
- The `-items:{<VolumesToRecover> | <AppsToRecover> | <FilesOrFoldersToRecover>}` parameter specifies a comma-delimited list of volumes, applications, files, or folders to be recovered, according to the item type you specify.
- The `-itemtype:{Volume | App | File}` parameter specifies the types of items to be recovered.

- The `-backuptarget` parameter specifies the storage location containing the backup that you want to recover.

For example, to recover a backup of volume `e:` that was taken at 8:00 a.m. on February 28, 2014, use the following command:

```
wbadmin start recovery -version:02/28/2014-08:00 -itemType:Volume
-items:e:
```

NOTE Additional parameters are available; for a complete description of this command and its available parameters, refer to "Wbadmin start recovery" at http://technet.microsoft.com/en-us/library/cc742070.aspx.

Recovering Files from OneDrive

We introduced Microsoft OneDrive (formerly SkyDrive) in Chapter 11. OneDrive is free cloud storage for your Windows 8.1 devices that integrates seamlessly with other local and network storage available in Windows.

NOTE You should be aware of how to maintain backups of your files if you are using OneDrive. Although OneDrive storage is integrated with Windows 8.1 and generally works like local storage, File History does not back up files that you have synced with OneDrive, even when they are in folders that File History backs up.

OneDrive and the Recycle Bin

The Microsoft OneDrive includes a Recycle bin that can be used to recover any deleted files. You should be aware of the retention policies for your OneDrive Recycle bin:

- Deleted files are kept for a maximum of 30 days. That means that no more than 30 days after the file is deleted, it is removed.
- If the Recycle bin reaches 10% of the total space for the OneDrive (which is 0.7 GB of the free 7 GB storage), files are deleted after 3 days, oldest files first, until the Recycle bin storage reaches less than 10% of the total space.

In Windows 8.1, the local PC's Recycle bin is also used for OneDrive. If you delete a file in OneDrive storage, it is moved to the PC's Recycle bin for easy recovery. This works regardless of whether the files are online only or available offline.

You can recover deleted files from either the local PC Recycle bin or the OneDrive.com Recycle bin. If you empty the Recycle bin on your local PC, you may still be able to recover your files from OneDrive.com using the following procedure:

1. From a web browser, sign into your OneDrive account at OneDrive.com.
2. In the lower-left corner, find the **Recycle bin** link and click on it. Any deleted files in your OneDrive Recycle bin show up in the list, as shown in Figure 20-13.

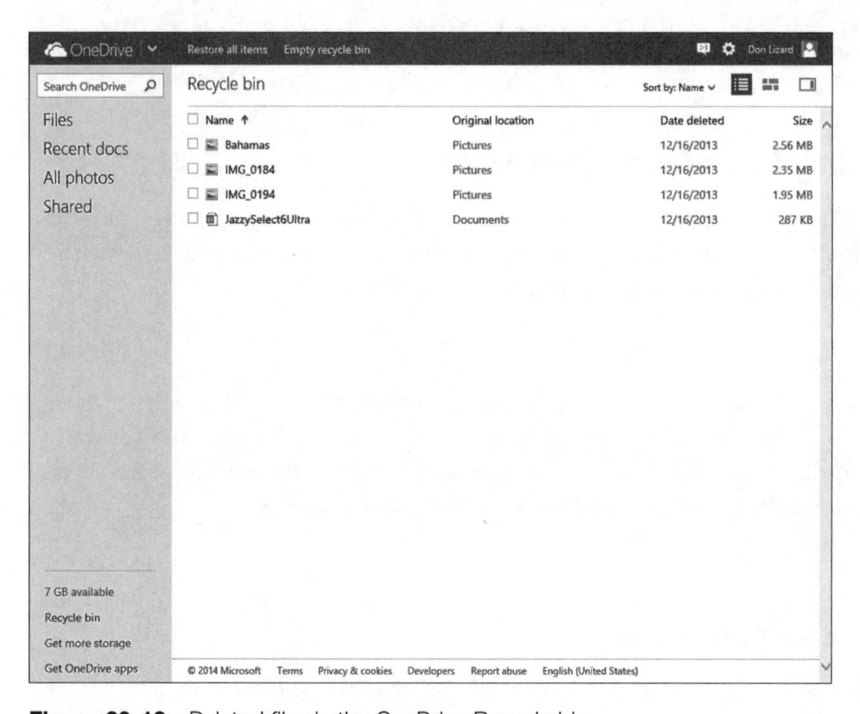

Figure 20-13 Deleted files in the OneDrive Recycle bin.

3. To restore all the files, select the **Restore all items** link at the top of the page. If you want to restore some files but not all of them, enable the check box to the left of each file by clicking it, as shown in Figure 20-14, and then select the **Restore** link at the top of the page.

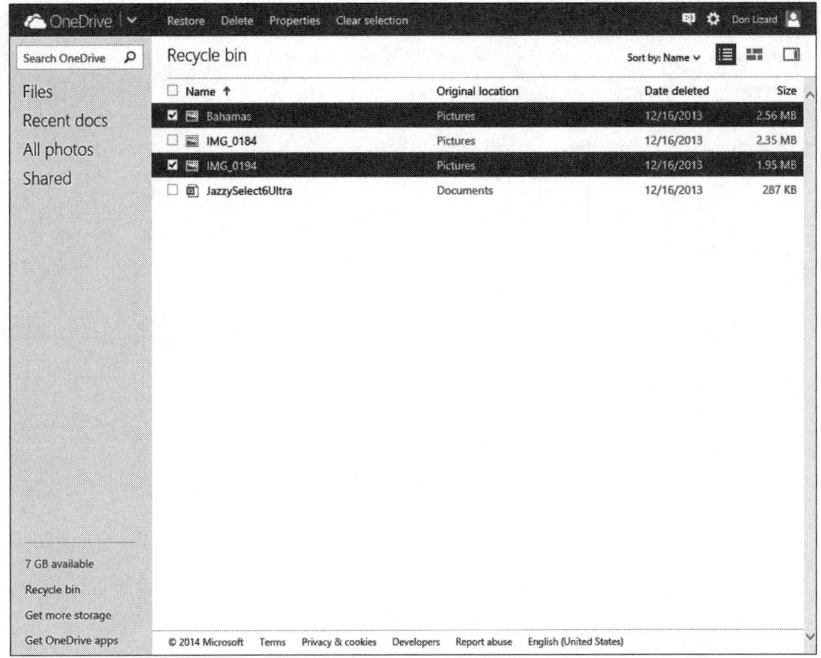

Figure 20-14 Restoring individual files from the OneDrive Recycle bin.

4. Check your OneDrive storage on Windows. The files should be restored there as well. Syncing your OneDrive storage may take a few minutes if you are using a slow network connection.

OneDrive Version History

Similar to the File History in Windows 8.1, OneDrive maintains multiple versions of your Office documents automatically. Each time you edit a document from OneDrive, whether directly from the OneDrive storage or OneDrive.com, a new version of the document is created.

OneDrive keeps track of up to 25 previous versions of each file. Note that you can access the previous versions only from OneDrive.com.

To access prior versions, sign in to your OneDrive.com account, locate your document, and right-click it. If changes have been made to the document since it was first added to that OneDrive folder, you see a Version history selection, as shown in Figure 20-15. Select the menu item to open the current document and view the previous versions.

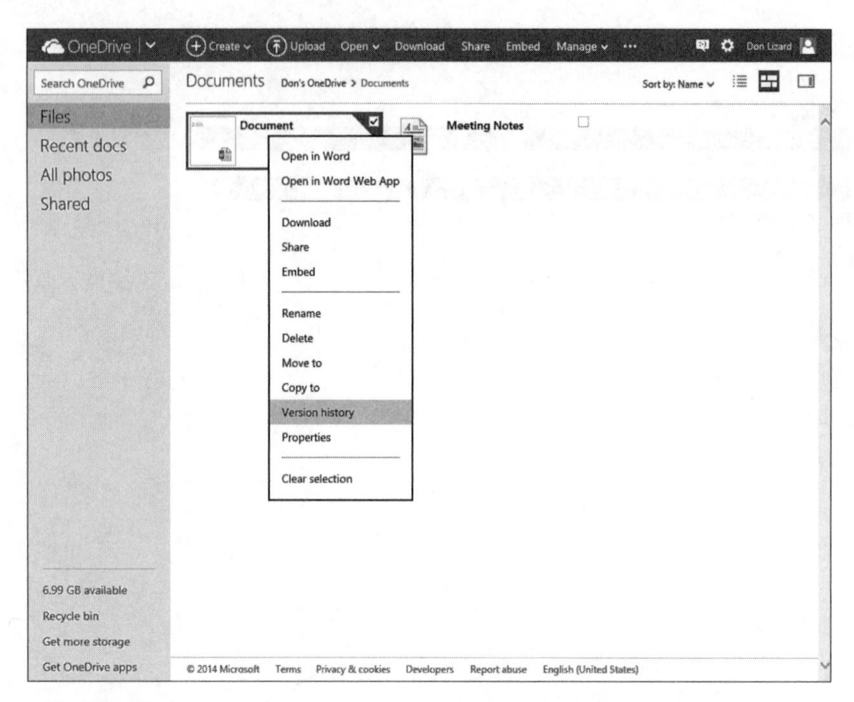

Figure 20-15 OneDrive maintains version history of Office documents.

Older versions of the document are displayed on the screen, along with the date and time each version was saved. When you select a previous version, OneDrive displays the name of the person who made the change (in case the file is shared with others). You also have the option to restore the file to the previous version or download the version to save on your PC.

NOTE Version history works only for MS Office files such as Word documents, Excel spreadsheets, and PowerPoint presentations. Version history is not maintained for other file types such as images and text files.

Exam Preparation Tasks

Review All the Key Topics

Review the most important topics in the chapter, noted with the key topics icon in the outer margin of the page. Table 20-2 lists a reference of these key topics and the page numbers on which each is found.

Table 20-2 Key Topics for Chapter 20

Key Topic Element	Description	Page Number(s)
Step List	Describes how to set up Windows File History	847-850
Figure 20-2	Shows how to set up File History	848
Figure 20-5	Shows several advanced File History options that specify how copies of files are retained	849
Step List	Shows how to restore files from File History	856-857
Figure 20-14	Shows how to select individual files for restoring from OneDrive	861

Definitions of Key Terms

Define the following key terms from this chapter and check your answers in the Glossary:

File History, OneDrive, Shadow copies, `wbadmin`

APPENDIX A

Answers to the "Do I Know This Already?" Quizzes

Chapter 1

1. **b.** The version of Windows designed for running on mobile platforms such as smartphones is known as Windows RT 8.1. Windows PE is the Windows PreBoot Execution Environment, which is created using the Windows Assessment and Deployment Kit (ADK) for Windows 8.1 and is associated with deployment of Windows. You will learn about Windows ADK in Chapter 2, "Installing Windows 8.1." Windows NT was the earlier 32-bit version of Windows used in the 1990s on many networks; modern Windows versions are descended from the original Windows NT. There is no such operating system as Windows 8.1 Home Basic; the Home Basic label existed only with Windows Vista and Windows 7.

2. **a, d.** You must have the Pro or Enterprise version of Windows 8.1 to join a Windows Server domain or encrypt files using EFS. You can run Windows Media Center or use more than one monitor on a computer running any version of Windows 8.1.

3. **b**. To access the Windows 8.1 charms, swipe your finger into the screen from either the top-right or bottom-right corner on a touch-screen device; on a conventional computer, move the pointer to either of these corners. The lower-left corner activates the Start screen when accessed from the desktop. The action of clicking **Start** does not work the same way in Windows 8 as it did in Windows 7 and earlier versions; it merely accesses the new Start screen. In Windows 8.1, it is possible to right-click **Start** and choose **Search**; this takes you to the Search charm but does not provide access to the other charms. There is no Charms option on the right-click menu from the Start screen or desktop.

4. **a, b, c, d, e, f.** You can perform all these tasks and several others from the new PC settings screen, which you can access by opening the **Settings** charm and selecting **Change PC settings** from the bottom of the charm.

5. **d.** To add tiles for Administrative Tools to the Start screen, open the Charms bar and select **Settings**. From the Settings bar, select **Tiles** and then toggle the switch under **Administrative Tools** to **On**. You can locate and open Administrative Tools from the Search charm, but these methods do not add tiles for these tools to the Start screen. The dialog box opened by clicking **Tools > Settings** from File Explorer does not include an option for adding tiles for Administrative Tools to the Start screen.
6. **a.** Windows 8.1 requires a 1 GHz processor. A higher processor speed will increase the speed of application execution but is not required for running Windows 8.1.
7. **d.** A 64-bit Windows 8.1 installation requires at least 20 GB of hard drive space on the system partition. You need additional hard drive space for your applications and data, but not for the Windows installation. Note that a 32-bit Windows 8.1 installation requires at least 16 GB of hard drive space.
8. **a, c, d.** Most 32-bit programs can run efficiently on a 64-bit machine; programs specifically designed to run on a 64-bit machine won't work on 32-bit Windows; and 64-bit device drivers are required on 64-bit machines. But device drivers written for 32-bit Windows will not work on a 64-bit machine.
9. **b.** An upgrade installation maintains all Windows settings, personal files, and applications from the previous Windows installation, whereas a clean installation of Windows 8.1 requires that you reinstall all programs and re-create all Windows settings. Clean installations do not maintain any settings, files, or applications from the previous Windows installation (except for files stored on a different partition). An upgrade installation does not require that you reinstall all programs and re-create all Windows settings.
10. **d.** The upgrade and full edition Windows 8.1 SKUs have identical features, but the upgrade SKU searches the computer for evidence of an older Windows installation before allowing the new Windows 8.1 to be activated. The upgrade SKU contains all the same Windows components including any that are unchanged since Windows 7. The installation of an upgrade SKU will start on a computer that does not have an older Windows installation, but it will not activate, nor will it ask you to provide a product code for an earlier Windows version.

Chapter 2

1. **a, b, c, d, f.** You should have all of these items on hand before beginning a Windows 8.1 installation. The Windows 8.1 installation media is on DVD and not CD, so you do not need a CD-ROM drive.

2. **a, c, d.** When installing Windows 8.1 from a DVD-ROM, you can configure the username and password; the date, time, and currency format; and the network settings type during installation. You would configure domain membership and the Charms bar after installation of Windows 8.1 is completed.

3. **a.** Windows System Image Manager (Windows SIM) is used to perform these actions. Windows AIK is the Automated Installation Kit, which was used to customize the installation and deployment of Windows Vista/7. Windows ADK, which includes Windows SIM, is the Windows Assessment and Deployment Kit for Windows 8.1, which replaces the Windows AIK. `sysprep` is a utility that prepares a computer running Windows with a set of installation applications for imaging and deployment to multiple target computers; its use is covered in Exam 70-688, "Supporting Windows 8.1."

4. **c.** When setting up a multiple-boot system, you should install the oldest operating system first. In this scenario, you would install Windows XP, then Windows 7, and finally Windows 8.1.

5. **d.** The `setupact.log` file records modifications performed on the system during Setup. The `netsetup.log` file reports the results of a computer attempting to join a workgroup or domain. The `setuperr.log` file records errors generated by hardware or driver issues during Windows installation. The `setupapi.log` file records data about Plug-and-Play devices and drivers, or about application installation.

6. **a, c, d, e, f, g.** You need to run the Windows Upgrade Assistant, ensure that all hardware is listed in the Windows Certification Program, check for available BIOS upgrades, scan your computer for viruses, remove or disable your antivirus program, and then install the latest service pack for Windows 7. The Windows Anytime Upgrade was used with Windows 7 to upgrade to a higher edition; it has been replaced by the Add features command in the Charms bar and is not associated with upgrading an older Windows operating system.

7. **d.** The simplest way is to insert the Windows 8.1 DVD and perform a clean install. It is not possible to upgrade Windows XP directly to any edition of Windows 8.1; it is also not possible to upgrade Windows XP directly to Windows 7. You could upgrade to Windows Vista and then to Windows 8.1, but this would require additional licensing costs and take much more time.

8. **b.** When you perform a clean installation of Windows 8.1 over Windows XP on the same partition without formatting this partition, a `Windows.old` folder is created and the Windows XP system files are placed in this folder. You would need to perform the clean installation on a different partition to create a dual-boot system.

9. **a.** The `Windows.old` folder also stores other Windows XP files, including all subfolders of the `Documents and Settings` folder. Fred can then access his documents and move them to the `Users\Fred\My Documents` folder. This would also be true when upgrading a Windows Vista/7 computer, except that the documents would be found in the `Users\Fred` subfolder. It should not be necessary to restore these files from backup; however, it is good practice to back them up before upgrading in case some type of failure occurs during the upgrade process.

10. **a.** You can easily accomplish the upgrade of Windows 8.1 to Windows 8.1 Pro by using the Add features command. This is true whether or not you've purchased the upgrade license; if you haven't purchased the license, you receive the option to purchase one. The Add features command is accessed from the Search utility in the Charms bar and not the Settings utility. You do not need to insert the Windows 8.1 DVD.

11. **d.** Windows To Go is a copy of Windows 8.1 imaged onto a USB device that enables a user to boot any computer with compatible hardware into the operating system on the USB device. It is a complete copy of operating system and application files and not simply a set of user credentials on the USB device. It is not a copy of Windows RT 8.1; nor is it a copy of Windows 8.1 located on a network drive.

12. **b.** Windows To Go is available only for Windows 8.1 Enterprise, which is required both for creating the Windows To Go workspace and for running Windows To Go on a USB drive.

13. **d.** Windows Recovery Environment is not available at all. BitLocker drive encryption can be used on the USB drive, but will use a boot password, not TPM. Windows App store and Hibernate are both disabled by default, but can be enabled by an administrator.

14. **b.** Although the USB drive must be USB 3.0 capable, Windows To Go can run on a USB 2.0 port in the computer. USB 3.0 will improve performance of Windows To Go.

15. **b, c, e.** The valid types of VHDs in Windows 8.1 are fixed, dynamic, and differencing. The other types of VHDs mentioned do not exist.

16. **a, b.** Use the Disk Management MMC or the DiskPart utility to create new VHDs. DISM can be used to mount and manage existing VHDs, but not to create or format them. You can load the Windows PE from a VHD with the environment installed, but you need to run DiskPart to create VHDs from the PE. `sysprep` is only for resetting the operating system environment, not for managing disks.

Chapter 3

1. **c.** Windows Easy Transfer provides a simple, wizard-based routine that enables a user to migrate documents and settings from an old computer to a new one. It replaces the Files and Settings Transfer Wizard, which was used with Windows XP but is no longer available. USMT would be used for migrating large numbers of users but not a single user (as in this scenario). Windows ADK is used to customize the installation and deployment of Windows 8.1, including the installation of USMT. It is not used in this situation.

2. **b.** USMT is suitable for a situation such as this one, where a large number of users are being migrated from old computers to new ones. It would be far more tedious and cumbersome to use Windows Easy Transfer, which would require migrating these users one at a time.

3. **a, b, d, f.** USMT 5.0 includes the `ScanState.exe`, `LoadState.exe`, `Usmtutils.exe`, and `MigApp.xml` components. `Migwiz.exe` is part of Windows Easy Transfer, and is not included with USMT 5.0. There is no such file as `Migapp.exe`.

4. **a.** The `ScanState.exe` utility is used to collect user settings and data from old computers when running USMT. `LoadState.exe` is used afterward to place these settings and data on the new Windows 8.1 computers. `Migwiz.exe` is part of Windows Easy Transfer and is not used in this situation. `Fastwiz.exe` was part of Windows XP's Files and Settings Transfer Wizard and is not used with more recent versions of Windows.

5. **b.** You would use `LoadState.exe` to transfer the user settings and data to the new Windows 8.1 computers. `ScanState.exe` is used to collect the settings and data from old computers and place them on the server. `Migwiz.exe` is part of Windows Easy Transfer and is not used in this situation. `Xcopy.exe` is an old DOS routine and is not used with any of the procedures described in this chapter.

6. **a, b, c, d.** These folders are all default library folders that you can redirect to another location such as a shared folder on a server. In addition, you can create additional library folders that can be redirected in the same way.

7. **b, c, e.** Domain-based folder redirection uses a Windows Server 2012 R2 computer configured as a domain controller plus a server configured with an accessible shared folder. You then create a GPO that specifies folder redirection settings. Note that a server running an older version of Windows Server can also be used, but some settings offered in Windows Server 2012 R2 might not be available. Neither a router nor a global catalog server is used with folder redirection.

8. **b.** A mandatory profile is stored on a server using the name `NTUser.man`. This profile is copied locally to any computer the user logs on to, and any changes are not saved when the user logs off. A roaming profile enables the user to make and save changes. A local profile is stored only on its local computer and is not available across the network. There is no such thing as a permanent profile (a temporary profile is available and is loaded if an error condition prevents a user from loading her normal profile).

9. **c.** You should click **Advanced System settings** in the System dialog box. In the System Properties dialog box that appears, select the **Advanced** tab and then click **Settings** under User Profiles. Then, in the User Profiles dialog box, select the default profile and click **Copy To**. Then type or browse to the desired location and click **OK**. The System Properties dialog box does not have a Profiles tab. It is not necessary to access the Default User settings from `%systemdrive%\Users`; in fact, this location does not have a Profiles subfolder.

Chapter 4

1. **a, b, c, d, e, f.** You can access Device Manager using any of these methods.

2. **b.** A disabled device is indicated in Device Manager by a red X appearing over the device icon. A black exclamation point icon on a yellow triangle background appearing next to the device icon indicates that a device is functioning but experiencing problems. A yellow question mark indicates that the device is not properly installed or is in conflict with another device in the system. A blue i on a white field indicates that the device has been configured manually with resource configurations.

3. **b.** By uninstalling a device driver, you remove the driver completely from the computer. You should do this only after you have actually removed the device because Windows will otherwise redetect the device at the next reboot and reinstall the driver. You should also select the **Delete the driver software for this device** check box. None of the other options provided will remove the driver completely.

4. **d.** New to Windows 8.1, the Events tab of the device's Properties dialog box displays a time-based list of actions that have occurred with regard to the device. None of the other tabs mentioned here provide this information.

5. **b.** The `sigverif.exe` utility is used to determine whether any unsigned drivers are present. The `sfc.exe` utility is the System File Checker, which checks the digital signature of system-protected files. `Msinfo32.exe` is the System Information utility, which provides a large amount of information on hardware and software on the computer but does not provide driver signature information. `Gpedit.exe` is the Local Group Policy Editor, which is used to apply policies to a computer or a series of computers.

6. **b.** If the device worked before you updated its driver, you can roll back the driver to restore the previous driver that worked with the device. A further update might solve the problem but would not likely be available because you already updated the driver. Uninstalling or disabling the driver would not work.

7. **c.** The Resources by type view displays the devices according to the resources used, including IRQ, DMA, and memory addresses. The other views do not provide this information directly, although the Resources by connection view displays which resources are currently available.

8. **a.** If the installation of a new device on your computer results in another device not working, this indicates that the two devices are attempting to use the same resource (such as an IRQ). Any of the other options provided could result in the new device (the Blu-ray writer) not working, but other devices would still work.

9. **a, e.** You can obtain information about the resources being used by a device by accessing the Resources tab of the device's Properties dialog box or from the Hardware Resources node of the System Information dialog box. The Components node of this dialog box provides information on hardware device properties, including driver information but not resource information. The General tab of the device's Properties dialog box provides the device's description and status. The Details tab provides a long list of property specifications, but not the resources used by the device.

10. **d.** The Conflicts/Sharing subnode of the Hardware Resources category in System Information provides information on device-related problems but does not provide tools for correcting these problems. Device Manager enables you to correct these problems. `Sigverif.exe` provides information on unsigned drivers but does not provide information on device-related problems. Action Center provides information on some device problems plus a link for corrective actions.

11. **d.** Creating a restore point will enable you to restore the computer to the point in time before the driver was installed. Although you can also do this with a system image, it is a much longer task and requires more resources than necessary.

12. **c, d.** These tools are useful for identifying the misbehaving driver. The `sigverif.exe` utility is used to determine whether any unsigned drivers are present. But it won't identify the specific driver causing the issue. You can disable suspect drivers with Advanced Startup options, but without your knowing which driver is at issue, it may take many rounds of troubleshooting. Driver Verifier allows you to debug groups of drivers at once, and the information from the crash report can be used to select which tests to run. You can search for conflicts with Device Manager, but if the system is crashing, there are

likely no conflicts that Device Manager can identify. Action Center can search the Internet for solutions to errors and will automatically prompt to search for the error after a crash.

13. **c.** Only drivers that have an Advanced tab have driver-specific settings that can be changed through the Device Manager. The Details tab will display such settings, but they cannot be changed in that dialog box.

Chapter 5

1. **a.** You should select **Run this program in compatibility mode for**, and select either **Windows XP Service Pack 2** or **Windows XP Service Pack 3**. Because the application has worked successfully on Windows XP, this is the most likely compatibility mode that would enable it to work with Windows 8.1.

2. **a, c, d.** Group Policy enables you to publish a package to users or assign a package to either users or computers. There is no option to publish an application package to computers.

3. **c.** You would use the command `msiexec /jm Program.msi` to advertise the `Program.msi` package to all users of the computer. The `msiexec /a` option creates an administrative installation package for deploying the application from a network share; it is not used with the `u` or `m` parameters. The `msiexec /ju` command advertises the package to a specific user of the computer, not to all users.

4. **b, c.** You should select **Default Programs** from the Programs applet in Control Panel and then select **Set your default programs**. From the list that appears, select **Firefox** and then click **Set this program as default**. This action automatically changes the default program for all web-based files to Firefox. You could also select **Set program access and computer defaults**. In the dialog box that appears, select **Custom** and then select **Mozilla Firefox**. If you select **Associate a file type or protocol with a program**, you could accomplish your task, but you would have to go through a long list of file types and select each one in turn, an action that would be time-consuming and error-prone. If you right-click any file with an `.htm` or `.html` extension and choose **Open with > Choose default program** and then select **Firefox** from the list that appears, only files with the chosen extension would open with Firefox. You would have to locate files with other extensions that might open in Internet Explorer and also change them, again a cumbersome and error-prone situation.

5. **a, d.** You can only install packaged apps from the Windows Store or using sideloading. The Programs and Features applet works only with Windows desktop applications, and "Apploading" does not exist.

6. **b.** Windows Store apps do not use "active icons." They display content using their tiles and can do so even when the app is not running. Apps do not use icons at all.

7. **c.** The Windows Store tile displays a number when updates are available indicating the number of updates available. The Windows Store screen tile also displays a link with the number when apps are available.

8. **d.** Because all clients are running Windows 8.1 Enterprise, and management is interested only in controlling the types of apps but not access to the Windows Store, AppLocker is the best tool to use. Policies can be used to restrict access to the Windows Store only. Software Restriction policies cannot be used to manage packaged apps.

9. **a, c, d, e.** You can configure any of these rule types in Software Restriction Policies. There is no such thing as an Operating System Version Rule.

10. **b, d.** AppLocker enables you to gather advanced data on software usage by implementing audit-only mode, and to create multiple rules at the same time with the help of a wizard. Disallowed, Basic User, and Unrestricted are the rule settings available with Software Restriction Policies; AppLocker uses Allow and Deny. You can use either Software Restriction Policies or AppLocker with Group Policy.

11. **d.** AppLocker policies are enforced only on Windows 8.1 Enterprise edition. You can use Windows 8.1 Pro to manage AppLocker polices, but they are not enforced on that SKU.

12. **a.** AppLocker rules for restricting apps must be Publisher rules. Unsigned apps cannot be loaded at all, and due to app updates and unpredictable installation paths, Path and File Hash rules cannot be enforced. AppLocker does not have "Registry" rules.

Chapter 6

1. **b, c, e, f.** The Start screen version of Internet Explorer offers a simplified browser that does not include the capability of using RSS feeds, compatibility view, and the ability to directly access the Internet Options dialog box. Further, you cannot pin websites to the taskbar, but you can pin websites to the Start screen to create tiles that automatically open the pinned websites. Both versions of IE support Adobe Flash and tabbed browsing, although the means of opening a new tab in the Start screen version is different (you must right-click an empty area in the currently displayed web page and choose the + icon).

2. **a, b, c, d, e.** These policy settings are available from the Compatibility View node of the Group Policy Object Editor. You can also configure settings for Turn on Internet Explorer Standards Mode for local intranet and Include updated website lists from Microsoft.
3. **b.** By default, all websites are placed in the Internet zone. You must manually configure the sites that will be placed in the other zones.
4. **d.** You should ensure that the SmartScreen Filter is enabled; it is enabled by default. This filter is an upgrade of the Phishing Filter first introduced in Internet Explorer 7, and it detects actions such as that described here. None of the other options perform this action.
5. **b.** The Pop-up Blocker Settings dialog box can be accessed by clicking the **Settings** button, which is found on the Privacy tab of Internet Options. None of the other tabs contain an access to this dialog box.
6. **b, c.** The Manage Add-ons dialog box enables you to configure search providers and accelerators. It also lets you configure toolbars and extensions as well as tracking protection, but you cannot manage InPrivate browsing or the SmartScreen filter from here.
7. **c.** The InPrivate Browsing feature sets up an isolated browser session that discards all personal types of browsing information after you close Internet Explorer, thereby ensuring that all traces of your actions have been removed. None of the other features mentioned enable this setting.
8. **c.** WebSocket applications use JavaScript in the browser to set up the connection and make calls. Disabling Active Scripting disables running any JavaScript in the browser and causes any WebSocket applications to fail. Note that the use of the High security disables Active Scripting.
9. **c.** The best option is to disable WebSockets using Group Policy settings. Option B also works, but it has the side effect of causing many other web applications and websites to also fail or not display properly. Windows Firewall blocks WebSockets, but because it uses the same port as all other website traffic, it also disables all access to websites.
10. **a.** Download Manager can be configured to save all downloads to the correct location, so no manual intervention is needed to copy or sync the downloaded files. SmartScreen Filter automatically checks the files but does not redirect them to a safe location.

Chapter 7

1. **b.** The new Hyper-V and Client Hyper-V virtual disk format is VHDX, and these files are created with the `.vhdx` extension.
2. **b, c, d.** These are all features of the new VHDX virtual disk format. The original VHD format supports up to 2 TB of space, but the new format files can store up to 64 TB.
3. **a, b, d.** Any and all of these tools can be used to create virtual hard disks, and they can create both `.vhd` and `.vhdx` files. BCDEdit is only used to edit a physical computer's boot loader and can add a VHD to the boot loader menu but cannot edit or modify `.vhd` files.
4. **b.** The computer appears to meet all the requirements for running Client Hyper-V, including processor support and BIOS features. Hyper-V does not run on 32-bit clients at all, however. Client Hyper-V requires a 64-bit version of Windows 8.1 Pro or Windows 8.1 Enterprise.
5. **a.** The Client Hyper-V services and management tools are included with Windows 8.1 Pro and Enterprise editions. It is not installed by default but can be enabled from the Control Panel's Programs applet by using the Windows Features installation tool.
6. **d.** The Client Hyper-V configuration settings for virtual machines always allow you to select the maximum amount of RAM that a VM can be assigned, which is limited to 1 TB. Note that unless the VM operating system can support it and the host actually has that amount of RAM, the actual memory used by the VM is less. In most cases, setting the maximum memory to the default of 1 TB simply means the VM is allowed to consume as much memory as is available.
7. **c.** Because other VMs are using enough processor resources that the application server does not have enough CPU left to run, the best option is to simply set a higher priority on processor resources to the VM serving the application. Doing so ensures that as processor resources become scarce, other VMs are cut back on resources before the application VM.
8. **c.** Hyper-V can assign virtual processors to each VM based on the total number of physical processor cores available on the host machine. The number of VMs hosted by the Hyper-V host computer does not affect this limit.
9. **c.** Checkpoints represent a point in time for the state of the virtual machine. When the checkpoint is deleted, the changes are not lost but are merged into the virtual machine's configuration. Deleting the checkpoint means you cannot revert the machine to that specific point in time.

10. **b.** The external virtual switch is the type of virtual switch that automatically provides Client Hyper-V virtual machines access to the host's network and external Internet.

11. **a.** Because an internal switch does not provide access to any network resources outside the Hyper-V host computer, you typically need to manually configure the VMs' network settings to enable communications among the VMs and with the host. Another potential method would be to create a single VM with a static IP address and host DHCP and DNS services on that VM to provide the other VMs with automatic network configuration. Note also that autoconfiguration addresses lock Windows 8.1 using only Public network settings, which disables sharing and uses stricter firewall rules.

Chapter 8

1. **a, b, d.** All these protocols are components of TCP/IP. Although it is used by TCP/IP-enabled computers, DHCP is not considered to be a component of TCP/IP.

2. **c.** The default gateway is the IP address of the router that connects your computer's subnet to other subnets on your company's network, as well as the Internet. Although important for your computer's TCP/IP configuration, the other items given here do not address this objective.

3. **b.** Any IP address in the range 128.0.0.0 to 191.255.255.255 belongs to class B. Class A addresses are in the range 1.0.0.0 to 126.255.255.255; Class C addresses are in the range 192.0.0.0 to 223.255.255.255; Class D addresses are in the range 224.0.0.0 to 239.255.255.255; Class E addresses are in the range 240.0.0.0 to 254.255.255.255.

4. **d.** CIDR enables you to specify the number of bits that are used for the subnet mask as part of the network address, in this case 24. WINS is not an address notation but is a protocol used for resolving NetBIOS names to IP addresses. Unicast and multicast are types of IPv6 addresses; this scenario deals with IPv4 addressing.

5. **a.** A global unicast address is a globally routable Internet address that is equivalent to a public IPv4 address. A link-local unicast address is used for communication between neighboring nodes on the same link; a site-local unicast address is used for communication between nodes located in the same site; a multicast address provides multiple interfaces to which packets are delivered; and anycast addresses are utilized only as destination addresses assigned to routers. None of these other address types are suitable for direct Internet contact.

6. **b.** A link-local IPv6 address has an address prefix of fe80::/64. This address is equivalent to an APIPA-configured IPv4 address. The other address types have different network prefixes.

7. **d.** Teredo is a tunneling communication protocol that enables IPv6 connectivity between IPv6/IPv4 nodes across Network Address Translation (NAT) interfaces, thereby improving connectivity for newer IPv6-enabled applications on IPv4 networks. It uses this prefix. The other address types use different prefixes.

8. **a, c.** To configure your computer to use DHCP, you should ensure that the **Obtain an IP address automatically** and **Obtain DNS server address automatically** options are selected. You would specify the other two options if you were configuring your computer to use static IP addressing.

9. **b.** If your computer is using an IPv4 address on the 169.254.0.0/16 network, it is configured to use APIPA. An address on this network is assigned when the computer is configured to receive an IP address automatically but is unable to reach a DHCP server. Private IPv4 addressing is in use if the IP address is on any of the 10.0.0.0/8, 172.16.0.0/16, or 192.168.0.0/24 networks. An alternate IP configuration is a separate static IP address that you can configure on a computer that is using DHCP; it would not be using this address.

10. **c.** The DNS tab of the Advanced TCP/IP Settings dialog box enables you to specify more than two DNS server addresses. It also allows you to sequence these server addresses in the order of most likely usage. The Internet Protocol (TCP/IP) Properties dialog box (either version 4 or 6) allows you to specify only two DNS server addresses. Another way you could solve this problem would be to add the first two DNS server addresses from this dialog box and then click **Advanced** to add the third DNS server address from the DNS tab as already described. The Alternate Configuration tab enables you to specify an alternate set of TCP/IP addressing parameters for use at a different location such as when using a portable computer; it does not allow the specification of additional DNS server addresses.

11. **a.** You should configure the public network profile option. Doing so performs a series of default options such as turning off network discovery, file and printer sharing, and media streaming. Simply turning off file and printer sharing is not sufficient to completely secure your computer against unauthorized users. The private network profile option turns on options such as those mentioned here and is used when your computer is connected to trusted networks and not the other way around. HomeGroup connections are used in a home or small office environment and not on a public network.

12. **b.** You should use the `ipconfig /renew` command. This command forces the computer to try again to connect to the DHCP server and obtain an IP address lease. In this case, the computer was unable to access the DHCP server and configured itself with an APIPA address. The `/release` parameter releases the current IP address configuration but does not contact the DHCP server. The `/flushdns` parameter flushes the contents of the DNS cache. You use this parameter when the computer connects to an incorrect network. The `/displaydns` parameter displays the contents of the DNS cache. This is also useful if the computer connects to an incorrect network.

13. **d, e.** The `tracert` and `pathping` commands both provide routing information. The route command provides routing table information or enables you to configure routers but does not provide the information requested in this scenario. The `netstat` command provides TCP/IP connection statistics. The `ping` command checks connectivity to a remote host but does not provide routing information.

14. **d, c, a, e, b.** You should perform the indicated actions in this sequence. Microsoft exams might ask you to select actions you must perform and place them in the required sequence.

15. **c.** If two computers on the network are configured with the same IP address, the first one connects properly, but the second one that attempts to connect will fail to do so, and this problem will result. If your computer is configured for static IP addressing, it never uses APIPA. If the subnet mask is incorrect, your computer will not connect to machines on another subnet at any time. If your computer is configured with static IP addressing, the alternate IP address option is unavailable.

Chapter 9

1. **a, b, d, e.** You can utilize wireless networks using any of these security protocols. Private is not a security protocol. Open is a security protocol type, but it provides no security. PEAP is not used to authenticate to an access point but can be used on a wireless network.

2. **c.** By default, Windows 8.1 uses WPA2-Personal to connect to ad hoc wireless networks because this is the most secure protocol available. WPA2-Enterprise cannot be used because it requires a RADIUS authentication server, which would not be available on an ad hoc network.

3. **a, d.** 802.11a uses 5 GHz frequency to communicate at all times. The 802.11n protocol can be configured to use either 2.4 GHz or 5 GHz, depending on the capabilities and configuration of the access points and the access devices.

4. **a, b, c, d.** You can encrypt data sent on a wireless connection by using any of TKIP, AES, WEP, WPA, or WPA2. The SSID is a network identifier that is broadcast by many wireless access points (WAPs) to enable you to locate available wireless networks; it does not provide data protection.

5. **d.** The 802.11n wireless networking protocol is compatible with devices using older protocols but enables a transmission speed of up to 150–600 Mbps. It has the best signal range and is most resistant to interference. Not one of the other protocol options offers this much transmission speed. Note, however, that an even newer protocol, 802.11ac, was approved in January 2014 and boasts even better transmission speeds; some devices supporting this protocol are becoming available and are expected to be widely available in 2015.

6. **b.** By default, the WPA2-Personal protocol uses AES encryption and requires a security key or passphrase. WPA-Personal and WPA-Enterprise both use TKIP encryption by default. Both WPA-Enterprise and WPA2-Enterprise do not require the user to type a security key or passphrase.

7. **c.** You should set the connection as a metered connection. When connected to a metered connection, Windows 8.1 limits the amount of data used by deferring noncritical updates and updates to Start screen tiles, choosing low-resolution images when available and other techniques. You can view usage statistics by showing estimated data usage, but not control it. Sharing affects only local network traffic.

8. **b.** Because only wireless networks currently in range are displayed in the Network list, out-of-range networks are hidden. You cannot access wireless profiles from the Network and Sharing Center, which is used only to manage network adapters and current connections. You can delete the profiles, but you must use the `netsh` command to view the list and delete each profile.

9. **b.** The conference room is currently the preferred wireless network because it is the network in range that you last connected to. Your home network was preferred, but it is not in range and Windows does not attempt a connection there. If you switch your connection to the engineering department, Windows moves that network to the top of the priority list.

10. **d.** When you access the network adapter's hardware properties from the Configure button through the connection, the Resources tab is not displayed. If you need to view or modify the resources the device uses, you must use the Device Manager.

11. **a, d.** The 802.11n mode is a wireless property, and Preferred band allows you to select the frequency for an 802.11n connection. Speed, duplex, transmit, and receive buffers are all properties available only for a wired network adapter.

12. **d.** The best option is to use the Location Aware Printing manager to simply change the default printer associated with the network at headquarters. The issue might resolve itself by deleting the original color printer, but the new printer would not automatically be selected. Turning off Location Aware Printing would simply use the same default printer at all times. The Printer Troubleshooting tool would likely find no issues at all because printing still works, just not to the desired printer.

Chapter 10

1. **c.** The Public or Guest network location locks down Windows Firewall so that others cannot access anything on your computer, although it can also limit your access to external resources. The Private network locations allow others to access any items you have configured for sharing on your computer. Wireless and Ethernet are incorrect here because both types of network connection can be either a Public or a Private location.

2. **b, c, e.** You can configure Windows Firewall to specify programs that are allowed to communicate, or you can configure Windows Firewall to block all incoming connections, from the Windows Firewall Control Panel applet. You can also specify firewall settings for home, work, and public networks from this location. However, you must use the Windows Firewall with Advanced Security snap-in to configure ports and logging. (The Windows Firewall applet in Windows Vista allowed specifying allowed ports, but this function was removed from this location in Windows 7 and 8.1.)

3. **c.** Windows Firewall with Advanced Security does not include any connection security rules by default. You can use the New Rules Wizard to set up connection security rules as well as additional rules for the other rule types.

4. **a.** You should run the New Inbound Rule Wizard, specify the path to Windows Media Player on the program page, and then specify the **Allow the connection if it is secure** option. The latter option permits only connections that have been authenticated using IPSec. You need an inbound rule, not an outbound rule. Connection security rules do not permit specifying programs that are allowed to connect. The Allowed Programs and Features list does not enable you to restrict connections to only those that have been authenticated using IPSec.

5. **d.** It is not possible to change a rule from Inbound to Outbound from any setting that is available in the rule's Properties dialog box. It is also not possible to drag a rule from one node to another in Windows Firewall with Advanced Security. You must create a new outbound rule to perform this action.

6. **a.** The Properties dialog box of Windows Firewall with Advanced Security enables you to perform this action for each of the Domain, Private, and Public profiles. You can access this dialog box by right-clicking **Windows Firewall with Advanced Security** at the top of the console tree and choosing **Properties.** None of the locations mentioned in the other options provide a Properties dialog box.
7. **b.** Because authentication credentials are requested and passed during the setup of the network connection, Windows prevents any authenticated exceptions to be associated with a firewall rule unless it is using a secure connection.
8. **a, b, c.** Windows 8.1 Network discovery can be enabled or disabled on any of the network profiles. Although it is not recommended, you may want to enable this feature even on a network that Windows detects as a public or guest network. Because the All Networks profile contains configuration settings that apply to all other profiles, Network discovery configuration settings are not included.
9. **a.** Configuring network discovery to automatically set up network-connected devices is only available on the Private network profile. You can still set up network devices on a Public or Guest network, but because of the risk of compromise, automatically installing devices from an unknown network is not recommended and cannot be enabled. Note that the Domain profile always enables this feature when Network discovery is turned on.
10. **b.** AES is considered a stronger form of encryption than TKIP and WEP. WEP has some significant vulnerabilities and should be avoided whenever any stronger encryption is available. Not an encryption type, 802.1x is, instead, an authentication protocol that uses RADIUS for two-layer authentication.
11. **e.** When Windows 8.1 connects to an ad hoc network, by default, it uses WPA2-Personal, which is the strongest authentication and uses the strongest encryption available on standard ad hoc network connections.

Chapter 11

1. **b.** By enabling the Public Folder Sharing option, you enable users at other computers to be able to access folders in your libraries. This is known as the Public Folder Sharing model. The File and Printer Sharing option enables you to share folders you have specifically configured for sharing, but you must specifically configure the required folders for sharing. Password-protected sharing limits the accessibility of shared folders to users who have a username and password. Media streaming enables sharing of media files with networked devices.

2. **b, d, e.** Administrative shares are created by default when you first install Windows 8.1. These shares are suffixed with the $ symbol and are visible from the Shares node of the Computer Management snap-in; they can be accessed by entering the UNC path to the share in the Run command. Because they are hidden, you cannot see them in an Explorer window, nor can you access them from the Network and Sharing Center.

3. **a, c, e.** You can specify any of Read, Change, or Full Control shared folder permissions. The Modify permissions and the Read & Execute permissions are NTFS security permissions; they are not shared folder permissions.

4. **d.** If the network location is set to Public, you cannot join a homegroup. You can join a homegroup even if your computer is joined to an AD DS domain; this facilitates working at home with a laptop that is moved between home and work locations. You can join a homegroup with any edition of Windows 8.1. A password is automatically created when you create a homegroup; this password is required for another computer to join the homegroup, but you cannot create a homegroup without a password.

5. **a.** Security (NTFS) permissions are cumulative; in other words, a user receives the least restrictive of the permissions that have been applied, so Bob has Full Control permission to the Documents folder.

6. **d.** While NTFS permissions are cumulative such that a user receives the least restrictive permission, an explicit denial of permission overrides all allowed permissions. Therefore, in this scenario, Jim does not have access to the Documents folder.

7. **c.** If a shared folder has both shared folder and NTFS permissions assigned to it and a user accesses this folder across the network, the most restrictive permission is the effective permission. Therefore, in this scenario, Carol has Read permission on the Documents folder.

8. **a.** When a user accesses a shared folder on the same computer on which it is located, the shared folder permission does not apply and the user receives only the NTFS permission that has been assigned to the folder. Therefore, in this scenario, Sharon has Full Control permission on the Documents folder.

9. **c.** When you copy a file or folder from one NTFS volume to another one, the copy inherits the permissions that are applied to the destination location. Therefore, the Accounts folder receives the Read permission that is applied to the `D:\Confidential` folder.

10. **a.** When you move a file from one folder to another folder on the same NTFS volume, the file retains its NTFS permissions. Therefore, in this scenario, Jennifer has Full Control permission to the `C:\Confidential\Projects.doc` file.

11. **b, c.** If you want to encrypt a file or folder, the file or folder must be located on a volume that is formatted with the NTFS file system. So you need to convert the volume to the NTFS file system or move the folder to another volume that is formatted with the NTFS file system. If you were to format the `D:\` volume with the NTFS file system, you would destroy the Confidential folder. The folder cannot be compressed because this is also a function of the NTFS file system.

12. **b.** By default, the administrator account created when Windows 8.1 is first installed is the default recovery agent for files or folders that have been encrypted on this computer, so you can decrypt the file if you log on with this account. Note that this account is disabled by default, so you need to log on with another account and enable the account first. If you re-create Peter's user account, the new account has a different security identifier (SID), so it does not have the capability of decrypting files encrypted with the old account.

13. **d.** It is not true that you are limited to the four default libraries in Windows 8.1; you can designate additional libraries outside these four defaults at any time. The other four answer options are true for libraries in Windows 8.1.

14. **b.** You should grant Kristin's user account the Manage This Printer permission. This permission enables her to do the required tasks. The Print permission grants only the ability to print documents on your printer. The Manage Documents permission enables her also to perform tasks such as modifying printer properties or permissions. Full Control is not included in the printer permissions; it is only a shared folder or NTFS permission.

15. **c.** You need to log in to the computer with the new account. OneDrive is tightly integrated with Windows 8.1, and you must be logged in to the computer with the correct Microsoft account to use the account's OneDrive. You cannot use OneDrive.com for Windows 8.1 computer accounts. There is no OneDrive applet in Control Panel, all settings are managed through the OneDrive app, and the OneDrive icon in the notification area is available only in older versions of Windows.

16. **b.** To automatically keep your OneDrive files and local copies up-to-date with any changes requires that you change the OneDrive configuration to make the files available offline. This is the way to sync OneDrive in Windows 8.1. You also can make the entire drive available offline, but if you want to sync only "a number of files," you can change this option selectively for specific folders and files. The Windows app allows you to copy files to and from your OneDrive, but it must be done manually. Your OneDrive.com account does not have access to any local computers running Windows 8.1. The mobile app works only on smartphones and tablets.

17. **d.** Disabling the built-in Proximity sharing firewall rule, which controls Proximity or Near Field Communications (NFC), is the most expedient and least disruptive method to use. Disabling Wi-Fi means the mobile users could not connect from coffee shops at all, not an acceptable solution to management. Because the Windows 8.1 computer is sharing information, it decrypts anything on the hard drive before transferring it, so encryption does not work. Disabling all app communication using a firewall rule is a sledgehammer solution and would make many of the apps entirely nonfunctional.

18. **a, f.** You need to ensure that the `D:\` drive is formatted with the NTFS file system; if this drive is formatted with the FAT32 file system, you cannot create disk quotas. Then, in the Add New Quota Entry dialog box, create a separate disk quota for each user in the Interns group that specifies the Limit disk space to option and the 500 MB limit. The Do not limit disk usage option does not allow you to set a limit; it merely allows tracking of disk usage without preventing users from exceeding any specified value. It is not possible to set a quota for a group; you need to specify separate quotas for each member of the group.

19. **b.** To fully configure object access auditing, you need to perform two actions: specify auditing in Group Policy and enable auditing for the folder or files whose access is to be tracked. Auditing logon events tracks attempts by others to log on to the boss's computer but does not track access to the sensitive documents. The boss is looking in the right location (the Security log) for audit events; they are not recorded in the System log. It might improve the security of the documents if you move the folder to a secured server, but this does not solve the problem of who is attempting to access them.

Chapter 12

1. **e.** The Store passwords using reversible encryption policy weakens security because it stores passwords in a format that is essentially the same as plain text. You should enable this policy only if needed for clients that cannot use normal encryption.

2. **b.** The Minimum password age policy enables you to prevent users from cycling rapidly through passwords and thereby defeating the Enforce password history policy. When this policy is enabled, a user cannot change her password again for the interval specified by this policy.

3. **c.** You should audit the Privilege use category in the Audit Policy node. This category tracks the use of a user right, such as changing the system time or time zone. The Account management category tracks the management of user accounts including password changes. The Policy change category tracks the

modification of policies such as user rights assignment, trust, and audit policies. The System events category tracks events such as improper shutdown of a computer or very little free space remaining on a disk.

4. **d.** The dimmed screen and request to confirm your intent is a UAC prompt, which was first introduced in Windows Vista and refined in Windows 7. Nothing is wrong with your Microsoft Office media and this does not indicate any need for configuring application compatibility options.

5. **b.** By default in Windows 8 or 8.1, as was the case in Windows 7, you receive a UAC prompt only if you are using a nonadministrative user account. In Windows Vista, you always received a UAC prompt; in Windows 7/8/8.1, this is true only if you change the UAC settings and select the **Always notify me when** option. You never have to log off from a standard user account and log back on as an administrator; you merely have to supply an administrative password. The latter option occurs only if you've configured the Never notify me option in the UAC settings.

6. **d.** The red title bar and shield indicate that the program is a high-risk program that Windows has blocked completely. You cannot run it in its present form. No command buttons are provided on this message box, so it is impossible to click **Yes** to run the program.

7. **c.** By enabling the **Admin Approval Mode for the Built-In Administrator account** policy in Group Policy, you configure the built-in Administrator account to display UAC prompts in the manner as governed by the User Account Settings Control Panel applet setting in use. Configuring options in this applet without enabling the Admin Approval Mode for the Built-In Administrator account policy does not change the behavior of the built-in Administrator account, which by default does not display any UAC prompts.

8. **c.** You should enable the **Behavior of the elevation prompt for standard users** policy and then select the **Automatically deny elevation requests** option. This option prevents any applications that require administrative credentials from running. Either of the Prompt for Credentials options would display a UAC prompt that requests an administrative password, but these would still allow these programs to run. Enabling the **Only elevate executables that are signed and validated** policy would perform public key infrastructure signature checks on programs requiring elevated privileges but would still allow programs that pass this check to run.

9. **a.** Secure Boot ensures that only authorized operating systems that have not been tampered with can be used during the computer's startup. Secure Boot checks the hash of the operating system being loaded with the signed image hash stored in the firmware. If a rootkit or boot sector virus attempts to install

itself in the boot loader, the signature does not match and the OS does not load. Although UEFI Boot is required to enable Secure Boot, UEFI alone does not enable signature checking by itself. DiskPart is a tool to partition hard disks, and BitLocker encrypts drives but cannot prevent boot sector viruses from loading.

10. **c.** The UEFI firmware, with Secure Boot enabled, does not allow an unrecognized operating system to load on the computer. Because it was manufactured for Windows 8.1, the OEM chose to recognize Windows 8.1 only for booting. This is true whether the boot device is the hard drive, DVD, or other storage device. Changing the firmware to use BIOS-compatibility mode will work, but then Windows 8.1 will probably not load. The best option is to disable Secure Boot in the computer's UEFI settings.

11. **b.** When running from UEFI, Windows 8.1 requires at least four partitions and will create the following four partitions during the default setup: Windows RE tools partition, system partition, Microsoft Reserved Partition (MSR), and a Windows partition.

12. **d.** As an administrator, you can select the **More Info** link and select the **Run anyway** option to run the application. Although you can turn off the SmartScreen from blocking any files, that is not a good option because it would allow untrusted, malicious software to run without warning you. A publisher's certificate signed by Microsoft will allow the application to run, but that process is long and too costly for every test version of the developer's executable.

13. **a, c, d.** SmartScreen protects your computer in all these ways, except scanning the files on the hard drive. SmartScreen checks files only when they are downloaded or opened.

Chapter 13

1. **c.** All other options are examples of authorization settings.

2. **b, c, d.** Windows 8.1 does not require Ctrl+Alt+Delete when joined to a domain by default, but you can change this through Group Policies. The Users section of PC Settings only allows users to manage their own account or create new ones. The Users and Groups section of the Computer Management snap-in must be used to change other user account settings.

3. **c.** Users can select three gestures in any combination of taps, circles, or straight lines. You must use exactly three gestures.

4. **b, c, d.** You cannot back up Web Credentials from Credential Manager, and there is no "Windows app" credential type; instead, Windows apps store their credentials as Generic Credentials.

5. **c.** Certificates used for authentication are in the Personal store of the User certificates store set. This is the only location that you can use with storing authentication settings with Credential Manager.

6. **c.** You can enable Windows Credentials for roaming within the AD domain; however, Web Credentials roam only between devices using the same Microsoft account. On domain-joined computers, Web Credential roaming is disabled.

7. **a.** If you lose the password to a Windows Credentials backup, there is no way to recover it, and the information in the backup is lost.

8. **c.** Windows manages certificates based for the current user, for service, and for the local computer. Each certificate store (user, services, and local computer) includes all the storage areas such as Personal, Enterprise Trust, Trusted Certificate Authorities, and so on.

9. **b.** Certificates are managed using the Certificates MMC snap-in. The other tools listed do not exist.

10. **c.** When you create a PIN for a smart card configured for Active Directory domain authentication, an administrator key is created for the domain administrators. You can use this key to reset the PIN on the smart card. The actual PIN is not stored outside the card and cannot be recovered, only reset.

11. **a, b, d.** These are all required for use of virtual smart cards, which use the built-in TPM chip on the computer instead of a physical smart card. With the TPM set up as a virtual smart card, no physical smart card is required. A smart card that supports Personal Identity Verification is not a requirement; it is a physical smart card standard only.

12. **b.** This is the most likely cause. By default, domain-joined computers do not allow domain logon using biometrics. You can enable the Group Policy Allow domain users to log on using biometrics on the domain, however, to allow this functionality on all domain-joined computers.

13. **c.** This is the most restrictive permission that will satisfy the technician's access requirement. Administrators group also works but provides more access than is needed. It may be possible to set all the necessary privileges using User Rights Assignment, but it results in the same privileges and is more difficult to implement, manage, and support.

14. **a, b, c, d.** All these are advantages to using a single Microsoft account for all Windows devices that can use it.

15. **c.** Using this Group Policy allows the company to manage all the Microsoft accounts used on computers centrally, without allowing users to create their own.

Chapter 14

1. **a.** Password Authentication Protocol (PAP) sends its credentials in clear-text (unencrypted) form, so it is the least secure method of authenticating a remote access connection. All of the other protocols mentioned provide some kind of credential security.

2. **d.** Extensible Authentication Protocol with Tunneled Transport Layer Security, or EAP-TTLS, uses a secure tunneled connection via TLS, and can interoperate with 802.1X authentication protocols and RADIUS servers. None of the other protocols use this type of connection security methodology.

3. **c.** Remote Desktop enables you to connect easily to a remote computer and display its desktop as though you were working directly on the remote computer. Hyper-V enables you to create virtual machines on your Windows 8.1 or Windows Server 2012 R2 computer. You would use Remote Assistance to invite an expert at another computer to assist you in overcoming some problem or learning how to perform a task. You would use VPN to make a connection to a server on a remote network.

4. **b.** Remote Assistance enables you to invite an expert at another computer to assist you in overcoming a problem that you are having difficulties with. Hyper-V enables you to create virtual machines on your Windows 8.1 or Windows Server 2012 R2 computer. You would use Remote Desktop to access another computer such as your work computer and work directly on this computer. You would use VPN to make a connection to a server on a remote network.

5. **c.** The computer to which you want to establish a Remote Desktop connection must run the Pro or Enterprise edition of Windows 8.1. The Remote Desktop Connection Software download enables older computers to make a Remote Desktop connection, but does not enable a computer running the base version of Windows 8.1 to receive a Remote Desktop connection from another computer. You can establish a Remote Desktop session with a Windows 7 Professional computer so you do not need to upgrade your work computer to Windows 8.1. This scenario uses Remote Desktop, and not Remote Assistance.

6. **a, c, d.** PowerShell cmdlets take the form verb-object, so `Get-process`, `Select-object`, and `Format-data` are valid cmdlets. `Value-output` and `Folder-create` start with nouns and therefore are not valid.

7. **c.** Because the error was a form of "Timeout," this indicates that the service is not started or the firewall is blocking access. Both of these are configured when PowerShell Remoting is enabled. If there were an authentication issue, some form of `Access Denied` error should be returned, and this would also be indicated if the computer was not in the list of Trusted Computers because

credentials could not be sent for authentication. PowerShell provides clear indication when the command syntax is incorrect or not recognized.

8. **a, b, d.** All of these snap-ins are available in the Computer Management tool except Windows Firewall with Advanced Security, which is a different snap-in.

9. **b.** Although L2TP can provide strong security with IPSec enabled, it has no encryption of its own built into the protocol. PPTP, SSTP, and IKEv2 provide their own encryption specifications and are part of the standards for these protocols.

10. **d.** The Networking tab enables you to specify protocols that will be used during your VPN session, including TCP/IPv4, TCP/IPv6, File and Printer Sharing for Microsoft Networks, and the Client for Microsoft Networks. None of the other tabs enable you to configure these options. Note that the Sharing tab enables you to configure Internet Connection Sharing (ICS).

11. **d.** IKEv2 is the protocol that is used by VPN Reconnect, which was first introduced in Windows 7 and has been continued in Windows 8 and 8.1, that enables you to automatically reestablish a VPN connection if it is temporarily disconnected. None of the other protocols can be used in this situation.

12. **c.** You should set up RD Gateway. Using RD Gateway allows remote users a simple way to connect to computers using the Remote Desktop protocol, without the overhead of a VPN. DirectAccess is an option but would require more resources and is not needed if only Remote Desktop connections are used. VPN Reconnect is a feature available to clients for VPN connections, and Internet Connection Sharing is only for clients on the local network to share a remote connection.

13. **d.** Using DirectAccess requires Windows 7 Ultimate, Windows 7 Enterprise, or Windows 8.1 Enterprise. It is not available on Windows 8.1 Pro or RT 8.1.

Chapter 15

1. **d.** You should select the **Always Available Offline** option. The Open Sync Center option enables you to configure certain file synchronization options but in itself does not automatically cache available files. The Disk Usage option merely specifies how much disk space can be used by cached files. The Sync Selected Offline Files option enables you to select which files are available offline.

2. **c, d.** The Optimized for performance option enables expanded caching of shared programs so that users can run them locally, thus providing enhanced performance. To select this option, you must have the **All files and programs**

that users open from the shared folder are automatically available offline option selected. The other two options do not optimize performance; in fact, the No files or programs from the shared folder are available offline option effectively disables Offline Files.

3. **b.** You should enable the **Enable Transparent Caching policy** setting. Transparent file caching enables Windows 8.1 computers to temporarily cache files obtained across a slow WAN link more aggressively, thereby reducing the number of times the client might have to retrieve the file across the slow link. The Configure Background Sync and Slow link mode settings control synchronization across WAN links but do not enable the transparent caching feature. The Administratively assigned offline files setting specifies network files and folders that are always available offline.

4. **b, c.** Either by choosing the **Power saver** power plan or by reducing the maximum power status of the processor from the Processor power management advanced power setting, you can reduce the processor power so that the battery lasts long enough to watch your movie. The Balanced power plan in itself does not accomplish this task. The Sleep setting would make your computer go to sleep during the movie, which is not what you want here. The Multimedia setting controls the sharing of multimedia with others.

5. **a, c, e.** You can perform any of these tasks by clicking links available from the battery meter. To enable presentation mode, you must access presentation settings from the Windows Mobility Center. To specify hard disk settings, you must configure a Group Policy setting in the Power Management subnode.

6. **a, c, d, e, f.** Wi-Fi Direct enables all these actions with Windows 8.1 computers. However, connections using Wi-Fi Direct are limited to two computers plus any number of other devices; you cannot connect more than two computers on one Wi-Fi Direct circuit.

7. **a.** In many computers equipped with TPM, you might first need to enable TPM in the BIOS before you can set up BitLocker. You need to enable TPM before you can configure a startup key. You do not need to use Group Policy before enabling TPM. You should contact your hardware manufacturer only if enabling TPM in the BIOS does not work or if the BIOS does not include an option to do so.

8. **a.** If you use BitLocker To Go to encrypt your USB flash drive containing the BitLocker recovery key, the recovery key may become inaccessible if your computer enters Recovery mode. On a domain computer, it is good practice to save copies of recovery keys to AD DS. It is possible to use BitLocker without additional keys on a computer that is equipped with a TPM, although this is less secure. If your computer is not equipped with a TPM, you must use Group Policy to enable BitLocker first.

9. **a, d.** You need to copy the BitLocker To Go reader to the Windows XP computers. You also need to enable the Allow Access to BitLocker-Protected Fixed Data Drives from Earlier Versions of Windows policy. These actions enable users of older computers to access data on BitLocker To Go–protected portable hard drives. You do not need to enable any of the other options mentioned here.

10. **a, b, c, d, e.** All these are possible locations to which a BitLocker recovery key can be saved or backed up.

11. **b.** The policy Require additional authentication at startup must be enabled before you can enable BitLocker on the system drive if the computer does not have a Trusted Platform Module. The Control Panel applet enables BitLocker on drives but does not work unless the policy is enabled. Signatures are written to any drive in order to manage them in Disk Management, but this does not affect BitLocker functionality.

12. **a.** BitLocker does not provide an option for saving the recovery key on a floppy disk; the only removable storage available is a USB drive. It can also be saved to the domain on a domain-joined computer or to a Microsoft account, a printed hard copy, or a local file.

13. **a, b, d.** Remote Wipe works on all these devices. Although you can use ActiveSync to remote wipe a Windows 8.1 laptop connected to a Microsoft Exchange Server, it wipes only Windows Mail information, contacts, and calendars. Other data on the laptop is not affected by the ActiveSync Remote Wipe. Windows Intune can selectively wipe corporate data on a Windows 8.1 laptop without affecting the user's personal data.

14. **a, b, c.** The Windows Location Platform uses GPS (if available), the computer's IP address, and any Wi-Fi triangulation to calculate the current location. The Windows Location Platform does not use the time zone, which can cover a very large area.

Chapter 16

1. **c.** An update roll-up is a packaged set of updates that fix problems with specific Windows components or software packages such as Microsoft Office. A critical security update is a single update that Microsoft issues to fix a problem that is critical for a computer's security. An optional update is a potentially useful non-security-related update. A service pack is a comprehensive operating system update that often adds new features or improvements to existing features.

2. **c.** By selecting the **Check for updates but let me choose whether to download and install them** option, you are notified that updates are available from the Windows Update website, but these updates are not downloaded or installed

until you click the icon that is displayed in the notification area. Thus, you can choose to download the updates at a time when Internet usage is minimized. Both the Install updates automatically and Download updates but let me choose whether to install them options download updates whenever they're available and do not provide the option for delaying the download until Internet usage has become minimized. You should never select the Never check for updates option because you won't receive any critical or important updates unless you check manually for update availability.

3. **e.** You should access Group Policy, enable the Configure Automatic Updates policy, and select the **4–Auto download and schedule the install** option. You should then specify a convenient time (the default is 3:00 a.m.). None of the other options listed in the question enable automatic installation of updates.

4. **c.** The Specify intranet Microsoft update service location policy enables you to specify a WSUS server on your network that client computers will access to receive software updates without accessing the Internet. With the other policies mentioned, client computers will still attempt to access the Internet for updates.

5. **b.** The View update history option displays a list of updates installed on your computer. From this location, you can double-click any update to provide detailed information including links to Microsoft websites that provide additional details. None of the other options mentioned here provide this information.

6. **b.** Windows Store apps can be updated only by using the Windows Store app. Windows Automatic updates is not aware of Store apps and does not update them.

7. **c.** You can use PowerShell to view app information and error logs. The Store app does not have an interface to view detailed error information, and errors are not logged in the Event Viewer logs. There is no Control Panel applet for managing Store apps.

Chapter 17

1. **b, c, g.** You can configure primary and extended partitions on a basic disk and create logical drives within an extended partition. The other volume types mentioned here require that you upgrade your basic disk to dynamic storage.

2. **c.** You should run the `convert gpt` command. This command converts the disk's partition style to GPT (GUID partition table), which enables a volume of more than 2 TB. By default, a disk uses the MBR (master boot record) partition table style, which enables volumes of up to 2 TB. It is not necessary to convert the disk to either basic or dynamic storage (it is basic by default) because you can have a 5 TB primary partition on a basic disk.

3. **b.** This procedure creates a spanned volume, which extends storage on one volume to additional disks without the need for an additional drive letter. A simple volume includes only a single disk. Mirrored and RAID-5 volumes contain 2 and 3–32 disks, respectively, but are created differently.

4. **b.** The Tools tab of a volume's Properties dialog box enables you to check the disk for errors, defragment it, or back it up. The General tab provides a pie chart of the disk's space allocation, specifies a volume name, and executes the Disk Cleanup utility. The Hardware tab displays hardware information for the computer's disk drives. The Quota tab enables you to configure disk quotas. The Customize tab enables you to optimize folders for specified purposes. None of these other tabs enable you to check your volume for errors.

5. **a.** When you move a disk from one computer to another, you need to initialize the disk in Disk Management before it can be accessed in the new operating system. The Resynchronize command resynchronizes members of a RAID-5 volume. You don't need to check the disk for errors unless you encounter other problems. It is definitely not necessary to format the disk and restore all the images from backup.

6. **c, d.** Mirroring (RAID-1) and striping with parity (RAID-5) are fault-tolerant and can withstand failure of a single disk without data loss. Spanning (which is not considered a RAID technology) and striping (RAID-0) are not fault-tolerant; loss of a single disk results in loss of the entire volume.

7. **a.** The maximum space that you can include in a RAID-5 volume is equal to the smallest amount of free space on a single disk multiplied by one less than the total number of disks. Here, the smallest amount of free space is 80 GB and the number of disks is 4, so you can have 80 × 3 = 240 GB. You require the space equivalent to one disk for parity; without parity, you could have 80 × 4 = 320 GB, but this is not the desired result. In this scenario, you could have created a three-disk striped volume without parity of 450 GB by using disks 0, 1, and 3 only, but this also is not the desired result. You cannot use all the space available when the sizes of the disks are different, so 530 GB is impossible.

8. **d.** The `add disk 1` command in DiskPart creates a mirror on disk 1 of the current volume. This is the only way you can create a fault-tolerant replica of your system and boot volumes. A striped volume is not fault-tolerant and cannot be used on the system and boot volumes. A RAID-5 volume is fault-tolerant, but you cannot use this technology on the system and boot volumes; further, this technology requires three disks. The `create volume mirror` command is invalid command syntax.

9. **a, b, c.** You should have at least 15% of free space on your disk so that the Optimize Drives can run in an optimal condition. Any of the first three options will increase the amount of free space.

10. **a, c.** You can either specify the volumes to be defragmented or use the `/E` parameter to specify the volumes that will not be defragmented. The `defrag /e:` command is incorrect syntax and will produce an error. The `defrag /E c: d:` command will defragment the E: volume but not the C: or D: volumes because it specifies to defragment all volumes except those mentioned.

11. **d.** You can create a storage space with any size; the pool capacity does not limit this setting. Because space is thin provisioned on the storage space, you can specify a larger amount than you currently have available and add disks to the storage pool when you want to actually use the space.

12. **b.** To use parity, at least three drives are required in the storage pool. A two-way mirror requires a minimum of two drives, and a three-way mirror requires a minimum of five drives.

13. **d.** You can change the size of the storage space at any time, and as long as you have enough capacity in the storage pool, you can use that space for files. You don't need to delete the "music" storage space because you can overallocate size on storage spaces regardless of the actual physical capacity on the storage pool.

Chapter 18

1. **d.** You should look in the Applications and Services logs for this type of information. These logs are located in their own subnode and provide information for single applications, as opposed to the Application log, which logs events related to all applications on the computer. The Security log records information on audited events, and the System log records events related to actions occurring on the computer in general.

2. **a.** By filtering the log to display only Critical, Warning, and Error events, you can reduce the number of visible events and more easily locate events of interest. Information events make up the vast bulk of events recorded in the System log and do not represent problematic situations. Configuring the log to overwrite events after 48 hours would reduce the number of events appearing in the log, but might cause loss of events indicating significant problems unless you always look at the logs more frequently. Event log subscriptions collect data from several computers and are not relevant here.

3. **b.** You should use a collector-initiated event subscription, which pulls events from the specified computers. A source-initiated event subscription is more appropriate where a large number of computers is configured with Group

Policy. A filter that views logs by event source displays logs according to Windows services, utilities, and components; this is not what is needed here. You could use a filter that views logs by user and computer, but this would be less convenient than creating an event log subscription.

4. **a, c.** You need to run the `Winrm` and `Wecutil` commands. The `Winrm` command initiates the Windows Remote Management service that enables a secure communication channel between source and collector computers. The `Wecutil` command enables you to create and manage subscriptions that are forwarded from remote computers. The `Wdsutil` command enables you to manage a Windows Deployment Services (WDS) server. The `Logman` command enables you to manage data collector sets in Performance Monitor. Neither of the latter two commands is associated with event log subscriptions.

5. **b, d.** You can use either Resource Monitor or Task Manager to terminate an unresponsive program although Task Manager is more convenient. To use Resource Monitor, you need to know the process name of the program to be terminated although this name is often intuitive (for example, `WINWORD.EXE` for Microsoft Word). The other tools mentioned here do not offer this functionality.

6. **c.** You should configure a Performance Counter Alert Data Collector Set. This feature logs conditions that you specify, such as a high processor utilization, and alerts you when such conditions occur. An Event Trace Data Collector Set creates trace logs that log data only when a specific activity takes place; however, this type of data collector set does not send messages for specific conditions. An event log is created by Event Viewer and logs a large number of events but not this type of message. A System Diagnostics Data Collector Set creates reports on local hardware resources, system response times, and processes on the computer along with system information and configuration data. It does not provide alerts.

7. **c.** You should check the Memory\Committed Bytes counter. This counter measures the amount of virtual memory that has been committed to either physical RAM or running processes. Although useful for determining whether additional RAM is needed, the other counters mentioned here do not provide this specific information.

8. **a, b, c, e.** The simplified interface of Task Manager enables you to perform all these tasks except for displaying performance statistics for a running program. Right-click the desired program and choose the appropriate option from the pop-up menu to perform these tasks. You need to click **More details** to see the advanced interface of Task Manager to display summary performance statistics on a running program.

9. **b.** You should access the advanced interface in Task Manager and select the **Startup** tab. Then right-click the required apps and choose **Disable**. There is no Run at startup check box in the Properties dialog box accessed from the simplified interface in Task Manager. You cannot disable apps from the Services tab in Task Manager; you can only start, stop, and restart them. The Startup tab in System Configuration is used to enable this task; now, it only redirects you to Task Manager. Always keep in mind that Microsoft expects you to know the changed features in the new operating system for the exam.

10. **a, b, d.** Action Center enables you to check for possible security-related alerts or solutions to possible maintenance problems. Action Center also enables you to configure the new File History feature. However, you cannot view alerts generated by data collector sets or close unresponsive applications in Action Center.

11. **a.** The Dependencies tab of the service's Properties dialog box, accessed from the Services snap-in, provides you with this information. The General tab of this dialog box does not provide this information. The System Configuration tool lets you disable services but does not provide this information. The Services subnode of the Software Environment node in the System Information tool provides information on all services on the computer including those that are running or stopped and their startup type, but this location does not provide the required information.

12. **b.** In the Indexing Options applet, you should click **Advanced**. Then in the Advanced Options dialog box, click **Rebuild**. This action deletes the current index and re-creates a new index. Modifying the locations in the Indexed Locations dialog box modifies where the indexing service searches; it does not enable an improved search for known items. Moving the index to a new location might help, but this should not be the first step in solving this problem. Modifying the file types searched on does not solve this problem.

Chapter 19

1. **c.** A USB recovery drive includes all the Windows files that are necessary to restore Windows from a hardware failure. This is the simplest way to accomplish the task required by this scenario. A system recovery disc was available in Windows 7; it enabled you to start the Windows Recovery Environment but did not include all the Windows files required to recover your computing environment completely. The USB recovery drive replaces the system recovery disc in Windows 8 and 8.1. A system state backup was used in Windows 2000/XP, and a Complete PC Backup was used in Windows Vista for this type of task, but neither is available in Windows 7, 8, or 8.1.

2. **a, b, c, f.** The System Restore program creates snapshots that include backups of the Registry, DLL cache folder, user profiles, and COM+ and WMI information.

In addition, certain monitored system files are backed up. However, user libraries and installed application executables are not backed up.

3. **d.** The System Restore feature restores your operating system, applications, and settings to the date and time that you have selected. It removes applications, drivers, and similar settings that have changed more recently. Simply rolling back the affected drivers does not fully complete this task. Restoring your profile does not remove bad drivers or applications. Restoring from a system image backup takes considerably more time and effort than using System Restore.

4. **a.** The device driver rollback feature enables you to rapidly restore an older driver to recover device functionality that has been lost. Downloading a new driver or using System Restore would work but would take far more time. Using a USB recovery drive is more drastic and would likely cause other changes as well.

5. **b.** The push-button reset feature restores your computer to the original factory image, and performing the reset without preserving your files (by choosing the **Remove everything and reinstall Windows** option) eliminates the virus infestation. Windows Complete PC Backup was a feature of Windows Vista, and Windows Backup and Restore was a feature of Windows 7; these have been replaced in Windows 8.1 by File History for recovering individual files and folders and the push-button recovery options for recovering your operating system. The USB recovery drive enables you to reboot your computer for recovery from a serious error but would not restore to manufacturer default functionality in this situation. System Restore would roll back recent changes to the operating system volume and any other volumes for which it has been configured; however, viruses that have affected other locations on the hard drive would remain.

6. **b, c, e.** You can access Advanced Startup Options by selecting **Change PC settings** from the Settings charm. Then from the PC settings window, click **General** and then click **Restart now**. You can also access these options from the logon screen by clicking the power icon in the bottom-right corner of this screen and then holding down the **Shift** key while clicking **Restart**. You can also boot your computer from the Windows 8.1 installation DVD. When the languages preferences screen appears, click **Next** and then click **Repair your computer**. Windows 8.1 boots too rapidly to allow you to access startup options by pressing **F8**, as was possible with older Windows operating systems, except if you have a dual-boot system, in which you can press **F8** when the boot loader menu is displayed. The options that appear when you press Ctrl+Alt+Delete do not enable access to startup options.

7. **a, b, c.** You can select options for Refreshing Windows (and preserving files), Reset your PC (deleting all settings), or Advanced options (which include System Restore and System Image Recovery) from the Troubleshoot Options. You can also choose to perform a Windows memory diagnostic or boot to a command prompt.

Recovery Console was used in Windows XP, but its function has been replaced with the Command Prompt option that is included under Advanced options.

8. **c.** You should select **Advanced options** from the Troubleshoot screen. Select **Startup settings** and then select **Enable low-resolution video**. Then perform a device driver rollback. This option starts the computer with a basic video driver at 640 x 480 screen resolution, thereby enabling you to log on and roll back the problematic driver. The Refresh and Reset options would solve the problem but would take far more effort. Safe Mode might work, but the low-resolution video option is designed for problems of this nature. You do not need to use System Restore to correct this problem.

9. **a.** The USB recovery drive provides a simple way to start your computer in this scenario and enables you to access a system image. The system image contains everything needed to replace Windows, your programs, and all your files, thereby restoring your computer to its previous condition. The Reinstall Windows option would reinstall Windows, but you would have to reinstall applications and restore files and settings separately. The System Restore option is not available when starting with a USB recovery drive. Performing an in-place upgrade would also require that you reinstall applications and restore files and settings separately.

10. **a.** You should use System Restore to manually create a restore point. If problems do occur after installing the application, you can use System Restore to restore your computer to the condition that existed immediately prior to the installation. Installing in Safe Mode doesn't help in any way. Using File History to back up your data would enable you to perform recovery options later but would take more effort than using System Restore. However, you might need to use a system image restore if System Restore does not succeed. Windows Backup and Restore was used in Windows 7 to perform this action but is no longer available in Windows 8.1. On the exam, choose the answer that enables you to perform the task at hand most easily.

Chapter 20

1. **a, c, e.** File History backs up files and folders stored in libraries, contacts, and desktop folders. File History also backs up favorites as configured in places such as Internet Explorer. However, File History does not back up operating system and application files.

2. **a, d, e.** File History enables you to back up files and folders to network folders, USB thumb drives, and external hard drives. You cannot use CD-ROMs or DVD-ROMs although you could use this option with the older Windows Backup program, which is no longer included in Windows 8.1. Although the Storage Spaces feature enables you to create a real-time mirror of your data, thereby providing protection against drive failure, File History does not *per se* back up to a Storage Spaces volume.

3. **b.** You can force Windows to create a backup of your files by selecting **Run now** from the File History dialog box in Control Panel. You can also check the date and time when the files were last copied. Restoring all the files is time-consuming and unnecessary, and may overwrite your current versions if you do not select a separate location. Searching for the files finds only the current version on disk. You can browse the backed-up files in the backup location, but you would need to compare each version to your current files, so forcing a new backup is the best option.

4. **c.** You should click **Clean up versions** and select the **All but the latest one** option and then click **Clean up** to proceed. This action ensures that only the most recent version of each file is retained. Neither the Until space is needed option nor the one-month interval option necessarily deletes all older file versions, although they free up quite a bit of disk space. The Keep saved versions setting does not contain an Until space is needed option.

5. **a, d.** From File Explorer, you should either add the `D:\workarea` folder to the Documents library or create a new library named Workarea. (Note that the new library is automatically named for the folder name, in this case, Workarea). You cannot add folders to File History by clicking **Select Folder**; the dialog box that appears only enables you to add libraries to File History. The File History app does not include an Add button that enables you to add a folder, only one that enables you to exclude folders.

6. **c.** The File History feature retains previous versions of a document and enumerates the available versions in the File History browser. By selecting the **Restore to** option, you can copy an older version of your report to a different location and then merge the missing section with your current document. If you select the **Restore** option, the older version overwrites your current version, losing your most recent changes. The approach of restoring from a backup and selecting the options indicated works but takes more effort. Previous Versions is no longer available in Windows 8.1, so that is not an option.

7. **b.** You should check the Recycle bin on OneDrive.com. Because your files were on the OneDrive storage, the OneDrive.com service has a copy of the files in its own Recycle bin, even after you have cleared the Recycle bin on your PC. After emptying the Recycle bin, you cannot recover files from there. OneDrive files are not backed up by File History. Volume Shadows are maintained only for local volumes, not OneDrive storage.

8. **d.** Because the Recycle bin is using more than 10% of your total storage (in this case, 0.7 GB), OneDrive starts to delete the oldest in only 3 days. When the Recycle bin storage falls under 10% of total space, no files are removed from the Recycle bin until 30 days after deletion.

Glossary

`.msi` file The installation file for an application that uses Windows Installer.

`.msp` file The installation file for a patch or hotfix used to update an application that uses Windows Installer.

`.mst` file A transform file that performs a scripting-like function for a Windows Installer package.

802.11 A set of protocol standards, defined by IEEE, for wireless digital communications. There have been several defined: 802.11a, 802.11b, 802.11g, and 802.11n.

Access control list (ACL) The list of permissions granted or denied that is attached to a file or folder.

Account lockout policy A policy setting that locks a user out of a computer if he enters a password incorrectly a specified number of times. This setting is designed to thwart an intruder who uses a password-cracking utility in an attempt to compromise a user account.

Action Center A Windows 8.1 tool that consolidates security, performance, and maintenance issues affecting your computer into a single panel and provides links to obtain more information and troubleshoot problems that might be affecting your computer.

Active partition A partition or volume on a hard disk that has been identified as the primary partition from which the operating system is booted.

Add-on Manager An Internet Explorer 11 tool that enables you to disable or allow browser add-ons or undesired ActiveX controls.

Add-ons Optional additional features that can be installed in Internet Explorer and provide enhanced functionality. Websites often download and install add-ons to your browser, sometimes without your knowledge and consent.

Address Resolution Protocol (ARP) A TCP/IP protocol that is used to resolve the IP address of the destination computer to the physical or Media Access Control (MAC) address.

Admin Approval mode The default action mode of Windows 8.1, in which all user accounts—even administrative ones—run without administrative privileges until such privileges are required. When this happens, the user is presented with a UAC prompt.

Administrative shares A series of shares that are automatically created when Windows 8.1 is first installed. These shares are useful for administrating remote computers on the network.

AES AES is the Advanced Encryption Standard, a cryptographic provider used in Windows for securing data on the network and at rest. The AES standard is an open standard defined by the National Institute of Science and Technology, and can utilize a number of strong encryption algorithms. AES supports key sizes of 128, 192, or 256 bits.

Alert A notification provided by the Data Collector Sets feature of Performance Monitor that informs you when the value of a counter has exceeded a preconfigured level.

Anycast IPv6 address A type of IPv6 address that is utilized only for a destination address assigned to a router.

Application compatibility The process of ensuring that a program or application written for a previous Windows operating system will function properly within Windows 8.1.

Application Compatibility Manager A component of the ACT that enables you to collect and analyze compatibility data so that you can remedy any issues before you deploy a new operating system such as Windows 8.1.

Application Compatibility Toolkit (ACT) A Microsoft resource that helps administrators identify the compatibility of their applications with Windows Vista, Windows 7, and Windows 8.1, thereby helping organizations to produce a comprehensive software inventory.

AppLocker An update to the older Software Restriction Policies, providing new enhancements that enable you to specify exactly what users are permitted to run on their desktops according to unique file identities. You can also specify the users or groups permitted to execute these applications.

Apps A series of programs included by default with Windows 8.1 that enable you to access information rapidly from the Internet, or features on your computer such as pictures, music, calendar, maps, Internet Explorer, and so on. You can add additional apps at any time from the Windows Store.

App-V An application virtualization technology used to stream applications without installing them locally. The only local installation required is the App-V client, which enables virtual applications to run on Windows computers.

Auditing A security process that tracks the usage of selected network resources, typically storing the results in a log file.

Authenticated Exceptions Windows firewall rules support authenticated exceptions to allow authenticated users or computers to use a network connection that is otherwise blocked.

Authentication A security process that confirms the identity of a user, service, or device.

Authorization The security process and settings that allow access to a specific resource to a specific account.

Automatic Private IP Addressing (APIPA) The dynamic IPv4 addressing system used when DHCP is unavailable.

Basic disk A disk partitioning scheme that uses partition tables supported by many other operating systems, containing primary partitions, extended partitions, and logical drives.

Basic Input/Output System (BIOS) The firmware application encoded in a computer that initializes the computer before the operating system is loaded. The BIOS manages basic hardware configuration.

Battery meter A small application that runs on mobile computers and displays the percentage of battery power remaining as well as the power plan currently in use.

BCDBoot A command-line tool that enables you to manage and create new BCD stores and BCD boot entries.

BCDEdit A command-line tool that enables you to manage boot configuration data (BCD) stores in Windows Vista/7/8/8.1, Server 2008, and Server 2012 R2.

Biometrics Technologies that measure and analyze human body characteristics, such as DNA, fingerprints, eye retinas and irises, voice patterns, and facial patterns, typically for authentication purposes.

BitLocker A feature of Windows 8.1 Pro and Enterprise that enables you to encrypt the entire contents of your system or data partition. It is useful for protecting data stored on laptops, which are susceptible to theft.

BitLocker To Go A component of BitLocker that enables you to encrypt the contents of a USB flash drive or portable hard drive.

CA Certificate authority is a trusted service that authenticates users and devices and signs certificates for identification and encryption purposes.

Cache A space on the computer's hard disk that is set aside for holding offline copies of shared files and folders from a computer on the network.

Certificate A method of granting access to a user based on unique identification. Certificates represent a distinctive way to establish a user's identity and credentials.

Challenge Handshake Authentication Protocol (CHAP) An authentication protocol that uses a hashed version of a user's password so that the user's credentials are not sent over the wire in clear text.

Charms A series of applications that lie along the right side of the Windows 8.1 interface. They enable you to access Search, Share, Start, Devices, and Settings.

Checkpoint A point-in-time state of a virtual machine, including hard disk, memory, and hardware configuration information.

Classless Inter-Domain Routing (CIDR) A flexible method of stating IP addresses and masks without needing to classify the addresses. An example of the CIDR format is 192.168.1.0/24.

Client Hyper-V The Microsoft virtualization technology included in Windows 8.1 Pro and Windows 8.1 Enterprise.

Cloud Applications, storage, shared resources, and other services available over the Internet. Services that are always available whenever a device is connected to the Internet from anywhere are typically referred to as being "in the cloud."

Compatibility View A feature of Internet Explorer 11 that enables websites designed for earlier versions of Internet Explorer to display properly in Internet Explorer 11.

Computer Management console A pre-built set of Microsoft Management snap-ins that provides users with the most common set of administrative tools, such as Task Scheduler, Event Viewer, Local Users and Groups, Performance Monitor, Device Manager, Services, and several others.

Credentials The discrete attributes that make up the total of items required to authenticate a user, service, or device. Credentials are typically made up of an account name and password but can include many other attributes.

Data Collector Sets A component of the Performance Monitor that records computer performance information into log files. This feature was known as Performance Logs and Alerts in Windows 2000/XP/Server 2003.

Data recovery agent A specially configured user account that has the ability to decrypt drives and partitions that have been encrypted using BitLocker.

Decryption Unscrambling the data in an encrypted file through use of an algorithm so that the file can be read.

Default gateway The term applied to the router that leads to other networks.

Default program The application that is associated with a file of a given extension so that Windows uses this program to open the file whenever you double-click any file with this extension.

DEP Data Execution Prevention, a security feature used to prevent buffer overflow exploits by marking memory with nonexecutable or data-only regions, and preventing any code execution from those regions.

Destination computer A computer on which Windows 8.1, together with applications, has been freshly installed and to which user settings and data are to be restored using the USMT.

Device driver The specialized software component of an operating system that interfaces with a particular hardware component.

Device Manager A tool from which you can manage all the hardware devices on your computer. It enables you to view and change device properties, update or roll back drivers, configure settings, and remove devices.

Device Stage A Windows 8.1 application that acts as a home page for your hardware devices, listing all devices and enabling you to perform management tasks.

Differencing VHD Also known as a child VHD, a VHD that contains only the differences between it and its parent VHD.

Direct Memory Access (DMA) The process of data bypassing the CPU and accessing RAM directly, designed as channels; for example, a floppy drive uses DMA channel 2.

DirectAccess DirectAccess is a new feature in Windows Server that enables seamless connectivity to an organization network through the Internet without requiring a VPN.

Disk Management snap-in A Microsoft Management Console snap-in that enables you to perform all management activities related to disks, partitions, and volumes.

Disk quotas A system of space limits for users on a volume formatted with NTFS. This is set up to ensure that all users have available space on which to store their files, preventing any one user from using all the available space.

DiskPart A command-line tool that enables you to perform all management activities related to disks, partitions, and volumes. You can use this tool to script actions related to disk management.

Domain Name System (DNS) A hierarchical naming system that is contained in a distributed database. DNS provides name resolution for IP addresses and DNS names.

Download Manager A tool available in Internet Explorer 11 for managing files downloaded from websites.

Driver package The complete set of files that make up all the components needed for working with a hardware device or peripheral.

Driver signing The digital signature that Microsoft adds to a third-party device driver to validate its usage.

Dual-factor authentication An authentication method that includes multiple methods for a single authentication transaction. Often referred to as "something you have and something you know," when the factors include a device such as a smart card and a secret such as a password or PIN.

Duplex A term referring to the simultaneity of communications. Simultaneous two-way communication is full duplex, while two-way communications that can occur in only one direction at a time is half duplex.

Dynamic disk A disk partitioning scheme supported by Windows XP, Vista, 7, 8, and 8.1 as well as Windows Server 2008 R2 and 2012 R2 that contains dynamic volumes.

Dynamic Host Configuration Protocol (DHCP) The protocol in the TCP/IP protocol stack that negotiates the lease of an IP address from a DHCP server.

Dynamic VHD A VHD that gradually increases in size toward a configured maximum as data is added to it.

EAP-TTLS Extensible Authentication Protocol with Tunneled Transport Layer Security is a new protocol for Windows Server 2012 R2 and Windows 8.1 that uses secure TLS connections to encrypt the authentication traffic during the VPN connection handshake.

Encrypting File System (EFS) An advanced attribute setting of Windows 2000/XP/Vista/7/8/8.1 and Windows Server 2003/2008 R2/2012 R2 for files and folders on an NTFS-formatted volume that provides certificate-based public key security for those files and folders. EFS encrypts and decrypts files in a manner that is transparent to users.

Encryption Scrambling and rearranging data in a file through use of an algorithm so the file cannot be read.

Event log subscription An Event Viewer feature that enables you to collect event logs from a number of computers in a single, convenient location that helps you keep track of events that occur on these computers.

Event Viewer An administrative tool that enables an administrator to view and/or archive event logs such as the Operating System, Application, Setup, and Security logs. In Windows 8.1, this tool also enables you to configure event log subscriptions that collect events from several monitored computers.

Extended partition One of the primary partitions that can be divided into multiple logical drives.

Fibre Channel A special, high-speed network connectivity standard and protocol using optical fiber cables.

File Explorer The basic window that displays contents of a drive or folder, previously called Windows Explorer.

File History A new feature in Windows 8.1 that preserves versions of user files in libraries, contacts, and favorites on a separate drive, typically every 10 minutes.

Firewall profile A means of grouping firewall rules so that they apply to the affected computers dependent on where the computer is connected.

Firewall rule A set of conditions used by Windows Firewall to determine whether a particular type of communication is permitted. You can configure inbound rules, outbound rules, and connection security rules from the Windows Firewall with Advanced Security snap-in.

FireWire Also known as IEEE 1394. FireWire is a fast, external bus technology that allows for up to 800 Mbps data transfer rates and can connect up to 63 devices. FireWire devices, although conforming to standards that Windows uses, usually require software from the manufacturer to utilize the specialized capabilities of the hardware.

Fixed VHD A VHD that maintains the same size regardless of how much data is contained in it.

Folder redirection The practice of moving library folders to a different location, which is often a shared folder on a server. Used to facilitate management of storage space on the network and to ensure proper backup of vital data.

Gesture A method of interacting with a touch screen using hand swipes or finger touches. Gestures can include taps, straight lines, circles, or other more complicated figures involving multitouch screen readers.

GIDS Generic Identity Device Specification; a standard used for smart cards.

Global unicast IPv6 address An IPv6 address that uses a global routing prefix of 45 bits to identify a specific organization's network, a 16-bit subnet ID, and a 64-bit interface ID. These addresses are globally routable on the Internet and are equivalent to public IPv4 addresses.

GPS Global Positioning System, a technology deployed by the U.S. Department of Defense that uses a series of satellites in geosynchronous orbit to allow a receiver to determine its location on the surface of the earth.

Hibernation A condition in which your computer saves everything to the hard disk and then powers down. When you restart your computer from hibernation, all open documents and programs are restored to the desktop.

Hidden shares A shared folder that does not broadcast its presence and is not browsable in the Network folder. A hidden share is indicated by a dollar sign ($) at the end of the folder name.

HomeGroup A small group of Windows 8.1 computers that can exchange shared information easily with each other.

host A computing device that has been assigned an IP address.

HTML5 sandbox attribute A new object type supported by HTML version 5 that enhances security by enabling restrictions for web pages containing untrusted content.

Hypervisor An additional layer of software below the operating system for running virtual computers.

Indexing A process in Windows 8.1 that facilitates the task of users searching data contained in files on the computer so that users can rapidly locate information.

Information bar A message that Internet Explorer displays at the top of the page under certain circumstances to alert you of possible security problems. These messages include attempts by a website to install an ActiveX control, open a pop-up window, download a file, or run active content.

InPrivate browsing A special browsing mode of Internet Explorer 11 that prevents user information, cookies, and browsing history from being retained on the computer. This feature is particularly useful for public computers that are accessed by many individuals.

Input/Output (I/O) port address Set of wires used to transmit data between a device and the system. As with IRQs, each component has a unique I/O port assigned. There are 65,535 I/O ports in a computer, and they are referenced by a hexadecimal address in the range of 0000h to FFFFh.

Integration Services A set of applications and software running on a virtual guest that enables the hypervisor to control certain features and performance of the guest operating system.

Internet Connection Sharing (ICS) The simplified system of routing Internet traffic through a Windows 8.1 computer so that other computers on the network that are not connected to the Internet can access the Internet.

Internet Control Message Protocol (ICMP) A TCP/IP protocol that enables hosts on a TCP/IP network to share status and error information. The `ping` command uses ICMP to check connectivity to remote computers.

Internet Key Exchange version 2 (IKEv2) A tunneling protocol that uses IPSec Tunnel Mode over UDP port 500. This combination of protocols also supports strong authentication and encryption methods.

Internet Protocol Security (IPSec) An encryption and authentication protocol that is used to secure data transmitted across a network.

Interrupt Request (IRQ) A set of wires that run between the CPU and devices in the computer; they enable devices to "interrupt" the CPU so that they can transmit data.

IP address A logical address that is used to identify both a host and a network segment. Each network adapter on an IP network requires a unique IP address.

IP version 4 (IPv4) The version of the Internet Protocol that has been in use for many years and provides a 32-bit address space formatted as four octets separated by periods.

IP version 6 (IPv6) A newer version of the Internet Protocol that provides a 128-bit address space formatted as eight 16-bit blocks, each of which is portrayed as a 4-digit hexadecimal number and is separated from other blocks by colons.

`ipconfig` The command-line utility that provides detailed information about the IP configuration of a Windows computer's network adapters.

ISO A file format representing an optical disk image such as a DVD or CD.

Jumbo Frames The term given to packaging TCP/IP packet data, wrapped by routing headers with a larger amount of data. Typical frames contain 1500 bytes of payload data, while jumbo frames can carry up to 9000 bytes of data.

Layer 2 Tunneling Protocol (L2TP) A protocol that is used to create VPN tunnels across a public network. This protocol is used in conjunction with IPSec for security purposes.

Library A set of virtual folders that is shared by default with other users of the computer. It is used to group documents of similar type in an easily accessible place.

Link-local IPv6 address A type of IPv6 address used for communication between neighboring nodes on the same link. Equivalent to IPv4 addresses configured using APIPA.

Link-Local Multicast Name Resolution (LLMNR) The capability of computers running IPv6 on the local subnet to resolve each other's names without the need for a DNS server. It is enabled by default in Windows 8.1 IPv6.

`LoadState.exe` A utility used by USMT to restore user settings and data to a new computer running Windows 8.1.

Local Security Policy The security-based Group Policy settings that apply to a local computer and its local users.

Local user profile The collection of Registry settings and files associated with a user's desktop interface that is created the first time a user logs on to a computer. This profile is stored on the local hard disk.

Location Aware A network service that can identify a specific local network currently in use and adjust behavior based on the network location.

Logical drive A segment of the extended partition that can be assigned a separate drive letter.

Mandatory profile A user profile that is renamed to `NTUser.man`. This profile is read-only, such that any changes made to the user profile are never saved when the user logs off. Useful for setting company-specific desktop settings that users are not permitted to modify.

Metered connection A metered connection is any network connection using a service that is charged based on the amount of data transferred. Many wireless broadband services, smartphone data plans, and satellite communication services use metered connections.

Metro The original term Microsoft used for the new Start screen during development and Preview, which performs well with touch-enabled monitors that are standard on tablet devices and are available on many laptops and desktop monitors. It also performs well with traditional monitors and mice. This term was discontinued by Microsoft before Windows 8 was officially released, and replaced with "Windows 8," "Start screen," or "modern."

Microsoft account Previously called a Windows Live account; a cloud service account used to access Windows devices and integrate with cloud services and synchronize multiple devices.

Microsoft Challenge Handshake Authentication Protocol version 2 (MS-CHAPv2) A Microsoft version of CHAP that uses the same type of challenge/response mechanism as CHAP but uses a nonreversible encrypted password. This is done by using MD4 algorithms to encrypt the challenge and the user's password.

Miracast Display A wireless display option, providing multidisplay capability for mobile devices.

Mirroring A method of duplicating data between two separate hard disks so that the failure of one disk will not cause the operating system to fail.

MMC Microsoft Management Console is the framework used for installing administrative tools, known as snap-ins, for various administrative tasks.

`Msconfig` The command that opens the System Configuration utility, which you can use to perform actions such as modifying the startup scheme, the default operating system that boots on a dual-boot computer, services that are enabled, and startup programs that run automatically. You can also launch several computer management tools from this utility.

`msinfo32` The command that opens the System Information program.

Multicast IPv6 address An IPv6 address that enables the delivery of packets to each of multiple interfaces.

Network Address Translation (NAT) A specification in TCP/IP that maps the range of private IP addresses (192.168.0.1–192.168.0.254) to the public IP address of an Internet-facing network adapter.

Network and Sharing Center A feature of Windows 8.1 that provides a centralized location from which you can manage all networking tasks such as connecting to networks and the Internet and sharing of files and folders with users at other computers.

Network Discovery Network discovery is a feature of Windows networking used to allow computers to advertise themselves and locate and connect to other computers and network resources.

NFC Near Field Communications is any set of enabling technologies for communicating between devices in very close proximity (a few inches).

NIC Network interface card, or the hardware device used to connect the computer system to a media access layer of a network. Although termed a "card," many NICs are now integrated components of computers and other devices.

NTFS permissions The security feature available in NTFS that allows you to grant or deny local access rights.

NUMA Nonuniform memory architecture is a memory allocation technology that groups memory locations and processors into nodes, to avoid performance issues caused by multiple processors attempting to access the same memory location, or accessing memory in a location slower to access for the processor that requests it.

OCSP Online Certificate Status Protocol is a network standard for verifying the status of certificates, retrieving revocation lists, and obtaining the certificate trust change of a X.509 certificate.

Offline files A feature built into Windows 2000/XP/Vista/7/8/8.1 that enables you to cache locally stored copies of shared files and folders so that you can work with them while offline and resynchronize your changes when you go back online.

OneDrive Microsoft's integrated cloud storage for Windows 8.1, previously named SkyDrive. OneDrive is a cloud-based, always-available storage and file-sharing solution for Windows users.

Packaged app A packaged app, also known as a Windows Store app, is a new kind of application with special characteristics. It runs full screen, makes use of tiles instead of icons, and can be installed and run without elevated privileges.

Paging file Virtual memory stored on disk that enables Windows 8.1 to run more applications at one time than would be allowed by the computer's physical memory (RAM).

Partition A configured section of a basic disk that is capable of being formatted with a file system and identified with a drive letter.

Password Authentication Protocol (PAP) The oldest remote access authentication protocol, which sends the user's credentials over the wire in clear text and can easily be sniffed off the wire by an attacker.

Password policy A series of Group Policy settings that determine password security requirements, such as length, complexity, and age.

PEAP Protected Extensible Authentication Protocol, or PEAP, is an authentication protocol using extensible authentication wrapped in a secure TLS tunnel for encryption.

Performance counter A statistical measurement associated with a performance object such as % disk time, queue length, and so on.

Performance Monitor A Microsoft Management Console (MMC) application that contains several tools for monitoring your computer's performance.

Performance object Hardware or software components that the Performance Monitor can use for tracking performance data.

Pervasive Device Encryption A Windows 8.1 disk encryption feature, supported on newer laptops and other mobile devices.

Phishing The use of a fake website that closely mimics a real website and contains a similar-looking URL. This site is intended to scam users into sending confidential personal information (such as credit card or bank account numbers, birthdates, Social Security numbers, and so on).

PIN Personal Identification Number refers to any of a series of digital confirmation numbers required for use of a device or to supplement authentication of a device user.

PIV Personal Identity Verification is a standard developed and published by the National Institute of Standards and Technology (NIST) to specify the security and encryption attributes of smart cards and their functions.

PKI Public Key Infrastructure is the term for the various services and security devices used to implement encryption and identity certificates in an enterprise. The basis for PKI in a Windows Active Directory domain is the Active Directory Certificate Services and related server roles.

Plug and Play (PnP) A standard developed by Microsoft and Intel that allows for automatic hardware installation detection and configuration in most Windows operating systems.

Point-to-Point Protocol (PPP) A dial-up protocol that supports TCP/IP and other protocols with advanced compression and encryption functions.

Point-to-Point Tunneling Protocol (PPTP) A protocol that is used to create VPN tunnels across a public network and includes encryption and authentication.

Pop-up windows Additional windows displayed on your browser by some websites that present advertisements or perform other actions, mostly of an undesirable nature. Internet Explorer 11 in Windows 8.1 includes a pop-up blocker that blocks the appearance of such windows and provides you with an option to display them if you desire.

Power plans A series of preconfigured power management options that control actions such as shutting off the monitor or hard disks or placing the computer in sleep mode or hibernation.

PowerShell Remoting PowerShell Remoting is the framework within PowerShell and enabled by WinRM that allows administrators to run cmdlets and commands on remote computers.

Primary partition A segment of the hard disk. A maximum of four primary partitions may exist on a single basic disk.

Private key A piece of data generated by an asymmetric algorithm that's used by the host to decrypt data (for example, by using EFS). A matching public key can be used to encrypt data to be decrypted with the private key.

Protected Extensible Authentication Protocol-Transport Layer Security (PEAP-TLS) A remote access authentication and security protocol that provides an encrypted authentication channel, dynamic keying material from TLS, fast reconnect using cached session keys, and server authentication that protects against the setup of unauthorized access points.

Protected Mode First introduced with Internet Explorer 7 in Windows Vista, this mode protects Internet Explorer by providing enhanced levels of security and protection from malware.

Public folder sharing A simple Windows 8.1 folder sharing model that allows others on the network to access files in your Public folders of each Windows library (Documents, Pictures, Videos, and Music).

Public key A piece of data generated by an asymmetric algorithm distributed to the public for general use. Used to encrypt data when using EFS. Such information can be decrypted only by the corresponding private key holder.

Push-button reset A feature in Windows 8.1 used to refresh the operating system back to the factory image. Push-button reset can optionally preserve user data, or it can be used to completely wipe any user files and settings from the device.

RADIUS RADIUS, or Remote Authentication Dial-In User Service, is a network protocol used to centralize authentication of remote access users.

RAID-5 A combination of disk striping with parity data interleaved across three or more disks. RAID-5 provides improved disk performance and is fault-tolerant.

Recovery agent A user account that has been granted the authority to decrypt encrypted files.

Reliability Monitor A monitoring tool that provides a trend analysis of your computer's system stability with time. It shows how events such as hardware or application failures, software installations or removals, and so on affect your computer's stability.

Remote Assistance A service available in Windows 8.1 that enables a user to share control of her computer with an administrator or other user to resolve a computer problem.

Remote Desktop A service available in Windows 8.1 Pro or Enterprise that allows a single remote control session of a computer running Windows XP, Vista, 7, or 8.1. Remote Desktop uses the Remote Desktop Protocol (RDP), which is the same protocol used in Terminal Services.

Remote Desktop Gateway (RD Gateway) A Windows Server feature that replaces the Terminal Services feature included with older versions of Windows Server. RD Gateway enables you to connect to remote servers on the corporate network from any computer that is connected to the Internet. You can publish applications to users on RD Gateway by using RemoteApp.

Remote Wipe The process of deleting all private and personal information on a device connected to the Internet or other network, without any physical or direct access to the device. Remote Wipe is enabled at the server managing the device, and the next time the device attempts to connect to a network service, it receives a signal and initiates the wipe and reset process.

RemoteApp RemoteApp is a technology that enables you to make programs that are accessed remotely through Remote Desktop Services appear as if they are running on the end user's local computer.

Resource Monitor A monitoring tool that provides a summary of CPU, disk, network, and memory performance statistics including mini-graphs of recent performance of these four components as well as tabulated data pertaining to each of these components.

Roaming profile A user profile that is stored on a shared folder on a server so that a user receives the Registry settings and files for his desktop interface regardless of the computer to which he logs on.

Safe Mode A method of starting Windows 8.1 with only the basic drivers enabled so that you can troubleshoot problems that prevent Windows from starting normally.

`ScanState.exe` A utility used by USMT to collect user settings and data on an old computer for purposes of migration to a Windows 8.1 computer.

Secure Boot Secure Boot is a technology in Windows 8.1 that protects the pre-OS environment of a computer, to ensure that all drivers and system loaders are authenticated and secure.

Secure Socket Tunneling Protocol (SSTP) A tunneling protocol that uses Secure Hypertext Transfer Protocol (HTTPS) over TCP port 443 to transmit traffic across firewalls and proxy servers that might block PPTP and L2TP traffic.

Secure Sockets Layer (SSL) A protocol used to secure data transmitted via HTTPS through the use of public key/private key encryption.

Service pack (SP) A collection of updates and fixes to a software package, usually available via download from the Internet. Service packs are available for download from Microsoft and when using the Microsoft automated update service.

Service Set Identifier (SSID) A network name that identifies a wireless access point.

`Setup.exe` The application that installs Windows 8.1 on a new computer or updates an older Windows computer to Windows 8.1. Also frequently used as a routine for installing applications.

Shadow copies Backup copies of files and folders automatically created by Windows as you work on them, enabling you to restore them should they become corrupted or deleted.

Shared folder permissions The security feature available when sharing files and folders across a network that allows you to grant or deny access rights to network users.

Shared folders Folders that are made available for access by users who are working at another computer on the network.

`Sigverif.exe` A utility that checks your computer for unsigned device drivers.

Site-local IPv6 address An IPv6 address that is private to the network on which it is located. This type of address cannot be accessed from locations external to its network, such as the Internet.

SLAT Second Level Address Translation is a processor feature, also known as Rapid Virtualization Indexing (RVI), that improves processor performance by managing memory with additional indexes or lookup tables.

Sleep mode A condition in which the computer consumes low power but is available for use. Sleep mode saves configuration information to memory and powers down the monitor, disks, and several other hardware components.

Smart card A device with an embedded microprocessor or data chip used for authentication and encryption.

Smart Paging A technique used in Hyper-V that minimizes the risk of running out of memory during virtual machine startup operations by swapping some of the requests for physical memory out to a special file on the disk drive.

SmartScreen SmartScreen is a feature in Windows 8.1 and Internet Explorer that works in conjunction with dynamically updated online databases to track malicious software and phishing sites to warn users of potential malware and identity theft sites.

SmartScreen Filter An enhancement of the antiphishing and antimalware tools first introduced with Internet Explorer 7 that compares website addresses to a database that is continuously updated to protect users from fraudulent websites that attempt to steal identity information or install malicious software.

Software Restriction Policies A series of settings included in Group Policy and Local Security Policy that can be used to limit the types of software that can run on a Windows XP/Vista/7/8.1 computer. You can limit users to running only those applications they need to do their jobs, and you can also prevent malicious applications from installing or running.

Source computer An old computer from which user settings and data are to be collected using the USMT, prior to repurposing or upgrading to Windows 8.1.

Special access permissions A granular set of NTFS security permissions that enables a single type of access only. Regular NTFS permissions are actually a combination of special access permissions.

Startup Repair A utility that provides a diagnostics-based, step-by-step troubleshooter that enables end users and tech support personnel to rapidly diagnose and repair problems that are preventing a computer from starting normally.

Storage pool A set of physical disk drives grouped together and used as the storage capacity for virtual storage spaces.

Storage space A virtual disk volume, optionally with resiliency, created from a pool of physical disks and used as a single disk drive.

Striping A method of segmenting data and interleaving it across multiple disks, which has the effect of improving disk performance, but is not fault-tolerant.

Subnet mask A set of numbers, 32-bits in length, that begins with 1s and ends with 0s in binary notation. The number of 1s represents the number of bits that are considered the subnet address. The bits that are 0s are the host address. Using a subnet mask, you can create more subnets with a smaller number of computers per subnet. All computers on a given subnet must have the same subnet mask. Using dotted decimal notation, you write a subnet mask as 255.255.0.0 (which is the default mask for a Class B address).

Sync Center A program on mobile computers that synchronizes data with other network devices, including servers, desktop computers, and other portable computers.

Synchronization conflicts Situation that occurs when two users have modified a file that is available offline and Windows detects that conflicting modifications have occurred. Windows 8.1's Sync Center enables you to save either or both of these versions.

Synchronizing files The act of copying files from a shared folder on the network to an offline files cache on a computer or copying the same files back to the shared folder after a user has modified them.

System access control list (SACL) A list of actions that trigger audit events.

System Configuration utility A tool that enables you to perform actions such as modifying the startup scheme, the default operating system that boots on a dual-boot computer, services that are enabled, and startup programs that run automatically. You can also launch several computer management tools from this utility. Started with the `Msconfig.exe` command.

System Protection A troubleshooting tool that provides several options for retaining copies of system files and settings so that you can configure how System Restore works to restore your computer to an earlier point in time.

System Restore A troubleshooting tool that enables you to restore your computer to an earlier time at which it was operating properly.

Task Manager A Windows 8.1 administrative utility that provides data about currently running processes, including their CPU and memory usage, and enables you to modify their priority or shut down misbehaving applications. You can also manage services, including starting, stopping, enabling, and disabling them; obtain information on network utilization; and display users with sessions running on the computer.

Teredo A tunneling communication protocol that enables IPv6 connectivity between IPv6/IPv4 nodes across Network Address Translation (NAT) interfaces, thereby improving connectivity for newer IPv6-enabled applications on IPv4 networks.

TKIP TKIP, or Temporal Key Integrity Protocol, is an encryption standard used for wireless networking. It was the first successor to the weaker WEP encryption standard and incorporates several features to ensure unique encryption keys for every data packet, making it a much more challenging encryption methodology compared to WEP.

TPM Trusted Platform Module is a hardware-level encryption and security device that works with firmware and operating systems to implement a complete secure environment from the hardware to the application layer.

UEFI The Unified Extensible Firmware Interface is a specification designed as a replacement for the older BIOS firmware on PCs. It defines the services and interface points between the computer firmware and the operating system.

Update roll-up A packaged set of updates that fixes problems with specific Windows components or software packages such as Microsoft Office.

USB recovery drive A USB thumb drive or portable hard drive on which copies of files required to start your computer are used if a problem has prevented your computer from starting properly.

User Account Control (UAC) A feature in Windows 8.1 that enables you to work with a nonadministrative user account. UAC displays a prompt that requests approval when you want to perform an administrative task. Should malicious software attempt to install itself or perform undesirable actions, you receive a prompt that you can use to prevent such actions from occurring. First introduced in Windows Vista, UAC has been updated in Windows 8.1 to provide new configuration options and reduce the number of prompts.

User profile A series of user-specific settings that is composed of desktop settings, files, application data, and the specific environment established by the user.

User State Migration Tool (USMT) A program that migrates a large number of users from an old computer to a new Windows 8.1 computer. This program uses two executables, `ScanState.exe` and `LoadState.exe`, together with a series of `.xml` configuration files, to migrate user files and settings. You can script this program to facilitate large migrations.

`Verify.exe` A utility used for low-level debugging of device driver issues.

VFD Virtual floppy disk, a representation of floppy disk images stored in a disk file.

VHD Virtual hard disk, a representation of a hard drive of specific geometry stored in a disk file.

VHDX A new format for virtual hard disks optimized for use by Hyper-V virtual machines.

Virtual hard disk (VHD) A file that includes all the files and folders that would be found on a hard disk partition.

Virtual machine A computer running inside another operating system or hypervisor, sharing the hardware resources of the host and behaving as it would running on a physical computer.

Virtual Private Network (VPN) A remote access connection technology that uses a protocol such as Point-to-Point Tunneling Protocol (PPTP) or L2TP with IPSec to tunnel through a public network to connect to a private network and maintain a secure connection.

Virtual switch A software representation of a network switch, configured in software and used to connect virtual machines in a Hyper-V environment.

Virtualization The process of creating software representations of physical computer components that behave like their physical counterparts.

VLAN Virtual local area networks (VLANs) are creating by use of special routing or virtual switches that tag network packets with VLAN ID numbers, which are then used to divide a network space into individual and separate LAN segments.

Volume A logical drive that has been formatted for use by a file system. Although often considered synonymous with "partition," a volume is most specifically a portion of a dynamic disk, or multiple sections of dynamic disks, that is capable of being formatted with a file system and being identified with a drive letter.

VT VT represents Intel's technology for virtualization on the x86 platform. Not all Intel processors support VT; support for VT may vary between different versions of the same model number. As of May 2011, the Intel CPU P6100 which is used in laptops does not support hardware virtualization.

WAP A wireless access point is a router or other device that broadcasts wireless signals to computers on a wireless local area network (WLAN). Also known as an access point (AP). Computers connecting through a WAP are members of an infrastructure (as opposed to ad hoc) wireless network.

`wbadmin` A command-line utility that provides a comprehensive system backup function in a scriptable form.

WDS Windows Deployment Services (WDS) is Microsoft's technology that enables deployment of Windows operating systems over the network, without requiring the use of a CD or DVD for each install.

WebSockets A new protocol and application programming interface (API) defined for HTML version 5 that allows for fast, two-way communication between a web-based application and a web server.

WEP WEP, or Wired Equivalent Privacy, is the original encryption standard used on 802.11 wireless networks. It has a number of vulnerabilities that have prompted security experts to recommend against its use whenever possible.

Wi-Fi Direct A new industry standard connectivity technology in Windows 8.1 that enables data and content sharing between devices and PCs on a peer-to-peer network that does not require separate Wi-Fi access points.

Wi-Fi Protected Access (WPA) A wireless authentication protocol that uses preshared network key encryption to ensure that only authorized users receive access to the network. There are several flavors, including WPA2-Personal and WPA2-Enterprise.

Wi-Fi triangulation A technique that sweeps the current area for Wi-Fi access points and cross-references the information, including the strength of each signal, with a database of locations to determine the location of a computer in range of those access points.

Windows 8.1 Upgrade Assistant A utility that you can download from Microsoft that determines what hardware or software problems you might encounter in upgrading an older Windows computer to Windows 8.1.

Windows Easy Transfer A program that facilitates the migration of user files from an old computer to a new Windows 8.1 computer. Windows Easy Transfer replaces the Files and Settings Transfer Wizard used with Windows XP.

Windows Firewall The personal firewall software incorporated in Windows 8.1 that filters incoming TCP/IP traffic. Windows Firewall was first introduced in Windows XP SP2.

Windows Firewall with Advanced Security A Microsoft Management Console (MMC) snap-in that enables you to configure comprehensive firewall rules specifying conditions for external connection to your computer. Default inbound, outbound, and connection security rules are provided; you can modify these rules or create new rules as required.

Windows Hardware Certification Program A Microsoft program that identifies all hardware certified to run properly on Windows 8.1 computers. It replaces the Windows Logo program previously used with Windows 7 computers.

Windows Mobility Center An application that runs on all Windows 8.1 mobile computers that provides a quick view of functions pertinent to mobile computers, such as battery status, wireless network connections, sync partnerships, presentation settings, and so on. You can configure common mobile computer settings, such as display settings, speaker volume, and battery status.

Windows PowerShell An enhanced task-based command-line scripting interface that enables you to perform a large number of remote management tasks.

Windows Recovery Environment (Windows RE) A parallel, minimum Windows installation that enables you to boot your computer when your Windows 8.1 installation will not start using any of the other advanced startup modes. You can perform advanced recovery operations after you boot into Windows RE.

Windows Remote Management (WinRM) Service The Microsoft implementation of the WS-Management Protocol, which is a protocol that assists you in managing hardware on a network that includes machines that run a diverse mix of operating systems including remote computers.

Windows RT 8.1 The version of Windows 8.1 especially designed for running on mobile platforms utilizing the ARM architecture, such as smartphones and tablets.

Windows Server Update Services (WSUS) A service that can be configured to run on a server, supplying updates, hotfixes, and other patches automatically to computers on a network. WSUS enables you to deploy and manage updates that are downloaded from the Microsoft Windows Update website to WSUS servers running on your own network. Client computers simply connect to the local WSUS server to download and install updates.

Windows To Go A bootable version of Windows 8.1 contained on a USB drive. It includes all operating system files, applications, and Windows settings, and can be used to boot a computer with the appropriate hardware into Windows 8.1, independently of the operating system installed on this computer.

Windows Update A service provided by Microsoft to keep Windows operating systems and software up-to-date, automatically by default, and to provide patches that keep the operating system and application secure when vulnerabilities are discovered.

Windows XP Mode The basic virtualization technology introduced in Windows Vista for running an instance of Windows XP within a Vista or Windows 7 operating system. Replaced by Client Hyper-V in Windows 8.1.

`Windows.old` A folder created when upgrading an older version of Windows to a newer one. It contains subfolders containing operating system files, user files, and program files, some of which you can migrate to your newer Windows operating system.

Wired Equivalent Privacy (WEP) A protocol that is used on 802.11-based wireless networks to encrypt data sent between computers on a wireless network or between a computer and its access point. WEP is better security than an open network but is considered less secure than WPA.

Wireless network profile A series of configuration settings that determine the extent of access to external computers according to your computer's location. Windows enables you to create profiles for Home, Work, and Public locations.

WLAN Wireless local area network is synonymous with a local area network (LAN) using wireless equipment and signaling.

WPA and WPA2 WPA, or Wi-Fi Protected Access (and the next version, WPA2), is a security protocol developed by the Wi-Fi Alliance to secure wireless networks. WPA2 incorporates stronger AES-based encryption, and devices are subject to security certification by the Wi-Fi Alliance.

Index

Numbers

3D printing, 10
6-to-4 addresses, 342
32-bit versus 64-bit, 59-60
802.1x authentication, 387
802.11a protocol, 385
802.11ac protocol, 385-386
802.11b protocol, 385
802.11g protocol, 385
802.11n protocol, 385

A

A address class, 336
accelerated graphics (Internet Explorer 11), 270
accelerators, 275
access
assigned
configuring, 245-246
editions included in, 10
biometrics, 578
devices, 578-579
disabling, 579
enabling, 579
fingerprint enrollment, 10
group policies, 579
new features, 17
Windows Biometric Framework (WBF), 578
DirectAccess, 635-637
benefits, 635-636
editions included in, 10
Microsoft Forefront Unified Access Gateway (UAG), 636
requirements, 636-637
local files/folders from OneDrive app, 493
object access auditing, 506
audited objects access attempts, displaying, 510
configuring, 506
enabling, 506-508
objects to be audited, choosing, 508-510
Security log space, 510
OneDrive, 492
permissions. *See* permissions
remote. *See* remote access
RRAS firewall exception, 413
tokens, 529-530
Windows Store, controlling, 228-229
Access Control Assistance Operators group, 583
accessibility, 42-44, 270
accounts
additional, creating, 36
administrator, renaming, 527
blocking, 527
domain, 587
local
built-in groups, 583
creating, 581
existing, managing, 582
lockout policies, 521-522
Microsoft, 585
advantages, 585
blocking, 588
creating, 586-587
disadvantages, 588
domain accounts, connecting, 587
email confirmation, 587
signing in, 79
passwords, configuring, 34-36

PINs, 579-580

enabling, 581

security, 581

policies, 519, 523

properties, configuring, 34-36

UAC, 528

Administrator group member authentication, 529-530

elevated privileges, 530, 534-535

improvements, 528

integrity levels, 530

nonadministrative user account prompts, 531

options, 536-537

policies, 537-541

prompts on taskbar, 532

tasks, 529-530

third-party application prompts, 532-534

troubleshooting, 541, 803

website, 528, 534

User Accounts and Family Safety category (Control Panel), 53

Accounts utility, 34-36

ACL Editor, 466-467

ACT (Application Compatibility Toolkit), 65, 205-207

Compatibility Administrator, 206

Configuration Wizard, 206

websites, 205, 207

Action Center, 48

drivers, troubleshooting, 188

editions included in, 10

opening, 802

troubleshooting performance, 802-803

action logs, 92-93

active command, 294

Active Directory Certificate Services Overview website, 574

Active Directory Domain Services. *See* AD DS

ActiveX controls, disabling, 272

AD DS (Active Directory Domain Services), 150

Always Offline mode, 655-657

folder redirection, 150-154

Group Policy settings warning, 153

implementing, 150-151

locations, 152

options, 151-152

Kerberos authentication, 598-600

roaming/mandatory user profiles, 157-158

adapters

Fibre Channel, 307

legacy network, 307

network

802.11n mode, 398

device properties, 396-398

enabling/disabling, 398

preferred bands, 398

speed, 398

troubleshooting, 398-401

VMs, 307, 308

wireless mode, 398

wireless, 663

Add an App dialog box, 414

Add command (App-V clients), 223

Add Counters dialog box, 782

Add a Device wizard, 173

Add New Quota Entry dialog box, 503

Add-on Manager (Internet Explorer 11), 260

add-ons, 271

accelerators, 275

disabling, 272

finding, 272

InPrivate Browsing mode, 275-277

Manage Add-ons dialog box, 271-272

search providers, configuring, 273-275

Add Recovery Agent Wizard, 486-487

Add Search Provider dialog box, 273

adding

applications to taskbar, 23

apps to firewall exceptions, 414

counters, 782-784

credentials, 565

devices, 33, 171-173

DNS servers, 355

drives

storage spaces, 753

system image backups, 852

folders to File History, 851

hardware to VMs, 307

indexing file types, 807

languages, 124-125
library folders, 29, 488
local accounts, 571
quota entries, 503
users
sharing lists, 451-452
special access permissions, 469
VHDs to older computers, 120
Address Resolution Protocol (ARP), 332, 368
addresses
6-to-4, 342
APIPA, 350-351
DNS server, 334
IP
alternate, 348
APIPA, 350-351
duplicate, troubleshooting, 375
dynamic, 343
incorrect, troubleshooting, 374-375
IP Address app, 372
multiple, 350
static, 334-337
IPv4, 334
address classes, 336
classes, 335
components, 334
IPv6 compatibility, 342
private, 338
static addressing, 335-337
IPv6
address classes/subclasses, 340-341
classes/subclasses, 340-341
IPv4 compatibility, 342
syntax, 339
types, 340
Teredo, 342
WINS, 334
ad-hoc wireless networks, 10
ADK (Assessment and Deployment Kit)
downloads website, 138
installing, 83-85
Admin Approval Mode (UAC)
all administrators, 540
built-in administrators, 538
administrators
accounts, renaming, 527
group, 529-530, 583
task approval prompt, 530
tools, 45-46, 49
UAC prompt behaviors, 539
Advanced Attributes dialog box, 483-484
Advanced Encryption Standard (AES), 387
Advanced Properties dialog box
elevated privileges, 535
IKEv2 tab, 631
Advanced Security Settings dialog box
Auditing tab, 508
effective permissions, displaying, 475
NTFS permissions
displaying, 468
inheritance, 473
taking ownership, 474
Advanced Sharing dialog box, 453
Advanced Sharing Settings dialog box, 359-361, 449
Advanced Subscription Settings dialog box, 774
Advanced tab (dialog boxes)
Device Properties, 178
Internet Properties, 269-271
Remote Desktop Connection, 611
Advanced TCP/IP Settings dialog box, 349, 352, 355
AES (Advanced Encryption Standard), 387
AJAX (Asynchronous JavaScript and XML), 277
all-user profiles, 393
Allow apps to communicate through Windows Firewall dialog box, 413
alternate IP addresses, 348
animations, configuring, 44
answer files
creating, 83-90
ADK, installing, 83-85
catalog file, creating, 87-88
completing, 89
components, adding, 88
errors, correcting, 89
image file, selecting, 86-87
packages, adding, 89
validating, 89

editing, 90
overview, 82
unattended installations, performing, 90
websites, 89
antihammering, 575
anycast addresses, 340-341
APIPA (Automatic Private Internet Protocol Addressing), 350-351
APIs (application programming interfaces), 212
App Connection Groups tab (App-V management console), 223
App history tab (Task Manager), 797
App sizes utility, 39
App to App Communication. *See* NFC
App-V, 220
command-line utilities, 222-224
deployment website, 221
installing, 221
management console, 222-223
overview, 220-221
Appearance Personalization category (Control Panel), 54
applets
Control Panel
Appearance and Personalization, 54
Clock, Language, and Region, 55
Ease of Access, 55
Hardware and Sound, 50-52
Network and Internet, 49-50
Programs, 52-53
System and Security category, 48-49
User Accounts and Family Safety, 53
Devices and Printers, 51, 489
Family Safety, 53, 269
Indexing Options, 805
Location Settings, 52
Network and Sharing Center. *See* Network and Sharing Center
Personalization, 54
Power Options, 659-660
Problem Reports and Solutions, 775
Programs and Features, 52
Speech Recognition, 55
Storage Spaces, 752
User Accounts, 53, 558, 582
Windows Firewall, opening, 412
Windows Update. *See* Update
Application Compatibility Toolkit. *See* ACT
application programming interfaces (APIs), 212
Application Virtualization. *See* App-V applications
applications
adding/removing to taskbar, 23
AppLocker, 15
App-V, 220
command-line utilities, 222-224
deployment website, 221
management console, 222-223
overview, 220-221
assigned access, configuring, 245-246
Bing
Food & Drink, 413
Health & Fitness, 413
Biometric Devices, 578
blocks, bypassing, 547
compatibility
ACT, 205-207
Application Compatibility mode, configuring, 203-205
control policies. *See* AppLocker
currently running
actions, 795
displaying, 795
default
file associations, configuring, 213-215
properties, 39
desktop, displaying, 26
elevated privileges, 534-535
file associations
default program settings, editing, 213-215
default programs, selecting, 219
extensions with specific programs, 215-219
firewall exceptions, 413-416
adding apps, 414
authenticated, configuring, 430-431
network profiles, 416
properties, displaying, 416
removing apps, 416
selecting, 413

installing
elevation prompts, 540
Windows Installer. See *Installer*
IP Address, 372
location settings, configuring, 696
logs, 767
Mail, Calendar, People and Messaging, 413
Maps, 413
Network, 344
OneDrive, 493-495
files, uploading, 494
local files/folders, accessing, 493
offline availability, 495
open, switching between, 20
Photos, 413
Programs, 52-53
restrictions, 230-231
application control policies. See *AppLocker*
benefits, 231
software, 231-236
sideloading, 230
sizes, 39
SkyDrive desktop, downloading, 496
Start screen, 20, 28-29
startup, troubleshooting, 801
switching between, 26
third-party prompts, 532-534
tile-based, closing, 20
UIAccess, 538, 540
uninstalling, 39
User Accounts
local accounts, managing, 582
Secure sign-in, 558
Windows Store, 225
access, controlling, 228-229
automatic updating, 10
characteristics, 225
content, managing, 228
editions supported, 10
error logs, 719
installing, 226
managing with PowerShell cmdlets, 719-720
NFC capabilities, 500
SmartScreen Filter, turning on/off, 547
updates. See *updates, Windows Store apps*

applications and services logs, 768
AppLocker, 15
app management website, 237
application control policies, 236-237
configuring, 238
creating, 241-244
default, 240
enforcement, 239
properties, 244
capabilities, 237
editions included in, 10
Properties dialog box, 239
software restriction policies, compared, 238
Windows Store access, 228
Apps view, 26
archived messages, displaying, 803
ARP (Address Resolution Protocol), 332, 368
Assessment and Deployment Kit. *See* ADK
assign letter command, 294
assigned access, 10
Asynchronous JavaScript and XML (AJAX), 277
attach command, 294
attended installations, 75-81
background color, 78
booting to setup, 76
computer names, 78
default settings, 79
finishing, 81
How should we set up your PC page, 80
installation type, choosing, 77
licensing, 76
Microsoft account sign-in, 79
partitions, choosing, 77
preparations, 75
product key, entering, 76
progress, tracking, 78
security code, 79
SkyDrive, 80
Windows Setup dialog box, 76
audio, 51
auditing
Auditpol utility, 510
new features, 16

object access, 506
audited objects access attempts, displaying, 510
configuring, 506
enabling, 506-508
objects to be audited, choosing, 508-510
Security log space, 510
policies, 523-526
account logon events, 526
completed action event log entries, triggering, 523
enabling, 523
event types, 525
success or failure actions, configuring, 525
website, 508
Auditing Entry dialog box, 508
Auditing tab (Advanced Security Settings dialog box), 508
Auditpol.exe utility, 510
authentication
Administrator group members, 529-530
biometrics, 578
devices, 578-579
disabling, 579
enabling, 579
group policies, 579
Windows Biometric Framework (WBF), 578
BYOD multifactor, 10
defined, 557
logons
lock screens, 557-559
picture passwords, 560-562
prompts, 557-559
multifactor, 557
remote
certificates, 597-598
group policies, 600
Kerberos, 598-600
NTLM, 598-600
planning, 596-597
protocols, 597
technologies, 597
smart cards
defined, 574
group policies, 577-578
new features website, 578
properties, 574-575
readers, 574
virtual, 575-577
VPN, 627
Windows Firewall exceptions, 430-431
wireless networks, 387, 436
Auto Complete (Internet Explorer 11), 269
autocorrecting misspelled words, 33
auto-dial, 361
Automatic Private Internet Protocol Addressing (APIPA), 350-351
automatic updates
auto-restart after installation, disabling, 713
delaying restarts, 713
detection frequency, 713
immediate installation, 713
properties, 710-712
rescheduling, 713
restart re-prompts, 713
scheduling, 712
Windows Store apps, 718-719
AutoPlay, 34, 51
availability
disk quota space, 505
NFC devices, 501
OneDrive offline, 495
Available Bytes counter, 789
Average Disk Bytes/Transfer counter, 793
Average Disk Sec/Transfer, 792
Avg. Disk Queue Length counter, 792

B

B address class, 336
backgrounds
displaying on start, 26
slide show, 663
wallpaper, 10
Backup Operators group, 583
Backup utility, 851
backups
Backup utility, 851
credentials, 567
DaRT, 855
EFS keys, 485

File History, 846
adding folders, 851
copies of files, saving, 850
damaged/deleted files, restoring, 856-858
drives, choosing, 847
event logs, 850
excluding folders, 848-849
features, 846
homegroups, 850
multiple versions of files, restoring, 858
offline cache size, 850
older versions of files/folders, deleting, 850
saved versions of files, keeping, 850
shadow copies, 855
Start screen app, 850
system images, creating, 852-854
turning on, 847
website, 852
recovery key, 690
system image, creating, 852-854
drives, adding, 852
network locations, 853
save locations, choosing, 852
verifying, 854
System Restore snapshots, 818
Wbadmin utility, 854-855
Balanced power plan, 661
basic disks, 729
converting
dynamic disks back, 737
to dynamic, 736-737
partitions
creating, 731-732
deleting, 735
extending, 733
properties, displaying, 734-735
shrinking, 733
Basic Input/Output System. *See* BIOS
basic user security level, 232
batteries
meters, 664-666
settings, 664
BCDBoot utility, 110
BCDEdit utility, 91, 110, 118-120
Bing
Food & Drink app, 413
Health & Fitness app, 413
searches, 10
Biometric Devices app, 578
biometrics, 578
devices, 578-579
disabling, 579
enabling, 579
fingerprint enrollment, 10
group policies, 579
new features, 17
Windows Biometric Framework (WBF), 578
BIOS (Basic Input/Output System)
compatibility, 59
VMs, configuring, 307
BitLocker, 16, 49
DRAs, 683-686
drive encryption, 672-674
Drive Encryption dialog box, 674
editions included in, 10
enabling, 674-675
managing, 677-678
new features, 673
overview, 672
partitions, encrypting, 676-677
policies, 680
fixed data drives, 682-683
operating system drives, 680
recovery keys, storing, 676
requirements, 58
startup keys, 672
TPM compatibility, 674
unlocking drives at startup, 675
websites, 674
Windows To Go workspaces, 105
without TPM preparations, 687-690
BitLocker To Go, 16, 672, 679-680
Block Inheritance dialog box, 473
blocking accounts, 527
blue screen of death (BSOD), 93-94
boot-sector viruses, 541
Boot tab (System Configuration utility), 800
Bootcfg.exe, 91

booting
advanced options, 832-833
boot management programs, 91
directly to desktop, 26
dual-booting, 90
advantages, 90
configuring, 91-92
logging, enabling, 832
management programs, 91
recovery options, 830
safe mode, 832
Secure Boot. *See* Secure Boot
troubleshooting
boot options, 800
diagnostic utilities, listing, 801
general options, 799
services, 800-801
startup applications, 801
trusted/secure, 15
VHDs, 111-112, 118-120
Windows To Go, 106
BranchCache, 10, 16
broadband connections
DirectAccess, 635-637
benefits, 635-636
editions included in, 10
Microsoft Forefront Unified Access Gateway (UAG), 636
requirements, 636-637
RD Gateway, 632
advantages, 633
group policies, 635
logon methods, 634
server settings, configuring, 633
website, 635
browsers
add-ons, 271
accelerators, 275
disabling, 272
finding, 272
InPrivate Browsing mode, 275-277
Manage Add-ons dialog box, 271-272
search providers, configuring, 273-275
default, configuring, 45
history, deleting, 258
Internet Explorer. *See* Internet Explorer 11
BSOD (blue screen of death), 93-94
buffers, 398
built-in local groups, 583
business data, removing remotely, 10, 17
BYOD multifactor authentication, 10

C

C address class, 336
caches
BranchCache, 10
offline, sizing, 850
transparent, 657
camera roll, 498
CAs, 572
catalog files
32-bit, 89
creating, 87-88
certificates
Active Directory Certificate Services Overview website, 574
Certificate Manager, opening, 570
EFS, 481
Export Wizard, 485
Internet Explorer 11, 269
properties, displaying, 570-571
remote authentication, 597-598
requesting, 572-574
virtual smart cards, 576-577
Change homegroup settings dialog box, 463
change permissions, 455, 471
CHAP (Challenge Handshake Authentication Protocol), 597
charms, 13
Charms panel
accessing, 19
Search button, 20-22
Settings button, 30
displaying/hiding, 26
Networks, 391
Settings, 389-390
checkpoints (VMs), 315-318
applying changes, 317-318
creating, 315-316
deleting, 317
file locations, 308

merging changes, 318
storing, 315
VHDs, expanding, 315
chkdsk.exe utility, 739
Choose Media Streaming Options for Computers and Devices dialog box, 459
CIDR (classless inter-domain routing), 338
cipher utility
decrypting files, 485
files, encrypting, 483
classes
IPv4, 335
IPv6, 340-341
classless inter-domain routing (CIDR), 338
clean installations
attended, 75-81
background color, 78
booting to setup, 76
computer name, 78
default settings, 79
finishing, 81
How should we set up your PC page, 80
installation type, choosing, 77
licensing, 76
Microsoft account sign-in, 79
partitions, choosing, 77
preparations, 75
product key, entering, 76
progress, tracking, 78
security code, 79
SkyDrive, 80
Windows Setup dialog box, 76
dual-booting, 90
advantages, 90
configuring, 91-92
refreshing, 92
troubleshooting
log files, 92-93
Stop errors, 93-94
stopped, 94
unattended, 81
answer files. See *answer files*
configuration passes, 82-83
upgrading, compared, 60-61
website resources, 95
clicking tiles/icons, 20
client-side targeting (updates), 713
clients
Hyper-V. *See* Hyper-V
Remote Desktop, 10
Clock, Language, and Region category (Control Panel), 55
closing tile-based apps, 20
cloud storage. *See* OneDrive
clusters, 747
collecting events, 771
collector-initiated event subscriptions, 771
COM ports, 308
commands
active, 294
App-V clients, 222-224
assign letter, 294
attach, 294
cipher, 485
Convert dynamic, 745
create partition primary, 294
create vdisk, 294
Defrag, 750
diskpart. *See* DiskPart utility
format fs, 294
list disk, 294, 745
Mount, 223
net share, 458-459
netsh wireless networking, 394
Select disk, 294, 745
Wecutil, 772
Winrm, 771
Committed Bytes counter, 789
compatibility
Administrator, 206
applications
ACT, 205-207
Application Compatibility mode, configuring, 203-205
hardware, 58-59
IPv4 and IPv6 addresses, 342
software, 63-65
Upgrade Assistant check, 61-62
Compatibility tab (application Properties dialog box), 203-204

Compatibility View (Internet Explorer), 256
browsing history, deleting, 258
configuring
Compatibility View Settings dialog box, 256-257
GPOs, 258
Compatibility View Settings dialog box, 257
Complete Media Center, 58
components included (editions), 10
Computer Management snap-in, 55
file/folder sharing security, 451
Local Users and Groups section, 582
computer names, 78
configuration passes, 82-83
Configure Automatic Updates dialog box, 710
configuring
accessibility options, 42-44
app sizes, 39
application compatibility
ACT, 205-207
Application Compatibility mode, 203-205
application restrictions
application control policies. See *AppLocker*
benefits, 231
software, 231-236
AppLocker rules, 238
assigned access, 245-246
Compatibility View Settings dialog box, 256-257
GPOs, 258
dates and times, 42
default apps, 39
default browser, 45
devices, 170-171, 177-178
disk quotas, 504-505
DNS
TCP/IPv4, 354-356
TCP/IPv6, 356-357
driver properties, 193-196
dual-booting, 91-92
Easy Connect, 608
file associations
default program settings, editing, 213-215
default programs, selecting, 219
extensions with specific programs, 215-219
Firewall
Advanced Security. See *Firewall, Advanced Security*
authenticated exceptions, 430-431
Group Policy, 428-429
multiple profiles, 418-420
new connection security rules, 424
new inbound/outbound rules, 420-424
notifications, 427-428
program exceptions, 413-416
Windows Firewall applet, opening, 412
homegroups, 463
ICS, 361-363
Internet Explorer 11
advanced security settings, 269-271
Auto Complete, 269
certificates, 269
cookies, 267
Download Manager. See *Download Manager*
family safety, 269
location services, 267
Pop-up Blocker, 268-269
Protected Mode, 263
RSS feeds/Web slices, 269
security, 260-261
security zones, 261-263
SmartScreen Filter, 264-265
languages, 124-125
listening ports, 613-614
Location Aware Printing, 401-402
lock screen, 32
mouse, 33
network connections
APIPA, 350-351
new, 358
TCP/IPv4, 346-350
TCP/IPv6, 351-353
networks
adapters, 396-398
profiles, 433
properties, 40-41
notifications, 39
NTFS permissions
special access, 468-472
standard, 466-467

object access auditing, 506
Offline Files
client computer, 646-648
server, 649-650
OneDrive, 36-37, 497
passwords, 34-36
picture passwords, 560-562
PINs, 579-580
power and sleep, 34
power plans, 665
printer sharing, 489-492
privacy, 39
recoveries, 44
Remote Assistance
accepting offers, 603-604
invitations to receive help, sending, 604-607
Remote Desktop servers, 612-613
resource sharing, 449-450
restore points, 838
search providers, 273-275
searches, 39
services performance, 803-804
sharing, 39
software restriction rules, 233
taskbar, 23
TCP/IPv4, 334
touchpad, 33
TPMs as virtual smart cards, 575-576
UAC policies, 537
updates, 44
user accounts, 34-36
VHD native boot, 111-112
VMs, 306-307
automatically starting/stopping, 309
BIOS, 307
checkpoint file locations, 308
COM ports, 308
diskette drives, 308
dynamic memory, 307
hardware, adding, 307
IDE controllers, 308-311
integration services, 308
memory, 307
names, 308
network adapters, 308
processors, 310
SCSI controllers, 308
Smart Paging, 308
WebSockets, 279
wireless network connections, 386-388
manually connecting, 386-388
new, 386
properties, 437
connections
DHCP server, troubleshooting, 375
DirectAccess, 635-637
benefits, 635-636
Microsoft Forefront Unified Access Gateway (UAG), 636
requirements, 636-637
file-sharing, encrypting, 450
Internet sharing. *See* ICS
IPv6, troubleshooting, 376
LANs, troubleshooting, 366
metered, 499
networks
APIPA, 350-351
displaying, 346
DNS, configuring, 354-356
existing, 359
host, sharing, 361-362
Network app, 344
Network and Sharing Center, 344-345
new, configuring, 358
properties, 41
TCP/IPv4, 346-350
TCP/IPv6, 351-353
testing, 372
troubleshooting, 365-372
RD Gateway, 632
advantages, 633
group policies, 635
logon methods, 634
server settings, configuring, 633
website, 635
remote
Easy Connect, 601, 608
listening ports, configuring, 613-614
types, 597
Windows XP, 614

Remote Desktop, creating, 610-611
TCP/IP, troubleshooting, 367-373
virtual switches, 319
VMs with virtual switches, 323-324
VPN, 624
authentication, 627
available network connections, displaying, 629
compatibility and interoperability, 625
establishing, 626-627
properties, 629-630
protocols, 625
reconnecting, 631
remote access, 625-626
security, 630
website, 632
Wi-Fi Direct, 670-671
connecting devices, 671
finding devices, 671
installing devices, 670
pairing devices, 671
properties, 670
proximity sensors, 671
website, 671
wireless, 386-388
automatic, stopping, 394
manually connecting, 386-388
metered, 391
new, 386
preferred, 392-393
security, 435-437
Content tab (Internet Properties dialog box), 269
Control Panel
Appearance and Personalization, 54
Clock, Language, and Region, 55
Computer and Management snap-in, 55
displaying, 46
Ease of Access category, 55
Hardware and Sound, 50-52
Network and Internet, 49-50
Programs category, 52-53
System and Security, 47-49, 536
User Accounts and Family Safety, 53
controllers
IDE, 308-311
SCSI, 307-308
Convert dynamic command, 745
Convert.exe utility, 482
cookies, handling, 267
copying
files/folders
NTFS permissions, 476-477
OneDrive, 494
user profiles, 157
core networking firewall exception, 413
Corners and Edges utility, 33
counters
adding, 782-784
defined, 781
highlighting, 784
LogicalDisk object, 793
Memory object, 789-790
PhysicalDisk object, 792
Processor object, 792
CPU performance statistics, displaying, 778-779
CPU tab (Resource Monitor), 779
Create and Attach Virtual Hard Disk dialog box, 112
Create Basic Task Wizard, 770
Create Custom View dialog box, 769-770
create files NTFS special access permission, 471
create folders NTFS special access permission, 471
Create a Homegroup Wizard, 460
Create New Data Collector Set Wizard, 785
create partition primary command, 294
create vdisk command, 294
Credential Manager, 53, 563
credentials
adding, 565
backing up, 567
deleting, 565
editing, 565
restoring, 568
Web Credentials, 568-569
roaming capabilities, 566

credentials
adding, 565
backing up, 567
Credential Manager, 563
deleting, 565
editing, 565
restoring, 568
roaming capabilities, 566
types, 564
Web, 568-569
Cryptographic Operators group, 583
cryptography, 583
Current Disk Queue Length counter, 793
cursor thickness, 44
Customize Allow if Secure Settings dialog box, 422
customizing
answer files, 90
Appearance and Personalization category (Control Panel), 54
credentials, 565
display, 32
paging files, 791
power plans, 662
profile paths, 156
shared folders
permissions, 455-456
properties, 453
Start screen tiles, 10
Windows Firewall rule properties, 426

D

D address class, 336
DaRT (Diagnostics and Recovery Toolset), 855
data
collector sets, 784
firewall exception, 413
manually, 787-788
names, 785
Performance Monitor, 788-789
from templates, 785-786
recovery agents (DRAs), 683-686
usage, displaying, 391
dates and times, 42
debugging mode, enabling, 832
decryption, 485
Default Programs applet, 53
default program settings, configuring, 213-215
file extension associations, 215-219
defaults
application file associations, configuring, 213-215
AppLocker rules, configuring, 240
browser, 45
Defaults utility, 39
Defender (Windows), 10
Defrag.exe, 750
defragmenting disks
clusters, 747
Defrag.exe, 750
Optimize Drives utility, 748-750
Delete Browsing History dialog box, 258
delete NTFS special access permission, 471
delete subfolders and files NTFS special access permission, 471
deleting
Administrative Tools tiles, 45-46
applications from taskbar, 23
AppLocker rules, 240
apps from firewall exceptions list, 416
browsing history, 258
business data remotely, 10, 17
checkpoints, 317
credentials, 565
indexing file types, 807
languages, 126
last username displayed, 559
library folders, 29, 488
older versions of files/folders, 850
partitions, 735
restore points, 838
shared folders, 452
updates, 715
user profiles, 157
wireless networking profiles, 394
denying permissions, 475
dependencies (services), 804

deploying
VMs, 309-314
wireless network profiles, 396
Deployment Image Servicing and Management (DISM), 110
desktop
apps, displaying, 26
background
displaying on start, 26
slide show, 663
wallpaper, 10
booting directly, 26
charms. *See* charms
four variable sized-windows, opening, 10
gadgets, 55
Internet Explorer 11
running, 253
Start screen version, compared, 255-256
navigating, 25-26
OneDrive, 496-497
previewing from taskbar, 25
remote
connections, creating, 610-611
editions included in, 10
firewall exception, 413
listening ports, configuring, 613-614
nonadministrative access, granting, 613
protocol (RDP), 609
server side, configuring, 612-613
Start screen version, 612
Terminal Services restriction, 609
Windows XP connections client software, 614
secure, 540
Start button, 10, 13
Start screen. *See* Start screen
tile, 19
Windows 7, displaying, 45
Details tab (dialog boxes)
device Properties, 178,
Task Manager, 797
Device Manager, 56
devices
installed, displaying, 176
Properties dialog box, 177-178
status, displaying, 176-177
drivers
disabling, 179
resource conflicts, troubleshooting, 185-187
uninstalling, 179
network adapter device properties, 396-398
opening, 175-176
Device Stage, 171-173
devices
biometrics, 578-579
drivers. *See* drivers
managing, 693-694
mobile. *See* mobile devices
network adapter properties, 396-398
NFC
availability, 501
capabilities, 500
Properties dialog box tabs, 178
Wi-Fi, connecting, 671
Wi-Fi Direct
finding, 671
installing, 670
pairing, 671
wireless networks, finding, 390
Devices charm, 13
Devices and Printers applet, 51, 489
Devices utility, 33
DHCP (Dynamic Host Configuration Protocol)
Allocators, 362
dynamic IP addressing, 343
server connections, troubleshooting, 375
Diagnostics and Recovery Toolset (DaRT), 855
dialog boxes
Add an app, 414
Add Counters, 782
Add New Quota Entry, 503
Add Search Provider, 273
Advanced Attributes, 483-484
Advanced Properties
elevated privileges, 535
IKEv2 tab, 631
Advanced Security Settings
Auditing tab, 508
effective permissions, displaying, 475

NTFS permissions, 468, 473
taking ownership, 474
Advanced Sharing, 453
Advanced Sharing Settings, 359-361, 449
Advanced Subscription Settings, 774
Advanced TCP/IP Settings, 349, 352, 355
Allow apps to communicate through Windows Firewall, 413
AppLocker Properties, 239
Auditing Entry, 508
BitLocker Drive Encryption, 674
Block Inheritance, 473
Certificate Properties, 571
Change homegroup settings, 463
Choose Media Streaming Options for Computers and Devices, 459
Compatibility View Settings, 257
Configure Automatic Updates, 710
Create and Attach Virtual Hard Disk, 112
Create Custom View, 769-770
Customize Allow if Secure Settings, 422
Delete Browsing History, 258
device Properties, 177-178
Disable Add-on, 272
Disks to Convert, 737
Download Options, 283
Driver Verifier Manager, 191
Edit Plan Setting, 662
Ethernet Properties, 346, 366
Exclude from File History, 848
File Sharing, 452
Home-File History, 856
Indexed Locations, 805
Internet Options, 261
Internet Properties
Advanced tab, 269-271
Content tab, 269
Privacy tab, 267
security, 260-261
LAN Settings, 363
Local Area Connection Properties dialog box, 354
Manage Add-ons, 271-272
Manage Default Printers, 401
Microsoft SmartScreen Filter, 265
Network Connection Details, 366
Network Connections, 346, 362
adapters, enabling/disabling, 398
LANs, troubleshooting, 366
New Path Rule, 234
Offline Files, 647
Offline Files Sync Schedule, 652
Offline Settings, 649
Performance Options, 791
Permission Entry, 469-470
Permissions for (folder name), 455
Pop-up Blocker Settings, 268
Quota Properties, 503
RD Gateway Server Settings, 633
Remote Assistance, 604
Remote Assistance Settings, 604
Remote Desktop Connection, 610
Remote Desktop Users, 613
Security Settings, 262
Select Folder, 849
Select Users or Groups, 242, 584
Select a Windows Image, 86
Set Program Access and Computer Defaults, 219
Set Up a Connection or Network, 627
Shrink (Volume), 733
Subscription Properties, 773
System Properties
Remote tab, 603
roaming, 159
System Restore, 818
Taskbar and Navigation Properties, 23
jump lists, 27
Navigation tab, 25-26
Taskbar tab, 24-25
toolbars, 27
TCP/IPv4 Properties, 347
TCP/IPv6 Properties, 351
Troubleshoot problems-Network and Internet, 365
User Account Control Settings, 536-537
Virtual Memory, 791
VPN Connection Properties
properties, 629-630
Security tab, 630

Windows Firewall, 602
Windows Firewall with Advanced Security on Local Computer Properties, 418
Windows Setup, 76
Wireless Network Properties, 391-392
differencing VHDs, 109-110
digital signatures
drivers, 180-183
requirements, 180-181
searching, 181
unsigned, 183
verifying, 181-183
website, 181
Internet Explorer 11, 260
Secure Boot, 541-542
updates, 713
direct memory access (DMA), 195
DirectAccess, 635-637
benefits, 635-636
editions included in, 10
Microsoft Forefront Unified Access Gateway (UAG), 636
requirements, 636-637
Disable Add-on dialog box, 272
disabling
add-ons, 272
auto-restart after automatic update installations, 713
biometrics, 579
device drivers, 179
drivers, 193
location settings, 695, 697
Microsoft accounts, 588
network adapters, 398
Network Location Wizard, 365
NFC, 501
Offline Files, 647
picture passwords, 562
scripting, 279
services, 804
SmartScreen Filter, 547
TCP/IPv6, 357
Windows Firewall, 412-413
Windows Store apps automatic updates, 718-719
disallowed security level, 231
discovery
firewall exception, 413
Network Discovery, 360, 432
Domain profile, 433
network profile options, 433
typical network profiles, 432-433
Disk Cleanup utility, 739
Disk Defragmenter, 739
Disk Management utility, 56, 728
actions, 729
converting basic disks to dynamic disks, 736-737
extending volumes, 738
mirrored volumes, creating, 744-745
opening, 728
partitions
creating, 731-732
deleting, 735
extending, 733
RAID-5 volumes, creating, 745
striped volumes, creating, 742-744
VHDs, 110, 112-114, 295
volume statuses, 740-741
Disk tab (Resource Monitor), 779
% Disk Time counter, 792-793
Disk Transfers/sec counter, 793
diskpart command, 294
diskette drives, 308
DiskPart utility, 739
MBR/GPT conversions, 730-731
VHDs, 110, 293-294
assigning, 294
attaching, 294
commands, 294
file, 294
formatting, 294
partitions, 294
volumes, creating, 745-746
website, 294
disks
basic, 729
converting dynamic disks back, 737
converting to dynamic, 736-737
creating partitions, 731-732
deleting partitions, 735
extending partitions, 733

partition properties, displaying, 734-735
shrinking partitions, 733
defragmentation
clusters, 747
Defrag.exe, 750
Optimize Drives utility, 748-750
dynamic
advantages, 729
basic disk conversions to, 736-737
converting to basic disks, 737
disadvantages, 730
extending volumes, 738
volumes, 737-738
EFS preparations, 482
error checking, 751
management utilities, listing of, 738-739
partition styles
converting between, 730-731
listing of, 730
performance optimization, 792
LogicalDisk counters, 793
PhysicalDisk counters, 792
statistics, displaying, 778-779
quotas, 502
adding entries, 503
available space, 505
configuration options, 504
enabling, 502-503
guidelines, 505-506
properties, 504-505
specific user entries, configuring, 503
storage pool drive failures, 756
storage spaces, 751-752
adding drives, 753
creating, 752-753
managing, 755
PowerShell management, 757
renaming drives, 755
resiliency options, 754
storage pools, compared, 754
troubleshooting, 739-741
full disks, 739
hard disk controller failures, 739
invalid media types, 739
missing operating systems, 739
non-system disk errors, 739
volume statuses, 740-741
volumes
creating with DiskPart, 745-746
mirrored, creating, 744-745
RAID. See *RAID volumes*
spanned, creating, 744
statuses, troubleshooting, 740-741
Disks to Convert dialog box, 737
DISM (Deployment Image Servicing and Management), 110
dismounting VHDs, 295
displaying
Administrative Tools tiles, 45-46
Apps view, 26
archived messages, 803
audited objects access attempts, 510
certificate properties, 570-571
charms, 26
Control Panel, 46
current NTFS permissions, 468
desktop apps, 26
desktop background on start, 26
device status, 176-177
downloads list, 282-283
effective permissions, 475
event logs in Event Viewer, 767-768
file extensions, 55
firewall exception app properties, 416
installed hardware, 176
large number of tiles, 20
last usernames at logon, 559
libraries, 488
network connections, 346
partition properties, 734-735
PowerShell version, 617
sync partnerships, 651
taskbar icons, 24-25
UAC prompts on taskbar, 532
updates, 708, 714
Windows
7 desktop, 45
Firewall applet, 412
Store apps updates available count, 715-716

wireless
data usage, 391
network profiles, 394
Display tab (Remote Desktop Connection dialog box), 610
displays
Control Panel applet, 51, 54
customizing, 32
high-contrast, configuring, 43
lock screen photo slide shows, 10
Miracast
editions included in, 10
hardware requirements, 66
installing, 122
website, 123
multiple, 10
Start screen, displaying, 26
taskbar, 25
navigating, 25-26
power settings, 664
resolution requirements, 58
Distributed COM users group, 583
Distributed Transaction Coordinator firewall exception, 413
DMA (direct memory access), 195
DNS
configuring
TCP/IPv4, 354-356
TCP/IPv6, 356-357
dynamic, 355, 357
FQDNs, 357
TCP/IPv4, 355
TCP/IPv6, 357
NetBIOS names, 356
overview, 354
servers
adding, 355
addresses, 334
Documents library, 29
domain accounts, 587
domain-based folder redirection, 150-154
Group Policy settings warning, 153
implementing, 150-151
locations, 152
options, 151-152
Domain profile, 418, 433
Download Manager
canceling, 281
files, saving, 281
GPOs, 284
list of downloads, displaying, 282-283
opening files, 281
options, 283
overview, 281
SmartScreen Filter, 281
Download Options dialog box, 283
dragging objects, 478
DRAs (data recovery agents), 683-686
Driver tab (device Properties dialog box), 178, 193
Driver Verifier Manager dialog box, 191
Driver Verifier utility, 191-193
drivers, 165
compatibility, 58
Device Manager
device Properties dialog box, 177-178
device status, displaying, 176-177
disabling drivers, 179
hardware, displaying, 176
opening, 175-176
uninstalling drivers, 179
device setup, 170-171
digital signatures, 180-183
requirements, 180-181
searching, 181
signing and staging website, 181
uninstalling, 179
updating, 174-175
verifying, 181-183
disabling, 179, 193
DMA, enabling, 195
Driver Verifier, 191-193
installing
device setup, 170-171
Device Stage, 171-173
permissions, 183
PnPUtil, 184-185
jumbo packet settings, 195
new support features, 169-170
overview, 169

packages, managing, 184-185
port settings, 195
properties, configuring, 193-196
advanced settings, 194-195
Driver tab (device Properties dialog box), 193
rolling back, 189-190, 193, 821-822
speed, 195
troubleshooting, 185
Action Center, 188
resource conflicts, 185-187
rolling back, 189-190
System Information utility, 189
UEFI. *See* UEFI
uninstalling, 193
unsigned, 183
updating, 193
drives
adding to storage spaces, 753
diskette, 308
encryption, 49
File History, choosing, 847
fixed data, 682-683
mapping, 457-458
operating system, 680
Storage Spaces applet, 49
system image backups, adding, 852
unlocking at startup, 688
USB
selective suspend setting, 663
Windows To Go, 103-104
USB recovery, 815-817
finishing, 817
Recovery Drive Wizard, 815
recovery partitions, creating, 817
Startup Repair, invoking, 836-837
USB drives, choosing, 816-817
website, 817
dual-booting, 90
advantages, 90
configuring, 91-92
duplex (network adapters), 398
dynamic disks
advantages, 729
basic disk conversions to, 736-737
converting to basic disks, 737
disadvantages, 730
volumes
extending, 738
properties, 738
types, 737
dynamic DNS, 355, 357
Dynamic Host Configuration Protocol. *See* DHCP
dynamic memory, 307
dynamic VHDs, 109

E

E address class, 336
EAP (Extensible Authentication Protocol), 597
EAP-TTLS (Extensible Authentication Protocol Tunneled Transport Layer Security), 597
Ease of Access Center, 42-44, 54-55
Easy Connect, 601
configuring, 608
troubleshooting, 608
Easy Transfer
collected files, saving to destination computer, 145-147
firewall exception, 413
overview, 142
source computer files, collecting, 142-145
collected data, storage options, 143
data, transferring, 144
wizard, starting, 142
website, 147
ECMAScript resource websites, 279
Edit Plan Settings dialog box, 662
editing. *See* customizing
editions
components included, 10
listing of, 9-10
upgrading, 100-101
Effective Access tab (Advanced Security Settings dialog box), 475
effective permissions, 474
displaying, 475
rules, 474-475

EFS (Encrypting File System), 10
certificates, 481
disk preparations, 482
editions included in, 10
keys
backing up, 485
overview, 481
NTFS requirement, 480
overview, 480
recovery agents, 486-487
resource website, 487
rules, 480-481
technology website, 481
elevated privileges, 534-535
elevation prompts, 530
behaviors, configuring, 539-540
executables, 540
secure desktop, 540
enabling
auditing, 523
biometrics, 579
BitLocker, 674-675
BitLocker To Go, 679
boot logging, 832
debugging mode, 832
disk quotas, 502-503
Hyper-V, 298-299
InPrivate Browsing, 275-277
location settings, 695
media streaming, 459
network adapters, 398
NFC, 501
object access auditing, 506-508
Offline Files, 647
PINs, 581
PowerShell Remoting, 620
Public folders, 450
recommended updates, 713
services, 804
SmartScreen Filter, 547
software
notifications, 713
restriction policies, 232
TPMs as virtual smart cards, 575-576
UEFI Secure Boot, 542-543
Windows
Firewall, 412
Store app automatic updates, 718-719
encrypted files, indexing, 807
Encrypting File System. *See* EFS
encryption
BitLocker
applet, 49
DRAs, 683-686
drive encryption, 672-674
enabling, 674-675
fixed data drives, 682-683
managing, 677-678
new features, 673
operating system drives policies, 680
overview, 672
partitions, encrypting, 676-677
policies, 680
recovery keys, storing, 676
startup keys, 672
TPM compatibility, 674
unlocking drives at startup, 675
websites, 674
without TPM preparations, 687-690
BitLocker To Go, 672, 679-680
decryption, 485
EFS
backing up keys, 485
certificates, 481
disk preparations, 482
editions included in, 10
encryption keys, 481
NTFS requirement, 480
overview, 480
recovery agents, 486-487
resource website, 487
rules, 480-481
technology website, 481
file-sharing connections, 450
files, 483-484
keys, 481
Offline Files, 648
Pervasive Device
hardware requirements, 66
installing, 123
website, 123

SSL, 260
VPN, 630
Windows To Go workspaces, 105
wireless networks, 387, 436
ENERGY STAR Qualified plan, 661
enforcement
AppLocker rules, 239
software policies, 235
Enhanced Protected Mode (Internet Explorer 11), 260
Enterprise edition, 9
errors
answer files, 89
disks, checking, 751
Error logs, 93
Stop, 93-94
Ethernet properties, 346
Ethernet Properties dialog box, 346, 366
event logs
displaying in Event Viewer, 767-768
Event Viewer, 766
File History, 850
Readers group, 583
subscriptions
advanced settings, 774
creating, 772-773
destination logs, 773
event types, selecting, 774
names, 773
overview, 771
source computers, selecting, 774
websites, 774
types of events recorded, 769
Event Viewer, 56, 766, 771
customizing, 769-770
event logs, displaying, 767-768
events
tasks, associating, 770
types of events recorded, 769
networks, troubleshooting, 375
opening, 766
subscriptions
advanced settings, 774
creating, 772-773
destination logs, 773
event types, selecting, 774
names, 773
overview, 771
source computers, selecting, 774
websites, 774
events
audit types, 525
forwarding/collecting, 771
tasks, creating from, 770
types recorded in event logs, 769
Events tab (device Properties dialog box), 178
exceptions (Windows Firewall), 413-416
apps
adding, 414
removing, 416
authenticated, configuring, 430-431
network profiles, 416
properties, displaying, 416
selecting, 413
Exceptions tab (AppLocker Properties dialog box), 244
Exclude from File History dialog box, 848
executables, elevating, 540
Experience tab (Remote Desktop Connection dialog box), 611
Extend Volume Wizard, 733, 738
extending
partitions, 733
volumes, 738
Extensible Authentication Protocol (EAP), 597
Extensible Authentication Protocol Tunneled Transport Layer Security (EAP-TTLS), 597
extensions
files
displaying, 55
program associations, configuring, 215-219
Installer supported, 208
external virtual switches, 319, 321

F

Family Safety applet, 53, 269
Fibre Channel adapters, 307

File and Printer Sharing firewall exception, 413
File Explorer window, 451-452
File Hash tab (AppLocker Properties dialog box), 244
File History, 846
drives, choosing, 847
event logs, 850
features, 846
files
copies, saving, 850
damaged/deleted, restoring, 856-858
older versions, deleting, 850
multiple versions, restoring, 858
saved versions, keeping, 850
folders
adding, 851
excluding, 848-849
older versions, deleting, 850
homegroups, 850
offline cache size, 850
shadow copies, 855
Start screen app, 850
system image backups, creating
drives, adding, 852
network locations, 853
save location, choosing, 852
verifying, 854
system images, creating, 852-854
turning on, 847
website, 852
File Sharing dialog box, 452
File Transfer Protocol. *See* FTP
files
answer
creating, 83-90
editing, 90
overview, 82
unattended installations, performing, 90
catalog
32-bit, 89
creating, 87-88
checkpoint locations, 308
collecting from source computers
USMT, 138-139
Windows Easy Transfer, 142-145
copying
NTFS permissions, 476-477
OneDrive, 494
damaged/deleted versions, restoring, 856-858
decrypting, 485
deleted, recovering
File History, 856-858
OneDrive, 860-861
encrypted, indexing, 807
encrypting. *See* EFS
extensions, displaying, 55
hash rules, 244
history. *See* File History
indexing, 805
accents/diacritical marks, 807
encrypted files, 807
file types, adding/deleting, 807
Indexing Options applet, opening, 805
locations, 805, 807
rebuilding, 807
websites, 808
Installer supported, 208
libraries. *See* libraries
log. *See* logs
migrating. *See* migrating
moving
NTFS permissions, 477-478
OneDrive, 494
.msi, 212
NTFS permissions, 465
Offline Files, 646
Always Offline mode, 655-657
client computer configuration, 646-648
disabling, 647
enabling, 647
encrypting, 648
network share files, caching, 648
policies, 653
server configuration, 649-650
server requirements, 646
storing, 646
Sync Center, 650-653
transparent caching, 657
website, 646

OneDrive, 37
access, 493
version history, 861-862
opening, 281
paging, editing, 791
previously backed up, recovering, 858-859
program associations, configuring
default settings, editing, 213-215
extensions, 215-219
Set Program Access and Computer Defaults dialog box, 219
recovering
after upgrades, 100
Wbadmin utility, 858-859
saving
Download Manager, 281
OneDrive, 497
sharing, 360-361
adding users to sharing list, 451-452
command-line administration, 458-459
configuring with Network and Sharing Center, 449-450
connections, encrypting, 450
drives, mapping, 457-458
firewall exception, 413
NTFS permissions. See *NTFS permissions*
password protecting, 459
properties, editing, 453
public, 449, 457
security, 451
standard, 449
taking ownership, 474
transform, 212
uploading to OneDrive, 494
USMT
executable/rule, 136
.xml, creating, 136
write failures, redirecting, 541

filters
keys, 43
packet, 410
SmartScreen. *See* SmartScreen Filter

finding. *See* searching

Firewall (Windows), 410
Advanced Security
connection security rules, 418
Group Policy, 428-429
inbound rules, 417
IPSec settings, 420
monitoring, 418
multiple profiles, configuring, 418-420
new connection security rules, configuring, 424
new inbound/outbound rules, configuring, 420-424
notifications, 427-428
opening, 416-417
outbound rules, 418
resource websites, 427
rule properties, editing, 426
authenticated exceptions, 430-431
Control Panel applet, 48
default settings, restoring, 416
disabling, 413
editions included in, 10
enabling/disabling, 412
new features, 17, 410-411
packet filtering, 410
program exceptions, 413-416
adding apps, 414
network profiles, 416
properties, displaying, 416
removing apps, 416
selecting programs, 413
Remote Assistance, allowing, 602-603
Windows Firewall applet, opening, 412

folders
adding to File History, 851
Control Panel applet, 54
damaged/deleted versions, restoring, 856-858
encrypting. *See* EFS
excluding from File History, 848-849
indexing, 805
accents/diacritical marks, 807
encrypted files, 807
file types, adding/deleting, 807
Indexing Options applet, opening, 805
locations, 805, 807

rebuilding, 807
websites, 808
libraries. *See* libraries
NTFS permissions
copying, 476-477
moving, 477-478
Offline Files, 646
Always Offline mode, 655-657
client computer configuration, 646-648
disabling, 647
enabling, 647
encrypting, 648
network share files, caching, 648
policies, 653
server configuration, 649-650
server requirements, 646
storing, 646
Sync Center, 650-653
transparent caching, 657
website, 646
OneDrive, 493
access, 493
offline availability, 495
selecting, 495
version history, 861-862
preserved/refreshed, 823-824
previously backed up, recovering, 858-859
public, 457, 449-450
redirection, 147
benefits, 147-148
domain-based, 150-154
library folders, 148-150
offline files website, 154
website, 147
sharing, 449, 451
adding users to sharing list, 451-452
command-line administration, 458-459
configuring with Network and Sharing Center, 449-450
deleting shared folders, 452
drives, mapping, 457-458
granular security permissions, 456
NTFS permissions. See *NTFS permissions*
password protecting, 459
permissions, editing, 455-456
properties, editing, 453
public folders, 449, 457
security, 451
standard, 449
taking ownership, 474
work
Control Panel applet, 49
editions included in, 10
website, 49
fonts, 54
format fs command, 294
formatting
partitions, 732
striped volumes, 743
VHDs, 294
forwarded events logs, 768
forwarding events, 771
four variable-sized windows, opening, 10
FQDNs (fully qualified domain names)
TCP/IPv4, 355
TCP/IPv6, 357
% Free Space counter, 793
fsutil.exe, 739
FTP (File Transfer Protocol)
passwords, 278
TCP/IP, troubleshooting, 368
full control permission, 455, 465, 471
fully qualified domain names. *See* FQDNs

G

gateways
default, 334
TCP/IPv4, 334, 350
General tab
dialog boxes
AppLocker Properties, 244
Device Properties, 178
System Configuration utility, 799
gestures, 561-562
Get command (App-V clients), 223
global unicast class, 340
GPOs (Group Policy Objects)
AD DS folder redirection, 150-154
biometrics, 579

BitLocker, 680
fixed data drives, 682-683
operating system drives, 680
Download Manager, 284
Firewall, 428-429
Installer, 208-209
Internet Explorer Compatibility View, configuring, 258
location settings, 697
Offline Files, 653
power management, 667-668
RD Gateway, 635
recovery agents, 486
remote authentication, 600
smart cards, 577-578
UAC, 537-541
Admin Approval Mode, 538, 540
administrative users prompt behaviors, 539
application installation detection, 540
configuring, 537
elevation prompt behaviors, 539-540
executables, elevating, 540
file/registry write failures, redirecting, 541
secure desktop prompting, 540
UIAccess application elevation, 538, 540
WebSockets configuring, 280
Windows Store access, 228-229
Windows Update, 710-714
automatic update behaviors, 710-712
automatic update detection frequency, 713
client-side targeting, 713
delaying restarts, 713
disabling auto-restart after automatic updates installation, 713
immediately installing automatic updates, 713
Install Updates and Shut Down, 712
intranet Microsoft update service locations, 712
non-administrator notifications, 713
recommended updates, 713
rescheduling automatic updates, 713
restart re-prompts, 713
signed updates, 713
software notifications, 713
waking up computers to install updates, 712
wireless network profiles, managing, 395

GPT (GUID partition tables) disks, 544, 730
converting to MBR, 731
MBR conversions, 730
website, 731
graphics processor requirements, 57
Group Policy Object Editor, opening, 710
Group Policy Objects. *See* GPOs
groups
built-in local, 583
guest, 583
homegroups. *See* homegroups
Guest group, 583
GUID partition table. *See* GPT disks

H

hard disks
power settings, 663
requirements, 57
virtual. *See* VHDs
hardware
32-bit versus 64-bit, 59-60
actions, displaying, 178
adding, 33
compatibility, 58-59
configuring, 170-171
Devices and Printers applet, 51, 489
diskette drives, 308
disks. *See* disks
drivers. *See* drivers
enrollment, 10
Hardware and Sound category (Control Panel), 50-52
installed, displaying, 176
Pervasive Encryption
installing, 123
requirements, 66
website, 123
power management, 178
Properties dialog box, 177-178
requirements
Hyper-V, 66
Miracast displays, 66
Pervasive Device Encryption, 66
Secure Boot, 66
virtual smart cards, 66
Windows 8.1, 57-58

smart cards, 599
specifications, displaying, 178
status, displaying, 176-177
system resources consumed, displaying, 178
Upgrade Assistant
compatibility check, 61-62
current installation options, keeping, 62
website, 61
upgrading versus clean installation, 60-61
USB. *See* USB devices
VHDs, 108
8.1, installing to, 114-116
adding to older computers, 120
best practices, 114-116
booting, 118-120
creating with DiskPart utility, 293-294
Disk Management snap-in, 112-114
features, 109
mounting/dismounting, 295-297
native boot configuration, 111-112
overview, 292
tools, 110-111
types, 109
VHDX format, 292-293
Virtual Hard Disk Test Drive Program website, 292
VM checkpoints, 315
WIM2VHD utility, 118
VMs, adding307
Windows Certification program, 58
Hardware and Sound category (Control Panel), 50-52, 658
HCK (Hardware Certification Kit), 58
help
Help and Support, 13
PowerShell, 619
Remote Assistance. *See* Remote Assistance
hibernation, 660
hiding
charms, 26
taskbar, 24
updates, 708
high contrast, configuring, 43
High performance power plan, 661
history
files. *See* File History
Windows
7, 8
8, 8
8.1, 9
95, 7
2000, 7
NT, 7
Phone 7, *8*
Vista, 7
XP Home/Professional editions, 7
Home-File History dialog box, 856
homegroups
applet, 50, 460
configuration options, 463
creating, 460
editions included in, 10
File History, 850
firewall exception, 413
joining, 462-463
library folders, sharing, 464
media streaming options, 463
membership, 10
properties, 41
sharing, 361
hotspot tethering, 10
How should we set up your PC page, 80
HTML5 sandbox attribute, 260
HTTP settings (Internet Explorer 11), 270
Hyper-V
Administrators group, 583
checkpoints, 315-318
applying changes, 317-318
creating, 315-316
deleting, 317
merging changes, 318
storing, 315
VHDs, expanding, 315
dynamic memory, 307
enabling, 298-299
hardware requirements, 66
installing, 121-122
processor configuration options, 310
requirements, 297-298

virtual switches
creating, 319-320
external, 321
internal, 322
private, 323
types, 319
VMs, connecting, 323-324
VMs, 300-301
deploying, 309-314
physical machine conversions, 314
Hyper-V Manager, 301-302. *See* also VMs, Hyper-V

I

icacls.exe utility, 468
ICF (Internet Connection Firewall). *See* Firewall
ICMP (Internet Control Message Protocol), 332
icons
clicking, 20
taskbar
displaying, 24-25
sizing, 24
ICS (Internet Connection Sharing), 361
client computers, configuring, 363-364
components, 361-362
host connection, sharing, 362-363
LAN settings, 363
troubleshooting, 364
website, 364
IDE controllers, 308-311
IKEv2 (Internet Key Exchange version 2), 625
IKEv2 tab (Advanced Properties dialog box), 631
important updates
automatic checking/installation, editing, 706
defined, 704
inbound rules, 417, 420-424
Indexed Locations dialog box, 805
indexing, 805
accents/diacritical marks, 807
encrypted files, 807
file types, adding/deleting, 807
Indexing Options applet, opening, 805
locations, 805, 807
rebuilding, 807
websites, 808
Indexing Options applet, 805
information bar (Internet Explorer 11), 260
inheritance (NTFS permissions), 473
InPrivate Browsing mode, 275-277
"Install, Deploy, and Migrate to Windows 8" website, 63
installations
ADK, 83-85
App-V client, 221
applications
elevation prompts, 540
Windows Installer. See *Installer*
attended, 75-81
background color, 78
booting to setup, 76
computer name, 78
default settings, 79
finishing, 81
How should we set up your PC page, 80
installation type, choosing, 77
licensing, 76
Microsoft account sign-in, 79
partitions, choosing, 77
preparations, 75
product key, entering, 76
progress, tracking, 78
security code, 79
SkyDrive, 80
Windows Setup dialog box, 76
clean versus upgrading, 60-61
device drivers
device setup, 170-171
Device Stage, 171-173
permissions, 183
PnPUtil, 184-185
dual-booting, 90
advantages, 90
configuring, 91-92
Hyper-V, 121-122
Miracast displays, 122
optional updates, 706
Pervasive Device Encryption, 123

refreshing, 92
Secure Boot, 124
troubleshooting
log files, 92-93
Stop errors, 93-94
stopped, 94
unattended, 81
answer files. See *answer files*
configuration passes, 82-83
upgrading 8 to 8.1, 99-100
upgrading older operating systems, 95
data, saving, 96
preparations, 97
process, 97-99
upgrade paths, 95
upgrading other 8.1 editions, 100-101
VHDs, 108
8.1, installing to, 114-116
adding to older computers, 120
best practices, 117-118
booting, 118-120
Disk Management snap-in, 112-114
features, 109
native boot configuration, 111-112
tools, 110-111
types, 109
virtual smart cards, 123
website resources, 95
Wi-Fi Direct devices, 670
Windows Store apps, 226, 717
Windows To Go, 102
exceptions, 102-103
host computers, 107-108
USB drive preparations, 103
workspaces, provisioning, 103-107

Installer
actions, 209-210
API, 212
file types supported, 208
GPOs, 208-209
installation rules, 212
.msi files, 212
Msiexec utility, 210-212
new features, 208
transform files, 212
website, 212

Integrated Scripting Environment (ISE), 620
integration services (VMs), 308
integrity levels, 530
interactive logons, 527
internal virtual switches, 319, 322
internationalization (Internet Explorer 11), 270
Internet
connections, sharing. *See* ICS
Control Panel applet, 50
firewall. *See* Firewall
hardware requirements, 58
Internet Connection Firewall (ICF). ***See*** **Firewall**
Internet Control Message Protocol (ICMP), 332
Internet Explorer 11
add-ons, 271
accelerators, 275
disabling, 272
finding, 272
InPrivate Browsing mode, 275-277
Manage Add-ons dialog box, 271-272
Compatibility View, 256
browsing history, deleting, 258
configuring with Compatibility View Settings dialog box, 256-257
configuring with GPOs, 258
desktop version, 253
Download Manager
canceling, 281
GPOs, 284
list of downloads, displaying, 282-283
opening files, 281
options, 283
overview, 281
saving files, 281
SmartScreen Filter, 281
editions included in, 10
Gallery, 272
interfaces, 255-256
JavaScript Timer frequency, 663
new features, 254
search providers, configuring, 273-275

security
accelerated graphics, 270
accessibility, 270
Add-on Manager, 260
Auto Complete, 269
browsing, 270
certificates, 269
configuring, 260-261
cookies, 267
digital signatures, 260
Enhanced Protected Mode, 260
family safety, 269
features, 260
HTML5 sandbox attribute, 260
HTTP settings, 270
information bar, 260
international settings, 270
location services, 267
media, 270
new features, 17
notifications, 260
Pop-up Blocker, 260, 268-269
privacy settings, 262
Protected Mode, 263
RSS feeds/Web slices, 269
SmartScreen Filter, 260, 264-265
SSL encryption, 260
zones, configuring, 261-263
SmartScreen Filter. *See* SmartScreen Filter
Start screen version, 253
switching between versions, 253
Web Credentials, 568-569
WebSockets, 277
configuring, 279
GPOs, 280
resources, accessing, 278
support, 278
website, 278
Internet Key Exchange version 2 (IKEv2), 625
Internet Options dialog box, 261
Internet Properties dialog box
Advanced tab, 269-271
Content tab, 269
Privacy tab, 266
security, 260-261
Interrupts/sec counter, 792
Intune Connector, 693-694
IP (Internet Protocol)
addresses
alternate, 348
APIPA, 350-351
duplicate, troubleshooting, 375
dynamic, 343
incorrect, troubleshooting, 374-375
IP Address app, 372
multiple, 350
static, 334-337
defined, 332
v4
address classes, 335
addressing components, 334
alternate configurations, troubleshooting, 375
classless inter-domain routing, 338
DNS, configuring, 354-356
incorrect addresses, troubleshooting, 374-375
private network addresses, 338
Properties dialog box, 347
resource websites, 339
static addressing, 335-337
troubleshooting, 373
version 6 compatibility, 342
v6, 339
address classes/subclasses, 339
benefits, 333-334
classes/subclasses, 340-341
connections, configuring, 351-353
connectivity, troubleshooting, 376
disabling, 357
DNS, configuring, 356-357
prefixes, 339
properties, 351
troubleshooting, 373
types of addresses, 340
version 4 compatibility, 342
website, 334, 341
IP Address app, 372
Ipconfig utility, 368-370
IPSec, 420

iSCSI service firewall exception, 413
ISE (Integrated Scripting Environment), 620
isolated cryptography, 575

J

joining homegroups, 462-463
Jumbo Frames, 398
jump lists, 27

K

Kerberos authentication, 598-600
Key Management service, 413
keyboard accessibility options, 43
keys
  EFS, 485
  encryption, 481

L

L2TP (Layer 2 Tunneling Protocol), 625
LAN connections, troubleshooting, 366
LAN Settings dialog box, 363
languages
  configuring, 124-125
  removing, 126
legacy network adapters, 307
libraries, 29-30
  accessing, 29
  creating, 30
  default, 487-488
  displaying, 488
  Documents, 29
  folders
    adding, 29
    redirecting, 148-150
  homegroup access, 464
  Music, 29
  Pictures, 29
  properties, 488
  sharing, 30
  subfolders, 488
  Videos, 29
licensing, 76
lid closures, 664
link-local unicast class, 340
list disk command, 294, 745
list folder contents permission, 465
list folder NTFS special access permission, 471
listening ports, configuring, 613-614
LoadState utility
  collected files, saving, 139-140
  website, 140
local accounts
  built-in groups, 583
  creating, 581
  managing, 582
Local Area Connection Properties dialog box, 354
Local Group Policy Editor
  classic logon, 558
  user rights, controlling, 584
Local Resources tab (Remote Desktop Connection dialog box), 610
local security policies
  account lockouts, 521-522
  accounts, 519
  audits, 523-526
    account logon events, 526
    completed action event log entries, triggering, 523
    enabling, 523
    event types, 525
    success or failure actions, configuring, 525
  local policies, 523
  Local Security Policy snap-in, 518-519
  passwords, 520-521
  security options, 526-527
  unlocking accounts, 523
Local Security Policy snap-in, 518-519
  accounts, 519
    lockouts, 521-522
    unlocking, 523
  audits, 523-526
  local policies, 523
  opening, 232
  passwords, 520-521
  security options, 526-527
Local Users and Groups utility, 56
local users profiles, 155

Location Aware Printing, 401-402
Location Settings applet, 52
locations
indexing, 805, 807
Internet Explorer 11 services, 267
networks
defined, 358
existing networks, 359
Internet connection sharing. See *ICS*
new connections, configuring, 358
sharing, 359-361
privacy settings, 40
settings, 694-695
enabling/disabling, 695
group policies, 697
Windows apps, 696
lock screens, 557-559
configuring, 32
photo slide shows, 10
lockout policies, 521-522
LogicalDisk object, 793
Logman utility, 794
logons
last usernames, displaying, 559
lock screens, 557-559
picture passwords, 560-562
disabling, 562
gestures, 561-562
PC Settings Sign-in options, 560
pictures, choosing, 561
switching to text passwords, 562
PINs
configuring, 579-580
enabling, 581
security, 581
prompts, 557-559
domain-joined computers, 558
non-domain-joined computers, 558
security policies, 527
User Accounts and Family Safety category (Control Panel), 53
logs
application, 767
applications and services, 768
event
displaying in Event Viewer, 767-768
File History, 850
subscriptions, 771-774
types of events recorded, 769
Event Viewer, 766
forwarded events, 768
installations, troubleshooting, 92-93
performance, 413
security, 510, 767
setup, 767
system, 767
Windows Firewall profiles, 419
Windows Store error, 719
loopback address class, 336
low-resolution video mode, 832

M

Magnifier, configuring, 43
Mail, Calendar, People and Messaging app, 413
mail app, 10
malware protection, 541
Protected Mode, 263
resistance, new features, 17
SmartScreen Filter, 260, 264-265
application blocks, bypassing, 547
Download Manager, 281
Internet Explorer features, 545-546
troubleshooting, 803
turning on/off, 547
Windows SmartScreen built-in feature, 546-547
Manage Add-ons dialog box, 271-272
Manage Default Printers dialog box, 401
mandatory user profiles, 155
Active Directory, 157-158
establishing, 161-162
Map Network Drive Wizard, 457-458
mapping drives, 457-458
Maps app, 413
MBR (Master Boot Record) disks
converting to GPT, 730
GPT conversions, 731
defined, 730

MDM support, 10
MDOP (Microsoft Desktop Optimization Pack), 855
media
AutoPlay, 34, 51
Complete Media Center, 58
Internet Explorer 11, 270
Media Player, 241-244
Music library, 29
OneDrive storage, 498
power settings, 664
sharing, 360
homegroup access, 463
media streaming, enabling, 459
streaming, 450
videos
conferencing requirements, 58
library, 29
OneDrive storage, 498
Videos library, 29
Media Center
editions included in, 10
Extenders, 413
Media Player, 241-244
memory
object counters, 789-790
performance
optimizing, 789-791
statistics, displaying, 778-779
VMs, 297
configuring, 307
dynamic, 307
Memory tab (Resource Monitor), 779
menu bar (Task Manager), 798
messaging, 10
metered connections, 37, 391, 499
microphone, 40
Microsoft
accounts, 585
advantages, 585
blocking, 588
creating, 586-587
disadvantages, 588
domain accounts, connecting, 587
email confirmation, 587
signing in, 79
Application Compatibility Toolkit, 65
Challenge Handshake Authentication Protocol version 2 (MS-CHAPv2), 597
DaRT, 855
Desktop Optimization Pack (MDOP), 855
Forefront Unified Access Gateway (UAG), 636
Management Console (MMC), 623-624
SmartScreen Filter dialog box, 265
MigApp.xml file, 136
MigDocs.xml file, 136
migrating
folder redirection, 147
benefits, 147-148
domain-based, 150-154
library folders, 148-150
website, 147
user profiles
Active Directory, 157-158
configuring, 154-157
copying, 157
deleting, 157
mandatory, 161-162
operating system versions, 162
paths, editing, 156
roaming, 158-161
types, 155
USMT
collected files, saving to destination computer, 139-140
executable/rule files, 136
overview, 135-136
running, 140-141
server preparations, 138
source computer files, collecting, 138-139
step-by-step website, 142
technician computer requirements, 138
Usmtutils utility, 136-137
.xml files, creating, 136
Windows Easy Transfer
collected files, saving to destination computer, 145-147
overview, 142
source computer files, collecting, 142-145
website, 147
MigUser.xml file, 136

Miracast displays
editions included in, 10
hardware requirements, 66
installing, 122
website, 123
mirrored volumes, creating, 737
Disk Management, 744-745
DiskPart, 745-746
dynamic, 738
misspelled words, autocorrecting, 33
MMC (Microsoft Management Console), 623-624
mobile devices
BitLocker
DRAs, 683-686
drive encryption, 672-674
enabling, 674-675
fixed data drives policies, 682-683
managing, 677-678
new features, 673
operating system drives policies, 680
overview, 672
partitions, encrypting, 676-677
policies, 680
recovery keys, storing, 676
startup keys, 672
TPM compatibility, 674
unlocking drives at startup, 675
websites, 674
BitLocker To Go, 672, 679-680
hotspot/Wi-Fi tethering, 10
Intune Connector, 693-694
location settings, 694-695
enabling/disabling, 695
group policies, 697
Windows apps, 696
Mobility Center, 52, 668-669
computer specific modules, 669
features, 669
opening, 668
mobility enhancements, 15
new features, 14
Offline Files, 646
Always Offline mode, 655-657
client computer configuration, 646-648
disabling, 647
enabling, 647
encrypting, 648
network share files, caching, 648
policies, 653
server configuration, 649-650
server requirements, 646
storing, 646
Sync Center, 650-653
transparent caching, 657
website, 646
power
airplane, 661
batteries, 664-666
customizing plans, 665
desktop background slide show, 663
display, 664
editing plans, 662
group policies, 667-668
hard disk inactivity, 663
hibernation, 660
JavaScript Timer frequency, 663
lid actions/settings, 662, 664
media, 664
passwords on wakeup, 662-663
PCI Express, 664
plans, 661
Power Options applet, 659-660
power/sleep buttons, 662, 664
processors, 664
shutdown settings, 662
sleep mode, 659-660, 663
turning off components after inactivity, 665
USB settings, 663
wireless adapters, 663
remote wipe, 692-693
startup key storage, 687
Syskey, 690-692
without TPM, 687-690
Wi-Fi Direct, 670-671
connecting devices, 671
finding devices, 671
installing devices, 670
pairing devices, 671
properties, 670
proximity sensors, 671
website, 671
Windows Phone 7, 8

Mobility Center, 52, 668-669
computer specific modules, 669
features, 669
opening, 668
mobility enhancements, 15
modify permission, 465
monitoring
performance
counters, 782-784
data collector sets, creating, 788-789
features, 781
opening, 782
terminology, 781
Users group, 583
website, 784
Windows Firewall, 418
monitors. *See* displays
Mount command (App-V clients), 223
mounting VHDs, 295-297
mouse
accessibility options, 44
configuring, 33
moving files/folders
NTFS permissions, 477-478
OneDrive, 494
MS-CHAPv2 (Microsoft Challenge Handshake Authentication Protocol version 2), 597
.msi files, 212
Msiexec utility, 210-212
multibooting, 90
multicast addresses, 340-341
multifactor authentication, 557
biometrics, 578
devices, 578-579
disabling, 579
enabling, 579
group policies, 579
Windows Biometric Framework (WBF), 578
smart cards
defined, 574
group policies, 577-578
new features website, 578
properties, 574-575
readers, 574
virtual, 575-577
multimedia. *See* media
multiple displays
editions included in, 10
Start screen, displaying, 26
taskbar, 25
Music library, 29

N

names
data collector sets, 785
FQDNs, 355, 357
NetBIOS, 356
resolution. *See* DNS
subscriptions, 773
virtual switches, 319
VMs, 308
Narrator, configuring, 43
NAT (Network Address Translation), 362
native boots, 111-112
navigation
Control Panel applet, 54
display/Start screen, 25-26
Nbtstat utility, 370
Near Field Communication. *See* NFC
net share command, 458-459
NetBIOS names, 356
Netlogon service, 413
netsh utility
IPv6, 353
websites, 356, 395
wireless networking commands, 394
Netstat utility, 370
Network Adapter Troubleshooting Wizard, 399-401
Network Address Translation (NAT), 362
Network app, 344
Network Configuration Operators group, 583
Network Connection Details dialog box, 366
Network Connection dialog box, 346, 362
adapters, enabling/disabling, 398
LANs, troubleshooting, 366
Network Discovery, 374
Network and Internet category (Control Panel), 49-50

Network Location Wizard, 365
Network and Sharing Center, 50, 344-345
network
adapter device properties, 396-398
connections, 358
problem troubleshooter, 365
sharing, 359-361
opening, 345
resource sharing, 449-450
TCP/IPv4, 346-350
advanced settings, 349
alternate IP addresses, 348
Ethernet properties, 346
gateways, 350
multiple IP addresses, 350
network connections, displaying, 346
properties, 347-348
TCP/IPv6 connections, 351-353
VPN connections, 627
wireless network connections, 386-388
Network tab (Resource Monitor), 780
Network utility, 40-41, 391
networks
adapters
802.11n mode, 398
device properties, 396-398
enabling/disabling, 398
preferred bands, 398
requirements, 58
speed, 398
troubleshooting, 398-401
VMs, 307-308
wireless mode, 398
connections
APIPA, 350-351
displaying, 346
existing, 359
host, sharing, 361-362
Network and Sharing Center, 344-345
Network app, 344
new, configuring, 358
properties, 41
TCP/IPv4, 346-350
TCP/IPv6, 351-353
testing, 372
Control Panel applets, 49-50
discovery, 360, 432
Domain profile, 433
firewall exception, 413
network profile options, 433
typical network profiles, 432
DNS
dynamic, 355, 357
FQDNs, 355
NetBIOS names, 356
overview, 354
servers, adding, 355
TCP/IPv4, 354-356
TCP/IPv6, 356-357
drives, mapping, 457-458
homegroups
configuration options, 463
Control Panel applet, 50
creating, 460
editions included in, 10
firewall exception, 413
joining, 462-463
library folders, sharing, 464
media streaming options, 463
membership, 10
properties, 41
sharing, 361
Location Aware Printing, 401-402
locations
defined, 358
existing networks, 359
Internet connection sharing. See *ICS*
new connections, configuring, 358
sharing options, 359-361
Network and Sharing Center, 50
performance statistics, displaying, 778, 780
printer sharing. *See* printing, sharing printers
profiles
configuration options, 433
Domain, 433
firewall app exceptions, 416
typical, 432
proxies, 41
remote access. *See* remote access
security. *See* Firewall

sharing. *See* sharing
TCP/IP. *See* TCP/IP
troubleshooting
DHCP server connections, 375
diagnostic tools, 365-367
duplicate IP addresses, 375
Event Viewer, 375
incorrect IPv4 addresses, 374-375
IPv6 connectivity, 376
Network Discovery, 374
subnet masks, 374-375
TCP/IP utilities, 367-372
TCP/IPv4 alternate configurations, 375
wireless
adapter properties, 398
ad-hoc wireless, 10
connections, configuring, 386-388
data usage, displaying, 391
devices, finding, 390
metered connections, 391
Network Properties dialog box, 391-392
preferred, 392-393
profiles, 393-396
properties, 391-392
protocols, 385
security. See *security, wireless*
Settings charm, 389-390
WLANs, 384
Workplace
joins, 10, 14
properties, 41
New Connection Security Rule Wizard, 424
new features
BitLocker, 673
Firewall, 410-411
Installer, 208
Internet Explorer 11, 254
PowerShell, 617
productivity, 12-15
charms, 13
Help and Support, 13
Hyper-V, 14
mobility, 14-15
OneDrive, 14
printing, 15
Start button, 13
Start screen, 13
To Go, 14
touch-screen capabilities, 12
Web Application Proxy, 14
Windows Store, 14
workplace join, 14
security, 15-17
AppLocker, 15
auditing, 16
biometrics, 17
BitLocker/BitLocker To Go, 16
BranchCache, 16
Firewall, 17
Internet Explorer security, 17
malware resistance, 17
picture passwords, 15
remote business data removal, 17
smart cards, 16
trusted/secure boots, 15
smart cards, 578
websites, 17
New Inbound Rule Wizard, 420
New Mirrored Volume Wizard, 745
New Outbound Rule Wizard, 420
New Path Rule dialog box, 234
New Raid-5 Volume Wizard, 745
New Simple Volume Wizard, 731
New Striped Volume Wizard, 742
New Technology File System (NTFS), 464, 480
New Virtual Machine Wizard, 303-305
NFC (Near Field Communication), 500
devices
availability, 501
capabilities, 500
disabling, 501
enabling, 501
Windows Store apps, 500
non-EAP remote authentication methods, 597
nonexportability (smart cards), 575
notifications
area, 25
Firewall, 427-428
Internet Explorer 11, 260
properties, 39

software, turning on, 713
updates, 712
utility, 39

NSLookup utility, 370

NTFS (New Technology File System), 464, 480

NTFS permissions, 465

applying, 466-467
denying, 475
dragging objects between locations, 478
effective, 474-475
displaying, 475
rules, 474-475
files/folders, 465
copying, 476-477
moving, 477-478
sharing, 478-479
inheritance, 473
special access, 468-472
advanced permissions, configuring, 469-470
change permissions, 471
create files, 471
create folders, 471
currently assigned, displaying, 468
delete, 471
delete subfolders and files, 471
full control, 471
list folder, 471
read attributes, 471
read extended attributes, 471
read permissions, 471
take ownership, 471-472
traverse folder, 471
users, adding, 469
write attributes, 471
write extended attributes, 471
taking ownership, 474

NTLM authentication, 598-600

O

objects

access auditing, 506
audited objects access attempts, displaying, 510
configuring, 506
enabling, 506-508
objects to be audited, choosing, 508-510
Security log space, 510
GPOs. *See* GPOs
LogicalDisk, 793
Memory, 789-790
performance, 781
PhysicalDisk, 792
Processor, 792

offline caches, sizing, 850

Offline Files, 646

Always Offline mode, 655-657
client computer configuration, 646-648
disabling, 647
enabling, 647
encryption, 648
network share files, caching, 648
policies, 653
server
configuration, 649-650
requirements, 646
storing, 646
Sync Center, 650-653
conflicts, 653
creating sync partnerships, 651
displaying sync partnerships, 651
features, 650
opening, 651
schedules, creating, 652-653
specific network shares, synchronizing, 651
transparent caching, 657
website, 646

Offline Files dialog box, 647

Offline Files Sync Schedule dialog box, 652

offline migration. *See* USMT

Offline Settings dialog box, 649

older operating systems, upgrading, 95

OneDrive

accessing, 492
app, 493-495
files, uploading, 494
folders, 493
local files/folders, accessing, 493
offline availability, 495
attended installation setup, 80

Camera Roll folder, 498
deleted files, recovering, 860-861
desktop, 496-497
files, 37
metered connections, 37, 499
overview, 14, 492
PC Recycle bin, 860
properties, configuring, 36-37
Recycle bin, 859
save location, editing, 497
settings, 497
storage amount, 36, 497
synchronization, 37, 498-499
version history, 861-862

open MDM support, 10

open wireless security, 436

opening
Certificate Manager, 570
Device Manager, 175-176
Event Viewer, 766
files, 281
Firewall with Advanced Security snap-in, 416-417
Group Policy Object Editor, 710
Indexing Options applet, 805
Local Security Policy snap-in, 232
Mobility Center, 668
Network and Sharing Center, 345
Performance Monitor, 782
RE, 831
Reliability Monitor, 776
Resource Monitor, 777
Sync Center, 651
System Restore, 818
Task Manager, 794-795
Update, 705
windows, 10
Windows To Go provisioning tool, 104

operating system drives, 680

Optimize Drives utility, 748-750

optimizing performance. *See* performance optimization

optional updates
defined, 704
installing, 706

outbound rules (Firewall), 418, 420-424

Overview tab
App-V management console, 222
Resource Monitor, 778

P

packages (driver), 184-185

packet filtering, 410

Packet InterNet Gopher (ping), 370-371

Page Faults/sec counter, 789

Pages/sec counter, 789

Paging File% Usage counter, 790

paging files, editing, 791

PAP (Password Authentication Protocol), 597

parental controls
editions included in, 10
Family Safety applet (Control Panel), 53

partitions. *See also* volumes
creating, 731-732
deleting, 735
extending, 733
formatting, 732
GPTs, 544
properties, displaying, 734-735
recovery, creating, 817
shrinking, 733
styles
converting between, 730-731
listing of, 730
UEFI Secure Boot, 544-545

Password Authentication Protocol (PAP), 597

passwords
Easy Connect, 608
FTP, 278
picture, 15, 560-562
disabling, 562
gestures, 561-562
PC Settings Sign-in options, 560
pictures, choosing, 561
switching to text, 562
policies, 520-521
recovery, 677, 690
sharing resources, 361, 450, 459
user accounts, configuring, 34-36
waking from sleep mode, 662-663

Patch Tuesday, 701
Path tab (AppLocker Properties dialog box), 244
pathping utility, 372
PC and Devices utility, 31-34
PCI Express, 664
PC info, 34
PC Settings utility, 30
Accounts, 34-36
Ease of Access, 42-44
editions included in, 10
languages, adding, 124-125
Network, 40-41
OneDrive, 36-37
PC and Devices, 31-34
Privacy, 39
Search and Apps, 37-39
Time and Language, 42
Update and Recovery, 44
PEAP (Protected Extensible Authentication Protocol with Transport Layer Security), 597
Peer Name Resolution Protocol (PNRP), 601
Performance Log Users group, 583
Performance Logs and Alerts. *See* data, collector sets
Performance Monitor
counters
adding, 782-784
highlighting, 784
data collector sets, creating, 788-789
features, 781
opening, 782
terminology, 781
Users group, 583
website, 784
performance optimization
Action Center, 802
command-line utilities, 794
counters, 781
data collector sets, 784
creating from templates, 785-786
manually creating, 787-788
Performance Monitor, 788-789
disks, 792
LogicalDisk counters, 793
PhysicalDisk counters, 792
instances, 781
logs, 413
memory
counters, 789-790
paging files, editing, 791
objects, 781
Performance Monitor
adding counters, 782-784
data collector sets, creating, 788-789
features, 781
highlighting counters, 784
opening, 782
terminology, 781
Users group, 583
website, 784
processor utilization, 792
Reliability Monitor, 775-777
list of problems, displaying, 777
opening, 776
Problem Reports and Solutions integration, 775
report categories, 776
System Stability Chart, 775-776
XML-based reports, exporting, 777
Resource Monitor
component information, displaying, 777
CPU tab, 779
Disk tab, 779
graphical displays, sizing, 779
Memory tab, 779
Network tab, 780
opening, 777
Overview tab, 778
unresponsive processes, ending, 780
website, 780
services, configuring, 803-804
solutions, checking, 777
System Configuration utility, 799
Boot tab, 800
General tab, 799
Services tab, 800-801
Startup tab, 801

Tools tab, 801
website, 801
Task Manager. *See* Task Manager
troubleshooting, 802-803
Performance Options dialog box, 791
Performance tab (Task Manager), 797
Performance utility, 56
Permission Entry dialog box, 469-470
permissions
device driver installations, 183
NTFS. *See* NTFS permissions
printer sharing, 490-492
shared folders, editing, 455-456
Permissions for (folder name) dialog box, 455
personal identification numbers. *See* PINs
Personal Identity Verification (PIV), 557
Personalization applet, 54
Pervasive Device Encryption
hardware requirements, 66
installing, 123
website, 123
phishing, 264-265
photos
lock screen slide shows, 10
OneDrive storage, 498
picture passwords, choosing, 561
Pictures library, 29
Photos app, 413
PhysicalDisk object, 792
picture passwords, 15, 560-562
disabling, 562
gestures, 561-562
PC Settings Sign-in options, 560
pictures, choosing, 561
switching to text, 562
Pictures library, 29
ping (Packet InterNet Gopher), 370-371
PINs (personal identification numbers), 557
configuring, 579-580
enabling, 581
security, 581
PIV (Personal Identity Verification), 557
PnPUtil utility, 184-185
PNRP (Peer Name Resolution Protocol), 601
Point-to-Point Tunneling Protocol (PPTP), 625
Point-to-Point (PPP) VPN protocol, 625
policies
accounts, 519
lockouts, 521-522
unlocking, 523
AppLocker, 236-237
configuring, 238
creating, 241-244
default, configuring, 240
enforcement, 239
properties, 244
audits, 523-526
account logon events, 526
completed action event log entries, triggering, 523
enabling, 523
event types, 525
success or failure actions, configuring, 525
BitLocker, 680
fixed data drives, 682-683
operating system drives, 680
local, 523
local security, 518-519
location settings, 697
Offline Files, 653
passwords, 520-521
power management, 667-668
security, 526-527
smart card group, 577-578
software restrictions, 231-236
AppLocker, compared, 238
enabling, 232
enforcement, 235
Local Security Policy snap-in. opening, 232
path rules, 234
rules, configuring, 233
security levels, 231-233
UAC, 537-541
Admin Approval Mode, 538, 540
administrative users prompt behaviors, 539
application installation detection, 540
configuring, 537

elevation prompt behaviors, 539-540
executables, elevating, 540
file/registry write failures, redirecting, 541
secure desktop prompting, 540
UIAccess applications elevation, 538, 540
Update, 710-714
automatic update behaviors, 710-712
automatic update detection frequency, 713
client-side targeting, 713
delaying restarts, 713
disabling auto-restart after automatic updates installation, 713
immediately installing automatic updates, 713
Install Updates and Shut Down, 712
intranet Microsoft update service locations, 712
non-administrator notifications, 713
recommended updates, 713
rescheduling automatic updates, 713
restart re-prompts, 713
signed updates, 713
software notifications, 713
waking up computers to install updates, 712

Pool Nonpaged Bytes counter, 789
Pop-up Blocker (Internet Explorer 11), 260, 268-269
Pop-up Blocker Settings dialog box, 268
portability. *See* mobile devices
portrait mode improvements, 10
ports
COM, 308
driver settings, configuring, 195
listening, configuring, 613-614
power
batteries, 664-666
buttons, 662, 664
configuring, 34
desktop background slide show, 663
Control Panel applet, 49, 51
devices, managing, 178
display, 664
group policies, 667-668
hard disk inactivity options, 663
hibernation, 660
JavaScript Timer frequency, 663
lid actions/settings, 662, 664
media, 664
passwords on wakeup, 662-663
PCI Express, 664
plans
customizing, 665
editing, 662
overview, 661
Power Options applet, 659-660
processor power levels, 664
shutdown settings, 662
sleep mode, 663
advantages, 659-660
airplanes, 661
button, 662
configuring, 34
passwords on wakeup, 663
settings, 663
waking from to install updates, 712
turning off components after inactivity, 664
USB selective suspend, 663
wireless adapters, 663

Power Management tab (device Properties dialog box), 178
Power Options applet, 659-660
Power saver plan, 661
Power Users group, 583
PowerShell
accessing, 26
App-V clients commands, 222-224
cmdlet verbs, 618
help, 619
ISE, 620
new features, 617
overview, 617
Remoting, 620-623
disk information queries, 622-623
enabling, 620
remote computers, managing, 622
restore points, specifying, 839
starting, 618
storage spaces, managing, 757-758
version, displaying, 617
websites, 617
Windows Store apps, managing, 719-720

PPP (Point-to-Point) VPN protocol, 625
PPTP (Point-to-Point Tunneling Protocol), 625
preferred wireless networks, 392-393
prefixes (IPv6), 339
preparations
attended installations, 75
EFS, 482
remote authentication, 596-597
upgrading older operating systems, 97
USB drives for Windows To Go, 103
USMT technician computer, 138
previewing desktop, 25
printing
3D, 10
Location Aware Printing, 401-402
new features, 15
sharing printers, 489-492
configuring, 489-490
firewall exception, 413
permissions, 490-492
Wi-Fi Direct wireless, 10
privacy settings (Internet Explorer 11), 262
cookies, 267
location services, 267
Pop-up Blocker, 268-269
Privacy tab (Internet Properties dialog box), 266
Privacy utility, 39
private IPv4 network addresses, 338
Private profile (Windows Firewall), 418
private virtual switches, 319, 323
Pro edition, 9
Problem Reports and Solutions applet, 775
processes
currently running
sorting, 797
summary performance information, 796
unresponsive, ending, 780
Processes tab (Task Manager), 796
Processor object, 792
% Processor Time counter, 792
processors
performance optimization, 792
power management, 664
requirements, 57
VMs, configuring, 310
productivity, new features, 12-15
charms, 13
Hyper-V, 14
Help and Support, 13
mobility, 14-15
OneDrive, 14
printing, 15
Start button, 13
Start screen, 13
To Go, 14
touch-screen capabilities, 12
Web Application Proxy, 14
Windows Store, 14
workplace join, 14
profiles
copying, 157
deleting, 157
Firewall, 418-420
mandatory
Active Directory, 157-158
establishing, 161-162
migrating, 154-157
networks
configuration options, 433
domain, 433
firewall app exceptions, 416
typical, 432
operating system versions, 162
paths, edition, 156
roaming
Active Directory, 157-158
implementing, 158-161
operating system incompatibility, 162
types, 155
wireless networks, 393-396
automatic connections, stopping, 394
deleting, 394
deploying, 396
displaying, 394
GPOs, 395
security key information, displaying, 394
types, 393
Program Compatibility Troubleshooter, 803

Programs category (Control Panel), 52-53, 215-219
Programs and Features applet, 52
Programs tab (Remote Desktop Connection dialog box), 611
properties
accessibility, 42-44
app sizes, 39
AppLocker, 239, 244
automatic updates, 710-712
certificates, displaying, 570-571
dates and times, 42
default apps, 39
devices, 177-178
disk quotas, 504-505
drivers, configuring, 193-196
advanced settings, 194-195
Driver tab (device Properties dialog box), 193
dynamic volumes, 738
Ethernet, 346
Firewall
exception apps, displaying, 416
rules, editing, 426
homegroups, 41
jump lists, 27
libraries, 488
network adapter devices, 396-398
networks, 40-41
notifications, 39
OneDrive, 36-37
partitions, displaying, 734-735
PC and Devices, 31-34
privacy, 39
recoveries, 44
search, 39
services, 804
shared folders, editing, 453
sharing, 39
smart cards, 574-575
taskbar, 24-25
TCP/IPv4, 347-348
TCP/IPv6, 351
toolbars, 27
updates, 44
user accounts, 34-36
virtual switches, 319-320
VPN connections, 629-630
Wi-Fi Direct, 670
wireless networks, 391-392, 437
Properties dialog box, tabs, 178
Protected Extensible Authentication Protocol with Transport Layer Security (PEAP), 597
Protected Mode (Internet Explorer 11), 263
protocols
ARP, 368
CHAP, 597
DHCP
Allocators, 362
dynamic IP addressing, 343
server connections, troubleshooting, 375
EAP, 597
EAP-TTLS, 597
FTP, 368
passwords, 278
TCP/IP, troubleshooting, 368
IKEv2, 625
L2TP, 625
MS-CHAPv2, 597
non-EAP, 597
NTLM authentication, 598
PAP, 597
PEAP, 597
PPP, 625
PPTP, 625
RDP, 609
remote authentication, 597
SSTP, 625
TCP/IP. *See* TCP/IP
TFTP, 368
VPN, 625
wireless networking, 385
wireless security, 435
proxies, 41
Public folders
enabling, 450
file sharing, 457
overview, 449
Public profile (Windows Firewall), 418
Publisher tab (AppLocker Properties dialog box), 244

push-button resets, 823
folders preserved/refreshed, 823-824
refreshing computers, 824-825
resetting to original installation condition, 827-829

Q

Quota Properties dialog box, 503
quotas (disks), 502
available space, 505
configuration options,
enabling, 502-503
entries
adding, 503
specific users, configuring, 503
guidelines, 505-506
properties, configuring, 504-505

R

RAID (Redundant Array of Independent Disks) volumes, 741-744
5, 737
Disk Management, 745
DiskPart, 745-746
dynamic, 738
fault-tolerance, 744
overview, 741-744
striped, creating
Disk Management, 742-744
DiskPart, 745-746
disks, selecting, 742
drive letters/mount paths, assigning, 743
formatting, 743
troubleshooting, 746-747
RAM requirements, 57
RD Gateway, 632
advantages, 633
group policies, 635
logon methods, 634
server settings, configuring, 633
website, 635
RD Gateway Server Settings dialog box, 633
RDP (Remote Desktop Protocol), 609
RE (Windows Recovery Environment), 830
actions, 830
opening, 831
troubleshooting options, 831-833
read attributes NTFS special access permission, 471
read & execute permission, 465
read permissions, 455, 465, 471
rebuilding indexing, 807
receive buffers, 398
recommended updates, 713
Reconnect (VPN), 631
recording steps that created problems, 607
recovery
advanced startup options, 830
DaRT, 855
device drivers, rolling back, 821-822
EFS recovery agents, 486-487
files
File History, 856-858
OneDrive, 860-862
after upgrades, 100
Wbadmin utility, 858-859
keys, storing, 676
partitions, creating, 817
passwords, 677, 690
push-button resets, 823
folders preserved/refreshed, 823-824
refreshing computers, 824-825
resetting to original installation condition, 827-829
restore points
automatically creating, 837-838
configuring, 838
deleting, 838
manually creating, 839
specifying as PowerShell cmdlet, 839
website, 839
services, 804
system image, 833-836
finishing, 836
restore options, 835
startup troubleshooting options, 834
system image backup, choosing, 835

System Restore, 818
backup snapshots, 818
date/time restore points, 820
interruptions, 821
opening, 818
points, 818
safe mode, 833
System Restore dialog box, 818
troubleshooting options, 831-833
Update and Recovery utility, 44
USB recovery drives, 815-817
finishing, 817
Recovery Drive Wizard, 815
recovery partitions, creating, 817
Startup Repair, invoking, 836-837
USB drives, choosing, 816-817
website, 817
Recovery Drive Wizard, 815
Recovery Environment. *See* RE
Recycle bin
OneDrive, 859
PC, 860
redirecting folders. *See* folders, redirection
Redundant Array of Independent Disks. *See* RAID volumes
refreshing installations, 92
registry write failures, redirecting, 541
Reliability Monitor, 775-777
list of problems, displaying, 777
opening, 776
Problem Reports and Solutions integration, 775
report categories, 776
solutions, checking, 777
System Stability Chart, 775-776
XML-based reports, exporting, 777
Relog utility, 794
remote access
authentication
certificates, 597-598
group policies, 600
Kerberos, 598-600
NTLM, 598-600
planning, 596-597
protocols, 597
technologies, 597
connection types, 597
DirectAccess, 635-637
benefits, 635-636
Microsoft Forefront Unified Access Gateway (UAG), 636
requirements, 636-637
Easy Connect, 601
configuring, 608
troubleshooting, 608
managing with MMC snap-ins, 623-624
PowerShell
cmdlet verbs, 618
help, 619
ISE, 620
new features, 617
overview, 617
Remoting, 620-623
resource websites, 617
starting, 618
version, displaying, 617
RD Gateway, 633
advantages, 633
group policies, 635
logon methods, 634
server settings, configuring, 633
website, 635
Remote Assistance, 601
accepting offers, configuring, 603-604
Firewall, 602-603
invitations to receive help, sending, 604-607
requirements, 602
shadow sessions, 607
steps that created problems, recording, 607
website, 607
Remote Desktop
connections, creating, 610-611
listening ports, configuring, 613-614
nonadministrative access, granting, 613
protocol, 609
server side, configuring, 612-613
Start screen version, 612
Terminal Services restriction, 609
Windows XP connections client software, 614
RSAT, 609

VPN, 624
authentication, 627
available network connections, displaying, 629
compatibility and interoperability website, 625
connection properties, 629-630
connections, establishing, 626-627
protocols, 625
Reconnect, 631
remote access connections, 625-626
security, 630
website, 632
WinRM, 614-616
WinRS, 616
Remote Assistance, 601
accepting offers, 603-604
Easy Connect
configuring, 608
troubleshooting, 608
Firewall, 413, 602-603
invitations to receive help, sending, 604-607
requirements, 602
shadow sessions, 607
steps that created problems, recording, 607
Remote Assistance dialog box, 604
Remote Assistance Settings dialog box, 604
remote business data removal, 10
Remote Desktop
connections, creating, 610-611
editions included in, 10
firewall exception, 413
listening ports, configuring, 613-614
nonadministrative access, granting, 613
protocol (RDP), 609
server side, configuring, 612-613
Start screen version, 612
Terminal Services restriction, 609
Windows XP connection client software, 614
Remote Desktop Connection dialog box, 610
Remote Desktop Users dialog box, 613
Remote Desktop Users group, 583
Remote Management (Windows), 413
remote (item) management, 413
Remote Management Users group, 583
Remote Server Administration Tools (RSAT), 609
Remote tab (System Properties dialog box), 603
remote wipe, 692-693
removing. *See* deleting
Replicator group, 583
requesting certificates, 572-574
requirements
DirectAccess, 636-637
driver signatures, 180-181
hardware
Hyper-V, 66
Miracast displays, 66
Pervasive Device Encryption, 66
Secure Boot, 66
virtual smart cards, 66
Windows 8.1, 57-58
Hyper-V, 297-298
Offline Files server, 646
Remote Assistance, 602
UEFI partitions, 544-545
USMT technician computer, 138
VM memory, 297
resiliency (storage spaces), 754
Resource Monitor
component information, displaying, 777
graphical displays, sizing, 779
opening, 777
tabs
CPU, 779
Disk, 779
Memory, 779
Network, 780
Overview, 778
unresponsive processes, ending, 780
website, 780
resources
accessing via browsers, 278
conflicts, 185-187
sharing. *See* sharing
Resources tab (device Properties dialog box), 178
Restore-Computer PowerShell cmdlet, 839
restore points, 818
automatically creating, 837-838
configuring, 838
deleting, 838

manually creating, 839
specific date/time, 820
specifying as PowerShell cmdlet, 839
website, 839

restoring. ***See also*** **recovery**
credentials, 568
Firewall default settings, 416
systems, 10

restrictions (applications), 230-231
application control policies. *See* AppLocker
benefits, 231
software, 231-236

roaming user profiles, 155
Active Directory, 157-158
implementing, 158-161
operating system incompatibility, 162

rolling back drivers, 189-190, 193, 821-822

routing, 338

RRAS (Routing and Remote Access), 413

RSAT (Remote Server Administration Tools), 609

RSS feeds, 269

RT 8.1 edition, 9

rules. ***See also*** **policies**
AppLocker
configuring, 238
creating, 241-244
default, configuring, 240
enforcement, 239
properties, 244
effective permissions, 474-475
EFS, 480-481
Firewall
connection security, 418
inbound, 417
new connection security, configuring, 424
new inbound/outbound, configuring, 420-424
outbound, 418
properties, editing, 426
software restrictions, 233

S

safe mode, 832
limitations, 833
System Restore combination, 833

saving
collected files to destination computers
USMT, 139-140
Windows Easy Transfer, 145-147
copies of files in File History, 850
data during upgrades, 96
files
Download Manager, 281
OneDrive, 497

ScanState utility, 138-139

schedules
synchronization, creating, 652-653
tasks, 55
updates, 712

scripting, disabling, 279

SCSI controllers, 307-308

Search (Windows)
accessing, 20
Apps view, 26
editions included in, 10
overview, 22
properties, 39

Search and Apps utilities, 37-39

Search button (Charms panel), 20-22

Search charm, 13

search providers, configuring, 273-275

searching
add-ons, 272
Bing, 10
Food & Drink app, 413
Health & Fitness app, 413
driver signatures, 181-183
Wi-Fi Direct devices, 671
wireless network devices, 390

Secure Boot, 15, 541
hardware requirements, 66
installing, 124
signatures, 541-542
UEFI
enabling, 542-543
partition requirements, 544-545
partition resource website, 545
specification, 542
website, 124

secure desktop, 540

Secure Sockets Layer (SSL), 260
Secure Socket Tunneling Protocol (SSTP), 625
security
advanced features support, 10
BitLocker
DRAs, 683-686
drive encryption, 672-674
enabling, 674-675
fixed data drives, 682-683
managing, 677-678
new features, 673
operating system drives policies, 680
overview, 672
partitions, encrypting, 676-677
policies, 680
recovery keys, storing, 676
startup keys, 672
TPM compatibility, 674
unlocking drives at startup, 675
websites, 674
without TPM preparations, 687-690
BitLocker To Go, 672, 679-680
certificates
Active Directory Certificate Services Overview website, 574
Certificate Manager, opening, 570
properties, viewing, 570-571
remote authentication, 597-598
requesting, 572-574
virtual smart cards, 576-577
Control Panel options, 47-49
credentials. *See* credentials
encryption. *See* encryption
file/folder sharing, 451, 456
Firewall. *See* Firewall
Internet Explorer 11
accelerated graphics, 270
accessibility, 270
Add-on Manager, 260
Auto Complete, 269
browsing, 270
certificates, 269
configuring, 260-261
cookies, 267
digital signatures, 260
Enhanced Protected Mode, 260
family safety, 269
features, 260
HTML5 sandbox attribute, 260
HTTP settings, 270
information bar, 260
international settings, 270
location services, 267
media, 270
notifications, 260
Pop-up Blocker, 260, 268-269
privacy settings, 262
Protected Mode, 263
RSS feeds/Web slices, 269
SmartScreen Filter, 260, 264-265
SSL encryption, 260
zones, configuring, 261-263
local policies, 523
account lockouts, 521-522
accounts, 519
audits, 523-526
Local Security Policy snap-in, 518-519
passwords, 520-521
security options, 526-527
unlocking accounts, 523
logons
lock screens, 557-559
picture passwords, 560-562
PINs, 579-581
prompts, 557-559
logs, 510, 767
malware, 541
Microsoft accounts, 588
Network Discovery, 432
Domain profile, 433
network profile options, 433
typical network profiles, 432
new features, 15-17
AppLocker, 15
auditing, 16
biometrics, 17
BitLocker/BitLocker To Go, 16
BranchCache, 16
Firewall, 17

Internet Explorer security, 17
malware resistance, 17
picture passwords, 15
remote business data removal, 17
smart cards, 16
trusted/secure boots, 15
parental controls, 53
passwords. *See* passwords
permissions. *See* permissions
PINs, 581
remote wipe, 692-693
Secure Boot. *See* Secure Boot
SmartScreen Filter
application blocks, bypassing, 547
Download Manager, 281
Internet Explorer features, 545-546
troubleshooting, 803
turning on/off, 547
Windows SmartScreen built-in feature, 546-547
software restriction levels, 231-232
VPN, 630
wireless, 384, 435
authentication, 387, 436
connection properties, 437
encryption, 387, 436
improvements, 384-385
keys, 387
protocols, 435
sharing, 437
types, 436
WEP disadvantages, 437
WPA types, choosing, 389, 437
Security Settings dialog box, 262
Security tab (VPN Connection Properties dialog box), 630
Select disk command, 294, 745
Select Folder dialog box, 849
Select Users or Groups dialog box, 242, 584
Select a Windows Image dialog box, 86
Server 2012 R2, 14
servers
DHCP
connections, troubleshooting, 375
dynamic IP addressing, 343
DNS
additional servers, adding, 355
addresses, 335
dynamic, 355, 357
FQDNs, 355, 357
NetBIOS names, 356
overview, 354
TCP/IPv4, 334, 354-356
TCP/IPv6, 356-357
Offline Files, 646, 649-650
RD Gateway
advantages, 633
group policies, 635
logon methods, 634
settings, configuring, 633
Remote Desktop, configuring, 612-613
WSUS, 710
service packs, 705
services
booting problems, troubleshooting, 800-801
dependencies, 804
enabling/disabling, 804
iSCSI, 413
Key Management, 413
logon accounts, 804
Netlogon, 413
Performance Logs and Alerts, 413
performance optimization, configuring, 803-804
properties, 804
recovery, 804
Services console, 803-804
Services tab
System Configuration utility, 800-801
Task Manager, 797
Services utility, 56
Set command (App-V clients), 223
Set Program Access and Computer Defaults dialog box, 219
Set Up a Connection or Network dialog box, 627
Set Up a Connection or Network Wizard, 358
Settings button (Charms panel), 30
Settings charm, 13, 389-390
setup logs, 767

shadow copies, 855
shadow sessions (Remote Assistance), 607
Share charm, 13
Share utility, 39
Shared Folders utility, 56
sharing, 449
adding users to sharing list, 451-452
command-line administration, 458-459
configuring with Network and Sharing Center, 449-450
drives, mapping, 457-458
file-sharing connections, 450
files, 360-361, 413
folders, 451
deleting shared folders, 452
granular security permissions, 456
NTFS permissions, 478-479
permissions, editing, 455-456
properties, editing, 453
homegroups, 361, 460
configuration options, 463
creating, 460
joining, 462-463
library folders, 464
media streaming options, 463
Internet connections. *See* ICS
libraries, 30
media, 360
homegroup access, 463
streaming, enabling, 450, 459
Network and Sharing Center, 50
networks, configuring, 359-361
password protecting, 361, 450, 459
printers, 360, 489-492
configuring, 489-490
firewall exception, 413
properties, 39
Public folders
enabling, 450
file sharing, 457
overview, 449
security, 451
standard, 449
wireless networks, 437
Shrink (Volume) dialog box, 733
shrinking partitions, 733
shutdown settings, 662
sideloading apps, 230
signatures. *See* digital signatures
signing in. *See* logons
sigverif utility, 182
SIM (System Image Manager), answer files, 82-90
ADK, installing, 83-85
catalog file, creating, 87-88
completing, 89
components, adding, 88
errors, correcting, 89
image file, selecting, 86-87
packages, adding, 89
validating, 89
simple volumes, 737
site-local unicast class, 341
sizes
apps, 39
taskbar icons, 24
VHDs, 113
SKUs, choosing, 65
SkyDrive. *See* OneDrive
sleep mode
advantages, 659-660
airplanes, 661
button, 662
configuring, 34
passwords on wakeup, 663
settings, 663
waking from to install updates, 712
smart cards, 599
defined, 557, 574
group policies, 577-578
new features, 16, 578
PIV, 557
properties, 574-575
readers, 574
remote authentication, 597
virtual, 575-577
certificates, 576-577
hardware requirements, 66
installing, 123
TPM, enabling, 575-576
website, 124

Smart Paging, 308
SmartScreen Filter, 260, 264-265
application blocks, bypassing, 547
Download Manager, 281
Internet Explorer features, 545-546
troubleshooting, 803
turning on/off, 547
Windows SmartScreen built-in feature, 546-547
software
compatibility, 63-65
notifications, turning on, 713
restriction policies, 231-236
AppLocker, compared, 238
enabling, 232
enforcement, 235
Local Security Policy snap-in opening, 232
path rules, 234
rules, configuring, 233
security levels, 231-232
sound, 51
source-initiated event subscriptions, 771
spanned volumes, 737
Disk Management, 744
dynamic, 737
special access NTFS permissions, 468-472
advanced permissions, configuring, 469-470
change permissions, 471
create files, 471
create folders, 471
currently assigned permissions, displaying, 468
delete, 471
delete subfolders and files, 471
full control, 471
list folder, 471
read attributes, 471
read extended attributes, 471
read permissions, 471
take ownership, 471-472
traverse folder, 471
users, adding, 469
write attributes, 471
write extended attributes, 471
Speech Recognition applet, 55
speed
drivers, 195
network adapters, 398
spelling, 33
SSL (Secure Sockets Layer), 260
SSTP (Secure Socket Tunneling Protocol), 625
stability. ***See*** **Reliability Monitor**
standard folder sharing, 449
Start button, 10, 13
Start charm, 13
Start screen
accessing, 19
Administrative Tools, 45-46
apps, 20, 28-29
background wallpaper, 10
Charms panel
accessing, 19
Settings button, 30
Control Panel, displaying, 46
controls, 10
desktop, accessing, 19
File History app, 850
Internet Explorer 11
desktop version, compared, 255-256
running, 253
jump lists, 27
multiple displays, 26
navigating, 25-26
new features, 13
old familiar desktop, accessing, 18
open programs, switching between, 20
Remote Desktop, 612
Search button, 20-22
taskbar
configuring, 23
properties, 24-25
tiles
accessing, 19
apps, closing, 20
customizing, 10
large number, displaying, 20
overview, 18
toolbar properties, 27
Update, running, 708-709
zooming, 20

startup applications, troubleshooting, 801
startup keys, 687
Syskey, 690-692
without TPM, 687-690
drives, unlocking at startup, 688
enabling BitLocker, 688
recovery key backups, 690
USB drives, 688-689
startup repair, 832-833, 836-837
Startup tab
System Configuration utility, 801
Task Manager, 797
state (Firewall profiles), 419
static addressing, 335-337
Steps Recorder, 607
sticky keys, 43
Stop errors, 93-94
storage
Offline Files, 646
OneDrive. *See* OneDrive
pools
drive failures, 756
drives, renaming, 755
managing, 755
storage spaces, compared, 754
recovery keys, 676
SkyDrive. *See* OneDrive
spaces, 751-752
applet, 49, 752
creating, 752-753
drive failures, 756
drives, adding, 753
drives, renaming, 755
editions included in, 10
managing, 755, 757-758
resiliency options, 754
storage pools, compared, 754
VM checkpoints, 315
Store (Windows), 14
access, controlling, 228-229
apps, 225
assigned access, configuring, 245-246
automatic updating, 10
characteristics, 225
editions supported, 10
error logs, 719
installing, 226
location settings, configuring, 696
managing with PowerShell cmdlets, 719-720
SmartScreen Filter, turning on/off, 547
updates. See *updates, Windows Store apps*
content, managing, 228
NFC capabilities, 500
website, 14
streaming media, 450, 459
striped volumes, 737
creating
Disk Management, 742-744
DiskPart, 745-746
disks, selecting, 742-744
drive letters/mount paths, assigning, 743
formatting, 743
dynamic, 738
fault-tolerance, 744
subnet masks
defined, 334
IPv4 static addressing, 337
TCP/IPv4, 334
troubleshooting, 374-375
Subscription Properties dialog box, 773
subscriptions (event log)
advanced settings, 774
creating, 772-773
destination logs, 773
event types, selecting, 774
names, 773
overview, 771
source computers, selecting, 774
websites, 774
Sync Center
conflicts, 653
features, 650
opening, 651
schedules, creating, 652-653
specific network shares, synchronizing, 651
sync partnerships
creating, 651
displaying, 651
Sync command (App-V clients), 223

synchronization
metered connections, 37
OneDrive, 37, 498-499
Sysprep utility, 110
System Configuration utility, 799
tabs
Boot, 800
General, 799
Services, 800-801
Startup, 801
Tools, 801
website, 801
System File Checker, 183
System Image Manager. *See* SIM, 82
system images
backups, creating, 852-854
drives, adding, 852
network locations, 853
save locations, choosing, 852
verifying, 854
recovery, 833-836
finishing, 836
restore options, 835
startup troubleshooting options, 834
system image backup, choosing, 835
System Information utility, 189
system logs, 767
System Properties dialog box
Remote tab, 603
roaming user profiles, 159
System Restore, 818
backup snapshots, 818
date/time restore points, 820
dialog box, 818
editions included in, 10
interruptions, 821
opening, 818
points, 818
safe mode combination, 833
System and Security category (Control Panel), 47-49, 536
system settings. *See* PC Settings utility
System Stability Chart, 775-776
SystemProcessor Queue Length counter, 792

T

take ownership NTFS special access permission, 471-472, 474
Task Manager
currently running apps
actions, 795
displaying, 795
currently running processes
sorting, 797
summary performance information, 796
editions included in, 10
menu bar, 798
opening, 794-795
tabs
App history, 797
Details, 797
Performance, 797
Processes, 796
Services, 797
Startup, 797
Users, 797
website, 798
Task Scheduler, 55
taskbar
configuring, 23
Control Panel applet, 54
desktop, previewing, 25
hiding, 24
icons
displaying, 24-25
sizing, 24
locking, 24
multiple displaying, 25
notification area, 25
placement, 24
properties, 24-25
thumbnail previews, 10
UAC prompts, displaying, 532
Taskbar and Navigation Properties dialog box, 23
jump lists, 27
tabs
Navigation, 25-26
Taskbar, 24-25
toolbars, 27

tasks
administrative
approval prompt, 530
privileges required, 530
creating from events, 770
elevated privileges, 534-535
scheduling, 55
UAC, 529
TCP (Transmission Control Protocol), 332
TCP/IP (Transmission Control Protocol/ Internet Protocol), 332
ARP, 332
dynamic IP addresses, 343
ICMP, 332
IP, 332
TCP, 332
troubleshooting, 367-372
ARP, 368
connectivity problems, 373
FTP/TFTP, 368
Ipconfig, 368-370
IPv4/IPv6 problems, 373
Nbtstat, 370
Netstat, 370
NSLookup, 370
pathping, 372
ping, 370-371
Tracert, 372
UDP, 332
version 4
addressing components, 334
alternate configurations, troubleshooting, 375
classes, 335
classless inter-domain routing, 338
connections, configuring, 346-350
DNS, configuring, 354-356
incorrect IP addresses, troubleshooting, 374-375
private network addresses, 338
Properties dialog box, 347
resource websites, 339
static addressing, 335-337
troubleshooting, 373
version 6 compatibility, 342
version 6, 339
address syntax, 339
benefits, 333-334
classes/subclasses, 340-341
connections, configuring, 351-353
connectivity, troubleshooting, 376
disabling, 357
DNS, configuring, 356-357
prefixes, 339
properties, 351
troubleshooting, 373
types of addresses, 340
version 4 compatibility, 342
website, 334, 341
templates (data collector sets), 785-786
Temporal Key Integrity Protocol (TKIP), 387
temporary user profiles, 155
Teredo addresses, 342
testing
drivers, 191-193
network connectivity, 372
TFTP (Trivial File Transfer Protocol), 368
third-party application prompts, 532-534
thumbnail previews (taskbar), 10
tiles (Start screen)
accessing, 19
apps, closing, 20
clicking, 20
displaying/removing, 45-46
frequently used, displaying, 46
large number, displaying, 20
overview, 18
Time and Language utility, 42
times, 42
TKIP (Temporal Key Integrity Protocol), 387
To Go (Windows), 14
editions included in, 10
exceptions, 102-103
host computers, 107-108
installing, 102
USB drives, preparing, 103
website, 107

workspaces, provisioning, 103-107
boot options, 106
encrypting, 105
image files, selecting, 104
provisioning tool, opening, 104
USB device selection, 104
workspace installation, 105
toggle keys, 43
tokens (access), 529-530
toolbar properties, 27
Tools tab (System Configuration utility), 801
touchpad, configuring, 33
touch-screen
capabilities, 12
clicking icons/tiles, 20
requirements, 58
TPM (Trusted Platform Module)
BitLocker
compatibility, 674
drive encryption, 672-674
as virtual smart cards, enabling, 575-576
Tracert utility, 372
transform files, 212
Transmission Control Protocol (TCP), 332
transmit buffers, 398
transparent caching, 657
traverse folder NTFS special access permission, 471
Trivial File Transfer Protocol (TFTP), 368
Troubleshoot problems-Network and Internet dialog box, 365
troubleshooting
alternate TCP/IPv4 configurations, 375
blue screen of death (BSOD), 93-94
booting performance
boot options, 800
diagnostic utilities, listing, 801
general, 799
services, 800-801
startup applications, 801
DHCP server connections, 375
disk performance, 792
LogicalDisk counters, 793
PhysicalDisk counters, 792
disks, 739-741
error checking, 751
full disks, 739
hard disk controller failures, 739
invalid media types, 739
missing operating systems, 739
non-system disk errors, 739
volume statuses, 740-741
drivers, 185
Action Center, 188
resource conflicts, 185-187
rolling back, 189-190
System Information utility, 189
Easy Connect, 608
ICS, 364
installations
log files, 92-93
Stop errors, 93-94
stopped, 94
IP addresses
duplicate, 375
incorrect, 374-375
IPv6 connections, 376
LAN connections, 366
memory performance
counters, 789-790
paging files, editing, 791
network connections
diagnostic tools, 365-367
TCP/IP utilities, 367-372
networks
adapters, 398-401
DHCP server connections, 375
duplicate IP addresses, 375
Event Viewer, 375
incorrect IPv4 addresses, 374-375
IPv6 connectivity, 376
Network Discovery, 374
subnet masks, 374-375
TCP/IPv4 alternate configurations, 375
performance, 802-803
processor performance, 792
RAID volumes, 746-747
steps that created problems, recording, 607
storage pool drive failures, 756

subnet masks, 374-375
system recovery, 831-833
TCP/IP, 367-372
ARP, 368
connectivity problems, 373
FTP/TFTP, 368
Ipconfig, 368-370
IPv4/IPv6 problems, 373
Nbtstat utility, 370
Netstat, 370
NSLookup, 370
pathping, 372
ping, 370-371
Tracert, 372
UAC, 541
Windows Store app errors, 719
trusted boots, 15
Trusted Platform Module. *See* TPM
Typeperf utility, 794
typing misspelled words, autocorrecting, 33

U

UAC (User Account Control), 528
Administrator group member authentication, 529-530
elevated privileges, 534-535
elevation prompts, 530
improvements, 528
integrity levels, 530
nonadministrative user account prompts, 531
options, 536-537
policies, 537-541
Admin Approval Mode, 538, 540
administrative users prompt behaviors, 539
application installation detection, 540
configuring, 537
elevation prompt behaviors, 539-540
executables, elevating, 540
file/registry write failures, redirecting, 541
secure desktop prompting, 540
UIAccess applications, elevating, 538, 540
prompts on taskbar, 532
tasks, 529-530
third-party application prompts, 532-534
troubleshooting, 803
websites
How User Account Control Works, 534
overview, 528
troubleshooting, 541
UAG (Microsoft Forefront Unified Access Gateway), 636
UDP (User Datagram Protocol), 332
UEFI (Unified Extensible Firmware Interface), 59
partition resource website, 545
Secure Boot
enabling, 542-543
partition requirements, 544-545
specification, 542
website, 542
UIAccess (User Interface Accessibility), 538, 540
unattended installations, 81
answer files
creating, 83-90
editing, 90
overview, 82
performing unattended installations, 90
configuration passes, 82-83
unicast addresses, 340
Unified Extensible Firmware Interface. *See* UEFI
uninstalling
8.1, 101
apps, 39
drivers, 179, 193
unique local IPv6 unicast address class, 341
unlocking accounts, 523
unresponsive processes, ending, 780
unrestricted security level, 232
unsigned drivers, 183
Update (Windows)
critical updates only option, 707
drivers, 174-175
editions included in, 10
features, 704
hiding/displaying, 708
notifications, 712
opening, 705
policies, 710-714

automatic update behaviors, 710-712
automatic update detection frequency, 713
client-side targeting, 713
delaying restarts, 713
disabling auto-restart after automatic updates installation, 713
immediately installing automatic updates, 713
Install Updates and Shut Down, 712
intranet Microsoft update service locations, 712
non-administrator notifications, 713
recommended updates, 713
rescheduling automatic updates, 713
restart re-prompts, 713
signed updates, 713
software notifications, 713
waking up computers to install updates, 712
running from Start screen, 708-709
troubleshooting, 781
updates
automatic checking/installation, 706
deleting, 715
history, reviewing, 714
manually checking for, 705
new, checking for, 710
optional, installing, 706
other Microsoft products, receiving, 707
scheduling, 712
supported, 704-705
WSUS, 710
Update and Recovery utility, 44
updates
automatic
auto-restart after installation, disabling, 713
checking/installation, editing, 706
delaying restarts, 713
detection frequency, 713
immediate installation, 713
properties, 710-712
rescheduling, 713
restart re-prompts, 713
scheduling, 712
Windows Store apps, 718-719
critical only option, 707
deleting, 715
drivers, 174-175, 193
hiding/displaying, 708
history, reviewing, 714
important, 704, 706
manually checking for, 705
new, checking for, 710
notifications, 712
optional, 704, 706
other Microsoft products, receiving, 707
Patch Tuesday, 701
recommended, 713
roll-ups, 705
scheduling, 712
service packs, 705
signed, 713
Update and Recovery utility, 44
Update supported, 704-705
Windows Store apps, 226-227, 715
automatic, 10, 718-719
available updates count, displaying, 715-716
choosing apps for updating, 716
installing updates, 717
PowerShell cmdlets management, 719-720
Upgrade Assistant
compatibility check, 61-62
current installation options, keeping, 62
website, 61
upgrades
8 to 8.1, 99-100
clean installation, compared, 60-61
file recovery, 100
older operating systems to 8.1, 95
data, saving, 96
preparations, 97
process, 97-99
upgrade paths, 95
other 8.1 editions, 100-101
SKUs, choosing, 65
uploading files to OneDrive, 494
USB devices
recovery drives, 815-817
finishing, 817
Recovery Drive Wizard, 815
recovery partitions, creating, 817

Startup Repair, invoking, 836-837
USB drives, choosing, 816-817
website, 817
selective suspend setting, 663
Windows To Go
preparations, 103
selecting, 104
User Account Control. *See* UAC
User Account Control Settings dialog box, 536-537
User Accounts applet, 53, 558, 582
User Accounts and Family Safety category (Control Panel), 53
User Datagram Protocol (UDP), 332
User Interface Accessibility (UIAccess), 538, 540
users
accounts
additional, creating, 36
blocking, 527
local security policies, 519
lockout policies, 521-522
passwords, configuring, 34-36
PINs, 579-581
properties, configuring, 34-36
sign-in options, 35-36
UAC. See *UAC*
unlock policies, 523
User Accounts and Family Safety category (Control Panel), 53
administrators
accounts, renaming, 527
group, 529-530, 583
task approval prompt, 530
tools, 45-46, 49
UAC prompt behaviors, 539
credentials
adding, 565
backing up, 567
Credential Manager, 563
deleting, 565
editing, 565
restoring, 568
roaming capabilities, 566
types, 564
Web, 568-569
migrating. *See* migrating
object access auditing, 506
audited objects access attempts, displaying, 510
configuring, 506
enabling, 506-508
objects to be audited, choosing, 508-510
Security log space, 510
profiles. *See* profiles
Remote Desktop access, granting, 613
rights, 581
built-in local groups, 583
controlling, 584
existing accounts, managing, 582
local accounts, creating, 581
sharing lists, adding, 451-452
special access permissions, adding, 469
UAC. *See* UAC
Users group, 583
Users tab (Task Manager), 797
USMT (User State Migration Tool), 135
collected files, saving to destination computer, 139-140
executable/rule files, 136
overview, 135-136
running, 140-141
source computer files, collecting, 138-139
step-by-step website, 142
technician computer
preparations, 138
requirements, 138
Usmtutils utility, 136-137
.xml files, creating, 136
Usmtutils utility, 136-137
utilities
Accounts, 34-36
ACL Editor, 466-467
App sizes, 39
App-V command-line, 222-224
Auditpol.exe, 510
Backup, 851
BCDEdit, 118-120
boot management, 91
chkdsk.exe, 739
cipher, 483

Computer Management snap-in, 55
    file/folder sharing security, 451
    Local Users and Groups section, 582
Convert, 482
Corners and Edges, 33
Defaults, 39
Defrag.exe, 750
Device Manager, 56, 396-398
Devices, 33
Disk Cleanup, 739
Disk Defragmenter, 739
Disk Management. *See* Disk Management utility
DiskPart, 739
    MBR/GPT conversions, 730-731
    VHDs, creating, 293-294
    volumes, creating, 745-746
    website, 294
Driver Verifier, 191-193
Ease of Access, 42-44
Event Viewer, 56, 375
fsutil.exe, 739
Hyper-V Manager, 301-302
icacls.exe, 468
Ipconfig, 368-370
LoadState
    collected files, saving, 139-140
    website, 140
Local Security Policy snap-in, 518-519
    account lockouts, 521-522
    accounts, 519
    audits, 523-526
    local policies, 523
    passwords, 520-521
    security options, 526-527
    unlocking accounts, 523
Local Users and Groups, 56
Logman, 794
Msiexec, 210-212
Nbtstat, 370
netsh
    IPv6, 353
    websites, 356, 395
    wireless networking commands, 394
Netstat, 370
Network, 40-41
Network Discovery, 374
Notifications, 39
NSLookup, 370
Optimize Drives, 748-750
pathping, 372
PC and Devices, 31-34
PC Settings, 30
    Accounts, 34-36
    Ease of Access, 42-44
    Network, 40-41
    OneDrive, 36-37
    PC and Devices, 31-34
    Privacy, 39
    Search and Apps, 37-39
    Time and Language, 42
    Update and Recovery, 44
Performance, 56
Performance Monitor
    adding counters, 782-784
    data collector sets, creating, 788-789
    features, 781
    highlighting counters, 784
    opening, 782
    terminology, 781
    website, 784
ping, 370-371
PnPUtil, 184-185
Privacy, 39
Reliability Monitor, 775-777
    list of problems, displaying, 777
    opening, 776
    Problem Reports and Solutions integration, 775
    report categories, 776
    solutions, checking, 777
    System Stability Chart, 775-776
    XML-based reports, exporting, 777
Relog, 794
Resource Monitor
    component information, displaying, 777
    CPU tab, 779
    Disk tab, 779
    graphical displays, sizing, 779
    Memory tab, 779

Network tab, 780
opening, 777
Overview tab, 778
unresponsive processes, ending, 780
website, 780
ScanState, 138-139
Search and Apps, 37-39
Services, 56
Share, 39
Shared Folders, 56
sigverif, 182
Syskey, 690-692
System Configuration, 799
Boot tab, 800
General tab, 799
Services tab, 800-801
Startup tab, 801
Tools tab, 801
website, 801
System File Checker, 183
System Information, 189
Task Scheduler, 55
TCP/IP troubleshooting, 367-372
ARP, 368
FTP/TFTP, 368
Ipconfig, 368-370
Nbtstat, 370
Netstat, 370
NSLookup, 370
pathping, 372
ping, 370-371
Tracert, 372
Time and Language, 42
Tracert, 372
Typeperf, 794
Update and Recovery, 44
Usmtutils, 136-137
VHD management, 110-111
Wbadmin
backing up data, 854-855
recovering data, 858-859
WIM2VHD, 118
WMI Control, 56

V

validating answer files, 89
VDI enhancements, 10
VHDs (virtual hard disks), 108
8.1, installing to, 114-116
adding to older computers, 120
best practices, 114-116
booting, 118-120
creating with DiskPart utility, 293-294
assigning, 294
attaching, 294
commands, 294
file, 294
formatting, 294
partitions, 294
Disk Management snap-in, 112-114
features, 109
mounting/dismounting, 295-297
native boot configuration, 111-112
overview, 292
tools, 110-111
types, 109
VHDX format, 292-293
Virtual Hard Disk Test Drive Program website, 292
VM checkpoints, 315
WIM2VHD utility, 118
videos
conferencing requirements, 58
library, 29
OneDrive storage, 498
Videos library, 29
views (Apps), 26
Virtual Apps tab (App-V management console), 223
virtual hard disks. *See* VHDs
virtual machines. *See* VMs
Virtual Memory dialog box, 791
Virtual Private Network. *See* VPN
virtual smart cards, 16
hardware requirements, 66
installing, 123
website, 124

virtual switches
creating, 319-320
external, 321
internal, 322
private, 323
types, 319
VMs, connecting, 323-324
virtualization
App-V, 220
command-line utilities, 222-224
deployment website, 221
management console, 222-223
overview, 220-221
file/registry write failures, redirecting, 541
hard disks. *See* VHDs
history, 287
Hyper-V
enabling, 298-299
Hyper-V Manager, 301-302
requirements, 297-298
VMs, creating, 300-301
overview, 287
smart cards, 575-577
certificates, 576-577
TPM, enabling, 575-576
virtual switches
creating, 319-320
external, 321
internal, 322
private, 323
types, 319
VMs, connecting, 323-324
VMs
checkpoints, 315-318
configuring. See *VMs, configuring*
creating, 303-306
deploying, 309-314
Hyper-V, creating, 300-301
memory requirements, 297
physical machine conversions, 314
support, 297
virtual switches, connecting, 323-324
viruses, 541
VLAN IDs, 320
VMs (virtual machines), 297
checkpoints, 315-318
applying changes, 317-318
creating, 315-316
deleting, 317
merging changes, 318
storing, 315
VHDs, expanding, 315
configuring, 306-307
automatically starting/stopping, 309
BIOS, 307
checkpoint file locations, 308
COM ports, 308
diskette drives, 308
hardware, adding, 307
IDE controllers, 311-308
integration services, 308
memory, 307
names, 308
network adapters, 308
processors, 310
SCSI controllers, 308
Smart Paging, 308
creating, 303-306
deploying, 309-314
dynamic memory, 307
Hyper-V
enabling, 298-299
Hyper-V Manager, 301-302
requirements, 297-298
VMs, creating, 300-301
memory requirements, 297
physical machine conversions, 314
support, 297
virtual switches, connecting, 323-324
Volume Shadow Storage (VSS), 855-858
volumes. *See also* partitions
creating with DiskPart, 745-746
dynamic
properties, 738
types, 737
extending, 738
mirrored, creating, 744-745
RAID, 741-744
5, creating, 745
overview, 741

striped, creating, 742-744
troubleshooting, 746-747
spanned, creating, 744
statuses, troubleshooting, 740-741
striped
Disk Management, 742-744
disks, selecting, 742-744
drive letters/mount paths, creating, 743
fault-tolerance, 744
formatting, 743
VPN (Virtual Private Network), 624
authentication, 627
compatibility and interoperability, 625
connections
available, displaying, 629
establishing, 626-627
properties, 629-630
protocols, 625
Reconnect, 631
remote access, 625-626
security, 630
website, 632
VPN Connection Properties dialog box
properties, 629-630
Security tab, 630
VSS (Volume Shadow Storage), 855-858

W

W3C (World Wide Web Consortium), 277
wallpapers, 10
Wbadmin utility
backing up data, 854-855
recovering data, 858-859
WBF (Windows Biometric Framework), 578
WDAC (Windows Data Access Components), 785-786
WDS (Windows Deployment Services), 118
Web
Application Proxy, 14
credentials, 568-569
slices, 269
Webcam privacy settings, 40
websites
802.11ac wireless networks, 385
ACT
download, 205
resources, 207
Active Directory Certificate Services Overview, 574
ADK download, 84, 138
Always Offline mode, 657
answer files, 89
Application Compatibility Toolkit, 65
AppLocker app management, 237
App-V deployment, 221
audit policies, 508
Auditpol.exe, 510
Backup utility, 851
battery properties, 666
Bcdedit.exe, 91
BitLocker, 674
DRAs, 686
policies, 680
Bootcfg.exe, 91
configuration passes, 83
DaRT, 855
device drivers signing and staging, 181
device setup, 173
DiskPart utility, 294
Driver Verifier, 193
ECMA Script resources, 279
EFS
recovery agents/backing up keys, 487
technology, 481
event subscriptions, 774
Event Viewer, 771
File History, 852
file recovery after upgrades, 100
folders
redirection, 147, 154
preserved/refreshed during push-button refreshes, 823-824
GPT disks, 731
Hyper-V, 122, 298
Icacls, 468
ICS, 364
indexing, 808

"Install, Deploy, and Migrate to Windows 8," 63
installation resources, 95
Internet Explorer 11
  new features, 254
  version comparison, 256
Intune Connector, 694
IP Address app, 372
IPv6, 334
  address compatibility, 342
  connectivity, troubleshooting, 376
  disabling, 357
  new features, 341
Kerberos authentication, 600
LoadState utility, 140
mandatory user profiles, 162
Miracast displays, 123
Msiexec.exe, 211
NAT, 362
netsh utility, 353, 356, 395
new features, 17
NTLM authentication, 600
Offline Files, 646
Performance Monitor, 784
Pervasive Device Encryption, 123
physical machine VM conversions, 314
PnPUtil, 185
PowerShell, 617, 758
printer permissions, 492
processor requirements, 57
RAID-5 volumes, 745
RD Gateway, 635
refreshing/resetting Pcs, 829
Remote Assistance, 607
Resource Monitor, 780
Restore-Computer PowerShell cmdlet, 839
restore points, 839
roaming profiles
  AD DS, 158
  operating system incompatibility, 162
RSAT, 609
ScanState Syntax, 139
Secure Boot, 124
Security Options (Local Security Policy snap-in), 527
sideloading apps, 230
SkyDrive desktop app download, 496
smart card new features, 578
startup repair, 833
System Configuration utility, 801
Task Manager, 798
TCP/IP version 4, 339
UAC
  How User Account Control Works, 534
  overview, 528
  troubleshooting, 541
UEFI, 60, 542, 545
uninstalling 8.1, 101
upgrade paths, 96
upgrading to 8.1, 65
USB drives
  recovery, 817
  Windows To Go, 103
USMT process, 142
Usmtutils utility, 137
Virtual Hard Disk Test Drive Program, 292
virtual smart cards, 124
VLAN IDs, 320
VPN, 625, 632
Wbadmin utility, 855, 859
WDAC, 786
WebSockets, 278
Wi-Fi Direct, 671
Windows
  8 to 8.1 upgrades, 100
  Easy Transfer, 147
  Firewall advanced security, 427
  Hardware Certification program, 58
  Installer, 212
  Store, 14
  To Go, 107
  XP client software download, 614
WinRM, 616
wireless network profiles, deploying, 396
work folders, 49
WebSockets, 277
configuring, 279
GPOs, 280
resources, accessing, 278
support, 278
website, 278

Wecutil command, 772
WEP (Wired Equivalent Privacy), 387, 437
"What is PAE, NX, and SSE2?" website, 57
Wi-Fi Direct, 670-671
devices
connecting, 671
finding, 671
installing, 670
pairing, 671
properties, 670
proximity sensors, 671
website, 671
Wi-Fi Protected Access. *See* WPA
WIM2VHD utility, 118
Windows
7, 8
interface, displaying, 45
upgrade requirements, 97
8, 8
8.1
components included, 10
development, 9
editions, 9-10
new features websites, 17
productivity improvements, 12-15
security improvements, 15-17
32-bit versus 64-bit, 59-60
95, 7
2000, 7
Biometric Framework (WBF), 578
Data Access Components (WDAC), 785-786
Defender, 10
Deployment Services (WDS), 118
Easy Transfer. *See* Easy Transfer
Firewall. *See* Firewall
To Go, 14
editions included in, 10
exceptions, 102-103
host computers, 107-108
installing, 102
USB drive preparations, 103
website, 107
workspaces, provisioning, 103-107
Hardware Certification program, 58
Installer
actions, 209-210
API, 212
file types supported, 208
GPOs, 208-209
installation rules, 212
.msi files, 212
Msiexec utility, 210-212
new features, 208
transform files, 212
website, 212
Internet Name Service. *See* WINS
NT, 7
PE, 110
Phone 7, 8
Recovery Environment. *See* RE
Remote Management (WinRM), 614-616, 623-624
Remote Shell (WinRS), 616
Search, 10
Server Update Services (WSUS), 710
Setup dialog box, 76
SkyDrive, 10
Store. *See* Store
Update. *See* Update
Vista, 7
XP Home/Professional editions, 7
windows, four variable-sized, opening, 10
Winload.exe, 91
Winresume.exe, 91
WinRM (Windows Remote Management), 614-616, 623-624
Winrm command, 771
WinRS (Windows Remote Shell), 616
WINS (Windows Internet Name Service)
overview, 335
TCP/IPv4, 334
Wired Equivalent Privacy (WEP), 387, 437
wired network connections
adapter properties, 398
APIPA, 350-351
Network app, 344
Network and Sharing Center, 344-345
TCP/IPv4, 346-350
advanced settings, 349
alternate IP addresses, 348

Ethernet properties, 346
gateways, 350
multiple IP addresses, 350
network connections, displaying, 346
properties, 347-348
TCP/IPv6, 351-353
Wireless Network Properties dialog box, 391-392
wireless networks
adapters
power savings, 663
properties, 398
ad-hoc networks, 10
connections, configuring, 386-388
manually connecting, 386-388
new, 386
data usage, displaying, 391
devices, finding, 390
metered connections, 391
Miracast displays, 10
preferred, 392-393
profiles, 393-396
automatic connections, stopping, 394
deleting, 394
deploying, 396
displaying, 394
GPOs, 395
security key information, displaying, 394
types, 393
properties, 391-392
protocols, 385
security, 384, 435
authentication, 387, 436
connection properties, 437
encryption, 387, 436
improvements, 384-385
keys, 387
protocols, 435
sharing, 437
types, 436
WEP disadvantages, 437
WPA types, choosing
settings
Network Properties dialog box, 391-392
Settings charm, 389-390
Wi-Fi
Direct wireless printing, 10
tethering, 10
WLANs, 384
wizards
ACT Configuration, 206
Add a Device, 173
Add Recovery Agent, 486-487
Certificate Export, 485
Create Basic Task, 770
Create a Homegroup, 460
Create New Data Collector Set, 785
Extend Volume, 733, 738
Map Network Drive, 457-458
Network Adapter Troubleshooting, 399-401
Network Location, 365
New Connection Security Rule, 424
New Inbound Rule, 420
New Mirrored Volume, 745
New Outbound Rule, 420
New RAID-5 volume, 745
New Simple Volume, 731
New Striped Volume, 742
New Virtual Machine, 303-305
Recovery Drive, 815
Set Up a Connection or Network, 358
Windows Easy Transfer
collected files, saving to destination computer, 145-147
source computer files, collecting, 142-144
WLANs, 384
WMI Control utility, 56
work folders
Control Panel applet, 49
editions included in, 10
website, 49
workplace
joins, 10, 14
properties, 41
workspaces (Windows To Go), 103-107
boot options, 106
encrypting, 105
image files, selecting, 104
provisioning tool, opening, 104
USB device selection, 104
workspace installation, 105

World Wide Web Consortium (W3C), 277
WPA (Wi-Fi Protected Access)
2-Enterprise, 387-388, 436
2-Personal, 387
choosing between types, 389, 437
encryption, 436
Enterprise, 387
Personal, 387
write attributes NTFS special access permission, 471
write extended attributes NTFS special access permission, 471
write permission, 465
WSUS (Windows Server Update Services), 710

X - Z

XML-based reliability reports, exporting, 777

zones (Internet Explorer security), 261-263
zooming (Start screen), 20